GEORGE WASHINGTON

GEORGE WASHINGTON

WRITINGS

THE LIBRARY OF AMERICA

The paper used in this publication meets the
minimum requirements of the American National Standard for
Information Sciences—Permanence of Paper for Printed
Library Materials, ANSI Z39.48—1984.

Distributed to the trade in the United States
by Penguin Books USA Inc
and in Canada by Penguin Books Canada Ltd.

Library of Congress Catalog Number: 96–9665
For cataloging information, see end of Index.
ISBN 1–883011–23–X

First Printing
The Library of America—91

Manufactured in the United States of America

JOHN RHODEHAMEL
SELECTED THE CONTENTS AND WROTE THE NOTES
FOR THIS VOLUME

*This volume has been published with support from
The John M. Olin Foundation*

Contents

THE COLONIAL PERIOD, 1747–1775

"Rules of Civility & Decent Behaviour in Company
and Conversation," *1747* 3

"A Journal of my Journey over the Mountains began Fryday
the 11th. of March 1747/8," *March 11–April 13, 1748* . . . 11

To Robin, *c. 1749–1750* 16

Design for a Coat, *c. 1749–1750* 17

Journey to the French Commandant,
January 16–17, 1754 17

To Richard Corbin, *January 28, 1754* 34

To Robert Dinwiddie, *April 25, 1754* 35

To Robert Dinwiddie, *May 18, 1754* 38

To Robert Dinwiddie, *May 29, 1754* 40

To Robert Dinwiddie, *May 29, 1754* 46

To John Augustine Washington, *May 31, 1754* 47

To William Fitzhugh, *November 15, 1754* 48

To Mary Ball Washington, *May 6, 1755* 50

To John Augustine Washington, *May 14, 1755* 51

To John Augustine Washington, *May 28, 1755* 51

To Sarah Cary Fairfax, *June 7, 1755* 53

To John Augustine Washington, *June 28, 1755* 54

To Robert Dinwiddie, *July 18, 1755* 58

To John Augustine Washington, *July 18, 1755* 59

To Mary Ball Washington, *August 14, 1755* 60

General Orders, *October 6, 1755* 60

To Christopher Gist, *October 10, 1755* 62

To Robert Dinwiddie, *October 11, 1755* 62

To Robert Dinwiddie, *December 5, 1755* 69

To Robert Hunter Morris, *April 9, 1756* 71

To Robert Dinwiddie, *April 18, 1756* 72

To Robert Dinwiddie, *April 22, 1756* 74

General Orders, *May 3, 1756* 76

General Orders, *May 21, 1756* 77

To Robert Dinwiddie, *May 23, 1756* 77

General Orders, *June 1, 1756*   80
To the Earl of Loudoun, *July 25, 1756*   80
To Robert Dinwiddie, *October 10, 1756*   81
To Robert Dinwiddie, *March 10, 1757*   85
To Richard Washington, *April 15, 1757*   88
To John Stanwix, *July 15, 1757*   89
To Robert Dinwiddie, *September 17, 1757*   91
To John Stanwix, *April 10, 1758*   93
To James Wood, *c. July 28, 1758*   95
To Francis Halkett, *August 2, 1758*   95
To Sarah Cary Fairfax, *September 12, 1758*   96
Farewell Address to the Virginia Regiment,
    January 10, 1759   98
To Robert Cary & Company, *May 1, 1759* 100
To Richard Washington, *September 20, 1759* 100
Diary Entry, *May 22, 1760* 101
Reward for Runaway Slaves, *August 11, 1761* 102
To Richard Washington, *October 20, 1761* 103
To Robert Cary & Company, *May 28, 1762* 105
To Charles Lawrence, *April 26, 1763* 107
To Robert Stewart, *April 27, 1763* 108
To Robert Cary & Company, *August 10, 1764* 110
To Robert Cary & Company, *September 20, 1765* 113
To Joseph Thompson, *July 2, 1766* 118
To John Posey, *June 24, 1767* 118
To Capel and Osgood Hanbury, *July 25, 1767* 122
To William Crawford, *September 17, 1767* 123
To Jonathan Boucher, *May 30, 1768* 126
To Robert Cary & Company, *June 6, 1768* 127
To William Ramsay, *January 29, 1769* 129
To George Mason, *April 5, 1769* 129
To Robert Cary & Company, *July 25, 1769* 132
To Charles Washington, *January 31, 1770* 134
To Thomas Johnson, *July 20, 1770* 137
To Jonathan Boucher, *July 9, 1771* 140
To Jonathan Boucher, *May 21, 1772* 143
To Benedict Calvert, *April 3, 1773* 144
To Burwell Bassett, *June 20, 1773* 146
To George Muse, *January 29, 1774* 147

To George William Fairfax, *June 10, 1774* 148
To Bryan Fairfax, *July 4, 1774* 152
To Bryan Fairfax, *July 20, 1774* 153
To Bryan Fairfax, *August 24, 1774* 157
To Robert McKenzie, *October 9, 1774* 159
To John West, *January 13, 1775* 161
To John Connolly, *February 25, 1775* 162
To George William Fairfax, *May 31, 1775* 163

COMMANDER OF THE CONTINENTAL ARMY, 1775–1783

Address to the Continental Congress,
 June 16, 1775 167
To Martha Washington, *June 18, 1775* 167
To Burwell Bassett, *June 19, 1775* 169
To John Augustine Washington, *June 20, 1775* 171
To the Officers of Five Virginia Companies,
 June 20, 1775 172
To Martha Washington, *June 23, 1775* 173
Address to the New York Provincial Congress,
 June 26, 1775 174
General Orders, *July 4, 1775* 174
To Richard Henry Lee, *July 10, 1775* 177
To John Augustine Washington, *July 27, 1775* 179
To Thomas Gage, *August 11, 1775* 181
To Thomas Gage, *August 19, 1775* 182
To Lund Washington, *August 20, 1775* 183
To the Inhabitants of Bermuda, *September 6, 1775* 186
To the Inhabitants of Canada, *c. September 14, 1775* . . . 187
To William Woodford, *November 10, 1775* 189
To Lund Washington, *November 26, 1775* 190
To Benedict Arnold, *December 5, 1775* 192
To Joseph Reed, *December 15, 1775* 193
General Orders, *January 1, 1776* 196
To Joseph Reed, *January 4, 1776* 198
To Joseph Reed, *January 14, 1776* 200
To Joseph Reed, *January 31, 1776* 205
To Joseph Reed, *February 1, 1776* 207
To John Hancock, *February 9, 1776* 208
To Joseph Reed, *February 10, 1776* 211
To Phillis Wheatley, *February 28, 1776* 216

To John Hancock, *March 19, 1776* 216

To John Augustine Washington, *March 31, 1776* 218

To John Augustine Washington, *May 31, 1776* 223

General Orders, *July 2, 1776* 225

General Orders, *July 9, 1776* 227

To John Hancock, *July 14, 1776* 228

To Adam Stephen, *July 20, 1776* 232

General Orders, *August 1, 1776* 233

To Lund Washington, *August 19, 1776* 234

General Orders, *August 23, 1776* 238

To John Hancock, *September 8, 1776* 240

To John Augustine Washington, *September 22, 1776* . . . 244

To John Hancock, *September 24, 1776* 248

To Lund Washington, *September 30, 1776* 248

To the Massachusetts General Court, *November 6, 1776* . . 251

To John Augustine Washington, *November 6, 1776* . . . 252

To John Hancock, *December 5, 1776* 256

To Lund Washington, *December 10, 1776* 258

To John Hancock, *December 27, 1776* 262

To Robert Morris, George Clymer, and George Walton,
   January 1, 1777 264

To John Hancock, *January 5, 1777* 266

Proclamation Concerning Loyalists, *January 25, 1777* . . 269

To Benedict Arnold, *April 3, 1777* 270

To Alexander Spotswood, *April 30, 1777* 271

To James Warren, *May 23, 1777* 271

To John Hancock, *September 11, 1777* 274

To Richard Henry Lee, *October 17, 1777* 275

To John Augustine Washington, *October 18, 1777* 276

To Israel Putnam, *October 19, 1777* 279

To Thomas Conway, *c. November 5, 1777* 280

General Orders, *December 17, 1777* 280

To Henry Laurens, *December 23, 1777* 281

To Henry Laurens, *January 2, 1778* 286

To Horatio Gates, *January 4, 1778* 287

To William Howe, *January 30, 1778* 289

To Henry Laurens, *January 31, 1778* 290

To William Gordon, *February 15, 1778* 291

To George Clinton, *February 16, 1778* 292

To Bryan Fairfax, *March 1, 1778* 293
General Orders, *March 1, 1778* 295
To John Banister, *April 21, 1778* 298
To John Augustine Washington, *May 1778* 305
General Orders, *May 5, 1778* 307
To Robert Morris, *May 25, 1778* 309
To Landon Carter, *May 30, 1778* 310
To Henry Laurens, *July 1, 1778* 313
To Thomas Nelson, *August 20, 1778* 319
To Comte d'Estaing, *September 11, 1778* 321
To Gouverneur Morris, *October 4, 1778* 325
To Henry Laurens, *November 14, 1778* 327
To Benjamin Harrison, *December 18, 1778* 330
To Lund Washington, *February 24, 1779* 334
To Thomas Nelson, *March 15, 1779* 336
To Henry Laurens, *March 20, 1779* 337
To George Mason, *March 27, 1779* 338
To James Warren, *March 31, 1779* 341
To Elias Boudinot, *May 3, 1779* 344
To William Maxwell, *May 7, 1779* 345
To Gouverneur Morris, *May 8, 1779* 347
Speech to the Delaware Chiefs, *May 12, 1779* 349
Circular to State Governments, *May 22, 1779* 352
To Marquis de Lafayette, *July 4, 1779* 354
To John Cochran, *August 16, 1779* 355
To Lund Washington, *August 17, 1779* 356
To John Jay, *September 7, 1779* 358
To Marquis de Lafayette, *September 30, 1779* 360
To Benjamin Harrison, *October 25, 1779* 366
To Robert Howe, *November 20, 1779* 369
To Joseph Jones, *May 14, 1780* 371
To Joseph Reed, *May 28, 1780* 373
To Joseph Jones, *May 31, 1780* 377
To John Augustine Washington, *June 6, 1780* 379
To Benedict Arnold, *August 3, 1780* 381
To Joseph Jones, *August 13, 1780* 382
Circular to State Governments, *August 27, 1780* 385
To Samuel Huntington, *September 26, 1780* 387

To Henry Clinton, *September 30, 1780* 388

Instructions to Spies Going into New York,
  c. September 1780 389

To John Cadwalader, *October 5, 1780* 390

To John Laurens, *October 13, 1780* 392

Circular to State Governments, *October 18, 1780* 393

To William Fitzhugh, *October 22, 1780* 400

To George Mason, *October 22, 1780* 401

To Benjamin Franklin, *December 20, 1780* 402

To James Duane, *December 26, 1780* 404

Circular to New England State Governments,
  January 5, 1781 406

To John Laurens, *January 15, 1781* 408

To Sarah Bache, *January 15, 1781* 412

To Robert Howe, *January 22, 1781* 413

Circular to State Governments, *January 22, 1781* 414

General Orders, *January 30, 1781* 415

To John Parke Custis, *February 28, 1781* 417

To Lund Washington, *April 30, 1781* 420

Journal of the Yorktown Campaign,
  May 1–November 5, 1781 421

To Charles Cornwallis, *October 17, 1781* 464

To Thomas McKean, *October 19, 1781* 464

To Thomas Nelson, *October 27, 1781* 466

To Thomas McKean, *November 15, 1781* 468

To Lewis Nicola, *May 22, 1782* 468

To John Price Posey, *August 7, 1782* 469

To Thomas Paine, *September 18, 1782* 471

To Benjamin Lincoln, *October 2, 1782* 472

To James McHenry, *October 17, 1782* 474

To Benjamin Franklin, *October 18, 1782* 476

To William Gordon, *October 23, 1782* 477

To Joseph Jones, *December 14, 1782* 478

To Tench Tilghman, *January 10, 1783* 480

To Bushrod Washington, *January 15, 1783* 482

To Nathanael Greene, *February 6, 1783* 484

To Thomas Jefferson, *February 10, 1783* 485

To Lund Washington, *February 12, 1783* 486

To Alexander Hamilton, *March 4, 1783* 487

General Orders, *March 11, 1783* 490

To Alexander Hamilton, *March 12, 1783* 491

To Joseph Jones, *March 12, 1783* 493

To Elias Boudinot, *March 12, 1783* 495

Speech to the Officers of the Army, *March 15, 1783* 496

To Elias Boudinot, *March 16, 1783* 500

To Joseph Jones, *March 18, 1783* 501

To Lund Washington, *March 19, 1783* 502

To Nathanael Greene, *March 31, 1783* 504

To Alexander Hamilton, *March 31, 1783* 504

To Theodorick Bland, *April 4, 1783* 506

To Marquis de Lafayette, *April 5, 1783* 508

To Guy Carleton, *April 9, 1783* 511

General Orders, *April 18, 1783* 512

To Tench Tilghman, *April 24, 1783* 515

Circular to State Governments, *June 8, 1783* 516

To John Augustine Washington, *June 15, 1783* 526

To Elias Boudinot, *June 17, 1783* 528

To William Gordon, *July 8, 1783* 530

To Robert Stewart, *August 10, 1783* 533

To James Duane, *September 7, 1783* 535

To Lund Washington, *September 20, 1783* 541

Farewell Address to the Armies of the United States,
November 2, 1783 542

To Thomas Mifflin, *December 20, 1783* 546

Address to Congress on Resigning Commission,
December 23, 1783 547

THE CONFEDERATION PERIOD, 1783–1789

To George Clinton, *December 28, 1783* 551

To Benjamin Harrison, *January 18, 1784* 551

To Marquis de Lafayette, *February 1, 1784* 553

To Tench Tilghman, *March 24, 1784* 555

To James Craik, *March 25, 1784* 556

To Marquise de Lafayette, *April 4, 1784* 557

To William Gordon, *May 8, 1784* 559

To Benjamin Harrison, *October 10, 1784* 559

To Richard Henry Lee, *December 14, 1784* 567

To William Gordon, *December 20, 1784* 569

To Benjamin Harrison, *January 22, 1785* 570
To George William Fairfax, *February 27, 1785* 572
To Francis Hopkinson, *May 16, 1785* 576
To Tench Tilghman, *June 2, 1785* 577
To William Goddard, *June 11, 1785* 578
To David Humphreys, *July 25, 1785* 579
To Marquis de Lafayette, *July 25, 1785* 582
To Edmund Randolph, *July 30, 1785* 586
To James McHenry, *August 22, 1785* 587
To George Mason, *October 3, 1785* 590
To James Warren, *October 7, 1785* 591
To Robert Morris, *April 12, 1786* 593
To Marquis de Lafayette, *May 10, 1786* 594
To William Fitzhugh, *May 15, 1786* 598
To John Jay, *May 18, 1786* 599
To Thomas Jefferson, *August 1, 1786* 600
To Arthur Young, *August 6, 1786* 602
To John Jay, *August 15, 1786* 605
To John Francis Mercer, *September 9, 1786* 607
To Henry Lee, *October 31, 1786* 608
Comments on David Humphreys' Biography
   of Washington, *c. October 1786* 610
To James Madison, *November 5, 1786* 621
To James Madison, *November 18, 1786* 623
To James Madison, *December 16, 1786* 624
To Edmund Randolph, *December 21, 1786* 627
To Henry Knox, *December 26, 1786* 628
To David Humphreys, *December 26, 1786* 631
To Henry Knox, *February 3, 1787* 634
To Mary Ball Washington, *February 15, 1787* 636
To Henry Knox, *February 25, 1787* 640
To Henry Knox, *March 8, 1787* 641
To John Jay, *March 10, 1787* 642
To Edmund Randolph, *March 28, 1787* 644
To James Madison, *March 31, 1787* 646
To Edmund Randolph, *April 9, 1787* 649
Contract with Philip Bater, *April 23, 1787* 650
To Marquis de Lafayette, *June 6, 1787* 651
To Alexander Hamilton, *July 10, 1787* 652

To John Cannon, *September 16, 1787* 653
To the Continental Congress, *September 17, 1787* 654
Diary Entry, *September 17, 1787* 655
To Patrick Henry, *September 24, 1787* 656
To David Humphreys, *October 10, 1787* 656
To Henry Knox, *October 15, 1787* 658
To Bushrod Washington, *November 9, 1787* 659
To Thomas Jefferson, *January 1, 1788* 663
To Edmund Randolph, *January 8, 1788* 666
To Marquis de Lafayette, *February 7, 1788* 667
To John Armstrong, *April 25, 1788* 670
To Marquis de Chastellux, *April 25, 1788* 674
To Marquis de Lafayette, *April 28, 1788* 676
To Marquis de Lafayette, *May 28, 1788* 680
To Marquis de Lafayette, *June 19, 1788* 682
To Richard Henderson, *June 19, 1788* 685
To Benjamin Lincoln, *June 29, 1788* 688
To Noah Webster, *July 31, 1788* 689
To Alexander Hamilton, *August 28, 1788* 691
To Edward Newenham, *August 29, 1788* 693
To Alexander Hamilton, *October 3, 1788* 696
To Benjamin Lincoln, *October 26, 1788* 698
Reflection on Slavery, *c. 1788–1789* 701
Fragments of a Draft of the First Inaugural Address,
  c. January 1789 702
To Marquis de Lafayette, *January 29, 1789* 716
To Richard Conway, *March 4, 1789* 719
To George Steptoe Washington, *March 23, 1789* 719
To James Madison, *March 30, 1789* 723
To Thomas Green, *March 31, 1789* 724
To Henry Knox, *April 1, 1789* 726

PRESIDENT, 1789–1797
Reply to Charles Thomson, *April 14, 1789* 729
To John Langdon, *April 14, 1789* 729
Diary Entries, *April 16 and 23, 1789* 730
First Inaugural Address, *April 30, 1789* 730
To James Madison, *May 5, 1789* 734
To Edward Rutledge, *May 5, 1789* 735

Reply to the House of Representatives, *May 8, 1789* 736

To John Adams, *May 10, 1789* 736

To the United Baptist Churches in Virginia, *May 1789* . . . 738

To Betty Washington Lewis, *September 13, 1789* 740

To Arthur St. Clair, *October 6, 1789* 743

To Gouverneur Morris, *October 13, 1789* 745

First Annual Message to Congress, *January 8, 1790* 748

To Catharine Macaulay Graham, *January 9, 1790* 751

To Thomas Jefferson, *January 21, 1790* 754

To David Stuart, *March 28, 1790* 756

To Comte de la Luzerne, *April 29, 1790* 758

To David Stuart, *June 15, 1790* 760

To Marquis de Lafayette, *August 11, 1790* 764

To the Hebrew Congregation in Newport,
   Rhode Island, *August 18, 1790* 766

To Henry Knox, *November 19, 1790* 767

Second Annual Message to Congress, *December 8, 1790* . . . 768

To the Chiefs of the Seneca Nation, *December 29, 1790* . . . 772

Message to the Congress Concerning the Seat of
   Government, *January 24, 1791* 776

To David Humphreys, *July 20, 1791* 777

To Marquis de Lafayette, *July 28, 1791* 780

To Gouverneur Morris, *July 28, 1791* 782

To Jean Baptiste Ternant, *September 24, 1791* 785

To Tobias Lear, *October 14, 1791* 785

Third Annual Message to Congress, *October 25, 1791* . . . 786

To Harriot Washington, *October 30, 1791* 793

To Alexander Martin, *November 14, 1791* 794

To Arthur Young, *December 5, 1791* 795

To Gouverneur Morris, *January 28, 1792* 799

To David Stuart, *April 8, 1792* 800

To Isaac Heard, *May 2, 1792* 802

To Comte de Ségur, *May 4, 1792* 803

To James Madison, *May 20, 1792* 804

To Marquis de Lafayette, *June 10, 1792* 807

To Thomas Jefferson, *July 17, 1792* 809

To Alexander Hamilton, *July 29, 1792* 809

To Tobias Lear, *July 30, 1792* 814

To Thomas Jefferson, *August 23, 1792* 815
To Alexander Hamilton, *August 26, 1792* 818
To Edmund Randolph, *August 26, 1792* 820
To John Francis Mercer, *September 26, 1792* 822
To Betty Washington Lewis, *October 7, 1792* 824
To Thomas Jefferson, *October 18, 1792* 825
Fourth Annual Message to Congress, *November 6, 1792* . . 826
Passport for Jean Pierre Blanchard, *January 9, 1793* 832
To Henry Lee, *January 20, 1793* 832
To the Members of the New Church in Baltimore,
   c. January 27, 1793 833
To Frances Bassett Washington, *February 24, 1793* 834
Second Inaugural Address, *March 4, 1793* 835
To Gouverneur Morris, *March 25, 1793* 836
To Thomas Jefferson, *April 12, 1793* 837
To the Earl of Buchan, *April 22, 1793* 837
Proclamation of Neutrality, *April 22, 1793* 840
To Henry Lee, *July 21, 1793* 840
To Edmund Pendleton, *September 23, 1793* 842
To William Pearce, *October 6, 1793* 844
Fifth Annual Message to Congress, *December 3, 1793* . . . 846
To Arthur Young, *December 12, 1793* 851
To William Pearce, *December 18, 1793* 859
To Thomas Jefferson, *January 1, 1794* 864
To Tobias Lear, *May 6, 1794* 865
Proclamation Calling Forth the Militia, *August 7, 1794* . . . 870
To Charles Mynn Thruston, *August 10, 1794* 873
To Henry Lee, *August 26, 1794* 875
To John Jay, *August 30, 1794* 879
To Elizabeth Parke Custis, *September 14, 1794* 881
Proclamation Concerning the "Whiskey Rebellion,"
   September 25, 1794 882
To Burges Ball, *September 25, 1794* 884
To Edmund Randolph, *October 16, 1794* 886
Sixth Annual Message to Congress, *November 19, 1794* . . . 887
To William Pearce, *November 23, 1794* 895
To Alexander Spotswood, *November 23, 1794* 899
To Eleanor Parke Custis, *January 16, 1795* 900

To Edmund Pendleton, *January 22, 1795* 903

To the Commissioners of the District of Columbia,
    January 28, 1795 905

To Charles Carter, *March 10, 1795* 907

To Thomas Jefferson, *March 15, 1795* 908

To William Pearce, *May 10, 1795* 910

To Alexander Hamilton, *July 3, 1795* 912

To Alexander Hamilton, *July 29, 1795* 914

To Henry Knox, *September 20, 1795* 916

To Patrick Henry, *October 9, 1795* 918

Seventh Annual Message to Congress, *December 8, 1795* . . 919

To Gouverneur Morris, *December 22, 1795* 924

To the Cabinet, *March 25, 1796* 929

To the House of Representatives, *March 30, 1796* 930

To Alexander Hamilton, *March 31, 1796* 933

To Alexander Hamilton, *May 8, 1796* 934

To Alexander Hamilton, *May 15, 1796* 938

Draft of the Farewell Address, *May 15, 1796* 940

To Alexander Hamilton, *June 26, 1796* 948

To Thomas Jefferson, *July 6, 1796* 951

To Alexander Hamilton, *August 25, 1796* 954

Address to the Cherokee Nation, *August 29, 1796* 956

To Alexander Hamilton, *September 1, 1796* 960

Farewell Address, *September 19, 1796* 962

Eighth Annual Message to Congress, *December 7, 1796* . . . 978

To John Greenwood, *January 20, 1797* 985

To Henry Knox, *March 2, 1797* 986

To Jonathan Trumbull, Jr., *March 3, 1797* 988

RETIREMENT, 1797–1799

To James McHenry, *April 3, 1797* 993

To William Heath, *May 20, 1797* 994

To James McHenry, *May 29, 1797* 996

To David Humphreys, *June 26, 1797* 997

To the Earl of Buchan, *July 4, 1797* 999

To Samuel Washington, *July 12, 1797* 1001

To Lawrence Lewis, *August 4, 1797* 1002

To Sarah Cary Fairfax, *May 16, 1798* 1003

To John Adams, *July 13, 1798* 1005

To John Adams, *September 25, 1798* 1007

To Landon Carter, *October 5, 1798* 1015

To Alexander Spotswood, *November 22, 1798* 1015

To Patrick Henry, *January 15, 1799* 1016

To James McHenry, *January 27, 1799* 1019

To James Welch, *April 7, 1799* 1021

Last Will and Testament, *July 9, 1799* 1022

To Jonathan Trumbull, Jr., *July 21, 1799* 1042

To James McHenry, *August 11, 1799* 1045

To Robert Lewis, *August 18, 1799* 1047

To Jonathan Trumbull, Jr., *August 30, 1799* 1048

To Burges Ball, *September 22, 1799* 1050

To Alexander Hamilton, *December 12, 1799* 1051

To James Anderson, *December 13, 1799* 1051

Chronology 1055

Note on the Texts 1076

Notes 1094

Index 1129

THE COLONIAL PERIOD
1747–1775

"Rules of Civility & Decent Behaviour In Company and Conversation"

1ˢᵗ Every Action done in Company, ought to be with Some Sign of Respect, to those that are Present.

2ᵈ When in Company, put not your Hands to any Part of the Body, not usualy Discovered.

3ᵈ Shew Nothing to your Freind that may affright him.

4 In the Presence of Others Sing not to yourself with a humming Noise, nor Drum with your Fingers or Feet.

5ᵗʰ If You Cough, Sneeze, Sigh, or Yawn, do it not Loud but Privately; and Speak not in your Yawning, but put Your handkercheif or Hand before your face and turn aside.

6ᵗʰ Sleep not when others Speak, Sit not when others stand, Speak not when you Should hold your Peace, walk not on when others Stop.

7ᵗʰ Put not off your Cloths in the presence of Others, nor go out your Chamber half Drest

8ᵗʰ At Play and at Fire its Good manners to Give Place to the last Commer, and affect not to Speak Louder than Ordinary

9ᵗʰ Spit not in the Fire, nor Stoop low before it neither Put your Hands into the Flames to warm them, nor Set your Feet upon the Fire especially if there be meat before it

10ᵗʰ When you Sit down, Keep your Feet firm and Even, without putting one on the other or Crossing them

11ᵗʰ Shift not yourself in the Sight of others nor Gnaw your nails

12ᵗʰ Shake not the head, Feet, or Legs rowl not the Eys lift not one eyebrow higher than the other wry not the mouth, and bedew no mans face with your Spittle, by approaching too near him when you Speak

13ᵗʰ Kill no Vermin as Fleas, lice ticks &c in the Sight of Others, if you See any filth or thick Spittle put your foot Dexteriously upon it if it be upon the Cloths of your Companions, Put it off privately, and if it be upon your own Cloths return Thanks to him who puts it off

14ᵗʰ Turn not your Back to others especially in Speaking, Jog not the Table or Desk on which Another reads or writes, lean not upon any one

3

15th Keep your Nails clean and Short, also your Hands and Teeth Clean yet without Shewing any great Concern for them

16th Do not Puff up the Cheeks, Loll not out the tongue rub the Hands, or beard, thrust out the lips, or bite them or keep the Lips too open or too Close

17th Be no Flatterer, neither Play with any that delights not to be Play'd Withal.

18th Read no Letters, Books, or Papers in Company but when there is a Necessity for the doing of it you must ask leave: come not near the Books or Writings of Another so as to read them unless desired or give your opinion of them unask'd also look not nigh when another is writing a Letter.

19th let your Countenance be pleasant but in Serious Matters Somewhat grave.

20th The Gestures of the Body must be Suited to the discourse you are upon.

21st Reproach none for the Infirmaties of Nature, nor Delight to Put them that have in mind thereof.

22[d] Shew not yourself glad at the Misfortune of another though he were your enemy.

23[d] When you see a Crime punished, you may be inwardly Pleased; but always shew Pity to the Suffering Offender

24th Do not laugh too loud or too much at any Publick Spectacle.

25th Superfluous Complements and all Affectation of Ceremonie are to be avoided, yet where due they are not to be Neglected

26th In Pulling off your Hat to Persons of Distinction, as Noblemen, Justices, Churchmen &c make a Reverence, bowing more or less according to the Custom of the Better Bred, and Quality of the Person. Amongst your equals expect not always that they Should begin with you first, but to Pull off the Hat when there is no need is Affectation, in the Manner of Saluting and resaluting in words keep to the most usual Custom

27th Tis ill manners to bid one more eminent than yourself be covered as well as not to do it to whom it's due Likewise he that makes too much haste to Put on his hat does not well, yet he ought to Put it on at the first, or at most the Second time of being ask'd; now what is herein Spoken, of Qualification in behaviour in Saluting, ought also to be observed in taking of Place, and Sitting down for ceremonies without Bounds is troublesome

28th If any one come to Speak to you while you are are Sitting Stand up tho he be your Inferiour, and when you Present Seats let it be to every one according to his Degree

29th When you meet with one of Greater Quality than yourself, Stop, and retire especially if it be at a Door or any Straight place to give way for him to Pass

30th In walking the highest Place in most Countrys Seems to be on the right hand therefore Place yourself on the left of him whom you desire to Honour: but if three walk together the mid Place is the most Honourable the wall is usually given to the most worthy if two walk together

31st If any one far Surpassess others, either in age, Estate, or Merit yet would give Place to a meaner than himself in his own lodging or elsewhere the one ought not to except it, So he on the other part should not use much earnestness nor offer it above once or twice.

32^{d} To one that is your equal, or not much inferior you are to give the cheif Place in your Lodging and he to who 'tis offered ought at the first to refuse it but at the Second to accept though not without acknowledging his own unworthiness.

33^{d} They that are in Dignity or in office have in all places Preceedency but whilst they are Young they ought to respect those that are their equals in Birth or other Qualitys, though they have no Publick charge.

34th It is good Manners to prefer them to whom we Speak before ourselves especially if they be above us with whom in no Sort we ought to begin.

35th Let your Discourse with Men of Business be Short and Comprehensive.

36th Artificers & Persons of low Degree ought not to use many ceremonies to Lords, or Others of high Degree but Respect and highly Honour them, and those of high Degree ought to treat them with affibility & Courtesie, without Arrogancy

37th In Speaking to men of Quality do not lean nor Look them full in the Face, nor approach too near them at lest Keep a full Pace from them

38th In visiting the Sick, do not Presently play the Physicion if you be not Knowing therein

39th In writing or Speaking, give to every Person his due Title According to his Degree & the Custom of the Place.

40th Strive not with your Superiers in argument, but always Submit your Judgment to others with Modesty

41st Undertake not to Teach your equal in the art himself Proffesses; it Savours of arrogancy

42[d] Let thy ceremonies in Courtesie be proper to the Dignity of his place with whom thou conversest for it is absurd to act y[e] same with a Clown and a Prince

43[d] Do not express Joy before one sick or in pain for that contrary Passion will aggravate his Misery.

44th When a man does all he can though it Succeeds not well blame not him that did it.

45th Being to advise or reprehend any one, consider whether it ought to be in publick or in Private; presently, or at Some other time in what terms to do it & in reproving Shew no Sign of Cholar but do it with all Sweetness and Mildness

46th Take all Admonitions thankfully in what Time or Place Soever given but afterwards not being culpable take a Time & Place convenient to let him him know it that gave them.

47th Mock not nor Jest at any thing of Importance break no Jest that are Sharp Biting and if you Deliver any thing witty and Pleasent abtain from Laughing thereat yourself.

48th Wherein wherein you reprove Another be unblameable yourself; for example is more prevalent than Precepts

49 Use no Reproachfull Language against any one neither Curse nor Revile

50th Be not hasty to beleive flying Reports to the Disparagment of any

51st Wear not your Cloths, foul, unript or Dusty but See they be Brush'd once every day at least and take heed that you approach not to any uncleaness

52[d] In your Apparel be Modest and endeavour to accomodate Nature, rather than to procure Admiration keep to the Fashion of your equals Such as are Civil and orderly with respect to Times and Places

53[d] Run not in the Streets, neither go too slowly nor with

Mouth open go not Shaking y^r Arms kick not the earth with y^r feet, go not upon the Toes, nor in a Dancing fashion.

54th Play not the Peacock, looking every where about you, to See if you be well Deck't, if your Shoes fit well if your Stokings Sit neatly, and Cloths handsomely.

55th Eat not in the Streets, nor in ye House, out of Season

56th Associate yourself with Men of good Quality if you Esteem your own Reputation; for 'tis better to be alone than in bad Company

57th In walking up and Down in a House, only with One in Company if he be Greater than yourself, at the first give him the Right hand and Stop not till he does and be not the first that turns, and when you do turn let it be with your face towards him, if he be a Man of Great Quality, walk not with him Cheek by Joul but Somewhat behind him; but yet in Such a Manner that he may easily Speak to you

58th Let your Conversation be without Malice or Envy, for 'tis a Sign of a Tractable and Commendable Nature: And in all Causes of Passion admit Reason to Govern

59th Never express anything unbecoming, nor Act agst ye Rules Moral before your inferiours

60th Be not immodest in urging your Freinds to Discover a Secret

61st Utter not base and frivilous things amongst grave and Learn'd Men nor very Difficult Questians or Subjects, among the Ignorant or things hard to be believed, Stuff not your Discourse with Sentences amongst your Betters nor Equals

62^d Speak not of doleful Things in a Time of Mirth or at the Table; Speak not of Melancholy Things as Death and Wounds, and if others Mention them Change if you can the Discourse tell not your Dreams, but to your intimate Friend

63^d A Man ought not to value himself of his Atchievements, or rare Qualities of wit; much less of his riches Virtue or Kindred

64th Break not a Jest where none take pleasure in mirth Laugh not aloud, nor at all without Occasion, deride no mans Misfortune, tho' there seem to be Some cause

65th Speak not injurious Words neither in Jest nor Earnest Scoff at none although they give Occasion

66th Be not froward but friendly and Courteous; the first to

Salute hear and answer & be not Pensive when it's a time to Converse

67th Detract not from others neither be excessive in Commanding

68th Go not thither, where you know not, whether you Shall be Welcome or not. Give not Advice whth being Ask'd & when desired do it briefly

69 If two contend together take not the part of either unconstrained; and be not obstinate in your own Opinion, in Things indiferent be of the Major Side

70th Reprehend not the imperfections of others for that belongs to Parents Masters and Superiours

71st Gaze not on the marks or blemishes of Others and ask not how they came. What you may Speak in Secret to your Friend deliver not before others

72^d Speak not in an unknown Tongue in Company but in your own Language and that as those of Quality do and not as ye Vulgar; Sublime matters treat Seriously

73^d Think before you Speak pronounce not imperfectly nor bring out your Words too hastily but orderly & distinctly

74th When Another Speaks be attentive your Self and disturb not the Audience if any hesitate in his Words help him not nor Prompt him without desired, Interrupt him not, nor Answer him till his Speech be ended

75th In the midst of Discourse ask not of what one treateth but if you Perceive any Stop because of your coming you may well intreat him gently to Proceed: If a Person of Quality comes in while your Conversing it's handsome to Repeat what was said before

76th While you are talking, Point not with your Finger at him of Whom you Discourse nor Approach too near him to whom you talk especially to his face

77th Treat with men at fit Times about Business & Whisper not in the Company of Others

78th Make no Comparisons and if any of the Company be Commended for any brave act of Vertue, commend not another for the Same

79th Be not apt to relate News if you know not the truth thereof. In Discoursing of things you Have heard Name not your Author always A Secret Discover not

80th Be not Tedious in Discourse or in reading unless you find the Company pleased therewith

81st Be not Curious to Know the Affairs of Others neither approach those that Speak in Private

82[d] Undertake not what you cannot Perform but be Carefull to keep your Promise

83[d] When you deliver a matter do it without Passion & with Discretion, however mean y[e] Person be you do it too

84th When your Superiours talk to any Body hearken not neither Speak nor Laugh

85th In Company of these of Higher Quality than yourself Speak not till you are ask'd a Question then Stand upright put of your Hat & Answer in few words

86 In Disputes, be not So Desireous to Overcome as not to give Liberty to each one to deliver his Opinion and Submit to y[e] Judgment of y[e] Major Part especially if they are Judges of the Dispute

87th Let thy carriage be such as becomes a Man Grave Settled and attentive to that which is spoken. Contradict not at every turn what others Say

88th Be not tedious in Discourse, make not many Digressions, nor repeat often the Same manner of Discourse

89th Speak not Evil of the absent for it is unjust

90 Being Set at meat Scratch not neither Spit Cough or blow your Nose except there's a Necessity for it

91st Make no Shew of taking great Delight in your Victuals, Feed not with Greediness; cut your Bread with a Knife, lean not on the Table neither find fault with what you Eat

92 Take no Salt or cut Bread with your Knife Greasy

93 Entertaining any one at table it is decent to present him w[t] meat, Undertake not to help others undesired by y[e] Master

94th If you Soak bread in the Sauce let it be no more than what you put in your Mouth at a time and blow not your broth at Table but Stay till Cools of it Self

95th Put not your meat to your Mouth with your Knife in your hand neither Spit forth the Stones of any fruit Pye upon a Dish nor Cast anything under the table

96 It's unbecoming to Stoop much to ones Meat Keep your Fingers clean & when foul wipe them on a Corner of your Table Napkin

97th Put not another bit into your Mouth til the former be Swallowed let not your Morsels be too big for the Gowls.

98th Drink not nor talk with your mouth full neither Gaze about you while you are a Drinking

99th Drink not too leisurely nor yet too hastily. Before and after Drinking wipe your Lips breath not then or Ever with too Great a Noise, for its uncivil

100 Cleanse not your teeth with the Table Cloth Napkin Fork or Knife but if Others do it let it be done w[t] a Pick Tooth

101st Rince not your Mouth in the Presence of Others

102[d] It is out of use to call upon the Company often to Eat nor need you Drink to others every Time you Drink

103[d] In Company of your Betters be not longer in eating than they are lay not your Arm but only your hand upon the table

104th It belongs to y[e] Chiefest in Company to unfold his Napkin and fall to Meat first, But he ought then to Begin in time & to Dispatch with Dexterity that y[e] Slowest may have time allowed him

105th Be not Angry at Table whatever happens & if you have reason to be so, Shew it not but on a Chearfull Countenance especially if there be Strangers for Good Humour makes one Dish of Meat a Feast

106th Set not yourself at y[e] upper of y[e] Table but if it be your Due or that y[e] Master of y[e] house will have it So, Contend not, least you Should Trouble y[e] Company

107th If others talk at Table be attentive but talk not with Meat in your Mouth

108th When you Speak of God or his Atributes, let it be Seriously & with Reverence. Honour & Obey your Natural Parents altho they be Poor

109th Let your Recreations be Manfull not Sinfull.

110th Labour to keep alive in your Breast that Little Spark of Celestial fire Called Conscience.

Finis

"A Journal of my Journey over the Mountains began Fryday the 11th. of March 1747/8"

Fryday March 11th. 1747/8.   Began my Journey in Company with George Fairfax Esqr.; we travell'd this day 40 Miles to Mr. George Neavels in Prince William County.

Saturday March 12th.   This Morning Mr. James Genn the surveyor came to us. We travel'd over the Blue Ridge to Capt. Ashbys on Shannondoa River. Nothing remarkable happen'd.

Sunday March 13.   Rode to his Lordships Quarter about 4 Miles higher up the River we went through most beautiful Groves of Sugar Trees & spent the best part of the Day in admiring the Trees & richness of the Land.

Monday 14th.   We sent our Baggage to Capt. Hites (near Frederick Town) went ourselves down the River about 16 Miles to Capt. Isaac Penningtons (the Land exceeding Rich & Fertile all the way produces abundance of Grain Hemp Tobacco &c.) in order to Lay of some Lands on Cates Marsh & Long Marsh.

Tuesday 15th.   We set out early with Intent to Run round the sd. Land but being taken in a Rain & it Increasing very fast obliged us to return. It clearing about one oClock & our time being too Precious to Loose we a second time ventured out & Worked hard till Night & then returnd to Penningtons we got our Suppers & was Lighted in to a Room & I not being so good a Woodsman as the rest of my Company striped my self very orderly & went in to the Bed as they call'd it when to my Surprize I found it to be nothing but a Little Straw—Matted together without Sheets or any thing else but only one Thread Bear blanket with double its Weight of Vermin such as Lice Fleas &c. I was glad to get up (as soon as the Light was carried from us) & put on my Cloths & Lay as my Companions. Had we not have been very tired, I am sure we should not have slep'd much that night. I made a Promise not to Sleep so from that time forward chusing rather to sleep in the open Air before a fire as will Appear hereafter.

Wednesday 16th.   We set out early & finish'd about one oClock & then Travell'd up to Frederick Town where our Baggage came to us. We cleaned ourselves (to get Rid of the Game we had catched the Night before) & took a Review of the Town & then return'd to our Lodgings where we had a good Dinner prepar'd for us Wine & Rum Punch in Plenty & a good Feather Bed with clean Sheets which was a very agreeable regale.

Thursday 17th.   Rain'd till Ten oClock & then clearing we reached as far as Major Campbells one of there Burgesses about 25 Miles from Town. Nothing Remarkable this day nor Night but that we had a Tolerable good Bed lay on.

Fryday 18th.   We Travell'd up about 35 Miles to Thomas Barwicks on Potomack where we found the River so excessively high by Reason of the Great Rains that had fallen up about the Allegany Mountains as they told us which was then bringing down the melted Snow & that it would not be fordable for severall Days it was then above Six foot Higher than usual & was Rising. We agreed to stay till Monday. We this day call'd to see the Fam'd Warm Springs. We camped out in the field this Night. Nothing Remarkable happen'd till sunday the 20th.

Sunday 20th.   Finding the River not much abated we in the Evening Swam our horses over & carried them to Charles Polks in Maryland for Pasturage till the next Morning.

Monday 21st.   We went over in a Canoe & Travell'd up Maryland side all the Day in a Continued Rain to Collo. Cresaps right against the Mouth of the South Branch about 40 Miles from Polks I believe the Worst Road that ever was trod by Man or Beast.

Tuesday 22d.   Continued Rain and the Freshes kept us at Cresaps.

Wednesday 23d.   Rain'd till about two oClock & Clear'd when we were agreeably surpris'd at the sight of thirty odd Indians coming from War with only one Scalp. We had some Liquor with us of which we gave them Part it elevating there Spirits put them in the Humour of Dauncing of whom we

had a War Daunce. There Manner of Dauncing is as follows
Viz. They clear a Large Circle & make a great Fire in the
Middle then seats themselves around it the Speaker makes a
grand Speech telling them in what Manner they are to Daunce
after he has finish'd the best Dauncer Jumps up as one awaked
out of a Sleep & Runs & Jumps about the Ring in a most
comicle Manner he is followd by the Rest then begins there
Musicians to Play the Musick is a Pot half of Water with a
Deerskin Streched over it as tight as it can & a goard with
some Shott in it to Rattle & a Piece of an horses Tail tied to
it to make it look fine the one keeps Rattling and the other
Drumming all the While the others is Dauncing.

Fryday 25th. 1748.   Nothing Remarkable on thursday but
only being with the Indians all day so shall slip it. This day
left Cresaps & went up to the Mouth of Patersons Creek &
there swum our Horses over got over ourselves in a Canoe &
travel'd up the following Part of the Day to Abram Johnstones
15 miles from the Mouth where we camped.

Saterday 26.   Travelld up the Creek to Solomon Hedges
Esqr. one of his Majestys Justices of the Peace for the County
of Frederick where we camped. When we came to Supper
there was neither a Cloth upon the Table nor a Knife to eat
with but as good luck would have it we had Knives of own.

Sunday 27th.   Travell'd over to the South Branch (attended with the Esqr.) to Henry Vanmetriss in order to go
about Intended Work of Lots.

Monday 28th.   Travell'd up the Branch about 30 Miles to
Mr. James Rutlidge's Horse Jockey & about 70 Miles from
the Mouth.

Tuesday 29th.   This Morning went out & Survey'd five
Hundred Acres of Land & went down to one Michael Stumps
on the So. Fork of the Branch. On our way Shot two Wild
Turkies.

Wednesday 30th.   This Morning began our Intended Business of Laying of Lots. We began at the Boundary Line of the
Northern 10 Miles above Stumps & run of two Lots & returnd to Stumps.

Thursday 31st.   Early this Morning one of our Men went out with the Gun & soon Returnd with two Wild Turkies. We then went to our Business. Run of three Lots & returnd to our Camping place at Stumps.

Fryday April the 1st. 1748.   This Morning Shot twice at Wild Turkies but killd none. Run of three Lots & returnd to Camp.

Saterday April 2d.   Last Night was a blowing & Rainy night. Our Straw catch'd a Fire that we were laying upon & was luckily Preserv'd by one of our Mens awaking when it was in a [   ] We run of four Lots this day which Reached below Stumps.

Sunday 3d.   Last Night was a much more blostering night than the former. We had our Tent Carried Quite of with the Wind and was obliged to Lie the Latter part of the Night without covering. There came several Persons to see us this day one of our Men Shot a Wild Turkie.

Monday 4th.   This morning Mr. Fairfax left us with Intent to go down to the Mouth of the Branch. We did two Lots & was attended by a great Company of People Men Women & Children that attended us through the Woods as we went shewing there Antick tricks. I really think they seem to be as Ignorant a Set of People as the Indians. They would never speak English but when spoken to they speak all Dutch. This day our Tent was blown down by the Violentness of the Wind.

Tuesday 5th.   We went out & did 4 Lots. We were attended by the same Company of People that we had the day before.

Wednesday 6th.   Last Night was so Intolerably smoaky that we were obliged all hands to leave the Tent to the Mercy of the Wind and Fire this day was attended by our aforesd. Company untill about 12 oClock when we finish'd we travell'd down the Branch to Henry Vanmetris's. On our Journey was catch'd in a very heavy Rain. We got under a Straw House untill the Worst of it was over & then continued our Journy.

Thursday 7th.   Rain'd Successively all Last Night. This

Morning one of our men Killed a Wild Turky that weight 20 Pounds. We went & Surveyd 15 Hundred Acres of Land & Returnd to Vanmetris's about 1 oClock. About two I heard that Mr. Fairfax was come up & at 1 Peter Casseys about 2 Miles of in the same Old Field. I then took my Horse & went up to see him. We eat our Dinners & Walked down to Vanmetris's. We stayed about two Hours & Walked back again and slept in Casseys House which was the first Night I had slept in a House since I came to the Branch.

Fryday 8th.   We breakfasted at Casseys & Rode down to Vanmetris's to get all our Company together which when we had accomplished we Rode down below the Trough in order to Lay of Lots there. We laid of one this day. The Trough is couple of Ledges of Mountain Impassable running side & side together for above 7 or 8 Miles & the River down between them. You must Ride Round the back of the Mountain for to get below them. We Camped this Night in the Woods near a Wild Meadow where was a Large Stack of Hay. After we had Pitched our Tent & made a very Large Fire we pull'd out our Knapsack in order to Recruit ourselves. Every was his own Cook. Our Spits was Forked Sticks our Plates was a Large Chip as for Dishes we had none.

Saterday 9th.   Set the Surveyors to work whilst Mr. Fairfax & myself stayed at the Tent our Provision being all exhausted & the Person that was to bring us a Recruit disappointing us we were obliged to go without untill we could get some from the Neighbours which was not till about 4 or 5 oClock in the Evening. We then took our Leaves of the Rest of our Company Road Down to John Colins in order to set off next Day homewards.

Sunday 10th.   We took our farewell of the Branch & travelld over Hills and Mountains to 1 Coddys on Great Cacapehon about 40 Miles.

Monday 11th.   We Travell'd from Coddys down to Frederick Town where we Reached about 12 oClock. We dined in Town and then went to Capt. Hites & Lodged.

Tuesday 12th.   We set of from Capt. Hites in order to go

over Wms. Gap about 20 Miles and after Riding about 20 Miles we had 20 to go for we had lost ourselves & got up as High as Ashbys Bent. We did get over Wms. Gap that Night and as low as Wm. Wests in Fairfax County 18 Miles from the Top of the Ridge. This day see a Rattled Snake the first we had seen in all our Journey.

Wednesday the 13th. of April 1748.   Mr. Fairfax got safe home and I myself safe to my Brothers which concludes my Journal.

To Robin

Dear Friend Robin

As its the greatest mark of friendship and esteem absent Friends can shew each other in Writing and often communicating their thoughts to his fellow companions makes me endeavour to signalize myself in acquainting you from time to time and at all times my situation and employments of Life and could Wish you would take half the Pains of contriving me a Letter by any oppertunity as you may be well assured of its meeting with a very welcome reception my Place of Residence is at present at his Lordships where I might was my heart disengag'd pass my time very pleasantly as theres a very agreeable Young Lady Lives in the same house (Colo. George Fairfax's Wife's sister) but as thats only adding Fuel to fire it makes me the more uneasy for by often and unavoidably being in Company with her revives my former Passion for your Low Land Beauty whereas was I to live more retired from yound Women I might in some measure eliviate my sorrows by burying that chast and troublesome Passion in the grave of oblivion or etarnall forgetfulness for as I am very well assured that's the only antidote or remedy that I ever shall be releivd by or only recess than can administer any cure or help to me as I am well convinced was I ever to attempt any thing I should only get a denial which would be only adding grief to uneasiness.

c. 1749–1750

Design for a Coat

Memorandum to have my Coat made by the following Directions to be made a Frock with a Lapel Breast the Lapel to Contain on each side six Button Holes and to be about 5 or 6 Inches wide all the way equal and to turn as the Breast on the Coat does to have it made very Long Waisted and in Length to come down to or below the Bent of the knee the Waist from the armpit to the Fold to be exactly as long or Longer than from thence to the Bottom not to have more than one fold in the Skirt and the top to be made just to turn in and three Button Holes the Lapel at the top to turn as the Cape of the Coat and Bottom to Come Parrallel with the Button Holes the Last Button hole in the Breast to be right opposite to the Button on the Hip.

c. 1749–1750

Journey to the French Commandant

On Wednesday the 31st. of October 1753 I was Commission'd & appointed by the Honble. Robert Dinwiddie Esqr. Governor &ca. of Virginia

To visit & deliver a Letter to the Commandant of the French Forces on the Ohio, & set out on the intended Journey the same Day. The next I arriv'd at Fredericksburg, & engag'd Mr. Jacob Vanbraam, Interpreter, & proceeded with him to Alexandria where we provided Necessaries. From thence we went to Winchester & got Baggage Horses &ca. & from there we pursued the new Road to Wills Creek, where we arriv'd the 14th: of November.

Here I engag'd Mr. Gist to Pilot us out, & also hired four others as Servitors (vizt.) Barnaby Currin, & John McGuier (Indian Traders) Henry Steward, & William Jenkins; & in Company with those Persons I left the Inhabitants the Day following. The excessive Rains & vast Quantity of Snow that had fallen prevented our reaching Mr. Frazer's, an Indian

Trader at the Mouth of Turtle Creek, on Monongehela, 'til Thursday.

22d: We were inform'd here, that Expresses were sent a few Day's ago to the Traders down the River to acquaint them with the General's Death, & return of Major Part of the French Army into Winter Quarters. The Waters were quite impassable, without Swimming our Horses, which oblig'd us to get the loan of a Canoe from Mr. Frazer, & to send Barnaby Currin & Henry Steward down Monongehela, with our Baggage to meet us at the Forks of Ohio, about 10 Miles to cross Allegany.

As I got down before the Canoe, I spent some Time in viewing the Rivers, & the Land in the Fork, which I think extreamly well situated for a Fort; as it has the absolute Command of both Rivers. The Land at the Point is 20 or 25 Feet above the common Surface of the Water; & a considerable Bottom of flat well timber'd Land all around it, very convenient for Building. The Rivers are each a quarter of a Mile, or more, across, & run here very nigh at Right Angles; Allegany bearing N: E: & Monongehela S: E: The former of these two is a very rapid swift running Water the other deep & still, with scarce any perceptable Fall. About two Miles from this, on the S: E: Side of the River, at the Place where the Ohio Company intended to erect a Fort; lives Singess, King of the Delawars; We call'd upon him to invite him to Council at the Logstown.

As I had taken a good deal of Notice Yesterday of the Situation at the Forks; my Curiosity led me to examine this more particularly; & my Judgement to think it greatly inferior, either for Defence or Advantages, especially the latter; For a Fort at the Forks wou'd be equally well situated on Ohio, & have the entire Command of Monongehela, which runs up to our Settlements & is extreamly well design'd for Water Carriage, as it is of a deep still Nature; besides a Fort at the Fork might be built at a much less Expence, than at the other Place. Nature has well contriv'd the lower Place for Water Defence, but the Hill whereon it must stand, being a quarter of a Mile in Length, & then descending gradually on the Land Side, will render it difficult & very expensive making a sufficient Fortification there. The whole Flat upon the Hill must be taken in, or the Side next the Descent made extreamly high;

or else the Hill cut away: otherwise the Enemy will raise Batteries within that Distance, without being expos'd to a single Shot from the Fort.

Singess attended us to Logstown, where we arriv'd between Sunsetting & Dark, the 25th: Day after I left Williamsburg. We travel'd over some extream good & bad Land to get to this Place. As soon as I came into Town, I went to Monacatoocha (as the Half King was out at his hunting Cabbin on little Bever Creek, about 15 Miles off) & inform'd him, by John Davison Interpreter that I was sent a Messenger to the French General, & was ordered to call upon the Sachems of the Six Nations, to acquaint them with it. I gave him a String of Wampum, & a twist of Tobacco, & desir'd him to send for the Half King; which he promis'd to do by a Runner in the Morning, & for other Sachems. I invited him & the other Great Men present to my Tent, where they stay'd an Hour & return'd.

According to the best Observations I cou'd make, Mr. Gist's new Settlement (which we pass'd by) bears about W: N: W: 70 Miles from Wills Creek, Shanapins, or the Forks N: B: W: or N: N: W: about 50 Miles from that; & from thence to the Logstown, the Course is nearly West, about 18 or 20 Miles; so that the whole Distance, as we went & computed it, is at least 135 or 40 Miles from our back Settlements.

25th: Came to Town four of ten French Men that Deserted from a Company at the Cuscusas, which lies at the Mouth of this River; I got the following Account from them. They were sent from New Orlians with 100 Men, & 8 Canoe load of Provisions, to this Place; where they expected to have met the same Number of Men, from the Forts this Side Lake Erie to convoy them, & the Horses up, but were not arriv'd when they ran off. I enquir'd into the Situation of the French on the Mississippi, their Number, & what Forts they had Built: They inform'd me that there were four small Forts between New Orlians, & the Black Islands, Garrison'd with about 30 or 40 Men, & a few small Pieces of Cannon in each. That at New Orlians, which is near the Mouth of the Mississippi, there is 35 Companies of 40 Men each, with a pretty strong Fort, mounting 8 large Carriage Guns; & at the Black Islands there is several Companies, & a Fort with 6 Guns. The Black Islands is about 130 Leagues above the Mouth of the Ohio, which is 150 above New Orlians: They also acquainted me, that there was a small Palisadoed Fort on the Ohio, at the Mouth of the Obaish, about 60 Leagues from the Mississippi: the Obaish heads near the West End of Lake Erie, & affords the Com-munication between the French on Mississippi, & those on the Lakes. These Deserters came up from the lower Shawnesse Town, with one Brown an Indian Trader, & were going to Philadelphia.

About 3 o'Clock this Evening the Half King came to Town; I went up & invited him & Davison privately to my Tent, & desir'd him to relate some of the Particulars of his Journey to the French Commandant, & reception there, & to give me an Account of the Way & Distance. He told me that the near-est & levelest Way was now impassable, by reason of the many large miry Savannas; that we must be oblig'd to go by Venan-go, & shou'd not get to the near Fort under 5 or 6 Nights Sleep, good Traveling. When he went to the Fort he said he was receiv'd in a very stern Manner by the late Commander, who ask'd him very abruptly, what he had come about, & to declare his Business; which he says he did in the following Speech.

FATHERS I am come to tell you your own Speeches, what your own Mouths have declar'd. FATHERS You in former Days set a Silver Bason before us wherein there was the Leg of a Beaver, and desir'd of all Nations to come & eat of it; to eat in Peace & Plenty, & not to be Churlish to one another; & that if any such Person shou'd be found to be a Disturber; I here lay down by the Edge of the Dish a rod, which you must Scourge them with; & if Me your Father shou'd get Foolish in my old Days, I desire you may use it upon me as well as others.

NOW FATHERS it is you that is the Disturber in this Land, by coming & building your Towns, and taking it away unknown to us & by Force. FATHERS We kindled a Fire a long Time ago at a Place call'd Morail, where we desir'd you to stay, & not to come & intrude upon our Land. I now desire you may dispatch to that Place;

for be it known to you Fathers, this is our Land, & not yours. FATHERS I desire you may hear me in Civilness; if not, We must handle that rod which was laid down for the Use of the obstropulous. If you had come in a peaceable Manner like our Brothers the English, We shou'd not have been against your trading with us as they do, but to come Fathers, & build great Houses upon our Land, & to take it by Force, is what we cannot submit to.

FATHERS Both you & the English are White. We live in a Country between, therefore the Land does not belong either to one or the other; but the GREAT BEING above allow'd it to be a Place of residence for us; so Fathers, I desire you to withdraw, as I have done our Brothers the English, for I will keep you at Arm's length. I lay this down as a Tryal for both, to see which will have the greatest regard to it, & that Side we will stand by, & make equal Sharers with us: Our Brothers the English have heard this, & I come now to tell it to you, for I am not affraid to discharge you off this Land. This, he said, was the Substance of what he said to the General, who made this Reply.

NOW MY CHILD I have heard your Speech. You spoke first, but it is my Time to speak now. Where is my Wampum that you took away, with the Marks of Towns in it? This Wampum I do not know, which you have discharg'd me off the Land with; but you need not put yourself to the Trouble of Speaking for I will not hear you: I am not affraid of Flies or Musquito's; for Indians are such as those; I tell you down that River I will go, & will build upon it according to my Command: If the River was ever so block'd up, I have Forces sufficient to burst it open, & tread under my Feet all that stand in Opposition together with their Alliances; for my Force is as the Sand upon the Sea Shoar: therefore here is your Wampum, I fling it at you. Child, you talk foolish; you say this Land belongs to you, but there is not the Black of my Nail yours, I saw that Land sooner than you did, before the Shawnesse & you were at War: Lead was the Man that went down, & took Possession of that River;

it is my Land, & I will have it let who will stand up for, or say against it. I'll buy & sell with the English (mockingly). If People will be rul'd by me they may expect Kindness but not else.

The Half King told me, he enquir'd of the General after two English Men that were made Prisoners, & receiv'd this Answer.

CHILD You think it is a very great Hardship that I made Prisoners of those two People at Venango, don't you concern yourself with it we took & carried them to Canada to get Intelligence of what the English were doing in Virginia.

He inform'd me that they had built two Forts, one on Lake Erie, & another on French Creek, near a small Lake about 15 Miles asunder, & a large Waggon Road between; they are both built after the same Model, but different in the Size; that on the Lake the largest; he gave me a Plan of them of his own drawing. The Indians enquir'd very particularly after their Brothers in Carolina Goal. They also ask'd what sort of a Boy it was that was taken from the South Branch; for they had, by some Indians heard, that a Party of French Indians had carried a White Boy by the Cuscusa Town, towards the Lakes.

26th: We met in council at the Long House, about 9 o'Clock, where I spoke to them as follows,

BROTHERS I have call'd you together in Council, by Order of your Brother the Governor of Virginia, to acquaint you that I am sent with all possible Dispatch to visit & deliver a Letter to the French Commandant of very great Importance to your Brothers the English: & I dare say to you their Friends & Allies. I was desir'd Brothers, by your Brother the Governor, to call upon you, the Sachems of the Six Nations, to inform you of it, & to ask your Advice & Assistance to proceed the nearest & best Road to the French. You see Brothers I have got thus far on my Journey. His Honour likewise desir'd me to apply to you for some of your young Men

to conduct and provide Provisions for us on our Way:
& to be a Safeguard against those French Indians, that
have taken up the Hatchet against us. I have spoke this
particularly to you Brothers, because His Hon. our Governor, treats you as good Friends & Allies, & holds you
in great Esteem. To confirm what I have said I give you
this String of Wampum.

After they had considered some Time on the above, the
Half King got up & spoke.

NOW MY BROTHERS. In Regard to what my Brother
the Governor has desir'd of me, I return you this Answer. I rely upon you as a Brother ought to do, as you
say we are Brothers, & one People. We shall put Heart
in Hand, & speak to our Fathers the French, concerning
the Speech they made to me, & you may depend that
we will endeavour to be your Guard.

BROTHER, as you have ask'd my Advice, I hope you
will be ruled by it, & stay 'til I can provide a Company
to go with you. The French Speech Belt is not here, I
have it to go for to my hunting Cabbin likewise the
People I have order'd are not yet come, nor can 'til the
third Night from this, 'till which Time Brother I must
beg you to stay. I intend to send a Guard of Mingoes,
Shawnesse, & Delawar's, that our Brothers may see the
Love and Loyalty We bear them.

As I had Orders to make all possible Dispatch, & waiting
here very contrary to my Inclinations; I thank'd him in the
most suitable Manner I cou'd, & told that my Business requir'd the greatest Expedition, & wou'd not admit of that
Delay: He was not well pleas'd that I shou'd offer to go before
the Time he had appointed, & told me that he cou'd not
consent to our going without a Guard, for fear some Accident
shou'd befall us, & draw a reflection upon him—besides says
he, this is a Matter of no small Moment, & must not be enter'd into without due Consideration, for I now intend to
deliver up the French Speech Belt, & make the Shawnesse &
Delawars do the same, & accordingly gave Orders to King

Singess, who was present, to attend on Wednesday Night with the Wampum, & two Men of their Nation to be in readiness to set off with us next Morning. As I found it impossible to get off without affronting them in the most egregious Manner, I consented to stay.

I gave them back a String of Wampum that I met with at Mr. Frazer's, which they had sent with a Speech to his Honour the Governor, to inform him, that three Nations of French Indians, (vizt.) Chippaway's, Ottaway's, & Arundacks, had taken up the Hatchet against the English, & desired them to repeat it over again; which they postpon'd doing 'til they met in full Council with the Shawnesse, & Delawar Chiefs.

27th: Runners were dispatch'd very early for the Shawness Chiefs, the Half King set out himself to fetch the French Speech Belt from his hunting Cabbin.

28th: He return'd this Evening, & came with Monacatoocha & two other Sachems to my Tent, & beg'd (as they had comply'd with his Honour the Governor's Request in providing Men, &ca.) to know what Business we were going to the French about? This was a Question I all along expected, & had provided as satisfactory Answers as I cou'd, which allay'd their Curiosity a little. Monacatoocha Informed me, that an Indian from Venango brought News a few Days ago; that the French had call'd all the Mingo's, Delawar's &ca. together at that Place, & told them that they intended to have been down the River this Fall, but the Waters were geting Cold, & the Winter advancing, which obliged them to go into Quarters; but they might assuredly expect them in the Spring, with a far greater Number; & desired that they might be quite Passive, & not intermeddle, unless they had a mind to draw all their Force upon them; for that they expected to fight the English three Years, (as they suppos'd there would be some Attempts made to stop them) in which Time they shou'd Conquer, but if they shou'd prove equally strong, that they & the English wou'd join to cut them off, & divide the Land between them: that though they had lost their General, & some few of their Soldiers, yet there was Men enough to reinforce, & make them Masters of the Ohio. This Speech, he said, was deliver'd to them by an Captn. Joncaire, their Interpreter in Chief, living at Venango, & a Man of Note in the Army.

29th: The Half King and Monacatoocha came very early & beg'd me to stay one Day more, for notwithstanding they had used all the Diligence in their Power, the Shawnesse Chiefs had not brought the Wampum they order'd, but wou'd certainly be in to Night, if not they wou'd delay me no longer, but send it after us as soon as they arriv'd: When I found them so pressing in their request; & knew that returning of Wampum, was the abolishing of Agreements; & giving this up was shaking of all Dependence upon the French, I consented to stay, as I believ'd an Offence offer'd at this Crisis, might have been attended with greater ill Consequence than another Day's Delay.

They also inform'd me that Singess cou'd not get in his Men, & was prevented from coming himself by His Wife's Sickness, (I believe by fear of the French) but that the Wampum of that Nation was lodg'd with Custaloga, one of their Chiefs at Venango. In the Evening they came again, & acquainted me that the Shawnesse were not yet come, but it shou'd not retard the Prosecution of our Journey. He deliver'd in my Hearing the Speeches that were to be made to the French by Jeskakake, one of their old Chiefs, which was giving up the Belt the late Commandant had ask'd for, & repeating near the same Speech he himself had done before. He also deliver'd a String of Wampum to this Chief, which was sent by King Singess to be given to Custaloga, with Orders to repair to, & deliver up the French Wampum. He likewise gave a very large String of black & white Wampum, which was to be sent immediately up to the Six Nations, if the French refus'd to quit the Land at this Warning, which was the third & last Time, & was the right of this Jeskakake to deliver.

30th: Last Night the great Men assembled to their Council House to consult further about this Journey, & who were to go; the result of which was, that only three of their Chiefs, with one of their best Hunters shou'd be our Convoy: the reason they gave for not sending more, after what had been propos'd in Council the 26th. was, that a greater Number might give the French Suspicion of some bad Design, & cause them to be treated rudely; but I rather think they cou'd not get their Hunters in.

We set out about 9 o'Clock, with the Half King, Jeskakake, White Thunder, & the Hunter; & travel'd on the road to Venango, where we arriv'd the 4th: of December, without any Thing remarkably happening, but a continued Series of bad Weather. This is an old Indian Town, situated on the Mouth of French Creek on Ohio, & lies near No. about 60 Miles from the Logstown, but more than 70 the Way we were oblig'd to come. We found the French Colours hoisted at a House where they drove Mr. John Frazer an English Subject from: I immediately repair'd to it, to know where the Commander resided: There was three Officers, one of which, Capt. Joncaire, inform'd me, that he had the Command of the Ohio, but that there was a General Officer at the next Fort, which he advis'd me to for an Answer.

He invited us to Sup with them, & treated with the greatest Complaisance. The Wine, as they dos'd themselves pretty plentifully with it, soon banish'd the restraint which at first appear'd in their Conversation, & gave license to their Tongues to reveal their Sentiments more freely. They told me it was their absolute Design to take Possession of the Ohio, & by G—— they wou'd do it, for tho' they were sensible, that the English cou'd raise two Men for their one; yet they knew their Motions were too slow & dilatory to prevent any Undertaking of theirs. They pretended to have an undoubted right to the river from a Discovery made by one La Sol 60 Years ago, & the use of this Expedition is to prevent our Settling on the River or Waters of it, as they have heard of some Families moving out in order thereto.

From the best Intelligence I cou'd get, there has been 1,500 Men this Side Oswago Lake, but upon the Death of the General, all were recall'd to about 6 or 7 Hundred, which were left to Garrison four Forts, 150 or thereabouts in each, the first of which is on French Creek, near a small Lake, about 60 Miles from Venango near N: N: W: the next lies on Lake Erie, where the greatest Part of their Stores are kept about 15 Miles from the other; from that it is 120 Miles from the Carrying Place, at the Fall of Lake Erie, where there is a small Fort, which they lodge their Goods at, in bringing them from

Morail, the Place that all their Stores come from; the next Fort lies about 20 Miles from this, on Oswago Lake; between this Fort & Morail there are three others; the first of which is near the English Fort Oswago. From the Fort on Lake Erie to Morail is about 600 Miles, which they say if good Weather, requires no more than 4 Weeks Voyage, if they go in Barks or large Vessells that they can cross the Lake; but if they come in Canoes, it will require five or six Weeks for they are oblig'd to keep under the Shoar.

5th: Rain'd successively all Day, which prevented our traveling. Capt. Joncaire sent for the half King, as he had but just heard that he came with me: He affected to be much Concern'd that I did not make free to bring him in before; I excused it in the best Manner I was capable, & told him I did not think their Company agreeable, as I had heard him say a good deal in dispraise of Indians in General. But another Motive prevented my bringing them into his Company: I knew that he was Interpreter, & a Person of very great Influence among the Indians, & had lately used all possible means to draw them over to their Interest; therefore I was desirous of giving no more Opportunity than cou'd be avoided. When they came in there was great Pleasure express'd at seeing them, he wonder'd how they cou'd be so near without coming to visit him, made several trifling Presents, & applied Liquors so fast, that they were soon render'd incapable of the Business they came about notwithstanding the Caution that was given.

6th: The Half King came to my Tent quite Sober, & insisted very much that I shou'd stay & hear what he had to say to the French. I fain wou'd have prevented his speaking any Thing 'til he came to the Commandant, but cou'd not prevail. He told me that at this Place Council Fire was kindled, where all their Business with these People were to be transacted, & that the Management of the Indian Affairs was left solely to Monsieur Joncaire. As I was desirous of knowing the Issue of this, I agreed to stay, but sent our Horses a little Way up French Creek, to raft over & Camp, which I knew wou'd make it near Night.

About 10 oClock they met in Council, the King spoke much the same as he had done to the General, & offer'd the French

Speech Belt which had before been demanded, with the Marks of four Towns in it, which Monsieur Joncaire refused to receive; but desired him to carry it to the Fort to the Commander.

7th: Monsieur La Force, Commissary of the French Stores, & three other Soldiers came over to accompany us up. We found it extreamly difficult getting the Indians off to Day; as every Stratagem had been used to prevent their going up with me. I had last Night left John Davison (the Indian Interpreter that I brought from Logstown with me) strictly charg'd not to be out of their Company, as I cou'd not get them over to my Tent (they having some Business with Custaloga, to know the reason why he did not deliver up the French Belt, which he had in keeping,) but was oblig'd to send Mr. Gist over to Day to fetch them, which he did with great Perswasion.

At 11 o'Clock we set out for the Fort, & was prevented from arriving there 'till the 11th: by excessive rains, Snows, & bad traveling, through many Mires & Swamps, which we were oblig'd to pass to avoid crossing the Creek, which was impassible either by Fording or Rafting, the Water was so high & rapid. We pass'd over much good Land since we left Venango, & through several extensive & very rich Meadows, one of which was near 4 Miles in length, & considerably wide in some Places.

12th: I prepar'd early to wait upon the Commander, & was receiv'd & conducted to him by the 2d. Officer in Command; I acquainted him with my Business, & offer'd my Commission & Letter, both of which he desir'd me to keep 'til the Arrival of Monsieur Riparti, Capt. at the next Fort, who was sent for & expected every Hour.

This Commander is a Knight of the Military Order of St: Lewis, & named Legadieur St. Piere, he is an elderly Gentleman, & has much the Air of a Soldier; he was sent over to take the Command immediately upon the Death of the late General, & arriv'd here about 7 Days before me. At 2 o'Clock the Gentleman that was sent for arriv'd, when I offer'd the Letters &ca. again, which they receiv'd, & adjourn'd into a private Appartment for the Captain to translate, who understood a little English, after he had done it, the Captain desir'd

I wou'd walk in & bring my Interpreter to peruse & correct it, which I did.

13th: The chief Officer retired to hold a Council of War, which gave me an Opportunity of taking the Dimensions of the Fort, & making what Observations I cou'd. It is situated on the South or West Fork of French Creek, near the Water, & is almost surrounded by the Creek, & a small Branch of it which forms a Kind of an Island, as may be seen by a Plan I have here annexed, it is built exactly in that Manner & of that Dimensions. 4 Houses compose the Sides; the Bastions are made of Piles drove into the Ground, & about 12 Feet above sharpe at Top, with Port Holes cut for Cannon & Small Arms to fire through; there are Eight 6 lb. Pieces Mounted, two in each Bastion, & one of 4 lb. before the Gate: In the Bastions are a Guard House, Chapel, Doctor's Lodgings, & the Commander's private Store, round which is laid Platforms for the Cannon & Men to stand on: there is several Barracks without the Fort for the Soldiers dwelling, cover'd some with Bark, & some with Boards, & made chiefly of Logs, there is also several other Houses such as Stables, Smiths Shop &ca: all of which I have laid down exactly as they stand, & shall refer to the Plan for Explanation.

I cou'd get no certain Account of the Number of Men here; but according to the best Judgement I cou'd form, there is an Hundred exclusive of Officers, which are pretty many. I also gave Orders to the People that were with me, to take an exact Account of the Canoes that were haled up, to convey their Forces down in the Spring, which they did, and told 50 of Birch Bark, & 170 of Pine; besides many others that were block'd out, in Readiness to make.

14th: As the Snow increased very fast, & our Horses daily got weaker, I sent them off unloaded, under the Care of Barnaby Currin & two others, to make all convenient Dispatch to Venango, & there wait our Arrival, if there was a Prospect of the Rivers Freezing, if not, then to continue down to Shanapin's Town at the Forks of Ohio, & there wait 'till we came to cross Allegany; intending my Self to go down by Water, as I had the Offer of a Canoe or two.

As I found many Plots concerted to retard the Indians Business, & prevent their returning with me, I endeavour'd all in my Power to frustrate their Schemes, & hurry them on to execute their intended Design. They accordingly pressed for admittance this Evening, which at length was granted them privately with the Commander, & one or two other Officers. The Half King told me that he offer'd the Wampum to the Commander, who evaded taking it, & made many fair Promises of Love & Friendship; said he wanted to live in Peace & trade amicably with them; as a Proof of which, he wou'd send some Goods immediately down to the Logstown for them, but I rather think the Design of that is to bring away all of our stragling traders that they may meet with; as I privately understood they intended to carry an Officer, &ca. with them; & what rather confirms this Opinion, I was enquiring of the Commander by what Authority he had taken & made Prisoners of several of our English Subjects. He told me the Country belong'd to them, that no English Man had a right to trade upon them Waters; & that he had Orders to make every Person Prisoner that attempted it on the Ohio or the Waters of it.

I enquir'd of Capt. Riparti about the Boy that was carried by, as it was done while the Command devolved upon him, between the Death of the late General & the Arrival of the Present. He acknowledg'd that a Boy had been carried past, & that the Indians had two or three white Scalps, (I was told by some of the Indians at Venango 8) but pretended to have forgot the Name of the Place that the Boy came from, & all the Particulars, tho' he Question'd him for some Hours as they were carrying him past. I likewise enquired where & what they had done with John Trotter, & James McClocklan, two Pensylvania Traders, which they had taken with all their Goods: they told me that they had been sent to Canada, but were now return'd Home.

This Evening I receiv'd an Answer to His Honour the Governor's Letter from the Commandant.

15th: The Commander order'd a plentiful Store of Liquor, Provisions & ca. to be put on board our Canoe, & appear'd to be extreamly complaisant, though he was ploting every Scheme that the Devil & Man cou'd invent, to set our Indians at Variance with us, to prevent their going 'till after our Departure. Presents, rewards, & every Thing that cou'd be suggested by him or his Officers was not neglected to do. I can't say that ever in my Life I suffer'd so much Anxiety as I did in this affair: I saw that every Stratagem that the most fruitful Brain cou'd invent: was practis'd to get the Half King won to their Interest, & that leaving of him here, was giving them the Opportunity they aimed at: I went to the Half King and press'd him in the strongest Terms to go. He told me the Commander wou'd not discharge him 'till the Morning; I then went to the Commander & desired him to do their Business, & complain'd of ill Treatment; for keeping them, as they were Part of my Company was detaining me, which he promis'd not to do, but to forward my Journey as much as he cou'd: He protested he did not keep them but was innocent of the Cause of their Stay; though I soon found it out. He had promis'd them a Present of Guns, &ca. if they wou'd wait 'till the Morning. As I was very much press'd by the Indians to wait this Day for them; I consented on a Promise that Nothing shou'd hinder them in the Morning.

16th: The French were not slack in their Inventions to keep the Indians this Day also; but as they were obligated, according to promise, to give the Present: they then endeavour'd to try the Power of Liquor; which I doubt not wou'd have prevail'd at any other Time than this, but I tax'd the King so close upon his Word that he refrain'd, & set off with us as he had engag'd. We had a tedious & very fatiguing Passage down the Creek, several Times we had like to have stove against Rocks, & many Times were oblig'd all Hands to get out, & remain in the Water Half an Hour or more, getting her over the Shoals: on one Place the Ice had lodg'd & made it impassable by Water; therefore we were oblig'd to carry our Canoe across a neck Land a quarter of a Mile over. We did not reach Venango 'till the 22d: where we met with our Horses. This Creek is extreamly crooked, I dare say the Distance between the Fort & Venango can't be less than 130 Miles to follow the Meanders.

23d: When I got Things ready to set off I sent for the Half King, to know whether they intended to go with us, or by Water. He told me that the White Thunder had hurt himself much, & was Sick & unable to walk, therefore he was oblig'd to carry him down in a Canoe: As I found he intended to stay a Day or two here, & knew that Monsieur Joncaire wou'd employ every Scheme to set him against the English, as he had before done; I told him I hoped he wou'd guard against his Flattery, & let no fine Speeches Influence Him in their Favour: He desired I might not be concern'd, for he knew the French too well, for any Thing to engage him in their Behalf, & though he cou'd not go down with us, he wou'd endeavour to meet at the Forks with Joseph Campbell, to deliver a Speech for me to carry to his Honour the Governor. He told me he wou'd order the young Hunter to attend us, & get Provision &ca. if wanted. Our Horses were now so weak & feeble, & the Baggage heavy; as we were oblig'd to provide all the Necessaries the Journey wou'd require, that we doubted much their performing it; therefore my Self & others (except the Drivers which were oblig'd to ride) gave up our Horses for Packs, to assist along with the Baggage; & put my Self into an Indian walking Dress, & continue'd with them three Day's, 'till I found there was no Probability of their getting in, in any reasonable Time; the Horses grew less able to travel every Day. The Cold increas'd very fast, & the Roads were geting much worse by a deep Snow continually Freezing; And as I was uneasy to get back to make a report of my Proceedings to his Honour the Governor; I determin'd to prosecute my Journey the nearest way through the Woods on Foot. Accordingly I left Mr. Vanbraam in Charge of our Baggage, with Money and Directions to provide Necessaries from Place to Place for themselves & Horses & to make the most convenient Dispatch in. I took my necessary Papers, pull'd off my Cloths; tied My Self up in a Match Coat; & with my Pack at my back, with my Papers & Provisions in it, & a Gun, set out with Mr. Gist, fitted in the same Manner, on Wednesday the 26th.

The Day following, just after we had pass'd a Place call'd the Murdering Town where we intended to quit the Path & steer across the Country for Shanapins Town, we fell in with a Party of French Indians, which had laid in wait for us, one of them fired at Mr. Gist or me, not 15 Steps, but fortunately missed. We took this Fellow into Custody, & kept him 'till about 9 o'Clock at Night, & then let him go, & then walked all the remaining Part of the Night without making any Stop; that we might get the start, so far as to be out of the reach of their Pursuit next Day, as were well assur'd they wou'd follow upon our Tract as soon as it was Light: The next Day we continued traveling 'till it was quite Dark, & got to the River about two Miles above Shanapins; we expected to have found the River Froze, but it was not, only about 50 Yards from each Shoar; the Ice I suppose had broke up above, for it was driving in vast Quantities.

There was no way for us to get over but upon a Raft, which we set about with but one poor Hatchet, & got finish'd just after Sunsetting, after a whole days Work: We got it launch'd, & on board of it, & sett off; but before we got half over, we were jamed in the Ice in such a Manner, that we expected every Moment our Raft wou'd sink, & we Perish; I put out my seting Pole, to try to stop the Raft, that the Ice might pass by, when the Rapidity of the Stream through it with so much Violence against the Pole, that it Jirk'd me into 10 Feet Water, but I fortunately saved my Self by catching hold of one of the Raft Logs. Notwithstanding all our Efforts we cou'd not get the Raft to either Shoar, but were oblig'd, as we were pretty near an Island, to quit our Raft & wade to it. The Cold was so extream severe, that Mr. Gist got all his Fingers, & some of his Toes Froze, & the Water was shut up so hard, that We found no Difficulty in getting off the Island on the Ice in the Morning, & went to Mr. Frazers. We met here with 20 Warriors that had been going to the Southward to War, but coming to a Place upon the Head of the Great Cunnaway, where they found People kill'd & Scalpt, all but one Woman with very Light Hair, they turn'd about; & ran back, for fear of the Inhabitants rising & takeing them as the Authors of the Murder: They report that the People were lying about the House, & some of them much torn & eat by Hogs; by the Marks that were left, they say they were French Indians of the Ottaway Nation, &ca. that did it.

As we intended to take Horse here, & it requir'd some Time to hunt them; I went up about 3 Miles to the Mouth of Yaughyaughgane to visit Queen Aliquippa, who had express'd great Concern that we pass'd her in going to the Fort. I made her a Present of a Match Coat; & a Bottle of rum, which was thought much the best Present of the two.

Tuesday 1st: Day of Jany: We left Mr. Frazers House, & arriv'd at Mr. Gists at Monangahela the 2d. where I bought Horse Saddle &ca. The 6th: We met 17 Horses loaded with Materials & Stores for a Fort at the Forks; & the Day after, a Family or two going out to settle; this Day we arriv'd at Wills Creek, after as fatiguing a Journey as it is possible to conceive, rendered so by excessive bad Weather: From the first Day of December 'till the 15th. there was but one Day, but what it rain'd or snow'd incessantly & throughout the whole Journey we met with nothing but one continued Series of cold wet Weather; which occasioned very uncumfortable Lodgings, especially after we had left our Tent; which was some Screen from the Inclemency of it.

On the 11th. I got to Belvoir, where I stop'd one Day to take necessary rest; & then set out for, & arrived at Williamsburg, the 16th. & waited upon His Honour the Governor with the Letter I had brought from the French Commandant, & to give an Account of the Proceedures of my Journey. Which I beg leave to do by offering the Foregoing, as it contains the most remarkable Occurrences that happen'd to me.

I hope it will be sufficient to satisfy your Honour with my Proceedings; for that was my Aim in undertaking the Journey: & chief Study throughout the Prosecution of it.

With the Assurance, & Hope of doing it, I with infinite Pleasure subscribe my Self Yr. Honour's most Obedt. & very Hble. Servant.

January 16–17, 1754

To Richard Corbin

Dear Sir:

In a conversation at Green Spring you gave me some room to hope for a commission above that of a Major, and to be ranked among the chief officers of this expedition. The command of the whole forces is what I neither look for, expect, nor desire; for I must be impartial enough to confess, it is a charge too great for my youth and inexperience to be intrusted with. Knowing this, I have too sincere a love for my country, to undertake that which may tend to the prejudice of it. But if I could entertain hopes that you thought me worthy of the post of Lieutenant-colonel, and would favour me so far as to mention it at the appointment of officers, I could not but entertain a true sense of the kindness.

I flatter myself that under a skilful commander, or man of sense, (which I most sincerely wish to serve under,) with my own application and diligent study of my duty, I shall be able to conduct my steps without censure, and in time, render myself worthy of the promotion that I shall be favoured with now.

January 28, 1754

To Robert Dinwiddie

Honble Sir, 25th April 1754 Wills Creek

Captain Trents Ensign Mr Ward this Day arrived from the Forks of Monongehele, and brings the disagreeable account that the Fort on the Seventeenth Instant was surrender'd at the summons of Captain Contrecour to a Body of French consisting of upwards of one Thousand Men, who came from Venago with Eighteen pieces of Cannon, Sixty Battoes, and three Hundred Canoes: they gave him liberty to bring off all his men and working Tools, which he accordingly did the same Day.

Immediately upon this Information I called a Council of War to advise on proper measures to be taken in this Exigence; a Copy of whose resolves, with the proceedings I herewith inclose by the Bearer, who I have continued Express to your Honour for more minute Intelligence.

Mr Ward has the Summons with him, and a speech from the Half King which I also inclose with the Wampum: He is accompanied by one of the Indians that is mentioned therein, who were sent to see where we were, what was our strength, and to know the time to expect us out; the other Young man

I have prevailed upon to return to the Half King with the following Speech.

"Sachems Warriours of the Six united Nations; Shanoahs and Delawares, our Friends and Brethren:

"I received by the Bucks Brother your speech, who came to us with the two young men five sleeps after leaveing you; We return you thanks from Hearts glowing with Affection for your steadfast adherence to us, for your kind speech, and for your wise Councils, and directions to the Bucks Brother.

The Young man will inform you where he met a small part of our army advancing towards you, Clearing the Roads for a great Number of our Warriours that are immediately to follow with our Great Guns, our Ammunition, and our Provisions.

I could not delay to let you know our Hearts and therefore have sent back one of the Young Men with this speech to acquaint you with them; while I have sent the other according to your desire to the Governour of Virginea with the Bucks Brother to deliver your speech and Wampum, And to be an Eye witness of the preparations we are makeing, to come in haste to support you, whose Interest is as dear to us as our Lives. We resent the usage of the treacherous French, and our Conduct henceforth will plainly shew to you how much we have it at Heart.

I cannot be easye without seeing you, before our Forces meet at the Fork of the Roads, and therefore have the greatest inclination that you and Esscruniata or one of you meet me on the Road as soon as possible to assist us in Council. To Assure you of the good will we bare you; and to confirm the truth of what has been said, I herewith present you this string of Wampum that you may thereby remember how much I am Your Brother and Friend

Go: Washington
als
Connotaucarious

To the Half King
Esscruneata & the Belt of Wampum

I hope my proceedings in these affairs will be Satisfactory to Your Honour, as I have to the Utmost of my knowledge consulted the Interest of the Expedition and good of my Country: whose Rights, while they are asserted in so just a Cause I will defend to the last remains of Life. Hitherto the difficulty I have met with in Marching has been greater than I expect to encounter on Ohio where probably I may be sur-round'd by the Enemy; and this occasion'd by those who had they acted as becometh every good Subject, would have ex-erted their Utmost abilitys to forward our just designs Out of Twenty four Waggons that were impress'd at Winchester, we got but Ten after waiting a week, and some of those so illy provided with Teams that we could not travel with them with-out the Soldiers assisting them up the Hills. when it was known they had better Teams at home. I doubt not but in some points I may have strained the Law, but I hope as my sole motive was to Expedite the March, I shall be supported in it should my authority be Questioned which at present I dont Apprehend will, unless some busy body intermeddles.

Your Honour will see by the resolves in Council that I am destin'd to Monongehele with all the diligent dispatch in My power. We will endeavour to make the Road sufficiently good for the heaviest Artillery to pass and when we Arrive at Red Stone Creek Fortifie ourselves as strongly as the short time will allow off. I doubt not but to maintain a possession there till we are Reinforced (If it seasonably Arrives) unless the wa-ters rising admit their Cannon to be convey'd up in Canoes and then I flatter myself we shall not be so wanting for In-telligence but to get timely notice of it and make a good Re-treat.

I hope your Honour will see the absolute Necessity there is for haveing as soon as our Forces are collected a Number of Cannon (some of heavy Mettle) with Mortors Granadoes &c. to attack the French, and put us on an equal footing with them.

Perhaps it may also be thought adviseable to Invite the Cherokees, Cawtabas, and Chicasaws to March to our Assis-tance (as we are informed that Six Hundred Chippoways & Ottaways are Marching down Sciodo Creek to join the French that are coming up Ohio). In that case I would beg leave to recommend their being Orderd to this Place first that a peace may be concluded between them and the Six Nations for I am informed by several hands that as there is no good harmony subsisting betwixt them that by comeing first to Ohio it may create great discords and turn much to our disadvantage.

As I had oppertunitys to the Governour's of Maryland and Pensylvania I wrote to both acquainting them with these advices, and inclosed the Summons and Indian speech, which I hope your Honour will not think me too forward in doing: I consider'd that the Assembly of Maryland was to sit in five days time, and the Pensylvania Assembly now Sitting and that by giveing them timely notice something might be done which would turn to the advantage of this Expedition which now requires all the Force we can Muster.

By the best information I can get I much doubt whether any of the Indians will be in to treat in May. I am with all due respect and regard Your Honours most Obt & Very Humle Servt

Query Whether the Indian Women and Children if they settle amongst us are to be maintained at our Expence or not, they will Expect it.

To Robert Dinwiddie

Sir,

Youghiogany
May 18, 1754.

I am heartily concerned, that the officers have such real cause to complain of the Committee's resolves; and still more to find my inclinations prone to second their just grievances.

I have endeavoured, as far as I was able, to see in the best light I could the trifling advantages that may accrue; yet nothing prevents their throwing down their commissions, (with gratitude and thanks to your Honor, whose good intentions of serving us we are all well assured of,) but the approaching danger, which has too far engaged their honor to recede till other officers are sent in their room, or an alteration made regarding their pay, during which time they will assist with their best endeavours voluntarily, that is, without receiving the gratuity allowed by the resolves of the Committee.

Giving up my commission is quite contrary to my intention. Nay, I ask it as a greater favor, than any amongst the many I have received from your Honor, to confirm it to me. But let me serve voluntarily; then I will, with the greatest pleasure in life, devote my services to the expedition without any other reward, than the satisfaction of serving my country; but to be slaving dangerously for the shadow of pay, through woods, rocks, mountains,—I would rather prefer the great toil of a daily laborer, and dig for a maintenance, provided I were reduced to the necessity, than serve upon such ignoble terms; for I really do not see why the lives of his Majesty's subjects in Virginia should be of less value, than of those in other parts of his American dominions; especially when it is well known, that we must undergo double their hardship.

I could enumerate a thousand difficulties that we have met with, and must expect to meet with, more than other officers who have almost double our pay; but as I know you reflect on these things, and are sensible of the hardships we must necessarily encounter, it would be needless to enlarge.

Besides, as I have expatiated fully (and, perhaps, too warmly) in a letter to Colonel Fairfax, who, I suppose, will accompany you to Winchester, upon the motives that occasion these my resolves, I shall not trouble you with them; for the subject leads me too far when I engage in it.

Another thing resolved by the Committee is, that only one sergeant and one corporal be allowed to a company; with whom it is as much impossible to do the necessary duty, as it is to conquer kingdoms with my handful of men.

Upon the whole, I find so many clogs upon the expedition, that I quite despair of success; nevertheless, I humbly beg it, as a particular favor, that your Honor will continue me in the post I now enjoy, the duty whereof I will most cheerfully execute as a volunteer, but by no means upon the present pay.

I hope what I have said will not be taken amiss; for I really believe, were it as much in your power, as it is your inclination, we should be treated as gentlemen and officers, and not have annexed to the most trifling pay, that ever was given to

English officers, the glorious allowance of soldier's diet—a pound of pork, with bread in proportion, per day. Be the consequence what it will, I am determined not to leave the regiment, but to be amongst the last men that quit the Ohio, even if I serve as a private volunteer, which I greatly prefer to the establishment we are now upon. I am, &c.

To Robert Dinwiddie

From our Camp at the Great Meadows
Honble Sir   29th of May 1754

To answer your Honour's Letter of the 25th by Mr Birney— I shall begin with assuring you, that nothing was farther from my intention than to recede, thô I then pressd and still desire that my Services may be voluntary rather than on the present Pay—I am much concernd that your Honour should seem to charge me with ingratitude for your generous, and my undeserved favours, for I assure you Honble Sir, nothing is a greater stranger to my Breast, or a Sin that my Soul more abhor's than that black and detestable one Ingratitude. I retain a true Sense of your kindnesses, and want nothing but oppertunity to give testimony of my willingness to oblige as far as my Life or fortune will extend.

I cou'd not object to the Pay before I knew it. I dare say your Honour remembers the first Estimation allowd a Lieutt Colo. 15/ and Majr 12/6 which I then complaind very much off; till your Honour assurd me that we were to be furnish'd with proper necessary's and offerd that as a reason why the pay was Less than British: after this when you were so kind to preferr me to the Comn I now have, and at the same time acquainted me that I was to have but 12/6—This, with some other Reason's induced me to acquaint Colo. Fairfax with my intention of Resigning, which he must well remember as it happd at Belhaven; and was there that he disswaded me from it and promised to represent the trifling pay to your Honour, who would endeavour (as I at the same time told him that the Speaker thought the Officr's pay too small) to have it enlarg'd.

As to the Number's that applied for Commission's and to whom we were preffer'd; I believe, had those Gentlemen been as knowing of this Country, and as Sensible of the difficulties that would attend a Campaign here as I then was—I concive your Honour wd not have been so troublesomly sollicited as you were; yet, I do not offer this as a reason for quitting the Service. for my own part I can answer, I have a Constitution hardy enough to encounter and undergo the most severe tryals, and I flatter myself resolution to Face what any Man durst, as shall be prov'd when it comes to the Test, which I believe we are upon the Border's off.

There is nothing Sir (I believe) more certain than that the Officer's on the Canada Expedition had British pay allowd, whilst they were in the Service, Lieutt Wagr Captn Trent, and several other's whom I have conversed with on tht Head, and were engagd in it, affirm it for truth: therefore Honble Sir, as this can't be allow'd; suffer me to serve a Volunteer which I assure you will be the next reward to British pay, for As my Services, so far as I have knowledge will equal those of the best Officer, I make it a point of Honr to serve for less and accept a medium.

Nevertheless, I have communicated your Honour's Sentiments to them; and as far as I could put on the Hipocrite, set forth the advantages that may accrue, and advis'd them to accept the Terms, as a refusal might reflect dishonour upon their Character; leaving it to the World to assign what reason's they please for quitting the Service—I am very sensible of the pernicious consequence that will attend their resigning, as they have by this gain'd some experience of the Military Art, have a tolerable knowledge of the Country, being sent most of them out at different times with partys: and now are accustom'd to the hardships and fatiegue of Living as we do, which I believe were it truely stated, wd prevent your Honour from many troublesome Sollicitations from others for Comns. This last motive, has, and will induce me to do what I can to reconcile matter's; thô I really believe there is some tht will not remain long witht an alteration.

They have promis'd to consider of it, and give your Honour an answer. I was not ignorant of the allowe which Colo. Fry has for his Table, but being a dependt there myself deprives me of the pleasure of inviting an Officer or Friend, which to me wd be more agreeable than the Nick Nacks I shall meet with there.

And here I cannot forbear answering one thing more in your Honrs Letter on this head; which (too) is more fully express'd in a paragraph of Colo. Fairfax's to me as follows "If on the British Establishment Officer's are allowd more Pay, the Regimentals they are oblig'd annually to furnish, their necessary Table and other Incidents being considerd, little or no savings will be their Portion"—I believe it is well known we have been at the expence of Regimentals (and it is still better known, that Regimentals, and every other necessary that we were under an indispensable necessity of purchasing for this Expedition, were not to be bought for less Virga curry, than British Officer's cd get for sterling money; which they ought to have been, to put us upon a parity in this respect, then Colo. Fairfax observes that their Table and other Incident charges prevents them frm saving much: if they dont save much, they have the enjoyment of their Pay which we neither have in one sense nor the other: We are debarr'd the pleasure of good Living, which Sir (I dare say with me you will concur) to one who has always been used to it; must go somewhat hard to be confin'd to a little salt provision and Water: and do duty, hard, laborious duty that is almost inconsistent with that of a Soldier, and yet have the same Reductions as if we were allowd luxuriously: My Pay accordg to the British Establisht & common exchange is near 22/ pr Day, in the Rm of that the Committee (for I can't in the least imagine yr Hr had any hd in it) has provided 12/6 so long as the Service requires me, whereas, one half of the other is ascertain'd to the British Officer's forever: now if we shd be fortunate enough to drive the French from Ohio—as far as your Honour wd please have them sent to—in any short time, our Pay will not be sufficient to discharge our first expences.

I would not have your Honour imagine from this, that I have said all these things to have the Pay encreas'd—but to justify myself, and shew your Honour that our complaints are not frivolous, but are founded upon strict Reason: for my own part, it is a matter almost indefferent whether I serve for full pay, or as a generous Volunteer; indeed, did my circumstances corrispond with my Inclination, I shd not hesitate a moment to prefer the Latter: for the motives that lead me here were pure and Noble I had no view of acquisition but that of Honour, by serving faithfully my King and Country.

As your Honour has recommended Mr Willis you may depend I shall with pleasure do all that I can for him.

But above all Sir, you may depend I shall take all possible means of procureing intelligence, and guarding against surprises, and be assur'd nothing but very unequal number's shall engage me to submit or Retreat.

Now Sir, as I have answer'd your Honour's Letter I shall beg leave to acqt you with what has happen'd since I wrote by Mr Gist; I then acquainted you that I had detach'd a party of 75 Men to meet with 50 of the French who we had Intelligence were upon their March towards us to Reconnoitre &ca. Abt 9 Oclock the same Night, I receivd an express from the Half King who was Incampd with several of His People abt 6 Miles of, that he had seen the Tract of two French Men xing the Road and believ'd the whole body were lying not far off, as he had an acct of that number passing Mr Gist—I set out with 40 Men before 10, and was from that time till near Sun rise before we reach'd the Indian's Camp, havg Marched in small path, & heavy Rain, and a Night as Dark as it is possible to concieve—we were frequently tumbling one over another, and often so lost that 15 or 20 Minutes search would not find the path again.

When we came to the Half King I council'd with him, and got his assent to go hand in hand and strike the French. accordingly, himself, Monacatoocha, and a few other Indians set out with us, and when we came to the place where the Tracts were, the Half King sent Two Indians to follow their Tract and discover their lodgment which they did abt half a mile from the Road in a very obscure place surrounded with Rocks. I thereupon in conjunction with the Half King & Monacatoocha, formd a disposion to attack them on all sides, which we accordingly did and after an Engagement of abt 15 Minutes we killd 10, wounded one and took 21 Prisoner's, amongst those that were killd was Monsieur De Jumonville the Commander, Principl Officers taken is Monsieur Druillong and Monsr Laforc, who your Honour has often heard me speak

of as a bold Enterprising Man, and a person of gt subtilty and
cunning with these are two Cadets—These Officers pretend
they were coming on an Embassy, but the absurdity of this
pretext is too glaring as your Honour will see by the Instructions and summons inclos'd: There Instructions were to reconnoitre the Country, Roads, Creeks &ca to Potomack;
which they were abt to do, These Enterpriseing Men were
purposely choose out to get intelligence, which they were to
send Back by some brisk dispatches with mention of the Day
that they were to serve the Summon's; which could be
through no other view, than to get sufficient Reinforcements
to fall upon us imediately after. This with several other Reasons induc'd all the Officers to beleive firmly that they were
sent as spys rather than any thing else, and has occasiond my
sending them as prisoners, tho they expected (or at least had
some faint hope of being continued as ambassadors) They
finding where we were Incamp'd, instead of coming up in a
Publick manner sought out one of the most secret Retire-
ments; fitter for a Deserter than an Ambassador to incamp
in—stayd there two or 3 days sent Spies to Reconnoitre our
Camp as we are told, tho they deny it—Their whole Body
movd back near 2 Miles, sent off two runnors to acquaint
Contracoeur with our Strength, and where we were Incamp'd &ca now 36 Men wd almost have been a Retinue for
a Princely Ambassador, instead of Petit, why did they, if there
design's were open stay so long within 5 Miles of us witht
delivering his Ambassy, or acquainting me with it; his waiting
cd be with no other design than to get Detachts to enforce
the Summons as soon as it was given, they had no occasion
to send out Spy's; for the Name of Ambassador is Sacred
among all Nations; but it was by the Tract of these Spy's they
were discoverd, and we got Intilligence of them—They wd
not have retird two Miles back witht delivering the Summons
and sought a sculking place (which to do them justice was
done with gt Judgment) but for some especial Reason: Besides
The Summon's is so insolent, & savour's so much of Gas-
coigny that if two Men only had come openly to deliver it. It
was too great Indulgence to have sent them back.

The Sense of the Half King on this Subject is, that they

have bad Hearts, and that this is a mere pretence, they never designd to have come to us but in a hostile manner, and if we were so foolish as to let them go again, he never would assist us in taking another of them. Besides, looseing La Force I really think wd tend more to our disservice than 50 other Men, as he is a person whose active Spirit, leads him into all parlys, and brought him acquainted with all parts, add to this a perfect use of the Indian Tongue, and gt influence with the Indian He Ingenuously enough confessd that as soon as he saw the commission & Instructions that he believd and then said he expected some such tendency tho he pretends to say he does not believe the Commander had any other but a good design.

In this Engagement we had only one Man killd, and two or three wounded, among which was Lieutt Waggener slightly—a most miraculous escape, as Our Right Wing was much exposd to their Fire and receivd it all.

The Half King receiv'd your Honour's speech very kind: but desird me to inform you that he could not leave his People at this time, thinking them in great Danger—He is now gone to the xing for their Familys to bring to our Camp & desird I wd send some Men and Horses to assist them up; which I have accordingly done—sent 30 Men & upwards of 20 Horses. He say's if your Honr has any thing to say you may communicate by me &ca; and that if you have a present for them it may be kept to another occasion, after sending up some things for their imediate use, He has declar'd to send these Frenchmens Scalps with a Hatchet to all the Nations of Indian's in union with them, and did that very day give a Hatchet and a large Belt of Wampum to a Delaware Man to carry to Shingiss: he promis'd me to send down the River for all the Mingo's & Shawnesse to our camp, where I expect him to Morrow with 30 or 40 Men with their wives & Children, to confirm what he has said here, he has sent your Honour a String of Wampum.

As these Runnors went of to the Fort on Sunday last, I shall expect every hour to be attackd and by unequal number's, which I must withstand if there is 5 to 1 or else I fear the Consequence will be we shall loose the Indians if we suffer ourselves to be drove Back, I dispatchd an express imediately to Colo. Fry with this Intelligence desiring him to send me Reinforcements with all imaginable dispatch.

Your Honour may depend I will not be surprizd, let them come what hour they will—and this is as much as I can promise—but my best endeavour's shall not be wanting to deserve more, I doubt not but if you hear I am beaten, but you will at the same hear that we have done our duty in fighting as long there was a possibility of hope.

I have sent Lieutt West accompanied with Mr Sprilldorph & a Guard of 20 Men to conduct the Prisoners in, and I believe the Officer's have acquainted him what answer to return yr Honour.

Monsiur La-Force, and Monsieur Druillong beg to be recommend to your Honour's Notice, and I have promis'd they will meet with all the favour that's due to Imprison'd Officer's: I have shew'd all the respect I cou'd to them here, and have given some necessary cloathing by which I have disfurnish'd myself, for having brought no more than two or three Shirts from Wills Ck that we might be light I was ill provided to furnish them I am Yr Honour's most Obt Hble Servt

NB I have neither seen nor heard any particular acct of the Twigtwees since I came on these Water's, we have already began a Palisadod Fort and hope to have it up tomorrow I must beg leave to acqt yr honr tht Captn Vanbraam & Monsr Peyrouney has behav'd extreamely well since they came out— & I hope will meet wth yr Honrs favr.

To Robert Dinwiddie

Honble Sir

Since writing the other, I have still stronger presumption, indeed almost confirmation that they were sent as Spyes, and were order'd to wait near us till they were truely informd of our Intention's, situation, strength, &ca and were to have acquainted the Commander therewith and laid lurking near for Reinforcements before they served the Summon's if it at all.

I doubt not but they will endeavour to amuse your Honour with many smooth Story's as they did me but were confuted in them all and by circumstances too plain to be denied almost made asham'd of their assertions—I dare say your Honour will treat them with respect which is due to all unfortunate Person in their Condition But I hope give no Ear to What they will have an oppertunity of displaying to the best advantage having none by to contradict their reports.

I have heard since they went away that they shd say they calld to us not to Fire, but that I know to be False for I was the first Man that approach'd them & the first whom they saw, and imediately upon it ran to their Arms and Fir'd briskly till they were defeated.

We have heard of another being killd by the Indian's that made his Escape from us, so that we are certain of 33 that are killd and taken I thought it expedient to acqt your Honr with the above as I fancy they will have the assurance of asking the Priviledges due to an Embassy when in strict Justice they ought to be hang'd for Spyes of the worst sort being authorizd by their Comr at the expence of a Character which shd be Sacred to all Nations and trifled with or used in an Equivocal way. I am Honble Sir Yr most Obt

May 29, 1754

To John Augustine Washington

Dr John

Since my last we have arrived at this place, where 3 days agoe we had an engagemt wth the French that is, between a party of theirs & Ours; Most of our men were out upon other detachments, so that I had scarcely 40 men under my Command, and about 10, or a doz. Indians, nevertheless we obtained a most signal Victory. The Battle lasted abt 10, or 15 minutes, sharp firing on both sides, when the French gave ground & run, but to no great purpose; there were 12 killed, among which was Monsr De Jumonville the Commandr, & taken 21 prisoners with whom are Monsieurs La Force, Druillong, together with 2 Cadets. I have sent them to his Honr the Governor at Winchester conducted by Lieut. West & a guard of 20 men. We had but one man killed, 2 or 3 wounded and a great many more within an Inch of being shott; among the wounded on our side was Lieut. Waggoner, but no danger will ensue.

We expect every Hour to be attacked by a superior Force, but shall if they stay one day longer be prepared for them; We have already got Intrenchments & are about a Pallisado'd Fort, which will I hope be finished today. The Mingo's have struck the French & I hope will give a good blow before they have done, I expect 40 odd of them here to night, wch with our Fort and some reinforcements from Colo. Fry, will enable us to exert our Noble Courage with Spirit. I am Yr Affe Bror

I fortunately escaped without a wound, tho' the right Wing where I stood was exposed to & received all the Enemy's fire and was the part where the man was killed & the rest wounded. I can with truth assure you, I heard Bulletts whistle and believe me there was something charming in the sound.

May 31, 1754

To William Fitzhugh

To Colo. William Fitzhugh.

Dear Sir,   Belvoir, November 15th 1754

I was favoured with your letter, from Rousby-Hall, of the 4th Instant. It demands my best acknowledgments, for the particular marks of Esteem you have expressed therein; and for the kind assurances of his Excellency, Governour Sharp's good wishes towards me. I also thank you, and sincerely, Sir, for your friendly intention of making my situation easy, if I return to the Service; and do not doubt, could I submit to the Terms, that I should be as happy under your command, in the absence of the General, as under any gentleman's whatever: but, I think, the disparity between the present offer of a Company, and my former Rank, too great to expect any real satisfaction or enjoyment in a Corps, where I once did, or thought I had a right to, command; even if his Excellency had power to suspend the orders received in the Secretary of Wars' Letter; which, by the bye, I am very far from thinking he either has or will attempt to do, without fuller Instructions than I believe he has: especially, too, as there has been a representation of this matter by Governour Dinwiddie, and, I believe, the Assembly of this State; we have advices, that it was received before Demmarree obtained his Letter.

All that I presume the General *can* do, is, to prevent the different Corps from interfering, which will occasion the Duty to be done by Corps, instead of Detachments; a very inconvenient way, as is found by experience.

You make mention in your letter of my continuing in the Service, and retaining my Colo.'s Commission. This idea has filled me with surprise: for if you think me capable of holding a Commission that has neither rank or emolument annexed to it; you must entertain a very contemptible opinion of my weakness, and believe me to be more empty than the Commission itself.

Besides, Sir, if I had time, I could enumerate many good reasons, that forbid all thoughts of my Returning; and which, to you, or any other, would, upon the strictest scrutiny, appear to be well-founded. I must be reduced to a very low Command, and subjected to that of many who have acted as my inferior Officers. In short, every Captain, bearing the King's Commission; every half-pay Officer, or other, appearing with such commission, would rank before me; for these reasons, I choose to submit to the loss of Health, which I have, however, already sustained (not to mention that of Effects) and the fatigue I have undergone in our first Efforts; than subject myself to the same inconveniences, and run the risque of a second disappointment. I shall have the consolation itself, of knowing, that I have opened the way when the smallness of our numbers exposed us to the attacks of a Superior Enemy; That I have hitherto stood the heat and brunt of the Day, and escaped untouched, in time of extreme danger; and that I have the Thanks of my Country, for the Services I have rendered it.

It shall not sleep in silence, my having received information, that those peremptory Orders from Home, which, you say, could not be dispensed with, for reducing the Regiments into Independant Companies, were generated, hatched, & brought from Will's-Creek. Ingenuous treatment, & plain dealing, I at least expected—It is to be hoped the project will answer; it shall meet with my acquiescence in every thing except personal Services. I herewith enclose Governour Sharp's Letter, which I beg you will return to him, with my Acknowledgments for the favour he intended me; assure him, Sir, as you truly may, of my reluctance to quit the Service, and of the pleasure I should have received in attending his Fortunes: also, inform him, that it was to obey the call of Honour, and the advice of my Friends, I declined it, and not to gratify any desire I had to leave the military line.

My inclinations are strongly bent to arms.

The length of this, & the small room I have left, tell me how necessary it is to conclude, which I will do as you always shall find—Truly & sincerely, Your most hble Servant,

Nov. 15th 1754

To Mary Ball Washington

To Mrs Washington
Honourd Madam

I came to this place last Saturday, and shall set out to-morrow with the General for Wills Creek; where I fear we shall wait some time for a sufficient number of Waggons to transport us over the Mountains.

I am very happy in the Generals Family, as I am treated with a complaisant Freedom which is quite agreeable; so that I have no reason to doubt the satisfaction I propos'd, in making the Campaigne.

As we have met with nothing yet worth relating I shall only beg my Love to my Brother's and Sister's; and Compliments to Friends. I am Honour'd Madam Yr most Dutiful & Obedt Son

Winchester May 6th 1755

To John Augustine Washington

To Colo. Auge Washington
Dear Brother

I left home the 24th of last Month, and overtook the General at Frederick Town in Maryland: from whence we proceeded by slow Marches to this place; where, I fear, we shall remain some-time for want of Horses and Carriages to convey our Baggage &ca over the Mountains; but more especially for want of Forage; as it cannot be imagin'd that so many Horses as we require, will be subsisted without [   ].

We hear nothing particular from the Ohio only that the French are in hourly expectation of being joind by a large body of Indians; but I fancy they will find themselves so warmly attackd in other places, that it will [   ].

I am treated with freedom and respect, by the General and his Family; so that I dont doubt but I shall spend my time very agreeably this Campaigne, tho' not advantageously; as I conceive a little experience will be my chief reward. Please to give my Love to my Sister &ca. I am Dr Sir Yr most Affecte Brother

Fort Cumberland 14th of May 1755

This Letter was not sent.

To John Augustine Washington

To Mr Jno. Auge Washington
Dear Jack

I came to this place last Night, and was greatly disappointed at not finding the Cavalry according to promise: I am obligd to wait till it does arrive, or till I can procure a guard from the Militia, either of which I suppose will detain me two days; as you may, with almost equal success, attempt to raize the Dead to Life again, as the force of this County; and that from Wills Creek cannot be expected in less than the aforementiond time without they are now upon their March.

The Droughth in this County, if possible, exceeds what we

see below; so that, it is very reasonably conjectur'd, they wont make Corn to suffice the People; and as for Tobacco, they decline all thoughts of making any.

The Inhabitants of this place abound in News, but as I apprehend it is founded upon as much truth as some I heard in my way down, I think it advisable to forego the recital till a little better authority confirms the report and then you may expect to have a succinct acct.

I shoud be glad to hear you live in Harmony and good fellowship with the family at Belvoir, as it is in their power to be very serviceable upon many occasion's to us as young beginner's: I woud advise your visiting often as one Step towards the rest, if any more is necessary, your own good sense will sufficient dictate; for to that Family I am under many obligations particularly to the old Gentleman.

Mrs Fairfax and Mrs Spearing expressd an Inclination to hear whether I had [   ] this place (with my charge safe) you may therefore acquaint them that, I met with no other Interruption, than the difficulty of gettg Horses after I found her's for want of Shoes grew lame, I was oblig'd to get a fresh horse every 15 or 20 Mile, which render'd the journey tiresome. I shoud have receivd greater relief from the fatiegues of my journey, and my time woud have been spent much more agreeably had I halted below rather than in this vile hole; but I little imagin'd I shoud have occasion to wait for a Guard who ought to have waited for me; if either must have waited at all.

I have given Colo. Fairfax an Order upon you for £8.17.5 which please to pay, as it is on acct of a horse wch I bought of Neale some time ago. You receive Inclosd, Bowee's receipt for Harry, and I shoud be glad, if you have any oppertunity, that you woud demand My Bond which I had given, and coud not receive at payment of the money; this receipt you may put into my receipt draw. My Compliments attend my Friends who I wish health and happiness to, very sincerely; I am Dear Jack Your most Affectionate Brother

P.S. As I understand your County is to be divided, and that Mr Alexander intends to decline serving it, I shoud be glad if you could fish out Colo. Fairfax's Intention's, and let me

know whether he purposes to offer himself a Candadite; If he does not, I shoud be glad to stand a pole, if I thought my chance tolerably good. Majr Carlyle mention'd it to me in Williamsburg in a bantering and askd how I shoud like to go, saying at the same time, he did not know but they might send me when I knew nothing of the matter, for one or 'tother of the Counties. I must own I shoud like to go for either, in that manner, but more particularly for Fairfax, as I am a resident there. I shoud be glad if you coud discover Major Carlyles real Sentimts also those of Mr Dalton, Ramsay, Mason, &ca wch I hope & think you may witht disclosing much of mine; as I know yr own good sense can furnish you with means enough without letting it proceed immediately from me. If you do any thing in this pray let me know by the first oppertunity how you have succeeded in it; & how those Gentlemen stand affected; if they seem inclinable to promote my Interest, and things shoud be drawing to a crisis you then may declare my Intentions & beg their assistance—If on the Contrary you find them more inclind to favour some other, I wd have the Affair entirely subside. Parson Green's, and Captn McCartys Interests in this woud be of Consequence; & I shoud be glad if you coud sound their Pulse upon that occasion; conduct the whole, till you are satisfied of the Sentimts of those I have mention'd, with an air of Indifference & unconcern; after that you may regulate your conduct accordingly. Captn West the present Burgess, and our Friend Jack West, coud also be servicable if they had a mind to assist the Interest of Dear Jack Your loving Brother
Winchester 28th May 1755

To Sarah Cary Fairfax

To Mrs Fairfax,
Dear Madam

When I had the pleasure to see you last, you expressd an Inclination to be informd of my safe arrival at Camp, with the charge that was entrusted to my care; but at the same time desird it might be communicated in a Letter to some body of your acquaintance: This I took as a Gentle rebuke and polite manner of forbidding my corrisponding with you; and conceive this opinion is not illy founded when I reflect that I have hitherto found it impracticable to engage one moment of your attention: If I am right in this, I hope you will excuse my present presumption and lay the imputation to elateness at my successfull arrival; If on the contrary these are fearfull apprehensions only, how easy is it to remove my suspicions, enliven my Spirits, and make me happier than the Day is long, by honouring me with a corrispondance which you did once partly promise.

Please to make my Complts to Miss Hannah, and to Mr Bryan to whom I shall do myself the pleasure of writing so soon as I hear he is returnd from Westmoreland. I am Madam Yr most Obedt & most Hble Servt
Fort Cumberd at Wills Creek 7th of June 1755

To John Augustine Washington

To Mr Jno. Auge Washington
Dear Jack

Immediately upon our leavg the C. at Geors. Ck the 14th Inst. (from whe I wrote to yo.) I was siezd wt violt Fevers & Pns in my hd wch cond wtout the lt Intermisn till the 23 follg when I was reliev'd by the Genls absolty ordering the Phyns to give me Doctr Jas Powder; wch is the most excelt mede in the W.) for it gave me immee ease, and removed my Fevrs & othr Compts in 4 Days time. My illness was too violent to suffer me to ride, therefore I was indebted to a coverd Waggon for some part of my Transpn; but even in this I cd not conte for the joltg was so gt that I was left upon the Road with a Guard and necessys, to wait the Arrl of Colo. Dunbars Detacht, whh was 2 days M. behind. The Genl giving me his wd and honr that I shd be brought up before he reachd the French Fort; this promise, and the Doctrs threats that if I perseverd it woud endanger my Life, determind my halting for the above Detacht.

As I expect the Comn betn this & Wills Ck will soon be too dangerous for single persons to pass, it will possibly stop the Interce of Lettrs in any measure; therefore I shall attempt (and will go through if I have strength,) to give you an acct of our proceedings, of our Situation, & of our prospects at present; which I desire yo. may come to Colo. Fairfax &ca my Corrispts; for I am too weak to write more than this Lettr. In the Lr wch I wrote fm Georges Ck I acqd you that unless the numr of Wagns were retrenchd & the carryg Hs incrd that we never shd be able to see Duquisne: This in 2 Days afterwards, wch was abt the time they got to the little Meadows with some of their F. Waggon's and strongest Teams, they themselves were convinced off, for they found that beside the almost imposy of gettg the Wagns along at all; that they had often a Rear of 3 or 4 Miles of Waggons; & tht the Soldrs Guarding these were so disunitd that if we had been attackd either in Front, Center or Rear that part so attackd, must have been cut of & totally defeatd before they coud be properly sustaind by any other Corps.

At the little Meadws there was a 2d Council calld, for there had been one wherein it was representd to all the Offrs of the difft Corps the gt necessity there was for Hs. & how laudable it wd be to retrench their Baggage and offer the Spare Hs. for the Publick Service. In order to encourage this I gave up my best Horse (wch I have nevr hd of since) & took no more baggage than half my Portmanteau cd easily contn. It was also sd tht the numbr was to be lessend, but this was only from 210 or 12, to 200 wch had no perceptable difference.

The Genl before they met in Council askd my prive Opinn concerng the Expn; I urgd it in the warmest terms I was master off, to push on; if we even did it with a chosn Detacht for that purpose, with the Artillery and such other things as were absolutely necessary; leavg the [   ] and other Convoys with the Remainder of the Army, to follw by slow and regular Marches, which they might do safely while we were advanced in Front. As one Reason to support this Opinion, I inform'd tht if we cd credt our Intelligence, the French were weak at the Forks but hourly expectd reinfts wch to my certain knowledge coud not arrive with Provns or any supplys durg the continuance of the Droughth—as the Buffaloe River down wch is their only commn to Venango, must be as Dry as we now fd the gt xing of the Yaughe; wch may be passd dry shod.

This was a Scheme that took, & it was detd that the Genl, with 1200 Chosen Men and Officers of all the differt Corps, with the following Field Officer's (vizt Sr Petr Halkett who acts as Brigadier, Lt Colo. Gage Lt C: Burton, and Majr Sparke, with such a certain number of Waggons as the Train wd absolutely require, shoud March as soon as things coud be got in readiness for them; which was compleated, and we on our March by the 19th, leavg Colo. Dunbar & Majr Chapman with the residue of the Regts, Companys most of the Women and in short every thing behind; except such Provision's & other necessarys as we took, and carried upon Horses.

We set out with less than 30 Carriages (Inclg all those that transported the Howetzers, 12 prs, 6 prs, &ca) & all of those strongly Horsed; which was a prospect that conveyd the most infinite delight to me, tho' I was excessively ill at the time. But this prospect was soon over turned, & all my Sanguine hopes brought very low when I found, that instead of pushing on with vigour, without regarding a little rough Road, they were halting to Level every Mold Hill, & to erect Bridges over every brook; by which means we were 4 Days gettg 12 Miles; where I was left by the Doctrs Advice, and the Genls absolute Orders, otherwise I woud not have been prevaild upon to remain behind, my own Detachmt as I then imagin'd, and believd I shall now find it not very easy to join my own Corps again, which is 25 Miles advanced before us; tho' I had the Genls word & Honr pledgd in the most Solemn manner, that I shd be bt up before he arrived at Duquisne. They have had frequent Alarms and several Men Scalp'd, but this is only done to retard the March; and harass the Men if they are to be turnd out every time a small party of them attack the Guards at Night; (for I am certain they have not sufficient strength to make head against the whole.

I have been now 6 Days with Colo. Dunbars Corps, who are in a misserable Condition for want of Horses; not havg now one half enough for their Wagns so that the only method he has of proceeding is to March on himself with as many

Waggon's as those will draw, and then Halt till the Remainder
are brought up which requires two Days more; and I believe,
shortly he will not be able to stir at all; but there has been
vile management in regard to Horses; and while I am men-
tiong this, I must not forget to desire, that you'll acqt Colo.
G. Fx that I have made the most strict enquiry after his Man
& Horses, but can hear nothing of either; at least nothing
that can be credited. I was told that the Fellow was taken ill
upon the Road while he was with Sr Jno. St Clairs Detachmt,
and [   ] the certainty of this I cant answer for, but I believe
there is nothing more certn than that he is not with any part
of the Army. And unless the Horses stray and make home
themselves I believe there is 1000 to 1 whether he ever sees
them again: for I gave up a horse only one Day, & never coud
see or hear of him afterwards: My strength wont admit me to
say more, tho I have not said half what I intended cong our
Affrs here. Business, I shall not think of but depd solely upon
yr mant of all my affrs, & doubt not but they will be well
conducted—You may thank my Fds for the Lettrs I have recd;
wch has not been *one* from *any Mortal* since I left Fairfax,
except yourself and Mr Dalton. It is a piece of regard & kindness which I shd endr to acknowe was I able, and sufferd to
write. All your Letters to me I wd have you send to Mr Cocks
of Winchester or to Govr Innis at Fort Cumberd, & then you
may be certn of their comg safe to hand; otherwise I cant say
as much. Make my Complimts to all who think me worthy of
their Enquirys. I am
Gt xing on the Yaughe June 28th 1755

P.S. Added afterwards, to the foregoing Letter as follows
    A Great Misfortune that attended me in my Sickness was,
looseing the use of my Servant, for poor Jno. was taken abt
the same time that I was, with near the same disorder; and
was confind as long; so that we did not see each other for
several Days. He is also tolerably well recoverd. We are now
advand almost as far as the gt Meadows; and I shall set out
tomorrow morning for my own Corps, with an Escort of 100
Men which is to guard some Provision's up; so that my Fears
and doubts on that head are quite removd.
    I had a Letter Yesterday from Orme, who writes me word

that they have passd the Yaughyangane for the last time, that
they have sent out Partys to scour the Country thereabouts,
and have Reason to believe that the French are greatly alarmd
at their approach.
2d July 1755

To Robert Dinwiddie

To The Honble Robt Dinwiddie Esqr.
Honble Sir

As I am favourd with an oppertunity, I shoud think myself
inexcusable, was I to omit givg you some acct of our late
Engagemt with the French on the Monongahela the 9th Inst.

We continued our March from Fort Cumberland to Frazer's (which is within 7 Miles of Duquisne) witht meetg with
any extraordinary event, havg only a stragler or two picked
Up by the French Indians. When we came to this place, we
were attackd, (very unexpectedly I must own) by abt 300
French and Indns; Our number's consisted of abt 1300 well
armd Men, chiefly regular's, who were immediately struck
with such a deadly Panick, that nothing but confusion and
disobedience of order's prevaild amongst them: The Officer's
in genl behavd with incomparable bravery, for which they
greatly sufferd, there being near 60 killd and woundd A large
Proportion out of the number we had! The Virginians behavd
like Men, and died like Soldier's; for I believe out of 3 Companys that were there that Day, scarce 30 were left alive: Captn
Peyrouny and all his Officer's down to a Corporal, were killd;
Captn Polson shard almost as hard a Fate, for only one of his
Escap'd: In short the dastardly behaviour of the English Soldier's exposd all those who were inclin'd to do their duty, to
almost certain Death; and at length, in despight of every effort
to the contrary, broke & run as Sheep before the Hounds,
leavg the Artillery, Ammunition, Provision, and every individual thing we had with us a prey to the Enemy; and when we
endeavourd to rally them in hopes of regaining our invaluable
loss, it was with as much success as if we had attempted to
have stopd the wild Bears of the Mountains.

The Genl was wounded behind the Shoulder, & into the Breast; of wch he died three days after; his two Aids de Camp were both wounded, but are in a fair way of Recovering; Colo. Burton and Sir Jno. St Clair are also wounded, and I hope will get over it; Sir Peter Halket, with many other brave Officers were killd in the Field: I luckily escapd witht a wound, tho I had four Bullets through my Coat and two Horses shot under me: It is supposed that we left 300 or more dead in the Field; abt that number we brought off wounded; and it is imagin'd (I believe with great justice too) that two thirds of both those number's receiv'd their shott from our own cowardly dogs of Soldier's, who gatherd themselves into a body contrary to orders 10 or 12 deep, woud then level, Fire, & shoot down the Men before them.

I Tremble at the consequences that this defeat may have upon our back setlers, who I suppose will all leave their habitation's unless their are proper measures taken for their security.

Colo. Dunbar, who commands at present, intends so soon as his Men are recruited at this place, to continue his March to Philia into *Winter* Quarter's; so that there will be no Men left here unless it is the poor remains of the Virginia Troops; who now are, & will be too small to guard our Frontiers. As Captn Orme is writg to yr honour I doubt not but he will give you a circumstantial acct of all things, which will make it needless for me to add more than that I am Honble Sir Yr most Obt & most Hble Servt

Fort Cumberland July 18th 1755

To John Augustine Washington

To Mr Jno. Auge Washington
Dear Jack

As I have heard since my arrivl at this place, a circumstantial acct of my death and dying Speech, I take this early oppertunity of contradicting both, and of assuring you that I [   ] of the livg by the miraculous care of Providence, that protected me beyond all human expectation; I had 4 Bullets through my Coat, and two Horses shot under and yet escaped unhurt.

We have been most scandalously beaten by a trifling body of men; but fatiegue, and the want of time, prevents me from [   ]ing any of the [   ] till I have the happiness of seeing you at home; which I now most ardently wishd for, since we are drove in thus far. A Weak, and Feeble State of Health, obliges me to halt here for 2 or 3 days, to recover a little strength, that I may thereby be enabled to proceed home-wards with more ease; You may expect to see me there on Saturday or Sunday Se'night, which is as soon as I can well be down as I shall take my Bullskin Plantation's in my way. Pray give my Compts to all my Fds. I am Dr Jack Yr most Affecte Brothr

Fort Cumberld 18th July 1755

To Mary Ball Washington

To Mrs Washington
Honourd Madam

If it is in my power to avoid going to the Ohio again, I shall, but if the Command is press'd upon me by the genl voice of the Country, and offerd upon such terms as can't be objected against, it woud reflect eternal dishonour upon me to refuse it; and that I am sure must, or ought, to give you greater cause of uneasiness than my going in an honourable Comd; for upon no other terms I will accept of it, if I do at all; at present I have no proposals, or any mention made abt it, only from private hands. I am Dr Mm &c.

Mount Vernon Augt 14th 1755

General Orders

As Captain George Mercer of the Virginia Forces, has been appointed aide de camp to Colonel Washington, and declared in Publick Orders at Fort Cumberland—To prevent any Disputes or delays of Orders, which may be issued by him. It is also thought proper to acquaint all Officers, &c. at this place, with the said appointment; and that all Orders which come from him, are to be as punctually obeyed, as those which may come from the Commander in Chief.

Every Officer of the Virginia Regiment is, as soon as possible, to provide himself with an uniform Dress, which is to be of fine Broad Cloath: The Coat Blue, faced and cuffed with Scarlet, and Trimmed with Silver: The Waistcoat Scarlet, with a plain Silver Lace, if to be had—the Breeches to be Blue, and every one to provide himself with a silver-laced Hat, of a Fashionable size.

A Detachment of one Lieutenant, one Ensign, three Sergeants, three Corporals, a Drummer, and Fifty private men, under the Command of Captain Woodward, are to march on Monday next, for Fort-Cumberland, and to proceed according to the following March Route: viz.

Monday, October the 13th To William Pickets
                      14. To Martin Hardens
                      15   To Joseph Nevils
                      16   To Halt
                      17   To Watts's
                      18   To the River
                      19   To Winchester
                 20 & 21   To Halt
                      22   To Jesse Pugh's
                      23   To Henry Enocks
                      24   To Friend Cox's
                      25   To Plumers, at Crisaps
                      26   To Fort Cumberland.

Lieutenant Lomax and Ensign Hubbard, are Subalterns appointed for this Detachment, being the eldest at present fit for Duty. All the Officers, except such as Major Lewis shall think fit to stay in Town, to take care of the Recruits, are to disperse themselves to different parts, and have a farther time, 'till the 20th of October, allowed them for Recruiting, on which Day, they are to Repair to their place of Rendezvous, without Failure, with what Recruits they can Raise.

October 6, 1755

To Christopher Gist

To Mr Gist.

Before I got to Williamsburgh, the Commissions were chiefly disposed of; yet having you strongly in my mind (which occasioned an earnest solicitation) I succeeded in procuring the only Commission that was vacant, i.e. to be Captain of a Company of Scouts. This is attended with equal Honour, Rank and Profit, with the other Captains; but will be accompanied with more Fatigue; which you will not regard, as you are greatly inured to it. It is intended, that your Company shall consist as much of active Woodsmen, capable of something adequate to your names; I must therefore desire you will Repair immediately thither, in order to receive Money and Instructions to Recruit them; and you may be assured, that I shall Endeavour to provide for your Son in the same Company.

I doubt not but you have heard of the Ravages committed by our inhuman Foes, on the back inhabitants; I am now upon my march against them, with full hopes, that I shall be able to get Satisfaction for their cruel Barbarities.

Never were Indians more wanted than at this time; I have therefore sent to Montour, inviting him, and all he can bring—and should be glad that you would come that way, and use all your interest (as I know you have much with him) to engage his coming—I will promise if he brings many, to do something handsome for him—You had better be silent on this head, though; least where you are, measures may be taken by the Pennsylvanians, to prevent him from bringing any Indians—I am &c.

Winchester October 10th 1755.

To Robert Dinwiddie

Honble Sir   Winchester Saturday Octr the 11th 1755

As I think it my indispensible duty to inform you particularly of my proceedings, and to give the most plain and authentic acct from time to time of our situation, I must acquaint your Honour that immediately after giving the necessary Orders at Fredericksburg and dispatching expresses to hurry the Recruits from Alexandria, I rid post to this place passing by Lord Fairfax's who was not at home, but here; where I arrivd Yesterday abt Noon, and found every thing in the greatest hurry and confusion by the back Inhabitants flocking in, and those of the Town removing out, which I have prevented as far as it was in my power.

I was desirous of proceeding immediatelly at the head of some Militia to put a stop to the Ravages of the Enemy believing their Numbers to be few, but was told by Colo. Martin who had attempted to raise the Militia for the same purpose that it was impossible to get above 20 or 25 Men, they having absolutely refus'd to stir, choosing as they say to die with their Wives and Family's—Finding this expedient was likely to prove abortive, I sent of expresses to hurry on the Recruits from below, and the Militia from Fairfax, Prince William, &ca which Lord Fairfax had ordered—and also hired Spies to go out and see to discover the Numbers of the Enemy, and to encourage the Rangers who we were told, are blocked up by the Indians in small fortresses—but if I may offer my opinion—I believe they are more encompassd by fear than by the Enemy: I have also Impressd Waggons and sent them to Conogogee for Flour, Musket Shott, and Flints; Powder, and a trifling quantity of Paper bought at extravagent prices for Cartridges, I expect from below. Six or eight Smiths are now at Work repairing the few Arms that are here, which is all that we have to depend upon. A man was hired the 24th of last Month to do the whole but neglected, and was just moving off in Wagns to Pennsylvania; I pressd his Waggon's, and compelld him by Force to assist in this Work.

In all things I meet with the greatest opposition no orders are obey'd but what a Party of Soldier's or my own drawn Sword Enforces; without this a single horse for the most urgent occasion cannot be had, to such a pitch has the insolence of these People arrivd by having every point hitherto submitted to them; however, I have given up none where his Majestys Service requires the Contrary, and where my proceedings are justified by my Instruction's, nor will I, unless they execute what they threaten i, e, "to blow out my brains."

I have invited the poor distressed People (who were drove from there Habitation's) to Lodge their Familys in some place of security, and to join our Partys in Scouring the Woods where the Enemy lie; and beleive some will chearfully assist. I also have, & shall continue to take every previous Step to forward the March of the Recruits &ca so soon as they arrive here, and your Honour may depend that nothing that is in my power to do, shall be wanting for the good of the Service.

I woud again hint the necessity of putting the Militia under better Regulation had I not mention'd it twice before, and a third time may seem Impertinent. but I must once more beg leave to declare, (for here I am more immediately concern'd), that unless the Assembly will Enact a Law, to enforce the Military Law in all its Parts, that I must with great regret decline the Honour that has been so generously intended me. and for this only reason I do it—The foreknowledge I have of failing in every point that might justly be expected from a person invested with full power to exert his Authority. I see the growing Insolence of the Soldiers, the Indolence, and Inactivity of the Officers, who are all sensible how confin'd their punishments are, in regard to what they ought to be. In fine, I can plainly see that under our present Establishment we shall become a Nusance; an insupportable charge to our Country, and never answer any one expectation of the Assembly: And here, I must assume the Freedom to express some surprise, that we alone shou'd be so tenacious of Liberty as not to invest a power, where Interest, and Politicks so unanswerably demand it; and from whence so much good must consequently ensue: do we not see that every Nation under the Sun find their accd therein; and without it no Order, no regularity can be observ'd Why then shoud it be expected from us (who are all young and unexperienced) to govern, and keep up a proper spirit of Discipline witht Laws, when the best, and most experienc'd can scarcely do it with—then if we consult our Interest—I am sure it is loudly calld for, For I can confidantly assert that the money expended in Recruiting, Cloathing, Arming, Maintaining, and Subsisting Soldiers who have deserted, has cost the Country an immense Sum, which might have been prevented were we under Restraints, that woud terrifie the Soldrs from such practices: One thing more on this head I will recommend, and then quit the subject, and that is, to have the Inhabitants liable to certain heavy Fines, or Corporal Punishments for Entertaining of Deserters; and a Reward for takg them up; if this was done, it woud be next to an impossibility for a Soldier to Escape—but on the contrary as things now stand, they are not only seduc'd to run away, but are also harbour'd and assisted with every necessary means to make their escape.

Sunday Noon

Last night at 8 o'clock, arrivd an express just spent with fatigue and fear, reporting that a Party of Indians were seen at the Plantation of one Isaac Julian's abt 12 Miles off, and that the Inhabitants were flying in the most promiscuous manner from their dwellings—I immediately order'd the Town Guards to be strengthned, Perkins's Lieut. to be in readiness with his Company, some Recruits (who had only arrivd abt half an hour before) to be Arm'd, and sent two men will acquainted with the woods to go up that road and lay wait, to see if they coud discover the Numbers & Motion of the Indian's, that we might have timely notice of their approach. This Morning before we coud parade the Men to March upon the last Alarm, arriv'd a Second Express ten times more terrified than the former; with information that the Indians had got within four Miles of the Town and were killing and destroying all before them. for that he—himself—had heard constant Firing, and the Shrieks of the unhappy Murder'd— upon this I immediately collected what Force I cou'd, which consisted only of 22 Men recruited for the Ranger's, and 19 of the Militia and Marchd therewith directly to the place where these horrid Murders were said to be committed— when we got there, who shoud we find occasioning all this disturbance, but 3 drunken Soldiers of the Light Horse carousing, firing their Pistols, and uttering the most unheard off Imprecation's, these we took and marchd Prisoner's to Town where we met the Men I sent out last Night, and learnt that the Party of Indian's discovered by Isaac Julian, provd to be a Mulatto and Negro seen hunting of Cattle by his Son, who alarmd the Father, and the Father the neighbourhd. These Circumstances are related only to shew, what a panick prevails among the People, how much they are alarmd at the most usual, and customary Cry's—and yet how impossible it is to get them to act in any respect for their common safety's; an Instance of this then appeard—Colo. Fairfax who arrivd in Town while we were upon the Scout, immediately sent to a Noble Captain (not far off) to repair with his Company forth-with to Winchester: with coolness and moderation, this great Captn answerd, that his Wife, Family, and Corn was at stake, so were those of his Soldrs therefore it was not possible for him to come, such is the Example of the Officer's! Such the behaviour of the Men! And such the unhappy Circumstances on which our Country depends!

Monday Morning

The Men I hired to bring Intelligence from the Branch, return'd last Night with Letter's from Captn Ashby and the other Partys up there, by which we learn that the Indians are gone off. Scouts having been dispersd upon those Water's for several days witht discovering tracts, or other Signs of the En-emy. I am also inform'd that it is believ'd their numbers amounted to 150—that 70 or near it of our People are killd, and missing, and that several houses and Plantations are de-stroy'd, but not so great havock made as was at first repre-sented—The Ranger's, and a small party of Militia ordered up there by Lord Fairfax I am given to understand intend to March down on Wednesday next, who will be immediately followd by all the Inhabitants of those parts that had gather'd under their protection: I have therefore sent Preemptory Or-der's to the Contrary, but what obedience will be paid to it— a little time will reveal. I have order'd those Men who were recruited for the Ranger's to join their Respective Company's, and there is also a party of 20 Militia marchd with them, under the Command of Captn Hardin.

Captn Waggener is this Instant arrivd with 30 Rects which he marched from Alexandria in less than three days a great march indeed! Majr Lewis and his Rects from Fredericksburg is expected in Tomorrow, when with these, and 22 Men of Captn Bells now here I shall proceed by quick Marches to

Fort Cumberland in order to strengthen the Garrison there. Besides these, I think it absolutely necessary that there shoud be two or 3 Companys exclusive of Ranger's to Guard the Potomack Water's, till such times as our Regiment is compleated; and indeed the Ranger's and volunteer Companys in Augusta, with some of their Militia shoud be properly disposd of on those Frontier's for fear of an Attack upon that Quarter: This thô is submitted to your honour's Judgement, & waits your Order's for execution if it shoud be thought expedient. Captn Waggener inform'd me, that it was with difficulty he passd the Ridge for the Crowds of People who were flying, as if every moment was death. he endeavourd, but in Vain to stop them, they firmly believg that Winchester was taken, and in Flames—I have sent expresses down the several Roads in hopes of bringing back the Inhabitants who are really frighted out of their Senses.

I dispatchd an express immediately upon my arrival to this place with a Copy of the Inclosd to Andw Montour, who I heard was at a place calld long Island with 300 Indians, to see if I coud engage him and them to join us. The Letter favours a little of flattery & &ca but this I hope is justifiable on such occasion's—I also wrote to Gist acquaintg him of the favour your Honour intended him, and desir'd he woud repair home in order to raise his Company of Scouts.

I shall defer writing to the Speaker and Committee upon any other head than that of Commissary, still hoping to be down by the time I mention'd in my last (provided no new disturbances happens) having some points to settle that I am uneasy and urgent abt—I have been oblig'd to do dutys quite foreign from my own, but that I shall never hesitate abt when other's do; and the good of the Service requires the Contrary—In a journey from Fort Cumberld to Fort Dinwiddie, which I made purposely to see the Situation of our Frontier's, how the Rangers were Posted, and how Troops might be disposd off for the defence of the Country, I purchased 650 fine Beeves to be deliverd at Fort Cumberland by the First day of Novr next, at 10/ pr hundd except a few that I was obligd to give Eleven Shilgs for, and have my own Bonds now out for performance of Covenants—this being the Commissarys business, who I am sorry to say has hitherto been of no use, but disservice to me, in neglecting my Orders, and leaving this place witht Flour, and Fredericksburg witht any Provision's for the Rects tho their was timely notice given: I must beg that if Mr Dick will not act, that some Person may be appointed that will, for if things remain in this uncertain Situation, the Season will pass witht havg any Provision made for the Winters or Summer's Campaign: whoever acts as Comy shoud be sent up immediately abt Salting the Provision's &ca, it will be difficult I believe to provide a quantity of Pork—I enquir'd as I rode thrô Hampshire, Augusta, &ca and cou'd not hear of much for Sale.

Most of the new appointed Officer's have been extreamly difficient in their Duty's by not repairing to their Rendezvouses according to appointment: Captn McKenzie, Lieutt King & Ensigns Milner and Dean, who were orderd to send their Recruits to Alexandria by the first of Octr were not arrived when Captn Waggener left that place: nor have we heard any thing of Captn Harrison whose Recruits shoud have been at Fredericksburg by the same time; and Captn Bell only sent his here on Saturday last—If these Practices are allowd off, we may as well quit altogether for no duty can ever be carried on, if there is not the greatest punctuality observ'd, one thing always depending so immediately upon Another.

I have appointed Captn George Mercer (whose seniority intitled him to it) my Aid de Camp, and Mr Kirkpatrick of Alexandria my Secretary, a young Man bred to business, of good character, well recommended, and a person whose Abilitys coud not be doubted—I hope your Honour will be kind enough to dispatch Colo. Stephen, with order's to repair here immediately, and excuse the Prolixity of this; I was willing to give a circumstantial acct of our Situation &ca that you may be the Better enabled to judge what Orders are necessary to give. I am Honble Sir Yr most Obt Servt
Winchester Octr 14th 1755

Majr Lewis is just arriv'd, and on Thursday I shall begin my March to Fort Cumberland allowg the Rects 1 day to Refresh themselves.

To Robert Dinwiddie

To the Honourable Robert Dinwiddie, Esquire; Governor.

I have sent the Bearer Captain John Mercer (who has accompts to settle with the Committee) to the Treasurer for the balance of that ten thousand pounds; and to acquaint your Honour, that meeting with Letters at Fredericksburgh, as I returned from Williamsburgh; informing me that all was peaceable above, and that nothing was so immediately wanting as Salt. I got what I could at that place, and hastened on here to engage more; to receive the Recruits that were expected in; and to wait the arrival of the Vessel with Arms, &c. from James River, in order to forward them up with the greater dispatch. The Vessel is not yet arrived.

I have impatiently expected to hear the result of your Honours Letter to General Shirley; and wish that the delays may not prove ominous. In that case, I shall not know how to act; for I can never submit to the command of Captain Dagworthy, since you have honoured me with the command of the Virginia Regiment, &c.

The Country has sustained inconceivable losses by delaying the Commissaries at Williamsburgh: Many of the Carolina Beeves are dead, through absolute poverty; and the chief part of them too poor to slaughter. We are at a loss how to act, for want of the mutiny Bill; and should be obliged to your Honour to have fifty or an hundred printed, and sent by the Bearer. There is a clause in that Bill, which if you are not kind enough to obviate, will prevent entirely the good intention of it: i.e. delaying the execution of Sentences, until your Honour shall be made acquainted with the proceedings of the Court.

This, at times when there is the greatest occasion for Expamples, will be morally impossible (I mean while we are on our march; perhaps near the Ohio) when none but strong parties can pass with safety: at all times it must be attended with great expence, trouble and inconveniency. This I represented to Colonel Corbin and some other Gentlemen of the Council, when I was down; who said that that objection to the Bill would be removed, by your Honours' giving Blank Warrants, to be filled up as occasion should require. This would effectually remedy all those Evils, and put things in their proper channel.

We suffer greatly for want of Kettles: those sent from below being Tin, are of small duration. We shall also, in a little time, suffer as much for want of Clothing; none can be got in these parts: those which Major Carlyle and Dalton contracted to furnish, we are disappointed off. Shoes and Stockings we have, and can get more if wanted, but nothing else. I should be glad your Honor would direct what is to be done in these cases; and that you would be kind enough to desire the Treasurer to send some part of the money in gold and silver: were this done, we might often get necessaries for the Regiment in Maryland or Pennsylvania, when they can not be had here. But with our money it is impossible; our paper not passing there.

The recruiting Service goes on extremely slow. Yesterday being a day appointed for Rendezvousing at this place, there came in ten Officers with twenty men only. If I had any other than paper money, and you approved of it; I would send to Pennsylvania and the Borders of Carolina: I am confident, men might be had there. Your Honor never having given any particular Directions about the Provisions; I should be glad to know, whether you would have more laid in than what will serve for twelve hundred men; that I may give Orders accordingly.

As I can not now conceive, that any great danger can be apprehended at Fort Cumberland this Winter; I am sensible, that my constant attendance there, can not be so serviceable as riding from place to place, making the proper Dispositions, and seeing that all our necessaries are forwarded up with dispatch. I therefore think it advisable to inform your Honour of it, hoping that it will correspond with your own opinion.

I forgot to mention when I was down, that Mr Livingston, the Fort-Major, was appointed adjutant to our Regiment: I knew of none else whose long servitude in a military way, had qualified better for the Office; he was appointed the 17th of September.

Captain Mercer's pay, as aid de camp, seems yet doubtful; I should be glad if your Honour would fix it: so is Captain Stewarts: If Captain Stewarts is encreased, I suppose all the

Officers belonging to the Light Horse will expect to have theirs augmented also. Colonel Stephens, in a late letter, discovered an inclination to go to the Creek and Cherokee Indians this Winter. I told him where to apply, if he had any such thoughts. I believe, on so useful a Business, he might be spared until the Spring. If your Honor think proper to Order the Act of Assembly for apprehending Deserters, and against harbouring them, to be published every Sunday in each parish Church, until the people were made acquainted with the Law, it would have a very good effect. The Commonalty in general, err more through ignorance than design: few of them are acquainted that such a Law exists: and there is no other certain way of bringing it to their knowledge. There are a great many of the men that did once belong to our Companies, deserted from the Regiments into which they were draughted, that would now gladly return, if they could be sure of indemnity. If your Honor would be kind enough to intimate this to General Shirley, or the Colonels of those Regiments, it would be of service to us: without leave we dare not receive them. &c. Alexandria: December 5th 1755

To Robert Hunter Morris

Dear Sir

I had scarce reachd Williamsburg, before an express was after me with news of the French & Indians advancing within our Settlements, and doing incredable mischief to the Inhabitants which obligd me to postpone my business there, and hurry to their assistance with all expedition: when I came to this place I found everythings in deep confusion: and the poor distressd Inhabitants under a general consternation. I therefore collected such force as I could immediately raise, and sent them in such parties, and to such places as twas judged most likely to meet with the Enemy: one of which, under the command of Mr Paris, luckily fell in with a small body of them as they were surrounding a small Fort on the No. River of Cacapehon; whom they engagd, and (after half an hour's close firing) put to flight with the loss of their commander Monsr

Donville (killd) & three or four more mortally wounded. The accident that has determined the fate of Monsieur; has, I believe, dispers'd his Party: for I dont hear of any mischief done in this Colony since, thô we are not without numbers who are makeing hourly discoverys.

I have sent you a copy of the Instructions that were found about this Officer: that you may see how bold and enterprising the Enemy have grown, how unconfind are these ambitious design's of the French: and how much it will be in their power, (if the Colonys continue in their fatal Lethargy) to give a final stab to liberty, & Property.

Nothing I more sincerely wish than a union to the Colonys in this time of Eminent danger: and that you may find your assembly in a temper of mind to act consistently with their preservation. What Maryland has, or will do I know not: but this I am certain off, that Virginia will do every thing that can be expected to promote the publick good.

I went to Williamsburg fully resolved to resign my Commission, but was disswaded from it, at least for a time. If the hurry of business in which I know your honour is genlly engagd: will admit of an oppertunity to murder a little time in writing to me. I shoud receive the favour as a mark of that esteem, which I coud wish to merit, by shewing at all times when its in my power, how much I am Dear Sir Yr honours most Obt & most Hble Servt

P.S. A Letter this instant arriving from Williamsburg, informs, that our Assembly have voted 20,000£s more and that their Forces shd be increas'd to 2000 Men. a laudable example this, and I hope not a singular one.

The inclosed to Colo. Gage I beg the favr of you to forward.

April 9, 1756

To Robert Dinwiddie

To the Honourable Robert Dinwiddie. Governour of Virginia. Honourable Sir,

It gave me infinite concern to find in yours by Governour

Innis, that any representations should inflame the Assembly against the Virginia Regiment; or give cause to suspect the morality and good Behaviour of the Officers. How far any of the individuals may have deserved such invidious reflections, I will not take upon me to determine; but this I am certain of; and can call my conscience, and what I suppose will still be a more demonstrable proof in the eyes of the World, my orders to witness how much I have, both by Threats and persuasive means, endeavoured to discountenance Gaming, drinking, swearing, and irregularities of every other kind. While I have, on the other hand, practised every artifice to inspire a laudable emulation in the Officers for the Service of their Country; and to encourage the Soldiers in the unerring exercise of their Duty—How far I have failed in this desirable end, I can not pretend to say—But it is nevertheless a point which does in my opinion merit some scrutiny, before it meets with a final condemnation. Yet I will not undertake to vouch for the conduct of many of the Officers: as I know there are some who have the seeds of idleness very strongly ingrafted in their natures: and I also know, that the unhappy difference about the command, which has kept me from Fort Cumberland; has consequently prevented me from *enforcing* the Orders, which I never failed to *send*.

However, if I continue in the Service, I shall take care to act with a little more rigor, than has hitherto been practised; since I find it so absolutely necessary.

I wrote your Honour in my last how unsuccessfully we attempted to raise the Militia; and that I was reduced to the necessity of waiting here the arrival of an Escort from Fort Cumberland—Should this escort arrive before Mr Kirkpatrick does from Williamsburgh (whom I hourly expect) I must yet wait a little longer; he being left with all my accompts and Papers to lay before the Committee: and were I to go up without him, it would put it out of my power to settle with the Recruiting Officers above, in order that I might make a final settlement with the Committee below.

The Garrison at Fort Cumberland is barely manned: The rest are out on Parties: yet the Indians continue to Hunt the Roads and pick up stragling persons. This your Honour may see by the enclosed from Captain John Mercer; who being

out with a scouting party of one hundred men I have ordered to search the warm-Spring mountain; where, it is lately reported, that the Indians Rendezvous. The Commission your Honor has sent for holding Courts Martial is yet insufficient, as it is copied (I suppose too literally) after Governor Innis's; who had no power to hold a General Court martial, or to try Commissioned Officers Having none either to hold a Court, or in short any to try. But this may be postponed until I come down, which will be in a short time after I arrive at Fort Cumberland. I am your Honor's &c.
Winchester, April 18th 1756.

To Robert Dinwiddie

To the Honorable Robert Dinwiddie, Governor.
Honorable Sir,

This encloses several letters, and the minutes of a Council of War, which was held upon the receipt of them. Your Honor may see to what unhappy straits the distressed Inhabitants as well as I, am reduced. I am too little acquainted, Sir, with pathetic language, to attempt a description of the peoples distresses; though I have a generous soul, sensible of wrongs, and swelling for redress—But what can I do? If bleeding, dying! would glut their insatiate revenge—I would be a willing offering to Savage Fury: and die by inches, to save a people! I *see* their situation, *know* their danger, and participate their *Sufferings*, without having it in my power to give them further relief, than uncertain promises. In short; I see inevitable destruction in so clear a light, that, unless vigorous measures are taken by the Assembly, and speedy assistance sent from below; the poor Inhabitants that are now in Forts, must unavoidably fall; while the remainder of the County are flying before the barbarous Foe. In fine; the melancholy situation of the people; the little prospect of assistance; The gross and scandalous abuses cast upon the Officers in general—which is reflecting upon me in *particular*, for suffering misconducts of such extraordinary kinds—and the distant prospects, if any, that I can see, of gaining Honor and Reputation in the Service—are motives which cause me to lament the hour that gave me a Commission: and would induce me at any other time than *this*, of imminent danger; to resign without one hesitating moment, a command, which I never expect to reap either Honor or Benefit from: But, on the contrary, have almost an absolute certainty of incurring displeasure below: While the murder of poor innocent Babes, and helpless families, may be laid to my account here!

The supplicating tears of the women; and moving petitions from the men, melt me into such deadly sorrow, that I solemnly declare, if I know my own mind—I could offer myself a willing Sacrifice to the butchering Enemy, provided that would contribute to the peoples ease.

Lord Fairfax has ordered men from the adjacent counties: But when they will come, or in what numbers, I can not pretend to determine—If I may judge from the success we have met with here, I have but little hopes; as three days incessant endeavours have produced but twenty men.

I have too often urged my opinion for vigorous measures—Therefore I shall only add; that besides the accounts you will receive in the Letters; we are told, from all parts, that the woods appear to be alive with Indians, who feast upon the Fat of the Land. As we have not more than a Barrel or two of Powder at this place; the rest being at Fort Cumberland; I could wish your Honor would send up some. I have wrote to Alexandria and Fredericksburgh, desiring that two Barrels may be sent from each place; but whether there is any at either, I know not. I have sent Orders to Captain Harrison to be diligent on the waters where he is posted; and to use his utmost endeavours to protect the People; and, if possible, to surprize the Enemy at their sleeping places. Ashbys Letter is a very extraordinary one. The design of the Indians was only, in my opinion to intimidate him into a Surrender—For which reason I have wrote him word, that if they do attack him, he must defend that place to the last extremity: and, when he is bereft of hope; then to lay a train to blow up the Fort, and retire by night to Cumberland. A small Fort which we have at the mouth of Pattersons Creek, containing an officer and thirty men, guarding Stores, was attacked smartly by the French and Indians; and were as warmly received; upon which they retired. Our men at present are dispersed into such small Bodies, guarding the People and Public Stores; that we are not able to make, or even form a Body. I am Your Honors &c. Winchester, April 22, 1756

General Orders

Evening Orders.

The General Court Martial, whereof Captain Stewart was President, is dissolved.

Colonel Washington approves of the Sentence of the Court—was unanimous in opinion, that Sergeant Nathan Lewis, for his misbehaviour, in running away with his Party, should suffer Death.

The three eldest Captains, eight Subalterns, ten Sergeants, one Drummer, and an hundred Rank & File, to hold themselves in readiness to march to morrow morning upon a Scout.

The Officers to examine the mens arms and ammunition; and see that they are in good order; and are completed with cartridges—This command to draw two days provision more to-night.

The Captains for this command, to see that these Orders are punctually complied with.

Of the Fairfax Militia one hundred men must march tomorrow for the South-Branch; under two Captains and four Subalterns—and to receive their Orders from Colonel Washington. The remainder of the Fairfax Militia, and the company of Volunteers, under Captain John Dalton; are to join the above party, ordered to Scout.

May 3, 1756

General Orders

Parole Westminster.   Winchester—Friday, May 21st 1756.
A Regimental Court Martial to sit immediately for trial of John McMillian.

An Order was lately given out for the Officers to see that the men kept their arms constantly in good repair: But as the *sense* of this order seems to have been mistaken, by its not being strictly complied with—(the Guns perhaps *may* fire;) but that is not all that is expected. Therefore Colonel Washington now expressly orders, that every Soldier who does not appear on the parade at the usual hours, with his Firelock bright and clean, and otherwise in good order, according to the custom of the Army; that he shall be immediately confined and tried by a Court Martial.

It is expected the Officers will see this order strictly complied with; as the sense of *it now*, can not be misconstrued: and if it is neglected to be duly executed; the Officer, to whom such Soldier belongs, must expect to answer Disobedience of orders.

Parole Yarmouth.   Winchester: Saturday, May 22, 1756.

To Robert Dinwiddie

To the Honourable Robert Dinwiddie esq. Governour of Virginia.

Honble Sir,

The method I shall use to inform your Honour of the proceedings of the Militia, is to enclose a Transcript of my Journal that relates to that Affair; and to send a copy of a Council of War held here by the Field Officers of these Counties you were pleased to order to our assistance—These, I hope, will be sufficient to discover the springs that actuated my Conduct.

The spirit of Desertion was so remarkable in the Militia, that it had a surprizing effect upon the Regiment, and encouraged many of the Soldiers to desert: but as I never had

failed in sending Officers on different roads upon the first
reports, so neither did I neglect it now; and luckily caught
two; who being brought to trial, were both convicted—as
your Honour will see by the Courts proceedings. James Thomas, one of them, was among the first of my followers; and
always behaved himself with great sobriety, honesty and diligence, so far as I have ever seen or heard. And I imagine, if
he did not lose the money, as he says in his defence; he might
be prevailed upon to spend a part in liquour—and then was
afraid to meet his officer with the rest.

The other criminal, Henry Campbell, is a most atrocious
villain, and richly merits an ignominious Death, for a former
as well as the present, offence. He was once a Sergeant, and
entrusted with some Goods from Alexandria; part of which
he embezzled; and because it could not be absolutely proved,
was *only* Reduced. After that, (in December last) he deserted,
and carried several men with him: and, upon the most solemn
promises of good Behaviour, was pardoned—But for this only
reason—we had no *power* to hold General Courts martial. and
now he was instrumental in carrying off seven others; two only
of whom were taken. For these reasons I hope your Honour
will think him as worthy an Example against Desertion, as
Lewis against Cowardice: whose execution I have delayed until the arrival of the Draughts. These Examples, and proper
encouragement for good Behaviour, will I hope, bring the
Soldiers under proper Discipline. I found it absolutely impossible to go to Fort Cumberland at this time, without letting
matters of greater importance suffer in my absence here: Such
a multiplicity of different kinds of Business am I at present
engaged in.

Governour Innes is gone up; who I hope will assist with his
advice in setting things to rights, if any irregularities have been
practised contrary to the custom of the army. But I can not
find, by any enquiries that I have been able to make, that there
have.

I have ordered a sufficiency of Officers to be left at Fort
Cumberland, and the rest to repair to this place; in order to
proceed to Fredericksburgh, agreeably to your Honours
Commands: and, as soon as the Gentlemen, Associators arrive
here, I shall take that place in my way to Williamsburgh, to

settle my accompts, and receive more money, which is already scarce with me.

I am heartily glad your Honour has fixed upon those Gentlemen to point out the place for erecting of Forts; but am sorry to find their motions are so slow—The summer season will be so far advanced, that if we meet with opposition in conducting the work; the difficulties and delays that must attend the execution, can not be described.

It gave me infinite concern to find the Assembly had levied their Troops until December only: By the time they shall have entered into the Service, they will claim a Discharge—To get the least smattering of the Duty, they can not; and we find by experience, that our poor and ragged Soldiers, would kill the most likely Militia in five days marching: so little are the latter acquainted with Fatigue. Men would almost as soon have entered the Service for *seventeen* months as for *seven*—and in that time I am convinced, we could have enlisted them all upon our own terms. as it is, some perhaps may be got: Pray does your Honour approve that they should? One of *those* would be of more worth than two of the *others.*

Your Honour, in a letter of the [   ] ultimo, approved of the Scheme I sent down for forming the Regiment into two Battalions of twenty companies (giving the Field Officers each one;) but never gave any directions concerning the appointment. Nor do I think there can be any plan judiciously concerted, until we know what number of Forts are to be built on our Frontiers; as the number of our Companies must in a great measure depend upon the Divisions of the Regiment. As the case now stands, there are several vacancies in the Regiment; and I have but one blank commission: Though if I had, I should not think it prudent to fill up more, until matters are a little better regulated.

At this place I have begun the Fort according to your Orders; and found, as little of the matter as I know myself, the *work* could not be conducted if I was away: which was one among many reasons, that detained me here—I have also ordered Captain Stewart, who commands at Conogochieg, to fortify that place as well as he can, with the Tools he *can* procure. And shall endeavour in all things, so far as I am capable, to act for the best.

Mr Dick (who is just returned from the northward) says, There are Orders for drawing out all the ammunition and other Stores that belong to the Train at Fort Cumberland; and to send them immediately round to New-York.

I have thought it expedient to give your Honour the earliest advice, that you may order accordingly: For should this be done, it will leave that place entirely defenceless; and stop the source that can supply us otherwise. I have given Colonel Stephen previous notice of it; and have desired he will work on the conductor of the Train (in whose care it is left) and have the Forts of Ashby, Cockes, &c. plentifully furnished before such an order arrives. I am &c.

Winchester—May 23, 1756.

General Orders

Parole, Integrity.   Winchester: Tuesday, June 1st 1756.

The Company of artificers being intended to assist in building a Fort at this place, are to do no Duty as Soldiers—They are to get their Tools in order, and go to work to-morrow morning.

A Return to be given in immediately of all the men fit for Duty in Town; mentioning those who are good Carpenters.

His Honour, Governour Dinwiddie, has approved of the Sentence of the General Court martial, held here the eighteenth day of may last, whereof Captain Woodward was President—which was of opinion, that James Thomas and Henry Campbell (for Desertion) should suffer death—But he has been pleased, upon James Thomas's former good behaviour, to pardon him—through Colonel Washingtons Recommendation.

To the Earl of Loudoun

Winchester in Virginia July 25th 1756
To the Right Honourable, John, Earl of Loudon—General and Commander in Chief of all His Majesty's Forces in North

America and Governor and Commander in Chief of His Majesty's Most antient Colony and Dominion of Virginia.

We the Officers of the Virginia Regiment beg Leave to congratulate Your Lordship on your safe Arrival in America: And to express the deep Sense We have of His Majesty's great Wisdom and paternal Care for his Colonies in sending your Lordship to their Protection at this critical Juncture. We likewise beg Leave to declare our singular Satisfaction and sanguine Hopes on your Lordship's immediate Appointment over our Colony, as it in a more especial Manner entitles Us to your Lordship's Patronage.

Full of Hopes that a perfect Union of the Colonies will be brought about by Your Lordship's Wisdom and Authority, and big with Expectations of seeing the extravagant Insolence of an Insulting Subtle and Inhuman Enemy restrained, and of having it in our Power to take our desired Revenge: We humbly represent to your Lordship, that We were the first Troops in Action on the Continent on Occasion of the present Broils, And that by several Engagements and continual Skirmishes with the Enemy, We have to our Cost acquired a Knowledge of Them, and of their crafty and cruel Practices, which We are ready to testify with the greatest Chearfulness and Resolution whenever We are so happy as to be honoured with the Execution of your Lordship's Commands. In Behalf of the Corps

Go: Washington, Colo.

To Robert Dinwiddie

To The Honble Robert Dinwiddie, Esquire; Governor of
  Virginia.
Honble Sir,

This day, within five miles of the Carolina line, as I was proceeding to the southermost Fort in Halifax; I met Major Lewis on his return from the Cherokees, with seven men, and three women only of that nation. The causes of this unhappy disappointment, I have desired him to communicate, that your Honor may take measures accordingly. This account is sent by Express, to give the earliest notice, while the Assembly

are sitting. I shall defer giving a particular detail of my remarks
and observations on the situation of our Frontiers, until I return to Winchester, as I expect by that time to be more intimately acquainted with the unhappy circumstances of the
people: Yet I shall not omit mentioning some occurrences
which have happened in my Tour to this place. I wrote your
Honor from Winchester, that I should set out the next day
for Augusta; I accordingly did with Captain McNeil; and hearing at the Court-house, that the Indians still continue their
depredations (although not so openly as at first)—I applied to
Colonel Stewart, then present, to raise a party of the militia,
and said I would head them, and march to Jackson's River,
to try to scour the woods, and if possible fall in with the
Enemy. He gave me very little encouragement to expect any
men, yet desired I would wait 4 days, until monday, and he
would use his endeavours to collect a body: until Tuesday I
waited, and only 9 men appeared. This being too inconsiderable a number to expose to a triumphant enemy; I was advised to apply to Colonel Buchanan for men, between whom
and Colo: Stewart there was contention about command. As
Col. Buchanan lived at Luneys ferry, on James River, 60 miles
along the road to Vass's, on Roanoak, where Captain Hogg
was building a fort; to which place I did intend, if I could
have got men to range along the Frontiers with me. I set out
immediately for his house, attended by Captain Preston; who
was kind enough to conduct me along, and acquainted the
Colonel with the motives that brought me thither. He told
me with very great concern, it was not in his power to raise
men; for that three days before, some of the militia in a fort,
about 15 miles above his house, at the head of Cattawba, commanded by one Colonel Nash, was attacked by the Indians
which occasioned all that Settlement to break up totally, even
to the ferry at Luneys: That he had ordered three companies
to repair thither, to march against the enemy, and not one
man came, except a Captain, Lieutenant, &c. and 7 or 8 men
from Bedford. Finding then that it was impossible to get a
party to range and scour the frontiers, it remained only to
proceed without men to see the situation of the Forts, or to
return back again: the latter I was loth to do, as I had got
this far; and was anxious to see what posture of defence they

were in. I therefore determined to come forward, at least to Vass's; and accordingly set out in company with Colonel Buchanan, who being desirous that I might see and relate their unhappy circumstances, undertook to accompany me. We got safe to Vass's, where Captain Hogg, with only 18 of his company, were building a fort which must employ him 'til Christmas, without more assistance. One Captain Hunt from Lunenburg, was there with 30 men; but none of them wou'd strike a stroke, unless I would engage to see them paid 40 lb's. Tobacco per day, which is provided by act of Assembly for militia Carpenters. This I certainly could not do; as your Honor (who I thought had ordered them purposely out for this Duty) had given no directions in the affair. Whatever expectations your Honor may have had from the militia assistance; I am told they never lent a hand, save a few, that first came out with Captain Hoy; who he has paid after the same rates with our men, at 6d. per diem. Vass's place is a pass of very great importance, being a very great inroad of the enemy, and secure, if it was strongly garrisoned. All Bedford, and the greatest part of this County, notwithstanding they have built three forts here, and *one* of them, if no more, erected in my opinion in a very out-of-the-way place—This they call Fort Trial. From Vass's I came off with a Servant and a Guide, to visit the range of forts in this county; and in less than two hours after, two men were killed along the same road; as will appear by Captain McNiel's letter, which I have just received, & herewith send, to let your Honor see by the account of Captain Hunts behaviour what dependance may be put in the militia. The Inhabitants are so sensible of their danger, if left to the protection of these people, that not a man will stay at his place—This I have from their own mouths, and the principal persons of Augusta-County. The militia are under such bad order and discipline, that they will go and come when and where they please; without regarding time, their officers, or the safety of the Inhabitants; but consulting solely their own inclinations. There shou'd be, according to your Honors orders, one-third of the militia of these parts, now on Duty at once; instead of that, I believe scarce $\frac{1}{13}$th is out. They are to be relieved every month—they are more than that time marching to & from their stations, and will not wait one day

longer than the limited time, whether they are relieved or not,
let the necessity for it be never so urgent. An instance of this
happened in my presence about 4 days ago, in the case of
Captain Daniel from Albemarle; who was entreated by Colonel Buchanan to stay, at the time he was gathering, or attempting to gather men, upon that alarm of the Catawba
Settlement, before mentioned—but his month was out, and
go he must and did: nay I believe I may venture to say, that
whether his month had been out or not, this wou'd have induced him to go: for this Gentlemen went away from Vass's,
because he thought it was a dangerous post, giving that for
his reason—and left Captain Hogg with 18 men, exposed to
the insults of the enemy. Perhaps it may be thought I am
partial in my relation, and reflect unjustly; I really do not, Sir;
I scorn to make unjust remarks on the behaviour of the militia, as much as I despise and contemn the persons who
detract from mine, and the character of the Regiment. Were
it not that I consulted the good of the public, and thought
these Garrisons merited redress I should not think it worth
my mention—I only want to make the Country sensible, how
ardently I have studied to promote her cause; & wish very
sincerely my Successor may fill my place, more to their satisfaction in every respect than I have been able to do. I mentioned in my last to your Honor, that I did not think a less
number than 2,000 men wou'd be sufficient to defend our
extensive and much exposed Frontiers, from the ravages of
the enemy—I have not had one reason yet to alter my opinion, but many to strengthen and confirm it. and I flatter myself the Country will, when they know my determinations, be
convinced that I have no sinister views, no vain motives of
commanding a number of men—that urge me to recommend
this number to your Honor; but that it proceeds from the
knowledge I have acquired of the country, people, &c. to be
defended.

Your Honor I hope will give directions about laying in provisions on our southern frontiers; it is not in my power to do
it, as I know not what Troops can or will be put there; for
the Regiment is at present too weak to allow any men to
march from the Quarter on which they are now stationed. I
set out this day on my return to the Fort, on the head of

Catawba, where Colonel Buchanan promised to meet me with a party to conduct me along our Frontiers, up Jackson's-River to Fort-Dinwiddie, and higher if needful. If he does not meet me, I shall immediately proceed to Winchester, as it will be impossible to do any thing without men. If your Honor thinks proper to advance the pay of the militia, in order to engage them to work, please to acquaint Captain Hogg therewith, and send him money for that purpose: and were there more men ordered to cover his party, and assist in the work, it wou'd be highly advisable; for he lies greatly exposed. Major Lewis is extremely unwell—This Express is refered to your Honor for pay—I have not money to do it. I am hurried a good deal; but have given a plain account of all those several matters, mentioned in the foregoing Sheet. I am &c.
Hallifax, October 10th 1756.

To Robert Dinwiddie

Honble Sir   Philadelphia March 10th 1757
    We may I think with great Propriety and Justice represent.
    That—The Virginia Regiment was the first in arms of any Troops upon the Continent, in the prest War. That—The three Years which they have Servd has been one continued Scene of Action. That—whilst other Troops have an agreeable recess in Winter Quarters, the Nature of the Service in which we are engagd, and the smallness of Our Numbers so unequal to the Task, keep us constantly in Motion—That nevertheless, all these Services have hitherto been performd with great Spirit and cheerfulness but That continuing in a Service precarious and uncertain: hazarding Life Fortune & health to the chances of War, for the present, and a bare Subsistance, is matter for serious, and melancholy reflection: It tends to promote langour and Indifference: It sickens that laudable and generous Emulation so necessary among Troops: It is nipping in the bud our rising hopes. Hopes that we have been led to cherish: It is discouraging to Merit, and, I can't help repeating, that it is in the highest degree dispiriting to the Officers, more especially those, who, having thrown themselves out of

other employments are now to look forward and see, that they are wasting the Prime of their Lives and Constitutions in a Service the most uncertain, and Precarious: In which they can expect to be continued no longer than hard blows, and continual Dangers require their Aid. and when those Causes Cease, are then dismissd, perhaps in a State of disability and Indigence from wounds, &ca.

These are reflections that must have due weight in every Breast, but the Idiots and Madman's, and have made Our Officers anxiously Solicituous to know their Fate—at once—and the full extent of their Dependances, that they may regulate their conduct accordingly.

We cant conceive, that being Americans shoud deprive us of the benefits of British Subjects; nor lessen our claim to preferment: and we are very certain, that no Body of regular Troops ever before Servd 3 Bloody Campaigns without attracting Royal Notice.

As to those Idle Arguments which are often times us'd—namely, You are Defending your own properties; I look upon to be whimsical & absurd; We are Defending the Kings Dominions, and althô the Inhabitants of Gt Britain are removd from (this) Danger, they are yet, equally with Us, concernd and Interested in the Fate of the Country, and there can be no Sufficient reason given why we, who spend our blood and Treasure in Defence of the Country are not entitled to equal prefermt.

Some boast of long Service as a claim to Promotion—meaning I suppose, the length of time they have pocketed a Commission—I apprehend it is the service done, not the Service engag'd in, that merits reward; and that their is, as equitable a right to expect something for three years hard & bloody Service, as for 10 spent at St James's &ca where real Service, or a field of Battle never was seen.

If it shou'd be said, the Troops of Virginia are Irregulars, and cannot expect more notice than other Provincials, I must beg leave to differ, and observe in turn, that we want nothing but Commissions from His Majesty to make us as regular a Corps as any upon the Continent—Because, we were regularly Enlisted attested and bound, during the King's or Colony's Pleasure—We have been regularly Regimented and trained, and have done as regular Duty for upwards of 3 Years as any regiment in His Majesty's Service—We are regularly and uniformly Cloathd; Officers & Soldiers—We have been at all the expence that regulars are in providing equipage for the Camp—and in few words I may say, we labour under every disadvantage, and enjoy not one benefit which regulars do.

How different from Us, the Establishment of all other Provincials is, may easily be discernd by considering, that they are raizd for a Season—assembled in the spring and are dismissd in the Fall. consequently are totally ignorant of regular Service—They know their Dependance, and had nothing to expect; therefore coud not be dissappointed. They are never cloathd, and are at little expence, as they act as Irregulars and paid exorbitantly. There remains one reason more, which of itself, is fully sufficient to obviate scrupples: & that is—we have been in constant Pay, & on constant Duty since the commencement of these Broils, which none others have.

And we flatter ourselves, it will evidently appear, that the Advantages gaind by the Enemy, and the Ravages committed on our Frontiers are not owing to the Inactivity of the V. Regt In proof of which, we appeal to the many bloody Skirmishes with the Enemy last Campagn to our Behar at Monogahela, & Services in the Campaign of 1754; To the number of Officers & Men killd in Battle, &ca &ca.

Recountg these Services is highly disagreeable to us—as it is repugnant to the Modesty becoming the Brave, but we are compelld thereto by the little Notice taken of Us—It being the General Opinion, that our Services are slighted, or have not been properly represented to His Majesty: otherwise the best of Kings woud have graciously taken Notice of Us in turn, while there are now Six Battalions raizd in America, and not an Officer of the Virginia Regiment Provided for. notwithstanding many of them had distinguishd themselves in the Service before Orders were Issued for raizing one of the Battalions above mentiond. Whereas, the disregarding the faithful services of any Body of His Majesty's Subjects, tends to discourage Merit and lessen that generous Emulation, spirit, and laudable ambition so necessary to prevail in an Army and which Contributes so much to the Success of Enterprize.

I, in behalf of the Officers of the Virginia Regt beg, that

your Honour will be pleas'd to take their Case into particular
Consideration, and as they think themselves particularly entitled to your Honours Patronage, give them Reason by your
earnest endeavours with His Lordship, to hope for a Soldiers
reward, and redress their Grievances in whatever manner shall
seem to your Honour most conducive to their Interest, and
His Majesty's Service—We are all Sensible, that nothing but
earnest application can obtain promotion, while there are so
many dependants; & we now hope, as justice and equity are
clear on our side, and as this seems to be the Crisis of our
Fate that no stone will be unturnd to bring this abt. I am
Honble Sir Yr most Obedt Hble Servt

To Richard Washington

Dear Sir,   Fort Loudoun April 15th 1757.
   After so long Silence it may be expected I shoud introduce
this Letter with an Apology for my seeming neglect, it is necessary to urge something in my defence I own Sir, that I may
satisfy you it proceeds from a very different cause than the
want of Inclination, and what can be so proper as the Truth.
   I have been posted then for twenty Months past upon our
cold and Barren Frontiers, to perform I think I may say im-
possibilitys that is, to protect from the cruel Incursions of a
Crafty Savage Enemy a line of Inhabitants of more then 350
Miles extent with a force inadequate to the taske, by this mean
I am become in a manner an exile and Seldom informd of
those oppertunitys which I might otherwise embrase of corrisponding with my friends.
   Experience Sir, has convincd every thinking Man in this
Colony that we must bid adieu to peace and safety whilst the
French are allowd to possess the Ohio, and to practice their
hellish Arts among the numerous Tribes of Indian Nations
that Inhabit those Regions. They are also convincd that it
must be attended with an expence infinitely greater to defend
our Possessions (as they ought to be defended) against the
Sculking Enemy than to remove the cause of our groundless
Fears in the Reduction of the Place—Fort Duquesne I mean,

Yet, from what strange Causes I know not, no attempt this Season will be made I fear, to destroy this Hold of Barbarians—for they deserve no better a name who have become a Terror to three populous Colonies—Virginia may justly say she was always willing to furnish her full proportion of Men and money for this desirable end—and I think I can venture to affirm that there never was, and verily I believe never will be, a more favourable time than now for an Enterprize of this kind while the Enemy's Troops are (doubtless) drawn of to the Northward to defend themselves at home against the more formidable attacks of Lord Loudoun.

I have now to add—That I am so little acquainted with the Business relative to my private Affairs that I can scarce give you any information concerning it—I know that I ought to have some Tobo and that it ought to be Shipd—that I have begd the favour of Colo. Carlyle on Potomack and Fielding Lewis Esqr. on Rappahannock to do this for me and that I desird them to write you in my behalf and draw for Sundry things which I am in want of but whether any part, or all of this is done I know not I shall therefore desire these two things of you first that you may put yourself to no real Inconvenience in providing Goods to greater amount than my Remittances will fetch because I by no means intended to be troublesome when I sollicited your Corrispondance—and secondly that whatever Goods you may send me where the prices are not absolutely limited you will let them be fashionable—neat—and good in their several kinds. Inclosd is a List of Sundries which I shoud be glad to receive agreeable to those Directions. I am Dr Sir Yr affecte & Obedt Friend

To John Stanwix

To Colo. Stanwix
Dear Sir,   July 15th 1757.
Your obliging favour of the 11th instant I received this morning. It will seem odd to send you three letters under one cover; and those so widely differring in their dates: But the truth only shall account for it.

Mr Atkin has told me day after day, since the date of my first, that his Express wou'd go off the next morning, as he wou'd the preceding evening be able to finish his dispatches to you. This prevented my enquiring after any other conveyance, and is the cause of the delay of my letters 'till now.

Militia, you will find, Sir, will never answer your expectation—No dependendance is to be placed upon them: They are obstinate and perverse; they are often egged on by the Officers, who lead them to acts of disobedience: And, when they are ordered to certain posts for the security of Stores, or the protection of the Inhabitants, will, on a sudden, resolve to leave them, and the united vigilance of their Officers can not prevent them. Instances of the above nature I have now before me, which put me to some difficulty.

No man I conceive was ever worse plagu'd than I have been with the Draughts that were sent from the several counties in this Government, to compleat its Regiment: out of 400 that were received at Fredericksburgh, and at this place, 114 have deserted; notwithstanding every precaution, except absolute confinement, has been used to prevent this infamous practice. I have used the most vigorous measures to apprehend those fellows who escaped from hence (which amounted to about 30;) and have succeeded so well, that they are taken, with the loss of one of their men, and a Soldier wounded. I have a Gallows near 40 feet high erected (which has terrified the *rest* exceedingly:) and I am determined, if I can be justified in the proceeding, to hang two or three on it, as an example to others.

An affair has happened at this place which may, I apprehend, be productive of very unhappy consequences: it is this. About 6 days ago came to this town, from Chota, in the cherokee nation, ten Indians; some of whom call themselves Mingo's tribe of the Six nations; others Cherokees, &c. But, as they gave no good account of their intentions, Mr Atkin suspected their loyalty; and taking them for Spies, has caused them to be put in close confinement, in which they now remain.

This proceedure greatly alarmed, and at the same time exasperated about 12 cherokees, who were at this place and knew all the prisoners; and has obliged Mr Atkin to send an Express to the South-Branch, to bring Outassity down, who now lies sick there, to clear the matter up. He is not yet arrived.

Nineteen Indians, and the Officer I mentioned in my last, marched from Fort Cumberland the 9th instant for Ft du Quesne. By their return, I hope I shall receive some intelligence worth transmitting to you: At present we are pretty peaceable.

The Philadelphia post, which formerly came to this place, being stopped, prevents our hearing any foreign news, but what are transmitted in the channel of friendly Letters. We greatly regret the loss of this post, and wou'd gladly keep it up by private subscription, from this to Carlyle, if it comes that length. I am Your &c.

To Robert Dinwiddie

To Governor Dinwiddie
Honble Sir,

A letter of the 22d ultimo from Captn Peachy, came to my hands the other day—contents as follows (here was inserted the letter.) I shou'd take it infinitely kind if your Honor would please to inform me, whether a report of this nature was ever made to you; and in that case, who was the author of it?

It is evident from a variety of circumstances, and especially from the change in your Honors conduct towards me, that some person as well inclined to detract, but better skilled in the art of detraction than the author of the above stupid scandal, has made free with my character. For I can not suppose, that malice so absurd, so bare-fac'd, so diametrically opposite to truth, to common policy; and in short, to every thing but villainy, as the above is, *cou'd* impress you with so ill an opinion of my honor and honesty!

If it be possible that Colonl Corbin (for my belief is staggered; not being conscious of having given the least cause to any one, much less to that Gentleman, to reflect so grossly;) I say, if it be possible, that Colo. Corbin cou'd descend so low as to be the propagator of this story; he must either be vastly ignorant in the state of affairs in this county at *that time*;

or else he must suppose, that the whole body of Inhabitants had combined with me, in executing the deceitful fraud. Or why did they almost to a man, forsake their dwellings in the greatest terror and confusion? And, while one half of them sought shelter in paltry forts (of their own building) the other shou'd flee to the adjacent counties for refuge; numbers of them even to Carolina; from whence they have never returned.

These are facts well known; but not better known, than that these wretched people, while they lay pent up in forts, destitute of the common supports of life (having in their precipitate flight forgotten, or were unable rather, to secure any kind of necessaries) did dispatch messengers of their own (thinking I had not represented their miseries in the piteous manner they deserved) with addresses to your Honor and the Assembly, praying relief. And did I ever send any alarming account, without also sending the original papers (or the copies) which gave rise to it?

That I have foibles, and perhaps many of them, I shall not deny; I shou'd esteem myself, as the world also wou'd, vain and empty, were I to arrogate perfection. Knowledge in military matters is to be acquired by practise and experience only: and if I have erred, great allowance should be made for my errors for want of it—unless those errors shou'd appear to be wilful: and then I conceive it wou'd be more generous to charge me with my faults, and let me stand or fall, according to evidence, than to stigmatize me behind my back.

It is uncertain in what light my Services may have appeared to your Honor—But this I know, and it is the highest consolation I am capable of feeling; that no man that ever was employed in a public capacity has endeavoured to discharge the trust reposed in him with greater honesty, and more zeal for the country's interest, than I have done: and if there is any person living, who can say with justice that I have offered any intentional wrong to the public, I will chearfully submit to the most ignominious punishment that an injured people ought to inflict! On the other hand; it is hard to have my character arraigned and my actions condemned, without a hearing.

I must therefore again beg, in *more plain*, and in very *earnest terms*, to know, if Colo. Corbin has taken the liberty of representing my character to your Honor, with such ungentlemanly freedom as the letter implies? Your condescension herein will be acknowledged a singular favour done. Your Honors' most obedt Hble Servant,
Fort Loudoun, Septem. 17th 1757.

To John Stanwix

To Brigadier-General Stanwix
Dear Sir,   Ft L April 10th 1758.

Permit me, at the same time I congratulate you (which I most sincerely do) upon the promotion you have met with, and justly merited; to express my Concern at the prospect of parting with you. I can truly say, it is a matter of no small regret to me! and that I shou'd have thought myself happy in serving this campaign under your immediate command. But every thing I hope, is ordered for the best; and it is our duty to submit to the will of our Superior. I must nevertheless beg, that you will add one more kindness to the many I have experienced, and that is, to mention me in favorable terms to General Forbes (if you are acquainted with that Gentleman) not as a person who would depend upon him for further recommendation to military preferment, for I have long conquered all such expectancies (and serve this campaign merely for the purpose of affording my best endeavours to bring matters to a conclusion) but as a person who would gladly be distinguished in some measure from the *common run* of provincial Officers; as I understand there will be a motley herd of us.

Nothing can contribute more to His Majesty's Interest in this Quarter, than an early campaign, or a speedy junction of the Troops to be employed in this Service. Without this, I fear the Indians with difficulty will be restrained from returning to their nation before we assemble; and in that event, no words can tell how much they will be missed. It is an affair of great importance, and ought to claim the closest attention of the Commanding Officer; for, on the assistance of these people, does the security of our march very much depend.

There should be great care taken, also, to lay in a supply of proper Goods for them: The Indians are mercenary; every service of theirs must be purchased: and they are easily offended, being thoroughly sensible of their own importance. Upwards of 5,00 are already come to this place, the greatest part of whom are gone to war: many others are daily expected, and we have neither arms nor clothes (proper) to give them: nor indeed is it reasonable to expect, that the whole expence accruing on account of these people, should fall upon this Government—which hath already in this, as well as in many other respects, exerted her utmost abilities for His Majestys Interest, and in the present case, shares *only* an equal proportion of the advantages arising from Indian Services. These crude thoughts are hastily thrown together: if you find any thing contained in them which may be useful, be pleased to improve them for his Majestys interest.

The latitude which you have hitherto allowed me—joined to my zeal for the Service, have encouraged me to use this freedom with You Sir, which I should not chuse to take, unasked, with another.

If it is not inconsistent, I should be glad, before I conclude to ask, what regular troops are to be employed under Brigad. Gen. Forbes, and when they may be expected? also, where they are to rendezvous? Ft Frederick, I hear, is mentioned for this purpose, &, in my humble opinion, a little improperly: In the first place, because the country people all around are fled, and the troops will, consequently, lack those refreshments so needful to Soldiers. In the next place; I am fully convinced there never can be a road made between Fort Frederick and Fort Cumberland that will admit the transportation of carriages: for I have passed it with many others, who were of the same opinion. And, lastly—because this is the place to which all Indian parties, either going to, or returning from war, will inevitably repair. I am, with most sincere Esteem, Dear Sir, Your most obedient, and obliged humble Servant,

To James Wood

My Dear Colonel

If thanks flowing from a heart replete with joy and Gratitude can in any Measure compensate for the fatigue anxiety & Pain you had at my Election be assurd you have them. tis a poor, but I am convincd welcome tribute to a generous Mind—such, I believe yours to be.

How I shall thank Mrs Wood for her favourable wishes? and how acknowledge my Sense of Obligations to the People in General for their choice of me I am at a loss to resolve on—but why—can I do it more effectually than by making there Interests (as it really is) my own and doing every thing that lyes in my little Power for the Honr and welfare of the County—I think not—and my best endeavours they may always Command—I promise this now, when promises may be regarded—before they might pass as words of Course.

I am extreme thankly to you & my other friends for entertaining the Freeholders in my name—I hope no exception were taken to any that voted against me but that all were alike treated and all had enough it is what I much desird—my only fear is that you spent with too sparing a hand.

I don't like to touch upon our Publick Affairs the Prospect is overspread by too many ill to give a favourable Acct. I will therefore say little—but yet say this, that backwardness appears in all things but the approach of Winter—that joggs on apace.

c. July 28, 1758

To Francis Halkett

To Francis Halkett—Brigade Mr
My dear Halkett.

I am just returnd from a Conference held with Colo. Bouquet. I find him fixd—I think I may say fix'd, upon leading you a New way to the Ohio; thro. a Road, every Inch of it to cut, at this advancd Season, when we have scarce time left to tread the beaten Tract; universally confessd to be the best Passage through the Mountains.

If Colo. Bouquet succeeds in this point with the General—all is lost!—All is lost by Heavens!—our Enterprize Ruind; & We stopd at the Laurel Hill for this Winter—not to gather Laurels by the by, desirable in their effects—The Southern Indians turn against Us—and these Colonies become desolate by such an Acquisition to the Enemy's Strength.

These are the Consequences of a Miscarriage. and a Miscarriage the Consequence of the Attempt—I have drawn my Reason's out at large, and now send them to Colo. Bouquet—He desir'd I woud do so that he might forward them to the General. shou'd this happen you may Judge of their weight.

I am uninfluencd by Prejudice—having no hope or fears but for the General Good—That be assurd of—and my Sincere Sentiments are spoke on this occasion. I am Dear Halkett Most Affectionately Yr Obedt
Camp at Ft Cumbd 2d of August 1758

To Sarah Cary Fairfax

Dear Madam,   Camp at Fort Cumberland 12th Septr 1758.

Yesterday I was honourd with your short, but very agreable favour of the first Instt. how joyfully I catch at the happy occasion of renewing a Corrispondance which I feard was disrelishd on your part, I leave to time, that never failing Expositor of All things.—and to a Monitor equally as faithful in my own Breast, to Testifie. In silence I now express my Joy.—Silence which in some cases—I wish the present—speaks more Intelligably than the sweetest Eloquence.

If you allow that any honour can be derivd from my opposition to Our present System of management, you destroy the merit of it entirely in me by attributing my anxiety to the annimating prospect of possessing Mrs Custis. When—I—need not name it.—guess yourself.—Shoud not my own Honour, and Country's welfare be the excitement? Tis true, I profess myself a Votary to Love—I acknowledge that a Lady is in the Case—and further I confess, that this Lady is known to you.—Yes Madam, as well as she is to one, who is too sensible of her Charms to deny the Power, whose Influence he feels and must ever Submit to. I feel the force of her amiable beauties in the recollection of a thousand tender passages that I coud wish to obliterate, till I am bid to revive them.—but experience alas! sadly reminds me how Impossible this is.—and evinces an Opinion which I have long entertaind, that there is a Destiny, which has the Sovereign controul of our Actions—not to be resisted by the strongest efforts of Human Nature.

You have drawn me my dear Madam, or rather have I drawn myself, into an honest confession of a Simple Fact—misconstrue not my meaning—'tis obvious—doubt it not, nor expose it,—the World has no business to know the object of my Love, declard in this manner to—you when I want to conceal it—One thing, above all things in this World I wish to know, and only one person of your Acquaintance can solve me that, or guess my meaning.—but adieu to this, till happier times, if I ever shall see them.—the hours at present are melancholy dull.—neither the rugged Toils of War, nor the gentler conflict of A—— B—s is in my choice.—I dare believe you are as happy as you say—I wish I was happy also—Mirth, good Humour, ease of Mind and.—what else? cannot fail to render you so; and consummate your Wishes.

If one agreable Lady coud almost wish herself a fine Gentleman for the sake of another; I apprehend, that many fine Gentlemen will wish themselves finer, e'er Mrs Spotswood is possest.—She has already become a reigning Toast in this Camp; and many there are in it, who intends—(fortune favouring)—to make honourable Scar's speak the fulness of their Merit, and be a messenger of their Love to Her.

I cannot easily forgive the unseasonable haste of my last Express, if he deprivd me thereby of a single word you intended to add.—the time of the present messenger is, as the last might have been, entirely at your disposal.—I cant expect to hear from my Friends more than this once, before the Fate of the Expedition will, some how or other be determind, I therefore beg to know when you set out for Hampton; & when you expect to Return to Belvoir again—and I shoud be glad to hear also of your speedy departure, as I shall thereby hope for your return before I get down; the disappointment of seeing your Family woud give me much concern.—From any thing I can yet see 'tis hardly possible to say when we shall finish—I dont think there is a probability of it till the middle of November. Your Letter to Captn Gist I forwarded by a safe hand the moment it came to me.—his answer shall be carefully transmitted.

Colo. Mercer to whom I deliverd your message and Compliments, Joins me very heartily in wishing you and the Ladies of Belvoir the perfect enjoyment of every Happiness this World affords.—be assured that I am Dr Madam with the most unfeigned regard, Yr Most Obedient & Most Obligd Hble Servt

N.B. Many Accidents happening (to use a vulgar saying) between the Cup and the Lip, I choose to make the Exchange of Carpets myself—since I find you will not do me the honour to accept of mine.

Farewell Address to the Virginia Regiment

To Captain Robert Steward and Gentlemen Officers of the
  Virginia Regiment.
My dear Gentlemen.   New Kent County 10th Janry 1759
  If I had words that could express the deep sense I entertain of your most obliging & affectionate address to me, I should endeavour to shew you that *gratitude* is not the smallest engredient of a character you have been pleased to celebrate; rather, give me leave to add, as the effect of your partiality & politeness, than of my deserving.
  That I have for some years (under uncommon difficulties, which few were thoroughly acquainted with) been able to conduct myself so much to your satisfaction, affords me the greatest pleasure I am capable of feeling; as I almost despared of attaining that end—so hard a matter is it to please, when one is acting under disagreeable restraints! But your having, nevertheless, so fully, so affectionately & so publicly declared your approbation of my conduct, during my command of the

Virginia Troops, I must esteem an honor that will constitute the greatest happiness of my life, and afford in my latest hours the most pleasing reflections. I had nothing to boast, but a steady honesty—this I made the invariable rule of my actions; and I find my reward in it.

I am bound, Gentlemen, in honor, by inclination & by every affectionate tye, to promote the reputation & interest of a Corps I was once a member of; though the Fates have disjoined me from it now, I beseech you to command, with equal confidence & a greater degree of freedom than ever, my best services. Your Address is in the hands of the Governor, and will be presented by him to the Council. I hope (but cannot ascertain it) that matters may be settled agreeable to your wishes. On me, depend for my best endeavours to accomplish this end.

I should dwell longer on this subject, and be more particular in my answer, did your address lye before me. Permit me then to conclude with the following acknowledgments: first, that I always thought it, as it really was, the greatest honor of my life to command Gentlemen, who made me happy in their company & easy by their conduct: secondly, that had every thing contributed as fully as your obliging endeavours did to render me satisfied, I never should have been otherwise, or have had cause to know the pangs I have felt at parting with a Regiment, that has shared my toils, and experienced every hardship & danger, which I have encountered. But this brings on *reflections* that fill me with grief & I must strive to forget them; in thanking you, Gentlemen, with uncommon sincerity & true affection for the honor you have done me—for if I have acquired any reputation, it is from you I derive it. I thank you also for the love & regard you have all along shewn me. It is in this, I am rewarded. It is herein I glory. And lastly I must thank you for your kind wishes. To assure you, that I feel every generous return of mutual regard—that I wish you every honor as a collective Body & every felicity in your private Characters, is, Gentlemen, I hope unnecessary—Shew me how I can demonstrate it, and you never shall find me otherwise than your Most obedient, most obliged and most affectionate

To Robert Cary & Company

Gentn   Williamsburg May 1. 1759.

The Inclosd is the Ministers Certificate of my Marriage with Mrs Martha Custis—properly as I am told—Authenticated, you will therefore for the future please to address all your Letters which relate to the Affairs of the late Danl Parke Custis Esqr. to me. as by Marriage I am entitled to a third part of that Estate, and Invested likewise with the care of the other two thirds by a Decree of our Genl Court which I obtain in order to Strengthen the Power I before had in consequence of my Wifes Administration.

I have many Letters of yours in my possession unanswerd, but at present this serves only to advise you of the above Change and at the sametime to acquaint you that I shall continue to make you the same Consignments of Tobo as usual, and will endeavour to encrease it in proportion as I find myself and the Estate benefitted thereby.

The Scarcity of the last Years Crop; and the high prices of Tobo consequent thereupon woud in any other Case, have inducd me to sell the Estates Crop (which indeed is only 16 Hhds) in the Country but for a present, & I hope small advantage only I did not care to break the Chain of Corrispondance that has so long Subsisted, and therefore have, according to your desire, given Captn Talman an offer of the whole.

On the other side is an Invoice of some Goods which I beg of you to send me by the first Ship bound either to Potomack or Rappahannock, as I am in immediate want of them, Let them be Insurd, and in case of accidents reshipd witht Delay. Direct for me at Mount Vernon Potomack River Virginia; the former is the name of my Seat the other the River on which 'tis Situated. I am Gentn Yr Most Obedt Hble Servt

To Richard Washington

Dear Sir,   Mount Vernon 20th September 1759

Inclosd you will receive a Bill (promisd in my last of the

7th May) which please to receive and place to my Credit—Since mine of the above date your agreable favour of the 26th March covering Invoice of Sundries pr the desire is come to hand as has the Goods also in good Order which is more than most of the Importers by that Ship can boast great part of her Cargoe being damagd—thrô the Negligence tis said of the Captain.

My Brother is safe arrivd but little benifitted in point of Health by his Trip to England. The longing desire, which for many years I have had of visiting the great Matrapolis of that Kingdom is not in the least abated by his prejudices because I think the Small share of Health he enjoyd while there must have given a Sensible Check to any pleasures he might figure to himself, and woud render any place Irksome—but, I am now tied by the Leg and must set Inclination aside.

The Scale of Fortune in America is turnd greatly in our favour, and Success is become the boon Companion of our Fortunate Generals—Twoud be folly in me to attempt particularising their Actions since you receive Accts in a Channel so much more direct than from hence.

I am now I beleive fixd at this Seat with an agreable Consort for Life and hope to find more happiness in retirement than I ever experiencd amidst a wide and bustling World—I thank you heartily for your Affectionate Wishes—Why wont you give me an occasion of congratulating you in the same manner? none woud do it with more cordiality, & true sincerity than Dear Sir Yr Most Obedt & Obligd Servt

Diary Entry

For an Experimt.

Take 7 Pots (Earthen) or 7 Boxes of equal size and number them.

Then put in No. 1 pld. Earth taken out of the Field below, which is intend. for Wheat—in No. 2, 3, 4, 5, 6 and 7 equal proportion's of the same Earth—to No. 2 put Cow dung—to 3 Marle, 4 with Mud from the Marshes & bottoms adjoining the [   ] Field, to 5 Mud taken out of the River immediately, to 6 the same Mud lain to Mellow sum time, and to 7 the Mud taken from the Shoreside at low Water where it appears to be unmixd with Clay. Of each an equal quantity—and at the proper Season of Sowing Oats put in each of these Pots or boxes 6 Grains of the largest and heaviest Oats planted at proper distances—and watch their growth and different changes till Harvest.

N.B. To preserve them from Accidents put them in the Garden and let the Pots be buried up to their brims.

May 22, 1760

Reward for Runaway Slaves

Fairfax County (*Virginia*) *August* 11, 1761. Ran away from a Plantation of the Subscriber's, on *Dogue Run* in *Fairfax*, on Sunday the 9th Instant, the following Negroes, *viz.*

Peros, 35 or 40 Years of Age, a well-set Fellow, of about 5 Feet 8 Inches high, yellowish Complexion, with a very full round Face, and full black Beard, his Speech is something slow and broken, but not in so great a Degree as to render him remarkable. He had on when he went away, a dark colour'd Cloth Coat, a white Linen Waistcoat, white Breeches and white Stockings.

Jack, 30 Years (or thereabouts) old, a slim, black, well made Fellow, of near 6 Feet high, a small Face, with Cuts down each Cheek, being his Country Marks, his Feet are large (or long) for he requires a great Shoe: The Cloathing he went off in cannot be well ascertained, but it is thought in his common working Dress, such as Cotton Waistcoat (of which he had a new One) and Breeches, and Osnabrig Shirt.

Neptune, aged 25 or 30, well set, and of about 5 Feet 8 or 9 Inches high, thin jaw'd, his Teeth stragling and fil'd sharp, his Back, if rightly remember'd, has many small Marks or Dots running from both Shoulders down to his Waistband, and his Head was close shaved: Had on a Cotton Waistcoat, black or dark colour'd Breeches, and an Osnabrig Shirt.

Cupid, 23 or 25 Years old, a black well made Fellow, 5 Feet

8 or 9 Inches high, round and full faced, with broad Teeth before, the Skin of his Face is coarse, and inclined to be pimpley, he has no other distinguishable Mark that can be recollected; he carried with him his common working Cloaths, and an old Osnabrigs Coat made Frockwise.

The two last of these Negroes were bought from an *African* Ship in *August* 1759, and talk very broken and unintelligible *English*; the second one, *Jack*, is Countryman to those, and speaks pretty good *English*, having been several Years in the Country. The other, *Peros*, speaks much better than either, indeed has little of his Country Dialect left, and is esteemed a sensible judicious Negro.

As they went off without the least Suspicion, Provocation, or Difference with any Body, or the least angry Word or Abuse from their Overseers, tis supposed they will hardly lurk about in the Neighbourhood, but steer some direct Course (which cannot even be guessed at) in Hopes of an Escape: Or, perhaps, as the Negro *Peros* has lived many Years about *Williamsburg*, and *King William* County, and *Jack* in *Middlesex*, they may possibly bend their Course to one of those Places.

Whoever apprehends the said Negroes, so that the Subscriber may readily get them, shall have, if taken up in this County, Forty Shillings Reward, beside what the Law allows; and if at any greater Distance, or out of the Colony, a proportionable Recompence paid them, by

GEORGE WASHINGTON.

N.B. If they should be taken separately, the Reward will be proportioned.

To Richard Washington

Dear Sir,   Mount Vernon October the 20th 1761.
Since my last of the 14th July I have in appearance been very near my last gasp—The Indisposition then spoken of Increasd upon me and I fell into a very low and dangerous State—I once thought the grim King woud certainly master my utmost efforts and that I must sink in spite of a noble

struggle but thank God I have now got the better of the disorder and shall soon be restord I hope to perfect health again.

I dont know that I can Muster up one tittle of News to communicate, in short the occurrances of this part of the World are at present scarce worth reciting for as we live in a state of peaceful tranquility ourselves, so we are at very little trouble to enquire after the operations against the Cherokees who are the only People that disturbs the repose of this great Continent and who I believe woud gladly accomodate Differences upon almost any Terms not I conceive from any Apprehensions they are under on account of our Arms but because they want the Supplys which we, and we only, can furnish them with—We catch the reports of Peace with gaping Mouths, and every Person seems anxious for a confirmation of that desirable Event provided it comes as no doubt it will, upon honourable terms.

On the other side is an Invoice of Cloaths which I beg the favour of you to purchase for me and to send them by the first Ship bound to this River—As they are designd for Waring Apparel for myself I have committed the choice of them to your fancy—having the best opinion of your taste—I want neither Lace nor Embroidery—plain Cloaths with a gold or Silver Button (if worn in genteel Dress) is all I desire—I have hitherto had my Cloaths made by one Charles Lawrence in old Fish Street but whether it be the fault of the Taylor, or the Measure sent I can't say but certain it is my Cloaths have never fitted me well. I therefore leave the choice of the Workman to your care likewise—I enclose a Measure, and for a further Insight I dont think it amiss to add that my stature is Six feet—otherwise rather slender than Corpulent. I am very sincerely Dr Sir Yr Most Affecte Hble Servt

To Robert Cary & Company

Gentlemen,   Mount Vernon 28th May 1762

Your unacknowledged favours of the 26th June 10th Augt 16 & 19th Septr and the 19th of Octr following now lye before—in that one of Augt 10th I perceive you bring the shortness of some of the Bundles of the Tobo Shipped in the Bland to acct for the lowness of the Price—That some of the Tobo was small I shall not undertake to dispute, but at the sametime I must observe that it was clean & neatly handled which I apprehended woud have rendered the other objection of very little weight—As to stemming my Tobo in the manner you recommend I woud readily do it if the returns woud be equivalent to the trouble, & loss of the Stem, and of this I shall be a tolerable judge as I am at no small pains this year to try the quality with the advantages & disadvantages of different kinds of Tobos and shall at the sametime find out the difference between a hhd of Leaf & a hhd of Stemmd Tobo by comparing then the loss of the one with the extra price of the other I shall be able to determine which is the best to pursue & follow that method which promises the most certain advantages.

Some of the Tobo which I put on board the Unity Captn Cuzzens got damaged in carrying to the Warehouses for Inspection & had a part cut of which will no doubt deface it a little but as this happened while I was at Williamsburg I am able to give you no exact Information concerning it—In this parcel of Tobo there are three kinds which please to give me yr opinions upon—No. 1 to 6 Inclusive are of one kind—from 9 to 14 are of another—& 15 & 16 are of a third sort—the rest are of the same kinds of these three but made on other Plantations.

As I have ever laid it down as an established Maxim to believe that every person is, (most certainly ought to be) the best judges of What relates to their own Interest & Concerns I very rarely undertake to propose Schemes to others which may be attended with uncertainty & miscarriage—this will at once acct for my being among the last who shoud advise your sending a Vessell into Potomack for the accomodation of your

Friends there. That I have often thought of it as a desirable thing for the Shippers, I will readily confess and have as often concluded that so soon as you found an established consignment formed here you woud do it of course—and sooner we ought not to expect it—Since you have proposed the matter yourself to me—I certainly must approve of it, and as you are so obliging to write that you shall direct the Matter to be under my notice I hope you will be perswaded to believe that I shall readily contribute my best advice and assistance towards his dispatch—The Tobacco's of most of your friends upon Potomack (or that Ships from thence) lyes within 15 Miles above & below this place, and as good, or the best harbour (Piscataway) is within sight of my Door—It has this great advantage besides good Anchorage & laying safe from the Winds that it is out of the way of the Worm which is very hurtful to Shipping a little lower down & lyes in a very plentiful part of the Country—I thought it incumbant upon me to mention these things after which do as you please. If I had receivd any Intimation of your sending a Vessell into this River I shoud not have engaged any part of my Tobo to Cuzzens, & while I remain in expectation of her arrival will not seek a freight else where for the residue of what I intend your house from this River which probably may amount to about 30 hhds more.

My Letter of the 25th of Jany will inform you how the Interest of the Bank stock is to be applied—as that fund was appropriated towards the payment of Miss Custis's Fortune I am informed that the Stock ought to be transferred to her. you will please therefore to have it done accordingly and whatever charges may arise in so doing place to her own Acct. I hope Messrs Hill & Co. will send the wine into this River for I had rather have it in Madeira than York.

Thus far had I wrote & was going to conclude when your favour of the 18th Jany was presented to me—I am sorry to hear the Accts given of the Tobo Shipped in Boyes but as you don't particularize the proprietor's names who suffered most I am in hopes my 70 hhds have pretty well escaped the general complaint—If it has not I confess it to be an Art beyond my skill, to succeed in making good Tobo as I have used my utmost endeavours for that purpose this two or 3 years past—& am once again urged to express my surprize at finding that

I do not partake of the best prices that are going—I saw an Acct rendered by Mr Athaws of some Tobo which he sold for Mr Fairfax at 12½d. the Tobo went from this River & I can aver was not better than 12 hhds of my Mountn Crop which you receivd in the Sarah & Bland last Summr—In fact Mr Fairfax's Plantation's & mine upon Shannondoah lye in the same neighbourhood—The Tobo brought to the same Inspection—and to be short, is in all respects exactly alike—none of mine however sold for more than 11d. or 3½ which you please while his went of a little before at the price of 12½ aforesaid—this is a difference really too great & I see it with concern—however Gentlemen I hope to find it otherwise for the time to come. I am Yr Most Obedt Hble Servt.

To Charles Lawrence

Mr Lawrence   Virginia 26th April 1763.

Be pleased to send me a genteel sute of Cloaths made of superfine broad Cloth handsomely chosen; I shoud have Inclosed you my measure but in a general way they are so badly taken here that I am convinced it woud be of very little service; I woud have you therefore take measure of a Gentleman who wears well made Cloaths of the following size—to wit—Six feet high & proportionably made; if any thing rather Slender than thick for a Person of that highth with pretty long arms & thighs—You will take care to make the Breeches longer than those you sent me last, & I woud have you keep the measure of the Cloaths you now make by you and if any alteration is required, in my next it shall be pointed out. Mr Cary will pay your Bill—& I am Sir Yr Very Hble Servt

Note for your further Government and knowledge of my size I have sent the Inclosed—and you must observe that from the Coat end To No. 1 & No. 3 is the size over the breast & hips.

No. 2 over the Belly—&

No. 4 round the Arm—& from the Breeches end

To No. a is for Waistband.

b thick of the Thigh
c upper button hole
d kneeband
e for length of Breeches
therefore if you take measure of a Person about 6 feet high
of this bigness, I think you can't go amiss—you must take
notice that the Inclosed is the exact size without any allowance
for Seams &ca. Yr &ca

To Robert Stewart

My dear Stewart
Your Letters of the 18th Jany & 2d of Mar. came to my
hands at the sametime about the 10th Instt. I knew of no ship
then on the point of Sailing for any part of Great Britain, and
therefore have been unavoidably silent till now; indeed I coud
have given but a very unsatisfactory answer before this. I participated in the pleasing prospect which seemed to flatter your
wishes about the time of writg your first Letter, as much as I
felt for its reverse in the next, but human Affairs are always
chequered, and Viscissitudes in this Life are rather to be expected than wondered at.

I wish my dear Stewart that the circumstances of my Affairs
woud have permitted me to have given you an order upon
any Person—in the world I might add—for £400 with as
much ease & propriety as you seem to require it, or even for
twice that Sum if it woud make you easy; but alas! to shew
my inability in this respect I inclose you a copy of Mr Carys
last Acct currt against me, which upon my honr and the faith
of a Christian is a true one, and transmitted to me with the
additional aggravation of a hint at the largeness of it. Messrs
Hanbury's have also a Balle against me, and I have no other
Corrispondants in England with whom I deal, unless it be
with a namesake for trifles such as Cloaths; & for these I do
not know whether the Balle is for or against me.

This upon my Soul is a genuine Acct of my Affairs in England—here they are a little better because I am not much in
debt. I doubt not but you will be surprized at the badness of

their condition unless you will consider under what terrible management and disadvantages I found my Estate when I retired from the Publick Service of this Colony; and that besides some purchases of Lands and Negroes I was necessitated to make adjoining me—(in order to support the Expences of a large Family)—I had Provision's of all kinds to buy for the first two or three years, and my Plantations to Stock—in short with every thing—Buildings to make, and other matters, which swallowed up before I well knew where I was, all the money I got by Marriage nay more, brought me in Debt, and I believe I may appeal to your own knowledge of my Circumstances before.

I do not urge these things my dear Sir in order to lay open the distresses of my own Affairs, on the contrary they shoud forever have remained profoundly secret to your knowledge did it not appear necessary at this time to acquit myself in yr esteem, & to evince my inability, of exceeding £300 a sum I am now labouring to procure by getting money to purchase Bills of that amt to remit to yourself, that Mr Cary may have no knowledge of the transaction since he expected this himself, and for which my regard for you will disappoint him—A Regard of that high nature that I coud never see you uneasy without feeling a part and wishing to remove the cause; and therefore when you complained of the Mortification of remaining a Subaltern in a Corp you had frequently commanded the Subs. of I wanted you out, and hoped it might be effected—but I shall have done on the Subject giving me leave to add only that in case you shoud not have a call for the money (and your Letter speaks of this) you will then be so good as to pay it to Mr Cary to whom I believe it will be no disagreable tender and advise me thereof—the Inclosd will inform you of what I have wrote to him on this head, which Letter you may deliver, or destroy at pleasure.

I am exceedingly obliged to you for your kind offer's of Services in London, but I have nothing to give you the trouble of. I write in very great haste, and know I may depend upon your Friendship to excuse any thing and every thing amiss in the Letter. With the most perfect regard I remain Dear Sir Yr Most Affecte & Most Obedt

April 27, 1763

To Robert Cary & Company

Gentn   Mount Vernon 10th August 1764.

Since my last of the first of May I have received the Goods by Boyes, likewise the Nails pr Watson, with the Letters Accounts of Sales Accounts Current &ca which accompanied them—as also another Letter of the 28th of March by Captn Hooper.

It might possibly answer very little purpose were I to enter into a minute detail of the Reasons that have caused me to fall so much in arrears to you and therefore I shall not trouble you fully with the particulars at this time but content myself with observing in as few words as the nature of the Subject will admit of that in whatsoever light it may appear to you, it is not less evidently certain that Mischances rather than Misconduct hath been the causes of it: For it was a misfortune that Seasons and chance shoud prevent my making even tolerable Crops in this part of the Country for three years successively and it was a misfortune likewise when they were made that I shoud get little or nothing for them—It may also be looked upon, as unlucky at least, that the Debts which I thought I had collected, and actually did remit to you shoud be paid in Bills void of credit, and as things have turned out (and you have such occasion for your money) it is unlucky likewise that I made some purchases of Lands & Slaves in this Country since it obliged me to apply more of the Currt money (which was due to the Estate here) towards the payment thereof than I expected and of consequence more of the Sterlg Balle in your hands to the credit of Master Custis in order to Assign him his full dividend of the personal Estate not conceiving in the least degree that I shoud have occasion for more of it than woud remain after such application was made—because, had these Bills been answerd—had my Crops proovd good, & sold well, the Balle I think coud never have been against me—Howevr to be as short as possible—To remove the seeming apprehension (expressd in yours of the 13th of February) of your suffering in point of Interest for the money you then discoverd you stood in advance for me I wrote you on the first of May following that I had no sort of

objections to allowing Interest from thence forward and desired you woud charge it accordingly untill the Debt was
Paid—not desiring that you, or any body else shoud suffer in
the most trivial Instances on my account—and I shall now in
consequence of your other Letter of the 28th of March beg
leave to inform you—in terms equally sincere and direct—that
it is not in my power, I shoud add in a manner convenient
and agreable to myself, to make remittances faster than my
Crops (& perhaps some few occasional Sums which may fall
in my way) will furnish me with the means: but if notwithstanding, you cannot be content with this mode of payments
you have only to advise me of it and I shall hit upon a method
(thô I woud choose to avoid it) that will at once discharge
the Debt, and effectually remove me from all further mention
of it—for I must confess, I did not expect that a corrispondant
so steady, & constant as I have proovd, & was willing to have
continued to your House while the advantages were in any
degree reciprocal woud be reminded in the Instant it was discovered how necessary it was for him to be expedious in his
payments—Reason and prudence naturally dictates to every
Man of common sense the thing that is right, & you might
have rested assured, that so fast as I coud make remittances
without distressing myself too much, my Inclinations woud
have prompted me to it: because in the first place it is but an
irksome thing to a free mind to be any ways hampered in
Debt; and in the next place, I think I have discovered no
intentions, Since I have found how the Balle was likely to turn,
of increasing that Debt (unless it shoud appear in the amount
of my Invoices last year which greatly indeed exceeded my
expectations but will be ballenced I hope by the contracted
one of this year): but on the contrary all the willingness I
coud, under the accidents that have happened, of decreasing
it to the utmost of my power—but I have already run into
much greater prolixity on this head than I promised, or intended—Your answer will determine my measures, and upon
this Issue it must Rest.

I shoud be glad to receive an Acct of Sales for the rest of
the Tobaccos which Master Custis and myself have in yr hands
that I may see more fully how the Ballances stand—All the
Tobacco which I had ready upon this River I have given to

Boyes amounting to 20 Hhds on which please to make such Insurance as you shall judge most advisable—in like manner do upon 21 Hhds of my York River Tobacco in the same Ship—and upon Sixty of Master Custis's which accompanies it—I have about 8 or 10 Hhds more on this River which shall be shipd by the first Vessell I can obtain liberty in after it is got from the Mountains where the disturbances that have been occasiond by the Indians renders it difficult to procure Waggon's for the transportation of it.

Some pains have I taken to satisfie myself of the equity of Mrs Pasavents claim of £5.8.6 or to convince you of the Injustice of it the latter of which I conceive can easily be done from the Inclosed papers and from Mrs Washingtons Assertion's who will if required give testimony that she never sent for such Goods as Mrs Passavent Charges the delivery of in 1758 (for the eviction of which it is only having recourse to the order's of the preceeding year) and moreover that she never did receive any such—Inclosed is Mrs Pasavents Note of Sundrys sent by Captn Coxen & charged in yr Invoice of March 1758—If any such Goods were had (as She now charges) woud they not have been included in this Bill? surely I think so, but further I can declare I nevr saw or heard of such things althô the Goods by Coxen arrivd a little before the time of my Marriage and in 1760 I wrote for the very Identical Articles, which She there charges, (except the French bead Stomacher & Sleeve knots) and had them in accordingly the year following as will appear by S. Rush's Note and your own Invoice and that at the very identical prices also which the other has chargd—it is very unlikely therefore that we shoud have occasion for Goods of this sort in the succession here chargd—on the contrary I think it must appear evident from the circumstances & assurances here given that Mrs Pasavents claim arises from a mistake, or that the charge is in itself unjustly made in either of which cases I cannot submit to a payment of the demand.

Miss Custis's Trunk which was missing last year is at length received: the contents in good order—Inclosd are Invoices of such Goods as I stand in need of for my Family's use & shoud be glad to receive by the first good oppertunity that offers to this River (Potomack): The usual quantity of Goods for our

Plantations on York River are yet to be added, but untill I see or hear from Mr Valentine I cannot form the Lists in the meantime am unwilling to slip the present occasion of forwarding my own.

Equally in behalf of Master and Miss Custis, and in favour of Mr Walter Magowan (their Tutor) I drew upon you the 6th Instt for £45.13.9 which is to be charged to them in equal proportion's—Miss Custis may not perhaps just at the time of offering this Bill have as much money in your hands arising from the Interest of Bank stock as will fully pay her half of it, and answer the order for Goods at the same time, but as the half years payment at Lady day next will soon follow, and I shall always be ready to make up any deficiency, I hope they will nevertheless meet with a ready acceptance. I am Gentn Yr Most Obedt Serv.

To Robert Cary & Company

Gentn   Mount Vernon 20th September 1765.

It cannot reasonably be imagined that I felt any pleasing Sensations upon the receipt of your Letter of the 13th of February covering accts of Sales for 153 Hhds of Master Custis's Tobo and 115 of mine.

That the Sales are pitifully low, needs no words to demonstrate—and that they are worse than many of my Acquaintance upon this River—Potomack—have got in the Out Posts, & from Mr Russel and other Merchants of London for common Aronoko Tobo, is a truth equally as certain—Nay not so good as I myself have got from Mr Gildart of Liverpool for light Rent Tobaccos (shipd him at the same time I did to you) of the meanest sort; such as you once complaind of as the worst of Maryland & not Saleable—Can it be otherwise than a little mortifying then to find, that we, who raise none but Sweetscented Tobacco, and endeavour I may venture to add, to be careful in the management of it, however we fail in the execution, & who by a close and fixed corrispondance with you, contribute so largely to the dispatch of your Ships in this Country shoud meet with such unprofitable returns? Surely I may answer No! Notwithstanding, you will again receive my own Crops this year, & 67 Hhds of Master Custis's; but Gentlemen you must excuse me for adding (As I cannot readily conceive that our Tobacco's are so much depreciated in quality as not only to sell much below other Marks of good repute, but actually for less, as I before observd, than the commonest kinds do) that justice to myself & ward will render it absolutely necessary for me to change my corrispondance unless I experience an alteration for the better.

I might take notice upon this occasion also, that my Tobo Netts a good deal less than Master Custis's, & why it shoud do so, I am really at a loss to discover: his 153 Hhds averaging £7.7.7 and my 115 only £5.17.6—perhaps it may be urged that some of mine was Potomack Tobacco, I grant it, but take these out and the Yorks then average £6.6.5 only—If you had allowed him the benefit of the Bonded Duties I shoud not have wonderd at the difference, but this I perceive is not done, and certain I am, my Tobacco ought not to have been inferior to his—in any respect—the Lands being the same, & my directions for making it good equally as express.

Tobacco I well perceive for a year or two past, had fallen in its value—from what causes I shall not take upon me to determine—and I am not so extravagent as to believe that my own and Master Custis's Crops shoud fetch their usual prices when other good Tobacco met with abatements; but I am really selfish enough to expect that we ought to come in for a part of the good prices that are going, from a belief that our Tobacco is of a quality not so much inferior to some that still sells well, and that so considerable a Consignment—when confined in a manner to one House, as ours is—woud lay claim to the best endeavours of the Merchant in the Sales, and in the return of Goods, for many Articles of which I pay exceeding heavily. another thing I cannot easily Account for, unless it is on a Presumption that they are bought at very long credits which by no means ought to be the case; for where a Person has money in a Merchants hands he shoud doubtless have all the benefits that can result from that money—and in like manner where he pays Interest for the use of the Merchants shoud he be entitled to the same advantages, otherwise it might well be asked for what purpose is it that

Interest is paid? Once upon my urging a complaint of this nature you wrote me, that the Goods ought to be sent back, and they shoud be returnd upon the Shopkeepers hands in cases of Imposition; but a moments reflection points out the Inconveniencies of such a measure unless (the Imposition be grossly abusive, or that) we coud afford to have a years stock before hand; how otherwise can a Person who Imports bear requisites only submit to lay a year out of any particular Article of Cloathing, or necessary for Family use, and have recourse to such a tedious & uncertain way of relief as this, when possibly a Tradesman woud deny the Goods & consequently refuse them—It is not to be done—we are obliged to acquiesce to the present loss & hope for future redress.

These Gentlemen are my Sentiments, fully, and candidly expressd, without any design—believe me—of giving you offence; but as the selling of our Tobacco's well, & purchasing of Our Goods upon the best Terms, are matters of the utmost consequence to our well doing, it behooves me to be plain and sincere in my declaration's on these points—previous to any change of measures—that I may stand acquitted of the Imputation of fickleness if I am at last forced to a discontinuance of my corrispondance with your House.

Twenty Hhds of my Tobacco from this River makes up Forty eight which I have in Boyes; the remainder (which is trifling) shall be sent by the first Ship that gives liberty; and as I have not been able to discover any advantages we obtain by our Tobaccos lying so long upon hand, unsold, I shoud be glad to have the present Crops (& so of others if more be sent) disposd of to the first good Chapmen, & the Sales returnd, unless there is a very probable certainty of a rise of price to warrant the keeping of it.

By this conveyance you will receive Invoices of Goods wanted for our Plantation's on York; and those for this River, will no longer I hope be sent in by Boyes for when they come into that River we really suffer by the strange mistakes that continually happen—Last year several parcels of Goods designd for York River were sent to this place and others for me left down there & in going backwards & forwards some were lost (things too of no inconsiderable value, for one of the parcels was a Bale of Linnen) and this year all my Plaid hose for this River came in a package to Mr Valentine & I have them to send for 150 Miles—These mistakes & Inconveniencies woud necessarily be avoided if the Goods were to come by Ships to the respective Rivers; and they woud also escape those frequent damages which is the consequence of shifting them from one Vessel to another, and transporting them from place to place—Oppertunities of doing this cannot be wanting as many Vessels comes to this River annually (from London) some of which lye at my Door.

It appears pretty evident to me from the prices I have generally got for my Tobacco in London, & from some other concomitant Circumstances, that it only suits the Interest of a few particular Gentlemen to continue their consignments of this commodity to that place, while others shoud endeavour to substitute some other Article in place of Tobacco, and try their success therewith. In order thereto you woud do me a singular favour in advising of the general price one might expect for good Hemp in your Port watered & prepared according to Act of Parliament, with an estimate of the freight, & all other Incident charges pr Tonn that I may form some Idea of the profits resulting from the growth—I shoud be very glad to know at the sametime how rough & undressd Flax has generally, and may probably sell; for this year I have made an Essay in both, and altho. I suffer pretty considerably by the attempt, owing principally to the severity of the Drougth, & my inexperience in the management I am not altogether discouraged from a further prosecution of the Scheme provided I find the Sales with you are not clogd with too much difficulty and expence.

The Stamp Act, imposed on the Colonies by the Parliament of Great Britain engrosses the conversation of the speculative part of the Colonists, who look upon this unconstitutional method of Taxation as a direful attack upon their Liberties, & loudly exclaim against the violation—What may be the result of this (I think I may add) ill Judgd measure, and the late restrictions of our Trade and other Acts to Burthen us, I will not undertake to determine; but this I think may be said— that the advantages accruing to the Mother Country will fall far short of the expectation's of the Ministry; for certain it is, that the whole produce of our labour hitherto has centred in

Great Britain—what more can they desire? and that all Taxes which contribute to lessen our Importation of British Goods must be hurtful to the Manufacturers of them, and to the Common Weal—The Eyes of our People (already beginning to open) will perceive, that many of the Luxuries which we have heretofore lavished our Substance to Great Britain for can well be dispensed with whilst the Necessaries of Life are to be procurd (for the most part) within ourselves—This consequently will introduce frugality; and be a necessary stimulation to Industry—Great Britain may then load her Exports with as Heavy Taxes as She pleases but where will the consumption be? I am apt to think no Law or usage can compel us to barter our money or Staple Commodities for their Manufacturies, if we can be supplied within ourselve upon the better Terms—nor will her Traders dispose of them without a valuable consideration and surety of Pay—where then lyes the utility of these Measures?

As to the Stamp Act taken in a single and distinct view; one, & the first bad consequence attending of it I take to be this— our Courts of Judicature will be shut up, it being morally impossible under our present Circumstances that the Act of Parliament can be complied with, were we ever so willing to enforce the execution; for not to say, which alone woud be sufficient, that there is not money to pay the Stamps there are many other Cogent Reasons to prevent it and if a stop be put to our Judicial proceedings it may be left to yourselves, who have such large demands upon the Colonies, to determine, who is to suffer most in this event—the Merchant, or the Planter.

I am very much obliged to you for your kind advice of corrisponding with Mr Dandridge—it is a piece of respect due to so near a Relation of my Wifes, & therefore I give you the trouble of the Inclosed; but I have not the least expectation of deriving any advantages from it for thô he has no nearer relatives than her, there are some to whom I believe he has given stronger proofs of his Inclinations of serving—but to you my thanks are equaly due, & I return them with cordiality for the goodness of your Intentions. I am Gentn Yr Most Obedt humble Servt

To Josiah Thompson

Sir,   Mount Vernon July 2d 1766.
    With this Letter comes a Negro (Tom) which I beg the
favour of you to sell, in any of the Islands you may go to, for
whatever he will fetch, & bring me in return for him
    One Hhd of best Molasses
    One Ditto of best Rum
    One Barrl of Lymes—if good & Cheap
    One Pot of Tamarinds—contg about 10 lbs.
    Two small Do of mixed Sweetmeats—abt 5 lb. each
    And the residue, much or little, in good old Spirits
    That this Fellow is both a Rogue & Runaway (tho. he was
by no means remarkable for the former, and never practised
the latter till of late) I shall not pretend to deny—But that he
is exceeding healthy, strong, and good at the Hoe, the whole
neighbourhood can testifie & particularly Mr Johnson and his
Son, who have both had him under them as foreman of the
gang; which gives me reason to hope he may, with your good
management, sell well, if kept clean & trim'd up a little when
offerd to Sale.
    I shall very chearfully allow you the customary Commis-
sions on this affair, and must beg the favour of you (least he
shoud attempt his escape) to keep him handcuffd till you get
to Sea—or in the Bay—after which I doubt not but you may
make him very useful to you.
    I wish you a pleasant and prosperous Passage, and a safe &
speedy return, being Sir, Yr Very Hble Servt

To John Posey

Sir,   Mt Vernon 24th June 1767.
    It is difficult for me to tell which was greatest, my Surprise,
or concern, at finding by your Letter of the 20th that instead
of being able with the money I agreed to lye somewhat longer
out of, to discharge your Debts, that you wanted to borrow
a further Sum of £500 to answer this purpose. I was in hopes,

and you gave me the strongest assurances to believe, that when I lent you (& very inconvenient it was for me to do it) the first Sum of £700 you coud therewith, not only discharge all your Creditors, but in two years time sink the principal which was lent to effect that end; how it comes to pass then, that instead of being prepared in twice two years to discharge my claim, you shoud require £500 more to satisfie others, is, as I at first said, entirely beyond my comprehension, and leaves but too much cause to apprehend, that if you coud be supplied with the further Sum required, it woud afford but temporary relief; and that at the end of any other prefixd period you woud be as unprepard and as reluctantly then, as now, part with yr effects to discharge this Debt; thinking it equally hard to be forced into compliance—for permit me to say again, if you have not been able in the course of 4 Years to lay up anything towards sinking even the Interest of a Sum which you said woud entirely clear you of all demands, what prospect can you possibly have to expect when £500 more (& probably this woud be insufficient) is added to the other surety of between eight and nine hundd, that you will have it in your power to effect this end, when even the Interest thereof is a pretty little Income, & woud be such a Moth in your Estate as woud inevitably destroy it, be your notions of saving & Industry extended to never so high a degree: Indeed Sir, the only purpose it coud possibly answer woud be to put the evil day of for a moment, in comparison, & then like most things swelld beyond their natural bounds, burst upon you like a torrent & redouble your distresses. Besides, you really deceive yourself greatly in estimating your Effects, as you will unhappily experience; you have viewed them but on one side, considering only what they cost you, not what they will sell at, which is a delusive way of calculating; for you will find that many things which you perhaps have lavishd large Sums in the purchase of, in order to gratify yr own taste, will neither suit, nor probably please others; so in respect to buildings which are rarely considered in the purchase of Lands, & principally I presume from the same causes, especially upon small bits of Land divested of Wood & Timber.

I wish with all my Heart you may be strengthned by some able and friendly hand in such a manner as to keep your effects

together; provided it may turn to your future good in ena
bling you to Work thrô the load of Debt you seem to be
entangled in, but that it is intirely out of my power without
selling part of my own Estate to contribute further thereto
you may easily be convincd of when I tell you, & affirm it
that I find it next to impossible to extract any part of the
money which is due to me; that I have struggled to the utmost
of my power for two years past, unsuccessfully to raise 4 or
£500 to lend a very particular friend of mine, who I know
must sell part of his Estate without it—& that I have not yet
dischargd the Sums you Involvd me in the payment of before,
having my Bond out to Mr Greens Estate for the £260 you
borrowd of him & cannot raise money to discharge it, altho'
I have used my true endeavours for that purpose—add to
these, some Engagements of my own which there is a necessity of complying with, or doing Acts of Injustice. How absurd and Idle woud it be then, under these Circumstances, to
enter myself security for the payment of yr Debts, unless I
foresaw some prospect of raising the money—true it is some
of yr Creditors might agree to wait, others tis presumeable
woud not, and certain it is pay day must come to all; what
then is to be done? to tell a Man who had been disappointed
from time to time, and at last had waited in confidence of
Receiving his money from me, that I was unprovided with the
means of satisfying his demand, woud be gauling to me—
unjust to him—& what I can by no means think of practising.
the only favour therefore that is in my power to shew you, is
to be easy & forbearing in my own demands, which I shall
endeavour to do as long as I can with any sort of convenience
to myself, notwithstanding I am in want of the money; & to
point out any Person who cd lend so much money even if
they liked the Security, I am equally at a loss to do: but few
there are I beleive, who woud choose to risque their money
(unless influenced by motives of compassion) upon such hazardous & perishable Articles as Negroes, Stock, & Chattels,
which are to be swept of by innumerable distempers, & subject to many accidents & misfortunes; so upon the whole yo.
will excuse me I hope if I am Inclid to offer yo. the same
advice I wd give to my Bror were he undr the same circumstans, & that is, if you find it impracticable to keep yr Estate

togethr for at least 3 or 4 Yrs till the Country, I mean the
Indebted part of it, can immerge a little from the distress it
must unavoidably fall into from the pressg of Creditors, &
want of Cash; then to sell of immedly (I mean this fall at
furthest) before Cash grows into greater demand wch it inevitably will do as our Currency is called in, & every thing of
consequence sell worse; therewith dischargg all yr Debts: be-
ging with the Sales of such things as can be best spared, & so
raising to Negroes, & even Land if requisite; for if the whole
shd go, there is a large Field before you—an opening prospect
in the back Country for Adventurers—where numbers resort
to—& where an enterprizing Man with very little Money may
lay the foundation of a Noble Estate in the New Settlemts
upon Monongahela for himself and posterity. the Surplus
money wch yo. might save after dischargg yr Debts, woud
possibly secure yo. as much Land as in the course of 20 yrs
wd sell for 5 times yr prest Estate—for proof of which only
look to Frederick, & see what Fortunes were made by the
Hite's & first takers up of those Lands: Nay how the greatest
Estates we have in this Colony were made; Was it not by
taking up & purchasing at very low rates the rich back Lands
which were thought nothing of in those days, but are now
the most valuable Lands we possess? Undoubtedly it was, &
to pursue this plan is the advice I wd offer my Br. were he in
yr Situation, but to yo. I only drop it as a hint for your serious
Reflectn; because I do not expect—nor woud by any means
wish—to see you adopt any Scheme of mine without duely
attending to it—weighing—& well considering of it in all
points & advising with your friends. I woud only ask whethr
it wd be bettr to labr undr a load of Debt where you are, wch
must inevitably keep yo. in continual Anxiety, & dread of yr
Creditors; be selling the produce of yr labour at under value,
(the never failg consequence of necessitous Circumstances)
with other evils too obvious to need innumeration, & which
must forever lend a helping hand to keep yo. low & distressed
or to Pluck up Resolution at once & disengage yourself of
these Incumbrances & Vexations—Abiding where you are if
you can save your Land & have a prospect of Reaping future
advantages from it, or to remove back, where there is a moral
certainty of laying the foundation of good Estates to yr Childn

I say I woud but ask wch of these two is the best, and leave
you to think of them at leizure, with this assurance on my
part, that what I have propounded to you on this Subject
proceeds from the utmost sincerity & Candour, And if you
will have recourse to the Publick Gazettes you may perceive
by the number of Estates wch are continually advertising for
Sale, that you are not the only one under Misfortune, and
that many good families are retiring into the Interior parts of
the Country for the benefit of ther Children—Some of the
best Gentlemen in the Country talk of doing so, who are not
drove by necessity, but adopt the Scheme from principals of
Gain—Whatever Resolution you may come to, I wish you success in it and am Sir Yr Very Hble Servt

To Capel and Osgood Hanbury

Gentn   Mount Vernon 25th July 1767.
    Since mine of the 28th of June, last year, I have been fa-
vour'd with your two Letters of the 27th of March, first of
July, and 21st of October in the past, and Sixth of April in the
present year. Had any thing material occurd—(worth giving
you the trouble of a Letter)—I shoud not have been silent till
this time; and even now, I have but little to say.
    The Accounts Currt transmitted by Necks were right, oth-
erwise I shoud have noted it sooner; and by Easton you will
receive two Tonns of Mr Custis's Tobacco, which when sold,
you will please to carry to the credit of the Young Gentleman's Acct who falling very short in his Crops last year is the
reason why Easton has only Eight Hhds of his Tobo this.
From the present face of things, there appears to be an almost
absolute certainty that the Crops of Tobacco this year will be
shorter than has been for many past, which I mention, that if
other Accts from different parts of this, and the other Tobo
Colony corrispond with it you may regulate the Sales in such
a manner as to obtain a good price for the Tobacco just
Shipped. I coud wish that it was a practice, to render an Acct
Currt of the dealings between us once a year, that if any Errors

shoud arise they may be rectified while the Transactions are recent.

Unseasonable as it may be, to take any notice of the repeal of the Stamp Act at this time, yet, I cannot help observing that a contrary measure woud have Introduced very unhappy Consequences: those therefore who wisely foresaw this, and were Instrumental in procuring the repeal of it, are, in my opinion, deservedly entitled to the thanks of the well wishers to Britain and her Colonies; & must reflect with pleasure that through their means, many Scenes of confusion and distress have been avoided: Mine they accordingly have, and always shall have, for their opposition to any Act of Oppression, for that Act coud be looked upon in no other light by every person who woud view it in its proper colours. I coud wish it was in my power to congratulate you with success, in having the Commercial System of these Colonies put upon a more enlargd and extensive footing than it is because I am well satisfied that it woud, ultimately, redound to the advantages of the Mother Country so long as the Colonies pursue trade and Agriculture, and woud be an effectual Let to Manufacturing among themselves—The Money therefore which they raise woud centre in Great Britain, as certain as the Needle will settle to the Poles. I am Gentn Yr Most Obedt Hble Servt

To William Crawford

Dear Sir   September 1767
From a sudden hint of your Brother Vale I wrote to you a few days ago in a hurry, since which having had more time for reflection, I am now set down in order to Write more deliberately, & with greater precission, to you on the Subject of my last Letter; desiring that if any thing in this shoud be found contradictory to that Letter you will wholely be governd by what I am now going to add.

I then desird the favour of you (as I understood Rights might now be had for the Lands which have fallen within the Pensylvania Line) to look me out a Tract of about 1500, 2000, or more acres somewhere in your Neighbourhood meaning

only by this that it might be as contiguous to your own Settlemt as such a body of good Land coud be found and about
Jacobs Cabbins or somewhere on those Waters I am told this
might be done. It will be easy for you to conceive that Ordinary, or even middling Land woud never answer my purpose
or expectation so far from Navigation & under such a load of
Expence as those Lands are incumbred with; No: A Tract to
please me must be rich (of which no Person can be a better
judge than yourself) & if possible to be good and level; Coud
such a piece of Land as this be found you woud do me a
singular favour in falling upon some method to secure it immediately from the attempts of any other as nothing is more
certain than that the Lands cannot remain long ungranted
when once it is known that Rights are to be had for them.
What mode of proceeding is necessary in order to accomplish
this design I am utterly at a loss to point out to you but as
your own Lands are under the same Circumstances self Interest will naturally lead you to an enquiry—I am told the Land,
or Surveyors Office is kept at Carlyle, if so I am of Opinion
that Colo. Armstrong (an Acquaintance of mine) has something to do in the management of it. & I am perswaded woud
readily serve me to him therefore at all events I will write by
the first oppertunity on that Subject that the way may be pre-
pard for your application if you shoud find it necessary to
make one to him. Whatever trouble or expence you may be
engagd in on my behalf you may depend upon being thankfully repaid. It is possible (but I do not know that it really is
the case) that Pensylvania Customs will not admit so large a
quantity of Land as I require, to be enterd together if so this
may possibly be evaded by making several Entrys to the same
amount if the expence of doing which is not too heavy but
this I only drop as a hint leaving the whole to your descretion
& good management. If the Land can only be securd from
others it is all I want at present the Surveying I woud choose
to postpone, at least till the Spring. when if you can give me
any Satisfactory Account of this matter and of what I am next
going to propose I expect to pay you a visit about the last of
April.

The other matter just now hinted at and which I proposd
in my last is to join you in attempting to secure some of the

most valuable Lands in the Kings part which I think may be accomplished after a while notwithstanding the Proclamation that restrains it at present & prohibits the Settling of them at all for I can never look upon that Proclamation in any other light (but this I say between ourselves) than as a temporary expedient to quiet the Minds of the Indians & must fall of course in a few years especially when those Indians are consenting to our Occupying the Lands. any Person therefore who neglects the present oppertunity of hunting out good Lands & in some measure Marking & distinguishing them for their own (in order to keep others from settling them) will never regain it. If therefore you will be at the trouble of seeking out the Lands I will take upon me the part of securing them so soon as there is a possibility of doing it & will moreover be at all the Cost & charges of Surveying Patenting &ca after which you shall have such a reasonable proportion of the whole as we may fix upon at our first meeting as I shall find it absolutely necessary & convenient for the better furthering of the design to let some few of my friends be concernd in the Scheme & who must also partake of the advantages. By this time it may be easy for you to discover, that my Plan is to secure a good deal of Land, You will consequently come in for a very handsome quantity and as you will obtain it without any Costs, or expences I am in hopes you will be encourag'd to begin this search in time. I woud choose if it were practicable, to get pretty large Tracts together, and it might be desirable to have them as near your Settlement, or Fort Pitt as we coud get them good; but not to neglect others at a greater distance if fine & bodies of it lye in a place. It may be a Matter worthy your enquiry to find out how the Maryland back line will run, and what is said about the laying of Neales (I think it is & Companys) Grant. I will enquire particularly concerning the Ohio Companys that one may know what to apprehend from them. For my own part I shoud have no objection to a Grant of Land upon the Ohio a good way below Pittsburg but woud willingly secure some good Tracts nearer hand first.

I woud recommend it to you to keep this whole matter a profound Secret, or Trust it only with those in whom you can confide & who can assist you in bringing it to bear by their discoveries of Land and this advice proceeds from several very good Reasons, and in the first place because I might be censurd for the opinion I have given in respect to the Kings Proclamation & then if the Scheme I am now proposing to you was known it might give the alarm to others & by putting them upon a Plan of the same nature (before we coud lay a proper foundation for success ourselves) set the different Interests a clashing and very probably in the end overturn the whole all which may be avoided by a Silent management & the Scheme snugly carried on by you under the pretence of hunting other Game which you may I presume effectually do at the same time you are in pursuit of Land which when fully discovered advise me of it & if there appears but a bear possibility of succeeding any time hence I will have the Lands immediately Surveyed to keep others off & leave the rest to time & my own Assiduity to Accomplish.

If this Letter shoud reach your hands before you set out I shoud be glad to have your thoughts fully expressd on the Plan I have proposd, or as soon afterwards as conveniently may be as I am desirous of knowing in time how you approve of the Scheme. I am Dr Sir Yr Very Hble Servt

September 17, 1767

To Jonathan Boucher

Revd Sir   May 30th 1768.

Mr Magowan who lived several years in my Family a Tutor to Master Custis (my Son in law & Ward) having taken his departure for England leaves the young Gentleman without any master at all at this time I shoud be glad there fore to know if it woud be convenient for you to add him to the number of your Pupils. He is a boy of good genius, about 14 yrs of age, untainted in his Morals, & of innocent Manners. Two yrs and upwards he has been reading of Virgil, and was (at the time Mr Magowan left him) entered upon the Greek Testament, thô I presume he has grown not a little rusty in both; having had no benefit of his Tutor since Christmas, notwithstanding he left the Country in March only.

If he comes, he will have a boy (well acquainted with House business, which may be made as useful as possible in your Family to keep him out of Idleness) and two Horses, to furnish him with the means of getting to Church, and elsewhere as you may permit; for he will be put entirely, and absolutely under your Tuition, and direction to manage as you think proper in all respects.

Now Sir, if you Incline to take Master Custis I shoud be glad to know what conveniencies it may be necessary for him to bring, & how soon he may come, for as to his Board & Schooling (Provendar for his Horses he may lay in himself) I do not think it necessary to enquire into, and will chearfully pay Ten or Twelve pounds a year extraordinary to engage your peculiar care of, and a watchful eye to him, as he is a promising boy—the last of his Family—& will possess a very large Fortune—add to this my anxiety to make him fit for more useful purposes, than a horse Racer &ca.

This Letter will be sent to you by my Brother at Fredericksburg, and I shoud be obligd to you for an answer by the first Post to Alexandria, near to which place I live; I am Sir Yr Most Obedt & Hble Servt

P.S. If it is necessary for him to provide a Bed, cou'd one be purchased in your Neighbourhood? it woud save a long carriage.

To Robert Cary & Company

Gentn   Mt Vernon 6th June 1768

My old Chariot havg run its race, & gone through as many stages as I coud conveniently make it travel, is now renderd incapable of any further Service; The intent of this Letter therefore is to desire you will bespeak me a New one, time enough to come out with the Goods (I shall hereafter write for) by Captn Johnstoun, or some other Ship.

As these are kind of Articles, that last with care a gt number of years, I woud willingly have the Chariot you may now send me made in the newest taste, handsome, genteel, & light; yet not slight & consequently unserviceable. To be made of the best Seasond Wood, & by a celebrated Workman. The last Importation which I have seen, besides the customary Steel springs have others that play in a Brass barrel, & contribute at one & the sametime to the ease & Ornament of the Carriage; One of these kind therefore woud be my choice; & Green being a colour little apt, as I apprehend, to fade, & grateful to the Eye, I woud give it the preference unless any other colour more in vogue & equally lasting is entitled to precedency in that case I woud be governd by fashion. A light gilding on the mouldings (that is round the Pannels) & any other Ornaments that may not have a heavy & tawdry look (together with my arms agreeable to the Impression here sent) might be added, by way of decoration. A lining of a handsome, lively cold leather of good quality, I shd also prefer; such as green, blew, or &ca as may best suit the colr of the outside. let the box that slips under Seat, be as large as it conveniently can be made (for the benefit of Stoage upon a journey) and to have a Pole (not Shafts) for the Wheel Horses to draw by—together with a handsome sett of Harness for four middle sized Horses orderd in such a manner as to suit either two Postilions (without a box) or a box & one Postilion—The Box being made to fix on, and take of occasionally, with a hammel Cloth &ca suitable to the lining. On the Harness let my Crest be engravd.

If such a Chariot as I have here describd cd be got at 2d hand little or nothg the worse of wear, but at the sametime a good deal under the first cost of a new one (& sometimes tho. perhaps rarely it happens so) it wd be very desirable; but if I am obligd to go to near the origl cost I wd e'en have one made; & have been thus particular, in hopes of gettg a handsome Chart through yr direction, good taste, & managt—Not of Copper howr for these do not stand the powerful heat of our sun.

Inclosd you will receive a Bill of Excha: on Laughlin Mcacleane Esqr. for £302 Sterg out of wch this Chart may be paid for, & the Balle carrd to the Credit of my Acct Currt—At the sametime you prest the Bill be pleasd to delivr the Letter also. I am Gentn Yr Most Hble Servt

P.S. The Origl of this was sent by the Keith to Glasgow and the Copies by Captn Johnstoun.

To William Ramsay

Dear Sir,   Mount Vernon 29th January 1769.

Frequently as I have seen you of late, I have always forgot to inform you, that Mr Adam, on whom I have depended for money, declare's his inability of supplying me; it is not only out of my power therefore to furnish you & Mr Fairfax with the sum asked, but to comply with sundry engagements of my own; for both of which I am really sorry.

Having once or twice of late heard you speak highly in praise of the Jersey College, as if you had a desire of sending your Son William there (who I am told is a youth fond of study & instruction, & disposed to a sedentary studious Life; in following of which he may not only promote his own happiness, but the future welfare of others) I shou'd be glad, if you have no other objection to it than what may arise from the expence, if you wou'd send him there as soon as it is convenient & depend upon me for Twenty five pounds this Currency a year for his support so long as it may be necessary for the completion of his Education—If I live to see the accomplishment of this term, the Sum here stipulated shall be annually paid, and if I die in the mean while, this letter shall be obligatory upon my Heirs or Executors to do it according to the true intent & meaning hereof—No other return is expected or wished for, for this offer than that you will accept it with the same freedom & good will with which it is made, & that you may not even consider it in the [   ] of an obligation, or mention it as such; for be assur'd that from me, it never will be known. I am Dr Sir Your most obedt Servant

To George Mason

Dear sir,   Mount Vernon 5th April 1769.

Herewith you will receive a letter and sundry papers which were forwarded to me a day or two ago by Doctor Ross of Bladensburg. I transmit them with the greater pleasure, as my own desire of knowing your sentiments upon a matter of this importance exactly coincides with the Doctrs inclinations.

At a time when our lordly Masters in Great Britain will be satisfied with nothing less than the deprivation of American freedom, it seems highly necessary that something shou'd be done to avert the stroke and maintain the liberty which we have derived from our Ancestors; but the manner of doing it to answer the purpose effectually is the point in question.

That no man shou'd scruple, or hesitate a moment to use a—ms in defence of so valuable a blessing, on which all the good and evil of life depends; is clearly my opinion; Yet A—ms I wou'd beg leave to add, should be the last resource; the denier resort. Addresses to the Throne, and remonstrances to parliament, we have already, it is said, proved the inefficacy of; how far then their attention to our rights & priviledges is to be awakened or alarmed by starving their Trade & manufactures, remains to be tryed.

The northern Colonies, it appears, are endeavouring to adopt this scheme—In my opinion it is a good one; & must be attended with salutary effects, provided it can be carried pretty generally into execution; but how far it is practicable to do so, I will not take upon me to determine. That there will be difficulties attending the execution of it every where, from clashing interests, & selfish designing men (ever attentive to their own gain, & watchful of every turn that can assist their lucrative views, in preference to any other consideration) cannot be denied; but in the Tobacco Colonies where the Trade is so diffused, and in a manner wholly conducted by Factors for their principals at home, these difficulties are certainly enhanced, but I think not insurmountably increased, if the Gentlemen in their several counties wou'd be at some pains to explain matters to the people, & stimulate them to a cordial agreement to purchase none but certain innumerated articles out of any of the Stores after such a period, nor import nor purchase any themselves. This, if it did not effectually withdraw the Factors from their Importations, wou'd at least make them extremely cautious in doing it, as the prohibited Goods could be vended to none but the non-associater, or those who wou'd pay no regard to their association; both of whom ought to be stigmatized, and made the objects of publick reproach.

The more I consider a Scheme of this sort, the more ardently I wish success to it, because I think there are private, as well as public advantages to result from it—the former certain, however precarious the other may prove; for in respect to the latter I have always thought that by virtue of the same power (for here alone the authority derives) which assume's the right of Taxation, they may attempt at least to restrain our manufactories; especially those of a public nature; the same equity & justice prevailing in the one case as the other, it being no greater hardship to forbid my manufacturing, than it is to order me to buy Goods of them loaded with Duties, for the express purpose of raising a revenue. But as a measure of this sort will be an additional exertion of arbitrary power, we cannot be worsted I think in putting it to the Test. On the other hand, that the Colonies are considerably indebted to Great Britain, is a truth universally acknowledged. That many families are reduced, almost, if not quite, to penury & want, from the low ebb of their fortunes, and Estates daily selling for the discharge of Debts, the public papers furnish but too many melancholy proofs of. And that a scheme of this sort will contribute more effectually than any other I can devise to immerge the Country from the distress it at present labours under, I do most firmly believe, if it can be generally adopted. And I can see but one set of people (the Merchants excepted) who will not, or ought not, to wish well to the Scheme; and that is those who live genteely & hospitably, on clear Estates. Such as these were they, not to consider the valuable object in view, & the good of others, might think it hard to be curtail'd in their living & enjoyments; for as to the penurious man, he saves his money, & he saves his credit; having the best plea for doing that, which before perhaps he had the most violent struggles to refrain from doing. The extravagant & expensive man has the same good plea to retrench his Expences—He is thereby furnished with a pretext to live within bounds, and embraces it—prudence dictated œconomy to him before, but his resolution was too weak to put it in practice; for how can I, *says he*, who have lived in

such & such a manner change my method? I am ashamed to
do it: and besides, such an alteration in the System of my
living, will create suspicions of a decay in my fortune, & such
a thought the world must not harbour; I will e'en continue
my course: till at last the course discontinues the Estate, a sale
of it being the consequence of his perseverance in error. This
I am satisfied is the way that many who have set out in the
wrong tract, have reasoned, till ruin stares them in the face.
And in respect to the poor & needy man, he is only left in
the same situation he was found; better I might say, because
as he judges from comparison, his condition is amended in
proportion as it approaches nearer to those above him.

Upon the whole therefore, I think the Scheme a good one,
and that it ought to be tryed here, with such alterations as
the exigency of our circumstances render absolutely necessary;
but how, & in what manner to begin the work, is a matter
worthy of consideration; and whether it can be attempted
with propriety, or efficacy (further than a communication of
sentiments to one another) before May, when the Court &
Assembly will meet together in Williamsburg, and a uniform
plan can be concerted, and sent into the different counties to
operate at the same time, & in the same manner every where,
is a thing I am somewhat in doubt upon, & shou'd be glad
to know your opinion of. I am Dr Sir Your most Obt humble
Servant

To Robert Cary & Company

Gentn   Mount Vernon July 25: 1769.
Inclosd you will receive Invoices of Goods wanted for myself & Master Custis for this place and our Plantations on York
River, as also for Miss Custis which I beg may be sent by
Captn Johnstoun if the Orders gets to hand in time, if not,
by any other Vessel bound to this River—But if there are any
Articles containd in either of the respective Invoices (Paper
only excepted) which are Taxd by Act of Parliament for the
purpose of Raising a Revenue in America, it is my express
desire and request, that they may not be sent, as I have very

heartily enterd into an Association (Copies of which I make
no doubt you have seen otherwise I shoud have Inclosed one)
not to import any Article which now is, or hereafter shall be
Taxed for this purpose until the said Act or Acts are repeald.
I am therefore particular in mentioning this matter as I am
fully determined to adhere religiously to it, and may perhaps
have wrote for some things unwittingly which may be under
these Circumstances.

Many of your Letters lying before me I shall take notice of
such parts of them as require answering and shall begin first
with Mr McLean because the trouble you have had with him
on my Acct deserves my particular acknowledgments; but
even here, I hope there is but little occasion to be explicit, as
he will undoubtedly have paid the Money before this Letter
can get to hand—True it is, the Draft arose in consequence
of a Debt due to me from Colo. Robt Stewart, and as true it
is, that I shoud have been unwilling to have done any thing
that might have distressd that Gentleman; but surely Mr Mc-
Lean will not pretend to say, that there was not time to have
rectified the mistake he attributes the Non-payment to, between the hour of his Acceptance of the Bill and the date of
your Letter of the first of March. Certain I am it woud give
Colo. Stewart a good deal of uneasiness to think I had met
with any obstacle in receiving the Money as I lent it to him
five or Six years ago without Security and without Interest,
having nothing but the Word of a Gentleman of no Estate to
repay it to me again.

I observe what you have mentioned in a Letter of the 12th
of August, last year in respect to the payment of the Duties
of Master Custis's Tobo and not doubting the justice of the
Remark, I have only to add, that I shall confide in your pursuing such measures as appears most conducive (under the
change of Circumstances which are often happening) to his
Interest.

By a Letter which I have just receivd from Mr Josh Valentine I am informd that 37 Hhds of Mastr Custis's Tobo and
all mine (amounting to 17 Hhds) are put on board Captn
Peterson to your Address, on both which parcels you will
please to Insure Ten pounds pr Hhd—I have no Tobo on this
River, having made none for two or three years past and be-

lieve I never shall again—There is, in my opinion, a very great appearance of another short Crop of Tobo owing to several concurrant Causes, but more especially to a Drought which has been severely felt in most parts of the Country during the whole Month of June, part of May, and till the middle of this Instt.

I am obligd to you for your notice of Mr Magowan, who is now returnd & got fixed in a valuable living in the Provence of Maryland not far from this place—As it is probable I shall have occasion to draw upon you at the next October Genl Court for some part (perhaps four, five, or Six hundd pounds) of Master Custis's Money, I take this oppertunity of mentioning of it to you and am Gentn Yr Most Hble Servt

To Charles Washington

Dr Charles,   Mount Vernon Jany 31st 1770

If you saw my Brother John in Stafford when you were down there at Christmas; if you had any Conversation with my Br. Saml on the Subject I mentioned to you; and if any time was proposed for your meeting at this place, I should be glad to know it, & beg you will write me a line by the first Post after this gets to hand informing me of it accordingly; as I want to prepare for my journey but am desirous before hand of knowing whether I am to go alone or in company as it will make some difference in my preparations.

As I expect it will now shortly be known, whether the Officers & Soldiers under the Kings Proclamation have any chance to come in for Lands West of the Alligany mountains I shoud be glad to know if any of them which may fall in your way woud sell their rights; and upon what terms; tho. I have little expectations that any of them will sell upon such terms as I woud buy, or any person coud afford to buy, unless they warranted the Land; for if the number of Grants (which are of older date to the King's Proclamation) shoud take place, as their is but too much reason to apprehend, if they do not by clashing with each other, destroy themselves; I woud hardly give any Officer a button for his Right: for besides a large

Tract of Country reserved for the Indian Traders, from Fort Pitt near 150 Miles down the Ohio, & up to the Laurell Hill, there appeard by a List laid before the House of Burgesses by Order of the Govr to be between 6 & 7,000,000 of Acres actually granted, & Petitioned for; & most of the Grants made in such generall, & indeterminate terms, that if confirmd, no man can lay off a foot of Land & be sure of keeping it, till they are servd.

Upon my shewing Mr Thruston (who was formerly a Lieutt, & thereby entitled to 2,000 Acres of Land) a Copy of the Grants, & proceedings of the House of Burgesses there-upon, he immediately sold his right (tho. otherwise very fond of it) to Lund Washington for Ten pounds—Now, coud I purchase 12 or 15,000 Acres upon the same terms, I woud do it, considering of it as a Lottery only; and my Reason's for so doing are these—Such a quantity of Land as this, added to what I may expect in my own Right, woud form a Tract of so great dignity as to render it worth my while to send out a Person for the discovery of Land, clear if possible of these numerous grants; and to be at some expence and trouble in seating and Saving it; for without this the Land woud soon be forfeited (which I beleive will be the case with half the Officers in this Colony) if they shoud actually obtain the Land. & again, it woud be worth my while thus situated, to buy of some who might under their Grants think I clash'd with them.

Upon the whole, as you are situated in a good place for seeing many of the Officers at different times, I shoud be glad if you woud (in a joking way, rather than in earnest at first) see what value they seem to set upon their Lands, and if you can buy any of the rights of those who continued in the Ser-vice till after the Cherokee Expedition, at the rate of about five, Six, or Seven pounds a thousand acres I shall be obligd to you, & will pay the money upon demand. I am of opinion that Chew, & some of those who may be in want of a little ready money, would gladly sell; nor is it much to be wondered at if they shoud, for if those large Grants which I have already mentiond shoud take place the purchaser will have sunk so much money to very little purpose; nor is the Officer's right under the Proclamation of any consequence to those who either does not resolve to go after the Land himself, or employ others to do it for him; the first I do not suppose many are inclind to, the last is hardly worth the expense for small tracts; & the Officer is as much obliged to find the Land as any other individual; nor is his Title, if he be not entitled to some degree of preference, a jot better than any other Man's who will go in pursuit of Lands himself, except that he is to enjoy it 10 years free of Quitrents.

If you shoud make any purchases, let it be done in your own name; for reason's I shall give you when we meet—take Bonds in large Penalties to convey all their Rights under the Kings Proclamation to you; and they shoud be obligd to suffer their names to be made use of to obtain the Land, as the Kings Proclamation requires a Personal application to the Govr & Council in order to entitle them to the Respective quantities granted. In looking over the List of Grants that were laid before the Ho. of Burgesses I perceivd one for 10,000 Acres to a certain Ambrose Powell (who I beleive lives in Culpeper County) lying above the Mouth of the great Kanhaway—this is comprehended within our Grant of 200,000 Acres, it is also fixed at a place where two or three other Grants are laid & I believe some of them older; but yet, as it lyes in the way of a scheme I have in view; and woud, in some small degree promote my Plan if I had it, I shoud be obligd to you if you woud enquire in a round about way who this Powell is, where he lives, &ca; & tell me who you think the most likely person for me to employ to purchase his right to the Grant—You need not let your reasons for enquiring after Powell be known, till you have given me what information you can concerning him, least it may give him or others cause to imagine that his grant is more valuable than it really is: In fact, I do not think that it is intrinsically worth a groat (tho. I woud give eight or Ten pounds for it, If I coud not get it for less) inasmuch as it is totally swallowed up in other Grants; but several of this sort may in some measure give me a prior claim to have my share of the 200,000 Acres laid of above the Mouth of the Gt Kanhaway where I am told the land is very fine, it is for this reason therefore I would even give a tittle for Powell's.

In the whole of your transactions, either with the Officers, or on this other matter; do not let it be known that I have any concern therein. I have Inclosd you a copy of the Bond I drew from Thruston to Lund Washington, which will serve you for a Precedent in case you shoud make any purchases— I have put your name in the place of Lund Washington's as I would have the title given to you, & not to me, till matters are riper than they appear to be at present. I shall take care to furnish you with money as you may find occasion to com- pleat the quantity I have mentioned. Show no part of this Letter, so that you can be drawn into no trouble or difficulty in the Affair. In the mean time I shoud be glad if you would write to me fully by the first post after this gets to hand. I am Yr Most Affecte Brother

P.S. Inclosd you will receive 30/ to pay the within Acct of James Browns—tho. I think it is a most enormous charge as I shoud be glad you would tell him.

To Thomas Johnson

Sir   Virginia 20th July 1770.
    I was honourd with your favour of the 18th of June about the last of that Month and read it with all the attention I was capable of but having been closely engaged with my Hay & Wheat Harvests from that time till now I have not been able to enquire into the Sentiments of any of the Gentlemen of this side in respect to the Scheme of opening the Inland Nav- igation of Potomack by private Subscription—in the manner you have proposed—and therefore, any opinion which I may now offer on this head will be considered I hope as the result of my own private thinking—not of the Publick.
    That no person more intimately concernd in this Event wishes to see an undertaking of the sort go forward with more facility and ardour than I do, I can truely assure you; and will, at all times, give any assistance in my power to promote the design; but I leave you to judge from the Tryal, which before this you undoubtedly have made, how few there are (not immediately benefited by it) that will contribute any thing

worthwhile to the work; and how many small sums are requisite to raise a large one.

Upon your Plan of raising money, it appears to me that
there will be found but two kinds of People who will Subscribe much towards it—Those who are actuated by motives
of Publick Spirit; and those again, who from their proximity
to the Navigation will reap the salutary effects of clearing the
River. The number of the latter, you must be a competent
judge of; those of the former, is more difficult to ascertain;
for wch reason I own to you, that I am not without my doubts
of your Schemes falling through, however sanguine your first
hopes may be from the rapidity of Subscribers; for it is to be
supposed, that your Subscription Papers will probably be
opend among those whose Interests naturally Incline them to
wish well to the undertaking & consequently will aid it; but
when you come to shift the Scene a little and apply to those
who are unconnected with the River & the advantages of its
Navigation how slowly will you advance?

This Sir, is my Sentiment, generally, upon your Plan of obtaining Subscriptions for extending the Navigation of Potomack; whereas I conceive, that if the Subscribers were vested
by the two Legislatures with a kind of property in the Navigation, under certain restrictions & limitation's, and to be
reimbursd their first advances with a high Interest thereon by
a certain easy Toll on all Craft proportionate to their respective Burthen's, in the manner that I am told works of this sort
are effected in the Inland parts of England—or, upon the Plan
of Turnpike Roads; you woud add thereby a third set of Men
to the two I have mentioned and gain considerable strength
by it: I mean the monied Gentry; who tempted by lucrative
views woud advance largely on Acct of the high Interest—
This I am Inclind to think is the only method by which this
desirable work will ever be accomplished in the manner it
ought to be; for as to its becoming an object of Publick Expence I never expect to see it—Our Interests (in Virginia, at
least) are too much divided—our Views too confind, if our
Finances were better, to suffer that, which appears to redound
to the advantage of a part of the Community only, to become
a Tax upon the whole—thô in the Instance before Us, there
is the strongest speculative Proof in the World of the immense

advantages which Virginia & Maryland might derive (and at a very small comparitive Expence) by making Potomack the Channel of Commerce between Great Britain and that immense Tract of Country which is unfolding to our view the advantages of which are too great, & too obvious I shoud think to become the Subject of serious debate but which thro. illtimed Parsimony & supiness may be wrested from us & conducted thro. other Channels such as the Susquehanna (which I have seen recommended by some writers) the Lakes &c.—how difficult it will be to divert it afterwards, time only can show. Thus far Sir I have taken the liberty of communicating my Sentiments on the different modes of establishing a fund but if from the efforts you have already made on the North side of Potomack it shoud be found that my fears are rather imaginary than real (as I heartily wish they may prove) I have no doubts but the same spirit may be stird up on the South side if Gentlemen of Influence in the Counties of Hampshire Frederick Loudoun & Fairfax will heartily engage in it and receive all occasional Sums from those who may wish to see a work of this sort undertaken, altho. they expect no benefit to themselves from it.

As to the manner in which you propose to execute the work, in order to avoid the Inconvenience which you seem to apprehend fr. Locks I profess myself to be a very incompetent Judge of it—It is a general receivd opinion I know, that by reducing one Fall you too frequently create many; but how far this Inconvenience is to be avoided by the method you speak of, those who have examind the [   ] Rifts, the depth of Water above, &ca must be infinitely the best qualified to determine. But I am inclind to think that, if you were to exhibit your Scheme to the Publick upon a more extensive Plan than the one now Printed, it woud meet with a more general approbation; for so long as it is considered as a partial Scheme so long will it be partially attended to—whereas, if it was recommended to Publick Notice upon a more enlargd Plan, and as a means of becoming the Channel of conveyance of the extensive & valuable Trade of a rising Empire; & the Operations to begin at the lower Landings (above the Great Falls) & to extend upwards as high as Fort Cumberland; or, as far as the expenditure of the money woud carry them; from whence the Portage to the Waters of Ohio must commence; I think many woud be envited to contribute their mite, that otherwise will not—It may be said the expence of doing this will be considerably augmented—I readily grant it, but believe that the Subscribers will encrease in proportion; at any rate I think that there will be at least an equal Sum raised by this means that the end of your plan will be as effectually answerd by it.

Your obliging offer in respect to Miss Custis we chearfully embrace, & Mrs Washington woud think herself much favourd in receiving those Simples, & direction's for the use of them, which your Brother Administers for Fitts—Miss Custis's Complaint has been of two years standing, & rather Increases than abates—Mr Boucher will do us the favour of forwarding the Medicine so soon as you can procure & commit them to his charge which it is hoped will be as soon as possible.

To Jonathan Boucher

Dear Sir,   MOUNT VERNON, 9 July, 1771

From several concurring causes, which have assembled upon the eve of my departure for Williamsburg, I have both my head and my hands too full of business to allow me time to write more than a hasty undigested answer to your letter of the 4th. This, however, I shall attempt to do.

In my last I informed you, (as well as I can recollect the contents of the letter) that the friends (I do not confine myself to the relations) of Mr. Custis, were divided in their opinions, of the propriety of his travelling, not on account of the advantages which might result from it, but on account of the expense, as he would set out with so heavy a charge, as you thought sufficient to induce you to accompany him, which would at once anticipate half his income. For his estate is of a kind, that rather comes under the denomination of a large than a profitable one. He has a good deal of land and a great many slaves, it is true, but the former is more to be esteemed for the situation than the produce, being of an indifferent quality and much worn, so that large crops cannot be made from them. These doubtful opinions was a sufficient cause, I added, for me to be circumspect in my conduct, as I had another tribunal to account to besides that in my own breast, for the part I was to act on this occasion. For you cannot but know, that every farthing, which is expended on this young gentleman, must undergo the inspection of the General Court, in their examination of my guardianship accounts, and that it would never answer for me to permit him to launch into any uncommon or extravagant tract, (especially at a time when a heavy and expensive chancery suit is just commenced against his estate,) without first knowing whether such an expence would be submitted to by those, who had a constitutional right to put a negative thereon.

These are the reasons why I said in my last, that my own inclinations were still as strong as ever for Mr. Custis's pursuing his travelling scheme, but that it was necessary the Court should approve of the expense, (I did not want their opinion of the utility of travelling) and provided, that it should appear, when his judgment is a little more matured, that he is desirous of undertaking this tour upon a plan of improvement, rather than a vague desire of gratifying an idle curiosity, or spending his money wantonly. For by the bye, if his mother does not speak her sentiments, rather than his, he is abundantly lukewarm in the scheme; and I cannot help giving it as my opinion, that his education, from what I have understood of his improvements, (however advanced it may be for a youth of his age,) is by no means ripe enough for a tour of travelling; not that I think his becoming a mere scholar is a desirable education for a gentleman, but I conceive a knowledge of books is the basis upon which other knowledge is to be built, and that it is men and things more than books he is to be acquainted with by travelling. At present, however well versed he may be in the principles of the Latin language (which is not to be at all wondered at, as he began the study of it as soon as he could speak), he is unacquainted with several of their classical authors, which might be useful to him to read. He is ignorant of the Greek, (which the advantages of understanding I do not pretend to judge), knows nothing of French, which is absolutely necessary to him as a traveller; little or nothing acquainted with arithmetic, and totally ignorant of the mathematics, than which, so much of it at least as relates to surveying, nothing can be more essentially necessary to any person possessed of a large landed estate, the bounds of some part or other of which is always in controversy.

Now, whether he has time between this and next spring to acquire a sufficient knowledge of these, or so much of them as are requisite, I leave you to judge of; and whether a boy of seventeen years old, which will be his age the last of November next, can have any just notions of the ends and designs of travelling? I have already given it as my opinion, that it would be precipitating this event, unless he was to go immediately to the university for a couple of years, and in this case he could see nothing of America; which might be a disadvantage to him, as it is to be expected that every man, who travels with a view of observing the laws and customs of other countries, should be able to give some description of the situation and government of his own.

Upon the whole, it is impossible for me at this time to give a more decisive answer, however strongly inclined I may be to put you upon an absolute certainty in this affair, than I have done; and I should think myself wanting in candor, if I concealed any circumstance from you, which leads me to fear, that there is a possibility, if not a probability, that the whole design may be totally defeated; and therefore I add, that before I ever thought myself at liberty to encourage this plan, I judged it highly reasonable and necessary, that the mother should be consulted. I laid your first letter and proposals before her, and desired that she would ponder well, before she resolved, as an unsteady behavior might be a disadvantage to you. Her determination was, that, if it appeared to be his inclination to undertake this tour, and if it should be adjudged for his benefit, she would not oppose it, whatever pangs it might give her to part with him. This declaration she still adheres to, but in so faint a manner, that I think, what with her fears and his indifference, (if he really is so) it will soon be declared he has no inclination to go, the consequence of which is too obvious to be mentioned. I do not say that this will be the case; I cannot speak positively. But as this is the result of my own reflection upon the matter, I thought it but fair to communicate it to you.

Several causes, I believe, have concurred to make her view his departure, as the time approaches, with more reluctance than she expected. The unhappy situation of her daughter has in some degree fixed her eyes upon him as her only hope. Add to this the doubts of her friends, &c., to what I have already said, I can only add, that my warmest wishes are to see him prosecute a plan, at a proper period, which I am sure will redound to his advantage, and that nothing shall be wanted on my part to aid and assist him in it. In the event of his going, I shoud think myself highly favored, and him much honored, by Governor Eden's letters of introduction. Such, with others that might be procured, can not fail of having their advantages.

You will please to make my compliments to Mr. Dulany, and assure him, that I have not the vestige of a house at the Frederic Springs, otherwise it should have been, if unengaged, much at his service. The two seasons I spent at those waters I stood indebted to Mr. Mercer for the use of his house.

I scarce know what answer to give to the papers you transmitted to me as an executor of the will of Col. Thos. Colvill, deceased. The affairs of that estate are unhappily involved with Mr. Semple, to whom Colo. Colvill in his life time sold a tract of land in Maryland, called Merryland, for (I think) £2600 sterling, and from whom we can neither get the money nor land. Till this matter is settled the executors are unable to pay off the legacies in this country, consequently can answer no demands of the residuary legatees in England, who only come in for the surplusage if any there be. I believe there will be more than sufficient to discharge the debts and legacies here, but the overplus will be trifling. I remain, &c.

To Jonathan Boucher

Dear Sir, Mount Vernon May 21st 1772

Inclination having yielded to Importunity, I am now, contrary to all expectation under the hands of Mr Peale; but in so grave—so sullen a Mood—and now and then under the influence of Morpheus, when some critical strokes are making,

that I fancy the skill of this Gentleman's Pencil, will be put
to it, in describing to the World what manner of Man I am.
I have no doubt of Mr Peales meeting with very good In-
couragement in a Tour to Williamsburg; for having mentioned
him to some Gentlemen at our Court, they seem desirous of
employing him in his way down.

Your excuse for denying us the pleasure of your Company
with Governr Eden & Lady, thô not strictly warranted by
Scripture, is nevertheless highly admissable, and I sincerely
congratulate you upon the prospect of happiness; as I think
there is a fair Field of it opening to your view, from the ju-
diciousness of your choice—Whether Mrs Washington ever
stretches as far as An[   ]ot, we shall certainly take
som[   ]ppertunity of making y[   ]n this occasion. In the
meanwhile with Compliments to yr self & Miss Boucher in
which she joins I am with very sincere regard Dr Sir Yr Most
Obedt Servt

To Benedict Calvert

Dear Sir,   Mount Vernon April 3d 1773.
    I am now set down to write to you on a Subject of Im-
portance, & of no small embarrassment to me. My Son in
Law & Ward, Mr Custis, has, as I have been informd, paid
his Addresses to your Second Daughter, & having made some
progress in her Affections required her in Marriage—How far
a union of this Sort may be agreeable to you, you best can
tell, but I should think myself wanting in Candour was I not
to acknowledge, that Miss Nellys amiable qualification's
stands confess'd at all hands; and that, an alliance with your
Family, will be pleasing to his.

    This acknowledgement being made, you must permit me
to add Sir, that at this, or in any short time, his youth, inexperience, and unripened Education is, & will be insuperable
obstacles in my eye, to the completion of the Marriage—As
his Guardian, I conceive it to be my indispensable duty (to
endeavour) to carry him through a regular course of Education, many Branches of which, sorry I am to add, he is totally

difficient of, and, to guard his youth to a more advancd age before an Event, on which his own Peace, & the happiness of another is to depend, takes place; not that I have any doubt of the warmth of his affection, nor I hope I may add, any fears of a change in them; but at present, I do not conceive that he is capable of bestowing that due attention to the Important consequences, of a Marriage State, which is necessary to be done by those who are Inclind to enter into it; & of course am unwilling he should do it till he is—If the affection which they have avowd for each other is fixd upon a Solid Basis, it will receive no diminution in the Course of two or three years, in which time he may prosecute his Studies, and thereby render himself more deserving of the Lady & useful to Society; If unfortunately (as they are both young) there should be an abatement of affection on either side, or both, it had better preceed, than follow after, Marriage.

Delivering my Sentiments thus, will not, I hope, lead you into a belief that I am desirous of breaking of the Match—to postpone it, is all I have in view; for I shall recommend it to the young Gentleman with the warmth that becomes a Man of honour (notwithstanding he did not vouchsafe to consult either his Mother, or me, on the occasion) to consider himself as much engagd to your Daughter as if the indissoluble Knot was tied; and, as the surest means of effecting this, to stick close to his Studies (in which I flatter myself you will join me) by which he will, in a great measure, avoid those little Flirtation's with other Girls which may, by dividing the attention, contribute not a little to divide the affection.

It may be expected of me perhaps, to say something of Fortune, But, to discend to particulars, at this time, may seem rather premature—In general therefore I shall inform you, that, Mr Custis's Estate consists of abt 15,000 Acres of Land, good part of it adjoing to the City of Wmsburg, & none 40 Miles from it; sevl Lotts in the said City; between two & three hundd Negroes; and about Eight or ten thousd Pounds upon Bond, & in the hands of his Merchts—this Estate he now holds independant of his Mothers Dower, wch will be an acquisition to it at her Death, & upon the whole such an one, as you will readily acknowledge ought to entitle him to a handsome Portion in a Wife; But, as I shd never require a

Child of my own to make a Sacrafice of himself to Interest, so, neither do I think it incumbt on me, to recommend it as a Guardian; but as I know you are full able, I should hope, & expect, if we were now upon the point of Settling these Preliminaries, that you would also be willing to do something genteel by your Daughter.

At all times when you, Mrs Calvert, or the young Ladies can make it convenient to favour us with a visit we should be happy in seeing you at this place. Mrs Washington & Miss Custis join me in respectful Compliments, and I am Dr Sir Yr Most Obedt Servt

To Burwell Bassett

Dear Sir   Mount Vernon June 20th 1773

It is an easier matter to conceive, than to describe, the distress of this Family; especially that of the unhappy Parent of our Dear Patcy Custis, when I inform you that yesterday removd the Sweet Innocent Girl into a more happy, & peaceful abode than any she has met with, in the afflicted Path she hitherto has trod.

She rose from Dinner about four Oclock, in better health and spirits than she appeard to have been in for some time; soon after which she was siezd with one of her usual Fits, & expird in it, in less than two Minutes without uttering a Word, a groan, or scarce a Sigh.—this Sudden, and unexpected blow, I scarce need add has almost reduced my poor Wife to the lowest ebb of Misery; which is encreas'd by the absence of her Son (whom I have just fixed at the College in New York, from whence I returnd the 8th Instt) and want of the balmy Consolation of her Relations; which leads me more than ever to wish she could see them, and that I was Master of Arguments powerful enough to prevail upon Mrs Dandridge to make this place her entire, & absolute home. I should think, as she lives a lonesome life (Betcy being Married) it might suit her well, & be agreeable, both to herself & my wife, to me most assuredly it would.

I do not purpose to add more at present, the end of my

writing being only to inform you of this unhappy change. Our Sincere Affections are offerd to Mrs Bassett, Mrs Dandridge, & all other Friends & I am very sincerely Yr Obedt & Affecte Hble St

To George Muse

Sir,   Mount Vernon 29th January 1774
   Your impertinent Letter of the 24th ulto, was delivered to me yesterday by Mr Smith—As I am not accustomed to receive such from any Man, nor would have taken the same language from you personally, without letting you feel some marks of my resentment; I would advise you to be cautious in writing me a second of the same tenour; for though I understand you were drunk when you did it, yet give me leave to tell you, that drunkeness is no excuse for rudeness; & that, but for your stupidity & sottishness you might have known, by attending to the public Gazettes, (particularly Rinds of the 14th of January last) that you had your full quantity of ten thousand acres of Land allow'd you; that is, 9073 acres in the great Tract of 51,302 acres, & the remainder in the small tract of 927 acres; whilst I wanted near 500 acres of my quantity, Doctr Craik 300 of his, and almost every other claimant little or much of theirs. But suppose you had really fallen short 73 acres of your 10,000, do you think your superlative merit entitles you to greater indulgences than others? or that I was to make it good to you, if it did? when it was at the option of the Governor & Council to have allowed you but 500 acres in the whole, if they had been inclin'd so to do. If either of these should happen to be your opinion, I am very well convinced you will stand singular in it; & all my concerns is, that I ever engag'd in behalf of so ungrateful & dirty a fellow as you are. But you may still stand in need of my assistance, as I can inform you that your affairs, in respect to these Lands, do not stand upon so solid a basis as you may imagine, & this you may take by way of hint; as your coming in for *any,* much less a *full share* may still be a disputed point, by a Gentleman who is not in this Country at this time, & who is exceedingly

dissatisfyed therewith. I wrote to you a few days ago concerning the other distribution, proposing an easy method of dividing our Lands; but since I find in what temper you are, I am sorry I took the trouble of mentioning the Land, or your name in a Letter, as I do not think you merit the least assistance from

G: Washington

To George William Fairfax

Dear Sir, Wmsburg June 10th 1774

In my way to this place I met with your Letter of the 10th of Jany at Dumfries—In consequence of which, I immediately wrote to Mr Willis (having an oppertunity so to do) desiring him to go to Belvoir, & after examining & considering every thing maturely, to give me his opinion of the Rent which ought to be set upon your Interest there (collectively or seperately) that I might, by knowing the opinion of others, be enabled, as I intended to advertise the Renting of it as soon as I came to this place, to give answers to any application's which should be made; what follows is his answer as I wrote both to Berkeley & Belvr as he was expected at the latter place.

Whether Mr Willis is under, or over the Notch, time only can determine—I wish he may not have exceeded it, although I apprehend you will be disappointed at his estimate for you will please to consider, that, there are very few People who are of ability to pay a Rent equivalent to the Interest of the Money which such buildings may have cost, who are not either already provided with a Seat, or would choose to buy one, in order to Improve it; chance indeed, may throw a Person peculiarly circumstanc'd in the way, by which means a good Rent may be had, but this is to be viewd in the light of a lucky hit not as a matter of expectation; for the generalty of Renters would not give, I conceive, any more rent for the mansion House than if the Land was totally divested of It; & as to your Fishery at the Racoon Branch, I think you will be disappointed there likewise as there is no Landing on this side

the River that Rents for more than half of what you expect
for that and those on the other side opposite to you (equally
good they say) to be had at £15 Maryld Curry however Sir
every notice that can, shall be given of their disposal, & nothing in my power, wanting to put them of to the best advantage in the manner desird. I have already advertizd the Publick
of this matter, also of the Sale of your Furniture, as you may
see, by the Inclosd Gazette, which I send, as it contains some
acct of our American transactions respecting the oppressive
and arbitrary Act of Parliament for stopping up the Port &
commerce of Boston; The Advertisements are in Mrs Rinds
Gazette also—& the one relative to Renting shall be put into
the Papers of Maryland & Pensylvania whilst the other is already printed in hand Bills, & shall be distributed in the several Counties & Parts round about us, that notice thereof may
be as general as possible. the other parts of your Letter relative
to the removal of your Negro's Stock &ca shall be complied
with & you may rely upon it that your Intention of not returning to Virginia shall never transpire from me though give
me leave to add by way of caution to you that a belief of this
sort generally prevails, & hath done so for sometime whether
from People, conjectures, or any thing you may have dropt I
know not. I have never heard the most distant Insinuation of
Lord Dunmore's wanting Belvoir nor am I inclind to think
he does as he talks much of a Place he has purchasd near the
warm Springs, In short I do not know of any Person at present
that is Inclind that way. I shall look for your Bonds when I
return, and do with them as directed—your Books of Accts I
found in your Escruitore, & never heard of a Ballances drawn
or Settlement thereof made by Messrs Adam & Campbell but
will now endeavour to do this myself.

Our Assembly met at this place the 4th Ulto according to
Proragation, and was dissolvd the 26th for entering into a
resolve of which the Inclosd is a Copy, and which the Govr
thought reflected too much upon his Majesty, & the British
Parliamt to pass over unnoticed—this Dissolution was as sudden as unexpected for there were other resolves of a much
more spirited Nature ready to be offerd to the House wch
would have been adopted respecting the Boston Port Bill as
it is call'd but were withheld till the Important business of the

Country could be gone through. As the case stands the assembly sat the 22 day's for nothing—not a Bill being passed the Council being adjournd from the rising of the Court to the day of the Dissolution & came either to advise, or in opposition to the measure. The day after this Event the Members convend themselves at the Raleigh Tavern & enterd into the Inclosd Association which being followed two days after by an Express from Boston accompanied by the Sentiments of some Meetings in our Sister Colonies to the Northwd the proceedings mentiond in the Inclos'd Papers were had thereupon & a general meeting requested of all the late Representatives in this City on the first of August when it is hopd, & expected that some vigorous measures will be effectually adopted to obtain that justice which is denied to our Petitions & Remonstrances; in short the Ministry may rely on it that Americans will never be tax'd without their own consent that the cause of Boston the despotick Measures in respect to it I mean now is and ever will be considerd as the cause of America (not that we approve their condt in destroyg the Tea) & that we shall not suffer ourselves to be sacrificed by piecemeal though god only knows what is to become of us, threatned as we are with so many hoverg evils as hang over us at present; having a cruel & blood thirsty Enemy upon our Backs, the Indians, between whom & our Frontier Inhabitants many Skirmishes have happend, & with whom a general war is inevitable whilst those from whom we have a right to Seek protection are endeavouring by every piece of Art & despotism to fix the Shackles of Slavry upon us—This Dissolution which it is said, & believd, will not be followed by an Election till Instructions are receivd from the Ministry has left us without the means of Defence except under the old Militia & Invasion Laws which are by no means adequate to the exigency's of the Country for from the best accts we have been able to get, there is a confederacy of the Western, & Southern Indian's formd against us and our Settlemt over the Alligany Mountains indeed in Hampshire Augusta &ca are in the utmost Consternation & distress, in short since the first Settlemt of this Colony the Minds of People in it never were more disturbd or our situation so critical as at present; arising as I have said before from an Invasion of our Rights & Priviledges by the Mother Country—& our lives and properties by the Savages whilst a Cruel Frost succeeded by as cruel a drought hath contributed not a little to our unhappy Situation, tho. it is now thought the Injury done to Wheat by the frost is not so great as was at first apprehended—the present opinion being that take the Country through half Crops will be made. to these may be added & a matter of no small moment they are that a total stop is now put to our Courts of Justice (for want of a Fee Bill, which expird the 12th of April last) & the want of Circulating cash amongst Us; for shameful it is that the meeting of Merchants which ought to have been at this place the 25th of April, never happend till about 10 days ago and I beleive will break up in a manner very dissatisfactory to every one if not injurious to their Characters.

I have lately been applied to by Mr Robt Rutherford to join (as your Attorney) in the Conveyance of the Bloomery Tract & Works; but as I never had any particular Instructions from you on this head, & know nothing of the Situation & Circumstances of the matter I have told him that I must receive direction's from you on the Subject before I do anything in it & I desired him therefore to relate the case as it stands which is Inclos'd in his own words. He is urgent to have this business executed & seems to signify that you can not expect any part of the money till you have joind in the Conveyance. June 15th My Patience is entirely exhausted in waiting till the business as they call it, is done, or in other words till the exchange is fix'd—I have therefore left your Money with Colo. Fieldg Lewis to dispose of for a Bill of £200 Sterg which I suppose will be near the amt of the Currt money in my hands as there are Advertisements, hand Bills, Bonds, & ca to pay for preparatory to the Sale of your Furniture and am now hurrying home, in order, if we have any wheat to Harvest that I may be present at it.

Mrs Fairfax's friends in this place & at Hampton are all well (I suppose she has long ago heard of the death of her Brothers Second Son) my best wishes attend her and you and I am Dr Sir Yr Most Obedt Servt

To Bryan Fairfax

DEAR SIR,   Mount Vernon, 4 July, 1774.

John has just delivered to me your favor of yesterday, which I shall be obliged to answer in a more concise manner, than I could wish, as I am very much engaged in raising one of the additions to my house, which I think (perhaps it is fancy) goes on better whilst I am present, than in my absence from the workmen.

I own to you, Sir, I wished much to hear of your making an open declaration of taking a poll for this county, upon Colonel West's publicly declining last Sunday; and I should have written to you on the subject, but for information then received from several gentlemen in the churchyard, of your having refused to do so, for the reasons assigned in your letter; upon which, as I think the country never stood more in need of men of abilities and liberal sentiments than now, I entreated several gentlemen at our church yesterday to press Colonel Mason to take a poll, as I really think Major Broadwater, though a good man, might do as well in the discharge of his domestic concerns, as in the capacity of a legislator. And therefore I again express my wish, that either you or Colonel Mason would offer. I can be of little assistance to either, because I early laid it down as a maxim not to propose myself, and solicit for a second.

As to your political sentiments, I would heartily join you in them, so far as relates to a humble and dutiful petition to the throne, provided there was the most distant hope of success. But have we not tried this already? Have we not addressed the Lords, and remonstrated to the Commons? And to what end? Did they deign to look at our petitions? Does it not appear, as clear as the sun in its meridian brightness, that there is a regular, systematic plan formed to fix the right and practice of taxation upon us? Does not the uniform conduct of Parliament for some years past confirm this? Do not all the debates, especially those just brought to us, in the House of Commons on the side of government, expressly declare that America must be taxed in aid of the British funds, and that she has no longer resources within herself? Is there any thing to be expected from petitioning after this? Is not the attack upon the liberty and property of the people of Boston, before restitution of the loss to the India Company was demanded, a plain and self-evident proof of what they are aiming at? Do not the subsequent bills (now I dare say acts), for depriving the Massachusetts Bay of its charter, and for transporting offenders into other colonies or to Great Britain for trial, where it is impossible from the nature of the thing that justice can be obtained, convince us that the administration is determined to stick at nothing to carry its point? Ought we not, then, to put our virtue and fortitude to the severest test?

With you I think it a folly to attempt more than we can execute, as that will not only bring disgrace upon us, but weaken our cause; yet I think we may do more than is generally believed, in respect to the non-importation scheme. As to the withholding of our remittances, that is another point, in which I own I have my doubts on several accounts, but principally on that of justice; for I think, whilst we are accusing others of injustice, we should be just ourselves; and how this can be, whilst we owe a considerable debt, and refuse payment of it to Great Britain, is to me inconceivable. Nothing but the last extremity, I think, can justify it. Whether this is now come, is the question.

I began with telling you, that I was to write a short letter. My paper informs me I have done otherwise. I shall hope to see you to-morrow, at the meeting of the county in Alexandria, when these points are to be considered. I am, dear Sir, your most obedient and humble servant.

To Bryan Fairfax

Dear Sir,   Mount Vernon July 20th 1774.
Your Letter of the 17th was not presented to me till after the Resolution's (which were adjudg'd advisable for this county to come to) had been revis'd, alterd, & corrected in the Committee; nor till we had gone into a general Meeting in the Court House, and my attention necessarily call'd every moment to the business that was before it; I did however

upon receipt of it (in that hurry & bustle) hastily run it over, and handed it round to the Gentlemen on the Bench, of which there were many; but as no person present seem'd in the least disposed to adopt your Sentiments—as there appeard a perfect satisfaction, & acquiescence to the measures propos'd (except from a Mr Williamson, who was for adopting your advise litterally, without obtaining a Second voice on his Side)—and as the Gentlemen to whom the Letter was shown, advis'd me not to have it read, as it was not like to make a Convert, & repugnant (some of them thought) to the very principle we were contending for, I forebore to offer it otherwise than in the manner abovementioned, which I shall be sorry for, if it gives you any dissatisfaction in not having your Sentiments read to the County at large, instead of communicating them to the first People in it, by offering them the Letter in the manner I did.

That I differ very widely from you, in respect to the mode of obtaining a repeal of the Acts so much, & so justly complaind of, I shall not hesitate to acknowledge; & that this difference in opinion may, probably, proceed from the different Construction's we put upon the Conduct, & Intention of the Ministry, may also be true; But as I see nothing on the one hand, to induce a belief that the Parliament would embrace a favourable oppertunity of Repealing Acts which they go on with great rapidity to pass, in order to enforce their Tyrannical System; and on the other, observe, or think I observe, that Government is pursuing a regular Plan at the expence of Law & justice, to overthrow our Constitutional Rights & liberties, how can I expect any redress from a Measure which hath been ineffectually tryd already—For Sir what is it we are contending against? Is it against paying the duty of 3d. pr lb. on Tea because burthensome? No, it is the Right only, we have all along disputed, & to this end we have already Petitiond his Majesty in as humble, & dutiful a manner as Subjects could do; nay more, we applied to the House of Lords, & House of Commons in their different Legislative Capacities setting forth that, as Englishmen, we could not be deprivd of this essential, & valuable part of our Constitution; If then (as the Fact really is) it is against the Right of Taxation we now do, & (as I before said) all along have contended, why should they suppose an exertion of this power would be less obnoxious now, than formerly? and what reasons have we to believe that, they would make a Second attempt whilst the same Sentiments fill'd the Breast of every American, if they did not intend to inforce it if possible? The conduct of the Boston People could not justify the rigour of their Measures, unless their had been a requisition of payment & refusal of it; nor did that measure require an Act to deprive the Governmt of Massachusets Bay of their Charter; or to exempt Offenders from tryal in the place, where Offences were Committed, as there was not, nor could not be, a single Instance produced to manifest the necessity of it—Are not all these things self evident proofs of a fixed & uniform Plan to Tax us? If we want further proofs, does not all the Debates in the House of Commons serve to confirm this? and hath not Genl Gage's Conduct since his arrival (in Stopping the Address of his Council, & Publishing a Proclamation more becoming a Turkish Bashaw than an English Govr & declaring it Treason to associate in any manner by which the Commerce of Great Britain is to be affected) exhibited unexampled Testimony of the most despotick System of Tyranny that ever was practiced in a free Government. In short what further proofs are wanting to satisfy one of the design's of the Ministry than their own Acts; which are uniform, & plainly tending to the same point—nay, if I mistake not, avowedly to fix the Right of Taxation—what hope then from Petitioning, when they tell us that now, or never, is the time to fix the matter—shall we after this whine & cry for releif, when we have already tried it in vain?, or shall we supinely sit, and see one Provence after another fall a Sacrafice to Despotism? If I was in any doubt as to the Right wch the Parliament of Great Britain had to Tax us without our Consents, I should most heartily coincide with you in opinion, that to Petition, & petition only, is the proper method to apply for relief; because we should then be asking a favour, & not claiming a Right wch by the Law of Nature & our Constitution we are, in my opinion, indubitably entitled to; I should even think it criminal to go further than this, under such an Idea; but none such I have, I think the Parliament of Great Britain hath no more Right to put their hands into my Pocket, without my consent, than I have to put my hands into your's, for money; and this being already urged to them in a firm, but decent manner by all the Colonies, what reason is there to expect any thing from their justice?

As to the Resolution for addressing the Throne, I own to you Sir I think the whole might as well have been expung'd; I expect nothing from the measure; nor shd my voice have accompanied it, if the non-Importation Scheme was intended to be Retarded by it; for I am convinc'd, as much as I am of my Existance, that there is no relief for us but in their distress; & I think, at least I hope, that there is publick Virtue enough left among us to deny ourselves every thing but the bare necessaries of Life to accomplish this end—this we have a Right to do, & no power upon Earth can compel us to do otherwise, till they have first reducd us to the most abject state of Slavery that ever was designd for Mankind. The Stopping our Exports would, no doubt, be a shorter Cut than the other, to effect this purpose, but if we owe Money to Great Britain, nothing but the last necessity can justify the Non-payment of it; and therefore, I have great doubts upon this head, & wish to see the other method, which is legal, & will facilitate these payments, first tried.

I cannot conclude, without expressing some concern that I should differ so widely in Sentiments from you in a matter of such great Moment, & general Import; & should much distrust my own judgment upon the occasion, if my Nature did not recoil at the thought of Submitting to Measures which I think Subversive of every thing that I ought to hold dear and valuable—and did I not find, at the sametime, that the voice of Mankind is with me. I must appologize for sending you so rough a sketch of my thoughts upon your Letter. when I look'd back and saw the length of my own, I could not, as I am also a good deal hurried at this time, bear the thoughts of making off a fair Copy. I am Dr Sir Yr Most Obedt Humble Servt

To Bryan Fairfax

Dear Sir   Mount Vernon Augt 24th 1774

Your Letter of the 5th Instt came to this place, forwarded by Mr Ramsay, a few days after my return from Williamsburg; and I delayed acknowledging of it sooner, in hopes that I should find time, before I began my other journey to Philadelphia, to answer it fully, if not satifactorily, but as much of my time has been engrossd since I came home by Company; by your Brother's Sale & the business consequent thereupon; In writing Letters to England; and now in attending to my own domestick affairs previous to my departure as above; I find it impossible to bestow so much time and attention to the Subject matter of your Letter as I could wish to do, & therefore must rely upon your good nature & candour in excuse for not attempting it. In truth, perswaded as I am that you have read all the Political Pieces which compose a large share of the Gazettes, at this time, I should think it, but for your request, a piece of inexcusable arrogance in me, to make the least essay towards a change in your Political Opinion's; for I am sure I have no new lights to throw upon the Subject, or any arguments to offer in support of my own doctrine than what you have seen; and could only in general add, that an Innate Spirit of freedom first told me, that the Measures which Administration hath for sometime been, and now are, most violently pursuing, are repugnant to every principle of natural justice; whilst much abler heads than my own, hath fully convinced me that it is not only repugnant to natural Right, but Subversive of the Laws & Constitution of Great Britain itself; in the Establishment of which some of the best Blood in the Kingdom hath been Spilt; Satisfied then that the Acts of a British Parliament are no longer Govern'd by the Principles of justice—that it is trampling upon the Valuable Rights of American's, confirmd to them by Charter, & the Constitution they themselves boast of; & convinc'd beyond the smallest doubt, that these Measures are the result of deliberation; & attempted to be carried into Execution by the hand of Power is it a time to trifle, or risk our Cause upon Petitions which with difficulty obtain access, and afterwards are thrown by with the utmost contempt—or should we, because heretofore unsuspicious of design and then unwilling to enter into disputes with the Mother Country go on to bear more, and forbear to innumerate our just causes of Complaint—For my own part, I shall not undertake to say where the Line between Great Britain and the Colonies should be drawn, but I am clearly of opinion that one ought to be drawn; & our Rights clearly ascertaind. I could wish, I own, that the dispute had been left to Posterity to determine, but the Crisis is arrivd when we must assert our Rights, or Submit to every Imposition that can be heap'd upon us; till custom and use, will make us as tame, & abject Slaves, as the Blacks we Rule over with such arbitrary Sway.

I intended to have wrote no more than an apology for not writing, but find I am Insensibly running into a length I did not expect, & therefore shall conclude with remarking, that if you disavow the Right of Parliament to Tax us (unrepresented as we are) we only differ in respect to the mode of opposition; and this difference principally arises from your belief that they (the Parliament I mean) want a Decent oppertunity to Repeal the Acts; whilst I am as fully convinc'd, as I am of my existance, that there has been a regular Systematick Plan formd, to enforce them; and that nothing but Unanimity in the Colonies (a stroke they did not expect) and firmness can prevent it; It seems, from the best advices from Boston, that Genl Gage is exceedingly disconcerted at the quiet & steady Conduct of the People of the Massachusets Bay, and at the Measures pursuing by the other Governments; as I dare say he expected to have forc'd those oppressd People into compliance, or irritated them to acts of violence before this, for a more colourable pretence of Ruling that, and the other Colonies with a high hand. But I am done.

I shall set off on Wednesday next for Philadelphia whither if you have any Commands I shall be glad to oblige you in them. being Dr Sir, with real regard Yr Most Obedt Servt

P.S. Pray what do you think of the Canada Bill?

To Robert McKenzie

Dear Sir,   Philadelphia 9th October 1774

Your letter of the 13th ulto from Boston, gave me pleasure, as I learnt thereby that you were well, and might be expected at Mount Vernon in your way to or from James river, in the course of the winter.

When I have said this, permit me with the freedom of a friend, (for you know I always esteemed you) to express my sorry at Fortunes placing you in a service that must fix curses to latest posterity upon the diabolical contrivers; and if success (which by the by is impossible) accompanies it, execrations upon all those who have been instrumental in the execution.

I do not mean by this to insinuate that an officer is not to discharge his duty, even when chance, not choice, has placed him in a disagreeable situation; but I conceive when you condemn the conduct of the Massachusetts People, you reason from effects, not causes; otherwise you would not wonder at a people who are every day receiving fresh proofs of a Systematic ascertion of an arbitrary power, deeply planned to overturn the Laws & Constitution of their country, & to violate the most essential & valuable rights of mankind; being irritated, & with difficulty restrained from acts of the greatest violence and intemperance. For my own part I confess to you candidly that I view things in a very different point of light to the one in which you seem to consider them, and though you are led to believe by venal men (for such I must take the liberty of calling those new fangled counsellors which fly to & surround you, & all others who for honorary or pecuniary gratifications will lend their aid to overturn the constitution, & introduce a system of arbitrary Government,) altho' you are taught, I say, by discoursing with such men, to believe that the people of Massachusetts are rebellious, setting up for independency, & what not; give me leave, my good friend, to tell you that you are abused—grossly abused; and this I advance with a degree of confidence, & boldness which may claim your belief; having better opportunities of knowing the real sentiments of the people you are among, from the Leaders of them, in opposition to the present measures of administration, than you have from those whose business it is not to disclose truths, but to misrepresent facts in order to justify as much as possible to the world, their own conduct; for give me leave to add, & I think I can announce it as a fact, that it is not the wish, or the interest of the Government, or any other upon this Continent, separately, or collectively, to set up for Independence; but this you may at the same time rely on, that none of them will ever submit to the loss of those valuable rights & priviledges which are essential to the happiness of every free State, and without which, Life, Liberty & property are rendered totally insecure.

These Sir, being certain consequences which must naturally result from the late acts of Parliament relative to America in general, & the Government of Massachusetts Bay in particular, is it to be wonder'd at, I repeat, that men who wish to avert the impendg blow, should attempt to oppose it in its progress, or perhaps for their defence, if it cannot be diverted? Surely I may be allowed to answer in the negative; & give me leave to add, as my opinion, that more blood will be spilt on this occasion (if the Ministry are determined to push matters to extremity) than history has ever yet furnished instances of in the annals of North America; and such a vital wound given to the peace of this great Country, as time itself cannot cure or eradicate the remembrance of. But I have done. I was involuntarily lead into a short discussion of this subject by your remarks on the conduct of the Boston people; & your opinion of their wishes to set up for independency. I am well satisfyed, as I can be of my existence, that no such thing is desired by any thinking man in all North America; on the contrary, that it is the ardent wish of the warmest advocates for liberty, that peace & tranquility, upon Constitutional grounds, may be restored, & the horrors of civil discord prevented.

I am very glad to hear that my friend Stewart was well when you left London. I have not had a letter from him these five years, nor heard of him, I think for two—I wish you had mentioned his employment. Poor Mercer! I often hear from him; much cause has he, I fear, to lament his having fallen into the accursed state of attendance & dependance. I remain with very great esteem Dr Sir Your most Obedt Servt

To John West

Sir, Mount Vernon January 13th 1775

Your Letter of the 8th, which is just handed to me, could not have given you more pain in writing, than it has done me in reading; Because I never deny, or even hesitate in granting any request that is made to me (especially by persons I esteem, and in matters of moment) without feeling inexpressable uneasiness—I do not wonder at your sollicitude on acct of your (only) Son—In Nurturing, and bringing him up in a proper Tract, is, no doubt, an object of great concern to you, as well as Importance to him; but two things are essentially necessary in the Man to whom this charge is committed—A Capacity of judging, with propriety, of Measures proper to be taken in the Government of a Youth—and leizure sufficient to attend the Execution of these Measures—That you are pleased to think favourably of me, in respect to the first, I shall take for granted, from the request you have made—but to shew my incapacity of attending to the latter, with that good faith which I think every man ought to do, who undertakes a trust of this Interesting nature, I can solemnly declare to you, that for this year or two past, there has been scarce a Moment that I can properly call my own: For what with my own business— my present Wards—My Mothers (which is wholely in my hands)—Colo. Colvills—Mrs Savages—Colo. Fairfax's— Colo. Mercers (for Colo. Tayloe though he accepted of the Trust jointly with myself, seems no ways inclined to take any part of the Execution of it)—and the little Assistance I have undertaken to give in the management of my Brother Augustines Affairs (for I have absolutely refused to qualify as an Executor) keeps me, together with the share I take in publick Affairs, constantly engaged in writing Letters—Settling Accts—and Negotiating one piece of business or another, in behalf of one or other of these Concerns; by which means I have really been deprivd of every kind of enjoyment, and had almost fully resolved, to engage in no fresh matter, till I had entirely wound up the old.

Thus much Sir, Candour, indeed the principles of common honesty, obliged me to relate to you; as it is not my wish to deceive any person by promising what I do not think it is in my power to perform, with that punctuallity & rectitude wch I conceive the nature of the trust would require of me—I do not however give a flat refusal to your request—I rather wish you to be fully informed of my Situation, that you may think, with me, or as I do, that if it should please the Almighty to take you to himself so soon as you apprehend (but I hope without just cause) that your Son may be placed in better hands than mine—If you think otherwise, I will do the best I can, merely as Guardian.

I think you will act very prudently in having your will Revised by some person knowing in the Law, as a Testators Intention is often defeated, by different Interpretations of Statutes, which require the whole business of a Man's life to be perfectly conversant In—and in such a case as yours where there are Children by different Ventures, it becomes still more necessary—I shall not, after what I have here said, add any thing more than my wishes, which are sincerely offered for your recovery, & that you may live to see the accomplishment of your Son's Education &ca being with very great esteem Sir Yr Most Obedt Hble Servt

To John Connolly

DEAR SIR,   MOUNT-VERNON, Feb. 25, 1775.

Your servant, on his return from Williamsburg, affords me occasion to answer your polite letter. I confess the state of affairs is sufficiently alarming; which our critical situation, with regard to the Indians does not diminish: but as you have wrote to Lord Dunmore, relative to the prisoners under your charge, there can be no doubt of his Lordship's having now transmitted you the necessary directions on that subject. I have only to express my most ardent wishes that every measure, consistent with reason and sound policy, may be adopted to keep those people, at this time, in good humour; for another rupture would not only ruin the external, but internal parts of this government. If the journal of your proceedings in the Indian war is to be published, I shall have an opportunity of seeing what I have long coveted. With us here, things wear a disagreeable aspect; and the minds of men are exceedingly disturbed at the measures of the British government. The King's Speech and Address of both Houses, prognosticate nothing favourable to us; but by some subsequent proceedings thereto, *as well as by private letters from London*, there is reason to believe, the Ministry would willingly change their ground, from a conviction the forcible measures will be inadequate to the end designed. A little time must now unfold the mystery, as matters are drawing to a point. I am, dear sir, your friend, and most obedient humble servant,

To George William Fairfax

Dear Sir,   Philadelphia May 31st 1775.

Since my last (dated about the first of April) I have received from Mr Craven Peyton the Sum of £193.6.10 (as you may see by the inclosed Account) with which, and the Balance of the former Money, I now remit you the following Bills; to wit, one drawn by Mr Thomas Contee on Mr Mollison, for £40 Sterling, and another drawn by Lyonel Bradstreet on Mr William Tippell of London for the like Sum (indorsed by Mr Contee; the strongest assurances being given me, that they are both good) Mr Contee is Mr Mollison's principal Factor, or Agent, in Maryland, and is besides a Man of property himself; but notwithstanding this, the times are so ticklish, that there is no such thing as answering for the payment of Bills. You must therefore, either take the chance of receiving bad ones, or suffer your Money to lay dead.

I have also, since my coming to this place, purchased a Bill from Messieurs Willing and Morris of £161.5.10 Sterling, which will, I believe, for I have not a state of our Account with me, about Balance it. With the Copy of Mr Peyton's Account, you will receive a List of the Rents which he collected since last settlement; and these, as I have not been favoured with a Line from you, since your Letter of June, is all I recollect at present worth communicating relative to your business.

Before this Letter can reach you, you must, undoubtedly,

have received an Account of the engagement in the Massachusetts Bay between the Ministerial Troops (for we do not,
nor cannot yet prevail upon ourselves to call them the King's
Troops) and the Provincials of that Government; But as you
may not have heard how that affair began, I inclose you the
several Affidavits that were taken after the action.

General Gage acknowledges, that the detachment under
Lieutenant Colonel Smith was sent out to destroy private
property; or, in other Words, to destroy a Magazine which
self preservation obliged the Inhabitants to establish. And he
also confesses, in effect at least, that his Men made a very
precipitate retreat from Concord, notwithstanding the reinforcement under Lord Piercy; the last of which may serve to
convince Lord Sandwich (and others of the same sentiment)
that the Americans will fight for their Liberties and property,
however pusilanimous, in his Lordship's Eye, they may appear
in other respects.

From the best accounts I have been able to collect of that
affair; indeed from every one, I believe the fact, stripped of
all colouring, to be plainly this, that if the retreat had not
been as precipitate as it was (and God knows it could not well
have been more so) the Ministerial Troops must have surrendered, or been totally cut off: For they had not arrived in
Charlestown (under cover of their Ships) half an hour, before
a powerful body of Men from Marblehead and Salem were at
their heels, and must, if they had happened to have been up
one hour sooner, inevitably intercepted their retreat to
Charlestown. Unhappy it is though to reflect, that a Brother's
Sword has been sheathed in a Brother's breast, and that, the
once happy and peaceful plains of America are either to be
drenched with Blood, or Inhabited by Slaves. Sad alternative!
But can a virtuous Man hesitate in his choice? I am, With
sincere Regard and Affectionate compliments to Mrs Fairfax,
Dear Sir, Your Most obt servant,

COMMANDER OF
THE CONTINENTAL ARMY
1775–1783

Address to the Continental Congress

The President informed Colo. Washington that the Congress had yesterday, Unanimously made choice of him to be General & Commander in Chief of the American Forces, and requested he would accept of that Appointment; whereupon Colo. Washington, standing in his place, Spake as follows.

"Mr. President, Tho' I am truly sensible of the high Honour done me in this Appointment, yet I feel great distress, from a consciousness that my abilities & Military experience may not be equal to the extensive & important Trust: However, as the Congress desire it I will enter upon the momentous duty, & exert every power I Possess In their service & for the Support of the glorious Cause: I beg they will accept my most cordial thanks for this distinguished testimony of their Approbation.

"But lest some unlucky event should happen unfavourable to my reputation, I beg it may be rememberd by every Gentn in the room, that I this day declare with the utmost sincerity, I do not think my self equal to the Command I am honoured with.

"As to pay, Sir, I beg leave to Assure the Congress that as no pecuniary consideration could have tempted me to have accepted this Arduous emploiment at the expence of my domestk ease & happiness I do not wish to make any proffit from it: I will keep an exact Account of my expences; those I doubt not they will discharge & that is all I desire."

June 16, 1775

To Martha Washington

My Dearest,   Philadelphia June 18th 1775.

I am now set down to write to you on a subject which fills me with inexpressable concern—and this concern is greatly aggravated and Increased when I reflect on the uneasiness I know it will give you—It has been determined in Congress, that the whole Army raised for the defence of the American

Cause shall be put under my care, and that it is necessary for me to proceed immediately to Boston to take upon me the Command of it. You may beleive me my dear Patcy, when I assure you, in the most solemn manner, that, so far from seeking this appointment I have used every endeavour in my power to avoid it, not only from my unwillingness to part with you and the Family, but from a consciousness of its being a trust too great for my Capacity and that I should enjoy more real happiness and felicity in one month with you, at home, than I have the most distant prospect of reaping abroad, if my stay was to be Seven times Seven years. But, as it has been a kind of destiny that has thrown me upon this Service, I shall hope that my undertaking of it, is designd to answer some good purpose—You might, and I suppose did perceive, from the Tenor of my letters, that I was apprehensive I could not avoid this appointment, as I did not even pretend to intimate when I should return—that was the case—it was utterly out of my power to refuse this appointment without exposing my Character to such censures as would have reflected dishonour upon myself, and given pain to my friends—this I am sure could not, and ought not to be pleasing to you, & must have lessend me considerably in my own esteem. I shall rely therefore, confidently, on that Providence which has heretofore preservd, & been bountiful to me, not doubting but that I shall return safe to you in the fall—I shall feel no pain from the Toil, or the danger of the Campaign—My unhappiness will flow, from the uneasiness I know you will feel at being left alone—I therefore beg of you to summon your whole fortitude & Resolution, and pass your time as agreeably as possible—nothing will give me so much sincere satisfaction as to hear this, and to hear it from your own Pen.

If it should be your desire to remove into Alexandria (as you once mentioned upon an occasion of this sort) I am quite pleased that you should put it in practice, & Lund Washington may be directed, by you, to build a Kitchen and other Houses there proper for your reception—if on the other hand you should rather Incline to spend good part of your time among your Friends below, I wish you to do so—In short, my earnest, & ardent desire is, that you would pursue any Plan that is most likely to produce content, and a tolerable degree of

Tranquility as it must add greatly to my uneasy feelings to hear that you are dissatisfied, and complaining at what I really could not avoid.

As Life is always uncertain, and common prudence dictates to every Man the necessity of settling his temporal Concerns whilst it is in his power—and whilst the Mind is calm and undisturbed, I have, since I came to this place (for I had not time to do it before I left home) got Colo. Pendleton to Draft a Will for me by the directions which I gave him, which Will I now Inclose—The Provision made for you, in case of my death, will, I hope, be agreeable; I have Included the Money for which I sold my own Land (to Doctr Mercer) in the Sum given you, as also all other Debts. What I owe myself is very trifling—Cary's Debt excepted, and that would not have been much if the Bank stock had been applied without such difficulties as he made in the Transference.

I shall add nothing more at present as I have several Letters to write, but to desire you will remember me to Milly & all Friends, and to assure you that I am with most unfeigned regard, My dear Patcy Yr Affecte

P.S. Since writing the above I have receivd your Letter of the 15th and have got two suits of what I was told was the prettiest Muslin. I wish it may please you—it cost 50/. a suit that is 20/. a yard.

To Burwell Bassett

Dear Sir,   Philadelphia, June 19th 1775.

I am now Imbarkd on a tempestuous Ocean from whence, perhaps, no friendly harbour is to be found. I have been called upon by the unanimous Voice of the Colonies to the Command of the Continental Army—It is an honour I by no means aspired to—It is an honour I wished to avoid, as well from an unwillingness to quit the peaceful enjoyment of my Family as from a thorough conviction of my own Incapacity & want of experience in the conduct of so momentous a concern—but the partiallity of the Congress added to some political motives, left me without a choice—May God grant therefore that my acceptance of it may be attended with some good to the common cause & without Injury (from want of knowledge) to my own reputation—I can answer but for three things, a firm belief of the justice of our Cause—close attention in the prosecution of it—and the strictest Integrety—If these cannot supply the places of Ability & Experience, the cause will suffer, & more than probable my character along with it, as reputation derives its principal support from success—but it will be rememberd I hope that no desire, or insinuation of mine, placed me in this situation. I shall not be deprivd therefore of a comfort in the worst event if I retain a consciousness of having acted to the best of my judgment.

I am at liberty to tell you that the Congress in Committee (which will, I daresay, be agreed to when reported) have consented to a Continental Currency, and have ordered two Million of Dollars to be struck for payment of the Troops, and other expences arising from our defence—as also that 15,000 Men are voted as a Continental Army, which will I daresay be augmented as more Troops are Imbark'd & Imbarking for America than was expected at the time of passing that Vote. As to other Articles of Intelligence I must refer you to the Gazettes as the Printers pick up every thing that is stirring in that way. The other Officers in the higher departments are not yet fixed—therefore I cannot give you their names. I set out to morrow for Boston where I shall always be glad to hear from you; my best wishes attend Mrs Bassett—Mrs Dandridge & all our Relations and friends—In great haste, as I have many Letters to write and other business to do I remain with the sincerest regard Dr Sir Yr Most Obedt & Affecte Hble Servt

P.S. I must Intreat you & Mrs Bassett, if possible, to visit at Mt Vernon as also my Wife's other friends—I could wish you to take her down, as I have no expectations of returning till Winter & feel great uneasiness at her lonesome Situation—I have sent my Chariot & Horses back.

To John Augustine Washington

Dear Brother,   Philadelphia June 20th 1775.

I am now to bid adieu to you, & to every kind of domestick ease, for a while. I am Imbarked on a wide Ocean, boundless in its prospect & from whence, perhaps, no safe harbour is to be found. I have been called upon by the unanimous Voice of the Colonies to take the Command of the Continental Army—an honour I neither sought after, nor desired, as I am thoroughly convinced; that it requires greater Abilities, and much more experience, than I am Master of, to conduct a business so extensive in its nature, and arduous in the execution, but the partiallity of the Congress, joind to a political motive, really left me without a Choice; and I am now Commissioned a Generl & Commander in Chief of all the Forces now raisd, or to be raisd, for the defence of the United Colonies—That I may discharge the Trust to the Satisfaction of my Imployers, is my first wish—that I shall aim to do it, there remains as little doubt of—how far I may succeed is another point—but this I am sure of, that in the worse event, I shall have the consolation of knowing (if I act to the best of my judgment) that the blame ought to lodge upon the appointers, not the appointed, as it was by no means a thing of my own seeking, or proceeding from any hint of my friends.

I am at liberty to inform you, that the Congress, in a Committee (which will I dare say be agreed to when reported) have converted to a Continental Currency—have ordered two Million of Dollars to be struck for payment of the Troops &ca and have voted 15,000 Men as a Continental Army—which number will be augmented, as the strength of the British Troops will be greater than was expected at the time of passing that vote. Genl Ward—Genl Lee—Genl Schuyler—and Genl Putnam—are appointed Major Genls under me—the Brigadier Genls are not yet appointed. Majr Gates Adjutant Genl— I expect to set out to morrow for Boston & hope to be joind there in a little time by Ten Companies of Rifle men from this Provence, Maryland, & Virginia—for other Articles of Intelligence, I shall refer you to the Papers, as the Printers are diligent in collecting every thing that is stirring.

I shall hope that my Friends will visit, & endeavour to keep up the Spirits of my Wife as much as they can, as my departure will, I know, be a cutting stroke upon her; and on this acct alone, I have many very disagreeable Sensations—I hope you & my Sister, (although the distance is great) will find as much leisure this Summer, as to spend a little time at Mt Vernon. My sincere regards attend you both as also the little ones and I am Dr Sir Yr most Affecte Brother

To the Officers of Five Virginia Companies

Gentlemen   Philadelphia June 20. 1775
I am now about to bid adieu to the Companies under your respective commands, at least for a while—I have launched into a wide & extensive field, too boundless for my abilities, & far, very far beyond my experience—I am called by the unanimous voice of the Colonies to the command of the Continental army: an honour I did not aspire to—an honor I was sollicitous to avoid upon full conviction of my inadequacy to the importance of the service; the partiallity of the Congress however, assisted by a political motive, rendered my reasons unavailing & I shall, to morrow, set out for the camp near Boston—I have only to beg of you therefore (before I go—especially as you did me the honor to place your Companies under my directions, and know not how soon you may be called upon in Virginia) for an exertion of your military skill, by no means to relax in the discipline of your Respective companies.

I am at liberty to inform you Gentlemen, That the Congress in a Committee, (which will, I dare say be agreed to when reported) have consented to a Continental currency—Ordered Two millions of Dollars to be struck & Voted 15,000 men; Which number I am Inclined to think will be augmented, as more Troops have embarked & are embarking for America, than were expected at the time of passing that Vote.

The Arrangement of Officers in the higher departments of

the army is not yet fixed, ultimately, but I beleive they will stand thus; Genl Ward, Genl Lee, Genl Putnam, & Genl Scyler—Major Genls—The Brigadier Genls are not yet proposed—Major Gates Adjutant Genl—For other articles of Intelligence, the Gazettes will furnish you with them more precisely than I can, as the printers let no news pass by them— The Chief end of my writing to you at this time being, to Recommend a diligent attention to the disciplining of your Companies, & Seeing that they are well provided with ammunition—I shall not Enlarge as I am very much hurried with one thing and another in consequence of my appointment— I shall only add therefore that I am with sincere regard & esteem Gentlemen Your Most Obedt & Hble servant

P.S. you will, I am persuaded, excuse my addressing a joint Letter to you, as I had it not in my power to write seperate ones, & could not think of departing without affording you this Testimonial of my regard. Yrs

To Martha Washington

My dearest,   Phila. June 23d 1775.
   As I am within a few Minutes of leaving this City, I could not think of departing from it without dropping you a line; especially as I do not know whether it may be in my power to write again till I get to the Camp at Boston—I go fully trusting in that Providence, which has been more bountiful to me than I deserve, & in full confidence of a happy meeting with you sometime in the Fall—I have not time to add more, as I am surrounded with Company to take leave of me—I retain an unalterable affection for you, which neither time or distance can change, my best love to Jack & Nelly, & regard for the rest of the Family concludes me with the utmost truth & sincerety Yr entire

Address to the
New York Provincial Congress

Gentlemen   June 26. 1775.

At the same time that with you I deplore the unhappy Necessity of such an Appointment, as that with which I am now honoured, I cannot but feel sentiments of the highest Gratitude for this affecting Instance of Distinction & Regard.

May your warmest wish be realized in the Success of America at this important and interesting Period; & be assured that, every Exertion of my worthy Colleagues & myself, will be equally extended to the re establishment of Peace & Harmony between the Mother Country and the Colonies. As to the fatal, but necessary Operations of War. When we assumed the Soldier, we did not lay aside the Citizen, & we shall most sincerely rejoice with you in that happy Hour, when the Establishment of American Liberty on the most firm, & solid Foundations, shall enable us to return to our private Stations in the bosom of a free, peaceful, & happy Country.

General Orders

Head Quarters, Cambridge, July 4th 1775.

Parole. Abington.   Countersign, Bedford.

Exact returns to be made by the proper Officers of all the Provisions, Ordnance, Ordnance stores, Powder, Lead, working Tools of all kinds, Tents, Camp Kettles, and all other Stores under their respective care, belonging to the Armies at Roxbury and Cambridge. The commanding Officer of each Regiment to make a return of the number of blankets wanted to compleat every Man with one at least.

The Hon: Artemus Ward, Charles Lee, Philip Schuyler, and Israel Putnam Esquires, are appointed Major Generals of the American Army and due Obedience is to be paid them as such. The Continental Congress not having compleated the appointments of the other officers in said army, nor had sufficient time to prepare and forward their Commissions; every

Officer is to continue to do duty in the Rank and Station he at present holds untill further orders.

Thomas Mifflin Esqr. is appointed by the General one of his Aid-de-Camps. Joseph Reed Esqr. is in like manner appointed Secretary to the General, and they are in future to be consider'd and regarded as such.

The Continental Congress having now taken all the Troops of the several Colonies, which have been raised, or which may be hereafter raised, for the support and defence of the Liberties of America; into their Pay and Service: They are now the Troops of the United Provinces of North America; and it is hoped that all Distinctions of Colonies will be laid aside; so that one and the same spirit may animate the whole, and the only Contest be, who shall render, on this great and trying occasion, the most essential service to the great and common cause in which we are all engaged.

It is required and expected that exact discipline be observed, and due Subordination prevail thro' the whole Army, as a Failure in these most essential points must necessarily produce extreme Hazard, Disorder and Confusion; and end in shameful disappointment and disgrace.

The General most earnestly requires, and expects, a due observance of those articles of war, established for the Government of the army, which forbid profane cursing, swearing & drunkeness; And in like manner requires & expects, of all Officers, and Soldiers, not engaged on actual duty, a punctual attendance on divine service, to implore the blessings of heaven upon the means used for our safety and defence.

All Officers are required and expected to pay diligent Attention, to keep their Men neat and clean—to visit them often at their quarters, and inculcate upon them the necessity of cleanliness, as essential to their health and service. They are particularly to see, that they have Straw to lay on, if to be had, and to make it known if they are destitute of this article. They are also to take care that Necessarys be provided in the Camps and frequently filled up to prevent their being offensive and unhealthy. Proper Notice will be taken of such Officers and Men, as distinguish themselves by their attention to these necessary duties.

The commanding Officer of each Regiment is to take particular care that not more than two Men of a Company be absent on furlough at the same time, unless in very extraordinary cases.

Col. Gardner is to be buried to morrow at 3, OClock, P: M. with the military Honors due to so brave and gallant an Officer, who fought, bled and died in the Cause of his country and mankind. His own Regiment, except the company at Malden, to attend on this mournful occasion. The places of those Companies in the Lines on Prospect Hill, to be supplied by Col. Glovers regiment 'till the funeral is over.

No Person is to be allowed to go to Fresh-water pond a fishing or on any other occasion as there may be danger of introducing the small pox into the army.

It is strictly required and commanded that there be no firing of Cannon or small Arms from any of the Lines, or elsewhere, except in case of necessary, immediate defence, or special order given for that purpose.

All Prisoners taken, Deserters coming in, Persons coming out of Boston, who can give any Intelligence; any Captures of any kind from the Enemy, are to be immediately reported and brought up to Head Quarters in Cambridge. Capt. Griffin is appointed Aid-de-Camp to General Lee and to be regarded as such.

The Guard for the security of the stores at Watertown, is to be increased to thirty men immediately.

A serjeant and six men to be set as a Guard to the Hospital, and are to apply to Doctor Rand.

Complaint having been made against John White Quarter Master of Col. Nixon's Regmt for misdemeanors in drawing out Provisions for more Men than the Regiment consisted of; A Court Martial consisting of one Captain and four Subalterns is ordered to be held on said White, who are to enquire, determine and report.

After Orders. 10 OClock

The General desires that some Carpenters be immediately set to work at Brattle's Stables, to fix up Stalls for eight Horses, and more if the Room will admit, with suitable racks, mangers &c.

To Richard Henry Lee

Dear Sir,   Camp at Cambridge July 10th 1775.

I was exceeding glad to receive a Letter from you, as I always shall be whenever it is convenient, though perhaps my hurry, till such time as matters are drawn a little out of the Chaos they appear in at present, will not suffer me to write you such full and satisfactory answers, or give such clear, and precise accts of our Situation & views, as I could wish, or you might expect.

After a journey, a good deal retarded, principally by the desire the different Townships through which I traveld, express'd of shewing respect to the Genl of your armies; I arrivd here on this day week; since which I have been labouring with as much assiduity by fair, and threatning means to obtain returns of our strength in this Camp and Roxbury, & their Dependencies, as a man could do, and never have been able to accomplish the matter till this day—now, I will not answer for the correctness of them, although I have sent several of the Regimental returns back more than once to have mistakes rectified. I do not doubt but the Congress will think me very remiss in not writing to them sooner but you may rely on it yourself, and I beg you to assure them, that it has never been in my power till this day, to comply with their orders. could I have conceivd, that which ought, and in a regular Army would have been done in an hour, would employ eight days, I should have sent an Express off the 2d Morning after I arrivd with a genl acct of things. but expecting in the Morning to receive the Returns in the Evening, and in the Evening surely to find them in the Morning (& at last getting them full of Imperfections) I have been drilled on from day to day, till I am ashamed to look back at the time which has elapsed since my arrival here.

You will perceive by the returns, that, we have but about 16,000. effective men in all this department, whereas by the accts which I receivd from even the first Officers in Command, I had no doubt of finding between 18. and 20,000—out of these there are only 14000 fit for duty—So soon as I was able to get this state of the army, & came to the knowledge of our Weakness, I immediately summond a Council of War, the result of which you will see, as it is Inclosed to the Congress. Between you and me I think we are in an exceeding dangerous Situation, as our Numbers are not much larger than we suppose, from the best accts we are able to get, those of the Enemy to be; theirs situated in such a manner as to be drawn to any point of attack without our having an hours previous notice of it (if the Genl will keep his own Council) whereas we are obliged to be guarded at all points, & know not where, with precission, to look for them—I should not, I think, have made choice of the present Posts in the first Instance altho. I beleive, the Communication between the Town and Country could not have been so well cut off without; but, as much labour has been bestowed in throwing up lines—making redoubts &ca—as Cambridge Roxbury and Watertown must be immediately exposed to the Mercy of the Enemy were we to retreat a little further in the Country—as it would give general dissatisfaction to this Colony—dispirit our own People, and Incourage the Enemy, to remove at this time to another place we have for these reasons resolved in Council to maintain our ground if we can—Our Lines on Winter & Prospect Hills, & those of the Enemy on Bunkers Hill, are in full view of each other, a Mile distant, our advanc'd guard much nearer, & the centries almost near enough to converse—At Roxbury & Boston Neck it is the same between these, we are obliged to guard sevl other Places at which the Enemy may Land. The Enemy have strongly fortified, or will in a few days, their Camp on Bunkers Hill; after which, & their new Landed Troops have got a little refreshd, we shall look for a visit, if they mean, as we are told they do, to come out of their Lines—their great Command of Artillery, & adequate Stores of Powder &ca gives them advantages which we have only to lament the want of—The abuses in this army, I fear, are considerable. and the new modelling of it, in the Face of an Enemy, from whom we every hour expect an attack exceedingly difficult, & dangerous—if things therefore should not turn out as the Congress would wish I hope they will make proper allowances—I can only promise & assure them, that, my whole time is devoted to their Service, & that as far as my judgment goes, they shall have no cause to complain.

I need not tell you that this Letter is written in much haste. The fact will sufficiently appear from the face of it; I thought a hasty Letter would please you better than no Letter, & therefore I shall offer no further appology, but assure you that with sincere regard for my fellow Labourers with you. Doctr Shippens Family &ca. I am Dr Sir Yr Most Affecte Servt

To John Augustine Washington

Camp at Cambridge about 5 Miles from Boston;
Dear Brother   July 27th 1775.
On the 2d Instt I arrived at this place after passing through a great deal of delightful Country, covered with grass (although the Season has been dry) in a very different manner to what our Lands in Virginia are. I found a mixed multitude of People here, under very little discipline, order, or Government—I found the Enemy in Possession of a place called Bunkers Hill, on Charles Town Neck, strongly Intrenched & Fortifying themselves: I found part of our Army on two Hills (called Winter & prospect Hills) about a Mile & quarter from the Enemy on Bunkers Hill, in a very insecure state—I found another part of the Army at this Village and a third part at Roxbury, guarding the Entrance in and out of Boston—My whole time since I came here has been Imployed in throwing up Lines of Defence at these three several places; to secure in the first Instance, our own Troops from any attempts of the Enemy, and in the next, to cut of all Communication between their Troops and the Country; For to do this, & to prevent them from penetrating into the Country with Fire and Sword, & to harrass them if they do, is all that is expected of me; and if effected, must totally overthrow the designs of Administration, as the whole Force of Great Britain in the Town and Harbour of Boston, can answer no other end than to sink her under the disgrace and weight of the expence—Their Force, including Marines Tories, &ca, are computed from the best Accts I can get, at abt 12,000 Men; ours including Sick, absent, &ca at about 16,000; but then we have a cemi Circle of Eight or nine Miles to guard; to every part of wch we are

obliged to be equally attentive, whilst they, situated as it were in the Centre of that Cemicircle, can bend their whole Force (having the entire command of the Water) against any one part of it with equal facility; this renders our Situation not very agreeable, though necessary, however, by incessant labour (Sundays not excepted) we are in a much better posture of defence now than when I first came. The Inclosed, though rough, will give you some small Idea of the Situation of Boston, & Bay on this side; as also of the Post they have Taken in Charles Town Neck, Bunkers Hill, and our Posts.

By very authentick Intelligence lately receivd out of Boston (from a Person who saw the returns) the number of Regulars (including I presume the Marines) the Morning of the action on Bunkers Hill amounted to 7533 Men—their killed & wounded on that occasion amounted to 1043, whereof 92 were Officers. our loss was 138 killed—36 Missing & 276 Wounded. The Enemy are sickly, and scarce of Fresh provisions—Beef, which is chiefly got by Slaughtering their Milch Cows in Boston, sells from one Shilling to 18d. Sterg pr lb.; & that it may not get cheaper, or more plenty, I have drove all the Stock within a considerable distance of this place, back into the Country, out of the Way of the Men of War Boats; In short I have, & shall continue to do, every thing in my power to distress them. The Transports are all arrived & their whole Re-inforcement Landed, so that I can see no reason why they should not if they ever attempt it, come boldly out and put the matter to Issue at once—if they think themselves not strong enough to do this, they surely will carry their Arms (having Ships of War & Transports ready) to some other part of the Continent, or relinquish the dispute; the last of which the Ministry, unless compeld will never agree to do—Our works, & those of the Enemy, are so near & quite open between that we see every thing that each other is doing—I recollect nothing more worth mentioning—I shall therefore conclude with my best wishes, and love to my Sister and the Family & Compliments to any enquiring Friends Yr Most affecte Brother.

To Thomas Gage

Sir   Cambridge August 11th 1775

I understand that the Officers engaged in the Cause of Liberty, and their Country, who by the Fortune of War, have fallen into your Hands have been thrown indiscriminately, into a common Gaol appropriated for Felons—That no Consideration has been had for those of the most respectable Rank, when languishing with Wounds and Sickness. That some have been even amputated, in this unworthy Situation.

Let your Opinion, Sir, of the Principle which actuates them be what it may, they suppose they act from the noblest of all Principles, a Love of Freedom, and their Country. But political Opinions I conceive are foreign to this Point, the Obligations arising from the Rights of Humanity, & Claims of Rank, are universally binding and extensive, except in Case of Retaliation. These, I should have hoped, would have dictated a more tender Treatment of those Individuals, whom Chance or War had put in your Power—Nor can I forbear suggesting, its fatal Tendency to widen that unhappy Breach, which you, and those Ministers under whom you act, have repeatedly declared you wish'd to see forever closed.

My Duty now makes it necessary to apprize you, that for the future I shall regulate my Conduct towards those Gentlemen who are or may be in our Possession, exactly by the Rule which you shall observe, towards those of ours, who may be in your Custody. If Severity, & Hardship mark the Line of your Conduct, (painful as it may be to me) your Prisoners will feel its Effects: But if Kindness & Humanity are shewn to ours, I shall with Pleasure consider those in our Hands, only as unfortunate, and they shall receive the Treatment to which the unfortunate are ever intitled.

I beg to be favoured with an Answer as soon as possible. And am, Sir, Your most Obedt & very Hbble Servt

To Thomas Gage

Sir   Head Quarters Cambridge Augt 19th 1775.

   I address'd you on the 11th Instant in Terms which gave the fairest Scope, for the Exercise of that Humanity & Politeness, which were supposed to form a Part of your Character— I remonstrated with you, on the unworthy Treatment shewn to the Officers, and Citizens of America, whom the Fortune of War, Chance, or a mistaken Confidence had thrown into your Hands. Whether British, or American Mercy, Fortitude, & Patience are most preeminent; whether our virtuous Citizens whom the Hand of Tyranny has forced into Arms, to defend their Wives, their Children, & their Property; or the mercenary Instruments of lawless Domination, Avarice, and Revenge best deserve the Appellation of Rebels, and the Punishment of that Cord, which your affected Clemency has forborne to inflict; Whether the Authority under which I act is usurp'd, or founded on the genuine Principles of Liberty, were altogether foreign to my Subject. I purposely avoided all political Disquisition; nor shall I now avail myself of those Advantages, which the sacred Cause of my Country, of Liberty, and human Nature give me over you. Much less shall I stoop to Retort, & Invective. But the Intelligence, you say, you have received from our Army requires a Reply. I have taken Time, Sir, to make a strict Inquiry, and find it has not the least Foundation in Truth. Not only your Officers, and Soldiers have been treated with a Tenderness due to Fellow Citizens, & Brethren; but even those execrable Parricides, whose Counsels & Aid have deluged their Country with Blood, have been protected from the Fury of a justly enraged Poeple. Far from compelling, or even permitting their Assistance, I am embarassed with the Numbers who crowd to our Camp animated with the purest Principles of Virtue, & Love of their Country.

   You advise me to give free Operation to Truth, to punish Misrepresentation & Falshood. If Experience stamps Value upon Counsel, yours must have a Weight which few can claim. You best can tell, how far the Convulsion which has brought such Ruin on both Countries, and shaken the mighty Empire of Brittain to its Foundation, may be traced to those malignant Causes.

You affect, Sir, to despise all Rank not derived from the same Source with your own. I cannot conceive any more honourable, than that which flows from the uncorrupted Choice of a brave and free Poeple—The purest Source & original Fountain of all Power. Far from making it a Plea for Cruelty, a Mind of true Magnanimity, & enlarged Ideas would comprehend & respect it.

What may have been the ministerial Views which precipitated the present Crisis, Lexington—Concord, & Charlestown can best declare—May that God to whom you then appealed, judge between America & you! Under his Providence, those who influence the Councils of America, and all the other Inhabitants of these united Colonies, at the Hazard of their Lives, are resolved to hand down to Posterity those just & invaluable Privileges which they received from their Ancestors.

I shall now, Sir, close my Correspondence with you, perhaps forever. If your Officers who are our Prisoners receive a Treatment from me, different from what I wish'd to shew them, they, & you, will remember the Occasion of it. I am Sir, Your very Hbble Servant

To Lund Washington

Dear Lund,   Camp at Cambridge Augt 20th 1775.
Your Letter by Captn Prince came to my hands last Night—I was glad to learn by it that all are well. the acct given of the behaviour of the Scotchmen at Port Tobacco & Piscataway surprizd & vexed me—Why did they Imbark in the cause? what do they say for themselves? what does other say of them? are they admitted into Company? or kicked out of it? what does their Countrymen urge in justification of them? they are fertile in invention, and will offer excuses where excuses can be made. I cannot say but I am curious to learn the reasons why men, who had subscribed, & bound themselves to each other, & their Country, to stand forth in defence of it, should lay down their arms the first moment they were called upon.

Although I never hear of the Mill under the direction of Simpson, without a degree of warmth & vexation at his extreame stupidity, yet, if you can spare money from other Purposes, I could wish to have it sent to him, that it may, if possible, be set agoing before the Works get ruined & spoilt, & my whole money perhaps totally lost. If I am really to loose Barraud's debt to me, it will be a pretty severe stroke upon the back of Adams, & the expence I am led into by that confounded fellow Simpson, and necessarily so in Seating my Lands under the Management of Cleveland.

Spinning should go forward with all possible dispatch, as we shall have nothing else to depend upon if these disputes continue another year—I can hardly think that Lord Dunmore can act so low, & unmanly a part, as to think of siezing Mrs Washington by way of revenge upon me; howevr as I suppose she is, before this time gone over to Mr Calverts, & will soon after retug, go down to New Kent, she will be out of his reach for 2 or 3 Months to come, in which time matters may, & probably will, take such a turn as to render her removal either absolutely necessary, or quite useless—I am nevertheless exceedingly thankful to the Gentlemen of Alexandria for their friendly attention to this point & desire you will if there is any sort of reason to suspect a thing of this kind provide a Kitchen for her in Alexandria, or some other place of safety elsewhere for her and my Papers.

The People of this Government have obtain a Character which they by no means deserved—their Officers generally speaking are the most indifferent kind of People I ever saw. I have already broke one Colo. and five Captain's for Cowardice, & for drawing more Pay & Provision's than they had Men in their Companies. there is two more Colos. now under arrest, & to be tried for the same Offences—in short they are by no means such Troops, in any respect, as you are led to believe of them from the Accts which are published, but I need not make myself Enemies among them, by this declaration, although it is consistent with truth. I daresay the Men would fight very well (if properly Officered) although they are an exceeding dirty & nasty people. had they been properly conducted at Bunkers Hill (on the 17th of June) or those that were there properly supported, the Regulars would have met with a shameful defeat; & a much more considerable loss than they did, which is now known to be exactly 1057 Killed & Wounded—it was for their behaviour on that occasion that the above Officers were broke, for I never spared one that was accused of Cowardice but brot 'em to immediate Tryal.

Our Lines of Defence are now compleated, as near so at least as can be—we now wish them to come out, as soon as they please, but they (that is the Enemy) discover no Inclination to quit their own Works of Defence; & as it is almost impossible for us to get to them, we do nothing but watch each other's motion's all day at the distance of about a Mile; every now and then picking of a stragler when we can catch them without their Intrenchments; in return, they often Attempt to Cannonade our Lines to no other purpose than the waste of a considerable quantity of Powder to themselves which we should be very glad to get.

What does Doctr Craik say to the behaviour of his Countrymen, & Townspeople? remember me kindly to him, & tell him that I should be very glad to see him here if there was any thing worth his acceptance; but the Massachusets People suffer nothing to go by them that they can lay hands upon.

I wish the money could be had from Hill, & the Bills of Exchange (except Colo. Fairfax's, which ought to be sent to him immediately) turnd into Cash; you might then, I should think, be able to furnish Simpson with about £300; but you are to recollect that I have got Cleveland & the hired People with him to pay also. I would not have you buy a single bushel of Wheat till you can see with some kind of certainty what Market the Flour is to go to—& if you cannot find sufficient Imployment in repairing the Mill works, & other things of this kind for Mr Roberts and Thomas Alferd, they must be closely Imployed in making Cask, or working at the Carpenters or other business otherwise they must be discharged, for it is not reasonable, as all Mill business will probably be at an end for a while, that I am to pay them £100 a year to be Idle. I should think Roberts himself must see, & be sensible of the reasonableness of this request, as I believe few Millers will find Imploymt if our Ports are shut up, & the Wheat kept in the Straw, or otherwise for greater Security.

I will write to Mr Milnor to forward you a good Country

Boulting Cloth for Simpson which endeavour to have contrived to him by the first safe conveyance. I wish you would
quicken Lanphire & Sears about the Dining Room Chimney
Piece (to be executed as mentioned in one of my last Letters)
as I could wish to have that end of the House compleatly
finished before I return. I wish you had done the end of the
New Kitchen next the Garden as also the old Kitchen with
rusticated Boards; however, as it is not, I would have the Corners done so in the manner of our New Church. (those two
especially which Fronts the Quarter.) What have you done
with the Well? is that walled up? have you any accts of the
Painter? how does he behave at Fredericksburg?

I much approve of your Sowing Wheat in clean ground,
although you should be late in doing it, & if for no other
purpose than a tryal—It is a growing I find, as well as a new
practice, that of overseers keeping Horses, & for what purpose, unless it be to make fat Horses at my expence, I know
not, as it is no saving of my own Horses—I do not like the
custom, & wish you would break it—but do as you will, as I
cannot pretend to interfere at this distance. Remember me
kindly to all the Neighbours who enquire after Yr Affecte
friend & Servt

To the Inhabitants of Bermuda

Gentlemen

In the great Conflict which agitates this Continent I cannot
doubt but the Assertors of Freedom & the Rights of the Constitution are possessed of your most favourable Regards &
Wishes for Success. As the Descendants of Freemen & Heirs
with us of the same glorious Inheritance we flatter ourselves
that tho. divided by our Situation we are firmly united in Sentiment. The Cause of Virtue & Liberty is confined to no Continent or Climate it comprehends within its capacious Limits
the wise & the good however dispersed & separated in Space
or Distance. You need not be informed that the Violence &
Rapacity of a tyrannick Ministry have forced the Citizens of
America your Brother Colonists into Arms. We equally detest

& lament the Prevalence of those Councils which have led to the Effusion of so much human Blood & left us no Alternative but a Civil War or a base Submission. The wise Disposer of all Events has hitherto smiled upon our virtuous Efforts, those mercenary Troops a few of whom lately boasted of subjugating this vast Continent, have been checked in their earliest Ravages, & are now actually encircled in a small Space their Arms disgraced & suffering all the Calamities of a Siege. The Virtue & Spirit & Union of the Provinces leave them nothing to fear but the Want of Ammunition: The Applications of our Enemies to foreign States & their Vigilance upon our Coasts are the only Efforts they have made against us with Success. Under these Circumstances & with these Sentiments we have turned our Eyes to you Gentlemen for Relief. We are informed that there is a large Magazine in your Island under a very feeble Guard. We would not wish to involve you in an Opposition in which from your Situation we should be unable to support you, we know not therefore to what Extent to sollicit your Assistance in availing ourselves of this Supply: but if your Favour & Friendship to North America & its Liberties have not been misrepresented I perswade myself you may consistent with your own Safety promote & favour this Scheme so as to give it the fairest Prospect of Success. Be assured that in this Case the whole Power & Exertion of my Influence will be made with the Honourable Continental Congress that your Island may not only be supplied with Provisions but experience every other Mark of Affection & Friendship which the grateful Citizens of a free Country can bestow on its Brethren & Benefactors.

September 6, 1775

To the Inhabitants of Canada

Friends and Brethren,

   The unnatural Contest between the English Colonies and Great-Britain, has now risen to such a Height, that Arms alone must decide it. The Colonies, confiding in the Justice of their Cause, and the Purity of their Intentions, have reluctantly appealed to that Being, in whose Hands are all human Events. He has hitherto smiled upon their virtuous Efforts—The Hand of Tyranny has been arrested in its Ravages, and the British Arms which have shone with so much Splendor in every Part of the Globe, are now tarnished with Disgrace and Disappointment.—Generals of approved Experience, who boasted of subduing this great Continent, find themselves circumscribed within the Limits of a single City and its Suburbs, suffering all the Shame and Distress of a Siege. While the trueborn Sons of America, animated by the genuine Principles of Liberty and Love of their Country, with increasing Union, Firmness and Discipline repel every Attack, and despise every Danger.

Above all, we rejoice, that our Enemies have been deceived with Regard to you—They have perswaded themselves, they have even dared to say, that the Canadians were not capable of distinguishing between the Blessings of Liberty, and the Wretchedness of Slavery; that gratifying the Vanity of a little Circle of Nobility—would blind the Eyes of the People of Canada.—By such Artifices they hoped to bend you to their Views, but they have been deceived, instead of finding in you that Poverty of Soul, and Baseness of Spirit, they see with a Chagrin equal to our Joy, that you are enlightned, generous, and virtuous—that you will not renounce your own Rights, or serve as Instruments to deprive your Fellow Subjects of theirs.—Come then, my Brethren, unite with us in an indissoluble Union, let us run together to the same Goal.—We have taken up Arms in Defence of our Liberty, our Property, our Wives, and our Children, we are determined to preserve them, or die. We look forward with Pleasure to that Day not far remote (we hope) when the Inhabitants of America shall have one Sentiment, and the full Enjoyment of the Blessings of a free Government.

Incited by these Motives, and encouraged by the Advice of many Friends of Liberty among you, the Grand American Congress have sent an Army into your Province, under the Command of General Schuyler; not to plunder, but to protect you; to animate, and bring forth into Action those Sentiments of Freedom you have disclosed, and which the Tools of Despotism would extinguish through the whole Creation.—To co-operate with this Design, and to frustrate those cruel and perfidious Schemes, which would deluge our Frontiers with the Blood of Women and Children; I have detached Colonel Arnold into your Country, with a Part of the Army under my Command—I have enjoined upon him, and I am certain that he will consider himself, and act as in the Country of his Patrons, and best Friends. Necessaries and Accommodations of every Kind which you may furnish, he will thankfully receive, and render the full Value.—I invite you therefore as Friends and Brethren, to provide him with such Supplies as your Country affords; and I pledge myself not only for your Safety and Security, but for ample Compensation. Let no Man desert his Habitation—Let no one flee as before an Enemy. The Cause of America, and of Liberty, is the Cause of every virtuous American Citizen; whatever may be his Religion or his Descent, the United Colonies know no Distinction but such as Slavery, Corruption and arbitrary Domination may create. Come then, ye generous Citizens, range yourselves under the Standard of general Liberty—against which all the Force and Artifice of Tyranny will never be able to prevail.

c. September 14, 1775

To William Woodford

Dear Sir,   Cambridge, 10 November, 1775.

Your favor of the 18th of September came to my hands on Wednesday last, through Boston, and open, as you may suppose. It might be well to recollect by whom you sent it, in order to discover if there has not been some treachery practised.

I do not mean to flatter, when I assure you, that I highly approve of your appointment. The inexperience you complain of is a common case, and only to be remedied by practice and close attention. The best general advice I can give, and which I am sure you stand in no need of, is to be strict in your discipline; that is, to require nothing unreasonable of your officers and men, but see that whatever is required be punctually complied with. Reward and punish every man according to his merit, without partiality or prejudice; hear his complaints; if well founded, redress them; if otherwise, discourage them, in order to prevent frivolous ones. Discourage vice in every shape, and impress upon the mind of every man, from the first to the lowest, the importance of the cause, and what it is they are contending for. For ever keep in view the necessity of guarding against surprises. In all your marches, at times, at least, even when there is no possible danger, move with front, rear, and flank guards, that they may be familiarized to the use; and be regular in your encampments, appointing necessary guards for the security of your camp. In short, whether you expect an enemy or not, this should be practised; otherwise your attempts will be confused and awkward, when necessary. Be plain and precise in your orders, and keep copies of them to refer to, that no mistakes may happen. Be easy and condescending in your deportment to your officers, but not too familiar, lest you subject yourself to a want of that respect, which is necessary to support a proper command. These, Sir, not because I think you need the advice, but because you have been condescending enough to ask it, I have presumed to give as the great outlines of your conduct.

As to the manual exercise, the evolutions and manoeuvres of a regiment, with other knowledge necessary to the soldier, you will acquire them from those authors, who have treated upon these subjects, among whom Bland (the newest edition) stands foremost; also an Essay on the Art of War; Instructions for Officers, lately published at Philadelphia; the Partisan; Young; and others.

My compliments to Mrs. Woodford; and that every success may attend you, in this glorious struggle, is the sincere and ardent wish of, dear Sir, your affectionate humble servant.

To Lund Washington

Novr 26th 1775.

I well know where the difficulty of accomplishing these things will lie. Overseers are already engaged (upon shares) to look after my business. Remote advantages to me, however manifest and beneficial, are nothing to them; and to engage standing Wages, when I do not know that any thing I have, or can raise, will command Cash, is attended with hazard; for which reason I hardly know what more to say than to discover my wishes. The same reason, although it may in appearance have the same tendency in respect to you, shall not be the same in its operation: For I will engage for the Year coming, and the Year following, if these troubles, and my absence continues, that your Wages shall be standing and certain, at the highest amount that any one years Crop has produced to you yet. I do not offer this as any Temptation, to Induce *you* to go on more chearfully in prosecuting *these* Schemes of *mine*. I should do ingustice to you, were I not to acknowledge that your conduct has ever appeard to me above every thing Sordid, but I offer it in consideration of the great charge you have upon your hands, and my entire dependance upon your Fidility and Industry. It is the greatest, indeed it is the only comfortable reflection I enjoy on this score, to think that my business is in the hands of a person in whose Integrity I have not a doubt, and on whose care I can rely— was it not for this I should feel very unhappy on acct of the Situation of my Affaers; but I am perswaded you will do for me as you would for yourself, & more than this I cannot expect.

I observe you mention something, in respect to the removal of my valuable Furniture, but where can you carry it? or what will be done with it? I wish the Wine could be secured, & the Rum in the Barn Sold—the last I should think might easily be done, & to a good Acct as the Importation will be stopped—If you are obligd to give Credit for this, or any thing else, be sure of your Men—I had rather take much less than be obliged to enter into letigeous disputes.

Let the Hospitality of the House, with respect to the Poor, be kept up; Let no one go hungry away—if any of these kind of People should be in want of Corn supply their necessities, provided it does not incourage them in Idleness; and I have no objection to your giving my money in Charity to the amount of Forty or Fifty pounds a year, when you think it well bestowd. What I mean by having no objection, is, that it is my desire that it should be done—you are to consider that neither myself, or wife are now in the way to do these good Offices. In all other respects I recommend it to you, and have no doubt of your observing, the greatest Oeconomy and frugality; as I suppose you know, that I do not get a farthing for my Services here, more than my Expences; it becomes necessary therefore for me to be saving at home.

Great as the length is, to which I have run this Letter, I will not conclude it without expressing my wish that something should be done this Winter to prevent Armed Vessels from running up the River, in order to destroy the property thereon in the Spring: If the Channel is too wide, & too deep for sinking of Cheveaux de Frieze, Hulks, or &ca Floating Batteries, or such kind of Armed Boats as they have Built in the Delaware, with Land Batteries would, though more expensive answer the purpose; & more than probable would be a very considerable saving of Property. I have no doubt of your using every endeavour to prevent the destruction of My Houses, if any attempts should be made thereon by the Men of War & their Cutters, but I would have you run no hazards about it, unless an oppertunity presents of doing some damage to the Enemy. The Height of the Hill—& the distance from the Channel gives it many advantages.

Remember me kindly to all friends and be assured that I am with sincere regards Yr Affecte friend & Servt

P.S. Acknowledge the receipt of this Letter that I may know whether it gets safe to hand or not.

To Benedict Arnold

Dear Sir,   Cambridge 5 Decr 1775

Your Letter of the 8 Ultimo with a Postscript of the 14 from Point Levi, I have had the pleasure to receive—It is not in the power of any man to command success, but you have done more—you have deserved it, & before this I hope, have met with the Laurels which are due to your Toils, in the possession of Quebec—My thanks are due, & sincerely offered to you, for your Enterprizing & persevering spirit—To your brave followers I likewise present them.

I was not unmindful of you or them in the Establishment of a new army—One out of 26 Regiments, (likely Genl Putnams) you are appointed to the Command of, and I have Ordered all the Officers with you, to the one or the other of these Regiments, in the Rank they now bear, that in case they chuse to continue in service, & no appointment take place, where they now are, no disappointment may follow—Nothing very material has happened in this Camp since you left it— Finding we were not likely to do much in the Land way, I fitted out several Privateers rather Armed Vessells in behalf of the Continent, with which we have taken several prizes, to the amount it is supposed of £15,000 Sterling—One of them a valuable Store Ship (but no powder in it) containing a fine Brass mortar 13 Inch—2000 Stand of Arms—Shot &c. &c.

I have no doubt but a juncture of your detachment with the Army under Genl Montgomerie, is effected before this: If so, you will put yourself under his Command and will I am persuaded give him all the Assistance in your power, to finish the Glorious work you begun—That the Almighty may preserve & prosper you in it, is the sincere & fervent prayer of Dr Sir &c.

P.S. You could not be more Surprized than I was, at Enos return with the Division under his Command. I immediately put him under Arrest & had him tried for Quitting the Detachmt without your Orders—He is acquitted on the Score of provision.

To Joseph Reed

Dear Sir, Cambridge 15th Decr 1775.
Since my last, I have had the pleasure of receiving your Favours of the 28th Ulto and 2d Instt. I must again express my gratitude for the attention shewn Mrs Washington at Philadelphia—It cannot but be pleasing, altho' it did in some measure, impede the progress of her journey on the Road.

I am much obliged to you for the hints contain in both of the above Letters respecting the jealousies which you say are gone abroad. I have studiously avoided in all Letters intended for the publick eye—I mean for that of the Congress—every expression that could give pain or uneasiness—and I shall observe the same rule with respect to private Letters, further than appears absolutely necessary for the illucidation of Facts, I cannot charge myself with incivility, or, what in my opinion is tantamount, ceremonious Civility, to the Gentlemen of this Colony; but if such my conduct appears, I will endeavour at a reformation, as I can assure you my dear Reed that I wish to walk in such a Line as will give most general Satisfaction. You knew, that it was my wish at first to Invite a certain number of the Gentlemen of this Colony every day to dinner, but, unintentionally I believe by any body, we some how or other missed of it; if this has given rise to the jealousy, I can only say that I am sorry for it, at the same time I add, that it was rather owing to inattention, or more properly too much attention to other matters, which caused me to neglect it. The Extracts of Letters from this Camp which so frequently appear in the Pensa Papers are not only written without my knowledge, but without my approbation, as I have always thought they must have a disagreeable tendency; but there is no restraining Mens tongues, or Pens, when charged with a little vanity, as in the Accounts given of or rather by the Rifflemen.

With respect to what you have said of yourself, & Situation, to what I have before said on this subject, I can only add, that whilst you leave the door open to my expectation of your return, I shall not think of supplying your place. if, ultimately, you resolve against coming, I should be glad to know it, as soon as you have determin'd upon it. The Congress have resolv'd well in respect to the pay of, and advance to the Men, but if they cannot get the Money Signers to dispatch their business it is of very little avail, for we have not at this time money enough in Camp to answer the Commissary's & Qur Masters accts much more to pay, and advance to the Troops—strange conduct this!

The Acct which you have givn of the Sentiments of People respecting my conduct is extreamely flattering—pray God I may continue to deserve them in the perplex'd and Intricate situation I stand in—Our Inlistment goes on Slow, by the Returns last Monday only 5917 Men are engaged for the Insuing Campaign, & yet we are told, that we shall get the Number wanted as they are only playing off to see what advantages are to be made, & whether a bounty cannot be extorted either from the Publick at large, or Individuals, in case of a draft. time only can discover this—I doubt the measure exceedingly.

The Fortunate Capture of the storeship has supplied us with Flints, & many other Articles we stood in need of—but we still have our wants—We are securing our Approach to Litchmores Point, unable upon any principle whatever to Acct for their Silence, unless it be to lull us into a fatal security to favour some attempt they may have in view about the time of the great change they expect will take place the last of this Month—If this be the drift, they deceive themselves for if possible it has Increas'd my Vigilance, & induced me to Fortify all the Avenues to our Camps to guard against any approaches upon the Ice.

If the Virginians are wise, that Arch Traitor to the Rights of Humanity, Lord Dunmore, should be instantly crushd, if it takes the force of the whole Colony to do it. otherwise, like a snow Ball in rolling, his army will get size—some through Fear—some through promises—and some from Inclination joining his Standard—But that which renders the measure indispensably necessary, is, the Negros; for if he gets formidable, numbers of them will be tempted to join who will be affraid to do it without. I am exceeding happy to find, that that Villain Connelly is siezed; I hope if there is any thing to convict him, that he will meet with the Punishment due to his demerit, & treachery.

We impatiently wait for Accts from Arnold—would to God we may hear he is in Quebec—& that all Canada is in our possession. My best respects to Mrs Reed I am Dr Sir Yr Affecte Hble Servt

P.S. The Small Pox is in every part of Boston—the Soldiers there who have never had it, are we are told under Innoculation—& consider'd as a Security against any attempt of ours.

A third ship load of People is come out to point Shirley—If we escape the Small Pox in this Camp, & the Country round about, it will be miraculous—Every precaution that can be, is taken to guard against this Evil both by the General Court & myself.

General Orders

Head Quarters, Cambridge, January 1st 1776
Parole The Congress.   Countersign, America.

This day giving commencement to the new-army, which, in every point of View is entirely Continental; The General flatters himself, that a laudable Spirit of emulation, will now take place, and pervade the whole of it; without such a Spirit, few Officers have ever arrived to any degree of Reputation, nor did any Army ever become formidable: His Excellency hopes that the Importance of the great Cause we are engaged in, will be deeply impressed upon every Man's mind, and wishes it to be considered, that an Army without Order, Regularity & Discipline, is no better than a Commission'd Mob; Let us therefore, when every thing dear and valuable to Freemen is at stake; when our unnatural Parent is threat'ning of us with destruction from every quarter, endeavour by all the Skill and Discipline in our power, to acquire that knowledge, and conduct, which is necessary in War—Our men are brave and good; Men who with pleasure it is observed, are addicted to fewer Vices than are commonly found in Armies; but it is Subordination & Discipline (the Life and Soul of an Army) which next under providence, is to make us formidable to our enemies, honorable in ourselves, and respected in the world; and herein is to be shewn the Goodness of the Officer.

In vain is it for a General to issue Orders, if Orders are not attended to, equally vain is it for a few Officers to exert themselves, if the same spirit does not animate the whole; it is therefore expected, (it is not insisted upon) that each Brigadier, will be attentive to the discipline of his Brigade, to the exercise of, and the Conduct observed in it, calling the Colonels, and Field Officers of every regiment, to severe Account for Neglect, or Disobedience of orders—The same attention is to be paid by the Field Officers to the respective Companies of their regiments—by the Captains to their Subalterns, and so on: And that the plea of Ignorance, which is no excuse for the Neglect of Orders (but rather an Aggravation) may not be offer'd, It is order'd, and directed, that not only every regiment, but every Company, do keep an Orderly-book, to which frequent recourse is to be had, it being expected that all standing orders be rigidly obeyed, until alter'd or countermanded—It is also expected, that all Orders which are necessary to be communicated to the Men, be regularly read, and carefully explained to them. As it is the first wish of the General to have the business of the Army conducted without punishment, to accomplish which, he assures every Officer, & Soldier, that as far as it is in his power, he will reward such as particularly distinguish themselves; at the same time, he declares that he will punish every kind of neglect, or misbehaviour, in an exemplary mannor.

As the great Variety of occurrences, and the multiplicity of business, in which the General is necessarily engaged, may withdraw his attention from many objects & things, which might be improved to Advantage; He takes this Opportunity of declaring, that he will thank any Officer, of whatsoever Rank, for any useful hints, or profitable Informations, but to avoid trivial matters; as his time is very much engrossed, he requires that it may be introduced through the channel of a General Officer, who is to weigh the importance before he communicates it.

All standing Orders heretofore issued for the Government of the late Army, of which every Regiment has, or ought to have Copies; are to be strictly complied with, until changed, or countermanded.

Every Regiment now upon the new establishment, is to give in signed by the Colonel, or commanding Officer, an exact List of the Commissioned Officers, in order that they may receive Commissions—particular Care to be taken that no person is included as an Officer, but such as have been appointed by proper authority; any Attempt of that kind in the new-Army, will bring severe punishment upon the author: The General will, upon any Vacancies that may happen, receive recommendations, and give them proper Consideration, but the Congress alone are competent to the appointment.

An exact Return of the strength of each Regiment, is to be given in, as soon as possible, distinguishing the Number of militia, and such of the old Regiments, as have joined for a Month only, from the established men of the regiment.

This being the day of the Commencement of the new-establishment, The General pardons all the Offences of the old, and commands all Prisoners (except Prisoners of war) to be immediately released.

To Joseph Reed

Dear Sir,   Cambridge 4th Jany 1776

Since my last, I have recd your obliging favours of the 19th & 23d Ulto & thank you for the Articles of Intelligence therein containd; as I also do for the Buttons which accompanied the last Letter, althô I had got a sett, better I think, made at Concord.

I am exceeding glad to find, that things wear a better face in Virginia than they did sometime ago; but I do not think that any thing less than the life, or liberty, will free the Colony from the effects, of Lord Dunmores Resentments and Villainies.

We are at length favourd with a sight of his Majesty's most gracious Speech, breathing sentiments of tenderness & compassion for his deluded American Subjects; the Eccho is not yet come to hand; but we know what it must be; and as Lord North said, & we ought to have believed (& acted accordingly) we now know the ultimatum of British Justice. the Speech I send you—a volume of them was sent out by the Boston Gentry—And, farcical enough, we gave great Joy to them (the red Coats I mean) without knowing or intending it, for on that day, the day which gave being to the New Army (but before the Proclamation came to hand) we had hoisted the Union Flag in compliment to the United Colonies, but behold! it was receivd in Boston as a token of the deep Impression the Speech had made upon Us, and as a signal of

Submission—so we learn by a person out of Boston last Night—by this time I presume they begin to think it strange that we have not made a formal surrender of our Lines. Admiral Shuldam is arrivd at Boston. the 55th and greatest part, if not all, the 17th Regiment, are also got in there—the rest of the 5 Regiments from Ireland were intended for Hallifax & Quebec; those for the first are arrived there, the others we know not where they are got to.

It is easier to conceive, than to describe the Situation of My Mind for sometime past, & my feelings under our present Circumstances; search the vast volumes of history through, & I much question whether a case similar to ours is to be found. to wit, to maintain a Post against the flower of the British Troops for Six Months together without _____ and at the end of them to have one Army disbanded and another to raise within the same distance of a Reinforced Enemy—it is too much to attempt—what may be the final Issue of the last Manouvre time only can tell—I wish this Month was well over our heads—The same desire of retiring into a Chimney Corner siez'd the Troops of New Hampshire, Rhode Island, & Massachusets (so soon as their time expired) as had Work'd upon those of Connecticut, notwithstanding many of them made a tender of their Services to continue till the Lines could be sufficiently strengthned—We are now left with a good deal less than half rais'd Regiments, and about 5000 Militia who only stand Ingaged to the middle of this Month; when, according to custom, they will depart, let the necessity of their stay be never so urgent. thus it is that for more than two Months past I have scarcely immerged from one difficulty before I have plunged into another—how it will end God in his great goodness will direct, I am thankful for his protection to this time. We are told that we shall soon get the Army compleated, but I have been told so many things which have never come to pass, that I distrust every thing.

I fear your Fleet has been so long in Fitting, and the destination of it so well known, that the end will be defeated, if the Vessels escape. how is the arrival of French Troops in the west Indies, & the hostile appearance there, to be reconciled with that part of the Kings Speech wherein he assures Parliament, "that, as well from the Assurances I have receivd, as from the general appearance of Affairs in Europe, I see no probability that the Measures which you may adopt will be interrupted by disputes with any foreign Power."

I hope the Congress will not think of adjourning at so Important, & critical a Juncture as this. I wish they would keep a watchful eye to New York—from Captn Searss Acct (now here) much is to be apprehended from that Quarter. A Fleet is now fitting out at Boston consisting of 5 Transports & two Bomb Vessels under Convoy of the Scarborough & Fowey Men of War—300 some say, others more, Troops are on board, with Flat bottom'd Boats—It is whisperd, as if designedly, that they are intended for New Port, but it is generally beleiv'd that they are bound either to long Island, or Virginia—the other Transports are taking In Water & a good deal of Bisquet is Baking—some say for the Shipping to lay in Nantasket Road to be out of the way of Ice, whilst others think a more Important move is in Agitation—all however is conjecture—I heartily wish you, Mrs Reed & Family the Complts of the Season, in wch the Ladies here, & Family, join—Be assured that I am with Sincere Affecte & Regard

To Joseph Reed

Dear Sir,   Cambridge 14th Jany 1776.

The bearer presents an oppertunity to me, of acknowledging the receipt of your favour of the 30th Ulto (which never came to my hands till last Night) and, if I have not done it before, of your other of the 23d preceeding.

The hints you have communicated from time to time not only deserve, but do most sincerely, and cordially meet with my thanks—you cannot render a more acceptable service, nor in my estimation give me a more convincing proof of your Friendship, than by a free, open, & undisguised account of every matter relative to myself, or conduct. I can bear to hear of imputed, or real errors; the Man who wishes to stand well in the opinion of others must do this, because he is thereby enabled to correct his faults, or remove the prejudices which are imbib'd against him; for this reason I shall thank you for giving me the opinion's of the world upon such points as you know me to be Interested In; for as I have but one capitol object in view, I could wish to make my conduct coincide with the wishes of Mankind as far as I can consistently—I mean without departing from that great line of Duty which, though hid under a cloud for sometime, from a peculiarity of Circumstances, may nevertheless bear a Scrutiny. My constant attention to the great, and perplexing objects which continually rise to my view, absorbs all lesser considerations & indeed scarcely allows me time to reflect that there is such a body in existance as the General Court of this Colony but when I am reminded of it by a Committee; nor can I, upon recollection, discover in what Instances (I wish they would be more explicit) I have been inattentive to, or slighted them. they could not, surely, conceive that there was a propriety in unbosoming the Secrets of an Army to them—that it was necessary to ask their opinion of throwing up an Intrenchment—forming a Battalion, &ca &ca, it must therefore be what I before hinted to you, & how to remedy it I hardly know, as I am acquainted with few of the Members, never go out of my own Lines, or see any of them in them.

I am exceeding sorry to hear that your little Fleet has been shut in by the frost. I hope it has Saild e'er this, & given you some proof of the Utility of it. and enabl'd the Congress to bestow a little more attention to the Affairs of this Army, which suffers exceedingly by their over much business—or too little attention to it. we are now without any Money in our treasury—Powder in our Magazines—Arms in Our Stores— We are without a Brigadier (the want of which has been twenty times urged)—Engineers—Expresses (though a Committee has been appointed these two Months to establish them)—and by & by, when we shall be called upon to take the Field, shall not have a Tent to lay in—a propos, what is doing with mine?

These are Evils, but small in comparison of those, which disturb my present repose. Our Inlistments are at a stand— the fears I ever entertaind are realiz'd—that is, the discontented Officers (for I do not know how else to acct for it) have thrown such difficulties, or Stumbling blocks in the way of Recruiting that I no longer entertain a hope of compleating

the Army by Voluntary Inlistments, & I see no move, or likelihood of one, to do it by other mean's—In the two last Weeks
we have Inlisted but abt 1000 Men, whereas I was confidently
bid to believe, by all the Officers I conversed with, that we
should, by this time, have had the Regiments nearly compleated—Our total number upon Paper amounts to abt 10500
but as a large portion of these are returnd not joind, I never
expect to receive them; as, an ineffectual Order has once Issued to call them In—another is now gone forth, peremptorily
requireng all Officers under pain of being Cashierd, & Recruits, as being treated as Deserters, to join their respective
Regiments by the first day of next Month that I may know
my real strength; but if my fears are not imaginary, I shall
have a dreadful acct of the advanc'd Months pay. In consequence of the Assurances given, & my expectation of having
at least Men enough Inlisted to defend our lines, to which
may be added my unwillingness of burthening the cause with
unnecessary expence, no relief of Militia has been order'd In
to supply the places of those who are releasd from their Ingagement To morrow, and on whom (thô many have promis'd to continue out the Month) their is no security of their
Stay.

Thus am I situated with respect to Men—with regard to
Arms I am yet worse of—before the dissolution of the old
Army I Issued an Order directing three judicious Men of each
Brigade to attend—review—and appraise the good Arms of
every Regiment—& finding a very great unwillingness in the
Men to part with their Arms, at the same time, not having it
in my power to pay them for the Months of Novr & Decr I
threatned, severely, that every Soldier who carried away his
Firelock, without leave, should never receive pay for those
Months; yet, so many have been carried of, partly by stealth,
but cheefly as condemn'd, that we have not, at this time, 100
Guns in the Stores of all that have been taken in the Prize
Ship, and from the Soldiery notwithstanding our Regiments
are not half compleat—at the same time I am told, and believe
it, that to restrain the Inlistment to Men with Arms you will
get but few of the former, & still fewer of the latter wch would
be good for any thing: How to get furnish'd I know not—I
have applied to this & the Neighbouring Colonies but with

what success, time only can tell. the reflection upon my Situation, & that of this Army, produces many an uneasy hour when all around me are wrapped in Sleep. Few People know the Predicament we are In, on a thousand Accts—fewer still will beleive, if any disaster happens to these Lines, from what causes it flows—I have often thought, how much happier I should have been, if, instead of accepting of a command under such Circumstances I had taken my Musket upon my Shoulder & enterd the Ranks, or, if I could have justified the Measure to Posterity, & my own Conscience, had retir'd to the back Country, & livd in a Wig-wam—If I shall be able to rise superior to these, and many other difficulties, which might be innumerated, I shall most religiously believe that the finger of Providence is in it, to blind the Eyes of our Enemys; for surely if we get well throw this Month, it must be for want of their knowing the disadvantages we labour under.

Could I have foreseen the difficulties which have come upon us—could I have known that such a backwardness would have been discoverd in the old Soldiers to the Service, all the Generals upon Earth should not have convincd me of the propriety of delaying an Attack upon Boston till this time. When it can now be attempted I will not undertake to Say, but thus much I will answer for, that no oppertunity can present itself earlier than my wishes—but—as this Letter discloses some Interesting truths, I shall be somewhat uneasy till I hear it gets to your hand although the conveyance is thought safe.

We made a successful attempt a few Nights ago upon the Houses near Bunker Hill—A Party under Majr Knolton crossd upon the Mill damn (the Night being Dark) and set fire to, and burnt down Eight, out of 14 which were standing, and which we found they were daily pulling down for Fuel—five Soldiers, & the Wife of one of them, Inhabiting one of the Houses, were brought of Prisoners; another Soldier was killed; none of ours hurt.

Having undoubted information of the Imbarkation of Troops (somewhere from three to 500) at Boston and being convinced that they were design'd either for New York Government (from whence we have some very disagreeable Accts of the Conduct of the Tories) or Virginia, I dispatched Genl Lee a few days ago in order to secure the City of New York from falling into their hands, as the consequences of such a blow might prove fatal to our Interests. He is also to enquire a little into the conduct of the Long Islanders, & such others, as have, by their conduct & declaration's, proved themselves Inemical to the common Cause. To effect these purposes he is to raise Volunteers in Connecticut, & call upon the Troops of New Jersey, if not contrary to any Order of Congress.

By a Ship just arrivd at Portsmouth (New Hampshire) we have London Prints to the 2d of Novr, containing the Addresses of Parliament, which contain little more than a repetition of the Speech, with assurances of standing by his Majesty with Lives and Fortunes—the Captns (for there were three or four of them Passengers) say that we have nothing to expect but the most vigorous exertions of Administration, who have a dead Majority upon all Questions, although the Duke of Grafton & General Conway have joind the Minority, as also the Bishop of Peterborough. These Captains affirm, confidently, that the 5 Regiments from Ireland cannot, any of them, have arriv'd at Hallifax; inasmuch, as that by a violent Storm on the 19th of October the Transports were forced (in a very distressful condition) into Milford haven (Wales) and were not in a Condition to Put to Sea when they left London and that the Weather has been such since as to prevent heavy loaded Ships from making a passage by this time. One or two Transports they add, were thought to be lost; but these arriv'd some considerable time ago at Boston with 3 Companies of the 17th Regiment.

Mr Sayre has been committed to the Tower upon the Information of a certain Lieutt or Adjutant Richardson (formerly of yr City) for treasonable practices—an Intention of Seizeing his Majesty & possessing himself of the Tower—it is said in the Crisis—but is admitted to Bail; himself in £500 & two Suretys in £250 each. What are the Conjectures of the wise ones with you, of the French Armament in the West Indies? but previous to this, is there any certainty of such an Armament? the Captains who are sensible Men, heard nothing of this when they left England, nor does there appear any apprehensions on this score in any of the measures, or Speeches of Administration—I should think the congress will not—ought not—to adjourn at this important Crisis—but it is highly necessary, when I am at the end of a Second Sheet of Paper, that I should adjourn my Acct of matters to another Letter. I shall therefore, in Mrs Washington's name thank you for yr good Wishes towards her & with her Complimts added to mine to Mrs Reed &ca conclude Dr Sir Yr Sincere & Affecte Servt

To Joseph Reed

My dear Sir,   Cambridge 31st of Jan: 1776.

In my last (date not recollected) by Mr John Adams, I communicated my distresses to you, on Acct of my want of your Assistance—since this, I have been under some concern at doing of it, least it should precipitate your return before you were ripe for it, or bring on a final resignation, which I am unwilling to think of, if your return can be made convenient and agreeable—True it is, that from a variety of Causes my business has been, & now is, multiplied & perplexed; whilst the means of execution is greatly contracted. this may be a cause for my wishing you here, but no Inducement to your coming, if you hesitated before.

I have now to thank you for your favours of the 15th 16th & 20th Instt; and for the several Articles of Intelligence which they convey—the Acct given of your Navy, at the sametime that it is exceedingly unfavourable to our wishes, is a little provoking to me; in as much as it has depriv'd us of a necessary Article which otherwise would have been sent hither; but which, a kind of fatality I fear will forever deprive us of— In the Instance of New York, we are not to receive a particle of what you expected would be sent from thence—the time and Season is passing away, as I believe the Troops in Boston also will, before the Season for taking the field arrives. I dare say they are preparing for it now, as we have undoubted Intelligence of Clintons leaving Boston with a number of Troops (by different Accts from four or five hundred to 10 Companies of Grenadiers, & nine of light Infantry) believd to be design'd for Long Island, or New York, in consequence of Assurances from Governor Tryon of a powerful Aid from the Tories there.

I hope my Countrymen (of Virginia) will rise superior to any losses the whole Navy of Great Britain can bring on them, & that the destruction of Norfolk, & threatned devastation of other places, will have no other effect than to unite the whole Country in one indissoluble Band against a Nation which seems to be lost to every sense of Virtue, and those feelings which distinguish a Civilized People from the most barbarous Savages. A few more of such flaming Arguments as were exhibited at Falmouth and Norfolk, added to the sound Doctrine, and unanswerable reasoning containd (in the pamphlet) Common Sense, will not leave numbers at a loss to decide upon the Propriety of a Seperation.

By a Letter of the 21st Instt from Wooster I find that Arnold was continuing the Blockade of Quebec the 19th which, under the heaviness of our loss there, is a most favourable Circumstance, & exhibits a fresh proof of Arnolds Ability and perseverence in the midst of difficulties. the re-inforcement ordered to him will, I hope, compleat the entire Conquest of Canada this Winter; and but for the loss of the Gallant Chief & his brave Followers I should think the re-buff rather favourable than otherwise; for had the Country been subdued by such a handful of Men 'tis more than probable that it would have been left to the defence of a few, & rescued from us in the Spring—Our Eyes will now, not only be open to the Importance of holding it, but the numbers which are requisite to that end.

In return for your two Beef & Poultry Vessels from New York, I can acquaint you that our Commodore, Manley, has just taken two Ships from Whitehaven to Boston with Coal & Potatoes & sent them into Plymouth, & fought a Tender (close by the Light House, where the Vessels were taken) long enough to give his Prizes time to get off, in short till she thought it best to quit the combat, & he to move of from the Men of War wch were Spectators of this Scene.

In my last I think I inform'd you of my sending Genl Lee to New York with Intention to secure the Tories of Long Island &ca; and to prevent, if possible, the Kings Troops from making a Lodgment there; but I fear the Congress will be duped by the Representations from that Government or yield to them in such a manner as to become Marplots to the Expedition. The City seems to be entirely under the Government of Tryon & the Captn of the Man of War.

Mrs Washington desires I will thank you for the Picture sent her. Mr Campbell whom I never saw (to my knowledge) has made a very formidable figure of the Commander in Chief giving him a sufficient portion of Terror in his Countenance. Mrs Washington also desires her Compliments to Mrs Reed &ca as I do—& with the sincerest regard & Affection I remain Dr Sir Yr Most Obedt Servt

To Joseph Reed

My dear Sir,   Cambridge Feby 1st 1776.
   I had wrote the Letter herewith Inclosed before your favour of the 21st came to hand—The Acct given of the behaviour of the Men under Genl Montgomerie is exactly consonant to the opinion I have form'd of these People, and such as they will exhibit abundant proofs of in similar cases whenever called upon—Place them behind a Parapet—a Breast Work—Stone Wall—or anything that will afford them Shelter, and from their knowledge of a Firelock, they will give a good Acct of their Enemy, but I am as well convinced as if I had seen it, that they will not March boldly up to a Work—or stand exposed in a plain—and yet, if we are furnished with the Means, and the Weather will afford us a Passage, and we can get in Men (for these three things are necessary) something must be attempted. The Men must be brought to face danger—they cannot allways have an Intrenchment, or a Stone Wall as a safe guard or Shield—and it is of essential Importance that the Troops In Boston should be destroyed if possible before they can be re-inforced, or remove—this is clearly my opinion—whether Circumstances will admit of the tryal—& if tryed what will be the Event, the all-wise disposer of them alone can tell.

   The Evils arising from short, or even any limited Inlistment of the Troops are greater, and more extensively hurtful than any person (not an eyewitness to them) can form any Idea of—It takes you two or three Months to bring New men in any tolerable degree acquainted with their duty—it takes a longer time to bring a People of the temper, and genius of these into such a subordinate way of thinking as is necessary for a Soldier—Before this is accomplished, the time approaches for their dismission, and your beginning to make Interest with them for their continuance for another limitted period; in the doing of which you are oblig'd to relax in your discipline, in order as it were to curry favour with them, by which means the latter part of your time is employd in undoing what the first was accomplishing and instead of having Men always ready to take advantage of Circumstances you must govern your Movements by the Circumstances of your Inlistment—this is not all—by the time you have got Men arm'd & equip'd—the difficulty of doing which is beyond description—and with every new sett you have the same trouble to encounter without the means of doing it. In short the disadvantages are so great, & apparent to me, that I am convinc'd, uncertain as the continuance of the War is, that the Congress had better determine to give a Bounty of 20, 30, or even 40 Dollars to every Man who will Inlist for the whole time, be it long or short—I intend to write my Sentiments fully on this Subject to Congress the first leizure time I have.

I am exceeding sorry to hear that Arnolds Wound is in an unfavourable way—his Letter to me of the 14th Ulto says nothing of this. I fancy Congress have given some particular direction respecting Genl Prescot—I think they ought for more reasons than one. I am Sincerely & Affectionately Yr Most Obedt Servt

To John Hancock

Sir,   Cambridge Feby 9th 1776.

The purport of this Letter, will be directed to a single object—through you I mean to lay it before Congress, and at the same time that I beg their serious attention to the subject, to ask pardon for intruding an opinion, not only unasked, but in some measure repugnant to their Resolves.

The disadvantages attending the limited Inlistment of Troops, is too apparent to those who are eye witnesses of them to render any animadversions necessary; but to Gentlemen at a distance, whose attention is engross'd by a thousand important objects, the case may be otherwise.

That this cause precipitated the fate of the brave, and much to be lamented Genl Montgomerie, & brought on the defeat which followed thereupon, I have not the most distant doubt of; for had he not been apprehensive of the Troops leaving him at so important a crisis, but continued the Blockade of Quebec, a Capitulation, from the best Accts I have been able to collect, must inevitably have followed. And, that we were not obliged at one time to dispute these Lines under disadvantageous Circumstances (proceeding from the same cause, to wit, the Troops disbanding of themselves before the Militia could be got in) is to me a matter of wonder & astonishment; and proves, that General Howe was either unacquainted with our Situation, or restraind by his Instructions from putting any thing to a hazard till his re-inforcements should arrive.

The Instance of General Montgomery—I mention it because it is a striking one—for a number of others might be adduced; proves that instead of having Men to take advantage of Circumstances, you are in a manner compell'd, Right or Wrong, to make Circumstances yield to a Secondary consideration—Since the first of December I have been devising every means in my power to secure these Incampments, and though I am sensible that we never have, since that period, been able to act upon the Offensive, and at times not in a condition to defend, yet the cost of Marching home one set of Men—bringing in another—the havock & waste occasioned by the first—the repairs necessary for the Second, with a thousand incidental charges and Inconveniencies which have arisen, & which it is scarce possible either to recollect or describe, amounts to near as much as the keeping up a respectable body of Troops the whole time—ready for any emergency—would have done.

To this may be added that you never can have a well Disciplined Army.

To bring Men well acquainted with the Duties of a Soldier, requires time—to bring them under proper discipline & Subordination, not only requires time, but is a Work of great difficulty; and in this Army, where there is so little distinction between the Officers and Soldiers, requires an uncommon degree of attention—To expect then the same Service from Raw, and undisciplined Recruits as from Veteran Soldiers is to expect what never did, and perhaps never will happen—Men who are familiarizd to danger meet it without shrinking; whereas those who have never seen Service often apprehend danger where no danger is—Three things prompt Men to a regular discharge of their Duty in time of Action, Natural bravery—hope of reward—and fear of punishment—The two first are common to the untutor'd, and the Disciplin'd Soldier; but the latter, most obviously distinguishes the one from the other. A Coward, when taught to believe, that if he breaks his Ranks, & abandons his Colours, will be punished with Death by his own party, will take his chance against the Enemy; but the Man who thinks little of the one, and is fearful of the other, acts from present feelings, regardless of consequences.

Again, Men of a days standing will not look forward, and from experience we find, that as the time approaches for their discharge they grow careless of their Arms, Ammunition, Camp Utensils, &ca; nay even the Barracks themselves have felt uncommon Marks of Wanton depredation, and lays us under fresh trouble, and additional expence, in providing for every fresh sett; when we find it next to impossible to procure such Articles as are absolutely necessary in the first Instance— To this may be added the Seasoning which new Recruits must have to a Camp—& the loss, consequent thereupon. But this is not all, Men ingaged for a short, limited time only, have the Officers too much in their power; for to obtain a degree of popularity, in order to induce a second Inlistment, a kind of familiarity takes place which brings on a relaxation of Discipline—unlicensed furloughs—and other Indulgences incompatable with order and good government; by which means, the latter part of the time for which the Soldier was engaged, is spent in undoing what you were aiming to inculcate in the first.

To go into an enumeration of all the Evils we have experienced in this late great change of the Army—and the expence incidental to it—to say nothing of the hazard we have run, and must run, between the discharging of one Army and Inlistment of another (unless an Inormous expence of Militia is incurrd) would greatly exceed the bounds of a Letter; what I have already taken the liberty of saying, will serve to convey a general Idea of the matter, & therefore I Shall, with all due deference, take the freedom to give it as my opinion, that if the Congress have any reason to believe that there will be occasion for Troops another year, and consequently of another Inlistment, they would save money, & have infinitely better Troops if they were, even at a bounty of twenty, thirty, or more Dollars to engage the Men already Inlisted (till Jany next) & such others as may be wanted to compleat to the Establishment, for and during the War. I will not undertake to say that the Men can be had upon these terms, but I am satisfied that it will never do to let the matter alone, as it was last year, till the time of Service was near expiring—The hazard is too great in the first place—In the next, the trouble and perplexity of disbanding one Army and raising another at the same Instant, & in such a critical Situation as the last was, is scarcely in the power of Words to describe, and such as no Man who has experienced it once will ever undergo again.

If Congress should differ from me in Sentiment upon this point, I have only to beg, that they will do me the justice to believe, that I have nothing more in view than what to me appears necessary, to advance the publick Weal, although in the first Instance it will be attended with a capitol expence— And, that I have the honour to be with all due deference & respect theirs, and Your Most & Obedient & faithful Hble Servt

To Joseph Reed

My dear Sir   Cambridge Feby 10th 1776.
  Your obliging favours of the 28th Ulto & 1st Instt are now before me, & claim my particular thanks for the polite atten-

tion you pay to my wishes, in an early, & regular Communication of what is passing in your Quarter.

If my dear Sir, you conceive that I took any thing wrong, or amiss, that was conveyed in any of your former Letters you are really mistaken—I only meant to convince you, that nothing would give me more real satisfaction than to know the Sentiments which are entertaind of me by the Publick, whether they be favourable, or otherwise—and, urged as a reason that the Man who wished to steer clear of Shelves & Rocks must know where they lay—I know—but to declare it unless to a friend, may be an argument of vanity—the Integrety of my own Heart—I know the unhappy predicament I stand in. I know, that much is expected of me—I know that without Men, without Arms, without Ammunition, without any thing fit for the accomodation of a Soldier that little is to be done—and, which is mortifying; I know, that I cannot stand justified to the World without exposing my own Weakness & injuring the cause by declaring my wants, which I am determined not to do further than unavoidable necessity brings every Man acquainted with them—If under these disadvantages I am able to keep above Water (as it were) in the esteem of Mankind I shall feel myself happy; but, if from the unknown, peculiarity of my Circumstances, I suffer in the opinion of the World I shall not think you take the freedom of a friend if you conceal the reflections that may be cast upon my conduct. My own Situation feels so irksome to me at times, that, if I did not consult the publick good more than my own tranquility I should long e're this have put every thing to the cast of a Dye—So far from my having an Army of 20,000 Men well Armd &ca I have been here with less than one half of it, including Sick, furloughd, & on Command, and those neither Arm'd or Cloathed, as they should be. In short my Situation has been such that I have been obligd to use art to conceal it from my own Officers.

The Congress as you observe, expect I believe, that I should do more than others; for whilst they compel me to Inlist men without a bounty they give 40/ to others; which will, I expect, put a stand to our Inlistments, for notwithstanding all the publick virtue which is ascribd to these people, there is no nation under the Sun (that I ever came across) pay greater adoration to money than they do—I am pleasd to find, that your Battalions are Cloathed and look well, and that they are filing of for Canada—I wish I could say that the Troops here had altered much in Dress or appearance—Our Regiments are little more than half compleat & Recruiting nearly at a stand—In all my Letters I fail not the mention of Tents & now perceive that notice is taken of the Applin.

I have been convinced by General Howes conduct that he has either been very ignorant of our Situation (which I do not believe) or, that he has received positive Orders (wch I think is natural to conclude) not to put any thing to the hazard till his reinforcements arrive—otherwise, there has not been a time since the first of December that we must have fought like men to have maintaind these Lines, so great in their extent—The Party to Bunkers Hill had some good, & some bad Men engaged in it—One or two Courts have been held on the Conduct of part of it—to be plain, these People—among friends—are not to be depended upon if exposed—and any Man will fight well if he thinks himself in no danger—I do not apply this to these People—I suppose it to be the case with all raw, & undisciplined Troops.

You may rely upon it, that Transports left Boston Six Weeks ago with Troops. where they are gone to (unless drove to the West Indias) I know not—you may also rely upon General Clintons Sailing from Boston about 3 Weeks ago with about four or five hundred Men—his destination I am also a stranger to. I am sorry to hear of the failures you speak of from France, but why will not Congress forward part of the Powder made in your provence? they seem to look upon this as the Season for Action, but will not furnish the means—but, I will not blame them—I dare say the demands upon them are greater than they can supply—the cause must be starved till our resources are greater, or more certain within ourselves.

With respect to myself, I have never entertaind an Idea of an Accomodation since I heard of the Measures which were adopted in consequence of the Bunkers Hill fight. The Kings Speech has confirmd the Sentiments I entertaind upon the News of that Affair—and, if every Man was of my Mind the Ministers of G. B. should know, in a few Words, upon what Issue the cause should be put. I would not be deceived by artful declarations, or specious pretences—nor would I be amused by unmeaning propositions. but in open, undisguised, and Manly terms proclaim our Wrongs & our Resolutions to be redressed. I would tell them, that we had born much—that we had long, & ardently sought for reconciliation upon honourable terms—that it had been denied us—that all our attempts after Peace had provd abortive and had been grossly misrepresented—that we had done every thing that could be expected from the best of Subjects—that the Spirit of Freedom beat too high in us, to Submit to Slavery; & that, if nothing else would satisfie a Tyrant & his diabolical Ministry, we were determined to shake of all Connexions with a State So unjust, & unnatural. This I would tell them, not under Covert, but in Words as clear as the Sun in its Meridian brightness.

I observe what you say, in respect to the Ardour of the Chimney Corner Hero's. I am glad their zeal is in some measure abated because if Circumstances will not permit us to make an Attempt upon B or if it Should be made and fail, we shall not appear altogether so culpable—I entertain the same opinion of the attempt now which I have ever done. I believe an Assault will be attended with considerable loss. and I believe it wd Succeed, if the Men should behave well—without it, unless there is equal bad behaviour on the other side, we cannot—As to an Attack upon B—— Hill (unless it could be carried by surprize) the loss, I conceive, would be greater in proportion than at Boston and if a defeat should follow would be discouraging to the Men, but highly animating if crown'd with Success. great good, or great evil, would consequently result from it. it is quite a different thing to what you left, being by odds the strongest Fortress they possess, both in Rear and Front.

The Congress having ordered all Captures to be tried in the Courts of Admiralty of the different Governments to which they are sent—& some irreconcaleable difference arising between the Resolves of Congress, & the Law of this Colony respecting the preceedings, or something or another, which always happens to procrastinate business here has put a total stop to the tryals to the no small injury of the publick as well as great grievance of Individuals whenever a condemnation shall take place I shall not be unmindful of your advice respecting the Hulls &ca.

Would to Heaven the Plan you Speak of for obtaining Arms may succeed—the acquisition would be great and give fresh life & vigour to our measures as would the arrival you speak of; Our expectations are kept alive, and if we can keep ourselves so and spirits up another Summer I have no fears of wanting the needful after that.

As the number of our Inlisted Men were too small to undertake any offensive Operation if the Circumstances of Weather &ca should favour I ordered in (by Application to this Govt Connecticut, & New Hampshire) as many Regiments of Militia as would enable us to attempt something, in some manner or other—they were to have been here by the first of the Month. but only a few stragling Companies are yet come in. The Bay towds Roxbury has been froze up once or twice pretty hard, and yesterday, Single Persons might have crossd I believe from Litchmores point by Picking his Way— a thaw I fear is again approaching.

We have had the most laborious piece of Work at Litchmores point on Acct of the Frost that ever you saw. We hope to get it finished on Sunday. It is within as Commanding a Distance of Boston, as Dorchester Hill tho' of a different part. Our Vessels now and then pick up a prize or two—our Commodore (Manley) was very near being catched about 8 days ago but happily escaped with Vessel & Crew after running a Shore Scutling, & defending her. I recollect nothing else worth giving you the trouble of, unless you can be amused by reading a Letter and Poem addressed to me by Mrs or Miss Phillis Wheatley—In searching over a parcel of Papers the other day, in order to destroy such as were useless, I brought it to light again—at first, With a view of doing justice to her great poetical Genius, I had a great Mind to publish the Poem, but not knowing whether it might not be considered rather as a mark of my own vanity than as a Compliment to her I laid it aside till I came across it again in the manner just mentioned.

I congratulate you upon your Election although I consider it as the Coup-de-grace to my expectation of ever seeing you a resident in this Camp again—I have only to regret the want of you, if that should be the case, & I shall do it more feelingly as I have experienced the good effects of your aid. I am with Mrs Washingtons Compliments to Mrs Reed, & my best respects added Dr Sir Yr Most Obedt & Affecte Hble Servt

To Phillis Wheatley

Mrs Phillis,   Cambridge February 28th 1776.
    Your favour of the 26th of October did not reach my hands 'till the middle of December. Time enough, you will say, to have given an answer ere this. Granted. But a variety of important occurrences, continually interposing to distract the mind and withdraw the attention, I hope will apologize for the delay, and plead my excuse for the seeming, but not real, neglect.
    I thank you most sincerely for your polite notice of me, in the elegant Lines you enclosed; and however undeserving I may be of such encomium and panegyrick, the style and manner exhibit a striking proof of your great poetical Talents. In honour of which, and as a tribute justly due to you, I would have published the Poem, had I not been apprehensive, that, while I only meant to give the World this new instance of your genius, I might have incurred the imputation of Vanity. This, and nothing else, determined me not to give it place in the public Prints.
    If you should ever come to Cambridge, or near Head Quarters, I shall be happy to see a person so favoured by the Muses, and to whom nature has been so liberal and beneficent in her dispensations. I am, with great Respect, Your obedt humble servant,

To John Hancock

Sir   Head Quarters Cambridge 19 March 1776
    It is with the greatest pleasure I inform you that on Sunday last, the 17th Instant, about 9 O'Clock in the forenoon, The

Ministerial Army evacuated the Town of Boston, and that the Forces of the United Colonies are now in actual possession thereof. I beg leave to congratulate you Sir, & the honorable Congress—on this happy Event, and particularly as it was effected without endangering the lives & property of the remaining unhappy Inhabitants.

I have great reason to imagine their flight was precipitated by the appearance of a Work which I had Order'd to be thrown up last Saturday Night, on an Eminence at Dorchester which lay nearest to Boston Neck, call'd Newks Hill. The Town, although it has suffer'd greatly is not in so bad a state as I expected to find it, and I have a particular pleasure in being able to inform you Sir, that your house has receiv'd no damage worth mentioning. Your furniture is in tolerable Order and the family pictures are all left entire and untouch'd. Capt. Cazneau takes Charge of the whole until he shall receive further Orders from you.

As soon as the Ministerial Troops had quitted the Town, I order'd a thousand Men (who had had the Small Pox) under Command of General Putnam to take possession of the Heighths, which I shall endeavour to fortify in such a manner as to prevent their return should they attempt it, but as they are still in the Harbour I thought it not prudent to march off with the Main Body of the Army until I should be fully satisfied they had quitted the Coast—I have therefore only detach'd five Regiments, beside the Rifle Battalion, to New York, and shall keep the remainder here till all Suspicion of their return ceases.

The Situation in which I found their Works evidently discovered that their retreat was made with the greatest precipitation—They have left their Barracks & other Works of Wood at Bunkers Hill &c. all standing, & have destroy'd but a small part of their Lines. They have also left a number of fine pieces of Cannon, which they first spik'd up, also a very large Iron Mortar, and (as I am inform'd) they have thrown another over the end of your Wharf—I have employ'd proper Persons to drill the Cannon & doubt not shall save the most of them. I am not yet able to procure an exact list of all the Stores they have left, as soon as it can be done I shall take care to transmit it to you. From an Estimate of what the Quarter Master

Gen'ral has already discover'd the Amount will be 25 or 30,000£.

Part of the Powder mention'd in yours of the 6th Instt, has already arriv'd—The remainder I have order'd to be stop'd on the Road as we shall have no occasion for it here. The Letter to General Thomas I immediately sent to him, he desir'd leave for three or four days to settle some of his private Affairs after which he will set out for his Command in Canada—I am happy that my Conduct in intercepting Lord Drummond's Letter is approv'd of by Congress. I have the honor to be, with sincere respect Sir Your most obedt Servt.

To John Augustine Washington

Dear Brother,   Cambridge 31st March 1776.

Your Letter of the 24th Ulto was duely forwarded to this Camp by Colo. Lee. and gave me the pleasure of hearing that you, my Sister and family were well. after your Post is established to Fredericksburg the Intercourse by Letter may become regular and certain (& when ever time, little of which God knows I have for friendly corrispondances, will permit, I shall be happy in writing to you)—I cannot call to mind the date of my last to you, but this I recollect, that I have wrote more Letters to than I have received from you.

The Want of Arms, Powder &ca, is not peculiar to Virginia—this Country of which doubtless, you have heard such large and flattering Accounts, is more difficient of each than you can conceive, I have been here Months together with what will scarce be believed—not 30 rounds of Musket Cartridges a Man. have been obliged to submit to all the Insults of the Enemy's Cannon for want of Powder, keeping what little we had for Pistol distance. Another thing has been done, which added to the above, will put it in the power of this Army to say what perhaps none other with justice ever could. We have maintain'd our Ground against the Enemy under the above want of Powder—and, we have disbanded one Army & recruited another, within Musket Shot of two and Twenty

Regimts, the Flower of the British Army when our strength
have been little if any, superior to theirs. and, at last have beat
them, in a shameful & precipitate manner out of a place the
strongest by Nature on this Continent—strengthen'd and fortified in the best manner, and at an enormous Expence.

As some Acct of the late Manouvres of both Armies, may
not be unacceptable, I shall, hurried as I always am, devote a
little time to it.

Having received a small supply of Powder then—very inadequate to our wants—I resolved to take possession of
Dorchester Point, laying East of Boston; looking directly into
it; and commanding (absolutely) the Enemys Lines on the
Neck (Boston)—To effect this, which I knew would force the
Enemy to an Ingagement, or subject them to be enphiladed
by our Cannon, it was necessary in the first Instance to possess
two heights (those mentioned in Genl Burgoynes Letter to
Lord Stanley in his Acct of the Battle of Bunkers hill) which
had the entire command of it—The grd at this time being
froze upwards of two feet deep, & as impenetrable as a Rock,
nothing could be attempted with Earth; we were oblig'd
therefore to provide an amazing quantity of Chandeliers and
Fascines for the Work, and on the Night of the 4th, after a
previous severe Cannonade & Bombardment for three Nights
together to divert the Enemy's attention from our real design,
removed every material to the spot under Cover of Darkness,
and took full possession of those heights without the loss of
a Single Man.

Upon their discovery of the Works next Morning great
preparations were made for attacking them, but not being
ready before the Afternoon and the Weather getting very tempestuous, much blood was Saved, and a very important blow
(to one side or the other) prevented—That this remarkable
Interposition of Providence is for some wise purpose I have
not a doubt; but as the principal design of the Manouvre was
to draw the Enemy to an Ingagement under disadvantages—
as a premeditated Plan was laid for this purpose, and seemed
to be succeeding to my utmost wish and as no Men seem'd
better disposed to make the Appeal than ours did upon that
occasion, I can scarce forbear lamenting the disappointment,

unless the dispute is drawing to an Accomodation, and the Sword going to be Sheathed.

But to return, the Enemy thinking (as we have since learnt) that we had got too securely posted before the Second Morning to be much hurt by them, and apprehending great annoyance from our new Works resolved upon a retreat, and accordingly Imbark'd in as much hurry, precipitation and confusion as ever Troops did, the 17th, not taking time to fit their transports, but leaving Kings property in Boston to the amount, as is supposed, of thirty or £40,000 in Provisions, Stores, &ca—Many Pieces of Cannon, some Mortars, and a number of Shot, Shells &ca are also left—and Baggage Waggons, Artillery Carts &ca which they have been Eighteen Months preparing to take the Field with, were found destroyed—thrown into the Docks—and drifted upon every Shore—In short, Dunbars destruction of Stores after Genl Braddocks defeat, which made so much noise, affords but a faint Idea of what was to be met with here.

The Enemy lay from the 17th to the 27th In Nantasket & Kings Roads abt Nine Miles from Boston to take in Water (from the Islands thereabouts, surrounded by their Shipping) & to fit themselves for Sea—whither they are now bound, & where their Tents will be next pitched, I know not; but as New York and the Hudson's River are the most important objects they can have in view, as the latter secures the communication with Canada, at the same time it seperates the Northern and Southern Colonies Armies; and the former is thought to abound in disaffected Persons who only wait a favourable oppertunity, and support, to declare themselves openly, it became equally important for us to prevent their gaining Possession of these advantages, & therefore, so soon as they Imbarked I detach'd a Brigade of Six Regimts to that Government. so soon as they Sailed, another Brigade compos'd of the same number, and to morrow another of Five will March—In a day or two more I shall follow myself & be in New York ready to receive all but the first.

The Enemy left all their Works standing in Boston, & on Bunkers hill, and formidable they are—the Town has shared a much better Fate than was expected—the damage done to the Houses being nothing equal to report—but the Inhabitants have sufferd a good deal by being plunder'd by the Soldiery at their departure. All those who took upon themselves the Style, & title of Government Men in Boston in short all those who have acted an unfriendly part in this great Contest have Shipped themselves off in the same hurry, but under still greater disadvantages than the Kings Troops have done; being obliged to Man their own Vessels (for Seamen could not be had for the Transports for the Kings use) and submit to every hardship that can be conciv'd—One or two have done, what a great many ought to have done long ago—committed Suicide—By all Accts there never existed a more miserable set of Beings than these wretched Creatures now are—taught to believe that the Power of Great Britain was superior to all opposition, and that foreign Aid (if not) was at hand, they were even higher, & more insulting in their opposition than the Regulars—when the Order Issued therefore for Imbarking the Troops in Boston, no Electric Shock—no sudden Clap of thunder—in a word the last Trump—could not have Struck them with greater Consternation. they were at their Wits end, and conscious of their black ingratitude chose to commit themselves in the manner I have above describ'd to the Mercy of the Waves at a tempestuous Season rather than meet their offended Countrymen. but with this declaration the choice was made that if they thought the most abject Submission would procure them Peace they never would have stir'd.

I believe I may, with great truth affirm, that no Man perhaps since the first Institution of Armys ever commanded one under more difficult Circumstances than I have done—to enumerate the particulars would fill a volume—many of my difficulties and distresses were of so peculiar a cast that in order to conceal them from the Enemy, I was obliged to conceal them from my friends, indeed from my own Army thereby subjecting my Conduct to interpretations unfavourable to my Character—especially by those at a distance, who could not, in the smallest degree, be acquainted with the Springs that govern'd it—I am happy however to find, and to hear from different Quarters, that my reputation stands fair—that my Conduct hitherto has given universal Satisfaction—the Addresses which I have received, and which I suppose will be published, from the general Court of this Colony (the same as our Genl Assembly) and from the Selectmen of Boston upon the evacuation of the Town & my approaching departure from the Colony, exhibits a pleasing testimony of their approbation of my conduct, and of their personal regard, which I have found in various other Instances; and wch, in retirement, will afford many comfortable reflections.

The share you have taken in these Publick disputes is commendable and praiseworthy—it is a duty we owe our Country—a Claim posterity has on us—It is not sufficient for a Man to be a passive friend & well wisher to the Cause. This, and every other Cause, of such a Nature, must inevitably perish under such an opposition. every person should be active in some department or other, without paying too much attention to private Interest, It is a great stake we are playing for, and sure we are of winning if the Cards are well managed—Inactivity in some—disaffection in others—and timidity in many, may hurt the Cause; nothing else can, for Unanimity will carry us through triumphantly in spite of every exertion of Great Britain, if link'd together in one indissoluble Band—this they now know, & are practising every strategem which Human Invention can devise, to divide us, & unite their own People—upon this principle it is, the restraining Bill is past, and Commissioners are coming over. The device to be sure is shallow—the covering thin—But they will hold out to their own People that the Acts (complaind of) are repealed, and Commissioners sent to each Colony to treat with us, neither of which will we attend to &ca—this upon weak Minds among us will have its effect—they wish for reconciliation—or in other Words they wish for Peace without attending to the Conditions.

General Lee, I expect, is with you before this—He is the first Officer in Military knowledge and experience we have in the whole Army—He is zealously attachd to the Cause—honest, and well meaning, but rather fickle & violent I fear in his temper however as he possesses an uncommon share of good Sense and Spirit I congratulate my Countrymen upon his appointment to that Department. The appointment of Lewis I think was also judicious, for notwithstanding the odium thrown upon his Conduct at the Kanhawa I always look'd upon him as a Man of Spirit and a good Officer—his experience is equal to any one we have. Colo. Mercer would have supplied the place well but I question (as a Scotchman) whether it would have gone glibly down. Bullet is no favourite of mine, & therefore I shall say nothing more of him, than that his own opinion of himself always kept pace with what others pleas'd to think of him—if any thing, rather run a head of it.

As I am now nearly at the end of my Eighth page, I think it time to conclude, especially as I set out with prefacing, the little time I had for friendly Corrispondances—I shall only add therefore my Affectionate regards to my Sister and the Children, & Compliments to any enquiring friends and that I am with every Sentiment of true Affection yr Loving Brother & faithful friend.

To John Augustine Washington

Dear Brother,   Philadelphia May 31st 1776
    Since my arrival at this place, where I came at the request of Congress, to settle some matters relative to the ensuing Campaign I have received your Letter of the 18th from Williamsburg, & think I stand indebted to you for another, which came to hand sometime ago, in New York.

    I am very glad to find that the Virginia Convention have passed so noble a vote, with so much unanimity—things have come to that pass now, as to convince us, that we have nothing more to expect from the justice of G: Britain—also, that She is capable of the most delusive Arts; for I am satisfied that no Commissioners ever were design'd, except Hessians & other Foreigners; and that the Idea was only to deceive, & throw us off our guard—the first it has too effectually accomplished, as many Members of Congress, in short, the representation of whole Provences, are still feeding themselves upon the dainty food of reconciliation; and thô they will not allow that the expectation of it has any influence upon their judgments (with respect to their preparions for defence) it is but too obvious that it has an operation upon every part of their conduct, and is a clog to their proceedings—it is not in

the nature of things to be otherwise, for no Man, that entertains a hope of seeing this dispute speedily, and equitably adjusted by Commissioners, will go to the same expence, and
run the same hazards to prepare for the worst event as he who
believes that he must conquer, or submit to unconditional
terms, & its concomitants, such as Confiscation, hanging,
&ca, &ca.

To form a new Government, requires infinite care, & unbounded attention; for if the foundation is badly laid the superstructure must be bad. too much time therefore, cannot
be bestowed in weighing and digesting matters well—we
have, no doubt, some good parts in our present constitution—many bad ones we know we have, wherefore no time
can be misspent that is imployed in seperating the Wheat from
the Tares—My fear is, that you will all get tired and homesick,
the consequence of which will be, that you will patch up some
kind of Constitution as defective as the present—this should
be avoided—every Man should consider, that he is lending his
aid to frame a Constitution which is to render Million's happy,
or Miserable, and that a matter of such moment cannot be
the Work of a day.

I am in hopes to hear some good Acct from No. Carolina—
If Clinton has only part of his force there, and not strongly
Intrenchd, I should think Genl Lee will be able to give a very
good Acct of those at Cape Fare—Surely Administration must
intend more than 5000 Men for the Southern district, otherwise they must have a very contemptable opinion of those
Colonies, or have great expectation of assistance from the Indians, Slaves, & Tories. We expect a very bloody Summer of
it at New York & Canada, as it is there I expect the grand
efforts of the Enemy will be aim'd; & I am sorry to say that
we are not, either in Men, or Arms, prepared for it. however,
it is to be hoped that if our cause is just, as I do most religiously believe it to be, the same Providence which has in
many Instances appeard for us, will still go on to afford its
aid.

Your Convention is acting very wisely in removing the
disaffected, Stock, &ca from the Counties of Princess Anne
& Norfolk; and are much to be commended for their Attention to the Manufacture of Salt, Salt Petre, Powder, &ca. No

time, nor expence should be spared to accomplish these things.

Mrs Washington is now under Innoculation in this City; & will, I expect, have the Small pox favourably—this is the 13th day, and she has very few Pustules—she would have wrote to my Sister but thought it prudent not to do so, notwithstanding there could be but little danger in conveying the Infection in this Manner. She joins me in love to you, her, and all the little ones—I am with every Sentiment of regard, Dr Sir Yr Most Affecte Brother

General Orders

                         Head Quarters, New York, July 2nd 1776.
Parole Armstrong.   Countersign Lee.

Genl Mifflin is to repair to the post near Kingsbridge and use his utmost endeavours to forward the works there—General Scott in the mean time to perform the duty required of General Mifflin in the orders of the 29th of June.

No Sentries are to stop or molest the Country people coming to Market or going from it but to be very vigilant in preventing Soldiers leaving the army.

Col. Cortlandt of the New-Jersey Brigade is to send over five-hundred of the Militia under his command to reinforce General Greene's Brigade; these troops are to be distinguished from the old Militia in future by being called New-Levies— The Quarter Master General to furnish them with Tents: The detachment from General Spencers Brigade to return when these get over. The Militia not under the immediate Command of General Heard are to be under that of Genl Mercer until the arrival of their own General Officer.

The time is now near at hand which must probably determine, whether Americans are to be, Freemen, or Slaves; whether they are to have any property they can call their own; whether their Houses, and Farms, are to be pillaged and destroyed, and they consigned to a State of Wretchedness from which no human efforts will probably deliver them. The fate of unborn Millions will now depend, under God, on the

Courage and Conduct of this army—Our cruel and unrelenting Enemy leaves us no choice but a brave resistance, or the most abject submission; this is all we can expect—We have therefore to resolve to conquer or die: Our own Country's Honor, all call upon us for a vigorous and manly exertion, and if we now shamefully fail, we shall become infamous to the whole world—Let us therefore rely upon the goodness of the Cause, and the aid of the supreme Being, in whose hands Victory is, to animate and encourage us to great and noble Actions—The Eyes of all our Countrymen are now upon us, and we shall have their blessings, and praises, if happily we are the instruments of saving them from the Tyranny meditated against them. Let us therefore animate and encourage each other, and shew the whole world, that a Freeman contending for Liberty on his own ground is superior to any slavish mercenary on earth.

The General recommends to the officers great coolness in time of action, and to the soldiers a strict attention and obedience, with a becoming firmness and spirit.

Any officer, or soldier, or any particular Corps, distinguishing themselves by any acts of bravery, and courage, will assuredly meet with notice and rewards; and on the other hand, those who behave ill, will as certainly be exposed and punished—The General being resolved, as well for the Honor and Safety of the Country, as Army, to shew no favour to such as refuse, or neglect their duty at so important a crisis.

The General expressly orders that no officer, or soldier, on any pretence whatever, without leave in writing, from the commanding officer of the regiment, do leave the parade, so as to be out of drum-call, in case of an alarm, which may be hourly expected—The Regiments are immediately to be under Arms on their respective parades, and should any be absent they will be severely punished—The whole Army to be at their Alarm posts completely equipped to morrow, a little before day.

Ensign Charles Miller, Capt. Wrisst's Company, and Colonel Wyllys's Regiment, charged with "absenting himself from his Guard" tried by a General Court Martial and acquitted—The General approves the sentence, and orders him to be dismissed from his arrest.

As there is a probability of Rain, the General strongly recommends to the officers, to pay particular attention, to their men's arms and ammunition, that neither may be damaged.

Lieut. Col. Clark who was ordered to sit on General Court Martial in the orders of yesterday being absent on command, Lieut. Col. Tyler is to sit in Court.

Evening Orders. 'Tis the General's desire that the men lay upon their Arms in their tents and quarters, ready to turn out at a moments warning, as their is the greatest likelihood of it.

General Orders

Head Quarters, New York, July 9th 1776.
Parole Manchester.   Countersign Norfolk.

John Evans of Capt: Ledyards Company Col. McDougall's Regiment—Hopkins Rice of Capt: Pierce's Company Col. Ritzema's Regiment having been tried by a General Court Martial whereof Col. Read was President and found guilty of "Desertion," were sentenced to receive each Thirty-nine Lashes. The General approves the Sentences and orders them to be executed at the usual time & place.

Passes to go from the City are hereafter to be granted by John Berrien, Henry Wilmot and John Ray Junr a Committee of the City appointed for that purpose—Officers of the Guards at the Ferries and Wharves, to be careful in making this regulation known to the sentries, who are to see that the passes are signed by one of the above persons, and to be careful no Soldier goes over the Ferry without a pass from a General officer.

The North River Guard to be removed to the Market House near the Ferry-Stairs, as soon as it is fitted up.

The Honorable Continental Congress having been pleased to allow a Chaplain to each Regiment, with the pay of Thirty-three Dollars and one third ⅌ month—The Colonels or commanding officers of each regiment are directed to procure Chaplains accordingly; persons of good Characters and exemplary lives—To see that all inferior officers and soldiers pay them a suitable respect and attend carefully upon religious exercises: The blessing and protection of Heaven are at all times necessary but especially so in times of public distress and danger—The General hopes and trusts, that every officer, and man, will endeavour so to live, and act, as becomes a Christian Soldier defending the dearest Rights and Liberties of his country.

The Honorable the Continental Congress, impelled by the dictates of duty, policy and necessity, having been pleased to dissolve the Connection which subsisted between this Country, and Great Britain, and to declare the United Colonies of North America, free and independent STATES: The several brigades are to be drawn up this evening on their respective Parades, at six OClock, when the declaration of Congress, shewing the grounds & reasons of this measure, is to be read with an audible voice.

The General hopes this important Event will serve as a fresh incentive to every officer, and soldier, to act with Fidelity and Courage, as knowing that now the peace and safety of his Country depends (under God) solely on the success of our arms: And that he is now in the service of a State, possessed of sufficient power to reward his merit, and advance him to the highest Honors of a free Country.

The Brigade Majors are to receive, at the Adjutant Generals Office, several of the Declarations to be delivered to the Brigadiers General, and the Colonels of regiments.

The Brigade Majors are to be execused from farther attendance at Head Quarters, except to receive the Orders of the day, that their time and attention may be withdrawn as little as possible, from the duties of their respective brigades.

To John Hancock

Sir   New York July the 14th 1776
My last of friday evening which I had the honor of addressing you, advised that Two of the Enemies Ships of War & three Tenders had run above our Batteries here and the Works at the upper end of the Island. I am now to Inform you, that Yesterday forenoon receiving Intelligence from Genl Mifflin

that they had past the Tanpan Sea and were trying to proceed higher up, by advice of R. R. Livingston Esqr. and other Gentn I dispatched expresses to Genl Clinton of Ulster and the Committee of Safety for Dutchess County, to take measures for securing the passes in the Highlands, lest they might have designs of Seizing them and have a force concealed for the purpose. I wrote the Evening before to the commanding Officer of the Two Garrisons there to be vigilant and prepared against any Attempts they or any disaffected persons might make against them, and to forward expresses all the way to Albany, that provision and other Vessells might be secured and prevented falling into their Hands. The information given Genl Mifflin was rather premature as to their having gone past the Sea: A Letter from the Committee of Orange County which came to hand this morning says they were there yesterday and that a Regiment of their Militia was under Arms to prevent their landing and making an Incursion. The Messenger who brought It, and to whom It refers for particulars, adds, that a party of them in two or three boats, had approched the Shore but were forced back by our people firing at them. Since the Manuvre of friday there have been no other movements in the Fleet.

Genl Sullivan in a Letter of the 2d Inst. informs me of his arrival with the Army at Crown point, where he is fortifying & throwing up Works. he adds that he has secured all the Stores, except three Cannon left at Chamblee, which in part is made up by taking a fine Twelve pounder out of the Lake— The Army is sickly, many with the small pox, and he is apprehensive the Militia ordered to Join them, will not escape the Infection. An Officer he had sent to reconnoitre had reported that he saw at St Johns about 150 Tents. 20 at St Rays & 15 at Chamblee and works at the first were busily carrying on.

I have Inclosed a General return of the Army here which will shew the whole of our strength. All the detached posts are Included.

A Letter from the Eastward by last nights post to Mr Hazard, post Master in this City, advises "That Two ships had been taken & carried into Cape Ann; One from Antigua consigned to Genl Howe with 439 puncheons of Rum—The other a Jamaicaman with 400 Hogsheads of Sugar, 200 puncheons of Rum. 39 Bales of Cotton. Pimento. Fustick &c. &c. Each mounted 2 Guns, Six pounders."

About 3 OClock this afternoon I was informed that a Flag from Ld Howe was coming up and waited with two of our Whale boats untill directions should be given. I immediately convened such of the Genl officers as were not upon other duty who agreed in opinion that I ought not to receive any Letter directed to me as a private Gentleman, but if otherwise and the Officer desired to come up to deliver the Letter himself as was suggested, he should come under a safe conduct— Upon this I directed Colo. Reed to go down & manage the affair under the above general Instruction. On his return he Informed me, after the common Civilities the Officer acquainted him that he had a Letter from Ld Howe to Mr Washington which he shewed under a superscription to George Washington Esqr. Col. Reed replied there was no such person in the Army and that a Letter Intended for the General could not be received under such a direction—The Officer expressed great concern, said It was a Letter rather of a civil than Military nature. That Lord Howe regretted he had not arrived sooner. That he (Ld Howe) had great Powers. the anxiety to have the Letter received was very evident, though the Officer disclaimed all Knowledge of Its contents. However Col. Reeds Instructions being positive they parted—after they had got some distance the Officer with the Flag again put about and asked under what direction Mr Washington chose to be addressed. to which Colo. Reed answered his station was well known and that certainly they could be at no loss how to direct to him. The Officer said they knew It & lamented It and again repeated his wish that the Letter could be received—Col. Reed told him a proper direction would obviate all difficulties & that this was no new matter. this subject having been fully discussed in the course of the last year, of which Ld Howe could not be ignorant upon which they parted.

I would not upon any occasion sacrifice Essentials to Punctilio, but in this Instance, the Opinion of Others concurring with my own, I deemed It a duty to my Country and my appointment to insist upon that respect which in any other than a public view I would willingly have waived. Nor do I doubt but from the supposed nature of the Message and the anxiety expressed they will either repeat their Flag or fall upon some mode to communicate the Import and consequence of It.

I have been duly honoured with your two Letters that of the 10th by Mr Anderson, and the 11th, with Its Inclosures. I have directed the Quarter Master to provide him with every thing he wants to carry his Scheme into execution: It is an Important One, and I wish It success but I am doubtfull that It will be better in Theory than practice.

The passage of the Ships of War and Tenders up the river, is a matter of great importance, and has excited much conjecture and spectulation; to me two things have occurred, as leading them to this proceeding; first, a design to seize on the narrow passes on both sides the river, giving almost the only Land Communication with Albany, and of consequence with our Northern Army, and for which purpose they might have troops concealed on board which they deemed competent of themselves as the defiles are narrow, or that they would be Joined by many dissaffected persons in that Quarter. Others have Added a probability of their having a large quantity of Arms on board to be in readiness to put into the hands of the Tories immediately on the arrival of the fleet, or rather at the time they Intend to make their attack. The second is to cut off entirely all Intercourse between this and Albany by Water and the upper Country & to prevent Supplies of every kind going and coming. These matters are truly alarming and of such Importance, that I have wrote to the Provincial Congress of New York and recommended to their serious consideration, the adoption of every possible expedient to guard against the two first, and have suggested the propriety of their employing the Militia or such part of them in the Counties in which these defiles are to keep the Enemy from possessing them till further provision can be made, and to write to the several leading persons on our side in that Quarter, to be attentive to all the movements of the Ships and the disaffected in order to discover and frustrate whatever pernicious Schemes they have in view.

In respect to the Second conjecture of my own & which seems to be generally adopted, I have the pleasure to Inform

Congress, That If their design is to keep the Armies from provision, that the Commissary has told me upon Inquiry, he has forwarded supplies to Albany, now there and above It, sufficient for 10,000 men for four Months. that he has a sufficency here for 20,000 men for three months, and an abundant quantity secured in different parts of the Jersey for the flying Camp, besides having about 4,000 Barrells of Flour in some neighbouring part of Connecticut. upon this head there is but little occasion for any apprehensions at least for a considerable time. I have the honor to be with Sentiments of great esteem Your Most Obedt Servt

P.S. I have sent Orders to the Commandg Officer of the Pensylvania Militia to march to Amboy as their remaing at Trenton can be of no service.

To Adam Stephen

Dear Sir,   New York July 20th 1776.
    Your Letter of the 4th Instt came duly to hand. I thank you for yr kind congratulations on the discovery of the vile Machinations of still viler Ministerial Agents. I hope the untimely fruit of their Intentions will in the end recoil upon their own heads—all the measures heretofore projected, has done so I think, except in Canada, where an unaccountable kind of fatality seems to have attended all our Movements since the death of poor Montgomery.
    We have a powerful Fleet under the Command of Lord Howe in full view of us—distant about 8 Miles from this City—the Troops (from the best Accts amounting to about Eight or nine thousand Men) are upon Staten Island, fortifying themselves and waiting the Re-inforcement from England, which every fair Wind is expected to bring. this Reinforcement from different Accts will be from Fifteen to 20,000 Men. Our Strength greatly inferior unless the New Levies come in much faster than they have done, which I hope will be the case as harvest will soon be over and that Plea, at an end.

Two Ships on the 12th, to wit the Phœnex of 44. Guns & Rose of 20, exhibited a proof of the incompetency of Batteries to stop a Ships passage with a brisk Wind & strong tide where there are no obstruction's in the Water to impede their motion—the above Ships pass'd through an incessant Fire from our Batteries without receiving much damage—they were each hulled several times & their Rigging a little damaged but not so as to retard their way up the River to what is called the Taupon bay a wide part of the River out of reach of Cannon Shot from either shore. here they now are, having cut of the Water Communication with Albany, & our Army on the Lakes, entirely.

I did not let the Anniversary of the 3d or 9th of this Instt pass of without a grateful remembrance of the escape we had at the Meadows and on the Banks of Monongahela. the same Provedence that protected us upon those occasions will, I hope, continue his Mercies, and make us happy Instruments in restoring Peace & liberty to this once favour'd, but now distressed Country. Give my Complimts to the Several of yr Corps of my acquaintances and believe me to be Dr Sir Yr Most Obedt Sert,

General Orders

Head Quarters, New York, August 1st 1776.
Parole Paris.   Countersign Reading.

It is with great concern, the General understands, that Jealousies &c: are arisen among the troops from the different Provinces, of reflections frequently thrown out, which can only tend to irritate each other, and injure the noble cause in which we are engaged, and which we ought to support with one hand and one heart. The General most earnestly entreats the officers, and soldiers, to consider the consequences; that they can no way assist our cruel enemies more effectually, than making division among ourselves; That the Honor and Success of the army, and the safety of our bleeding Country, depends upon harmony and good agreement with each other; That the Provinces are all United to oppose the common enemy, and all distinctions sunk in the name of an American; to make this honorable, and preserve the Liberty of our Country, ought to be our only emulation, and he will be the best Soldier, and the best Patriot, who contributes most to this glorious work, whatever his Station, or from whatever part of the Continent, he may come: Let all distinctions of Nations, Countries, and Provinces, therefore be lost in the generous contest, who shall behave with the most Courage against the enemy, and the most kindness and good humour to each other—If there are any officers, or soldiers, so lost to virtue and a love of their Country as to continue in such practices after this order; The General assures them, and is directed by Congress to declare, to the whole Army, that such persons shall be severely punished and dismissed the service with disgrace.

To Lund Washington

Dear Lund,   New York Augt 19th 1776.

Very unexpectedly to me, another revolving Monday is arrived before an Attack upon this City, or a movement of the Enemy—the reason of this is incomprehensible, to me—True it is (from some late informations) they expect another arrival of about 5000 Hessians; but then, they have been stronger than the Army under my Command; which will now, I expect, gain strength faster than theirs, as the Militia are beginning to come in fast, and have already augmented our numbers in this City and the Posts round about, to about 23,000 Men. The Enemy's numbers now on the Island and in the Transports which lay off it, are by the lowest Accts 20,000 Men by the greatest 27,000 to these the expected (5000) Hessians are to be added.

There is something exceedingly misterious in the conduct of the Enemy—Lord Howe takes pains to throw out, upon every occasion, that he is the Messenger of Peace—that he wants to accomodate matters—nay, has Insinuated, that he thinks himself authorized to do it upon the terms mentioned in the last Petition to the King of G: Britain—But has the

Nation got to that, that the King, or his Ministers will openly dispense with Acts of Parliament—And if they durst attempt it, how is it to be accounted for that after running the Nation to some Millions of Pounds Sterlg to hire and Transport Foreigners, and before a blow is struck, they are willing to give the terms proposed by Congress before they, or we, had encountered the enormous expence that both are now run to— I say, how is this to be accounted for but from their having received some disagreeable advices from Europe; or, by having some Manouvre in view which is to be effected by procrastination. What this can be the Lord knows—we are now passed the Middle of August and they are in possession of an Island only, which it never was in our power, or Intention to dispute their Landing on. this is but a small step towards the Conquest of this Continent.

The two Ships which went up this River about the middle of the past Month, came down yesterday, sadly frightned I believe, the largest of them, the Phœnex (a 44. Gun Ship) having very narrowly escaped burning the Night before by two Fire ships which I sent up; one of which was grapnal'd to her for Ten Minutes, in a light blaze, before the Phœnex could cut away so as to clear herself. the other Fire ship run on board of the Tender near the Phœnex, & soon reduced her to Ashes. We lost no lives in the Attempt unless the Captn of the Ship which made the attempt upon the Phœnex perish'd. We have not heard of him since, but it is thought he might have made his escape by Swimming, which was the Plan he had in contemplation.

As the Collection of Mercers Bonds has not been put into the hands of Colo. Peyton, I have no objection to your undertaking of it if Colo. Tayloe has none; accordingly, I inclose you a Letter to him on this Subject, which you may forward, & act agreeable to his Instructions, and appointment. I do not recollect enough of the Tenor of the Bonds to decide absolutely in the case of Majr Powell. true it is the design of making the Bonds carry Interest from the date, was to enforce the punctual payment of them; or, to derive an advantage if they were not. The Circumstances attending his going to Hampton, & the time when he did, I know not. He knew that those Bonds were payable to Tayloe & me—he knew that they became due (to the best of my recollection) the first of December, & should have tendered the Money at that time in strictness—however if you have the Collection, in all matters of that kind take Colo. Tayloe's, or (which I believe will be the same thing) Mr Jas Mercer's opinion as it will be impossible for me to determine these matters at the distance I am, and under the hurry of business I am Ingaged In.

There is no doubt but that the Honey locust if you could procure Seed enough, & that Seed would come up, will make (if sufficiently thick) a very good hedge—so will the Haw, or thorn, and if you cannot do better I wish you to try these—but Cedar or any kind of ever Green, would look better; howr, if one thing will not do, we must try another, as no time ought to be lost in rearing of Hedges, not only for Ornament but use.

Adams's Land you will continue to Rent to the best advantage, for I believe it will turn out, that I made bad worse, by attempting to save myself by taking that pretty youths debts upon myself. As Lord Dunmore and his Squadron have joind the Fleet at Staten Island, you will, I should think, have a favourable oppertunity of sending of your Flour, Midlings, Ship stuff &ca—Corn will, more than probably, sell well sometime hence—especially if your Crops should be as short as you apprehend—If your Ship stuff & Middlings should have turnd Sower it will make exceeding good Bisquet notwithstanding. Your Works abt the Home House will go on Slowly I fear as your hands are reduced, & especially if Knowles fails. remember that the New Chimneys are not to smoke. Plant Trees in the room of all dead ones in proper time this Fall. and as I mean to have groves of Trees at each end of the dwelling House, that at the South end to range in a line from the South East Corner to Colo. Fairfax's, extending as low as another line from the Stable to the dry well, and towards the Coach House, Hen House, & Smoak House as far as it can go for a Lane to be left for Carriages to pass to, & from the Stable and Wharf. from the No. Et Corner of the other end of the House to range so as to Shew the Barn &ca. in the Neck—from the point where the old Barn used to Stand to the No. Et Corner of the Smiths Shop, & from thence to the Servants Hall, leaveng a passage between the

Quarter & Shop, and so East of the Spinning & Weaving House (as they used to be called) up to a Wood pile, & so into the yard between the Servts Hall & the House newly erected—these Trees to be Planted without any order or regularity (but pretty thick, as they can at any time be thin'd) and to consist that at the North end, of locusts altogether. & that at the South, of all the clever kind of Trees (especially flowering ones) that can be got, such as Crab apple, Poplar, Dogwood, Sasafras, Lawrel, Willow (especially yellow & Weeping Willow, twigs of which may be got from Philadelphia) and many others which I do not recollect at present— these to be interspersed here and there with ever greens such as Holly, Pine, and Cedar, also Ivy—to these may be added the Wild flowering Shrubs of the larger kind, such as the fringe Tree & several other kinds that might be mentioned. It will not do to Plant the Locust Trees at the North end of the House till the Framing is up, cover'd in, and the Chimney Built—otherwise it will be labour lost as they will get broke down, defaced and spoil'd, But nothing need prevent planting the Shrubery at the other end of the House. Whenever these are Planted they should be Inclosd, which may be done in any manner till I return—or rather by such kind of fencing as used to be upon the Ditch running towards Hell hole—beginning at the Kitchen & running towards the Stable & rather passing the upper Corner—thence round the Dry Well—below the necessary House, & so on to the Hollow by the Wild Cherry tree by the old Barn—thence to the Smiths Shop & so up to the Servants Hall as before described. If I should ever fulfil my Intention it will be to Inclose it properly—the Fence now described is only to prevent Horses &ca. injuring the young Trees in their growth.

As my Greys are almost done, and I have got two or three pretty good Bays here, I do not Incline to make an absolute Sale of the bay horse you mention—But if Mr Custis wants him, & you and he can fix upon a price, he may take him at such valuation; paying the Money and using him as his own; subject however to return him to me if I should hereafter want him and will repay him his money—by this means he will (if it should not prove an absolute Sale) have the use of the Horse and I, the use of the money.

Before I conclude I must beg of you to hasten Lanphire about the addition to the No. End of the House, otherwise you will have it open I fear in the cold & wet Weather, and the Brick work to do at an improper Season, neither of which shall I be at all desirous of. My best wishes to Milly Posey and all our Neighbours and friends. with sincere regard I remain Dr Lund, Yr affecte Friend

General Orders

Head Quarters, New York, August 23rd 1776.
Parole Charlestown.   Countersign Lee.

The Commissary General is directed to have five days Bread baked, and ready to be delivered: If the Commissary should apply to the commanding officers of regiments, for any Bakers, they are to furnish them without waiting for a special order.

The General was sorry yesterday to find, that when some troops were ordered to march, they had no provisions, notwithstanding the Orders that have been issued. The men must march, if the service requires it, and will suffer very much if not provided: The General therefore directs, all the Troops to have two days hard Bread, and Pork, ready by them; and desires the officers will go through the encampment, and quarters, to see that it be got and kept.

The General would be obliged to any officer, to recommend to him, a careful, sober person who understands taking care of Horses and waiting occasionally. Such person being a Soldier will have his pay continued, and receive additional wages of twenty Shillings ℔ Month—He must be neat in his person, and to be depended on for his honesty and sobriety.

The officers of the militia are informed, that twenty-four Rounds are allowed to a man, and two Flints; that the Captains of each Company should see that the Cartridges fit the bore of the gun; they then are to be put up in small Bundles; All the Cartridges except six; writing each mans name on his bundle, and keep them safely 'till the Alarm is given, then deliver to each man his bundle; the other six to be kept for common use. In drawing for ammunition, the commanding officers should, upon the regimental parade, examine the state of their regiments, and then draw for Cartridges, and Flints, agreeable to the above regulation. Capt: Tilton will assist them in their business, and unless in case of alarm, they are desired not to draw for every small number of men, who may be coming in.

The Enemy have now landed on Long Island, and the hour is fast approaching, on which the Honor and Success of this army, and the safety of our bleeding Country depend. Remember officers and Soldiers, that you are Freemen, fighting for the blessings of Liberty—that slavery will be your portion, and that of your posterity, if you do not acquit yourselves like men: Remember how your Courage and Spirit have been despised, and traduced by your cruel invaders; though they have found by dear experience at Boston, Charlestown and other places, what a few brave men contending in their own land, and in the best of causes can do, against base hirelings and mercenaries—Be cool, but determined; do not fire at a distance, but wait for orders from your officers—It is the General's express orders that if any man attempt to skulk, lay down, or retreat without Orders he be instantly shot down as an example, he hopes no such Scoundrel will be found in this army; but on the contrary, every one for himself resolving to conquer, or die, and trusting to the smiles of heaven upon so just a cause, will behave with Bravery and Resolution: Those who are distinguished for their Gallantry, and good Conduct, may depend upon being honorably noticed, and suitably rewarded: And if this Army will but emulate, and imitate their brave Countrymen, in other parts of America, he has no doubt they will, by a glorious Victory, save their Country, and acquire to themselves immortal Honor.

The Brigade Majors are immediately to relieve the Guards out of the regiments order'd to Long Island, from other regiments of the brigade, and forward such Guards to the regiments.

Major Newbury's Col. Hinmans, Major Smiths, Col. Cook's, Col. Talcots, Col. Baldwin's and Major Strong's Regiments of Connecticut Militia to parade this evening precisely at five OClock on the Grand parade—Major Henly will attend and shew them their alarm posts, and direct them in manning the lines.

When any of the Field Officers for Picquet, or Main Guard, are sick, or otherwise incapable of the duty, they are immediately to signify it to their Brigade Major—but the General hopes that triffling excuses will not be made, as there is too much reason to believe has been the case.

To John Hancock

Sir   New York Head Qrs Septr 8th 1776

Since I had the honour of addressing you on the 6th Instt I have called a Council of the General Officers in order to take a full & comprehensive view of our situation & thereupon form such a plan of future defence as may be immediately pursued & subject to no other alteration than a change of Operations on the Enemy's side may occasion. Before the Landing of the Enemy on Long Island, the point of Attack could not be known or any satisfactory Judgemt formed of their Intentions—It might be on Long Island—on Bergen, or directly on the City, this made It necessary to be prepared for each and has occasiond an expence of labour which now seems useless & is regretted by those who form a Judgement from after knowledge: But I trust men of discernment will think differently, and see that by such works & preparations we have not only delayed the Operations of the Campaign till It is too late to effect any capital Incursion into the Country, but have drawn the Enemy's forces to one point and obliged them to decline their plan, so as to enable us to form our defence on some certainty. It is now extremely obvious from all Intelligence—from their movements, & every other circumstance that having landed their whole Army on Long Island, (except about 4,000 on Staten Island) they mean to inclose us on the Island of New York by taking post in our Rear, while the Shipping effectually secure the Front; and thus either by cutting off our Communication with the Country oblige us to fight them on their own Terms or Surrender at discretion, or by a Brilliant stroke endeavour to cut this Army in peices & secure the collection of Arms & Stores which they will know we shall not be able soon to replace. Having therefore their System unfolded to us, It became an important consideration how It could be most successfully opposed—On every side there is a choice of difficulties, & every measure on our part, (however painfull the reflection is from experience) to be formed with some apprehension that all our Troops will not do their duty. In deliberating on this great Question, it was impossible to forget that History—our own experience—the advice of our ablest Friends in Europe—The fears of the Enemy, and even the Declarations of Congress demonstrate that on our side the War should be defensive, It has been even called a War of posts, that we should on all occasions avoid a general Action or put anything to the risque unless compelled by a necessity into which we ought never to be drawn. The Arguments on which such a System was founded were deemed unanswerable & experience has given her sanction—With these views & being fully persuaded that It would be presumption to draw out our young Troops into open Ground against their superiors both in number and discipline, I have never spared the Spade & Pickax: I confess I have not found that readiness to defend even strong posts at all hazards which is necessary to derive the greatest benefit from them. The honour of making a brave defence does not seem to be a sufficient stimulus when the success is very doubtfull and the falling into the Enemy's hands probable: But I doubt not this will be gradually attained. We are now in a strong post but not an Impregnable one, nay acknowledged by every man of Judgement to be untenable unless the Enemy will make the Attack upon Lines when they can avoid It and their Movements Indicate that they mean to do so—To draw the whole Army together in order to arrange the defence proportionate to the extent of Lines & works would leave the Country open for an approach and put the fate of this Army and Its stores on the Hazard of making a successfull defence in the City or the issue of an Engagement out of It—On the other hand to abandon a City which has been by some deemed defensible and on whose Works much Labor has been bestowed has a tendency to dispirit the Troops and enfeeble our Cause: It has

also been considered as the Key to the Northern Country,
But as to that I am fully of opinion that the establishing of
Strong posts at Mount Washington on the upper part of this
Island and on the Jersey side opposite to It with the assistance
of the Obstructions already made, & which may be improved
in the Water, that not only the Navigation of Hudsons River
but an easier & better communication may be more effectually
secured between the Northern & Southern States. This I beleive every one acquainted with the situation of the Country
will readily agree to, and will appear evident to those who
have an Opportunity of recurring to good Maps. These and
the many other consequences which will be involved in the
determination of our next measure have given our minds full
employ & led every One to form a Judgement as the various
Objects presented themselves to his view. The post at Kingsbridge is naturally strong & is pretty well fortified, the
Heights about It are commanding and might soon be made
more so. These are Important Objects, and I have attended
to them accordingly—I have also removed from the City All
the Stores & Ammunition except what was absolutely necessary for Its defence and made every Other disposition that did
not essentially interfere with that Object, carefully keeping in
view untill It should be absolutely determined on full consideration, how far the City was to be defended at all events. In
resolving points of such Importance many circumstances peculiar to our own Army also occur, being only provided for a
Summers Campaign, their Cloaths, Shoes and Blankets will
soon be unfit for the change of weather which we every day
feel—At present we have not Tents for more than ⅔d, many
of them old & worn out, but if we had a plentiful supply the
season will not admit of continuing in them long—The Case
of our Sick is also worthy of much consideration—their number by the returns forms at least ¼ of the Army. policy and
Humanity require they should be made as comfortable as possible—With these and many other circumstances before them,
the whole Council of Genl Officers met yesterday in order to
adopt some Genl line of conduct to be pursued at this Important crisis. I intended to have procured their separate
Opinions on each point, but time would not admit, I was
therefore Obliged to collect their sense more generally than I

could have wished. All agreed the Town would not be tenable If the Enemy resolved to bombard & cannonade It—But the difficulty attending a removal operated so strongly, that a course was taken between abandoning It totally & concentring our whole strength for Its defence—Nor were some a little Influenced in their opinion to whom the determn of Congress was known, against an evacuation totally, as they were led to suspect Congress wished It to be maintained at every hazard—It was concluded to Arrange the Army under Three Divisions, 5000 to remain for the defence of the City, 9000 to Kingsbridge & Its dependancies as well to possess & secure those posts as to be ready to attack the Enemy who are moving Eastward on Long Island, If they should attempt to land on this side—The remainder to occupy the intermediate space & support either—That the Sick should be immediately removed to Orange Town, and Barracks prepared at Kingsbridge with all expedition to cover the Troops.

There were some Genl Officers in whose Judgemt and opinion much confidence is to be reposed, that were for a total and immediate removal from the City, urging the great danger of One part of the Army being cut off before the other can support It, the Extremities being at least Sixteen miles apart—that our Army when collected is inferior to the Enemy's—that they can move with their whole force to any point of attack & consequently must succeed by weight of Numbers if they have only a part to oppose them—That by removing from hence we deprive the Enemy of the Advantage of their Ships which will make at least one half of the force to attack the Town—That we should keep the Enemy at Bay—put nothing to the hazard but at all events keep the Army together which may be recruited another Year, that the unspent Stores will also be preserved & in this case the heavy Artillery can also be secured—But they were overruled by a Majority who thought for the present a part of our force might be kept here and attempt to maintain the City a while longer.

I am sensible a retreating Army is encircled with difficulties, that the declining an Engagemt subjects a General to reproach and that the Common cause may be affected by the discouragement It may throw over the minds of many. Nor am I insensible of the contrary Effects if a brilliant stroke could be made with any probability of Success, especially after our Loss upon Long Island—But when the Fate of America may be at Stake on the Issue, when the wisdom of Cooler moments & experienced men have decided that we should protract the War, if possible, I cannot think it safe or wise to adopt a different System when the Season for Action draws so near a Close—That the Enemy mean to winter in New York there can be no doubt—that with such an Armament they can drive us out is equally clear. The Congress having resolved that It should not be destroyed nothing seems to remain but to determine the time of their taking possession—It is our Interest & wish to prolong It as much as possible provided the delay does not affect our future measures.

The Militia of Connecticut is reduced from 8000 to less than 2,000 and in a few days will be merely nominal—The arrival of some Maryland troops &c. from the flying Camp has in a great degree supplied the loss of men, but the Ammunition they have carried away will be a loss sensibly felt— the impulse for going Home was so irresistable it answered no purpose to oppose It—tho I would not discharge, I have been obliged to acquiesce & It affords one more melancholy proof how delusive such dependencies are.

Inclosed I have the honor to transmit a Genl Return, the first I have been able to procure for some time—Also a report of Captn Newell from Our Works at Horn's Hook or Hell Gate—their situation is extremely low and the Sound so very narrow that the Enemy have 'em much within their Command. I have the Honor to be with great respect Sir Yr Most Obed. Servt

P.S. The Inclosed Informatn this minute came to Hand, I am in hopes we shall henceforth get regular Intelligence of the Enemies Movements.

To John Augustine Washington

Dear Brother,　　　　　　　　Heights of Harlem Sepr 22—76
　　My extreame hurry for some time past has rendered it ut-

terly impossible for me to pay that attention to the Letters of my Friends which Inclination, and natural Affection always Inclines me to. I have no doubt therefore of meeting with their excuse, tho' with respect to yourself, I have had no Letter from you since the date of my last saving the one of Septr the 1st.

With respect to the Attack and Retreat from Long Island the public Papers would furnish you with Accts nearly true. I shall only add, that in the former we lost abt 800 Men, more than three fourths of which were taken Prisoners—This misfortune happened in a great measure by two Detachments of our People who were Posted in two Roads leading thrô a Wood in order to intercept the Enemy in their March, suffering a Surprize, and making a precepitate Retreat, which enabled the Enemy to lead a great part of their force against the Troops Commanded by Lord Sterling which formed a third detachment; who behaved with great bravery and resolution.

As to the Retreat from the Island, under the Circumstances we then were, it became absolutely necessary, and was effected without loss of Men, and with but very little baggage. A few heavy Cannon were left, not being movable, on Acct of the Grounds being soft and Miry thro' the heavy & incessant Rains which had fallen. The Enemys loss in killed we could never ascertain, but have many reasons to believe that it was pretty considerable and exceeded ours a good deal—Our Retreat from thence as I said before was absolutely necessary, the Enemy having landed the main body of their Army to Attack us in Front while their Ships of War were to cut off all communication with the City, from whence resources of Men, Provisions &ca were to be drawn.

Having made this Retreat, not long after we discovered by the movements of the Enemy and the information we received from Deserters and others, that they declin'd attacking our Lines in the City, and were forming a plan to get in our Rear with their Land Army, by crossing the Sound above us, and thereby cut of all Intercourse with the Country and every necessary supply. The Ships of War were to cooperate, possess the North River and prevent Succours from the Jerseys &ca. this Plan appearing probable and but too practicable in its execution, it became necessary to guard agt the fatal consequences that must follow if their scheme was affected; for which purpose I caused a removal of a part of our Stores, Troops, &ca from the City, and a Council of General Officers determined on thursday the 12th that it must be entirely abandoned; as we had, with an Army Weaker than theirs, a line of Sixteen or 18 Miles to defend, to keep open our Communication with the Country, besides the defence of the City—We held up however every show and appearance of defence till our Sick and all our Stores could be brought away—the evacuation being resolved on every exertion in our power was made to baffle their designs, and effect our own. the sick were numerous (amounting to more than the fourth of our whole Army) and an object of great Importance, happily we got them away; but before we could bring off all our Stores, on Sunday Morning Six or Seven Ships of War which had gone up the East River some few days before began a most severe and heavy Canonade to scour the Ground and effect a Landing of their Troops—Three Ships of War also ran up the North River that Morning above the City, to prevent our Boats and Small Craft carrying away our Baggage &ca.

I had gone the Evening before to the Main body of our Army which was Posted about these Heights & the Plains of Harlem, where it seemed probable from the movements, and disposition of the Enemy they meant to Land & make an Attack the next Morning. However the Event did not happen. Immediately on hearing the Cannonade I rode with all possible expedition towards the place of Landing, and where Breast Works had been thrown up to secure our Men, & found the Troops that had been posted there to my great surprize & Mortification, and those ordered to their Support (consisting of Eight Regiments) notwithstanding the exertions of their Generals to form them, running away in the most Shameful and disgraceful manner—I used every possible effort to rally them but to no purpose, & on the appearance of a small part of the Enemy (not more than 60 or 70) they ran off without firing a Single Gun—Many of our heavy Cannon wd inevitably have fallen into the Enemy's hands as they landed so soon, but this scandalous conduct occasioned a loss of many Tents, Baggage & Camp Equipage, which would have been easily secured had they made the least opposition.

The Retreat was made with the loss of a few men only—We Incamp'd, and still are on, the Heights of Harlem which are well calculated for Defence against their approaches. On Monday Morning they advanced in sight in several large bodys but attempted nothing of a general Nature tho' there were smart Skirmishes between their advancd parties and some Detachments from our lines which I sent out—In these our Troops behaved well, putting the Enemy to flight in open Ground, and forcing them from Posts they had siezed two or three times—A Sergeant who deserted from them says they had as he was told 89 Wounded and Missing besides Slain, but other Accts make the wounded much greater.

Our loss in killed and Wounded was about 60—but the greatest loss we sustaind was in the death of Lt Colo. Knolton, a brave and Gallant Officer—Majr Leitch of Weedons Regiment had three Balls through his Side, & behaved exceedingly well—he is in a fair way of recovery—Nothing material has happend since this—the Enemy it is said are bringing up their heavy Cannon, so that We are to expect another Attack soon—both by Land & Water, as we are upon the Hudson (or North River) at the place where we have attempted to stop the Navigation by sinking obstructions in the River & erecting Batteries.

The Dependance which the Congress has placed upon the Militia, has already greatly injured—& I fear will totally ruin, our Cause—Being subject to no controul themselves they introduce disorder among the Troops you have attempted to discipline while the change in their living brings on sickness—this makes them Impatient to get home, which spreads universally & introduces abominable Desertions—In short, it is not in the power of Words to describe the task I have to Act. £50,000 Should not induce me again to undergo what I have done—Our Numbers by Sickness, desertion, &ca is greatly reduced—I have been trying these 4 or 5 days to get a return but have not yet succeeded—I am sure however we have not more than 12 or 14,000 Men fit for duty, whilst the Enemy (who it is said are very healthy) cannot have less than near 25,000. My Sincere love to my Sister and the Family & Complimts to any enquiring Friends concludes me Dr Sir Yr most Affecte Brother

To John Hancock

Sir   Head Qrs Harlem Heights Septr 24th 1776
     The post being about to depart I have only time to add,
That no event of importance has taken place on this side Hudson's River since my last of the 22d Instt.

     The Inclosed Letter received last night from Genl Greene,
who now commands in the Jerseys, will give Congress all the
information I have respecting the evacuation of powles Hook
and the landing of the Enemy to possess It.

     I this minute obtained a Copy of the Genl Return of our
Force, the first I have been able to procure for some time
past, which I do myself the honor of transmitting for the satisfaction of Congress. I am Sir with the greatest respect Yr
Most Obedt Servt

P.S. The Thirteen Militia Regiments from Connecticut being
reduced to a little more than Seven Hundred Men Rank &
file, fit for duty, I have thought proper to discharge the whole,
to save the States the immense charge that would arise for
Officer's pay—There are too, many Militia that have just come
in & on their way from that State, none of which are provided
with a Tent or a Single Camp Utensil. This distresses me beyond measure.

To Lund Washington

                         Col. Morris's, on the Heights of Harlem,
Dear Lund,   30 September, 1776.
     Your letter of the 18th, which is the only one received and
unanswered, now lies before me. The amazement which you
seem to be in at the unaccountable measures which have been
adopted by —— would be a good deal increased if I had time
to unfold the whole system of their management since this
time twelve months. I do not know how to account for the
unfortunate steps which have been taken but from that fatal
idea of conciliation which prevailed so long—fatal, I call it,

because from my soul I wish it may not prove so, though my fears lead me to think there is too much danger of it. This time last year I pointed out the evil consequences of short enlistments, the expenses of militia, and the little dependence that was placed in them. I assured —— that the longer they delayed raising a standing army, the more difficult and chargeable would they find it to get one, and that, at the same time that the militia would answer no valuable purpose, the frequent calling them in would be attended with an expense, that they could have no conception of. Whether, as I have said before, the unfortunate hope of reconciliation was the cause, or the fear of a standing army prevailed, I will not undertake to say; but the policy was to engage men for twelve months only. The consequence of which, you have had great bodies of militia in pay that never were in camp; you have had immense quantities of provisions drawn by men that never rendered you one hour's service (at least usefully), and this in the most profuse and wasteful way. Your stores have been expended, and every kind of military destroyed by them; your numbers fluctuating, uncertain, and forever far short of report—at no one time, I believe, equal to twenty thousand men fit for duty. At present our numbers fit for duty (by this day's report) amount to 14,759, besides 3,427 on command, and the enemy within stone's throw of us. It is true a body of militia are again ordered out, but they come without any conveniences and soon return. I discharged a regiment the other day that had in it fourteen rank and file fit for duty only, and several that had less than fifty. In short, such is my situation that if I were to wish the bitterest curse to an enemy on this side of the grave, I should put him in my stead with my feelings; and yet I do not know what plan of conduct to pursue. I see the impossibility of serving with reputation, or doing any essential service to the cause by continuing in command, and yet I am told that if I quit the command inevitable ruin will follow from the distraction that will ensue. In confidence I tell you that I never was in such an unhappy, divided state since I was born. To lose all comfort and happiness on the one hand, whilst I am fully persuaded that under such a system of management as has been adopted, I cannot have the least chance for reputation, nor those allowances made which the nature of the case requires; and to be told, on the other, that if I leave the service all will be lost, is, at the same time that I am bereft of every peaceful moment, distressing to a degree. But I will be done with the subject, with the precaution to you that it is not a fit one to be publicly known or discussed. If I fall, it may not be amiss that these circumstances be known, and declaration made in credit to the justice of my character. And if the men will stand by me (which by the by I despair of), I am resolved not to be forced from this ground while I have life; and a few days will determine the point, if the enemy should not change their plan of operations; for they certainly will not—I am sure they ought not—to waste the season that is now fast advancing, and must be precious to them. I thought to have given you a more explicit account of my situation, expectation, and feelings, but I have not time. I am wearied to death all day with a variety of perplexing circumstances—disturbed at the conduct of the militia, whose behavior and want of discipline has done great injury to the other troops, who never had officers, except in a few instances, worth the bread they eat. My time, in short, is so much engrossed that I have not leisure for corresponding, unless it is on mere matters of public business.

I therefore in answer to your last Letter of the 18th shall say

With respect to the chimney, I would not have you for the sake of a little work spoil the look of the fireplaces, tho' that in the parlor must, I should think, stand as it does; not so much on account of the wainscotting, which I think must be altered (on account of the door leading into the new building,) as on account of the chimney piece and the manner of its fronting into the room. The chimney in the room above ought, if it could be so contrived, to be an angle chimney as the others are: but I would not have this attempted at the expence of pulling down the partition.—The chimney in the new room should be exactly in the middle of it—the doors and every thing else to be exactly answerable and uniform—in short I would have the whole executed in a masterly manner.

You ought surely to have a window in the gable end of the

new cellar (either under the Venitian window, or one on each side of it).

Let Mr. Herbert know that I shall be very happy in getting his brother exchanged as soon as possible, but as the enemy have more of our officers than we of theirs, and some of ours have been long confined (and claim ye right of being first exchanged,) I do not know how far it may be in my power at this time, to comply with his desires.

Remember me to all our neighbors and friends, particularly to Colo. Mason, to whom I would write if I had time to do it fully and satisfactorily. Without this, I think the correspondence on my part would be unavailing—I am with truth and sincerity, Dr Lund yr affect'e friend.

To the Massachusetts General Court

Gentn   White plains Novr the 6th 1776

The situation of our Affairs is critical and truly alarming; The dissolution of our Army is fast approaching and but little, if any prospect of levying a New one in a reasonable time. A large part of it under the denomination of New Levies, are now on the eve of their departure, and this at a time when the Enemy have a very numerous & formidable force, watching an Opportunity to execute their plans, and to spread ruin and devastation among us. Impressed with the importance of these matters, I this day laid them before a Council of General Officers with a view of obtaining their Opinion upon the same, and of the measures which in their Judgement should be immediately adopted. The result was, that I should apply to several of the States for supplies of Militia, and that your Honble Assembly should be requested to furnish as soon as possible, Four thousand as their Quota to be properly accoutred and equipped with every necessary to supply the place of those who are now here under Genl Lincoln, and who I fear will not be prevailed on to stay longer than the time they engaged for at first. The hope and probability of raising a New Army within a convenient time, are so little, and the consequences so evidently alarming if a sufficient force is not kept up to counteract the designs of the Enemy in the mean time, that the Council and myself have unanimously agreed, that the Militia should be engaged if possible to continue 'till the 1st of March unless their return can be sooner dispensed with. we flatter ourselves by that time, if not long before, such an Army will be levyed, as to render any future claims upon them unless in cases of the most pressing emergency, altogether unnecessary.

From the experience I have had of your past exertions in times of difficulty, I know that nothing in your power to effect will be wanting, and with the greatest confidence I trust that the present requisition will have your most ready approbation and compliance, being in some degree anticipated by the Inquiry you have directed to be made into the State of our Affairs, and whether any further Aid will be necessary. I have the Honor to be with great respect Gentn Yr most Obedt Servt

To John Augustine Washington

Dear Brother,   White plains Novr 6th 1776.

I have had the pleasure to receive your Letter of the 6th Ulto. We have, I think, by one Manouvre and another, and with a parcel of—but it is best to say nothing more about them—Mixed, & ungovernable Troops, spun the Campaign out to this time without coming to any decisive Action, or without letting Genl How obtain any advantage which, in my opinion, can contribute much to the completion of the business he is come upon, or to the Honour and glory of the British Arms, and those of their Auxilaries—Our numbers from the Beginning have been disjointed and confused, and much less than were apprehended. had we ever hazarded a general Action with them therefore, unless it had been in our Works at New York, or Harlem heights, we undoubtedly should have risked a good cause upon a very unfavourable Issue.

Whilst we lay at the upper end of York Island (or the heights of Harlem) How suddenly Landed from the best Accts we cd get, about 16,000 Men above us, on a place called Frogs point on the East River, or Sound, this obliged Us, as his design was evidently to surround us, & cut of our Communication with the Country, thereby stopping all Supplies of Provisions (of which we were very scant) to remove our Camp and out Flank him, which we have done, & by degrees got Strongly posted on advantageous Grounds at this place.

It is not in my power to furnish you with so extensive a Draft as you require, as I have none but printed Maps of the Country you want to see deleniated, & have no person about me that has time enough to Copy one, but a rough sketch of the Country in wch we have been Manouvreing, & which I had taken off to carry in my pocket, I enclose you, as it will afford some Idea of the parts adjacent to New York.

Novr 19th at Hackensac: I began this Letter at the White plains as you will see by the first part of it; but by the time I had got thus far the Enemy advanced a Second time (for they had done it once before, & after engaging some Troops which I had posted on a Hill, & driving them from it with the loss of abt 300 killed & wounded to them, & little more than half the number to us) as if they meant a genel Attack but finding us ready to receive them, & upon such ground as they could not approach without loss, they filed of & retreated towards New York.

As it was conceived that this Manouvre was done with a design to attack Fort Washington (near Harlem heights) or to throw a body of Troops into the Jerseys, or what might be still worse, aim a stroke at Philadelphia, I hastend over on this side with abt 5000 Men by a round about March (wch we were obliged to take on Acct of the shipping opposing the passage at all the lower Ferries) of near 65 Miles, but did not get hear time enough to take Measures to save Fort Washington tho I got here myself a day or two before it surrendered, which happened on the 16th Instt after making a defence of about 4 or 5 hours only.

We have no particular Acct of the loss on either side, or of the Circumstances attending this matter, the whole Garrison after being drove from the out lines & retiring within the Fort surrendered themselves Prisoners of War, and giving me no

Acct of the terms. By a Letter wch I have just receivd from
Genl Greene at Fort Lee (wch is opposite to Fort Washington) I am informd that "one of the Train of Artillery came
across the River last Night on a Raft—by his Acct the Enemy
have suffered greatly on the North side of Fort Washington—
Colo. Rawlings's Regiment (late Hugh Stephenson's) was
posted there, and behaved with great Spirit—Colo. Magaw
could not get the Men to Man the Lines, otherwise he would
not have given up the Fort."

This is a most unfortunate affair and has given me great
Mortification as we have lost not only two thousand Men that
were there, but a good deal of Artillery, & some of the best
Arms we had. And what adds to my Mortification is, that this
Post after the last Ships went by it, was held contrary to my
Wishes & opinion; as I conceived it to be a dangerous one:
but being determind on by a full Council of General Officers,
& receiving a resolution of Congress strongly expressive of
their desires, that the Channel of the River (which we had
been labouring to stop a long while at this place) might be
obstructed, if possible; & knowing that this could not be done
unless there were Batteries to protect the Obstruction I did
not care to give an absolute Order for withdrawing the Garrison till I could get round & see the Situation of things &
then it became too late as the Fort was Invested. I had given
it, upon the passing of the last Ships, as my opinion to Genl
Greene under whose care it was, that it would be best to
evacuate the place—but—as the order was discretionary, & his
opinion differed from mine, it unhappyly was delayd too long,
to my great grief, as I think Genl Howe considering his Army
& ours, would have had but a poor tale to have told without
it & would have found it difficult, unless some Southern Expedition may prove successful, to have reconciled the People
of England to the Conquest of a few pitiful Islands, none of
wch were defensable considering the great number of their
ships & the power they have by Sea to Surround & render
them unapproachable.

Your Letter of the 30th of Octr was delivered to me a few
days ago by Colo. Woodford—It is a matter of great grief and
surprize to me, to find the different States so slow, and inattentive to that essential business of levying their quota's of

Men—In ten days from this date, there will not be above 2000 Men, if that, on this Side Hudson's River (of the fixed & establish'd Regiments) to oppose Howes whole Army, and very little more on the other to secure the Eastern Colonies and the Important Passes leading through the Highlands to Albany & the Country about the Lakes. In short it is impossible for me in the compass of a Letter to give you any Idea of our Situation—of my difficulties—& the constant perplexities & mortifications I constantly meet with, derived from the unhappy policy of short enlistments, & delaying them too long. Last fall or Winter; before the Army which was then to be raised, was set about, I represented in clear & explicit terms the evils wch would arise from short Inlistments—the expence that must attend the raising of an Army every year—the futility of such an Army when raised; and, in a word, if I had spoke with a prophetick spirit, could not have foretold the evils with more accuracy than I did—all the year since I have been pressing them to delay no time in engaging Men upon such terms as would Insure success, telling them that the longer it was delayed the more difficult it would grow; but the measure was not set about till it was too late to be effected, & then in such a manner as to bid adieu to every hope of getting an Army from which any Services are to be expected. the different States without regard to the merits or qualifications of an Officer, quarrelling about the appointments; & nominating such as are not fit to be Shoe Blacks from the local attachments of this or that Member of Assembly.

I am wearied almost to death with the retrograde Motions of things, and Solemnly protest that a pecuniary rewd of 20,000 £s a year would not induce me to undergo what I do; and after all perhaps, to loose my Character as it is impossible, under such a variety of distressing Circumstances to conduct Matters agreeable to public expectation or even of those who employ me—as they will not make proper allowances for the difficulties their own errors have occasioned.

I am glad to find by your last Letter that your family are tolerably well recoverd from the Indispositions they labourd under. God grant you all health & happiness—nothing in this world would contribute so much to mine as to be once more

fixed among you in the peaceable enjoymt of my own vine,
& fig Tree. Adieu my dear Sir—remember me Affectionately
to my Sister & the Family, & give my Compliments to those
who enquire after Yr Sincerely Affectionate Brother

To John Hancock

Sir   Trenton Decr 5th 1776
   As nothing but necessity obliged me to retire before the
Enemy, & leave so much of the Jerseys unprotected, I conceive it my duty, and it corresponds with my Inclination to
make head against them so soon as there shall be the least
probability of doing it with propriety. That the Country might
in some measure be covered, I left two Brigades consisting of
the Five Virginia Regiments and that of Delaware, containing
in the whole about 1200 Men fit for duty, under the command
of Lord Stirling & Genl Stephen at Princeton, till the Baggage
& Stores could cross the Delaware, or the Troops under their
respective commands should be forced from thence. I shall
now, having removed the greatest part of the above Articles,
face about with such Troops as are here fit for service, and
march back to Princeton and there govern myself by circumstances and the movements of Genl Lee. At any event the
Enemy's progress may be retarded by this means, if they intend to come on, & the Peoples fears in some measure qui-
eted, if they do not. Sorry I am to observe however, that the
frequent calls upon the Militia of this State—the want of exertion in the Principal Gentlemen of the Country—or a fatal
supineness and insensibility of danger, till it is too late to prevent an evil, that was not only foreseen, but foretold, have
been the causes of our late disgraces. If the Militia of this State
had stepped forth in Season, and timely notice they had, we
might have prevented the Enemy's crossing the Heckenseck,
although without some previous notice of the time & place it
was impossible to have done this at the North River. We might
with equal probability of success, have made a stand at Brunswic on the Rariton; but as both these Rivers were fordable in
a variety of Places, (knee deep only) it required many men

to defend the passes & these we had not. At Heckenseck our force was insufficient, because a part was at Elizabeth Town, Amboy & Brunswick, guarding a Coast which I thought most exposed to danger—and at Brunswic, because I was disappointed in my expectation of Militia, and because on the day of the Enemy's approach, and probably the occasion of it, the term of the Jersey & Maryland Brigades service expired, neither of which would consent to stay an hour longer.

These among Ten thousand other Instances might be adduced to shew the disadvantages of Short inlistments & the little dependance upon Militia in times of real danger; But as yesterday cannot be recalled, I will not dwell upon a Subject which no doubt has given much uneasiness to Congress, as well as extreme pain and anxiety to myself. My first wish is, That Congress may be convinced of the impropriety of relying upon the Militia, and of the necessity of raising a larger standing Army than what they have voted. The saving in the article of Stores, Provisions and in a thousand other things, by having nothing to do with Militia unless in cases of extraordinary exigency, & such as could not be expected in the common course of events, would amply support a large Army, which well officered would be daily improving, instead of continuing a destructive, expensive, disorderly Mob.

I am clear in Opinion, that if 40,000 Men had been kept in constant pay since the first commencement of Hostilities, and the Militia had been excused doing duty during that period, the Continent would have saved Money. When I reflect on the losses we have sustained for want of good Troops, the certainty of this is placed beyond a doubt in my mind. In such case the Militia, who have been harrassed & tired by repeated calls upon them, and farming & manufactures in a manner suspended, would upon any pressing emergency have run with alacrity to Arms, Whereas the cry now is, they may be as well ruined in one way as another, & with difficulty are obtained. I mention these things to shew, that in my Opinion, if any dependance is placed in the Militia another year, Congress will be deceived. When danger is a little removed from them, they will not turn out at all—When it comes Home to 'em, the well affected instead of flying to Arms to defend themselves, are busily employed in removing their Families & Effects, whilst the disaffected are concerting measures to make their submission & spread terror & dismay all around to induce others to follow the example. daily experience & abundant proofs warrant this information.

I shall this day reinforce Lord Stirling with about 1200 Men which will make his Numbers about 2400—to morrow I mean to repair to Princeton myself & shall order the Pensylvania Troops (who are not yet arrived, except part of the German Batallion & a Company of Light Infantry), to the same place.

By my last advices the Enemy are still at Brunswic, and the Account adds that Genl Howe was expected at Elizabeth Town with a reinforcement to erect the King's Standard and demand a submission of this State. I can only give this as a report brought from the Enemys Camp by some of the Country people. I have the Honor to be with great respect Sir Yr Most Obedt Servt

To Lund Washington

Falls of Delaware So. Side
Dear Lund,   10th Decr 1776.

Hurried as I am and distressed by a number of perplexing circumstances I will write you a few Lines in acknowledgment of yr Letters of the 20th & 26th Ulto.

I wish to Heaven it was in my power to give you a more favourable Acct of our situation than it is—our numbers, quite inadequate to the task of opposing that part of the Army under the Command of Genl Howe, being reduced by Sickness, Desertion, & Political Deaths (on & before the first Instt, & having no assistance from the Militia) were obliged to retire before the Enemy, who were perfectly well informd of our Situation till we came to this place, where I have no Idea of being able to make a stand, as My numbers, till joind by the Philadelphia Militia did not exceed 3000 Men fit for duty—now we may be about 5000 to oppose Howes whole Army, that part of it excepted which saild under the Comd. of General Clinton. I tremble for Philadelphia, nothing in my opinion but General Lee's speedy arrival, who has been long expected, thô still at a distance (with about 3000 Men) can save it. We have brought over, and destroyed, all the Boats we could lay our hands on, upon the Jersey Shore for many Miles above and below this place; but it is next to impossible to guard a Shore for 60 Miles with less than half the Enemys numbers; when by force, or Stratagem they may suddenly attempt a passage in many different places. at present they are Incamp'd or quarterd along the other shore above & below us (rather this place for we are obliged to keep a face towards them) for fifteen Miles.

If you can get some Holly Trees to plant upon the Circular Banks in the manner, or rather thicker than I did a year or two ago I should be glad of it—or if good & well set Holly can not be had then young & strait bodied Pines will do. If you have a mind to try the Sycamore upon some of the cross Banks in the Neck, or elsewhere I have no objection to the experiment; but it runs in my head that I have heard of some objection to the Sycamore—near to, or upon the Land of Colo. Warner Lewis in Gloucester, I have seen neglected hedges of it; but to what cause I know not. perhaps Colo. Fieldg Lewis (who I think it was told me they did not answer) can tell. The honey locust must, I should think, be better, if to be had.

If you can get a good match (and a young horse) for the Stallion, I should like it very well—but let the match be good, & the Horse handsome. the hurried situation I am in at present allows me no time, or indeed any body to spare, to send the Horses I promis'd—Mrs Washington must therefore make the old greys serve her a little while longer, I think if there can be any possible shift made, without buying Linnen for the Negros at the enormous price you speak of, it ought to be attempted, as the price is too heavy to be borne with (if it be possible to avoid it) without making the poor Negros suffer too much—this I would not do to save any expence, as they certainly have a just claim to their Victuals and cloaths, if they make enough to purchase them.

Decr 17th Ten Miles above the Falls. This Letter was wrote in order to send you by the last Post, but in the multiplicity & hurry of my business I forgot that I had wrote it, and therefore it was not sent.

I have since moved up to this place to be more convenient to our great and extensive defence of this River. hitherto by our destruction of the Boats, and vigilance in watching the Fords of the River above the Falls (which are now rather high) we have prevented them from crossing; but how long we shall be able to do it, God only knows, as they are still hovering about the River, and if every thing else fails will wait till the first of Jany when their will be no other Men to oppose them but Militia, none of which but those from Philadelphia mentiond in the first part of this Letter, are yet come (tho I am told some are expected from the back Counties) when I say none but Militia, I am to except the Virginia Regiments & the shatterd remains of Smallwoods which by fatiegue, want of Cloaths &ca &ca are reduced to nothing; Weedons which was the strongest, not having more than between One hundd & thirty & 40 Men fit for duty; the rest being in the Hospitals. The unhappy policy of short Inlistments, and a dependance upon Militia will, I fear, prove the downfall of our cause, tho early pointed out with an almost Prophetick Spirit.

Our Cause has also receivd a severe blow in the Captivity of General Lee—Unhappy Man! taken by his own Imprudence! going three or four Miles from his own Camp to lodge, & within 20 of the Enemy; notice of which by a rascally Tory being given, a party of light Horse siez'd him in the Morning after travelling all Night & carried him off in high triumph, and with every Mark of Indignity—not even suffering him to get his Hat, or Sartout Coat. the Troops that were under his Command are not yet come up with us, though I think they may be expected to morrow. A large part of the Jerseys have given every proof of disaffection that a people can do, & this part of Pensylvania are equally inemical; in short your immagination can scarce extend to a situation more distressing than mine—Our only dependance now, is upon the Speedy Inlistment of a New Army; if this fails us, I think the game will be pretty well up, as from disaffection, and want of spirit & fortitude, the Inhabitants instead of resistance, are offering Submission, & taking protections from Genl Howe in Jersey.

I send you by Mr Mercer a very pretty Mare, but rather too small (if she had ever been broke to it) for the draft—I also send you a very likely, as well as a very good Horse to match the Bay you have for Mrs Washington; but as he has been badly cut, he is exceeding troublesome, being very vicious; as much so I think after Mares, as any Stallion I ever met with— buy the Horse you spoke of, & if you have any Money to spare, of mine, I should be glad to have it laid out in young Mares for Breeders.

Matters to my view, but this I say in confidence to you, as a friend, wears so unfavourable an aspect (not that I apprehend half so much danger from Howes Army, as from the disaffection of the three States of New York, Jersey & Pensylvania) that I would look forward to unfavorable Events, & prepare Accordingly in such a manner however as to give no alarm or suspicion to any one; as one step towards it, have my Papers in such a Situation as to remove at a short notice in case an Enemy's Fleet should come up the River—When they are removd let them go immediately to my Brothers in Berkeley.

Since writing the above I have determind to send Mrs Washington another Horse for her Chariot, which with the one before mentiond, the one you have, and the one you are to buy, will make a very good set, if you can purchase a good one and likely—the two I send are exceeding good Horses, and Young, the lightest of the two Bays is an exceeding tough, hardy horse as any in the World, but rather lazy—he will do well for the Postilian before.

My best remembrance to all friends with sincere regard I am Yr Affecte friend

P.S. If you could exchange the old Greys for young Mares, it would be a good way of getting quit of them. If I never did, in any of my Letters, desire you to Plant locusts across from the New Garden to the Spinning House as the Wall is to run from the end of the Sunk Wall (& on that side of it next the Quarter) as also as the other Wall from the old Garden gate to the Smoke House or Hen House (and on the lower side of it) I must request it now in this Letter. let them be tall and strait bodyed and about Eight or ten feet to the first Limbs— plant them thick enough for the limbs to Interlock when the Trees are grown for Instance 15 or 16 feet a part.

The young Gentlemen who carry my Horses home should be assisted by you in getting to Fredericksburg—may be they would purchase some of yr Greys.

To John Hancock

Sir   Head Quarters Newtown 27th Decemr 1776.

I have the pleasure of congratulating you upon the Success of an Enterprize, which I had formed against a Detatchment of the Enemy lying in Trenton, and which was executed yesterday Morning.

The Evening of the 25th I ordered the Troops intended for this Service to parade back of McKonkey's Ferry, that they might begin to pass as soon as it grew dark, imagining we should be able to throw them all over, with the necessary Artillery, by 12 OClock, and that we might easily arrive at Trenton by five in the Morning, the distance being about nine Miles. But the quantity of Ice, made that Night, impeded the passage of Boats so much, that it was three OClock before the Artillery could all be got over, and near four, before the Troops took up their line of march.

This made me despair of surprizing the Town, as I well knew we could not reach it before the day was fairly broke, but as I was certain there was no making a Retreat without being discovered, and harassed on repassing the River, I determined to push on at all Events. I formed my Detachment into two divisions one to march by the lower or River road, the other, by the upper or Pennington Road. As the Divisions had nearly the same distance to march, I ordered each of them, immediately upon forcing the out Guards, to push directly into the Town, that they might charge the Enemy before they had time to form. The upper division arrived at the Enemys advanced post, exactly at eight OClock, and in three Minutes after, I found from the fire on the lower Road that, that Division had also got up. The Out Guards made but small Opposition, tho', for their Numbers, they behaved very well, keeping up a constant retreating fire from behind Houses.

We presently saw their main Body formed, but from their Motions, they seem'd undetermined how to act.

Being hard pressed by our Troops, who had already got possession of part of their Artillery, they attempted to file off by a road on their right leading to Princetown, but perceiving their Intention, I threw a Body of Troops in their Way which immediately checked them. Finding from our disposition, that they were surrounded, and that they must inevitably be cut to peices if they made any further Resistance, they agreed to lay down their Arms. The Number, that submitted in this manner, was 23 Officers and 886 Men. Colo. Rall the commanding Officer and seven others were found wounded in the Town. I dont exactly know how many they had killed, but I fancy not above twenty or thirty, as they never made any regular Stand. Our Loss is very trifling indeed, only two Officers and one or two privates wounded.

I find, that the Detatchment of the Enemy consisted of the three Hessian Regiments of Lanspatch, Kniphausen and Rohl amounting to about 1500 Men, and a Troop of British Light Horse; but immediately, upon the beginning of the Attack, all those, who were not killed or taken, pushed directly down the Road towards Bordentown. These would likewise have fallen into our hands, could my plan have been compleatly carried into Execution. Genl Ewing was to have crossed before day at Trenton Ferry, and taken possession of the Bridge leading out of Town, but the Quantity of Ice was so great, that tho' he did every thing in his power to effect it, he could not get over. This difficulty also hindered Genl Cadwallader from crossing, with the Pennsylvania Militia, from Bristol, he got part of his Foot over, but finding it impossible to embark his Artillery, he was obliged to desist. I am fully confident, that could the Troops, under Generals Ewing and Cadwallader, have passed the River, I should have been able, with their Assistance, to have driven the Enemy from all their posts below Trenton. But the Numbers I had with me, being inferior to theirs below me, and a strong Battalion of Light Infantry being at Princetown above me, I thought it most prudent to return the same Evening, with the prisoners and the Artillery we had taken. We found no Stores of any Consequence in the Town.

In justice to the Officers and Men, I must add, that their Behaviour upon this Occasion, reflects the highest honor upon them. The difficulty of passing the River in a very severe Night, and their March thro' a violent Storm of Snow and Hail, did not in the least abate their Ardour. But when they came to the Charge, each seemed to vie with the other in pressing forward, and were I to give a preferance to any particular Corps, I should do great injustice to the others.

Colo. Baylor, my first Aid de Camp, will have the honor of delivering this to you, and from him you may be made acquainted with many other particulars; his spirited Behaviour upon every Occasion, requires me to recommend him to your particular Notice. I have the Honor to be with great Respect Sir Your most obt Servt

Inclosed you have a particular List of the Prisoners, Artillery and other Stores.

To Robert Morris, George Clymer, and George Walton

Head Quarters, Trenton, January 1, 1777.

Gentn.: I have the honor and pleasure of acknowledging your favors of the 28th and 31st December and Mr. Morris's of the 30th and 31st. The Messenger delivered me the two parcels of hard Money, which I suppose will turn out agreeable to the list, having not had time to count it.

The Sum that is lodged at Ticonderoga shall be ordered down, provided the Commander in the Northern Department, finds no better use for it there, than I can make of it here.

The Accounts you give me, in yours of the 28 Ulto. of the good effects that are likely to flow from our Success at Trenton, add not a little to the Satisfaction I have felt on that occasion. You are pleased to pay me many personal Compliments, as if the Merit of that affair, was due solely to me; but

I assure you, the other General Officers, who assisted me in the plan and Execution, have full as good a right to your Encomiums as myself. We are devising such Measures, as I hope, if they succeed, will add as much or more to the distress of the Enemy, than their defeat at Trenton, and I promise myself the greatest Advantages from having engaged a number of the Eastern Troops, to stay Six Weeks beyond their time of Inlistment, upon giving a Bounty of Ten dollars. This I know is a most extravagant price, when compared to the time of Service; but the Example was set by the State of Pennsylvania, with respect to their Militia, and I thought it no time to stand upon Trifles, when a Body of firm Troops, inured to danger, were absolutely necessary to lead on the more raw and undisciplined.

I shall know this day how many of Colo Glover's Regt. are willing to continue in the land Service. I dont expect many will be prevailed upon to stay, and I will endeavour to procure the rest for the purpose of fitting out the Frigates upon the best terms I can.

The future and proper disposition of the Hessian Prisoners, struck me in the same light in which you view it, for which Reason I advised the Council of Safety to seperate them from their Officers, and canton them in the German Counties. If proper pains are taken to convince them, how preferable the Situation of their Countrymen, the Inhabitants of those Counties is to theirs, I think they may be sent back in the Spring, so fraught with a love of Liberty and property too, that they may create a disgust to the Service among the remainder of the foreign Troops and widen that Breach which is already opened between them and the British.

Yours of the 31st of last Month, incloses me sundry Resolves of Congress, by which I find they have done me the honor to intrust me with powers, in my Military Capacity, of the highest nature and almost unlimited in extent. Instead of thinking myself free'd from all *civil* Obligations, by this mark of their Confidence, I shall constantly bear in mind, that as the Sword was the last Resort for the preservation of our Liberties, so it ought to be the first thing laid aside, when those Liberties are firmly established. I shall instantly set about making the most necessary Reforms in the Army; but it will not be in my power to make so great a progress, as if I had a little leisure time upon my Hands.

Mr. Morris has my sincere thanks for the advice and Assistance he promises to give Mr. Commissary Wharton, and I beg he would remind him, that all his Exertions will be necessary, to Support an Army in this exhausted Country. I have &ca.

P.S. My best thanks to Mr. Morris for procuring the Qr. Cask Wine, which is not yet got to hand.

To John Hancock

Pluckamin, January 5, 1777.

Sir: I have the honor to inform you, that since the date of my last from Trenton I have remov'd with the Army under my Command to this place. The difficulty of crossing the Delaware on Acct. of the Ice made our passage over it tedeous, and gave the Enemy an oppertunity of drawing in their Several Cantonments, and assembling their whole Force at Princeton. Their large Picquets, advanc'd towards Trenton; their great preparations, and some Intelligence I had received, added to their knowledge that the first of Janry. brought on a dissolution of the best part of our Army, gave me the strongest reasons to conclude that an attack upon us was meditating.

Our Situation was most critical and our strength small; to remove immediately, was again destroying every dawn of hope which had begun to revive in the breasts of the Jersey Militia, and to bring those Troops which had first cross'd the Delaware, and were laying at Crosswixs under Genl. Cadwallader, and those under Genl. Mifflin at Bordenton (amounting in the whole to abt. 3600) to Trenton, was bringing of them to an exposed place; one or the other however, was unavoidable; the latter was prefered, and these Troops orderd to join us at Trenton which they did by a Night March on the first Instt.

On the Second, according to my expectation, the Enemy began to advance upon us, and after some skirmishing, the head of their Column reach'd Trenton about 4 O'Clock whilst their rear was as far back as Maidenhead; they attempted to pass Sanpinck Creek (which runs through Trenton) at different places, but finding the Fords guarded, halted, and kindled their Fires. We were drawn up on the other Side of the Creek. In this Situation we remain till dark canonading the Enemy, and receiving the Fire of their Field pieces, which did us but little damage.

Having by this time discoverd that the Enemy were greatly Superior in Numbers, and that their drift was to surround us. I orderd all our Baggage to be removd silently to Burlington soon after dark, and at twelve O'Clock (after renewing our Fires, and leaving Guards at the Bridge in Trenton, and other passes on the same stream above March'd by a round about road to Princeton where I knew they could not have much force left, and might have Stores. One thing I was sure of, that it would avoid the appearance of a Retreat, which (was of Consequence) or to run the hazard of the whole Army's being cut of was unavoidable whilst we might, by a fortunate stroke withdraw Genl. Howe from Trenton, give some reputation to our Arms; happily we succeeded. We found Princeton about Sunrise with only three Regiments of Infantry and three Troops of Light Horse in it, two of which were upon their March for Trenton; these three Regiments (especially the two first) made a gallant resistance and in killed, wounded and Prisoners must have lost near 500 Men upwards of one hundred of them were left dead in the Field, and with what I have with me, and what was taken in the pursuit, and carried across the Delaware, there are near 300 Prisoners, 14 of wch. are Officers, all British.

This piece of good fortune, is counterballanced by the loss of the brave and worthy Genl. Mercer, and several other valuable Officers who were slain in the Field and have since died of their Wounds. Our whole loss cannot be ascertained, as many who were in pursuit of the Enemy (who were chased three or four Miles) are not yet come in. Our Slain in the Field was about 30.

The rear of the Enemy's army laying at Maidenhead (not more than five or Six Miles from Princeton) were up with us before our pursuit was over, but as I had the precaution to destroy the Bridge over Stony Brooke (about half a Mile from the Field of Action) they were so long retarded there, as to give us time to move of in good order for this place. We took two Brass Field pieces from them, but for want of Horses could not bring them of. We also took some Blankets, Shoes, and a few other trifling Articles, Burnt the Hay and destroyed such other things as the Shortness of the time would admit of.

My original plan when I set out from Trenton was to have pushed on to Brunswick, but the harrassed State of our own Troops (many of them having had no rest for two Nights and a day) and the danger of loosing the advantage we had gaind by aiming at too much, Induced me, by the advice of my Officers, to relinquish the attempt but in my judgment Six or Eight hundred fresh Troops upon a forcd March would have destroyed all their Stores, and Magazines; taken (as we have since learnt) their Military Chest containing 70,000 £ and put an end to the War. The Enemy from the best Intelligence I have been able to get, were so much alarmed at the apprehension of this, that they March'd immediately to Brunswick without Halting (except at the Bridges, for I also took up those on Millstone on the different routs to Brunswick) and got there before day.

From the best Information I have received, Genl. Howe has left no Men either at Trenton or Princeton; the truth of this I am endeavouring to ascertain that I may regulate my movements accordingly. The Militia are taking Spirit, and, I am told, are coming in fast from this State; but I fear those from Philadelphia will scarce Submit to the hardships of a Winter Campaign much longer, especially as they very unluckily sent their Blankets with their Baggage to Burlington; I must do them the justice however to add, that they have undergone more fatigue and hardship than I expected Militia (especially Citizens) would have done at this Inclement Season. I am just moving to Morristown where I shall endeavour to put them under the best cover I can, hitherto we have lain without any, many of our poor Soldiers quite bearfoot and ill clad in other respects. I am &c.

Proclamation Concerning Loyalists

Whereas several persons, inhabitants of the United States of America, influenced by inimical motives, intimidated by the threats of the enemy, or deluded by a Proclamation issued the 30th of November last, by Lord and General Howe, stiled the King's Commissioners for granting pardons, &c. (now at open war, and invading these states), have been so lost to the interest and welfare of their country, as to repair to the enemy, sign a declaration of fidelity, and in some instances have been compelled to take oaths of allegiance to and engage not to take up arms, or encourage others so to do, against the King of Great-Britain; And whereas it has become necessary to distinguish between the friends of America and those of Great-Britain, inhabitants of these States; and that every man who receives protection from, and as a subject of any State, (not being conscientiously scrupulous against bearing arms), should stand ready to defend the same against hostile invasion; I do therefore, in behalf of the United States, by virtue of the powers committed to me by Congress, hereby strictly command and require every person, having subscribed such declaration, taken such oath, and accepted such protection and certificates from Lord and General Howe or any person under their authority forthwith to repair to Head-Quarters, or to the quarters of the nearest general officer of the Continental Army, or Militia, (until further provision can be made by the Civil Authority,) and there deliver up such protections, certificates and passports, and take the oath of allegiance to the United States of America. Nevertheless hereby granting full Liberty to all such as prefer the interest and protection of Great-Britain to the freedom and happiness of their country, forthwith to withdraw themselves and families within the enemy's lines; and I do hereby declare, that all and every person, who may neglect or refuse to comply with this order, within Thirty days from the date hereof, will be deemed adherents to the King of Great-Britain, and treated as common enemies of the American States.

Given at Head-Quarters, Morris-Town, January 25, 1777.

To Benedict Arnold

Head Quarters, Morris Town, April 3, 1777.

Dear Sir: I was this day favoured with yours of the 26th. last Month and a few days ago with that of the 11th.

It is needless for me to say much upon a Subject, which must undoubtedly give you a good deal of uneasiness. I confess I was surprised, when I did not see your name in the list of Major Generals, and was so fully of opinion that there was some mistake in the matter, that I (as you may recollect) desired you not to take any hasty Step, before the intention of Congress was fully known. The point does not now admit of a doubt, and is of so delicate a nature, that I will not even undertake to advise, your own feelings must be your guide. As no particular charge is alledged against you, I do not see upon what ground you can demand a Court of inquiry. Besides, public Bodies are not amenable for their Actions; They place and displace at pleasure, and all the satisfaction that an individual can obtain, when he is overlooked, is, if innocent, a consciousness that he has not deserved such treatment for his honest exertions. Your determination, not to quit your present Command, while any danger to the public might ensue from your leaving it, deserves my thanks, and justly entitles you to the thanks of your Country.

General Greene, who has lately been at Philadelphia, took occasion to inquire upon what principle the Congress proceeded in their late promotion of General Officers. He was informed, that the Members from each State seemed to insist upon having a proportion of Genl. Officers, adequate to the number of Men which they furnish, and that as Connecticut had already two Major Generals, it was their full share. I confess this is a strange mode of reasoning, but it may serve to shew you, that the promotion which was due to your Seniority, was not overlooked for want of Merit in you. I am etc.

To Alexander Spotswood

Head Quarters, Morris Town, April 30, 1777.
Sir: I want to form a Company for my Guard. In doing this I wish to be extremely cautious; because it is more than probable, that in the Course of the Campaign, my Baggage, Papers, and other Matters of great public Import, may be committed to the Sole care of these Men. This being premised, in order to impress you with proper attention in the Choice, I have to request that you will immediately furnish me with four Men of your Regiment, And, as it is my further wish, that this Company should look well and be nearly of a Size, I desire that none of the Men may exceed in Stature 5 feet 10 Inches, nor fall Short of 5 feet 9 Inches, Sober, Young, Active and well made. When I recommend care in your Choice, I would be understood to mean Men of good Character in the Regiment, that possess the pride of appearing clean and Soldierlike. I am satisfied there can be no absolute security for the fidelity of this Class of people, but yet I think it most likely to be found in those who have Family Connections in the Country. You will therefore send me none but Natives, and Men of some property, if you have them. I must insist, that in making this Choice, you give no Intimation of my preference of Natives, as I do not want to create any invidious Distinction between them and the Foreigners. I am etc.

To James Warren

Head Quarters, Morris Town, May 23, 1777.
Dear Sir: Your favor of the 4th. instant was duly handed me. I am fully sensible of the zeal, your State has demonstrated, in the instances you recite, and in many more. With you, I consider them as great exertions, and as a decisive evidence of your inclination to do every thing in your power to advance the Common Cause. At the same time, whatever efforts have been, or can be made, are not more than adequate

to the exigency of our Situation. Tho' over sanguine and un-informed people may think differently, this is a most interesting and critical period, and will not countenance the least want of Activity or attention in any quarter. I have the highest confidence, that your State will not let the great object, we are contending for, be lost, or endangered, more than is unavoidable, by any such deficiency on their part.

Your repealing the offensive part of the Act you mention, is a proof of your justice and regard to the Sense of your Sister States. It certainly bore the features of a monopoly, and was liable to the interpretation put upon it; and, though I am ready to believe, it proceeded from impolitick, rather than Selfish, motives,—I am happy the Cause of complaint is removed, and the matter placed upon a more liberal footing.

I observe, your State is not a little alarmed at the prospect of an immediate invasion. Notwithstanding the intelligence from Europe, in some measure, warrants the Supposition of such an event and makes it proper not intirely to disregard it; yet I am clearly of opinion, it is not much to be apprehended.—It is by no means an eligible way to the conquest of this country; your State, from its union, numbers and Situation, being capable of a much better defence than perhaps any other; and it is presumable, the Enemy will make their attacks where Circumstances promise the greatest likelihood of Success. But, be this as it may, I cannot help disapproving the project of raising Colonial regiments for your defence, at least till the Continental are filled. It is easy to perceive, as you have yourself hinted, that it will have a direct tendency to defeat your endeavours, for compleating your quota of the United Army; and it would be the most wretched policy to weaken the hands of the Continent, under the mistaken Idea of Strengthening your own. It would also be well to consider, how far it might be consistent with propriety, in the pursuit of partial schemes, to put it out of your own power to fulfill what is required of you by the Continent.

If the Several States, by levying Troops on the particular establishment of each, leave but a Small Continental Army in the Field, it will be impossible effectually to watch the Motions of the Enemy, and oppose them where they may in reality direct their operations;—the consequences of which must be inevitably fatal. But if we have a sufficient Continental force on foot, we shall be able to watch them narrowly and counteract them wherever they may attempt to move.—Every State will find its Security in such an Army, whose sole business it will be to oppose the Enemy, wherever it is most requisite.—It cannot be imagined, that if your State were seriously attacked, a proportionate part of the Continental force would not be detached to Succour and protect it. My duty, inclination, and a regard to the safety of the whole would equally compel me to it.—What valuable end can then be answered to you, in the Step you propose to take, which can compensate for the irretrivable injury the common cause might sustain, from our not having a Sufficient Army in the field for the purposes of general opposition? The measure, injurious in every view, can only serve to burthen the State, with an unnecessary expence, which will be intirely its own; as the Troops intended to be raised will be for local and Colonial uses, and in diminution of the common force.

I see no advantage you can derive from such an impolitic Step, which would not be fully produced, by what I assured the Assembly, on a former occasion, should be done; which is,—That the Supernumerary Regiments adopted by you, should remain in your State, 'till the designs of the Enemy became so evident, as to convince us, their continuance would be no longer expedient, or useful. This assurance I repeat; and I beg you will communicate it in my name to them; earnestly recommending it to them, to relinquish the Scheme. Indeed Sir, on a Cool, dispassionate Survey of all Circumstances, it will be found replete with impolicy and danger; and I am persuaded that, either they have already, on mature deliberation laid it aside, or on a reconsideration of the matter will coincide with me in opinion, and correct the mistake. With great regard and respect, I am &c.

To John Hancock

At Midnight, Chester, September 11, 1777.

Sir: I am sorry to inform you, that in this day's engagement, we have been obliged to leave the enemy masters of the field. Unfortunately the intelligence received of the enemy's advancing up the Brandywine, and crossing at a ford about six miles above us, was uncertain and contradictory, notwithstanding all my pains to get the best. This prevented my making a disposition, adequate to the force with which the Enemy attacked us on the right; in consequence of which the troops first engaged, were obliged to retire before they could be reinforced. In the midst of the attack on the right, that body of the Enemy which remained on the other side of Chad's Ford, crossed it, and attacked the division there under the command of General Wayne and the light troops under General Maxwell who, after a severe conflict, also retired. The Militia under the command of Major Genl. Armstrong, being posted at a ford, about two miles below Chad's, had no opportunity of engaging. But though we fought under many disadvantages, and were from the causes, above mentioned obliged to retire, yet our loss of men is not, I am persuaded, very considerable, I beleive much less than the enemy's. We have also lost about seven or eight pieces of cannon, according to the best information I can at present obtain. The baggage having been previously moved off, is all secure, saving the men's Blankets, which being at their backs, many of them doubtless are lost.

I have directed all the Troops to Assemble behind Chester, where they are now arranging for this Night. Notwithstanding the misfortune of the day, I am happy to find the troops in good spirits; and I hope another time we shall compensate for the losses now sustained. The Marquis La Fayette was wounded in the leg, and Genl. Woodford in the hand. Divers other Officers were wounded and some Slain, but the number of either cannot now be ascertained. I have &ca.

P.S. It has not been in my power to send you earlier intelligence; the present being the first leisure moment I have had since the action.

To Richard Henry Lee

Matuchen Hill, Phila. Cty, October 17, 1777.
Dear Sir: Your favour of the 5th. Instant, as also that of the 11th. by Baron de Kalb, are both at hand. It is not in my power, at present, to answer your Query respecting the appointment of this Gentleman: But, Sir, if there is any truth in a report which has been handed to me; Vizt., that Congress hath appointed, or, as others say, are about to appoint, Brigadier Conway a Major General in this Army, it will be as unfortunate a measure as ever was adopted. I may add (and I think with truth) that it will give a fatal blow to the existence of the Army. Upon so interesting a subject, I must speak plain: The duty I owe my Country; the Ardent desire I have to promote its true Interests, and justice to Individuals requires this of me. General Conway's merit, then, as an Officer, and his importance in this Army, exists more in his own imagination, than in reality: For it is a maxim with him, to leave no service of his own untold, nor to want any thing which is to be obtained by importunity: But, as I do not mean to detract from him any merit he possesses, and only wish to have the matter taken up upon its true Ground, after allowing him every thing that his warmest Friends will contend for, I would ask, why the Youngest Brigadier in the service (for I believe he is so) should be put over the heads of all the Eldest? and thereby take Rank, and Command Gentlemen, who but Yesterday, were his Seniors; Gentlemen, who, I will be bold to say (in behalf of some of them at least) of sound judgment and unquestionable Bravery? If there was a degree of conspicuous merit in General Conway, unpossessed by any of his Seniors, the confusion which might be occasioned by it would stand warranted upon the principles of sound policy; for I do readily agree that this is no time for trifling; But, at the same time, I cannot subscribe to the fact, this truth I am very well assured of (though I have not directly, nor indirectly, exchanged a Word with any one of the Brigadiers on the subject; nor am I certain that any one of them has heard of the Appointment) that they will not serve under him. I leave you to guess, therefore, at the situation this Army would be in at

so important a Crisis, if this event should take place. These Gentlemen have feelings as Officers, and though they do not dispute the Authority of Congress to make Appointments, they will judge of the propriety of acting under them. In a Word, the service is so difficult, and every necessary so expensive, that almost all our Officers are tired out: Do not, therefore, afford them good pretexts for retiring: No day passes over my head without application for leave to resign; within the last six days, I am certain, twenty Commissions, *at least*, have been tendered to me. I must, therefore, conjure you, to conjure Congress to consider this matter well, and not by a real Act of injustice, compel some good Officers to leave the service, and thereby incur a train of evils unforeseen and irremidiable.

To Sum up the whole, I have been a Slave to the service: I have undergone more than most Men are aware of, to harmonize so many discordant parts; but it will be impossible for me to be of any further service, if such insuperable difficulties are thrown in my way.

You may believe me, my good Sir, that I have no Earthly views, but the public good, in what I have said. I have no prejudice against General Conway, nor desire to serve any other Brigadier, further than I think the cause will be benefitted by it; to bring which to a speedy and happy conclusion, is the most fervent wish of my Soul.

With respect to the wants of the Militia in the Articles of Clothing, you must be well convinced, that it is not in my power to supply them, in the smallest degree, when near one half of our own Men are rendered unfit for service for want of these Things. I can add no more at present, than that I am, etc.

To John Augustine Washington

Philadelphia County, October 18, 1777.
Dear Brother: Your kind and Affectionate Letters of the 21st. of Septr. and 2d. Instt. came Safe to hand. When my last to you was dated I know not, for truely I can say, that my

whole time is so much engross'd that I have scarce a moment (but sleeping ones) for relaxation, or to endulge myself in writing to a friend. The anxiety you have been under, on Acct. of this Army, I can easily conceive; would to God there had been less Cause for it; or, that our Situation at present, was such, as to promise much from it. The Enemy crossed the Schuylkill, which, by the by, above the Falls (and the Falls you know is only five Miles from the City) is as easily crossed in any place as Potomack Run, Aquia, or any other broad and Shallow Water. rather by stratagem; tho' I do not know that it was in our power to prevent it, as their Manœuvres made it necessary for us to attend to our Stores which lay at Reading, towards which they seemed bending their course, and the loss of which must have proved our Ruin. After they had crossed, we took the first favourable oppertunity of attacking them; this was attempted by a Nights March of fourteen Miles to Surprize them (which we effectually did) so far as reaching their Guards before they had notice of our coming, and but for a thick Fog rendered so infinitely dark at times, as not to distinguish friend from Foe at the distance of 30 Yards, we should, I believe, have made a decisive and glorious day of it. But Providence or some unaccountable something, designd it otherwise; for after we had driven the Enemy a Mile or two, after they were in the utmost confusion, and flying before us in most places, after we were upon the point, (as it appeard to every body) of grasping a compleat Victory, our own Troops took fright and fled with precipitation and disorder. how to acct. for this I know not, unless, as I before observed, the Fog represented their own Friends to them for a Reinforcement of the Enemy as we attacked in different Quarters at the same time, and were about closing the Wings of our Army when this happened. one thing indeed contributed not a little to our Misfortune, and that was want of Ammunition on the right wing, which began the Ingagement, and in the course of two hours and 40 Minutes which it lasted, had (many of them) expended the 40 Rounds which they took into the Field.

After the Ingagement we removd to a place about 20 Miles from the Enemy, to collect our Force together, to take care of our Wounded, get furnished with necessaries again, and be in a better posture, either for offensive, or defensive operations. We are now advancing towards the Enemy again, being at this time within 12 Miles.

Our loss in the late action was, in killed, wounded, and Missing, about 1000, but of the missing, many, I dare say took advantage of the times, and deserted. Genl. Nash of No. Carolina was Wounded and died two or three days after. Many valuable Officers of ours was also wounded and some killed. The Enemys loss is variously reported; none make it less than 1500 (killed and wounded) and many estimate it much larger. Genl. Agnew of theirs was certainly killed, many Officers wounded among whom some of distinction; this we certainly know that the Hospital at Philadelphia and several large Meeting Houses are filled with their wounded besides private Houses with the Horses. In a word, it was a bloody day; would to Heaven I could add, that it had been a more fortunate one for us.

Our distress on Acct. of Cloathing is great, and in a little time must be very Sensibly felt, unless some expedient can be hit upon to obtain them. We have since the Battle got in abt. 1200 Militia from Virginia; about the same number have gone off from this State and Jersey but others are promised in lieu of them, with truth however it may be said, that this State acts most infamously, the People of it I mean as we derive little or no assistance from them. In short they are, in a manner, totally, disaffected, or in a kind of Lethargy.

The Enemy are making vigorous efforts to remove the obstructions in the Delaware, and to possess themselves of the Works which have been constructed for the Defence of them. I am doing all I can in my present situation to save them, God only, knows which will succeed.

I very sincerely congratulate you on the change in your Family. tell the young couple, after wishing them joy of their union, that it is my sincere hope, that it will be as happy, and lasting as their present joys are boundless. the Inclosed Letter of thanks to my Sister for her elegant present you will please to deliver; and with sincere Affection for you all, I am, &c.

P.S. I had scarce finish'd this Letter when by express from the State of New York, I received the Important and glorious News which follows.

I most devoutly congratulate you, my Country, and every well wisher to the Cause on this Signal Stroke of Providence. Yrs. as before.

To Israel Putnam

Camp, 20 Miles from Philada., October 19, 1777.
Dear Sir: Your favor of the 16th. I received Yesterday morning, and was much obliged by the interesting contents. The defeat of Genl. Burgoyne is a most important event, and such as must afford the highest satisfaction to every well affected American breast. Should providence be pleased to crown our Arms in the course of the Campaign, with one more fortunate stroke, I think we shall have no great cause for anxiety respecting the future designs of Britain. I trust all will be well in his good time. The obvious intention of Sr. Henry Clinton, was to relieve Genl. Burgoyne and being disappointed in that by his surrender, I presume he will make an expeditious return. I am happy to find you at the Head of so respectable a force and flatter myself, if he should Land with a view to Action, tho I do not expect it, you will give us a happy account of him. I believe, from the bravery of the Garrison of Fort Montgomery, he purchased victory at no inconsiderable expence. Genl. Campbell was certainly killed. This they mention in their own printed account, but call him Colo. of the 52d Regt. He was a Genl. on the American Establishment, so declared in one of the Orderly Books which fell into our hands.

I have but little to add respecting the Situation of affairs here. They remain much as they were when I wrote you last. To remove the Obstructions in the River, seems to be a Capital object with the Enemy. Their attempts hitherto have not succeeded and I hope will not.

I am extremely sorry for the death of Mrs. Putnam and Sympathise with you upon the occasion. Remembering that all must die, and that she had lived to an honourable age, I hope you will bear the misfortune with that fortitude and complacency of mind, that become a Man and a Christian. I am etc.

To Thomas Conway

Sir: A Letter which I receivd last Night, contain the following paragraph.

In a Letter from Genl. Conway to Genl. Gates he says: "Heaven has been determind to save your Country; or a weak General and bad Councellors would have ruind it."

I am Sir Yr. Hble Servt.

c. November 5, 1777

General Orders

Head Quarters, at the Gulph, December 17, 1777. Parole Warwick.   Countersigns Woodbridge, Winchester.

The Commander in Chief with the highest satisfaction expresses his thanks to the officers and soldiers for the fortitude and patience with which they have sustained the fatigues of the Campaign. Altho' in some instances we unfortunately failed, yet upon the whole Heaven hath smiled on our Arms and crowned them with signal success; and we may upon the best grounds conclude, that by a spirited continuance of the measures necessary for our defence we shall finally obtain the end of our Warfare, Independence, Liberty and Peace. These are blessings worth contending for at every hazard. But we hazard nothing. The power of America alone, duly exerted, would have nothing to dread from the force of Britain. Yet we stand not wholly upon our ground. France yields us every aid we ask, and there are reasons to believe the period is not very distant, when she will take a more active part, by declaring war against the British Crown. Every motive therefore, irresistably urges us, nay commands us, to a firm and manly perseverance in our opposition to our cruel oppressors, to slight difficulties, endure hardships, and contemn every danger. The General ardently wishes it were now in his power, to conduct the troops into the best winter quarters. But where are these to be found? Should we retire to the interior parts of the State, we should find them crowded with virtuous citizens, who, sacrificing their all, have left Philadelphia, and fled thither for protection. To their distresses humanity forbids us to add. This is not all, we should leave a vast extent of fertile country to be despoiled and ravaged by the enemy, from which they would draw vast supplies, and where many of our firm friends would be exposed to all the miseries of the most insulting and wanton depredation. A train of evils might be enumerated, but these will suffice. These considerations make it indispensibly necessary for the army to take such a position, as will enable it most effectually to prevent distress and to give the most extensive security; and in that position we must make ourselves the best shelter in our power. With activity and diligence Huts may be erected that will be warm and dry. In these the troops will be compact, more secure against surprises than if in a divided state and at hand to protect the country. These cogent reasons have determined the General to take post in the neighbourhood of this camp; and influenced by them, he persuades himself, that the officers and soldiers, with one heart, and one mind, will resolve to surmount every difficulty, with a fortitude and patience, becoming their profession, and the sacred cause in which they are engaged. He himself will share in the hardship, and partake of every inconvenience.

To morrow being the day set apart by the Honorable Congress for public Thanksgiving and Praise; and duty calling us devoutely to express our grateful acknowledgements to God for the manifold blessings he has granted us. The General directs that the army remain in it's present quarters, and that the Chaplains perform divine service with their several Corps and brigades. And earnestly exhorts, all officers and soldiers, whose absence is not indispensibly necessary, to attend with reverence the solemnities of the day.

To Henry Laurens

Valley Forge, December 23, 1777.

Sir: Full as I was in my representation of matters in the Commys. departmt. yesterday, fresh, and more powerful reasons oblige me to add, that I am now convinced, beyond a doubt that unless some great and capital change suddenly takes place in that line, this Army must inevitably be reduced to one or other of these three things. Starve, dissolve, or disperse, in order to obtain subsistence in the best manner they can; rest assured Sir this is not an exaggerated picture, but that I have abundant reason to support what I say.

Yesterday afternoon receiving information that the Enemy, in force, had left the City, and were advancing towards Derby with apparent design to forage, and draw Subsistance from that part of the Country, I order'd the Troops to be in readiness, that I might give every opposition in my power; when, behold! to my great mortification, I was not only informed, but convinced, that the Men were unable to stir on Acct. of Provision, and that a dangerous Mutiny begun the Night before, and with difficulty was suppressed by the spirited exertion's of some officers was still much to be apprehended on acct. of their want of this Article.

This brought forth the only Comy. in the purchasing Line, in this Camp; and, with him, this Melancholy and alarming truth; that he had not a single hoof of any kind to Slaughter, and not more than 25. Barls. of Flour! From hence form an opinion of our Situation when I add, that, he could not tell when to expect any.

All I could do under these circumstances was, to send out a few light Parties to watch and harrass the Enemy, whilst other Parties were instantly detached different ways to collect, if possible, as much Provision as would satisfy the present pressing wants of the Soldiery. But will this answer? No Sir: three or four days bad weather would prove our destruction. What then is to become of the Army this Winter? and if we are as often without Provisions now, as with it, what is to become of us in the Spring, when our force will be collected, with the aid perhaps of Militia, to take advantage of an early Campaign before the Enemy can be reinforced? These are considerations of great magnitude, meriting the closest attention, and will, when my own reputation is so intimately connected, and to be affected by the event, justifie my saying that the present Commissaries are by no means equal to the execution or that the disaffection of the People is past all belief.

The misfortune however does in my opinion, proceed from both causes, and tho' I have been tender heretofore of giving any opinion, or lodging complaints, as the change in that departmt. took place contrary to my judgment, and the consequences thereof were predicted; yet, finding that the inactivity of the Army, whether for want of provisions, Cloaths, or other essentials, is charged to my Acct., not only by the common vulgar, but those in power, it is time to speak plain in exculpation of myself; with truth then I can declare that, no Man, in my opinion, ever had his measures more impeded than I have, by every department of the Army. Since the Month of July, we have had no assistance from the Quarter Master Genl. and to want of assistance from this department, the Commissary Genl. charges great part of his deficiency; to this I am to add, that notwithstanding it is a standing order (and often repeated) that the Troops shall always have two days Provisions by them, that they may be ready at any sudden call, yet, no oppertunity has scarce ever yet happened of taking advantage of the Enemy that has not been either totally obstructed or greatly impeded on this Acct., and this tho' the great and crying evil is not all. Soap, Vinegar and other Articles allowed by Congress we see none of nor have seen I believe since the battle of brandywine; the first indeed we have now little occasion of few men having more than one Shirt, many only the Moiety of one, and Some none at all; in addition to which as a proof of the little benefit received from a Cloathier Genl., and at the same time as a further proof of the inability of an Army under the circumstances of this, to perform the common duties of Soldiers (besides a number of Men confind to Hospitals for want of Shoes, and others in farmers Houses on the same Acct.) we have, by a field return this day made no less than 2898 Men now in Camp unfit for duty because they are bare foot and otherwise naked and by the same return it appears that our whole strength in continental Troops (Including the Eastern Brigades which have joined us since the surrender of Genl. Burgoyne) exclusive of the Maryland Troops sent to Wilmington amount to no more than 8200 In Camp fit for duty. Notwithstanding which, and that, since the 4th Instt. our Numbers fit for duty from the hardships and exposures they have undergone, particularly on Acct. of Blankets (numbers being obliged and do set up all Night by fires, instead of taking comfortable rest in a natural way) have decreased near 2000 Men. we find Gentlemen without knowing whether the Army was really going into Winter Quarters or not (for I am sure no resolution of mine would warrant the remonstrance) reprobating the measure as much as if they thought Men were made of Stocks or Stones and equally insensible of frost and Snow and moreover, as if they conceived it practicable for an inferior Army under the disadvantages I have describ'd our's to be wch. is by no means exagerated to confine a superior one (in all respects well appointed, and provided for a Winters Campaign) within the City of Phila., and cover from depredation and waste the States of Pensa., Jersey, &ca. but what makes this matter still more extraordinary in my eye is, that these very Gentn. who were well apprized of the nakedness of the Troops, from occular demonstration thought their own Soldiers worse clad than others, and advised me, near a Month ago, to postpone the execution of a Plan, I was about to adopt (in consequence of a resolve of Congress) for seizing Cloaths, under strong assurances that an ample supply would be collected in ten days agreeably to a decree of the State, not one Article of wch., by the bye, is yet come to hand, should think a Winters Campaign and the covering these States from the Invasion of an Enemy so easy a business. I can assure those Gentlemen that it is a much easier and less distressing thing to draw remonstrances in a comfortable room by a good fire side than to occupy a cold bleak hill and sleep under frost and Snow without Cloaths or Blankets; however, although they seem to have little feeling for the naked, and distressed Soldier, I feel superabundantly for them, and from my Soul pity those miseries, wch. it is neither in my power to relieve or prevent.

It is for these reasons therefore I have dwelt upon the Subject, and it adds not a little to my other difficulties, and distress, to find that much more is expected of me than is possible to be performed, and that upon the ground of safety and policy, I am obliged to conceal the true State of the Army from Public view and thereby expose myself to detraction and Calumny.

The Honble. Comee of Congress went from Camp fully

possessed of my Sentiments respecting the Establishment of this Army, the necessity of Auditors of Accts, appointment of Officers, new arrangements, &ca. I have no need therefore to be prolix on these Subjects, but refer to them after adding a word or two to shew, first, the necessity of some better provision for binding the Officers by the tye of Interest to the Service (as No day, nor scarce an hour passes without the offer of a resignd Commission) otherwise I much doubt the practicability of holding the Army together much longer. In this I shall, probably, be thought more sincere, when I freely declare that I do not, myself, expect to derive the smallest benefit from any establishment that Congress may adopt, otherwise than as a Member of the Community at large in the good which I am perswaded will result from the measure by making better Officers and better Troops, and Secondly to point out the necessity of making the Appointments, arrangements, &ca. without loss of time. We have not more than 3 Months to prepare a great deal of business in; if we let these slip, or waste, we shall be labouring under the same difficulties all next Campaign as we have done this, to rectifie mistakes and bring things to order. Military arrangements and movements in consequence, like the Mechanism of a Clock, will be imperfect, and disorderd, by the want of a part; in a very sensible degree have I experienced this in the course of the last Summer, Several Brigades having no Brigadiers appointed to them till late and some not at all; by which means it follows that an additional weight is thrown upon the Shoulders of the Commander in chief to withdraw his attention from the great line of his duty. The Gentlemen of the Comee. when they were at Camp talk'd of an expedient for adjusting these matters, which I highly approved and wish to see adopted namely, that two or three Members of the Board of War or a Comee of Congress should repair immediately to Camp where the best aid can be had and with the Commanding Officer, or a Comee of his appointing prepare and digest the most perfect plan that can be devised for correcting all abuses, making new arrangements, considering what is to be done with the weak and debelitated regiments (if the States to wch they belong, will not draft men to fill them, for as to enlisting Soldiers it seems to me to be totally out of the question) together with many other things that would occur in the course of such a conference, and after digesting matters in the best manner they can to submit the whole to the ultimate determination of Congress. If this measure is approved of I would earnestly advise the immediate execution of it and that the Comy. General of Purchases whom I rarely see, may be directed to form Magazines without a Moments delay, in the Neighbourhood of this Camp in order to secure Provision for us in case of bad weather; the Quarter Mr. Genl. ought also to be busy in his department; in short there is as much to be done in preparing for a Campaign as in the active part of it; in fine, every thing depends upon the preparation that is made in the several departments in the course of this Winter and the success, or misfortunes of next Campaign will more than probably originate with our activity, or supineness this Winter. I am &ca.

To Henry Laurens

Valley Forge, January 2, 1778.

Sir: I take the liberty of transmitting you the Inclosed Copies of a Letter, from me to Genl. Conway, since his return from York to Camp, and Two Letters from him to me, which you will be pleased to lay before Congress. I shall not in this Letter animadvert upon them, but after making a single observation submit the whole to Congress.

If General Conway means, by cool receptions mentioned in the last paragraph of his Letter of the 31st Ulto., that I did not receive him in the language of a warm and cordial Friend, I readily confess the charge. I did not, nor shall I ever, till I am capable of the arts of dissimulation. These I despise, and my feelings will not permit me to make professions of friendship to the man I deem my Enemy, and whose system of conduct forbids it. At the same time, Truth authorizes me to say, that he was received and treated with proper respect to his Official character, and that he has had no cause to justify the assertion, that he could not expect any support for fulfilling the duties of his Appointment. I have the honor, etc.

P.S. The Inclosed Extract from the proceedings of a Council

of Genl. Officers will shew, the Office of Inspector Genl. was a matter not of such modern date as Genl. Conway mentions it to be, and that it was one of the Regulations in view for the reform of the Army. The Foreign Officers who had Commissions and no Commands and who were of ability, were intended to be recommended to execute it; particularly the Baron D'Arendt with whom the Idea originated, and whose capacity seemed to be well admitted.

To Horatio Gates

Valley Forge, January 4, 1778.

Sir: Your Letter of the 8th. Ulto. came to my hands a few days ago; and, to my great surprize informed me, that a Copy of it had been sent to Congress, for what reason, I find myself unable to acct.; but, as some end doubtless was intended to be answered by it, I am laid under the disagreeable necessity of returning my answer through the same channel, lest any Member of that honble. body, should harbour an unfavourable suspicion of my having practiced some indirect means, to come at the contents of the confidential Letters between you and General Conway.

I am to inform you then, that Colo. Wilkenson, in his way to Congress in the Month of Octobr. last, fell in with Lord Stirling at Reading, and, not in confidence that I ever understood, inform'd his Aid de Camp Majr. McWilliams that General Conway had written thus to you,

Heaven has been determined to save your Country; or a weak General and bad Counsellors would have ruined it.

Lord Stirling from motives of friendship, transmitted the acct. with this remark.

The inclosed was communicated by Colonl. Wilkinson to Majr. McWilliams, such wicked duplicity of conduct I shall always think it my duty to detect.

In consequence of this information, and without having any

thing more in view than merely to shew that Gentn. that I
was not unapprized of his intrieguing disposition, I wrote him
a Letter in these Words.

> Sir. A Letter which I received last night contained the
> following paragraph.
>
> In a Letter from Genl. Conway to Genl. Gates he says,
> "Heaven has been determined to save your Country; or
> a weak General and bad Counsellors would have ruined
> it."
>
> I am Sir &ca.

Neither this Letter, nor the information which occasioned
it, was ever, directly, or indirectly communicated by me to a
single Officer in this Army (out of my own family) excepting
the Marquis de la Fayette, who, having been spoken to on
the Subject by Genl. Conway, applied for, and saw, under in-
junctions of secrecy, the Letter which contained Wilkenson's
information; so desirous was I, of concealing every matter that
could, in its consequences, give the smallest Interruption to
the tranquility of this Army, or afford a gleam of hope to the
enemy by dissentions therein.

Thus Sir, with an openess and candour which I hope will
ever characterize and mark my conduct have I complied with
your request; the only concern I feel upon the occasion (finding how matters stand) is, that in doing this, I have necessarily
been obliged to name a Gentn. whom I am perswaded (although I never exchanged a word with him upon the Subject)
thought he was rather doing an act of Justice, than committing an act of infidility; and sure I am, that, till Lord Stirlings
Letter came to my hands, I never knew that General Conway
(who I viewed in the light of a stranger to you) was a corrispondant of yours, much less did I suspect that I was the subject of your confidential Letters; pardon me then for adding,
that so far from conceiving that the safety of the States can
be affected, or in the smallest degree injured, by a discovery
of this kind, or, that I should be called upon in such solemn
terms to point out the author, that I considered the information as coming from yourself; and given with a friendly
view to forewarn, and consequently forearm me, against a
secret enemy; or, in other words, a dangerous incendiary; in

which character, sooner or later, this Country will know Genl. Conway. But, in this, as in other matters of late, I have found myself mistaken. I am, etc.

To William Howe

Head Quarters, January 30, 1778.

Sir: I have duly received your Letter of the 19th. Inst. It is unnecessary to enter minutely into its contents; since the inclosed Resolutions of Congress will shew you, that the Matter is now put upon a footing different from that mentioned by Mr. Boudinot; which, at the same time, you will be pleased to consider, as final and decisive, and to regulate your Measures accordingly.

I shall be glad as soon as possible to be favoured with your determinations in consequence, especially on those parts numbered in the Margin of the Resolves, to which I must request a speedy and explicit answer.

There is one passage of your Letter, which I cannot forbear taking particular notice of. No expressions of personal politeness to me can be acceptable, accompanied by reflections on the Representatives of a free People, under whose Authority I have the Honor to act. The delicacy I have observed in refraining from every thing offensive in this way, entitled me to expect a similar Treatment from you. I have not indulged myself in invective against the present Rulers of Great Britain, in the course of our Correspondence, nor will I even now avail myself of so fruitful a Theme.

The Quarter Masters permitted to go with the Cloathing, appeared to me sufficient for the purpose. For tho' the Prisoners are in different places, yet they lie chiefly on a direct communication. If upon any future occasion you should conceive a greater number requisite, you will inform me of it previous to their coming, and I shall be ready to comply, as far as I think myself justified.

Whether your sending out more than one British Quarter Master was an encroachment upon the spirit of the Agreement between us, shall not now be a matter of discussion, but can it be said there is anything in it, that can reconcile the coming out of Captn. McCleod. I have the Honor, etc.

To Henry Laurens

Valley Forge, January 31, 1778.

Sir: I this morning received your favor of the 27th. Ulto.

I cannot sufficiently express the obligation I feel to you for your friendship and politeness upon an occasion in which I am so deeply interested. I was not unapprized that a malignant faction had been for sometime forming to my prejudice; which, conscious as I am of having ever done all in my power to answer the important purposes of the trust reposed in me, could not but give me some pain on a personal account; but my chief concern arises from an apprehension of the danger-ous consequences, which intestine dissentions may produce to the common cause.

As I have no other view than to promote the public good, and am unambitious of honours not founded in the appro-bation of my Country, I would not desire in the least degree to suppress a free spirit of enquiry into any part of my conduct that even faction itself may deem reprehensible.

The anonymous paper handed you exhibits many serious charges, and it is my wish that it should be submitted to Con-gress; this I am the more inclined to, as the suppression, or concealment, may possibly involve you in embarrassments hereafter; since it is uncertain how many, or who may be privy to the contents.

My Enemies take an ungenerous advantage of me; they know the delicacy of my situation, and that motives of policy deprive me of the defence I might otherwise make against their insiduous attacks. They know I cannot combat their in-sinuations, however injurious, without disclosing secrets, it is of the utmost moment to conceal. But why should I expect to be exempt from censure; the unfailing lot of an elevated station? Merits and talents, with which I can have no preten-sions of rivalship, have ever been subject to it. My Heart tells me it has been my unremitted aim to do the best circumstances would permit; yet, I may have been very often mistaken in my judgment of the means, and may, in many instances deserve the imputation of error.

I cannot forbear repeating that I have a grateful sense of the favourable disposition you have manifested to me in this affair, and beg you will believe me to be, with sentiments of real Esteem, etc.

To William Gordon

Valley-forge, February 15, 1778.

Dear Sir: Since my last to you abt. the end of Jany. I have been favourd with your Letter of the 12th. of that Month, which did not reach my hands 'till within these few days. The question there put was, in some degree, solved in my last. But to be more explicit, I can assure you that no person ever heard me drop an expression that had a tendency to resignation. the same principles that led me to imbark in the opposition to the Arbitrary Claims of Great Britn. operate with additional force at this day; nor is it my desire to withdraw my Services while they are considered of importance in the present contest; but to report a design of this kind, is among the Arts wch those who are endeavouring to effect a change, are practising, to bring it to pass. I have said, and I still do say, that there is not an Officer in the Service of the United States that would return to the sweets of domestic life with more heart felt joy than I should; but I would have this declaration, accompanied by these Sentiments, that while the public are satisfied with my endeavours I mean not to shrink in the cause; but, the moment her voice, not that of faction, calls upon me to resign, I shall do it with as much pleasure as ever the weary traveller retired to rest. This my dear Doctor, you are at liberty to assert; but in doing it, I would have nothing formal. All things will come right again and soon recover their proper tone as the design is not only seen thro but reprobated.

With sincere esteem and regard I am etc.

P.S. Mrs. Washington who is now with me joins in best respects to Mrs. Gordon.

To George Clinton

Head Quarters, Valley Forge, February 16, 1778.
Dear Sir: It is with great reluctance, I trouble you on a subject, which does not properly fall within your province; but it is a subject that occasions me more distress, than I have felt, since the commencement of the war; and which loudly demands the most zealous exertions of every person of weight and authority, who is interested in the success of our affairs. I mean the present dreadful situation of the army for want of provisions, and the miserable prospects before us, with respect to futurity. It is more alarming than you will probably conceive, for, to form a just idea, it were necessary to be on the spot. For some days past, there has been little less, than a famine in camp. A part of the army has been a week, without any kind of flesh, and the rest three or four days. Naked and starving as they are, we cannot enough admire the incomparable patience and fidelity of the soldiery, that they have not been ere this excited by their sufferings, to a general mutiny and dispersion. Strong symptoms, however, of discontent have appeared in particular instances; and nothing but the most active efforts every where can long avert so shocking a catastrophe.

Our present sufferings are not all. There is no foundation laid for any adequate relief hereafter. All the magazines provided in the States of New Jersey, Pensylvania, Delaware and Maryland, and all the immediate additional supplies they seem capable of affording, will not be sufficient to support the army more than a month longer, if so long. Very little has been done to the Eastward, and as little to the Southward; and whatever we have a right to expect from those quarters, must necessarily be very remote; and is indeed more precarious, than could be wished. When the forementioned supplies are exhausted, what a terrible crisis must ensue, unless all the energy of the Continent is exerted to provide a timely remedy?

Impressed with this idea, I am, on my part, putting every engine to work, that I can possibly think of, to prevent the fatal consequences, we have so great reason to apprehend. I am calling upon all those, whose stations and influence enable them to contribute their aid upon so important an occasion; and from your well known zeal, I expect every thing within the compass of your power, and that the abilities and resources of the state over which you preside, will admit. I am sensible of the disadvantages it labours under, from having been so long the scene of war, and that it must be exceedingly drained by the great demands to which it has been subject. But, tho' you may not be able to contribute materially to our relief, you can perhaps do something towards it; and any assistance, however trifling in itself, will be of great moment at so critical a juncture, and will conduce to keeping the army together till the Commissary's department can be put upon a better footing, and effectual measures concerted to secure a permanent and competent supply. What methods you can take, you will be the best judge of; but, if you can devise any means to procure a quantity of cattle, or other kind of flesh, for the use of this army, to be at camp in the course of a month, you will render a most essential service to the common cause. I have the honor etc.

To Bryan Fairfax

Valley forge, March 1, 1778.

Dear Sir: Your favor of the 8th. of Decr. came safe to my hands after a considerable delay in its passage. The sentiments you have expressed of me in this Letter are highly flattering, meriting my warmest acknowledgements, as I have too good an Opinion of your sincerity and candour to believe that you are capable of unmeaning professions and speaking a language foreign from your Heart. The friendship I ever professed, and felt for you, met with no diminution from the difference in our political Sentiments. I know the rectitude of my own intentions, and believing in the sincerity of yours, lamented, though I did not condemn, your renunciation of the creed I had adopted. Nor do I think any person, or power, ought to do it, whilst your conduct is not opposed to the general Interest of the people and the measures they are pursuing; the latter, that is our actions, depending upon ourselves, may be

controuled, while the powers of thinking originating in higher
causes, cannot always be moulded to our wishes.

The determinations of Providence are all ways wise; often
inscrutable, and though its decrees appear to bear hard upon
us at times is nevertheless meant for gracious purposes; in this
light I cannot help viewing your late disappointment; for if
you had been permitted to have gone to england, unrestrained
even by the rigid oaths which are administred on those occns.
your feelings as a husband, Parent, &ca. must have been considerably wounded in the prospect of a long, perhaps lasting
seperation from your nearest relatives. What then must they
have been if the obligation of an oath had left you without a
Will? Your hope of being instrumental in restoring Peace
would prove as unsubstantial as mist before the Noon days
Sun and would as soon dispel: for believe me Sir great Britain
understood herself perfectly well in this dispute but did not
comprehend America. She meant as Lord Campden in his late
speech in Parlt. clearly, and explicitly declared, to drive America into rebellion that her own purposes might be more fully
answered by it but take this along with it, that this Plan originating in a firm belief, founded on misinformation, that no
effectual opposition would or could be made, they little
dreamt of what has happened and are disappd. in their views;
does not every act of administration from the Tea Act to the
present Session of Parliament declare this in plain and self
evidt. Characters? Had the Comrs. any powers to treat with
America? If they meant Peace, would Lord Howe have been
detaind in England 5 Months after passing the Act? Would the
powers of these Comrs. have been confined to mere acts of
grace, upon condition of absolute submission? No, surely, No!
they meant to drive us into what they termed rebellion, that
they might be furnished with a pretext to disarm and then
strip us of the rights and privileges of Englishmen and Citizens. If they were actuated by principles of justice, why did
they refuse indignantly to accede to the terms which were
humbly supplicated before hostilities commenced and this
Country deluged in Blood; and now make their principal Officers and even the Comrs. themselves say, that these terms
are just and reasonable; Nay that more will be granted than
we have yet asked, if we will relinquish our Claim to Inde-

pendency. What Name does such conduct as this deserve? and what punishment is there in store for the Men who have distressed Millions, involved thousands in ruin, and plunged numberless families in inextricable woe? Could that wch. is just and reasonable now, have been unjust four Years ago? If not upon what principles, I say does Administration act? they must either be wantonly wicked and cruel, or (which is only anr. mode of describing the same thing) under false colours are now endeavouring to deceive the great body of the people, by industriously propagating a belief that G. B. is willing to offer any, and that we will accept of no terms; thereby hoping to poison and disaffect the Minds of those who wish for peace, and create feuds and dissentions among ourselves. In a word, having less dependance now, in their Arms than their Arts, they are practising such low and dirty tricks, that Men of Sentiment and honr. must blush at their Villainy, among other manœuvres, in this way they are counterfeiting Letters, and publishing them, as intercepted ones of mine to prove that I am an enemy to the present measures, and have been led into them step by step still hoping that Congress would recede from their present claims. I am, etc.

General Orders

Head-Quarters, V. Forge, Sunday, March 1, 1778.
Parole Arnold.　　　　　　Countersigns Ashford, Almbury.
　　The Commander in Chief again takes occasion to return his warmest thanks to the virtuous officers and soldiery of this Army for that persevering fidelity and Zeal which they have uniformly manifested in all their conduct. Their fortitude not only under the common hardships incident to a military life, but also under the additional sufferings to which the peculiar situation of these States have exposed them, clearly proves them worthy the enviable privilege of contending for the rights of human nature, the *Freedom and Independence* of their Country. The recent Instance of uncomplaining Patience during the scarcity of provisions in Camp is a fresh proof that they possess in an eminent degree the spirit of soldiers and

the magninimity of Patriots. The few refractory individuals who disgrace themselves by murmurs it is to be hoped have repented such unmanly behaviour, and resolved to emulate the noble example of their associates upon every trial which the customary casualties of war may hereafter throw in their way. Occasional distress for want of provisions and other necessaries is a spectacle that frequently occurs in every army and perhaps there never was one which has been in general so plentifully supplied in respect to the former as ours. Surely we who are free Citizens in arms engaged in a struggle for every thing valuable in society and partaking in the glorious task of laying the foundation of an *Empire*, should scorn effeminately to shrink under those accidents and rigours of War which mercenary hirelings fighting in the cause of lawless ambition, rapine and devastation, encounter with cheerfulness and alacrity, we should not be merely equal, we should be superior to them in every qualification that dignifies the man or the soldier in proportion as the motive from which we act and the final hopes of our Toils, are superior to theirs. Thank Heaven! our Country abounds with provision and with prudent management we need not apprehend want for any length of time. Defects in the Commissaries department, Contingencies of weather and other temporary impediments have subjected and may again subject us to a deficiency for a few days, but soldiers! American soldiers! will despise the meanness of repining at such trifling strokes of Adversity, trifling indeed when compared to the transcendent *Prize* which will undoubtedly crown their Patience and Perseverence, Glory and Freedom, Peace and Plenty to themselves and the Community; The Admiration of the World, the Love of their Country and the Gratitude of Posterity!

Your General unceasingly employs his thoughts on the means of relieving your distresses, supplying your wants and bringing your labours to a speedy and prosperous issue. Our Parent Country he hopes will second his endeavors by the most vigorous exertions and he is convinced the faithful officers and soldiers associated with him in the great work of rescuing our Country from Bondage and Misery will continue in the display of that patriotic zeal which is capable of smoothing every difficulty and vanquishing every Obstacle.

At a Brigade Court Martial Feby. 27th. whereof Lt. Colo. Burr was President Lieutt. Blackall William Ball of 12th. Pennsylvania Regiment tried for disobedience of orders, Insolence and ungentlemanlike behavior. The Court after mature deliberation on the evidence produced are clearly and unanimously of opinion that Lieutt. Ball is not guilty and do therefore unanimously acquit him with the highest honor of all and every of the Articles exhibited against him. The Court do further agree and determine that the charges each and all of them are groundless, frivilous and malicious, that Lt. Ball's behaviour was truly gentlemanlike, his attention and obedience to orders exemplary and his Conduct rather deserving applause than Censure.

The Commander in Chief confirms the opinion of the Court and orders Lieutt. Ball to be immediately released from his arrest.

At a General Court Martial whereof Colonel Cortland was President, Feby. 25th. Philip Bocker an Inhabitant of this State tried for attempting to carry Provision in to the Enemy at Philadelphia and unanimously acquitted of the charge.

At the same Court Joseph De Haven, an Inhabitant of this State tried for repeatedly going into Philadelphia since the Enemy have been in possession of it and acquitted.

Also Michael Milanberger an Inhabitant of this State tried for Supporting the Enemy with Provision and acquitted.

The Commander in Chief confirms the aforegoing opinions of the Court and orders the three last mentioned Prisoners to be immediately released from confinement.

At the same Court Jacob Cross an Inhabitant of this State tried for stealing Calves and carrying them into Philadelphia, found guilty of stealing two Calves one of which he carried into Philadelphia, the other he was carrying in when taken, being a breach of a resolution of Congress dated October 8th, '77 extended by another dated December 29th. and do Sentence him to receive two hundred lashes on his bare back well laid on.

The Commander in Chief approves the sentence and orders it to be put in Execution on the Grand-Parade tomorrow morning at guard mounting.

At a General Court Martial whereof Colo. Cortland was

President Feby. 24th, '78, Joseph Worrell an Inhabitant of the State of Pennsylvania tried for giving intelligence to the Enemy and for acting as guide and pilot to the Enemy; The Court are of opinion the Prisoner is guilty of acting as a guide to the Enemy (and do acquit him of the other charge against him) being a breach of a resolution of Congress dated Octr. 8th, '77, extended by another resolution of Congress dated december 29th, 1777, and they do (upwards of two thirds agreeing) sentence him to suffer death.

His Excellency the Commander in Chief approves the sentence and orders Joseph Worrell to be executed next tuesday at 10 o'Clock in the forenoon.

To John Banister

Valley Forge, April 21, 1778.

Dear Sir: On Saturday Evening, I had the pleasure to receive your favour of the 16th. Instant.

I thank you very much, for your obliging tender of a friendly intercourse between us; and you may rest assured, that I embrace it with chearfulness, and shall write you freely, as often as leisure will permit, of such points as appear to me material and interesting.

I am pleased to find, that you expect the proposed establishment of the Army will succeed; though it is a painful consideration, that matters of such pressing importance and obvious necessity meet with so much difficulty and delay. Be assured the success of the measure is a matter of the most serious moment, and that it ought to be brought to a conclusion, as speedily as possible. The spirit of resigning Commissions has been long at an alarming height, and increases daily. Applications from Officers on furlough are hourly arriving, and Genls. Heath, of Boston, McDougal on the No. River, and Mason of Virginia are asking what they are to do with the appliants to them.

The Virginia Line has sustained a violent shock in this instance; not less than Ninety havg. resigned already, to me, the same conduct has prevailed among the Officers from the other

States, though not yet to so considerable a degree; and there are but too just Grounds to fear, that it will shake the very existence of the Army, unless a remedy is soon, very soon, applied. There is none, in my opinion, so effectual, as the one pointed out. This, I trust, will satisfy the Officers, and, at the same time, it will produce no present additional emission of Money. They will not be persuaded to sacrifice all views of present interest, and encounter the numerous vicissitudes of War, in the defence of their Country, unless she will be generous enough, on her part, to make a decent provision for their future support, I do not pronounce absolutely, that we shall have no Army, if the establishment fails: But the Army, we may have, will be without discipline, without energy, incapable of acting with vigor, and destitute of those cements necessary to promise success, on the one hand, or to withstand the shocks of adversity, on the other. It is indeed hard to say how extensive the evil may be, if the measure should be rejected, or much longer delayed. I find it a very arduous task to keep the Officers in tolerable humour, and to protract such a combination in quitting the service, as might possibly undo us forever. The difference between our service and that of the Enemy, is very striking. With us, from the peculiar, unhappy situation of things, the Officer, a few instances excepted, must break in upon his private fortune for present support, without a prospect of future relief. With them, even Companies are esteemed so honourable and so valuable, that they have sold of late from 15 to 2,200 £ Sterling, and I am credibly informed, that 4,000 Guineas have been given for a Troop of Dragoons: You will readily determine how this difference will operate; what effects it must produce. Men may speculate as they will; they may talk of patriotism; they may draw a few examples from ancient story, of great atchievements performed by its influence; but whoever builds upon it, as a sufficient Basis for conducting a long and bloody War, will find themselves deceived in the end. We must take the passions of Men as Nature has given them, and those principles as a guide which are generally the rule of Action. I do not mean to exclude altogether the Idea of Patriotism. I know it exists, and I know it has done much in the present Contest. But I will venture to assert, that a great and lasting War can never be supported on this principle alone. It must be aided by a prospect of Interest or some reward. For a time, it may, of itself push Men to Action; to bear much, to encounter difficulties; but it will not endure unassisted by Interest.

The necessity of putting the Army upon a respectable footing, both as to numbers and constitution, is now become more essential than ever. The Enemy are beginning to play a Game more dangerous than their efforts by Arms, tho' these will not be remitted in the smallest degree, and which threatens a fatal blow to American Independence, and to her liberties of course: They are endeavouring to ensnare the people by specious allurements of Peace. It is not improbable they have had such abundant cause to be tired of the War, that they may be sincere, in the terms they offer, which, though far short of our pretensions, will be extremely flattering to Minds that do not penetrate far into political consequences: But, whether they are sincere or not, they may be equally destructive; for, to discerning Men, nothing can be more evident, than that a Peace on the principles of dependance, however limited, after what has happened, would be to the last degree dishonourable and ruinous. It is, however, much to be apprehended, that the Idea of such an event will have a very powerful effect upon the Country, and, if not combatted with the greatest address, will serve, at least, to produce supineness and dis-union. Men are naturally fond of Peace, and there are Symptoms which may authorize an Opinion, that the people of America are pretty generally weary of the present War. It is doubtful, whether many of our friends might not incline to an accommodation on the Grounds held out, or which may be, rather than persevere in a contest for Independence. If this is the case, it must surely be the truest policy to strengthen the Army, and place it upon a substantial footing. This will conduce to inspire the Country with confidence; enable those at the head of affairs to consult the public honour and interest, notwithstanding the defection of some and temporary inconsistency and irresolution of others, who may desire to compromise the dispute; and if a Treaty should be deemed expedient, will put it in their power to insist upon better terms, than they could otherwise expect.

Besides, the most vigorous exertions at Home, to increase

and establish our Military force upon a good Basis; it appears to me advisable, that we should immediately try the full extent of our interest abroad and bring our European Negotiations to an Issue. I think France must have ratified our Independence, and will declare War immediately, on finding that serious proposals of accommodation are made; but lest, from a mistaken policy, or too exalted an Opinion of our powers, from the representations she has had, she should still remain indecisive, it were to be wished proper persons were instantly dispatched, or our envoys, already there, instructed, to insist pointedly on her coming to a final determination. It cannot be fairly supposed, that she will hesitate a moment to declare War, if she is given to understand, in a proper manner, that a reunion of the two Countries may be the consequence of procrastination. An European War, and an European Alliance would effectually answer our purposes. If the step I now mention, should be eligible, despatches ought to be sent at once, by different conveyances, for fear of accidents. I confess it appears to me, a measure of this kind could not but be productive of the most salutary consequences. If possible, I should also suppose it absolutely necessary, to obtain good intelligence from England, pointing out the true springs of this manœuvre of Ministry; the preparations of force they are making; the prospects there are of raising it; the amount, and when it may be expected.

It really seems to me, from a comprehensive view of things, that a period is fast approaching, big with events of the most interesting importance. When the councils we pursue and the part we act, may lead decisively to liberty, or to Slavery. Under this Idea, I cannot but regret, that inactivity, that inattention, that want of something, which unhappily, I have but too often experienced in our public Affairs. I wish that our representation in Congress was compleat and full from every State, and that it was formed of the first Abilities among us. Whether we continue to War, or proceed to Negotiate, the Wisdom of America in Council cannot be too great. Our situation will be truly delicate. To enter into a Negotiation too hastily, or to reject it altogether, may be attended with consequences equally fatal. The wishes of the people, seldom founded in deep disquisitions, or resulting from other reasonings than their present feeling, may not intirely accord with our true policy and interest. If they do not, to observe a proper line of conduct, for promoting the one, and avoiding offence to the other, will be a Work of great difficulty. Nothing short of Independence, it appears to me, can possibly do. A Peace, on other terms, would, if I may be allowed the expression, be a Peace of War. The injuries we have received from the British Nation were so unprovoked; have been so great and so many, that they can never be forgotten. Besides the feuds, the jealousies; the animosities that would ever attend a Union with them. Besides the importance, the advantages we should derive from an unrestricted commerce; Our fidelity as a people; Our gratitude; Our Character as Men, are opposed to a coalition with them as subjects, but in case of the last extremity. Were we easily to accede to terms of dependence, no nation, upon future occasions, let the oppressions of Britain be never so flagrant and unjust, would interpose for our relief, or at least they would do it with a cautious reluctance and upon conditions, most probably, that would be hard, if not dishonourable to us. France, by her supplies, has saved us from the Yoke thus far, and a wise and virtuous perseverence, would and I trust will, free us entirely.

I have sent Congress, Lord North's Speech and two Bills offered by him to Parliament. They are spreading fast through the Country, and will soon become a subject of general notoriety. I therefore think, they had best be published in our papers, and persons of leisure and ability set to Work, to counteract the impressions, they may make on the Minds of the people.

Before I conclude, there are one or two points more upon which I will add an Observation or two. The first is, the indecision of Congress and the delay used in coming to determinations in matters referred to them. This is productive of a variety of inconveniences; and an early decision, in many cases, though it should be against the measure submitted, would be attended with less pernicious effects. Some new plan might then be tried; but while the matter is held in suspence, nothing can be attempted. The other point is, the *jealousy* which Congress unhappily entertain of the Army, and which, if reports are right, some Members labour to establish. You may be assured, there is nothing more injurious, or more unjustly founded. This jealousy stands upon the common, received Opinion, which under proper limitations is certainly true, that standing Armies are dangerous to a State, and from forming the same conclusion of the component parts of all, though they are totally dissimilar in their Nature. The prejudices in other Countries has only gone to them in time of *Peace*, and these from their not having, in general cases, any of the ties, the concerns or interests of Citizens or any other dependence, than what flowed from their Military employ; in short, from their being Mercenaries; hirelings. It is our policy to be prejudiced against them in time of *War*, and though they are Citizens having all the Ties, and interests of Citizens, and in most cases property totally unconnected with the Military Line. If we would pursue a right System of policy, in my Opinion, there should be none of these distinctions. We should all be considered, Congress, Army, &c. as one people, embarked in one Cause, in one interest; acting on the same principle and to the same End. The distinction, the Jealousies set up, or perhaps only incautiously let out, can answer not a single good purpose. They are impolitic in the extreme. Among Individuals, the most certain way to make a Man your Enemy, is to tell him, you esteem him such; so with public bodies; and the very jealousy, which the narrow politics of some may affect to entertain of the Army, in order to a due subordination to the supreme Civil Authority, is a likely mean to produce a contrary effect; to incline it to the pursuit of those measures which that may wish it to avoid. It is unjust, because no Order of Men in the thirteen States have paid a more sanctimonious regard to their proceedings than the Army; and, indeed, it may be questioned, whether there has been that scrupulus adherence had to them by any other, for without arrogance, or the smallest deviation from truth it may be said, that no history, now extant, can furnish an instance of an Army's suffering such uncommon hardships as ours have done, and bearing them with the same patience and Fortitude. To see Men without Cloathes to cover their nakedness, without Blankets to lay on, without Shoes, by which their Marches might be traced by the Blood from their feet, and almost as often without Provisions as with; Marching through frost and

Snow, and at Christmas taking up their Winter Quarters within a day's March of the enemy, without a House or Hutt to cover them till they could be built and submitting to it without a murmur, is a mark of patience and obedience which in my opinion can scarce be parallel'd.

There may have been some remonstrances or applications to Congress, in the stile of complaint from the Army and slaves indeed should we be, if this privilidge was denied, on Account of their proceedings in particular instances; but these will not Authorize nor even excuse a jealousy, that they are therefore aiming at unreasonable powers; or making strides, dangerous, or subversive of Civil Authority. Things should not be viewed in that light, more especially, as Congress, in some cases, have relieved the injuries complained of, and which had flowed from their own Acts.

I refer you to my Letter to yourself and Colonel Lee which accompanies this, upon the subject of Money for such of the Old Virginia Troops, as have or may reinlist.

In respect to the Volunteer Plan I scarce know what opinion to give at this time. The propriety of a requisition on this head, will depend altogether, on our operations. Such kind of Troops should not be called for, but upon the spur of the occasion and at the moment of executing an Enterprise. They will not endure a long service; and, of all Men in the Military Line, they are the most impatient of restraint and necessary Government.

As the propositions, and the Speech of Lord North must be founded in the despair of the Nation of succeeding against us, or, from a rupture in Europe that has actually happend, or that certainly will; or from some deep political Manœuvre; or from what I think, still more likely, a composition of the whole, would it not be good policy, in this day of uncertainty and distress to the Tories to avail ourselves of the occn. and for the sevl. States to hold out Pardon &ca. to all delinquents returng. by a certain day? They are frightned, and that is the time to operate upon them. Upon a short consideration of the matter it appears to me that such a measure wd. detach the Tories from the Enemy, and bring things to a much speed-ier conclusion and of course be a mean of saving much public treasure.

I will now be done, and I trust that you excuse not only the length of my Letter, but the freedom with which I have delivered my sentiments in the course of it upon several occasions. The subjects struck me as important and interesting, and I have only to wish, that they may appear to you in the same light. I am etc.

To John Augustine Washington

Valley-forge, May   , 1778.

Dear Brother: Your letter of the 27th. of Mar. from Bush-field came safe to hand, and gave me the pleasure of hearing, or rather inferring (for you are not explicit) that my Sister and the rest of your family were well. I thank you for your intelligence respecting the pamphlet of forged Letters which Colo. Lee has, and said to be written by me; not one sentence of which you may rely on it, did I ever write; although so many little family circumstances are interspersed through the whole performance to give it the air of authenticity. The Arts of the enemy, and the low dirty tricks which they are daily practising is an evincing proof that they are lost to all Sense of virtue and honor, and that they will stick at nothing however incompatible with truth and manliness to carry their points. They have lately forged, and industriously circulated, a resolve for Congress, purporting (after reciting with great propriety, and plausibility, the inconveniencies of short enlistments) that all Soldiers who have been drafted for periods short of the War, shall nevertheless continue in Service during it; and by their emissaries have endeavoured, and effected the injury of the Service by this means, alarming the fears of the Soldiery and Country.

I am mistaken if we are not verging fast to one of the most important periods that ever America saw; doubtless before this reaches you, you will have seen the Draughts of two Bills intended to be enacted into Laws, and Lord North's Speech upon the occasion; these our accts. from Phila. say, will be immediately followed by the Commissioners; and Lord Amherst, Adml. Keppel, and General Murray are said to be the

Commissioners. These Gentlemen I presume, are to move in a civil and Military Line, as Genl. Howe is certainly recalled, and report adds, Lord Howe also. Be this as it may, it will require all the skill, the wisdom, and policy, of the first abilities of these States, to manage the helm, and steer with judgment to the haven of our wishes through so many Shelves and Rocks, as will be thrown in our way. This, more than ever, is the time for Congress to be replete with the first characters in every State, instead of having a thin Assembly, and many States totally unrepresented, as is the case at present. I have often regretted the pernicious (and what appears to me, fatal) policy of having our able Men engaged in the formation of the more local Governments, and filling Officers in their respective States, leaving the great national concern, on wch. the superstructure of all, and every of them does absolutely depend, and without which none can exist, to be managed by Men of more contracted abilities, indeed those at a distance from the Seat of War live in such perfect tranquility that they conceive the dispute to be at an end in a manner, and those near hand it, are so disaffected that they only serve as embarrassments; between the two, therefore, time Slips away without the necessary means for opening the Campaign in time, or with propriety.

Your accts. of the high prices of fresh Provisions in Philadelphia are true, but it affects the Inhabitants more than the Soldiery, who have plenty of Salt Meat, Pease &ca.

Since I began this Letter, authentic accts. have come to my hands of France having declared the United States free and Independant, and guaranteeing to them all the Territory formerly ceeded by them to Great Britain. My acct. (from the Gentleman who was going on to Congress with the Treaty) adds, that France have done this in the most generous manner, and to our utmost wish. This is great, 'tis glorious News. and must put the Independency of America out of all manner of dispute. and accts. for the gentle gales which have succeeded rude Boreas, of late. A publication of this important intelligence will no doubt be directed by Congress and diffused through the Continent as speedily as possible, I shall add nothing further therefore on the Subject.

It would have been a happy circumstance if the several

States had been industrious in pushing their recruits into the field, early; but I see little prospect of it at present, if ever. My love and best wishes, in which Mrs. Washington joins me attend My Sister and the rest of your family and with great truth I subscribe myself Yr., etc.

General Orders

Head Quarters, V. Forge, Tuesday, May 5, 1778.
Parole Europe.   Countersigns Exeter, Eltham.

Aaron Ogden Esquire is appointed Brigade Major in General Maxwell's Brigade and is to be obeyed and respected accordingly.

Mr. Davis Bevan is appointed by the Quarter Master General to superintend the Artificers and to deliver out boards, Plank &c. in future therefore when boards or Plank are wanting or Artificers are necessary to do any Jobbs in the Army an order signed by a General Officer, Officers commanding Brigades or Brigade Quarter Masters and directed to Mr. Bevan at Sullivan's Bridge will be duly attended to.

If there are any Comb-makers in the Army, the Brigadiers and Officers commanding Brigades are desired to make return of them to the Adjutant General.

A Flag goes into Philadelphia next Friday.

At a General Court Martial whereof Majr. Tyler was President at the Gulph Mills May 2nd. A.D. 1778. John Morrel a soldier in Colo. Henry Jackson's Regiment tried for desertion from his Post while on Centry and unanimously found guilty of a breach of Article 1st. Section 6th. and Article 6th Section 13th. of the Articles of War and unanimously sentenced to be hung by the neck 'till he is dead.

At a Brigade Court Martial whereof Colonel Bicker was President April 24th. 1778, Thomas Hartnet a soldier in the Second Pennsylvania Regiment tried for desertion to the Enemy, found guilty and unanimously sentenced to be hung by the Neck 'till he is dead.

His Excellency the Commander in Chief approves the

aforegoing sentences. The General Court Martial whereof Major Tyler is President is dissolved.

It having pleased the Almighty ruler of the Universe propitiously to defend the Cause of the United American-States and finally by raising us up a powerful Friend among the Princes of the Earth to establish our liberty and Independence up lasting foundations, it becomes us to set apart a day for gratefully acknowledging the divine Goodness and celebrating the important Event which we owe to his benign Interposition.

The several Brigades are to be assembled for this Purpose at nine o'Clock tomorrow morning when their Chaplains will communicate the Intelligence contain'd in the Postscript to the Pennsylvania Gazette of the 2nd. instant and offer up a thanksgiving and deliver a discourse suitable to the Occasion. At half after ten o'Clock a Cannon will be fired, which is to be a signal for the men to be under Arms. The Brigade Inspectors will then inspect their Dress and Arms, form the Battalions according to instructions given them and announce to the Commanding Officers of Brigades that the Battalions are formed. The Brigadiers or Commandants will then appoint the Field Officers to command the Battalions, after which each Battalion will be ordered to load and ground their Arms.

At half after eleven a second Cannon be fired as a signal for the march upon which the several Brigades will begin their march by wheeling to the right by Platoons and proceed by the nearest way to the left of their ground in the new Position; this will be pointed out by the Brigade Inspectors. A third signal will be given upon which there will be a discharge of thirteen Cannon; When the thirteen has fired a runing fire of the Infantry will begin on the right of Woodford's and continue throughout the whole front line, it will then be taken on the left of the second line and continue to the right. Upon a signal given, the whole Army will Huzza! "Long Live the King of France." The Artillery then begins again and fires thirteen rounds, this will be succeeded by a second general discharge of the Musquetry in a runing fire. Huzza! "And long live the friendly European Powers." Then the last dis-

charge of thirteen Pieces of Artillery will be given, followed
by a General runing fire and Huzza! "To the American
States."

There will be no Exercise in the morning and the guards
of the day will not parade 'till after the feu de joie is finished,
when the Brigade Major will march them out to the Grand
Parade. The Adjutants then will tell off their Battalions into
eight Platoons and the commanding officer will reconduct
them to their Camps marching by the Left.

Major General Lord Stirling will command on the right,
the Marquis De la fayette on the left and Baron De Kalb the
second line. Each Major General will conduct the first Brigade
of his Command to its ground, the other Brigades will be
conducted by their commanding Officers in separate Columns. The Posts of each Brigade will be pointed out by Baron
De Steuben's Aids. Majr. Walker will attend Lord Stirling—
Major DeEponsien the Marquis De la Fayette and Captain
Lanfant the Baron De Kalb. The line is to be formed with the
Interval of a foot between the files.

Each man is to have a Gill of rum. The Quarter Masters of
the several Brigades are to apply to the Adjutant General for
an order on the Commissary of Military Stores for the number
of blank Cartridges that may be wanted.

To Robert Morris

Valley-forge, May 25, 1778.

Dear Sir: Your favor of the 9th Inst informed me of the
acceptable present which your friend Mr Governeur (of Cur-
racoa) was pleased to intend for me, and for which he will,
through you. accept my sincere thanks, these are also due to
you my good sir, for the kind Communication of the matter,
and for the trouble you have had in ordering the Wine forward.

I rejoice most sincerely with you, on the glorious change
in our prospects, Calmness and serenity, seems likely to succeed in some measure, those dark and tempestuous clouds
which at times appeared ready to overwhelm us, The game,

whether well or ill played hitherto, seems now to be verging fast to a favourable issue, and cannot I think be lost, unless we throw it away by too much supineness on the one hand, or impetuosity on the other, God forbid that either of these should happen at a time when we seem to be upon the point of reaping the fruits of our toil and labour, A stroke, and reverse, under such circumstances, would be doubly distressing.

My best respects in which Mrs. Washington joins, are offered to your Lady, and with sincere thanks for your kind wishes, etc.

To Landon Carter

Valley Forge, May 30, 1778.

My Dear Sir: Your favors of the 10th of March (ended the 20th) and 7th inst. came safe to hand after a good deal of delay.

I thank you much for your kind and affectionate remembrance and mention of me, and for that solicitude for my welfare, which breathes through the whole of your letters. Were I not warm in my acknowledgments for your distinguished regard, I should feel that sense of ingratitude, which I hope will never constitute a part of my character, nor find a place in my bosom. My friends therefore may believe me sincere in my professions of attachment to them, whilst Providence has a joint claim to my humble and grateful thanks, for its protection and direction of me, through the many difficult and intricate scenes, which this contest hath produced; and for the constant interposition in our behalf, when the clouds were heaviest and seemed ready to burst upon us.

To paint the distresses and perilous situation of this army in the course of last winter, for want of cloaths, provisions, and almost every other necessary, essential to the well-being, (I may say existence,) of an army, would require more time and an abler pen than mine; nor, since our prospects have so miraculously brightened, shall I attempt it, or even bear it in remembrance, further than as a memento of what is due to the great Author of all the care and good, that have been extended in relieving us in difficulties and distress.

The accounts which you had received of the accession of Canada to the Union were premature. It is a measure much to be wished, and I believe would not be displeasing to the body of that people; but, while Carleton remains among them, with three or four thousand regular troops, they dare not avow their sentiments, (if they really are favorable,) without a strong support. Your ideas of its importance to our political union coincide exactly with mine. If that country is not with us, it will, from its proximity to the eastern States, its intercourse and connexion with the numerous tribes of western Indians, its communion with them by water and other local advantages, be at least a troublesome if not a dangerous neighbor to us; and ought, at all events, to be in the same interests and politics, of the other States.

If all the counties in Virginia had followed the example of yours, it would have been a fortunate circumstance for this army; but instead of fifteen hundred men, under the first draft, and two thousand from the latter, we have by an accurate return made me four days ago received only twelve hundred and forty-two in the whole. From hence, unless you can conceive our country possessed of less virtue, or less knowledge in the principles of government than other States, you may account for the multitude of men, which undoubtedly you have heard our army consisted of, and consequently for many things, which, without such a key, would seem mysterious.

With great truth I think I can assure you, that the information you received from a gentleman at Sabine Hall, respecting a disposition in the northern officers to see me superseded in my command by General G—s is without the least foundation. I have very sufficient reasons to think, that no officers in the army are more attached to me, than those from the northward, and of those, none more so than the gentlemen, who were under the immediate command of G—s last campaign. That there was a scheme of this sort on foot, last fall, admits of no doubt; but it originated in another quarter; with three men, who wanted to aggrandize themselves; but finding no support, on the contrary, that their conduct and views, when seen into, were likely to undergo severe rep-

rehension, they slunk back, disavowed the measure, and professed themselves my warmest admirers. Thus stands the
matter at present. Whether any members of Congress were
privy to this scheme, and inclined to aid and abet it, I shall
not take upon me to say; but am well informed, that no whisper of the kind was ever heard in Congress.

The draughts of bills as mentioned by you, and which have
since passed into acts of British legislation, are so strongly
marked with folly and villany, that one can scarce tell which
predominates, or how to be surprised at any act of a British
minister. This last trite performance of Master North's is neither more nor less than an insult to common sense, and shows
to what extremity of folly wicked men in a bad cause are
sometimes driven; for this rude Boreas, who was to bring
America to his feet, knew at the time of draughting these bills,
or had good reason to believe, that a treaty had actually been
signed between the court of France and the United States. By
what rule of common sense, then, he could expect that such
an undisguised artifice would go down in America I cannot
conceive. But, thanks to Heaven, the tables are turned; and
we, I hope, shall have our independence secured, in its fullest
extent, without cringing to this Son of Thunder, who I am
persuaded will find abundant work for his troops elsewhere;
on which happy prospect I sincerely congratulate you and
every friend to American liberty.

The enemy seem to be upon the point of evacuating Philadelphia, and I am persuaded are going to New York, whether
as a place of rendezvous of their whole force, for a general
imbarkation, or to operate up the North River, or to act from
circumstances is not quite so clear. My own opinion is, that
they must either give up the Continent or the Islands; which
they will do, is not clear; and yet, I think, they will endeavor
to retain New York, if they can by any means spare troops
enough to garrison it. Reinforcements will, undoubtedly, be
sent to Canada, Nova Scotia, &c.; and I presume must go
from their army in America, as I trust full employment will be
found for their subscription, and other Troops in England and
Ireland. Equally uncertain is it, whether the Enemy will move
from Philadelphia by Land or Water. I am inclined to think
the former, and lament that the number of our sick (under

inoculation, &c.), the situation of our stores, and other matters, will not allow me to make a large detachment from this army till the enemy have actually crossed the Delaware and began their march for South Amboy, then it will be too late; so that we must give up the idea of harassing them *much* in their march through the Jerseys, or attempt it at the hazard of this Camp, and the stores which are covered by the army that lays in it, if we should divide our forces, or remove it wholly, which by the by, circumstanced as the Quartermaster's department is, is impracticable.

I am sorry it is not in my power to furnish you with the letter required, which, (with many others,) was written to show, that I was an enemy to independence, and with a view to create distrust and jealousy. I never had but one of them, and that I sent to Mrs. Washington, to let her see what obliging folks there were in the world. As a sample of it, I enclose you another letter, written for me to Mr. Custis, of the same tenor, and which I happen to have by me. It is no easy matter to decide, whether the villany or artifice of these letters is greatest. They were written by a person, who had some knowledge or information of the component parts of my family, and yet so deficient in circumstances and facts, as to run into egregious misrepresentations of both.

I have spun out a long letter, and send it to you in a very slovenly manner; but, not having time to give it with more fairness, and flattering myself into a belief, that you had rather receive it in this dress than not at all, I shall make no other apology for the interlineations and scratches you will find in it, than you will please to allow my hurried situation. I am, dear Sir, &c.

To Henry Laurens

English Town, July 1, 1778.

Sir: I embrace the first moment of leisure, to give Congress a more full and particular account of the movements of the Army under my command, since its passing the Delaware, than the situation of our Affairs would heretofore permit.

I had the honor to advise them, that on the appearance of the enemy's intention to march thro' Jersey becoming serious, I had detached General Maxwells Brigade, in conjunction with the Militia of that State, to interrupt and impede their progress, by every obstruction in their power; so as to give time to the Army under my command to come up with them, and take advantage of any favorable circumstances that might present themselves. The Army having proceeded to Coryell's ferry and crossed the Delaware at that place, I immediately sent off Colo. Morgan with a select Corps of 600 Men to reinforce General Maxwell, and marched with the main Body towards Princetown.

The slow advance of the Enemy had greatly the air of design, and led me, with others, to suspect that General Clinton desirous of a general Action was endeavouring to draw us down, into the lower Country, in order by a rapid movement to gain our Right, and take possession of the strong Grounds above us. This consideration, and to give the troops time to repose and refresh themselves from the fatigues they had experienced from rainy and excessive hot Weather, determined me to halt at Hopewell Township, about five Miles from Princetown, where we remained till the Morning of the 25th. On the proceeding day I made a second detachment of 1500 chosen troops under Brigadier Genl. Scott, to reinforce those already in the vicinity of the Enemy, the more effectually to annoy and delay their march. The next day the Army moved to Kingston, and having received intelligence that the Enemy were prosecuting their Rout towards Monmouth Court House, I dispatched a thousand select Men, under Brigadier General Wayne, and sent the Marquis de la Fayette to take the command of the whole advanced Corps, including Maxwells Brigade and Morgans light Infantry; with orders to take the first fair opportunity of attacking the Enemy's Rear. In the evening of the same day, the whole Army marched from Kingston where our Baggage was left, with intention to preserve a proper distance for supporting the advanced Corps, and arrived at Cranberry early the next morning. The intense heat of the Weather, and a heavy storm unluckily coming on made it impossible to resume our march that day without great inconvenience and injury to the troops. Our advanced Corps, being differently circumstanced, moved from the position it had held the night before, and took post in the evening on the Monmouth Road, about five Miles from the Enemy's Rear; in expectation of attacking them the next morning on their march. The main Body having remained at Cranberry, the advanced Corps was found to be too remote, and too far upon the Right to be supported either in case of an attack upon, or from the Enemy, which induced me to send orders to the Marquis to file off by his left towards English Town, which he accordingly executed early in the Morning of the 27th.

The Enemy, in Marching from Allen Town had changed their disposition and placed their best troops in the Rear, consisting of all the Grenadiers, Light Infantry, and Chasseurs of the line. This alteration made it necessary to increase the number of our advanced Corps; in consequence of which I detached Major General Lee with two Brigades to join the Marquis at English Town, on whom of course the command of the whole devolved, amounting to about five thousand Men. The main Body marched the same day and encamped within three Miles of that place. Morgans Corps was left hovering on the Enemy's right flank and the Jersey Militia, amounting at this time to about 7 or 800 Men under General Dickinson on their left.

The Enemy were now encamped in a strong position, with their right extending about a Mile and a half beyond the Court House, in the parting of the Roads leading to Shrewsbury and Middletown, and their left along the Road from Allen Town to Monmouth, about three miles on this side the Court House. Their Right flank lay on the skirt of a small-wood, while their left was secured by a very thick one, and a Morass running towards their rear, and their whole front covered by a wood, and for a considerable extent towards the left with a Morass. In this situation they halted till the morning of the 28th.

Matters being thus situated, and having had the best information, that if the Enemy were once arrived at the Heights of Middletown, ten or twelve Miles from where they were, it would be impossible to attempt any thing against them with a prospect of success I determined to attack their Rear the moment they should get in motion from their present Ground. I communicated my intention to General Lee, and ordered him to make his disposition for the attack, and to keep his Troops constantly lying upon their Arms, to be in readiness at the shortest notice. This was done with respect to the Troops under my immediate command.

About five in the Morning General Dickinson sent an Express, informing that the Front of the Enemy had began their march, I instantly put the Army in motion, and sent orders by one of my Aids to General Lee to move on and attack them, unless there should be very powerful Reason's to the contrary; acquainting him at the same time, that I was marching to support him and for doing it with the greater expedition and convenience, should make the men disincumber themselves of their packs and Blankets.

After marching about five Miles, to my great surprise and mortification, I met the whole advanced Corps retreating, and, as I was told, by General Lee's orders, without having made any opposition, except one fire given by a party under the command of Colo. Butler, on their being charged by the Enemy's Cavalry, who were repulsed. I proceeded immediately to the Rear of the Corps, which I found closely pressed by the Enemy, and gave directions for forming part of the retreating troops, who by the brave and spirited conduct of the Officers, and aided by some pieces of well served Artillery, checked the Enemy's advance, and gave time to make a disposition of the left wing and second line of the Army upon an eminence, and in a wood a little in the Rear covered by a morass in front. On this were placed some Batteries of Cannon by Lord Stirling who commanded the left Wing, which played upon the Enemy with great effect, and seconded by parties of Infantry detached to oppose them, effectually put a stop to their advance.

General Lee being detached with the advanced Corps, the command of the Right Wing, for the occasion, was given to General Greene. For the expedition of the march, and to counteract any attempt to turn our Right, I had ordered him to file off by the new Church two miles from English Town, and fall into the Monmouth Road, a small distance in the Rear of the Court House, while the rest of the Column moved directly on towards the Court House. On intelligence of the Retreat, he marched up and took a very advantageous position on the Right.

The Enemy by this time, finding themselves warmly opposed in front made an attempt to turn our left Flank; but they were bravely repulsed and driven back by detached parties of Infantry. They also made a movement to our Right, with as little success, General Greene having advanced a Body of Troops with Artillery to a commanding piece of Ground, which not only disappointed their design of turning our Right, but severely infiladed those in front of the left Wing. In addition to this, General Wayne advanced with a Body of Troops and kept up so severe and well directed a fire that the Enemy were soon compelled to retire behind the defile where the first stand in the beginning of the Action had been made.

In this situation, the Enemy had both their Flanks secured by thick Woods and Morasses, while their front could only be approached thro a narrow pass. I resolved nevertheless to attack them, and for that purpose ordered General Poor with his own and the Carolina Brigade, to move round upon their Right, and General Woodford upon their left, and the Artillery to gall them in front: But the impediments in their way prevented their getting within reach before it was dark. They remained upon the Ground, they had been directed to occupy, during the Night, with intention to begin the attack early the next morning, and the Army continued lying upon their Arms in the Field of Action, to be in readiness to support them. In the meantime the Enemy were employed in removing their wounded, and about 12 OClock at Night marched away in such silence, that tho' General Poor lay extremely near them, they effected their Retreat without his Knowledge. They carried off all their wounded except four Officers and about Fifty privates whose wounds were too dangerous to permit their removal.

The extreme heat of the Weather, the fatigue of the Men from their march thro' a deep, sandy Country almost entirely destitute of Water, and the distance the Enemy had gained by marching in the Night, made a pursuit impracticable and fruitless. It would have answered no valuable purpose, and would have been fatal to numbers of our Men, several of whom died the preceeding day with Heat.

Were I to conclude my account of this day's transactions without expressing my obligations to the Officers of the Army in general, I should do injustice to their merit, and violence to my own feelings. They seemed to vie with each other in manifesting their Zeal and Bravery. The Catalogue of those who distinguished themselves is too long to admit of particularising individuals; I cannot however forbear mentioning Brigadier General Wayne whose good conduct and bravery thro' the whole action deserves particular commendation.

The Behaviour of the troops in general, after they recovered from the first surprise occasioned by the Retreat of the advanced Corps, was such as could not be surpassed.

All the Artillery both Officers and Men that were engaged, distinguished themselves in a remarkable manner.

Inclosed Congress will be pleased to receive a Return of the killed, wounded and missing. Among the first were Lieut. Colo. Bunner of Penna. and Major Dickinson of Virginia, both Officers of distinguished merit and much to be regretted. The Enemys slain left on the Field and buried by us, according to the Return of the persons assigned to that duty were four Officers and Two hundred and forty five privates. In the former number was the Honble. Colo Monckton. Exclusive of these they buried some themselves, as there were several new Graves near the field of Battle. How many Men they may have had wounded cannot be determined; but from the usual proportion to the slain, the number must have been considerable. There were a few prisoners taken.

The peculiar Situation of General Lee at this time requires that I should say nothing of his Conduct. He is now in arrest. The Charges against him, with such Sentence as the Court Martial may decree in his Case, shall be transmitted for the approbation or disapprobation of Congress as soon as it shall have passed.

Being fully convinced by the Gentlemen of this Country that the Enemy cannot be hurt or injured in their embarkation at Sandy Hook the place to which they are going, and being unwilling to get too far removed from the North River, I put the Troops in motion early this morning and shall proceed that way, leaving the Jersey Brigade, Morgan's Corps and other light parties (the Militia being all dismissed) to hover about them, countenance desertion and to prevent their depredations, as far as possible. After they embark the former will take post in the Neighbourhood of Elizabeth Town. The latter rejoin the Corps from which they were detached. I have the Honor etc.

To Thomas Nelson

Camp at the White-plains, August 20, 1778.

My dear Sir: In what terms can I sufficiently thank you for your polite attention to me, and agreeable present? and, which is still more to the purpose, with what propriety can I deprive you of a valuable, and favourite Horse? You have pressed me once, nay twice, to accept him as a gift; as a proof of my sincere attachment to, and friendship for you, I obey, with this assurance, that from none but a Gentn. for whom I have the highest regard, would I do this, notwithstanding the distressed situation I have been in for want of one.

I am heartily disappointed at a late resolution of Congress for the discontinuance of your Corps, because I pleased myself with the prospect of seeing you, and many other Gentn. of my acquaintance from Virginia, in Camp. As you had got to Philadelphia, I do not think the saving, or difference of expense (taking up the matter even upon that ground, which under present circumstances I think a very erroneous one) was by any means an object suited to the occasion.

The arrival of the French Fleet upon the Coast of America is a great, and striking event; but the operations of it have been injured by a number of unforeseen and unfavourable circumstances, which, tho they ought not to detract from the merit, and good intention of our great Ally, has nevertheless lessened the importance of their Services in a great degree. The length of the passage in the first instance was a capital misfortune, for had even one of common length taken place, Lord Howe with the British Ships of War and all the Transports in the River Delaware must, inevitably, have fallen; and

Sir Harry must have had better luck than is commonly dispensed to Men of his profession, under such circumstances, if he and his Troops had not shared (at least) the fate of Burgoyne. The long passage of Count D'Estaing was succeeded by an unfavourable discovery at the hook, which hurt us in two respects; first in a defeat of the enterprize upon New York; the Shipping, and Troops at that place; and next, in the delay that was used in ascertaining the depth of Water over the Bar; which was essential to their entrance into the Harbour of New York, and lastly, after the enterprize upon Rhode Island had been planned, and was in the moment of execution, that Lord Howe with the British Ships should interpose, merely to create diversion, and draw the French fleet from the Island was again unlucky, as the Count had not return'd on the 17th. to the Island, tho drawn of from it the 10th; by which means the Land operations were retarded, and the whole subject to a miscarriage in case of the arrival of Byrons Squadron.

I do not know what to make of the enemy at New York; whether their stay at that place is the result of choice, or the effect of necessity, proceeding from an inferiority in the Fleet, want of Provision, or other Causes, I know not, but certain it is that, if it is not an act of necessity it is profoundly misterious unless they look for considerable reinforcements and are waiting the arrival of them to commence their operations, time will shew.

It is not a little pleasing, nor less wonderful to contemplate, that after two years Manœuvring and undergoing the strangest vicissitudes that perhaps ever attended any one contest since the creation both Armies are brought back to the very point they set out from and, that that, which was the offending party in the beginning is now reduced to the use of the spade and pick axe for defence. The hand of Providence has been so conspicuous in all this, that he must be worse than an infidel that lacks faith, and more than wicked, that has not gratitude enough to acknowledge his obligations, but, it will be time enough for me to turn preacher, when my present appointment ceases; and therefore, I shall add no more on the Doctrine of Providence; but make a tender of my best respects to your good Lady; the Secretary and other friends and assure you that with the most perfect regard I am etc.

P.S. Since writing the foregoing, I have been favoured with your Letter of the 25th. Ulto. from Baltimore, and 9th. Instt. from Philadelphia. The method you propose to take with the Public Horses in your volunteer Corps will be very proper and agreeable to me.

To Comte d'Estaing

Head Quarters, September 11, 1778.
Sir: I have had the honor of receiving your Letter of the 5th. inst: accompanied by a Copy of two Letters to Congress and Genl. Sullivan. The confidence which you have been pleased to shew in communicating these papers engage my sincere thanks. If the deepest regret that the best concerted enterprise and bravest exertions should have been rendered fruitless by a disaster which human prudence is incapable of foreseeing or preventing can alleviate disappointment, you may be assured that the whole Continent sympathizes with you; it will be a consolation to you to reflect that the thinking part of Mankind do not form their judgment from events; and that their equity will ever attach equal glory to those actions which deserve success, as to those which have been crowned with it. It is in the trying circumstances to which your Excellency has been exposed, that the virtues of a great Mind are displayed in their brightest lustre; and that the General's Character is better known than in the moment of Victory; it was yours, by every title which can give it, and the adverse element which robbed you of your prize, can never deprive you of the Glory due to you. Tho your success has not been equal to your expectations yet you have the satisfaction of reflecting that you have rendered essential Services to the common cause.

I exceedingly lament that in addition to our misfortunes, there has been the least suspension of harmony and good understanding between the Generals of allied Nations, whose views, must like their interests be the same. On the first intimation of it I employed my influence in restoring what I regard as essential to the permanence of an Union founded on mutual inclination and the strongest ties of reciprocal advantage. Your Excellencys offer to the Council of Boston had a powerful tendency to promote the same end, and was distinguished proof of your zeal and magnanimity.

The present superiority of the enemy in Naval force, must, for a time, suspend all plans of offensive cooperation between us; it is not easy to foresee what change may take place by the arrival of Succours to you from Europe or what opening the enemy may give you to resume your activity; in this moment therefore, every consultation on this subject would be premature. But it is of infinite importance that we should take all the means that our circumstances will allow for the defence of a Squadron, which is so precious to the common cause of france and America, and which may have become a capital object with the enemy. Whether this really is the case can be only matter of Conjecture; the original intention of the reinforcement sent to Rhode island, was obviously the Relief of the Garrison at that post. I have to lament that, tho seasonably advised of the movement, it was utterly out of my power to counteract it. A naval force alone could have defeated the attempt; how far their views may since have been enlarged by the arrival of Byron's fleet, Your Excellency will be best able to judge. Previous to this event, I believe Genl. Clinton was waiting orders from his court, for the conduct he was to pursue; in the mean time embarking his Stores and heavy baggage in order to be the better prepared for a promt evacuation, if his instructions should require it.

But as the present posture of affairs may induce a change of operations, and tempt them to carry the war eastward for the ruin of your Squadron, it will be necessary for us to be prepared to oppose such an enterprise. I am unhappy that our situation will not admit of our contributing more effectually to this important end; but assure you at the same time, that what ever can be attempted without losing sight of objects equally essential to the interests of the two Nations, shall be put in execution.

A Candid view of our affairs which I am going to exhibit, will make you a judge of the difficulties, under which we labour. Almost all our supplies of flour and no inconsiderable part of our meat, are drawn from the States westward of

Hudson's River; this renders a secure communication across that River indispensably necessary both to the support of your Squadron and the Army. The enemy being masters of that navigation, would interrupt this essential intercourse between the States. They have been sensible of these advantages, and by the attempts which they have made, to bring about a separation of the Eastern from the Southern States, and the facility which their superiority by Sea had hitherto given him, have always obliged us besides garrisoning the Forts that immediately defend the passage, to keep a force at least, equal to that which they have had posted in New York and its dependencies.

It is incumbent upon us at this time to have a greater force in this quarter than usual, from the concentred State of the enemy's strength and the uncertainty of their designs; in addition to this it is to be observed that they derive an inestimable advantage from the facility of transporting their troops from one point to another; these rapid movements enable them to give us uneasiness for remote unguarded parts, in attempting to succour which we should be exposed to ruinous marches, and after all perhaps be the dupes of a feint. if they could by any demonstration in another part draw our attention and strength from this important point, and by anticipating our return, possess themselves of it, the consequences would be fatal. Our dispositions must therefore have equal regard to cooperating with you in a defensive plan, and securing the North River; which, the remoteness of the two objects from each other, renders peculiarly difficult. Immediately upon the change which happened in your naval affairs, my attention was directed to conciliating these two great ends.

The necessity of transporting magazines, collected relatively to our present position, and making new arrangements for ulterior operations, has hitherto been productive of delay. these points are now nearly accomplished and I hope in a day or two to begin a general movement of the Army eastward, as a commencement of this, one division marched this morning under Major General Gates towards Danbury, and the rest of the army will follow as speedily as possible.

The following is a general Idea of my disposition: The Army will be thrown into several divisions, one of which consisting of a force equal to the Enemy's in New York, will be posted about thirty miles in the rear of my present camp, and in the vicinity of the North River with a view to its defence; the other will be pushed on at different stages, as far towards Connecticut River, as can be done consistently with preserving a communication, and having them within supporting distance of each other; so as that when occasion may require, they may form a junction, either for their own immediate defence, or to oppose any attempts that may be made on the North River. The facility which the enemy have of collecting their whole force and turning it against any point they choose, will restrain us from extending ourselves so far as will either expose us to be beaten by detachment or endanger the Security of the North River.

This disposition will place the American forces as much in measure for assisting in the defence of your Squadron and the Town of Boston, as is compatible with the other great objects of our care.

It does not appear to me probable that the Enemy would hazard the penetrating to Boston by land, with the force which they at present have to the eastward. I am rather inclined to believe that they will draw together their whole Land and Naval strength, to give the greater probability of Success. in order to this, New York must be evacuated, an event which cannot take place without being announced by circumstances impossible to conceal and I have reason to hope that the time which must necessarily be exhausted in embarking and transporting their troops and Stores, would be sufficient for me to advance a considerable part of my army in measure for opposing them.

The observations which Your Excellency makes relative to the necessity of having intelligent Spies, are perfectly just; every measure that circumstances would admit has been to answer this valuable end, and our intelligence has in general been as good as could be expected from the situation of the Enemy.

The distance at which we are from our posts of observation in the first instance, and the long Journey which is afterwards to be performed before a letter can reach your Excellency hinder my communicating intelligence with such celerity as I could wish.

The letter which I sent giving an account of Lord Howes movement, was dispatched as soon as the fact was ascertained; but it did not arrive 'till you had gone to Sea, in pursuit of the British Squadron.

As your Excellency does not mention the letters which I last had the honor of writing to you, I am apprehensive of some delay, or miscarriage; their dates were the 3rd. and 4th. inst.

The sincere esteem and regard which I feel for Your Excellency, make me set the highest value upon every expression of friendship with which you are pleased to honor me; I entreat you to accept the most cordial returns on my part.

I shall count it a singular felicity if in the course of possible operations above alluded to, personal intercourse shd afford me the means of cultivating a closer intimacy with you, and of proving more particularly the respect and attachment with which I have the honor etc.

P.S. My dispatches were going to be closed when your Excellency's Letter of the 8th. was delivered to me.

The State of Byron's Fleet from the best intelligence I have been able to obtain, is as follows:

Six Ships, the names of which are mentioned in the paper I had the honor of transmitting the 3rd. have arrived at New York with their Crews in very bad health.

Two vizt. The Cornwall of *74* and Monmouth of *64*, had joined Lord Howe; *two* One of which the Admirals Ship, were missing. One had put back to Portsmouth.

To Gouverneur Morris

Fish-kill, October 4, 1778.

Dear Sir: My public Letters to the President of Congress will inform you of the Wind that wafted me to this place; nothing more therefore need be said on that head.

Your Letter of the 8th. Ulto. contains three questions and

answers, to wit: Can the Enemy prosecute the War? Do they mean to stay on the Continent? And is it our interest to put impediments in the way of their departure? To the first you answer in the Negative; to the second you are decided in opinion that they do not; And to the third, say, clearly No.

Much, my good Sir, may be said in favor of these answers; and *some* things against the two first of them. By way therefore of dissertation on the first, I will also beg leave to put a question, and give it an answer. Can *we* carry on the War much longer? certainly *NO*, unless some measures can be devised, and speedily executed, to restore the credit of our Currency, restrain extortion, and punish forestallers.

Without these can be effected, what funds can stand the present expences of the Army? And what Officer can bear the weight of prices, that every necessary Article is now got to? A Rat, in the shape of a Horse, is not to be bought at this time for less than £200; a Saddle under thirty or Forty; Boots twenty, and Shoes and other articles in like proportion. How is it possible therefore for Officers to stand this, without an increase of pay? And how is it possible to advance their Pay when Flour is selling (at different places) from five to fifteen pounds pr. Ct., Hay from ten to thirty pounds pr. Tunn, and Beef and other essentials, in this proportion.

The true point of light then to place, and consider this matter in, is not simply whether G. Britain can carry on the War, but whose Finances (theirs or ours) is most likely to fail: which leads me to doubt *very much* the infalibility of the answer given to your Second question, respecting the Enemy's leaving the Continent; for I believe, that they will not do it, while ever *hope* and the chapter of *accidents* can give them a *chance* of bringing us to terms short of *Independance*. But this *you* perhaps will say, they are now bereft of. *I* shall acknowledge that many things favor the idea; but add, that upon a comparative view of circumstances there is abundant matter to puzzle and confound the judgment. To your third answer, I subscribe with hand and heart. the opening is now fair, and God grant they may embrace the oppertunity of bidding an eternal adieu to our, once quit of them, happy Land. If the Spaniards would but join their Fleets to those of France, and commence hostilities, my doubts would all subside. Without it, I fear the British Navy has it too much in its power to counteract the Schemes of France.

The high prices of every necessary. The little, indeed no benefit, which Officers have derived from the intended bounty of Congress in the article of Cloathing, The change in the establishment, by which so many of them are discontinued. The unfortunate delay of this business, which kept them too long in suspence, and set a number of evil spirits to work. The unsettled Rank, and contradictory modes of adjusting it, with other causes which might be enumerated, have conspired to sour the temper of the Army exceedingly; and has, I am told, been productive of a Memorial, or representation of some kind, to Congress, which neither directly, nor indirectly did I know, or ever hear was in agitation, till some days after it was dispatched; owing, as I apprehend, to the secrecy with which it was conducted to keep it from my knowledge, as I had in a similar instance last Spring, discountenanced and stifled a child of the same illigitimacy in its birth. If you have any News worth communicating, do not put it under a bushel, but transmit it to Dr. Sir, Yrs. sincerely.

To Henry Laurens

Fredericksburgh, November 14, 1778.

Dear Sir: This will be accompanied by an official letter on the subject of the proposed expedition against Canada. You will perceive I have only considered it in a military light; indeed I was not authorised to consider it in any other; and I am not without apprehensions, that I may be thought, in what I have done, to have exceeded the limits intended by Congress. But my solicitude for the public welfare which I think deeply interested in this affair, will I hope justify me in the eyes of all those who view things through that just medium.

I do not know, Sir, what may be your sentiments in the present case; but whatever they are I am sure I can confide in your honor and friendship, and shall not hesitate to unbosom myself to you on a point of the most delicate and important Nature.

The question of the Canadian expedition in the form it now stands appears to me one of the most interesting that has hitherto agitated our National deliberations. I have one objection to it, untouched in my public letter, which is in my estimation, insurmountable, and alarms all my feelings for the true and permanent interests of my country. This is the introduction of a large body of French troops into Canada, and putting them in possession of the capital of that Province, attached to them by all the ties of blood, habits, manners, religion and former connexion of government. I fear this would be too great a temptation, to be resisted by any power actuated by the common maxims of national policy. Let us realize for a moment the striking advantages France would derive from the possession of Canada; the acquisition of an extensive territory abounding in supplies for the use of her Islands; the opening a vast source of the most beneficial commerce with the Indian nations, which she might then monopolize; the having ports of her own on this continent independent on the precarious good will of an ally; the engrossing the whole trade of New found land whenever she pleased, the finest nursery of seamen in the world; the security afforded to her Islands; and finally, the facility of awing and controuling these states, the natural and most formidable rival of every maritime power in Europe. Canada would be a solid acquisition to France on all these accounts and because of the numerous inhabitants, subjects to her by inclination, who would aid in preserving it under her power against the attempt of every other.

France acknowledged for some time past the most powerful monarchy in Europe by land, able now to dispute the empire of the sea with Great Britain, and if joined with Spain, I may say certainly superior, possessed of New Orleans, on our Right, Canada on our left and seconded by the numerous tribes of Indians on our Rear from one extremity to the other, a people, so generally friendly to her and whom she knows so well how to conciliate; would, it is much to be apprehended have it in her power to give law to these states.

Let us suppose, that when the five thousand french troops (and under the idea of that number twice as many might be introduced,) were entered the city of Quebec; they should declare an intention to hold Canada, as a pledge and surety for the debts due to France from the United States, or, under other specious pretences hold the place till they can find a bone for contention, and in the meanwhile should excite the Canadians to engage in supporting their pretences and claims; what should we be able to say with only four or five thousand men to carry on the dispute? It may be supposed that France would not choose to renounce our friendship by a step of this kind as the consequence would probably be a reunion with England on some terms or other; and the loss of what she had acquired, in so violent and unjustifiable a manner, with all the advantages of an Alliance with us. This in my opinion is too slender a security against the measure to be relied on. The truth of the position will intirely depend on naval events. If France and Spain should unite and obtain a decided superiority by Sea, a reunion with England would avail very little and might be set at defiance. France, with a numerous army at command might throw in what number of land forces she thought proper to support her pretensions; and England without men, without money, and inferior on her favourite element could give no effectual aid to oppose them. Resentment, reproaches, and submission seem to be all that would be left us. Men are very apt to run into extremes; hatred to England may carry some into an excess of Confidence in France; especially when motives of gratitude are thrown into the scale. Men of this description would be unwilling to suppose France capable of acting so ungenerous a part. I am heartily disposed to entertain the most favourable sentiments of our new ally and to cherish them in others to a reasonable degree; but it is a maxim founded on the universal experience of mankind, that no nation is to be trusted farther than it is bound by its interest; and no prudent statesman or politician will venture to depart from it. In our circumstances we ought to be particularly cautious; for we have not yet attained sufficient vigor and maturity to recover from the shock of any false step into which we may unwarily fall.

If France should even engage in the scheme, in the first instance with the purest intentions, there is the greatest danger that, in the progress of the business, invited to it by circumstances and, perhaps, urged on by the solicitations and wishes of the Canadians, she would alter her views.

As the Marquis clothed his proposition when he spoke of it to me, it would seem to originate wholly with himself; but it is far from impossible that it had its birth in the Cabinet of France and was put into this artful dress, to give it the readier currency. I fancy that I read in the countenances of some people on this occasion, more than the disinterested zeal of allies. I hope I am mistaken and that my fears of mischief make me refine too much, and awaken jealousies that have no sufficient foundation.

But upon the whole, Sir, to wave every other consideration; I do not like to add to the number of our national obligations. I would wish as much as possible to avoid giving a foreign power new claims of merit for services performed, to the United States, and would ask no assistance that is not indispensible. I am, etc.

To Benjamin Harrison

Head Qrs., Middle Brook, December 18, 1778.
My dear Sir: You will be so obliging as to present the inclosed to the House when oppertunity, and a suitable occasion offers. I feel very sensibly the late honorable testimony of their remembrance; to stand well in the good opinion of my Countrymen constitutes my chiefest happiness; and will be my best support under the perplexities and difficulties of my present Station.

The mention of my lands in the back Country was more owing to accident than design; the Virga. Officers having sollicited leave for Colo. Wood to attend the Assembly of that commonwealth with some representation of theirs respecting their claims, or wishes, brought my own matters (of a similar nature) to view; but I am too little acquainted with the minutiæ of them to ground an application on or give any trouble to the Assembly concerning them. Under the proclamation of 1763, I am entitled to 5000 Acres of Land in my own right;

and by purchase from Captn. Roots, Posey, and some other Officers, I obtained rights to several thousands more, a small part of wch. I patented during the Admn. of Lord Dunmore; another part was (I believe) Surveyed, whilst the major part remains in locations; but where (without having recourse to my Memms.) and under what circumstances, I know not at this time any more than you do, nor do I wish to give trouble abt. them.

I can assign but two causes for the enemys continuance among us, and these balance so equally in my Mind, that I scarce know which of the two preponderates. The one is, that they are waiting the ultimate determination of Parliament; the other, that of our distresses; by which I know the Commissioners went home not a little buoyed up; and sorry I am to add, not without cause. What may be the effect of such large and frequent emissions, of the dissentions, Parties, extravagance, and a general lax of public virtue Heaven alone can tell! I am affraid even to think of It; but it appears as clear to me as ever the Sun did in its meredian brightness, that America never stood in more eminent need of the wise, patriotic, and Spirited exertions of her Sons than at this period and if it is not a sufficient cause for genl. lamentation, my misconception of the matter impresses it too strongly upon me, that the States seperately are too much engaged in their local concerns, and have too many of their ablest men withdrawn from the general Council for the good of the common weal; in a word, I think our political system may, be compared to the mechanism of a Clock; and that our conduct should derive a lesson from it for it answers no good purpose to keep the smaller Wheels in order if the greater one which is the support and prime mover of the whole is neglected. How far the latter is the case does not become me to pronounce but as there can be no harm in a pious wish for the good of ones Country I shall offer it as mine that each State wd. not only choose, but absolutely compel their ablest Men to attend Congress; that they would instruct them to go into a thorough investigation of the causes that have produced so many disagreeable effects in the Army and Country; in a word that public abuses should be corrected, and an entire reformation worked; without these it does not, in my judgment, require the spirit of

divination to foretell the consequences of the present Administration, nor to how little purpose the States, individually, are
framing constitutions, providing laws, and filling Offices with
the abilities of their ablest Men. These, if the great whole is
mismanaged must sink in the general wreck and will carry with
it the remorse of thinking that we are lost by our own folly
and negligence, or the desire perhaps of living in ease and
tranquility during the expected accomplishment of so great a
revolution in the effecting of which the greatest abilities and
the honestest Men our (i.e. the American) world affords
ought to be employed. It is much to be feared my dear Sir
that the States in their seperate capacities have very inadequate
ideas of the present danger. Removed (some of them) far distant from the scene of action and seeing, and hearing such
publications only as flatter their wishes they conceive that the
contest is at an end, and that to regulate the government and
police of their own State is all that remains to be done; but it
is devoutly to be wished that a sad reverse of this may not fall
upon them like a thunder clap that is little expected. I do not
mean to designate particular States. I wish to cast no reflections upon any one. The Public believes (and if they do believe
it, the fact might almost as well be so) that the States at this
time are badly represented, and that the great, and important
concerns of the nation are horribly conducted, for want either
of abilities or application in the Members, or through discord
and party views of some individuals; that they should be so,
is to be lamented more at this time, than formerly, as we are
far advanced in the dispute and in the opinn. of many drawg.
to a happy period; have the eyes of Europe upon us, and I
am perswaded many political Spies to watch, discover our situation, and give information of our weaknesses and wants.

The story you have related of a proposal to redeem the
paper money at its present depreciated value has also come to
my ears, but I cannot vouch for the authenticity of it. I am
very happy to hear that the Assembly of Virginia have put the
completion of their Regiment upon a footing so apparently
certain, but as one great defect of your past Laws for this
purpose, has lain in the mode of getting the Men to the Army,
I shall hope that effectual measures are pointed out in the
present, to remedy the evil and bring forward all that shall be

raised. The Embargo upon Provisions is a most salutary measure as I am affraid a sufficiency of flour will not easily be
obtained even with money of higher estimation than ours.
adieu my dear Sir.

P.S. Phila. 30th. This Letter was to have gone by Post from
Middle brook but missed that conveyance, since which I have
come to this place at the request of Congress whence I shall
soon return.

I have seen nothing since I came here (on the 22d. Instt.)
to change my opinion of Men or Measrs. but abundant reason
to be convinced, that our Affairs are in a more distressed,
ruinous, and deplorable condition than they have been in
Since the commencement of the War. By a faithful labourer
then in the cause. By a Man who is daily injuring his private
Estate without even the smallest earthly advantage not common to all in case of a favourable Issue to the dispute. By one
who wishes the prosperity of America most devoutly and sees
or thinks he sees it, on the brink of ruin, you are beseeched
most earnestly my dear Colo. Harrison, to exert yourself in
endeavouring to rescue your Country, by, (let me add) sending your ablest and best Men to Congress; these characters
must not slumber, nor sleep at home, in such times of pressing
danger; they must not content themselves in the enjoyment
of places of honor or profit in their own Country, while the
common interests of America are mouldering and sinking into
irretrievable (if a remedy is not soon applied) ruin, in which
theirs also must ultimately be involved. If I was to be called
upon to draw A picture of the times, and of Men; from what
I have seen, heard, and in part know I should in one word
say that idleness, dissipation and extravagance seem to have
laid fast hold of most of them. That Speculation, peculation,
and an insatiable thirst for riches seems to have got the better
of every other consideration and almost of every order of
Men. That party disputes and personal quarrels are the great
business of the day whilst the momentous concerns of an empire, a great and accumulated debt; ruined finances, depreciated money, and want of credit (which in their consequences
is the want of every thing) are but secondary considerations
and postponed from day to day, from week to week as if our
affairs wore the most promising aspect; after drawing this

picture, which from my Soul I believe to be a true one I need not repeat to you that I am alarmed and wish to see my Countrymen roused. I have no resentments, nor do I mean to point at any particular characters; this I can declare upon my honor for I have every attention paid me by Congress than I can possibly expect and have reason to think that I stand well in their estimation but in the present situation of things I cannot help asking: Where is Mason, Wythe, Jefferson, Nicholas, Pendleton, Nelson, and another I could name; and why, if you are sufficiently impressed with your danger, do you not (as New Yk. has done in the case of Mr. Jay) send an extra Member or two for at least a certain limited time till the great business of the Nation is put upon a more respectable and happy establishmt. Your Money is now sinking 5 pr. Ct. a day in this City; and I shall not be surprized if in the course of a few months a total stop is put to the currency of it. And yet an assembly, a concert, a Dinner, or Supper (that will cost three or four hundred pounds) will not only take Men of from acting in but even from thinking of this business while a great part of the Officers of your Army from absolute necessity are quitting the Service and the more virtuous few rather than do this are sinking by sure degrees into beggery and want. I again repeat to you that this is not an exaggerated acct.; that it is an alarming one I do not deny, and confess to you that I feel more real distress on acct. of the prest. appearances of things than I have done at any one time since the commencement of the dispute; but it is time to bid you once more adieu. Providence has heretofore taken us up when all other means and hope seemed to be departing from us, in this I will confide. Yr. &ca.

To Lund Washington

Middle Brook, February 24, 1779.

Dear Lund: I wrote to you by the last post, but in so hasty a manner as not to be so full and clear as the importance of the subject might require. In truth, I find myself at a loss to do it to my own satisfaction in this hour of more leisure and thought, because it is a matter of much importance and requires a good deal of judgment and foresight to time things in such a way as to answer the purposes I have in view.

The advantages resulting from the sale of my negroes, I have very little doubt of; because, as I observed in my last, if we should ultimately prove unsuccessful (of which I am under no apprehension unless it falls on us as a punishment for our want of public, and indeed private virtue) it would be a matter of very little consequence to me, whether my property is in Negroes, or loan office Certificates, as I shall neither ask for, nor expect any favor from his most gracious Majesty, nor any person acting under his authority; the only points therefore for me to consider, are, first, whether it would be most to my interest, in case of a fortunate determination of the present contest, to have negroes, and the Crops they will make; or the sum they will now fetch and the interest of the money. And, secondly, the critical moment to make this sale.

With respect to the first point (if a negro man will sell at, or near one thousand pounds, and woman and children in proportion) I have not the smallest doubt on which side the balance, placed in the scale of interest, will preponderate: My scruples arise from a reluctance in offering these people at public vendue, and on account of the uncertainty of timeing the sale well. In the first case, if these poor wretches are to be held in a state of slavery, I do not see that a change of masters will render it more irksome, provided husband and wife, and Parents and children are not separated from each other, which is not my intentions to do. And with respect to the second, the judgment founded in a knowledge of circumstances, is the only criterion for determining when the tide of depreciation is at an end; for like the flux and reflux of the water, it will no sooner have got to its full ebb or flow, but an immediate turn takes place, and every thing runs in a contrary direction. To hit this critical moment then, is the point; and a point of so much nicety, that the longer I reflect upon the subject, the more embarrassed I am in my opinion; for if a sale takes place while the money is in a depreciating state, that is, before it has arrived at the lowest ebb of depreciation; I shall lose the difference, and if it is delayed, 'till some great and important event shall give a decisive turn in favor of our affairs, it may be too late. Notwithstanding, upon a full consideration of the whole matter; if you have done nothing in consequence of my last letter, I wou'd have you wait 'till you hear further from me on this subject. I will, in the meanwhile, revolve the matter in my mind more fully, and may possibly be better able to draw some more precise conclusions than at present, while you may be employed in endeavouring to ascertain the highest prices Negroes sell at, in different parts of the Country, where, and in what manner it would be best to sell them, when such a measure is adopted, (which I think will very likely happen in the course of a few months.)

Inclosed is my Bond for conveyance of the Land purchased of the Ashfords &c. It is as well drawn as I can do it, and I believe it to be effectual.

February 26, 1779.

Your Letter of the 17th. inst: is just come to hand, your apprehensions on account of my health are groundless; the irregularity of the Post, and stoppage of your letters, or miscarriages of them, were the principal causes of my long silence. My last letter to you was full on the subject of corn; I shall not touch upon it therefore in this. I then desired, and again repeat my wish, that you would sell every thing about the house and plantations, that is not essentially necessary. Mr. Custis wrote to me for an Anchor, to be sold or lent, the former I prefer, as I wish to get quit of all those kind of things; the money arising from all which, the sale of Flour &c, I would have put in the continental loan office. I am glad to hear your success in Lambs is so great. Mrs. Washington joins in remembrance to yourself and Milly, with Dr. Lund, Your affecte. Servant.

To Thomas Nelson

Middle brook, March 15, 1779.

My dear Sir: I have to thank you for your friendly letter of the 9th., and for your obliging, tho unsuccessful endeavours to procure the Horses I am indebted to my Country for. At present I have no immediate call for them, as we find it rather difficult to support the few we keep at Camp, in forage.

It gives me very singular pleasure to find that you have again taken a Seat in Congress; I think there never was a time when cool and dispassionate reasoning; strict attention and application, great integrity, and (if it was in the nature of things, unerring) wisdom were more to be wished for than the present. Our Affairs, according to my judgment, are now come to a crisis, and require no small degree of political skill, to steer clear of those shelves and Rocks which tho deeply buried, may wreck our hopes, and throw us upon some inhospitable shore. Unanimity in our Councils, disinterestedness in our pursuits, and steady perseverence in our national duty, are the only means to avoid misfortunes; if they come upon us after these we shall have the consolation of knowing that we have done our best, the rest is with the Gods.

Shall I hope to have the pleasure of seeing you at Camp, when the weather gets a little settled? I can assure you that it will be a gratification of my wishes. Mrs. Washington salutes you most cordially, and offers her thanks for the letter you was kind enough to send her. I am, etc.

To Henry Laurens

Middle brook, March 20, 1779.

Dear Sir: I have to thank you, and I do it very sincerely, for your obliging favors of the 2d. and 16th Inst.; and for their several inclosures, containing articles of intelligence. I congratulate you most cordially on Campbells precipitate retreat from Fort Augusta. What was this owing to? it seems to have been a surprize even upon Williamson. but I rejoice much more on acct. of his disappointed application to the Creek Indians; this I think, is to be considered as a very important event, and may it not be the conjectural cause of his (Campbells) hasty return; this latter circumstance cannot but be a fresh proof to the disaffected (in that Country) that they are leaning upon a broken reed; severe examples should, in my judgment, be made of those who were forgiven former offences and again in Arms against us.

The policy of our arming Slaves is, in my opinion, a moot point, unless the enemy set the example; for should we begin to form Battalions of them, I have not the smallest doubt (if the War is to be prosecuted) of their following us in it, and justifying the measure upon our own ground; the upshot then must be, who can arm fastest, and where are our Arms? besides, I am not clear that a discrimination will not render Slavery more irksome to those who remain in it; most of the good and evil things of this life are judged of by comparison; and I fear a comparison in this case will be productive of much discontent in those who are held in servitude; but as this is a subject that has never employed much of my thoughts, these are no more than the first crude Ideas that have struck me upon the occasion.

I had not the smallest intimation of Monsr. Gerards passing through Jersey till I was favoured with your Letter, and am now ignorant of the cause, otherwise than by conjecture. The inclosed I return, as Mr. Laurens left this some days ago for Philadelphia, on his way to the Southward.

Mrs. Washington joins me in respectful compliments to you, and with every sentiment of regard and attachment. I am etc.

To George Mason

Dear Sir,   Camp at Middlebrook March 27th 1779

By some interruption of the last Weeks Mail your favor of the 8th. did not reach my hands till last Night. Under cover of this Mr. Mason (if he should not have Sailed, &) to whom I heartily wish a perfect restoration of health, will receive two letters; one of them to the Marqs. de la Fayette & the other to Doctr. Franklin; in furnishing which I am happy, as I wish for instances in which I can testify the sincerity of my regard for you.

Our Commissary of Prisoners hath been invariably, & pointedly instructed to exchange those Officers first who were first captivated, as far as Rank will apply; and I have every reason to believe he has obeyed the order; as I have refused a great many applications for irregular exchanges in consequence—and I did it because I would not depart from my principle, & thereby incur the charge of partiality. It sometimes happens, that Officers later in captivity than others, have been exchanged before them; but it is in cases where the rank of the Enemys Officers in our possession, do not apply to the latter. There is a prospect now I think of a general exchange taking place, which will be very pleasing to the parties and their connexions; and will be a mean of relieving much distress to individuals—though it may not, circumstanced as we are at this time, be advantageous to us, considered in a rational & political point of view. Partial exchanges have, for sometime past, been discontinued by the Enemy.

Though it is not in my power to devote much time to private correspondences, owing to the multiplicity of public letters (and other business) I have to read, write, & transact; yet I can with great truth assure you, that it would afford me very singular pleasure to be favoured at all times with your sentiments in a leizure hour, upon public matters of general concernment as well as those which more immediately respect yr. own State (if proper conveyance wd. render prudent a free communication). I am particularly desirous of it at this time, because I view things very differently, I fear, from what people in general do who seem to think the contest is at an end; and to make money, and get places, the only things now remaining to do. I have seen without dispondency (even for a moment) the hours which America have stiled her gloomy ones, but I have beheld no day since the commencement of hostilities that I have thought her liberties in such eminent danger as at present. Friends and foes seem now to combine to pull down the goodly fabric we have hitherto been raising at the expence of so much time, blood, and treasure—and unless the bodies politick will exert themselves to bring things back to first principles—correct abuses—& punish our internal foes, inevitable ruin must follow. Indeed we seem to be verging so fast to destruction, that I am filled with sensations to which I have been a stranger till within these three Months. Our Enemy beholds with exultation & joy how effectually we labour for their benefit; & from being in a state of absolute dispair, & on the point of evacuating America, are now on tiptoe—nothing therefore in my judgment can save us but a total reformation in our own conduct, or some decisive turn to affairs in Europe. The former alas! to our shame be it spoken! is less likely to happen than the latter, as it is now consistent with the views of the Specalators—various tribes of money makers—& stock jobbers of all denominations, to continue the War for their own private emolument, with out considering that their avarice, & thirst for gain must plunge every thing (including themselves) in one common Ruin.

Were I to indulge my present feelings & give a loose to that freedom of expression which my unreserved friendship for you would prompt me to, I should say a great deal on this subject—but letters are liable to so many accidents, and the sentiments of Men in office sought after by the enemy with so much avidity, and besides conveying useful knowledge (if they get into their hands) for the super structure of their plans, is often perverted to the worst of purposes, that I shall be somewhat reserved, notwithstanding this Letter goes by a private hand to Mt. Vernon. I cannot refrain lamenting however in the most poignant terms, the fatal policy too prevalent in most of the states, of employing their ablest Men at home in posts of honor or profit, till the great national Interests are fixed upon a solid basis. To me it appears no unjust simile to compare the affairs of this great continent to the Mechanism of a Clock, each State representing some one or other of the smaller parts of it, which they are endeavouring to put in fine order without considering how useless & unavailing their labour, unless the great wheel, or spring which is to set the whole in motion, is also well attended to & kept in good order. I allude to no particular state nor do I mean to cast reflections upon any one of them. Nor ought I, it may be said, to do so upon their representatives, but as it is a fact too notorious to be concealed, that C—— is rent by party—that much business of a trifling nature & personal concernment withdraws their attention from matters of great national moment at this critical period. When it is also known that idleness and dissipation takes place of close attention and application, no man who wishes well to the liberties of his Country &

desires to see its rights established, can avoid crying out where
are our Men of abilities? Why do they not come forth to save
their Country? Let this voice my dear Sir call upon you—
Jefferson & others—do not from a mistaken opinion that we
are about to set down under our own Vine and our own fig
tree let our hitherto noble struggle end in ignominy. Believe
me when I tell you there is danger of it. I have pretty good
reasons for thinking, that Administration a little while ago had
resolved to give the matter up, and negotiate a peace with us
upon almost any terms, but I shall be much mistaken if they
do not now from the present state of our Currency dissentions
& other circumstances, push matters to the utmost extremity.
Nothing I am sure will prevent it but the interposition of
Spain & their disappointed hopes from Russia.

I thank you most cordially for your kind offer of rendering
me Services. I shall without reserve as heretofore, call upon
you whenever instances occur that may require it, being with
the sincerest regard, Dr Sir Yr. Most Obed & affecte. H:
Servt.

To James Warren

Middlebrook, March 31, 1779.
Dear Sir: I beseech you not to ascribe my delay in answering
your obliging favor of the 16th. of Decr. to disrespect, or want
of inclination to continue a corrispondence in which I have
always taken pleasure, and thought myself honord.

Your Letter of the above date came to my hands in Philadelphia where I attended at the request of Congress to settle
some important matters respecting the army and its future
operations; and where I was detained till some time in Feby.,
during that period my time was so much occupied by the
immediate and pressing business which carried me down, that
I could attend to little else; and upon my return to Camp I
found the ordinary business of the Army had run so much
behind hand, that, together with the arrangements I had to
carry into execution, no leizure was left me to endulge myself
sooner in making the acknowledgment I am now about to do,

of the pleasure I felt at finding that I still enjoyed a share of your confidence and esteem, and now and then am to be informed of it by Letter. believe me Sir when I add, that this proof of your holding me in remembrance is most acceptable and pleasing.

Our conflict is not likely to cease so soon as every good Man would wish. The measure of iniquity is not yet filled; and unless we can return a little more to first principles, and act a little more upon patriotic ground, I do not know when it will, or, what may be the Issue of the contest. Speculation, Peculation, Engrossing, forestalling with all their concomitants, afford too many melancholy proofs of the decay of public virtue; and too glaring instances of its being the interest and desire of too many who would wish to be thought friends, to continue the War.

Nothing I am convinced but the depreciation of our Currency proceeding in a great measure from the foregoing Causes, aided by Stock jobbing, and party dissensions has fed the hopes of the Enemy and kept the B. Arms in America to this day. They do not scruple to declare this themselves, and add, that we shall be our own conquerers. Cannot our common Country Am. possess virtue enough to disappoint them? Is the paltry consideration of a little dirty pelf to individuals to be placed in competition with the essential rights and liberties of the present generation, and of Millions yet unborn? Shall a few designing men for their own aggrandizement, and to gratify their own avarice, overset the goodly fabric we have been rearing at the expence of so much time, blood, and treasure? and shall we at last become the victims of our own abominable lust of gain? Forbid it heaven! forbid it all and every State in the Union! by enacting and enforcing efficacious laws for checking the growth of these monstrous evils, and restoring matters, in some degree to the pristine state they were in at the commencement of the War. Our cause is noble, it is the cause of Mankind! and the danger to it, is to be apprehended from ourselves. Shall we slumber and sleep then while we should be punishing those miscreants who have brot. these troubles upon us and who are aimg. to continue us in them, while we should be striving to fill our Battalions, and devising ways and means to appreciate the currency; on the credit of wch. every thing depends? I hope not. Let vigorous measures be adopted; not to limit the prices of Articles, for this I believe is inconsistent with the very nature of things, and impracticable in itself, but to punish Speculaters, forestallers, and extortioners, and above all to sink the money by heavy taxes. To promote public and private œconomy; Encourage Manufactures &ca. Measures of this sort gone heartily into by the several States would strike at once at the root of all our evils and give the coup de grace to British hope of subjugating this Continent, either by their Arms or their Arts. The first, as I have before observed, they acknowledge is unequal to the task; the latter I am sure will be so if we are not lost to every thing that is good and virtuous.

A little time now, must unfold in some degree, the Enemys designs. Whether the state of affairs in Europe will permit them to augment their Army with more than recruits for the Regiments now on the Continent and therewith make an active and vigorous compaign, or whether with their Florida and Canadian force they will aid and abet the Indians in ravaging our Western Frontier while their Shipg. with detachments harrass (and if they mean to prosecute the predatory War threatened by Administration through their Commissioners) burn and destroy our Sea Coast; or whether, contrary to expectation, they should be more disposed to negotiate than to either is more than I can determine; the latter will depend very much upon their apprehensions from the Court of Spain, and expectations of foreign aid and powerful alliances; at present we seem to be in a Chaos but this cannot last long as I suppose the ultimate determination of the British Court will be developed at the meeting of Parliament after the Hollidays.

Mrs. Washington joins me in cordial wishes, and best respects to Mrs. Warren; she would have done herself the pleasure of writing but the present convayance was sudden. I am, etc.

To Elias Boudinot

Head Quarters, Middle brook, May 3, 1779.
Dear Sir: The many and important matters which pressed
upon me while you were in Camp, prevented my consulting
you on an affair which I have a good deal at heart, and which
I wished to make the Subject of a personal, rather than an
epistolary conversation—To come to the point.—It is a matter
of great importance to have early and good intelligence of the
enemys strength and motions, and as far as possible, designs.
and to obtain them through different channels. Do you think
it practicable to come at these by means of ——? I shall not
press it upon him; but you must be sensible that to obtain
intelligence from a man of observation near the head Quarters
of an Army from whence all orders flow and every thing originates must be a most desirable thing.

The person rendering such Service will entitle himself not
only to thanks but reward, at a proper season.

If —— is inclined to engage in a business of this kind, I
shall leave it to you and him to fix upon such a mode of
corrisponding as will convey intelligence in the most speedy,
safe, and effectual manner. To guard against possible evils,
your corrispondence might be under fictitious names, by
numbers (to represent men and things), in characters, or other
ways, as you shall agree. It is in my power, I believe, to procure a liquid which nothing but a counter liquor (rubbed over
the paper afterwards) can make legible. Fire which will bring
lime juice, Milk and other things of this kind to light, has no
effect on it. A letter upon trivial matters of business, written
in common Ink, may be fitted with important intelligence
which cannot be discovered without the counter part, or liquid here mention'd.

I shall add no more on this subject; enough has been said
for you to found a negotiation on, at least to hint the matter
to the person mentioned, for tryal of his willingness to engage
in a corrispondence of this kind. No person but you, he, and
I, and such as he shall make choice of to convey the intelligence to you, will be privy to this matter. Your letters to me
inclosing his Accts. may be under an outer cover with the

usual address, the inner cover may be directed on private Service, which will prevent any of my own family from opening it. and even under these circumstances and caution, the name of —— may be avoided.

I am very sincerely and respectfully Yrs. etc.

To William Maxwell

Head Quarters, Middle Brook, May 7, 1779.

Sir: I have received your two favors of yesterdays date; one of them with infinite concern. There is nothing, which has happened in the course of the war that has given me so much pain as the remonstrance you mention from the officers of the 1st. Jersey Regiment. I cannot but consider it as a hasty and imprudent step, which on more cool consideration they will themselves condemn. I am very sensible of the inconveniences under which the officers of the army labor and I hope they do me the justice to believe, that my endeavours to procure them relief are incessant. There is however more difficulty in satisfying their wishes than perhaps they are aware; our resources have been hitherto very limited; the situation of our money is no small embarrassment, for which, though there are remedies, they cannot be the work of a moment. Government is not insensible of the merits and sacrifices of the officers, nor, I am persuaded, unwilling to make a compensation; but it is a truth, of which a little observation must convince us, that it is very much straitened in the means. Great allowances ought to be made on this account for any delay and seeming backwardness which may appear. Some of the states indeed have done as generously as it is at this juncture in their power, and if others have been less expeditious it ought to be ascribed to some peculiar cause, which a little time aided by example will remove. The patience and perseverance of the army have been under every disadvantage such as to do them the highest honor both at home and abroad; and have inspired me with an unlimited confidence in their virtue, which has consoled me amidst every perplexity and reverse of fortune, to which our affairs in a struggle of this nature were necessarily exposed. Now that we have made so great a progress to the attainment of the end we have in view, so that we cannot fail without a most shameful desertion of our own interests, any thing like a change of conduct would imply a very unhappy change of principles and a forgetfulness as well of what we owe to ourselves as to our country. Did I suppose it possible this could be the case even in a single regiment of the army, I should be mortified and chagrined beyond expression. I should feel it as a wound given to my own honor, which I consider as embarked with that of the army at large. But this I believe to be impossible. Any corps that was about to set an example of the kind would weigh well the consequences and no officer of common discernment and sensibility would hazard them. If they should stand alone in it, independent of other consequences, what would be their feelings on reflecting that they had held themselves out to the world in a point of light inferior to the rest of the army? Or if their example should be followed and become general how would they console themselves for having been the foremost in bringing ruin and disgrace upon their country? They would remember that the army would share a double portion of the general infamy and distress; and that the character of an american officer would become as despicable as it is now glorious.

I confess the appearances in the present instance are disagreeable; but I am convinced they seem to mean more than they really do. The Jersey officers have not been outdone by any others in the qualities either of citizens or soldiers; and I am confident no part of them would seriously intend anything that would be a stain to their former reputation. The gentlemen cannot be in earnest, they have only *reasoned wrong about the means of obtaining a good end*, and on Consideration I hope and flatter myself they will renounce what must appear improper. At the opening of a campaign, when under marching orders, for an important service, their own honor, duty to the public and to themselves, a regard to military propriety will not suffer them to persist in a measure which would be a violation of them all. It will even wound their delicacy cooly to reflect that they have hazarded a step which has an air of dictating terms to their country, by taking advantage of the necessity of the moment.

The declaration they have made to the state at so critical a time, that unless they obtain relief in the short period of three days, they must be considered out of the service has very much the aspect; and the seeming relaxation of continuing till the state can have a *reasonable* time to provide other officers will be thought only a superficial veil. I am now to request that you will convey my sentiments to the Gentlemen concerned and endeavour to make them sensible that they are in an error. The service for which the Regiment was intended will not admit of delay; it must at all events march on Monday morning in the first place to this camp and further directions will be given when it arrives. I am sure I shall not be mistaken in expecting a prompt and chearful obedience. I am etc.

To Gouverneur Morris

Hd. Qrs. Middle Brook, May 8, 1779.
Monsieur Gerard did me the honor to deliver me your favour of the 26th. I shall always be obliged to you, my dear Sir, for a free communication of your sentiments on whatsoever subject may occur.

The objects of your letter were important. Mr. Gerard I dare say has made it unnecessary for me to recapitulate what passed between him and myself and has informed you of the alternative I proposed for improving the important event announced by him. From what he told me it appears that sufficient assurances cannot be given of points which are essential to justify the great undertaking you had in view at the expense of other operations very interesting. And indeed though I was desirous to convince the Minister that we are willing to make every effort in our power for striking a decisive blow; yet my judgment rather inclined to the second plan as promising more certain success, without putting so much to the hazard. The relief of the Southern States appears to me an object of the greatest magnitude and what may lead to still more important advantages. I feel infinite anxiety on their account; their internal weakness, disaffection, the want of energy, the general languor that has seized the people at large makes me apprehend the most serious consequences; it would seem too, as if the enemy meant to transfer the principal weight of the war that way. If it be true that a large detachment has lately sailed from New York and that Sir Henry Clinton is gone with it, in which several accounts I have received agree (though I do not credit the latter) and these should be destined for the Southward as is most probable, there can be little doubt that this is the present plan. Charles town it is likely will feel the next stroke. This if it succeeds will leave the enemy in full possession of Georgia by obliging us to collect our forces for the defence of South Carolina and, will consequently open new sources for Men and supplies and prepare the way for a further career. The climate, I am aware is an obstacle but perhaps not so great as is imagined and, when we consider the difference in our respective means of preserving health it may possibly be found more adverse to our troops than to theirs. In this critical situation, I hardly know any resource we have unless it be in the *event expected*; and the supposed reinforcement now on its way, for want of a competent land force on our part, may make even this dependence precarious. If it should fail, our affairs which have a very sickly aspect in many respects will receive a stroke they are little able to bear.

As a variety of accidents may disappoint our hopes here it is indispensable we should make every exertion on our part to check the enemy's progress. This cannot be done to effect, if our reliance is solely or principally on militia, for a force continually fluctuating is incapable of any material effort. The states concerned ought by all means to endeavour to draw out men for a length of time; a smaller number, on this plan would answer their purpose better; a great deal of expence would be avoided and agriculture would be much less impeded. It is to be lamented that the remoteness and weakness of this army, would make it folly to attempt to send any succour from this quarter. Perhaps for want of knowing the true state of our Foreign expectations and prospects of finance, I may be led to contemplate the glomy side of things. But I confess they appear to me to be in a very disagreeable train. The rapid decay of our currency, the extinction of public spirit, the increasing rapacity of the times, the want of harmony in our councils, the declining zeal of the people, the discontents and distresses of the officers of the army; and I may add, the prevailing security and insensibility to danger, are symptoms, in my eye of a most alarming nature. If the enemy have it in their power to press us hard this campaign I know not what may be the consequence. Our army as it now stands is but little more than the skeleton of an army and I hear of no steps that are taking to give it strength and substance. I hope there may not be great mistakes on this head, and that our abilities in general are not overrated. The applications for succour, are numerous; but no pains are taken to put it in my power to afford them. When I endeavour to draw together the Continental troops for the most essential purposes I am embarrassed with complaints of the exhausted defenceless situation of particular states and find myself obliged either to resist solicitations, made in such a manner and with such a degree of emphasis, as scarcely to leave me a choice; or to sacrifice the most obvious principles of military propriety and risk the general safety.

I shall conclude by observing, that it is well worthy the ambition of a patriot Statesman at this juncture, to endeavour to pacify party differences, to give fresh vigor to the springs of government, to inspire the people with confidence, and above all to restore the credit of our currency. With very great regard I am, etc.

Speech to the Delaware Chiefs

Head Quarters, Middle Brook, May 12, 1779.
Brothers: I am happy to see you here. I am glad the long Journey you have made, has done you no harm; and that you are in good health: I am glad also you left All our friends of the Delaware Nation well.

Brothers: I have read your paper. The things you have said are weighty things, and I have considered them well. The Delaware Nation have shown their good will to the United States. They have done wisely and I hope they will never repent. I rejoice in the new assurances you give of their friendship. The things you now offer to do to brighten the chain, prove your sincerity. I am sure Congress will run to meet you, and will do every thing in their power to make the friendship between the people of these States, and their Brethren of the Delaware nation, last forever.

Brothers: I am a Warrior. My words are few and plain; but I will make good what I say. 'Tis my business to destroy all the Enemies of these States and to protect their friends. You have seen how we have withstood the English for four years; and how their great Armies have dwindled away and come to very little; and how what remains of them in this part of our great Country, are glad to stay upon Two or three little Islands, where the Waters and their Ships hinder us from going to destroy them. The English, Brothers, are a boasting people. They talk of doing a great deal; but they do very little. They fly away on their Ships from one part of our Country to an other; but as soon as our Warriors get together they leave it and go to some other part. They took Boston and Philadelphia, two of our greatest Towns; but when they saw our Warriors in a great body ready to fall upon them, they were forced to leave them.

Brothers: We have till lately fought the English all alone. Now the Great King of France is become our Good Brother and Ally. He has taken up the Hatchet with us, and we have sworn never to bury it, till we have punished the English and made them sorry for All the wicked things they had in their Hearts to do against these States. And there are other Great Kings and Nations on the other side of the big Waters, who love us and wish us well, and will not suffer the English to hurt us.

Brothers: Listen well to what I tell you and let it sink deep into your Hearts. We love our friends, and will be faithful to them, as long as they will be faithful to us. We are sure our Good brothers the Delawares will always be so. But we have sworn to take vengeance on our Enemies, and on false friends. The other day, a handful of our young men destroyed the settlement of the Onondagas. They burnt down all their Houses, destroyed their grain and Horses and Cattle, took their Arms away, killed several of their Warriors and brought off many prisoners and obliged the rest to fly into the woods.

This is but the beginning of the troubles which those Nations, who have taken up the Hatchet against us, will feel.

Brothers: I am sorry to hear that you have suffered for want of necessaries, or that any of our people have not dealt justly by you. But as you are going to Congress, which is the great Council of the Nation and hold all things in their hands, I shall say nothing about the supplies you ask. I hope you will receive satisfaction from them. I assure you, I will do every thing in my power to prevent your receiving any further injuries, and will give the strictest orders for this purpose. I will severely punish any that shall break them.

Brothers: I am glad you have brought three of the Children of your principal Chiefs to be educated with us. I am sure Congress will open the Arms of love to them, and will look upon them as their own Children, and will have them educated accordingly. This is a great mark of your confidence and of your desire to preserve the friendship between the Two Nations to the end of time, and to become One people with your Brethren of the United States. My ears hear with pleasure the other matters you mention. Congress will be glad to hear them too. You do well to wish to learn our arts and ways of life, and above all, the religion of Jesus Christ. These will make you a greater and happier people than you are. Congress will do every thing they can to assist you in this wise intention; and to tie the knot of friendship and union so fast, that nothing shall ever be able to loose it.

Brothers: There are some matters about which I do not open my Lips, because they belong to Congress, and not to us warriors; you are going to them, they will tell you all you wish to know.

Brothers: When you have seen all you want to see, I will then wish you a good Journey to Philadelphia. I hope you may find there every thing your hearts can wish, that when you return home you may be able to tell your Nation good things of us. And I pray God he may make your Nation wise and Strong, that they may always see their own true interest and have courage to walk in the right path; and that they never may be deceived by lies to do any thing against the people of these States, who are their Brothers and ought always to be one people with them.

Circular to State Governments

Head Quarters, Middle Brook, May 22, 1779.

Sir: The situation of our affairs at this period appears to me peculiarly critical, and this I flatter myself will apologise for that anxiety which impels me to take the liberty of addressing you on the present occasion. The state of the army in particular is alarming on several accounts, that of its numbers is not among the least. Our battalions are exceedingly reduced, not only from the natural decay incident to the best composed armies; but from the expiration of the term of service for which a large proportion of the men were engaged. The measures hitherto taken to replace them, so far as has come to my knowledge have been attended with very partial success; and I am ignorant of any others in contemplation that afford a better prospect. A reinforcement expected from Virginia, consisting of new levies and reinlisted men is necessarily ordered to the Southward. Not far short of one third of our whole force must be detached on a service undertaken by the direction of Congress and essential in itself. I shall only say of what remains, that when it is compared with the force of the enemy now actually at New York and Rhode Island, with the addition of the succours, they will in all probability receive from England, at the lowest computation, it will be found to justify very serious apprehensions and to demand the zealous attention of the different legislatures.

When we consider the rapid decline of our currency, the general temper of the times the disaffection of a great part of the people, the lethargy that overspreads the rest, the increasing danger to the Southern States, we cannot but dread the consequences of any misfortune in this quarter; and must feel the impolicy of trusting our security, to a want of activity and enterprise in the Enemy.

An expectation of peace and an opinion of the Enemys inability to send more troops to this country, I fear, have had too powerful an influence in our affairs. I have never heard of any thing conclusive to authorise the former, and present appearances are in my opinion against it. The accounts we receive from Europe uniformly announce vigorous preparations to continue the war, at least another campaign. The debates and proceedings in Parliament wear this complexion. The public papers speak confidently of large reinforcements destined for America. The minister in his speech asserts positively that reinforcements will be sent over to Sir Henry Clinton; though he acknowledges the future plan of the war will be less extensive than the past. Let it be supposed, that the intended succours will not exceed five thousand men. This will give the Enemy a superiority very dangerous to our safety, if their strength be properly exerted, and our situation not materially altered for the better.

These considerations and many more that might be suggested to point to the necessity of immediate and decisive exertions to complete our battalions and to make our military force more respectable. I thought it my duty to give an idea of its true state and to urge the attention of the States to a matter in which their safety and happiness are so interested. I hope a concern for the public good will be admitted as the motive and excuse of my importunity.

There is one point which I beg leave to mention also. The want of system, which has prevailed in the clothiers department has been a source of innumerable evils; defective supplies, irregular and unequal issues, great waste loss and expence to the public, general dissatisfaction in the army, much confusion and perplexity, an additional load of business to the officers commanding make but a part of them. I have for a long time past most ardently desired to see a reformation. Congress by a resolve of the 23d of March has established an ordinance for regulating this department. According to this, there is a sub or state clothier to be appointed by each state. I know not what instructions may have been given relative to these appointments; but, if the matter now rests with the particular States, I take the liberty to press their execution without loss of time. The service suffers amazingly from the disorder in this department, and the regulations for it cannot possibly be too soon carried into effect. I have the honor, etc.

To Marquis de Lafayette

New Windsor, July 4, 1779.

My dear Marqs: Since my last which was written (to the best of my recollection for not having my Papers with me I can not have recourse to dates) in March, both Armies continued quiet in their Winter cantonments till about the first of May when a detachmt. of abt. 2000 of the Enemy under the command of General Matthews conveyed by Sir George Collier made a sudden invasion of a Neck of land comprehending Portsmouth and Suffolk in Virginia, and after plundering and destroying the property (chiefly private) in those places and stealing a number of Negroes returned to New York the moment they found the Country rising in Arms to oppose them.

This exploit was immediately followed by a movement of Sir Henry Clinton up the North River the beginning of June. what the real object of this expedition was, I cannot with certainty inform you. Our Posts in the highlands were supposed to be his aim because they were of importance to us, and consonant to his former plan for prosecuting the War; but whether upon a nearer approach he found them better provided and more difficult of access than he expected, or whether his only view was to cut off the communication between the East and West side of the River below the highlands I shall not undertake to decide; certain it is however that he came up in full force, disembarked at Kings ferry and there began to fortify the points on each side which to all intents and purposes are Islands and by nature exceedingly strong.

This movement of the enemy and my solicitude for the security of our defences on the River, induced me to March the Troops which were cantoned at Middle brook, immediately to their support and for the further purpose of strengthening the defences by additional Works. in this business I have been employed near three weeks, while the enemy have not been idle in establishing themselves as above. They have reinforced their main army with part of the garrison at Rhode Island.

General Sullivan commands an Expedition against the Six Nation's which aided by Butlar and Brandt, with their Tory

Friends, and some force from Canada have greatly infested our Frontrs. He has already Marched to the Susquehanna with about 4000 Men, all Continental Soldiers and I trust will destroy their Settlements and extirpate them from the Country which more than probably will be effected by their flight as it is not a difficult matter for them to take up their Beds and Walk.

We have received very favourable Accts. from South Carolina, by wch. it appears that the British Troops before Charles town have met with a defeat and are in a very perilous situation. We have this matter from such a variety of hands that it scarcely admits of a doubt and yet no official information is received of it.

When my dear Marquis shall I embrace you again? Shall I ever do it? or have the charms of the amiable and lovely Marchioness, or the smiles and favors of your Prince withdrawn you from us entirely? At all times, and under all circumstances, I have the honor to be with the greatest regard, personal attachment and affection, Yr., etc.

To John Cochran

West-point, August 16, 1779.

Dr. Doctr: I have asked Mrs. Cockran and Mrs. Livingston to dine with me to morrow; but ought I not to apprize them of their fare? As I hate deception, even where the imagination only is concerned; I will.

It is needless to premise, that my table is large enough to hold the ladies; of this they had occular proof yesterday. To say how it is usually covered is rather more essential, and this, shall be the purport of my Letter. Since our arrival at this happy spot, we have had a Ham (sometimes a shoulder) of Bacon, to grace the head of the table; a piece of roast Beef adorns the foot; and, a small dish of Greens or Beans (almost imperceptable) decorates the center.

When the Cook has a mind to cut a figure (and this I presume he will attempt to do to morrow) we have two Beef-stake-Pyes, or dishes of Crabs in addition, one on each side the center dish, dividing the space, and reducing the distance between dish and dish to about Six feet, which without them, would be near twelve a part. Of late, he has had the surprizing luck to discover, that apples will make pyes; and it's a question if, amidst the violence of his efforts, we do not get one of apples instead of having both of Beef.

If the ladies can put up with such entertainment, and will submit to partake of it on plates, once tin but now Iron; (not become so by the labor of scowering) I shall be happy to see them. I am, etc.

To Lund Washington

August 17, 1779.

Some time ago (but how long I can not remember) you applied to me to know if you should receive payment of Genl. Mercer's Bonds; and after this, of the bond due from the deceased Mr. Mercers Estate to me; and was, after animadverting a little upon the subject; authorized to do so; of course I presume the money has been received. I have since considered this matter in every point of view my judgment enables me to place it, and am resolved to receive no more old debts; such I mean as were contracted and ought to have been paid before the War at the present nominal value of the money, unless compelled to it, or it is the practice of others to do it. Neither justice, reason, nor policy requires it. The law, undoubtedly, was well designed; it was intended to stamp a value and give a free circulation, to the paper bills of credit; but it never was nor could be intended to make a man take a Shilling or Six pence in the pound for a just debt, wch. he is well able to pay, thereby involving himself in ruin. I am as willing now as I ever was to take paper money for *every* kind of debt, and at its present depreciated value for those debts which have been contracted since the money became so; but I will not in future receive the nominal sum for such old debts as come under the above description, except as before excepted. The fear of injuring by any example of mine the credit of our paper currency if I attempted to discriminate between the real and nominal value of Paper money, has already sunk me a large Sum if the Bonds beforementd. are paid off; the advantage taken in doing which no Man of honor or common honesty can reconcile to his own feelings and conscience; not as it respects me do I mean but transactions of this kind generally. The thing which induced me to mention the matter to you at present, is the circumstance you have related respecting the Wages of Roberts, which you say (according to his demands) will amount to upwards of £2000, and comes to as much for the Service of a *common* Miller for *one year only*, as I shall get for 600 acres of land sold Mercer in the best of times and in the most valuable part of Virginia, that ought to have been pd. for before the money began to depreciate; nay years before the War. This is such a manifest abuse of reason and justice that no Arguments can reconcile it to common sense, or common honesty. Instead of appealing to me who have not the means of informatn. or knowledge of common usage and practice in matters of this kind in the State or the Laws that govern there, I wish you would consult Men of honor, honesty, and firm attachment to the cause, and govern yourself by their advice or by their conduct. If it be customary with others to receive money in this way, that is 6 d. or 1 / in the pound for old debts; if it is thought to be advansive of the great cause we are imbarked in for individuals to do so thereby ruining themselves while others are reaping the benefit of such distress. if the Law imposes this, and it is thought right to submit, I will not say aught against it, or oppose another word to it. No man has, nor no man will go further to serve the Public than myself, if sacrificing my whole Estate would effect any valuable purpose I would not hesitate one moment in doing it. but my submitting to matters of this kind unless it is done so by others, is no more than a drop in the bucket, in fact it is not serving the public but enriching individuals and countenancing dishonesty for sure I am that no honest Man would attempt to pay 20 /. with one or perhaps half a one In a word I had rather make a present of the Bonds than receive payment of them in so shameful a way.

To John Jay

West point, September 7, 1779.
Dr Sir: I have received Your obliging Favors of the 25th.
and 31st. of last month and thank you for them.

It really appears impossible to reconcile the conduct Britain
is pursuing, to any system of prudence or policy. For the reasons you assign, appearances are against her deriving aid from
other powers; and if it is truly the case, that she has rejected
the mediation of Spain, without having made allies, it will
exceed all past instances of her infatuation. Notwithstanding
appearances, I can hardly bring myself fully to believe that it
is the case; or that there is so general a combination against
the interests of Britain among the European powers, as will
permit them to endanger the political ballance. I think it probable enough, that the conduct of France in the affairs of the
Porte and Russia will make an impression on the Empress;
but I doubt whether it will be sufficient to counterballance
the powerful motives she has to support England; and the
Porte has been perhaps too much weakened in the last war
with Russia to be overfond of renewing it. The Emperor is
also the natural ally of England notwithstanding the connexions of Blood between his family and that of France; and he
may prefer reasons of National policy to those of private attachment. Tis true his finances may not be in the best state,
though one campaign could hardly have exhausted them, but
as Holland looks up to him for her chief protection, if he
should be inclined to favor England, it may give her Councils
a decided biass the same way. She can easily supply what is
wanting in the Article of money; and by this aid, give sinews
to that confederacy. Denmark is also the natural ally of England; and though there has lately been a family bickering,
her political interest may outweigh private animosity. Her marine assistance would be considerable. Portugal too, though
timid and cautious at present, if she was to see connexions
formed by England able to give her countenance and security,
would probably declare for her interests. Russia, Denmark,
The Emperor, Holland, Portugal and England would form a
respectable counterpoise to the opposite scale. Though all the

maritime powers of Europe were interested in the independence of this Country, as it tended to diminish the overgrown power of Britain, yet they may be unwilling to see too great a preponderacy on the side of her rivals; and when the question changes itself from the separation of America to the ruin of England as a Naval power, I should not be surprised at a proportionable change in the sentiments of some of those States which have been heretofore unconcerned Spectators or inclining to our side. I suggest these things rather as possible than probable; it is even to be expected that the decisive blow will be struck, before the interposition of the Allies England may acquire can have effect. But still as possible events, they ought to have their influence and prevent our relaxing in any measures necessary for our safety, on the supposition of a speedy peace or removal of the War from the present Theatre in America.

The account which Mr. Wharton received, of the reinforcement that came with Adml. Arbuthnot, corresponds pretty well, with respect to number, with the best information I have been able to obtain upon the subject. Some recent advices make it about Three thousand, and say that these Troops are rather in a sickly condition. It is generally said, that they are Recruits; but whether there is so great a proportion of them Scotch as his intelligence mentions, is not ascertained by any accounts I have received.

With respect to the person you recommended last Winter, he was employed in consequence; and I have not the smallest doubt of his attachment and integrity. But he has not had it in his power, and indeed it is next to impossible that any one should circumstanced as he is, to render much essential service in the way it was intended to employ him. You will readily conceive the difficulties in such a case. The business was of too delicate a nature for him to transact it frequently himself, and the Characters, he has been obliged occasionally to confide it to, have not been able to gain any thing satisfactory or material. Indeed, I believe it will seldom happen, that a person acting in this way, can render any essential advantages more than once or twice at any rate; and that what he will be compelled to do to preserve the pretended confidence of the other party, will generally counterbalance any thing he may effect.

The greatest benefits are to be derived from persons who live with the other side; whose local circumstances, without subjecting them to suspicions, give them an opportunity of making observations and comparing and combining things and Sentiments. It is with such I have endeavoured to establish a correspondence, and on whose reports I shall most rely. From these several considerations, I am doubtful whether it will be of any advantage for the person to continue longer in the way he has acted. The points to which he must have alluded in his Letter, were the movements up the North River and against Charles Town and the expedition to Virginia. I believe the first certain information of the first of these events came from him. He has never received any thing from me. The Gentleman who employed him first, had some Money deposited with him for confidential purposes; but I cannot tell how much he may have paid him.

With every sentiment of esteem etc.

To Marquis de Lafayette

West-point, September 30, 1779.

My dear Marqs: A few days ago I wrote you a letter in much haste. the cause a sudden notification of Monsr. Gerards having changed the place of his embarkation from Boston (as was expected) to Philadelphia, and the hurry Monsir. de la Colombe was in to reach the latter before the Minister should have left it. Since that, I have been honourd with the company of the Chevr. de la Luzerne, and by him was favour'd with your obliging letter of the 12th. of June which filled me with equal pleasure and surprise; the latter at hearing that you had not received one of the many letters I had written to you, since you left the American Shore. I cannot at this time charge my memory with the precise dates of these letters but the first, which ought and I expected would have reached you at Boston and I much wished it to do so because it contained a Letter from me to Doctr Franklin expressive of the Sentiments I entertained of your Services and merit was put into the hands of a Captn. McQueen of Charles Town, who was to

Sail from Phila. soon after. In March I wrote you once or twice, and in June or the first of July following, (when it was reported that Monsr. Gerard was about to leave us I took the liberty of committing to his care another of my lettrs. to you,) which sevl. efforts though they may have been unsuccessful will exhibit no bad specimen of my having kept you constantly in remembrance and a desire of giving you proofs of it.

It gave me infinite pleasure to hear from yourself of the favourable reception you met with from your Sovereign, and of the joy which your safe arrival in France had diffused among your friends. I had no doubt but that this wou'd be the case; to hear it from yourself adds pleasure to the acct. and here My dear friend let me congratulate you on your new, honourable and pleasing appointment in the Army commanded by the Count de Vaux which I shall accompy. with an assurance that none can do it with more warmth of Affection, or sincere joy than myself. Your forward zeal in the cause of liberty; Your singular attachment to this infant World; Your ardent and persevering efforts, not only in America but since your return to France to serve the United States; Your polite attention to Americans, and your strict and uniform friendship for *me*, has ripened the first impressions of esteem and attachment which I imbibed for you into such perfect love and gratitude that neither time nor absence can impair which will warrant my assuring you, that whether in the character of an Officer at the head of a Corps of gallant French (if circumstances should require this) whether as a Major Genl. commanding a division of the American Army; Or whether, after our Swords and Spears have given place to the plough share and pruning hook, I see you as a private Gentleman, a friend and Companion, I shall welcome you in all the warmth of friendship to Columbia's shore; and in the latter case, to my rural Cottage, where homely fare and a cordial reception shall be substituted for delicacies and costly living. this from past experience I know *you* can submit to; and if the lovely partner of your happiness will consent to participate with *us* in such rural entertainment and amusemts. I can undertake in behalf of Mrs. Washington that she will do every thing in her power to make Virginia agreeable to the Marchioness. My inclination and endeavours to do this cannot be doubted when I assure you that I love everybody that is dear to you. consequently participate in the pleasure you feel in the prospt. of again becoming a parent and do most Sincerely congratulate you and your Lady on this fresh pledge she is about to give you of her love.

I thank you for the trouble you have taken, and your polite attention in favouring me with a Copy of your letter to Congress; and feel as I am perswaded they must do, the force of such ardent zeal as you there express for the interest of this Country. The propriety of the hint you have given them must carry conviction and I trust will have a salutary effect; tho' there is not, I believe, the same occasion for the admonition now, there was some months ago; many late changes have taken place in that honourable body which has removed in a very great degree, if not wholly, the discordant spirit which it is said prevailed in the Winter, and I hope measures will also be taken to remove those unhappy and improper differences which have extended themselves elsewhere to the prejudice of our affairs in Europe.

You enquire after Monsr. de la Colombe, and Colo. Neville; the first (who has been with Baron de Kalb) left this a few days ago, as I have already observed, for Phila., in expectation of a passage with Monsr. Gerard. Colo. Neville called upon me about a Month since and was to have dined with us the next day but did not come, since which I have not seen him, nor do I know at this time where he is; he had then but just returned from his own home; and it was the first time I had seen him since he parted with you at Boston. It is probable he may be with the Virginia Troops which lye at the mouth of Smiths clove abt. 30 Miles from hence.

I have had great pleasure in the visit which the Chevalier de la Luzerne and Monsr. Marbois did me the honor to make at this Camp; for both of whom I have imbibed the most favourable impressions, and thank you for the honourable mention you made of me to them. The Chevr. till he had announced himself at Congress, did not choose to be received in his public character. If he had, except paying him Military honors, It was not my intention to depart from that plain and simple manner of living which accords with the real Interest and policy of Men struggling under every difficulty for the attainment of the most inestimable blessing of life, *Liberty*; the Chevalier was polite enough to approve my principle, and condescended to appear pleased with our Spartan living. In a word he made us all exceeding happy by his affability and good humour, while he remained in Camp.

You are pleased my dear Marquis to express an earnest desire of seeing me in France (after the establishment of our Independancy) and do me the honour to add, that you are not singular in your request. let me entreat you to be perswaded, that to meet you anywhere after the final accomplishment of so glorious an event would contribute to my happiness; and that, to visit a country to whose generous aid we stand so much indebted, would be an additional pleasure; but remember my good friend, that I am unacquainted with your language. that I am too far advanced in years to acquire a knowledge of it. and that to converse through the medium of an interpreter upon common occasions, especially with the *Ladies* must appr. so extremely aukward, insipid, and uncouth, that I can scarce bear it in idea. I will therefore hold myself disengaged for the *present* and when I see you in Virginia, we will talk of this matter and fix our plans.

The declaration of Spain in favour of France has given universal joy to every Whig, while the poor Tory droops like a withering flower under a declining Sun.

We are anxiously expecting to hear of great and important events on your side the Atlantic. At prest. the immagination is left in the wide field of conjecture. Our eyes one moment are turned to an Invasion of England. then of Ireland. Minorca, Gibralter, &ca. In a word we hope every thing, but know not what to expect or where to fix.

The glorious successes of Count DEstaing in the West Indies at the sametime that it adds dominion to France and fresh lustre to her Arms is a source of *new* and unexpected misfortune to our *tender* and *generous parent* and must serve to convince her of the folly of quitting the substance in pursuit of a shadow; and as there is no experience equal to that which is bought I trust she will have a superabundance of this kind of knowledge and be convinced as I hope all the World, and every tyrant in it will that the best and only safe road to honour, glory, and true dignity, is *justice*.

We have such repeated advices of Count D'Estaings being in these Seas that (though I have no official information of the event) I cannot help giving entire credit to the report and looking for his arrival every moment and am preparing accordingly. The enemy at New York also expect it, and to guard agt. the consequences as much as it is in their power to do, are repairing and strengthening all the old fortifications and adding New ones in the vicinity of the City; their fear however does not retard an embarkation which was making (and generally believed) to be for the West Indies or Charles Town. It still goes forward, and by my intelligence will consist of a pretty large detachment. About 14 days ago one british Regiment (the 44th. compleated) and 3 Hessian Regiments were embarked and are gone, as is supposed, to Hallifax. Under convoy of Admiral Arbuthnot about the 20th. of last month the Enemy recd. a reinforcement consisting of two new raised Scotch Regts. some drafts and a few Recruits amounting altogether to about 3000 Men and a few days ago Sir Andw. Hammond arrived with (as it is said) abt. 2000 more; many of these new Troops died on their passage and since landing, the rest are very sickly as indeed their whole Army is while ours keeps remarkably healthy.

The Operations of the enemy this campaign have been confined to the establishment of works of defence. taking a post at Kings ferry, and burning the defenceless towns of New haven, Fairfield, Norwalk, &ca. on the sound within reach of their Shipping where little else was, or could be opposed to them than the cries of distressed Women and helpless children; but these were offered in vain; since these notable exploits they have never stepped out of their Works or beyond their lines. How a conduct of this kind is to effect the conquest of America the wisdom of a North, a Germaine, or Sandwich best can tell. it is too deep and refined for the comprehension of common understandings and general run of politicians.

Colo. Fleury who I expect will have the honour of presenting this letter to you, and who acted an important and honourable part in the event, will give you the particulars of the assault and reduction of Stony point the capture of the G. consg. of 600 men with their Colours, Arms, Baggage, Stores, 15 pieces of valuable ordnance, &ca. He led one of the columns; struck the colours of the garrison with his own hands; and in all respects behaved with that intrepidity and intelligence which marks his conduct upon all occasions.

Since that event we surprized and took Paulus hook a very strong fortified post of the enemys, opposite to the city of New York and within reach of the batteries of that place. The garrison consisting of about 160 Men with the colors were brought off, but none of the stores could be removed on acct. of its insular situation and the difficulty of removing them; the first of these enterprizes was made under the command of General Wayne; the other was conducted by Majr. Lee of the light Horse both of whom have acquired much honor by their gallant behaviour in the respective attacks.

By my last advices from Genl. Sullivan of the 9th. Instt. I am led to conclude that ere this he has completed the entire destruction of the whole Country of the Six nations, excepting so much of it as is inhabited by the Oneidas who have always lived in amity with us; and a few towns belonging to the Cayugas and Onondago's who were disposed to be friendly. At the time these advices came away he had penetrated to the heart of their settlements after having defeated in a general engagement the united force of Indians, Tories, and regulars from Niagara. Burnt between 15 and 20 Towns, destroyed their Crops and every thing that was to be found. He was then advancing to the exterior Towns with a view to complete the desolation of the whole Country, and Remove the cruel inhabitants of it to a greater distance, who were then fleeing in the utmost confusion, consternation and distress towards Niagara, distant 100 Miles through an uninhabited wilderness; experiencing a little of that distress, but nothing of those cruelties which they have exercised on our unhappy frontier Settlers, who (Men, Women and Children) have been deliberately murdered, in a manner shocking to humanity.

But to conclude, you requested from me a long letter, I have given you one; but methinks my dear Marquis, I hear you say, there is reason in all things; that this is too long. I am clearly in sentiment with you, and will have mercy on you in my next. But at present must pray your patience a while longer, till I can make a tender of my most respectful compliments to the Marchioness. Tell her (if you have not made a mistake, and offered your *own love* instead of *hers* to me) that I have a heart susceptible of the tenderest passion, and that it is already so strongly impressed with the most favourable ideas of her, that she must be cautious of putting loves torch to it; as you must be in fanning the flame. But here again methinks I hear you say, I am not apprehensive of danger. My wife is young, you are growing old and the atlantic is between you. All this is true, but know my good friend that no distance can keep *anxious* lovers long asunder, and that the Wonders of former ages may be revived in this. But alas! will you not remark that amidst all the wonders recorded in holy writ no instance can be produced where a young Woman from *real inclination* has prefered an old man. This is so much against me that I shall not be able *I fear* to contest the prize with you, yet, under the encouragement you have given me I shall enter the list for so inestimable a Jewell.

I will now reverse the scene, and inform you, that Mrs. Washington (who set out for Virginia when we took the field in June) often has in, her letters to me, enquired if I had heard from you, and will be much pleased at hearing that you are well, and happy. In her name (as she is not here) I thank you for your polite attention to her; and shall speak her sense of the honor confered on her by the Marchioness.

When I look back to the length of this letter I am so much astonished and frightened at it myself, that I have not the courage to give it a careful reading for the purpose of correction. You must therefore receive it with all its imperfections, accompanied with this assurance that though there may be many incorrections in the letter, there is not a single defect in the friendship of my dear Marquis Yr., etc.

To Benjamin Harrison

West-point, October 25, 1779.

My dear Sir: Letters of a private nature and for the mere purposes of friendly intercourse are, with me, the production of too much haste to allow time (generally speaking) to take, or make fair copies of them; and my memory (unfortunately for me) is of too defective a frame to furnish the periods at which they were written. But I am much mistaken if I have not, since I came to the prest. Incampmt. wrote you a full acct. of the situation of things in this quarter. Your last letter to me was in May.

The Pensylvania Gazettes, which I presume you regularly receive, will have conveyed official accts. to the public of all occurrances of any importance. A repetition would be unnecessary and tedious. But it may not be amiss to observe, that excepting the plundering expedition to Virginia, and the burning one in Connecticut the enemy have wasted another Campaign (till this stage of it at least) in their ship-bound Islands, and strong-holds, without doing a single thing advancive of the end in view, unless by delays and placing their whole dependance in the depreciation of our money, and the wretched management of our finances, they expect to accomplish it.

In the meanwhile they have suffered, I do not know what other term to give it, a third part of the Continental Troops wch. altogether was inferior to theirs, to be employed in the total destruction of all the Country inhabited by the hostile tribes of the Six Nations, their good and faithful Allies! While the other two thirds without calling upon the Militia for the aid of a single man excepting upon the Inhabitants in the vicinity of this Post (and that for a few days only) at the time Genl. Clinton moved up the River in the Spring and before we could reach it restrained their foraging parties, confined them within very circumscribed bounds at the same time bestowing an immensity of labour on this Post, more important to us, considered in all its consequences, than any other in America.

There is something so truly unaccountable in all this that I do not know how to reconcile it with their own views, or to any principle of common sense; but the fact is nevertheless true. The latter end of May as I have hinted already Genl. Clinton moved up to Kings-ferry in force, and possessed himself of Stony and Verplanks points; alarmed at this (for I conceived these works, and the command of the river in conseque. was really the object, and the other only an advance to it) I hastened to its succour; but the return of the enemy

towards the last of June, after having fortified and garrisoned
the points, convinced me that that was not their design, or
that they had relinquished it, till their reinforcemts. shd. have
arriv'd since which these Posts have changed Masters frequently and after employing the enemy a whole campaign,
costing them near a thousand men in Prisoners by desertion,
and otherways, and infinite labour is at length in Statu-quo
that is, simply, a continental Ferry again.

The reinforcements from G: Britain under Convoy of Adml.
Arbuthnot and Sir Andw. Hammend from the best Acct. we
have received amounted to about 4000 Men, mostly new recruits, and sickly; many having died on their passage and since
their arrival.

We are now in appearances, launching into a wide and
boundless field, puzzled with mazes and o'er spread with difficulties; a glorious object is in view, and God send we may
attain it. Some time ago it was much within the reach of probability; but the Season, and the incessant labour of the enemy
to secure the City and harbour of New York are much opposed to us, and serve to lessen my hopes in proportion as
time rolls on. It is now 30 days since Congress gave me official
notice of Count D'Estaing's intended co-operation, and no
authentic acct. of him is since come to hand. The probability
therefore is, that we shall have hot work in a cold season.

I have called upon Massachusetts bay, Connecticut, New
York, New Jersey, and Pensa. for Militia, and every thing being in a proper train for a capitol enterprize, to the Gods and
our best endeavours the event is committed.

Verplanks and Stony points as I have before observed are
already evacuated and from every acct. and appeares the like
will happen at Rhode Isld., things being in a train for it. Their
whole force then will be concentred at New York, and in
regular Troops only, will amount to at least 18,000, besides
Seamen from near 1000 Sail of Vessels of different kinds.
Refugees, and the Militia of those Islands wch. are actually in
their power, and which they have had employed on their
works of defence ever since the first rumour of the french
fleets being in these Seas.

I have no doubt but that the Assembly of Virginia, at its
last session, had cogent reasons for opening the Land Office;

but so far as it respects the Army, the measure is to be lamented; for I believe, from what I have heard, that it will be a means of breaking up the Virginia line.

I have never read the Act with any degree of attention, and at this time, have but an imperfect recollection of the purport of it. But in general conversation I learn from the Officers, that by some clause in this or an antecedant Act those who have already taken pains, and have been at expence to secure Lands in that Country, will receive little benefit from either the one or the other unless some requisites before Commissioners are complied with; and this they add is not to be done (if I understand them properly) otherwise than by personal attendance. While this operates powerfully upon the minds of all those who have already taken measures to secure an Interest in that new world a desire prevails universally amongst the whole of them to become adventurers before the Cream is skimmed.

I am informed that the New York Assembly which is now sitting, mean to make an offer of Land to the Officers and Soldiers of other States, equally with their own, who may incline to take the Continental bounty in it; the policy of this measure may not be unworthy of consideration by the Assembly of Virginia. If it is conceived, that this great Country will long continue to be part of the present government of that commonwealth, no measure that can be adopted will, in my opinion, give it a more vigorous growth than the opening of this door and add more to its population which ever has been considered the riches of a Country.

To any enquiring friends you will please to make a tender of my compliments and do me the justice to believe that in truth and sincerity I am, etc.

To Robert Howe

West-point, November 20, 1779.
Dear Sir: Herewith you will receive Mr. Pulteney's lucubrations, and my thanks for the perusal of them. He has made I perceive, the dependance of America essential to the existance

of Great Britain as a powerful Nation. This I shall not deny; because I am in sentiment with him in thinking her fallen state in consequence of the seperation too obvious to be disputed. It was of magnitude sufficient to have made a wise and just people look before they leaped. But I am glad to find that he has placed the supplies necessary to support that dependance upon three things which I am perswaded will never again exist in his nation; namely Public virtue, public œconomy, and public union in her grand Council.

Stock Jobbing, speculation dissipation luxury and venality with all their concomitants are too deeply rooted to yield to virtue and the public good. *We* that are not yet hackneyed in vice, but infants as it were in the arts of corruption, and the knowledge of taking advantage of public necessity (tho' I am much mistaken if we shall not soon become very great adepts at them), find it almost, if not quite impossible to preserve virtue enough to keep the body politic and corporate in tolerable tune. It is scarcely to be expected therefore that a people who have reduced these things to a system and have actually interwoven them into their constitution should at once become immaculate.

I do not know which rises highest, my indignation or contempt for the Sentiments which pervade the Ministerial writings of this day; these hireling scribblers labour to describe and prove the ingratitude of America in not breaking faith with France, and returning to her Allegiance to the Crown of Great Britain after its having offered such advantageous terms of accommodation. Such Sentiments as these are insulting to common sense and affrontive to every principle of sound policy and common honesty. Why has She offered these terms? because after a bloody contest, carried on with unrelenting and savage fury on her part the issue (which was somewhat doubtful while we stood alone) is now become certain by the aid we derive from our Alliance; notwithstanding the manifest advantages of which, and the blood and treasure which has been spent to resist a tyranny which was unremitted as long as there remained a hope of subjugation we are told with an effrontery altogether unparrallelled that every cause of complaint is now done away by the generous offers of a tender parent; that it is ungrateful in us not to accept the proffered terms; and impolitic not to abandon a power (dangerous I confess to her but) which held out a Saving hand to us in the hour of our distress. What epithet does such Sentiments merit? How much shd. a people possessed of them be despised? From my Soul I abhor them! A Manly struggle, had it been conducted upon liberal ground; an honest confession that they were unequal to conquest, and wished for our friendship, would have had its proper weight; but their cruelties, exercised upon those who have fallen within their power; the wanton depredations committed by themselves and their faithful Allies the Indians; their low and dirty practices of Counterfeiting our money, forging letters, and condescending to adopt such arts as the meanest villain in private life would blush at being charged with has made me their fixed enemy.

I have received your letter by Colo. Moylan of yesterdays date. The Instructions given to —— are full and compleat. I have no thought of withdrawing the effective horse till the other Troops go into quarters. I am, etc.

To Joseph Jones

(Private)

Morris-Town, May 14, 1780.

Dear Sir: I received the acct. of your delegation with much satisfaction and was greatly pleased to hear of your arrival in Philadelphia; as I have ever placed you among the number of my friends I mean to take this early oppertunity of giving you a mark of my confidence in an interesting moment.

The arrival of the Marquis de la Fayette opens a prospect wch. offers the most important advantages to these States if proper measures are adopted to improve it. He announces an intention of his Court to send a Fleet and Army to co-operate effectually with us.

In the present state of our Finances, and in the total emptiness of our magazines a plan must be concerted to bring out the resources of the Country with vigor and decision; this I think you will agree with me cannot be effected if the measures to be taken should depend on the slow deliberations of a body so large as Congress admitting the best disposition in every member to promote the object in view. It appears to me of the greatest importance, and even of absolute necessity that a *small* Committee should be immediately appointed to reside near head Quarters vested with all the powers which Congress have so far as respects the purpose of a full co-operation with the French fleet and Army on the *Continent.* There authority should be Plenipotentiary to draw out men and supplies of every kind and give their sanction to any operations which the Commander in chief may not think himself at liberty to undertake without it as well beyond, as within the limit of these States.

This Committee can act with dispatch and energy, by being on the spot it will be able to provide for exigencies as they arise and the better to judge of their nature and urgency. The plans in contemplation may be opened to them with more freedom and confidence than to a numerous body. Where secrecy is impossible, where the indiscretion of a single member by disclosing may defeat the project.

I need not enlarge on the advantages of such a measure as I flatter myself they will occur to you and that you will be ready to propose and give it your support. The conjuncture is one of the most critical and important we have seen, all our prudence and exertions are requisite to give it a favourable issue. Hesitancy and delay would in all probability ruin our Affairs; circumstanced as we are the greatest good or the greatest ill must result. We shall probably fix the independence of America if we succeed and if we fail the abilities of the State will have been so strained in the attempt that a total relaxation and debility must ensue and the worst is to be apprehended.

These considerations should determine Congress to forego all inferior objects and unite with mutual confidence in those measures which seem best calculated to insure success. There is no man who can be more useful as a member of the Committee than General Schuyler. His perfect knowledge of the resources of the Country, the activity of his temper, His fruitfulness of expedients and his sound Military sense make me wish above all things he may be appointed. A well composed Committee is of primary importance, I need not hint that the delicacy of these intimations fits them only for your private ear.

The opinion I have of your friendship induces me thus freely and confidentially to impart my sentiments on the occasion and I shall be very happy you may agree with me in judgment. I am with the greatest esteem and regard Dr. Sir etc.

To Joseph Reed

Morris Town, May 28, 1780.

Dear Sir: I am much obliged to you for your favour of the 23. Nothing could be more necessary than the aid given by your state towards supplying us with provision. I assure you, every Idea you can form of our distresses, will fall short of the reality. There is such a combination of circumstances to exhaust the patience of the soldiery that it begins at length to be worn out and we see in every line of the army, the most serious features of mutiny and sedition. All our departments, all our operations are at a stand, and unless a system very different from that which has for a long time prevailed, be immediately adopted throughout the states our affairs must soon become desperate beyond the possibility of recovery. If you were on the spot my Dear Sir, if you could see what difficulties surround us on every side, how unable we are to administer to the most ordinary calls of the service, you would be convinced that these expressions are not too strong, and that we have every thing to dread. Indeed I have almost ceased to hope. The country in general is in such a state of insensibility and indifference to its interests, that I dare not flatter myself with any change for the better.

The Committee of Congress in their late address to the several states have given a just picture of our situation. I very much doubt its making the desired impression, and if it does not I shall consider our lethargy as incurable. The present juncture is so interesting that if it does not produce correspondent exertions, it will be a proof that motives of honor public good and even self preservation have lost their influence upon our minds. This is a decisive moment; one of the most I will go further and say *the* most important America has seen. The Court of France has made a glorious effort for our deliverance, and if we disappoint its intentions by our supineness we must become contemptible in the eyes of all mankind; nor can we after that venture to confide that our allies will persist in an attempt to establish what it will appear we want inclination or ability to assist them in.

Every view of our own circumstances ought to determine us to the most vigorous efforts; but there are considerations of another kind that should have equal weight. The combined fleets of France and Spain last year were greatly superior of those of the enemy: The enemy nevertheless sustained no material damage, and at the close of the campaign have given a very important blow to our allies. This campaign the difference between the fleets from every account I have been able to collect will be inconsiderable, indeed it is far from clear that there will not be an equality. What are we to expect will be the case if there should be another campaign? In all probability the advantage will be on the side of the English and then what would become of America? We ought not to deceive ourselves. The maritime resources of Great Britain are more substantial and real than those of France and Spain united. Her commerce is more extensive than that of both her rivals; and it is an axiom that the nation which has the most extensive commerce will always have the most powerful marine. Were this argument less convincing the fact speaks for itself; her progress in the course of the last year is an incontestible proof.

It is true France in a manner created a Fleet in a very short space and this may mislead us in the judgment we form of her naval abilities. But if they bore any comparison with those of great Britain how comes it to pass, that with all the force of Spain added she has lost so much ground in so short a time, as now to have scarcely a superiority. We should consider what was done by France as a violent and unnatural effort of the government, which for want of sufficient foundation, cannot continue to operate proportionable effects.

In modern wars the longest purse must chiefly determine

the event. I fear that of the enemy will be found to be so. Though the government is deeply in debt and of course poor, the nation is rich and their riches afford a fund which will not be easily exhausted. Besides, their system of public credit is such that it is capable of greater exertions than that of any other nation. Speculatists have been a long time foretelling its downfall, but we see no symptoms of the catastrophe being very near. I am persuaded it will at least last out the war, and then, in the opinion of many of the best politicians it will be a national advantage. If the war should terminate successfully the crown will have acquired such influence and power that it may attempt any thing, and a bankruptcy will probably be made the ladder to climb to absolute authority. Administration may perhaps wish to drive matters to this issue; at any rate they will not be restrained by an apprehension of it from forcing the resources of the state. It will promote their present purposes on which their all is at stake and it may pave the way to triumph more effectually over the constitution. With this disposition I have no doubt that ample means will be found to prosecute the war with the greatest vigor.

France is in a very different position. The abilities of her present Financier have done wonders. By a wise administration of the revenues aided by advantageous loans he has avoided the necessity of additional taxes. But I am well informed, if the war continues another campaign he will be obliged to have recourse to the taxes usual in time of war which are very heavy, and which the people of France are not in a condition to endure for any duration. When this necessity commences France makes war on ruinous terms; and England from her individual wealth will find much greater facility in supplying her exigencies.

Spain derives great wealth from her mines, but not so great as is generally imagined. Of late years the profits to government is essentially diminished. Commerce and industry are the best mines of a nation; both which are wanting to her. I am told her treasury is far from being so well filled as we have flattered ourselves. She is also much divided on the propriety of the war. There is a strong party against it. The temper of the nation is too sluggish to admit of great exertions, and tho' the Courts of the two kingdoms are closely linked together, there never has been in any of their wars a perfect harmony of measures, nor has it been the case in this; which has already been no small detriment to the common cause.

I mention these things to show that the circumstances of our allies as well as our own call for peace; to obtain which we must make one great effort this campaign. The present instance of the friendship of the Court of France is attended with every circumstance that can render it important and agreeable; that can interest our gratitude or fire our emulation. If we do our duty we may even hope to make the campaign decisive on this Continent. But we must do our duty in earnest, or disgrace and ruin will attend us. I am sincere in declaring a full persuasion, that the succour will be fatal to us if our measures are not adequate to the emergency.

Now my Dear Sir, I must observe to you, that much will depend on the State of Pennsylvania. She has it in her power to contribute without comparison more to our success than any other state; in the two essential articles of flour and transportation. New York, Jersey, Pensylvania and Maryland are our flour countries: Virginia went little on this article the last crop and her resources are call'd for to the southward. New York by legislative coercion has already given all she could spare for the use of the army. Her inhabitants are left with scarcely a sufficiency for their own subsistence. Jersey from being so long the place of the army's residence is equally exhausted. Maryland has made great exertions; but she can still do something more. Delaware may contribute handsomely in proportion to her extent. But Pennsylvania is our chief dependence. From every information I can obtain she is at this time full of flour. I speak to you in the language of frankness and as a friend. I do not mean to make any insinuations unfavourable to the state. I am aware of the embarrassments the government labours under, from the open opposition of one party and the underhand intrigues of another. I know that with the best dispositions to promote the public service, you have been obliged to move with circumspection. But this is a time to hazard and to take a tone of energy and decision. All parties but the disaffected will acquiesce in the necessity and give their support. The hopes and fears of the people at large may be acted upon in such a manner as to make them approve and second your views.

The matter is reduced to a point. Either Pensylvania must give us all the aid we ask of her, or we can undertake nothing. We must renounce every idea of cooperation, and must confess to our allies that we look wholly to them for our safety. This will be a state of humiliation and bitterness against which the feelings of every good American ought to revolt. Your's I am convinced will; nor have I the least doubt that you will employ all your influence to animate the Legislature and the people at large. The fate of these states hangs upon it. God grant we may be properly impressed with the consequences.

I wish the Legislature could be engaged to vest the executive with plenipotentiary powers. I should then expect every thing practicable from your abilities and zeal. This is not a time for formality or ceremony. The crisis in every point of view is extraordinary and extraordinary expedients are necessary. I am decided in this opinion.

I am happy to hear that you have a prospect of complying with the requisitions of Congress for specific supplies; that the spirit of the city and state seems to revive and the warmth of party decline. These are good omens of our success. Perhaps this is the proper period to unite.

I am obliged to you for the renewal of your assurances of personal regard; my sentiments for you, you are so well acquainted with as to make it unnecessary to tell you with how much esteem etc.

I felicitate you on the increase of your family. Mrs. Washington does the same and begs her particular respects and congratulations to Mrs. Reed, to which permit me to add mine.

To Joseph Jones

Morris-Town, May 31, 1780.

Dear Sir: I have been honored with your favor in answer to my letter respecting the appointment of a Comee.; and with two others of later date. the last containing Genl. Woodfords acct. of the situation of things at Charles Town at the time of his writing. I thank you for them all. Unhappily that place (Chs. Town), the garrison in it, &ca. (As appears by the New York account which I have transmitted to Congress) have been in the enemys hands since the 12th. Instt.

Certain I am that unless Congress speaks in a more decisive tone; unless they are vested with powers by the several States competent to the great purposes of War, or assume them as matter of right; and they, and the states respectively, act with more energy than they hitherto have done, that our Cause is lost. We can no longer drudge on in the old way. By ill-timing the adoption of measures, by delays in the execution of them, or by unwarrantable jealousies, we incur enormous expences, and derive no benefit from them. One state will comply with a requisition of Congress, another neglects to do it. a third executes it by halves, and all differ either in the manner, the matter, or so much in point of time, that we are always working up hill, and ever shall be (while such a system as the present one, or rather want of one prevails) unable to apply our strength or resources to any advantage.

This my dear Sir is plain language to a member of Congress; but it is the language of truth and friendship. It is the result of long thinking, close application, and strict observation. I see one head gradually changing into thirteen. I see one Army branching into thirteen; and instead of looking up to Congress as the supreme controuling power of the united States, are considering themselves as dependent on their respective States. In a word, I see the powers of Congress declining too fast for the consequence and respect which is due to them as the grand representative body of America, and am fearful of the consequences of it.

Till your letter of the 23d. came to hand I thought General Weedon had actually resigned his Commission; but be this as it may, I see no possibility of giving him any command out of the line of his own State. He certainly knows that every state that has Troops enough to form a Brigade claims, and has exercised, uniformly, the previledge of having them commanded by a Brigr. of its own, nor is it in my power to depart from this system without convulsing the Army; which at all times is hurtful, and may be ruinous at this. I am, etc.

To John Augustine Washington

Morris-Town, June 6 1780.

My dear Brother: Your letter of the 10th. of March came safe, but was rather long on its passage. I have also received the other letter refered to, dated at Mt. Vernon last fall. I do not at this time recollect the date of my last letter to you, because, however agreeable it may be to me, I have little leizure for private corrispondencies being, in a manner, wearied to death by the multiplicity of public matters I am obliged to attend to. I can only say, and I say it with much truth, that I derive much pleasure in hearing from you, although it is not in my power to response as often as I could wish.

I am glad to find that you did not dispose of your land. the Paper currency of this Continent has, for sometime past, been upon too fluctuating a scale to receive in return for real property, unless it was to be bartered off immediately for something else of permanent value. To say when the hour of apreciation will arrive, is (if not beyond the reach of human ken) very difficult; it depends upon a variety of causes; more virtue; more exertion; more œconomy and a better knowledge of our true situation. While the interested man, who makes every thing yield to his lust for gain, the Speculator, which is only another term for the same thing, and the disaffected, though acting upon different principles to effect the same end, are practising every art that human craft and cunning can devise to counteract the struggles of the virtuous part of the community I think our money is upon too unstable a footing and fluctuating to part with Land for, when the latter we are certain will become more valuable every day. It ever was my opinion, though candor obliges me to confess it is not consistent with national policy, to have my property as much as possible in Lands. I have seen no cause to change this opinion; but abundant reason to confirm me in it; being persuaded that a few years Peace will inundate these States with emigrants and of course enhaunce the price of Land. far above the comn. Intt. of Money.

July 6th. 1780.

I begun this letter, and had written nearly thus far when

advice came to me that the enemy had landed at Elizabeth Town point, and was advancing in force upon us. Unable as we were to oppose them, I thought it best to put on a good countenance and advance towards them; which being done; and the partial engagements which followed being published, makes it unnecessary for me to detail them again. It is to be lamented, bitterly lamented, and in the anguish of Soul I do lament, that our fatal and accursed policy should bring the 6th. of June upon us and not a single recruit to the Army, tho' the consequences were foretold last Fall, and pressed with as much precision as if the opinion had been the result of inspiration; but it has ever been our conduct and misfortune to Slumber and Sleep while we should be deligent in preparation; and when pressed by irresistable necessity and when we can delay no longer, then to bring ourselves to the brink of destruction by expensive and temporary expedients. In a word, we have no system, and seem determined not to profit by experience. We are, during the winter, dreaming of Independance and Peace, without using the means to become so. In the Spring, when our Recruits should be with the Army and in training, we have just discovered the necessity of calling for them. and by the Fall, after a distresed, and inglorious campaign for want of them, we begin to get a few men, which come in just time enough to eat our Provisions, and consume our Stores without rendering any service; thus it is, one year Rolls over another, and with out some change, we are hastening to our Ruin.

To tell a person at the distance of three or 400 Miles that an Army reduced almost to nothing (by the expiration of short enlistments) should, sometimes, be five or Six days together without Bread, then as many without Meat, and once or twice, two or three without either; that the same Army should have had numbers of Men in it with scarcely cloaths enough to cover their nakedness, and a full fourth of it without even the shadow of a blanket severe as the Winter was, and that men under these circumstances were held together, is hardly within the bounds of credibility, but is nevertheless true, it is no difficult matter therefore under this view of things (which is not sufficiently coloured to the life) to form some idea of my situation.

The States, under an expectation of hourly succour from France, are *now* called upon in pointed and pressing terms for Men and Supplies to co-operate with them; but in what manner they will give them; when they will arrive, and what may be the result, the womb of time only can reveal, I cannot. Our whole re-inforcement as yet is about 250 Men.

The Enemy after leaving the Jerseys, made demonstrations towards our Posts in the Highlands (on the North River) as if a visit was intended them; this occasioned my moving that way; but after hovering upon the Water for two or three days, in the River, they debarked on the East side of it, and are foraging that Ground which we ought to preserve if we had the power to accomplish it; meanwhile we lye on the West side of the River, distant from it abt. 18 Miles, with a view of refreshing our Troops, waiting the arrival of the French-fleet, and our own Reinforcements. My affectionate regards are presented to my Sister and all the family. with much truth I can assure that I am Yrs., etc.

To Benedict Arnold

Head Quarters at Peekskill, August 3, 1780.

Sir: You are to proceed to West point and take the command of that post and its dependencies, in which are included all from Fishkill to Kings Ferry. The Corps of Infantry and Cavalry advanced towards the Enemy's lines on the East side of the River will also be under your orders and will take directions from you, and you will endeavour to obtain every intelligence of the Enemy's Motions. The Garrison of West point is to consist of the Militia of New Hampshire and Massachusetts, for which reason, as soon as the number from those States amounts to twelve hundd the New York Militia under the command of Colo. Malcom are to join the Main Army on the West side of the River, and when the number from Massachusetts-bay alone shall amount to fifteen hundred Rank and file, the Militia of New Hampshire will also march to the Main Army. Colo. James Livingstons Regiment is, till further orders, to garrison the Redoubts at Stoney and Verplanks points.

Claverac upon the North River is appointed for the place of rendezvous of the Militia of New Hampshire and Massachusetts, from whence you will have them brought down as fast as they arrive. A supply of provision will be necessary at that place, which you will order from time to time as there may be occasion.

You will endeavour to have the Works at West point carried on as expeditiously as possible by the Garrison, under the direction and superintendance of the Engineers. The Stores carefully preserved, and the provision safely deposited and often inspected, particularly the salted Meat. A certain quantity of provision has been constantly kept in each Work, to be ready against a sudden attack. Where there are Bomb proofs, they serve for Magazines; but in the smaller Works where there are none, you will have places erected sufficiently tight to preserve the provision from damage and pillage.

You will, as soon as possible, obtain and transmit an accurate Return of the Militia which have come in, and inform me regularly of their increase.

Should any Levies, from the State of New York or those to the Eastward of it, intended for the Continental Army arrive at West point, you will immediately forward them to the Lines to which they respectively belong.

The difficulties we shall certainly experience on the score of provisions render the utmost œconomy highly necessary. You will therefore attend frequently to the daily Issues, and by comparing them with your Returns, will be able to check any impositions.

To Joseph Jones

Head Qrs. Tappan, August 13, 1780.

Dear Sir: The subject of this letter will be confined to a single point. I shall make it as short as possible, and write it with frankness. If any sentiment therefore is delivered which may be displeasing to you *as a member of Congress*, ascribe it to the freedom which is taken with you by a friend, who has nothg. in view but the public good.

In your letter without date, but which came to hand yesterday, an idea is held up as if the acceptance of General Green's resignation of the Qr. Mrs. department was not all that Congress meant to do with him. If by this it is in contemplation to suspend him from his command in the line (of which he made an express reservation at the time of entering on the other duty) and it is not already enacted, let me beseech you to consider *well* what you are about before you resolve.

I shall neither condemn, or acquit Genl. Greens conduct for the act of resignation, because all the antecedents are necessary to form a right judgment of the matter, and possibly, if the affair is ever brought before the public, you may find him treading on better ground than you seem to imagine; but this by the by. My sole aim at present is to advertise you of what I think would be the consequences of suspending him from his command in the line (a matter distinct from the other), without a proper tryal. A proceedure of this kind must touch the feelings of every Officer; it will shew in a conspicuous point of view the uncertain tenure by which they hold their Commissions. In a word it will exhibit such a specimen of power that I question much if there is an Officer in the whole line that will hold a Commission beyond the end of the Campaign if they do till then. Such an Act in the most Despotic Government would be attended at least with loud complaints.

It does not require, I am sure, with you argument at this time of day to prove, that there is no set of Men in the United States (considered as a body) that have made the same sacrafices of their Interest in support of the common cause as the Officers of the American Army; that nothing but a love of their Country, of honor, and a desire of seeing their labours crowned with success could possibly induce them to continue one moment in Service. That no Officer can live upon his pay, that hundreds having spent their little all in addition to their scant public allowance have resigned, because they could no longer support themselves as Officers; that numbers are, at this moment, rendered unfit for duty for want of Cloathing, while the rest are wasteing their property and some of them verging fast to the gulph of poverty and distress. Can it be supposed that men under these circumstances who can derive at best if the Contest ends happily, only the advantages which attend in equal proportion with Others will sit patient under such a precedent? surely they will not, for the measure, not the man, will be the subject of consideration and each will ask himself this question if Congress by its mere fiat, without enquiry and without tryal, will suspend one Officer to day; an officer of such high rank, may it not be my turn to morrow and ought I to put it in the power of any man or body of men to sport with my Commission and character and lay me under the necessity of tamely acquiescing, or by an appeal to the public expose matters which must be injurious to its interests? The suspension of Genls. Schuyler and St. Clair, tho it was preceded by the loss of Ticonderoga which contributed not a little for the moment to excite prejudices against them, was by no means viewed with a satisfactory eye by many discerning Men, and tho it was in a manner supported by the public clamor; and the one in contemplation I am almost morally certain will be generally reprobated by the Army. Suffer not my Friend, if it is within the compass of your abilities to prevent it, so disagreeable an event to take place. I do not mean to justify; to countenance or excuse in the most distant degree any expressions of disrespect which the Gentn. in question, if he has used any, may have offered to Congress, no more than I do any unreasonable matters he may have required respecting the Q. M. G. department, but as I have already observed, my Letter is to prevent his suspension, because I *fear*, because I *feel* it must lead to very disagreeable and injurious consequences. Genl Greene has his numerous Friends out of the Army as well as in it, and from his Character and consideration in the world, he might not, when he felt himself wounded in so summary way, withhold from a discussion that could not at best promote the public cause. As a Military Officer he stands very fair and very deservedly so, in the opinion of all his acquaintance.

These sentiments are the result of my own reflections on the matter and, I hasten to inform you of them. I do not know that Genl. Greene has ever heard of the matter and I hope he never may; nor am I acquainted with the opinion of a single Officer in the whole Army upon the subject. Nor will any tone be given by me. It is my wish to prevent the proceeding; for sure I am it cannot be brought to a happy issue if it takes place. I am &c.

Circular to State Governments

Head Quarters, near the Liberty Pole, in
Bergen County, August 27, 1780.

Sir: The Honble: the Committee of Co-operation having returned to Congress, I am under the disagreeable necessity of informing you that the Army is again reduced to an extremity of distress for want of provision. The greater part of it had been without Meat from the 21st. to the 26th. To endeavour to obtain some relief, I moved down to this place, with a view of stripping the lower parts of the County of the remainder of its Cattle, which after a most rigorous exaction is found to afford between two and three days supply only, and those, consisting of Milch Cows and Calves of one or two years old. When this scanty pittance is consumed, I know not what will be our next resource, as the Commissary can give me no certain information of more than 120 head of Cattle expected from pennsylvania and about 150 from Massachusetts. I mean in time to supply our immediate wants. Military coercion is no longer of any avail, as nothing further can possibly be collected from the Country in which we are obliged to take a position, without depriving the inhabitants of the last morsel. This mode of subsisting, supposing the desired end could be answered by it, besides being in the highest degree distressing to individuals, is attended with ruin to the Morals and discipline of the Army; during the few days which we have been obliged to send out small parties to procure provision for themselves, the most enormous excesses have been committed.

It has been no inconsiderable support of our cause, to have

had it in our power to contrast the conduct of our Army with that of the enemy, and to convince the inhabitants that while their rights were wantonly violated by the British Troops, by ours they were respected. This distinction must unhappily now cease, and we must assume the odious character of the plunderers instead of the protectors of the people, the direct consequence of which must be to alienate their minds from the Army and insensibly from the cause. We have not yet been absolutely without Flour, but we have *this* day but *one* days supply in Camp, and I am not certain that there is a single Barrel between this place and Trenton. I shall be obliged therefore to draw down one or two hundred Barrels from a small Magazine which I have endeavoured to establish at West point, for the security of the Garrison in case of a sudden investiture.

From the above state of facts it may be foreseen that this army cannot possibly remain much longer together, unless very vigorous and immediate measures are taken by the States to comply with the requisitions made upon them. The Commissary General has neither the means nor the power of procuring supplies; he is only to receive them from the several Agents. Without a speedy change of circumstances, this dilemma will be involved; either the Army must disband, or what is, if possible, worse, subsist upon the plunder of the people. I would fain flatter myself that a knowledge of our situation will produce the desired relief; not a relief of a few days as has generally heretofore been the case, but a supply equal to the establishment of Magazines for the Winter. If these are not formed before the Roads are broken up by the weather, we shall certainly experience the same difficulties and distresses the ensuing Winter which we did the last. Altho' the troops have upon every occasion hitherto borne their wants with unparralled patience, it will be dangerous to trust too often to a repetition of the causes of discontent. I have the honor etc.

To Samuel Huntington

Robinson's House in the Highlands,
September 26, 1780.

Sir: I have the honor to inform Congress that I arrived here yesterday about 12 o'clock on my return from Hartford. Some hours previous to my arrival Major General Arnold went from his quarters which were at this place; and as it was supposed over the river to the garrison at West-point, whether I proceeded myself in order to visit the post. I found General Arnold had not been there during the day, and on my return to his quarters, he was still absent. In the mean time a packet had arrived from Lt. Colonel Jamison announcing the capture of a John Anderson who was endeavouring to go to New-York, with the several interesting and important papers mentioned below, all in the hand writing of General Arnold. This was also accompanied with a letter from the prisoner avowing himself to be Major John André Adjt: General of the British army, relating the manner of his capture, and endeavouring to shew that he did not come under the description of a spy. From these several circumstances, and information that the General seemed to be thrown into some degree of agitation on receiving a letter a little time before he went from his quarters, I was led to conclude immediately that he had heard of Major André's captivity, and that he would if possible escape to the enemy, and accordingly took such measures as appeared the most probable to apprehend him. But he had embarked in a barge, and proceeded down the river under a flag to the vulture ship of war, which lay at some miles below Stony and Verplank's points. He wrote me after he got on board a letter, of which the inclosed is a copy. Major André is not arrived yet, but I hope he is secure and that he will be here to-day. I have been and am taking proper precautions, which I trust will prove effectual, to prevent the important consequences which this conduct on the part of General Arnold was intended to produce. I do not know the party that took Major André; but it is said, it consisted only of a few militia, who acted in such a manner upon the occasion as does them the highest honor and proves them to be men of great virtue. They were offered, I am informed, a large sum of money for his release, and as many goods as they would demand, but without any effect. Their conduct gives them a just claim to the thanks of their country, and I also hope they will be otherwise rewarded. As soon as I know their names I shall take pleasure in transmitting them to Congress. I have taken such measures with respect to the Gentlemen of General Arnolds family as prudence dictated; but from every thing that has hitherto come to my knowledge, I have the greatest reason to believe they are perfectly innocent. I early secured, Joshua Smith, the person mentioned in the close of General Arnolds letter, and find him to have had a considerable share in this business. I have the honor etc.

To Henry Clinton

Head Quarters, September 30, 1780.
Sir: In answer to Your Excellency's Letter of the 26th Instant, which I had the honor to receive, I am to inform You, that Major André was taken under such circumstances as would have justified the most summary proceedings against him. I determined however to refer his case to the examination and decision of a Board of General Officers, who have reported, on his free and voluntary confession and Letters; "That he came on Shore from the Vulture Sloop of war in the night of the Twenty first of September Instant on an interview with General Arnold in a private and secret manner. Secondly that he changed his dress within our lines, and under a feigned name and in a disguised habit passed our Works at Stoney and Verplanks points the Evening of the Twenty second of September Instant, and was taken the morning of the Twenty third of September Instant, at Tarry Town, in a disguised habit, being then on his way to New York, and when taken he had in his possession Several papers which contained intelligence for the Enemy. The Board having maturely considered these Facts do also report to His Excellency General Washington, that Major André Adjutant General to the British Army ought to be considered as a Spy from the Enemy,

and that agreable to the Law and usage of Nations it is their opinion he ought to suffer death"

From these proceedings it is evident Major André was employed in the execution of measures very foreign to the Objects of Flags of truce and such as they were never meant to authorise or countenance in the most distant degree; and this Gentleman confessed with the greatest candor in the course of his examination, "that it was impossible for him to suppose he came on shore under the sanction of a Flag." I have the Honor etc.

Instructions to Spies Going into New York

Get into the City.

There, in the best manner possible, learn the designs of the Enemy.

Whether they mean to evacuate New York wholly in part, or continue the Army there. A discovery of this kind will be best made by attending a little to the conduct of Delancy, Bayard, Matthews &ca., as they, more than probably, will be preparing for a Removal if the City is to be left, wholly, or in any considerable degree.

Or Secondly, whether they have any views of Operating against this Army, which will be best known by their preparations of Waggons, Horses &ca., these will want Shoeing, repairing, &ca. Collecting together.

Enquire whether the Transports are Wooding and Watering. Whether the Stores are removing from the City into them, and whether any Regimental Baggage is Imbarked. Enquire also, how the Enemy are off for Provisions; whether the Cork Fleet is arrived and the number of Provision Ships it consists of.

Enquire also if Admiral Byrons Fleet is arrived. Where Lord Howe and the New York Fleet is; whether within Sandy hook, or gone out to Sea, and for what purpose.

Whether any Troops have been Imbarked lately and for what place. Whether any have arrived from England lately, or are expected.

Whether the Merchants who came from Europe and those who have been attached to Government are packing up or selling off their goods. Attend particularly to Coffin and Anderson who keep a large dry good Store and supply their Officers and Army.

c. September 1780

To John Cadwalader

Head Qrs., Tappan, October 5, 1780.

Dear Sir: I have to acknowledge and thank you for your obliging and friendly letter of the 20th Ulto. It came to this place in my absence from the Army and during my necessary detention at West point on a very interesting but disgraceful incident in our Military occurrences.

Altho I have but little leizure for the gratification of private corrispondencies, I beg you to be assured, that from a warmth of friendship, any letters of yours will be gratefully accepted. and it is with much pleasure I receive fresh assurances of your regard and attachment to me.

We are now drawing an inactive Campaign to a close. The beginning of which appeared pregnant with events, of a favourable complexn, I hoped, but hoped in vain, that a prospect was displaying which wd. enable me to fix a period to my military pursuits, and restore me to domestic life. The favourable disposition of Spain; the promised succour from France; the combined force in the West Indies; The declaration of Russia (acceded to by other powers of Europe, humiliating to the Naval pride and power of Great Britain); the Superiority of France and Spain by Sea in Europe; The Irish claims and English disturbances, formed in the agregate, an opinion in my breast (which is not very susceptable of peaceful dreams) that the hour of deliverance was not far distant; for that however unwilling Great B: might be to yield the point, it would not be in her power to continue the contest. but alas! these prospects, flattering as they were, have prov'd delusory, and I see nothing before us but accumulating distress. We have been half of our time without provision and are like to continue so. We have no Magazines, nor money to form them, and in a little time we shall have no Men, if we had money to pay them. We have lived upon expedients till we can live no longer. In a word, the history of the War is a history of false hopes and temporary devices, instead of system and œconomy. It is in vain however to look back, nor is it our business to do so. Our case is not desperate, if virtue exists in the people and there is wisdom among our rulers; but to suppose that this great revolution can be accomplished by a temporary army; that this Army will be subsisted by State supplies, and that taxation alone is adequate to our wants, is, in my Opinion absurd and as unreasonable as to expect an Inversion in the order of nature to accommodate itself to our views. If it was necessary, it could easily be proved to any person of a moderate share of understanding, that an annual Army, or any Army raised on the spur of the occasion, besides being unqualified for the end designed, is, in various ways which could be enumerated, ten times more expensive than a permanent body of Men, under good organization and military discipline, which never was, nor never will be the case of New Troops. A thousand arguments, resulting from experience and the nature of things, might also be adduced to prove, that the Army, if it is to depend upon State supplies, must disband or starve; and that taxation alone (especially at this late hour) cannot furnish the mean to carry on the War. Is it not time then to retract from error, and benefit by experience? or do we want further proof of the ruinous system we have pertinaciously adhered to?

You seem to regret not having accepted the appointment of Congress to a command in the American Army. It is a circumstance that ever was, most sincerely, regretted by me, and it is the more to be lamented as we find an Officer high in rank, and Military reputation capable of turning apostate, and attempting to sell his Country. Men of independent spirit and firmness of mind, must step forth to rescue our affairs from the embarrassments they have fallen into, or they will suffer in the general Wreck. I do not mean to apply this more to the Military than civil line. We want the best, and ablest men in both.

To tell you, if any event shd. ever bring you to the army,

and you have no *commd.* in it equal to your merit; nor *place* more agreeable to your wishes than being a member of my family, that I should be happy in seeing you there, would only be announcing a truth which has often been repeated and wch. I hope you are convinced of.

My best respects attend Mrs. Cadwalader, and compliments of congratulation to both of you on the increase of your family. With sentiments of the most sincere regard etc.

To John Laurens

Hd. Qrs., Passaic Falls, October 13, 1780.
My dear Laurens: Your friendly and Affectione. letter of the 4th. came to my hands on the 10th. and would have been acknowledged yesterday by the Baron de Steuben but for some important business I was preparing for Congress.

In no instance since the commencement of the War has the interposition of Providence appeared more conspicuous than in the rescue of the Post and Garrison of West point from Arnolds villainous perfidy. How far he meant to involve me in the catastrophe of this place does not appear by any indubitable evidence, and I am rather inclined to think he did not wish to hazard the more important object of his treachery by attempting to combine two events the lesser of which might have marred the greater. A combination of extraordinary circumstances. An unaccountable deprivation of presence of Mind in a man of the first abilities, and the virtuous conduct of three Militia men, threw the Adjutant General of the British forces in America (with full proofs of Arnolds treachery) into our hands; and but for the egregious folly, or the bewildered conception of Lieutt. Colo. Jameson who seemed lost in astonishment and not to have known what he was doing I should as certainly have got Arnold. André has met his fate, and with that fortitude which was to be expected from an accomplished man, and gallant Officer. But I am mistaken if at *this time*, Arnold is undergoing the torments of a mental Hell. He wants feeling! From some traits of his character which have lately come to my knowledge, he seems to have been so hackneyed in villainy, and so lost to all sense of honor and shame that while his faculties will enable him to continue his sordid pursuits there will be no time for remorse.

Believe me sincere when I assure you, that my warmest wishes accompany Captn. Wallops endeavours and your expectations of exchange; and that nothing but the principle of Justice and policy wch. I have religiously adhered to of exchanging Officers in the order of their Captivity (where rank would apply) has prevented my every exertion to obtain your release and restoration to a family where you will be receiv'd with open arms by every individual of it; but from none with more cordiality and true affection than Your Sincere friend etc.

P. S. The Baron not setting out as I expected becomes the bearer of this letter.

Circular to State Governments

Head Quarters, near Passaic Falls, October 18, 1780.
Sir: In obedience to the orders of Congress, I have the honor to transmit you the present state of the troops of your line, by which you will perceive how few Men you will have left after the 1st of Jany. next. When I inform you also that the Regiments of the other Lines will be in general as much reduced as yours, you will be able to judge how exceedingly weak the Army will be at that period, and how essential it is the states should make the most vigorous exertions to replace the discharged Men as early as possible.

Congress are now preparing a plan for a new establishment of their Army which when finished they will transmit to the several States with requisitions for their respective quotas. I have no doubt it will be a primary object with them to have the Levies for the War, and this appears to me a point so interesting to our Independence that I cannot forbear entering into the motives which ought to determine the States without hesitation or alternative to take their measures decisively for that object.

I am religiously persuaded that the duration of the War and

the greatest part of the misfortunes and perplexities we have hitherto experienced, are chiefly to be attributed to the System of temporary enlistments. Had we in the commencement raised an Army for the War, such as was within the reach of the Abilities of these States to raise and maintain we should not have suffered those military Checks which have so frequently shaken our cause, nor should we have incurred such enormous expenditures as have destroyed our paper Currency and with it all public credit. A moderate compact force on a permanent establishment capable of acquiring the discipline essential to military operations would have been able to make head against the enemy without comparison better than the throngs of Militia which at certain periods have been, not in the field, but in their way to and from the Field; for from that want of perseverance which characterises all Militia, and of that coercion which cannot be exercised upon them, it has always been found impracticable to detain the greatest part of them in service even for the term, for which they have been called out, and this has been commonly so short, that we have had a great proportion of the time two sets of Men to feed and pay, one coming to the Army and the other going from it. From this circumstance and from the extraordinary waste and consumption of provisions, stores, Camp equipage, Arms, Cloaths and every other Article incident to irregular troops, it is easy to conceive what an immense increase of public expence has been produced from the source of which I am speaking. I might add the diminution of our Agriculture by calling off at critical Seasons the labourers employed in it, as has happened in instances without number.

In the enumeration of Articles wasted, I mention Cloathes. It may be objected that the terms of engagements of the Levies do not include this, but if we want service from the Men particularly in the cold Season we are obliged to supply them notwithstanding, and they leave us before the Cloaths are half worn out.

But there are evils still more striking that have befallen us. The intervals between the dismission of one Army and the collection of another have more than once threatened us with ruin, which humanly speaking nothing but the supineness or folly of the enemy could have saved us from. How did our cause totter at the close of 76, when with a little more than two thousand Men we were driven before the enemy thro' Jersey and obliged to take post on the other side of the Delaware to make a shew of covering Philadelphia while in reallity nothing was more easy to them with a little enterprise, and industry than to make their passage good to that City and dissipate the remaining force which still kept alive our expiring opposition! What hindered them from dispersing our little Army and giving a fatal Blow to our affairs during all the subsequent winter, instead of remaining in a state of torpid inactivity and permitting us to hover about their Quarters when we had scarcely troops sufficient to mount the ordinary Guard? After having lost two Battles and Philadelphia in the following Campaign for want of those numbers and that degree of discipline which we might have acquired by a permanent force in the first instance, in what a cruel and perilous situation did we again find ourselves in the Winter of 77 at Valley Forge, within a days march of the enemy, with a little more than a third of their strength, unable to defend our position, or retreat from it, for want of the means of transportation? What but the fluctuation of our Army enabled the enemy to detach so boldly to the southward in 78 and 79 to take possession of the two States Georgia and South Carolina, while we were obliged here to be idle Spectators of their weakness; set at defiance by a Garrison of six thousand regular troops, accessible every where by a Bridge which nature had formed, but of which we were unable to take advantage from still greater weakness, apprehensive even for our own safety? How did the same Garrison insult the main Army of these States the ensuing Spring and threaten the destruction of all our Baggage and Stores, saved by a good countenance more than by an ability to defend them? And what will be our situation this winter, our Army by the 1st. of January diminished to a little more than a sufficient Garrison for West point, the enemy at liberty to range the Country wherever they please, and, leaving a handful of Men at N York, to undertake Expeditions for the reduction of other States, which for want of adequate means of defense will it is much to be dreaded add to the number of their conquests and to the examples of our want of energy and wisdom?

The loss of Canada to the Union and the fate of the brave Montgomery compelled to a rash attempt by the immediate prospect of being left without Troops might be enumerated in the catalogue of evils that have sprang from this fruitful source. We not only incur these dangers and suffer these losses for want of a constant force equal to our exigencies, but while we labor under this impediment it is impossible there can be any order or œconomy or system in our finances. If we meet with any severe blow the great exertions which the moment requires to stop the progress of the misfortune oblige us to depart from general principles to run into any expence or to adopt any expedient however injurious on a larger scale to procure the force and means which the present emergency demands. Every thing is thrown into confusion and the measures taken to remedy immediate evils perpetuate others. The same is the case if particular conjunctions invite us to offensive operations; we find ourselves unprepared without troops, without Magazines, and with little time to provide them. We are obliged to force our resources by the most burthensome methods to answer the end, and after all it is but half answered: the design is announced by the occasional effort, and the enemy have it in their power to counteract and elude the blow. The prices of every thing, Men provisions &ca. are raised to a height to which the Revenues of no Government, much less ours, would suffice. It is impossible the people can endure the excessive burthen of bounties for annual drafts and substitutes increasing at every new experiment: whatever it might cost them once for all to procure Men for the War would be a cheap bargain.

I am convinced our System of temporary inlistments has prolonged the War and encouraged the enemy to persevere. Baffled while we had an Army in the field, they have been constantly looking forward to the period of its reduction, as the period to our opposition, and the season of their successes. They have flattered themselves with more than the event has justified; for they believed when one Army expired, we should not be able to raise another: undeceived however in this expectation by experience, they still remained convinced, and to me evidently on good grounds, that we must ultimately sink under a system which increases our expense beyond calculation, enfeebles all our measures, affords the most inviting opportunities to the enemy, and wearies and disgusts the people. This has doubtless had great influence in preventing their coming to terms and will continue to operate in the same way, The debates on the ministerial side have frequently manifested the operation of this motive, and it must in the nature of things have had great weight.

The interpositions of Neutral powers may lead to a negociation this winter: Nothing will tend so much to make the Court of London reasonable as the prospect of a permanent Army in this Country, and a spirit of exertion to support it.

Tis time we should get rid of an error which the experience of all mankind has exploded, and which our own experience has dearly taught us to reject; the carrying on a War with Militia, or, (which is nearly the same thing) temporary levies against a regular, permanent and disciplined force. The Idea is chimerical, and that we have so long persisted in it is a reflection on the judgment of a Nation so enlightened as we are, as well as a strong proof of the empire of prejudice over reason. If we continue in the infatuation, we shall deserve to lose the object we are contending for.

America has been almost amused out of her liberties. We have frequently heard the behavior of the Militia extolled upon one and another occasion by Men who judge only from the surface, by Men who had particular views in misrepresenting, by visionary Men whose credulity easily swallowed every vague story in support of a favorite Hypothesis. I solemnly declare I never was witness to a single instance that can countenance an opinion of Militia or raw troops being fit for the real business of fighting. I have found them useful as light parties to skirmish the Woods, but incapable of making or sustaining a serious attack. This firmness is only acquired by habit of discipline and service. I mean not to detract from the merit of the Militia; their zeal and spirit upon a variety of occasions have intitled them to the highest applause; but it is of the greatest importance we should learn to estimate them rightly. We may expect everything from ours that Militia is capable of, but we must not expect from any, service for which Regulars alone are fit. The late Battle of Campden is a melancholy comment upon this doctrine. The Militia fled at the first fire, and left the Continental troops surrounded on every side and overpowered by numbers to combat for safety instead of Victory. The enemy themselves have witnessed to their Valor.

An ill effect of short enlistments which I have not yet taken notice of, is that the constant fluctuation of their Men is one of the sources of disgust to the Officers. Just when by great trouble fatigue and vexation (with which the training of Recruits is attended) they have brought their Men to some kind of order, they have the mortification to see them go home, and to know that the drudgery is to recommence the next Campaign, In Regiments so constituted, an Officer has neither satisfaction nor credit in his command

Every motive which can arise from a consideration of our circumstances, either in a domestic or foreign point of view calls upon us to abandon temporary expedients and substitute something durable, systematic and substantial. This applies as well to our civil administration as to our military establishment. It is as necessary to give Congress, the common Head, sufficient powers to direct the common Forces as it is to raise an Army for the War; but I should go out of my province to expatiate on Civil Affairs. I cannot forbear adding a few more remarks.

Our finances are in an alarming state of derangement. Public credit is almost arrived at its last Stage. The People begin to be dissatisfied with the feeble mode of conducting the War, and with the ineffectual burthens imposed upon them, which tho' light in comparison to what other nations feel are from their novelty heavy to them. They lose their confidence in Government apace. The Army is not only dwindling into nothing, but the discontents of the Officers as well as the Men have matured to a degree that threatens but too general a renunciation of the service, at the end of the Campaign. Since January last we have had registered at Head Quarters more than one hundred and sixty resignations, besides a number of others that were never regularly reported. I speak of the Army in this Quarter. We have frequently in the course of the Campaign experienced an extremity of want. Our Officers are in general indecently defective in Cloathing. Our Men are almost naked, totally unprepared for the inclemency of the approaching season. We have no magazines for the Winter; the mode of procuring our supplies is precarious, and all the reports of the Officers employed in collecting them are gloomy.

These circumstances conspire to show the necessity of immediately adopting a plan that will give more energy to Government, more vigor and more satisfaction to the Army. Without it we have every thing to fear. I am persuaded of the sufficiency of our resources if properly directed.

Should the requisitions of Congress by any accident not arrive before the Legislature is about to rise, I beg to recommend that a plan be devised, which is likely to be effectual, for raising the Men that will be required for the War, leaving it to the Executive to apply it to the Quota which Congress will fix, I flatter myself however the requisition will arrive in time.

The present Crisis of our Affairs appears to me so serious as to call upon me as a good Citizen to offer my sentiments freely for the safety of the Republic. I hope the motive will excuse the liberty I have taken. I have the honor etc.

TO BE ADDED TO THE LETTER OF DELAWARE

P.S. The foregoing is circular to the several states. Having received no return of your regiment since the affair of Campden, I have it not in my power to transmit any. I can only observe that my accounts make it probable it is greatly reduced. There are in Lee's corps Thirty eight men belonging to your state. I beg leave to suggest that the readiest way to obtain a perfect Return will be by application of your Excellency to the commanding Officer with the Regt.

P.S. to the State of Maryland.

The foregoing is Circular to the several States. I have it not in my power to transmit a very accurate return of the Troops of your State, but I send the best I have received since the late affair at Campden; in which however the remains of the Delaware Regiment are included without being distinguished. I beg leave to suggest that the readiest way to obtain a more perfect one, will be by application from your Excellency to Major General Smallwood.

P.S. to the States of Virginia and North Carolina.

The foregoing is circular to the several states. The circumstances of your line put it out of my power to transmit a return.

P.S. To Pensylvania.

The foregoing is circular to the several states. The observation I make in the first paragraph respecting the comparative strength of the troops would mislead, if applied to your line; for you have a much larger proportion of troops for the war than most of the other states. The Men belonging to Pensylvania in Hazen's regiment is not included in the return I send you, because I believe it will be the intention of Congress to keep this regiment up upon a distinct establishment.

To William Fitzhugh

Hd. Qrs. Passaic Falls, October 22, 1780.

Dear Sir: The Gentn. who will have the honor of presenting you with this letter, is Majr. Genl. Greene, a particular friend of mine, and one who I would beg leave to recommend to your civilities. He is going to take command of the Southern Army, and calls at Annapolis to make some arrangements with the State respecting its supplies which are turned into that direction.

This Gentleman is so intimately acquainted with our situation and prospects, and can relate them with such accuracy, that I shall not trouble you with them. My best respects attend Mrs. Fitzhugh and the young Officer, whose final exchange is, I hope, not far distant; if the Prisoners we have in this quarter will reach the date of his captivity in the exchange we are about to make. The Comy. is now gone in with powers to effect this purpose. I am etc.

PS. I hope the Assemblies that are now sitting, or are about to sit, will not rise till they put three things in a fair and proper train

First, to give full and ample powers to Congress, competent to all the purposes of War.

Secondly, by Loans and Taxes to put our finances upon a more respectable footing than they are at present. and

Thirdly, that they will endeavour to establish a permanent

force. These things will secure our Independency beyond dispute, but to go on in our present Systemn; Civil as well as military is a useless and vain attempt. Tis idle to suppose that raw and undisciplined Men are fit to oppose regular Troops, and if they were, our present Military System is too expensive, for any funds except that of an Eastern Nabob; and in the Civil line instead of one head and director we have, or soon shall have, thirteen, which is as much a monster in politicks as it would be in the human form. Our prest. distresses, and future prospects of distress, arising from these and similar causes, is great beyond the powers of description and without a change must end in our ruin.

To George Mason

Head Quarters, Passaic Falls, October 22, 1780.
Dear Sir: In consequence of a resolve of Congress directing an enquiry into the conduct of Genl. Gates, and authorising me to appoint some other Officer in his place during this enquiry, I have made choice of Majr. Genl. Greene who will, I expect, have the honor of presenting you with this Letter.

I can venture to introduce this Gentn. to you as a man of abilities bravery and coolness. He has a comprehensive knowledge of our affairs, and is a man of fortitude and resources. I have not the smallest doubt therefore, of his employing all the means which may be put into his hands to the best advantage; nor of his assisting in pointing out the most likely ones to answer the purposes of his command. With this character, I take the liberty of recommending him to your civilities and support; for I have no doubt, from the embarrassed situation of Southern affairs; of his standing much in need of the latter from every Gentn. of Influence in the Assemblies of those States.

As General Greene can give you the most perfect information, in detail of our present distresses, and future prospects, I shall content myself with giving the agregate acct. of them; and with respect to the first, they are so great and complicated, that it is scarcely within the powers of description to give an adequate idea of them; with regard to the second, unless there is a material change both in our military, and civil policy, it will be in vain to contend much longer.

We are without money, and have been so for a great length of time, without provision and forage except what is taken by Impress; without Cloathing; and shortly shall be (in a manner) without Men. In a word, we have lived upon expedients till we can live no longer, and it may truly be said that, the history of this War is a history of false hopes, and temporary devices, instead of System, and œconomy which results from it.

If we mean to continue our struggles (and it is to be hoped we shall not relinquish our claim) we must do it upon an entire new plan. We must have a permanent force; not a force that is constantly fluctuating and sliding from under us as a pedestal of Ice would do from a Statue in a Summers day. Involving us in expence that baffles all calculation, an expence which no funds are equal to. We must at the same time contrive ways and means to aid our Taxes by Loans, and put our finance upon a more certain and stable footing than they are at prest. Our Civil government must likewise undergo a reform, ample powers must be lodged in Congress as the head of the Federal Union, adequate to all the purposes of War. Unless these things are done, our efforts will be in vain, and only serve to accumulate expence, add to our perplexities, and dissatisfy the people without a prospect of obtaining the prize in view. but these Sentimts. do not appear well in a hasty letter, without digestion or order. I have not time to give them otherwise; and shall only assure you that they are well meant, however crude they may appear. With sincere Affectn. and esteem etc.

To Benjamin Franklin

Hd. Qrs., New Windsor, December 20, 1780.
Sir: A few days since, by the Chevr. De Chatteleaux, I had the honor to receive your favor of the 19th. of March introductory of him, and thank you for bringing me acquainted with a gentn. of his merit, knowledge, and agreeable manners.

I spent several days very happily with him, at our Camp near the great Falls of Passaic in New Jerseys before the Army seperated for its cantonments, the principle of which is at West point in the vicinity of this place where I make my own Quarters.

Disappointed of the second division of French Troops; but more especially in the expected Naval superiority which was the pivet upon wch. every thing turned, we have been compelled to spend an inactive Campaign after a flattering prospect at the opening of it, and vigorous struggles to make it a decisive one on our part. Latterly we have been obliged to become Spectators of a succession of detachments from the Army at New York, in aid of Lord Cornwallis; while our Naval weakness, and the political dissolution of a large part of our Army, puts it out of our power to counteract them at the Southward, or take advantage of them here.

The movements of Lord Cornwallis during the last Month or two have been retrogade; what turn the late reinforcements which have been sent to him may give to his Affairs, remains to be known. I have reinforc'd also, principally with Horse, but the length of the March is so much opposed to the measure, that evy. corps, in a greater or lesser degree, is ruined that encounters it.

I am happy however in assurg. you, that a better disposition never prevailed in the Legislatures of the several States than does at this time. The folly of temporary expedients are seen into and exploded, and vigorous efforts will be used to obtain a permanent Army, and carry on the War systematically, if the obstinacy of Great Britain should compel us to continue it. We want nothing but the aid of a loan to enable us to put our Finance into a tolerable train. The Country does not want resources, but we the means of drawing them forth.

It is unnecessary for me to go into a more detail acct. of our affairs, as you are doubtless officially advised of every material occurrence. I shall therefore only add my Compliments to Mr. Adams, and the strongest assurances of being, With the greatest esteem etc.

To James Duane

New Windsor, December 26, 1780.

My dear Sir: I received with much thankfulness your confidential letter of the 9th. Instt. and am greatly obliged by the affectionate expressions of personl. regard wch are contained in it. An unreserved communication of Sentiments, accompanying such information as you are at liberty to give, will ever be pleasing to me, and cannot fail of being useful, in this light I view, and value, your last letter; some parts of wch are new, agreeable and instructive, while that part of it wch. relates to the transactn. at the Ct. of V——— is wonderfully astonishing.

There are two things (as I have often declared) which in my opinion, are indispensably necessary to the well being and good Government of our public Affairs; these are, greater powers to Congress, and more responsibility and permanency in the executive bodies. If individual States conceive themselves at liberty to reject, or alter any act of Congress, which in a full representation of them, has been solemnly debated and decided on; it will be madness in us, to think of prosecuting the War. And if Congress suppose, that Boards composed of their own body, and always fluctuating, are competent to the great business of War (which requires not only close application, but a constant and uniform train of thinking and acting) they will most assuredly deceive themselves. Many, many instances might be adduced in proof of this, but to a mind as observant as yours there is no need to enumerate them. One however, as we *feelingly* experience it, I shall name. It is the want of cloathing, when I have every reason to be convinced that the expence wch. the Public is run to in this article would Cloath our Army as well as any Troops in Europe; in place of it, we have enumerable objects of distresg. want.

Necessity alone can justify the present mode of obtaining supplies; for besides the hazard and difficulty we meet with in procuring them, I am well convinced, that the public is charged with dble. what it receives, and what it receives is doubly charged so expensive and precarious is the prest. System. When the Army marched for Winter Quarters, I visited the Hospitals and back communication from Pensa. to this place. In the Neighbourhood of Pitts town, I fell in with a parcel of Cattle that were going to be slaughtered and Salted; and can assure you upon my honor, that besides being immensely poor, they were so small that I am convinced they would not average 175 lbs. the 4 nett quarters. some could not exceed One hundd. weight, and others were mere Calves. These pass by the head and the State, or States that furnish them, will have the reputation of supplying that Numbr. of Merchantable Bullocks, when the fact is, that next Summer a starving man wd. scarce eat the Beef they were about to put up after the Salt had extracted the little fat and juices that were in it; there were about 100 in the drove I saw, and my information extended to abt. 8 or 900 more of the same kind, in the neighbourhood. I directed the Commissary to select the *best* for Salting, and let the others be eaten fresh, as it would be a waste of Salt, Barrels and time to put it up. I relate this as a matter coming under my own observation, many other instances of a similar nature might be given from information, but I avoid it.

This letter will accompany one to Congress on the subject of promotion. That of lineal, instead of Regimental, I am perswaded, as well from the opinions I have heard, as from the reason and nature of the thing; will be most consistt. with justice and most pleasing to each State line. With respect to the rise of Colonels and promotion of General Officers, I have no wish to gratify, except that which I have expressed in my public letter of fixing some principle, to avoid discontent and the consequences which flow from it. Irregular promotion, unless there is obvious cause for it, is not only injurious in any Service, but in ours is derogatory of the dignity of Congress for the Officer who is superceded and afterwards restored, is hurt by the first act and does not feel himself obliged by the latter (considering it as an act of justice only); while the two acts stands as an undeniable proof on record, that there is an establishd principle wanting, or that there is a want of information, or a want of firmness in Congress to resist importunity because the restoring act, as I have obsd. is an incontestable proof of one or the other of these three things.

At present we are in no want of Major Generals, in this part of the Army at least; but while I am on the subject of promotion, and while the thing is in my mind, I will beg leave to mention, that if at any time hereafter, there should be a Brigr., junr. to Genl. Knox, promoted before him, he will be lost to the Service; tho' he should, thereafter, be restored to his place. I mention it because under the idea of State promotion he can never rise, and because I am well perswaded that the want of him at the head of the Artillery, would be irrepairable.

I cannot conclude without mentioning the case of Lt. Colo. Smith as deserving of notice, if a remedy can be applied. This Gentn. is of the remaining Sixteen Regiments, and though one of the oldest and (without disparagement to others) one of the best *Battalion* Officers of the whole line, must quit the Service without a chance of staying altho' he is extremely anxious to do so. He has, during the last Campaign, been in the Inspectorate department where *I think* he may still be continued in his present Rank without injury to any one, to his own satisfaction, and the public benefit, without locating his services to any particular Corps, but to be employed as circumstances may require.

Mrs. Washington, impressed with a grateful sence of your kind intention of accompanying her to Trenton, joins me in thanks for it, and complimts. to you. Mr. Tilghman (the only person of my family at this momt. with me) also prests. his compts. with every Sentimt. of estm. etc.

Circular to
New England State Governments

Head Quarters, New Windsor, January 5, 1781.
Sir: It is with extreme anxiety, and pain of mind, I find myself constrained to inform Your Excellency that the event I have long apprehended would be the consequence of the complicated distresses of the Army, has at length taken place. On the night of the 1st instant a mutiny was excited by the

Non Commissioned Officers and Privates of the Pennsylvania Line, which soon became so universal as to defy all opposition; in attempting to quell this tumult, in the first instance, some Officers were killed, others wounded, and the lives of several common Soldiers lost. Deaf to the arguments, entreaties, and utmost efforts of *all their Officers* to stop them, the Men moved off from Morris Town, the place of their Cantonment, with their Arms, and six pieces of Artillery: and from Accounts just received by Genl. Wayne's Aid De Camp, they were still in a body, on their March to Philadelphia, to demand a redress of their grievances. At what point this defection will stop, or how extensive it may prove God only knows; at present the Troops at the important Posts in this vicinity remain quiet, not being acquainted with this unhappy and alarming affair; but how long they will continue so cannot be ascertained, as they labor under some of the pressing hardships, with the Troops who have revolted.

The aggravated calamities and distresses that have resulted, from the total want of pay for nearly twelve Months, for want of cloathing, at a severe season, and not unfrequently the want of provisions; are beyond description. The circumstances will now point out much more forcibly what ought to be done, than any thing that can possibly be said by me, on the subject.

It is not within the sphere of my duty to make requisitions, without the Authority of Congress, from individual States: but at such a crisis, and circumstanced as we are, my own heart will acquit me; and Congress, and the States (eastward of this) whom for the sake of dispatch, I address, I am persuaded will excuse me, when once for all I give it decidedly as my opinion, that it is in vain to think an Army can be kept together much longer, under such a variety of sufferings as ours has experienced: and that unless some immediate and spirited measures are adopted to furnish at least three Months pay to the Troops, in Money that will be of some value to them; And at the same time ways and means are devised to cloath and feed them better (more regularly I mean) than they have been, the worst that can befall us may be expected.

I have transmitted Congress a Copy of this Letter, and have in the most pressing manner requested them to adopt the measure which I have above recommended, or something similar to it, and as I will not doubt of their compliance, I have thought proper to give you this previous notice, that you may be prepared to answer the requisition.

As I have used every endeavour in my power to avert the evil that has come upon us, so will I continue to exert every means I am possessed of to prevent an extension of the Mischief, but I can neither foretell, or be answerable for the issue.

That you may have every information that an officer of rank and abilities can give of the true situation of our affairs, and the condition and temper of the Troops I have prevailed upon Brigadier Genl Knox to be the bearer of this Letter, to him I beg leave to refer your Excellency for many Matters which would be too tedious for a Letter. I have the honor etc.

To John Laurens

New Windsor, January 15, 1781.

Dear Sir: In compliance with your request I shall commit to writing the result of our conferences on the present state of American affairs; in which I have given you my ideas, with that freedom and explicitness, which the objects of your commission, my intire confidence in you, and the exigency demand. To me it appears evident:

1st. That, considering the diffused population of these states, the consequent difficulty of drawing together its resources; the composition and temper of *a part* of its inhabitants; the want of a sufficient stock of national wealth as a foundation for Revenue and the almost total extinction of commerce; the efforts we have been compelled to make for carrying on the war, have exceeded the natural abilities of this country and by degrees brought it to a crisis, which renders immediate and efficacious succours from abroad indispensable to its safety.

2dly. That, notwithstanding from the confusion, always attendant on a revolution, from our having had governments to frame, and every species of civil and military institution to create; from that inexperience in affairs, necessarily incident to a nation in its commencement, some errors may have been committed in the administration of our finances, to which a part of our embarrassments are to be attributed, yet they are principally to be ascribed to an essential defect of means, to the want of a sufficient stock of wealth, as mentioned in the first article; which, continuing to operate, will make it impossible, by any merely interior exertions, to extricate ourselves from those embarrassments, restore public credit, and furnish the funds requisite for the support of the war.

3dly. That experience has demonstrated the impracticability, long to maintain a paper credit without funds for its redemption. The depreciation of our currency was, in the main, a necessary effect of the want of those funds; and its restoration is impossible for the same reason; to which the general diffidence, that has taken place among the people, is an additional, and in the present state of things, an insuperable obstacle.

4thly. That the mode, which for want of money has been substituted for supplying the army; by assessing a proportion of the productions of the earth, has hitherto been found ineffectual, has frequently exposed the army to the most calamitous distress, and from its novelty and incompatibility with ancient habits, is regarded by the people as burthensome and oppressive; has excited serious discontents, and, in some places, alarming symptoms of opposition. This mode has besides many particular inconveniences which contribute to make it inadequate to our wants, and ineligible, but as an auxiliary.

5thly. That from the best estimates of the annual expence of the war, and the annual revenues which these states are capable of affording, there is a large ballance to be supplied by public credit. The resource of domestic loans is inconsiderable because there are properly speaking few monied men, and the few there are can employ their money more profitably otherwise; added to which, the instability of the currency and the deficiency of funds have impaired the public credit.

6thly. That the patience of the army from an almost uninterrupted series of complicated distress is now nearly exhausted; their discontents matured to an extremity, which has recently had very disagreeable consequences, and which demonstrates the absolute necessity of speedy relief, a relief not

within the compass of our means. You are too well acquainted
with all their sufferings, for want of cloathing, for want of
provisions, for want of pay.

7thly. That the people being dissatisfied with the mode of
supporting the war, there is cause to apprehend, evils actually
felt in the prosecution, may weaken those sentiments which
begun it; founded not on immediate sufferings, but in a speculative apprehension of future sufferings from the loss of their
liberties. There is danger that a commercial and free people,
little accustomed to heavy burthens, pressed by impositions
of a new and odious kind, may not make a proper allowance
for the necessity of the conjuncture, and may imagine, they
have only exchanged one tyranny for another.

8thly. That from all the foregoing considerations result:

1st. The absolute necessity of an immediate, ample and efficacious succour of money; large enough to be a foundation
for substantial arrangements of finance, to revive public credit
and give vigor to future operations.

2dly. The vast importance of a decided effort of the allied
arms on this Continent, the ensuing campaign, to effectuate
once for all the great objects of the alliance; the liberty and
independence of these states.

Without the first, we may make a feeble and expiring effort
the next campaign, in all probability the period to our opposition. With it, we should be in a condition to continue the
war, as long as the obstinacy of the enemy might require. The
first is essential to the last; both combined would bring the
contest to a glorious issue, crown the obligations, which
America already feels to the magnanimity and generosity of
her ally, and perpetuate the union, by all the ties of gratitude
and affection, as well as mutual advantage, which alone can
render it solid and indissoluble.

9thly. That next to a loan of money a constant naval superiority on these coasts is the object most interesting. This
would instantly reduce the enemy to a difficult defensive, and
by removing all prospect of extending their acquisitions,
would take away the motives for prosecuting the war. Indeed
it is not to be conceived, how they could subsist a large force
in this country, if we had the command of the seas, to interrupt the regular transmission of supplies from Europe. This

superiority (with an aid of money) would enable us to convert the war into a vigorous offensive. I say nothing of the advantages to the trade of both nations, nor how infinitely it would facilitate our supplies. With respect to us, it seems to be one of *two* deciding points; and it appears too, to be the interest of our allies, abstracted from the immediate benefits to this country, to transfer the naval war to America. The number of ports friendly to them, hostile to the British; the materials for repairing their disabled ships; the extensive supplies towards the subsistence of their fleet, are circumstances which would give them a palpable advantage in the contest of these seas.

10thly. That an additional succour of troops would be extremely desirable. Besides a reinforcement of numbers, the excellence of the French troops, that perfect discipline and order in the corps already sent, which have so happily tended to improve the respect and confidence of the people for our allies; the conciliating disposition and the zeal for the service, which distinguish every rank, sure indications of lasting harmony, all these considerations evince the immense utility of an accession of force to the corps now here. Correspondent with these motives, the inclosed minutes of a conference between Their Excellencies The Count De Rochambeau, The Chevalier De Ternay and myself will inform you that an augmentation to fifteen thousand men was judged expedient for the next campaign; and it has been signified to me, that an application has been made to the Court of France to this effect. But if the sending so large a succour of troops, should necessarily diminish the pecuniary aid, which our allies may be disposed to grant, it were preferable to diminish the aid in men; for the same sum of money, which would transport from France and maintain here a body of troops with all the necessary apparatus, being put into our hands to be employed by us would serve to give activity to a larger force within ourselves, and its influence would pervade the whole administration.

11thly. That no nation will have it more in its power to repay what it borrows than this. Our debts are hitherto small. The vast and valuable tracts of unlocated lands, the variety and fertility of climates and soils; the advantages of every kind, which we possess for commerce, insure to this country a rapid advancement in population and prosperity and a certainty, its independence being established, of redeeming in a short term of years, the comparitively inconsiderable debts it may have occasion to contract.

That notwithstanding the difficulties under which we labour and the inquietudes prevailing among the people, there is still a fund of inclination and resource in the country equal to great and continued exertions, provided we have it in our power to stop the progress of disgust, by changing the present system and adopting another more consonant with the spirit of the nation, and more capable of activity and energy in public measures; of which a powerful succour of money must be the basis. The people are discontented, but it is with the feeble and oppressive mode of conducting the war, not with the war itself. They are not unwilling to contribute to its support, but they are unwilling to do it in a way that renders private property precarious, a necessary consequence of the fluctuation of the national currency, and of the inability of government to perform its engagements, oftentimes coercively made. A large majority are still firmly attached to the independence of these states, abhor a reunion with great Britain, and are affectionate to the alliance with France, but this disposition cannot supply the place of means customary and essential in war, nor can we rely on its duration amidst the perplexities, oppressions and misfortunes, that attend the want of them.

If the foregoing observations are of any use to you I shall be happy. I wish you a safe and pleasant voyage, the full accomplishment of your mission and a speedy return; being with sentiments of perfect friendship etc.

To Sarah Bache

Head Quarters, New Windsor, January 15, 1781.
Dear Madam: I should have done myself the pleasure to acknowledge the receipt of the Letter you did me the favor to write on the 26th of Decr: at the moment of its receipt; had not some affairs of a very unusual nature, (which are too recent and notorious to require explanation) engaged my

whole attention. I pray you now to be persuaded, that a sense of the Patriotic Exertions of yourself and the Ladies who have furnished so handsome and useful a gratuity for the Army, at so critical and severe a season, will not easily be effaced, and that the value of the donation will be greatly enhanced by a consideration of the hands by which it was made and presented.

Amidst all the distresses and sufferings of the Army, from whatever sources they have arisen, it must be a consolation to our *Virtuous Country Women* that they have never been accused of with holding their most zealous efforts to support the cause we are engaged in, and encourage those who are defending them in the Field. The Army do not want gratitude, nor do they Misplace it in this instance.

Although the friendship of your Father may oblige him to see some things through too partial a Medium, Yet the indulgent manner in which he is pleased to express himself respecting me, is indeed very pleasing. For nothing in human life, can afford a liberal Mind, more rational and exquisite satisfaction, than the approbation of a Wise, a great and virtuous Man.

Mrs Washington requests me to present her Compliments to Mr Bache and yourself, with which you will be pleased to accept of mine and believe me to be etc.

To Robert Howe

West Point, January 22, 1781.

Sir: You are to take the command of the detachment, which has been ordered to march from this post against the mutineers of the Jersey line. You will rendezvous the whole of your command at Ringwood or Pompton as you find best from circumstances. The object of your detachment is to compel the mutineers to unconditional submission, and I am to desire you will grant no terms while they are with arms in their hands in a state of resistance. The manner of executing this I leave to your discretion according to circumstances. If you succeed in compelling the revolted troops to a surrender you will instantly execute a few of the most active and most incendiary leaders.

You will endeavour to collect such of the Jersey troops to your standard as have not followed the pernicious example of their associates, and you will also try to avail yourself of the services of the Militia, representing to them how dangerous to civil liberty the precedent is of armed soldiers dictating terms to their country.

You will open a correspondence with Colonels Dayton and Shreve of the Jersey line and Col Freelinghuosen of the Militia or any others.

Circular to State Governments

Head Quarters, New Windsor, January 22, 1781.

Sir: I have received the disagreeable intelligence that a part of the Jersey Line had followed the example of that of Pennsylvania; and when the advices came away it was expected the revolt would be general. The precise intention of the Mutineers was not known, but their complaints and demands were similar to those, of the Pennsylvanians.

Persuaded that without some decisive effort, at all hazards to suppress this dangerous spirit it would speedily infect the whole Army. I have ordered as large a Detachment as we could spare from these Posts to march under Major General Howe with Orders to compel the Mutineers to unconditional submission; to listen to no terms while they were in a state of resistance, and on their reduction to execute instantly a few of the most active, and most incendiary Leaders. I am not certain what part the Troops detached for this purpose will act, but I flatter myself they will do their duty. I prefer any extremity to which the Jersey Troops may be driven, to a compromise.

The weakness of the Garrison but still more its embarrassing distress for want of Provisions made it impossible to prosecute such measures with the Pennsylvanians, as the nature of the case demanded, and while we were making arrangements, as far as practicable to supply these defects, an accommodation took place, which will not only subvert the Pennsylvania Line, but have a very pernicious influence on the whole Army. I mean however by these remarks only to give an idea of the miserable situation we are in, not to blame a measure which perhaps in our circumstances was the best that could have been adopted. The same embarrassments operate against coercion at this moment, but not in so great a degree; the Jersey Troops not being from their numbers so formidable as were the Pennsylvanians.

I dare not detail the risks we run from the present scantiness of supplies. We have received few or no Cattle for some time past, nor do we know of any shortly to be expected. The salted Meat we ought to have reserved in the Garrison, is now nearly exhausted. I cannot but renew my sollicitations with Your State, to exert every expedient for contributing to our immediate relief. With perfect Respect I have the honor etc.

General Orders

Head Quarters, New Windsor,
Tuesday, January 30, 1781.

Parole ——. Countersigns ——.

The General returns his thanks to Major General Howe for the judicious measures he pursued and to the officers and men under his command for the good conduct and alacrity with which they executed his orders for suppressing the late Mutiny in a part of the New Jersey line. It gave him inexpressible pain to have been obliged to employ their arms upon such an occasion and convinced that they themselves felt all the Reluctance which former Affection to fellow Soldiers could inspire. He considers the patience with which they endured the fatigues of the march through rough and mountainous roads rendered almost impassable by the depth of the Snow and the cheerfulness with which they performed every other part of their duty as the strongest proof of their Fidelity, attachment to the service, sense of subordination and abhorrence of the principles which actuated the Mutineers in so daring and atrocious a departure from what they owed to their Country, to their Officers to their Oaths and to themselves.

The General is deeply sensible of the sufferings of the army. He leaves no expedient unessayed to relieve them, and he is persuaded Congress and the several States are doing every thing in their power for the same purpose. But while we look to the public for the fullfilment of its engagements we should do it with proper allowance for the embarrassments of public affairs. We began a Contest for Liberty and Independence ill provided with the means for war, relying on our own Patriotism to supply the deficiency. We expected to encounter many wants and distresses and We should neither shrink from them when they happen nor fly in the face of Law and Government to procure redress. There is no doubt the public will in the event do ample justice to men fighting and suffering in its defence. But it is our duty to bear present Evils with Fortitude looking forward to the period when our Country will have it more in its power to reward our services.

History is full of Examples of armies suffering with patience extremities of distress which exceed those we have suffered, and this in the cause of ambition and conquest not in that of the rights of humanity of their country, of their families of themselves; shall we who aspire to the distinction of a patriot army, who are contending for every thing precious in society against every thing hateful and degrading in slavery, shall We who call ourselves citizens discover less Constancy and Military virtue than the mercenary instruments of ambition? Those who in the present instance have stained the honor of the American soldiery and sullied the reputation of patient Virtue for which they have been so long eminent can only atone for their pusillanimous defection by a life devoted to a Zealous and examplary discharge of their duty. Persuaded that the greater part were influenced by the pernicious advice of a few who probably have been paid by the enemy to betray their Associates; The General is happy in the lenity shewn in the execution of only two of the most guilty after compelling the whole to an unconditional surrender, and he flatters himself no similar instance will hereafter disgrace our military History. It can only bring ruin on those who are mad enough to make the attempt; for lenity on any future occasion would be criminal and inadmissible.

The General at the same time presents his thanks to Major General Parsons for the prudent and Military dispositions he made and to Lieutenant Colonel Hull and the officers and Men under his command for the good conduct address and Courage with which they executed the enterprize against a Corps of the enemy in West Chester, having destroyed their Barracks and a large quantity of Forage, burnt a bridge across Haerlem, under the protection of one of their redoubts, brought off fifty two prisoners and a number of Horses and Cattle with inconsiderable Loss except in the death of Ensign Thompson of the 6th. Massachusett's regiment an active and enterprizing officer.

The General also thanks Colonel Hazen and his party for their Conduct and bravery in covering Lieutenant Colonel Hull's retreat and repelling the Enemy and Colonels Scammell and Sherman and in general all the Officers and men of General Parsons's command for their good Conduct in supporting the advanced Corps.

To John Parke Custis

New Windsor, February 28, 1781.

Dear Custis: If you will accept a hasty letter in return for yours of last month I will devote a few moments for this purpose, and confine myself to an interesting point, or two.

I do not suppose that so young a Senator, as you are, little versed in political disquisitions can yet have much influence in a populous assembly; composed of Gentn. of various talents and of different views. But it is in your power to be punctual in your attendance (and duty to the trust reposed in you exacts it of you), to hear dispassionately, and determine cooly all great questions. To be disgusted at the decision of questions because they are not consonant to your own ideas, and to withdraw ourselves from public assemblies, or to neglect our attendance at them upon suspicion that there is a party

formed who are enimical to our Cause, and to the true interest of our Country is wrong because these things may originate in a difference of opinion; but supposing the fact is
otherwise and that our suspicions are well founded it is the
indispensable duty of every patriot to counteract them by the
most steady and uniform opposition. This advice is the result
of information, that you and others being dissatisfied at the
proceedings of the Virginia Assembly and thinking your attendance of little avail (as their is a majority for measures
which you and a minority conceive to be repugnant to the
interest of your Country) are indifferent about the Assembly.

The next and I believe the last thing I shall have time to
touch upon is our military establishment. and here if I
thought the conviction of having a permanent force had not,
ere this, flashed upon every mans mind I could write a volume
in support of the utility of it; for no day, nor hour arrives
unaccompd. with proof of some loss, some expence, or some
misfortune consequent of the want of it. No operation of War
offensive or defensive can be carried on, for any length of time
without it. No funds are adequate to the supplies of a fluctuating army; tho' it may go under the denomination of a
regular one; much less are they competent to the support of
Militia. In a word, for it is, unnecessary to go into all the
reasons the subject will admit of, we have brought a cause
which might have been happily terminated years ago by the
adoption of proper measures to the verge of ruin by temporary enlistments and a reliance on Militia. The sums expended
in bounties, waste of Arms, consumption of Military Stores,
Provisions, Camp Utensils &ca.; to say nothing of Cloathing
which temporary Soldiers are always receiving, and always in
want of, are too great for the resources of any Nation; and
prove the falacy and danger of temporary expedients which
are no more than Mushrooms and of as short duration, but
leave a sting (that is a debt) which is continually revolving
upon us behind them.

It must be a settled plan, founded on System, order and
œconomy that is to carry us triumphantly through the war.
Supiness, and indifference to the distresses and cries of a sister
State when danger is far of, and a general but momentary
resort to arms when it comes to our doors, are equally im-

politic and dangerous, and proves the necessity of a controuling power in Congress to regulate and direct all matters of
general concern; without it the great business of war never
can be well conducted, if it can be conducted at all; while the
powers of congress are only recommendatory; while one State
yields obedience, and another refuses it; while a third muti-
lates and adopts the measure in part only, and all vary in time
and manner, it is scarcely possible our affairs should prosper,
or that any thing but disappointmt. can follow the best concerted plans; the willing States are almost ruined by their exertions, distrust and jealousy succeeds to it; hence proceed
neglect and ill-timed compliances (one state waiting to see
what another will do), this thwarts all our measures after a
heavy tho' ineffectual expence is incurred.

Does not these things shew then in the most striking point
of view the indispensable necessity, the great and good policy
of each State's sending its ablest and best men to Congress?
Men who have a perfect understanding of the constitution of
their Country, of its policy and Interests, and of vesting that
body with competent powers. Our Independence depends
upon it; our respectability and consequence in Europe depends upon it; our greatness as a Nation, hereafter, depends
upon it. the fear of giving sufficient powers to Congress for
the purposes I have mentioned is futile, without it, our Independence fails, and each Assembly under its present Constitution will be annihilated, and we must once more return
to the Government of G: Britain, and be made to kiss the rod
preparing for our correction. a nominal head, which at present
is but another name for Congress, will no longer do. That
honble body, after hearing the interests and views of the several States fairly discussed and explained by their respective
representatives, must dictate, not merely recommend, and
leave it to the States afterwards to do as they please, which,
as I have observed before, is in many cases, to do nothing at
all.

When I began this letter I did not expect to have filled more
than one side of the sheet but I have run on insensibly. If you
are at home, give my love to Nelly and the Children. if at
Richmond present my complimts. to any enquiring friends.
Sincerely and affectly. I am etc.

P S. The Public Gazettes will give you all the news and occurrances of this Quarter, our eyes are anxiously turned towards the South for events.

To Lund Washington

New Windsor, April 30, 1781.

Dear Lund: Your letter of the 18th. came to me by the last Post. I am very sorry to hear of your loss; I am a little sorry to hear of my own; but that which gives me most concern, is, that you should go on board the enemys Vessels, and furnish them with refreshments. It would have been a less painful circumstance to me, to have heard, that in consequence of your non-compliance with their request, they had burnt my House, and laid the Plantation in ruins. You ought to have considered yourself as my representative, and should have reflected on the bad example of communicating with the enemy, and making a voluntary offer of refreshments to them with a view to prevent a conflagration.

It was not in your power, I acknowledge, to prevent them from sending a flag on shore, and you did right to meet it; but you should, in the same instant that the business of it was unfolded, have declared, explicitly, that it was improper for you to yield to the request; after which, if they had proceeded to help themselves, *by force*, you could but have submitted (and being unprovided for defence) this was to be prefered to a feeble opposition which only serves as a pretext to burn and destroy.

I am thoroughly perswaded that you acted from your best judgment; and believe, that your desire to preserve my property, and rescue the buildings from impending danger, were your governing motives. But to go on board their Vessels; carry them refreshments; commune with a parcel of plundering Scoundrels, and request a favor by asking the surrender of my Negroes, was exceedingly ill-judged, and 'tis to be feared, will be unhappy in its consequences, as it will be a precedent for others, and may become a subject of animadversion.

I have no doubt of the enemys intention to prosecute the plundering plan they have begun. And, unless a stop can be put to it by the arrival of a superior naval force, I have as little doubt of its ending in the loss of all my Negroes, and in the destruction of my Houses; but I am prepared for the event, under the prospect of which, if you could deposit, in safety, at some convenient distance from the Water, the most valuable and least bulky articles, it might be consistent with policy and prudence, and a mean of preserving them for use hereafter. such, and so many things as are necessary for common, and present use must be retained and run their chance through the firy trial of this summer.

Mrs. Washington joins me in best and affectionate regard for you, Mrs. Washington and Milly Posey; and does most sincerely regret your loss. I do not know what Negros they may have left you; and as I have observed before, I do not know what number they will have left me by the time they have done; but this I am sure of, that you shall never want assistance, while it is in my power to afford it. I am etc.

Journal of the Yorktown Campaign

I begin, at this Epoch, a concise Journal of Military transactions &ca. I lament not having attempted it from the commencement of the War, in aid of my memory and wish the multiplicity of matter which continually surround me and the embarrassed State of our affairs which is momently calling the attention to perplexities of one kind or another, may not defeat altogether or so interrupt my present intention, & plan, as to render it of little avail.

To have the clearer understanding of the entries which may follow, it would be proper to recite, in detail, our wants and our prospects but this alone would be a Work of much time, and great magnitude. It may suffice to give the sum of them—wch., I shall do in a few words—viz.—

Instead of having Magazines filled with provisions, we have a scanty pittance scattered here & there in the different States. Instead of having our Arsenals well supplied with Military

Stores, they are poorly provided, & the Workmen all leaving them. Instead of having the various articles of Field equipage in readiness to deliver, the Quarter Master General (as the denier resort, according to his acct.) is but now applying to the several States to provide these things for their Troops respectively. Instead of having a regular System of transportation established upon credit or funds in the Qr. Masters hands to defray the contingent Expences of it, we have neither the one nor the other and all that business, or a great part of it, being done by Military Impress, we are daily & hourly oppressing the people—souring their tempers and alienating their affection. Instead of having the Regiments compleated to the New establishment (and which ought to have been So by the of   agreeably to the requisitions of Congress, scarce any State in the Union has, at this hour, an eighth part of its quota in the field and little prospect, that I can see, of ever getting more than half. In a word—instead of having everything in readiness to take the Field, we have nothing—and instead of having the prospect of a glorious offensive campaign before us, we have a bewildered, and gloomy defensive one—unless we should receive a powerful aid of Ships—Land Troops and Money from our generous allies & these, at present, are too contingent to build upon.

May 1st. Induced by pressing necessity—the inefficacy, & bad tendency of pushing Military Impresses too far and the impracticability of keeping the Army supplied without *it*, or *money*, to pay the transportation I drew for 9000 dollars of the Sum sent on by the State of Massachusetts for payment of their Troops; and placed it in the hands of the QM General with the most positive orders to apply it solely to this purpose.

Fixed with Ezekiel Cornell Esqr. a member of the Board of War (then on a tour to the Eastward to inspect some of the Armoury's &ca.) on certain articles of Cloathing—arms and Military Stores which might be sent from hence to supply the wants of the Southern Army.

Major Talmadge was requested to press the C——s Senr. & Junr. to continue their correspondence and was authorized to assure the elder C—— that he should be repaid the Sum of 100 Guineas, or more, with interest; provided he advanced the same for the purpose of defraying the expence of the correspondence, as he had offered to do.

Colo. Dayton was also written to, and pressed to establish a correspondence with New York, by way of Elizabeth Town for the purpose of obtaining intelligence of the Enemys movemts. and designs; that by a comparison of Accts. proper & just conclusions may be drawn.

May 2d. No occurrence of note. A very fresh and steady gale of Wind all day from the So. East. Upon its shifting (about dusk) it blew violently, & continued boisterous through the Night or greatest part of it.

4th. A Letter of the Baron de Steuben's from Chesterfield Court House Virga. dated the 21st. Ulto. informs that 12 of the Enemys Vessels but with what Troops he knew not, had advanced up James River as high as Jamestown—that few Militia were in arms and few arms to put into their hands—that he had moved the public Stores from Richmond &ca. into the interior Country.

A Letter from the Marqs. de la Fayette, dated at Alexandria on the 23d., mentioned his having commenced his march that day for Fredericksburg—that desertion had ceased, & that his detachment were in good Spirits.

5th. Accounts from Brigadr. Genl. Clinton at Albany, dated the 30th. ulto. & 1st. Inst., filled me with anxious fears that the Garrison of fort Schuyler would be obliged to evacuate the Post for want of Provisions and that a Mutiny in the other Troops was to be apprehended. In consequence of this alarming information, I directed the Q. M. Gl. to send 50 Barls. of flour & the like qty. of Salted Meat immy. up for the Garrison of Fort Schuyler—but of the latter there being only 24 in Store, no more could be sent.

6th. Colo. Menonville, one of the Adjutt. Generals in the French Army came to Head Quarters by order of Count de Rochambeau to make arrangements for supplying the Troops of His Most Christian Majesty with certain provisions contracted for by Doctr. Franklin. This demand, tho' the immediate compliance with it, was not insisted upon, comports illy with our circumstances; & is exceedingly embarrassing.

The D Q M at Sussex Ct House, conceiving that the Provision Magazine, & other stores at that place were exposed to a surprize, and in danger of being destroyed by the Indians & Tories who were infesting the Settlement at Minisink, I directed Colo. Dayton to send a guard there from the Jersey Brigade near Morristown.

Mr. John Flood (at present a liver at lower Salem) whom I had sent for to obtain from him an acct. of the Harbours in the Sound from Frogs point Eastward, arrived; and gave the information wch. is filed in my Office.

Other letters arriving this Evening late (more expressive of the wants of the York Troops at Albany, & the Posts above) I ordered 100, out of 131 Barrls. of Flour which were in Store, to be immediately sent up; & again called upon the Q. M. Genl. in the most pointed terms to send active men to forward on, by every means they could devise, the Salted provs. in Connecticut; & flour from Sussex Ct. Ho. &ca.

That the States might not only know our Wants, which my repeated & pressing letters had recently, & often communicated, but, if possible, be impressed with them and adopt some mode of Transporting it to the Army, I resolved to send Genl. Heath (2d. Offr. in Commd.) to make to the respective legislatures East of York State, pointed representations; & to declare explicitly that unless measures are adopted to supply transportation, it will be impossible to subsist & keep the Troops together.

7th. The Wind which blew with great force from the So. East the last two days was accompanied this day by incessant Rain and was a most violent Storm & is supposed to have done damage to Ships on the Coast.

9th. Went to the Posts at West point, and found by enquiry of General Heath, that all the Meat deposited in the advanced redoubts for contingent purposes would not, if served out, serve the Army two days—that the Troops had drawn none that day & that none remained in the common Magazine.

10th. The Q. M. Genl. representing, that it was not in his power to get the Salt Meat of Connecticut transported—even for the Money that was put into his hands for this purpose—

the people now alledging that they had no forage—when the badness of the roads was an excuse when they were called upon by the Executive of their State in the Month of March and that nothing but Military force could affect the transport for our present wants. Parties were ordered out accordingly and the Officers commanding them directed to receive their Instructions from him.

11th. Major Genl. Heath set out this day for the Eastn. States, provided with Instructions, and letters couched in strong terms—representing the distresses of the Army for want of provisions and the indispensable necessity of keeping up regular supplies by the adoption of a plan, which will have system & permanency in't.

This day also I received advice from Colo. Dayton that 10 Ships of the line, and 3 or 4000 Troops had sailed from New York. The intelligence was immediately communicated to Congress, and to the French Genl. & Admiral at R. Isld.

12th. Colo. Dayton's intelligence, so far as respected the Sailing of Troops, was confirmed by two sensible deserters from Kingsbridge; which place they left yesterday Morning at two Oclock. They add the detachment consisted of the Grenadrs. (Bh.)—the Corps. of Anspach (two Battalions) & the 37th. & 43d. British regiments, amounting, as is supposed, to about 2000 Men under the Command of Majr. Genl. Redeisel.

13th. Received Letters from Count de Rochambeau advising me of the arrival of his Son & from Count de Barras informing me of his appointment to the Command of the French Squadron at Rhode Island—both solliciting an Interview with me as soon as possible. Appointed, in answer, Monday the 21st. Inst. & Wethersfield, as the time & place of Meeting.

14th. About Noon, intelligence was recd. from Genl. Patterson at West point, that the Enemy were on the No. side of Croton in force—that Colo. Green, Majr. Flag, & some other officers with 40 or 50 Men were surprized & cut off at the Bridge & that Colo. Scammell with the New Hampshire Troops had Marched to their assistance. I ordered the Connecticut Troops to move in & support those of New Hampshire.

In the evening, information was brot. that the enemy (consisting of about 60 horse, & 140 Infantry) had retreated precipitately & that several of our Soldiers had been inhumanly murdered.

15th. Information, dated 12 oclock yesterday reports 15 Sail of Vessels & a number of Flatboats to be off Fort Lee. Ordered a detachment of 200 Men to March immediately to support the Post at Dobbs's. ferry—countenance the Militia, & cover the Country in that Neighbourhood.

Intelligence from C—— Senr., dated 729 —a detachment is expected to Sail tomorrow from New York, & said to consist of the Anspach Troops's 43d. B. Regiment, remainder of the 76th., 80th., 17th. Dragoons, & Infantry of the same—to be conveyed by 7 Ships of the line, 2 fifties, & 3 forty fours which are to cruize of the Capes of Virginia. He gives it as the opinion of C—— Junr. that the above detachmt. does not exceed 2000 Men—that not more than 4000 remain—wch. is only (he adds) to be accounted for on the supposition of their expecting a reinforcement immediately from Europe.

16th. Went to the Posts at West point. Received a particular acct. of the surprize of Colo. Green & the loss we sustained which consisted of himself & Major (Flag) killed—three officers & a Surgeon taken prisoners (the latter & two of the former wounded)—a Sergeant & 5 R & F killed—5 left wounded & 33 made Prisoners & missing—in all 44 besides Officers.

The report of the number of Shipping &ca. at Fort Lee was this day contradicted in part—the number of Vessels being reduced, & said to be no higher than Bulls ferry. In consequence of this intelligence Lt. Colo. Badlam who marched with the detachment of 200 Men pursuant to the order of Yesterday & had reached Stony point halted—but was directed not to return till the designs of the enemy were better understood.

17th. Received a letter from Captn. Lawrence, near Dobbss ferry, informing me that abt. 200 Refugees were building a block house & raising other works at Fort Lee. Order'd the detachment which had halted at Kings Ferry & another forming under Colo. Scammel to advance down & endeavour to annoy, if they could not prevent them.

A Letter from Genl. Foreman of Monmouth (dated the 14th. Instt.) informs me that the British fleet from New York consisting of Seven Ships of 60 Guns & upwards—12 large Transport Vessels, & 10 topsail Schooners & Sloops made Sail from Sandy hook the 12th., with the wind at So. East. but veering round to the Southward, & Westward, it returned within the hook & lay there till 10 o'clock next day when it again Sailed. By two oclock it was clear of the hook and steering Southward.

18th. Received Letters from Generals Schuyler and Clinton giving an acct. of the threatened Invasion of the Northern Frontier of this State from Canada, and of the unfavourable prospects from Vermont and of the destruction of the Post of Fort Schuyler—the indefensible State of the Works occasioned thereby & submitting for considn. the propriety of removing the Garrison to the German Flatts which he (that is Clinton) was requested to do if it appear'd to be the sense of the Governor & other principal Gentn. of the State that it would be eligable.

Set out this day for the Interview at Weathersfield with the Count de Rochambeau & Admiral Barras. Reached Morgans Tavern 43 Miles from Fishkill Landing after dining at Colo. Vandebergs.

19th. Breakfasted at Litchfield—dined at Farmington & lodged at Weathersfield at the House of Joseph Webb Esqr. (the Quarters wch. were taken for me & my Suit).

20th. Had a good deal of private conversation with Govr. Trumbull who gave it to me as his opinion that if any important offensive operation should be undertaken he had little doubt of our obtaining Men & Provision adequate to our wants. In this opinion Colo. Wadsworth & others concurr'd.

21st. The Count de Rochambeau with the Chevr. de Chastellux arrived about Noon. The appearance of the British Fleet (under Adml. Arbuthnot) off Block Island prevented the attendance of the Count de Barras.

22nd. Fixed with Count de Rochambeau upon a plan of Campaign—in Substance as follows. That the French Land force (except 200 Men) should March so soon as the Squadron could Sail for Boston—to the North River & there, in conjunction with the American, to commence an operation against New York (which in the present reduced State of the Garrison it was thought would fall, unless relieved; the doing which wd. enfeeble their Southern operations, and in either case be productive of capital advantages) or to extend our views to the Southward as circumstances and a Naval superiority might render more necessary & eligable. The aid which would be given to such an operation in this quarter—the tardiness with which the Regiments would be filled for any other—the insurmountable difficulty & expence of Land transportation—the waste of Men in long marches (especially where there is a disinclination to the Service—objections to the climate &ca.) with other reasons too numerous to detail, induced to this opinion. The heavy Stores & Baggage of the French Army were to be deposited at Providence under Guard of 200 Men (before mentioned) & Newport Harbour & Works were to be secured by 500 Militia.

23d. Count de Rochambeau set out on his Return to Newport, while I prepared and forwarded dispatches to the Governors of the four New England States calling upon them in earnest & pointed terms, to compleat their Continental Battalions for the Campaign, at least, if it could not be done for the War or 3 Years—to hold a body of Militia (according to the Proportion given them) ready to march in one Week after being called for and to adopt some effectual mode to supply the Troops when assembled with Provisns. & Transportation.

I also sollicited the Governors of the States of Massachusetts & Connecticut earnestly for a Loan of Powder & the means of Transporting it to the Army.

A Letter from Genl. St. Clair came to hand with accts. of an apparent intention of the enemy to evacuate New York.

24th. Set out on my return to New Windsor—dined at Farmington and lodged at Litchfield.

25th. Breakfasted at Squire Cogswells—dined at Colo. Vandeburgs & reached head Quarters about Sunset where I found letters from Generls. Schuyler & Clinton, full of uncertain information respecting the enemys landing at Crown point & intention to penetrate on the Hudson & Mohawk Rivers. This uncertainty respects the number, not the fact—the latter seeming to be beyond a doubt. In consequence of this information I ordered the Companies of Vanscaicks Regiment at West point to hold themselves in readiness to Move at an hours warning.

26th. Received a Letter from the Honble. Jno. Laurens Minister from the United States of America at the Court of Versailles—informing me that the Sum of 6,000,000 of Livres was granted as a donation to this Country—to be applied in part to the purchase of Arms—Cloaths &ca. for the American Troops and the ballance to my orders, & draughts at long sight and that a Fleet of 20 Sail of the Line was on its departure for the West Indies 12 of which were to proceed to this Coast where it was probable they might arrive in the Month of July. He also added that the Courts of Petersbg. & Vienna had offered their Mediation in settling the present troubles wch. the King of France, tho' personally pleas'd with, could not accept without consulting his Allies. A Letter from Doctr. Lee—inclosing extracts of one from his Brother Wm. Lee Esqr. dated the 20th. of Feby. holds out strong assurances of Peace being restored in the course of this Yr.

28th. The Commanding Officer of Artillery & the chief Engineer were called upon to give in estimates of their wants for the intended operation against New York. The intention of doing this was also disclosed to the Q. M. General who was desired to give every attention toward the Boats, that a number of them might be prepared; & provide other matters necessary to such an undertaking—especially those things which might be called for by the Artillery, & the Engineering departments.

31st. A Letter from Count de Rochambeau informed me that the British fleet had left Block Island—that Adml. de Barras would Sail with the first fair Wind for Boston (having 900 of his Soldiers on Board to Man his fleet) and that he should commence his March as soon as possible, but would be under the necessity of Halting a few days at Providence.

A Letter from Major Talmage, inclosing one from C—— Senr. & another from S. G. dated the 27th. were totally silent on the subject of an evacuation of New York; but speak of an order for Marching the Troops from Long Island and the Countermand of it after they had commenced their March; the cause for either they could not assign. Neither C. Senr. nor S. G. estimate the Enemys regular force at New York or its dependencies at more than 4500 men including the New Levies; but C—— says it is reported that they can command five & some add 6,000 Militia & refugees. S. G. disposes of the Enemys force as follow.

At Fort Washington & towards New York	
—2 Hessn. Regts.	2
Laurel Hill—Fort George. 57th B.	1
Haerlam—at a place called Laurel Hill	
—38 Do.	1
At Hornes hook, & towds. the City—22d. & 42d.	
B. Regts.	2
In the City Hessian Regimts.	2
On Staten Island	2
Total on this Isld 1200	
On Long Island	
1st. B. Grenadrs. . . . New Town	1
2d. . . . . Ditto . . . Jamaica	1
Worms Hessian Yagers	
(called by him 6 or 700) No. side	
of the Plains	1
Light Dragns. . . . 17th. Regt.	
at Hempstead Plains	1
Loyds Neck—detachmets. from New Corps	
Abt. 6, or 700	14

The detachment which left Sandy hook the 13th Instt. according to the S. G.'s acct.—consisted of the Troops on the other side—though it is thought he must be mistaken in naming the 46th. & 86th. Regimts.—the first of them being a convention Regimt. and the other not in America. By Accts.

from Deserters the 37th. Regt. went with the detachment and must be in place of the 46th. as the 80th. must be that of the 86th.

	suppos'd
43 British Regiments	300
Anspach—2 Battalions	700
part of the 86th	150
part of the 46th	150
Hessian Yagers—abt.	150
	1450

1st. Received Letters from Generals Schuyler & Clinton, containing further but still indistinct accts, of the enemys force at Crown point. Letters from Doctr. Smith of Albany, & —— Shepherd principal armourer at that place, were intercepted, going to the enemy with acct. of our distresses—the strength & dispositon of our Troops—The disaffection of particular Settlements—the provision these Settlemts. had made to subsist them—their readiness to join them—the genl. temper of the people and their earnest wishes for their advance in force—assuring them of the happy consequences which would derive to the Kings arms if they would move rapidly to Albany. In consequence of this information I directed the Q. M. General to provide Craft for, & the 6 Companies of Vanscaicks Regiment & Hazens to proceed immediately to Albany & put themselves under General Clintons orders.

4th. Letters from the Marqs. de la Fayette of the 25th Ulto. informs that Lord Cornwallis had formed a junction with Arnold at Petersbourg—that with their United force he had Marched to City point on James River and that the detachment which sailed from New York the 13th of May had arrived in James River and were debarking at Westover and that he himself had removed from Wilton to Richmond.

The Duke de Lauzen arrived this afternoon with Letters from Count de Rochambeau & Admiral Count de Barras, with the proceedings of a Council of War held on Board the Duke de Burgoyne proposing to continue the Fleet at Rhode Island under the protection of 400 French Troops & 1000 Militia in preference to the plan adopted at Weathersfield; requiring my opinion thereon which was given to the effect—that I conceived the first plan gave a more perfect security to the Kings fleet than the latter, & consequently left the Land force more at liberty to act, for which reason I could not change my former opinion but shou'd readily acquiesce to theirs if upon a re-consideration of the matter they adhered to it. Accordingly, that delay might be avoided, I inclosed letters (under flying Seals) to the Governors of Rd. Island & Massachusetts, to be made use of or not, requesting the Militia; & pressed the March of the Land Troops as soon as circumstances would admit of it.

5th. Governor Rutlidge of South Carolina came to Head Qrs. with representations of the situation of Southern affairs, & to sollicit aids. I communicated the plan of Campaign to him & candidly exposed the true State of our Circumstances which convinced him—or seemed to do so—that no relief cd. be given from this army till we had acquired a Naval Superiority and cd. transport Troops by Water.

7th. A Letter from the Govr. of Virginia dated at Charlottesville the 28th. Ulto. representing the distressed State of Virginia & pressing my repairng thither, was received—other letters (but not official) speak of Lord Cornwallis's advance to Hanover Court House—that the Marquis was retreating before him towards Fredericksburg and that General Leslie was embarked in James River with about 1200 Men destined, as was supposed, to Alexandria whither it was conjectured by the letter writers Lord Cornwallis was pointing his March.

Accts. from Pittsburg were expressive of much apprehension for that quarter as a force from Canada was expected thither by way of the Lakes and the Alligany River.

A Letter from the Executive of Pennsylvania afforded little hope of assistance in the article of Provision or other things from that State and was more productive of what they had done, than what they meant to do.

9th. A Captn. Randolph—sent by General Clarke from Pittsburg, arrived here with letters & representations of his disappointments of Men, and the prospect of failure in his intended Expedition against Detroit unless he could be aided

by the 9th. Virginia Regiment & Heths Company at Pittsburg—but the weakness of the Garrison & other considerations would not admit this—nor did it appear to me that this
reinforcement would enable him to undertake & prosecute
the Plan.

11th. Received Letters from the Marqs. de la Fayette, containing information of Lord Cornwallis's movements from Westover, and that, at the date of his letter—the 3d. Instt.—he had
advanced to the North Anna—but his design was not sufficiently understood—supposed Fredericksburg. The Marqs.
was retreating before him with abt. 3000 Men Militia included—the Enemys force exclusive of Leslies detachment being estimated at five or 6000 Men, 600 of wch. were Horse.

13th. To facilitate the building, and repairing of Boats, a number of Carpenters was ordered from the line of the army to
the Q. M. G. to aid the artificers of his department in this
important business and Major Darby with a Captain 5 Subs &
6 Sergts. and 100 Rank & file were drawn from the army in
order to collect and take care of the public Boats.

14th. Received agreeable acts. from General Greene, of his
Successes in South Carolina—viz.—that Lord Rawden had
abandoned Cambden with precipitation, leaving all our
wounded taken in the action of the 25th. of April last, together
with 58 of his own too bad to remove—that he had destroy'd
his own Stores—burnt many buildings and in short left the
Town little better than a heap of Rubbish—That Orangeburg,
Forts Mott. & Granby, had surrendered; their Garrisons including officers consisting of near 700 Men—That Ninety Six
& Fort Augusta were invested—that he was preparing to
March to the Former and that, Lord Rawden was at Nelsons
ferry removing the Stores from that place which indicated an
Evacuation thereof.

16th. Directed that no more Invalids be transferred till further
Orders—that a detachment be formed of the weakliest Men
for garrisoning of West point & that a Camp be marked out
by the Chief Engineer & Q. M. Genl. near Peekskill to assemble the Troops on.

18th. Brigaded the Troops, and made an arrangement of the

Army, which is to March for the New Camp in three divisions—the 1st. on Thursday the 21st.—the 2d. on the 23d. and the 3d. on the 24th. Instt. To strengthen the detachment intended for the Garrison of West point, I had previously called upon the State of Connecticut for 800 Militia.

20th. Recd. Letters from Genl. Clinton at Albany inclosing the examination of two Prisoners taken at Crown point by wch. and other intelligence it appears that no Troops had landed at that place and that the enemys Shipping *only*, had ever been there. In consequence, the Continental Troops to the Noward were ordered to be in readiness to join the army on the shortest notice & Governor Clinton informed thereof that the New levies of the State, & nine months, men might be hastened to relieve them.

24th. A Letter from the Count de Rochambeau dated at Windham the 20th. advises me of his having reached that Town, that day, with the first division of his army—that the other 3 divisions were following in regular succession—that he expected to Halt the Troops two days at Hartford, but would come on to my Camp from that place after the arrival of the division with which he was.

By a Letter from Govr. Trumbull it appear'd that the assembly of Connecticut had passed some salutary Laws for filling their Battalions, & complying with my requisition—but it is to be feared that their list of deficiencies, which the respective Towns are called upon to make good by drafts to compleat the Battalions is short of the number wanting for this purpose.

25th. A Letter from Genl. Heath of the 18th. holds up favourable Ideas of the disposition prevaling in the State of Massachusetts Bay to comply with every thing required of them.

Joined the Army at its Encampment at Peekskill. Mrs. Washington set out at the same time towards Virginia but with an intention to Halt at Philadelphia if from information & circumstances it was not likely she should remain quietly at Mt. Vernon.

A Letter from Count de Rochambeau informs me that he shall be with his first division at Newtown on the 28th. where he purposed to assemble his force & March in Brigades while the Duke de Lauzens Legion continues to move on his Left flank.

Had an interview with Govr. Clinton, Lieut. Govr. Courtlandt, & Generals Schuyler & Tenbrook; in which I pressed the necessity of my recalling the Continental Regiments from Albany, & the Posts above, & of the States hastening up their Levies for 3 Years & Nine months and agreed to order 600 Militia (part of the quota required of Massachusetts bay) from the Counties of Berkshire and Hampshire to March immediately to Albany which was accordingly done & Govr. Hancock advised of it.

Genl. Stark was directed to repair to Saratoga & take command of the Troops on the Northern & western frontier and Genl. Clinton called upon in pointed terms to have the Continental Troops under his command in the most perfect readiness to join the Army.

Recd. a Letter from the Minister of France advising me of the arrival of between 3 & 4000 Troops abt. the 4th. Inst. at Charles Town—that 2000 of them had debarked & that the rest were said to be destined for St. Augustine & New York—that George Town was evacuated & the Enemy in Charles town weak (not exceeding 450 Men before the reinforcement arrived—which latter must be a mistake, as the Ministers informant added, that Lord Rawden had got there after a precipitate retreat from a Post above and that the American parties were within 5 Miles of the Town. Lord Rawdens Troops alone amounted to more than the Number here mentioned).

Having suggested to the Count de Rochambeau the advantages which might be derived to the common cause in general and the Southern States in particular, if by arming the Fantasque & bringing the 50 gun ship to Rhode Isld. (which then lay at Boston) the fleet of his most Christian Majesty at Newport could appear in Chesapeak bay. I received an answer from the French Admiral through the General that he was disposed to the measure provided he could obtain a loan of the French Guard (of 400 Men which were left at Newport & which were granted) and 4 pieces of heavy artillery at Brentons point which the Count could not spare but that the fleet could not bc ready to Sail under 20 days from the date of his letter (the 21st.)—thus, uncertain, the matter stands.

28th. Having determined to attempt to surprize the Enemys Posts at the No. end of Yk. Island, if the prospt. of success continued favourable, & having fixed upon the Night of the 2d. of July for this purpose and having moreover combined with it an attempt to cut off Delancy's And other light Corps without Kingsbridge and fixed upon Genl. Lincoln to Commd. the first detachment & the Duke de Lauzen the 2d. every thing was put in train for it and the Count de Rochambeau requested to file of from Ridgebury to Bedford & hasten his March—while the Duke de Lauzen was to do the same & to assemble his command (which was to consist of abt. 3 or 400 Connecticut State Troops under the Command of Genl. Waterbury—abt. 100 York Troops under Captn. Sacket—Sheldons Legion of 200, & his own proper Corps.). Genl. Lincolns command was to consist of Scammells light Troops and other detachments to the amt. of 800 Rank & file properly officerd—150 watermen and 60 artillerists.

29th. Recd. a letter from the Marqs. de la Fayette informing me that Lord Cornwallis after having attempted to surprise the Virginia Assembly at Charlottesville and destroy some Stores at the Forks of James River in which he succeeded partially had returned to Richmond without having effected any valuable purpose by his manoeuvers in Virginia. In a private letter he complains heavily of the conduct of the Baron de Steuben whom he observes has rendered himself extremely obnoxious in Virga.

July 2d. Genl. Lincoln's detachment embarked last Night after dark, at or near Tellers point; and as his operations were to be the movement of two Nights he was desired to repair to Fort Lee this day & reconnoitre the enemy's Works—Position and strength as well as he possibly could & take his ultimate determination from appearances—that is to attempt the surprize if the prospect was favourable or to relinquish it if it was not, and in the latter case to land above the Mouth of Spikendevil & cover the Duke in his operation on Delancys Corps.

At three o'clock this Morning I commenced my March with the Continental Army in order to cover the detached Troops and improve any advantages which might be gained by them. Made a small halt at the New bridge over Croton abt. 9 Miles from Peekskill—another at the Church by Tarry Town till Dusk (9 Miles more) and compleated the remaining part of the March in the Night—arriving at Valentines Hill (at Mile square) about Sun rise.

Our Baggage & Tents were left standing at the Camp at Peekskill.

3d. The length of Duke Lauzens March & the fatiegue of his Corps, prevented his coming to the point of Action at the hour appointed. In the meantime Genl. Lincolns Party who were ordered to prevent the retreat of Delancy's Corps by the way of Kg. Bridge & prevent succour by that Rout were attacked by the Yagers and others but on the March of the Army from Valentines Hill retired to the Island. Being disappointed in both objects from the Causes mentioned I did not care to fatiegue the Troops any more but suffered them to remain on their Arms while I spent good part of the day in reconnoitering the Enemys works.

In the afternoon we retired to Valentines Hill & lay upon our Arms. Duke Lauzen & Waterbury lay on the East side of the Brunxs river on the East Chester road. Our loss in this days skirmishing was as follows—viz.—

4th. Marched & took a position a little to the left of Dobbes ferry & marked a Camp for the French Army upon our left. Duke Lauzen Marched to the Whitepln & Waterbury to Horseneck.

5th. Visited the French Army which had arrived at Northcastle.

6th. The French Army formed the junction with the American on the Grounds marked out. The Legion of Lauzen took a position advanced of the plains on Chittendens hill west of the River Brunx. This day also the Minister of France arrived in Camp from Philadelphia.

8th. Began a Work at Dobbs's ferry with a view to establish a communication there for the transportation of provision and Stores from Pensylvania.

9th. Received a Letter from the Marqs. de la Fayette informing me of Cornwallis's retreat to Williamsburg—that he had pushed his rear and had obtained advantages—having killed 60 & wounded an hundred with small loss.

Southern accts. though not official speak of the reduction of Augusta and Ninety Six by the arms of Major Genel. Greene.

10th. A Letter from Governor Trumbull, inclosing the proceedings of a convention of Eastern Deligates gives better hope of a regular supply of provision than we have been accustomed to for more than two years as the business seem to be taken up Systematically and regular modes adopted to furnish supplies at stated periods.

General Heath also writes very favourably of the disposition of the Eastn. States but still we are without the reinforcements of Men required of them.

The Boats undertaken by General Schuyler, are, by his letters, in a promising way—as those at Wappings Creek also are by the Q. Mr. Genls. report.

Hazen's, and the 1st. York Regimt. who had been ordered to West point arrived there, but not till the latter had mutinied on acct. of their pay & several had deserted. The other York Regiment were detained at Albany to bring down the Boats & boards.

13th. The Jersey Troops arrived at Dobbs's Ferry agreeable to orders. Some French Frigates made an attempt on the Enemy's Post at Loyds Neck but without success not being able to Land in the Night.

14th. Near 5000 Men being ordered to March for Kings bridge, to cover and secure a reconnoitre of the Enemys Works on the No. end of York Island, Harlaem river, & the Sound were prevented doing so by incessant rain.

15th. The Savage Sloop of War of 16 Guns—the Ship Genl. Washington, lately taken by the Enemy—a row Galley and two other small armed Vessels passed our post at Dobbs Ferry (which was not in a condition to oppose them). At the same time three or four river Vessels with 4 Eighteen pounders—stores &ca. had just arrivd at Tarry town and with infinite difficulty, & by great exertion of Colo. Sheldon, Captn. Hurlbut, (who got wounded)—Captn. Lieutt. Miles of the artillery & Lt. Shayler were prevented falling into the hands of the Enemy as they got a ground 100 yards from the Dock and were set fire to by the Enemy but extinguished by the extraordinary activity & spirit of the above Gentn. Two of the Carriages however were a good deal damaged by the fire. The Enemy however by sending their armed Boats up the River took the Vessel of a Captn. Dobbs laden with Bread for the French Army—Cloathing for Sheldons Regiment & some passengers. This was done in the Night—it being after Sunset before the Vessels passed the Post at Dobs ferry.

16th. The Cannon & Stores were got out of the Vessels & every thing being removed from Tarry town, two french twelve pounders, & one of our 18 prs. were brought to bear upon the Ships which lay of Tarry town, distant about a Mile, and obliged them to remove lower down & move over to the West shore.

17th. The Vessels being again fired at in the position they took yesterday run up the River to Tellers point & there came to burning the House of the Widow Noyell.

18th. I passed the North River with Count de Rochambeau Genl. de Beville his Qr. Mr. Genl. & Genl. Duportail in order to reconnoitre the Enemy Posts and Encampments at the North end of York Island. Took an Escort of 150 Men from the Jersey Troops on the other side.

   From different views the following discoveries were made—viz.—

   That two Ships of 20 Guns & upwards lay opposite to the Mouth of spikendevil—one pretty near the East Shore the other abt. the same distance from the West; the first is intended to guard the Mouth of Spikendevil equally with the No. River. Below these, & directly opposite to Fort Washington (or Knyphausen) lay two transports with about 6 Guns & few Men in each. The Eastermost Ship seems designed to

Guard the landing at the little bay above Jefferys Rock. About
the center of the Ground leading to Jeffreys Rock or point a
Guard Mounts. It appears to be no more than a Sergeants
guard with one centry in front where there is a small Work—
the Guard House standing within.

These are all the Guards and all the security I could discover
upon the No. River—on the right flank of the Enemy. The
Shore from Jeffreys rock downwards, was quite open, and
free—without Hutts of any kind—Houses or Troops—none
being encamped below the heights. There did not even appear
springs, or washing places any where on the face of the Hill
which were resorted to.

The Island is totally stripped of Trees, & wood of every
kind; but low bushes (apparently as high as a Mans waste)
appear in places which were covered with Wood in the year
1776.

The Side of the Hill from the Barrier below Fort Tryon, to
the Bay opposite to fort Knyphausen, is difficult of access; but
there seems to be a place abt. 200 yds. above the bay, which
has the best appearance of a landing, and is most private—but
a hut or two on the heights abt. 200 yds. above Fort Knyphausen, & a little above the old long Battery, which was
thrown up in 1776 must be avoided by leaving it on the left
in getting to the Fort last mentioned.

In the hollow below Morris's heights (between that &
Haerlam) is a good place to land but near the York Road
opposite there appeared to be a few Tents and many Dragoon
Horses seemed to be at Pasture in the low land between the
heights. A landing perfectly concealed, but not so good,
might be made a little higher up the river, and nearer to those
heights which ought to be immediately occupied—(between
the old American lines and the aforesaid hollow).

From the point within the Mouth of Spiken devil, the way
to the Fort on Cox's Hill seems difficult, and the first part of
it covered with bushes. There is a better way up from the
outer point, but too much exposed to a discovery from the
Ship which lays opposite to it, and on acct. of its being less
covered with wood.

The ground round the Fort on Cox's hill is clear of Bushes.
There is an abatis round the Work, but no friezing; nor could

I discover whether there is a ditch. At the No. Et. corner there appeared to be no Parapet & the whole seemed to be in a decaying State. The gate is next the No. River.

Forts Tryon, Knyphausen & Ft. George on Laurell, with the Batteries in the line of Pallisading across from River to river appeared to be well friezed, ditched & abattied—In a word to be strong and in good repair.

Fort No. 8 is also abatied & friezed at the Top. The gate is next Haerlam River. There are no Houses or Huts on the side of the Hill from this work till you come near old Fort Independence.

On McGowans heights there appears (by the extent of the Tents) to be two Battns. Encamped—supposed to be the British Grenadiers. A little in the rear of this, and on the (enemys) left, are a number of Huts but whether they are Inhabited or not could not be ascertained there being different opinions on this point, from the nearest view we could get of it. On the height opposite to Morris's white House there appeared to be another Regt. (supposed to be the 38th. British). Between this and Fort Knyphausen (abt. half way) are two small Encampments contiguous to each other—both together containing two or 3 and 40 Tents—Hessians. On Laurel Hill near Fort George is another Encampment in view abt. 40 Tents & huts which appear to be Inhabited also—by (it is said)—the 57th. Regiment. The other, and only remaining Encampment in View, & discoverable from the West side of the river, is betwn. the Barrier and Kings bridge—in the Hollow between Cox's hill and the heights below. One hundred Tents could be counted in view at the same time, and others might be hid by the Hills. At this place it is said the Jagers—Hessian & Anspach lay.

19th. The Enemys Shipping run down the river, and left the Navigation of it above once more free for us. In passing our Battery at Dobbs's where were 2 Eighteen & 2 twelve pounders and two Howitzers, they recd. considerable damage; especially the Savage Sloop of War which was frequently hulled, and once set on fire; occasioning several of her people, and one of our own (taken in Dobbes Sloop, and) who gives the Acct. to jump over board. Several people he says were killed

& the ship pierced through both her sides in many places and in such a manner as to render all their pumps necessary to free the Water.

20th. Count de Rochambeau having called upon me, in the name of Count de Barras, for a definitive plan of Campaign, that he might communicate it to the Count de Grasse—I could not but acknowledge, that the uncertainties under which we labour—the few Men who have joined (either as recruits for the Continental Battns. or Militia) & the ignorance in which I am kept by some of the States on whom I mostly depended—especially Massachusetts from whose Govr. I have not received a line since I addressed him from Weathersfd. the 23d. of May last—rendered it impracticable for me to do more than to prepare, first, for the enterprize against New York as agreed to at Weathersfield and secondly for the relief of the Southern States if after all my efforts, & earnest application to these States it should be found at the arrivl. of Count de Grasse that I had neither men, nor means adequate to the first object. To give this opinion I was further induced from the uncertainty with respect to the time of the arrival of the French Fleet & whether Land Troops would come in it or not as had been earnestly requested by me & inforced by the Minister of France.

The uncertainty of sufficient aids, of Men & Means from the States to whom application had been made, and the discouraging prospects before me of having my requisitions complied with—added to an unwillingness to incur any expence that could be avoided induced me to desire Genl. Knox to suspend the Transport of the heavy Cannon & Stores from Philadelphia lest we should have them to carry back again or be encumbd. with them in the field.

21st. Wrote to the Count de Grasse in a Cypher of the Count de Rochambeau's, giving information of the junction of the allied armys—the Position they had taken—our strength and that of the enemy's—our hopes & fears & what we expected to do under different circumstances. This letter was put under cover to Genl. Forman, who was requested to have look outs on the heights of Monmouth, and deliver it himself upon the arrival of the Fleet and who was also requested, to establish a chain of Expresses for quick communication between Monmouth and Dobbs's ferry—the Expence of which I would see paid.

Again ordered abt. 5000 Men to be ready to March at 8 oclock, for the purpose of reconnoitering the enemys Posts at Kings bridge and to cut off, if possible, such of Delancys Corps as should be found without their lines.

At the hour appointed the March commenced in 4 Columns, on different roads. Majr. Genl. Parsons with the Connecticut Troops & 25 of Sheldon's horse formed the right column (with two field pieces) on the No. River road. The other Two divisions of the Army, under the Majr. Generals Lincoln & Howe, together with the Corps of Sappers and Miners, and 4 field pieces, formed the next column on the Sawmill river road. The right column of the French (on our left) consisted of the Brigade of Bourbonnis, with the Battn. of Grenadiers and Choissairs, 2 field pieces & 2 twelve pounders. Their left column was composed of the Legion of Lauzen—one Battn. of Grenadiers, & Choissairs of Soussonnis, 2 field pieces & 2 Howitzers. General Waterbury with the Militia and State Troops of Connecticut, were to March on the East chester Road and to be joined at that place by the Cavalry of Sheldon, for the purpose of Scouring Frogs Neck. Sheldons Infantry was to join the Legion of Lauzen for the purpose of Scouring Morrissania, and to be covered by Scammells light Infantry who were to advance thro' the fields & way lay the Roads—stop all communication & prevent Intelligence getting to the Enemy.

At Mile Square (Valentine's hill) The left column of the American Troops, and right of the french formed their junction, as did the left of the French also, by *mistake* as it was intended it should cross the Brunx by Garrineaus, & recross it at Williams's bridge.

The whole Army (Parson's division first) arrived at Kingsbridge about day light & formed on the heights back of Fort Independance—extending towards delancy's Mills—While the Legion of Lauzen & Waterbury proceeded to scour the Necks of Morrissania & throgs to little effect, as most of the Refugees were fled, & hid in such obscure places as not to be discovered; & by stealth got over to the Islands adjacent, &

to the enemys shipping which lay in the East River. A few however were caught and some cattle & Horses brought off.

22d. The enemy did not appear to have had the least intelligence of our movement or to know we were upon the height opposite to them till the whole Army were ready to display.

After having fixed upon the ground, & formed our line, I began, with General Rochambeau and the Engineers, to reconnoitre the enemy's position and Works first from Tippets hill opposite to their left and from hence it was evident that the small redoubt (Fort Charles) near Kings bridge would be absolutely at the command of a battery which might be erected thereon. It also appeared equally evident that the Fort on Cox's hill was in bad repair, & little dependence placed in it. There is neither ditch nor friezing to it, and the No. East Corner appears quite easy of access (occasioned as it would seem by a Rock). The approach from the inner Point (mentioned in the Reconnoitre from the Jersey shore) is secured by a ledge of Rocks which would conceal a party from the observation & view of the ship till it got within abt. 100 Yds. of the Fort round which for that, or a greater distance the ground has little covering upon it of bushes. There is a house on this side under Tippets hill but out of view, I conceive of the crossing place most favourable to a partizan stroke. From this view, and every other I could get of Forts Tryon, Knyphausen & Laurel hill the Works are formidable.

There is no Barracks or huts on the East side of the Hill on which Fort Tryon and Knyphausen stands—nor are there any on the hill opposite except those by Fort George. Near the Blew bell there is a number of Houses but they have more the appearance of Stables than Barracks. In the hollow, near the Barrier gate, are about 14 or 15 Tents; which is the only Encampment I could see without the line of Pallisading as the large one discovered on the 18th. through the brake of the Hill betwn. Fort Tryon & Coxss hill was not to be seen from any view I had.

A continued Hill from the Creek, East of Haerlam River, & a little below Morris's White House, has from every part of it, the command of the opposite shore, & all the plain adjoining, within range of shot from batteries which may be erected thereon. The general width of the river along this range of Hills, appears to be from one to two hundred yards. The opposite shore (tho' more or less marshy) does not seem miry, & the banks are very easy of access. How far the Battery, under cover of the block Ho on the hill No. West of Harlaem town is capable of scouring the plain, is difficult to determine from this side, but it would seem as if the distance was too great to be within the range of its shot on that part of the plain nearest the Creek before mentioned & which is also nearest the height back of our old lines thrown up in the year 1776. It unfortunately happens that in the rear of the (continued) hill before mentioned, there is a deep swamp, and the grounds East of that swamp, are not so high as the heights near Harlaem river. In the rear of this again is the Brunx which is not be crossed without Boats below De Lancys Mills.

23d. Went upon Frogs Neck, to see what communication could be had with Long Isld. The Engineers attending with Instrumts. to measure the distance across found it to be Yards.

Having finished the reconnoitre without damage—a few harmless shot only being fired at us—we Marched back about Six o'clock by the same routs we went down & a reversed order of March and arrived in Camp about Midnight.

This day letters from Genls. Greene and the Marqs. de la Fayette came to hand, the first informing of his having taken all the Enemy's posts in Georgia except Savanna and all those in So. Carolina except Charles Town & Ninety Six—the last of wch. he was obliged to abandon the siege of, on acct. of the relief which was marching to it, consequent of the late reinforcemt. received at Charles Town. The second, that Waynes affair with Lord Cornwallis on the 6th. Instt. was partial on our side, as a part of our force was opposed to the enemys whole Army—that on our Side the loss in killed, wounded & missing, amounted to 5 Capt. 1 Captn. Lieutt. 4 Lieutts. 11 Sergts. & 118 R. & file—that the enemys loss was computed at 300 at least—that our loss of two field pieces proceeded, from the horses belonging to them being killed and that Lord Cornwallis had retreated to the South side of James River from the Peninsula at James Town.

29th. A Letter from the Marqs. de la Fayette (commanding in Virginia) informed me that after Lord Cornwallis had crossed James River he detached Tarlton with a body of horse into Amelia County with a view, as was supposed, to destroy some Stores which had been deposited there but which had been previously removed—that after this the enemys whole force removed to Portsmouth with a design it was said to embark part of them and that he had detached Generl. Wayne to the South side of James River to cover the Country, while the enemy lay in it, & to March Southerly if they did not— he himself with the Main body of his Army having taken a position at a place called Malvin hill not far from Shirley.

Part of the Second York Regiment came down from Albany with such of the Boats as had been undertaken by Gen. Schuyler, & were finished. The light Infantry Company of the Regiment were ordered down with the next Boats & the remainder of the Regiment to bring down the rest when done.

About this time, the discontents in the Connecticut State line, occasioned by some disappointment of a Committee sent from it to the Assembly, in settling an Acct. of Subsistence &ca. began to increase, & put on a more serious face; which induced me to write a second letter to the Govr. of that State. The distress of the Line for want of a small portion of the pay due it contributed not a little to irritate them.

30th. Ordered the Jersey Militia, who were directed to Assemble in the first instance at Morristown to Dobbs ferry and there join the remains of the Jersey Brigade and receiving Letters from Govr. Clinton & Genl. Clinton complaining that none of the Massachusetts Militia had repaired to Albany agreeable to my requisition I again addressed Govr. Hancock in pointed terms to send them on & complained of not having recd. answers from him to any of my letters since the Conference with Count de Rochambeau and a communication of the plan of operation which was agreed on at Weathersfield the 22d. of May last.

Received a Letter from the Count de Barras, refering me to one written by him to Genl. Rochambeau in Cypher; pointing, in stronger terms than heretofore, his disinclination to leave Newport till the arrival of Adml. de Grass. This induced me to desist from further representing the advantages which would result from preventing a junction of the enemy's force at New York; & blocking up those which are now in Virginia, lest in the Attempt any disaster should happen, & the loss of, or damage to his fleet, should be ascribed to my obstinacy in urging a measure to which his own judgment was oppos'd, & the execution of which might impede his junction with the West India fleet, & thwart the views of the Count de Grasse upon this Coast—especially as he gave it as a clear opinion, that the West India fleet might be expected by the 10th. of Next Month.

31st. Governor Trumbull informed me, that in order to facilitate the Collection of a Specie Tax for the purpose of sending Money to the Troops of the Connecticut line Gentlemen were sent to the different Towns of the State to try by personal influence & exertion to hasten it to the Army and that he & some of his Council had removed to Hartford to forward on the Recrts. for the Continental Regiments and the Militia and in a word to promote the operations of the Campaign as much as in them lay.

1st. By this date all my Boats were ready—viz.—One hundred New ones at Albany (constructed under the direction of Genel. Schuyler) and the like number at Wappings Creek by the Qr. Mr. Genel.; besides old ones which have been repaired. My heavy ordnance & Stores from the Eastward had also come on to the North Rivr. and every thing would have been in perfect readiness to commense the operation against New York, if the States had furnished their quotas of men agreeably to my requisitions but so far have they been from complying with these that of the first, not more than half the number asked of them have joined the Army; and of 6200 of the latter pointedly & timously called for to be with the Army by the 15th. of last Month, only 176 had arrived from Connecticut, independant of abt. 300 State Troops under the Command of Genel. Waterbury, which had been on the lines before we took the field, & two Companies of York levies (abt. 80 Men) under similar circumstances.

Thus circumstanced, and having little more than general assurances of getting the succours called for and energetic

Laws & resolves or Laws & resolves energetically executed, to depend upon—with little appearance of their fulfillment, I could scarce see a ground upon wch. to continue my preparations against New York—especially as there was much reason to believe that part (at least) of the Troops in Virginia were recalled to reinforce New York and therefore I turned my views more seriously (than I had before done) to an operation to the Southward and, in consequence, sent to make enquiry, indirectly, of the principal Merchants to the Eastward what number, & in what time, Transports could be provided to convey a force to the Southward if it should be found necessary to change our plan & similar application was made in a direct way to Mr. Morris (Financier) to discover what number cd. be had by the 20th. of this Month at Philadelphia or in Chesapeak bay. At the sametime General Knox was requested to turn his thoughts to this business and make every necessary arrangement for it in his own Mind—estimating the ordnance & Stores which would be wanting & how many of them could be obtained without a transport of them from the North River. Measures were also taken to deposit the Salt provisions in such places as to be Water born. More than these, while there remained a hope of Count de Grasses bringing a land force with him, & that the States might yet put us in circumstances to prosecute the original plan could not be done without unfolding matters too plainly to the enemy & enabling them thereby to Counteract our Schemes.

4th. Fresh representations of the defenceless State of the Northern frontier, for want of the Militia so long called for and expected from Massachusetts bay; accompanied by a strong expression of the fears of the People that they should be under the necessity of abandoning that part of the Country & an application that the Second York Regiment (Courtlandts) at *least* should be left for their protection induced me to send Major Genl. Lincoln (whose influence in his own State was great) into the Counties of Berkshire & Hampshire to enquire into the causes of these delays & to hasten on the Militia. I wrote at the same time to the Governor of this State consenting to suffer the 4 Companies of Courtlandts Regiment (now at Albany) to remain in that Quarter till the Militia did come in, but observed that if the States instead of filling their Battalions & sending forth their Militia were to be calling upon, & expecting me to dissipate the sml. operating force under my command for local defences that all offensive operations must be relinquished and we must content ourselves (in case of compliance) to spend an inactive and injurious Campaign which might—at this critical moment—be ruinous to the common cause of America.

6th. Reconnoitred the Roads and Country between the North River and the Brunxs from the Camp to Philip's and Valentines Hill and found the ground every where strong—the Hills 4 in Number running parallel to each other with deep ravines between them—occasioned by the Saw Mill river—the Sprain branch and another more Easterly. These hills have very few interstices or Breaks in them, but are more prominent in some places than others. The Saw mill River, & the Sprain branch occasion an entire seperation of the hills above Philips's from those below commonly called Valentines hills. A strong position might be taken with the Saw Mill (by the Widow Babcocks) in Front, & on the left flank and the No. River on the right Flank and this position may be extended from the Saw Mill river over the sprain Branch.

A Letter from the Marqs. de la Fayette of the 26th. Ulto. gives the following acct.—That the two Battalions of light Infantry—Queens Rangers—the Guards & one or two other Regiments had Embarked at Portsmouth & fallen down to Hampton Rd. in 49 Transports—that he supposed this body of Troops could not consist of less than 2000 Men—That Chesapeak bay & Potomack River were spoken of as the destination of this detachment—but he was of opinion that it was intended as a reinforcement to New York. Horses were laid for the speedy communication of Intelligence and an officer was to be sent with the acct. of the Fleets Sailing.

7th. Urged Governor Greene of Rhode Island to keep up the number of Militia required of that State at Newport & to have such arrangements made of the rest as to give instant & effectual support to the Post, & the Shipping in the harbour, in case any thing should be enterprized against the latter upon the arrival of Rodney; who, with the British fleet, is said to be expected at New York, & in conjuction with the Troops which are Embarked in Virginia & their own Marines are sufficient to create alarms.

8th. The light Company of the 2d. York Regiment (the first having been down some days) having joined the Army, were formed with two Companies of Yk. levies into a Battn. under the Command of Lieutt. Colo. Hamilton & Major Fish & placed under the orders of Colo. Scammell as part of the light Troops of the Army.

9th. A Letter from the Marqs. de la fayette of the 30th. Ulto., reports, that the Embarkation in Hampton Road still remained there—that there were 30 Ships full of Troops chiefly red Coats in the fleet—that Eight or ten other Vessels (Brigs) had Cavalry on Board—that the Winds had been extremely favourable—notwithstanding which they still lay at anchor & that the Charon & several other frigates (some said Seven) were with them as an escort. The Troops which he now speaks of as composing the detachment are the light Infantry—Queens Rangers and he thinks two British & two German Regiments—no mention of the Guards as in his former Acct.

10th. Ordered the first York, and Hazens Regiments immediately to this place from West point—The Invalids having got in both from Philadelphia & Boston and more Militia got in from Connecticut, as also some from Massachusetts bay giving with 4 Companies of Courtlandts Regiment in addition to the detachment left there upon the March of the Army perfect security to the Posts.

11th. Robt. Morris Esqr. Superintendant of Finance & Richd. Peters Esqr. a Member of the Board of War, arrived at Camp to fix with me the number of Men necessary for the next Campaign and to make the consequent arrangements for their establishment and Support.

A Fleet consisting of about 20 Sail, including 2 frigates & one or two prizes, arrived within the harbour of New York with German recruits—to the amount—by Rivington—of

2880 but by other, & better information to abt. 1500 sickly Men.

12. By accounts this day received from the Marqs. de la Fayette it appeared that the Transports in Hampton road had stood up the Bay & came too at the distance of 15 Miles and, in conseqe. he had commenced his March toward Fredericksburg that he might more readily oppose his operations on Potomack or up Chesapeak bay.

14th. Received dispatches from the Count de Barras announcing the intended departure of the Count de Grasse from Cape Francois with between 25 & 29 Sail of the line & 3200 land Troops on the 3d. Instant for Chesapeake bay and the anxiety of the latter to have every thing in the most perfect readiness to commence our operations in the moment of his arrival as he should be under a necessity from particular engagements with the Spaniards to be in the West Indies by the Middle of October—At the same time intimating his (Barras's) Intentions of enterprizing something against Newfoundland, & against which both Genl. Rochambeau and myself remonstrated as impolitic & dangerous under the probability of Rodneys coming upon this Coast.

Matters having now come to a crisis and a decisive plan to be determined on—I was obliged, from the Shortness of Count de Grasses premised stay on this Coast—the apparent disinclination in their Naval Officers to force the harbour of New York and the feeble compliance of the States to my requisitions for Men, hitherto, & little prospect of greater exertion in future, to give up all idea of attacking New York; & instead thereof to remove the French Troops & a detachment from the American Army to the Head of Elk to be transported to Virginia for the purpose of cooperating with the force from the West Indies against the Troops in that State.

15. Dispatched a Courier to the Marquis de la Fayette with information of this matter—requesting him to be in perfect readiness to second my views & to prevent if possible the retreat of Cornwallis toward Carolina. He was also directed to Halt the Troops under the Command of General Wayne if

they had not made any great progress in their March to join the Southern Army.

16th. Letters from the Marqs. de la Fayette & others, inform that Lord Cornwallis with the Troops from Hampton Road, had proceeded up York River & landed at York & Gloucester Towns where they were throwing up Works on the 6th. Inst.

19th. The want of Horses, or bad condition of them in the French army delayed the March till this day. The same causes, it is to be feared, will occasion a slow and disagreeable March to Elk if fresh horses cannot be procured & better management of them adopted.

The detachment from the American is composed of the light Infantry under Scammell—two light companies of York to be joined by the like Number from the Connecticut line— the remainder of the Jersey line—two Regiments of York— Hazens Regiment & the Regiment of Rhode Island—together with Lambs regiment of Artillery with Cannon and other Ordnance for the field & Siege.

Hazens regiment being thrown over at Dobbs's ferry was ordered with the Jersey Troops to March & take Post on the heights between Spring field & Chatham & Cover a french Battery at the latter place to veil our real movement & create apprehensions for Staten Island. The Quarter Master Genl. was dispatched to Kings ferry—the only secure passage—to prepare for the speedy transportation of the Troops across the River.

Passed Singsing with the American column. The French column marched by the way of Northcastle, Crompond & Pinesbridge being near ten miles further.

20th. The head of the Americans arrived at Kings ferry about ten O'clock & immediately began to cross.

21st. In the course of this day the whole of the American Troop, all their baggage, artillery & Stores, crossed the river. Nothing remained of ours but some Waggons in the Commissary's & Qr. Mr. Generals departmt., which were delayed, that no interruption might be given to the passage of the French Army.

During the passing of the French Army I mounted 30 flat

Boats (able to carry about 40 Men each) upon carriages—as well with a design to deceive the enemy as to our real movement, as to be useful to me in Virginia when I get there.

Some of the french Artillery wch. preceeded their Infantry got to the ferry & crossed it also.

22d. 23d. 24th. & 25th. Employed in transporting the French Army, its baggage & Stores over the river.

The 25th. the American Troops marched in two Columns—Genl. Lincoln with the light Infantry & first York Regiment pursuing the rout by Peramus to Springfield—while Colo. Lamb with his Regiment of Artillery—the Parke—Stores and Baggage of the Army covered by the Rhode Island Regt. proceeded to Chatham by the way of Pompton & the two bridges.

The Legion of Lauzen & the Regiments of Bourbonne & Duponts with the heavy Parke of the French Army also Marched for percipony by Suffrans Pompton &   .

The 26th. the remainder of the French army, its baggage & Stores, moved from the ferry and arrived at Suffrans—the ground the others had left.

28th. The American columns and 1st. division of the French Army arrived at the places assigned them.

29th. The Second division of French joined the first. The whole halted—as well for the purpose of bringing up our rear—as because we had heard not of the arrival of Count de Grasse & was unwilling to discover our real object to the enemy.

30th. As our intentions could be concealed one March more (under the idea of Marching to Sandy hook to facilitate the entrance of the French fleet within the Bay), the whole Army was put in motion in three columns—the left consisted of the light Infantry, first York Regiment, and the Regiment of Rhode Island—the Middle column consisted of the Parke Stores & Baggage—Lambs Regt. of Artillery—Hazens & the Corps of Sappers & Miners—the right column consisted of the whole French army, Baggage Stores &ca. This last was to march by the rout of Morristown—Bullions Tavern—Somer-

set Ct House & Princeton. The middl. was to go by Bound
brooke to Somerset &ca. and the left to proceed by the way
of Brunswick to Trenton, to which place the whole were to
March Transports being ordered to meet them there.

I set out myself for Philadelphia to arrange matters there—
provide Vessels & hasten the transportation of the Ordnance
Stores, &ca.—directing before I set out, the secd. York Regiment (which had not all arrived from Albany before we left
Kings ferry) to follow with the Boats—Intrenching Tools &ca.
the French Rear to Trenton.

31st. Arrived at Philadelphia to dinner and immediately hastened up all the Vessels that could be procured—but finding
them inadequate to the purpose of transporting both Troops
& Stores, Count de Rochambeau & myself concluded it
would be best to let the Troops March by land to the head
of Elk, & gave directions accordingly to all but the 2d. York
Regiment which was ordered (with its baggage) to come
down in the Batteaux they had in charge to Christiana bridge.

5th. The rear of the French army having reached Philadelphia
and the Americans having passed it—the Stores having got up
& every thing in a tolerable train here; I left this City for the
head of Elk to hasten the Embarkation at that place and on
my way—(at Chester)—received the agreeable news of the
safe arrival of the Count de Grasse in the Bay of Chesapeake
with 28 Sail of the line & four frigates—with 3000 land Troops
which were to be immediately debarked at James town &
form a junction with the American Army under the command
of the Marqs. de la Fayette.

Finding upon my arrival at the head of Elk a great deficiency
of Transports, I wrote many letters to Gentn. of Influence on
the Eastern shore, beseeching them to exert themselves in
drawing forth every kind of Vessel which would answer for
this purpose and agreed with the Count de Rochambeau that
about 1000 American Troops (including the Artillery Regiment) and the Grenadiers & Chasseurs of the Brigade of
Bourbonne with the Infantry of Lauzen's legion should be
the first to Embark and that the rest of the Troops should
continue their march to Baltimore proceeding thence by
Land, or Water according to circumstances. The Cavalry of

Lauzen, with the Saddle horses & such teams of both armies as the Qr. Masters thereof might judge necessary to go round by Land to the place of operation.

Judging it highly expedient to be with the army in Virginia as soon as possible, to make the necessary arrangements for the Siege, & to get the Materials prepared for it, I determined to set out for the Camp of the Marqs. de la Fayette without loss of time and accordingly in Company with the Count de Rochambeau who requested to attend me, and the Chevr. de Chastellux set out on the

8th. and reached Baltimore where I recd. and answered an address of the Citizens.

9th. I reached my own Seat at Mount Vernon (distant 120 Miles from the Hd. of Elk) where I staid till the 12th. and in three days afterwards that is on the 14th. reached Williamsburg. The necessity of seeing, & agreeing upon a proper plan of cooperation with the Count de Grasse induced me to make him a visit at Cape Henry where he lay with his fleet after a partial engagement with the British Squadron off the Capes under the Command of Admiral Graves whom he had driven back to Sandy hook.

17th. In company with the Count de Rochambeau—the Chevr. Chastellux—Genls. Knox & Duportail, I set out for the Interview with the Admiral & arrived on board the Ville de Paris (off Cape Henry) the next day by Noon and having settled most points with him to my satisfaction except not obtaining an assurance of sending Ships above York and one that he could not continue his fleet on this Station longer than the first of November I embarked on board the Queen Charlotte (the Vessell I went down in) but by hard blowing; & contrary Winds, did not reach Williamsburg again till the 22d.

22d. Upon my arrival in Camp I found that the 3d. Maryland Regiment had got in (under the Command of Colo. Adam) and that all except a few missing Vessels with the Troops from the head of Elk were arrived, & landing at the upper point of the College Creek—where Genl. Choisy with 600 Fr. Troops who had from R. Isld. had arrived in the Squadron of Count de Barras

had done before them during my absence.

25th. Admiral de Barras having Joined the Count de Grasse with the Squadron and Transports from Rhode Island, & the latter with some Frigates being sent to Baltimore for the remr. of the French army arrived this day at the usual port of debarkation above the College Creek and began to land the Troops from them.

28th. Having debarked all the Troops and their Baggage— Marched and Encamped them in Front of the City and having with some difficulty obtained horses & Waggons sufficient to move our field Artillery—Intrenching Tools & such other articles as were indispensably necessary—we commenced our March for the Investiture of the Enemy at York.

The American Continental, and French Troops formed one column on the left—the first in advance—the Militia composed the right column & marched by the way of Harwoods Mill. Half a mile beyond the halfway Ho the French & Americans seperated. The former continued on the direct road to York, by the Brick House. The latter filed of to the right for Murfords bridge, where a junction with the Militia was to be made. About Noon the head of each column arrived at its ground, & some of the enemys Picquets were driven in on the left by a Corps of French Troops, advanced for the purpose, which afforded an oppertunity of reconnoitering them on their right. The enemy's Horse on the right were also obliged to retire from the ground they had Encamped on, & from whence they were employed in reconnoitering the right column.

The line being formed, all the Troops—Officers & Men— lay upon their arms during the Night.

29th. Moved the American Troops more to the right, and Encamped on the East side of Bever dam Creek, with a Morass in front, about Cannon shot from the enemys lines. Spent this day in reconnoitering the enemys position, & determining upon a plan of attack & approach which must be done without the assistance of Shipping above the Town as the Admiral (notwithstanding my earnest sollicitation) declined hazarding any Vessells on that Station.

30th. The Enemy abandoned all their exterior works, & the position they had taken without the Town; & retired within their Interior works of defence in the course of last Night—immediately upon which we possessed them, & made those on our left (with a little alteration) very serviceable to us. We also began two inclosed Works on the right of Pidgeon Hill—between that & the ravine above Mores Mill.

From this time till the 6th. of October nothing occurred of Importance—much deligence was used in debarking, & transporting the Stores—Cannon &ca. from Trebells Landing (distant 6 Miles) on James Riv., to Camp; which for want of Teams went on heavily and in preparing Fascines, Gabions, &ca. for the Siege—as also in reconnoitering the Enemys defences, & their situation as perfectly as possible, to form our parallels & mode of attack.

The Teams which were sent round from the head of Elk, having arrived about this time, we were enabled to bring forward our heavy Artillery & Stores with more convenience and dispatch and every thing being prepared for opening Trenches 1500 Fatiegue men & 2800 to cover them, were ordered for this Service.

6th. Before Morning the Trenches were in such forwardness as to cover the Men from the enemys fire. The work was executed with so much secresy & dispatch that the enemy were, I believe, totally ignorant of our labor till the light of the Morning discovered it to them. Our loss on this occasion was extremely inconsiderable, not more than one Officer (french) & about 20 Men killed & Wounded—the Officer & 15 of which were on our left from the Corps of the Marqs. de St. Simond, who was betrayed by a deserter from the Huzzars that went in & gave notice of his approaching his parrallel.

7th. & 8th. Was employed in compleating our Parallel—finishing the redoubts in them and establishing Batteries.

9th. About 3 o'clock P.M. the French opened a battery on

our extreme left, of 4 Sixteen pounders, and Six Morters & Hawitzers and at 5 oclock an American battery of Six 18s & 24s; four Morters & 2 Hawitzers, began to play from the extremity of our right—both with good effect as they compelled the Enemy to withdraw from their ambrazures the Pieces which had previously kept up a constant firing.

10th. The French opened two batteries on the left of our front parallel—one of 6 twenty four pounders, & 2 Sixteens with 6 Morters & Hawitzers—the other of 4 Sixteen pounders and the Americans two Batteries between those last mentioned & the one on our extreme right the left of which containing 4 Eighteen pounders—the other two Mortars.

The whole of the batteries kept an incessant fire—the Cannon at the Ambrazures of the enemy, with a view to destroy them—the Shells into the Enemy's Works, where by the information of deserters they did much execution.

The French battery on the left, by red hot shot, set fire to (in the course of the Night) the Charon frigate & 3 large Transports which were entirely consumed.

11th. The French opened two other batteries on the left of the parallel, each consisting of 3 Twenty four pounders. These were also employed in demolishing the Ambrazures of the enemys Works & advancd Redoubts.

Two Gentlemen—a Major Granchien & Captn. D'Avilion being sent by Admiral de Grasse to reconnoiter the Enemys Water defences, & state of the River at and near York, seemed favourably disposed to adopt the measure which had been strongly urged of bringing Ships above the Town & made representations accordingly to the Count de Grasse.

12th. Began our second parallel within abt. 300 yards (& in some places less) of the enemys lines and got it so well advanced in the course of the Night as to cover the Men before morning. This business was conducted with the same secresy as the former & undertaken so much sooner than the enemy expected (we should commence a second parallel) that they did not by their conduct, & mode of firing, appear to have had any suspicion of our Working parties till day light discovered them to their Picquets; nor did they much annoy the Trenches in the course of this day (the Parallel being opened last Night from the ravene in front, and on the right flank of the Enemy till it came near to the intersection of the line of fire from the American 4 Gun Battery to the enemy's advanced redoubts on their left. The french Batteries fired over the second parallel.

13th. The fire of the enemy this Night became brisk—both from their Cannon and royals and more injurious to us than it had been; several Men being killed, and many wounded in the Trenches, but the works were not in the smallest degree retarded by it. Our Batteries were begun in the course of the Night and a good deal advanced.

14th. The day was spent in compleating our parallel, and maturing the Batteries of the second parallel. The old batteries were principally directed against the abattis & salient angles of the enemys advanced redoubts on their extreme right & left to prepare them for the intended assault for which the necessary dispositions were made for attacking the two on the left and,

At half after Six in the Evening both were carried—that on their left (on the Bank of the river) by the Americans and the other by the French Troops. The Baron Viominel commanded the left attack & the Marqs. de la fayette the right on which the light Infantry were employed.

In the left redoubt (assaulted by the Americans) there were abt. 45 men under the command of a Major Campbell; of which the Major a Captn. & Ensign, with 17 Men were made Prisoners—But few were killed on the part of the Enemy & the remainder of the Garrison escaped. The right Redoubt attacked by the French, consisted of abt. 120 Men, commanded by a Lieutenant Colo.—of these 18 were killed, & 42 taken Prisoners—among the Prisoners were a Captain and two Lieutenants. The bravery exhibited by the attacking Troops was emulous and praiseworthy—few cases have exhibited stronger proofs of Intripidity coolness and firmness than were shown upon this occasion. The following is our loss in these attacks and since the Investiture of York.

American

Periods	Killed						Wounded							Total
	Colo.	Lt. Colo.	Maj.	Captn.	C. Lieu	Lieut.	Sergt. R & F	Colo.	Lt. Colo.	Majr.	Captn.	C. Lt.	Lieut.	Sergt. R & F	
From the Investe. to openg. 1st. parall.	1					1	4							8	14
To the opening of the 2d. parl.							2							6	8
To the Storm on the 14th.				1			6				1			14	22
At the Storm							8	2	1	2	1	1	1	28	44
Total	1		1			1	20	2	1	3	1	1	1	56	88

The loss of the French from the Investiture to the Assault of the Redoubts Inclusive, is as follow—viz.—

```
Officers—killed . . . . . . . . . . .      2
             Wounded . . . . . . . . . .   7  . . .
                                                        9
Soldiers  . . .  Killed . . . . . . .     50
                 Wounded . . . . . .     127
                                                      177
             Total . . . . . . . . . . . . . . 186
```

15th. Busily employed in getting the Batteries of the Second parallel compleated, and fixing on New ones contiguous to the Redoubts which were taken last Night. Placed two Hawitzers in each of the Captured Redoubts wch. were opened upon the enemy about 5 oclock in the Afternoon.

16th. About four O'clock this Morning the enemy made a Sortee upon our Second parallel and spiked four French pieces of Artillery & two of ours—but the guards of the Trenches advancing quickly upon them they retreated precipitately. The Sally being made upon that part of the parallel which was guarded by the French Troops they lost an officer & 12 Men killed and 1 Officer taken prisoner. The American loss was one Sergeant of Artillery (in the American battery) Wounded. The Enemy, it is said, left 10 dead and lost 3 Prisoners.

About 4 Oclock this afternoon the French opened two Batteries of 2. 24s. & four 16s. each. 3 pieces from the American grand battery were also opened—the others not being ready.

17th. The French opened another Battery of four 24s. & two 16s. and a Morter Battery of 10 Morters and two Hawitzers. The American grand Battery consisting of 12 twenty fours and Eighteen prs.—4 Morters and two Hawitzers.

About ten Oclock the Enemy beat a parley and Lord Cornwallis proposed a cessation of Hostilities for 24 hours, that Commissioners might meet at the house of a Mr. Moore (in the rear of our first parallel) to settle terms for the surrender of the Posts of York and Gloucester. To this he was answered, that a desire to spare the further effusion of Blood would readily incline me to treat of the surrender of the above Posts but previous to the meeting of Commissioners I wished to have his proposals in writing and for this purpose would grant a cessation of hostilities two hours—Within which time he sent out A letter with such proposals (tho' some of them were inadmissable) as led me to believe that there would be no great difficulty in fixing the terms. Accordingly hostilities were suspended for the Night & I proposed my own terms to which if he agreed Commissioners were to meet to digest them into form.

18th. The Commissioners met accordingly; but the business was so procrastinated by those on their side (a Colo. Dundas & a Majr. Ross) that Colo. Laurens & the Viscount De Noailles who were appointed on our part could do no more than make the rough draft of the Articles which were to be submitted for Lord Cornwallis's consideration.

19th. In the Morning early I had them copied and sent word to Lord Cornwallis that I expected to have them signed at 11 Oclock and that the Garrison would March out at two O'clock—both of which were accordingly done. Two redoubts on the Enemys left being possessed (the one by a detachment of French Grenadiers, & the other by American

Infantry) with orders to prevent all intercourse between the army & Country and the Town—while Officers in the several departments were employed in taking acct. of the public Stores &ca.

20th. Winchester & Fort Frederick in Maryland, being the places destined for the reception of the Prisoners they were to have commenced their March accordingly this day, but were prevented by the Commissary of Prisoners not having compleated his Accounts of them & taken the Paroles of the Officers.

21st. The prisoners began their March & set out for the Fleet to pay my respects, & offer my thanks to the Admiral for his important Services and to see if he could not be induced to further co-operations before his final departure from this Coast. Despairing from the purport of my former conferences with him, & the tenor of all his letters, of obtaining more than a Convoy, I contented myself with representing the import, consequences and certain prospect of an attempt upon Charles town and requesting if his orders or other Engagements would not allow him to attend to that great object, that he would nevertheless transport a detachment of Troops to, & cover their debarkation at Wilmington that by reducing the enemy's post there we might give peace to another State with the Troops that would afterwards join the Southern army under the Command of Majr. Genl. Greene.

Having promised the Command of the detachment destined for the Enterprize against Wilmington to the Marqs. de la Fayette in case he could engage the Admiral to convey it & secure the debarkation I left him on Board the Ville de Paris to try the force of his influence to obtain these.

23d. The Marqs. returned with assurances from the Admiral, that he would countenance, & protect with his fleet, the Expedition against Wilmington. Preparations were immediately begun for Embarking Wayne's & Gists Brigades with a sufficiency of Artillery, Stores, & provisions for this purpose.

24th. Received advice, by Express from General Forman, of the British Fleet in the Harbour of New York consisting of 26 Sail of the line, some 50s. & 44s.—Many frigates—fire Ships

& Transports mounting in the whole to 99 Sail had passed the Narrows for the hook, & were as he supposd, upon the point of Sailing for Chesapeak. Notice was immediately communicated to the Count de grasse.

From this time to the 28th. was employed in collecting and taking an acct. of the different species of Stores which were much dispersed and in great disorder.

All the Vessels in public employ in the James River were ordered round for the purpose of receiving and transporting Stores &ca. to the Head of Elk.

28th. Began to Embark the Ordnance and Stores for the above purpose.

Received a Letter from the Count de Grasse, declining the Convoy he had engaged to give the detachment for Wilmington & assigning his reasons for it. This after a suspence & consequent delay of 6 or 7 days obliged me to prepare to March the Troops by Land under the command of M. Genl. St. Clair.

In the Evening of this day Intilligence was received from the Count de Grasse that the British fleet was off the Capes, & consisted of 36 Ships 25 of which were of the line & that he had hove out the Signal for all his People to come on board & prepare to Sail—but many of his Boats & hands being on Shore it could not be effected.

29th. The British Fleet still appeared in the offing without the Capes, but the Wind being unfavourable, and other causes preventing, the French Fleet kept to their Moorings within. In the Evening of this day the former fleet disappeared, & Count de Grasse engaged to remain a few days in the Bay to cover the Water transport of our Stores & Troops up the Bay to the River Elk.

From this time to the 5th. of Novr. was employed in embarking the ordnance & Stores, & the Troops which were returning to the Northward—preparing the detachment for the Southward—providing Cloathing & Stores for the Army commanded by Majr. Genl. Greene—depositing a Magazine at Westham for the use of the Southern States and making other necessary arrangements previous to the division of the army and my return to the North river—also in marching off

467 Convalescents from the British Hospital under escort of Courtlandts York Regiment for Fredericksburg on their way to join their respective Regiments at Winchester & Fort Frederick in Maryland.

5th. The detachment for the Southward, consisting as has been before observed, of Waynes & Gists Brigades (excepting such Men of the Maryland & Virginia lines whose terms of Service would expire before the first of Jany.). Began their March and were to be joined by all the Cavalry that could be equiped of the first—third & fourth Regiments at   .

To Charles Cornwallis

Camp before York, October 17, 1781.

My Lord: I have had the Honor of receiving Your Lordship's Letter of this Date.

An Ardent Desire to spare the further Effusion of Blood, will readily incline me to listen to such Terms for the Surrender of your Posts and Garrisons of York and Gloucester, as are admissible.

I wish previously to the Meeting of Commissioners, that your Lordship's proposals in writing, may be sent to the American Lines: for which Purpose, a Suspension of Hostilities during two Hours from the Delivery of this Letter will be granted. I have the Honor etc.

To Thomas McKean

Head Quarters near York, October 19, 1781.

Sir: I have the Honor to inform Congress, that a Reduction of the British Army under the Command of Lord Cornwallis, is most happily effected. The unremitting Ardor which actuated every Officer and Soldier in the combined Army on this Occasion, has principally led to this Important Event, at an earlier period than my most sanguine Hopes had induced me to expect.

The singular Spirit of Emulation, which animated the whole Army from the first Commencement of our Operations, has filled my Mind with the highest pleasure and Satisfaction, and had given me the happiest presages of Success.

On the 17th instant, a Letter was received from Lord Cornwallis, proposing a Meeting of Commissioners, to consult on Terms for the Surrender of the Posts of York and Gloucester. This Letter (the first which had passed between us) opened a Correspondence, a Copy of which I do myself the Honor to inclose; that Correspondence was followed by the Definitive Capitulation, which was agreed to, and Signed on the 19th. Copy of which is also herewith transmitted, and which I hope, will meet the Approbation of Congress.

I should be wanting in the feelings of Gratitude, did I not mention on this Occasion, with the warmest Sense of Acknowledgements, the very chearfull and able Assistance, which I have received in the Course of our Operations, from his Excellency the Count de Rochambeau, and all his Officers of every Rank, in their respective Capacities. Nothing could equal this Zeal of our Allies, but the emulating Spirit of the American Officers, whose Ardor would not suffer their Exertions to be exceeded.

The very uncommon Degree of Duty and Fatigue which the Nature of the Service required from the Officers of Engineers and Artillery of both Armies, obliges me particularly to mention the Obligations I am under to the Commanding and other Officers of those Corps.

I wish it was in my Power to express to Congress, how much I feel myself indebted to The Count de Grasse and the Officers of the Fleet under his Command for the distinguished Aid and Support which have been afforded by them; between whom, and the Army, the most happy Concurrence of Sentiments and Views have subsisted, and from whom, every possible Cooperation has been experienced, which the most harmonious Intercourse could afford.

Returns of the Prisoners, Military Stores, Ordnance Shipping and other Matters, I shall do myself the Honor to transmit to Congress as soon as they can be collected by the Heads of Departments, to which they belong.

Colo. Laurens and the Viscount de Noiailles, on the Part of the combined Army, were the Gentlemen who acted as Commissioners for formg and settg the Terms of Capitulation and Surrender herewith transmitted, to whom I am particularly obliged for their Readiness and Attention exhibited on the Occasion.

Colo Tilghman, one of my Aids de Camp, will have the Honor to deliver these Dispatches to your Excellency; he will be able to inform you of every minute Circumstance which is not particularly mentioned in my Letter; his Merits, which are too well known to need my observations at this time, have gained my particular Attention, and could wish that they may be honored with the Notice of your Excellency and Congress.

Your Excellency and Congress will be pleased to accept my Congratulations on this happy Event, and believe me to be With the highest Respect etc.

P.S. Tho' I am not possessed of the Particular Returns, yet I have reason to suppose that the Number of Prisoners will be between five and Six thousand, exclusive of Seamen and others.

To Thomas Nelson

Head Quarters near York, Virginia, October 27, 1781.

Dear Sir: As the Assembly of Your State are now sitting, I cannot omit so favorable an occasion to suggest to your Excellency some measures, which I conceive our present circumstances and prospects require should be immediately adopted.

To recruit the Regiments assigned as the quota of this State, to their full establishment, and put them on a respectable footing, is in my opinion, the first great object, which demands the attention of your Legislature. The Arguments, which have formerly been so frequently urged to enforce the expediency of this Measure, must I presume, have carried conviction with them; but unhappily for us, the situation of affairs, especially in the States which were the immediate seat of War, was so perplexed; and the embarrassments of Government so numerous and great, that there could be hitherto but a partial compliance with the Requisitions of Congress on this subject. Many of these difficulties are now removed, and the present moment, which is certainly very favorable to the recruiting service, ought to be eagerly embraced for the purpose.

I will candidly confess to Your Excellency, that my only apprehension (which I wish may be groundless) is, lest the late important success, instead of exciting our exertions, as it ought to do, should produce such a relaxation in the prosecution of the War, as will prolong the calamities of it. While on the other hand, it appears to me to be our only sound policy (let that of the Enemy be what it will) to keep a well-appointed, formidable Army in the field, as long as the War shall continue. For should, the British Cabinet still persevere in their hostile designs and the powers of Europe interpose in their behalf this is a measure of absolute necessity; or should a negociation soon take place, the small expence which will be incurred by raising and keeping up a respectable force, for a short time, will be more than compensated by the advantages to be derived from it, at the pacification.

Since this State, is at present, intirely liberated from the ravages of War, I must take the liberty of recommending, in the most earnest manner, that every possible aid and assistance may be given by it, to the Southern States which are yet invaded, and that General Greene may meet, with that effectual support, from its resources, which he will now have a right to expect.

Had I not considered the present period, too precious to be suffered to pass unimproved for the public good; and that vigorous and decisive efforts ought to be made without a moment's loss of time, for augmenting our force and reducing the power of the Enemy in the Southern States, I should rather have delayed this address, until the sentiments of Congress could have been communicated to you; but the importance of the occasion, will I flatter myself be a sufficient apology to them and your Excellency, for the liberty I am now taking. I have the honor etc.

To Thomas McKean

Mount Vernon, November 15, 1781.

Sir: I have the Honor to acknowledge the Receipt of your Favor. of the 31st. ulto. covering the Resolutions of Congress of 29th. and a Proclamation for a Day of public Prayer and Thanksgiving; And have to thank you Sir! most sincerely for the very polite and affectionate Manner in which these Inclosures have been conveyed. The Success of the Combined Arms against our Enemies at York and Gloucester, as it affects the Welfare and Independence of the United States, I viewed as a most fortunate Event. In performing my Part towards its Accomplishment, I consider myself to have done only my Duty and in the Execution of that I ever feel myself happy. And at the same Time, as it agurs well to our Cause, I take a particular Pleasure in acknowledging, that the interposing Hand of Heaven in the various Instances of our extensive Preparations for this Operation, has been most conspicuous and remarkable.

After the Receipt of your Favor I received Official Information, thro' the Secretary of Congress, of the new Choice of their President. While I congratulate you Sir on a Release from the Fatigues and Trouble of so arduous and important a Task: I beg you to accept my sincere Thanks for the Pleasure and Satisfaction which I have received in the Correspondence with which you have honored me, and the many Interesting Communications of Intelligence with which you have favored me. I am etc.

To Lewis Nicola

Newburgh, May 22, 1782.

Sir: With a mixture of great surprise and astonishment I have read with attention the Sentiments you have submitted to my perusal. Be assured Sir, no occurrence in the course of the War, has given me more painful sensations than your information of there being such ideas existing in the Army as you have expressed, and I must view with abhorrence, and reprehend with severity. For the present, the communicatn. of them will rest in my own bosom, unless some further agitation of the matter, shall make a disclosure necessary.

I am much at a loss to conceive what part of my conduct could have given encouragement to an address which to me seems big with the greatest mischiefs that can befall my Country. If I am not deceived in the knowledge of myself, you could not have found a person to whom your schemes are more disagreeable; at the same time in justice to my own feelings I must add, that no Man possesses a more sincere wish to see ample justice done to the Army than I do, and as far as my powers and influence, in a constitutional way extend, they shall be employed to the utmost of my abilities to effect it, should there be any occasion. Let me conjure you then, if you have any regard for your Country, concern for yourself or posterity, or respect for me, to banish these thoughts from your Mind, and never communicate, as from yourself, or any one else, a sentiment of the like Nature. With esteem I am.

To John Price Posey

Head Qrs. Newburgh, August 7, 1782.

Sir: With a mixture of surprize, concern, and even horror; have I heard of your treatment of the deceased Mr. Custis; in the abuse, and misapplication of the Estate which he had committed, with much confidence I am sure, and I believe personal regard, to your management.

If what I have heard, or the half of it be true, you must not only be lost to the feelings of virtue, honor and common honesty; but you must have suffered an unwarrantable thirst of gain to lead you into errors which are so pregnant with folly and indiscretion, as to render you a mark for every mans arrow to level at. Can you suppose Sir, that a Manager, can dissipate his Employers Estate with impunity? That there are not Laws in every free Country by which justice is to be obtained? or, that the Heirs of Mr. Custis will not find friends who will pursue you to the end of the Earth in order to come at it? If you do, you are proceeding upon exceedingly mistaken principles. but, for a moment only let us suppose that you have taken the advantage of an unsuspecting friend; for such I am sure Mr. Custis was *to you*. and, that you have acted so covertly, as to elude the Law; do you believe that in the hours of cool reflection, in the moment perhaps, when you shall find that ill-gotten pelf can no longer avail you; that your conscience will not smite you severely for such complicated inequity as arises not only from acts of injustice, but the horrors of ingratitude; in abusing the confidence of a man who supposed you incapable of deceiving him, and who was willing, and I believe did, in a great degree, commit his whole property to your care?

But this by the by, I do not mean to put this matter upon the footing of Conscience. Conscience, must have been kicked out of doors before you could have proceeded to the length of selling another Mans Negros for your own emolument and this too after having applyed the greatest part, or the whole of the profits of his Estate to your own benefit. Conscience again seldom comes to a Mans aid while he is in the zenith of health, and revelling in pomp and luxury upon ill gotten spoils; it is generally the *last* act of his life and comes too late to be of much service to others here, or to himself hereafter. But Sir, the footing I expect to see you put this matter upon, is, to settle without delay, such Accts. with the Administrator of Mr. Custis's Estate, whose duty it is to have it done, as you can support by authentic vouchers. That you will show by what authority you have sold any of his Negros, and to what purposes the money has been applied. and lastly, what Crops you have made, what Stocks you have raisd and how they have been disposed of. A settlement of this kind, altho' it should appear by it, that you have applied the greatest part, or even the whole of the money arising fm. the sales of them to your own purposes, will be the next best thing to never having committed the wrong.

How far Mr. Dandridge, as an Administrator, may chuse to push matters, I cannot undertake (never having heard from him on the subject) to say. but this you may *rely on*, that this affair shall be most critically investigated, and probed to the bottom; let the trouble and cost of doing it be what it may;

as a Man therefore who wishes for your own sake as well as that of an injurd family to see you act properly, I advise, and warn you of the consequences of a contrary conduct, being Sir Yr. etc.

To Thomas Paine

Head Quarters, September 18, 1782.

Sir: I have the pleasure to acknowledge your favor of the 7th. instant, informg of your proposal to present me with fifty Copies of your last publication, for the Amusement of the Army.

For this Intention you have my sincere thanks, not only on my own Acco, but for the pleasure, I doubt not, the Gentlemen of the Army will receive from the perusal of your Pamphlets.

Your Observation on the *Period of Seven Years*, as it applies itself to and affects British Minds, are ingenious, and I wish it may not fail of its Effects in the present Instance.

The Measures and the policy of the Enemy are at present in great perplexity and Embarrassment. But I have my fears, whether their Necessities (which are the only operating motive with them) are yet arrived to that point, which must drive them unavoidably into what they will esteem disagreeable and dishonourable Terms of peace; such for Instance as an absolute, unequivocal Admission of American Independence, on the Terms upon which she can accept it.

For this Reason, added to the Obstinancy of the King, and the probable consonant principle of some of his principal Ministers, I have not so full Confidence in the Success of the present Negotiation for peace, as some Gentlemen entertain.

Should Events prove my Jealousies to be illfounded, I shall make myself happy under the Mistake, consoling myself with the Idea of havg erred on the safest Side, and enjoying with as much Satisfaction as any of my Countrymen, the pleasing Issue of our severe Contest.

The case of Capt Asgill has indeed been spun out to a great

Length. But with you, I hope, that its termination will not be unfavourable to this Country. I am &c.

To Benjamin Lincoln

Head Quarters, October 2, 1782.

My dear Sir: Painful as the task is to describe the dark side of our affairs, it some times becomes a matter of indispensable necessity. Without disguize or palliation, I will inform you candidly of the discontents which, at this moment, prevail universally throughout the Army.

The Complaint of Evils which they suppose almost remediless are, the total want of Money, or the means of existing from One day to another, the heavy debts they have already incurred, the loss of Credit, the distress of their Families (i e such as are Maried) at home, and the prospect of Poverty and Misery before them. It is vain Sir, to suppose that Military Men will acquiesce *contently* with bare rations, when those in the Civil walk of life (unacquainted with half the hardships they endure) are regularly paid the emoluments of Office; while the human Mind is influencd by the same passions, and have the same inclinations to endulge it cannt. be. A Military Man has the same turn to sociability as a person in Civil life; he conceives himself equally called upon to live up to his rank; and his pride is hurt when circumstans. restrain him. Only conceive then, the mortification they (even the Genl. Officers) must suffer when they cannot invite a French Officer, a visiting friend, or travelling acquaintance to a better repast than stinking Whiskey (and not always that) and a bit of Beef without Vegitables, will afford them.

The Officers also complain of other hardships which they think might and ought to be remedied without delay, viz, the stopping Promotions where there have been vacancy's open for a long time, the withholding Commissions from those who are justly entitled to them and have Warrants or Certificates of their Appointments from the Executive of their States, and particularly the leaving the compensation for their services, in a loose equivocal state, without ascertaining their claims upon the public, or making provision for the future payment of them.

While I premise, that tho' no one that I have seen or heard of, appears opposed to the principle of reducing the Army as circumstances may require; Yet I cannot help fearing the Result of the measure in contemplation, under present circumstances when I see such a Number of Men goaded by a thousand stings of reflexion on the past, and of anticipation on the future, about to be turned into the World, soured by penury and what they call the ingratitude of the Public, involved in debts, without one farthing of Money to carry them home, after having spent the flower of their days and many of them their patrimonies in establishing the freedom and Independence of their Country, and suffered every thing human Nature is capable of enduring on this side of death; I repeat it, these irritable circumstances, without one thing to sooth their feelings, or frighten the gloomy prospects, I cannot avoid apprehending that a train of Evils will follow, of a very serious and distressing Nature. On the other hand could the Officers be placed in as good a situation as when they came into service, the contention, I am persuaded, would be not who should continue in the field, but who should retire to private life.

I wish not to heighten the shades of the picture, so far as the real life would justify me in doing, or I would give Anecdotes of patriotism and distress which have scarcely ever been paralleled, never surpassed in the history of Mankind; but you may rely upon it, the patience and long sufferance of this Army are almost exhausted, and that there never was so great a spirit of Discontent as at this instant: While in the field, I think it may be kept from breaking out into Acts of Outrage, but when we retire into Winter Quarters (unless the Storm is previously dissipated) I cannot be at ease, respecting the consequences. It is high time for a Peace.

To you, my dear Sir, I need not be more particular in describing my Anxiety and the grounds of it. You are too well acquainted, from your own service, with the real sufferings of the Army to require a longer detail; I will therefore only add that exclusive of the common hardships of a Military life, Our Troops have been, and still are obliged to perform more services, foreign to their proper duty, without gratuity or reward, than the Soldiers of any other Army; for example, the immense labours expended in doing the duties of Artificers in erecting Fortifications and Military Works; the fatigue of building themselves Barracks or Huts annually; And of cutting and transporting Wood for the use of all our Posts and Garrisons, without any expence whatever to the Public.

Of this Letter, (which from the tenor of it must be considered in some degree of a private nature) you may make such use as you shall think proper. Since the principal objects of it were, by displaying the Merits, the hardships, the disposition and critical state of the Army, to give information that might eventually be useful, and to convince you with what entire confidence and esteem. I am etc.

To James McHenry

Verplanks point, October 17, 1782.
My dear Sir: In a visit to the Post of Dobbs's Ferry last Saturday, I accidentally met with Majr. Lynch at that place and received from him your letter of the 30th. Ulto.

In a time like this, of general uncertainty with respect to the designs of the British Court, It is not at all wonderful to find men enquiring at every corner for News; the North sends to the South, and the South to the North, to obtain it. but at present, all, I believe, are equally ignorant. My opinion of the matter is, that you could learn nothing decisive from the Cabinet itself. I have long thought, and still think, they are trying the Chapter of Accidents; and the good or ill success alone of this Campaign, will fix their Councils. If they can obtain any advantages at Sea or in the Indies, East or West no matter where, I am of opinion they will continue the War; if their affairs on the other hand stand still, or continue to retrograde, their stomachs will come to, and they will think seriously of Peace.

In a long letter I had from the Marqs. De la Fayette of the 29th. of June, nothing more could be collected than that doubts and darkness prevailed; that the business of Mr. Greenville seemed to be that of procrastination. In a word, that nothing was fixed; and that the cause of his stay was to see matters in such a train as to see his way clear before he left France.

In New York they are as impatient as us for News, expecting the August Packet to remove all their doubts; but herein they will be mistaken, as later advices than the Packet will bring, leave the Negotiations at Paris in as doubtful a state as ever. A letter which I have just received from Boston gives me the Inclosed as an extract of a letter from Mr. Adams of the 20th. of Augt. at the Hague; the Boston Gazette says the combined Fleets had left the Channel, and that the Jamaica fleet got in four days after. it also gives an Acct. of an Action in the East Indies between the French and British fleets; in wch. it is said to have been a hard fought battle, but in favor of the English. this however being the British Acct. acknowledging that Admiral Hughes was unable (from the shattered condn. of his Ships) to pursue, not much I think, is to be feared from it.

You will recollect the opinion I gave you upon the receipt of Carletons letter of the 2d. of Augt; subsequent events, as far as they have come to my knowledge, prove it was well founded, and I wish future ones may not evince, that to gain time, was all that the British Ministry had in view. the impolicy therefore of suffering ourselves to be lulled by expectations of Peace, because we wish it, and because it is the Interest of great Britain to hold up the idea of it will, more than probably, prove the ruin of our cause; and the disbanding of the Army; for it really appears, from the conduct of the States, that they do not conceive it necessary for the Army to receive any thing but hard knocks; to give them pay is a matter wch. has been long out of the question and we were upon the very point of trying our hand at how we could live without subsistence, as the Superintendant was no longer able to fulfill his Contract with the Victuallers of the Army, and they relinquishing it, till fortunately for us, we met with Gentn, who for an advanced price pr. Ration, have saved us from starvation, or disbandment, by giving a credit; our Horses have long been without every thing their own thriftiness could not supply.

Let any Man, who will allow reason fairplay, ask himself what must be the inevitable consequences of such policy. Have not Military Men the same feelings of those in Civil line? why then shd. the one set receive the constant wages of Service, and the other be continually without them? do the former deserve less for their watchings and toils, for enduring heat and cold, for standing in Sunshine and in Rain, and for the dangers they are continually exposed to for the sake of their Country, and by which means the Man in civil life sits quiet under his own vine and his figtree solacing himself in all the comforts, pleasures and enjoyments, of life, free and unrestrained? let impartiality answer the question. These are matters worthy of serious consideration, the patience, the fortitude, the long and great sufferings of this Army is unexampled in History; but there is an end to all things, and I fear we are very near one to this, which, more than probably, will oblige me to stick very close to the Troops this Winter and to try like a careful physician to prevent if possible the disorders getting to an incurable height. I am etc.

To Benjamin Franklin

Head Quarters, October 18, 1782.

Sir: I have been honored with two Favors of your Excellency; One presented by the Count de Segur, of the 2d. of April, the other delivered by the Prince de Broglie, of the 8th. both which were rendered doubly agreeable, by the pleasure I had in receiving them from the Hands of two such amiable and accomplished Young Gentlemen.

Independent of my Esteem for your Excellency. Be assured Sir! that my respect and Regard for the french Nation at large, to whom this Country is under so great Obligations, as well as the very favorable Impressions I have conceived for their particular Characters, will secure my warmest attention to the persons of these distinguished young Noblemen.

I am much obliged by the political Information, which you have taken the trouble to convey to me; but feel myself much embarrassed in my Wish to make you a Return in kind. At the first of the Season, the Expectations of America were much raised, in Consequence of the Change of the British

Ministry and the Measures of Parliament; but Events have shewn, that their Hopes have risen too high. The Death of the Marquis of Rockingham, the Advancement of the Earl of Shelburne, and the Delays of Negotiation, have given us very different Impressions from those we at first conceived. We now begin again to reflect upon the persevering Obstinacy of the King, the wickedness of his Ministry, and the haughty Pride of the Nation, which Ideas recall to our Minds very disagreeable prospects, and a probable Continuance of our present Trouble.

The military Operations of the Campaign, are drawing to a Close, without any very important Events, on this Side the Water, unless the Evacuation of Charlestown, which is generally expected, but not yet known to me, should take place and form a paragraph in the Page of this Years History.

The British Fleet from the West Indies, still continues in N York. I have not been able yet to decide on the Enemy's Intentions there. It is generally tho't that a detachment of their Troops will sail with them when the fleet returns to the West Indies, where it is conjectured their Efforts for the Winter, will be prosecuted with Vigor. I have the honr etc.

To William Gordon

Verplanks point, October 23, 1782.

Dear Sir: I have been honored with your favor of the 2d. Instt. and thank you for the extract of Mr. Adams's letter.

I never was among the sanguine ones, consequently shall be less disappointed than People of that description, if our Warfare should continue. From hence (it being the opinion of some Men that our expectations have an accordance with our wishes) it may be infered that mine are for a prolongation of the War. But maugre this doctrine, and the opinion of others that a continuation of the War till the Powers of Congress, our political systems, and general form of Government are better established, I can say, with much truth, that there is not a Man in America that more Fervently wishes for Peace, and a return to private life than I do. Nor will any man go back to the rural and domestick enjoyments of it with more Heart felt pleasure than I shall. It is painful to me therefore to accompany this declaration with an opinion that while the present King can maintain the influence of his Crown, and extort Men and Money from his Subjects, so long will the principles by which he is governed push him on in his present wild career. The late change in his Ministry is an evidence of this; and other changes which I suspect will soon take place, will convince us, I fear, of the falacy of our hopes.

It appears to me impracticable for the best Historiographer living, to write a full and correct history of the present revolution who has not free access to the Archives of Congress, those of Individual States, the Papers of the Commander in Chief, and Commanding Officers of seperate departments. Mine, while the War continues, I consider as a species of Public property, sacred in my hands; and of little Service to any Historian who has not that general information which is only to be derived with exactitude from the sources I have mentioned. When Congress then shall open their registers, and say it is proper for the Servants of the public to do so, it will give me much pleasure to afford all the Aid to your labors and laudable undertaking which my Papers can give; 'till one of those periods arrive I do not think myself justified in suffering an inspection of, and any extracts to be taken from my Records.

You will please to accept my sincere and grateful thanks for the kind wishes, and generous Sentiments you express for me. My best respects to Mrs. Gordon. I am etc.

To Joseph Jones

Newburgh, December 14, 1782.

Dear Sir: In the course of a few days Congress will, I expect, receive an Address from the Army on the subject of their grievances.

This Address, tho' couched in very respectful terms, is one of those things which tho' unpleasing is just now unavoidable;

for I was very apprehensive once, that matters would have taken a more unfavourable turn, from the variety of discontents which prevailed at this time.

The temper of the Army is much soured, and has become more irritable than at any period since the commencement of the War. This consideration alone, prevented me (for every thing else seemed to be in a state of inactivity and almost tranquility) from requesting leave to spend this Winter in Virginia, that I might give some attention to my long neglected private concerns.

The dissatisfactions of the Army had arisen to a great and alarming height, and combinations among the Officers to resign, at given periods in a body, were beginning to take place when by some address and management their resolutions have been converted into the form in which they will now appear before Congress. What that Honble. Body can, or will do in the matter, does not belong to me to determine; but policy, in my opinion, should dictate soothing measures; as it is an uncontrovertible fact, that no part of the community has undergone equal hardships, and borne them with the same patience and fortitude, that the Army has done.

Hitherto the Officers have stood between the lower order of the Soldiery and the public. and in more instances than one, at the hazard of their lives, have quelled very dangerous mutinies. But if their discontents should be suffered to rise equally high, I know not what the consequences may be.

The spirit of enthusiasm, which overcame every thing at first, is now done away; it is idle therefore to expect more from Military men, than from those discharging the Civil departments of Government. If both were to fare equally alike with respect to the emoluments of Office, I would answer for it that the Military character should not be the first to complain. But it is an inviduous distinction, and one that will not stand the test of reason or policy, the one set should receive all, and the other no part (or that wch. is next to it) of their pay. In a word, the experiment is dangerous, and if it succeeded would only prove that, the one is actuated by more Zeal than the other, not that they have less occasion for their money. I am etc.

To Tench Tilghman

Newburgh, January 10, 1783.

My dear Sir: I have been favored with your letters of the 22d. and 24th. of last Month from Philadelphia, and thank you for the trouble you have had with my small Commissions. I have sent Mr. Rittenhouse the Glass of such Spectacles as Suit my Eyes, that he may know how to grind his Christals.

Neither Du Portail nor Gouvion are arrived at this place. To the latter, I am refer'd by the Marqs. de la Fayette for some matters which he did not chuse to commit to writing. the sentiments however which he has delivered (with respect to the negociations for Peace) accord precisely with the Ideas I have entertained of this business, ever since the Secession of Mr Fox; viz: that no Peace would be concluded before the meeting of the British Parliament, and that if it did not take place within a Month afterwards, we might lay our Accts. for one more Campaign, at *least*.

The obstinacy of the King, and his unwillingness to acknowledge the Independency of this Country, I have ever looked upon as the greatest obstacles in the way of a Peace. Lord Shelburne, who is not only at the head of the Administration, but has been introducing others of similar sentiments to his own, has declared that nothing but *dire necessity* should ever force the measure. Of this necessity, Men will entertain different opinions. Mr Fox it seems thought the period had arrived some time ago; but Peace is not yet made nor will it, I conceive if the influence of the Crown can draw forth fresh Supplies from the Nation for the purpose of carrying on the War.

By the meeting of Parliament, Lord Shelburne wd have been able to ascertain two things; first, the best terms on which G. Britain cou'd obtain Peace from the Belligerent Powers. Secondly, the ground on which he himself stood. If he found it slippery, and that the voice of the People was for pacific measures, he wou'd then have informd the Parliamt. that after many Months spent in Negociations such were the best terms he cou'd obtain; and that the alternative of accepting them, or preparing vigorously for the prosecution of the War was submitted to their consideration being an extraordy case and decision; A little time therefore, if I have formed a just opinion of the matter, will disclose the result of it. consequently, we shall either soon have peace, or not the most agreeable prospect of War before us; as it appears evident to me that the States, *generally,* are sunk into the most profound lethargy, while *some of them* are running quite retrograde.

The King of G B by his Letters Patent (wch. I have seen) has Authorised Mr. Oswald to treat with any Comr. or Commissioners from the *United States* of America, who shall appear with proper Powers; this certainly, is a capital point gained. It is at least breaking ground on *their* part; and I dare say proved a bitter pill to Royalty; but, it was indispensably necessary to answer one of the points above mentioned, as the American Commissioners would enter on *no business* with Mr. Oswald till his powers were made to answer their purpose; upon the whole I am fixed in an opinion that Peace, or, a pretty long continuance of the War will have been determined on before the adjournment for the Hollidays, and as it will be the middle or last of Feby. before we shall know the result time will pass heavily on in this dreary mansion in which we are fast locked by frost and Snow.

Nothing new has happened in this quarter since you left it, except the abuse of me in a New York paper for having given *false information* to the Count de Vergennes, which says the writer was the occasion of the insinuatn. in *His Letter to me* of a want of B. Justice. I have not seen the Paper, but am told the author of the piece is *quite* in a passion at my want of ingenuity, and ascribes the release of Captn. Asgill to a *peremptory order* from the Ct. of France (in whose Service he places me) notwithstanding the soft and complaisant language of the French Minisr.

Mrs. Washington has received the Shoes you ordered for her and thanks you for your attention to her request. I receive with great sensibility and pleasure your assurances of affection and regard. It would be but a renewal of what I have often repeated to you, that there are few men in the world to whom I am more sincerely attached by inclination than I am to you. With the cause, I hope, most devoutly hope, there will soon be an end to my Military Services. When, as our places of residence will not be far apart, I shall never be more happy than when I see you at Mount Vernon. I shall always be glad to hear from, and keep up a corrispondence with you.

Mrs. Washington joins me in every wish that tends to your happiness. Humphrys and Walker who are the only Gentlemen of the family, with me at present, will speak for themselves. If this finds you at Baltimore I pray my respects to Mr. Caroll and Family. with the greatest esteem etc.

To Bushrod Washington

Newburgh, January 15, 1783.

Dear Bushrod: You will be surprized perhaps at receiving a letter from me; but if the end is answered for which it is written, I shall not think my time miss-spent.

Your Father, who seems to entertain a very favorable opinion of your prudence, and I hope you merit it: in one or two of his letters to me, speaks of the difficulty he is under to make you remittances. Whether this arises from the scantiness of his funds, or the extensiveness of your demands, is matter of conjecture, with me. I hope it is not the latter, because common prudence, and every other consideration which ought to have weight in a reflecting mind is opposed to your requiring more than his conveniency and a regard to his other Children will enable him to pay; and because he holds up no idea in his Letter, which would support me in the conclusion. yet when I take a view of the inexperience of Youth, the temptations in, and vices of Cities; and the distresses to which our Virginia Gentlemen are driven by an accumulation of Taxes and the want of a market; I am almost inclined to ascribe it, in part to both. Therefore, as a friend, I give you the following advice.

Let the object, which carried you to Philadelphia, be always before your Eyes; remember, that it is not the mere study of the Law, but to become eminent in the Profession of it which is to yield honor and profit; the first was your choice, let the second be your ambition. and that dissipation is incompatible with both.

That the Company in which you will improve most, will be least expensive to you; and yet I am not such a Stoic as to suppose you will, or to think it right that you ought, always to be in Company with Senators and Philosophers; but, of the young and juvenile kind let me advise you to be choice. It is easy to make acquaintances, but very difficult to shake them off, however irksome and unprofitable they are found after we have once committed ourselves to them; the indiscretions, and scrapes which very often they involuntarily lead one into, proves equally distressing and disgraceful.

Be courteous to all, but intimate with few, and let those few be well tried before you give them your confidence; true friendship is a plant of slow growth, and must undergo and withstand the shocks of adversity before it is entitled to the appellation.

Let your *heart* feel for the affliction, and distresses of every one, and let your *hand* give in proportion to your purse; remembering always, the estimation of the Widows mite. But, that it is not every one who asketh, that deserveth charity; all however are worthy of the enquiry, or the deserving may suffer.

Do not conceive that fine Clothes make fine Men, any more than fine feathers make fine Birds. A plain genteel dress is more admired and obtains more credit than lace and embroidery in the Eyes of the judicious and sensible.

The last thing I shall mention, is first of importance. and that is, to avoid Gaming. This is a vice which is productive of every possible evil. equally injurious to the morals and health of its votaries. It is the child of Avarice, the brother of inequity, and father of Mischief. It has been the ruin of many worthy familys; the loss of many a man's honor; and the cause of Suicide. To all those who enter the list, it is equally fascinating; the Successful gamester pushes his good fortune till it is over taken by a reverse; the loosing gamester, in hopes of retrieving past misfortunes, goes on from bad to worse; till grown desperate, he pushes at every thing; and looses his all. In a word, few gain by this abominable practice (the profit, if any, being diffused) while thousands are injured.

Perhaps you will say my conduct has anticipated the advice, and that "not one of these cases apply to me." I shall be heartily glad of it. It will add not a little to my happiness, to find those, to whom I am so nearly connected, pursuing the right walk of life; it will be the sure road to my favor, and to those honors, and places of profit, which their Country can bestow, as merit rarely goes unrewarded. I am, etc.

To Nathanael Greene

Newburgh, February 6, 1783.

My dear Sir: I have the pleasure to inform you that your Packet for Govr. Greene which came inclosed to me (in your private Letter of the 12th. of December) was forwarded in an hour after it came to my hands by a Gentleman returning to Rhode Island (Welcome Arnold Esquire); there can be no doubt therefore of its having got safe to the Governor.

It is with a pleasure which friendship only is susceptible of, I congratulate you on the glorious end you have put to hostilities in the Southern States; the honor and advantage of it, I hope, and trust, you will live long to enjoy. when this hemisphere will be equally free is yet in the womb of time to discover; a little while, however 'tis presumed, will disclose the determinations of the British Senate with respect to Peace or War as it seems to be agreed on all hands, that the present Premeir (especially if he should find the opposition powerful) intends to submit the decision of these matters to Parliament. The Speech, the Addresses, and Debates for which we are looking in every direction, will give a data from which the bright rays of the one, or the gloomy prospect of the other, may be discovered.

If Historiographers should be hardy enough to fill the page of History with the advantages that have been gained with unequal numbers (on the part of America) in the course of this contest, and attempt to relate the distressing circumstances under which they have been obtained, it is more than probable that Posterity will bestow on their labors the epithet and marks of fiction; for it will not be believed that such a force as Great Britain has employed for eight years in this Country could be baffled in their plan of Subjugating it by numbers infinitely less, composed of Men oftentimes half starved; always in Rags, without pay, and experiencing, at times, every species of distress which human nature is capable of undergoing.

I intended to have wrote you a long letter on sundry matters but Majr. Burnett popped in unexpectedly, at a time when I was preparing for the Celebration of the day; and was just going to a review of the Troops, previous to the Fue de joy. As he is impatient, from an apprehension of the Sleighing failing. and as he can give you the occurrences of this quarter more in detail than I have time to do, I will refer you to him. I cannot omit informing you however, that I let no oppertunity slip to enquire after your Son George at Princeton, and that it is with pleasure I hear he enjoys good health, and is a fine promising boy.

Mrs. Washington joins me in most Affectionate regards, and best wishes for Mrs Greene and yourself. With great truth and sincerity and every sentiment of friendship. I am etc.

To Thomas Jefferson

Dear Sir   Newburgh 10th. Feby. 1783.

I have been honored with your favor of the 22d. of Jany. from Philadelphia. I feel myself much flattered by your kind remembrance of me in the hour of your departure from this Continent and for the favourable Sentiments you are pleased to entertain of my Services for this our common Country. To merit the approbation of good and virtuous Men is the height of my ambition; and will be a full compensation for all my toils and sufferings in the long and painful contest we have been engaged.

It gave me great pleasure to hear that, the call upon you from Congress, to pass the Atlantic in the Character of one of their Ministers for Negociating Peace, had been repeated. But I hope you will have found the business already done. The speech of his Britainic Majesty is strongly indicative of the Olive branch; and yet, as he observes, unforeseen events may place it out of reach.

At present, the prospect of Peace absorbs, or seems to do so, every other consideration among us; and would, it is to be feared, leave us in a very unprepared state to continue the War if the Negociation at Paris should terminate otherwise than in a general pacification. But I will hope that it is the dearth of other News that fills the Mouths of every person with Peace, while their Minds are employed in contemplating on the Means for prosecuting the War if necessity should drive us to it.

You will please accept my grateful thanks for your obliging offer of Services during your stay in France. To hear frequently from you, will be an honor and very great satisfaction to Dr Sir, Yr Most Obedt and Most Hble Servt.,

To Lund Washington

Newburgh, February 12, 1783.

Dear Lund: Your letter of the 29th. of Jany. came by the last Post. You do not seem to have considered the force and tendency of the words of yr. letter when you talk of the probability *only* of sending me "the long promised account" "the irregularity of them"; not you add "for want of knowledge in keeping them but neglect; your aversion to writing" &ca. &ca. These are but other words for saying, "as I am not fond of writing, and it is *quite* immaterial whether you have any knowledge or information of your private concerns or whether the accts. are kept properly or not, I have delayed, and do not know how much longer I may continue to delay bringing you acquainted with these accts. irregular as they are."

Delicacy hitherto, and a hope that you long ago would have seen into the propriety of the measure, without a hint of it from me, has restrained me from telling you that annual Accts. of my Crops, together with the receipts and expenditure of my money, state of my stocks, &ca. ought to have been sent to me as regularly as the year came about. It is not to be supposed, that all the avocations of my public duties, great and laborious as they have been, could render me totally insensible to the *only means* by which myself and family; and the character I am to maintain in life hereafter, is to be supported, or that a precise acct. of these matters would not have been exceedingly satisfactory to me. Instead of this, except the Acct. rendered at Valley forge in the year 1778 I have received none since I left home; and not till after two or 3 applications in the course of last year could I get any acct. of the Crop of the preceeding one; and then only of the Corn by the Post on Sunday last.

I have often told you, and I repeat it with much truth; that the entire confidence which I placed in your integrity made me easy, and I was always happy at thinking that my Affairs were in your hands, which I could not have been, if they had been under the care of a common Manager; but this did not exempt me from the desires which all men have, of knowing the exact state of them. I have now to beg that you will not only send me the Account of your receipts, and expenditures of Specie; but of every kind of money subsequent to the Acct. exhibited at Valley Forge, which ended sometime in April 1778.

I want to know before I come home (as I shall come home with empty pockets whenever Peace shall take place) how Affairs stand with me, and what my dependence is.

I wish to know also, what I have to expect from the Wheat of 1781 and 82, as you say the two Crops are so blended that they cannot be rendered seperately? How are settlements to be made with and justice done to the several Parties Interested under these circumstances?

To Alexander Hamilton

Newburgh 4th. Mar: 1783

Dear Sir,

I have received your favor of February   & thank you for the information & observations it has conveyed to me. I shall always think myself obliged by a free communication of sentiments, & have often thought (but suppose I thought wrong as it did not accord with the practice of Congress) that the public interest might be benefitted, if the Commander in Chief of the Army was let more into the political & pecuniary state of our affairs than he is. Enterprises, & the adoption of Military & other arrangements that might be exceedingly proper in some circumstances, would be altogether improper in others. It follows then by fair deduction, that where there is a want of information there must be chance medley; & a man may be upon the brink of a precipice before he is aware of his danger—when a little foreknowledge might enable him to avoid it. But this by the by. The hint contained in your letter, and the knowledge I have derived from the public Gazettes respecting the nonpayment of Taxes contain all the information I have received of the danger that stares us in the face, on acct. of our funds, and so far was I from conceiving that our finances were in so deplorable a state, *at this time*, that I had imbibed ideas from some source or another, that with the prospect of a loan from Holland we should be able to rub along.

To you, who have seen the danger, to which the Army has been exposed, to a political dissolution for want of subsistence, & the unhappy spirit of licentiousness which it imbibed by becoming in one or two instances its own proveditors, no observations are necessary to evince the fatal tendency of such a measure; but I shall give it as my opinion, that it would at this day be productive of Civil commotions & end in blood. Unhappy situation this! God forbid we should be involved in it.

The predicament in which I stand as Citizen & Soldier, is as critical and delicate as can well be conceived. It has been the subject of many contemplative hours. The sufferings of a complaining army on one hand, and the inability of Congress and tardiness of the States on the other, are the forebodings of evil; & may be productive of events which are more to be depricated than prevented; but I am not without hope, if there is such a disposition shewn as prudence & policy dictates, to do justice, your apprehensions, in case of Peace, are greater than there is cause for. In this however I may be mistaken, if those ideas, which you have been informed are propagated in the Army, should be extensive; the source of which may be easily traced; as the old leven, *it is said*, for I have no proof of it, is again beginning to work, under the mask of the most perfect dissimulation & apparent cordiallity.

Be these things as they may, I shall pursue the same steady line of conduct which has governed me hitherto; fully convinced that the sensible, and discerning part of the army, cannot be unacquainted (although I never took pains to inform them) of the services I have rendered it, on more occasions than one. This, and pursuing the suggestions of your letter, which I am happy to find coincides with my own practice for several months past, & which was the means of directing the business of the Army into the Channel it now is, leaves me under no *great* apprehension of its exceeding the bounds of reason & moderation, nothwithstanding the prevailing sentiment in the Army is, that the prospect of compensation for past Services will terminate with the War.

The just claims of the Army ought, and it is to be hoped will, have their weight with every sensible Legislature in the Union, if Congress point to their demands; shew (if the case is so) the reasonableness of them, and the impracticability of complying with them without their aid. In any other point of view it would, in my opinion, be impolitic to introduce the Army on the Tapis; lest it should excite jealousy, and bring on its concomitants. The States cannot, surely, be so devoid of common sense, common honesty, & common policy as to refuse their aid on a full, clear, & candid representation of facts from Congress; more especially if these should be enforced by members of their own body; who might demonstrate what the inevitable consequences of failure must lead to.

In my opinion it is a matter worthy of consideration how far an Adjournment of Congress for a few months is advisable. The Delegates in that case, if they are in unison themselves respecting the great defects of their Constitution may represent them fully & boldly to their Constituents. To me, who know nothing of the business which is before Congress, nor of the arcanum, it appears that such a measure would tend to promote the public weal; for it is clearly my opinion, unless Congress have powers competent to all *general* purposes, that the distresses we have encountered, the expences we have incurred, and the blood we have spilt in the course of an Eight years war, will avail us nothing.

The contents of your letter is known only to myself and your prudence will direct what should be done with this. With great esteem and regard I am Dr Sir Yr. Most Obedt. Servt

General Orders

Head Quarters, Newburgh, Tuesday, March 11, 1783. Parole Quebec.   Countersigns Richmond, Sunbury.

For the day tomorrow Major Reading.

For duty the 5th. Massachusetts regiment.

The Commander in Chief having heard that a General meeting of the officers of the Army was proposed to be held this day at the Newbuilding in an anominous paper which was circulated yesterday by some unknown person conceives (altho he is fully persuaded that the good sense of the officers would induce them to pay very little attention to such an irregular invitation) his duty as well as the reputation and true interest of the Army requires his disapprobation of such disorderly proceedings, at the same time he requests the General and Field officers with one officer from each company and a proper representative of the staff of the Army will assemble at 12 o'clock on Saturday next at the Newbuilding to hear the report of the Committee of the Army to Congress.

After mature deliberation they will devise what further measures ought to be adopted as most rational and best calculated to attain the just and important object in view. The senior officer in Rank present will be pleased to preside and report the result of the Deliberations to the Commander in Chief.

Congress have been pleased to promote Captain Job Sumner of the 3d Massachusetts regiment to be a Major in the Army and to take rank from the 1st. of October 1782.

To Alexander Hamilton

Newburgh 12th. Mar. 1783.

Dear Sir,

When I wrote to you last we were in a state of tranquility, but after the arrival of a certain Gentleman, who shall be nameless at present, from Philadelphia, a storm very suddenly arose with unfavourable prognostics; which tho' diverted for a moment is not yet blown over, nor is it in my power to point to the issue.

The Papers which I send officially to Congress, will super-cede the necessity of my remarking on the tendency of them. The notification and address, both appeared at the same in-stant, on the day preceding the intended meeting. The first of these I got hold of the same afternoon; the other, not till next morning.

There is something very misterious in this business. It ap-pears, reports have been propagated in Philadelphia, that dan-gerous combinations were forming in the Army; and this at a time when there was not a syllable of the kind in agitation in Camp. It also appears, that upon the arrival in Camp of the Gentleman above alluded to such sentiments as these were immediately circulated: That it was universally expected the army would not disband untill they had obtained justice; That the public creditors looked up to them for Redress of their own grievances, wd afford them every aid, and even join them in the Field if necessary; That some members of Congress wished the measure might take effect, in order to compel the public, particularly the delinquent States, to do justice; with many other suggestions of a similar nature.

From this, and a variety of other considerations, it is firmly believed, by *some*, the scheme was not only planned but also digested and matured in Philadelphia; but in my opinion shall be suspended till I have a better ground to found one on. The matter was managed with great art; for as soon as the Minds of the Officers were thought to be prepared for the transac-tion, the anonymous invitations and address to the Officers were put in circulation, through every state line in the army. I was obliged therefore, in order to arrest on the spot, the

foot that stood wavering on a tremendous precipice; to prevent the Officers from being taken by surprize while the passions were all inflamed, and to rescue them from plunging
themselves into a gulph of Civil horror from which there
might be no receding, to issue the order of the 11th. This was
done upon the principle that it is easier to divert from a
wrong, and point to a right path, than it is to recall the hasty
and fatal steps which have been already taken.

It is commonly supposed if the Officers had met agreeably
to the anonymous summons, with their feelings all alive, Resolutions might have been formed the consequences of which
may be more easily conceived than described. Now they will
have leizure to view the matter more calmly, and will act more
seriously. It is to be hoped they will be induced to adopt more
rational measures, and wait a while longer for a settlement of
their accts., the postponing of which, appears to be the most
plausible and almost the only article of which designing men
can make an improper use, by insinuating (which they really
do) that it is done with design that Peace may take place and
prevent any adjustment of accts. which say they would inevitably be the case if the war was to cease tomorrow. Or supposing the best, you would have to dance attendance at public
Offices at great distances perhaps, and equally great expences
to obtain a settlement, which would be highly injurious, nay
ruinous to you. This is their language.

Let me beseech you therefore, my good Sir, to urge this
matter earnestly, and without further delay. The situation of
these Gentlemen I do verily believe, is distressing beyond description. It is affirmed to me, that a large part of them have
no better prospect before them than a Goal, if they are turned
loose without liquidation of accts. and an assurance of that
justice to which they are so worthily entitled. To prevail on
the Delegates of those States through whose means these difficulties occur, it may, in my opinion, with propriety be suggested to them, if any disastrous consequences should follow,
by reason of their delinquency, that they must be answerable
to God & their Country for the ineffable horrors which may
be occasioned thereby.

I am Dear Sir Yr. Most Obedt. Serv

P.S. I have received your letter of the 5th. & have put that matter in train which was mentioned in it.

I am this instant informed, that a second address to the Officers, distinguished No. 2, is thrown into circulation. The Contents, evidently prove that the Author is in, or near Camp; and that the following words, erased in the second page of this Letter, ought not to have met with this treatment. viz: "By others, that it is the illegitimate offspring of a person in the army."

To Joseph Jones

Newburgh, March 12, 1783.

Dear Sir: I have received your letter of the 27th. Ulto., and thank you for the information and freedom of your communications.

My Official Letter to Congress of this date will inform you of what has happened in this Quarter, in addition to which, it may be necessary it should be known to you, and to such others as you may think proper, that the temper of the Army, tho. very irritable on acct. of their long-protracted sufferings has been apparently extremely quiet while their business was depending before Congress untill four days past. In the mean time, it should seem reports have been propagated in Philadelphia that dangerous combinations were forming in the Army; and this at a time when there was not a syllable of the kind in agitation in Camp.

It also appears, that upon the arrival of a certain Gentleman from Phila. in Camp, whose name, I do not, at present, incline to mention such sentiments as these were immediately and industriously circulated. That it was universally expected the Army would not disband untill they had obtained Justice. That the public creditors looked up to them for redress of their Grievances, would afford them every aid, and even join them in the Field, if necessary. That some Members of Congress wished the Measure might take effect, in order to compel the Public, particularly the delinquent States, to do justice. With many other suggestions of a Similar Nature; from whence, and a variety of other considerations it is generally believ'd the Scheme was not only planned, but also digested and matured in Philadelphia; and that some people have been playing a double game; spreading at the Camp and in Philadelphia Reports and raising jealousies equally void of Foundation untill called into being by their vile Artifices; for as soon as the Minds of the Army were thought to be prepared for the transaction, anonymous invitations were circulated, requesting a general Meeting of the Officers next day; at the same instant many Copies of the Address to the Officers of the Army was scattered in every State line of it.

So soon as I obtained knowledge of these things, I issued the order of the 11th. (transmitted to Congress;) in order to rescue the foot, that stood wavering on the precipice of despair, from taking those steps which would have lead to the abyss of misery while the passions were inflamed, and the mind trimblingly alive with the recollection of past sufferings, and their present feelings. I did this upon the principle that it is easier to divert from a wrong to a right path, than it is to recall the hasty and fatal steps which have been already taken.

It is commonly supposed, if the Officers had met agreeable to the anonymous Summons, resolutions might have been formed, the consequences of which may be more easily conceived than expressed. Now, they will have leisure to view the matter more calmly and seriously. It is to be hoped they will be induced to adopt more rational measures, and wait a while longer for the settlemts. of their Accts.; the postponing of which gives more uneasiness in the Army than any other thing. there is not a man in it, who will not acknowledge that Congress have not the means of payment; but why not say they, one and all, liquidate the Accts. and certifie our dues? are we to be disbanded and sent home without this? Are we, afterwards, to make individual applications for such settlements at Philadelphia, or any Auditing Office in our respective states; to be shifted perhaps from one board to another; dancing attendence at all, and finally perhaps be postponed till we loose the substance in pursuit of the shadow. While they are agitated by these considerations there are not wanting insiduous characters who tell them, it is neither the wish nor the intention of the public to settle your accounts; but to delay this business under one pretext or another till Peace wch. we are upon the eve of, and a seperation of the Army takes place when it is well known a generl settlement never can be effected and that individual loss, in this instance, becomes a public gain.

However derogatory these ideas are with the dignity, honor, and justice of government yet in a matter so interesting to the Army, and at the same time so easy to be effected by the Public, as that of liquidating the Accounts, is delayed without any apparent, or obvious necessity, they will have their place in a mind that is soured and irritated. Let me entreat you therefore my good Sir to push this matter to an issue, and if there are Delegates among you, who are really opposed to doing justice to the Army, scruple not to tell them, if matters should come to extremity, that they must be answerable for all the ineffable horrors which may be occasioned thereby. I am etc.

To Elias Boudinot

Head Quarters, March 12, 1783.

Sir: It is with inexpressible concern, I make the followg Report to your Excellency.

Two Days ago, anonymous papers were circulated in the Army, requesting a general meeting of the Officers on the next Day. A Copy of one of these papers is inclosed, No. 1. About the same Time, another anonymous paper purporting to be an Address to the Officers of the Army, was handed about in a clandestine manner: a Copy of this is mark'd No 2 To prevent any precipitate and dangerous Resolutions from being taken at this perilous moment, while the passions were all inflamed; as soon as these things came to my knowledge, the next Morng. I issued the inclosed Order No. 3. And in this situation the Matter now rests.

As all opinion must be suspended until after the meeting on Saturday, I have nothing further to add, except a Wish, that the measures I have taken to dissipate a Storm, which had gathered so suddenly and unexpectedly, may be acceptable to Congress: and to assure them, that in every vicisitude of Circumstances, still actuated with the greatest zeal in their Service, I shall continue my utmost Exertions to promote the wellfare of my Country under the most lively Expectation, that Congress have the best Intentions of doing ample Justice to the Army, as soon as Circumstances will possibly admit. With the highest Respect etc.

PS. Since writing the foregoing another anonymous paper is put in Circulation, Copy of which is inclosed, No. 4

Speech to the Officers of the Army

Head Quarters, Newburgh, March 15, 1783.

Gentlemen: By an anonymous summons, an attempt has been made to convene you together; how inconsistent with the rules of propriety! how unmilitary! and how subversive of all order and discipline, let the good sense of the Army decide.

In the moment of this Summons, another anonymous production was sent into circulation, addressed more to the feelings and passions, than to the reason and judgment of the Army. The author of the piece, is entitled to much credit for the goodness of his Pen and I could wish he had as much credit for the rectitude of his Heart, for, as Men see thro' different Optics, and are induced by the reflecting faculties of the Mind, to use different means, to attain the same end, the Author of the Address, should have had more charity, than to mark for Suspicion, the Man who should recommend moderation and longer forbearance, or, in other words, who should not think as he thinks, and act as he advises. But he had another plan in view, in which candor and liberality of Sentiment, regard to justice, and love of Country, have no part; and he was right, to insinuate the darkest suspicion, to effect the blackest designs.

That the Address is drawn with great Art, and is designed to answer the most insidious purposes. That it is calculated to impress the Mind, with an idea of premeditated injustice in the Sovereign power of the United States, and rouse all those resentments which must unavoidably flow from such a belief. That the secret mover of this Scheme (whoever he may be) intended to take advantage of the passions, while they were warmed by the recollection of past distresses, without giving time for cool, deliberative thinking, and that composure of Mind which is so necessary to give dignity and stability to measures is rendered too obvious, by the mode of conducting the business, to need other proof than a reference to the proceeding.

Thus much, Gentlemen, I have thought it incumbent on me to observe to you, to shew upon what principles I opposed the irregular and hasty meeting which was proposed to have been held on Tuesday last: and not because I wanted a disposition to give you every oppertunity consistent with your own honor, and the dignity of the Army, to make known your grievances. If my conduct heretofore, has not evinced to you, that I have been a faithful friend to the Army, my declaration of it at this time wd. be equally unavailing and improper. But as I was among the first who embarked in the cause of our common Country. As I have never left your side one moment, but when called from you on public duty. As I have been the constant companion and witness of your Distresses, and not among the last to feel, and acknowledge your Merits. As I have ever considered my own Military reputation as inseperably connected with that of the Army. As my Heart has ever expanded with joy, when I have heard its praises, and my indignation has arisen, when the mouth of detraction has been opened against it, it can *scarcely be supposed*, at this late stage of the War, that I am indifferent to its interests. But, how are they to be promoted? The way is plain, says the anonymous Addresser. If War continues, remove into the unsettled Country; there establish yourselves, and leave an ungrateful Country to defend itself. But who are they to defend? Our Wives, our Children, our Farms, and other property which we leave behind us. or, in this state of hostile seperation, are we to take the two first (the latter cannot be removed), to perish in a Wilderness, with hunger, cold and nakedness? If Peace takes place, never sheath your Swords Says he untill you have obtained full and ample justice; this dreadful alternative, of either deserting our Country in the extremest hour of her distress, or turning our Arms against it, (which is the apparent object, unless Congress can be compelled into instant compliance) has something so shocking in it, that humanity revolts at the idea. My God! what can this writer have in view, by recommending such measures? Can he be a friend to the Army? Can he be a friend to this Country? Rather, is he not an insidious Foe? Some Emissary, perhaps, from New York, plotting the ruin of both, by sowing the seeds of discord and seperation between the Civil and Military powers of the Continent? And what a Compliment does he pay to our Understandings, when he recommends measures in either alternative, impracticable in their Nature?

But here, Gentlemen, I will drop the curtain, because it wd. be as imprudent in me to assign my reasons for this opinion, as it would be insulting to your conception, to suppose you stood in need of them. A moment's reflection will convince every dispassionate Mind of the physical impossibility of carrying either proposal into execution.

There might, Gentlemen, be an impropriety in my taking notice, in this Address to you, of an anonymous production, but the manner in which that performance has been introduced to the Army, the effect it was intended to have, together with some other circumstances, will amply justify my observations on the tendency of that Writing. With respect to the advice given by the Author, to suspect the Man, who shall recommend moderate measures and longer forbearance, I spurn it, as every Man, who regards that liberty, and reveres that justice for which we contend, undoubtedly must; for if Men are to be precluded from offering their Sentiments on a matter, which may involve the most serious and alarming consequences, that can invite the consideration of Mankind, reason is of no use to us; the freedom of Speech may be taken away, and, dumb and silent we may be led, like sheep, to the Slaughter.

I cannot, in justice to my own belief, and what I have great reason to conceive is the intention of Congress, conclude this Address, without giving it as my decided opinion, that that Honble Body, entertain exalted sentiments of the Services of the Army; and, from a full conviction of its merits and sufferings, will do it compleat justice. That their endeavors, to discover and establish funds for this purpose, have been unwearied, and will not cease, till they have succeeded, I have not a doubt. But, like all other large Bodies, where there is a variety of different Interests to reconcile, their deliberations are slow. Why then should we distrust them? and, in consequence of that distrust, adopt measures, which may cast a shade over that glory which, has been so justly acquired; and tarnish the reputation of an Army which is celebrated thro' all Europe, for its fortitude and Patriotism? and for what is this done? to bring the object we seek nearer? No! most certainly, in my opinion, it will cast it at a greater distance.

For myself (and I take no merit in giving the assurance, being induced to it from principles of gratitude, veracity and justice), a grateful sence of the confidence you have ever placed in me, a recollection of the chearful assistance, and prompt obedience I have experienced from you, under every vicissitude of Fortune, and the sincere affection I feel for an Army, I have so long had the honor to Command, will oblige me to declare, in this public and solemn manner, that, in the attainment of compleat justice for all your toils and dangers, and in the gratification of every wish, so far as may be done consistently with the great duty I owe my Country, and those powers we are bound to respect, you may freely command my Services to the utmost of my abilities.

While I give you these assurances, and pledge myself in the most unequivocal manner, to exert whatever ability I am possessed of, in your favor, let me entreat you, Gentlemen, on your part, not to take any measures, which, viewed in the calm light of reason, will lessen the dignity, and sully the glory you have hitherto maintained; let me request you to rely on the plighted faith of your Country, and place a full confidence in the purity of the intentions of Congress; that, previous to your dissolution as an Army they will cause all your Accts. to be fairly liquidated, as directed in their resolutions, which were published to you two days ago, and that they will adopt the most effectual measures in their power, to render ample justice to you, for your faithful and meritorious Services. And let me conjure you, in the name of our common Country, as you value your own sacred honor, as you respect the rights of humanity, and as you regard the Military and National character of America, to express your utmost horror and detestation of the Man who wishes, under any specious pretences, to overturn the liberties of our Country, and who wickedly attempts to open the flood Gates of Civil discord, and deluge our rising Empire in Blood. By thus determining, and thus acting, you will pursue the plain and direct road to the attainment of your wishes. You will defeat the insidious designs of our Enemies, who are compelled to resort from open force to secret Artifice. You will give one more distinguished proof of unexampled patriotism and patient virtue, rising superior to the pressure of the most complicated sufferings; And you will, by the dignity of your Conduct, afford occasion for Posterity to say, when speaking of the glorious example you have exhibited to Mankind, "had this day been wanting, the World had never seen the last stage of perfection to which human nature is capable of attaining."

To Elias Boudinot

Head Quarters, March 16, 1783.

Sir: I have the Honor to inform your Excellency, for the satisfaction of Congress, that the meeting of the Officers, which was mentioned in my last, has been held Yesterday: and, that it has terminated in a manner, which I had reason to expect, from a knowledge of that good Sense and steady Patriotism of the Gentlemen of the Army, which, on frequent Occasions, I have discovered.

The Report of the Meeting, with the other papers, which will be necessary to accompany it, I shall do myself the Honor to transmit to Congress, as soon as they can possibly be prepared. With the highest Respect etc.

To Joseph Jones

Newburgh, March 18, 1783.

The storm which seemed to be gathering with unfavourable prognostics, when I wrote to you last, is dispersed; and we are again in a state of tranquility. But do not, My dear Sir, suffer this appearance of tranquility to relax your endeavors to bring the requests of the Army to an issue. believe me, the Officers are too much pressed by their present wants, and rendered too sore by the recollection of their past sufferings to be touched much longer upon the string of forbearance, in matters wherein they can see no cause for delay. Nor would I have further reliance placed on any influence of mine to dispel other Clouds if any should arise, from the causes of the last.

By my official Letter to Congress, and the Papers inclosed in it, you will have a full view of my assurances to, and the expectations of the Army; and I perswade myself that the well wishers to both, and of their Country, will exert themselves to the utmost to irradicate the Seeds of distrust, and give every satisfaction that justice requires, and the means which Congress possess, will enable them to do.

In a former letter I observed to you, that a liquidation of Accts, in order that the Ballances might be ascertained, is the great object of the Army; and certainly nothing can be more reasonable. To have these Ballances discharged at this, or in any short time; however desirable, they know is impracticable, and do not expect it; altho', in the meantime, they must labour under the pressure of those sufferings; which is felt more sensibly by a comparison of circumstances.

The situation of these Gentlemen merit the attention of every thinking and grateful mind. As Officers, they have been *obliged* to dress, and appear in character, to effect which, they have been *obliged* to anticipate their pay, or participate their Estates. By the first, debts have been contracted. by the latter, their patrimony is injured. To disband Men therefore under these circumstances, before their Accts. are liquidated, and the Ballances ascertained, would be, to sett open the doors of the Goals, and then to shut them upon Seven Years faithful and

painful Services. Under any circumstances which the nature
of the case will admit, they must be considerable Sufferers;
because necessity will compell them to part with their certificates for whatever they will fetch; to avoid the evil I have
mentioned above: and how much this will place them in the
hands of unfeeling, avaricious speculators a recurrence to past
experience will sufficiently prove.

It may be said by those who have no disposition to compensate the Services of the Army, that the Officers have too
much penetration to place dependance (in any alternative)
upon the strength of their own Arm; I will readily concede to
these Gentlemen that no good could result from such an attempt; but I hope they will be equally candid in acknowledging, that much mischief may flow from it. and that nothing is
too extravagent to expect from men, who conceive they are
ungratefully, and unjustly dealt by; especially too if they can
suppose that characters are not wanting, to foment every passion which leads to discord, and that there are—but—time
shall reveal the rest.

Let it suffice, that the very attempt, wd. imply a want of
justice, and fix an indelible stain upon our national character;
as the whole world, as well from the enemies publication
(without any intention to serve us) as our own, must be
strongly impressed with the sufferings of this army from hunger, cold and nakedness. in allmost every stage of the War.
Very sincerely etc.

To Lund Washington

Newburg, March 19, 1783.

Dear Lund: I did not write to you by the last Post. I was
too much engaged at the time, in counteracting a most insidious attempt to disturb the repose of the army, and sow the
seeds of discord between the civil and military powers of the
continent, to attend to small matters. The author of this attempt, whoever he may be, is yet behind the curtain; and as
conjectures might be wrong, I shall be silent at present. The
good sense, the virtue, and patient forbearance of the army,

on this, as upon every other trying occasion which has happened to call them into action, has again triumphed: and appear'd with more lustre than ever. But if the States will not furnish the supplies required by Congress, thereby enabling the Superintendant of Finance to feed, clothe, and pay the army; if they suppose the war can be carried on without money, or that money can be borrowed without permanent funds to pay the interest of it; if they have no regard to justice, because it is attended with expence; if gratitude to men, who have rescued them from the jaws of danger and brought them to the haven of Independence and Peace, is to subside, as danger is removed; If the sufferings of the army, who have borne, and forborne more than any other class of men in the Ud. States; expending their health; and many of them their all, in an unremitted service of near eight years in the field, encountering hunger, cold and nakedness, are to be forgotten; if it is presumed there is no bounds to the patience of the army; or that when peace takes place, their claims for pay due, and rewards promised may die with the military non-existence of its member. If such, I say, should be the sentiments of the States; and that their conduct, or the conduct of some, does but too well warrant the conclusion, well may another anonymous addresser step forward, and with more effect than the last did, say with him, "You have arms in your hands, do justice to yourselves, and never sheath the sword, 'till you have obtained it." How far men, who labour under the pressure of accumulated distress, and are irritated by a belief that they are treated with neglect, ingratitude, and injustice in the extreme, might be worked upon by designing men, is worthy of very serious consideration. But justice, policy, yea common Sense, must tell every man that the creditors of the continent, cannot receive payments unless funds are provided for it, and that our national character, if these are much longer neglected, must be stamped with indelible infamy in every Nation of the world where the fact is known. I am etc.

To Nathanael Greene

Head Quarters, March 31, 1783.

Dear Sir: I have the pleasure to inclose to you a letter from the Marquis de la fayette, which came under cover to me, by the Packet Triumph, dispatched by the Marquis and the Count de Estaing from Cadiz to Phila.

All the Accounts which this Vessel has bro't, of a Conclusion of a General Peace, you will receive before this can reach you.

You will give the highest Credit to my Sincerity, when I beg you to accept my warmest Congratulations on this glorious and happy Event, an Event which crowns all our Labors and will sweeten the Toils which we have experienced in the Course of Eight Years distressing War. The Army here, universally participate in the general Joy which this Event has diffused, and, from this Consideration, together with the late Resolutions of Congress, for the Commutation of the Half pay, and for a Liquidation of all their Accounts, their Minds are filled with the highest Satisfaction. I am sure you will join with me in this additional occasion of joy.

It remains only for the States to be Wise, and to establish their Independence on that Basis of inviolable efficacious Union, and firm Confederation, which may prevent their being made the Sport of European Policy; may Heaven give them Wisdom to adopt the Measures still necessary for this important Purpose. I have the honor etc.

To Alexander Hamilton

Dear Sir,   Newburgh 31st. March 1783

I have duly received your favors of the 17th. & 24th. ulto. I rejoice most exceedingly that there is an end to our warfare, and that such a field is opening to our view as will, with wisdom to direct the cultivation of it, make us a great, a respectable, and happy People; but it must be improved by other means than State politics, and unreasonable jealousies & prejudices; or (it requires not the second sight to see that) we shall be instruments in the hands of our Enemies, & those

European powers who may be jealous of our greatness in Union to dissolve the confederation; but to attain this, altho the way seems extremely plain, is not so easy.

My wish to see the Union of these States established upon liberal & permanent principles, & inclination to contribute my mite in pointing out the defects of the present Constitution, are equally great. All my private letters have teemed with these Sentiments, & whenever this topic has been the subject of conversation, I have endeavoured to diffuse & enforce them; but how far any further essay, by me, might be productive of the wished for end, or appear to arrogate more than belongs to me, depends so much upon popular opinion, & the temper & disposition of People, that it is not easy to decide. I shall be obliged to you however for the thoughts which you have promised me on this subject, and as soon as you can make it convenient.

No man in the United States is, or can be more deeply impressed with the necessity of a reform in our present Confederation than myself. No man perhaps has felt the bad effects of it more sensibly; for to the defects thereof, & want of Powers in Congress may justly be ascribed the prolongation of the War, & consequently the Expences occasioned by it. More than half the perplexities I have experienced in the course of my command, and almost the whole of the difficulties & distress of the Army, have there origin here; but still, the prejudices of some, the designs of others, and the mere machinery of the majority, makes address & management necessary to give weight to opinions which are to Combat the doctrine of those different classes of men, in the field of Politics.

I would have been more full on this subject but the bearer (in the clothing department) is waiting. I wish you may understand what I have written.

I am Dr Sir Yr. Most Obedt Servt

Honble. Alexr Hamilton.

The inclosed extract of a Letter to Mr Livingston, I give you in confidence. I submit it to your consideration, fully persuaded that you do not want inclination to gratify the Marquis's wishes as far as is consistent with our National honor.

To Theodorick Bland

Newburgh, April 4, 1783.

Dear Sir; On Sunday last the Baron de Steuben handed me your obliging favor of the 22d. Ulto. permit me to offer you my unfeigned thanks for the clear and candid opinions which you have given me of European politics. your reasonings upon the conduct of the different Powers at War would have appeard conclusive had not the happy event which has been since announced to us, and on which I most sincerely congratulate you, proved how well they were founded. Peace has given rest to speculative opinions respecting the time, and terms of it. the first has come as soon as we could well have expected under the disadvantages we have labd. and the latter, is abundantly satisfactory. It is now the bounden duty of every one, to make the blessing thereof as diffusive as possible.

Nothing would so effectually bring this to pass as the removal of those local prejudices which intrude upon and embarrass that great line of policy which alone can make us a free, happy, and powerful people. Unless our Union can be fixed upon such a basis as to accomplish these ends certain I am we have toiled, bled and spent our treasure to very little purpose.

We have now a National character to establish; and it is of the utmost importance to stamp favourable impressions upon it; let justice then be one of its characteristics, and gratitude another. Public Creditors of every denomination will be comprehended in the first. the Army in a particular manner will have a claim to the latter; to say that no distinction can be made between the claims of public Creditors, is to declare that there is no difference in circumstances or, that the Services of all Men are equally alike. This Army, is of near 8 years standing; 6 of which they have spent in the field, without any other shelter from the inclemency of the Seasons than Tents, or such Houses as they could build for themselves, without expence to the public. they have encountered hunger, cold and Nakedness. they have fought many Battles, and bled freely. they have lived without pay, and in consequence of it, Officers as well as Men have been obliged to subsist upon their Rations:

they have often, very often been reduced to the necessity of eating Salt Porke or Beef not for a day or a week only but months together without Vegetables of any kind or money to buy them; or a cloth to wipe on. Many of them, to do better and to dress as Officers, have contracted heavy Debts, or spent their Patrimonies; the first see the doors of Goals opening to receive them whilst those of the latter are shut against them. Is there no discrimination then, no extra exertion to be made in favor of men under these Circumstances in the hour of their Military dissolution? Or, if no worse comes of it, are they to be turned a drift soured and discontented, complaining of the ingratitude of their Country, and under the irritation of these passions to become fit subjects for unfavourable impressions and unhappy dissentions? for permit me to add, tho' every Man in the Army feels the distress of his situatn it is not every one that reasons to the cause of it.

I would not, from the observatns. here made, be understood to mean that Congress should (because I know they cannot, nor does the Army expect it) pay the full arrearages due to them till Continental or State funds are established for the purpose; they would, from what I can learn, go home contented; nay *thankful*, to receive what I have mentioned in a more public Letter of this date, and in the manner there expressed. and surely this may be effected with proper exertions; or what possibility was there of keeping the Army together if the war had continued when the victualling, clothing and other exps were to have Another thing Sir, (as I mean to be frank and free in my communications on this subject) I will not conceal from you, it is dissimilarities in the payments of Men in Civil and Military life. the first receive every thing, the other get nothing, but bare subsistence. They ask what this is owing to? and reasons have been assigned, which say they, amount to this: that Men in Civil life have stronger passions and better pretensions to indulge them or less virtue and regd. for their Country than us; otherwise, as we are all contending for the same prize and equally interested in the attainment of it, why is not the burthen borne equally.

These, and other comparisons, which are unnecessary to enumerate, give a keener edge to their feelings, and contribute not a little to sour their tempers.

As it is the first wish of my Soul to see the war happily and speedily terminated, and those who are now in Arms return to Citizenship with good dispositions, I think it a duty which I owe to candor and to friendship to point you to such things as will have a tendency to harmony and to bring them to pass. With great esteem etc.

To Marquis de Lafayette

Head Qrs., Newburgh, April 5, 1783.
My dear Marqs.: It is easier for you to conceive than for me to express the sensibility of my Heart at the communications in your letter of the 5th. of Feby. from Cadiz. It is to these communications we are indebted for the only acct. yet recd of a general Pacification. My mind upon the receipt of this news was instantly assailed by a thousand ideas, all of them contending for pre-eminence, but believe me my dear friend none could supplant, or ever will eradicate that gratitude, which has arisen from a lively sense of the conduct of your Nation: from my obligations to many illustrious characters of it, among whom (I do not mean to flatter, when) I place you at the head of them; And from my admiration of the Virtues of your August Sovereign; who at the same time that he stands confessed the Father of his own people, and defender of American rights has given the most exalted example of moderation in treating with his Enemies.

We now stand an Independent People, and have yet to learn political Tactics. We are placed among the Nations of the Earth, and have a character to establish; but how we shall acquit ourselves time must discover; the probability, at least I fear it is, that local, or state Politics will interfere too much with that more liberal and extensive plan of government which wisdom and foresight, freed from the mist of prejudice, would dictate; and that we shall be guilty of many blunders in treading this boundless theatre before we shall have arrived at any perfection in this Art. In a word that the experience which is purchased at the price of difficulties and distress, will alone convince us that the honor, power, and true Interest of this

Country must be measured by a Continental scale; and that every departure therefrom weakens the Union, and may ultimately break the band, which holds us together. To avert these evils, to form a Constitution that will give consistency, stability and dignity to the Union; and sufficient powers to the great Council of the Nation for general purposes is a duty which is incumbent upon every Man who wishes well to his Country, and will meet with my aid as far as it can be rendered in the private walks of life; for hence forward my Mind shall be unbent; and I will endeavor to glide down the stream of life 'till I come to that abyss, from whence no traveller is permitted to return.

The Armament wch. was preparing at Cadiz, and in which you were to have acted a distinguished part would have carried such conviction with it, that it is not to be wondered at, that Great Britain should have been impressed with the force of such reasoning. To this cause I am perswaded, the Peace is to be ascribed. Your going to Madrid from thence, instead of coming immediately to this Country, is another instance My Dear Marquis of your Zeal for the American Cause; and lays a fresh claim to the gratitude of her Sons, who will, at all times, receive you with open Arms; but as no Official dispatches are yet received, either at Phila. or New York of the completion of the treaty, nor any measures taken for the reduction of the Army, my detention therewith is quite uncertain; to say then (at this time) where I may be at the epoch for your intended visit to this Continent is too vague even for conjecture; but nothing can be more true than that the pleasure with which I shall receive you, will be equal to your wishes. I shall be better able to determine *then* than now, on the practicability of accompanying you to France. A Country to which I shall ever feel a Warm Affection; and if I do not pay it that tribute of respect which is to be derived from a visit it may be ascribed with more justice to any other cause, than a want of inclination; or the pleasure of going there under the auspices of your friendship.

I have already observed, that the determinations of Congress, if they have come to any, respecting the Army, is yet unknown to me; but as you wish to be informed of *every thing* that concerns it, I do, for your satisfaction, transmit authentic documents of some very interesting occurrences, which have happened within the last Six Months. but I ought first to have premised, that from accumulated sufferings, and little or no prospect of relief, the discontents of the Officers last Fall put on the threatning appearance of a total resignation, till the business was diverted into the channel which produced the Address and Petition to Congress which stands first on the file herewith inclosed. I shall make no comment on these proceedings; to one as well acquainted with the sufferings of the American Army as you are, it is unnecessary, it will be sufficient to observe, that the more Virtue and forbearance of it is tried, the more resplendent it appears. My hopes, that the military exit of this valuable class of the community will exhibit such a proof of Amor patriæ as will do them honor in the page of history.

These papers with my last letter (which was intended to go by Colo. Gouvion, containing extensive details of Military Plans) will convey to you every information I can give, in the present uncertainty, worthy of attention. If you should get sleepy, and tired of reading them, recollect, for my exculpation, that it is in compliance with your request, I have run into such prolixity.

I made a proper use of the confidential part of your Letter of the 5th. of Feby.

The scheme, my dear Marqs. which you propose as a precedent, to encourage the emancipation of the black people of this Country from that state of Bondage in wch. they are held, is a striking evidence of the benevolence of your Heart. I shall be happy to join you in so laudable a work; but will defer going into a detail of the business, 'till I have the pleasure of seeing you.

Lord Stirling is no more; he died at Albany in Jany. last, very much regretted. Colo. Barber was snatched from us about the same time; in a way equally unexpected, sudden and distressing; leaving many friends to bemoan his fate.

Tilghman is on the point of Matrimony with a namesake and Couzin; Sister to Mrs. Carroll of Baltimore. It only remains for me now, My dear Marqs., to make a tender of my respectful Compliments in which Mrs. Washington unites, to Madame La Fayette; and to wish you, her, and your little

offspring, all the happiness this life can afford. I will extend
my Compliments to the Gentlemen, with whom I have the
honor of an Acquaintance, in your circle. I need not add how
happy I shall be to see you in America, and more particularly
at Mount Vernon; or with what truth and warmth of Affection
I am etc.

To Guy Carleton

Head Quarters, April 9, 1783.

Sir: I feel great satisfaction from your Excellency's Dispatches by Capt Stapleton, conveying to me the Joyful enun-
ciation of your having received Official Accounts of the
Conclusion of a general Peace, and a cessation of Hostilities.

Without official Authority from Congress, but perfectly
relying on your Excellency's Communication, I can at this
Time, only issue my Orders to the American Outposts to suspend all Acts of Hostilities until further Orders; this shall be
instantly done; And I shall be happy in the momentary Expectation of having it in my power to publish, to the American
Army, a general Cessation of all Hostilities between G Britain
and America.

To your Excellency's Observations respecting particular Articles of the Peace, I am obliged to reply, that it rests with
Congress to direct Measures for the Observance of all the
Articles contained in the provisional Treaty. Your Excellency
may be assured that as soon as I receive my Instructions from
the Sovereign power of the United States, I shall rejoice, in
giving every facility in my power to carry it into compleat
Execution, that Article of the Treaty which respects the Restitution of all prisoners of War, being perfectly disposed to
contribute to the diffusing, as much as possible, the happy
Effects of this great Event.

I thank your Excellency for the Assurances you are pleased
to express of your readiness to cultivate that spirit of perfect
good Will and Conciliation, which you wish should take place
between the King of G Britain and the United States and the
Citizens and Subjects of both Countries. And I beg Sir, that

you will please to accept a Tender from me of reciprocal good Will and Attention; accompanied with sincere Congratulations to your Excellency on this joyful Restoration of Peace and general Tranquility, with an earnest Wish, that, resting on the firm Basis of mutual Interest and good Will, it may prove as lasting as it is happy. I have the Honor etc.

General Orders

Friday, April 18, 1783.
Parole Kenalal.   Countersigns Litchfield, Montreal.
Brigadier Genl. Stark.
For the day tomorrow
Brigd. Qr. Mr. York Brigade.
The Jersey regiment gives the Guards and the Jersey battalion the fatigues tomorrow.

The Commander in Chief orders the Cessation of Hostilities between the United States of America and the King of Great Britain to be publickly proclaimed tomorrow at 12 o'clock at the Newbuilding, and that the Proclamation which will be communicated herewith, be read tomorrow evening at the head of every regiment and corps of the army. After which the Chaplains with the several Brigades will render thanks to almighty God for all his mercies, particularly for his over ruling the wrath of man to his own glory, and causing the rage of war to cease amongst the nations.

Although the proclamation before alluded to, extends only to the prohibition of hostilities and not to the annunciation of a general peace, yet it must afford the most rational and sincere satisfaction to every benevolent mind, as it puts a period to a long and doubtful contest, stops the effusion of human blood, opens the prospect to a more splendid scene, and like another morning star, promises the approach of a brighter day than hath hitherto illuminated the Western Hemisphere; on such a happy day, a day which is the harbinger of Peace, a day which compleats the eighth year of the war, it would be ingratitude not to rejoice! it would be insensibility not to participate in the general felicity.

The Commander in Chief far from endeavouring to stifle the feelings of Joy in his own bosom, offers his most cordial Congratulations on the occasion to all the Officers of every denomination, to all the Troops of the United States in General, and in particular to those gallant and persevering men who had resolved to defend the rights of their invaded country so long as the war should continue. For these are the men who ought to be considered as the pride and boast of the American Army; And, who crowned with well earned laurels, may soon withdraw from the field of Glory, to the more tranquil walks of civil life.

While the General recollects the almost infinite variety of Scenes thro which we have passed, with a mixture of pleasure, astonishment, and gratitude; While he contemplates the prospects before us with rapture; he can not help wishing that all the brave men (of whatever condition they may be) who have shared in the toils and dangers of effecting this glorious revolution, of rescuing Millions from the hand of oppression, and of laying the foundation of a great Empire, might be impressed with a proper idea of the dignifyed part they have been called to act (under the Smiles of providence) on the stage of human affairs: for, happy, thrice happy shall they be pronounced hereafter, who have contributed any thing, who have performed the meanest office in erecting this steubendous *fabrick* of *Freedom* and *Empire* on the broad basis of Indipendency; who have assisted in protecting the rights of humane nature and establishing an Asylum for the poor and oppressed of all nations and religions. The glorius task for which we first fleu to Arms being thus accomplished, the liberties of our Country being fully acknowledged, and firmly secured by the smiles of heaven, on the purity of our cause, and the honest exertions of a feeble people (determined to be free) against a powerful Nation (disposed to oppress them) and the Character of those who have persevered, through every extremity of hardship; suffering and danger being immortalized by the illustrious appellation of the *patriot Army*. Nothing now remains but for the actors of this mighty Scene to preserve a perfect, unvarying, consistency of character through the very last act; to close the Drama with applause; and to retire from the Military Theatre with the same approbation of Angells and men which have crowned all their former vertuous Actions. For this purpose no disorder or licentiousness must be tolerated, every considerate and well disposed soldier must remember it will be absolutely necessary to wait with patience untill peace shall be declared or Congress shall be enabled to take proper measures for the security of the public stores &ca.; as soon as these Arrangements shall be made the General is confident there will be no delay in discharging with every mark of distinction and honor all the men enlisted for the war who will then have faithfully performed their engagements with the public. The General has already interested himself in their behalf; and he thinks he need not repeat the assurances of his disposition to be useful to them on the present, and every other proper occasion. In the mean time he is determined that no Military neglects or excesses shall go unpunished while he retains the command of the Army.

The Adjutant General will have such working parties detailed to assist in making the preperations for a general rejoycing as the Chief Engineer with the Army shall call for, and the Quarter Master Genl. will also furnish such materials as he may want.

The Quarter Master General will without delay procure such a number of Discharges to be printed as will be sufficient for all the men enlisted for the War; he will please to apply to Head Quarters for the form.

An extra ration of liquor to be issued to *every* man tomorrow, to drink Perpetual Peace, Independence and Happiness to the United States of America.

The Inspection of the Army for the month of March will take place in the following manner and on the following days: The Maryland Detachment and Jersey brigade on Monday the 21st; York brigade and Hampshire, 22d; 1st Massachusetts Brigade, 23d; 2d, do, 24th; 3d, do, 25th; The regiments of Artillery at Westpoint, Sappers and Miners, Col. Swifts regimt. and Invalids, 28th; Connecticut brigade, 29th.

Inspection Rolls may be had at Colonel Stewarts Quarters.

Lieutenant Samuel Mellish of the 3d. Massachusetts regiment is appointed Aid de Camp to Brigadier General Greaton and is to be respected accordingly. This appointment to take place from the 7th. day of January last.

To Tench Tilghman

Newburgh, April 24, 1783.

Dear Sir: I received with much pleasure the kind congratulations contained in your letter of the 25th. Ulto. from Philadelphia, on the honorable termination of the War. No Man, indeed, can relish the approaching Peace with more heart felt, and grateful satisfaction than myself. A Mind always upon the stretch, and tortured with a diversity of perplexing circumstances, needed a respite; and I anticipate the pleasure of a little repose and retirement. It has been happy for me, always to have Gentlemen about me willing to share my troubles, and help me out of difficulties. to none of these can I ascribe a greater share of merit than to you.

I can scarce form an idea at this moment, when I shall be able to leave this place. the distresses of the Army for want of Money; the embarrassments of Congress, and the conseqt. delays, and disappointments on all sides, encompass me with difficulties; and produce, every day, some fresh source for uneasiness. But as I now see the Port opening to which I have been steering, I shall persevere till I have gained admittence. I will then leave the States to improve their present constitution, so as to make the Peace and Independency for which we have fought and obtained, a blessing to Millions yet unborn; but to do this, liberallity must supply the place of prejudice, and *unreasonable* jealousies must yield to that confidence, which *ought* to be placed in the sovereign Power of these States. In a word the Constitution of Congress must be competent to the *general purposes of Government*; and of such a nature as to bind us together. otherwise, we may well be compared to a rope of Sand, and shall as easily be broken and in a short time become the sport of European politics, altho' we might have no *great* inclination to jar among ourselves.

From the intimation in your Letter, and what I have heard from others I presume this letter will find you in the State of Wedlock. On this happy event I pray you, and your Lady, to accept of my best wishes, and sincerest congratulations; in which Mrs. Washington joins hers most cordially. With the most Affectionate esteem, etc.

Circular to State Governments

Head Quarters, Newburgh, June 8, 1783.

Sir: The great object for which I had the honor to hold an appointment in the Service of my Country, being accomplished, I am now preparing to resign it into the hands of Congress, and to return to that domestic retirement, which, it is well known, I left with the greatest reluctance, a Retirement, for which I have never ceased to sigh through a long and painful absence, and in which (remote from the noise and trouble of the World) I meditate to pass the remainder of life in a state of undisturbed repose; But before I carry this resolution into effect, I think it a duty incumbent on me, to make this my last official communication, to congratulate you on the glorious events which Heaven has been pleased to produce in our favor, to offer my sentiments respecting some important subjects, which appear to me, to be intimately connected with the tranquility of the United States, to take my leave of your Excellency as a public Character, and to give my final blessing to that Country, in whose service I have spent the prime of my life, for whose sake I have consumed so many anxious days and watchfull nights, and whose happiness being extremely dear to me, will always constitute no inconsiderable part of my own.

Impressed with the liveliest sensibility on this pleasing occasion, I will claim the indulgence of dilating the more copiously on the subjects of our mutual felicitation. When we consider the magnitude of the prize we contended for, the doubtful nature of the contest, and the favorable manner in which it has terminated, we shall find the greatest possible reason for gratitude and rejoicing; this is a theme that will afford infinite delight to every benevolent and liberal mind, whether the event in contemplation, be considered as the source of present enjoyment or the parent of future happiness; and we shall have equal occasion to felicitate ourselves on the lot which Providence has assigned us, whether we view it in a natural, a political or moral point of light.

The Citizens of America, placed in the most enviable condition, as the sole Lords and Proprietors of a vast Tract of

Continent, comprehending all the various soils and climates of the World, and abounding with all the necessaries and conveniencies of life, are now by the late satisfactory pacification, acknowledged to be possessed of absolute freedom and Independency; They are, from this period, to be considered as the Actors on a most conspicuous Theatre, which seems to be peculiarly designated by Providence for the display of human greatness and felicity; Here, they are not only surrounded with every thing which can contribute to the completion of private and domestic enjoyment, but Heaven has crowned all its other blessings, by giving a fairer oppertunity for political happiness, than any other Nation has ever been favored with. Nothing can illustrate these observations more forcibly, than a recollection of the happy conjuncture of times and circumstances, under which our Republic assumed its rank among the Nations; The foundation of our Empire was not laid in the gloomy age of Ignorance and Superstition, but at an Epocha when the rights of mankind were better understood and more clearly defined, than at any former period, the researches of the human mind, after social happiness, have been carried to a great extent, the Treasures of knowledge, acquired by the labours of Philosophers, Sages and Legislatures, through a long succession of years, are laid open for our use, and their collected wisdom may be happily applied in the Establishment of our forms of Government; the free cultivation of Letters, the unbounded extension of Commerce, the progressive refinement of Manners, the growing liberality of sentiment, and above all, the pure and benign light of Revelation, have had a meliorating influence on mankind and increased the blessings of Society. At this auspicious period, the United States came into existence as a Nation, and if their Citizens should not be completely free and happy, the fault will be intirely their own.

Such is our situation, and such are our prospects: but notwithstanding the cup of blessing is thus reached out to us, notwithstanding happiness is ours, if we have a disposition to seize the occasion and make it our own; yet, it appears to me there is an option still left to the United States of America, that it is in their choice, and depends upon their conduct, whether they will be respectable and prosperous, or contempt-

able and miserable as a Nation; This is the time of their political probation, this is the moment when the eyes of the
whole World are turned upon them, this is the moment to
establish or ruin their national Character forever, this is the
favorable moment to give such a tone to our Federal Government, as will enable it to answer the ends of its institution, or
this may be the ill-fated moment for relaxing the powers of
the Union, annihilating the cement of the Confederation, and
exposing us to become the sport of European politics, which
may play one State against another to prevent their growing
importance, and to serve their own interested purposes. For,
according to the system of Policy the States shall adopt at this
moment, they will stand or fall, and by their confirmation or
lapse, it is yet to be decided, whether the Revolution must
ultimately be considered as a blessing or a curse: a blessing or
a curse, not to the present age alone, for with our fate will
the destiny of unborn Millions be involved.

With this conviction of the importance of the present Crisis,
silence in me would be a crime; I will therefore speak to your
Excellency, the language of freedom and of sincerity, without
disguise; I am aware, however, that those who differ from me
in political sentiment, may perhaps remark, I am stepping out
of the proper line of my duty, and they may possibly ascribe
to arrogance or ostentation, what I know is alone the result
of the purest intention, but the rectitude of my own heart,
which disdains such unworthy motives, the part I have hitherto acted in life, the determination I have formed, of not
taking any share in public business hereafter, the ardent desire
I feel, and shall continue to manifest, of quietly enjoying in
private life, after all the toils of War, the benefits of a wise and
liberal Government, will, I flatter myself, sooner or later convince my Countrymen, that I could have no sinister views in
delivering with so little reserve, the opinions contained in this
Address.

There are four things, which I humbly conceive, are essential to the well being, I may even venture to say, to the existence of the United States as an Independent Power:

1st. An indissoluble Union of the States under one Federal
Head.

2dly. A Sacred regard to Public Justice.

3dly. The adoption of a proper Peace Establishment, and

4thly. The prevalence of that pacific and friendly Disposition, among the People of the United States, which will induce them to forget their local prejudices and policies, to make those mutual concessions which are requisite to the general prosperity, and in some instances, to sacrifice their individual advantages to the interest of the Community.

These are the Pillars on which the glorious Fabrick of our Independency and National Character must be supported; Liberty is the Basis, and whoever would dare to sap the foundation, or overturn the Structure, under whatever specious pretexts he may attempt it, will merit the bitterest execration, and the severest punishment which can be inflicted by his injured Country.

On the three first Articles I will make a few observations, leaving the last to the good sense and serious consideration of those immediately concerned.

Under the first head, altho' it may not be necessary or proper for me in this place to enter into a particular disquisition of the principles of the Union, and to take up the great question which has been frequently agitated, whether it be expedient and requisite for the States to delegate a larger proportion of Power to Congress, or not, Yet it will be a part of my duty, and that of every true Patriot, to assert without reserve, and to insist upon the following positions, That unless the States will suffer Congress to exercise those prerogatives, they are undoubtedly invested with by the Constitution, every thing must very rapidly tend to Anarchy and confusion, That it is indispensable to the happiness of the individual States, that there should be lodged somewhere, a Supreme Power to regulate and govern the general concerns of the Confederated Republic, without which the Union cannot be of long duration. That there must be a faithfull and pointed compliance on the part of every State, with the late proposals and demands of Congress, or the most fatal consequences will ensue, That whatever measures have a tendency to dissolve the Union, or contribute to violate or lessen the Sovereign Authority, ought to be considered as hostile to the Liberty and Independency of America, and the Authors of them treated accordingly, and lastly, that unless we can be enabled by the concurrence of the States, to participate of the fruits of the Revolution, and enjoy the essential benefits of Civil Society, under a form of Government so free and uncorrupted, so happily guarded against the danger of oppression, as has been devised and adopted by the Articles of Confederation, it will be a subject of regret, that so much blood and treasure have been lavished for no purpose, that so many sufferings have been encountered without a compensation, and that so many sacrifices have been made in vain. Many other considerations might here be adduced to prove, that without an entire conformity to the Spirit of the Union, we cannot exist as an Independent Power; it will be sufficient for my purpose to mention but one or two which seem to me of the greatest importance. It is only in our united Character as an Empire, that our Independence is acknowledged, that our power can be regarded, or our Credit supported among Foreign Nations. The Treaties of the European Powers with the United States of America, will have no validity on a dissolution of the Union. We shall be left nearly in a state of Nature, or we may find by our own unhappy experience, that there is a natural and necessary progression, from the extreme of anarchy to the extreme of Tyranny; and that arbitrary power is most easily established on the ruins of Liberty abused to licentiousness.

As to the second Article, which respects the performance of Public Justice, Congress have, in their late Address to the United States, almost exhausted the subject, they have explained their Ideas so fully, and have enforced the obligations the States are under, to render compleat justice to all the Public Creditors, with so much dignity and energy, that in my opinion, no real friend to the honor and Independency of America, can hesitate a single moment respecting the propriety of complying with the just and honorable measures proposed; if their Arguments do not produce conviction, I know of nothing that will have greater influence; especially when we recollect that the System referred to, being the result of the collected Wisdom of the Continent, must be esteemed, if not perfect, certainly the least objectionable of any that could be devised; and that if it shall not be carried into immediate execution, a National Bankruptcy, with all its deplorable consequences will take place, before any different Plan can possibly be proposed and adopted; So pressing are the present circumstances! and such is the alternative now offered to the States!

The ability of the Country to discharge the debts which have been incurred in its defence, is not to be doubted, an inclination, I flatter myself, will not be wanting, the path of our duty is plain before us, honesty will be found on every experiment, to be the best and only true policy, let us then as a Nation be just, let us fulfil the public Contracts, which Congress had undoubtedly a right to make for the purpose of carrying on the War, with the same good faith we suppose ourselves bound to perform our private engagements; in the mean time, let an attention to the chearfull performance of their proper business, as Individuals, and as members of Society, be earnestly inculcated on the Citizens of America, that will they strengthen the hands of Government, and be happy under its protection: every one will reap the fruit of his labours, every one will enjoy his own acquisitions without molestation and without danger.

In this state of absolute freedom and perfect security, who will grudge to yield a very little of his property to support the common interest of Society, and insure the protection of Government? Who does not remember, the frequent declarations, at the commencement of the War, that we should be compleatly satisfied, if at the expence of one half, we could defend the remainder of our possessions? Where is the Man to be found, who wishes to remain indebted, for the defence of his own person and property, to the exertions, the bravery, and the blood of others, without making one generous effort to repay the debt of honor and of gratitude? In what part of the Continent shall we find any Man, or body of Men, who would not blush to stand up and propose measures, purposely calculated to rob the Soldier of his Stipend, and the Public Creditor of his due? and were it possible that such a flagrant instance of Injustice could ever happen, would it not excite the general indignation, and tend to bring down, upon the Authors of such measures, the aggravated vengeance of Heaven? If after all, a spirit of disunion or a temper of obstinacy and perverseness, should manifest itself in any of the States, if such an ungracious disposition should attempt to frustrate all the happy effects that might be expected to flow from the Union, if there should be a refusal to comply with the requisitions for Funds to discharge the annual interest of the public debts, and if that refusal should revive again all those jealousies and produce all those evils, which are now happily removed, Congress, who have in all their Transaction shewn a great degree of magnanimity and justice, will stand justified in the sight of God and Man, and the State alone which puts itself in opposition to the aggregate Wisdom of the Continent, and follows such mistaken and pernicious Councils, will be responsible for all the consequences.

For my own part, conscious of having acted while a Servant of the Public, in the manner I conceived best suited to promote the real interests of my Country; having in consequence of my fixed belief in some measure pledged myself to the Army, that their Country would finally do them compleat and ample Justice; and not wishing to conceal any instance of my official conduct from the eyes of the World, I have thought proper to transmit to your Excellency the inclosed collection of Papers, relative to the half pay and commutation granted by Congress to the Officers of the Army; From these communications, my decided sentiment will be clearly comprehended, together with the conclusive reasons which induced me, at an early period, to recommend the adoption of the measure, in the most earnest and serious manner. As the proceedings of Congress, the Army, and myself are open to all, and contain in my opinion, sufficient information to remove the prejudices and errors which may have been entertained by any; I think it unnecessary to say any thing more, than just to observe, that the Resolutions of Congress, now alluded to, are undoubtedly as absolutely binding upon the United States, as the most solemn Acts of Confederation or Legislation. As to the Idea, which I am informed has in some instances prevailed, that the half pay and commutation are to be regarded merely in the odious light of a Pension, it ought to be exploded forever; that Provision, should be viewed as it really was, a reasonable compensation offered by Congress, at a time when they had nothing else to give, to the Officers of the Army, for services then to be performed. It was the only means to prevent a total dereliction of the Service, It was a part of their hire, I may be allowed to say, it was the price of their blood and of your Independency, it is therefore more than a common debt, it is a debt of honour, it can never be considered as a Pension or gratuity, nor be cancelled until it is fairly discharged.

With regard to a distinction between Officers and Soldiers, it is sufficient that the uniform experience of every Nation of the World, combined with our own, proves the utility and propriety of the discrimination. Rewards in proportion to the aids the public derives from them, are unquestionably due to all its Servants; In some Lines, the Soldiers have perhaps generally had as ample a compensation for their Services, by the large Bounties which have been paid to them, as their Officers will receive in the proposed Commutation, in others, if besides the donation of Lands, the payment of Arrearages of Cloathing and Wages (in which Articles all the component parts of the Army must be put upon the same footing) we take into the estimate, the Bounties many of the Soldiers have received and the gratuity of one Year's full pay, which is promised to all, possibly their situation (every circumstance being duly considered) will not be deemed less eligible than that of the Officers. Should a farther reward, however, be judged equitable, I will venture to assert, no one will enjoy greater satisfaction than myself, on seeing an exemption from Taxes for a limited time, (which has been petitioned for in some instances) or any other adequate immunity or compensation, granted to the brave defenders of their Country's Cause; but neither the adoption or rejection of this proposition will in any manner affect, much less militate against, the Act of Congress, by which they have offered five years full pay, in lieu of the half pay for life, which had been before promised to the Officers of the Army.

Before I conclude the subject of public justice, I cannot omit to mention the obligations this Country is under, to that meritorious Class of veteran Non-commissioned Officers and Privates, who have been discharged for inability, in consequence of the Resolution of Congress of the 23d of April 1782, on an annual pension for life, their peculiar sufferings, their singular merits and claims to that provision need only be known, to interest all the feelings of humanity in their behalf:

nothing but a punctual payment of their annual allowance can rescue them from the most complicated misery, and nothing could be a more melancholy and distressing sight, than to behold those who have shed their blood or lost their limbs in the service of their Country, without a shelter, without a friend, and without the means of obtaining any of the necessaries or comforts of Life; compelled to beg their daily bread from door to door! suffer me to recommend those of this discription, belonging to your State, to the warmest patronage of your Excellency and your Legislature.

It is necessary to say but a few words on the third topic which was proposed, and which regards particularly the defence of the Republic, As there can be little doubt but Congress will recommend a proper Peace Establishment for the United States, in which a due attention will be paid to the importance of placing the Militia of the Union upon a regular and respectable footing; If this should be the case, I would beg leave to urge the great advantage of it in the strongest terms. The Militia of this Country must be considered as the Palladium of our security, and the first effectual resort in case of hostility; It is essential therefore, that the same system should pervade the whole; that the formation and discipline of the Militia of the Continent should be absolutely uniform, and that the same species of Arms, Accoutrements and Military Apparatus, should be introduced in every part of the United States; No one, who has not learned it from experience, can conceive the difficulty, expence, and confusion which result from a contrary system, or the vague Arrangements which have hitherto prevailed.

If in treating of political points, a greater latitude than usual has been taken in the course of this Address, the importance of the Crisis, and the magnitude of the objects in discussion, must be my apology: It is, however, neither my wish or expectation, that the preceding observations should claim any regard, except so far as they shall appear to be dictated by a good intention, consonant to the immutable rules of Justice; calculated to produce a liberal system of policy, and founded on whatever experience may have been acquired by a long and close attention to public business. Here I might speak with the more confidence from my actual observations, and, if it would not swell this Letter (already too prolix) beyond the bounds I had prescribed myself: I could demonstrate to every mind open to conviction, that in less time and with much less expence than has been incurred, the War might have been brought to the same happy conclusion, if the resourses of the Continent could have been properly drawn forth, that the distresses and disappointments which have very often occurred, have in too many instances, resulted more from a want of energy, in the Continental Government, than a deficiency of means in the particular States. That the inefficiency of measures, arising from the want of an adequate authority in the Supreme Power, from a partial compliance with the Requisitions of Congress in some of the States, and from a failure of punctuality in others, while it tended to damp the zeal of those which were more willing to exert themselves; served also to accumulate the expences of the War, and to frustrate the best concerted Plans, and that the discouragement occasioned by the complicated difficulties and embarrassments, in which our affairs were, by this means involved, would have long ago produced the dissolution of any Army, less patient, less virtuous and less persevering, than that which I have had the honor to command. But while I mention these things, which are notorious facts, as the defects of our Federal Constitution, particularly in the prosecution of a War, I beg it may be understood, that as I have ever taken a pleasure in gratefully acknowledging the assistance and support I have derived from every Class of Citizens, so shall I always be happy to do justice to the unparalleled exertion of the individual States, on many interesting occasions.

I have thus freely disclosed what I wished to make known, before I surrendered up my Public trust to those who committed it to me, the task is now accomplished, I now bid adieu to your Excellency as the Chief Magistrate of your State, at the same time I bid a last farewell to the cares of Office, and all the imployments of public life.

It remains then to be my final and only request, that your Excellency will communicate these sentiments to your Legislature at their next meeting, and that they may be considered as the Legacy of One, who has ardently wished, on all occasions, to be useful to his Country, and who, even in the shade of Retirement, will not fail to implore the divine benediction upon it.

I now make it my earnest prayer, that God would have you, and the State over which you preside, in his holy protection, that he would incline the hearts of the Citizens to cultivate a spirit of subordination and obedience to Government, to entertain a brotherly affection and love for one another, for their fellow Citizens of the United States at large, and particularly for their brethren who have served in the Field, and finally, that he would most graciously be pleased to dispose us all, to do Justice, to love mercy, and to demean ourselves with that Charity, humility and pacific temper of mind, which were the Characteristicks of the Divine Author of our blessed Religion, and without an humble imitation of whose example in these things, we can never hope to be a happy Nation.

To John Augustine Washington

Newburgh, June 15, 1783.

My dear Brother: I have received your favor of the 12th. of April from Berkley, and am obliged to you for the Acct. contained in it of our deceased Brothers affairs. I have since heard that his Widow survived him but a little while. I am also obliged to you for taking upon you the direction of my mothers Interest at the little Fall Quarter, which I believe has been under most wretched Management. equally burthensome to me, and teazing to her.

In answer to the question you have propounded to me, respecting our Nephew Ferdinand, I must observe to you, that the *presumption* is, for I cannot speak with certainty, that our Navy, if it can be called one, will be laid up, or otherwise disposed of; consequently there can be no birth for Ferdinand there. It follows then, that there is only the other alternative of getting him on board a Merchant Ship, and this, possibly, may be the best of the two; your knowledge, together with that of his mothers friends, of the Trade, and Trading people of Virginia (where his Connections and Interest lyes) will point him much better than I can do, to the proper channel for employment.

I wait here with much impatience, the arrival of the Definitive Treaty; this event will put a period not only to my Military Service, but also to my public life; as the remainder of my natural one shall be spent in that kind of ease and repose which a man enjoys that is free from the load of public cares, and subject to no other Controul than that of his own judgment, and a proper conduct for the walk of private Life.

It is much to be wished (but I think a good deal to be doubted) that the States would adopt a liberal and proper line of Conduct for the Government of this Country. It should be founded in justice. prejudices, unreasonable jealousies, and narrow policy should be done away. competent powers for all *general* purposes should be vested in the Sovereignty of the United States, or Anarchy and Confusion will soon succeed. Liberty, when it degenerates into licenciousness, begets confusion, and frequently ends in Tyranny or some woeful catastrophe, and to suppose that the Affairs of this Continent can be conducted by thirteen distinct Sovereignties, or by one without adequate powers, are mere solecisms in politicks. It is in our United capacity we are known, and have a place among the Nations of the Earth. depart from this, and the States seperately would stand as unknown in the World and as contemptable (comparatively speaking) as an individual County in any one State is to the State itself; and in others perhaps, has never been heard of and would be as little attended to but for the sport of Politicians to answer their sinister views, or the purposes of designing Courts, if they should grow jealous of our rising greatness as an Empire, and wish to play off one State against another. We are a young Nation and have a character to establish. It behoves us therefore to set out right for first impressions will be lasting, indeed are all in all. If we do not fulfil our public engagement, if we do not religeously observe our Treaties. If we shall be faithless to, and regardless of those who have lent their money, given their personal Services, and spilt their Blood; and who are now returning home poor and pennyless; in what light shall we be considered? and that there is but too much reason to apprehend these, none who see the daily publications, and will attend to the conduct of some of the States, can hardly have any doubt of. so far therefore as the claims of the Army are concerned, and the Half pay or commutation of it is to be effected, I have suffered Extracts of Original Papers, in my possession, to be published; to shew the justice, œconomy, and even the necessity that Congress were under of granting this, to keep the Army in the Field at so early a period as 1778. One of these I herewith send you.

My love, in which Mrs. Washington joins me, is offered to my Sister and your family; present my Complimts. to all enquiring friends, and be assured etc.

To Elias Boudinot

Head Quarters, Newburgh, June 17, 1783.
Sir: I have the honor of transmitting to your Excellency for the consideration of Congress, a Petition from a large number of Officers of the Army in behalf of themselves, and such other Officers and Soldiers of the Continental Army as are entitled to rewards in lands, and may choose to avail themselves of any Priviledges and Grants which shall be obtained in consequence of the present solicitation. I enclose also the Copy of a Letter from Brigr. General Putnam in which the sentiments and expectations of the Petitioners are more fully explained; and in which the ideas of occupying the Posts in the western Country will be found to correspond very nearly with those I have some time since communicated to a Committee of Congress, in treating on the subject of a Peace Establishment. I will beg leave to make a few more observations on the general benefits of the location and Settlement now proposed; and then submit the justice and policy of the measure to the wisdom of Congress.

Altho' I pretend not myself to determine, how far the district of unsettled Country which is described in the Petition is free from the claim of every State, or how far this disposal of it may interfere with the views of Congress; Yet it appears to me this is the Tract which from its local position and peculiar advantages ought to be the first settled in preference to any other whatever and I am perfectly convinced that it cannot be so advantageously settled, by any other Class of Men, as by the disbanded Officers and Soldiers of the Army, to whom the faith of Government hath long since been pledged, that lands should be granted at the expiration of the War, in certain proportions agreeably to their respective grades.

I am induced to give my sentiments thus freely on the advantages to be expected from this plan of Colonization, because it would connect our Governments with the frontiers, extend our Settlements progressively, and plant a brave, a hardy and respectable Race of People, as our advanced Post, who would be always ready and willing (in case of hostility) to combat the Savages, and check their incursions. A Settlement formed by such Men would give security to our frontiers, the very name of it would awe the Indians, and more than probably prevent the murder of many innocent families, which frequently, in their usual mode of extending our Settlements and Encroachments on the hunting grounds of the Natives, fall the hapless Victims to savage barbarity. Besides the emoluments which might be derived from the Peltry Trade at our Factories, if such should be established; the appearance of so formidable a Settlement in the vicinity of their Towns (to say nothing of the barrier it would form against our other Neighbours) would be the most likely means to enable us to purchase upon equitable terms of the Aborigines their right of preoccupancy; and to induce them to relinquish our Territories, and to remove into the illimitable regions of the West.

Much more might be said of the public utility of such a Location, as well as of the private felicity it would afford to the Individuals concerned in it. I will venture to say it is the most rational and practicable Scheme which can be adopted by a great proportion of the Officers and Soldiers of our Army, and promises them more happiness than they can expect in any other way. The Settlers, being in the prime of life, inured to hardship and taught by experience to accommodate themselves in every situation, going in a considerable body; and under the patronage of Government, would enjoy in the first instance *advantages* in procuring subsistence, and all the necessaries for a comfortable beginning, superior to any common class of Emigrants and quite unknown to those who have heretofore extended themselves beyond the Apalachian Mountains; they may expect after a little perseverance, *Competence and Independence* for themselves, a pleasant retreat in old age, and the fairest prospects for their Children. I have the honor etc.

To William Gordon

Head Qrs., Newburgh, July 8, 1783.

Dear Sir: Your favor of the 19th. of June came to my hands on Sunday last by the Southern Mail; from this circumstance, and the date of it I conclude it has been to Philadelphia, a mistake not very unusual for the Post master at Fishkiln to commit.

I delayed not a moment to forwd. the letters which came to me under your cover of the 26th. of Feby. to New York. I did not answer the letter which accompanied them in due Season; not so much from the hurry of business, as because my Sentiments on the essential part of it had been communicated to you before; and because the Annunciation of Peace, which came close upon the heels of it, put an end to all speculative opinions with respect to the time and terms of it.

I now thank you for your kind congratulations on this event. I feel sensibly the flattering expressions, and fervent wishes with which you have accompanied them, and make a tender of mine, with much cordiality, in return. It now rests with the Confederated Powers, by the line of conduct they mean to adopt, to make this Country great, happy, and respectable; or to sink it into littleness; worse perhaps, into Anarchy and Confusion; for certain I am, that unless adequate Powers are given to Congress for the *general* purposes of the Federal Union that we shall soon moulder into dust and become contemptable in the Eyes of Europe, if we are not made the sport of their Politicks; to suppose that the general concern of this Country can be directed by thirteen heads, or one head without competent powers, is a solecism, the bad effects of which every Man who has had the practical knowledge to judge from, that I have, is fully convinced of; tho' none perhaps has felt them in so forcible, and distressing a degree. The People at large, and at a distance from the theatre of Action, who only know that the Machine was kept in motion, and that they are at last arrived at the first object of their Wishes are satisfied with the event, without investigating the causes of the slow progress to it, or of the Expences which have accrued and which they now seem unwilling to pay; great part of which has arisen from that want of energy in the Federal Constitution which I am complaining of, and which I wish to see given to it by a Convention of the People, instead of hearing it remarked that as we have worked through an arduous Contest with the Powers Congress already have (but which, by the by, have been gradually diminishing) why should they be invested with more?

To say nothing of the invisible workings of Providence, which has conducted us through difficulties where no human foresight could point the way; it will appear evident to a close Examiner, that there has been a concatenation of causes to produce this Event; which in all probability at no time, or under any Circumstances, will combine again. We deceive ourselves therefore by this mode of reasoning, and what would be much worse, we may bring ruin upon ourselves by attempting to carry it into practice.

We are known by no other character among Nations than as the United States; Massachusetts or Virginia is no better defined, nor any more thought of by Foreign Powers than the County of Worcester in Massachusetts is by Virginia, or Glouster County in Virginia is by Massachusetts (respectable as they are); and yet these Counties, with as much propriety might oppose themselves to the Laws of the State in wch. they are, as an Individual State can oppose itself to the Federal Government, by which it is, or ought to be bound. Each of these Counties has, no doubt, its local polity and Interests. these should be attended to, and brought before their respective legislatures with all the force their importance merits; but when they come in contact with the general Interest of the State; when superior considerations preponderate in favor of the whole, their Voices should be heard no more; so should it be with individual States when compared to the Union. Otherwise I think it may properly be asked for what purpose do we farcically pretend to be United? Why do Congress spend Months together in deliberating upon, debating, and digesting plans, which are made as palatable, and as whole-some to the Constitution of this Country as the nature of things will admit of, when some States will pay no attention to them, and others regard them but partially; by which means all those evils which proceed from delay, are felt by the whole; while the compliant States are not only suffering by these ne-glects, but in many instances are injured most capitally by their own exertions; which are wasted for want of the United effort. A hundd. thousand men coming one after another cannot move a Ton weight; but the united strength of 50 would trans-port it with ease. so has it been with great part of the expence which has been incurred this War. In a Word, I think the blood and treasure which has been spent in it has been lav-ished to little purpose, unless we can be better Cemented; and that is not to be effected while so little attention is paid to the recommendations of the Sovereign Power.

To me it would seem not more absurd, to hear a traveller, who was setting out on a long journey, declare he would take no Money in his pocket to defray the Expences of it but rather depend upon chance and charity lest he should misapply it, than are the expressions of so much fear of the powers and means of Congress. For Heavens sake who are Congress? are they not the Creatures of the People, amenable to them for their Conduct, and dependant from day to day on their breath? Where then can be the danger of giving them such Powers as are adequate to the great ends of Government, and to all the general purposes of the Confederation (I repeat the word *genl*, because I am no advocate for their having to do with the particular policy of any State, further than it concerns the Union at large). What may be the consequences if they have not these Powers I am at no loss to guess; and deprecate the worst; for sure I am, we shall, in a little time, become as contemptable in the great Scale of Politicks as we now have it in our power to be respectable; and that, when the band of Union gets once broken, every thing ruinous to our future prospects is to be apprehended; the best that can come of it, in my humble opinion is, that we shall sink into obscurity, unless our Civil broils should keep us in remembrance and fill the page of history with the direful consequences of them.

You say that, Congress loose time by pressing a mode that does not accord with the genius of the People, and will thereby, endanger the Union; and that it is the quantum they want. Permit me to ask if the quantum has not already been demanded? Whether it has been obtained? and whence proceed the accumulated evils, and poignant distresses of many of the public Creditors, particularly in the Army? For my own part I hesitate not a moment to confess, that I see nothing wherein the Union is endangered by the late requisition of that body; but a prospect of much good, justice, and propriety from the compliance with it. I know of no Tax more convenient; none so agreeable, as that which every man may pay, or let it alone as his convenience, abilities, or Inclination shall prompt. I am therefore a warm friend to the Impost.

I can only repeat to you, that whenever Congress shall think proper to open the door of their Archives to you, (which can be best known, and with more propriety discovered through the Delegates of your own State), All my Records and Papers shall be unfolded to your View, and I shall be happy in your Company at Mt. Vernon, while you are taking such Extracts from them, as you may find convenient. It is a piece of respect wch. I think is due to the Sovereign Power to let it take the lead in this business (without any interference of mine). and another reason why I choose to withhold mine, to this epoch is, that I am positive no History of the Revolution can be perfect if the Historiographer has not free access to that fund of Information.

Mrs. Washington joins me in Compliments to Mrs. Gordon and I am etc.

To Robert Stewart

State of New York, August 10, 1783.
Dear Sir: I received with much pleasure by the last Mail from Philadelphia, your favor of the 19th. of April from

London. For the Affectionate, and flattering expressions contained therein you will please to accept my warmest and most grateful acknowledgments.

This Letter removed an apprehension wch. I had long laboured under, of your having taken your departure for the Land of Spirits. How else could I acct. for a Silence of fully 15 years; for I think it must be at least that number since I heard *from* you, and not less than 9 or 10 since I could hear a tittle of you; altho' when I had oppertunity, I made it a point to enquire.

You may be assured Sir that I should ever feel pleasure in rendering you any Service in my power; but I will not be so uncandid as to flatter your expectations, or give you any hope of my doing it in the way you seem to expect. In a Contest, long, arduous and painful; which has brought forth the abilities of men in Military and Civil life and exposed them with Halters abt. their Necks, not only to common danger but many of them to the verge of poverty and the very brink of ruin, justice requires, and a grateful Governmt. certainly will bestow, those places of honor and profit which necessity must create upon those who have risked life fortune and Health to support its cause; but independent of these considerations I have never interfered in any Civil Appointments; and I only wait (and with anxious impatience) the arrival of the Definitive Treaty, that I may take leave of my Military Employments and by bidding adieu to Public life, for ever, enjoy the Shades of retirement that ease and tranquillity to which, for more than Eight years, I have been an entire stranger and for which a Mind which has been constantly on the stretch during that period and perplexed with a thousand embarrassing Circumstances, oftentimes without ray of light to guide it; stands much in need.

Gratitude to a Nation to whom I think America owes much, and an ardt. desire to see the Country and Customs of the French People, are strong inducemts. to make a visit to France; but a consideration more powerful than these will I dare say, be an insuperable Bar to such a tour. An impaired fortune (much injured by this Contest) must turn me into those walks of retirement, where perhaps the consciousness of having discharged to the best of my Abilities the great trust reposed in me and the duty I owed my Country must supply the place of other gratifications and may perhaps afford as rational and substantial entertainment as the gayer scenes of a more enlarged theatre.

I shall always be happy to see you at Mt Vernon. Mrs. Washington who enjoys but a very moderate share of health, unites in best wishes for your health and prosperity with Dr. Sir, etc.

To James Duane

Rocky Hill, September 7, 1783.

Sir: I have carefully perused the Papers which you put into my hands relative to Indian Affairs.

My Sentiments with respect to the proper line of Conduct to be observed towards these people coincides precisely with those delivered by Genl. Schuyler, so far as he has gone in his Letter of the 29th. July to Congress (which, with the other Papers is herewith returned), and for the reasons he has there assigned; a repetition of them therefore by me would be unnecessary. But independant of the arguments made use of by him the following considerations have no small weight in my Mind.

To suffer a wide extended Country to be over run with Land Jobbers, Speculators, and Monopolisers or even with scatter'd settlers, is, in my opinion, inconsistent with that wisdom and policy which our true interest dictates, or that an enlightened People ought to adopt and, besides, is pregnant of disputes both with the Savages, and among ourselves, the evils of which are easier, to be conceived than described; and for what? but to aggrandize a few avaricious Men to the prejudice of many, and the embarrassment of Government. for the People engaged in these pursuits without contributing in the smallest degree to the support of Government, or considering themselves as amenable to its Laws, will involve it by their unrestrained conduct, in inextricable perplexities, and more than probable in a great deal of Bloodshed.

My ideas therefore of the line of Conduct proper to be observed not only towards the Indians, but for the government of the Citizens of America, in their Settlement of the Western Country (which is intimately connected therewith) are simply these.

First and as a preliminary, that all Prisoners of whatever age or Sex, among the Indians shall be delivered up.

That the Indians should be informed, that after a Contest of eight years for the Sovereignty of this Country G: Britain has ceded all the Lands of the United States within the limits discribed by the   arte. of the Provisional Treaty.

That as they (the Indians) maugre all the advice and admonition which could be given them at the commencemt; and during the prosecution of the War could not be restrained from acts of Hostility, but were determined to join their Arms to those of G Britain and to share their fortune; so, consequently, with a less generous People than Americans they would be made to share the same fate; and be compelld to retire along with them beyond the Lakes. But as we prefer Peace to a state of Warfare, as we consider them as a deluded People; as we perswade ourselves that they are convinced, from experience, of their error in taking up the Hatchet against us, and that their true Interest and safety must now depend upon *our* friendship. As the Country, is large enough to contain us all; and as we are disposed to be kind to them and to partake of their Trade, we will from these considerations and from motives of Compn., draw a veil over what is past and establish a boundary line between them and us beyond which we will *endeavor* to restrain our People from Hunting or Settling, and within which they shall not come, but for the purposes of Trading, Treating, or other business unexceptionable in its nature.

In establishing this line, in the first instance, care should be taken neither to yield nor to grasp at too much. But to endeavor to impress the Indians with an idea of the generosity of our disposition to accommodate them, and with the necessity we are under, of providing for our Warriors, our Young People who are growing up, and strangers who are coming from other Countries to live among us. and if they should make a point of it, or appear dissatisfied at the line we may find it necessary to establish, compensation should be made them for their claims within it.

It is needless for me to express more explicitly because the tendency of my observns. evinces it is my opinion that if the Legislature of the State of New York should insist upon expelling the Six Nations from all the Country they Inhabited previous to the War, within their Territory (as General Schuyler seems to be apprehensive of) that it will end in another Indian War. I have every reason to believe from my enquiries, and the information I have received, that they will not suffer their Country (if it was our policy to take it before we could settle it) to be wrested from them without another struggle. That they would compromise for a part of it I have very little doubt, and that it would be the cheapest way of coming at it, I have no doubt at all. The same observations, I am perswaded, will hold good with respect to Virginia, or any other state which has powerful Tribes of Indians on their Frontiers; and the reason of my mentioning New York is because General Schuyler has expressed his opinion of the temper of its Legislature; and because I have been more in the way of learning the Sentimts. of the Six Nations, than of any other Tribes of Indians on this Subject.

The limits being sufficiently extensive (in the New Ctry.) to comply with all the engagements of Government and to admit such emigrations as may be supposed to happen within a given time not only from the several States of the Union but from Foreign Countries, and moreover of such magnitude as to form a distinct and proper Government; a Proclamation in my opinion, should issue, making it Felony (if there is power for the purpose and if not imposing some very heavy restraint) for any person to Survey or Settle beyond the Line; and the Officers Commanding the Frontier Garrison should have pointed and peremptory orders to see that the Proclamation is carried into effect.

Measures of this sort would not only obtain Peace from the Indians, but would, in my opinion, be the surest means of preserving it. It would dispose of the Land to the best advantage; People the Country progressively, and check Land Jobbing and Monopolizing (which is now going forward with great avidity) while the door would be open, and the terms known for every one to obtain what is reasonable and proper for himself upon legal and constitutional ground.

Every advantage that could be expected or even wished for would result from such a mode of proceedure our Settlements would be compact, Government well established, and our Barrier formidable, not only for ourselves but against our Neighbours, and the Indians as has been observed in Genl Schuylers Letter will ever retreat as our Settlements advance upon them and they will be as ready to sell, as we are to buy; That it is the cheapest as well as the least distressing way of dealing with them, none who are acquainted with the Nature of Indian warfare, and has ever been at the trouble of estimating the expence of one, and comparing it with the cost of purchasing their Lands, will hesitate to acknowledge.

Unless some such measures as I have here taken the liberty of suggesting are speedily adopted one of two capital evils, in my opinion, will inevitably result, and is near at hand; either that the settling, or rather overspreading the Western Country will take place, by a parcel of Banditti, who will bid defiance to all Authority while they are skimming and disposing of the Cream of the Country at the expence of many suffering officers and Soldiers who have fought and bled to obtain it, and are now waiting the decision of Congress to point them to the promised reward of their past dangers and toils, or a renewal of Hostilities with the Indians, brought about more than probably, by this very means.

How far agents for Indian Affrs. are indispensably necessary I shall not take upon me to decide; but if any should be appointed, their powers in my opinion should be circumscribed, accurately defined, and themselves rigidly punished for every infraction of them. A recurrence to the conduct of these People under the British Administration of Indian Affairs will manifest the propriety of this caution, as it will there be found, that self Interest was the principle by which their Agents were actuated; and to promote this by accumulating Lands and passing large quantities of Goods thro their hands, the Indians were made to speak any language they pleased by their representation; were pacific or hostile as their purposes were most likely to be promoted by the one or the other. No purchase under any pretence whatever should be made by any other authority than that of the Sovereign power, or the Legislature of the State in which such Lands may happen to be. Nor should the Agents be permitted directly or indirectly to trade; but to have a fixed, and ample Salary allowed them as a full compensation for their trouble.

Whether in practice the measure may answer as well as it appears in theory to me, I will not undertake to say; but I think, if the Indian Trade was carried on, on Government Acct., and with no greater advance than what would be necessary to defray the expence and risk, and bring in a small profit, that it would supply the Indians upon much better terms than they usually are; engross their Trade, and fix them strongly in our Interest; and would be a much better mode of treating them than that of giving presents; where a few only are benefitted by them. I confess there is a difficulty in getting a Man, or set of Men, in whose Abilities and integrity there can be a perfect reliance; without which, the scheme is liable to such abuse as to defeat the salutary ends which are proposed from it. At any rate, no person should be suffered to Trade with the Indians without first obtaining a license, and giving security to conform to such rules and regulations as shall be prescribed; as was the case before the War.

In giving my Sentiments in the Month of May last (at the request of a Committee of Congress) on a Peace Establishmt. I took the liberty of suggesting the propriety, which in my opinion there appeared, of paying particular attention to the French and other Settlers at Detroit and other parts within the limits of the Western Country; the perusal of a late Pamphlet entitled "Observations on the Commerce of the American States with Europe and the West Indies" impresses the necessity of it more forcibly than ever on my Mind. The author of that Piece strongly recommends a liberal change in the Government of Canada, and tho' he is too sanguine in his expectations of the benefits arising from it, there can be no doubt of the good policy of the measure. It behooves us therefore to counteract them, by anticipation. These People have a disposition towards us susceptible of favorable Impressions; but as no Arts will be left unattempted by the British to withdraw them from our Interest, the prest. moment should be employed by us to fix them in it, or we may loose them forever; and with them, the advantages, or disadvantages consequent of the choice they may make. From the best information and Maps of that Country, it would appear that from the Mouth of the Great Miami River wch. empties into the Ohio to its confluence with the Mad River, thence by a Line to the Miami Fort and Village on the other Miami River wch. empties into Lake Erie, and Thence by a Line to include the Settlement of Detroit would with Lake Erie to the No. ward Pensa. to the Eastwd. and the Ohio to the Soward form a Governmt. sufficiently extensive to fulfill all the public engagements, and to receive moreover a large population by Emigrants, and to confine The Settlement of the New States within these bounds would, in my opinion, be infinitely better even supposing no disputes were to happen with the Indians and that it was not necessary to guard against those other evils which have been enumerated than to suffer the same number of People to roam over a Country of at least 500,000 Square Miles contributing nothing to the support, but much perhaps to the Embarrassment of the Federal Government.

Was it not for the purpose of comprehending the Settlement of Detroit within the Jurisdn. of the New Governmt a more compact and better shaped district for a State would be for the line to proceed from the Miami Fort and Village along the River of that name to Lake Erie. leaving In that case the Settlement of Detroit, and all the Territory No. of the Rivers Miami and St. Josephs between the Lakes Erie, St. Clair, Huron, and Michigan to form, hereafter, another State equally large compact and water bounded.

At first view, it may seem a little extraneous, when I am called upon to give an opinion upon the terms of a Peace proper to be made with the Indians, that I should go into the formation of New States; but the Settlemt. of the Western Country and making a Peace with the Indians are so analogous that there can be no definition of the one without involving considerations of the other. for I repeat it, again, and I am clear in my opinion, that policy and œconomy point very strongly to the expediency of being upon good terms with the Indians, and the propriety of purchasing their Lands in preference to attempting to drive them by force of arms out of their Country; which as we have already experienced is like driving the Wild Beasts of the Forest which will return us soon as the pursuit is at an end and fall perhaps on those that are left there; when the gradual extension of our Settlements will as certainly cause the Savage as the Wolf to retire; both being beasts of prey tho' they differ in shape. In a word there is nothing to be obtained by an Indian War but the Soil they live on and this can be had by purchase at less expence, and without that bloodshed, and those distresses which helpless Women and Children are made partakers of in all kinds of disputes with them.

If there is any thing in these thoughts (which I have fully and freely communicated) worthy attention I shall be happy and am Sir Yr. etc.

P. S. A formal Address, and memorial from the Oneida Indians when I was on the Mohawk River, setting forth their Grievances and distresses and praying relief, induced me to order a pound of Powder and 3 lbs. of Lead to be issued to each Man, from the Military Magazines in the care of Colo. Willet; this, I presume, was unknown to Genl. Schuyler at the time he recommended the like measure in his Letter to Congress.

To Lund Washington

Rocky Hill, September 20, 1783.

Dear Lund: Mrs. Custis has never suggested in any of her Letters to Mrs. Washington (unless ardent wishes for her return, that she might then disclose it to her, can be so construed) the most distant attachment to D. S.; but if this should be the case, and she wants advice upon it; a Father and Mother, who are at hand, and competent to give it, are at the same time most proper to be consulted on so interesting an event. For my own part, I never did, nor do I believe I ever shall give advice to a woman who is setting out on a matrimonial voyage; first, because I never could advise one to marry without her own consent; and secondly, because I know it is to no purpose to advise her to refrain, when she has obtained it. A woman very rarely asks an opinion or requires advice on such an occasion, 'till her resolution is formed; and then it is with the hope and expectation of obtaining a sanction, not that she means to be governed by your disapprobation, that she applies. In a word, the plain english of the application may be summed up in these words; "I wish you to think as I do; but if unhappily you differ from me in opinion, my heart, I must confess is fixed, and I have gone too far *now* to retract."

If Mrs. Custis should ever suggest any thing of this kind to me, I will give her my opinion of the *measure*, not of the *man*, with candour, and to the following effect. I never expected you would spend the residue of your days in widowhood; but in a matter so important, and so interesting to yourself, children and connexions; I wish you would make a prudent choice; to do which, many considerations are necessary; such as the family and connexions of the man, his fortune (which is not the *most* essential in my eye), the line of conduct he has observed, and disposition and frame of his mind. You should consider, what prospect there is of his proving kind and affectionate to you; just, generous and attentive to your children; and, how far his connexions will be agreeable to you; for when they are once formed, agreeable or not, the die being cast, your fate is fixed. Thus far, and no farther I shall go in my opinions. I am etc.

Farewell Address to the Armies of the United States

Rock Hill, near Princeton, November 2, 1783.

The United States in Congress assembled after giving the most honorable testimony to the merits of the fœderal Armies, and presenting them with the thanks of their Country for their long, eminent, and faithful services, having thought proper by their proclamation bearing date the 18th. day of October last. to discharge such part of the Troops as were engaged for the war, and to permit the Officers on furlough to retire from service from and after to-morrow; which proclamation having been communicated in the publick papers for the information and government of all concerned; it only remains for the Comdr in Chief to address himself once more, and that for the last time, to the Armies of the U States (however widely dispersed the individuals who compose them may be) and to bid them an affectionate, a long farewell.

But before the Comdr in Chief takes his final leave of those he holds most dear, he wishes to indulge himself a few moments in calling to mind a slight review of the past. He will then take the liberty of exploring, with his military friends, their future prospects, of advising the general line of conduct, which in his opinion, ought to be pursued, and he will conclude the Address by expressing the obligations he feels himself under for the spirited and able assistance he has experienced from them in the performance of an arduous Office.

A contemplation of the compleat attainment (at a period earlier than could have been expected) of the object for which we contended against so formidable a power cannot but inspire us with astonishment and gratitude. The disadvantageous circumstances on our part, under which the war was undertaken, can never be forgotten. The singular interpositions of Providence in our feeble condition were such, as could scarcely escape the attention of the most unobserving; while the unparalleled perseverence of the Armies of the U States, through almost every possible suffering and discouragement for the space of eight long years, was little short of a standing miracle.

It is not the meaning nor within the compass of this address to detail the hardships peculiarly incident to our service, or to describe the distresses, which in several instances have resulted from the extremes of hunger and nakedness, combined with the rigours of an inclement season; nor is it necessary to dwell on the dark side of our past affairs. Every American Officer and Soldier must now console himself for any unpleasant circumstances which may have occurred by a recollection of the uncommon scenes in which he has been called to Act no inglorious part, and the astonishing events of which he has been a witness, events which have seldom if ever before taken place on the stage of human action, nor can they probably ever happen again. For who has before seen a disciplined Army form'd at once from such raw materials? Who, that was not a witness, could imagine that the most violent local prejudices would cease so soon, and that Men who came from the different parts of the Continent, strongly disposed, by the habits of education, to despise and quarrel with each other, would instantly become but one patriotic band of Brothers, or who, that was not on the spot, can trace the steps by which such a wonderful revolution has been effected, and such a glorious period put to all our warlike toils?

It is universally acknowledged, that the enlarged prospects of happiness, opened by the confirmation of our independence and sovereignty, almost exceeds the power of description. And shall not the brave men, who have contributed so essentially to these inestimable acquisitions, retiring victorious from the field of War to the field of agriculture, participate in all the blessings which have been obtained; in such a republic, who will exclude them from the rights of Citizens and the fruits of their labour. In such a Country, so happily circumstanced, the pursuits of Commerce and the cultivation of the soil will unfold to industry the certain road to competence. To those hardy Soldiers, who are actuated by the spirit of adventure the Fisheries will afford ample and profitable employment, and the extensive and fertile regions of the West will yield a most happy asylum to those, who, fond of domestic enjoyments are seeking for personal independence. Nor is it possible to conceive, that any one of the U States will prefer a national bankruptcy and a dissolution of the union, to a compliance with the requisitions of Congress and the payment of its just debts; so that the Officers and Soldiers may expect considerable assistance in recommencing their civil occupations from the sums due to them from the public, which must and will most inevitably be paid.

In order to effect this desirable purpose and to remove the prejudices which may have taken possession of the minds of any of the good people of the States, it is earnestly recommended to all the Troops that with strong attachments to the Union, they should carry with them into civil society the most conciliating dispositions; and that they should prove themselves not less virtuous and useful as Citizens, than they have been persevering and victorious as Soldiers. What tho, there should be some envious individuals who are unwilling to pay the debt the public has contracted, or to yield the tribute due to merit; yet, let such unworthy treatment produce no invective or any instance of intemperate conduct; let it be remembered that the unbiassed voice of the few Citizens of the United States has promised the just reward, and given the merited applause; let it be known and remembered, that the reputation of the fœderal Armies is established beyond the reach of malevolence; and let a conscientiousness of their achievements and fame still unite the men, who composed them to honourable actions; under the persuasion that the private virtues of œconomy, prudence, and industry, will not be less amiable in civil life, than the more splendid qualities of valour, perseverance, and enterprise were in the Field. Every one may rest assured that much, very much of the future happiness of the Officers and Men will depend upon the wise and manly conduct which shall be adopted by them when they are mingled with the great body of the community. And, altho the General has so frequently given it as his opinion, in the most public and explicit manner, that, unless the principles of the federal government were properly supported and the powers of the union increased, the honour, dignity, and justice of the nation would be lost forever. Yet he cannot help repeating, on this occasion, so interesting a sentiment, and leaving it as his last injunction to every Officer and every Soldier, who may view the subject in the same serious point of light, to add his best endeavours to those of his worthy fellow Citizens towards effecting these great and valuable purposes on which our very existence as a nation so materially depends.

The Commander in chief conceives little is now wanting to enable the Soldiers to change the military character into that of the Citizen, but that steady and decent tenor of behaviour which has generally distinguished, not only the Army under his immediate command, but the different detachments and seperate Armies through the course of the war. From their good sense and prudence he anticipates the happiest consequences; and while he congratulates them on the glorious occasion, which renders their services in the field no longer necessary, he wishes to express the strong obligations he feels himself under for the assistance he has received from every Class, and in every instance. He presents his thanks in the most serious and affectionate manner to the General Officers, as well for their counsel on many interesting occasions, as for their Order in promoting the success of the plans he had adopted. To the Commandants of Regiments and Corps, and to the other Officers for their great zeal and attention, in carrying his orders promptly into execution. To the Staff, for their alacrity and exactness in performing the Duties of their several Departments. And to the Non Commissioned Officers and private Soldiers, for their extraordinary patience in suffering, as well as their invincible fortitude in Action. To the various branches of the Army the General takes this last and solemn opportunity of professing his inviolable attachment and friendship. He wishes more than bare professions were in his power, that he were really able to be useful to them all in future life. He flatters himself however, they will do him the justice to believe, that whatever could with propriety be attempted by him has been done, and being now to conclude these his last public Orders, to take his ultimate leave in a short time of the military character, and to bid a final adieu to the Armies he has so long had the honor to Command, he can only again offer in their behalf his recommendations to their grateful country, and his prayers to the God of Armies. May ample justice be done them here, and may the choicest of heaven's favours, both here and hereafter, attend those who, under the devine auspices, have secured innumerable blessings for others; with these wishes, and this benediction, the Commander in Chief is about to retire from Service. The Curtain of seperation will soon be drawn, and the military scene to him will be closed for ever.

To Thomas Mifflin

Annapolis, December 20, 1783.

Sir: I take the earliest opportunity to inform Congress of my arrival in this City, with the intention of asking leave to resign the Commission I have the honor of holding in their Service. It is essential for me to know their pleasure, and in what manner it will be most proper to offer my resignation, whether in writing, or at an Audience; I shall therefore request to be honored with the necessary information, that being apprized of the sentiments of Congress I may regulate my Conduct accordingly. I have the honor etc.

Address to Congress on Resigning Commission

Mr. President: The great events on which my resignation depended having at length taken place; I have now the honor of offering my sincere Congratulations to Congress and of presenting myself before them to surrender into their hands the trust committed to me, and to claim the indulgence of retiring from the Service of my Country.

Happy in the confirmation of our Independence and Sovereignty, and pleased with the oppertunity afforded the United States of becoming a respectable Nation, I resign with satisfaction the Appointment I accepted with diffidence. A diffidence in my abilities to accomplish so arduous a task, which however was superseded by a confidence in the rectitude of our Cause, the support of the Supreme Power of the Union, and the patronage of Heaven.

The Successful termination of the War has verified the most sanguine expectations, and my gratitude for the interposition of Providence, and the assistance I have received from my Countrymen, encreases with every review of the momentous Contest.

While I repeat my obligations to the Army in general, I should do injustice to my own feelings not to acknowledge in this place the peculiar Services and distinguished merits of the Gentlemen who have been attached to my person during the War. It was impossible the choice of confidential Officers to compose my family should have been more fortunate. Permit me Sir, to recommend in particular those, who have continued in Service to the present moment, as worthy of the favorable notice and patronage of Congress.

I consider it an indispensable duty to close this last solemn act of my Official life, by commending the Interests of our dearest Country to the protection of Almighty God, and those who have the superintendence of them, to his holy keeping.

Having now finished the work assigned me, I retire from the great theatre of Action; and bidding an Affectionate farewell to this August body under whose orders I have so long acted, I here offer my Commission, and take my leave of all the employments of public life.

Annapolis, December 23, 1783

THE
CONFEDERATION PERIOD
1783–1789

To George Clinton

Mount Vernon, December 28, 1783.

My dear Sir: After as prosperous a Journey as could be expected at this late season of the year, I arrived at my Seat the day before Christmas, having previously divested myself of my official character. I am now a private Citizen on the banks of the Powtowmack, where I should be happy to see you if your public business would ever permit, and where in the meantime I shall fondly cherish the remembrance of all your former friendship.

Altho I scarcely need tell you how much I have been satisfied with every instance of your public conduct, yet I could not suffer Col Walker whose merits are too well known to you to need a recommendation of him from me if any thing should cast up favorable to his wishes to depart for N York, without giving your Excellency one more testimony of the obligations I consider myself under for the spirited and able assistance, I have often derived from the State under your Administration. The Scene is at last closed. I feel myself eased of a load of public Care. I hope to spend the remainder of my Days in cultivating the affections of good Men, and in the practice of the domestic Virtues; permit me still to consider you in the Number of my friends, and to wish you every felicity.

Mrs. Washington joins me in presentg the Complts of the Season with our best respects to Mrs. Clinton and the family. I have the honor etc.

To Benjamin Harrison

My Dear Sir,   Mount Vernon 18th Jany 1784

I have just had the pleasure to receive your letter of the 8th—for the friendly & affectionate terms in which you have welcomed my return to this Country & to private life; & for the favourable light in which you are pleased to consider, &

express your sense of my past services, you have my warmest
& most grateful acknowledgments.

That the prospect before us is, as you justly observe, fair,
none can deny; but what use we shall make of it, is exceedingly
problematical; not but that I believe, all things will come right
at last; but like a young heir, come a little prematurely to a
large inheritance, we shall wanton and run riot until we have
brought our reputation to the brink of ruin, & then like him
shall have to labor with the current of opinion when *compelled*
perhaps, to do what prudence & common policy pointed out
as plain as any problem in Euclid, in the first instance.

The disinclination of the individual States to yield competent powers to Congress for the Fœderal Government—their
unreasonable jealousy of that body & of one another—& the
disposition which seems to pervade each, of being all-wise &
all-powerful within itself, will, if there is not a change in the
system, be our downfal as a Nation. This is as clear to me as
the A, B.C.; & I think we have opposed Great Britain, & have
arrived at the present state of peace & independency, to very
little purpose, if we cannot conquer our own prejudices. The
powers of Europe begin to see this, & our newly acquired
friends the British, are already & professedly acting upon this
ground; & wisely too, if we are determined to persevere in
our folly. They know that individual opposition to their measures is futile, & *boast* that we are not sufficiently united as a
Nation to give a general one! Is not the indignity alone, of
this declaration, while we are in the very act of peace-making
& conciliation, sufficient to stimulate us to vest more extensive & adequate powers in the sovereign of these United
States? For my own part, altho' I am returned to, & am now
mingled with the class of private citizens, & like them must
suffer all the evils of a Tyranny, or of too great an extension
of fœderal powers; I have no fears arising from this source; in
my mind, but I have many, & powerful ones indeed which
predict the worst consequences from a half starved, limping
Government, that appears to be always moving upon crutches,
& tottering at every step. Men, chosen as the Delegates in
Congress are, cannot officially be dangerous—they depend
upon the breath—nay, they are so much the creatures of the
people, under the present Constitution, that they can have no

views (which could possibly be carried into execution), nor any interests, distinct from those of their constituents. My political creed therefore is, to be wise in the choice of Delegates—support them like Gentlemen while they are our representatives—give them competent powers for all fœderal purposes—support them in the due exercise thereof—& lastly, to compel them to close attendance in Congress during their delegation. These things under the present mode for, & termination of elections, aided by annual instead of constant Sessions, would, or I am exceedingly mistaken, make us one of the most wealthy, happy, respectable & powerful Nations, that ever inhabited the terrestrial Globe—without them, we shall in my opinion soon be every thing which is the direct reverse of them.

I shall look for you, in the first part of next month, with such other friends as may incline to accompany you, with great pleasure, being with best respects to Mrs Harrison, in which Mrs Washington joins me, Dear Sir, Your Most Obedt & affecte hble servant

To Marquis de Lafayette

Mount Vernon 1st Feby 1784

At length my Dear Marquis I am become a private citizen on the banks of the Potomac, & under the shadow of my own Vine & my own Fig tree, free from the bustle of a camp & the busy scenes of public life, I am solacing myself with those tranquil enjoyments, of which the Soldier who is ever in pursuit of fame—the Statesman whose watchful days & sleepless Nights are spent in devising schemes to promote the welfare of his own—perhaps the ruin of other countries, as if this Globe was insufficient for us all—& the Courtier who is always watching the countenance of his Prince, in hopes of catching a gracious smile, can have very little conception. I am not only retired from all public employments, but I am retireing within myself; & shall be able to view the solitary walk, & tread the paths of private life with heartfelt satisfaction—Envious of none, I am determined to be pleased with all. & this my dear friend, being the order for my march, I will move gently down the stream of life, until I sleep with my Fathers.

Except an introductory letter or two, & one countermanding my request respecting Plate, I have not written to you since the middle of Octobr by Genl Duportail. To inform you at this late hour, that the City of New York was evacuated by the British forces on the 25th of Novembr—that the American Troops took possession of it the same day, & delivered it over to the civil authority of the State—that good order, contrary to the expectation & predictions of Gl Carleton, his Officers & all the loyalists, was immediately established—and that the harbour of New York was finally cleared of the British flag about the 5th or 6th of Decemr, would be an insult to your intelligence. And to tell you that I remained eight days in New York after we took possession of the City—that I was very much hurried during that time, which was the reason I did not write to you from thence—that taking Phila. in my way, I was obliged to remain there a week—that at Annapolis, where Congress were then, and are now sitting, I did, on the 23d of December present them my Commission, & made them my last bow—& on the Eve of Christmas entered these doors an older man by near nine years, than when I left them, is very uninteresting to any but myself. Since that period we have been fast locked up in frost & snow, & excluded in a manner from all kinds of intercourse, the winter having been, & still continues to be, extremely severe.

I have now to acknowledge, and thank you for your favors of the 22d of July & 8th of September, both of which, altho' the first is of old date, have come to hand since my letter to you of October. The accounts contained therein of the political & commercial state of affairs as they respect America, are interesting, & I wish I could add that they were altogether satisfactory; & the Agency, you have had in both, particularly with regard to the Free ports in France, is a fresh evidence of your unwearied endeavours to serve this Country; but there is no part of your Letters to Congress My Dear Marquis, which bespeaks the excellence of your heart more plainly than that, which contains those noble & generous sentiments on the justice which is due to the faithful friends & Servants of the public; but I must do Congress the justice to declare, that as a body, I believe there is every disposition in them, not only to acknowledge the merits, but to reward the services of the army: there is a contractedness, I am sorry to add, in some of the States, from whence all our difficulties on this head, proceed; but it is to be hoped, the good sense & perserverance of the rest, will ultimately prevail, as the spirit of meanness is beginning to subside.

From a letter which I have just received from the Governor of this State I expect him here in a few days, when I shall not be unmindful of what you have written about the bust, & will endeavour to have matters respecting it, placed on their proper basis. I thank you most sincerely My Dear Marqs for your kind invitation to your house, if I should come to Paris. At present I see but little prospect of such a voyage, the deranged situation of my private concerns, occasioned by an absence of almost nine years, and an entire disregard of all private business during that period, will not only suspend, but may put it forever out of my power to gratify this wish. This not being the case with you, come with Madame la Fayette & view me in my domestic walks—I have often told you, & I repeat it again, that no man could receive you in them with more friendship & affection than I should do; in which I am sure Mrs Washington would cordially join me. We unite in respectful compliments to your Lady, & best wishes for your little flock. With every sentiment of esteem, Admiration & Love, I am, My Dr Marqs Your Most Affecte friend

To Tench Tilghman

Dear Sir,   Mount Vernon Mar. 24th 1784

I am informed that a Ship with Palatines is gone up to Baltimore, among whom are a number of Tradesmen. I am a good deal in want of a House Joiner & Bricklayer, (who really understand their profession) & you would do me a favor by purchasing one of each, for me. I would not confine you to Palatines. If they are good workmen, they may be of Assia, Africa, or Europe. They may be Mahometans, Jews, or Christian of any Sect—or they may be Athiests—I would however prefer middle aged, to young men. and those who have good countenances & good characters on ship board, to others who have neither of these to recommend them—altho, after all, the proof of the pudding must be in the eating. I do not limit you to a price, but will pay the purchase money on demand— This request will be in force 'till complied with, or counter-manded, because you may not succeed at this moment, and have favourable ones here after to do it in. My best respects, in which Mrs Washington joins, are presented to Mrs Tilgh-man & Mrs Carroll—and I am Dr Sir Yr Affecte Hble Servt

To James Craik

Dear Sir,   Mount Vernon 25th March 1784

In answer to Mr Bowie's request to you, permit me to as-sure that Gentleman, that I shall at all times be glad to see him at this retreat—That whenever he is here, I will give him the perusal of any public papers antecedent to my appoint-ment to the command of the American army—that he may be laying up materials for his work. And whenever Congress shall have opened *their* Archives to any Historian for infor-mation, that he shall have the examination of all others in my possession which are subsequent thereto, but that 'till this epoch, I do not think myself at liberty to unfold papers which contain all the occurrences & transactions of my *late* com-mand; first, because I conceive it to be respectful to the sov-ereign power to let them take the lead in this business—& next, because I have, upon this principle, refused Doctr Gor-don & others who are about to write the History of the rev-olution this priviledge.

I will frankly declare to you, My Dr Doctor that any mem-oirs of my life, distinct & unconnected with the general his-tory of the war, would rather hurt my feelings than tickle my pride whilst I lived. I had rather glide gently down the stream of life, leaving it to posterity to think & say what they please of me, than by an act of mine to have vanity or ostentation imputed to me—And I will furthermore confess that I was rather surprized into a consent, when Doctr Witherspoon (very unexpectedly) made the application, than considered the tendency of that consent. It did not occur to me at that moment, from the manner in which the question was propounded—that no history of my life, without a very great deal of trouble indeed, could be written with the least degree of accuracy—unless recourse was had to me, or to my papers for information—that it would not derive sufficient authenticity without a promulgation of this fact—& that such a promulgation would subject me to the imputation I have just mentioned—which would hurt me the more, as I do not think vanity is a trait of my character.

It is for this reason, & candour obliges me to be explicit, that I shall stipulate against the publication of the memoirs Mr Bowie has in contemplation to give the world, 'till I shou'd see more probability of avoiding the darts which *I think* would be pointed at me on such an occasion; and how far, under these circumstances, it wou'd be worth Mr Bowie's while to spend time which might be more usefully employed in other matters, is with him to consider; as the practicability of doing it efficiently, without having free access to the documents of this War, which must fill the most important pages of the Memoir, & which for the reasons already assigned cannot be admitted at present, also is. If nothing happens more than I at present foresee, I shall be in Philadelphia on or before the first of May; where 'tis probable I may see Mr Bowie & converse further with him on this subject—in the mean while I will thank you for communicating these Sentiments. I am very truly Your affectionate friend & Servt

To Marquise de Lafayette

Madam,   Mount Vernon 4th April 1784
It is now, more than ever, I want words to express the sensibility & gratitude with which the honor of your felicitations of the 26th of Decr has inspired me. If my expression was equal to the feelings of my heart the homage I am about to render you, would appear in a more favourable point of view,

than my most sanguine expectations will encourage me to hope for. I am more inclined therefore to rely upon the continuence of your indulgent sentiments of me, & that innate goodness for which you are remarked—than upon any merit I possess, or any assurances I could give of my sense of the obligation I am under for the honor you have conferred upon me by your correspondence.

Great as your claim is, as a French, or American woman; or as the wife of my amiable friend, to my affectionate regards; you have others to which the palm must be yielded. The charms of your person, & the beauties of your mind, have a more powerful operation—These Madam, have endeared you to me, & every thing which partakes of your nature will have a claim to my affections—George & Virginia (the offspring of your love), whose names do honor to my Country, & to myself, have a double claim & will be the objects of my vows.

From the clangor of arms & the bustle of a camp—freed from the cares of public employment, & the responsibility of Office—I am now enjoying domestic ease under the shadow of my own Vine, & my own Fig tree; & in a small Villa, with the implements of Husbandry & Lambkins around me, I expect to glide gently down the stream of life, 'till I am emtombed in the dreary mansions of my Fathers.

Mrs Washington is highly honored by your participations, & feels very sensibly the force of your polite invitation to Paris; but she is too far advanced in life, & is too much immersed in the care of her little progeny to cross the Atlantic. This my Dr Marchioness (indulge me with this freedom) is not the case with you. You have youth (& if you should not incline to bring your children, can leave them with all the advantages to Education)—and *must* have a curiosity to see the Country, young, rude & uncultivated as it is; for the liberties of which your husband has fought, bled, & acquired much glory—Where every body admires, every body loves him—Come then, let me entreat it, & call my Cottage your home; for your own doors do not open to you with more readiness, than mine wou'd. You will see the plain manner in which we live; & meet the rustic civility, & you shall taste the simplicity of rural life—It will diversify the Scene & may give you a higher relish for the gaieties of the Court, when you return to Versailles. In these wishes, & in most respectful compliments Mrs Washington joins me. With sentiments of strong attachment, & very great regard I have the honor to be Madam Your most obedt & much obliged Servt

To William Gordon

Revd Sir,   Philada May 8th 1784.
Every aid which can be derived from my official papers, I am willing to afford, & shall with much pleasure lay before you, whenever the latter can be unfolded with propriety.

It ever has been my opinion however, that no Historian can be possessed of sufficient materials to compile a *perfect* history of the revolution, who has not free access to the archives of Congress—to those of the respective States—to the papers of the commander in chief, & to those of the officers who have been employed in separate Departments. Combining & properly arranging the information which is to be obtained from these sources must bring to view all the material occurrences of the War. Some things probably will never be known.

Added to this, I have always thought, that it would be respectful to the Sovereign power of these United States, to *follow*, rather than to take the lead of them in disclosures of this Kind: but if there should be political restraints, under which Congress are not inclined at this time to lay open their papers; & these restraints do not in their opinion extend to mine—the same being signified by that honorable Body to me, my objections to your request will cease. I shall be happy then, as at all times, to see you at Mount Vernon, & will lay before you with chearfulness, my *public* papers for your information. With great esteem & regard, I am Dr Sir Your Most Obt &c.

To Benjamin Harrison

Dear Sir,   Mount Vernon 10th October 1784
Upon my return from the western Country a few days ago,

I had the pleasure to receive your favor of the 17th ulto—It has always been my intention to pay my respects to you before the chance of *another* early & hard winter should make a warm fire side too comfortable to be relinquished. and I shall feel an additional pleasure in offering this tribute of friendship & respect to you, by having the company of the Marqs de la Fayette, when he shall have revisited this place from his Eastern tour; now, every day to be expected.

I shall take the liberty now, my dear sir, to suggest a matter, which would (if I am not too short sighted a politician) mark your administration as an important œra in the Annals of this Country, if it should be recommended by you, & adopted by the Assembly.

It has been long my decided opinion, that the shortest, easiest & least expensive communication with the invaluable & extensive Country back of us, would be by one, or both of the rivers of this State which have their sources in the apalachian mountains. Nor am I singular in this opinion—Evans, in his Map and Analysis of the middle Colonies which (considering the early period at which they were given to the public) are done with amazing exactness. And Hutchins since, in his topographical description of the Western Country, (good part of which is from actual surveys)—are decidedly of the same sentiments; as indeed are all others who have had opportunities, & have been at the pains to investigate, & consider the subject.

But that this may not stand as mere matter of opinion or assertion, unsupported by facts (such at least as the best Maps now extant, compared with the oral testimony, which my opportunities in the course of the war have enabled me to obtain); I shall give you the different routs & distances from Detroit, by which all the trade of the North Western parts of the United territory, must pass; unless the Spaniards, contrary to their present policy, should engage part of it; or the British should attempt to force nature by carrying the trade of the upper Lakes by the river Outawaies into Canada, which I scarsely think they will or could effect. Taking Detroit then (which is putting ourselves in as unfavourable a point of view as we can be well placed, because it is upon the line of the British territory) as a point by which, as I have already observed, all that part of the trade must come, it appears from the statement enclosed, that the tide waters of this State are nearer to it by 168 miles than that of the river St Lawrence; or than that of the Hudson at Albany by 176 miles.

Maryland stands upon similar ground with Virginia. Pennsylvania altho' the Susquehanna is an unfriendly water, much impeded it is said with rocks & rapids, & nowhere communicating with those which lead to her capital; have it in contemplation to open a communication between Toby's Creek (which empties into the Alleghany river, 95 miles above Fort Pitt) & the west branch of Susquehanna; & to cut a Canal between the waters of the latter, & the Schuylkill; the expence of which is easier to be conceived than estimated or described by me. A people however, who are possessed of the spirit of Commerce—who see, & who will pursue their advantages, may atchieve almost anything. In the meantime, under the uncertainty of these undertakings, they are smoothing the roads & paving the ways for the trade of that Western World. That New York will do the same so soon as the British Garrisons are removed; which are at present insurmountable obstacles in *their* way, no person who knows the temper, genius & policy of those people as well as I do, can harbour the smallest doubt.

Thus much with respect to rival States—let me now take a short view of our own; & being aware of the objections which are in the way; I will enumerate, in order to contrast them with the advantages.

The first & principal one is, the *unfortunate Jealousy*, which ever has & it is to be feared ever will prevail, lest one part of the State should obtain an advantage over the other part (as if the benefits of trade were not diffusive & beneficial to all)—then follow a train of difficulties viz:—that our people are already heavily taxed—that we have no money; that the advantages of this trade are remote; that the most *direct* rout for it is thro' *other* States, over whom we have no controul; that the routs over which we have controul, are as distant as either of those which lead to Philadelphia, Albany or Montreal; that a sufficient spirit of commerce does not pervade the Citizens of this Commonwealth; that we are in fact doing for others, what they ought to do for themselves.

Without going into the investigation of a question, which has employed the pens of able politicians, namely, whether trade with Foreigners is an advantage or disadvantage to a country. This State as a part of the confederated States (all of whom have the spirit of it very strongly working within them) must adopt it, or submit to the evils arising therefrom without receiving its benefits—common policy therefore points clearly & strongly, to the propriety of our enjoying all the advantages which nature & our local situation afford us; and evinces clearly that unless this spirit could be totally eradicated in other States, as well as in this, and every man made to become either a cultivator of the Land, or a manufacturer of such articles as are prompted by necessity, such stimulas should be employed as will *force* this spirit; by shewing to our Countrymen the superior advantages we possess beyond others; & the importance of being upon a footing with our Neighbours.

If this is fair reasoning, it ought to follow as a consequence, that we should do our part towards opening the communication with the fur & peltry trade of the Lakes; & for the produce of the Country which lies within; & which will, so soon as matters are settled with the Indians, & the terms on which Congress mean to dispose of the Land, & found to be favourable, are announced—settle faster than any other ever did, or any one would imagine. This then when considered in an interested point of view, is alone sufficient to excite our endeavours; but in my opinion, there is a political consideration for so doing, which is of still greater importance.

I need not remark to you Sir, that the flanks & rear of the United States are possessed by other powers—& formidable ones, too; nor, how necessary it is to apply the cement of interest, to bind all parts of the Union together by indissoluble bonds—especially that part of it, which lies immediately west of us, with the middle States. For, what ties, let me ask, shou'd we have upon those people? How entirely unconnected with them shall we be, and what troubles may we not apprehend, if the Spaniards on their right, & Gt Britain on their left, instead of throwing stumbling blocks in their way as they now do, should hold out lures for their trade and alliance. What, when they get strength, which will be sooner than most people conceive (from the emigration of foreigners who will have no particular predilection towards us, as well as from the removal of our own Citizens) will be the consequence of their having formed close connexions with both, or either of those powers in a commercial way? It needs not, in my opinion, the gift of prophecy to foretell.

The Western settlers, (I speak now from my own observation) stand as it were upon a pivot—the touch of a feather, would turn them any way—They have look'd down the Mississippi, until the Spaniards (very impoliticly I think, for themselves) threw difficulties in their way; & they looked that way for no other reason, than because they could glide gently down the stream; without considering perhaps, the fatigues of the voyage back again, & the time necessary to perform it in: & because they have no other means of coming to us but by a long Land transportation & unimproved roads. These causes have hitherto checked the industry of the present settlers; for except the demand for provisions, occasioned by the increase of population, & a little flour which the necessities of Spaniards compel them to buy, they have no excitements to labour. But smooth the road once, & make easy the way for them, & then see what an influx of articles will be poured in upon us— how amazingly our exports will be encreased by them, & how amply we shall be compensated for any trouble & expence we may encounter to effect it.

A combination of circumstances makes the present conjuncture more favourable for Virginia, than for any other State in the Union, to fix these matters. The jealous & untoward disposition of the Spaniards on one hand, & the private views of some individuals, coinciding with the general policy of the Court of Great Britain, on the other, to retain as long as possible the Posts of Detroit, Niagara, Oswego &c. (which, tho' they are done under the letter of the Treaty, is certainly an infraction of the spirit of it, & injurious to the union) may be improved to the greatest advantage by this State; if she would open her avenues to the trade of that Country, & embrace the present moment to establish it—It only wants a beginning—the Western Inhabitants wou'd do their part towards its execution. weak as they are, they would meet us at least half way, rather than be *driven* into the arms of, or be made dependant upon foreigners; which would, eventually, either bring on a separation of them from us, or a War between the United States & one or the other of those powers—most probably with the Spaniards. The preliminary steps to the attainment of this great object, would be attended with very little expence; & might, at the same time that it served to attract the attention of the Western Country, & to convince the wavering Inhabitants thereof of our disposition to connect ourselves with them & to facilitate their commerce with us, would be a mean of removing those jealousies which otherwise might take place among ourselves.

These, in my opinion, are; to appoint Commissioners, who from their situation, integrity & abilities, can be under no suspicion of prejudice or predilection to one part more than to another. Let these Commissioners make an actual survey of James River & Potomack from tide water to their respective sources—Note with great accuracy the kind of navigation, & the obstructions in it; the difficulty & expence attending the removal of these obstructions; the distances from place to place thro' the whole extent; and the nearest & best Portages between these waters & the Streams capable of improvment which run into the Ohio; traverse these in like manner to *their* junction with the Ohio, & with equal accuracy—The navigation of this river (i.e. the ohio) being well known, they will have less to do in the examination of it; but nevertheless, let the courses & distances of it be taken to the mouth of the Muskingum, & up that river (notwithstanding it is in the ceded lands) to the carrying place with Cayahoga—down Cayahoga to Lake Erie, & thence to Detroit. Let them do the same with big Bever creek, although part of it is in the State of Pennsylvania; and with the Scioto also—In a word, let the Waters East & West of the Ohio, which invite our notice by their proximity, & the ease with which Land transportation may be had between them & the Lakes on one side, & the rivers Potomac & James on the other, be explored—accurately delineated, & a correct & connected Map of the whole be presented to the public. These things being done, I shall be mistaken if prejudice does not yield to facts; jealousy to candour—& finally, that reason & nature thus aided, will dictate what is right & proper to be done.

In the mean while, if it should be thought that the lapse of time which is necessary to effect this work, may be attended with injurious consequences, could not there be a sum of money granted towards opening *the best*, or if it should be deemed *more eligible*, two of the nearest communications, one to the Northward & another to the Southward, with the settlements to the westward? And an act be passed (if there should not appear a manifest disposition in the Assembly to make it a public undertaking) to incorporate, & encourage private Adventurers if any should associate & sollicit the same, for the purpose of extending the navigation of Potomac or James river? and, in the former case, to request the concurrence of Maryland in the measure—It will appear from my statement of the different routs (and as far as my means of information have extended, I have done it with the utmost candour) that all the produce of the settlements about Fort Pitt, can be brought to Alexandria by the Yohoghaney in 304 Miles; whereof only 31 is land transportation. And by the Monongahela and Cheat river in 360 miles; 20 only of which are land carriage. Whereas the common road from Fort Pitt to Philadelphia is 320 Miles, all Land transportation; or 476 miles, if the Ohio, Toby's Creek, Susquehanna & Schuylkill are made use of for this purpose: how much of this by land, I know not; but from the nature of the Country it must be very considerable. How much the interests & feelings of people thus circumstanced would be engaged to promote it, requires no illustration.

For my own part, I think it highly probable, that upon the strictest scrutiny (if the Falls of the Great Kanhawa can be made navigable, or a short portage had there)—it will be found of equal importance & convenience to improve the navigation of both the James & Potomac. The latter I am fully persuaded affords the nearest communication with the Lakes; but James river may be more convenient for all the settlers below the mouth of the Gt Kanhawa, & for some distance perhaps above, & west of it: for I have *no* expectation that any part of the trade *above* the falls of the Ohio will go down that river & the Mississippi, much less that the returns will ever come up them; unless our want of foresight & good management is the occasion of it. Or upon trial, if it should be found that these rivers, from the before-mentioned Falls, will admit the descent of Sea vessels; in which case, & the navigation of the former's becoming free, it is probable that both vessels & cargoes will be carried to foreign markets & sold; but the returns for them will never in the natural course of things, ascend the long & rapid current of that river; which with the Ohio to the Falls, in their meanderings, is little if any short of 2000 miles. Upon the whole, the object, in my estimation is of vast commercial and political importance: in these lights I think posterity will consider it, & regret (if our conduct should give them cause) that the present favourable moment to secure so great a blessing for them, was neglected.

One thing more remains, which I had like to have forgot, and that is the supposed difficulty of obtaining a passage thro' the State of Pennsylvania. How an application to its Legislature would be relished, in the first instance, I will not undertake to decide; but of one thing I am almost certain, such an application would place that body in a very delicate situation. There is in the State of Pennsylvania at least 100,000 souls west of the Laurel hill, who are groaning under the inconveniencies of a long land transportation; they are wishing, indeed they are looking for the improvement & extension of inland navigation; & if this cannot be made easy for them, to Philada (at any rate it must be lengthy), they will seek a Mart elsewhere—the consequence of which would be, that the State, tho' contrary to the policy & interests of its Sea-ports, must submit to the loss of so much of its trade, or hazard not only the trade but the loss of the Settlement also: for an opposition on the part of Government to the extension of water transportation, so consonant with the essential interests of a large body of people, or any extraordinary impositions upon the exports or imports to, or from another State, would ultimately bring on a separation between its Eastern & Western Settlements—towards which, there is not wanting a disposition at this moment in that part of it, which is beyond the mountains.

I consider Rumsey's discovery for working Boats against stream, by mechanical powers (principally) as not only a very fortunate invention for these States in general, but as one of those circumstances which have combined to render the present epocha favourable above all others for fixing, if we are disposed to avail ourselves of them, a large portion of the trade of the Western Country in the bosom of this State irrevocably.

Lengthy as this letter is, I intended to have written a fuller & more digested one, upon this important subject, but have met with so many interruptions since my return home, as almost to have precluded my writing at all—what I now give is crude; but if you are in sentiment with me, I have said enough; if there is not an accordance of opinion I have said too much, & all I pray in the latter case is, that you will do me the justice to believe my motives are pure, however erroneous my judgment may be on this matter, & that I am with the most perfect esteem & friendship Dr Sir Yrs &c. &c. &c.

To Richard Henry Lee

Dear Sir,   Mount Vernon 14th Decr 84

The letter which you did me the honor to write to me on the 20th of last Month, only came to my hands by the Post preceeding the date of this.

For the copy of the treaty held with the Six Nations at Fort Stanwix, you will please to accept my thanks. These people have given, I think, all that the United States could reasonably have asked of them; more perhaps than the State of New York conceive ought to have been required from them, by any other, than their own Legislature. I wish they were better satisfied. Individual States opposing the measures of the United States—encroaching upon the territory of one another—and setting up old and obsolete claims, is verifying the predictions of our enemies; and, in reallity, is truly unfortunate. If the Western tribes are as well disposed to treat with us as the Northern Indians have been, & will cede a competent district of Country North West of the Ohio, to answer our present purposes, it would be a circumstance as unexpected, as pleasing to me; for it was apprehended, if they agreed to the latter at all, it would be reluctantly. but the example of the Six Nations who (if they have not relinquished their claim) have pretensions to a large part of those Lands, may have a powerful influence on the Western gentry, & smooth the way for the Commissioners, who have proceeded to Fort Pitt.

It gave me pleasure to find by the last Gazettes, that a sufficient number of States had Assembled to form a Congress, and that you had been placed in the Chair of it—On this event, permit me to offer my Compliments of congratulation. To whatever causes the delay of this meeting may have been ascribed, it most certainly has an unfavorable aspect—contributes to lessen—(already too low)—the dignity and importance of the fœderal government. and is hurtful to our National character, in the eyes of Europe.

It is said (how founded I know not) that our Assembly have repealed their former act respecting British debts. If this be true, & the State of New York have not acted repugnant to the terms of the treaty, the British government can no longer hold the western posts under that cover; but I shall be mistaken if they do not intrench themselves behind some other expedient, to effect it; or, will appoint a time for surrendering them, of which we cannot avail ourselves—the probable consequence whereof will be, the destruction of the Works.

The Assemblies of Virginia and Maryland have now under consideration the extension of the inland navigation of the rivers Potomack & James; and opening a communication between them, and the Western Waters. They seem fully impressed with the political, as well as the commercial advantages which would result from the accomplishment of these great objects; & I hope will embrace the present moment to put them in a train for execution—Would it not at the same time, be worthy the wisdom, & attention of Congress to have the Western Waters well explored; the Navigation of them fully ascertained; accurately laid down; and a complete & perfect Map made of the Country; at least as far Westerly—as the Miamies, running into the Ohio & Lake Erie; and to see how the Waters of these communicates with the river St Joseph, which emptys into the Lake Michigan, & with the Wabash? for I cannot forbear observing that the Miami village in Hutchins Map, if it and the Waters are laid down with accuracy points to a very important Post for the Union—The expence attending such an undertaking could not be great—the advantages would be unbounded—for sure I am Nature has made such a display of her bounties in those regions that the more the Country is explored the more it will rise in estimation—consequently greater will the revenue be, to the Union.

Would there be any impropriety do you think Sir, in reserving for special Sale, all Mines, Minerals & Salt Springs in the general grants of land, from the United States? The public, instead of the few knowing ones might, in that case, receive the benefits which would proceed from the Sale of them; without infringing any rule of justice that occurs to me, or their own laws—but on the contrary, inflict just punishment upon those who, in defiance of the latter, have dared to create enemies to disturb the public tranquility, by roaming over the Country marking & Surveying the valuable spots in it, to the great disquiet of the Western tribes of Indians, who have viewed these proceedings with jealous indignation.

To hit upon a happy medium price for the Western Lands, for the prevention of Monopoly on one hand—and not discouraging useful Settlers on the other, will, no doubt, require consideration; but ought not in my opinion to employ too much time before the terms are announced. The Spirit of emigration is great—People have got impatient—and tho' you cannot stop the road, it is yet in your power to mark the way; a little while, & you will not be able to do either—It is easier to prevent, than to remedy an evil.

I shall be very happy in the continuation of your correspondence—& with sentiments of great esteem & respect I have the honor to be Dr Sir Yr Most Obedt Hble Servt

To William Gordon

Dear sir,   Mount Vernon 20th Decr 1784.

I am indebted to you for several letters; & am as much so for the Fish you kindly intended, as if it had actually arrived, & I was in the act of paying my respects to it at table—the chance, however, of doing this would be greater, was it at Boston, than in York-town in this State, where, I am informed it was landed at the time the Marqs de la Fayette did; who proceeded from thence to richmond, where I met him, & conducted him to Annapolis on his way to New York; the place of his intended embarkation for France, about the middle of this month.

I am glad to hear that my old acquaintance Colo. Ward is yet under the influence of vigorous passions—I will not ascribe the intrepidity of his late enterprize to a mere *flash* of desires, because, in his military career he would have learnt how to distinguish between false alarms & a serious movement. Charity therefore induces me to suppose that like a prudent general, he had reviewed his *strength*, his arms, & ammunition before he got involved in an action—But if these have been neglected, & he has been precipitated into the measure, let me advise him to make the *first* onset upon his fair del Tobosa, with vigor, that the impression may be deep, if it cannot be lasting, or frequently renewed.

We are all well at this time except Miss Custis, who still feels the effect, & sometimes the return of her fever—Mrs Lund Washington has added a daughter to her family—She, child and husband are well, & become house keepers at the distance of about four miles from this place.

We have a dearth of News, but the fine weather keeps us busy, & we have leisure for cogitation. All join in best wishes for you. Doctr & Mrs Stuart are of those who do it. I am Dr sir yrs &c.

To Benjamin Harrison

My Dr Sir,   Mount Vernon 22d Jan. 1785.

It is not easy for me to decide by which my mind was most affected upon the receipt of your letter of the 6th inst.—surprize or gratitude: both were greater than I have words to express. The attention & good wishes which the Assembly have evidenced by their act for vesting in me 150 shares in the navigation of each of the rivers Potomac & James, is more than mere compliment—there is an unequivocal & substantial meaning annexed—But believe me sir, notwithstanding these, no circumstance has happened to me since I left the walks of public life, which has so much embarrassed me. On the one hand, I consider this act, as I have already observed, as a noble and unequivocal proof of the good opinion, the affection, & disposition of my Country to serve me; & I should be hurt, if by declining the acceptance of it, my refusal should be construed into disrespect, or the smallest slight put upon the generous intention of the Country: or, that an ostentatious display of disinterestedness or public virtue, was the source of the refusal.

On the other hand, it is really my wish to have my mind, & the actions which are the result of contemplation, as free & independent as the air, that I may be more at liberty (in things which my opportunities & experience have brought me to the knowledge of) to express my sentiments, & if necessary, to suggest what may occur to me, under the fullest conviction, that altho' my judgment may be arraigned, there will be no suspicion that sinister motives had the smallest influence in the suggestion. Not content then with the bare consciousness of my having, in all this navigation business, acted upon the clearest conviction of the political importance of the measure; I would wish that every individual who may hear that it was a favorite plan of mine, may know also that I had no other motive for promoting it than the advantage I conceived it would be productive of to the Union, & to this State in particular, by cementing the Eastern and Western Territory together, at the same time that it will give vigor & encrease to our Commerce, & be a convenience to our Citizens.

How would this matter be viewed then by the eye of the world; and what would be the opinion of it, when it comes to be related that G: W——n exerted himself to effect this work—and G.W. has received 20,000 Dollars, and £5,000 Sterling of the public money as an interest therein? Would not this in the estimation of it (if I am entitled to any merit for the part I have acted; & without it there is no foundation for the act) deprive me of the principal thing which is laudable in my conduct? Would it not, in some respects, be considered in the same light as a pension? And would not the apprehension of this make me more reluctantly offer my sentiments in future? In a word, under what ever pretence, & however customary these gratuitous gifts are made in other Countries, should I not thence forward be considered as a dependant? one moments thought of which would give me more pain, than I should receive pleasure from the product of all the tolls, was every farthing of them vested in me: altho' I consider it as one of the most certain & increasing Estates in the Country.

I have written to you with an openess becoming our friendship—I could have said more on the subject; but I have already said enough to let you into the State of my mind. I wish to know whether the ideas I entertain occurred to, & were expressed by any member in or out of the House. Upon the whole, you may be assured my Dr Sir, that my mind is not a little agitated—I want the best information & advice to settle it. I have no inclination (as I have already observed) to avail myself of the generosity of the Country: nor do I want to appear ostentatiously disinterested, (for more than probable my refusal would be ascribed to this motive) or that the Country should harbour an idea that I am disposed to set little value on her favours—the manner of granting which is as flattering as the grant is important. My present difficulties however shall be no impediment to the progress of the undertaking. I will receive the full & frank opinions of my friends with thankfulness. I shall have time enough between this & the sitting of the next Assembly to consider the tendency of the act—& in this, as in all other matters, will endeavor to decide for the best.

My respectful compliments & best wishes, in which Mrs Washington & Fanny Bassett (who is much recovered) join, are offered to Mrs Harrison & the rest of your family. It would give us great pleasure to hear that Mrs Harrison had her health restored to her. With every sentiment of esteem, regard & friendship, I am My Dr Sir &c. &c.

To George William Fairfax

My Dr Sir,   Mount Vernon 27th Feby 1785.
    In a letter of old date, but lately received, from the Countess of Huntington, she refers me to a letter which her Lady-

ship says you obligingly undertook to forward to me: never having received one from her to the purport she mentions, there can be no doubt but that this letter with your cover to it, have met the fate of some of mine to you; as I have wrote several within the last twelve or eighteen months, without any acknowledgement of them from you.

The only letters I recollect to have received from you since my retirement are dated the 9th of Decr 1783, and 10th of June 1784. the first, relates to the heir of Mr Bristow—the second, to a case with pictures, which you were so obliging as to commit to the care of the revd Mr Bracken; & which has not yet got to hand. In Novr last at richmond, I happened in company with this gentleman who told me it was then in his possession at Wmsburgh, and that it should be forwarded by the first safe conveyance to this place—for your kind & polite attention in this matter, I pray you to receive my sincere thanks.

As soon as your letter of the 9th of Decr, abovementioned (accompanied by one from Mrs Bristow, & the memorial from the Executors of the Will of her deceased husband) came to my hands, I transmitted them to the Govr, who laid them before the Assembly which was then sitting; but what the result of it was, I have never yet heard, precisely. The case was involved in the general confiscation of British property, which makes discrimination difficult—How far the Law on national ground is just—or the expediency of it in the political scale, Wise & proper, I will not undertake to determine; but of this I am well convinced, that the most wretched management of the sales has pervaded every State; without, I believe a single exception in favor of any one of them.

I cannot at this moment recur to the contents of those letters of mine to you which I suspect have miscarried; further than that they were all expressive of an earnest wish to see you & Mrs Fairfax once more fixed in this country; & to beg that you would consider Mt Vernon as your home until you could build with convenience—in which request Mrs Washington joins very sincerely. I never look towards Belvoir, without having this uppermost in my mind. But alas! Belvoir is no more! I took a ride there the other day to visit the ruins —& ruins indeed they are. The dwelling house & the two brick buildings in front, underwent the ravages of the fire; the walls of which are very much injured: the other Houses are sinking under the depredation of time & inattention, & I believe are now scarcely worth repairing. In a word, the whole are, or very soon will be a heap of ruin. When I viewed them—when I considered that the happiest moments of my life had been spent there—when I could not trace a room in the house (now all rubbish) that did not bring to my mind the recollection of pleasing scenes; I was obliged to fly from them; & came home with painful sensations, & sorrowing for the contrast—Mrs Morton still lives at your Barn quarters—The management of your business is entrusted to one Muse (son to a Colonel of that name, whom you cannot have forgotten)—he is, I am told, a very active & industrious man; but in what sort of order he has your Estate, I am unable to inform you, never having seen him since my return to Virginia.

It may be & I dare say is presumed that if I am not returned to my former habits of life, the change is to be ascribed to a preference of ease & indolence, to exercise & my wonted activity: But be assured my dear sir, that at no period of the War have I been obliged *myself* to go thro' more drudgery in writing, or have suffered so much confinement to effect it, as since what is called my retirement to domestic ease & tranquillity. Strange as it may seem, it is nevertheless true—that I have been able since I came home, to give very little attention to my own concerns, or to those of others, with which I was entrusted—My accounts stand as I left them near ten years ago; those who owed me money, a very few instances excepted, availed themselves of what are called the tender Laws, & paid me off with a shilling & sixpence in the pound—Those to whom I owed I have now to pay under heavy taxes with specie, or its equivalent value. I do not mention these matters by way of complaint, but as an apology for not having rendered you a full & perfect statement of the Accot as it may stand between us, 'ere this. I allotted this Winter, supposing the drearyness of the season would afford me leisure to overhaul & adjust all my papers (which are in sad disorder, from the frequent hasty removals of them, from the reach of our transatlantic foes, when their Ships appeared): but I reckoned without my host; company, & a continual reference of old military matters, with which I ought to have no concerns; applications for certificates of service &c.—copies of orders & the Lord knows what besides—to which whether they are complied with or not, some response must be made, engross nearly my whole time. I am now endeavoring to get some person as a Secretary or Clerk to take the fatigueing part of this business off my hands—I have not yet succeeded, but shall continue my enquiries 'till one shall offer, properly recommended.

Nothing has occurred of late worth noticing, except the renewed attempts of the Assemblies of Virginia & Maryland to improve & extend the navigation of the river Potomac as far as it is practicable—& communicating it by good roads (at the joint & equal expence of the two States) with the waters of the amazing territory behind us—A copy of this Act (exactly similar in both States) I do myself the honor to enclose you. One similar to it passed the Legislature of this State for improving & extending the navigation of James river, & opening a good road between it & Green-briar. These acts were accompanied by another of the Virginia Assembly very flattering & honorable for me—not more so for the magnitude of the gift, than the avowed gratitude, & delicacy of its expression, in the recital to it—The purport of it is, to vest 100 shares (50 in each navigation) in me & my heirs forever. But it is not my intention to accept of it; altho', were I otherwise disposed, I should consider it as the foundation of the *greatest* & most *certain* income that the like sum can produce in any speculation whatever. So certain is the accomplishment of the work, if the sum proposed should be raised to carry it on— & so inconceivably will the tolls increase by the accumulating produce which will be water borne on the navigation of these two rivers; which penetrate so far & communicate so nearly, with the navigable waters to the Westward.

At the same time that I determine not to accept the generous & gratuitous offer of my Country, I am at a loss in what manner to decline it, without an apparent slight or disrespect to the Assembly on the one hand, or exposing myself to the imputation of pride, or an ostentatious display of disinterestedness on the other—neither have an existence in my breast,

& neither would I wish to have ascribed to me. I shall have time however to think of the matter, before the next session; for as if it was meant that I should have no opportunity to decline the offer at the *last*, it was the closing act thereof, without any previous intimation, or suspicion in my mind, of the intention. Admitting that Companies should be incorporated for the purposes mentioned in the Act, do you conceive my good Sir, that a person perfectly skilled in works of this sort, could be readily obtained from England? and upon what terms?

It is unnecessary I persuade myself, to use arguments to convince Mrs Fairfax & yourself, of the sincere regard & attachment & affection Mrs Washington and I have for you both, or to assure you how much, I am, My Dr Sir &c. &c.

P.S. Do you think it would be in your power, with ease & convenience, to procure for me, a male & female Deer or two. the cost of transportation I would gladly be at. If I should ever get relieved from the drudgery of the pen, it would be my wish to engage in these kind of rural amusements—raising of shrubberies &c. After what I have said in the body of this letter, I will not trouble you with an apology for such a scrawl as it now exhibits—You must receive it, my good Sir, as we have done better things—better for worse.

To Francis Hopkinson

Dear Sir,   Mount Vernon May 16th 1785

In for a penny, in for a pound, is an old adage. I am so hackneyed to the touches of the Painters pencil, that I am *now* altogether at their beck, and sit like patience on a Monument whilst they are delineating the lines of my face.

It is a proof among many others, of what habit & custom can effect. At first I was as impatient at the request, and as restive under the operation, as a Colt is of the Saddle—The next time, I submitted very reluctantly, but with less flouncing. Now, no dray moves more readily to the Thill, than I do to the Painters Chair. It may easily be conceived therefore that

I yielded a ready obedience to your request, and to the views of Mr Pine.

Letters from England, recommendatory of this Gentleman, came to my hand previous to his arrival in America—not only as an Artist of acknowledged eminence, but as one who had discovered a friendly disposition towards this Country—for which, it seems, he had been marked.

It gave me pleasure to hear from you—I shall always feel an interest in your happiness—and with Mrs Washingtons compliments, & best wishes joined to my own, for Mrs Hopkinson & yourself, I am—Dr Sir, Yr Most Obedt & Affecte Hble Servant

To Tench Tilghman

Dear Sir,   Mount Vernon June 2d 1785

As your letter of the 30th Ulto did not reach me until late this afternoon, and the Post goes from Alexaa at 4 Oclock in the morning, I have scarcely a moment (being also in company) to write you a reply.

I was not sufficiently explicit in my last. The terms upon which Mr Falconer came to this Country are too high for my finances—and (to you, my dear Sir, I will add) numerous expences. I do not wish to reduce his (perhaps well founded) expectations; but it behoves me to consult my own means of complying with them.

I had been in hopes, that a young man of no great expectations, might have begun the world, with me, for about fifty or Sixty pounds Virga Curry pr Ann.—but for one qualified in all respects to answer my purposes, I would have gone as far as Seventy five—more would rather distress me.

My purposes are these. To write Letters agreeably to what shall be dictated. Do all other writing which shall be entrusted to him—Keep Accts—Examine, arrange, & properly methodize my Papers, which are in great disorder. ride, at my expence, to do such business as I may have in different parts of this, or the other States, if I should find it more convenient to send, than attend my self, to the execution thereof. And, which was not hinted at in my last, to inetiate two little children (a girl of six, & a boy of 4 years of age, descendent's of the deceased Mr Custis, who live with me, and are very promising) in the first rudiments of education. This to both parties, would be mere amusement, because it is not my wish that the Children should be confined.

If Mr Falconer should incline to accept the above stipend in addition to his board, washing & mending, and *you* (for I would rather have *your opinion* of the Gentleman than the *report* of a thousand others in his favor) upon a close investigation of his character, Temper, & moderate political tenets (for supposing him an English man, he may come with the prejudices, & Doctrines of his Country) the sooner he comes, the better my purposes would be promoted.

If I had had time, I might have added more, but to you it would have been unnecessary. You know my wants—you know my disposition—and you know what kind of a man would suit them. In haste I bid you adieu. With assurances of great regard & sincere friendship, I am—Dr Sir Yr Affecte Hble Servt

To William Goddard

sir,   Mt Vernon 11th June 1785.

On the 8th inst: I received the favor of your letter of the 30th of May: In answer to it I can only say, that your own good judgement must direct you in the publication of the manuscript papers of Genl Lee—I can have no request to make concerning the work.

I never had a difference with that Gentleman but on public ground, & my conduct towards him upon this occasion, was such only, as I conceived myself indispensably bound to adopt in discharge of the public trust reposed in me. If this produced in him unfavourable sentiments of me, I yet can never consider the conduct I pursued, with respect to him, either wrong or improper; however I may regret that it may have been differently viewed by him, & that it excited his censure and animadversions. Should there appear in Genl Lee's writings anything injurious or unfriendly to me, the impartial & dispassionate world, must decide how far I deserved it from the general tenor of my conduct.

I am gliding down the stream of life, & wish as is natural, that my remaining Days may be undisturbed and tranquil; & conscious of my integrity, I would willingly hope that nothing would occur tending to give me anxiety; but should anything present itself in this or in any other publication, I shall never undertake the painful task of recrimination—nor do I know that I shall even enter upon my justification.

I consider the communication you have made as a mark of great attention, & the whole of your letter as a proof of your esteem. I am &c.

To David Humphreys

My dear Humphreys   Mount Vernon July 25th 1785.

Since my last to you I have received your letters of the 15th of Jany and (I believe) that of the 11th of Novr; & thank you for them both—It always gives me pleasure to hear from you; and I should think, if amusements would spare you, business could not so much absorb your time as to prevent your writing to me more frequently; especially as there is a regular & safe conveyance once a month, by the Packett.

As the complexion of European politics seem now (from the letters I have received from the Marquisses de la Fayette & Chastellux—the Chevr de la Luzerne, &ca) to have a tendency to Peace, I will say nothing of War, nor make any animadversions upon the contending Powers—otherwise I might possibly have added, that the retreat from it seemed impossible, after the explicit declarations of the Parties.

My first wish is, to see this plague to Mankind banished from the Earth; & the Sons & daughters of this World employed in more pleasing & innocent amusements than in preparing implements, & exercising them for the destruction of the human race. Rather than quarrel abt territory, let the poor, the needy, & oppressed of the Earth; and those who want Land, resort to the fertile plains of our Western Country, to the second Land of promise, & there dwell in peace, fulfilling the first & great Commandment.

In a former letter I informed you, My dear Humphreys, that if I had talents for it, I have not leizure to devote my time & thoughts to commentaries. I am conscious of a defective education, & want of capacity to fit me for such an undertaking. What with Company, letters, & other Matters, many of them extraneous, I have not yet been able to arrange my own private concerns so as to rescue them from that disordered state into which they have been thrown, by the War; and to do which, is become indispensibly necessary for my support, whilst I remain on this stage of human action.

The sentiment of your last letter on this subject gave me great pleasure. I should indeed be pleased to see you undertake this business. Your abilities as a writer—Your discernment respecting the principles which lead to the decision by Arms—Your personal knowledge of many facts as they occurred, in the progress of the War—Your disposition to justice, candour & impartiallity, and your diligence in investigating truth, combining, fits you, in the vigor of life, for this task. and I should with great pleasure not only give you the perusal of all my Papers, but any oral information of circumstances which cannot be obtained from the latter, that my memory will furnish. And I can with great truth add, that my House would not only be at your Service during the period of your preparing this work, but (and without an unmeaning compliment I say it) I shoud be exceedingly happy if you would make it your home. You might have an Apartment to yourself in which you could command your own time. You would be considered, & treated as one of the family. And would meet with that cordial reception & entertainment, which are characteristic of the sincerest friendship.

To reverberate European News would be idle; and we have little of a domestic kind worthy of attention. We have held treaties indeed with the Indians, but they were so unseasonably delayed that these people from our last accts from the Westward are in a discontented mood—supposed by many to be instigated thereto by our late enemy—now, to be sure, good & fast friends; who, from anything I can learn, under the indefinite expression of the treaty, hold, & seem resolved to retain, possession of our Western Posts. Congress have also—after long & tedeous deliberation—passed an Ordinance for laying of the Western territory into States, & for disposing of the Land; but in a manner, and on terms, which few people (in the Southern States) conceive can be accomplished. Both sides are sure, & the event is appealed to—time must decide. It is to be regretted however, that local politics, & self interested views, obtrude themselves into every measure of public utility. But on such characters, be the obloquy—My attention is more immediately engaged in a project which I think is big with great political, as well as Commercial consequences to these States, especially the middle ones. It is, by removing the obstructions—and extending the inland Navigations of our Rivers, to bring the States on the Atlantic in close connection with those forming to the Westward, by a short & easy Land transportation. Without this is effected, I can readily conceive that the Western Settlers will have different views—seperate interests—and other connections.

I may be singular in my ideas, but they are these, that to open the front door to, & make easy the way for those Settlers to the Westward (which ought to progress regularly & compactly) before we make any stir about the Navigation of the Mississipi, and before our settlements are far advanced towards that River would be our true line of policy. It can I think be demonstrated, that the produce of the Western territory (if the Navigations which are now in hand succeed, and of which I have no doubt) as low down the Ohio as the Great Kanhawa (I believe to the Falls) and between the parts above, & the Lakes, may be brought to the highest shipping Port either on this, or James River, at a less expence, with more ease (including the return) and in a much shorter time than it can be carried to New Orleans, if the Spaniards, instead of restrictions were to throw open their ports, & envite our trade—But if the commerce of that Country shd embrace this channel, and connections be formed, experience has taught us (and there is a very recent one in proof, with Great Britain) how next to impracticable it is to divert it—and if that shd be the case, the Atlantic States (especially as those to the Westward will, in a great degree, fill with foreigners) except to excite—perhaps with too much cause—our fears that the

Country of California, which is still more to the Westward, & belonging to another Power. Mrs Washington presents her compliments to you, and with every wish for your happiness I am—My dear Humphreys Yr sincere friend and Affectionate Hble Servt

To Marquis de Lafayette

My Dear Marquis,   Mount Vernon 25th July 1785.

I have to acknowledge & thank you for your several favors of the 9th of February—19th of March & 16th of April, with their enclosures; all of which (the last only yesterday) have been received since I had the honor to address you in February.

I stand before you as a Culprit; but to *repent* & *be forgiven* are the precepts of Heaven: I do the former—do you practise the latter, & it will be participating of a divine attribute. Yet I am not barren of excuses for this seeming inattention; frequent absences from home—a round of company when at it, & the pressure of many matters, might be urged as apologies for my long silence; but I disclaim all of them, & trust to the forbearance of friendship & your wonted indulgence: indeed so few things occur, in the line on which I now move, worthy of attention—that this also might be added to the catalogue of my excuses; especially when I further add, that one of my letters, if it is to be estimated according to its length, would make three of yours.

I now congratulate you, & my heart does it more effectually than my pen, on your safe arrival at Paris, from your voyage to this Country, & on the happy meeting with Madame la Fayette & your family in good health—May the blessing of this long continue to them—& may every day add increase of happiness to yourself. As the clouds which overspread your hemisphere are dispersing, & peace with all its concomitants is dawning upon your Land, I will banish the sound of War from my letter: I wish to see the sons & daughters of the world in Peace & busily employed in the more agreeable amusement, of fulfilling the first and great commandment—

Increase & Multiply: as an encouragement to which we have opened the fertile plains of the Ohio to the poor, the needy & the oppressed of the Earth; any one therefore who is heavy laden, or who wants land to cultivate, may repair thither & abound, as in the Land of promise, with milk & honey: the ways are preparing, & the roads will be made easy, thro' the channels of Potomac & James river.

Speaking of these navigations, I have the pleasure to inform you that the subscriptions, (especially for the first) at the surrender of the books, agreeably to the Act which I enclosed you in my last, exceeded my most sanguine expectation: for the latter, that is James river, no comparison of them has yet been made.

Of the £50,000 Sterlg required for the Potomac navigation, upwards of £40,000, was subscribed before the middle of May, & encreasing fast. A President & four Directors, consisting of your hble Servant, Govrs Johnson & Lee of Maryland, & Colo. Fitzgerald & Gilpin of this State, were chosen to conduct the undertaking. The first dividend of the money was paid in on the 15th of this month; & the work is to be begun the first of next, in those parts which require least skill: leaving the more difficult 'till an Engineer of abilities & practical knowledge can be obtained; which reminds me of the question which I propounded to you in my last, on this subject, & on which I should be glad to learn your sentiments. This project, if it succeeds & of which I have no doubt, will bring the Atlantic States & the Western Territory into close connexion, & be productive of very extensive commercial & political consequences; the last of which gave the spur to my exertions, as I could foresee many, & great mischiefs which would naturally result from a separation—& that a separation would inevitably take place, if the obstructions between the two Countries remained, & the navigation of the Mississippi should be made free.

Great Britain, in her commercial policy is acting the same unwise part, with respect to herself, which seems to have influenced all her Councils; & thereby is defeatg her own ends: the restriction of our trade, & her heavy imposts on the staple commodities of this Country, will I conceive, immediately produce powers in Congress to regulate the Trade of the

Union; which, more than probably would not have been obtained without in half a century. The mercantile interests of the *whole* Union are endeavouring to effect this, & will no doubt succeed; they see the necessity of a controuling power, & the futility, indeed the absurdity, of each State's enacting Laws for this purpose independant of one another. This will be the case also, after a while, in all matters of common concern. It is to be regretted, I confess, that Democratical States must always *feel* before they can *see*: it is this that makes their Governments slow—but the people will be right at last.

Congress after long deliberation, have at length agreed upon a mode for disposing of the Lands of the United States in the Western territory—it may be a good one, but it does not comport with my ideas. The ordinance is long, & I have none of them by me, or I would send one for your perusal. They seem in this instance, as in almost every other, to be surrendering the little power they have, to the States individually which gave it to them. Many think the price which they have fixed upon the Lands too high; and all to the Southward I believe, that disposing of them in Townships, & by square miles alternately, will be a great let to the sale: but experience, to which there is an appeal, must decide.

Soon after I had written to you in Feby, Mr Jefferson, & after him Mr Carmichael informed me that in consequence of an application from Mr Harrison for permission to export a Jack for me from Spain, his Catholic Majesty had ordered *two* of the first race in his Kingdom (lest an accident might happen to *one*) to be purchased and presented to me as a mark of his esteem. Such an instance of condescension & attention from a crowned head is very flattering, and lays me under great obligation to the King; but neither of them is yet arrived: these I presume are the two mentioned in your favor of the 16th of April; one as having been shipped from Cadiz—the other as expected from the Isle of Malta, which you would forward. As they have been purchased since December last, I began to be apprehensive of accidents; which I wish may not be the case with respect to the one from Cadiz, if he was actually shipped at the time of your account: should the other pass thro' your hands you cannot oblige me more, than by requiring the greatest care, & most particular attention to be paid to him. I have long endeavoured to procure one of a good size & breed, but had little expectation of receiving two as a royal gift.

I am much obliged to you My dear Marquis, for your attention to the Hounds, & not less sorry that you should have met the smallest difficulty, or experienced the least trouble in obtaining them: I was no way anxious about these, consequently should have felt no regret, or sustained no loss if you had not succeeded in your application. I have commissioned three or four persons (among whom Colo. Marshall is one) to procure for me in Kentucke, for the use of the Kings Garden's at Versailles or elsewhere, the seeds mentioned in the list you sent me from New York, & such others as are curious, & will forward them as soon as they come to my hands; whch cannot be 'till after the growing Crop has given its seeds.

My best wishes will accompany you to Potsdam, & into the Austrian Dominions whenever you set out upon that tour. As an unobserved spectator, I should like to take a peep at the troops of those Monarch's at their manœuverings upon a grand field day; but as it is among the unattainable things, my philosophy shall supply the place of curiosity, & set my mind at ease.

In your favor of the 19th of March you speak of letters which were sent by a Mr Williams; but none such have come to hand. The present for the little folks did not arrive by Mr Ridouts Ship as you expected; to what cause owing I know not. Mrs Washington has but indifferent health; & the late loss of her Mother, & only brother Mr Barthw Dandridge (one of the Judges of our supreme Court) has rather added to her indisposition. My mother & friends enjoy good health—George has returned after his peregrination thro' the West Indies, to Burmuda, the Bahama Islands, & Charlestown; at the last place he spent the winter. He is in better health than when he set out, but not quite recovered: He is now on a journey to the Sweet Springs, to procure a stock sufficient to fit him for a matrimonial voyage in the Frigate F. Bassett, on board which he means to embark at his return in October: how far his case is desperate, I leave you to judge—if it is so, the remedy however pleasing at first, will certainly be violent.

The latter end of April I had the pleasure to receive in good order, by a Ship from London, the picture of your self, Madame la Fayette & the children, which I consider as an invaluable present, & shall give it the best place in my House. Mrs Washington joins me in respectful compliments, & in every good wish for Madame de la Fayette, yourself & family; all the others who have come under your kind notice present their compliments to you. For myself, I can only repeat the sincere attachment, & unbounded affection of My Dr Marqs &c. &c. &c.

To Edmund Randolph

Dear Sir, Mount Vernon July 30th 1785.

Altho' it is not my intention to derive any pecuniary advantage from the generous vote of the Assembly of this State, consequent of its gratuitous gift of fifty shares in each of the navigations of the rivers Potomac and James; yet, as I consider these undertakings as of vast political & commercial importance to the States on the Atlantic, especially to those nearest the centre of the Union, & adjoining the Western Territory, I can let no act of mine impede the progress of the work: I have therefore come to the determination to hold the shares which the Treasurer was directed to subscribe on my account, in trust for the use & benefit of the public; unless I shall be able to discover, before the meeting of the Assembly, that it would be agreeable to it to have the product of the Tolls arising from these shares, applied as a fund on which to establish two Charity schools, one on each river, for the Education & support of the Children of the poor & indigent of this Country who cannot afford to give it; particularly the children of those men of this description, who have fallen in defence of the rights & liberties of it. If the plans succeed, of which I have no doubt, I am sure it will be a very productive & encreasing fund, & the monies thus applied will be a beneficial institun.

I am aware that my non-acceptance of these shares will have various motives ascribed to it, among which an ostentatious display of disinterestedness—perhaps the charge of disrespect or slight of the favors of my Country, may lead the van: but under a consciousness that my conduct herein is not influenced by considerations of this nature—& that I shall act more agreeably to my own feelings, & more consistent with my early declarations, by declining to accept them; I shall not only hope for indulgence, but a favorable interpretation of my conduct: my friends, I persuade myself, will acquit me, the World I hope will judge charitably.

Perceiving by the Advertisement of Messrs Cabell, Buchanan and Southall that half the sum required by the Act, for opening & extending the navigation of James river, is subscribed; & the 20th of next month appointed for the subscribers to meet at Richmond, I take the liberty, of giving a power to act for me on that occasion. I would (having the accomplishment of these navigations much at heart) have attended in person; but, the President and Directors of the Potomac Company by their own appointment, are to commence the survey of this river in the early part of next month; for which purpose I shall leave home tomorrow. Besides which, if the Ejectments which I have been obliged to bring for my Land in Pennsylva. are to be tried at the September Term, as Mr Smith, my Lawyer, conceived they would, & is to inform me—I shall find it necessary I fear, to attend the trial; an intermediate journey therefore, in addition, to Richmond would be impracticable for me to accomplish. I am Sir &c. &c.

To James McHenry

Dear Sir,   Mount Vernon 22d Augt 1785.

Your letter of the 1st Instt came to this place whilst I was absent on a tour up the Potomack, or an earlier acknowledgement of it would have been given. The inclosure shall, either by this, or the next Post, be sent to Doctr Gordon for his information, and that justice may be done to a character so deserving of American gratitude, & the pen of a Historiographer as that of the Marquis de la Fayette's.

I am very glad to hear that Congress is relieved from the

embarrassment which originated with Longchamp; had the demand of him been persisted in, it might have involved very serious consequences. It is better that the Court of France should be a little miffed than for it to have persevered in their demand of him.

As I have ever been a friend to adequate powers in Congress, without wch it is evident to me we never shall establish a National character, or be considered on a respectable footing by the powers of Europe, I am sorry I cannot agree with you in sentiment not to enlarge them for the regulation of Commerce. I have neither time nor abilities to enter upon a full discussion of this subject; but it should seem to me, that, your arguments against it—principally—that some States may be more benefitted than others by a Commercial regulation, applies to every matter of general utility; for where is the case in which this argument may not be used, in a greater, or less degree. We are either a United people under one head, & for Fœderal purposes, or, we are thirteen independent Sovereignties, eternally counteracting each other. If the former, whatever such a Majority of the States, as the Constitution requires, conceives to be for the benefit of the whole, should, in my humble opinion, be submitted to by the Minority. Let the Southern States always be represented. Let them Act more in unison—Let them declare freely, & boldly what is for the interest, & what is prejudicial to their Constituents, and there will—there must be, an accomodating spirit. In the establishment of an Act for Navigation, this, in a particular manner ought, & will, doubtless, be attended to; and if the assent of nine (or as some propose, of Eleven) States is necessary to give validity to a Commercial system, it insures this measure, or the Act cannot be obtained—Wherein then lyes the danger? but if your fears are in danger of being reallized, cannot certain provisos in the Law guard against the evil? I see no difficulty in this if the Southern Delegates would give their attendance in Congress, and follow the example, if such an one should beset them, of hanging together to counteract combinations.

I confess to you candidly that I can foresee no evil greater, than disunion—than those unreasonable jealousies (I say *unreasonable*, because I would have a proper jealousy always awake, and the United States always upon the watch, to prevent individual States from infracting the Constitution, with impunity) which are continually poisoning our minds, and filling them with imaginary evils, to the prevention of real ones. As you have asked the question, I answer, I do not know that we can enter a War of Imposts with G. Britain, or any other foreign Power, but we are certain that this War has been waged against us by the former, *professedly*, upon a belief that we never could unite in opposition to it. and I believe there is no way of putting an end to—at least of stopping the increase of it, but to convince them of the contrary. Our Trade in all points of view is as essential to G.B., as hers is to us—and she will exchange it upon reciprocal & liberal terms, if an advantage is not to be obtained. It can hardly be supposed, I think, that the carrying business will devolve wholly on the States you have named; or remain long with them if it should—for either G.B. will depart from her present selfish system, or the policy of the Southern States in forming a general Act of Navigation, or by Laws individually passed by their respective Legislatures, will devise ways & means to encourage seamen for the transportation of their own produce—or for the encouragement of Manufactures; but admitting the contrary, if the Union is considered as permanent, and on this I presume all superstructures are built, had we not better encourage Seamen among ourselves with less imports, than divide it with foreigners & by encreasing them, ruin our Merchants; & greatly injure the mass of our Citizens?

To sum up the whole, I foresee, or think I do it, many advantages which will result from giving powers of this kind to Congress (if a sufficient number of States are required to exercise them) without any evil save those which may proceed from inattention or want of wisdom in the formation of the Act. whilst without them, we stand, I conceive, in a ridiculous point of view in the eyes of the Nations of the Earth; with whom we are attempting to enter into Commercial Treaties without means of carrying them into effect and who must see, & feel, that the Union, or the States individually, are Sovereigns, as it best suits their purposes. In a word that we are one Nation today, & thirteen tomorrow—Who will treat with us on such terms? But perhaps I have gone too far, & there-

fore shall only add that, with great esteem & regard I am—
Dear Sir Yr Most Obedt & Affecte Hble Servt

P.S. Mrs Washington offers her Compliments & best wishes
for you.

To George Mason

Dr Sir   Mount Vernon 3d Octr 1785.

I have this moment received yours of yesterday's date enclosing a memorial & remonstrance against the assessment
Bill, which I will read with attention; at *present* I am unable
to do it, on account of company. The Bill itself I do not recollect ever to have read: with *attention* I am certain I never
did—but will compare them together.

Altho' no mans sentiments are more opposed to *any kind*
of restraint upon religious principles than mine are; yet I must
confess, that I am not amongst the number of those who are
so much alarmed at the thoughts of making people pay
towards the support of that which they profess, if of the
denominations of Christians; or declare themselves Jews,
Mahomitans or otherwise, & thereby obtain proper relief. As
the matter now stands, I wish an assessment had never been
agitated—& as it has gone so far, that the Bill could die an
easy death; because I think it will be productive of more quiet
to the State, than by enacting it into a Law; which, in my
opinion, wou'd be impolitic, admitting there is a decided majority for it, to the disgust of a respectable minority. In the
first case the matter will soon subside; in the latter it will ran-
kle, & perhaps convulse the State. The Dinner Bell rings, &
I must conclude with an expression of my concern for your
indisposition. Sincerely & affectionately I am &c. &c.

To James Warren

Dear Sir,   Mount Vernon Octr 7th 1785.

The assurances of your friendship, after a silence of more than six years, is extremely pleasing to me. Friendships formed under the circumstances that ours commenced are not easily eradicated, and I can assure you that mine has undergone no diminution. Every occasion therefore of renewing it, will give me pleasure; and I shall be happy, at all times, to hear of yr welfare.

The War, as you have very justly observed, has terminated most advantageously for America—and a large & glorious field is presented to our view. But I confess to you, my dear Sir, that I do not think we possess wisdom, or justice enough to cultivate it properly. Illiberality, Jealousy, & local policy mix too much in all our public Councils for the good government of the Union. In a word, the Confederation appears to me to be little more than an empty sound, and Congress a nugatory body; the ordinances of it being very little attended to.

To me, it is a solecism in politics, indeed it is one of the most extraordinary things in nature, that we should Confederate for National purposes, and yet be affraid to give the rulers thereof who are the Creatures of our own making— appointed for a limited and short duration—who are amenable for every action—recallable at any moment—and subject to all the evils they may be instrumental in producing, sufficient powers to order & direct the affairs of that Nation.

By such policy as this the wheels of government are clogged; & our brightest prospects, and that high expectation which was entertained of us by the wondering world, is turned into astonishment. and from the high ground on which we stood we are descending into the Valleys of confusion & darkness. That we have it in our power to be one of the most respectable Nations upon Earth, admits not, in my humble opinion, of a doubt, if we would pursue a wise, Just, & liberal policy towards one another—and would keep good faith with the rest of the World. That our resources are ample, & encreasing, none can deny; But whilst they are grudgingly applied, or not applied at all, we give the vital stab to public credit, and must sink into contempt in the eyes of Europe.

It has long been a speculative question amongst Philosophers and wise men, whether foreign Commerce is of advantage to any Country—that is, whether the luxury, effeminacy, & corruption which are introduced by it, are counterballanced by the conveniencies and wealth of which it is productive. But the right decision of this question is of very little importance to us. We have abundant reason to be convinced, that the spirit of Trade which pervades these States is not to be restrained. it behoves us therefore to establish it upon just principles; and this, any more than other matters of national concern cannot be done by thirteen heads, differently constructed; The necessity therefore of a controuling power is obvious, and why it should be with-held is beyond comprehension.

The Agricultural Society—lately established in Philadelphia—promises extensive usefulness, if it is prosecuted with spirit—I wish most sincerely that every State in the Union would institute similar ones; and that these Societies would corrispond fully, & freely with each other; & communicate all useful discoveries founded on practice, with a due attention to climate, Soil, and Seasons, to the public.

The great Works of improving and extending the inland navigations of the two large Rivers Potomack & James, which interlock with the Western Waters, are already begun; and I have little doubt of their success. The consequences to the Union, in my judgment, are immense—& more so in a political, than in a Commercial point; for unless we can connect the New States, which are rising to our view in the Regions back of us, with those on the Atlantic by interest, the only cement that will bind, and in this case no otherways to be effected than by opening such communications as will make it easier & cheaper for them to bring the product of their labour to our Markets, instead of carrying them to the Spaniards Southwardly, or the British Northwardly, they will be quite a distinct People, and ultimately may be very troublesome neighbours to us. In themselves, considered merely as a hardy race, this may happen; how much more so if linked with either of those Powers in Politics, & Commerce?

It would afford me great pleasure to go over (with a mind more at ease) those grounds in your State which I travelled in the years 1775 and Six; and to congratulate, on the happy change, with those characters who participated of the anxious cares with which those moments were filled; and for whom I entertain a sincere regard; but I do not know whether to flatter myself with the enjoyment of it. The deranged state of my affairs from an absence, and total neglect of them for almost nine years, & a pressure of other matters, allow me little leizure for gratifications of this sort. Mrs Washington offers compliments & best wishes to Mrs Warren, to which be so good as to present those of Dear Sir Yr Most Obedt Hble Servt

To Robert Morris

Dr Sir,   Mt Vernon 12th April 1786

I give you the trouble of this letter at the instance of Mr Dalby of Alexandria; who is called to Philadelphia to attend what he conceives to be a vexatious law-suit respecting a slave of his, which a Society of Quakers in the City (formed for such purposes) have attempted to liberate. The merits of this case will no doubt appear upon trial; but from Mr Dalby's state of the matter, it should seem that this Society is not only acting repugnant to justice so far as its conduct concerns strangers, but, in my opinion extremely impolitickly with respect to the State—the City in particular; & without being able (but by Acts of tyranny & oppression) to accomplish their own ends. He says the conduct of this society is not sanctioned by Law: had the case been otherwise, whatever my opinion of the Law might have been, my respect for the policy of the State would on this occasion have appeared in my silence; because against the penalties of promulgated Laws one may guard; but there is no avoiding the snares of individuals, or of private societies—and if the practice of this Society of which Mr Dalby speaks, is not discountenanced, none of those whose *misfortune* it is to have slaves as attendants will visit the City if they can possibly avoid it; because by so doing they hazard their property—or they must be at the expence (& this will not always succeed) of providing servants of another description for the trip.

I hope it will not be conceived from these observations, that it is my wish to hold the unhappy people who are the subject of this letter, in slavery. I can only say that there is not a man living who wishes more sincerely than I do, to see a plan adopted for the abolition of it—but there is only one proper and effectual mode by which it can be accomplished, & that is by Legislative authority: and this, as far as my suffrage will go, shall never be wanting.

But when slaves who are happy & content to remain with their present masters, are tampered with & seduced to leave them; when masters are taken at unawares by these practices; when a conduct of this sort begets discontent on one side and resentment on the other, & when it happens to fall on a man whose purse will not measure with that of the Society, & he looses his property for want of means to defend it—it is oppression in the latter case, & not humanity in any; because it introduces more evils than it can cure.

I will make no apology for writing to you on this subject; for if Mr Dalby has not misconceived the matter, an evil exists which requires a remedy; if he has, my intentions have been good though I may have been too precipitate in this address. Mrs Washington joins me in every good & kind wish for Mrs Morris & your family, and I am &c.

To Marquis de Lafayette

My Dear Marquis,   Mount Vernon 10th May 1786.

The Letter which you did me the favor to write to me by Mr Barratt dated the 6th of Feby, together with the parcel & packages which accompanied it, came safely to hand; & for which I pray you to accept my grateful acknowledgments.

The account given of your tour thro' Prussia & other States of Germany, to Vienna & back; & of the Troops which you saw reviewed, in the pay of those Monarchs, at different places, is not less pleasing than it is interesting; & must have been as instructive as entertaining to yourself. Your reception at the Courts of Berlin, Vienna, & elsewhere must have been pleasing to you: to have been received by the King of Prussia, & Prince Henry his brother, (who as soldiers & politicians can yield the palm to none) with such marks of attention & distinction, was as indicative of their discernment, as it is of your merit, & will encrease my opinion of them. It is to be lamented however that great characters are seldom without a blot. That one man should tyranise over millions, will always be a shade in that of the former; whilst it is pleasing to hear that a due regard to the rights of mankind, is characteristic of the latter: I shall revere & love him for this trait of his character. To have viewed the several fields of Battle over which you passed, could not, among other sensations, have failed to excite this thought—here have fallen thousands of gallant spirits to satisfy the ambition of, or to support their sovereigns perhaps in acts of oppression or injustice!—melancholy reflection! For what wise purposes does Providence permit this? Is it as a scourge for mankind, or is it to prevent them from becoming too populous? If the latter, would not the fertile plains of the Western world receive the redundancy of the old.

For the several articles of intelligence with which you have been so good as to furnish me, & for your sentimts on European politics, I feel myself very much obliged—on these I can depend. Newspaper Accounts are too sterile, vague & contradictory, on which to form any opinion, or to claim even the smallest attention. The account of, & observations which you have made on the policy & practice of Great Britain at the other Courts of Europe, respecting those States; I was but too well informed & convinced of before. Unhappily for us, tho' their Accounts are greatly exaggerated, yet our conduct has laid the foundation for them. It is one of the evils of democratical governments that the people, not always seeing & frequently mislead, must often feel before they can act right—but then evils of this nature seldom fail to work their own cure. It is to be lamented nevertheless that the remedies are so slow, & that those who may wish to apply them seasonably are not attended to before they suffer in person, in interest & in reputation. I am not without hopes that matters will soon take a favourable turn in the fœderal constitution—

the discerning part of the community have long since seen the necessity of giving adequate powers to Congress for national purposes; & the ignorant & designing must yield to it 'ere long. Several late Acts of the different Legislatures have a tendency thereto; among these, the Impost which is now acceded to by every State in the Union, (tho' cloggd a little by that of New York) will enable Congress to support the national credit in pecuniary matters better than it has been; whilst a measure, in which this state has taken the lead at its last session, will it is to be hoped give efficient powers to that Body for all commercial purposes. This is a nomination of some of its first characters to meet other Commissioners from the several States in order to consider of & decide upon such powers as shall be necessary for the sovereign Power of them to act under; which are to be reported to the respective Legislatures at their autumnal sessions for, it is to be hoped, final adoption: thereby avoiding those tedious & futile deliberations which result from recommendations & partial concurrences; at the same time that it places it at once in the power of Congress to meet European Nations upon decisive & equal ground. All the Legislatures which I have heard from have come into the proposition, & have made very judicious appointments. much good is expected from this measure, and it is regretted by many that more objects were not embraced by the Meeting. A General Convention is talked of by many for the purpose of revising & correcting the defects of the fœderal Government, but whilst this is the wish of some, it is the dread of others from an opinion that matters are not yet sufficiently ripe for such an event.

The British still occupy our Posts to the Westward, & will, I am persuaded, continue to do so under one pretence or another, no matter how shallow, as long as they can: of this, from some circumstances which had occurred, I have been convinced since August 1783 & gave it as my opinion at that time, if not officially to Congress as the sovereign, at least to a number of its members that they might act accordingly. It is indeed evident to me, that they had it in contemplation to do this at the time of the Treaty; the expression of the Article which respects the evacuation of them, as well as the tenor of their conduct since relative to this business, is strongly masked with deception. I have not the smallest doubt but that every secret engine in their power is continually at work to inflame the Indian mind, with a view to keep it at variance with these States for the purpose of retarding our settlements to the Westward, & depriving us of the fur & peltry trade of that Country.

Your assurances my dear Marquis, respecting the male & female asses, are highly pleasing to me; I shall look for them with much expectation & great satisfaction, as a valuable acquisition, & important service. The Jack which I have already received from Spain, in appearance is fine; but his late royal master, tho' past his grand climacteric, cannot be less moved by female allurements than he is, or when prompted, can proceed with more deliberation & majestic solemnity to the work of procreation. The other Jack perished at Sea.

Mr Littlepage in his dispute with Mr Jay seems to have forgot his former situation. It is a pity, for he appears to be a young man of abilities—At the next meeting of the Potomac Company (which I believe will not be 'till August) I will communicate to them your sentiments respecting the terms on which a good Ingénieur des ponts & chaussées may be had & take their opinion thereon.

The benevolence of your heart my Dr Marqs is so conspicuous upon all occasions, that I never wonder at any fresh proofs of it; but your late purchase of an Estate in the Colony of Cayenne with a view of emancipating the slaves on it, is a generous and noble proof of your humanity. Would to God a like spirit would diffuse itself generally into the minds of the people of this country, but I despair of seeing it—some petitions were presented to the Assembly at its last Session, for the abolition of slavery, but they could scarcely obtain a reading. To set them afloat at once would, I really believe, be productive of much inconvenience & mischief; but by degrees it certainly might, & assuredly ought to be effected & that too by Legislative authority.

I give you the trouble of a letter to the Marqs de St Simon, in which I have requested to be presented to Mr de Menonville. The favourable terms in which you speak of Mr Jefferson gives me great pleasure: he is a man of whom I early imbibed the highest opinion—I am as much pleased therefore to meet confirmations of my discernment in these matters, as I am mortified when I find myself mistaken.

I send herewith the copies of your private Letters to me, promised in my last, & which have been since copied by your old aid. As Mrs Washington & myself have both done ourselves the honor of writing to Madame de la Fayette, I shall not give you the trouble at this time of presenting my respects to her; but pray you to accept every good wish which this family can render for your health & every blessing this life can afford you. I cannot conclude without expressing to you the earnest enquiries & ardent wishes of your friends (among whom I claim to stand first) to see you in America, & of giving you repeated assurances of the sincerity of my friendship, & of the Affectionate regard with which I am &c. &c.

P.S. I had like to have forgotten a promise which I made in consequence of the enclos'd application from Colo. Carter— It was, that I would write to you for the wolf hound if to be had conveniently. The inducements, & the services you would render by this Act, will be more evident from the expression of the letter than from any thing I can say.

The vocabulary for her imperial Majesty, I will use my best endeavours to have compleated—but she must have a little patience—the Indian tribes on the Ohio are numerous, dispersed & distant from those who are most likely to do the business properly.

To William Fitzhugh

Dear Sir,   Mount Vernon 15th May 1786
    Your favor of the 13th came to me this day. Particular attention shall be paid to the Mares which your Servant brought; and when my Jack is in the humour they shall derive all the benefits of his labours—for labour it appears to be. At present, tho' young, he follows what one may suppose to be the example of his late royal Master, who cannot, tho' past his grand climacterick, perform seldomer, or with more Majestic solemnity, than he does. However, I am not without

hope, that when he becomes a little better acquainted with republican enjoyments, he will amend his manners, and fall into a better & more expeditious mode of doing business. If the case should be otherwise, I should have no disinclination to present his Catholic Majesty with as good a thing, as he gave me.

I am very sorry to hear of the accident which befel Colo. Fitzhugh in his late trip to Virginia; but, from the effect of it, I hope he will soon be perfectly recovered. I am happy in having it in my power to furnish the Colo. with a Bushel of the Barley, requested in your letter. A propos, are there any persons in your neighbourhood who raise Lambs for sale? My stock of sheep were so much neglected during my absence, that I would gladly buy one, or two hundred ewe lambs, and allow a good price for them, in order to get it up again. A line from you, when convenient, in answer to this query, would be obliging—Mrs Washington & the rest of the family join me in every good wish to the Colo. his Lady & yourself. I am—Dr Sir Yr Most Obedt Servt

P.S. Please to present me to Colo. & Mrs Plater when you see them.

To John Jay

Dear Sir,   Mount Vernon 18th May 1786.

In due course of Post, I have been honoured with your favours of the 2d & 16th of March; since which I have been a good deal engaged, and pretty much from home.

For the inclosure which accompanied the first, I thank you. Mr Littlepage seems to have forgot what had been his situation—What was due to you—and indeed what was necessary for his own character. And his Guardian I think, seems to have forgot every thing.

I coincide perfectly in sentiment with you, my dear Sir, that there are errors in our National Government which call for correction; loudly I will add; but I shall find my self happily mistaken if the remedies are at hand. We are certainly in a delicate situation, but my fear is that the people are not yet sufficiently misled to retract from error! To be plainer, I think there is more wickedness than ignorance, mixed with our councils. Under this impression, I scarcely know what opinion to entertain of a general Convention. That it is necessary to revise, and amend the articles of Confederation, I entertain *no* doubt; but what may be the consequences of such an attempt *is* doubtful. Yet, something must be done, or the fabrick must fall. It certainly is tottering! Ignorance & design, are difficult to combat. Out of these proceed illiberality, *improper* jealousies, and a train of evils which oftentimes, in republican governments, must be sorely felt before they can be removed. The former, that is ignorance, being a fit soil for the latter to work in, tools are employed which a generous mind would disdain to use; and which nothing but time, and their own puerile or wicked productions, can show the inefficacy and dangerous tendency of. I think often of our situation, and view it with concern. From the high ground on which we stood—from the plain path which invited our footsteps, to be so fallen!—so lost! is really mortifying. But virtue, I fear, has, in a great degree, taken its departure from our Land, and the want of disposition to do justice is the sourse of the national embarrassments; for under whatever guise or colourings are given to them, this, I apprehend, is the origin of the evils we now feel, & probably shall labour for sometime yet. With respectful Complimts to Mrs Jay—and sentiments of sincere friendship—I am—Dear Sir Yr most Obedt Hble Servt

P.S. Will you do me the favor to forward the enclosed, with any dispatches of your own, for England?

To Thomas Jefferson

Dear Sir,   Mount Vernon Augt 1st 1786.
    The letters you did me the favor to write to me on the 4th & 7th of Jany have been duly received.
    In answer to your obliging enquiries respecting the dress, attitude &ca which I would wish to have given to the Statue

in question—I have only to observe that not having a sufficient knowledge in the art of sculpture to oppose my judgment to the taste of Connoisseiurs, I do not desire to dictate in the matter—on the contrary I shall be perfectly satisfied with whatever may be judged decent and proper. I should even scarcely have ventured to suggest that perhaps a servile adherence to the garb of antiquity might not be altogether so expedient as some little deviation in favor of the modern custom, if I had not learnt from Colo. Humphreys that this was a circumstance hinted in conversation by Mr West to Houdon. This taste, which has been introduced in painting by West, I understand is received with applause & prevails extensively.

I have taken some pains to enquire into the facts respecting the medals of the Cincinnati, which Majr L'Enfant purchased in France. It seems that when he went to Europe in 1783 he had money put into his hands to purchase a certain number, and that conceiving it to be consonant with the intentions of the Society, he purchased to a still greater amount—insomuch that a Committee of the Genl Meeting, upon examining his Acct reported a balle due to him of Six hundred & thirty dollars, wch report was accepted. This money is still due, and is all that is due from the Society of the Cincinnati as a Society. General Knox has offered to pay the amount to Majr L'Enfant, but as it has become a matter of some public discussion, the latter wished it might remain until the next Genl Meeting, which will be in May next. In the meantime Genl Knox (who is Secretary Genl) has, or will write fully on the Subject to the Marquis de la Fayette, from whom he has had a letter respecting the business.

We have no news of importance And if we had, I should hardly be in the way of learning it; as I divide my time between the superintendence of opening the navigations of our rivers & attention to my private concerns. Indeed I am too much secluded from the world to know with certainty, what sensation the refusal of the British to deliver up the Western posts, has made on the public mind. I fear the edge of its sensibility is somewhat blunted. Fœderal measures are not yet universally adopted. New York, wch was as well disposed a State as any in the Union is said to have become in a degree antifœderal. Some other States are, in my opinion, falling into very foolish & wicked plans of emitting paper money. I cannot however give up my hopes & expectations that we shall 'ere long adopt a more liberal system of policy. What circumstances will lead, or what misfortunes will compel us to it, is more than can be told without the spirit of prophecy.

In the meantime the people are industrious, œconomy begins to prevail, and our internal governments are, in general, tolerably well administered.

You will probably have heard of the death of Genl Greene before this reaches you, in which case you will, in common with your Countrymen, have regretted the loss of so great and so honest a man. Genl McDougall, who was a brave Soldier & a disinterested patriot, is also dead—he belonged to the Legislature of his State, the last act of his life, was (after being carried on purpose to the Senate) to give his voice against the emission of a paper currency. Colo. Tilghman, who was formerly of my family, died lately & left as fair a reputation as ever belonged to a human character. Thus some of the pillars of the revolution fall. Others are mouldering by insensible degrees. May our Country never want props to support the glorious fabrick! With sentiments of the highest esteem & regard, I have the honor to be Dear Sir Yr Most Obedt & very Hble Servt

To Arthur Young

Sir,   Mount Vernon 6th Augt 1786

I have had the honor to receive your letter of the 7th of Jany from Bradford-Hall, in Suffolk, and thank you for the favor of opening a correspondence, the advantages of which will be so much in my favor.

Agriculture has ever been amongst the most favourite amusements of my life, though I never possessed much skill in the art, and nine years total inattention to it, has added nothing to a knowledge which is best understood from practice, but with the means you have been so obliging as to furnish me, I shall return to it (though rather late in the day) with hope & confidence.

The system of Agriculture (if the epithet of system can be applied to it) which is in use in this part of the United States, is as unproductive to the practitioners as it is ruinous to the landholders. Yet it is pertinaciously adhered to. To forsake it; to pursue a course of husbandry which is altogether different & new to the gazing multitude, ever averse to novelty in matters of this sort, & much attached to their old customs, requires resolution; and without a good practical guide, may be dangerous, because of the many volumes which have been written on this subject, few of them are founded on experimental knowledge—are verbose, contradictory, & bewildering. Your annals shall be this guide. The plan on which they are published, gives them a reputation which inspires confidence; and for the favor of sending them to me I pray you to accept my very best acknowledgments. To continue them, will add much to the obligation.

To evince with what avidity, and with how little reserve I embrace the polite & friendly offer you have made me of supplying me with "Men, Cattle, Tools, seeds, or any thing else that may add to my rural amusement," I will give you, Sir, the trouble of providing, and sending to the care of Wakelin Welch, Esqr. of London, Mercht the following articles.

Two of the simplest, & best constructed Plows for land which is neither very heavy nor Sandy. To be drawn by two horses. To have spare shares & Colters—and a mold on which to form new irons when the old ones are worn out, or will require repairing.

I shall take the liberty in this place to observe, that some years ago, from a description, or recommendation of what was then called the Rotheram; or Patent Plow, I sent to England for one of them, and till it began to wear, & was ruined by a bungling Country Smith that no plow could have done better work, or appeared to have gone easier with two horses; but for want of a Mold (wch I had neglected to order with the Plow), it became useless after the irons which came in with it were much worn.

A little of the best kind of Cabbage seeds, for field culture.

20 lbs. of the best Turnip-Seeds, for Do.

10 Bushels of Sainfoin Seeds.

8 Bushls of the Winter Vetches.

2 Bushls of Rye-grass Seeds.
50 lbs of Hop clover seeds.
and

If it is decided (for much has been said for and against it), that Burnet, as an early food, is valuable, I should be glad of a bushel of this seed also. Red clover seeds are to be had on easy terms in this Country, but if there are any other kinds of grass-seeds (not included in the above) that you may think valuable, especially for early feeding or cutting, you would oblige me by adding a small quantity of the seeds, to put me in stock. Early grasses, unless a species can be found that will stand a hot Sun, and oftentimes severe droughts in the summer months, without much expence of cultivation, would suit our climate best.

You see, Sir, that without ceremony, I avail myself of your kind offer; but if you should find in the course of our correspondence, that I am likely to become troublesome you can easily check me. Inclosed I give you an order on Wakelin Welch, Esqr. for the cost of such things as you may have the goodness to send me. I do not at this time ask for any other implements of Husbandry than the Plows; but when I have read your annals (for they are but just come to hand) I may request more. In the meanwhile, permit me to ask what a good Plowman might be had for, annual wages, to be found (being a single man) in board, washing, & lodging? The writers upon Husbandry estimate the hire of labourers so differently in England, that it is not easy to discover from them whether one of the class I am speaking of would cost Eight, or Eighteen pounds a year. A good Plowman at low wages, would come very opportunely with the Plows here requested.

By means of the application I made to my friend Mr Fairfax, of Bath, & through the medium of Mr Rack, a bailiff is sent to me, who, if he is acquainted with the best courses of cropping, will answer my purposes as a director or superintendant of my Farms. He has the appearance of a plain honest Farmer; is industrious; and, from the character given of him by a Mr Peacy (with whom he has lived many years) is understanding in the management of Stock, & of most matters for which he is employed. How far his abilities may be equal to a pretty extensive concern, is questionable. And what is still worse, he has come over with improper ideas; for instead of preparing his mind to meet a ruinous course of Cropping, exhausted Lands, and numberless inconveniencies into which we had been thrown by an eight years War, he seems to have expected that he was coming to well organized Farms, & that he was to have met Plows, Harrows, and all the other impliments of Husbandry in as high taste as the best farming Counties in England could have exhibited them. How far his fortitude will enable him to encounter these disappointments, or his patience & perseverence will carry him towards the work of reform, remains to be decided. With great esteem, I have the Honor to be, Sir, Yr Most Obedt Hble Servt

To John Jay

Dear Sir   Mount Vernon 15th Augt 1786
I have to thank you very sincerely for your interesting letter of the 27th of June, as well as for the other communications you had the goodness to make at the same time.

I am sorry to be assured, of what indeed I had little doubt before, that we have been guilty of violating the treaty in some instances. What a misfortune it is the British should have so well grounded a pretext for their palpable infractions?—and what a disgraceful part, out of the choice of difficulties before us, are we to act?

Your sentiments, that our affairs are drawing rapidly to a crisis, accord with my own. What the event will be is also beyond the reach of my foresight. We have errors to correct. We have probably had too good an opinion of human nature in forming our confederation. Experience has taught us, that men will not adopt & carry into execution, measures the best calculated for their own good without the intervention of a coercive power. I do not conceive we can exist long as a nation, without having lodged somewhere a power which will pervade the whole Union in as energetic a manner, as the authority of the different state governments extends over the several States. To be fearful of vesting Congress, constituted as that body is, with ample authorities for national purposes, appears to me the very climax of popular absurdity and madness. Could Congress exert them for the detriment of the public without injuring themselves in an equal or greater proportion? Are not their interests inseperably connected with those of their constituents? By the rotation of appointment must they not mingle frequently with the mass of citizens? Is it not rather to be apprehended, if they were possessed of the powers before described, that the individual members would be induced to use them, on many occasions, very timidly & inefficatiously for fear of loosing their popularity & future election? We must take human nature as we find it. Perfection falls not to the share of mortals. Many are of opinion that Congress have too frequently made use of the suppliant humble tone of requisition, in applications to the States, when they had a right to assume their imperial dignity and command obedience. Be that as it may, requisitions are a perfect nihility, where thirteen sovereign, independent, disunited States are in the habit of discussing & refusing compliance with them at their option. Requisitions are actually little better than a jest and a bye word through out the Land. If you tell the Legislatures they have violated the treaty of peace and invaded the prerogatives of the confederacy they will laugh in your face. What then is to be done? Things cannot go on in the same train forever. It is much to be feared, as you observe, that the better kind of people being disgusted with the circumstances will have their minds prepared for any revolution whatever. We are apt to run from one extreme into another. To anticipate & prevent disasterous contingencies would be the part of wisdom & patriotism.

What astonishing changes a few years are capable of producing! I am told that even respectable characters speak of a monarchical form of government without horror. From thinking proceeds speaking, thence to acting is often but a single step. But how irrevocable & tremendous! What a triumph for the advocates of despotism to find that we are incapable of governing ourselves, and that systems founded on the basis of equal liberty are merely ideal & falacious! Would to God that wise measures may be taken in time to avert the consequences we have but too much reason to apprehend.

Retired as I am from the world, I frankly acknowledge I

cannot feel myself an unconcerned spectator. Yet having happily assisted in bringing the ship into port & having been fairly discharged; it is not my business to embark again on a sea of troubles. Nor could it be expected that my sentiments and opinions would have much weight on the minds of my Countrymen—they have been neglected, tho' given as a last legacy in the most solemn manner. I had then perhaps some claims to public attention. I consider myself as having none at present. With sentiments of sincere esteem & friendship I am, my dear Sir, Yr most Obedt & Affecte Hble Servant

To John Francis Mercer

Dear Sir,   Mount Vernon 9th Sep. 1786.

Your favor of the 20th ulto did not reach me till about the first inst. It found me in a fever, from which I am now but sufficiently recovered to attend to business. I mention this to shew that I had it not in my power to give an answer to your propositions sooner.

With respect to the first, I never mean (unless some particular circumstances should compel me to it) to possess another slave by purchase; it being among my first wishes to see some plan adopted, by the legislature by which slavery in this Country may be abolished by slow, sure, & imperceptable degrees. With respect to the 2d, I never did, nor never intend to purchase a military certificate; I see no difference it makes with you (if it is one of the funds allotted for the discharge of my claim) who the purchaser is. If the depreciation is 3 for 1 only, you will have it in your power whilst you are at the receipt of Custom—Richmond—where it is said the great regulator of this business (Greaves) resides, to convert them into specie at that rate. If the difference is more, there would be no propriety, if I inclined to deal in them at all, in my taking them at that exchange.

I shall rely upon your promise of two hundred pounds in five weeks from the date of your letter. It will enable me to pay the workmen which have been employed abt this house all the Spring & Summer, (some of whom are here still). But there are two debts, which press hard upon me. One of which, if there is no other resource, I must sell Land or Negroes to discharge. It is owing to Govr Clinton of New York, who was so obliging as to borrow, & became my Security for £2500 to answer some calls of mine. This sum was to be returned in twelve months from the conclusion of Peace. For the remains of it, about eight hundred pounds York Cy I am now paying an interest of seven Pr Ct; but the high interest (tho' more than any estate can bear) I should not regard, if my credit was not at stake to comply with the conditions of the loan. The other debt, tho' I know the person to whom it is due wants it, and I am equally anxious to pay it, might be put off a while longer. This sum is larger than the other. I am Dr Sir Yr Most Obedt Hble Servt

To Henry Lee

Dear Sir,   Mount Vernon 31st October 1786.
    I am indebted to you for your several favors of the 1st 11th & 17th instt, and shall reply to them in the order of their dates: But first let me thank you for the interesting communications imparted in them.
    The picture which you have drawn, & the accts which are published, of the commotions & temper of numerous bodies in the Eastern States, are equally to be lamented and deprecated. They exhibit a melancholy proof of what our trans atlantic foe have predicted; and of another thing perhaps, which is still more to be regretted, and is yet more unaccountable; that mankind left to themselves are unfit for their own government. I am mortified beyond expression whenever I view the clouds which have spread over the brightest morn that ever dawned upon any Country. In a word, I am lost in amazement, when I behold what intriegueing; the interested views of desperate characters; Jealousy; & ignorance of the Minor part, are capable of effecting as a scurge on the major part of our fellow citizens of the Union: for it is hardly to be imagined that the great body of the people tho' they will not act can be so enveloped in darkness, or short sighted as not

to see the rays of a distant sun through all this mist of intoxication & folly.

You talk, my good Sir, of employing influence to appease the tumults in Massachusetts—I know not where that influence is to be found; and if attainable, that it would be a proper remedy for the disorders. Influence is no government. Let us have one by which our lives, liberties, and properties will be secured, or let us know the worst at once. Under these impressions, my humble opinion is, that there is a call for decision. Know precisely what the Insurgents aim at. If they have real grievances, redress them, *if possible*, or acknowledge the justice of their complaints and your inability of doing it, in the present moment. If they have not, employ the force of government against them at once. If this is inadequate, *all* will be convinced that the superstructure is bad, or wants support. To be more exposed in the eyes of the world & more contemptible than we already are, is hardly possible. To delay one of the other of these, is to exasperate in one case, and to give confidence in the other; and will add to their numbers; for like Snow-balls, such bodies encrease by every movement, unless there is something in the way to obstruct, & crumble them before the weight is too great & irrisistable.

These are my sentiments. Precedents are dangerous things. Let the reins of government then be braced in time & held with a steady hand; & every violation of the constitution be reprehended. If defective, let it be amended, but not suffered to be trampled on whilst it has an existence.

With respect to the navigation of the Mississipi, you already know my sentiments thereon. They have been uniformly the same, and as I have observed to you in a former letter, are controverted by one consideration *only* of weight; and that is the operation the occlusion of it may have on the minds of the Western Settlers; who will not consider the subject in a relative point of view, or on a comprehensive scale; and may be influenced by the demagagues of the Country to acts of extravagence & desperation, under a popular declamation that their interests are sacraficed. Colonel Mason is at present in a fit of the Gout, what his sentiments on the subject are, I know not, nor whether he will be able to attend the Assembly during the present Session. For some reasons (unnecessary to mention) I am inclined to believe he will advocate the navigation of that river. But in all matters of great national moment the only true line of conduct—in my opinion—is dispassionately to compare the advantages & disadvantages of the measure proposed, and decide from the ponderancy. The lesser evil (where there is a choice of them) should always yield to the greater. What benefits (more than we now enjoy) are to be derived from such a Treaty as you have delineated with Spain, I am not enough of a Commercial man to give any opinion on.

The China came to hand without much damage; and I thank you for your attention in procuring & forwarding of it to me. Mrs Washington joins me in best wishes for Mrs Lee and yourself and I am very affectionately Dear Sir Yr most Obedt & Obliged Hble Servant

Comments on David Humphreys' Biography of Washington

REMARKS

Page 1st. (1) It was rather the wish of my eldest brother (on whom the general concerns of the family devolved) that this shd. take place and the matter was contemplated by him. My father died when I was only 10 years old.

(2) He was not appointed Adjutant General of the Militia of Virginia untill after his return from the expedition to Cathagena. Nor did he Command the Colonial troops on that occasion. these were under the Orders of Sir Wm. Gouch Lt. Govr. of Virginia. He was no more than the Senior Officer of those which were raised in this Colony and wch. with those of the other Colonies formed what was called the American Brigade, under Sir William Gouch; he was scarcely of age when he went on this expedn.

(3) And from whom he had received many distinguished marks of patronage and favor.

(4) Not all, for the second Son (Augustine) left many

childn., sevl. of whom are now living; and inherit a very large portion of his Fathers Estate. perhaps the best part.

Page 2. (1) Before he was 20 years of age.

(2) He was then more than 21 years, as will appear from dates.

Page 3. (1) At a most inclement Season, for he travelled over the Apalacheon Mountains, and passed 200 miles thro an un-inhabited Country (except by a few tribes of Indians settled on the Banks of the Ohio) to Presque Isle within 15 miles of Lake Erie in the depth of winter while the face of the Earth was covered with snow and the waters covered with Ice; The whole diste. from Wmsburgh the then seat of Governmt. at least 500 miles.

(2) It was on this occasion he was named by the half-King (as he was called) and the tribes of Nations with whom he treated, Caunotaucarius (in English) the Town taker; which name being registered in their Manner and communicated to other Nations of Indians, has been remembered by them ever since in all their transactions with him during the late War.

Page 4th (1) This is a task to which GW. feels himself very incompetent (with any degree of accuracy) from the badness of his memory, loss of Papers, mutilated state, in which those of that date were preserved, and the derangement of them by frequent removals in the late war and want of time to collect and methodize them since. However accordg. to the best of his recollection: By the indefatigable Industry of the Lt. Colo. and the Officers who seconded his measures the Regiment was in great forwardness at Alexandria (the place of general ren-dezvous) early in the spring of 1754. and without waiting till the whole should be compleated, or for a detachment from the Independant Companies of regulars in the Southern Prov-ences (which had been reqsd. by the Executive of Virginia for this Service) or for troops which were raising in North Car-olina and destined in conjunction to oppose the Incroachment of the French on our Western frontiers. He began his march in the Month of May in order to open the Roads; (and this he had to do almost the whole distance *from Winchester* (in the County of Frederick, not more than 80 miles from Alex-andria to the Ohio). Form deposits, &ca., and for the especiall purpose of siezing, if possible, before the French shd. arrive at it, the important Post at the conflux of the Alligany and Monangahela; with the advantages of which he was forcibly struck the preceeding year; and earnestly advised the securing of, with Militia, or some other temporary force. But notwithstanding all his exertions, the New, and uncommon difficulties he had to encounter (made more intolerable by incessant Rains and swelled waters of which he had many to cross) he had but just ascended the Laurel Hill 50 M: short of his object: after a March of 230 Miles from Alexa. when he received information from his Scouts that the French had, in force, siezed the Post he was pushing to obtain; having descended from Presque Isle by the Rivers Lebeauf and Alligany to this Place by Water with Artillery &ca. &ca. The object of his precipitate advance being thus defeated. The detachmt. of Regulars, wch had arrived at Alexa. (by Water) and under his orders being far in his rear, and no Acct. of the Troops from No. Carolina, it was thought advisable to fall back a few miles; to a place known by the name of the great Meadows. abounding in Forage more convenient for the purpose of forming a Magazine and bringing up the Rear, and to advance from (if we should ever be in force to do it) to the attack of the Post which the enemy now occupied; and had called Du Quesne. At this place, some days after we were joined by the above detachment of Regulars; consisting (before they were reduced on the march by desertion, Sickness &ca.) of a Captn. (McKay a brave and worthy Officer), three Subalterns, and 100 Rank and file. But previous to this junction the French sent a detachment to reconnoitre our Camp and obtain intelligence of our Strength and position; notice of which being given by the Scouts G W marched at the head of a party, attacked, killed 9. or 10; and captured 20 odd. This, as soon as the enemy had assembled their Indian Allies, brought their whole force upon him; consisting, according to their own compared with the best accts. that could be obtained from others of about 1500 Men. His force consisted of the detachment above mentioned, and between two and 300 Virginians; for the few Indians which till now had attended him; and who by reconnoitering the enemy in their March had got terrified at their numbers and resolved to Retreat as they advised us to do also but which was impracticable without abandoning our Stores, Baggage, &ca. as the horses which had brought them to this place had returned for Provision had left us previous to the Attack. About 9 Oclock on the 3d. of July the Enemy advanced with Shouts, and dismal Indian yells to our Intrenchments, but was opposed by so warm, spirited, and constant a fire, that to force the works in *that way* was abandoned by them; they then, from every little rising, tree, stump, Stone, and bush kept up a constant galding fire upon us; which was returned in the best manner we could till late in the Afternn. when their fell the most tremendous rain that can be conceived, filled our trenches with Water, Wet, not only the Ammunition in the Cartouch boxes and firelocks, but that which was in a small temporary Stockade in the middle of the Intrenchment called Fort Necessity erected for the sole purpose of its security, and that of the few stores we had; and left us nothing but a few (for all were not provided with them) Bayonets for defence. In this situation and *no* prospt. of bettering it terms of capitulation were offered to us by the enemy wch. with some alterations that were insisted upon were the more readily acceded to, as we had no Salt provisions, and but indifferently supplied with fresh; which, from the heat of the weather, would not keep; and because a full third of our numbers Officers as well as privates were, by this time, killed or wounded. The next Morning we marched out with the honors of War, but were soon plundered contrary to the Articles of capitulation of great part of our Baggage by the Savages. Our Sick and wounded were left with a detachment under the care, and command of the worthy Doctr. Craik (for he was not only Surgeon to the Regiment but a lieutt. therein) with such necessaries as we could collect and the Remains of the Regimt., and the detachment of Regulars, took up their line for the interior Country. And at Winchester met 2 Companies from No. Carolina on their March to join them. These being fresh, and properly provided, were ordered to proceed to Wills's Creek and establish a post (afterwards called Fort Cumberland) for the purpose of covering the Frontiers. Where they were joined by a Company from Maryland, which, about this time, had been raized, Captn. McKay with his detachment remd. at Winchester; and the Virginia Regiment proceedd. to

Alexandria in order to recruit, and get supplied with cloathing and necessarys of which they stood much in need. In this manner the Winter was employed, when advice was recd. of the force destined for this Service under the ordrs. of G. B. and the arrival of Sir Jno. St. Clair the Q: Mastr. Genl with some new arrangement of Rank by which no Officer who did not *immediately* derive his Comn. from the *King* could command one *who did*. This was too degrading for G. W to submit to; accordingly, he resigned his Military employment; determining to serve the next campaign as a Volunteer; but upon the arrival of Genl. Braddock he was very particularly noticed by that General; taken into his family as an extra-Aid; offered a Captns. Comn. by *brevet* (which was the highest Grade he had it in his power to bestow and had the compliment of several blank Ensigncies given him to dispose of to the Young Gentlemen of his acqe. to supply the vacancies in the 44 and 48 Regts. which had arrived from Ireland.

In this capacity he commenced his second Campaign; and used every proper occasion till he was taken Sick and left behind in the vicinity of Fort Cumberland to impress the Genl., and the principal Officers around him, with the necessity of opposing the nature of his defence, to the mode of attack which, more than probably, he would experience from the *Canadian* French, and their Indians on his March through the Mountains and covered Country but so prepossessed were they in favr. of *regularity* and *discipline* and in such absolute contempt were *these people held*, that the admonition was suggested in vain.

About the middle of June, this Armament consisting of the two Regiments from Ireland, some Independant Companies and the Provincial troops of Virga. Maryld. and North Carolina, began to move from Fort Cumberland whither they had assembled. After several days March; and difficulties to which they had never been accustomed in regular Service, in Campaign Countries; and of whh. they seemed to have had very little idea. the Genl. resolved to divide his force, and at the head of the first division which was composed of the flower of his Army, to advance; and leave Colo. Dunbar with the second division and the heavy Baggage and Stores, to follow after. By so doing, the first division approached the Monon-

gahela 10 miles short of Fort Duquesne the 8th. of July; and
which time and place having so far recovered from a severe
fever and delerium from which he had been rescued by
James's powder, administed by the positive order of the Genl.
as to travel in a covered Waggon, he joined him and the next
day tho' much reduced and very weak mounted his horse on
cushions, and attended as one of his aids.

About 10 Oclock on the 9th., after the Van had crossed
the Monongahela the *second time*, to avoid an ugly defile (the
season being very dry and waters low) and the rear yet in the
River the front was attacked and by the unusual Hallooing
and whooping of the enemy, whom they could not see were
so disconcerted and confused as soon to fall into irretrievable
disorder. The rear was forced forward to support them, but
seeing no enemy, and themselves falling every moment from
the fire, a general panic took place among the Troops from
which no exertions of the Officers could recover them. In the
early part of the Action some of the Irregulars (as they were
called) without direcns. advanced to the right, in loose order,
to attack; but this, *unhappily* from the unusual appearance of
the movement being mistaken for cowardice and a running
away was discountenanced. and before it was *too late*, and the
confusion became general an offer was made by G. W to head
the Provincials and engage the enemy in their own way; but
the propriety of it was not seen into until it was too late for
execution. After this, many attempts were made to dislodge
the enemy from an eminence on the Right but they all proved
ineffectual; and fatal to the Officers; who by great exertions
and good examples endeavourd to accomplish it. In one of
these the Genl. recd. the Wd. of which he died; but previous
to it, had several horses killed and disabled under him. Captns.
Orme and Morris his two Aids de Camp. having received
wounds which rendered them unable to attd. G W. remained
the sole Aid through the day, to the Genl.; he also had one
horse killed, and two wounded under him. A ball through his
hat, and several through his clothes, but escaped unhurt. Sir
Peter Halket (secd. in Command) being early killed, Lieutt.
Colo. Burton and Sir Jno. St. Clair (who had the Rank of Lt.
Colo. in the Army) being badly wounded, Lieutt. Colo. Gage
(afterwards Genl Gage) having recd. a contusion. No person

knowing in the disordered State things were, who the surviving Senr. Officer was. and the Troops by degrees going off in
confusion; without a ray of hope left of further opposition
from those that remained; G W. placed the Genl. in a small
covered Cart, which carried some of his most essential equipage, and in the best order he could, with the best Troops
(who only contind. to be fired at) brought him over the *first*
ford of the Monongahela; where they were formed in the best
order circumstances would admit on a piece of rising ground;
after wch., by the Genls. order, he rode forward to halt those
which had been earlier in the retreat: Accordingly, after
crossing the Monongahela the *second time* and ascending the
heights, he found Lieutt. Colo. Gage engaged in this business
to whom he delivered the Genls order and then returned to
report the situation he found them in. When he was again
requested by the Genl. whom he met coming on, in his litter
with the first halted troops, to proceed (it then being after
sundown) to the second division under the command of Colo.
Dunbar, to make arrangements for covering the retreat, and
forwarding on provisions and refreshments to the retreating
and wounded Soldiery. To accomplish this, for the 2d. division
was 40 odd miles in the rear it took up the whole night and
part of the next Morning, which from the weak state in which
he was, and the fatigues, and anxiety of the last 24 hours,
rendered him in a manner wholly unfit for the execution of
the duty he was sent upon when he arrived at the Dunbars
Camp. To the best of his power however he discharged it, and
remained with the secd. division till the other joined it. The
shocking Scenes which presented themselves in this Nights
March are not to be described. The dead, the dying, the
groans, lamentation, and crys along the Road of the wounded
for help (for those under the latter descriptions endeavoured
from the first commencement of the action, or rather confusion to escape to the 2d. divn.) were enough to pierce a heart
of adamant. the gloom and horror of which was not a little
encreased by the impervious darkness occasioned by the close
shade of thick woods which in places rendered it impossible
for the two guides which attended to know when they were
in, or out of the track but by groping on the ground with
their hands.

Happy was it for him, and the remains of the first division that they left such a quantity of valuable and enticing baggage on the field as to occasion a scramble and contention in the seizure and distribution of it among the enemy for had a pursuit taken place, by passing the defile which we had avoided; and they had got into our rear, the whole, except a few woodsmen, would have fallen victims to the merciless Savages. Of about 12 or 13 hundred which were in this action eight or 9 hundd. were either killed or wounded; among whom a large proportion of brave and valuable Officers were included. The folly and consequence of opposing compact bodies to the sparse manner of Indian fighting, in woods, which had in a manner been predicted, was now so clearly verified that from hence forward another mode obtained in all future operations.

As soon as the two divisions united, the whole retreated towards Fort Cumberland; and at an Incampment near the Great Meadows the brave, but unfortunate Genl. Braddock breathed his last. He was interred with the honors of war, and as it was left to G W. to see this performed, and to mark out the spot for the reception of his remains, to guard against a savage triumph, if the place should be discovered, they were deposited in the Road over which the Army, Waggons &ca. passed to hide every trace by which the entombment could be discovered. thus died a man, whose good and bad qualities were intimately blended. He was brave even to a fault and in regular Service would have done honor to his profession. His attachments were warm, his enmities were strong, and having no disguise about him, both appeared in full force. He was generous and disinterested, but plain and blunt in his manner even to rudeness. After this event, the Troops continued their March for, and soon arrived at Fort Cumberland without molestation; and all except the Prals immediately resolved to proceed to Philadelphia; by which means the Frontiers of *that* State but *more especially* those of Virginia and Maryland were laid *entirely* open by the *very avenue* which had been prepared. Of the direful consequences of this measure G W, in a visit wch. he immediately made to Williamsburgh for the purpose brought the Govr. and Council of Virga. acquainted. But in vain did they remonstrate against the March of the B. Troops to that place of the officer Comg. them. They next proceeded to augment their own; the command of which under a very enlarged and dignified Commission, to Command *all* the Troops now raised, or to be raised in the Colony, was given to him with very extensive powers, and blank Commissions to appoint all new Officers. About this time also or soon after it the discontents and clamours of the Provincial Officers, and the remonstrance of G W. in person, to Genl. Shirley, the then Comr. in chief of the British Forces in America and through the Govr. and Council to the King's Minister with respect to the degrading Situation in which they were placed a new arrangement took place by the Kings Order, by which every Provincial Officer was to rank according to the Comn. he bore, but to be Junrs. to those of the same grade in the established Corps.

As G W foresaw, so it happened, the frontiers were continually harrassed, but not having force enough to carry the war to the gates of Du Quesne, he could do no more than distribute the Troops along the Frontiers in the Stockaded Forts; more with a view to quiet the fears of the Inhabitants than from any expectation of giving securities in so extensive a line to the settlements. During this interval in one of his tours along the frontier posts, he narrowly escaped, according to the acct. afterwards given by some of our People who were Prisoners with them, and eye witness at the time, [   ] falling by an Indian party who had waylaid (for another purpose) the communication along which with a small party of horse only he was passing, the road in this place formed a curve, and the prey they were in weight for being expected at the reverse part, the Captn. of the party had gone across to observe the number and manner of their movemt. &ca. in order that he might make his disposition accordingly, leaving orders for the party not to take notice of any passengers the other views till he returned to them, in the meantime in the opposite direction I passed and escaped almt. certain destruction for the weather was raining and the few Carbines unfit for use if we had escaped the first fire. This happened near Fort Vass. Never ceasing in the meantime in his attempts, to demonstrate to the Legislature of Virga., to Lord Loudoun, &ca. that the only means of preventing the devastations to which the middle states were exposed, was to remove the Cause. But the war by this time raging in another quarter of the Continent all applications were unheeded till the year 1758 when an Expedition against Fort Du Quesne was concerted, and undertaken under the conduct of Genl. Forbes; who tho a brave and good Officer, was so much debilitated by bad health, and so illy supplied with the means to carry on the expedition, that it was November before the Troops got to Loyal hanning 50 or 60 miles short of Du Quesne and even then was on the very point of abandoning the Expedition when some seasonable supplies arriving the Army was formed into three Brigades took up its March, and moved forward; the Brigade Commanded by G. W. being the leading one.

Previous to this and during the time the Army lay at Loyal haning a circumstance occurred wch. involved the life of G W in as much jeopardy as it had ever been before or since the enemy sent out a large detachment to reconnoitre our Camp, and to ascertain our strength; in consequence of Intelligence that they were within 2 Miles of the Camp a party commanded by Lt. Colo Mercer of the Virga. line (a gallant and good Officer) was sent to dislodge them between whom a severe conflict and hot firing ensued which lasting some time and appearing to approach the Camp it was conceived that our party was yielding the ground upon which G W. with permission of the Genl. called (for dispatch) for Volunteers and immediately marched at their head to sustain, as was conjectured the retireing troops. led on by the firing till he came within less than half a mile, and it ceasing, he detached Scouts to investigate the cause and to communicate his approach to his friend Colo. Mercer, advancing slowly in the meantime. But it being near dusk and the intelligence not having been fully dissiminated among Colo. Mercer's Corps, and they taking us, for the enemy who had retreated approaching in another direction commenced a heavy fire upon the releiving party which drew fire in return in spite of all the exertions of the Officers one of whom and several privates were killed and many wounded before a stop could be put to it. to accomplish which G W never was in more imminent danger. by being between two fires, knocking up with his sword the presented pieces.

When the Army had got within about 12 or 15 Miles of the

Fort the enemy dispairing of its defence, blew it up having first embarked their Artillery, Stores and Troops, and retreated by water down the Ohio to their Settlements below. Thus ended that Campaign, a little before Christmas in very inclement weather and the last one made during that War by G W whose health by this time (as it had been declining for many months before, occasioned by an inveterate disorder in his Bowels) became so precarious as to induce him (having seen quiet restored by this event to the Frontiers of his own Country which was the principal inducement to his taking arms) to resign his Military appointments. The sollicitation of the Troops which he commanded to Continue, their Affecte. farewell address to him, when they found the Situation of his health and other circumstances would not allow it. affected him exceedingly and in grateful sensibility he expressed the warmth of his attachmt. to them on that, and his inclination to serve them on every other future occasion.

Page 8 (1). I believe about 7,000 Bushls. of Wheat and 10000 bushels of Indn. Corn which was more the staple of the farm

Page 11 (2) Whether it be necessary to mention that my time and Services were given to the public without compensation, and that every direct and indirect attempt afterwards, to reward them (as appeared by the Letter of G. Mifflin, and the vote of 50 shares in each of the Navigations of Potomack and James River by the State of Virga. who knew that I would refuse anything that should carry with it the appearance of reward, you can best judge.

Page 14 (1). Once a week is his fixed hunts tho sometimes he goes oftner.

(2) And many others in this Country

(3) remarking the state of the Weather, nature of the Soil &ca.

The information given in these sheets, tho related from Memory, it is I believe to be depended upon. It is hastily and incorrectly related; but not so much for these reasons, as some others, it is earnestly requestd. that after Colo. Humphrey, has extracted what he shall judge necessary, and given it in his own language, that the *whole* of what Is here contained may be returned to G W, or committed to the flames. some of the enumerations are trifling; and perhaps more important circumstances omitted; but just as they occurred to the memory, they were committed. If there are any grains among them Colo. H can easily separate them from the chaff.

c. October 1786

To James Madison

My dear Sir,   Mount Vernon 5th Novr 1786.
  I thank you for the communications in your letter of the first instt. The decision of the House on the question respecting a paper emission, is portentous I hope, of an auspicious Session. It may certainly be classed among the important questions of the present day; and merited the serious consideration of the Assembly. Fain would I hope, that the great, & most important of all objects—the fœderal governmt—may be considered with that calm & deliberate attention which the magnitude of it so loudly calls for at this critical moment.
  Let prejudices, unreasonable jealousies, and local interest yield to reason and liberality. Let us look to our National character, and to things beyond the present period. No Morn ever dawned more favourable than ours did—and no day was ever more clouded than the present! Wisdom, & good examples are necessary at this time to rescue the political machine from the impending storm. Virginia has now an opportunity to set the latter, and has enough of the former, I hope, to take the lead in promoting this great & arduous work. Without some alteration in our political creed, the superstructure we have been seven years raising at the expence of much blood and treasure, must fall. We are fast verging to anarchy & confusion! A letter which I have just received from Genl Knox, who had just returned from Massachusetts (whither he had been sent by congress consequent of the commotion in that State) is replete with melancholy information of the temper & designs of a considerable part of that people. among other things he says, "there creed is, that the property of the United States, has been protected from confiscation of Britain by the joint exertions of *all*, and therefore ought to be the *common prop-*

erty of all. And he that attempts opposition to this creed is an enemy to equity & justice, & ought to be swept from off the face of the Earth." again "They are determined to anihilate all debts public & private, and have Agrarian Laws, which are easily effected by the means of unfunded paper money which shall be a tender in all cases whatever." He adds. "The numbers of these people amount in Massachusetts to about one fifth part of several populous Counties, and to them may be collected, people of similar sentiments from the States of Rhode Island, Connecticut, & New Hampshire so as to constitute a body of twelve or fifteen thousand desperate, and unprincipled men. They are chiefly of the young & active part of the Community.

How melancholy is the reflection that in so short a space, we should have made such large strides towards fulfilling the prediction of our transatlantic foes!—"leave them to themselves, and their government will soon dissolve." Will not the wise & good strive hard to avert this evil? Or will their supineness suffer ignorance, and the arts of selfinterested designing disaffected & desperate characters, to involve this rising empire in wretchedness & contempt? What stronger evidence can be given of the want of energy in our governments than these disorders? If there exists not a power to check them, what security has a man of life, liberty, or property? To you, I am sure I need not add aught on this subject, the consequences of a lax, or inefficient government, are too obvious to be dwelt on. Thirteen Sovereignties pulling against each other, and all tugging at the fœderal head, will soon bring ruin on the whole; whereas a liberal, and energetic Constitution, well guarded & closely watched, to prevent incroachments, might restore us to that degree of respectability & consequence, to which we had a fair claim, & the brightest prospect of attaining—With sentiments of the sincerest esteem & regard I am—Dear Sir Yr Most Obedt & Affecte Hble Servt

To James Madison

My Dr Sir,   Mount Vernon 18th Novr 1786.

Not having sent to the Post Office with my usual regularity, your favor of the 8th did not reach me in time for an earlier acknowledgment than of this date.

It gives me the most sensible pleasure to hear that the Acts of the present Session, are marked with wisdom, justice & liberality. They are the palladium of good policy, & the only paths that lead to national happiness. Would to God every State would let these be the leading features of their constituent characters: those threatening clouds which seem ready to burst on the Confederacy, would soon dispel. The unanimity with which the Bill was received, for appointing Commissioners agreeably to the recommendation of the Convention at Annapolis; and the uninterrupted progress it has met with since, are indications of a favourable issue. It is a measure of equal necessity & magnitude; & may be the spring of reanimation.

Altho' I have bid a public adieu to the public walks of life, & had resolved never more to tread that theatre; yet, if upon an occasion so interesting to the well-being of the Confederacy it should have been the wish of the Assembly that I should have been an associate in the business of revising the fœderal System; I should, from a sense of the obligation I am under for repeated proofs of confidence in me, more than from any opinion I should have entertained of my usefulness, have obeyed its call; but it is now out of my power to do this with any degree of consistency—the cause I will mention.

I presume you heard Sir, that I was first appointed & have since been rechosen President of the Society of the Cincinnati; & you may have understood also that the triennial Genl Meeting of this body is to be held in Philada the first monday in May next. Some particular reasons combining with the peculiar situation of my private concerns; the necessity of paying attention to them; a wish for retirement & relaxation from public cares, and rheumatic pains which I begin to feel very sensibly, induced me on the 31st ulto to address a circular letter to each State society informing them of my intention not to be at the next Meeting, & of my desire not to be rechosen President. The Vice President is also informed of this, that the business of the Society may not be impeded by my absence. Under these circumstances it will readily be perceived that I could not appear at the same time & place on any other occasion, with out giving offence to a very respectable & deserving part of the Community—the late officers of the American Army.

I feel as you do for our acquaintance Colo. Lee; better never have delegated, than left him out; unless some glaring impropriety of conduct has been ascribed to him. I hear with pleasure that you are in the new choice. With sentiments of the highest esteem & affectn I am &c.

To James Madison

My dear Sir,   Mount Vernon Decr 16th 1786.

Your favor of the 7th came to hand the evening before last. The resolutions which you say are inserted in the Papers, I have not yet seen. The latter come irregularly, tho' I am a subscriber to Hays Gazette.

Besides the reasons which are assigned in my circular letter to the several State Societies of the Cincinnati, for my nonattendance at the next General meeting to be holden in Philadelphia the first Monday of May, there exists one of a political nature, which operates more *forceably* on my mind than all the others; and which, in confidence, I will now communicate to you.

When this Society was first formed, I am persuaded not a member of it conceived that it would give birth to those Jealousies, or be chargeable with those dangers (real or imaginary) with which the minds of many, & some of respectable characters, were filled. The motives which induced the Officers to enter into it were, I am confident, truly & frankly recited in the Institution: one of which, indeed the principal, was to establish a charitable fund for the relief of such of their compatriots—the Widows—and dependants of them—as were fit subjects for their support; & for whom no *public* provision had been made. But the trumpet being sounded, the alarm was spreading far & wide; I readily perceived therefore that unless a modification of the plan could be effected (—to ani-hilate the Society altogether was impracticable, on acct of the foreign Officers who had been admitted)—that irritations wd arise which would soon draw a line betwn the Society, & their fellow Citizens. To prevent this—To conciliate the affec-tions—And to convince the World of the purity of the plan—I exerted myself, and with much difficulty, effected the changes which appeared in the recommendation from the General Meeting to those of the States; the accomplishment of which was not easy; & I have since heard, that whilst some States acceded to the recommendation, others are not dis-posed thereto, alledging that, unreasonable prejudices and ill founded jealousies ought not to influence a measure laudable in its institution, & salutary in its objects & operation. Under these circumstances, there will be no difficulty in conceiving, that the part I should have had to have acted, would have been delicate. On the one hand, I might be charged with dereliction to the Officers, who had nobly supported, and had treated me with uncommon marks of attention and attach-ment. On the other, with supporting a measure incompatible (some say) with republican principles. I thought it best there-fore without assigning this (the principal reason) to decline the Presidency, and to excuse my attendance at the meeting on the ground, which is firm & just; the necessity of paying attention to my private concerns; the conformity to my de-termination of passing the remainder of my days in a state of retirement—and to indisposition; occasioned by Rheumatick complaints with which, at times, I am a good deal afflicted. Professing at the same time my entire approbation of the in-stitution as altered, and the pleasure I feel at the subsidence of those Jealousies which yielded to the change. *Presuming*, on the general adoption of them.

I have been thus particular to shew, that under circum-stances like these, I should feel myself in an awkward situation to be in Philadelphia on another public occasion during the sitting of this Society. That the present æra is pregnant of great, & *strange* events; none who will cast their eyes around them, can deny—what may be brought forth between this and the first of May to remove the difficulties which at present labour in my mind, against the acceptance of the honor, which has lately been conferred on me by the Assembly, is not for me to predict; but I should think it incompatible with that candour which ought to characterize an honest mind, not to declare that under my present view of the matter, I should be too much embarrassed by the meetings of these two bodies in the same place, in the same moment (after what I have written) to be easy in the situation; and consequently, that it wd be improper to let my appointment stand in the way of any other.

Of this, you who have had the whole matter fully before you, will judge; for having received no other than private intimation of my election, and unacquainted with the formalities which are, or ought to be used on these occasions, silence may be deceptious, or considered as disrespectful; The imputation of both, or either, I would wish to avoid. This is the cause of the present disclosure, immediately on the receipt of your letter, which has been locked up by Ice; for I have had no communication with Alexandria for many days, till the day before yesterday.

My Sentiments are decidedly against Commutables; for sure I am it will be found a tax without a revenue. That the people will be burthened—The public expectation deceived—and a few Speculators *only* enriched—Thus the matter will end, after the morals of *some*, are more corrupted than they now are—and the minds of *all*, filled with more leaven, by finding themselves taxed, and the public demands in full force. Tobacco, on acct of the public places of deposit, and from the accustomed mode of negotiating the article, is certainly better fitted for a commutable than any other production of this Country; but if I understand the matter rightly (I have it from report only) will any man pay five pound in specie for five taxables, when the same sum (supposing Tobo not to exceed 20/ pr Ct) will purchase 500 lbs. of Tobo & thus, if at 28/ will discharge the tax on Seven? And will not the man who neither makes, nor can easily procure this commodity, complain of the inequality of such a mode, especially when he finds that the revenue is diminished by the difference be it what it may, between the real & nominal price and that he is again to be taxed to make this good? These, & such like things, in my humble opinion, are extremely hurtful, and are among the principal causes of the present depravity & corruption without accomplishing the object in view for it is not the shadow, but the substance with which Taxes must be paid, if we mean to be honest. With sentiments of sincere esteem & regard—I am—Dear Sir—Yr most Obedt & Affe. Servt

To Edmund Randolph

Sir,

I had not the honor of receiving your Excellency's favor of the 6th, with its enclosures, till last night.

Sensible as I am of the honor conferred on me by the General Assembly, in appointing me one of the Deputies to a Convention proposed to be held in the City of Philadelphia in May next, for the purpose of revising the Fœderal Constitution; and desirous as I am on all occasions, of testifying a ready obedience to the calls of my Country—yet, Sir, there exists at this moment, circumstances, which I am persuaded will render my acceptance of this fresh mark of confidence incompatible with other measures which I had previously adopted; and from which, seeing little prospect of disengaging myself, it would be disengenuous not to express a wish that some other character, on whom greater reliance can be had, may be substituted in my place; the probability of my non-attendance being too great to continue my appointment.

As no mind can be more deeply impressed than mine is with the awful situation of our Affairs—resulting in a great measure from the want of efficient powers in the fœderal head, and due respect to its Ordinances—so, consequently, those who do engage in the important business of removing these defects, will carry with them every good wish of mine, which the best dispositions towards the attainment, can bestow. I have the honr to be with very grt respect—Your Excellys Most Obedt Hble Servt

December 21, 1786

To Henry Knox

My dear Sir,   Mount Vernon 26th Decr 1786

Nothing but the pleasing hope of seeing you under this roof in the course of last month, and wch I was disposed to extend even to the present moment, has kept me till this time from acknowleging the receipt of your obliging favor of the 23d of October. Despairing now of that pleasure, I shall thank you for the above letter, and the subsequent one of the 17th instt, which came to hand yesterday evening.

Lamentable as the conduct of the Insurgents of Massachusetts is, I am exceedingly obliged to you for the advices respecting them; & pray you, most ardently, to continue the acct of their proceedings; because I can depend upon them from you without having my mind bewildered with those vague & contradictory reports which are handed to us in Newspapers; and which please one hour, only to make the moments of the next more bitter.

I feel, my dear Genl Knox, infinitely more than I can express to you, for the disorders which have arisen in these states. Good God! who besides a tory could have foreseen, or a Briton predicted them! were these people wiser than others, or did they judge of us from the corruption, and depravity of their own hearts? The latter I am persuaded was the case, and that notwithstanding the boasted virtue of America, we are far gone in every thing ignoble & bad. I do assure you, that even at this moment, when I reflect on the present posture of our affairs, it seems to me to be like the vision of a dream. My mind does not know how to realize it, as a thing in actual existence, so strange—so wonderful does it appear to me! In this, as in most other matters, we are too slow. When this spirit first dawned, probably it might easily have been checked; but it is scarcely within the reach of human ken, at this moment, to say when—where—or how it will end. There are combustibles in every State, which a spark may set fire to. In this state, a perfect calm prevails at present, and a prompt disposition to support, and give energy to the fœderal system is discovered, if the unlucky stirring of the dispute respecting the navigation of the Mississipi does not become a leaven that will ferment & sour the mind of it.

The resolutions of the prest session respecting a paper emission, military certificates—&ca—have stamped justice & liberality on the proceedings of the Assembly, & By a late act, *it* seems very desirous of a General Convention to revise and amend the fœderal Constitution—apropos, what prevented the Eastern states from attending the September meeting at Annapolis? Of all the states in the Union it should have seemed to me, that a measure of this sort (distracted as they were with internal commotions, and experiencing the want of energy in government) would have been most pleasing to them. What are the prevailing sentiments of the one now proposed to be held at Philadelphia, in May next? & how will it be attended? You are at the fountain of intelligence, and where the wisdom of the Nation, it is to be presumed, has concentered; consequently better able (as I have had abundant experience of your intelligence, confidence, & candour) to solve these questions. The Maryland Assembly has been violently agitated by the question for a paper emission. It has been carried in the House of Delegates, but what has, or will be done with the Bill in the Senate I have not yet heard. The partisans in favor of the measure in the lower House, threaten, it is said, a secession if it is rejected by that Branch of the Legislature—Thus are we advancing.

In regretting, which I have often done with the deepest sorrow, the death of our much lamented frd General Greene, I have accompanied it of late with a quaere; whether he would not have preferred such an exit to the scenes which it is more than probable many of his compatriots may live to bemoan.

In both your letters you intimate, that the men of reflection, principle & property in New England feeling the inefficacy of their present government, are contemplating a change; but you are not explicit with respect to the nature of it. It has been supposed, that, the Constitution of the State of Massachusetts was amongst the most energetic in the Union—may not these disorders then be ascribed to an endulgent exercise of the powers of Administration? If your laws authorized, and your powers were adequate to the suppression of these tumults, in the first appearance of them, delay & temporizing expedients were, in my opinion improper, these are rarely well applied, & the same causes would produce similar effects in any form of government, if the powers of it are not enforced. I ask this question for information, I know nothing of the facts.

That G.B. will be an unconcerned spectator of the present insurrections (if they continue) is not to be expected. That she is at this moment sowing the Seeds of jealousy & discontent among the various tribes of Indians on our frontier admits of no doubt, in my mind. And that she will improve every opportunity to foment the spirit of turbulence within the bowels of the United States, with a view of distracting our governments, & promoting divisions, is, with me, not less certain. Her first Manœuvres will, no doubt, be covert, and may remain so till the period shall arrive when a decided line of conduct may avail her. Charges of violating the treaty, & other pretexts, will not then be wanting to colour overt acts, tending to effect the grt objects of which she has long been in labour. A Man is now at the head of their American Affairs well calculated to conduct measures of this kind, & more than probably was selected for the purpose. We ought not therefore to sleep nor to slumber—vigilence in the watching, & vigour in acting, is, in my opinion, become indispensably necessary. If the powers are inadequate amend or alter them, but do not let us sink into the lowest state of humiliation & contempt, & become a byword in all the earth—I think with you that the Spring will unfold important & distressing Scenes, unless much wisdom & good management is displayed in the interim. Adieu—be assured no man has a higher esteem & regard for you than I have—none more sincerely Your friend, and More Affectly yr Hble Servt

P.S. Mrs Washington joins me in every good wish for you & Mrs Knox, and in congratulatory Compts on the late addition to your family. Will you be so obliging as to give the enclosed a safe conveyance—I have recd one or two very obliging letters from Genl Tupper whilst he was in the Western Country and wish to thank him for them—but know not in what part of Massachusetts he lives.

To David Humphreys

My dear Humphreys   Mount Vernon Decr 26th 1786
    I am much indebted to you for your several favors of the
1st 9th & 16th of November. The last came first. Mr Morse
keeping in Mind the old proverb, was determined not to make
more haste than good speed in prosecuting his journey to
Georgia—so I got the two first but lately.

    For your publication respecting the confinement of Captn
Asgill, I am exceedingly obliged to you. The manner of making it was as good as could be devised; and the matter, will
prove the injustice, as well as illiberality of the reports which
have been circulated on that occasion, and which are fathered
on that Officer, as the author.

    It is with the deepest, and most heart felt concern, I per-
ceive by some late paragraphs extracted from the Boston Gazettes, that the Insurgents of Massachusetts—far from being
satisfied with the redress offered by their General Court—are
still acting in open violation of Law & Government; & have
obliged the Chief Magistrate in a decided tone, to call upon
the militia of the State to support the Constitution. What,
gracious God, is man! that there should be such inconsistency
& perfidiousness in his conduct? It is but the other day we
were shedding our blood to obtain the Constitutions under
which we now live—Constitutions of our own choice and
framing—and now we are unsheathing the Sword to overturn
them! The thing is so unaccountable, that I hardly know how
to realize it, or to persuade my self that I am not under the
vision of a dream.

    My mind previous to the receipt of your letter of the first
Ulto had often been agitated by thoughts similar to those you
have expressed, respecting an old frd of yours; but heaven
forbid that a crisis should arrive when he shall be driven to
the necessity of making choice of either of the alternatives
therementioned. Let me entreat you, my dear Sir, to keep me
advised of the situation of Affairs in your quarter. I can depend upon your Accts. Newspaper paragraphs unsupported by
other testimony, are often contradictory & bewildering. At
one time these insurgents are represented as a mere Mob—

At other times as systematic in all their proceedings. If the first, I would fain hope that like other Mobs, it will, however formidable, be of short duration. If the latter, there surely are men of consequence and abilities behind the Curtain, who move the puppits. The designs of whom may be deep & dangerous. They may be instigated by British Councils—actuated by ambitious motives—or being influenced by dishonest principles, had rather see the Country plunged in civil discord than do what Justice would dictate to an honest mind.

Private and Confidential

I had hardly dispatched my circular letters to the several State Societies of the Cincinnati, when I received Letters from some of the principal members of our Assembly, expressing a wish that they might be permitted to name me as one of the Deputies to the Convention proposed to be held at Philadelphia, the first of May next. I immediately wrote to my particular friend Madison (& similarly to the rest) the answer contained in the extract No. 1—In reply I got No. 2—This obliged me to be *more* explicit & confidential with him, on points which a recurrence to the conversations we have had on this Subject will bring to your mind without my hazarding the recital of them in a letter—Since this interchange, I have received from the Governor the letter No. 4 to whom I returned the answer No. 5. If this business should be further prest (which I hope it will not, as I have no inclination to go) what had I best do? *You*, as an *indifferent person*—& one who is much better acquainted with the Sentiments, & views of the Cincinnati than I am (for in this State, where the recommendations of the General meeting have been acceded to, hardly any thing is said about it) as also with the temper of the people, and the state of Politics at large, can determine upon fuller evidence, & better ground than myself—especially as you will know in what light the States to the Eastward consider *the Convention* & the measures they are pursuing to contravene, or give efficacy to it. On the last occasion, only five States were represented—none East of New York. Why the New England Governments did not appear I am yet to learn; for of all others the distractions & turbulent temper of their people would, I should have thought, have afforded the strongest evidence of the *necessity* of competent powers some-where. That the fœderal Government is nearly, if not quite at a stand none will deny: The question then is, can it be propt— or shall it be anihilated? If the former, the proposed Conven-tion is an object of the first magnitude, and should be supported by all the friends of the present Constitution. In the other case, if on a full and dispassionate revision thereof, the continuances shall be adjudged impracticable, or unwise, would it not be better for such a meeting to suggest some other to avoid, if possible, civil discord, or other impending evils. Candour however obliges me to confess that as we could not remain quiet more than three or four years (in time of peace) under the constitutions of our own choice, which it was believed, in many instances, were formed with delibera-tion & wisdom, I see little prospect either of our agreeing upon any other, or that we should remain long satisfied under it if we could—Yet I would wish to see *any thing* and every thing essayed to prevent the effusion of blood, and to avert the humiliating, & contemptible figure we are about to make, in the Annals of Mankind.

If this second attempt to convene the States for the pur-poses proposed in the report of the partial representation at Annapolis in September last, should also prove abortive it may be considered as an unequivocal proof that the States are not likely to agree in any general measure which is to pervade the Union, & consequently, that there is an end put to Fœderal Government. The States therefore who make this last dying essay to avoid the misfortune of a dissolution would be mor-tified at the issue: and their deputies would return home cha-greened at their ill success & disappointment. This would be a disagreeable predicament for any of them to be in, but more particularly so for a person in my situation. If no further ap-plication is made to me, of course I do not attend. If there is, I am under no obligation to do it; but as I have had so many proofs of your friendship—know your abilities to judge—and your opportunities of learning the politicks of the day, on the points I have enumerated, you would oblige me by a *full* & *confidential* communication of your sentiments thereon.

Peace & tranquility prevail in this State. The Assembly by

a very great Majority, and in very emphatical terms have rejected an application for paper money; and spurned the idea of fixing the value of Military certificates by a scale of depreciation. In some other respects too, the proceedings of the present Session have been marked with Justice, and a strong desire of supporting the fœderal system.

Although I lament the effect, I am pleased at the cause which has deprived us of your aid in the Attack of Christmas Pyes. We had one yesterday on which all the company (and pretty numerous it was) were hardly able to make an impression. Mrs Washington, George & his wife (Mr Lear I had occasion to send into the Western Country) join in affectionate regard for you—& with sentiments of the warmest friendship I am—sincerely Yours

To Henry Knox

My dear Sir,   Mount Vernon 3d Feby 1787
  I feel my self exceedingly obliged to you for the full, & friendly communications in your letters of the 14th 21st & 25th ult.; and shall (critically as matters are described in the latter) be extremely anxious to know the issue of the movements of the forces that were assembling, the one to support, the other to oppose the constitutional rights of Massachusetts. The moment is, indeed, important! If government shrinks, or is unable to enforce its laws; fresh manœuvres will be displayed by the insurgents—anarchy & confusion must prevail—and every thing will be turned topsy turvey in that State; where it is not probable the mischiefs will terminate.

  In your letter of the 14th you express a wish to know my intention respecting the Convention, proposed to be held at Philada in May next. In *confidence* I inform you, that it is not, at this time, my purpose to attend it. When this matter was first moved in the Assembly of this State, some of the principal characters of it wrote to me, requesting to be permitted to put my name in the delegation. To this I objected—They again pressed, and I again refused; assigning among other reasons my having declined meeting the Society of the Cincinnati at that place, about the same time; & that I thought it would be disrespectfull to that body (to whom I ow'd much) to be there on any other occasion. Notwithstanding these intimations, my name was inserted in the Act; and an official communication thereof made by the Executive to me; to whom, at the same time that I expressed my sense of the confidence reposed in me, I declared, that as I saw no prospect of my attending, it was my wish that my name might not remain in the delegation, to the exclusion of another. To this I have been requested, in emphatical terms, not to decide absolutely, as no inconvenience would result from the non-appointment of another, at least for some time. Thus the matter stands, which is the reason of my saying to you in *confidence* that at present I retain my first intention—not to go. In the meanwhile as I have the fullest conviction of your friendship for, and attachment to me; know your abilities to judge; and your means of information, I shall receive any communications from you, respecting this business, with thankfulness. My first wish is, to do for the best, and to act with propriety; and you know me too well, to believe that reserve or concealment of any circumstance or opinion, would be at all pleasing to me.

The legality of this Convention I do not mean to discuss—nor how problematical the issue of it may be. That powers are wanting, none can deny. Through what medium they are to be derived, will, like other matters, engage public attention. That which takes the shortest course to obtain them, will, in my opinion, under present circumstances, be found best. Otherwise, like a house on fire, whilst the most regular mode of extinguishing it is contending for, the building is reduced to ashes. My opinion of the energetic wants of the federal government are well known—publickly & privately, I have declared it; and however constitutionally it may be for Congress to point out the defects of the fœderal System, I am strongly inclined to believe that it would not be found the most efficatious channel for the recommendation, more especially the alterations, to flow—for reasons too obvious to enumerate.

The System on which you seem disposed to build a national government is certainly more energetic, and I dare say, in every point of view is more desirable than the present one; which, from experience, we find is not only slow—debilitated—and liable to be thwarted by every breath, but is defective in that secrecy, which for the accomplishment of many of the most important national purposes, is indispensably necessary; and besides, having the Legislative, Executive & Judiciary departments concentered, is exceptionable. But at the same time I give this opinion, I believe that the political machine will yet be much tumbled & tossed, and possibly be wrecked altogether, before such a system as you have defined, will be adopted. The darling Sovereignties of the States individually, The Governors elected & elect. The Legislators—with a long train of etcetera whose political consequence will be lessened, if not anihilated, would give their weight of opposition to such a revolution. But I may be speaking without book, for scarcely ever going off my own farms I see few people who do not call upon me; & am very little acquainted with the Sentiments of the great world; indeed, after what I have seen, or rather after what I have heard, I shall be surprized at nothing; for if three years ago, any person had told me that at this day, I should see such a formidable rebellion against the laws & constitutions of our own making as now appears I should have thought him a bedlamite—a fit subject for a mad house. Adieu, you know how much, and how sincerely I am, ever, Yr Affecte & most Obedt Servant

Mrs Washington joins me in every good wish for yourself—Mrs Knox and the family.

To Mary Ball Washington

Hond Madam,   Mount Vernon February 15 1787

    In consequence of your communication to George Washington, of your want of money, I take the (first safe) conveyance by Mr John Dandridge to send you 15 Guineas which believe me is all I have and which indeed ought to have been paid many days ago to another agreeable to my own assurances. I have now demands upon me for more than 500£ three hundred and forty odd of which is due for the tax of 1786; and I know not where, or when I shall receive one shilling

with which to pay it. In the last two years I made no Crops.
In the first I was obliged to buy Corn and this year have none
to sell, and my wheat is so bad I cannot neither eat it myself
nor sell it to others, and Tobaca I make none. Those who owe
me money cannot or will not pay it without Suits and to sue
is like doing nothing, whilst my expences, not from any extravagance, or an inclination on my part to live splendidly but
for the absolute support of my family and the visitors who are
constantly here are exceedingly high; higher indeed than I can
support, without selling part of my estate which I am disposed
to do rather than run in debt or continue to be so but this I
cannot do, without taking much less than the lands I have
offered for sale are worth. This is really and truely my situation—I do not however offer it as any excuse for not paying
you what may really be due—for let this be little or much I
am willing; however unable to pay to the utmost farthing; but
it is really hard upon me when you have taken every thing
you wanted from the Plantation by which money could be
raised—When I have not received one farthing, directly nor
indirectly from the place for more than twelve years if ever—
and when, in that time I have paid, as appears by Mr Lund
Washingtons account against me (during my absence) Two
hundred and Sixty odd pounds, and by my own account Fifty
odd pounds out of my own Pocket to you. besides (if I am
rightly informed) every thing that has been raised by the
Crops on the Plantation. who to blame, or whether any body
is to blame for these things I know not, but these are facts.
and as the purposes for which I took the Estate are not answered nor likely to be so but dissatisfaction on all sides have
taken place, I do not mean to have any thing more to say to
your Plantation or Negros since the first of January except the
fellow who is here, and who will not, as he has formed connections in this neighbourhood leave it as experience has
proved him I will hire. of this my intention I informed my
brother John some time ago, whoes death I sincerely lament
on many Accounts and on this painful event condole with you
most sincerely. I do not mean by this declaration to with hold
any aid or support I can give from you; for whilst I have a
shilling left you shall have part, if it is wanted, whatever my
own distresses may be. what I shall then give I shall have

creadit for. now I have not for tho' I have received nothing
from your Quarter, and am told that every farthing goes to
you, and have moreover paid between 3 & 4 hundred pounds
besides out of my own pocket I am viewed as a delinquent.
& considered perhaps by the world as unjust and undutiful
Son. My advice to you therefore, is, to do one of two things
with the Plantation—either let your grandson Bushrod Washington, to whom the land is given by his Father have the
whole interest there, that is lands and negros, at a reasonable
rent—or, next year (for I presume it is too late this, as the
overseer may be engaged) to let him have the land at a certain
yearly rent during your life; and hire out the negros—this
would ease you of all care and trouble—make your income
certain—and your support ample. Further, my sincere, and
pressing advice to you is, to break up housekeeping, hire out
all the rest of your servants except a man and a maid and live
with one of your Children. This would relieve you entirely
from the cares of this world, and leave your mind at ease to
reflect, undisturbedly on that which aught to come. On this
subject I have been full with my Brother John and it was
determined he should endeavor to get you to live with him—
He alas is no more & three only of us remain—My House is
at your service, & would press you most sincerely & most
devoutly to accept it, but I am sure and candour requires me
to say it will never answer your purposes, in any shape whatsoever—for in truth it may be compared to a well resorted
tavern, as scarcely any strangers who are going from north to
south, or from south to north do not spend a day or two at
it—This would, were you to be an inhabitant of it, oblige you
to do one of 3 things, 1st to be always dressing to appear in
company, 2d to come into in a dishabille or 3d to be as it were
a prisoner in your own chamber The first yould not like, indeed for a person at your time of life it would be too fateigu-
ing. The 2d I should not like because those who resort here
are as I observed before strangers and people of the first distinction. and the 3d, more than probably, would not be pleasing to either of us—nor indeed could you be retired in any
room in my house; for what with the sitting up of Company;
the noise and bustle of servants—and many other things you
would not be able to enjoy that calmness and serenity of mind,

which in my opinion you ought now to prefer to every other consideration in life. If you incline to follow this advice the House and lotts on which you now live you may rent, and enjoy the benefit of the money arising there from as long as you live—this with the rent of the land at the little falls & the hire of your negros would bring you in an income which would be much more than sufficient to answer all your wants and make ample amends to the child you live with; for myself I should desire nothing, if it did not, I would, most chearfully contribute more. a man, a maid, The Phæten and two horses, are all you would want—to lay in a sufficiency for the support of these would not require 1/4 of your income, the rest would purchase every necessary you could possibly want, and place it in your power to be serviceable to those wth whom you may live, which no doubt, would be agreeable to all parties.

There are such powerful reasons in my mind for giving this advice, that I cannot help urging it with a degree of earnestness which is uncommon for me to do. It is I am convinced, the only means by which you can be happy. the cares of a family without any body to assist you—The charge of an estate the proft of which depend upon wind weather—a good Overseer—an honest man—and a thousand other circumstance, cannot be right, or proper at your advanced age & for me, who am absolutely prevented from attending to my own plantations which are almost within call of me to attempt the care of yours would be folly in the extreme; but the mode I have pointed out, you may reduce your income to a certainty, be eased of all trouble—and, if you are so disposed, may be perfectly happy—for happiness depends more upon the internal frame of a persons own mind—than on the externals in the world. of the last if you will pursue the plan here recommended I am sure you can want nothing that is essential—the other depends wholy upon your self, for the riches of the Indies cannot purchase it.

Mrs Washington, George & Fanny Join me in every good wish for you and I am honored Madam, Yr most dutiful & affe. Son

To Henry Knox

Mount Vernon 25th Feb. 1787

Accept, my dear General Knox my affectionate thanks for your obliging favors of the 29th, 30th, & 31st of Jany and 1st 8th & 12th of the present month.

They were indeed, exceedingly satisfactory, and relieving to my mind which has been filled with great & anxious uneasiness for the issue of General Lincoln's operations, and the dignity of Government.

On the prospect of the happy termination of this insurrection I sincerely congratulate you; hoping that good may result from the cloud of evils which threatned not only the hemisphere of Massachusetts but by spreading its baneful influence, the tranquillity of the Union. Surely Shays must be either a weak man—the dupe of some characters who are yet behind the curtain—or has been deceived by his followers. Or which may yet be more likely, he did not conceive that there was energy enough in the Government to bring matters to the crisis to which they have been pushed. It is to be hoped the General Court of that State concurred in the report of the Committee, that a rebellion did actually exist. This woud be decisive, and the most likely means of putting the finishing stroke to the business.

We have nothing new in this quarter except the dissentions which prevailed in, and occasioned the adjournment of, the Assembly of Maryland; that an appeal might be made to the people for their sentiments on the conduct of their representatives in the Senate & Delegates respecting a paper emission; which was warmly advocated by the latter and opposed by the former—and which may be productive of great, and perhaps dangerous divisions. Our Affairs, generally, seem really, to be approaching to some awful crisis. God only knows what the result will be. It shall be my part to hope for the best; as to see this Country happy whilst I am gliding down the stream of life in tranquil retirement is so much the wish of my Soul, that nothing on this side Elysium can be placed in competition with it.

I hope the postponement of your journey to this State does

not amount to a relinquishment of it—and that it is unnecessary to assure you of the sincere pleasure I should have at seeing you under this roof. Mrs Washington unites with me in every good wish for Mrs Knox yourself and family. With sentiments of the warmest friendship I am—Yrs most Affectionately

P.S. I had wrote this letter & was on the point of sending it with others to the Post Office when your favor of the 15th instt was handed to me. The spirit & decision of the Court is very pleasing & I hope will be attended with happy consequences. G.W.

To Henry Knox

My dear Sir,   Mount Vernon 8th Mar. 1787
   Will you permit me to give you the trouble of making an indirect, but precise enquiry, into the alligations of the enclosed letters. I flatter myself that from the vicinity of Elizabeth Town to New York, and the constant intercourse between the two, you will be able to do it without much trouble. It is but little in my power to afford the pecuniary aids required by the letter writer; but if the facts as set forth be true, I should feel very happy in offering my mite, and rendering any services in my power on the occasion. Be so good, when you write to me on this subject, to return the letters & translations.
   The observations contained in your letter of the 22d Ulto (which came duly to hand) respecting the disfranchisement of a number of the Citizens of Massachusetts for their rebellious conduct, may be just; and yet, without exemplary punishment, similar disorders may be excited by other ambitious and discontented characters. Punishment however ought to light on the principals.
   I am glad to hear that Congress are about to remove some of the stumbling blocks which lay in the way of the proposed Convention. A Convention I wish to see tried—after which, if the present government is not efficient, conviction of the

propriety of a change will dessiminate through every rank, and class of people and may be brought about in peace—till which, however necessary it may appear in the eyes of the more discerning, my opinion is, that it cannot be effected without great contention, and much confusion. It is among the evils, and perhaps is not the smallest, of democratical governments, that the people must *feel*, before they will *see*. When this happens, they are roused to action—hence it is that this form of government is so slow. I am indirectly, and delicately pressed to attend this convention. Several reasons are opposed to it in my mind, and not the least my having declined attending the General Meeting of the Cincinnati, which is to be holden in Philadelphia at the same time, on account of the disrespect it might *seem* to offer to that Society, to be there on another occasion. A thought however has lately run through my mind, which is attended with embarrassment. It is, whether my non-attendance in this Convention will not be considered as a dereliction to republicanism—nay more— whether other motives may not (however injuriously) be ascribed to me for not exerting myself on this occasion in support of it. Under these circumstances let me pray you, my dear Sir, to inform me confidentially, what the public expectation is on this head—that is, whether I will, or ought to be there? You are much in the way of obtaining this knowledge. and I can depend upon your friendship—candour—and judgment in the communication of it, as far as it shall appear to you—My final determination (if what I have already given to the Executive of this State is not considered in that light) cannot be delayed beyond the time necessary for your reply. With great truth I am yrs most Affectly

To John Jay

Dear Sir,   Mount Vernon Mar: 10th 1787
    I am indebted to you for two letters: The first, introductory of Mr Anstey needed no apology—nor will any be necessary on future occasions. The other, of the 7th of Jany is on a very interesting subject, deserving very particular attention.

How far the revision of the fœderal system, and giving more adequate powers to Congress may be productive of an efficient government, I will not, under my present view of the matter, presume to decide. That many inconveniencies result from the present form, none can deny. Those enumerated in your letter are so obvious, & sensibly felt that no logick can controvert, nor is it probable that any change of conduct will remove them. And that all attempts to alter or amend it will be like the propping of a house which is ready to fall, and which no shoars can support (as many seem to think) may also be true.

But, is the public mind matured for such an important change as the one you have suggested? What would be the consequences of a premature attempt?

My opinion is, that this Country have yet to *feel*, and *see* a little more, before it can be accomplished. A thirst for power, and the bantling—I had like to have said monster—sovereignty, which have taken such fast hold of the States individually, will, when joined by the many whose personal consequence in the line of State politics will in a manner be annihilated, form a strong phalanx against it; and when to these the few who can hold posts of honor or profit in the National government are compared with the many who will see but little prospect of being noticed, and the discontents of others who may look for appointments the opposition would be altogether irrisistable till the mass as well as the more discerning part of the Community shall see the Necessity.

Among men of reflection few will be found I believe, who are not *beginning* to think that our system is better in theory than practice—and that, notwithstanding the boasted virtue of America it is more than probable we shall exhibit the last melancholy proof that Mankind are not competent to their own government without the means of coercion in the Sovereign.

Yet, I would try what the wisdom of the proposed Convention will suggest; and what can be effected by their Councils. It may be the last peaceable mode of essaying the practicability of the prest form, without a greater lapse of time than the exigency of our Affairs will admit. In strict propriety a Convention so holden may not be legal—Congress however may give it a colouring by recommendation, which would fit it more to the taste, without proceeding to a definition of powers. This, however Constitutionally it might be done, would not, in my opinion, be expedient; for delicacy on the one hand, and Jealousy on the other would produce a mere nihil.

My name is in the delegation to this Convention; but it was put there contrary to my desire, and remains there contrary to my request. Several reasons at the time of this appointment and which yet exist combined to make my attendance inconvenient, perhaps improper tho. a good deal urged to it—With sentiments of great regard & friendship I have the honor to be—Dr Sir Yr Most Obedt and Affecte Hble Servt

P.S. Since writing this letter I have seen the resolution of Congress recommendatory of the Convention proposed to be held in Philadela the 2d Monday in May.

To Edmund Randolph

Dear Sir,   Mount Vernon 28th Mar. 1787

Your favor of the 11th did not come to my hand till the 24th; and since then, till now, I have been too much indisposed to acknowledge the receipt of it. To what cause to ascribe the detention of the letter I know not, as I never omit sending once, and oftener twice a week to the Post Office—In Alexandria.

It was the decided intention of the letter I had the honor of writing to your Excellency the 21st of December last, to inform you, that it would not be convenient for me to attend the Convention proposed to be holden in Philadelphia in May next; and I had entertained hopes that another had been, or soon would be, appointed in my place; inasmuch as it is not only inconvenient for me to leave home, but because there will be, I apprehend, too much cause to charge my conduct with inconsistency, in again appearing on a public theatre after a public declaration to the contrary; and because it will, I fear, have a tendency to sweep me back into the tide of public affairs, when retirement and ease is so essentially necessary for, and is so much desired by me.

However, as my friends, with a degree of sollicitude which is unusual, seem to wish my attendance on this occasion, I have come to a resolution to go if my health will permit, provided, from the lapse of time between the date of your Excellencys letter and this reply, the Executive may not—the reverse of which wd be highly pleasing to me—have turned its thoughts to some other character—for independantly of all other considerations, I have, of late, been so much afflicted with a rheumatic complaint in my shoulder that at times I am hardly able to raise my hand to my head, or turn myself in bed. This, consequently, might prevent my attendance, and eventually a representation of the State; which wd afflict me more sensibly than the disorder which occasioned it.

If after the expression of these sentiments, the Executive should consider me as one of the Delegates, I would thank your Excellency for the earliest advice of it; because if I am able, and should go to Philadelpa, I shall have some previous arrangements to make, and would set of for that place the first, or second day of May, that I may be there in time to account, personally, for my conduct to the General Meeting of the Cincinnati which is to convene on the first Monday of that month—My feelings would be much hurt if that body should otherwise, ascribe my attendance on the one, and not on the other occasion, to a disrespectful inattention to the Society; when the fact is, that I shall ever retain the most lively and affectionate regard for the members of which it is composed, on acct of their attachment to, and uniform support of me, upon many trying occasions; as well as on acct of their public virtues, patriotism, and sufferings.

I hope your Excellency will be found among the *attending* delegates. I should be glad to be informed who the others are—and cannot conclude without once more, and in emphatical terms, praying that if there is not a *decided* representation in *prospect*, without me, that another, for the reason I have assigned, may be chosen in my room without ceremony and without delay; for it would be unfortunate indeed if the State which was the mover of this Convention, should be unrepresented in it. With great respect I have the honor to be Yr Excellys Most Obedt Ser.

To James Madison

My dear Sir,   Mount Vernon 31st. Mar: 1787.

At the same time that I acknowledge the receipt of your obliging favor of the 21st. Ult. from New York, I promise to avail myself of your indulgence of writing only when it is convenient to me. If this should not occasion a relaxation on your part, I shall become very much your debtor—and possibly like others in similar circumstances (when the debt is burthensome) may feel a disposition to apply the spunge—or, what is nearly a-kin to it—pay you off in depreciated paper, which being a legal tender, or what is tantamount, being *that* or *nothing*, you cannot refuse. You will receive the nominal value, & that you know quiets the conscience, and makes all things easy—with the debto.

I am glad to find that Congress have recommended to the States to appear in the Convention proposed to be holden in Philadelphia in May. I think the reasons in favor, have the preponderancy of those against the measure. It is idle in my opinion to suppose that the Sovereign can be insensible of the inadequacy of the powers under which it acts—and that seeing, it should not recommend a revision of the Fœderal system, when it is considered by many as the *only* Constitutional mode by which the defects can be remedied. Had Congress proceeded to a delineation of the Powers, it might have sounded an alarm—but as the case is, I do not conceive that it will have that effect.

From the acknowledged abilities of the Secretary for Foreign Affairs, I could have had no doubt of his having ably investigated the infractions of the Treaty on both sides. Much is it to be regretted however, that there should have been any on ours. We seem to have forgotten, or never to have learnt, the policy of placing ones enemy in the wrong. Had we observed good faith on our part, we might have told our tale to the world with a good grace; but complts. illy become those who are found to be the first agressors.

I am fully of opinion that those who lean to a Monarchical governmt. have either not consulted the public mind, or that they live in a region where the levelling principles in which they were bred, being entirely irradicated, is much more productive of Monarchical ideas than are to be found in the Southern States, where from the habitual distinctions which have always existed among the people, one would have expected the first generation, and the most rapid growth of them. I also am clear, that even admitting the utility;—nay necessity of the form—yet that the period is not arrived for adopting the change without shaking the Peace of this Country to its foundation.

That a thorough reform of the present system is indispensable, none who have capacities to judge will deny and with hand and heart I hope the business will be essayed in a full Convention. After which, if more powers, and more decision is not found in the existing form—If it still wants energy and that secresy and dispatch (either from the non-attendance, or the local views of its members) which is characteristick of good Government—And if it shall be found (the contrary of which however I have always been more affrd. of, than of the abuse of them) that Congress will upon all proper occasions exercise the powers with a firm and steady hand, instead of frittering them back to the Individual States where the members in place of viewing themselves in their National character, are too apt to be looking—I say after this essay is made if the system proves inefficient, conviction of the necessity of a change will be dissiminated among all classes of the People. Then, and not till then, in my opinion can it be attempted without involving all the evils of civil discord.

I confess however that my opinion of public virtue is so far changed that I have my doubts whether any system without the means of coercion in the Sovereign, will enforce obedience to the Ordinances of a Genl. Government; without which, every thing else fails. Laws or Ordinances unobserved, or partially attended to, had better never have been made; because the first is a mere nihil—and the 2d is productive of much jealousy & discontent. But the kind of coercion you may ask?

This indeed will require thought; though the non-compliance of the States with the late requisition, is an evidence of the necessity.

It is somewhat singular that a State (New York) which used to be foremost in all fœderal measures, should now turn her face against them in almost every instance.

I fear the State of Massachusetts have exceeded the bounds of good policy in its disfranchisements—punishment is certainly due to the disturbers of a government, but the operations of this act is too extensive. It embraces too much—& probably may give birth to new, instead of destroying the old leven.

Some Acts passed at the last Session of our Assembly respecting the trade of this Country, has given great, and general discontent to the Merchants of it. An application from the whole body of those at Norfolk has been made, I am told, to convene the assembly.

———

I had written thus far, and was on the point of telling you how much I am your obliged Servant, when your favor of the 18th. calls upon me for additional acknowledgments.

I thank you for the Indian Vocabalary which I dare say will be very acceptable in a general comparison. Having taken a copy, I return you the original with thanks.

It gives me pleasure to hear that there is a probability of a full Representation of the States in Convention, but if the delegates come to it under fetters, the salutary ends proposed will in my opinion be greatly embarrassed & retarded, if not altogether defeated. I am anxious to know how this matter really is, as my wish is, that the Convention may adopt no temporising expedient, but probe the defects of the Constitution to the bottom, and provide radical cures, whether they are agreed to or not. A conduct like this, will stamp wisdom and dignity on the proceedings, and be looked to as a luminary, which sooner or later will shed its influence.

I should feel pleasure, I confess, in hearing that Vermont is received into the Union upon terms agreeable to all parties. I took the liberty years ago to tell some of the first characters in the State of New York, that sooner or later it would come to that. That the longer it was delayed the terms on their part, would, probably be more difficult—and that the general interest was suffering by the suspence in which the business was held; as the asylum wch. it afforded, was a constant drain from the Army in place of an aid which it offered to afford. And lastly, considering the proximity of it to Canada if they were not with us, they might become a sore thorn in our sides, wch. I verily believe would have been the case if the War had continued. The Western Settlements without good & wise management of them, may be equally troublesome. With sentimts. of the sincerest friendship I am Dear Sir Yr Affect. Servt

Be so good as to forward the enclosed. Mrs. Washington intended to have sent it by Colo. Carrington, but he did not call here.

To Edmund Randolph

My dear Sir,   Mount Vernon April 9th 1787

In reply to your favor of the 2d I have to request that you will not be at the trouble of forwarding any money to me from the treasury.

If I should attend the Service, it will suit me as well to receive it from you in Philadelphia as at this place. If I should not, I have no business with it at all.

It gives me pleasure to find by your letter that there will be so full a representation from this State. If the case had been otherwise I would in emphatical terms have urged again that, rather then depend upon my going, another might be chosen in my place; for as a friend, and in confidence, I declare to you that my assent is given contrary to my judgment; because the act will, I apprehend, be considered as inconsistent with my public declaration dilivered in a solemn manner at an interesting Æra of my life, never more to intermeddle in public matters. This declaration not only stands on the files of Congress, but is I believe registered in almost all the Gazettes and magazines that are published—and what adds to the embarrassment is, I had previous to my appointment, informed by circular letter the several State Societies of the Cincinnati of my intention to decline the Presidency of that order & excused myself from attending the next General meeting at Philadelphia on the first Monday in May—assigning reasons for so doing which apply as well in the one case as the other. Add to these, I very much fear that all the States will not appear in Convention, and that some of them will come fettered so as to impede rather than accelerate the great ends of their calling which, under the peculiar circumstances of my case, would place me in a disagreeable Situation which no other member present would stand in. As I have yielded however to what appeared to be the earnest wishes of my friends, I will hope for the best; and can assure you of the sincere and Affect. regard with which I am Dr Sir yr Obed. Servant

Contract with Philip Bater

April 23, 1787.

Articles of Agreement made this twelveth day of April Anno Domini one thousand seven hundred and eighty seven, by and between George Washington Esqr. of the Parish of Truro, in the County of Fairfax, State of Virginia, on the one part, and Philip Bater, Gardner, on the other Witness, that the said Philip Bater, for and in consideration of the covenants herein, hereafter, mentioned, doth promise and agree to serve the sd. George Washington, for the term of one year, as a Gardner, and that he will, during said time, conduct himself soberly, diligently and honestly, that he will faithfully and industriously perform all, and every part of his duty as a Gardner, to the best of his knowledge and abilities, and that he will not, at any time, suffer himself to be disguised with liquor, except on the times hereafter mentioned.

In Consideration of these things being well and truly performed on the part of the sd. Philip Bater, the said George Washington doth agree to allow him (the sd. Philip) the same kind and quantity of provisions as he has heretofore had; and likewise, annually, a decent suit of clothes befitting a man in his station; to consist of a Coat, Vest and breeches; a working

Jacket and breeches, of homespun, besides; two white Shirts; three Check Do; two pair of yarn Stockings; two pair of Thread Do; two linnen Pocket handkerchiefs; two pair linnen overalls; as many pair of Shoes as are actually necessary for him; four Dollars at Christmas, with which he may be drunk 4 days and 4 nights; two Dollars at Easter to effect the same purpose; two Dollars also at Whitsontide, to be drunk two days; A Dram in the morning, and a drink of Grog at Dinner or at Noon.

For the true and faithful performance of all and each of these things the parties have hereunto set their hands this twenty third day of April Anno Domini 1787.

To Marquis de Lafayette

My dear Marqs   Philadelphia June 6th 1787.

Not till within this hour was I informed of the intention of Mr Rutledge (son to the Governor Rutledge of South Carolina whom I believe you know) to embark in the Packet for France, or that he was to set out in the morning for New York, to take shipping the day after. Tho' totally unprepared (immersed as I am in the business of the Convention) I cannot let this Gentleman depart without a remembrance of my friendship for you. It was, when I came here, and still is, my intention, to write you a long letter from this place before I leave it, but the hour is not yet come when I can do it to my own Satisfaction or for your information. I therefore shall wait till the result of the present meeting is more matured, and till the members who constitute it are at liberty to communicate the proceedings more freely before I attempt it.

You will I dare say, be surprized my dear Marquis to receive a letter from me at this place, you will probably, be more so, when you hear that I am again brought, contrary to my public declaration, and intention, on a public theatre—such is the viscissitude of human affairs, and such the frailty of human nature that no man I conceive can well answer for the resolutions he enters into.

The pressure of the public voice was so loud, I could not

resist the call to a convention of the States which is to determine whether we are to have a Government of respectability under which life—liberty, and property secured to us, or whether we are to submit to one which may be the result of chance or the moment, springing perhaps from anarchie Confusion, and dictated perhaps by some aspiring demagogue who will not consult the interest of his Country so much as his own ambitious views. What may be the result of the present deliberations is more than I am able, at present, if I was at liberty, to inform & therefore I will make this letter short, and even assurance of being more particular when I can be more satisfactory—to this period also I refer more than to acknowledge the receipt of your obliging favours of the 7 of February inst.

Every good wish that can flow from a warm and sincere heart, much attached to you, and every one connected with you, is presented to Madam de la Fayette and your little flock; and with sentiments of encreasing friendship and love I am my dear Marquis Yr Most obliged, and Affecte Servant

To Alexander Hamilton

Dear Sir,   Philadelphia 10th. July 87.

I thank you for your communication of the 3d. When I refer you to the State of the Councils which prevailed at the period you left this City—and add, that they are now, if possible, in a worse train than ever; you will find that little ground on which the hope of a good establishment can be formed. In a word, I *almost* dispair of seeing a favourable issue to the proceedings of the Convention, and do therefore repent having had any agency in the business.

The Men who oppose a strong & energetic government are, in my opinion, narrow minded politicians, or are under the influence of local views. The apprehension expressed by them that the *people* will not accede to the form proposed is the *ostensible*, not the *real* cause of the opposition—but admitting that the present sentiment is as they prognosticate, the question ought nevertheless to be, is it or is it not, the best form?

If the former, recommend it, and it will assuredly obtain mauger opposition.

I am sorry you went away. I wish you were back. The crisis is equally important and alarming, and no opposition under such circumstances should discourage exertions till the signature is fixed. I will not, at this time trouble you with more than my best wishes and sincere regards.

I am Dear Sir Yr Obedt Servt

To John Cannon

Sir,   Philadelphia Sept. 16th 1787

I was suprized to find by your letter of the 8th of may, dated in this City (received after I came to it) that you had not got the letter I wrote to you sometime before under cover to Colo. Bayard of Pittsburg especially as the Colonel has acknowledged the receipt of it, and promised that it should be carefully forwarded to your house.

In that letter, to the best of my recollection, I requested that you would take charge of all my concerns—as well as those in Fayette, as Washington Counties & act for me as you would do for yourself. To this, if my memory serves me, your powers already extend—if not, I now give them to you by this letter.

I cannot consent to take two dollars a acre for the Land in Washington County. If the Government of this Country gets well toned, and property perfectly secured, I have no doubt of obtaining the price I have fixed on the land, and that in a short time, in the mean while, I had rather rent it from year to year than give leases for a term of years as the latter will certainly impede the Sale.

For the Land in Fayette County, I have been offered the price I had fixed on it—viz. Forty Shillings pr Acre—by a number of New Jersey people but we have differed with respect to the mode of payment and perhaps shall never agree I would not therefore have you Slip an opportunity of disposing of that Tract, if that price and the payment thereof is well secured. I would, as I think you have already been informed; be content with one fourth of the money paid down—the remainder in four annual payments with interest.

I am willing to take usual allowance of the Crops which were on the ground and hope you have taken your measures accordingly less than this, the Tenants cannot I should conceive think of giving—as the whole of them might have been demanded. I am Sir Yr Most Obed. Servant

To the Continental Congress

In Convention, September 17, 1787.

SIR, WE have now the honor to submit to the consideration of the United States in Congress assembled, that Constitution which has appeared to us the most adviseable.

The friends of our country have long seen and desired, that the power of making war, peace and treaties, that of levying money and regulating commerce, and the correspondent executive and judicial authorities should be fully and effectually vested in the general government of the Union: but the impropriety of delegating such extensive trust to one body of men is evident—Hence results the necessity of a different organization.

It is obviously impracticable in the fœderal government of these States; to secure all rights of independent sovereignty to each, and yet provide for the interest and safety of all—Individuals entering into society, must give up a share of liberty to preserve the rest. The magnitude of the sacrifice must depend as well on situation and circumstance, as on the object to be obtained. It is at all times difficult to draw with precision the line between those rights which must be surrendered, and those which may be reserved; and on the present occasion this difficulty was encreased by a difference among the several States as to their situation, extent, habits, and particular interests.

In all our deliberations on this subject we kept steadily in our view, that which appears to us the greatest interest of every true American, the consolidation of our Union, in which is involved our prosperity, felicity, safety, perhaps our national existence. This important consideration, seriously and deeply impressed on our minds, led each State in the Convention to be less rigid on points of inferior magnitude, than might have been otherwise expected; and thus the Constitution, which we now present, is the result of a spirit of amity, and of that mutual deference and concession which the peculiarity of our political situation rendered indispensible.

That it will meet the full and entire approbation of every State is not perhaps to be expected; but each will doubtless consider, that had her interests been alone consulted, the consequences might have been particularly disagreeable or injurious to others; that it is liable to as few exceptions as could reasonably have been expected, we hope and believe; that it may promote the lasting welfare of that country so dear to us all, and secure her freedom and happiness, is our most ardent wish.

With great respect, WE have the honor to be SIR, Your Excellency's most Obedient and humble servants.

> George Washington, President.
> By unanimous Order of the
> Convention

Diary Entry

Monday 17th. Met in Convention when the Constitution received the Unanimous assent of 11 States and Colo. Hamilton's from New York (the only delegate from thence in Convention) and was subscribed to by every Member present except Govr. Randolph and Colo. Mason from Virginia & Mr. Gerry from Massachusetts. The business being thus closed, the Members adjourned to the City Tavern, dined together and took a cordial leave of each other—after which I returned to my lodgings—did some business with, and received the papers from the secretary of the Convention, and retired to meditate on the momentous wk. which had been executed, after not less than five, for a large part of the time Six, and sometimes 7 hours sitting every day, sundays & the ten days adjournment to give a Comee. opportunity & time to arrange the business for more than four Months.

September 17, 1787

To Patrick Henry

Dear Sir,   Mount Vernon Sept. 24th 1787

In the first moments after my return I take the liberty of sending you a copy of the Constitution which the Fœderal Convention has submitted to the People of these States.

I accompany it with no observations—your own Judgment will at once descover the good, and the exceptionable parts of it. and your experience of the difficulty's which have ever arisen when attempts have been made to reconcile such variety of interests, and local prejudices as pervade the severeal States will render explanation unnecessary. I wish the Constitution which is offered had been made more perfect, but I sincerely believe it is the best that could be obtained at this time—and as a constitutional door is opened for amendment hereafter—the adoption of it under present circumstances of the Union is in my opinion desirable.

From a variety of concurring accounts it appears to me that the political concerns of this Country are, in a manner, suspended by a thread. That the Convention has been looked up to by the reflecting part of the community with a Sollicitude which is hardly to be conceived, and that, if nothing had been agreed on by that body, anarchy would soon have ensued—the seeds being reiply sown in every soil. I am &c.

To David Humphreys

My dear Humphreys,   Mount Vernon Octr 10th 1787.

Your favor of the 28th Ult. came duly to hand, as did the other of June. With great pleasure I received the intimation of your spending the Winter under this roof. The invitation was not less sincere than the reception will be cordial. The convention shall be, that in all things you shall do as you please—I will do the same—No ceremony shall be observed—nor any restraint be imposed on any one.

The Constitution that is submitted, is not free from inperfections; but there are as few radical defects in it as could well be expected, considering the heterogenious mass of which the Convention was composed—and the diversity of interests which were to be reconciled. A Constitutional door being opened, for future alterations and amendments, I think it would be wise in the People to adopt what is offered to them; and I wish it may be by as great a majority of them as in the body that decided on it; but this is hardly to be expected, because the importance, and sinister views of too many characters will be affected by the change. Much will depend however on literary abilities, & the recommendation of it by good pens, should it be openly, I mean publicly attacked in the Gazettes. Go matters however as they may, I shall have the consolation to reflect, that no objects but the public good, and that peace & harmony which I wished to see prevail in the Convention, ever obtruded, even for a moment, in my mind, during the whole session lengthy as it was. What reception this State will give to the proceedings (thro' the great territorial extent of it) I am unable to inform you. In these parts of it, it is advocated beyond my expectation. The great opposition, if great is given, will come from the Counties Southward and Westward; from whence I have not, as yet, heard much that can be depended on.

I condole with you on the loss of your parents, but as they lived to a good old age you could not be unprepared for the shock; tho' there is something painful in bidding an adieu to those we love, or revere, when we know it is a final one. Reason, religion & Philosophy may soften the anguish, but time *alone* can irradicate it.

As I am beginning to look for you, I shall add no more at present, but the best wishes of the family, and the affecte regards of your Sincere friend and Obedt Hble Servt

To Henry Knox

My dear Sir,   Mount Vernon October 15th 1787
Your favor of the 3d instt came duly to hand.

The fourth day after leaving Phila. I arrived at home, and found Mrs Washington and the family tolerably well, but the fruits of the Earth almost entirely destroyed by one of the severest droughts (in this neighbourhood) that ever was experienced. The Crops generally, below the Mountains are injured; but not to the degree that mine, & some of my Neighbours, are here.

The Constitution is now before the judgment seat. It has, as was expected, its adversaries, and its supporters; which will preponderate is yet to be decided. The former, it is probable, will be most active because the Major part of them it is to be feared, will be governed by sinester and self important considerations on which no arguments will work conviction—the opposition from another class of them (if they are men of reflection, information and candour) may perhaps subside in the solution of the following plain, but important questions. 1. Is the Constitution which is submitted by the Convention preferable to the government (if it can be called one) under which we now live? 2. Is it probable that more confidence will, at this time, be placed in another Convention (should the experiment be tried) than was given to the last? and is it likely that there would be a better agreement in it? Is there not a Constitutional door open for alterations and amendments, & is it not probable that real defects will be as readily discovered after, as before, trial? and will not posterity be as ready to apply the remedy as ourselves, if there is occasion for it, when the mode is provided? To think otherwise will, in my judgment, be ascribing more of the amor patria—more wisdom—and more foresight to ourselves, than I conceive we are entitled to.

It is highly probable that the refusal of our Govr and Colo. Mason to subscribe to the proceedings of the Convention will have a bad effect in this State; for as you well observe, they *must* not only assign reasons for the justification of their conduct, but it is highly probable these reasons will appear in terrific array, with a view to alarm the people—Some things are already addressed to their fears and will have their effect. As far however as the sense of *this* part of the Country has been taken it is strongly in favor of the proposed Constitution. further I cannot speak with precision—If a powerful opposition is given to it the weight thereof will, I apprehend, come from the Southward of James River, & from the Western Counties.

Mrs Washington & the family join me in every good wish for you and Mrs Knox—and with great and sincere regard I am, My dear Sir Yr Affecte

To Bushrod Washington

Dear Bushrod,   Mount Vernon Novr 9th 1787.
In due course of Post, I received your letters of the 19th & 26th Ult.; and since, the one which you committed to the care of Mr Powell. I thank you for the communications therein, & for a continuation, in matters of importance, I shall be obliged to you.

That the Assembly would afford the people an opportunity of deciding on the proposed Constitution I had hardly a doubt; the only question with me was, whether it would go forth under favourable auspices, or be branded with the mark of disapprobation. The opponents, I expected, (for it has ever been, that the adversaries to a measure are more active than its friends) would endeavour to give it an unfavourable complexion, with a view to biass the public mind. This, evidently, is the case with the writers in opposition; for their objections are better calculated to alarm the fears, than to convince the judgment of their readers. They build them upon principles which do not exist in the Constitution—which the known & litteral sense of it, does not support them in; and this too, after being flatly told that they are treading on untenable ground and after an appeal has been made to the letter, & spirit thereof, for proof: and then, as if the doctrine was uncontrovertable, draw such consequences as are necessary to rouse the apprehensions of the ignorant, & unthinking. It is not the interest of the major part of these characters to be convinced; nor will their local views yield to arguments which do not accord with their present, or future prospects; and yet, a candid solution of a single question, to which the understanding of almost every man is competent, must decide the point in dispute—namely—is it best for the States to unite, or not to unite?

If there are men who prefer the latter, then, unquestionably, the Constitution which is offered, must, in their estimation, be inadmissible from the first Word to the last signature, inclusively. But those who may think differently, and yet object to parts of it, would do well to consider, that it does not lye with *one* State, nor with a *minority* of the States, to superstruct a Constitution for the *whole*. The seperate interests, as far as it is practicable, must be consolidated—and local views as far as the general good will admit, must be attended to. Hence it is that *every* state has some objection to the *proposed* form; and that these objections are directed to different points. That which is most pleasing to one, is obnoxious to another, and vice versa. If then the Union of the whole is a desirable object, the parts which compose it, must yield a little in order to accomplish it; for without the latter, the former is unattainable. For I again repeat it, that not a single state nor a minority of the States, can force a Constitution on the majority. But admitting they had (from their importance) the power to do it, will it not be granted that the attempt would be followed by civil commotions of a very serious nature? But to sum up the whole, let the opponants of the proposed Constitution, *in this State*, be asked—it is a question they ought certainly to have asked themselves; What line of conduct they would advise it to adopt, if nine other States should accede to it, of which I think there is little doubt? Would they recommend that it should stand on its own basis—seperate & distinct from the rest? Or would they connect it with Rhode Island, or even say two others, checkerwise, & remain with them as outcasts from the Society, to shift for themselves? or will they advise a return to our former dependence on Great Britain for their protection & support? or lastly would they prefer the mortification of comg in, when they will have no credit there from? I am sorry to add in this place that Virginians entertain *too* high an opinion of the importance of their own Country. In extent of territory—In number of Inhabitants (*of all descriptions*) & In wealth I will readily grant that it certainly stands first in the Union; but in point of *strength*, it is, comparitively, weak. To this point, my opportunities authorise me to speak, decidedly; and sure I am, in every point of view, in which the subject can be placed, it is not (considering also the Geographical situation of the State) more the interest of any one of them to confederate, than it is the one in which we live.

The warmest friends to and the best supporters of the Constitution, do not contend that it is free from imperfections; but these were not to be avoided, and they are convinced if evils are likely to flow from them, that the remedy must come thereafter; because, in the *present moment* it is not to be obtained. And as there is a Constitutional door open for it, I think the people (for it is with them to judge) can, as they will have the aid of experience on their side, decide with as much propriety on the alterations and amendments wch shall be found necessary, as ourselves; for I do not conceive that we are more inspired—have more wisdom—or possess more virtue than those who will come after us. The power under the Constitution will always be with the people. It is entrusted for certain defined purposes and for a certain limited period to representatives of their own chusing; and whenever it is exercised contrary to their interests, or not according to their wishes, their Servants can, and undoubtedly will be, recalled. There will not be wanting those who will bring forward complaints of mal-administration whensoever they occur. To say that the Constitution *may be strained*, and an *improper* interpretation given to some of the clauses or articles of it, will apply to any that can be framed—in a word renders any one nugatory—for not one, more than another, can be binding, if the spirit and letter of the expression is disregarded. It is agreed on all hands that no government can be well administred without powers; and yet, the instant these are delegated, altho those who are entrusted with the Administration are taken from the people—return shortly to them again—and must feel the bad effect of oppressive measures—the persons holding them, as if their natures were immediately metamorphosed, are denominated tyrants and no disposition is allowed them, but to do wrong. Of these things in a government so constituted and guarded as the proposed one is, I can have no idea; and do firmly believe that whilst many ostensible reasons are held out against the adoption of it the true ones are yet behind the Curtain; not being of a nature to appear in open day. I believe further, supposing these objections to be founded in purity itself that as great evils result from too much jealousy, as from the want of it. And I adduce several of the Constitutions of these States, as proof thereof. No man is a warmer advocate for *proper* restraints, and *wholesome* checks in every department of government than I am; but neither my reasoning, nor my experience, has yet been able to discover the propriety of preventing men from doing good, because there is a possibility of their doing evil.

If Mr Ronald can place the finances of this Country upon so respectable a footing as he has intimated, he will deserve its warmest, and most grateful thanks. In the attempt, my best wishes—which is all I have to offer—will accompany him.

I hope there remains virtue enough in the Assembly of this State, to preserve inviolate public treaties, and private contracts. If these are infringed, farewell to respectability, and safety in the Government.

I never possessed a doubt, but if any had ever existed in my breast, re-iterated proofs would have convinced me of the impolicy, of all commutable taxes. If wisdom is not to be acquired from experience, where is it to be found? But why ask the question? Is it not believed by every one that *these* are time-serving jobs by which a few are enriched, at the public expence! but whether the plan originates for this purpose, or is the child of ignorance, oppression is the result.

You have, I find, broke the ice (as the saying is). one piece of advice only I will give you on the occasion (if you mean to be a respectable member, and to entitle yourself to the Ear of the House)—and that is—except in local matters which respect your Constituants and to which you are obliged, by duty, to speak, rise but seldom—let this be on important matters—and then make yourself thoroughly acquainted with the subject. Never be agitated by *more than* a decent *warmth*, & offer your sentiments with modest diffidence—opinions thus given, are listened to with more attention than when delivered in a dictatorial stile. The latter, if attended to at all, altho they may *force* conviction, is sure to convey disgust also.

Your aunt, and the family here join me in every good wish for you. and I am with sentiments of great regd and Affecte. —Yours

P.S. The letter you sent by Mr Powell for Nancy was forwarded next day to Doctr Brown, for the best conveyance that should offer from alexandria.

To Thomas Jefferson

Dear Sir   Mount Vernon January 1st. 1788

I have received your favor of the 15th. of August, and am sorry that it is not in my power to give you any further information relative to the practicability of opening a communication between Lake Erie and the Ohio, than you are already possessed of. I have made frequent enquiries since the time of your writing to me on that subject while Congress were sitting at Annapolis, but could never collect any thing that was decided or satisfactory. I have again renewed them, and flatter myself with better prospect of success.

The accounts generally agree as to its being a flat country between the Waters of Lake Erie and Big Beaver; but differ very much with respect to the distance between their sources, their navigation, and the inconveniencies which would attend the cutting a canal between them.

From the best information I have been able to obtain of that Country, the sources of the Muskingham and Cayohoga approach nearer to each other than any water of Lake Erie does to Big Beaver: But a communication by this River would be more circuitous and difficult, having the Ohio in a greater extent, to ascend; unless the latter could be avoided by opening a communication between James River and the Great Kanhawa, or between the little Kanhawa and the West branch of Monongahela, which is said to be very practicable by a short portage. As testimony thereof, the States of Virginia and Maryland have opened (for I believe it is compleated) a road from the No. branch of Potomack, commencing at, or near the mouth of Savage River, to the Cheat River, from whence the former are continuing it to the navigable Water of the little Kanhawa.

The distance between Lake Erie and the Ohio, through the Big Beaver, is, however, so much less than the rout through the Muskingham, that it would, in my opinion, operate very strongly in favor of opening a canal between the source of the nearest water of the Lake and Big Beaver, altho the distance between them should be much greater and the operation more difficult than to the Muskingham. I shall omit no opportunity of gaining every information relative to this important subject; and will, with pleasure, communicate to you whatever may be worthy of your attention.

I did myself the honor to forward to you the plan of Government formed by the Convention, the day after that body rose; but was not a little disappointed, and mortified indeed (as I wished to make the first offering of it to you) to find by a letter from Commode. Jones, dated in New York the 9th. of Novr. that it was, at that time, in his possession. You have, undoubtedly, received it, or some other 'ere now, and formed an opinion upon it. The public attention is, at present, wholly engrossed by this important subject. The Legislatures of those States (Rhode Island excepted) which have met since the Constitution has been formed, have readily assented to its being submitted to a Convention chosen by the People. Pensylvania, New Jersey and Delaware are the only States whose Conventions have as yet decided upon it. In the former it was adopted by 46 to 23 and in the two latter unanimously. Connecticut and Massachusetts are to hold their Conventions on the 1st. and 2d. tuesdays of this Month, Maryland in April, Virginia in June, and upon the whole, it appears, so far as I have had an opportunity of learning the opinions of the people in the several States, that it will be received. There will, undoubtedly, be more or less opposition to its adoption in most of the States; and in none a more formidable one than in this; as many influencial characters here have taken a decided part against it, among whom are Mr. Henry, Colo. Mason, Govr. Randolph and Colo. R. H. Lee; but from every information which I have been able to obtain, I think there will be a majority in its favor notwithstanding their dissention. In New York a considerable opposition will also be given.

I am much obliged to you, my dear Sir, for the account which you gave me of the general state of affairs in Europe. I am glad to hear that the Assembleé des Notables has been productive of good in France. The abuse of the finances being disclosed to the King, and the Nation, must open their eyes, and lead to the adoption of such measures as will prove beneficial to them in future. From the public papers it appears that the Parliaments of the several Provinces, and particularly that of Paris, have acted with great spirit and resolution. Indeed the rights of Mankind, the priviledges of the people, and the true principles of liberty seem to have been more generally discussed and better understood throughout Europe since the American revolution than they were at any former period.

Altho' the finances of France and England were such as led you to suppose, at the time you wrote to me, would prevent a rupture between those two powers, yet, if we credit the concurrent accounts from every quarter, there is little doubt but that they have commenced hostilities before this. Russia and the Porte have formally began the contest, and from appearances (as given to us) it is not improbable but that a pretty general war will be kindled in Europe. Should this be the case, we shall feel more than ever the want of an efficient general Government to regulate our Commercial concerns, to give us a national respectability, and to connect the political views and interests of the several States under one head in such a manner as will effectually prevent them from forming a seperate, improper, or indeed any connection, with the European powers which can involve them in their political disputes. For our situation is such as makes it not only unnecessary, but extremely imprudent for us to take a part in their quarrels; and whenever a contest happens among them, if we wisely and properly improve the advantages which nature has given us, we may be benefitted by their folly—provided we conduct ourselves with circumspection, and under proper restrictions, for I perfectly agree with you, that an extensive speculation, a spirit of gambling, or the introduction of any thing which will divert our attention from Agriculture, must be extremely prejudicial, if not ruinous to us. But I conceive under an energetic general Government such regulations might be made, and such measures taken, as would render this Country the asylum of pacific and industrious characters from all parts of Europe, would encourage the cultivation of the Earth by the high price which its products would command, and would draw the wealth, and wealthy men of other Nations, into our own bosom, by giving security to property, and liberty to its holders.

I have the honor to be With great esteem & regard Dear Sir Yr. most obed. & most Hble Servt,

To Edmund Randolph

Mount Vernon, January 8, 1788.

Dear Sir: The letter, which you did me the honor of writing to me on the 27th Ulto. with the enclosure, came duly to hand. I receive them as a fresh instance of your friendship and attention. For both I thank you.

The diversity of Sentiments upon the important matter which has been submitted to the People, was as much expected as it is regretted, by me. The various passions and motives, by which men are influenced are concomitants of fallibility, engrafted into our nature for the purposes of unerring wisdom; but had I entertained a latent hope (at the time you moved to have the Constitution submitted to a second Convention) that a more perfect form would be agreed to, in a word that any Constitution would be adopted under the impressions and instructions of the members, the publications, which have taken place since would have eradicated every form of it. How do the sentiments of the influential characters in *this* State who are opposed to the Constitution, and have favoured the public with their opinions, quadrate with each other? Are they not at variance on some of the most important points? If the opponents in the *same* State cannot agree in *their* principles what prospect is there of a coalescence with the advocates of the measure when the different views, and jarring interests of so wide and extended an Empire are to be brought forward and combated?

To my Judgment, it is more clear than ever, that an attempt to amend the Constitution which is submitted, would be productive of more heat and greater confusion than can well be conceived. There are some things in the new form, I will readily acknowledge, wch. never did, and I am persuaded never will, obtain my *cordial* approbation; but I then did conceive, and do now most firmly believe, that, in the aggregate, it is the best Constitution that can be obtained at this Epocha, and that this, or a dissolution of the Union awaits our choice, and are the only alternatives before us. Thus believing, I had not, nor have I now any hesitation in deciding on which to lean.

I pray your forgiveness for the expression of these sentiments. In acknowledging the receipt of your Letter on this subject, it was hardly to be avoided, although I am well disposed to let the matter rest entirely on its own merits, and mens minds to their own workings. With very great esteem &c.

To Marquis de Lafayette

Mount Vernon, February 7, 1788.

My dear Marqs: You know it always gives me the sincerest pleasure to hear from you, and therefore I need only say that your two kind letters of the 9th and 15th of Octr. so replete with personal affection and confidential intelligence, afforded me inexpressible satisfaction. I shall myself be happy in forming an acquaintance and cultivating a friendship with the new Minister Plenipotentiary of France, whom you have commended as a "sensible and honest man;" these are qualities too rare and too precious not to merit one's particular esteem. You may be persuaded, that he will be well received by the Congress of the United States, because they will not only be influenced in their conduct by his individual merits, but also by their affection for the nation of whose Sovereign he is the Representative. For it is an undoubted fact, that the People of America entertain a grateful remembrance of past services as well as a favourable disposition for commercial and friendly connections with your Nation.

You appear to be, as might be expected from a real friend to this Country, anxiously concerned about its present political situation. So far as I am able I shall be happy in gratifying that friendly solicitude. As to my sentiments with respect to the merits of the new Constitution, I will disclose them without reserve, (although by passing through the Post offices they should become known to all the world) for, in truth, I have nothing to conceal on that subject. It appears to me, then, little short of a miracle, that the Delegates from so many different States (which States you know are also different from each other in their manners, circumstances and prejudices) should unite in forming a system of national Government, so little liable to well founded objections. Nor am I yet such an enthusiastic, partial or undiscriminating admirer of it, as not to perceive it is tinctured with some real (though not radical) defects. The limits of a letter would not suffer me to go fully into an examination of them; nor would the discussion be entertaining or profitable, I therefore forbear to touch upon it. With regard to the two great points (the pivots upon which the whole machine must move,) my Creed is simply,

1st. That the general Government is not invested with more Powers than are indispensably necessary to perform the functions of a good Government; and, consequently, that no objection ought to be made against the quantity of Power delegated to it.

2ly. That these Powers (as the appointment of all Rulers will for ever arise from, and, at short stated intervals, recur to the free suffrage of the People) are so distributed among the Legislative, Executive, and Judicial Branches, into which the general Government is arranged, that it can never be in danger of degenerating into a monarchy, an Oligarchy, an Aristocracy, or any other despotic or oppressive form, so long as there shall remain any virtue in the body of the People.

I would not be understood my dear Marquis to speak of consequences which may be produced, in the revolution of ages, by corruption of morals, profligacy of manners, and listlessness for the preservation of the natural and unalienable rights of mankind; nor of the successful usurpations that may be established at such an unpropitious juncture, upon the ruins of liberty, however providently guarded and secured, as these are contingencies against which no human prudence can effectually provide. It will at least be a recommendation to the proposed Constitution that it is provided with more checks and barriers against the introduction of Tyranny, and those of a nature less liable to be surmounted, than any Government hitherto instituted among mortals, hath possessed. We are not to expect perfection in this world; but mankind, in modern times, have apparently made some progress in the science of government. Should that which is now offered to the People of America, be found on experiment less perfect than it can be made, a Constitutional door is left open for its amelioration.

Some respectable characters have wished, that the States, after having pointed out whatever alterations and amendments may be judged necessary, would appoint another federal Convention to modify it upon those documents. For myself I have wondered that sensible men should not see the impracticability of the scheme. The members would go fortified with such Instructions that nothing but discordant ideas could prevail. Had I but slightly suspected (at the time when the late Convention was in session) that another convention would not be likely to agree upon a better form of Government, I should now be confirmed in the fixed belief that they would not be able to agree upon any System whatever. So many, I may add, such contradictory, and, in my opinion unfounded objections have been urged against the System in contemplation; many of which would operate equally against every efficient Government that might be proposed. I will only add, as a further opinion founded on the maturest deliberation, that there is no alternative, no hope of alteration, no intermediate resting place, between the adoption of this, and a recurrence to an unqualified state of Anarchy, with all its deplorable consequences.

Since I had the pleasure of writing to you last, no material alteration in the political state of affairs has taken place to change the prospect of the Constitution's being adopted by nine States or more, Pennsylvania, Delaware, New Jersey and Connecticut have already done it. It is also said Georgia has acceded. Massachusetts, which is perhaps thought to be rather more doubtful than when I last addressed you, is now in convention.

A spirit of emigration to the western Country is very predominant. Congress have sold, in the year past, a pretty large quantity of lands on the Ohio, for public Securities, and thereby diminished the domestic debt considerably. Many of your military acquaintances such as the Generals Parsons, Varnum, and Putnam, the Colos. Tupper, Sprout and Sherman, with many more, propose settling there. From such beginnings much may be expected.

The storm of war between England and your Nation, it seems, is dissipated. I hope and trust the political affairs in France are taking a favorable turn. If the Ottomans wod. suffer themselves to be precipitated into a war, they must abide the consequences. Some Politicians speculate on a triple Alliance between the two Imperial Courts and Versailles. I think it was rather fortunate, than otherwise, that the incaution of Ambassador and the rascality of a Rhinegrave prevented you from attempting to prop a falling fabric.

It gives me great pleasure to learn that the present ministry of France are friendly to America; and that Mr. Jefferson and yourself have a prospect of accomplishing measures which will mutually benefit and improve the commercial intercourse between the two Nations. Every good wish attend you and yrs. I am, &c.

To John Armstrong

Mount Vernon, April 25, 1788.

Dear Sir: From some cause or other which I do not know your favor of the 20th of February did not reach me till very lately. This must apologize for its not being sooner acknowledged. Altho' Colo Blaine forgot to call upon me for a letter before he left Philadelphia, yet I wrote a few lines to you previous to my departure from that place; whether they ever got to your hands or not you best know.

I well remember the observation you made in your letter

to me of last year, "that my domestic retirement must suffer an interruption." This took place, notwithstanding it was utterly repugnant to my feelings, my interests and my wishes; I sacrificed every private consideration and personal enjoyment to the earnest and pressing solicitations of those who saw and knew the alarming situation of our public concerns, and had no other end in view but to promote the interests of their Country; and conceiving, that under those circumstances, and at so critical a moment, an absolute refusal to act, might, on my part, be construed as a total dereliction of my Country, if imputed to no worse motives. Altho' you say the same motives induce you to think that another tour of duty of this kind will fall to my lot, I cannot but hope that you will be disappointed, for I am so wedded to a state of retirement and find the occupations of a rural life so congenial; with my feelings, that to be drawn into public at my advanced age, could be a sacrifice that would admit of no compensation.

Your remarks on the impressions which will be made on the manners and sentiments of the people by the example of those who are first called to act under the proposed Government are very just; and I have no doubt but (if the proposed Constitution obtains) those persons who are chosen to administer it will have wisdom enough to discern the influence which their example as rulers and legislators may have on the body of the people, and will have virtue enough to pursue that line of conduct which will most conduce to the happiness of their Country; as the first transactions of a nation, like those of an individual upon his first entrance into life, make the deepest impression, and are to form the leading traits in its character, they will undoubtedly pursue those measures which will best tend to the restoration of public and private faith and of consequence promote our national respectability and individual welfare.

That the proposed Constitution will admit of amendments is acknowledged by its warmest advocates; but to make such amendments as may be proposed by the several States the condition of its adoption would, in my opinion amount to a complete rejection of it; for upon examination of the objections, which are made by the opponents in different States and the amendments which have been proposed, it will be found that what would be a favorite object with one State, is the very thing which is strenuously opposed by another; the truth is, men are too apt to be swayed by local prejudices and those who are so fond of amendments which have the particular interest of their own States in view cannot extend their ideas to the general welfare of the Union; they do not consider that for every sacrifice which they make they receive an ample compensation by the sacrifices which are made by other States for their benefit; and that those very things, which they give up operate to their advantage through the medium of the general interest.

In addition to these considerations it should be remembered that a constitutional door is open for such amendments as shall be thought necessary by nine States. When I reflect upon these circumstances I am surprised to find that any person who is acquainted with the critical state of our public affairs, and knows the variety of views, interests, feelings and prejudices which must be consulted in framing a general Government for these States, and how little propositions in themselves so opposite to each other, will tend to promote that desirable end, can wish to make amendments the ultimatum for adopting the offered system.

I am very glad to find, that the opposition in your State, however formidable it has been represented, is, generally speaking, composed of such characters, as cannot have an extensive influence; their fort, as well as that of those in the same class in other States seems to lie in misrepresentation, and a desire to inflame the passions and to alarm the fears by noisy declamation rather than to convince the understanding by sound arguments or fair and impartial statements. Baffled in their attacks upon the constitution they have attempted to vilify and debase the Characters, who formed it, but even here I trust they will not succeed. Upon the whole I doubt whether the opposition to the Constitution will not ultimately be productive of more good than evil; it has called forth, in its defence, abilities which would not perhaps have been otherwise exerted that have thrown new light upon the science of Government, they have given the rights of man a full and fair discussion, and explained them in so clear and forcible a manner, as cannot fail to make a lasting impression upon those who read the best publications on the subject, and particularly the pieces under the signature of Publius. There will be a greater weight of abilities opposed to the system in the convention of this State than there has been in any other, but notwithstanding the unwearied pains which have been taken, and the vigorous efforts which will be made in the Convention to prevent its adoption, I have not the smallest doubt but it will obtain here.

I am sorry to hear, that the College in your neighbourhood is in so declining a state as you represent it, and that it is likely to suffer a further injury by the loss of Dr. Nisbet whom you are afraid you shall not be able to support in a proper manner on account of the scarcity of Cash which prevents parents from sending their Children thither. This is one of the numerous evils which arise from the want of a general regulating power, for in a Country like this where equal liberty is enjoyed, where every man may reap his own harvest, which by proper attention will afford him much more than is necessary for his own consumption, and where there is so ample a field for every mercantile and mechanical exertion, if there cannot be money found to answer the common purposes of education, not to mention the necessary commercial circulation, it is evident that there is something amiss in the ruling political power which requires a steady, regulating and energetic hand to correct and control. That money is not to be had, every mans experience tells him, and the great fall in the price of property is an unequivocal and melancholy proof of it; when, if that property was well secured, faith and justice well preserved, a stable government well administered, and confidence restored, the tide of population and wealth would flow to us, from every part of the Globe, and, with a due sense of the blessings, make us the happiest people upon earth. With sentiments of very great esteem &c.

To Marquis de Chastellux

Mount Vernon, April 25, 1788.
My dear Marquis: In reading your very friendly and acceptable letter of 21st. December 1787, which came to hand by the last mail, I was, as you may well suppose, not less delighted than surprised to come across that plain American word "my wife." A wife! well my dear Marquis, I can hardly refrain from smiling to find you are caught at last. I saw, by the eulogium you often made on the happiness of domestic life in America, that you had swallowed the bait and that you would as surely be taken (one day or another) as you was a Philosopher and a Soldier. So your day has, at length, come. I am glad of it with all my heart and soul. It is quite good enough for you. Now you are well served for coming to fight in favor of the American Rebels, all the way across the Atlantic Ocean, by catching that terrible Contagion, domestic felicity, which time like the small pox or the plague, a man can have only once in his life: because it commonly lasts him (at least with us in America, I dont know how you manage these matters in France) for his whole life time. And yet after all the maledictions you so richly merit on the subject, the worst wish which I can find in my heart to make against Madame de Chastellux and yourself is, that you may neither of you ever get the better of this same domestic felicity during the entire course of your mortal existence.

If so wonderful an event should have occasioned me, my dear Marquis, to have written in a strange style, you will understand me as clearly as if I had said (what in plain English, is the simple truth) do me the justice to believe that I take a heartfelt interest in whatever concerns your happiness. And in this view, I sincerely congratulate you on your auspicious Matrimonial connection. I am happy to find that Madame de Chastellux is so intimately connected with the Dutchess of Orleans, as I have always understood that this noble lady was an illustrious pattern of connubial love, as well as an excellent model of virtue in general.

While you have been making love, under the banner of Hymen, the great Personages in the North have been making war, under the inspiration, or rather under the infatuation of Mars. Now, for my part, I humbly conceive, you have had much the best and wisest of the bargain. For certainly it is more consonant to all the principles of reason and religion (natural and revealed) to replenish the earth with inhabitants, rather than to depopulate it by killing those already in existence, besides it is time for the age of Knight-Errantry and mad-heroism to be at an end. Your young military men, who want to reap the harvest of laurels, don't care (I suppose) how many seeds of war are sown; but for the sake of humanity it is devoutly to be wished, that the manly employment of agriculture and the humanizing benefits of commerce, would supersede the waste of war and the rage of conquest; that the swords might be turned into plough-shares, the spears into pruning hooks, and, as the Scripture expresses it, "the nations learn war no more."

Now I will give you a little news from this side of the water, and then finish. As for us, we are plodding on in the dull road of peace and politics. We, who live in these ends of the earth, only hear of the rumors of war like the roar of distant thunder. It is to be hoped, that our remote local situation will prevent us from being swept into its vortex.

The Constitution, which was proposed by the fœderal Convention, has been adopted by the States of Massachusetts, Connecticut, Jersey, Pennsylvania, Delaware, and Georgia. No State has rejected it. The Convention of Maryland is now sitting and will probably adopt it; as that of South Carolina is expected to do in May. The other Conventions will assemble early in the summer. Hitherto there has been much greater unanimity in favour of the proposed government than could have reasonably been expected. Should it be adopted (and I think it will be) America will lift up her head again and in a few years become respectable among the nations. It is a flattering and consolatory reflection, that our rising Republics have the good wishes of all the Philosophers, Patriots, and virtuous men in all nations: and that they look upon them as a kind of Asylum for mankind. God grant that we may not disappoint their honest expectations, by our folly or perverseness.

With sentiments of the purest attachment &c.

P.S. If the Duke de Lauzun is still with you, I beg you will thank him, in my name, for his kind remembrance of me, and make my Compliments to him.

May 1st. Since writing the above I have been favoured with a duplicate of your letter in the hand-writing of a lady, and cannot close this without acknowledging my obligations for the flattering Postscript of the fair Transcriber. In effect, my dear Marquis, the Characters of this interpreter of your sentiments are so much fairer than those through which I have been accustomed to decypher them, that I already consider myself as no small gainer by your Matrimonial connection. Especially, as I hope, your amiable amanuensis will not forget, at sometimes, to add a few annotations of her own to your original text.

To Marquis de Lafayette

Mount Vernon, April 28, 1788.

I have now before me, my dear Marqs. your favor of the 3d of August in the last year; together with those of the 1st. of January, the 2d. of January and the 4th. of February in the present. Though the first is of so antient a date, they all come to hand lately, and nearly at the same moment. The frequency of your kind remembrance of me, and the endearing expressions of attachment, are by so much the more satisfactory, as I recognise them to be a counterpart of my own feelings for you. In truth, you know I speak the language of sincerity and not of flattery, when I tell you, that your letters are ever most welcome and dear to me.

This I lay out to be a letter of Politics. We are looking anxiously across the Atlantic for news and you are looking anxiously back again for the same purpose. It is an interesting subject to contemplate how far the war, kindled in the north of Europe, may extend its conflagrations, and what may be the result before its extinction. The Turk appears to have lost his old and acquired a new connection. Whether England has not, in the hour of her pride, overacted her part and pushed matters too far for her own interest, time will discover: but, in my opinion (though from my distance and want of minute information I should form it with diffidence) the affairs of that nation cannot long go on in the same prosperous train: in spite of expedients and in spite of resources, the Paper bubble will one day burst. And it will whelm many in the ruins. I hope the affairs of France are gradually sliding into a better state. Good effects may, and I trust will ensue, without any public convulsion. France, were her resources properly managed and her administrations wisely conducted, is (as you justly observe) much more potent in the scale of empire, than her rivals at present seem inclined to believe.

I notice with pleasure the additional immunities and facilities in trade, which France has granted by the late Royal arret to the United States. I flatter myself it will have the desired effect, in some measure, of augmenting the commercial intercourse. From the productions and wants of the two countries, their trade with each other is certainly capable of great amelioration, to be actuated by a spirit of unwise policy. For so surely as ever we shall have an efficient government established, so surely will that government impose retaliating restrictions, to a certain degree, upon the trade of Britain. at present, or under our existing form of Confederations, it would be idle to think of making commercial regulations on our part. One State passes a prohibitory law respecting some article, another State opens wide the avenue for its admission. One Assembly makes a system, another Assembly unmakes it. Virginia, in the very last session of her Legislature, was about to have passed some of the most extravagant and preposterous Edicts on the subject of trade, that ever stained the leaves of a Legislative Code. It is in vain to hope for a remedy of these and innumerable other evils, untill a general Government shall be adopted.

The Conventions of Six States only have as yet accepted the new Constitution. No one has rejected it. It is believed that the Convention of Maryland, which is now in session; and that of South Carolina, which is to assemble on the 12th of May, will certainly adopt it. It is, also, since the elections of Members for the Convention have taken place in this State, more generally believed that it will be adopted here than it was before those elections were made. There will, however, be powerful and eloquent speeches on both sides of the question in the Virginia Convention; but as Pendleton, Wythe, Blair, Madison, Jones, Nicholas, Innis and many other of our first characters will be advocates for its adoption, you may suppose the weight of abilities will rest on that side. Henry and Mason are its great adversaries. The Governor, if he opposes it at all will do it feebly.

On the general merits of this proposed Constitution, I wrote to you, some time ago, my sentiments pretty freely. That letter had not been received by you, when you addressed to me the last of yours which has come to my hands. I had never supposed that perfection could be the result of accommodation and mutual concession. The opinion of Mr. Jefferson and yourself is certainly a wise one, that the Constitution ought by all means to be accepted by nine States before any attempt should be made to procure amendments. For, if that acceptance shall not previously take place, men's minds will be so much agitated and soured, that the danger will be greater than ever of our becoming a disunited People. Whereas, on the other hand, with prudence in temper and a spirit of moderation, every essential alteration, may in the process of time, be expected.

You will doubtless, have seen, that it was owing to this conciliatory and patriotic principle that the Convention of Massachusetts adopted the Constitution in toto; but recommended a number of specific alterations and quieting explanations, as an early, serious and unremitting subject of attention. Now, although it is not to be expected that every individual, in Society, will or can ever be brought to agree upon what is, exactly, the best form of government; yet, there are many things in the Constitution which only need to be explained, in order to prove equally satisfactory to all parties. For example: there was not a member of the convention, I believe, who had the least objection to what is contended for by the Advocates for a *Bill of Rights* and *Tryal by Jury*. The first, where the people evidently retained every thing which they did not in express terms give up, was considered nugatory as you will find to have been more fully explained by Mr. Wilson and others: And as to the second, it was only the difficulty of establishing a mode which should not interfere with the fixed modes of any of the States, that induced the Convention to leave it, as a matter of future adjustment.

There are other points on which opinions would be more likely to vary. As for instance, on the ineligibility of the same person for President, after he should have served a certain course of years. Guarded so effectually as the proposed Constitution is, in respect to the prevention of bribery and undue influence in the choice of President: I confess, I differ widely myself from Mr. Jefferson and you, as to the necessity or expediency of rotation in that appointment. The matter was fairly discussed in the Convention, and to my full convictions; though I cannot have time or room to sum up the argument in this letter. There cannot, in my judgment, be the least danger that the President will by any practicable intrigue ever be able to continue himself one moment in office, much less perpetuate himself in it; but in the last stage of corrupted morals and political depravity: and even then there is as much danger that any other species of domination would prevail. Though, when a people shall have become incapable of governing themselves and fit for a master, it is of little consequence from what quarter he comes. Under an extended view of this part of the subject, I can see no propriety in precluding ourselves from the services of any man, who on some great emergency shall be deemed universally, most capable of serving the Public.

In answer to the observations you make on the probability of my election to the Presidency (knowing me as you do) I need only say, that it has no enticing charms, and no fascinating allurements for me. However, it might not be decent for me to say I would refuse to accept or even to speak much about an appointment, which may never take place: for in so doing, one might possibly incur the application of the moral resulting from that Fable, in which the Fox is represented as inveighing against the sourness of the grapes, because he could not reach them. All that it will be necessary to add, my dear Marquis, in order to show my decided predilection, is, that, (at my time of life and under my circumstances) the encreasing infirmities of nature and the growing love of retirement do not permit me to entertain a wish beyond that of living and dying an honest man on my own farm. Let those follow the pursuits of ambition and fame, who have a keener relish for them, or who may have more years, in store, for the enjoyment.

Mrs. Washington, while she requests that her best compliments may be presented to you, joins with me in soliciting that the same friendly and affectionate memorial of our constant remembrance and good wishes may be made acceptable to Madame de la Fayette and the little ones. I am &c.

P. S. May 1st. Since writing the foregoing letter, I have received Authentic Accounts that the Convention of Maryland have ratified the new Constitution by a Majority of 63 to 11.

To Marquis de Lafayette

Mount Vernon, May 28, 1788.
My dear Marquis: I have lately had the pleasure to receive the two letters by which you introduced to my acquaintance M. Du Pont and M. Vanderkemp and altho' those gentlemen have not as yet been to visit me, you may be persuaded that whensoever I shall have the satisfaction of receiving them, it will be with all that attention to which their merits and your recommendations entitle them.

Notwithstanding you are acquainted with Mr. Barlow in person, and with his works by reputation, I thought I would just write you a line by him, in order to recommend him the more particularly to your civilities. Mr. Barlow is considered by those who are good Judges to be a genius of the first magnitude; and to be one of those Bards who hold the keys of the gate by which Patriots, Sages and Heroes are admitted to immortality. Such are your Antient Bards who are both the priest and door-keepers to the temple of fame. And these, my dear Marquis, are no vulgar functions. Men of real talents in Arms have commonly approved themselves patrons of the liberal arts and friends to the poets of their own as well as former times. In some instances by acting reciprocally, heroes have made poets, and poets heroes. Alexander the Great is said to have been enraptured with the Poems of Homer and to have lamented that he had not a rival muse to celebrate his actions. Julius Cæsar is well known to have been a man of a highly cultivated understanding and taste. Augustus was the professed and magnificent rewarder of poetical merit, nor did he lose the return of having his atcheivments immortalized in song. The Augustan age is proverbial for intellectual refinement and elegance in composition; in it the harvest of laurels and bays was wonderfully mingled together. The age of your Louis the fourteenth, which produced a multitude of great Poets and great Captains, will never be forgotten: nor will that of Queen Ann in England, for the same cause, ever cease to reflect a lustre upon the Kingdom. Although we are yet in our cradle, as a nation, I think the efforts of the human mind with us are sufficient to refute (by incontestable facts) the doctrines of those who have asserted that every thing degenerates in America. Perhaps we shall be found, at this moment, not inferior to the rest of the world in the performances of our poets and painters; notwithstanding many of the incitements are wanting which operate powerfully among older nations. For it is generally understood, that excellence in those sister Arts has been the result of easy circumstances, public encouragements and an advanced stage of society. I observe that the Critics in England, who speak highly of the American poetical geniuses (and their praises may be the more relied upon as they seem to be reluctantly extorted,) are not pleased with the tribute of applause which is paid to your nation. It is a reason why they should be the more caressed by your nation. I hardly know how it is that I am drawn thus far in observations on a subject so foreign from those in which we are mostly engaged, farming and politics, unless because I had little news to tell you.

Since I had the pleasure of writing to you by the last Packet, the Convention of Maryland has ratified the federal Constitution by a majority of 63 to 11 voices. That makes the seventh State which has adopted it, next Monday the Convention in Virginia will assemble; we have still good hopes of its adoption here: though by no great plurality of votes. South Carolina has probably decided favourably before this time. The plot thickens fast. A few short weeks will determine the political fate of America for the present generation and probably produce no small influence on the happiness of society through a long succession of ages to come. Should every thing proceed with harmony and consent according to our actual wishes and expectations; I will confess to you sincerely, my dear Marquis; it will be so much beyond any thing we had a right to imagine or expect eighteen months ago, that it will demonstrate as visibly the finger of Providence, as any possible event in the course of human affairs can ever designate it. It is impracticable for you or any one who has not been on the spot, to realise the change in men's minds and the progress towards rectitude in thinking and acting which will then have been made.

Adieu, my dear Marquis, I hope your affairs in France will subside into a prosperous train without coming to any violent crisis. Continue to cherish your affectionate feelings for this country and the same portion of friendship for me, which you are ever sure of holding in the heart of your most sincere, &c.

To Marquis de Lafayette

Mount Vernon, June 19, 1788.
I cannot account for your not having received some of my letters, my dear Marquis, before you wrote yours of the 18th of March, as I have been writing to you, at short intervals, constantly since last autumn. To demonstrate the satisfaction I enjoy on the receipt of your favours; I always answer them almost as soon as they arrive. Although, on account of my retirement from the busy scenes of life and the want of diversity in the tenour of our affairs, I can promise to give you little novelty or entertainment in proportion to what I expect in return. Were you to acknowledge the receipt of my letters, and give the dates of them when you write to me, I should be able to ascertain which of them had reached you, and which of them had miscarried. I am left in doubt whether the Indian Vocabularies &c. &c. have got to you or not.

There seems to be a great deal of bloody work cut out for

this summer in the North of Europe. If war, want and plague are to desolate those huge armies that are assembled, who that has the feelings of a man can refrain from shedding a tear over the miserable victims of Regal Ambition? It is really a strange thing that there should not be room enough in the world for men to live, without cutting one anothers throats. As France, Spain and England have hardly recovered from the wounds of the late war, I would fain hope they will hardly be dragged into this. However, if the war should be protracted (and not end in a campaign as you intimate it possibly may) there seems to be a probability of other powers being engaged on one side or the other. by the British papers (which are our principal source of intelligence, though not always to be relied upon, as you know) it appears that the Spaniards are fitting out a considerable fleet and that the English Ministry have prohibited the subjects of their Kingdom from furnishing transports for the Empress of Russia. France must be too intent on its own domestic affairs to wish to interfere, and we have not heard that the King of Prussia, since his exploits in Holland, has taken it into his head not to meddle with other people's business. I cannot say that I am sorry to hear that the Algerines and other piratical powers are about to assist the Porte, because I think Russia will not forget and that she will take some leisure moment, just to keep her fleets in exercise, for exterminating those nests of Miscreants.

I like not much the situation of affairs in France. The bold demands of the parliaments, and the decisive tone of the King, shew that but little more irritation would be necessary to blow up the spark of discontent into a flame, that might not easily be quenched. If I were to advise, I would say that great moderation should be used on both sides. Let it not, my dear Marquis, be considered as a derogation from the good opinion, that I entertain of your prudence, when I caution you, as an individual desirous of signalizing yourself in the cause of your country and freedom, against running into extremes and prejudicing your cause. The King, though, I think from every thing I have been able to learn, he is really a good-hearted tho' a warm-spirited man, if thwarted injudiciously in the execution of prerogatives that belonged to the Crown, and in plans which he conceives calculated to promote the national good, may disclose qualities he has been little thought to possess. On the other hand, such a spirit seems to be awakened in the Kingdom, as, if managed with extreme prudence, may produce a gradual and tacit Revolution much in favor of the subjects, by abolishing Lettres de Cachet and defining more accurately the powers of government. It is a wonder to me, there should be found a single monarch, who does not realize that his own glory and felicity must depend on the prosperity and happiness of his People. How easy is it for a sovereign to do that which shall not only immortalize his name, but attract the blessings of millions.

In a letter I wrote you a few days ago by Mr. Barlow (but which might not possibly have reached New York until after his departure) I mentioned the accession of Maryland to the proposed government, and gave you the state of politics to that period. Since which the Convention of South Carolina has ratified the Constitution by a great majority: that of this State has been setting almost three weeks; and so nicely does it appear to be ballanced, that each side asserts that it has a preponderancy of votes in its favour. It is probable, therefore, the majority will be small, let it fall on whichever part it may; I am inclined to believe it will be in favour of the adoption. The Conventions of New York and New Hampshire assemble both this week; a large proportion of members, with the Governor at their head, in the former, are said to be opposed to the government in contemplation: New Hampshire it is thought will adopt it without much hesitation or delay. It is a little strange that the men of large property in the South, should be more afraid that the Constitution will produce an Aristocracy or a Monarchy, than the genuine democratical people of the East. Such are our actual prospects. The accession of one State more will complete the number, which by the Constitutional provision, will be sufficient in the first instance to carry the Government into effect.

And then, I expect, that many blessings will be attributed to our new government, which are now taking their rise from that industry and frugality into the practice of which the people have been forced from necessity. I really believe, that there never was so much labour and economy to be found before in the country as at the present moment. If they persist in the habits they are acquiring, the good effects will soon be distinguishable. When the people shall find themselves secure under an energetic government, when foreign nations shall be disposed to give us equal advantages in commerce from dread of retaliation, when the burdens of war shall be in a manner done away by the sale of western lands, when the seeds of happiness which are sown here shall begin to expand themselves, and when every one (under his own vine and fig-tree) shall begin to taste the fruits of freedom, then all these blessings (for all these blessings will come) will be referred to the fostering influence of the new government. Whereas many causes will have conspired to produce them. You see I am not less enthusiastic than ever I have been, if a belief that peculiar scenes of felicity are reserved for this country, is to be denominated enthusiasm. Indeed, I do not believe, that Providence has done so much for nothing. It has always been my creed that we should not be left as an awful monument to prove, "that Mankind, under the most favourable circumstances for civil liberty and happiness, are unequal to the task of Governing themselves, and therefore made for a Master."

We have had a backward spring and summer, with more rainy and cloudy weather than almost ever has been known: still the appearance of crops in some parts of the country is favorable, as we may generally expect will be the case, from the difference of soil and variety of climate in so extensive a region; insomuch that, I hope, some day or another, we shall become a storehouse and granary for the world. In addition to our former channels of trade, salted provisions, butter, cheese &c. are exported with profit from the eastern States to the East Indies. In consequence of a Contract, large quantities of flour are lately sent from Baltimore for supplying the garrison of Gibraltar. With sentiments of tenderest affection etc.

To Richard Henderson

Mount Vernon, June 19, 1788.
Sir: Your favour of the 5th. instant was lodged at my house, while I was absent on a visit to my Mother. I am now taking

the earliest opportunity of noticing its contents, and those of its Enclosure. Willing as I am to give satisfaction so far as I am able, to every reasonable enquiry (and this is certainly not only so, but may be highly important and interesting,) I must however, rather deal in general than particular observations: as I think you will be able, from the length of your residence in the country, and the extensiveness of your acquaintance with its affairs, to make the necessary applications and add the proper details. Nor would I choose that my interference in the business should be transmitted, lest, in a malicious world, it might be represented that I was officiously using the arts of seduction to depopulate other countries, for the sake of peopling our own.

In the first place it is a point conceded, that America, under an efficient government, will be the most favorable Country of any in the world for persons of industry and frugality, possessed of a moderate capital, to inhabit. It is also believed, that it will not be less advantageous to the happiness of the lowest class of people because of the equal distribution of property the great plenty of unoccupied lands, and the facility of procuring the means of subsistence. The scheme of purchasing a good tract of freehold estate and bringing out a number of able-bodied men, indented for a certain time appears to be indisputably a rational one.

All the interior arrangements of transferring the property and commencing the establishment you are as well acquainted with as I can possibly be. It might be considered as a point of more difficulty, to decide upon the place which should be most proper for a settlement. Although, I believe that Emigrants from other countries to this, who shall be well-disposed, and conduct themselves properly, would be treated with equal friendship and kindness in all parts of it; yet, in the old settled States, land is so much occupied, and the value so much enhanced by the contiguous cultivation, that the price would, in general be an objection. The land in western country, or that on the Ohio, like all others, has its *advantages and disadvantages.* The neighborhood of the Savages and the difficulty of transportation were the great objections. The danger of the first will soon cease by the strong establishments now taking place; the inconveniences of the second will be, in a great degree, remedied by opening the internal Navigation. No Colony in America was ever settled under such favorable auspices, as that which has just commenced at the Muskingum. Information, property and strength, will be its characteristics. I know many of the settlers personally and that there never were men better calculated to promote the welfare of such a community.

If I was a young man, just preparing to begin the world or if advanced in life, and had a family to make a provision for, I know of no country where I should rather fix my habitation than in some part of that region, for which the writer of the quæries seems to have a predilection. he might be informed that his namesake and distant relation, Genl. St. Clair, is not only in high repute, but that he is Governor of all the Territory westward of the Ohio, and that there is a gentleman (to wit Mr. Joel Barlow) gone from New York by the last French Packet, who will be in London in the course of this year, and who is authorized to dispose of a very large body of land in that Country. The author of the quæries may then be referred to the "Information for those who would wish to remove to America:" and published in Europe in the year 1784, by the great Philosopher Dr. Franklin. Short as it is, it contains almost every thing, that needs to be known on the subject of migrating to this Country. You may find that excellent little Treatise in "Carey's American Museum, for September, 1787." It is worthy of being republished in Scotland, and every other part of Europe.

As to the European Publications respecting the United States, they are commonly very defective. The Abbe Raynal is quite erroneous. Guthrie, though somewhat better informed, is not absolutely correct. There is now "an American Geography preparing for the press by a Mr. Morse of New Haven in Connecticut" which, from the pains the Author has taken in travelling through the States and acquiring information from the principal characters in each, will probably be much more exact and useful. of books at present existing, Mr. Jefferson's "Notes on Virginia" will give the best idea of this part of the Continent to a Foreigner: and the "American Farmer's Letters," written by Mr. Crevecœur (commonly called Mr. St. John) the French Consul in New York (who actually resided twenty years as a farmer in that State) will afford a great deal of profitable and amusing information, respecting *the private Life* of the Americans; as well as the progress of agriculture, manufactures, and arts in their Country. Perhaps the picture he gives, though founded on fact, is in some instances embellished with rather too flattering circumstances. I am, &c.

To Benjamin Lincoln

Mount Vernon, June 29, 1788.

My dear Sir: I beg you will accept my thanks for the communications handed to me in your letter of the 3d. instant, and my congratulations on the encreasing good dispositions of the Citizens of your State of which the late elections are strongly indicative. No one *can* rejoice more than I do at every step the people of this great Country take to preserve the Union, establish good order and government, and to render the Nation happy at home and respectable abroad. No Country upon Earth ever had it more in its power to attain these blessings than United America. Wondrously strange then, and much to be regretted indeed would it be, were we to neglect the means, and to depart from the road which Providence has pointed us to, so plainly; I cannot believe it will ever come to pass. The great Governor of the Universe has led us too long and too far on the road to happiness and glory, to forsake us in the midst of it. By folly and improper conduct, proceeding from a variety of causes, we may now and then get bewildered; but I hope and trust that there is good sense and virtue enough left to recover the right path before we shall be entirely lost.

You will, before this letter can have reached you, have heard of the Ratification of the new Government by this State. The final question without previous amendments was taken the 25th. Ayes, 89. Noes, 79; but something recommendatory, or declaratory of the rights, accompanied the ultimate decision. This account and the news of the adoption by New Hampshire arrived in Alexandria nearly about the same time on

Friday evening; and, as you will suppose, was cause for great rejoicing among the Inhabitants who have not I believe an Antifederalist among them. Our Accounts from Richmond are, that the debates, through all the different Stages of the business, though brisk and animated, have been conducted with great dignity and temper; that the final decision exhibited an awful and solemn scene, and that there is every reason to expect a perfect acquiescence therein by the minority; not only from the declaration of Mr. Henry, the great leader of it, who has signified that though he can never be reconciled to the Constitution in its present form, and shall give it every *constitutional* opposition in his power yet that he will submit to it peaceably, as he thinks every good Citizen ought to do when it is in exercise and that he will both by precept and example inculcate this doctrine to all around him.

There is little doubt entertained here *now* of the ratification of the proposed Constitution by North Carolina; and however great the opposition to it may be in New York the leaders thereof will, I should conceive, consider well the consequences before they reject it. With respect to Rhode Island, the power that governs there has so far baffled all calculation on this question that no man would chuse to hazard an opinion lest he might be suspected of participating in its phrensy. You have every good wish of this family and the sincere regard of your affectionate, &c.

To Noah Webster

Mount Vernon, July 31, 1788.

Sir: I duly received your letter of the 14th. instant, and can only answer very *briefly*, and generally from *memory*: that a combined operation of the land and naval forces of France in America, for the year 1781, was preconcerted the year before: that the point of attack was not absolutely agreed upon, because it would be easy for the Count de Grasse, in good time before his departure from the West Indies, to give notice by Express, at what place he could most conveniently first touch to receive advice, because it could not be foreknown where

the enemy would be most susceptible of impression; and because we (having the command of the water with sufficient
means of conveyance) could transport ourselves to any spot
with the greatest celerity: that it was determined by me (nearly
twelve months beforehand) at all hazards to give out and
cause it to be believed by the highest military as well as civil
Officers that New York was the destined place of attack, for
the important purpose of inducing the Eastern and Middle
States to make greater exertions in furnishing specific supplies
than they otherwise would have done, as well as for the interesting purpose of rendering the enemy less prepared elsewhere: that, by these means and these alone, artillery, Boats,
Stores and Provisions were in seasonable preparation to move
with the utmost rapidity to any part of the Continent; for the
difficulty consisted more in providing, than knowing how to
apply the military apparatus: that before the arrival of the
Count de Grasse it was the fixed determination *to strike the
enemy in the most vulnerable quarter* so as to ensure success
with moral certainty, as our affairs were then in the most
ruinous train imaginable: that New York was thought to be
beyond our effort and consequently the only hesitation that
remained was between an attack upon the British army in Virginia or that in Charleston: and finally that (by the intervention of several communications and some incidents which
cannot be Detailed in a letter; and wch. were *altogether unknown* to the late Quartermaster General of the Army, who
was informed of nothing but what related to the immediate
duties of his own department) the hostile Post in Virginia,
from being a *provisional and strongly expected* became the *definitive and certain object* of the Campaign. I only add, that
it never was in contemplation to attack New York, unless the
Garrison should first have been so far disgarnished to carry
on the southern operations, as to render our success in the
siege of that place as infallible as any future military event can
ever be made. For I repeat it, and dwell upon it again and
again, some splendid advantage (whether upon a larger or
smaller scale was almost immaterial) was so essentially necessary to revive the expiring hopes and languid exertions of the
Country, at the crisis in question, that I never would have
consented to embark in any enterprize; wherein, from the

most rational plan and accurate calculations, the favourable issue should not have appeared as clear to my view, as a ray of light. The failure of an attempt agst. the Posts of the enemy, could, in no other possible situation during the war, have been so fatal to our cause.

That much trouble was taken and finesse used to misguide and bewilder Sir Henry Clinton in regard to the real object, by fictitious communications, as well as by making a deceptive provision of Ovens, Forage and Boats in his Neighborhood, is certain. Nor were less pains taken to deceive our own Army; for I had always conceived, when the imposition did not completely take place at home, it could never sufficiently succeed abroad.

Your desire of obtaining truth is very laudable, I wish I had more leizure to gratify it: as I am equally solicitious the undisguised verity should be known. Many circumstances will unavoidably be misconceived and misrepresented. Notwithstanding most of the Papers which may properly be deemed official are preserved; yet the knowledge of innumerable things, of a more delicate and secret nature, is confined to the perishable remembrance of some few of the present generation. With esteem I am.

To Alexander Hamilton

Dear Sir,   Mount Vernon Augt. 28th. 1788
I have had the pleasure to receive your letter dated the 13th.—accompanied by one addressed to General Morgan. I will forward the letter to General Morgan by the first conveyance, and add my particular wishes that he would comply with the request contained in it. Although I can scarcely imagine how the Watch of a British Officer, killed within their lines, should have fallen into his hands (who was many miles from the scene of action) yet, if it so happened, I flatter myself there will be no reluctance or delay in restoring it to the family.

As the perusal of the political papers under the signature of Publius has afforded me great satisfaction, I shall certainly consider them as claiming a most distinguished place in my library. I have read every performance which has been printed on one side and the other of the great question lately agitated (so far as I have been able to obtain them) and, without an unmeaning compliment I will say that I have seen no other so well calculated (in my judgment) to produce conviction on an unbiassed mind, as the *Production* of your *Triumvirate*—when the transient circumstances & fugitive performances which attended this *crisis* shall have disappeared, that work will merit the notice of Posterity; because in it are candidly discussed the principles of freedom & the topics of government, which will be always interesting to mankind so long as they shall be connected in Civil Society.

The Circular Letter from your Convention, I presume, was the equivalent by wch. you obtained an acquiescence in the proposed Constitution: Notwithstanding I am not very well satisfied with the tendency of it; yet the Fœderal affairs have proceeded, with few exceptions, in so good a train, that I hope the political Machine may be put in motion, without much effort or hazard of miscarrying.

On the delicate subject with which you conclude your letter, I can say nothing; because the event alluded to may never happen; and because, in case it should occur, it would be a point of prudence to defer forming one's ultimate and irrevocable decision, so long as new data might be afforded for one to act with the greater wisdom & propriety. I would not wish to conceal my prevailing sentiment from you. For you know me well enough, my good Sir, to be persuaded that I am not guilty of affectation, when I tell you, it is my great and sole desire to live and die, in peace and retirement, on my own farm. Were it ever indispensable, a different line of conduct should be adopted; while you and some others who are acquainted with my heart would *acquit*, the world and Posterity might probably *accuse* me of *inconsistency* and *ambition*. Still I hope I shall always possess firmness and virtue enough to maintain (what I consider the most enviable of all titles) the character of *an honest man*, as well as prove (what I desire to be considered in reality) that I am, with great sincereity & esteem, Dear Sir Your friend and Most obedient Hble Ser

To Edward Newenham

Mount Vernon, August 29, 1788.

Dear Sir: I beg you will be persuaded that it always gives me singular pleasure to hear from you; and that your obliging letter of the 22nd and 25th of March afforded me particular satisfaction. I am also to thank you for the Irish Parliamentary Papers which have come safe to hand. The Edition of Cooke's Voyage, which you mention to have forwarded by a former occasion, has not been so successfull in its voyage to me; any more than the *New Books* wch. (in a letter of the 13th of Novr. 1786) you say had been sent to me by the Mary Captn. Mathews; or I should not have neglected the acknowledgement of them.

I am heartily glad to find that the prosperity of Ireland is on the encrease. It was afflicting for the Philanthropic mind, to consider the mass of People, inhabiting a Country naturally fertile in productions and full of resources, sunk to an abject degree of penury and depression. Such has been the picture we have received of the Peasantry. Nor do their calamities seem to be entirely removed yet, as we may gather from the Spirited speech of Mr. Gratton on the commutation of tythe. But I hope, ere long, matters will go right there and in the rest of the World. For instead of the disconsolatory idea that every thing is growing worse, I would fain cheer myself with a hope that every thing is beginning to mend. As you observe, if Ireland was 500 miles farther distant from Great Britain the case with respect to the former would be as speedily as materially changed for the better.

But what shall we say of Wars and the appearances of Wars in the rest of the World? Mankind are not yet ripe for the Millenial State. The affairs of some of the greatest Potentates appear to be very much embroiled in the North of Europe. The question is, whether the Turks will be driven out of Europe or not? One would suppose, if discipline and arrangement are to be calculated upon in preference to ignorance and brutal force, that the Porte must recede before the two Imperial Powers. But in the game of War, there are so many contingencies that often prevent the most probable events from taking place; and in the present instance, there are so many causes that may kindle the hostile conflagration into a general flame, that we need not be over hasty and sanguine in drawing our conclusions. Let us see how far the sparks of hostility have been scattered. The almost open rupture between the Emperor of Germany and his subjects in the Low Countries; the interference of Prussia in Holland and the disordered condition of that republic; the new alliances on the part of that republic with England and Prussia; the humiliating dereliction (or rather sacrafice) which France has been obliged to make of the Dutch Patriots in consequence of the derangement of her finances; the troubles, internally, which prevail in France, together with the ill-temper she must feel towards England on acct. of the terms lately dictated by the latter; the animosity of Britain and Morocco, in conjunction with several smaller subjects of National discussion, leave but too much ground to apprehend that the tranquility of Europe will not be of long continuance. I hope the United States of America will be able to keep disengaged from the labyrinth of European politics and Wars; and that before long they will, by the adoption of a good national government, have become respectable in the eyes of the world so that none of the maritime Powers, especially none of those who hold possessions in the New World or the West Indies shall presume to treat them with insult or contempt. It should be the policy of United America to administer to their wants, without being engaged in their quarrels. And it is not in the ability of the proudest and most potent people on earth to prevent us from becoming a great, a respectable and a commercial Nation, if we shall continue United and faithful to ourselves.

Your sollicitude that an efficient and good government may be established in this Country, in order that it may enjoy felicity at home and respectibility abroad serves only to confirm me in the opinion I have always entertained of your disinterested and ardent friendship for this Land of freedom. It is true, that, for the want of a proper Confœderation, we have not yet been in a situation fully to enjoy those blessings which God and Nature seemed to have intended for us. But I begin to look forward, with a kind of political faith, to scenes of National happiness, which have not heretofore been offered for the fruition of the most favoured Nations. The natural political, and moral circumstances of our Nascent empire justify the anticipation. We have an almost unbounded territory whose natural advantages for agriculture and Commerce equal those of any on the globe. In a civil point of view we have unequalled previledge of choosing our own political Institutions and of improving upon the experience of Mankind in the formation of a confœderated government, where due energy will not be incompatible with unalienable rights of freemen. To complete the picture, I may observe, that the information and morals of our Citizens appear to be peculiarly favourable for the introduction of such a plan of government as I have just now described.

Although there were some few things in the Constitution recommended by the Fœderal Convention to the determination of the People, which did not full accord with my wishes; yet, having taken every circumstance seriously into consideration, I was convinced it approached nearer to perfection than any government hitherto instituted among Men. I was also convinced, that nothing but a genuine spirit of amity and accomodation could have induced the members to make those mutual concessions and to sacrafice (at the shrine of enlightened liberty) those local prejudices, which seemed to oppose an insurmountable barrier, to prevent them from harmonising in any system whatsoever.

But so it has happened by the good pleasure of Providence, and the same happy disposition has been diffused and fostered among the people at large. You will permit me to say, that a greater Drama is now acting on this Theatre than has heretofore been brought on the American Stage, or any other in the World. We exhibit at present the Novel and astonishing Spectacle of a whole People deliberating calmly on what form of government will be most conducive to their happiness; and deciding with an unexpected degree of unanimity in favour of a System which they conceive calculated to answer the purpose.

It is only necessary to add for your satisfaction, that, as all the States, which have yet acted and which are ten in number, have adopted the proposed Constitution; and as the concurrence of nine States was sufficient to carry it into effect in the first inste. it is expected the government will be in complete organization and execution before the commencement of the ensuing year.

I failed not, on the receipt of your letter, to make the best arrangements in my power for obtaining the Opossums and birds you mentioned. But I shall not be able to succeed in time for this conveyance. Having heard of a Male and female Opossum, with several young ones, at the house of one of my friends in Maryland, I sent for them, but unfortunately they were all dead. I may probably be more successful in Autumn.

I please myself with the hope that the impediments which have prevented your visiting America will soon be removed, and that we shall have the satisfaction of witnessing to you personally our veneration for the Patriots of other Countries. In the interim Mrs. Washington desires that I will not fail to blend her best respects with mine for Lady Newenham and yourself. It is with pleasure I sieze occasions to assure you with how much truth I have the honor etc.

To Alexander Hamilton

Dear Sir,   Mount Vernon October 3d 1788

In acknowledging the receipt of your canded and kind letter by the last Post; little more is incumbent upon me, than to thank you sincerely for the frankness with which you communicated your sentiments, and to assure you that the same manly tone of intercourse will always be more than barely wellcome, Indeed it will be highly acceptable to me. I am particularly glad, in the present instance; you have dealt thus freely and like a friend. Although I could not help observing from several publications and letters that my name had been sometimes spoken of, and that it was possible the *Contingency* which is the subject of your letter might happen; yet I thought it best to maintain a guarded silence and to lack the *counsel* of my best friends (which I certainly hold in the highest estimation) rather than to hazard an imputation unfriendly to the delicacy of my feelings. For, situated as I am, I could hardly bring the question into the slightest discussion, or ask an opinion even in the most confidential manner; without betraying, in my Judgment, some impropriety of conduct, or without feeling an apprehension that a premature display of anxiety, might be construed into a vainglorious desire of pushing myself into notice as a Candidate. Now, if I am not grossly deceived in myself, I should unfeignedly rejoice, in case the Electors, by giving their votes in favor of some other person, would save me from the dreaded Dilemma of being forced to accept or refuse. If that may not be—I am, in the next place, earnestly desirous of searching out the truth, and of knowing whether there does not exist a probability that the government would be just as happily and effectually carried into execution, without my aid, as with it. I am *truly* solicitous to obtain all the previous information which the circumstances will afford, and to determine (when the determination can with propriety be no longer postponed) according to the principles of right reason, and the dictates of a clear conscience; without too great a referrence to the unforeseen consequences, which may affect my person or reputation. Untill that period, I may fairly hold myself open to conviction— though I allow your sentiments to have weight in them; and I shall not pass by your arguments without giving them as dispassionate a consideration, as I can possibly bestow upon them.

In taking a survey of the subject in whatever point of light I have been able to place it; I will not surpress the acknowledgment, my Dr Sir that I have always felt a kind of gloom upon my mind, as often as I have been taught to expect, I might, and perhaps must ere long be called to make a decision. You will, I am well assured, believe the assertion (though I have little expectation it would gain credit from those who are less acquainted with me) that if I should receive the appointment and if I should be prevailed upon to accept it; the acceptance would be attended with more diffidence and reluctance than ever I experienced before in my life. It would be, however, with a fixed and sole determination of lending whatever assistance might be in my power to promote the public, weal, in hopes that at a convenient and an early period, my services might be dispensed with, and that I might be permitted once more to retire—to pass an unclouded evening,

after the stormy day of life, in the bosom of domestic tranquility. But why these anticipations? if the friends to the Constitution conceive that my administering the government will
be a means of its acceleration and strength, is it not probable
that the adversaries of it may entertain the same ideas? and of
course make it an object of opposition? That many of this
description will become Electors, I can have no Doubt of: any
more than that their oppinion will extend to any character
who (from whatever cause) would be likely to thwart their
measures—It might be impolite in them to make this declaration *previous* to the Election, but I shall be out in my
conjectures if they do not act conformably thereto—and from
that the seeming moderation by which they appear to be actuated at present is neither more nor less than a finesse to lull
and deceive. Their plan of opposition is systemised, and a regular intercourse, I have much reason to believe between the
Leaders of it in the several States is formed to render it more
effectual. With sentiments of sincere regard and esteem—I
have, the honor to be &c.

To Benjamin Lincoln

My dear Sir,   Mount Vernon Oct: 26th 1788
    I have been lately favored with the receipt of your letters of
the 24th and 30th of September, with their enclosure, & thank
you sincerely for your free & friendly communications.

As the period is now rapidly approaching which must decide
the fate of the new Constitution as to the manner of its being
carried into execution & probably as to its usefulness, it is not
wonderful that we should all feel an unusual degree of anxiety
on the occasion. I must acknowledge my fears have been
greatly, but still I am not without hopes. From the good beginning that has been made in Pensylvania a State from which
much was to be feared, I cannot help foreboding well of the
others. That is to say, I flatter myself a majority of them will
appoint fœderal Members to the several branches of the New
Government. I hardly should think that Massachusetts, Connecticut, New Jersey, Delaware, Maryland, South Carolina &

Georgia, would be for attempting premature amendments. Some of the rest may, also, in all probability be apprehensive of throwing our affairs into confusion, by such ill-timed expedients. There will, however, be no room for the advocates of the Constitution to relax in their exertions; for if they should be lulled into security, appointments of Antifœderal men may probably take place; and the consequences, which you so justly dread, be realised. Our Assembly is now in session; it is represented to be rather antifœderal, but we have heard nothing of its doings. Mr Patrick Henry, R. H. Lee & Madison are talked of for the Senate. Perhaps as much opposition, or, in other words, as great an effort for early amendments, is to be apprehended from this State, as from any but New York. The constant report is, that North Carolina will soon accede to the New Union. A New Assembly is just elected in Maryland, in which it is asserted the number of Fœderalists greatly predominates; and that being the case, we may look for favorable appointments, in spite of the rancour & activity of a few discontented, and I may say *apparently* unprincipled men.

I would willingly pass over in silence that part of your letter, in which you mention the persons who are Candidates for the two first offices in the Executive, if I did not fear the omission might seem to betray a want of confidence. Motives of delicasy have prevented me hitherto from conversing or writing on this Subject, when ever I could avoid it with decency. I may, however, with great sincerity & I believe without offending against modesty or propriety, *say* to *you* that I most heartily wish the choice to which you allude might not fall upon me: and that, if it should, I must reserve to my self the right of making up my final decision, at the last moment when it can be no longer postponed; when all the circumstances can be brought into one view, & when the expediency & inexpediency of a *refusal* can be more judiciously determined than at present. But be assured, my dear Sir, if from any inducement I shall be persuaded ultimately to accept, it will not be (so far as I know my own heart) from any of a private or personal nature. Every personal consideration conspires to rivet me (if I may use the expression) to retirement. At my time of life and under my circumstances, nothing in this world can ever draw me from

it, unless it be a *conviction* that the partiality of my Countrymen had made my services absolutely necessary, joined to a
fear that my refusal might induce a belief that I prefered the
conservation of my own reputation & private ease to the good
of my Country. After all, if I should conceive my self in a
manner constrained to accept, I call Heaven to witness, that
this very act would be the greatest sacrafice of my personal
feelings & wishes that ever I have been called upon to make.
It would be to fore go repose and domestic enjoyment; for
trouble, perhaps; for public obloquy: for I should consider
myself as entering upon an unexplored field, enveloped on
every side with clouds & darkness.

From this embarrassing situation, I had naturally supposed
that my declarations at the close of the War would have saved
me; and that my sincere intentions, then publicly made
known, would have effectually precluded me for ever afterwards from being looked upon as a candidate for any Office.
This hope, as a last anchor of worldly happiness in old age, I
had still carefully preserved; untill the public papers & private
letters from my Corrispondents in almost every quarter,
taught me to apprehend that I might soon be obliged to answer the question, whether I would go again into public, or
not?

You will see, My dear Sir, from this train of reflections, that
I have lately had enough of my own perplexities to think of,
without adverting much to the affairs of others. So much have
I been otherwise occupied, and so little agency did I wish to
have in electioneering, that I have never entered into a single
discussion with any person, nor expressed a single sentiment
orally or in writing respecting the appointment of a Vice-
President. From the extent & respectability of Massachusetts
it might reasonably be expected that he would be chosen from
that State. But having taken it for granted, that the person
selected for that important place would be a true Fœderalist;
in that case, I was altogether disposed to acquiesce in the
prevailing sentiments of the Electors without giving any unbecoming preference or incurring any unnecessary ill-will.
Since it here seems proper to touch a little more fully upon
that point, I will frankly give you my manner of thinking; and
what, under certain circumstances, would be my manner of

acting. For this purpose I must speak again hypothetically for argument sake & say, supposing I should be appointed to the Administration & supposing I should accept it, I most solemnly declare, that whosoever shall be found to enjoy the confidence of the States so far as to be elected Vice President, cannot be disagreeable to me, in that Office. And even if I had any predeliction, I flatter myself, I possess patriotism enough to sacrafice it at the shrine of My Country; where, it will be unavoidably necessary for me to have made infinitely greater sacrafices, before I can find myself in the supposed predicament—that is to say—before I can be connected with others, in any possible political relation. In truth I believe that I have no prejudices on this subject; and that it would not be in the power of any evil-minded persons, who wished to disturb the harmony of those connected in the government, to infuse them into my mind. For, to continue the same hypothesis one step farther, supposing myself to be connected in Office with any Gentleman of character, I would most certainly treat him with perfect sincerity and the greatest candour in every respect. I would give him my full confidence & use my utmost endeavours to co-operate with him, in promoting & rendering permanent the national prosperity—this should be my great—my only aim—under the fixed & irrevocable resolution of leaving to other hands the helm of the State, as soon as my services could possibly with propriety be dispensed with.

I have thus, my dear Sir, insensibly been led into a longer detail than I intended; and have used more egotism than I could have wished—for which I urge no other apology, but my opinion of your friendship, discretion and candour. With sentiments of real esteem & regard I am—My dear Sir, Your Most Obedt & Affecte Servt

Reflection on Slavery

The unfortunate condition of the persons, whose labour in part I employed, has been the only unavoidable subject of regret. To make the Adults among them as easy & as com-

fortable in their circumstances as their actual state of ignorance & improvidence would admit; & to lay a foundation to
prepare the rising generation for a destiny different from that
in which they were born; afforded some satisfaction to my
mind, & could not I hoped be displeasing to the justice of
the Creator.—

c. 1788–1789

Fragments of a Draft of the First Inaugural Address

We are this day assembled on a solemn and important occasion—

———

not as a ceremony without meaning, but with a single reference to our dependence upon the Parent of all good—it becomes a pleasing commencement of my Office to offer my
heart-felt congratulations on the happy

———

We are not to take upon ourselves the conduct of that government. But before we entered upon the performance of our
several functions, it seemed to be our indispensable part, as
rational Beings

———

fairs. It will doubtless be conceded

———

been happily diffused & fostered among their

———

reputation and a decent respect for the sentiments of others,
require that something should be said by way of apology for
my

———

At the beginning of the late War with Great Britain, when
we thought our selves justifiable in resisting to blood, it was
known to those best acquainted with the different condition
of the combatants & the probable cost of the prize in dispute,
that the expence in comparison with our circumstances as Col-

onists must be enormous—the struggle protracted, dubious & severe. It was known that the resources of Britain were, in a manner, inexhaustible, that her fleets covered the Ocean, and that her troops had harvested laurels in every quarter of the globe. Not then organised as a nation, or known as a people upon the earth—we had no preparation—Money, the nerve of War, was wanting. The Sword was to be forged on the Anvil of necessity: the treasury to be created from nothing. If we had a secret resource of an nature unknown to our enemy, it was in the unconquerable resolution of our Citizens, the conscious rectitude of our cause, and a confident trust that we should not be forsaken by Heaven. The people willingly Offered

———

offered themselves to the battle; but the means of arming, clothing & subsisting them; as well as of procuring the implements of hostility were only to be found in anticipations of our future wealth. Paper bills of credit were emitted: monies borrowed for the most pressing emergencies: and our brave trps in the field unpaid for their services. In this manner, Peace, attended with every circumstance that could gratify our reasonable desires, or even inflate us with ideas of national importance, was at length obtained. But a load of debt was left upon us. The fluctuations of and speculations in our paper currency, had, but in too many instances, occasioned vague ideas of property, generated licencious appetites & corrupted the morals of men. To these immediate consequences of a fluctuating medium of commerce, may be joined a tide of circumstances that flowed together from sources mostly opened during and after the war. The ravage of farms, the conflagration of towns, the diminution

———

affairs were seen to decline. I will ask your patience for a moment, while I speak on so unpleasant a subject as the rotten part of our old Constitution. It is not a matter for wonder that the first projected plan of a fœderal government, formed on the defective models of some foreign Confederacies, in the midst of a war, before we had much experience; and while, from the concurrence of external danger and

———

But Congress, constituted in most respects as a diplomatic body, possessed no power of carrying into execution a simple Ordinance, however strongly dictated by prudence, policy or justice. The individual States, knowing there existed no power of coertion, treated with neglect, whenever it suited their convenience or caprice, the most salutary measures of the most indispensable requisitions of Congress. Experience taught

———

situation could be so agreeable to me as the condition of a private citizen. I solemnly assert and appeal to the searcher of hearts to witness the truth of it, that my leaving home to take upon myself the execution of this Office was the greatest personal sacrifice I have ever, in the course of my existence, been called upon to make. Altho' when the last war had become inevitable, I heartily concurred in the measures taken by my country for repelling force by force; yet it is known, I was so far from aspiring to the chief Military command, that I accepted it with unfeigned reluctance. My fellow-soldiers of the late patriotic Army will bear me testimony that when I accepted that appointment, it was not to revel in luxury, to grow proud of rank, to eat the bread of idleness, to be insensible to the sufferings, or to refuse a share in the toils and dangers to which they were exposed. I need not say what were the complicated cares, the cruel reverses or the unusual perplexities inseparable from my office, to

———

to prove that I have prematurely grown old in the Service of my Country. For in truth, I have now arrived at that sober age, when, aside of any extraordinary circumstances to deter me from encountering new fatiegues, & when, without having met with any particular shocks to injure the constitution the love of retirement naturally encreases; while the objects of human pursuit, which are most laudable in themselves and most

———

as in their consequences, lose much [   ]n captivating lustre—It is then high [   ] to have learnt [   ] the vanity of this [   ]ish dream of life. It is then high [   ] to contract the sphere of action, to [   ] the remnant of [   ] our days *peculiarly* [   ]wn, and to compensate for inquietude of turbulent scenes by the tranquility of domestic repose. After

I had rendered an account of my military trust to congress and retired to my farm, I flattered myself that this unenviable lot was reserved for my latter years. I was delighted with agricultural affairs and excepting a few avocations

———

myself with the idea it was all that would ever be expected at my hand. But in this I was disappointed. The Legislature of Virginia in opposition to my express desire signified in the clearest terms to the Governor of that State, appointed me a Delegate to the federal Convention. Never was my embarrassment or hesitation more extreme or distressing. By letters from some of the wisest & best men in almost every quarter of the Continent, I was advised, that it was my indispensable duty to attend, and that, in the deplorable condition to which our affairs were reduced, my refusal would be considered a desertion of

———

rest, neither life or reputation has been accounted dear in my sight. And, from the bottom of my Soul, I know, that my motives on no former occasion were more innocent than in the present instance—At my time of life & in my situation I will not suppose that many moments need

———

need be bestowed in exculpating myself from any suggestions, which might be made "that the incitement of pleasure or grandeur, or power have wrought a change in my resolution." Small indd must be the resources for happiness in the mind of that man, who cannot find a refuge from the tediousness of solitude but in a round of dissipation, the pomp of State, or the homage of his fellow Men. I am not conscious of being in that predicament. But if there should be single citizen of the United States, to whom the tenour of my life is so little known, that he could imagine me capable of being so smitten with the allurements of sensual gratification, the frivolities of ceremony or the baubles of ambition, as to be induced from such motives to accept a public appointment: I shall only lament his imperfect acquaintance with my heart, and leave him until another retirement (should Heaven spare my life for a little space) shall work a conviction

———

viction of his error. In the meantime it may not, perhaps, be improper to mention one or two circumstances wch will serve to obviate the jealousies that might be entertained of my having accepted this Office, from a desire of enriching myself or aggrandising my posterity. In the first place, if I have formerly served the community without a wish for pecuniary compensation, it can hardly be suspected that I am at present influenced by avaricious schemes. In the next place, it will be recollected, that the Divine Providence hath not seen fit, that my blood should be transmitted or my name perpetuated by the endearing, though sometimes seducing channel of immediate offspring. I have no child for whom I could wish to make a provision—no family to build in greatness upon my Country's ruins. Let then the Adversaries to this Constitution—let my personal enemies if I am so unfortunate as to have deserved such a return from

———

from any one of my countrymen, point to the sinester object, or to the earthly consideration beyond the hope of rendering some little service to our parent Country, that could have persuaded me to accept this appointment

———

to any favoured nation. We have purchased wisdom by experience. Mankind are believed to be naturally averse to the coertions of government. But when our Countrymen had experienced the inconveniences, arising from the feebleness of our

———

when they shall witness the return of more prosperous times. I feel the consolatory joys of futurity in contemplating the immense desarts, yet untrodden by the foot of man, soon to become fair as the garden of God, soon to be animated by the activity of multitudes & soon to be made vocal with the praises of the *Most High*. Can it be imagined that so many peculiar advantages, of soil & of climate, for agriculture & for navigation were lavished in vain—or that this Continent was not created and reserved so long undiscovered as a Theatre, for those glorious displays of Divine Munificence, the salutary consequences of which shall flow to another Hemisphere & extend through the interminable series of ages! Should not our Souls exult in the prospect! Though I shall not survive to perceive with these bodily senses, but a small portion of the blessed effects which our Revolution will occasion in the rest of the world; yet I enjoy the progress of human society & human happiness in anticipation. I

———

I rejoice in a belief that intellectual light will spring up in the dark corners of the earth; that freedom of enquiry will produce liberality of conduct; that mankind will reverse the absurd position that *the many* were made for *the few*; and that they will not continue slaves in one part of the globe, when they can become freemen in another.

Thus I have explained the general impressions under which I have acted: omitting to mention untill the last, a principal reason which induced my acceptance. After a consciousness that all is right within and an humble hope of approbation in Heaven—nothing can, assuredly, be so grateful to a virtuous man as the good opinion of his fellow citizens. Tho' the partiality of mine led them to consider my holding the Chief Magistracy as a matter of infinitely more consequence than it really is; yet my acceptance must be ascribed rather to an honest willingness to satisfy that partiality, than to an overweening presumption upon my own capacity. Whenever a government is to be instituted or changed by Consent of the people, confidence in the person placed at the head of it, is, perhaps, more peculiarly necessary

———

set up my judgment as the standard of perfection? And shall I arrogantly pronounce that whosoever differs from me, must discern the subject through a distorting medium, or be influenced by some nefarious design? The mind is so formed in different persons as to contemplate the same object in different points of view. Hence originates the difference on questions of the greatest import, both human & divine. In all Institutions of the former kind, great allowances are doubtless to be made for the fallibility & imperfection of their authors. Although the agency I had in forming this system, and the high opinion I entertained of my Colleagues for their ability & integrity may have tended to warp my judgment in its favour; yet I will not pretend to say that it appears absolutely perfect to me, or that there may not be many faults which have escaped my discernment. I will only say, that, during and since the Session of the Convention, I have attentively heard and read every

———

every oral & printed information on both sides of the question that could be procured. This long & laborious investigation, in which I endeavoured as far as the frailty of nature would permit to act with candour has resulted in a fixed belief that this Constitution, is really in its formation a government of the people; that is to say, a government in which all power is derived from, and at stated periods reverts to them—and that, in its operation, it is purely, a government of Laws made & executed by the fair substitutes of the people alone. The election of the differt branches of Congress by the Freemen, either directly or indirectly is the pivot on which turns the first wheel of the government—a wheel which communicates motion to all the rest. At the sametime the exercise of this right of election seems to be so regulated as to afford less opportunity for corruption & influence; & more for stability & system than has usually been incident to popular governments. Nor can the members of Congress exempt themselves from the consequences of

———

of any unjust & tyranical acts which they may impose upon others. For in a short time they will mingle with the mass of the people. Their interests must therefore be the same, and their feelings in sympathy with those of their Constituents. Besides, their re-election must always depend upon the good reputation which they shall have maintained in the judgment of their fellow citizens. Hence I have been induced to conclude that this government must be less obnoxious to well-founded objections than most which have existed in the world. And in that opinion I am confirmed on three accounts: *first*—because every government ought to be possessed of powers adequate to the purposes for which it was instituted: Secondly, because no other or greater powers appear to me to be delegated to this government than are essential to accomplish the objects for which it was instituted, to wit, the safety

& happiness of the governed: and thirdly because it is clear to my conception that no government before

———

before introduced among mankind ever contained so many checks & such efficatious restraints to prevent it from degenerating into any species of oppression. It is unnecessary to be insisted upon, because it is well known, that the impotence of Congress under the former confederation, and the inexpediency of trusting more ample prerogatives to a single Body, gave birth to the different branches which constitute the present general government. Convinced as I am that the balances, arising from the distribution of the Legislative—Executive—& Judicial powers, are the best that have been instituted; I presume not to assert, that better may not still be devised. On the article of proposed amendments I shall say a few words in another place. But if it was a point acknowledged on all parts that the late federal government could not have existed much longer; if without some speedy remedy a dissolution of the Union must have ensued, if without adhering to the Union we

———

on the one hand and an unalterable habit of error on the other, are points in policy equally desirable; though, I believe, a power to effect them never before existed. Whether the Constitutional door that is opened for amendments in ours, be not the wisest and apparently the happiest expedient that has ever been suggested by human prudence I leave to every unprejudiced mind to determine.

Under these circumstances I conclude it has been the part of wisdom to adopt it. I pretend to no unusual foresight into futurity, & therefore cannot undertake to decide, with certainty, what may be its ultimate fate. If a promised good should terminate in an unexpected evil, it would not be a solitary example of disappointment in this mutable state of existence. If the blessings of Heaven showered thick around us should be spilled on the ground or converted to curses, through the fault of those for whom they were intended, it would not be the first instance of folly

———

folly or perverseness in short-sighted mortals. The blessed Religion revealed in the word of God will remain an eternal and awful monument to prove that the best Institutions may be abused by human depravity; and that they may even, in some instances be made subservient to the vilest of purposes. Should, hereafter, those who are intrusted with the management of this government, incited by the lust of power & prompted by the supineness or venality of their Constituents, overleap the known barriers of this Constitution and violate the unalienable rights of humanity: it will only serve to shew, that no compact among men (however provident in its construction & sacred in its ratification) can be pronounced everlasting and inviolable—and if I may so express myself, that no wall of words—that no mound of parchmt can be so formed as to stand against the sweeping torrent of boundless ambition on the one side, aided by the sapping current of corrupted morals on the other. But

————

It might naturally be supposed that I should not silently pass by the subject of our defence. After excepting the unprovoked hostility committed against us by one of the Powers of Barbary, we are now at peace with all the nations of the globe. Seperated as we are from them, by intervening Oceans, an exemption from the burden of maintaining numerous fleets and Armies must ever be considered as a singular felicity in our National lot. It will be in our choice to train our youths to such industrious & hardy professions as that they may grow into an unconquerable force, without our being obliged to draw unprofitable Drones from the hive of Industry. As our people have a natural genius for Naval affairs & as our materials for navigation are ample; if we give due encouragement to the fisheries and the carrying trade, we shall possess such a nursery of Seamen & such skill in maratime operations as to enable us to create a navy

————

navy almost in a moment. But it will be wise to anticipate events & to lay a foundation in time. Whenever the circumstances will permit, a grand provision of warlike stores, arsenals and dockyards ought to be made.

As to any invasion that might be meditated by foreigners

against us on the land, I will only say, that, if the Mighty Nation with which we lately contended could not bring us under the yoke, no nation on the face of the earth can ever effect it; while we shall remain United & faithful to ourselves. A well organised Militia would constitute a strong defence; of course, your most serious attention will be turned to such an establishment. In your recess, it will give me pleasure, by making such reviews, as opportunities may allow, to attempt to revive the antient military spirit. During the present impoverished state of our Finances I would not wish to see any expence incurred by augmenting our regular

———

of this government, it may be proper to give assurances of our friendly dispositions to other Powers. We may more at our leisure, meditate on such Treaties of Amity & Commerce, as shall be judged expedient to be propounded to or received from any of them.

In all our appointments of persons to fill domestic & foreign offices, let us be careful to select only such as are distinguished for morals & abilities—Some attention should likewise be paid, when ever the circumstances will conveniently admit, to the distribution of Offices among persons, belonging to the different parts of the Union. But my knowledge of the characters of persons, through an extent of fifteen hundred miles, must be so imperfect as to make me liable to fall into mistakes: which, in fact, can only be avoided by the disinterested aid of my coadjutors. I forbear to enlarge on the delicacy there certainly will be, in discharging this part of our trust with fidelity, and without giving occasion for uneasiness. It

———

It appears to me, that it would be a favorable circumstance, if the characters of Candidates could be known, without their having a pretext for coming forward themselves with personal applications. We should seek to find the Men who are best qualified to fill Offices: but never give our consent to the creation of Offices to accomodate men

Certain propositions for taking measures to obtain explanations & amendments on some articles of the Constitution, with the obvious intention of quieting the minds of the good people of these United States, will come before you & claim a dispassionate consideration. Whatever may not be deemed incompatible with the fundamental principles of a free & efficient government ought to be done for the accomplishment of so desirable an object. The reasoning which have been used, to prove

———

prove that amendments could never take place after this Constitution should be adopted, I must avow, have not appeared conclusive to me. I could not understand, by any mathematical analogy, why the whole number of States in Union should be more likely to concur in any proposed amendment, than three fourths of that number: before the adoption, the concurrence of the former was necessary for effecting this measure—since the adoption, only the latter. Here I will not presume to dictate as to the time, when it may be most expedient to attempt to remove all the redundances or supply all the defects, which shall be discovered in this complicated machine. I will barely suggest, whether it would not be the part of prudent men to observe it fully in movement, before they undertook to make such alterations, as might prevent a fair experiment of its effects?—and whether, in the meantime, it may not be practicable for this Congress (if their proceedings shall meet with the approbation of three fourths of the Legislatures) in such manner to secure to the people all their justly-

———

justly-esteemed priviledges as shall produce extensive satisfaction?

The complete organization of the Judicial Department was left by the Constitution to the ulterior arrangement of Congress. You will be pleased therefore to let a supreme regard for equal justice & the inherent rights of the citizens be visible in all your proceedings on that important subject.

I have a confident reliance that your wisdom & patriotism will be exerted to raise the supplies for discharging the interest on the national debt & for supporting the government during the current year, in a manner as little burdensome to the people as possible. The necessary estimates will be laid before you. A general, moderate Impost upon imports; together with a higher tax upon certain enumerated articles, will, undoubtedly, occur to you in the course

———

of the soil and the Sea, for the wares and merchandize of other Nations is open to all. Notwithstanding the embarassments under which our trade has hitherto laboured, since the peace, the enterprising spirit of our citizens has steered our Vessels to almost every region of the known world. In some distant & heretofore unfrequented countries, our new Constellation has been received with tokens of uncommon regard. An energetic government will give to our flag still greater respect: While a sense of reciprocal benefits will serve to connect us with the rest of mankind in stricter ties of amity. But an internal commerce is more in our power; and may be of more importance. The surplus of produce in one part of the United States, will, in many instances, be wanted in another. An intercourse of this kind is well calculated to multiply Sailors, exterminate prejudices, diffuse blessings, and encrease the friendship of the inhabitants of one State for those of another. While

———

While the individual States shall be occupied in facilitating the means of transportation, by opening canals & improving roads: you will not forget that the purposes of business & Society may be vastly promoted by giving cheapness, dispatch & security to communications through the regular Posts. I need not say how satisfactory it would be, to gratify the useful curiosity of our citizens by the conveyance of News Papers & periodical Publications in the public vehicles without expence.

Notwithstanding the rapid growth of our population, from the facility of obtaining subsistence, as well as from the accession of strangers, yet we shall not soon become a manufacturing people. Because men are even better pleased with labouring on their farms, than in their workshops. Even the mechanics who come from Europe, as soon as they can procure a little land of their own, commonly turn Cultivators. Hence it will be found more beneficial, I believe, to continue to exchange

———

change our Staple commodities for the finer manufactures we

may want, than to undertake to make them ourselves. Many articles, however, in wool, flax, cotton, & hemp; and all in leather, iron, fur and wood may be fabricated at home with great advantage. If the quantity of wool, flax, cotton & hemp should be encreased to ten-fold its present amount (as it easily could be) I apprehend the whole might in a short time be manufactured. Especially by the introduction of machines for multiplying the effects of labour, in diminishing the number of hands employed upon it. But it will rest with you to investigate what proficiency we are capable of making in manufactures, and what encouragement should be given to particular branches of them. In almost every House, much Spinning might be done by hands which otherwise would be in a manner idle

————

It remains for you to make, out of a Country poor in the precious metals and comparatively thin of inhabitants a flourishing State. But here it is particularly incumbent on me to express my idea of a flourishing state with precision; and to distinguish between happiness & splendour. The people of this Country may doubtless enjoy all the great blessings of the social State: and yet United America may not for a long time to come make a brilliant figure as a nation, among the nations of the earth. Should this be the case, and should the people be actuated by principles of true magnanimity, they will not suffer their ambition to be awakened. They should guard against ambition as against their greatest enemy. We shou'd not, in imitation of some nations which have been celebrated for a false kind of patriotism, wish to aggrandize our own Republic at the expence of the freedom & happiness of the rest of mankind. The prospect that the Americans will not act upon so narrow a scale affords the most comfortable

————

ble reflections to a benevolent mind. As their remoteness from other nations in a manner precludes them from foreign quarrels: so their extent of territory & gradual settlement, will enable them to maintain something like a war of posts, against the invasion of luxury, dissipation, & corruption. For after the large cities & old establishments on the borders of the Atlantic, shall, in the progress of time, have fallen a prey to those

Invaders; the Western States will probably long retain their primaeval simplicity of manners & incorruptible love of liberty. May we not reasonably expect, that, by those manners & this patriotism, uncommon prosperity will be entailed on the civil institutions of the American world? And may you not console yourselves for any irksome circumstances which shall occur in the performance of your task, with the pleasing consideration, that you are now employed in laying the foundation of that durable prosperity

———

It belongs to you especially to take measures for promoting the general welfare. It belongs to you to make men honest in their dealings with each other, by regulating the coinage & currency of money upon equitable principles as well as by establishing just weights and measures upon an uniform plan. Whenever an opportunity shall be furnished to you as public or as private men, I trust you will not fail to use your best endeavors to improve the education and manners of a people; to accelerate the progress of arts & Sciences; to patronize works of genius; to confer rewards for inventions of utility; and to cherish institutions favourable to humanity. Such are among the best of all human employments. Such exertion of your talents will render your situations truly dignified & cannot fail of being acceptable in the sight of the Divinity.

By a series of disinterested services it will be in our power to shew, that we have nothing

———

While others in their political conduct shall demean themselves as may seem dear to them, let us be honest. Let us be firm. Let us advance directly forward in the path of our duty. Should the path at first prove intricate & thorny, it will grow plain and smooth as we go. In public as in private life, let the eternal line that seperates right from wrong, be the fence to

———

I have now again given way to my feelings, in speaking without reserve, according to my best judgment, the words of soberness & affection. If any thing indiscreet or foreign to the occasion has been spoken, your candour, I am convinced will not impute it to an unworthy motive. I come now to a conclusion by addressing my humble petition to the which will conduce to their temporal & eternal peace—I most earnestly supplicate that Almighty God, to whose holy keeping I commend my dearest Country, will never offer so fair an inheritance to become a prey to avar

c. January 1789

To Marquis de Lafayette

My dear Marqs   Mount Vernon Jany 29 1789

By the last Post, I was favored with the receipt of your letter, dated the 5th of September last. Notwithstanding the distance of its date, it was peculiarly welcome to me: for I had not, in the mean time received any satisfactory advices respecting yourself or your country. By that letter, my mind was placed much more at its ease, on both those subjects, than it had been for many months.

The last letter, which I had the pleasure of writing to you, was forwarded by Mr Gouverneur Morris. Since his departure from America, nothing very material has occurred. The minds of men, however, have not been in a stagnant State. But patriotism, instead of faction, has generally agitated them. It is not a matter of wonder, that, in proportion as we approached to the time fixed for the organization and operation of the new government, their anxiety should have been encreased, rather than diminished. The choice of Senators, Representatives and Electors, whh (excepting in that of the last description) took place at different times, in the different States, has afforded abundant topics for domestic News, since the beginning of Autumn. I need not enumerate the several particulars, as I imagine you see most of them detailed, in the American Gazettes. I will content myself with only saying, that the elections have been hitherto vastly more favorable than we could have expected, that federal sentiments seem to be growing with uncommon rapidity, and that this encreasing unanimity is not less indicative of the good disposition than the good sense of the Americans. Did it not savour so much of partiality for my Countrymen I might add, that I cannot help flattering

myself the new Congress on account of the self-created respectability and various talents of its Members, will not be
inferior to any Assembly in the world. From these and some
other circumstances, I really entertain greater hopes, that
America will not finally disappoint the expectations of her
Friends, than I have at almost any former period. Still however, in such a fickle state of existence, I would not be too
sanguine in indulging myself with the contemplation of scenes
of uninterupted prosperity; lest some unforeseen mischance
or perverseness should occasion the greater mortification, by
blasting the enjoyment in the very bud.

I can say little or nothing new, in consequence of the repetition of your opinion, on the expediency there will be, for
my accepting the office to which you refer. Your sentiments,
indeed, coincide much more nearly with those of my other
friends, than with my own feelings. In truth my difficulties
encrease and magnify as I drew towards the period, when,
according to the common belief, it will be necessary for me
to give a definitive answer, in one way or another. Should the
circumstances render it, in a manner inevitably necessary, to
be in the affirmative: Be assured, my dear Sir, I shall assume
the task with the most unfeigned reluctance, and with a real
diffidence for which I shall probably receive no credit from
the world. If I know my own heart, nothing short of a conviction of duty will induce me again to take an active part in
public affairs—and, in that case, if I can form a plan for my
own conduct, my endeavours shall be unremittingly exerted
(even at the hazard of former fame or present popularity) to
extricate my country from the embarrassments in which it is
entangled, through want of credit; and to establish, a general
system of policy, which, if pursued will insure permanent felicity to the Commonwealth. I think, I see a *path*, as clear
and as direct as a ray of light, which leads to the attainment
of that object. Nothing but harmony, honesty, industry and
frugality are necessary to make us a great and happy people.
Happily the present posture of affairs and the prevailing disposition of my countrymen promise to co-operate, in establishing those four great and essential pillars of public felicity.

What has been considered at the moment as a disadvantage,
will probably turn out for our good. While our commerce has

been considerably curtailed, for want of that extensive credit formerly given in Europe, and for fault of remittance; the usefull arts have been almost imperceptibly pushed to a considerable degree of perfection. Though I would not force the introduction of manufactures, by extravagant encouragements, and to the prejudice of agriculture; yet, I conceive, much might be done in that way by woman, children & others; without taking one really necessary hand from tilling the earth. Certain it is, great savings are already made in many articles of apparel, furniture and consumption. Equally certain it is, that no diminution in agriculture has taken place, at the time when greator and more substantial improvements in manufactures were making, than were ever before known in America. In Pennsylvania they have attended particularly to the fabrication of cotten cloths, hats, and all articles in leather. In Massachusetts they are establishing factories of Duck, Cordage, Glass and several other extensive and useful branches. The number of shoes made in one town and nails in another is incredible. In that State and Connecticut are also factories of superfine and other broad cloths. I have been writing to our friend Genl Knox this day, to procure me homespun broad cloth, of the Hartford fabric, to make a suit of cloaths for myself. I hope it will not be a great while, before it will be unfashionable for a gentleman to appear in any other dress. Indeed we have already been to long subject to British prejudices. I use no porter or cheese in my family, but such as is made in America—both those articles may now be purchased of an excellent quality.

While you are quarreling among yourselves in Europe—while one King is running mad—and others acting as if they were already so, by cutting the throats of the subjects of their neighbours: I think you need not doubt, My Dear Marquis we shall continue in tranquility here—And that population will be progressive so long as there shall continue to be so many easy means for obtaining a subsistence, and so ample a field for the exertion of talents and industry.

All my family join in Compliments to Madam la Fayette and yours. Adieu, my dear Marqs believe me, what I am—With &c.

To Richard Conway

Dear Sir,   Mount Vernon March 4th 1789
    Never 'till within these two yrs have I experienced the want
of money. Short Crops, & other causes not entirely within my
Controul, make me feel it now, very sensibly. To collect
money without the intervention of Suits (and those are tedious) seems impracticable. And Land, which I have offered for
Sale, will not command cash but at an under value.
    Under this statement I am inclined to do what I never ex-
pected to be reduced to the necessity of doing—that is, to
borrow money upon interest. Five hundred pounds would enable me to discharge what I owe in Alexandria &ca; and to
leave the State (if it shall not be permitted me to remain at
home in retirement) without doing this, would be exceedingly
disagreeable to me. Having thus fully & candidly explained
myself—permit me to ask if it is in your power to supply me
with the above, or a smaller sum? Any security you may best
like, I can give; and you may be assured, that it is no more
my inclination, than it can be yours, to let it remain long
unpaid. Could I get in one fourth part of the money which
is due to me by Bonds—or sell any of the landed property
which I am inclined to dispose of, I could do it with ease; but
independently of these—my Crops and Rents if I am tolerably
successful in the first, or have common justice done me in the
latter would enable me to do it. Your answer will much
oblige—Dr Sir Yr most Obedt Servt

To George Steptoe Washington

Dear George,   Mount Vernon 23d March 1789
    As it is probable I shall soon be under the necessity of quit-
ting this place, and entering once more into the bustle of
publick life, in conformity to the voice of my Country, and
the earnest entreaties of my friends, however contrary it is to
my own desires or inclinations; I think it incumbent on me

as, your Uncle & friend, to give you some advisory hints, which, if properly attended to, will, I conceive, be found very useful to you in regulating your conduct and giving you respectability not only at present but through every period of Life.

You have now arrived to that age when you must quit the trifling amusements of a boy, and assume the more dignified manners of a man. At this crisis your conduct will attract the notice of those who are about you; and as the first impressions are generally the most lasting, your doings now may mark the leading traits of your Character through life. It is therefore, absolutely necessary, if you mean to make any figure upon the Stage, that you should take the first steps right. What these steps are—and what general line is to be pursued to lay the foundation of an honorable and happy progress, is the part of age and experience to point out. This I shall do, as far as is in my power, with the utmost chearfulness; and I trust, that your own good sense will shew you the necessity of following it.

The first and great object with you at present is to acquire, by industry and application, such knowledge as your situation enables you to obtain, and as will be useful to you in life. In doing this two other important objects will be gained besides the acquisition of knowledge—namely, a habit of industry, and a disrelish of that profusion of money & dissipation of time which are ever attendant upon idleness. I do not mean by a close application to your Studies that you should never enter into those amusements which are suited to your age and station. They may be made to go hand in hand with each other—and, used in their proper seasons, will ever be found to be a mutual assistance to each other. But what amusements are to be taken, and when, is the great matter to be attended to. Your own judgement, with the advice of your *real* friends who may have an opportunity of a personal intercourse with you can point out the particular manner in which you may best spend your moments of relaxation, much better than I can at a distance. One thing, however, I would strongly impress upon you, viz., that when you have leisure to go into Company that it should always be of the best kind that the place you are in will afford; by this means you will be constantly improving your manners and cultivating your mind while you are relaxing from your books; and good Company will always be found much less expensive than bad. You cannot offer, as an excuse for not using it, that you cannot gain admission there—or that you have not a proper attention paid you in it; this is an apology made only by those whose manners are disgusting, or whose character is exceptionable; neither of which I hope, will ever be said of you.

I cannot enjoin too strongly upon you a due observance of economy & frugality—as you well know yourself the present state of your property & finances will not admit of any unnecessary expense. The article of clothing is now one of the chief expenses you will incur; and in this, I fear, you are not so economical as you should be. Decency & cleanliness will always be the first objects in the dress of a judicious & sensible man. A conformity to the prevailing fashion in a certain degree is necessary—but it does not follow from thence that a man should always get a new Coat, or other clothes, upon every trifling change in the mode, when, perhaps, he has two or three very good ones by him. A person who is anxious to be a leader of the fashion, or one of the first to follow it, will certainly appear, in the eyes of judicious men, to have nothing better than a frequent change of dress to recommend him to notice. I would always wish you to appear sufficiently decent to entitle you to admission into any company where you may be; but I cannot too strongly enjoin it upon you—and your own knowledge must convince you of the truth of it—that you should be as little expensive in this respect as you properly can; you should always keep some clothes to wear to Church, or on particular occasions, which should not be worne every day; this can be done without any additional expense; for whenever it is necessary to get new Clothes, those which have been kept for particular occasions will then come in as every day ones, unless they should be of a superior quality to the new. What I have said, with respect to Clothes, will apply, perhaps, more pointedly to Lawrence than to you; and as you are much older than he is, and more capable of judging of the propriety of what I have here observed, you must pay attention to him, in this respect, and see that he does not wear his clothes improperly or extravagantly.

Much more might be said to you, as a young man, upon the necessity of paying a due attention to the moral virtues; but this may, perhaps, more properly be the subject of a future letter when you are about to enter into the world. If you comply with the advise herein given to pay a diligent attention to your studies, and employ your time of relaxation in proper company, you will find but few opportunities and little inclination, while you continue at an Academy, to enter into those scenes of vice & dissipation which too often present themselves to youth in every place, & particularly in towns. If you are determined to neglect your books, and plunge into extravagance & dissipation nothing I could now say would prevent it—for you must be employed, and if it is not in pursuit of those things which are profitable it must be in pursuit of those which are destructive.

As your time of continuing with Mr Hanson will expire the last of this month, and I understand Doctor Craik has expressed an inclination to take you & Lawrence to board with him, I shall know his determination respecting the matter; and if it is agreeable to him & Mrs Craik to take you I shall be pleased with it, for I am certain that nothing will be wanting on their part to make your situation agreeable & useful to you. Should you live with the Doctor I shall request him to take you both under his peculiar care—provide such clothes for you, from time to time, as he shall judge necessary—and do by you in the same manner as he would if you were his own children; which if he will undertake, I am sensible, from the knowledge which I have of him, and the very amiable Character & disposition of Mrs Craik, that they will spare no proper exertions to make your situation pleasing and profitable to you; should you or Lawrence, therefore, behave in such a manner as to occasion any complaints being made to me—you may depend upon losing that place which you now have in my affections—and any future hopes you may have from me. But if, on the contrary, your conduct is such as to merit my regard you may always depend upon the warmest attachment & sincere regard of Your affectionate friend & Uncle

To James Madison

My dear Sir,   Mount Vernon March 30th 1789
    I have been favored with your Letter of the 19th by which
it appears that a quoram of Congress was hardly to be expected until the beginning of the *past* week. As this delay must
be very irksome to the attending members, and every days
continuance of it (before the Government is in operation) will
be more sensibly felt, I am resolved, no interruption shall proceed from me that can well be avoided (after notice of the
Election is announced); and therefore take the liberty of requesting the favor of you to engage Lodgings for me previous
to my arrival. Colo. Humphreys, I presume will be of my
party; and Mr Lear who has already lived three years with me
as a private Secretary, will accompany, or preceed me in the
Stage.
    On the subject of lodgings I will frankly declare, I mean to
go into none but hired ones. If these cannot be had tolerably
convenient (I am not very nice) I would take rooms in the
most decent Tavern, till a house can be provided for the more
permanent reception of the President. I have already declined
a very polite & pressing offer from the Governer, to lodge at
his house till a place could be prepared for me; after which
should any other of a similar nature be made, there would be
no propriety in the acceptance.
    But as you are fully acquainted with sentiments on this sub-
ject, I shall only add, that as I mean to avoid private families
on the one hand, so on another, I am not desirous of being
placed *early* in a Situation for entertaining. Therefore, hired
(private) lodging would not only be more agreeable to my
own wishes, but, possibly, more consistent with the dictates
of sound policy. For, as it is my wish & intention to conform
to the public desire and expectation, with respect to the style
proper for the Chief Magistrate to live in, it might be well to
know (as far as the nature of the case will admit) what these
are before he enters upon it.
    After all, something may perhaps have been decided upon,
with respect to the accommodations of the President, before
this letter wd have reached you that may render this applica-

tion nugatory. If otherwise, I will sum up all my wishes in one word, and that is to be placed in an independent situation, with the prospect I have alluded to, before me. With strong, and affectionate friendship I am ever Yours

To Thomas Green

Mount Vernon 31st March 1789

I am about to leave my home whether for a length of time, is more than I can tell at present. But be this as it may I expect the agreement to which we have subscribed, will be as strictly complied with on your part as it shall be punctually fulfilled on mine to enable you to do this, you would do well to keep two things always in remembrance—First that all Bargains are intended, for the Mutual benefit of and are equally binding on both the Parties, and are either binding in all their parts or are of no use at all—If then a man receives pay for his labour and he withholds that labour or if he trifles away that time for which he is paid, it is a robbery—and a robbery of the worst kind because it is not only a fraud but a dishonourable, unmanly and a deceitful fraud—but it is unnecessary to dwell on this because there is no Man so ignorant of the common obligations of Justice, as not to know it—altho' there are hundreds who do not scruple to practice it at the same time that they would think hard, on the other hand if they were to be deprived of their money. The other matter which—I advise you to keep always in remembrance is the good name which common policy as well as common honesty, makes it necessary for every workman who wishes to pass thro' life with reputation and to secure employment—Having said thus much by way of exhortation I shall inform you in the most serious and positive terms that I have left strict orders with the Major my Nephew, who is vested with full powers to transact all my business, that if he should find you unfaithful to your engagements—either from the love of liquor from a disposition to be running about—or from proneness to idle when at your work—to discard you immediately and to remove your family from their present abode. The sure means to avoid this evil is—first to refrain from drink which is the source of all evil—and the ruin of half the workmen in this Country—and next to avoid bad Company which is the bane of good morals œconomy and industry you have every inducement to do this—Reputation—the care and support of a growing family—and society which this family affords within your own doors whch may not be the case with some of the idle (to say nothing worse of them) characters who may lead you into temptation—Were you to look back, and had the means, either from recollection, or accounts to ascertain the cost of the liquor you have expended it would astonish you— In the manner this expence is generally incurred that is by getting a little now—a little then the impropriety of it is not seen in as much as it passes away without much thought. But view it in the aggregate you will be convinced at once whether any man who depends upon the labour of his hands not only for his own support but have that of an encreasing family can afford such a proportion of his wages to that article. But the expence is not the worst consequence that attends it for it naturally leads a man into the company of those who encourage dissipation and idleness by which he is led to by degrees to the perpetration of acts which may terminate in his Ruin— but supposing this not to happen a disordered frame—and a body debilitated, renders him unfit (even if his mind was disposed to discharge the duties of his station with honor to himself or fidility to his employer) from the execution of it. an aching head and trimbling limbs which are the inevitable effects of drinking disincline the hands from work hence begins sloth and that Lestessness which end in idleness—but which are no reasons for withholding that labour for which money is paid.

I have no other inducement for giving you this advice (in this my hour of hurry) but your own good—for the wages and priviledges which you have I well know would obtain for me the best workmen in this Country which the charges of such a family as yours but as it has been a custom with me through life to give a preference to those who have long lived with me and my wish to see them do well I have taken the trouble of writing You this letter. if you have gratitude, or a mind capable of reflection, it will make such an impression on it as may be serviceable to you thro life—if not, I have my labour for my pains.

Whilst the Negro Carpenters work at the same spot where you are, they will be subject to your inspection and orders—and at other times if it should be found necessary to put them under yr care it will be expected that you see that they do their duty. I am &ca

To Henry Knox

My dear Sir,   Mount Vernon April 1st 1789

The Mail of the 30th brought me your favor of the 23d—For which, & the regular information you have had the goodness to transmit of the state of things in New York, I feel myself very much obliged, and thank you accordingly.

I feel for those Members of the new Congress, who, hitherto, have given an unavailing attendance at the theatre of business. For myself, the delay may be compared to a reprieve; for in confidence I can assure *you*—with the *world* it would obtain *little credit*—that my movements to the chair of Government will be accompanied with feelings not unlike those of a culprit who is going to the place of his execution: so unwilling am I, in the evening of a life nearly consumed in public cares, to quit a peaceful abode for an Ocean of difficulties, without that competency of political skill—abilities & inclination which is necessary to manage the helm. I am sensible, that I am embarking the voice of my Countrymen and a good name of my own, on this voyage, but what returns will be made for them—Heaven alone can foretell. Integrity & firmness is all I can promise—these, be the voyage long or short; never shall forsake me although I may be deserted by all men. For of the consolations which are to be derived from these (under any circumstances) the world cannot deprive me. With best wishes for Mrs Knox, & sincere friendship for yourself—I remain Your affectionate

PRESIDENT
1789–1797

Reply to Charles Thomson

Sir, I have been long accustomed to entertain so great a respect for the opinion of my fellow citizens, that the knowledge of their unanimous suffrages having been given in my favour scarcely leaves me the alternative for an Option. Whatever may have been my private feelings and sentiments, I believe I cannot give a greater evidence of my sensibility for the honor they have done me than by accepting the appointment.

I am so much affected by this fresh proof of my country's esteem and confidence, that silence can best explain my gratitude—While I realize the arduous nature of the task which is conferred on me and feel my inability to perform it, I wish there may not be reason for regreting the choice. All I can promise is only that which can be accomplished by an honest zeal.

Upon considering how long time some of the gentlemen of both houses of Congress have been at New York, how anxiously desirous they must be to proceed to business and how deeply the public mind appears to be impressed with the necessity of doing it immediately I cannot find myself at liberty to delay my Journey—I shall therefore be in readiness to set out the day after to morrow, and shall be happy in the pleasure of your company. For you will permit me to say that it was a peculiar gratification to have received the communication from you.

April 14, 1789

To John Langdon

Sir,   Mount Vernon April 14th 1789.
I had the honor to receive your Official Communication, by the hand of Mr Secretary Thompson, about one o'clock this day. Having concluded to obey the important & flattering call of my Country, and having been impressed with an idea of the expediency of my being with Congress at as early a period as possible; I propose to commence my journey on

thursday morning which will be the day after to morrow. I have the honor to be with sentiments of esteem Sir Your most obedt Servt

Diary Entries

About ten o'clock I bade adieu to Mount Vernon, to private life, and to domestic felicity; and with a mind oppressed with more anxious and painful sensations than I have words to express, set out for New York in company with Mr. Thompson, and colonel Humphries, with the best dispositions to render service to my country in obedience to its call, but with less hope of answering its expectations.

The display of boats which attended and joined us on this occasion, some with vocal and some with instrumental music on board; the decorations of the ships, the roar of cannon, and the loud acclamations of the people which rent the skies, as I passed along the wharves, filled my mind with sensations as painful (considering the reverse of this scene, which may be the case after all my labors to do good) as they are pleasing.

April 16 and 23, 1789

First Inaugural Address

Fellow Citizens of the Senate and
of the House of Representatives
    Among the vicissitudes incident to life, no event could have filled me with greater anxieties than that of which the notification was transmitted by your order, and received on the fourteenth day of the present month. On the one hand, I was summoned by my Country, whose voice I can never hear but with veneration and love, from a retreat which I had chosen with the fondest predilection, and, in my flattering hopes, with an immutable decision, as the asylum of my declining years: a retreat which was rendered every day more necessary

as well as more dear to me, by the addition of habit to inclination, and of frequent interruptions in my health to the gradual waste committed on it by time. On the other hand, the magnitude and difficulty of the trust to which the voice of my Country called me, being sufficient to awaken in the wisest and most experienced of her citizens, a distrustful scrutiny into his qualifications, could not but overwhelm with despondence, one, who, inheriting inferior endowments from nature and unpractised in the duties of civil administration, ought to be peculiarly conscious of his own deficiencies. In this conflict of emotions, all I dare aver, is, that it has been my faithful study to collect my duty from a just appreciation of every circumstance, by which it might be affected. All I dare hope, is, that, if in executing this task I have been too much swayed by a grateful remembrance of former instances, or by an affectionate sensibility to this transcendent proof, of the confidence of my fellow-citizens; and have thence too little consulted my incapacity as well as disinclination for the weighty and untried cares before me; my *error* will be palliated by the motives which misled me, and its consequences be judged by my Country, with some share of the partiality in which they originated.

Such being the impressions under which I have, in obedience to the public summons, repaired to the present station; it would be peculiarly improper to omit in this first official Act, my fervent supplications to that Almighty Being who rules over the Universe, who presides in the Councils of Nations, and whose providential aids can supply every human defect, that his benediction may consecrate to the liberties and happiness of the People of the United States, a Government instituted by themselves for these essential purposes: and may enable every instrument employed in its administration, to execute with success, the functions allotted to his charge. In tendering this homage to the Great Author of every public and private good, I assure myself that it expresses your sentiments not less than my own; nor those of my fellow-citizens at large, less than either: No People can be bound to acknowledge and adore the invisible hand, which conducts the Affairs of men more than the People of the United States. Every step, by which they have advanced to the character of an independent nation, seems to have been distinguished by some token of providential agency. And in the important revolution just accomplished in the system of their United Government, the tranquil deliberations, and voluntary consent of so many distinct communities, from which the event has resulted, cannot be compared with the means by which most Governments have been established, without some return of pious gratitude along with an humble anticipation of the future blessings which the past seem to presage. These reflections, arising out of the present crisis, have forced themselves too strongly on my mind to be suppressed. You will join me I trust in thinking, that there are none under the influence of which, the proceedings of a new and free Government can more auspiciously commence.

By the article establishing the Executive Department, it is made the duty of the President "to recommend to your consideration, such measures as he shall judge necessary and expedient." The circumstances under which I now meet you, will acquit me from entering into that subject, farther than to refer to the Great Constitutional Charter under which you are assembled; and which, in defining your powers, designates the objects to which your attention is to be given. It will be more consistent with those circumstances, and far more congenial with the feelings which actuate me, to substitute, in place of a recommendation of particular measures, the tribute that is due to the talents, the rectitude, and the patriotism which adorn the characters selected to devise and adopt them. In these honorable qualifications, I behold the surest pledges, that as on one side, no local prejudices, or attachments; no seperate views, nor party animosities, will misdirect the comprehensive and equal eye which ought to watch over this great Assemblage of communities and interests: so, on another, that the foundations of our national policy, will be laid in the pure and immutable principles of private morality; and the pre-eminence of free Government, be exemplified by all the attributes which can win the affections of its Citizens, and command the respect of the world. I dwell on this prospect with every satisfaction which an ardent love for my Country can inspire: since there is no truth more thoroughly established, than that there exists in the œconomy and course of nature, an indissoluble union between virtue and happiness, between duty and advantage, between the genuine maxims of an honest and magnanimous policy, and the solid rewards of public prosperity and felicity: Since we ought to be no less persuaded that the propitious smiles of Heaven, can never be expected on a nation that disregards the eternal rules of order and right, which Heaven itself has ordained: And since the preservation of the sacred fire of liberty, and the destiny of the Republican model of Government, are justly considered as *deeply*, perhaps as *finally* staked, on the experiment entrusted to the hands of the American people.

Besides the ordinary objects submitted to your care, it will remain with your judgment to decide, how far an exercise of the occasional power delegated by the Fifth article of the Constitution is rendered expedient at the present juncture by the nature of objections which have been urged against the System, or by the degree of inquietude which has given birth to them. Instead of undertaking particular recommendations on this subject, in which I could be guided by no lights derived from official opportunities, I shall again give way to my entire confidence in your discernment and pursuit of the public good: For I assure myself that whilst you carefully avoid every alteration which might endanger the benefits of an United and effective Government, or which ought to await the future lessons of experience; a reverence for the characteristic rights of freemen, and a regard for the public harmony, will sufficiently influence your deliberations on the question how far the former can be more impregnably fortified, or the latter be safely and advantageously promoted.

To the preceding observations I have one to add, which will be most properly addressed to the House of Representatives. It concerns myself; and will therefore be as brief as possible. When I was first honoured with a call into the service of my Country, then on the eve of an arduous struggle for its liberties, the light in which I contemplated my duty required that I should renounce every pecuniary compensation. From this resolution I have in no instance departed—And being still under the impressions which produced it, I must decline as inapplicable to myself, any share in the personal emoluments, which may be indispensably included in a permanent provision for the Executive Department; and must accordingly pray that the pecuniary estimates for the Station in which I am placed, may, during my continuance in it, be limited to such actual expenditures as the public good may be thought to require.

Having thus imparted to you my sentiments, as they have been awakened by the occasion which brings us together, I shall take my present leave; but not without resorting once more to the benign Parent of the human race, in humble supplication that since he has been pleased to favour the American people, with opportunities for deliberating in perfect tranquility, and dispositions for deciding with unparellelled unanimity on a form of Government, for the security of their Union, and the advancement of their happiness; so this divine blessing may be equally *conspicuous* in the enlarged views—the temperate consultations, and the wise measures on which the success of this Government must depend.

April 30, 1789

To James Madison

My dear Sir,   New York May 5th 1789.

Notwithstanding the conviction I am under of the labour which is imposed upon you by Public Individuals as well as public bodies—yet, as you have begun, so I could wish you to finish, the good work in a short reply to the Address of the House of Representatives (which I now enclose) that there may be an accordance in this business.

Thursday 12 Oclock, I have appointed to receive the Address. The proper place is with the House to determine. As the first of everything, in *our situation* will serve to establish a Precedent, it is devoutly wished on my part, that these precedents may be fixed on true principles. With affectionate regard I am ever Yours

To Edward Rutledge

My dear Sir,   New York May 5th 1789.

I cannot fail of being much pleased with the friendly part you take in every thing which concerns me; and particularly with the just scale on which you estimate this last great sacrafice which I consider myself as having made for the good of my Country. When I had judged, upon the best appreciation I was able to form of the circumstances which related to myself, that it was my duty to embark again on the tempestuous & uncertain Ocean of public life, I gave up all expectations of private happiness in this world: You know, my dear Sir, I had concentered all my schemes, all my views, all my wishes, within the narrow circle of domestic enjoyment. Though I flatter myself the world will do me the justice to believe, that, at my time of life & in my circumstances, nothing but a conviction of duty could have induced me to depart from my resolution of remaining in retirement; yet I greatly apprehend that my Countrymen will expect too much from me. I fear, if the issue of public measures should not corrispond with their sanguine expectations, they will turn the extravagant (and I may say undue) praises which they are heaping upon me at this moment, into equally extravagant (though I will fondly hope unmerited) censures. So much is expected, so many untoward circumstances may intervene, in such a new and critical situation, that I feel an insuperable diffidence in my own abilities—I feel, in the execution of the duties of my arduous Office, how much I shall stand in need of the countenance & aid of every friend to myself, of every friend to the Revolution—and of every lover of good Government. I thank you, my dear Sir, for your affectionate expressions on this point.

I anticipate that one of the most difficult & delicate parts of the duty of my office will be that which relates to nominations for appointments. I receive with the more satisfaction the strong testimonials in behalf of Mr Hall because I hope they will tend to supercede the difficulty in this instance. Though from a system which I have prescribed to myself I can say nothing decisive on particular appointments; yet I may be allowed to observe in general, that nothing could be more agreeable to me than to have one Candidate brought forward for every Office of such clear pretensions as to secure him against competition.

Mrs Washington is not here, but is shortly expected; on her arrival I will offer the Compliments of Mrs Rutledge & yourself to her. In the meantime, I pray you to believe that, I am with sentiments of the purest esteem and highest consideration My dear Sir Yr Most Obedt Servt

Reply to the House of Representatives

Gentlemen,

Your very affectionate Address produces emotions which I know not how to express. I feel that my past endeavours in the Service of Country are far overpaid by its goodness: and I fear much that my future ones may not fulfil your kind anticipation. All that I can promise is, that they will be invariably directed by an honest and an ardent zeal. Of this resource my heart assures me. For all beyond, I rely on the wisdom and patriotism of those with whom I am to co-operate, and a continuance of the blessings of Heaven on our beloved Country.

May 8, 1789

To John Adams

The President of the United States wishes to avail himself of your sentiments on the following points.

1st Whether a line of conduct, equally distant from an association with all kinds of company on the one hand and from a total seclusion from Society on the other, ought to be adopted by him? and, in that case, how is it to be done?

2d What will be the least exceptionable method of bringing any system, which may be adopted on this subject, before the Public and into use?

3d Whether, after a little time, one day in every week will not be sufficient for receiving visits of Compliment?

4th Whether it would tend to prompt impertinent applications & involve disagreeable consequences to have it known, that the President will, every Morning at 8 Oclock, be at leisure to give Audiences to persons who may have business with him?

5th Whether, when it shall have been understood that the President is not to give general entertainment in the manner the Presidents of Congress have formerly done, it will be practicable to draw such a line of discrimination in regard to persons, as that Six, eight or ten official characters (including in the rotation the members of both Houses of Congress) may be invited informally or otherwise to dine with him on the days fixed for receiving Company, without exciting clamours in the rest of the Community?

6th Whether it would be satisfactory to the Public for the President to make about four great entertainmts in a year on such great occasions as—the Anniversary of the Declaration of Independence, the Alliance with France—the Peace with Great Britain—the Organization of the general government: and whether arrangements of these two last kinds could be in danger of diverting too much of the Presidents time from business, or of producing the evils which it was intended to avoid by his living more recluse than the Presidents of Congress have heretofore lived.

7th Whether there would be any impropriety in the Presidents making informal visits—that is to say, in his calling upon his Acquaintances or public Characters for the purposes of sociability or civility—and what (as to the form of doing it) might evince these visits to have been made in his private character, so as that they might not be construed into visits from the President of the United States? and in what light would his appearance *rarely* at *Tea* parties be considered?

8th Whether, during the recess of Congress, it would not be advantageous to the interests of the Union for the President to make the tour of the United States, in order to become better acquainted with their principal Characters & internal Circumstances, as well as to be more accessible to numbers of well-informed persons, who might give him useful informations and advices on political subjects?

9th If there is a probability that either of the arrangements may take place, which will eventually cause additional expenses, whether it would not be proper that these ideas should come into contemplation, at the time when Congress shall make a permanent provision for the support of the Executive.

Remarks

On the one side no augmentation can be effected in the pecuniary establishment which shall be made, in the first instance, for the support of the Executive—on the other, all monies destined to that purpose beyond the actual expenditures, will be left in the Treasury of the United States or sacredly applied to the promotion of some national objects.

Many things which appear of little importance in themselves and at the beginning, may have great and durable consequences from their having been established at the commencement of a new general Government. It will be much easier to commence the administration, upon a well adjusted system built on tenable grounds, than to correct errors or alter inconveniences after they shall have been confirmed by habit. The President in all matters of business & etiquette, can have no object but to demean himself in his public character, in such a manner as to maintain the dignity of Office, without subjecting himself to the imputation of superciliousness or unnecessary reserve. Under these impressions, he asks for your candid and undisguised opinions.

May 10, 1789

To the United Baptist Churches of Virginia

Gentlemen,

I request that you will accept my best acknowledgments for your congratulation on my appointment to the first office in the nation. The kind manner in which you mention my past conduct equally claims the expression of my gratitude.

After we had, by the smiles of Heaven on our exertions, obtained the object for which we contended, I retired at the conclusion of the war, with an idea that my country could have no farther occasion for my services, and with the intention of never entering again into public life: But when the exigence of my country seemed to require me once more to engage in public affairs, an honest conviction of duty superseded my former resolution, and became my apology for deviating from the happy plan which I had adopted.

If I could have entertained the slightest apprehension that the Constitution framed in the Convention, where I had the honor to preside, might possibly endanger the religious rights of any ecclesiastical Society, certainly I would never have placed my signature to it; and if I could now conceive that the general Government might ever be so administered as to render the liberty of conscience insecure, I beg you will be persuaded that no one would be more zealous than myself to establish effectual barriers against the horrors of spiritual tyranny, and every species of religious persecution—For you, doubtless, remember that I have often expressed my sentiment, that every man, conducting himself as a good citizen, and being accountable to God alone for his religious opinions, ought to be protected in worshipping the Deity according to the dictates of his own conscience.

While I recollect with satisfaction that the religious Society of which you are Members, have been, throughout America, uniformly, and almost unanimously, the firm friends to civil liberty, and the persevering Promoters of our glorious revolution; I cannot hesitate to believe that they will be the faithful Supporters of a free, yet efficient general Government. Under this pleasing expectation I rejoice to assure them that they may rely on my best wishes and endeavors to advance their prosperity.

In the meantime be assured, Gentlemen, that I entertain a proper sense of your fervent supplications to God for my temporal and eternal happiness.

May 1789

To Betty Washington Lewis

My dear Sister,   New York, September 13th 1789

Colonel Ball's letter gave me the first account of my Mother's death—since that I have received Mrs Carter's letter written at your request—and previous to both I was prepared for the event by some advices of her illness communicated to your Son Robert.

Awful, and affecting as the death of a Parent is, there is consolation in knowing that Heaven has spared ours to an age, beyond which few attain, and favored her with the full enjoyment of her mental faculties, and as much bodily strength as usually falls to the lot of four score. Under these considerations and a hope that she is translated to a happier place, it is the duty of her relatives to yield due submission to the decrees of the Creator—When I was last at Fredericksburg, I took a final leave of my Mother, never expecting to see her more.

It will be impossible for me at this distance, and circumstanced as I am, to give the smallest attention to the execution of her will. nor indeed is much required if, as she directs, no security should be given or appraisement made of her estate; but that the same should be allotted to the Devisees with as little trouble and delay as may be. How far this is legal I know not—Mr Mercer can, and I have no doubt would, readily advise you, if asked, which I wish you to do. If the ceremony of inventorying appraising, &ca can be dispensed with, all the rest, (as the will declares, that few or no debts are owing) can be done with very little trouble—Every person may in that case immediately receive what is specifically devised.

The Negroes who are engaged in the crop, and under an Overseer must remain I conceive on the Plantation until the crop is finished (which ought to be as soon as possible) after which the horses, stock of all sorts, and every species of property, not disposed of by the will, (the debts, if any, being first paid) must by law be equally divided into five parts, one of which you, another my Brother Charles, and a third myself, are entitled to—the other two thirds fall to the share of the children of our deceased Brothers Samuel and John. Were it not that the specific legacies which are given to me by the Will are meant, and ought to be considered and received as mementos of parental affection, in the last solemn act of life, I should not be desirous of receiving or removing them, but in this point of view I set a value on them much beyond their intrinsic worth. Whilst it occurs to me, it is necessary it should be known that there is a fellow belonging to that estate now at my house, who never stayed elsewhere, for which reason, and because he has a family I should be glad to keep him— He must I should conceive be far short in value of the fifth of the other negroes which will be to be divided, but I shall be content to take him as my proportion of them—and, if from a misconception either of the number or the value of these negroes it should be found that he is of greater value than falls to my lot I shall readily allow the difference, in order that the fellow may be gratified, as he never would consent to go from me.

Debts, if any are due, should be paid from the sale of the crops, Plantation utensils, Horses and stock; and the sooner an account is taken of the latter and they can conveniently be disposed of, the better it will be for two reasons; first because the Overseer (if he is not a very honest Man) may take advantage of circumstances, and convert part of these things to his own use—and secondly because the season is now fast approaching when without feeding (which would lessen the sale of the corn and fodder) the stock will fall off, and consequently sell to a disadvantage. Whether my Mother has kept any accounts that can be understood is more than I am able to say—If any thing is owing to her it should be received— and, if due from her, paid after due proof thereof is made— She has had a great deal of money from me at times, as can be made appear by my books, and the accounts of Mr L. Washington during my absence—and over and above this has not only had all that was ever made from the Plantation but got her provisions and every thing else she thought proper from thence. In short to the best of my recollection I have never in my life received a copper from the estate—and have paid many hundred pounds (first and last) to her in cash— However I want no retribution—I conceived it to be a duty whenever she asked for money, and I had it, to furnish her notwithstanding she got all the crops or the amount of them, and took every thing she wanted from the plantation for the support of her family, horses &ca besides.

As the accounts for or against the Estate must not only from the declaration in the will, but from the nature of the case, be very trifling and confined I should suppose to the town of Fredericksburg, it might be proper therefore in that paper to require in an advertisement all those who have any demands to bring them in properly attested immediately, and those who are owing to pay forthwith: The same advertisement might appoint a day for selling the stock, and every thing, excepting Negroes, at the plantation, that is not devised by the will, as it will be more convenient I should suppose for the heirs to receive their respective dividends of the money arising from the sales than to be troubled with receiving a cow, a calf, or such like things after the debts (which must be the case) have been first paid. It might be well in fixing the day of sale, to consult the Overseer, to know when the business of the plantation will admit the Cart, Team, and Utensils to be taken from it.

As the number of articles to be sold cannot be many and will be of small value, I think they had better be sold for ready money and so advertised, for though they would fetch more on credit, there would more than probable be bad debts contracted, and at any rate delay, if not law suits before the money could be collected, and besides if there are debts to be paid money will be wanted for the purpose, and in no way can be so readily and properly obtained as by a ready money sale, and from the crops.

If you think this business will be too troublesome for you with the aid of your sons—Mr Carter and Colonel Ball—who I am persuaded will give each of us assisstance, and you will let me know it, I will desire Major George Washington to attend.

As the land at the Little-falls Plantation goes to Mr Bushrod Washington he should be apprised in time of the breaking of it up, otherwise there may be injury to the houses and fencing if left without some person to attend to them. Have particular care taken of her papers, the letters to her &ca.

I should prefer selling the houses and lotts on which my

Mother lived to renting of them—and would give a year or two years credit to the purchasers paying interest—and not being acquainted with the value of lotts in Fredericksburg, I would leave the price to any three indifferent and impartial Gentlemen to say what they are worth, and that sum I will take.

If they cannot be sold and soon I would rent them from year to year to any orderly Tenant on a moderate rent—If they are not disposed of on sale or by tennanting before the weather gets cool the paling will, I expect, be soon burnt up.

Give my love to Mrs Carter and thank her for the letter she wrote to me—I would have done this myself had I more time for private correspondencies. Mrs Washington joins in best wishes for her, yourself, and all other friends, and I am, with the most sincere regard, Your affectionate Brother

To Arthur St. Clair

Sir,

Congress having by their Act of the 29th of September last empowered me to call forth the Militia of the States respectively, for the protection of the frontiers from the incursions of the hostile Indians, I have thought proper to make this communication to you, together with the instructions herein contained.

It is highly necessary that I should as soon as possible possess full information whether the Wabash and Illinois Indians are most inclined for war or peace—If for the former it is proper that I should be informed of the means which will most probably induce them to peace—If a peace can be established with the said indians on reasonable terms, the interests of the United States dictate that it should be effected as soon as possible.

You will therefore inform the said indians of the dispositions of the general government on this subject, and of their reasonable desire that there should be a cessation of hostilities as a prelude to a treaty—If however notwithstanding your intimations to them, they should continue their hostilities, or meditate any incursions against the frontiers of Virginia and Pennsylvania, or against any of the troops or posts of the United States, and it should appear to you the time of execution would be so near as to forbid your transmitting the information to me, and receiving my further orders thereon, then you are hereby authorised and empowered in my name to call on the Lieutenants of the nearest Counties of Virginia and Pennsylvania for such detachments of Militia as you may judge proper, not exceeding however one thousand from Virginia and five hundred from Pennsylvania.

I have directed Letters to be written to the Executives of Virginia and Pennsylvania, informing them of the before recited Act of Congress, and that I have given you these conditional directions, so that there may not be any obstructions to such measures as shall be necessary to be taken by you for calling forth the militia agreeably to the instructions herein contained.

The said militia to act in conjunction with the federal troops in such operations, offensive or defensive, as you and the Commanding officer of the troops conjointly shall judge necessary for the public service, and the protection of the inhabitants and the posts.

The said Militia while in actual service to be on the Continental establishment of pay and rations—they are to arm and equip themselves, but to be furnished with public ammunition if necessary—and no charge for the pay of said Militia will be valid unless supported by regular musters, made by a field or other Officer of the federal troops to be appointed by the commanding Officer of the troops.

I would have it observed forcibly that a War with the Wabash Indians ought to be avoided by all means consistently with the security of the frontier inhabitants, the security of the troops and the national dignity—In the exercise of the present indiscriminate hostilities, it is extremely difficult if not impossible to say that a war without further measures would be just on the part of the United States.

But if after manifesting clearly to the indians the dispositions of the general government for the preservation of peace, and the extension of a just protection to the said indians, they should continue their incursions, the United States will be constran'd to punish them with severity.

You will also proceed as soon as you can with safety to execute the orders of the late Congress, respecting the inhabitants at St Vincennes and at the Kaskaskies, and the other Villages on the Mississippi—It is a circumstance of some importance that the said inhabitants should as soon as possible possess the lands to which they are entitled by some known and fixed principles.

I have directed a number of copies of the treaty made by you at Fort Harmar with the Wyandots &c: on the 9th of January last to be printed, and forwarded to you, together with the ratification, and my Proclamation enjoining the observance thereof.

As it may be of high importance to obtain a precise and accurate knowledge of the several Waters which empty into the Ohio on the North West—and of those which discharge themselves into the lakes Erie and Michigan; the length of the portages between, and the nature of the ground, an early and pointed attention thereto is earnestly recommended. Given under my hand in the City of New-York, this 6th day of October, in the year of our Lord One thousand seven hundred and eighty nine, and in the thirteenth year of the sovereignty and Independence of the United States.

October 6, 1789

To Gouverneur Morris

Dear Sir,   New York, October 13th 1789.

In my first moments of leisure I acknowledge the receipt of your several favors of the 23 of February, 3 of March and 29 of April.

To thank you for the interesting communications contained in those letters, and for the pains you have taken to procure me a watch, is all, or nearly all I shall attempt in this letter— for I could only repeat things, were I to set about it, which I have reason to believe have been regularly communicated to you in detail, at the periods which gave birth to them.

It may not however be unpleasing to you to hear in one word that the national government is organized, and as far as my information goes, to the satisfaction of all parties—That opposition to it is either no more, or hides its head.

That it is hoped and expected it will take strong root, and that the non acceding States will very soon become members of the union—No doubt is entertained of North Carolina, nor would there be of Rhode Island had not the majority of that People bid adieu, long since to every principle of honor—common sense, and honesty. A material change however has taken place, it is said, at the late election of representatives, and confident assurances are given from that circumstance of better dispositions in their Legislature at its next session, now about to be held.

The revolution which has been effected in France is of so wonderful a nature that the mind can hardly realise the fact—If it ends as our last accounts to the first of August predict that nation will be the most powerful and happy in Europe; but I fear though it has gone triumphantly through the first paroxysm, it is not the last it has to encounter before matters are finally settled.

In a word the revolution is of too great magnitude to be effected in so short a space, and with the loss of so little blood—The mortification of the King, the intrigues of the Queen, and the discontents of the Princes, and the Noblesse will foment divisions, if possible, in the national assembly, and avail themselves of every faux pas in the formation of the constitution if they do not give a more open, active opposition.

To these the licentiousness of the People on one hand and sanguinary punishments on the other will alarm the best disposed friends to the measure, and contribute not a little to the overthrow of their object—Great temperance, firmness, and foresight are necessary in the movements of that Body. To forbear running from one extreme to another is no easy matter, and should this be the case, rocks and shelves not visible at present may wreck the vessel.

This letter is an evidence, though of a trifling sort, that in the commencement of any work one rarely sees the progress or end of it. I declared to you in the beginning that I had little to say. I have got beyond the second page, and find I have a good deal to add; but that no time or paper may be wasted in a useless preface I will come to the point.

Will you then, my good Sir, permit me to ask the favor of you to provide and send to me by the first Ship, bound to this place, or Philadelphia mirrors for a table, with neat and fashionable but not expensive ornaments for them—such as will do credit to your taste—The mirrors will of course be in pieces that they may be adapted to the company, (the size of it I mean) the aggregate length of them may be ten feet—the breadth two feet—The panes may be plated ware, or any thing else more fashionable but not more expensive. If I am defective recur to what you have seen on Mr Robert Morris's table for my ideas *generally*. Whether these things can be had on better terms and in a better style in Paris than in London I will not undertake to decide. I recollect however to have had plated ware from both places, and those from the latter came cheapest—but a single instance is no evidence of a general fact.

Of plated ware may be made I conceive handsome and useful Coolers for wine *at* and *after* dinner. Those I am in need of viz. *eight* double ones (for madeira and claret the wines usually drank at dinner) each of the apertures to be sufficient to contain a pint decanter, with an allowance in the depth of it for ice at bottom so as to raise the neck of the decanter above the cooler—between the apertures a handle is to be placed by which these double coolers may with convenience be removed from one part of the table to another. For the wine *after* dinner *four* quadruple coolers will be necessary each aperture of which to be of the size of a *quart* decanter or quart bottle for four sorts of wine—These decanters or bottles to have ice at bottom, and to be elevated thereby as above—a central handle here also will be wanting—Should my description be defective your imagination is fertile and on this I shall rely. One idea however I must impress you with and that is in whole or part to avoid extravagance. For extravagance would not comport with my own inclination, nor with the example which ought to be set—The reason why I prefer an aperture for *every* decanter or bottle to coolers that would contain two and four is that whether full or empty the bottles will always stand upright and never be at variance with each other.

The letter enclosed with your draught accompanying it will provide the means for payment—The clumsy manner in which Merchants (or rather their Tradesmen) execute commissions, where taste is required, for persons at a distance must be my apology, and the best that can be offered by Dear Sir Your most obedient and affecte humble Servant

Mrs Washington presents her compliments to you.
P.S. I was in the very act of sealing this letter when yours of the 31st of July from Dieppe was put into my hands—accept my sincere thanks for the important communications contained in it, and for the tables which accompanied. I shall add no more now, except that in the morning I commence a tour, though rather late in the season, through the States eastward of this. Adieu, yours

First Annual Message to Congress

United States January 8th 1790
Fellow Citizens of the Senate, and House of Representatives.

I embrace with great satisfaction the opportunity, which now presents itself, of congratulating you on the present favourable prospects of our public affairs. The recent accession of the important State of North Carolina to the Constitution of the United States (of which official information has been recieved)—the rising credit and respectability of our Country—the general and increasing good will towards the Government of the Union—and the concord, peace and plenty, with which we are blessed, are circumstances, auspicious, in an eminent degree to our national prosperity.

In resuming your consultations for the general good, you cannot but derive encouragement from the reflection, that the measures of the last Session have been as satisfactory to your Constituents, as the novelty and difficulty of the work allowed you to hope. Still further to realize their expectations, and to secure the blessings which a Gracious Providence has placed within our reach, will in the course of the present important Session, call for the cool and deliberate exertion of your patriotism, firmness and wisdom.

Among the many interesting objects, which will engage your attention, that of providing for the common defence will merit particular regard. To be prepared for war is one of the most effectual means of preserving peace.

A free people ought not only to be armed but disciplined; to which end a Uniform and well digested plan is requisite: And their safety and interest require that they should promote such manufactories, as tend to render them independent on others, for essential, particularly for military supplies.

The proper establishment of the Troops which may be deemed indispensible, will be entitled to mature consideration. In the arrangements which may be made respecting it, it will be of importance to conciliate the comfortable support of the Officers and Soldiers with a due regard to œconomy.

There was reason to hope, that the pacific measures adopted with regard to certain hostile tribes of Indians would have relieved the inhabitants of our Southern and Western frontiers from their depredations. But you will percieve, from the information contained in the papers, which I shall direct to be laid before you (comprehending a communication from the Commonwealth of Virginia) that we ought to be prepared to afford protection to those parts of the Union; and, if necessary, to punish aggressors.

The interests of the United States require, that our intercourse with other nations should be facilitated by such provisions as will enable me to fulfil my duty in that respect, in the manner, which circumstances may render most conducive to the public good: And to this end, that the compensations to be made to the persons, who may be employed, should, according to the nature of their appointments, be defined by law; and a competent fund designated for defraying the expenses incident to the conduct of foreign affairs.

Various considerations also render it expedient, that the terms on which foreigners may be admitted to the rights of Citizens, should be speedily ascertained by a uniform rule of naturalization.

Uniformity in the Currency, Weights and Measures of the United States is an object of great importance, and will, I am persuaded, be duly attended to.

The advancement of Agriculture, commerce and Manufactures, by all proper means, will not, I trust, need recommendation. But I cannot forbear intimating to you the expediency of giving effectual encouragement as well to the introduction of new and useful inventions from abroad, as to the exertions of skill and genius in producing them at home; and of facilitating the intercourse between the distant parts of our Country by a due attention to the Post-Office and Post Roads.

Nor am I less pursuaded, that you will agree with me in opinion, that there is nothing, which can better deserve your patronage, than the promotion of Science and Literature. Knowledge is in every Country the surest basis of public happiness. In one, in which the measures of Government recieve their impression so immediately from the sense of the Community as in our's, it is proportionably essential. To the security of a free Constitution it contributes in various ways: By convincing those, who are entrusted with the public administration, that every valuable end of Government is best answered by the enlightened confidence of the people: And by teaching the people themselves to know and to value their own rights; to discern and provide against invasions of them; to distinguish between oppression and the necessary exercise of lawful authority; between burthens proceeding from a disregard to their convenience and those resulting from the inevitable exigencies of Society; to discriminate the spirit of liberty from that of licentiousness, cherishing the first, avoiding the last, and uniting a speedy, but temperate vigilence against encroachments, with an inviolable respect to the laws.

Whether this desirable object will be best promoted by affording aids to Seminaries of Learning already established—by the institution of a national University—or by any other expedients, will be well worthy of a place in the deliberations of the Legislature.

Gentlemen of the House of Representatives.

I saw with peculiar pleasure, at the close of the last Session, the resolution entered into by you expressive of your opinion, that an adequate provision for the support of the public Credit is a matter of high importance to the national honor and prosperity. In this sentiment, I entirely concur. And to a perfect confidence in your best endeavours to divise such a provision, as will be truly consistent with the end, I add an equal reliance on the chearful co-operation of the other branch of the Legislature. It would be superfluous to specify inducements to a measure in which the character and permanent interests of the United States are so obviously and so deeply concerned; and which has recieved so explicit a sanction from your declaration.

Gentlemen of the Senate and House of Representatives.

I have directed the proper Officers to lay before you respectively such papers and estimates as regard the affairs particularly recommended to your consideration, and necessary to convey to you that information of the state of the Union, which it is my duty to afford.

The welfare of our Country is the great object to which our cares and efforts ought to be directed. And I shall derive great satisfaction from a co-operation with you, in the pleasing though arduous task of ensuring to our fellow Citizens the blessings, which they have a right to expect, from a free, efficient and equal Government.

To Catharine Macaulay Graham

Madam,   New York Jany 9th 1790

Your obliging letter, dated in October last, has been received; and, as I do not know when I shall have more Leisure than at present to throw together a few observations in return for yours, I take up my Pen to do it by this early occasion.

In the first place, I thank you for your congratulatory sentiments on the event which has placed me at the head of the American Government; as well as for the indulgent partiality, which it is to be feared however, may have warped your judgment too much in my favor. But you do me no more than Justice, in supposing that, if I had been permitted to indulge my first & fondest wish, I should have remained in a private Station. Although, neither the present age or Posterity may possibly give me full credit for the feelings which I have experienced on this subject; yet I have a consciousness, that nothing short of an absolute conviction of duty could ever have brought me upon the scenes of public life again. The establishment of our new Government seemed to be the last great experiment, for promoting human happiness, by reasonable compact, in civil Society. It was to be, in the first instance, in a considerable degree, a government of accomodation as well as a government of Laws. Much was to be done by *prudence*, much by *conciliation*, much by *firmness*. Few, who are not philosophical Spectators, can realise the difficult and delicate part which a man in my situation had to act. All see, and most admire, the glare which hovers round the external trappings of elevated Office. To me, there is nothing in it, beyond the lustre which may be reflected from its connection with a power of promoting human felicity. In our progress towards political happiness my station is new; and, if I may use the expression, I walk on untrodden ground. There is scarcely any action, whose motives may not be subject to a double interpretation. There is scarcely any part of my conduct wch may not hereafter be drawn into precedent. Under such a view of the duties inherent to my arduous office, I could not but feel a diffidence in myself on the one hand; and an anxiety for the Community that every new arrangement should be made in the best possible manner on the other. If after all my humble but faithful endeavours to advance the felicity of my Country & Mankind; I may endulge a hope that my labours have not been altogether without success, it will be the only real compensation I can receive in the closing Scenes of life.

On the actual situation of this Country, under its new Government, I will, in the next place, make a few remarks. That the Government, though not absolutely perfect, is one of the best in the World, I have little doubt. I always believed that an unequivocally free & equal Representation of the People in the Legislature; together with an efficient & responsable Executive were the great Pillars on which the preservation of American Freedom must depend. It was indeed next to a Miracle that there should have been so much unanimity, in points of such importance, among such a number of Citizens, so widely scattered and so different in their habits in many respects, as the Americans were. Nor are the growing unanimity and encreasing good will of the Citizens to the Government less remarkable than favorable circumstances. So far as we have gone with the new Government (and it is completely organized and in operation) we have had greater reason than the most sanguine could expect to be satisfied with its success. Perhaps a number of accidental circumstances have concurred with the real effects of the Government to make the People uncommonly well pleased with their situation and prospects. The harvests of Wheat have been remarkably good—the demand for that article from abroad is great—the encrease of Commerce is visible in every Port—and the number of new Manufactures introduced in one year is astonishing. I have lately made a tour through the Eastern States. I found the Country, in a great degree, recovered from the ravages of War—the Towns flourishing—& the People delighted with a government instituted by themselves & for their own good. The same facts I have also reason to believe, from good authority, exist in the Southern States.

By what I have just observed, I think you will be persuaded that the ill-boding Politicians, who prognosticated that America would never enjoy any fruits from her Independence & that She would be obliged to have recourse to a foreign Power for protection, have at least been mistaken. I shall sincerely rejoice to see that the American Revolution has been productive of happy consequences on both sides of the Atlantic. The renovation of the French Constitution is indeed one of the most wonderful events in the history of Mankind: and the agency of the Marquis de la Fayette in a high degree honorable to his character. My greatest fear has been, that the Nation would not be sufficiently cool & moderate in making arrangements for the security of that liberty, of which it seems to be fully possessed.

Mr Warville, the French Gentleman you mention, has been in America & at Mount Vernon; but has returned, sometime since to France.

Mrs Washington is well and desires her Compliments may be presented to you. We wish the happiness of your fire side;

as we also long to enjoy that of our own at Mount Vernon. Our wishes, you know, were limited; and I think that our plans of living will now be deemed reasonable by the considerate part of our species. Her wishes coincide with my own as to simplicity of dress, and every thing which can tend to support propriety of character without partaking of the follies of luxury and ostentation. I am with great regard Madam. Your Most Obedient and Most Humble Servant

To Thomas Jefferson

Dear Sir   New York Jany 21st 1790

I had the pleasure to receive duly your letter dated the 15th of Decr last; but I thought proper to delay answering or mentioning the contents of it, until after the arrival of Mr Madison, who I understood had been with you. He arrived yesterday, and I now take the earliest opportunity of mentioning to you the result of my reflections; and the expediency of your deciding, at as early a period as may consist with your convenience, on the important subject before you.

Previous to any remarks on the nature of the Office to which you have been recently appointed, I will premise, that I feel such delicacy & embarrassment in consequence of the footing on which you have placed your final determination, as to make it necessary for me to recur to the first ground on which I rested the matter. In confidence, therefore, I will tell you plainly that I wish not to oppose your inclinations; and that, after you shall have been made a little farther acquainted with the light in which I view the Office of Secretary of State, it must be at your option to determine relative to your acceptance of it, or continuance in your Office abroad.

I consider the successful Administration of the general Government as an object of almost infinite consequence to the present and future happiness of the Citizens of the United States. I consider the Office of Secretary for the Department of State as *very* important on many accts: and I know of no person, who, in my judgment, could better execute the Duties of it than yourself. Its duties will probably be not quite so arduous & complicated in their execution, as you might have been led at the first moment to imagine. At least, it was the opinion of Congress, that, after the division of all the business of a domestic nature between the Department of the Treasury, War and State, that those wch would be comprehended in the latter might be performed by the same Person, who should have the charge of conducting the Department of foreign Affairs. The experiment was to be made; and if it shall be found that the fact is different, I have little doubt that a farther arrangement or division of the business in the Office of the Department of State will be made, in such manner as to enable it to be performed, under the superintendance of one man, with facility to himself, as well as with advantage & satisfaction to the Public. These observations, however, you will be pleased to remark are merely matters of opinion. But, in order that you may be the better prepared to make your ultimate decision on good grounds, I think it necessary to add one fact, which is this, so far as I have been able to obtain information from all quarters, your late appointment has given very extensive and very great satisfaction to the Public. My original opinion & wish may be collected from my nomination.

As to what you mention in the latter part of your letter, I can only observe, I do not know that any alteration is likely to take place in the Commission from the United States to the Court of France. The necessary arrangements with regard to our intercourse with Foreign Nations have never yet been taken up on a great scale by the Government: because the Department which comprehended affairs of that nature has never been properly organised, so as to bring the business well and systematically before the Executive. If you shd finally determine to take upon yourself the duties of the Department of State, it would be highly requisite for you to come on immediately, as many things are required to be done while Congress is in Session rather than at any other time; and as, in that case, your presence might doubtless be much better dispensed with after a little time than at the present moment. Or, in all events, it will be essential that I should be informed of your conclusive option, so that, if you return to France, another Person may be, at as early a day as possible, nominated to fill the Department of State. With sentiments of the highest regard and esteem I am, Dear Sir Your Most Obedt Hble Servt

To David Stuart

Dear Sir,   New York March 28th 1790.
    Your letter of the 15th enclosing the Act of Assembly authorising an agreement with Mr Alexander came to my hand in the moment my last to you was dispatched.

I am sorry such jealousies as you relate should be gaining ground, & poisoning the minds of the Southern people. But, admit the fact which is alledged as the cause of them, and give it full scope, does it amount to more than what was known to every man of information before, at, and since the adoption of the Constitution? Was it not always believed that there are some points which peculiarly interest the Eastern States? And did any one who reads human nature, & more especially the character of the Eastern people, conceive that they would not pursue them steadily by a combination of their force? Are there not other points which equally concern the Southern States? If these States are less tenacious of their interest, or, if whilst the Eastern move in a solid phalanx to effect their purposes, the Southern are always divided, which of the two is most to be blamed? That there is diversity of interests in the Union none has denied. That this is the case also in every State is equally certain—and that it extends even to Counties, can be as readily proved. Instance the Southern & Northern parts of Virginia—the upper & lower parts of So. Carolina &ca—have not the interests of these always been at varience? Witness the County of Fairfax, has not the interests of the people thereof varied, or the Inhabitants been taught to believe so? These are well known truths, and yet it did not follow that seperation was to result from the disagreement.

To constitute a dispute there must be two parties. To understand it well both the parties & all the circumstances must be fully understood. And to accomodate differences good temper & mutual forbearance is requisite. Common danger brought the States into Confederacy, and on their Union our safety & importance depend. A spirit of accomodation was the basis of the present Constitution; can it be expected then that the Southern or the Eastern part of the Empire will succeed in all their Measures? certainly not. but I will readily grant that more points will be carried by the latter than the former, and for the reason which has been mentioned—namely—that in all great national questions they move in unison, whilst the others are divided; but I ask again which is most blameworthy, those who see & will steadily pursue their interests, or those who cannot see, or seeing, will not act wisely? and I will ask another question (of the highest magnitude in my mind) and that is, if the Eastern & Northern States are dangerous *in Union*, will they be less so *in seperation*? If self interest is their governing principle, will it forsake them, or be less restrained by such an event? I hardly think it would. Then, independent of other considerations what would Virginia (and such other States as might be inclined to join her) gain by a seperation? Would they not, most unquestionably, be the weaker party?

Men who go from hence without *feeling* themselves of so much consequence as they wished to be considered—disappointed expectants—and malignant designing characters that miss no opportunity to aim a blow at the Constitution, paint highly on one side without bringing into view the arguments which are offered on the other. It is to be lamented that the Editors of the several Gazettes of the Union do not more generally & more connectedly publish the debates in Congress on all great National questions that affect different interests instead of stuffing their papers with scurrility & malignant declamation, which few would read if they were apprised of the contents. That they might do this with very little trouble is certain. The principles upon which the difference in opinion arises, as well as the decision, would, in that case, come fully before the public, & afford the best data for its judgment.

Mr Madison, on the question of discrimination, was actuated, I am persuaded, by the purest motives; & most heartfelt conviction; but the Subject was delicate, & perhaps had better not have been stirred. The assumption of the State debts by the United States is another subject that has given birth to long and laboured debates without having yet taken a final form. The Memorial of the Quakers (& a very mal-apropos one it was) has at length been put to sleep, from which it is not [   ] it will awake before the year 1808. With much truth I am Sir Yr Affecte Hble Servt

To Comte de la Luzerne

Sir.   New York April 29th 1790.
    Your letter of the 17th of Janry, replete with politeness to myself & useful informations respecting public affairs, has but lately been received.
    In making my acknowledgments for the distinguished place I hold in your remembrance & for the obliging terms in which you allude to my conduct in war & peace; I should do injustice to conceal the favorable sentiments which were always entertained by myself & my Countrymen of your private deportment, & ministerial agency, while you resided in America. Those times, in which we always found you a sincere friend, were truly times of peril & distress. Now our situation is indeed much more eligible, & our prospects perhaps as good as could reasonably have been expected. We are recovering slowly from the calamities & burdens with which we were almost overwhelmed by a long & expensive war. Our Crops the year past have been more abundant, & our markets much better than usual. These circumstances will assist in enabling our Citizens to extricate themselves from their private & public debts. I hope a disposition will be found to prevail among us, for doing justice (as far as the nature of the case will admit) to all who afforded us their assistance in the hour of adversity. In the arrangement of such new & complicated business, as must inevitably come before our general Government, it is reasonably to be expected, that the proceedings will be slow— It is devoutly to be wished that they may terminate in such just & wise measures, as will fully establish our happiness at home & credit abroad. I am much pleased with the interest you take in our national reputation, and the information you

give that our credit is becoming so respectable in Europe, under the influence of our new Government.

You are right in conceiving that nothing can be indifferent to me, which regards the welfare of the French Nation. So far removed from that great Theatre of political action, & so little acquainted with many of the minute circumstances which may induce important decisions, as I am; it would be imprudent for me to hazard opinions which might possibly be unfounded. Indeed the whole business is so extraordinary in its commencement, so wonderful in its progress & may be so stupendous in its consequences, that I am almost lost in the contemplation. Of one thing, however, you may rest perfectly assured, that nobody is more anxious for the happy issue of that business than I am; as nobody can wish more sincerely for the prosperity of the French Nation than I do. Nor is it without the most sensible pleasure I learn, that our friend the Marquis de la Fayette, has, in acting the arduous part which has fallen to his share, conducted himself with so much wisdom & apparently to such general satisfaction.

We, at this great distance from the northern parts of Europe, hear of wars & rumours of wars—as if they were the events or reports of another Planet. What changes the death of the Emperor will occasion in the other Cabinets of Europe, time is yet to inform us. A spirit for political improvements seems to be rapidly & extensively spreading through many of the European Countries. I shall rejoice in seeing the condition of the Human Race happier than ever it has hitherto been. But I should be sorry to see, that those who are for prematurely accelerating those improvements, were making *more haste than good speed*, in their innovations. So much prudence, so much perseverance, so much disinterestedness & so much patriotism are necessary among the Leaders of a Nation, in order to promote the national felicity, that sometimes my fears nearly preponderate over my expectations. Better, however, will it be for me to leave such foreign matters to those who are more competent to manage them: and to do as much good as I can, in the little sphere where I am destined to move at present. With sentiments of the highest esteem & consideration I have the honor to be Your Excellency's &c. &c. &c.

To David Stuart

Dear Sir,   New York June 15th 1790

Your letter of the 2d Instant came duly to hand. If there are any Gazettes among my files at Mount Vernon which can be of use to you they are at your Service.

Your description of the public mind, in Virginia, gives me pain. It seems to be more irritable, sour & discontented than (from the information I receive) it is in any other state in the Union, except Massachusetts; which, from the same causes, but on quite different principles, is tempered like it.

That Congress does not proceed with all that dispatch which people at a distance expect; and which, were they to hurry business, they possibly might; is not to be denied. That measures have been agitated wch are not pleasing to Virginia; and others, pleasing perhaps to her, but not so to some other States; is equally unquestionable. Can it well be otherwise in a Country so extensive, so diversified in its interests? And will not these different interests naturally produce in an assembly of Representatives who are to Legislate for, and to assimilate & reconcile them to the general welfare, long, warm & animated debates? most undoubtedly; and if there was the same propensity in Mankind to investigate the motives, as there is for censuring the conduct of public characters, it would be found that the censure so freely bestowed is oftentimes unmerited, and uncharitable—for instance, the condemnation of Congress for sitting only four hours in the day. The fact is, by the established rules of the House of Representatives, no Committee can sit whilst the House is sitting; and this is, and has been for a considerable time, from ten o'clock in the forenoon until three, often later, in the afternoon, before & after which the business is going on in Committees—If this application is not as much as most Constitutions are equal to I am mistaken. Many other things which undergo malignant constructions wd be found, upon a candid examination, to wear other faces than are given to them. The misfortune is, that the enemies to the Government—always more active than its friends, and always upon the watch to give it a stroke—neglect no opportunity to aim one. If they tell truth, it is not the whole truth; by which means one side only of the picture appears; whereas if both sides were exhibited it might, and probably would assume a different form in the opinions of just & candid men who are disposed to measure matters by a Continental Scale. I do not mean however, from what I have here said, to justify the conduct of Congress in all its movements; for some of these movements in my opinion, have been injudicious, & others unseasonable, whilst the questions of assumption—Residence—and other matters have been agitated with a warmth & intemperence; with prolixity & threats; which it is to be feared has lessened the dignity of that body, & decreased that respect which was once entertained for it. And this misfortune is encreased by many members, even among those who wish well to the Government, ascribing in letters to their respective States when they are unable to carry a favourite measure, the worst motives for the conduct of their opponants; who, viewing matters through a different medium may, & do retort in their turn; by which means jealousies & distrusts are spread most impolitickly, far & wide; & will, it is to be feared have a most unhappy tendency to injure our public affairs—which, if wisely conducted might make us (as we are now by Europeans thought to be) the happiest people upon Earth. As an evidence of it, our reputation has risen in every part of the Globe; and our credit, especially in Holland, has got higher than that of *any* Nation in Europe (& where our funds are above par) as appears by *Official* advices just received. But the conduct we seem to be pursuing will soon bring us back to our late disreputable condition.

The introductions of the (Quaker) Memorial, respecting Slavery, was to be sure, not only an ill-judged piece of business, but occasioned a great waste of time. The final decision thereon, however, was as favourable as the proprietors of that species of property could well have expected considering the great dereliction to Slavery in a large part of this Union.

The question of assumption has occupied a great deal of time, & no wonder; for it is certainly a very important one; and, under *proper* restrictions, & scrutiny into accounts will be found, I conceive, to be just. The Cause in which the expences of the War was incurred, was a Common Cause. The States (in Congress) declared it so at the beginning, and pledged themselves to stand by each other. If then, some States were harder pressed than others, or from particular or local circumstances contracted heavier debts, it is but reasonable when this fact is ascertained (though it is a sentiment I have not made known here) that an allowance ought to be made them when due credit is given to others—Had the invaded, and hard pressed States believed the case would have been otherwise; opposition in them would very soon, I believe, have changed to submission; and given a different termination to the War.

In a letter of last year to the best of my recollection, I informed you of the motives, which *compelled* me to allot a day for the reception of idle and ceremonious visits (for it never has prevented those of sociability and friendship in the afternoon, or at any other time) but if I am mistaken in this, the history of this business is simply and shortly as follows—Before the custom was established, which now accommodates foreign characters, Strangers, and others who from motives of curiosity, respect, to the Chief Magistrate, or any other cause, are induced to call upon me—I was unable to attend to any business *whatsoever*; for Gentlemen, consulting their own convenience rather than mine, were calling from the time I rose from breakfast—often before—until I sat down to dinner—This, as I resolved not to neglect my public duties, reduced me to the choice of one of these alternatives, either to refuse them *altogether*, or to appropriate a time for the reception of them—The first would, I well knew, be disgusting to many—The latter, *I expected*, would undergo animadversion, and blazoning from those who would find fault, *with*, or *without* cause. To please every body was impossible—I therefore adopted that line of conduct which combined public advantage with private convenience, and which in my judgment was unexceptionable in itself. That I have not been able to make bows to the taste of poor Colonel Bland, (who by the by I believe never saw one of them) is to be regretted especially too as (upon those occasions) they were indiscriminately bestowed, and the best I was master of—would it not have been better to have thrown the veil of charity over them, ascribing their stiffness to the effects of age, or to the unskilfulness of my teacher, than to pride and dignity of office, which God knows has no charms for me? for I can truly say I had rather be at Mount Vernon with a friend or two about me, than to be attended at the Seat of Government by the Officers of State and the Representatives of every Power in Europe—These visits are optional—They are made without invitation—Between the hours of three and four every Tuesday I am prepared to receive them—Gentlemen—often in great numbers—come and go—chat with each other—and act as they please. A Porter shews them into the room, and they retire from it when they please, and without ceremony. At their *first* entrance they salute me, and I them, and as many as I can talk to I do— what pomp there is in all this I am unable to discover— Perhaps it consists in not sitting—To this two reasons are opposed, first it is unusual—secondly, (which is a more substantial one) because I have no room large enough to contain a third of the chairs, which would be sufficient to admit it—If it is supposed that ostentation, or the fashions of courts (which by the by I believe originates oftener in convenience, not to say necessity than is generally imagined) gave rise to this custom, I will boldly affirm that *no* supposition was ever more erroneous; for, if I was to give indulgence to my inclinations, every moment that I could withdraw from the fatigues of my station should be spent in retirement—That they are not proceeds from the sense I entertain of the propriety of giving to every one as free access, as consists with that respect which is due to the chair of government—and that respect I conceive is neither to be acquired or preserved but by observing a just medium between much state and too great familiarity.

Similar to the above, but of a more familiar and sociable kind are the visits every friday afternoon to Mrs Washington where I always am—These public meetings and a dinner once a week to as many as my table will hold with the references *to* and *from* the different Departments of State, and *other* communications with *all* parts of the Union is as much, if not more, than I am able to undergo, for I have already had within less than a year, two *severe* attacks—the last worse than the first—a third more than probable will put me to sleep with my fathers; at what distance this may be I know not. Within the last twelve months I have undergone more, and severer sickness than thirty preceding years afflicted me with, put it altogether—I have abundant reason however to be thankful that I am so well recovered; though I still feel the remains of the violent affection of my lungs—The cough, pain in my breast, and shortness in breathing not having entirely left me. I propose in the recess of Congress to visit Mount Vernon— but when this recess will happen is beyond my ken, or the ken I believe of any of its members. I am dear Sir &ca

To Marquis de Lafayette

My dear Marquis,   New York August 11th 1790.
    I have received your affectionate letter of the 17 of March by one conveyance, and the token of victory gained by Liberty over Despotism by another: for both which testimonials of your friendship and regard I pray you to accept my sincerest thanks.

In this great subject of triumph for the new World, and for humanity in general, it will never be forgotten how conspicuous a part you bore, and how much lustre you reflected on a country in which you made the first displays of character.

Happy am I, my good friend, that, amidst all the tremendous benefits which have assailed your political Ship, you have had address and fortitude enough to steer her hitherto safely through the quick-sands and rocks, which threatened instant destruction on every side; and your young King in all things seems so well disposed to conform to the wishes of the Nation. In such an important, such a hazardous voyage, when every thing dear and sacred is embarked, you know full well my best wishes have never left you for a moment—Yet I will avow the accounts we received through the English papers (which were sometimes our only channels for information) caused our fears of a failure almost to exceed our expectations of success. How much will the *Concerned* be indebted to the exertions of the principal Pilot, when the Ship shall, at the end of her dangerous course, be securely harboured in the haven of national tranquillity, freedom, and glory, to which she is destined, and which I hope she is near attaining.

Congress, after having been in session ever since last fall, are to adjourn in two or three days. Though they have been much perplexed and delayed in their proceedings on some questions of a local and intricate nature; yet they have done a great deal of important business, and will leave the public affairs in as satisfactory a state as could reasonably have been expected. One of the last acts of the executive has been the conclusion of a treaty of Peace and Friendship with the Creek Nation of Indians, who have been considerably connected with the Spanish Provinces and hostile to the Georgian frontiers since the war with Great Britain. McGillivray and about thirty of the Kings and Head Men are here: This event will leave us in peace from one end of our borders to the other; except where it may be interrupted by a small refugee banditti of Cherokees and Shawanese, who can be easily chastised or even extirpated if it shall become necessary: But this will only be done in an inevitable extremity; since the *basis* of our proceedings with the Indian Nations has been, and shall be *justice*, during the period in which I may have any thing to do in the administration of this government.

Our negotiations and transactions, though many of them are on a small scale as to the objects, ought to be governed by the immutable principles of equity, as much as your European politics, which are more extended in their compass. How your wars proceed in the North or in whose favor they are likely to terminate; what probability there may be that the misunderstandings between Britain and Spain should issue in an open rupture, and what other powerful nations, in that event, will be drawn in to take an active part on one side or the other, are subjects of vast magnitude, on which we, in these distant regions, must abstain from deciding positively even in our own minds, until we shall have more unequivocal data to go upon. It seems to be our policy to keep in the situation in which nature has placed us, to observe a strict neutrality, and to furnish others with those good things of subsistence, which they may want, and which our fertile land abundantly produces, if circumstances and events will permit us so to do. This letter is committed to Colonel Humphreys to carry to London, whither he is going. Should he, by any accident be in France, he will be able to give you a full state of our affairs and prospects. Gradually recovering from the distresses in which the war left us, patiently advancing in our task of civil government, unentangled in the crooked politics of Europe, wanting scarcely any thing but the free navigation of the Mississippi (which we must have and as certainly shall have as we remain a Nation)—I have supposed, that, with the undeviating exercise of a just, steady, and prudent national policy, we shall be the gainers, whether the powers of the old world may be in peace or war; but more especially in the latter case. In that case our importance will certainly encrease, and our friendship be courted. Our dispositions would not be indifferent to Britain or Spain. Why will not Spain be wise and liberal at once? It would be easy to annihilate all causes of quarrels between that Nation and the United States at this time. At a future period that may be far from being a fact. Should a war take place between Great Britain and Spain, I conceive from a great variety of concurring circumstances there is the highest probability that the Floridas will soon be in the possession of the former. Adieu, my dear Marquis! Believe me to be assuredly and affectionately Your friend and humble Servant

P.S. Not for the value of the thing, my dear Marquis, but as a memorial and because they are the manufacture of this City, I send you herewith a pair of shoe buckles.

To the Hebrew Congregation in Newport, Rhode Island

Gentlemen

While I receive, with much satisfaction, your Address replete with expressions of affection and esteem; I rejoice in the opportunity of assuring you, that I shall always retain a grateful remembrance of the cordial welcome I experienced in my visit to Newport, from all classes of Citizens.

The reflection on the days of difficulty and danger which are past is rendered the more sweet, from a consciousness that they are succeeded by days of uncommon prosperity and security. If we have wisdom to make the best use of the advantages with which we are now favored, we cannot fail, under the just administration of a good Government, to become a great and a happy people.

The Citizens of the United States of America have a right to applaud themselves for having given to mankind examples of an enlarged and liberal policy: a policy worthy of imitation. All possess alike liberty of conscience and immunities of citizenship. It is now no more that toleration is spoken of, as if it was by the indulgence of one class of people, that another enjoyed the exercise of their inherent natural rights. For happily the Government of the United States, which gives to bigotry no sanction, to persecution no assistance requires only that they who live under its protection should demean themselves as good citizens, in giving it on all occasions their effectual support.

It would be inconsistent with the frankness of my character not to avow that I am pleased with your favorable opinion of my Administration, and fervent wishes for my felicity. May the Children of the Stock of Abraham, who dwell in this land, continue to merit and enjoy the good will of the other Inhabitants; while every one shall sit in safety under his own vine and figtree, and there shall be none to make him afraid. May the father of all mercies scatter light and not darkness in our paths, and make us all in our several vocations useful here, and in his own due time and way everlastingly happy.

August 18, 1790

To Henry Knox

(Private)

My dear Sir,   Mount Vernon Novr 19th 1790.

I have received your letter of the 10th instt, and will declare to you without reserve, that my forebodings with respect to the Expedition against the Wabash Indians are of disappointment; and a disgraceful termination under the conduct of B. Genl Harmer.

I expected *little* from the moment I heard he was *a drunk-ard*. I expected *less* as soon as I heard that on *this account* no confidence was reposed in him by the people of the Western Country—And I gave up *all hope* of Success, as soon as I heard that there were disputes with *him* about command.

The latter information is from report *only*; but the report of *bad* news is rarely without foundation. If the issue of this Expedition is honorable to the Concerters of it, & favorable to our *Arms*, it will be *double* pleasing to me; but my mind, from the silence which reigns, and other circumstances, is prepared for the worst; that is—for expence without honor or profit.

If any thing *more* than the statement of *this* business for the information of Congress should occur to you, previous to my arrival, be so good as to digest it, for it is my wish to have every matter which may occur to the heads of Departments as well as to myself, ready, if proper to lay before that body, at the opening of the Session. With sincere friendship, & affecte regard I am—ever Yrs

P.S. I expect to commence my journey for Philadelphia on Monday—but from the State of the Roads after the incessant and heavy rains which have fallen, my progress must be slow.

Second Annual Message to Congress

Fellow citizens of the Senate and House of Representatives: In meeting you again I feel much satisfaction in being able to repeat my congratulations on the favorable prospects which continue to distinguish our public Affairs. The abundant fruits of another year have blessed our Country with plenty, and with the means of a flourishing commerce. The progress of public credit is witnessed by a considerable rise of American Stock abroad as well as at home. And the revenues allotted for this and other national purposes, have been productive beyond the calculations by which they were regulated. This latter circumstance is the more pleasing as it is not only a proof of the fertility of our resources, but as it assures us of a further increase of the national respectability and credit; and let me add, as it bears an honorable testimony to the patriotism and integrity of the mercantile and marine part of our Citizens. The punctuality of the former in discharging their engagements has been exemplary.

In conforming to the powers vested in me by acts of the last Session, a loan of three millions of florins, towards which some provisional measures had previously taken place, has been completed in Holland. As well the celerity with which it has been filled, as the nature of the terms, (considering the more than ordinary demand for borrowing created by the situation of Europe) gives a reasonable hope that the further execution of those powers may proceed with advantage and success. The Secretary of the Treasury has my directions to communicate such further particulars as may be requisite for more precise information.

Since your last Sessions, I have received communications by which it appears, that the District of Kentucky, at present a part of Virginia, has concurred in certain propositions contained in a law of that State; in consequence of which the District is to become a distinct member of the Union, in case the requisite sanction of Congress be added. For this sanction application is now made. I shall cause the papers on this very important transaction to be laid before you. The liberality and harmony, with which it has been conducted will be found to do great honor to both the parties; and the sentiments of warm attachment to the Union and its present Government expressed by our fellow citizens of Kentucky cannot fail to add an affectionate concern for their particular welfare to the great national impressions under which you will decide on the case submitted to you.

It has been heretofore known to Congress, that frequent incursions have been made on our frontier settlements by certain banditti of Indians from the North West side of the Ohio. These with some of the tribes dwelling on and near the Wabash have of late been particularly active in their depredations; and being emboldened by the impunity of their crimes, and aided by such parts of the neighboring tribes as could be seduced to join in their hostilities or afford them a retreat for their prisoners and plunder, they have, instead of listening to the humane overtures made on the part of the United States, renewed their violences with fresh alacrity and greater effect. The lives of a number of valuable Citizens have thus been sacrificed, and some of them under circumstances peculiarly shocking; whilst others have been carried into a deplorable captivity.

These aggravated provocations rendered it essential to the safety of the Western Settlements that the aggressors should be made sensible that the Government of the Union is not less capable of punishing their crimes, than it is disposed to respect their rights and reward their attachments. As this object could not be effected by defensive measures it became necessary to put in force the Act, which empowers the President to call out the Militia for the protection of the frontiers. And I have accordingly authorized an expedition in which the regular troops in that quarter are combined with such drafts of Militia as were deemed sufficient. The event of the measure is yet unknown to me. The Secretary of war is directed to lay before you a statement of the information on which it is founded, as well as an estimate of the expence with which it will be attended.

The disturbed situation of Europe, and particularly the critical posture of the great maritime powers, whilst it ought to make us more thankful for the general peace and security enjoyed by the United States, reminds us at the same time of the circumspection with which it becomes us to preserve these blessings. It requires also that we should not overlook the tendency of a war and even of preparations for a war, among the Nations most concerned in active Commerce with this Country, to abridge the means, and thereby at least enhance the price of transporting its valuable productions to their proper markets. I recommend it to your serious reflexion how far and in what mode, it may be expedient to guard against embarrassments from these contingencies, by such encouragements to our own Navigation as will render our commerce and agriculture less dependent on foreign bottoms, which may fail us in the very moments most interesting to both of these great objects. Our fisheries, and the transportation of our own produce offer us abundant means for guarding ourselves against this evil.

Your attention seems to be not less due to that particular branch of our trade which belongs to the Mediterranean. So many circumstances unite in rendering the present state of it distressful to us, that you will not think any deliberations misemployed, which may lead to its relief and protection.

The laws you have already passed for the establishment of a Judiciary System have opened the doors of Justice to all descriptions of persons. You will consider in your wisdom, whether improvements in that system may yet be made; and particularly whether a uniform process of execution on sentences issuing, from the federal Courts be not desireable through all the states.

The patronage of our commerce, of our merchants and Seamen, has called for the appointment of Consuls in foreign Countries. It seems expedient to regulate by law the exercise of that Jurisdiction and those functions which are permitted them, either by express Convention, or by a friendly indulgence in the places of their residence. The Consular Convention too with his most Christian Majesty has stipulated in certain cases, the aid of the national authority to his Consuls established here. Some legislative provision is requisite to carry these stipulations into full effect.

The establishment of the Militia; of a mint; of Standards of weights and measures; of the Post Office and Post Roads are subjects which (I presume) you will resume of course, and which are abundantly urged by their own importance.

Gentlemen of the House of Representatives: The sufficiency of the Revenues you have established for the objects to which they are appropriated, leaves no doubt that the residuary provisions will be commensurate to the other objects for which the public faith stands now pledged. Allow me, moreover, to hope that it will be a favorite policy with you not merely to secure a payment of the Interest of the debt funded, but, as far and as fast as growing resources of the Country will permit, to exonerate it of the principal itself. The appropriation you have made of the Western Lands explains your dispositions on this subject: And I am persuaded the sooner that valuable fund can be made to contribute along with other means to the actual reduction of the public debt, the more salutary will the measure be to every public interest, as well as the more satisfactory to our Constituents.

Gentlemen of the Senate and House of Representatives: In pursuing the various and weighty business of the present Session I indulge the fullest persuasion that your consultations will be equally marked with wisdom, and animated by the love of your Country. In whatever belongs to my duty, you shall have all the co-operation which an undiminished zeal for its welfare can inspire. It will be happy for us both, and our best reward, if by a successful administration of our respective trusts we can make the established Government more and more instrumental in promoting the good of our fellow Citizens, and more and more the object of their attachment and confidence.

December 8, 1790

To the Chiefs of the Seneca Nation

Philadelphia, December 29, 1790.

I the President of the United States, by my own mouth, and by a written Speech signed with my own hand and sealed with the Seal of the U S Speak to the Seneka Nation, and desire their attention, and that they would keep this Speech in remembrance of the friendship of the United States.

I have received your Speech with satisfaction, as a proof of your confidence in the justice of the United States, and I have attentively examined the several objects which you have laid before me, whether delivered by your Chiefs at Tioga point in the last month to Colonel Pickering, or laid before me in the present month by the Cornplanter and the other Seneca Chiefs now in Philadelphia.

In the first place I observe to you, and I request it may sink deep in your minds, that it is my desire, and the desire of the United States that all the miseries of the late war should be forgotten and buried forever. That in future the United States and the six Nations should be truly brothers, promoting each other's prosperity by acts of mutual friendship and justice.

I am not uninformed that the six Nations have been led into some difficulties with respect to the sale of their lands since the peace. But I must inform you that these evils arose before the present government of the United States was established, when the separate States and individuals under their authority, undertook to treat with the Indian tribes respecting the sale of their lands.

But the case is now entirely altered. The general Government only has the power, to treat with the Indian Nations, and any treaty formed and held without its authority will not be binding.

Here then is the security for the remainder of your lands. No State nor person can purchase your lands, unless at some public treaty held under the authority of the United States. The general government will never consent to your being defrauded. But it will protect you in all your just rights.

Hear well, and let it be heard by every person in your Nation, That the President of the United States declares, that the general government considers itself bound to protect you in all the lands secured you by the Treaty of Fort Stanwix, the 22d of October 1784, excepting such parts as you may since had fairly sold to persons properly authorized to purchase of you.

You complain that John Livingston and Oliver Phelps have obtained your lands, assisted by Mr. Street of Niagara, and they have not complied with their agreement.

It appears upon enquiry of the Governor of New York, that John Livingston was not legally authorized to treat with you, and that every thing he did with you has been declared null and void, so that you may rest easy on that account.

But it does not appear from any proofs yet in the possession of government, that Oliver Phelps has defrauded you.

If however you should have any just cause of complaint against him, and can make satisfactory proof thereof, the federal Courts will be open to you for redress, as to all other persons.

But your great object seems to be the security of your remaining lands, and I have therefore upon this point, meant to be sufficiently strong and clear.

That in future you cannot be defrauded of your lands. That you possess the right to sell, and the right of refusing to sell your lands.

That therefore the sale of your lands in future, will depend entirely upon yourselves.

But that when you may find it for your interest to sell any parts of your lands, the United States must be present by their Agent, and will be your security that you shall not be defrauded in the bargain you may make.

It will however be important, that before you make any further sales of your land that you should determine among yourselves, who are the persons among you that shall give sure conveyances thereof as shall be binding upon your Nation and forever preclude all disputes related to the validity of the sale.

That besides the before mentioned security for your land, you will perceive by the law of Congress, for regulating trade and intercourse with the Indian tribes, the fatherly care the United States intend to take of the Indians. For the particular meaning of this law, I refer you to the explanations given thereof by Colonel Pickering at Tioga, which with the law, are herewith delivered to you.

You have said in your Speech "That the game is going away from among you, and that you thought it the design of the great Spirit, that you should till the ground, but before you speak upon this subject, you want to know whether the United States meant to leave you any land to till?"

You now know that all the lands secured to you by the Treaty of Fort Stanwix, excepting such parts as you may since have fairly sold are yours, and that only your own acts can convey them away; speak therefore your wishes on the subject of tilling the ground. The United States will be happy to afford you every assistance in the only business which will add to your numbers and happiness.

The murders that have been committed upon some of your people, by the bad white men I sincerely lament and reprobate, and I earnestly hope that the real murderers will be secured, and punished as they deserve. This business has been sufficiently explained to you here, by the Governor of Pennsylvania, and by Colonel Pickering on behalf of the United States, at Tioga.

The Senekas may be assured, that the rewards offered for apprehending the murderers, will be continued until they are secured for trial, and that when they shall be apprehended, that they will be tried and punished as if they had killed white men.

Having answered the most material parts of your Speech, I shall inform you, that some bad Indians, and the outcast of several tribes who reside at the Miamee Village, have long continued their murders and depredations upon the frontiers, lying along the Ohio. That they have not only refused to listen to my voice inviting them to peace, but that upon receiving it, they renewed their incursions and murders with greater violence than ever. I have therefore been obliged to strike those bad people, in order to make them sensible of their madness. I sincerely hope they will hearken to reason, and not require to be further chastised. The United States desire to be the friends of the Indians, upon terms of justice and humanity. But they will not suffer the depredations of the bad Indians to go unpunished.

My desire is that you would caution all the Senekas and six Nations, to prevent their rash young men from joining the Miamee Indians. For the United States cannot distinguish the tribes to which bad Indians belong, and every tribe must take care of their own people.

The merits of the Cornplanter, and his friendship for the United States are well known to me, and shall not be forgotten. And as a mark of the esteem of the United States, I have directed the Secretary of war to make him a present of Two hundred and Fifty Dollars, either in money or goods, as the Cornplanter shall like best. And he may depend upon the future care and kindness of the United States. And I have also directed the Secretary of War to make suitable presents to the other Chiefs present in Philadelphia. And also that some further tokens of friendship to be forwarded to the other Chiefs, now in their Nation.

Remember my words Senekas, continue to be strong in your friendship for the United States, as the only rational ground of your future happiness, and you may rely upon their kindness and protection.

An Agent shall soon be appointed to reside in some place convenient to the Senekas and six Nations. He will represent the United States. Apply to him on all occasions.

If any man brings you evil reports of the intentions of the United States, mark that man as your enemy, for he will mean to deceive you and lead you into trouble. The United States will be true and faithful to their engagements.

Message to Congress Concerning the Seat of Government

United States, January 24, 1791.

Gentlemen of the Senate and House of Representatives: In execution of the powers with which Congress were pleased to invest me by their Act intitled "An Act for establishing the temporary and permanent seat of the Government of the United States" and on mature consideration of the advantages and disadvantages of the several positions, within the limits prescribed by the said Act, I have, by Proclamation, bearing date this day, a copy of which is herewith transmitted, directed Commissioners, appointed in pursuance of the Act, to survey and limit a part of the territory of ten miles square, on both sides the river Potomack, so as to comprehend George Town in Maryland, and to extend to the Eastern branch. I have not by this first Act given to the said territory the whole extent of which it is susceptible in the direction of the River; because I thought it important that Congress should have an opportunity of considering whether by an amendatory law, they would authorize the location of the residue at the lower end of the present, so as to comprehend the Eastern branch itself, and some of the Country on its lower side in the State of Maryland, and the town of Alexandria in Virginia. If, however, they are of opinion that the federal territory should be bounded by the water edge of the Eastern-branch, the location of the residue will be to be made at the upper end of what is now directed. I have thought best to await a survey of the territory before it is decided on what particular spot on the North Eastern side of the River the public buildings shall be erected.

To David Humphreys

Philadelphia, July 20, 1791.

My dear Sir: I have received your letters of the 16 of February and 3 of May, and am much obliged by your observations on the situation, manners, customs and dispositions of the Spanish nation. In this age of free inquiry and enlightened reason it is to be hoped that the condition of the people in every Country will be bettered, and the happiness of mankind promoted. Spain appears to be so much behind the other Nations of Europe in liberal policy that a long time will undoubtedly elapse before the people of that kingdom can taste the sweets of liberty, and enjoy the natural advantages of their Country.

In my last I mentioned my intention of visiting the southern States, which I have since accomplished, and have the pleasure to inform you, that I performed a journey of 1887 miles without meeting with any interruption by sickness, bad weather, or any untoward accident. Indeed so highly were we favored that we arrived at each place, where I proposed to make any halt, on the very day I fixed upon before we set out. The same horses performed the whole tour, and, altho' much reduced in flesh, kept up their full spirits to the last day.

I am much pleased that I have taken this journey as it has enabled me to see with my own eyes the situation of the country thro' which we travelled, and to learn more accurately the disposition of the people than I could have done by any information.

The country appears to be in a very improving state, and industry and frugality are becoming much more fashionable than they have hitherto been there. Tranquillity reigns among the people, with that disposition towards the general government which is likely to preserve it. They begin to feel the good effects of equal laws and equal protection. The farmer finds a ready market for his produce, and the merchant calculates with more certainty on his payments. Manufacturers have as yet made but little progress in that part of the country, and it will probably be a long time before they are brought to that state to which they have already arrived in the middle and eastern parts of the Union.

Each days experience of the Government of the United States seems to confirm its establishment, and to render it more popular. A ready acquiescence in the laws made under it shews in a strong light the confidence which the people have in their representatives, and in the upright views of those who administer the government. At the time of passing a law imposing a duty on home made spirits, it was vehemently affirmed by many, that such a law could never be executed in the southern States, particularly in Virginia and North Carolina. As this law came in force only on the first of this month little can be said of its effects from experience; but from the best information I could get on my journey respecting its operation on the minds of the people (and I took some pains to obtain information on this point) there remains no doubt but it will be carried into effect not only without opposition, but with very general approbation in those very parts where it was foretold that it would never be submitted to by any one. It is possible, however, and perhaps not improbable that some Demagogue may start up, and produce and get signed some resolutions declaratory of their disapprobation of the measure.

Our public credit stands on that ground which three years ago it would have been considered as a species of madness to have foretold. The astonishing rapidity, with which the newly instituted Bank was filled gives an unexampled proof (here) of the resources of our Countrymen and their confidence in public measures. On the first day of opening the subscription the whole number of shares (20,000) were taken up in one hour, and application made for upwards of 4000 shares more than were granted by the Institution, besides many others that were coming in from different quarters.

For some time past the western frontiers have been alarmed by depredations committed by some hostile tribes of Indians; but such measures are now in train as will, I presume, either bring them to sue for peace before a stroke is struck at them, or make them feel the effects of an enmity too sensibly to provoke it again unnecessarily, unless, as is much suspected, they are countenanced, abetted, and supported in their hostile views by the B——h. Tho' I must confess I cannot see much prospect of living in tranquillity with them so long as a spirit of land jobbing prevails, and our frontier Settlers entertain the opinion that there is not the same crime (or indeed no crime at all) in killing an Indian as in killing a white man.

You have been informed of the spot fixed on for the seat of Government on the Potomac, and I am now happy to add that all matters between the Proprietors of the soil and the public are settled to the mutual satisfaction of the Parties, and that the business of laying out the city, the grounds for public buildings, walks &c. is progressing under the inspection of Major L'Enfant with pleasing prospects.

Thus much for our american affairs; and I wish I could say as much in favor of circumstances in Europe. But our accounts from thence do not paint the situation of the Inhabitants in very pleasing colours. One part exhibits war and devastation; another preparations for war; a third commotions; a fourth direful apprehensions of commotions; and indeed there seems to be scarcely a nation enjoying uninterrupted, unapprehensive tranquillity.

The example of France will undoubtedly have its effects on other Kingdoms. Poland, by the public papers, appears to have made large and unexpected strides towards liberty, which, if true, reflects great honor on the present King, who seems to have been the principal promoter of the business.

By the by, I have never received any letter from Mr. Littlepage, or from the King of Poland, which you say Mr. Carmichael informed you were sent to me last summer.

I yesterday had Mr. Jaudennes, who was in this country with Mr. Gardoqui, and is now come over in a public character, presented to me, for the first time by Mr. Jefferson. Colonel Ternant is expected here every day as minister from France.

I am glad to learn that the air of Lisbon agrees so well with you. I sincerely hope you may long, very long enjoy the blessing of health, accompanied with such other blessings as may contribute to your happiness. I have been in the enjoyment of very good health during my journey, and have rather gained flesh upon it. Mrs. Washington desires her best wishes may be presented to you. You are always assured of those of, my dear Sir, etc.

To Marquis de Lafayette

Philadelphia, July 28, 1791.

I have, my dear Sir, to acknowledge the receipt of your favors of the 7 of March and 3 of May, and to thank you for the communications which they contain relative to your public affairs. I assure you I have often contemplated, with great anxiety, the danger to which you are personally exposed by your peculiar and delicate situation in the tumult of the times, and your letters are far from quieting that friendly concern. But to one, who engages in hazardous enterprises for the good of his country, and who is guided by pure and upright views, (as I am sure is the case with you) life is but a secondary consideration.

To a philanthropic mind the happiness of 24 millions of people cannot be indifferent; and by an American, whose country in the hour of distress received such liberal aid from the french, the disorders and incertitude of that Nation are to be peculiarly lamented. We must, however, place a confidence in that Providence who rules great events, trusting that out of confusion he will produce order, and, notwithstanding the dark clouds, which may threaten at present, that right will ultimately be established.

The tumultous populace of large cities are ever to be dreaded. Their indiscriminate violence prostrates for the time all public authority, and its consequences are sometimes extensive and terrible. In Paris we may suppose these tumults are peculiarly disastrous at this time, when the public mind is in a ferment, and when (as is always the case on such occasions) there are not wanting wicked and designing men, whose element is confusion, and who will not hesitate in destroying the public tranquillity to gain a favorite point. But until your Constitution is fixed, your government organized, and your representative Body renovated, much tranquillity cannot be expected; for, until these things are done, those who are unfriendly to the revolution, will not quit the hope of bringing matters back to their former state.

The decrees of the National Assembly respecting our tobacco and oil do not appear to be very pleasing to the people of this country; but I do not presume that any hasty measures will be adopted in consequence thereof; for we have never entertained a doubt of the friendly disposition of the french Nation toward us, and are therefore persuaded that if they have done any thing which seems to bear hard upon us, at a time when the Assembly must have been occupied in very important matters, and which perhaps would not allow time for a due consideration of the subject, they will, in the moment of calm deliberation, alter it and do what is right.

I readily perceive, my dear Sir, the critical situation in which you stand, and never can you have greater occasion to show your prudence, judgment, and magnanimity.

On the 6 of this month I returned from a tour through the southern States, which had employed me for more than three months. In the course of this journey I have been highly gratified in observing the flourishing state of the Country, and the good dispositions of the people. Industry and economy have become very fashionable in these parts, which were formerly noted for the opposite qualities, and the labours of man are assisted by the blessings of Providence. The attachment of all Classes of citizens to the general Government seems to be a pleasing presage of their future happiness and respectability.

The complete establishment of our public credit is a strong mark of the confidence of the people in the virtue of their Representatives, and the wisdom of their measures; and, while in Europe, wars or commotions seem to agitate almost every nation, peace and tranquillity prevail among us, except on some parts of our western frontiers, where the Indians have been troublesome, to reclaim or chastise whom proper measures are now pursuing. This contrast between the situation of the people of the United States, and those of Europe is too striking to be passed over, even by the most superficial observer, and may, I believe, be considered as one great cause of leading the people here to reflect more attentively on their own prosperous state, and to examine more minutely, and consequently approve more fully of the government under which they live, than they otherwise would have done. But we do not wish to be the only people who may taste the sweets of an equal and good government; we look with an anxious eye to the time, when happiness and tranquillity shall prevail in your country, and when all Europe shall be freed from commotions, tumults, and alarms.

Your friends in this country often express their great attachment to you by their anxiety for your safety. Knox, Jay, Hamilton, Jefferson remember you with affection; but none with more sincerity and true attachment than etc.

To Gouverneur Morris

Philadelphia, July 28, 1791.

Dear Sir: I have now before me your favors of the 22 of November 1 and 24 of December 1790, and of the 9 of March 1791.

The Plateaux which you had the goodness to procure for me arrived safe, and the account of them has been settled, as you desired, with Mr. Robert Morris. For this additional mark of attention to my wishes you must accept my thanks.

The communications in your several letters, relative to the state of affairs in Europe, are very gratefully received; and I should be glad if it was in my power to reply to them more in detail than I am able to do. But my public duties, which are at all times sufficiently numerous, being now much accumulated by an absence of more than three months from the seat of government, make the present a very busy moment for me.

The change of systems, which have so long prevailed in Europe, will, undoubtedly, affect us in a degree proportioned to our political or commercial connexions with the several nations of it. But I trust we shall never so far lose sight of our own interest and happiness as to become, unnecessarily, a party in their political disputes. Our local situation enables us to keep that state with them, which otherwise could not, perhaps, be preserved by human wisdom. The present moment seems pregnant with great events; But, as you observe, it is beyond the ken of mortal foresight to determine what will be the result of those changes which are either making or contemplated in the general system of Europe. Altho' as fellow-men we sincerely lament the disorders, oppressions, and incertitude which frequently attend national events, and which our European brethren must feel; yet we cannot but hope that it will terminate very much in favor of the Rights of man; and that a change there will be favorable to this Country I have no doubt. For, under the former system we were seen either in the distresses of war, or viewed after the peace in a most unfavorable light through the medium of our distracted state. In neither point could we appear of much consequence among Nations. And should affairs continue in Europe in the same state they were when these impressions respecting us were received, it would not be an easy matter to remove the prejudices imbibed against us. A change of system will open a new view of things, and we shall then burst upon them, as it were with redoubled advantages.

Should we under the present state of affairs form connexions, other than we now have, with any European powers, much must be considered in effecting them, on the score of our increasing importance as a Nation; and, at the same time, should a treaty be formed with a Nation whose circumstances may not at this moment be very bright much delicacy would be necessary in order to shew that no undue advantages were taken on that account. For unless treaties are mutually beneficial to the Parties, it is in vain to hope for a continuance of them beyond the moment when the one which conceives itself to be overreached is in a situation to break off the connexion. And I believe it is among nations as with individuals, the party taking advantage of the distresses of another will lose infinitely more in the opinion of mankind and in subsequent events than he will gain by the stroke of the moment.

In my late tour through the southern States I experienced great satisfaction in seeing the good effects of the general Government in that part of the Union. The people at large have felt the security which it gives and the equal justice which it administers to them. The Farmer, the Merchant, and the Mechanic have seen their several interests attended to, and from thence they unite in placing a confidence in their representatives, as well as in those in whose hands the execution of the laws is placed. Industry has there taken place of idleness, and economy of dissipation. Two or three years of good crops, and a ready market for the produce of their lands, has put every one in good humour; and, in some instances they even impute to the Government what is due only to the goodness of Providence.

The establishment of public credit is an immense point gained in our national concerns. This I believe exceeds the expectation of the most sanguine among us; and a late instance, unparalleled in this Country, has been given of the confidence reposed in our measures by the rapidity with which the subscriptions to the Bank of the United States were filled. In two hours after the books were opened by the Commissioners the whole number of shares were taken up, and 4000 more applied for than were allowed by the Institution. This circumstance was not only pleasing as it related to the confidence in government; but as it exhibited an unexpected proof of the resources of our Citizens.

In one of my letters to you the account which I gave of the number of inhabitants which would probably be found in the United States on enumeration, was too large. The estimate was then founded on the ideas held out by the Gentlemen in Congress of the population of their several States, each of whom (as was very natural) looking thro' a magnifying glass would speak of the greatest extent, to which there was any probability of their numbers reaching. Returns of the Census have already been made from several of the States and a tolerably just estimate has been formed now in others, by which it appears that we shall hardly reach four millions; but one thing is certain our *real* numbers will exceed, greatly, the official returns of them; because the religious scruples of some, would not allow them to give in their lists; the fears of others that it was intended as the foundation of a tax induced them to conceal or diminished theirs, and thro' the indolence of the people, and the negligence of many of the Officers numbers are omitted. The authenticated number however is far greater,

I believe, than has ever been allowed in Europe, and will have no small influence in enabling them to form a more just opinion of our present and growing importance than has yet been entertained there.

This letter goes with one from Mr. Jefferson, to which I must refer you for what respects your public transactions, and I shall only add to it the repeated assurances of regard and affection etc.

To Jean Baptiste Ternant

Mount Vernon, September 24, 1791.

Sir: I have not delayed a momt. since the receipt of your communications of the 22d. instant, in dispatching orders to the Secretary of the Treasury to furnish the money, and to the Secretary of War to deliver the Arms and Ammunition, which you have applied to me for.

Sincerely regretting, as I do, the cause which has given rise to this application; I am happy in the opportunity of testifying how well disposed the United States are to render every aid in their power to our good friends and Allies the French to quell "the alarming insurrection of the Negros in Hispaniola" and of the ready disposition to effect it, of the Executive authority thereof.

To Tobias Lear

Mount Vernon, October 14, 1791.

Dear Sir: Your letter of the 9th. was forwarded to me yesterday morning by the Post-Master in Alexandria (having sent no person to that place the evening before).

I am glad of the intimation given of the intentions of the Minister of France; and pleased, tho' distressed at the same time, at the information that, the 24th. instt. is the day fixed on for the meeting of Congress. I had no more idea of this than I had of its being dooms-day. Supposing the 31st. to be the day, I meant to have spent Monday, and possibly Tuesday, at George-Town; and then to have proceeded leizurely on; but as the case is I shall endeavor to reach Bladensburgh *at least*, the first night (that is Monday) and delay no time on the Road afterwards that can be avoided; as I shall have scarce any time to prepare my communications for the opening of the Session on the 24th. if there should be punctuality in the Members. This unexpected event makes it more essentially necessary to look, without delay, and with accuracy, into the Speeches and Laws (at the past Sessions) agreeably to my former directions; that, among other matters, they may be considered of when I arrive. If any thing else should have occurred to you, fit for recommendation, or communication in the Speech, note it, that, in case it shd. not be among my memorandums, it may be ready for consideration.

There is a mistery attending the Engraving of the Federal City which I do not comprehend. It appears somewhat singular, that the incorrectness of the Plan should not have been discovered till now, when Major L'Enfant was detained many days in Philadelphia to prepare and fit it for the purpose.

If the Memorial of Messrs. Triol Roux and Co. has not already been sent it may await my arrival in Philadelphia as I shall have no leizure to give it a consideration until after my Communications have been prepared for Congress. Being much hurried I have only time to wish you and Mrs. Lear well, and to assure you of the sincere esteem etc.

Third Annual Message to Congress

October 25, 1791.

Fellow Citizens of the Senate and House of Representatives:

I meet you, upon the present occasion, with the feelings which are naturally inspired by a strong impression of the prosperous situation of our common Country, and by a persuasion equally strong that the labours of the present Session, which has just commenced, will, under the guidance of a spirit no less prudent than patriotic, issue in measures, conducive to the stability and increase of national prosperity.

Numerous as are the Providential blessings which demand our grateful acknowledgments; the abundance with which another year has again rewarded the industry of the husbandman is too important to escape recollection.

Your own observations, in your respective situations, will have satisfied you of the progressive state of Agriculture, Manufactures, Commerce and Navigation: In tracing their causes, you will have remarked, with particular pleasure, the happy effects of that revival of confidence, public as well as private, to which the Constitution and Laws of the United States have so eminently contributed: And you will have observed, with no less interest, new and decisive proofs of the increasing reputation and credit of the Nation. But you nevertheless, cannot fail to derive satisfaction from the confirmation of these circumstances, which will be disclosed, in the several official communications, that will be made to you in the course of your deliberations.

The rapid subscriptions to the Bank of the United States, which completed the sum allowed to be subscribed, in a single day, is among the striking and pleasing evidences which present themselves, not only of confidence in the Government, but of resource in the community.

In the interval of your recess due attention has been paid to the execution of the different objects which were specially provided for by the laws and Resolutions of the last Session.

Among the most important of these is the defence and security of the Western Frontiers. To accomplish it on the most humane principles was a primary wish.

Accordingly, at the same time that treaties have been provisionally concluded, and other proper means used to attach the wavering, and to confirm in their friendship, the well-disposed tribes of Indians; effectual measures have been adopted to make those of a hostile description sensible that a pacification was desired upon terms of moderation and justice.

These measures having proved unsuccessful, it became necessary to convince the refractory of the power of the United States to punish their depredations. Offensive operations have therefore been directed; to be conducted however, as consistently as possible with the dictates of humanity. Some of these have been crowned with full success, and others are yet depending. The expeditions which have been completed were carried on under the authority, and at the expense of the United States by the Militia of Kentucke; whose enterprise, intripidity and good conduct, are entitled to peculiar commendation.

Overtures of peace are still continued to the deluded Tribes, and considerable numbers of individuals belonging to them, have lately renounced all further opposition, removed from their former situations, and placed themselves under the immediate protection of the United States.

It is sincerely to be desired that all need of coercion, in future, may cease; and that an intimate intercourse may succeed; calculated to advance the happiness of the Indians, and to attach them firmly to the United States.

In order to this it seems necessary: That they should experience the benefits of an impartial administration of justice. That the mode of alienating their lands the main source of discontent and war, should be so defined and regulated, as to obviate imposition, and, as far as may be practicable, controversy concerning the reality, and extent of the alienations which are made. That commerce with them should be promoted under regulations tending to secure an equitable deportment towards them, and that such rational experiments should be made, for imparting to them the blessings of civilization, as may, from time to time suit their condition. That the Executive of the United States should be enabled to employ the means to which the Indians have been long accustomed for uniting their immediate Interests with the preservation of Peace. And that efficatious provision should be made for inflicting adequate penalties upon all those who, by violating their rights, shall infringe the Treaties, and endanger the peace of the Union.

A System corrisponding with the mild principles of Religion and Philanthropy towards an unenlightened race of Men, whose happiness materially depends on the conduct of the United States, would be as honorable to the national character as conformable to the dictates of sound policy.

The powers specially vested in me by the Act laying certain duties on distilled spirits, which respect the subdivisions of the districts into Surveys, the appointment of Officers, and the assignment of compensations, have likewise been carried into effect. In a matter in which both materials and experience were wanting to guide the calculation, it will be readily conceived that there must have been difficulty in such an adjustment of the rates of compensation as would conciliate a reasonable competency with a proper regard to the limits prescribed by the law. It is hoped that the circumspection, which has been used will be found in the result to have secured the last of the two objects; but it is probable, that with a view to the first, in some instances, a revision of the provision will be found adviseable.

The impressions with which this law has been received by the community, have been, upon the whole, such as were to be expected among enlightened and well-disposed Citizens, from the propriety and necessity of the measure. The novelty, however of the tax, in a considerable part of the United States, and a misconception of some of its provisions, have given occasion, in particular places to some degree of discontent. But it is satisfactory to know that this disposition yields to proper explanations and more just apprehensions of the true nature of the law. and I entertain a full confidence, that it will, in all, give way to motives which arise out of a just sense of duty, and a virtuous regard to the public welfare.

If there are any circumstances, in the law, which consistently with its main design, may be so varied as to remove any well intentioned objections, that may happen to exist, it will consist with a wise moderation to make the proper variations. It is desirable on all occasions, to unite with a steady and firm adherence to constitutional and necessary Acts of Government, the fullest evidence of a disposition, as far as may be practicable, to consult the wishes of every part of the Community, and to lay the foundations of the public administration in the affection of the people.

Pursuant to the authority contained in the several Acts on that subject, a district of ten miles square for the permanent seat of the Government of the United States has been fixed, and announced by proclamation; which district will comprehend lands on both sides of the River Potomack, and the towns of Alexandria and George Town. A City has also been laid out agreeably to a plan which will be placed before Congress: And as there is a prospect, favoured by the rate of sales which have already taken place, of ample funds for carrying on the necessary public buildings, there is every expectation of their due progress.

The completion of the Census of the Inhabitants, for which provision was made by law, has been duly notified (excepting in one instance in which the return has been informal, and another in which it has been omitted or miscarried) and the returns of the Officers, who were charged with this duty, which will be laid before you, will give you the pleasing assurance that the present population of the United States borders on four Millions of persons.

It is proper also to inform you that a further loan of two millions and a half of Florins has been completed in Holland; the terms of which are similar to those of the one last announced, except as to a small reduction of charges. Another on like terms, for six Millions of Florins, had been set on foot under circumstances that assured immediate completion.

Gentlemen of the Senate:

Two treaties, which have been provisionally concluded with the Cherokees and Six Nations of Indians, will be laid before you for your consideration and ratification.

Gentlemen of the House of Representatives:

In entering upon the discharge of your legislative trust, you must anticipate with pleasure, that many of the difficulties, necessarily incident to the first arrangements of a new Government, for an extensive Country, have been happily surmounted by the zealous, and judicious exertions of your predecessors, in co-operation with the other branch of the legislature. The important objects, which remain to be accomplished, will, I am persuaded, be conducted upon principles equally comprehensive, and equally well calculated for the advancement of the general weal.

The time limited for receiving subscriptions to the loans proposed by the Act making provision for the debt of the United States having expired, statements from the proper department will, as soon as possible, apprize you of the exact result. Enough, however is already known, to afford an assurance that the views of that Act have been substantially fulfilled. The subscription in the domestic debt of the United States, has embraced by far the greatest proportion of that debt; affording at the same time proof of the general satisfaction of the public Creditors with the System which has been proposed to their acceptance, and of the spirit of accommodation to the convenience of the Government with which they are actuated. The subscriptions in the debts of the respective States, as far as the provisions of the law have permitted, may be said to be yet more general. The part of the debt of the United States, which remains unsubscribed, will naturally engage your further deliberations.

It is particularly pleasing to me to be able to announce to you, that the revenues which have been established, promise to be adequate to their objects; and may be permitted, if no unforeseen exigency occurs, to supercede, for the present, the necessity of any new burthens upon our Constituents.

An Object which will claim your early attention, is, a provision for the current service of the ensuing year, together with such ascertained demands upon the Treasury as require to be immediately discharged; and such casualties as may have arisen in the execution of the public business, for which no specific appropriations may have yet been made; of all which a proper estimate will be laid before you.

Gentlemen of the Senate,
and of the House of Representatives:

I shall content myself with a general reference to former communications for several objects, upon which the urgency of other affairs has hitherto postponed any definite resolution. Their importance will recall them to your attention; and I trust that the progress already made in the most arduous arrangements of the Government, will afford you leisure to resume them with advantage.

There are, however, some of them of which I cannot forbear a more particular mention. These are, the Militia; the Post-Office and Post-roads; the Mint; Weights and Measures; a provision for the sale of the vacant lands of the United States.

The first is certainly an object of primary importance,

whether viewed in reference to the national security, to the satisfaction of the community, or to the preservation of order. In connection with this, the establishment of competent Magazines and Arsenals, and the fortification of such places as are peculiarly important and vulnerable, naturally present themselves to consideration. The safety of the United States, under Divine protection, ought to rest on the basis of systematic and solid arrangements; exposed as little as possible to the hazard of fortuitous circumstances.

The importance of the Post-Office and Post-Roads, on a plan sufficiently liberal and comprehensive, as they respect the expedition, safety and facility of communication, is increased by the instrumentality in diffusing a knowledge of the laws and proceedings of the government; which, while it contributes to the security of the people, serves also to guard them against the effects of misrepresentation and misconception. The establishment of additional cross-posts, especially to some of the important points in the Western and Northern parts of the Union, cannot fail to be of material Utility.

The disorders in the existing currency, and especially the scarcity of small change, a scarcity so peculiarly distressing to the poorer classes, strongly recommend the carrying into immediate effect the resolution already entered into concerning the establishment of a Mint. Measures have been taken, pursuant to that Resolution, for procuring some of the most necessary Artists, together with the requisite Apparatus.

An uniformity in the weights and measures of the Country is among the important objects submitted to you by the Constitution, and if it can be derived from a standard at once invariable and universal, must be no less honorable to the public Councils than conducive to the public convenience.

A provision for the sale of the vacant lands of the United States is particularly urged, among other reasons, by the important considerations that they are pledged as a fund for reimbursing the public debt; that if timely and judiciously applied, they may save the necessity of burthening our citizens with new taxes for the extinguishment of the principal; and that being free to discharge the principal but in a limited proportion no opportunity ought to be lost for availing the public of its right.

To Harriot Washington

Philadelphia, October 30, 1791.
Dear Harriot: I have received your letter of the 21st. instant, and shall always be glad to hear from you. When my business will permit inclination will not be wanting in me to acknowledge the receipt of your letters, and this I shall do more cheerfully as it will afford me opportunities at those times of giving you such occasional advice, as your situation may require.

At present I could plead a better excuse for curtailing my letter to you than you had for shortening of yours to me, having a multitude of business before me while you have nothing to do, consequently you might, with equal convenience to yourself, have set down to write your letter an hour or two, or even a day sooner, as to have delayed it until your Cousin was on the point of sending to the Post-Office. I make this remark for no other reason than to shew you it is better to offer no excuse than a bad one, if at any time you should happen to fall into an error.

Occupied as my time now is, and must be during the sitting of Congress, I nevertheless will endeavor to inculcate upon your mind the delicacy and danger of that period, to which you are now arrived under peculiar circumstances. You are just entering into the state of womanhood, without the watchful eye of a Mother to admonish, or the protecting aid of a Father to advise and defend you; you may not be sensible that you are at this moment about to be stamped with that character which will adhere to you through life; the consequence of which you have not perhaps attended to, but be assured it is of the utmost importance that you should.

Your cousins, with whom you live are well qualified to give you advice, and I am sure they will if you are disposed to receive it. But if you are disobliging, self-willed, and untowardly it is hardly to be expected that they will engage themselves in unpleasant disputes with you, especially Fanny, whose mild and placid temper will not permit her to exceed the limits of wholesome admonition or gentle rebuke. Think then to what dangers a giddy girl of 15 or 16 must be exposed in circumstances like these. To be under but little or no controul may be pleasing to a mind that does not reflect, but this pleasure cannot be of long duration, and reason, too late perhaps, may convince you of the folly of mis-spending time. You are not to learn, I am certain, that your fortune is small; supply the want of it then with a well cultivated mind; with dispositions to industry and frugality; with gentleness of manners, obliging temper, and such qualifications as will attract notice, and recommend you to a happy establishment for life.

You might instead of associating with those from whom you can derive nothing that is good, but may have observed every thing that is deceitful, lying, and bad, become the intimate companion of and aid to your Cousin in the domestic concerns of the family. Many Girls before they have arrived at your age have been found so trustworthy as to take the whole trouble of a family from their Mothers; but it is by a steady and rigid attention to the rules of propriety that such confidence is obtained, and nothing would give me more pleasure than to hear that you had acquired it. The merits and benefits of it would redound more to your advantage in your progress thro' life, and to the person with whom you may in due time form a matrimonial connexion than to any others; but to none would such a circumstance afford more real satisfaction, than to Your affectionate Uncle.

To Alexander Martin

Philadelphia, November 14, 1791.

Sir: I have had the pleasure to receive your Excellency's private letter of the 27th of September, which accompanied your public communication of the cession of certain pieces of land in North Carolina for the purpose of building lighthouses thereon.

I request your Excellency will receive my thanks for the kind Congratulations which you express on my return from my southern tour in perfect health; and at the same time I beg you to be assured, that the reception which I met with among the Citizens of North Carolina, as well as those of the other states which I visited, was in the highest degree pleasing and satisfactory. My object in that journey was not to be received with parade and an ostentatious display of opulence. It was for a nobler purpose. To see with my own eyes the situation of the Country, and to learn on the spot the condition and disposition of our Citizens. In these respects I have been highly gratified, and to a sensible mind the effusions of affection and personal regard which were expressed on so many occasions is no less grateful, than the marks of respect shewn to my official Character were pleasing in a public view. I am etc.

To Arthur Young

Philadelphia, December 5, 1791.

Sir: In a letter which I addressed to you on the 15th. of August, acknowledging the receipt of your favor dated the 25th. of January preceeding, I promised to answer the queries contained in it, in detail.

Accordingly, I took measures for that purpose, by writing to some of the most intelligent Farmers in the States of New York, New Jersey, Pennsylvania, Maryland and Virginia; as you will perceive by the circular letter herewith enclosed: and have obtained the answers from the three last mentioned States that are thereunto annexed. I did not extend my enquiries to the Northward of New York, nor to the Southward of Virginia; because in neither extremity of the Union, in my opinion, is the climate, Soil, or other circumstances well adapted to the pursuits of a *mere* Farmer, or congenial to the growth of the smaller Grains.

I have delayed the information I am about to give you, in expectation of receiving answers which have been promised me from the States of New York and New Jersey; but as they are not yet arrived, and a Vessel is on the point of Sailing for London, I shall put this Packet under cover to Joshua Johnson Esqr. our Consul at that Port; with a request to him, that it may be forwarded to you, by a safe conveyance. The others shall follow as opportunities may present; it being my wish to give you a comprehensive view of the different parts of this

Country: although I have no hesitation in giving it at the sametime as my opinion, if I had a new establishment to make in it, that it would be, under the knowledge I entertain of it at present (and I have visited all parts from New Hampshire to Georgia inclusively) in one of the three States of which you are furnished with particular Accounts. New York and New Jersey do not differ much in Soil, or Climate, from the Northern parts of Pennsylvania. Both are pleasant, and both are well improved, particularly the first. But the Country beyond these, to the Eastward, (and the farther you advance that way it is still more so) is unfriendly to Wheat, which is subject to a blight or mill-dew, and of late years, to a fly, which has almost discouraged the growth of it. The lands, however, in the New England States are strong, and productive of other Crops; are well improved; populously seated; and as pleasant as it can be in a Country fast locked in Snow sevl. months in the year.

To the Southward of Virginia the climate is not well adapted to Wheat; and less and less so as you penetrate the warmer latitudes; nor is the Country so thickly settled, or well cultivated. In a word, as I have already intimated, was I to commence my career of life anew, I shd. not seek a residence north of Pennsylvania, or South of Virginia: nor, but this I desire may be received with great caution, for I may, without knowing I am so, be biassed in favor of the River on which I live should I go more than 25 miles from the margin of the Potomac, in less than half that distance, in some places I might seat myself either in Pennsylvania, Maryland or Virginia, as local circumstances might prompt me.

Having said thus much, some of the reasons which lead to this opinion, may be expected in support of it. Potomac River then, is the centre of the Union. It is between the extremes of heat and cold. It is not so far to the south as to be unfriendly to grass, nor so far north as to have the produce of the Summer consumed in the length, and severity of the winter. It waters that soil, and runs in that climate, which is most congenial to English grains, and most agreeable to the Cultivators of them.

It is the River, more than any other, in my opinion, which must, in the natural progress of things, connect by its inland navigation (now nearly compleated 190 measured miles up to Fort Cumberland, at the expence of £50,000 Sterlg. raised by private subscription) the Atlantic States with the vast region which is populating (beyond all conception) to the Westward of it. It is designated by law for the seat of the Empire; and must, from its extensive course through a rich and populous country become, in time, the grand Emporium of North America. To these reasons may be added, that, the lands within, and surrounding the district of Columbia are as high, as dry, and as healthy as any in the United States; and that those above them, in the Counties of Berkeley in Virginia, Washington in Maryland, and Franklin in Pennsylvania (adjoining each other) at the distance of from Sixty to 100 miles from Columbia, are inferior in their natural state to none in America.

The general Map of North America, which is herewith enclosed, will shew the situation of this district of the United States. And on Evans's Map of the Middle Colonies, which is on a larger scale, I have marked the district of Columbia with double red lines; and the Counties adjacent to, and above it, of which particular mention has been made, with single red lines.

The last mentioned Map shews the proximity of the Potowmac (which is laid down from actual Survey) to the Western Waters, and it is worthy of observation, that the Shenandore, in an extent of 150 miles from its confluence, through the richest tract of land in the State of Virginia, may (as is supposed) be made navigable for less than £2,000. The South branch of Potowmac (100 miles higher up, and) for a hundred miles of its extent, may be made navigable for a much less sum. And the intermediate waters on the Virginia side, in that proportion, according to their magnitude. On the Maryland side (the river Potowmac to the head of the North branch being the boundary between the two States) the Monocasy and Conogocheag are capable of improvement to a degree which will be convenient and benificial to the Inhabitants of that State, and to parts of Pennsylvania.

The local, or State taxes, are enumerated in the answers to the circular letter; and these from the nature of the Government, will probably decrease. The taxes of the General

Government will be found in the Revenue laws, which are contained in the volume that accompanies this letter.

"The Pennsylvania Mercury, and Philadelphia Price current" is sent that you may see what is, and has been, the prices of the several enumerated Articles which have been bought, and sold in this market at different periods, within the last twelve months.

An English farmer must entertain a contemptible opinion of our husbandry, or a horrid idea of our lands, when he shall be informed that not more than 8 or 10 bushels of Wheat is the yield of an Acre; but this low produce may be ascribed, and principally too, to a cause which I do not find touched by either of the Gentlemen whose letters are sent to you, namely, that the aim of the farmers in this Country (if they can be called farmers) is not to make the most they can from the land, which is, or has been cheap, but the most of the labour, which is dear, the consequence of which has been, much ground has been *scratched* over and none cultivated or improved as it ought to have been; Whereas a farmer in England, where land is dear and labour cheap, finds it his interest to improve and cultivate highly, that he may reap large crops from a small quantity of ground. That the last is the true, and the first an erroneous policy, I will readily grant, but it requires time to conquer bad habits, and hardly anything short of necessity is able to accomplish it. That necessity is approaching by pretty rapid strides.

If from these communications you shall derive information or amusement, it will be but a small return for the favors I have received from you; and I shall feel happy in having had it in my power to render them. As they result from your letter of the 25th. of January, and are intended for your private satisfaction it is not my wish that they should be promulgated as coming from me. With very great esteem I am etc.

To Gouverneur Morris

(Private)

Philadelphia, January 28, 1792.

My dear Sir: Your favor of the 30th of September came duly to hand, and I thank you for the important information contained in it.

The official communications from the Secretary of State, accompanying this letter, will convey to you the evidence of my *nomination*, and *appointment* of you to Minister Plenipotentiary for the United States at the Court of France; and my assurance, that both were made with *all my heart*, will, I am persuaded, satisfy you as to that fact. I wish I could add that the *advice* and *consent* flowed from a similar source. Candour forbids it, and friendship requires, that I should assign the causes, as far as they have come to my knowledge.

Whilst your abilities, knowledge in the affairs of this Country, and disposition to serve it, were adduced and asserted on one hand; you were charged on the other hand, with levity and imprudence of conversation and conduct. It was urged that your habits of expression indicated a *hauteur* disgusting to those, who happen to differ from you in sentiment; and among a people, who study civility and politeness more than any other nation, it must be displeasing; that in France you were considered as a favorer of Aristocracy, and unfriendly to its Revolution (I suppose they meant constitution). That under this impression, you could not be an acceptable public character, of consequence would not be able, however willing, to promote the interest of this Country in an essential degree. That in England you indiscreetly communicated the purport of your Mission in the first instance, to the Minister of France, at that Court, who availing himself in the same moment of the occasion, gave it the appearance of a movement through his Court. This, and other circumstances of a similar nature, added to a close intercourse with the opposition Members, occasioned distrust, and gave displeasure to the Ministry; which was the cause, it is said, of that reserve which you experienced in negotiating the business which had been intrusted to you.

But not to go further into detail, I will place the ideas of your political adversaries, in the light which their arguments have presented them to me: vizt. That the promptitude, with which your lively and brilliant imagination is displayed, allows too little time for deliberation and correction; and is the primary cause of those sallies, which too often offend, and of that ridicule of characters, which begets enmity not easy to be forgotten, but which might easily be avoided, if it was under the control of more caution and prudence. In a word, that it is indispensably necessary, that more circumspection should be observed by our representatives abroad, than they conceive you are inclined to adopt.

In this statement you have the pros and cons; by reciting them, I give you a proof of my friendship if I give none of my policy or judgment. I do it on the presumption, that a mind conscious of its own rectitude fears not what is said of it, but will bid defiance to and despise shafts that are not barbed with accusations against honor or integrity. And because I have the fullest confidence (supposing the allegations to be founded in whole or part) that you would find no difficulty, being apprized of the exceptionable light in which they are viewed, and considering yourself as the representative of this Country, to effect a change, and thereby silence, in the most unequivocal and satisfactory manner, your political opponents.

Of my good opinion, and of my friendship and regard, you may be assured, and that I am etc.

To David Stuart

Philadelphia, April 8, 1792.

Dear Sir: The letter from the Commissioners to Mr. Jefferson of the   has been laid before me, and I have desired him to approve the Contract respecting the bridge over Rockcreek: but in future, it would be more agreeable to me, after a plan, or the principles leading to the measure, is approved, not to have the details or the execution suspended for a reference to me. Because, to judge properly of the matter must (in many instances) depend upon calculation; upon accustomed modes; established prices, and usages of different places; none of which my time and avocations will allow me to investigate with promptness; consequently the business must be delayed (if I take time for examination) or I must decide in the dark, if I do not.

This has actually been the case with respect to the Bridge above mentioned; for if I had been called upon to say what such a bridge wou'd cost, I should have guessed less than the contract price. And though the Items which form the aggregate, may contain no more materials than are indispensably necessary; and the prices of them, and rates of work, not more than usual, yet, from a want of knowledge in these matters, both appear high to me.

Not for this reason, but because you have jealous and ill-disposed people about you, my advice to you, is to act with caution in all your contracts: and I give it with the freedom of friendship, because it has been insinuated, before the contract was made, that sufficient notice had not been given; and of course you would have no competitors for the undertaking of the Bridge.

Did Major L'Enfant assign any reason for his rejection of the compensation which had been offered him? Has any person applied for the Office of Superintendant? A Mr. Blodget has been recommended by some of the Proprietors; but except being pretty deeply interested in the City, having been a pretty considerable traveller in European Countries, and an observant man with some taste, it is said, I can say nothing of his qualifications for such a trust. How far he is a man of industry, arrangement, and integrity I know not, having a very slight acquaintance with him personally, and less knowledge of his abilities.

There is such an intimate connection in political and pecuniary considerations between the federal district and the inland navigation of the Potowmac, that no exertions, in my opinion, shou'd be dispensed with to accomplish the latter. For, in proportion as this advances, the City will be benefited. Public and private motives therefore combine to hasten this work. My best wishes to Mrs. Stuart and the family. I am etc.

To Isaac Heard

Philadelphia, May 2, 1792.

Sir: Your letter of the 7th. of December was put into my hands by Mr. Thornton; and I must request you will accept my acknowledgments, as well for the polite manner in which you express your wishes for my happiness, as for the trouble you have taken in making genealogical collections relative to the family of Washington.

This is a subject to which I confess I have paid very little attention. My time has been so much occupied in the busy and active scenes of life from an early period of it that but a small portion of it could have been devoted to researches of this nature, even if my inclination or particular circumstances should have prompted the enquiry. I am therefore apprehensive that it will not be in my power (circumstanced as I am at present) to furnish you with materials to fill up the sketch which you have sent me, in so accurate a manner as you could wish. We have no Office of Record in this Country in which exact genealogical documents are preserved; and very few cases, I believe, occur where a recurrence to pedigree for any considerable distance back has been found necessary to establish such points as may frequently arise in older Countries.

On comparing the Tables which you sent with such documents as are in my posession, and which I could readily obtain from another branch of the family with whom I am in the habits of corrispondence I find it to be just. I have often heard others of the family, older than myself, say that our ancestors who first settled in this Country came from some one of the Northern Counties of England, but whether from Lancashire, Yorkshire or one still more northerly I do not precisely remember. The Arms enclosed in your letter are the same that are held by the family here, though I have also seen, and have used as you may perceive by the Seal to this Packet a flying Griffen for the Crest.

If you can derive any information from the enclosed lineage which will enable you to complete your Table, I shall be well pleased in having been the mean to assist you in those researches which you have had the politeness to undertake, and shall be glad to be informed of the result, and of the ancient pedigree of the family, some of whom I find intermixed with the Ferrers &ca.

Lawrence Washington, from whose Will you enclose an abstract was my Grand father; the other abstracts (which you sent) do not, I believe, relate to the family of Washington in Virginia; but of this I cannot speak positively. With due consideration I am etc.

To Comte de Ségur

Philadelphia, May 4, 1792.

Sir: I received with much satisfaction the information of your having made an acquisition in this Country, and of your intentions to take up your residence among us. Your letter of the 30th. of September, giving me this information, did not get to my hands 'till some time in the last month.

The United States open, as it were, a new world to those who are disposed to retire from the noise and bustle of the old, and enjoy tranquility and security.

And we shall always consider men of your character as among our most valuable acquisitions.

Our connection with France, formed in a gloomy and distressful hour, must ever interest us in the happiness of that nation.

We have seen, with true commiseration, those outrages, inseparable from a Revolution, which have agitated the Kingdom, and we have not ceased our most fervent wishes that, their termination may be as happy as their progress has been distressing. With great esteem I am etc.

To James Madison

My dear Sir,   Mount Vernon May 20th. 1792.

As there is a possibility if not a probability, that I shall not see you on your return home; or, if I should see you, that it may be on the Road and under circumstances which will prevent my speaking to you on the subject we last conversed upon; I take the liberty of committing to paper the following thoughts, & requests.

I have not been unmindful of the sentiments expressed by you in the conversations just alluded to: on the contrary I have again, and again revolved them, with thoughtful anxiety; but without being able to dispose my mind to a longer continuation in the Office I have now the honor to hold. I therefore still look forward to the fulfilment of my fondest and most ardent wishes to spend the remainder of my days (which I can not expect will be many) in ease & tranquility.

Nothing short of conviction that my deriliction of the Chair of Government (if it should be the desire of the people to continue me in it) would involve the Country in serious disputes respecting the chief Magestrate, & the disagreeable consequences which might result therefrom in the floating, & divided opinions which seem to prevail at present, could, in any wise, induce me to relinquish the determination I have formed: and of this I do not see how any evidence can be obtained previous to the Election. My vanity, I am sure, is not of that cast as to allow me to view the subject in this light.

Under these impressions then, permit me to reiterate the request I made to you at our last meeting—namely—to think of the proper time, and the best mode of anouncing the intention; and that you would prepare the latter. In revolving this subject myself, my judgment has always been embarrassed. On the one hand, a previous declaration to retire, not only carries with it the appearance of vanity & self importance, but it may be construed into a Manœuvre to be invited to remain. And on the other hand, to say nothing, implys consent; or, at any rate, would leave the matter in doubt; and to decline afterwards might be deemed as bad, & uncandid.

I would fain carry my request to you farther than is asked

above, although I am sensible that your compliance with it must add to your trouble; but as the recess may afford you leizure, and I flatter myself you have dispositions to oblige me, I will, without apology desire (if the measure in itself should strike you as proper, & likely to produce public good, or private honor) that you would turn your thoughts to a Valadictory address from me to the public; expressing in plain & modest terms—that having been honored with the Presidential Chair, and to the best of my abilities contributed to the Organization & Administration of the government—that having arrived at a period of life when the private Walks of it, in the shade of retirement, becomes necessary, and will be most pleasing to me; and the spirit of the government may render a rotation in the Elective Officers of it more congenial with their ideas of liberty & safety, that I take my leave of them as a public man; and in biding them adieu (retaining no other concern than such as will arise from fervent wishes for the prosperity of my Country) I take the liberty at my departure from civil, as I formerly did at my military exit, to invoke a continuation of the blessings of Providence upon it—and upon all those who are the supporters of its interests, and the promoters of harmony, order & good government.

That to impress these things it might, among other things be observed, that we are *all* the Children of the same country—A Country great & rich in itself—capable, & promising to be, as prosperous & as happy as any the Annals of history have ever brought to our view. That our interest, however deversified in local & smaller matters, is the same in all the great & essential concerns of the Nation. That the extent of our Country—the diversity of our climate & soil—and the various productions of the States consequent of both, are such as to make one part not only convenient, but perhaps indispensably necessary to the other part; and may render the whole (at no distant period) one of the most independant in the world. That the established government being the work of our own hands, with the seeds of amendment engrafted in the Constitution, may by wisdom, good dispositions, and mutual allowances; aided by experience, bring it as near to perfection as any human institution ever aproximated; and therefore, the only strife among us ought to be, who should be foremost in facilitating & finally accomplishing such great & desirable objects; by giving every possible support, & cement to the Union. That however necessary it may be to keep a watchful eye over public servants, & public measures, yet there ought to be limits to it; for suspicions unfounded, and jealousies too lively, are irritating to honest feelings; and oftentimes are productive of more evil than good.

To enumerate the various subjects which might be introduced into such an Address would require thought; and to mention them to you would be unnecessary, as your own judgment will comprehend *all* that will be proper; whether to touch, specifically, any of the exceptionable parts of the Constitution may be doubted. All I shall add therefore at present, is, to beg the favor of you to consider—1st. the propriety of such an Address. 2d. if approved, the several matters which ought to be contained in it—and 3d. the time it should appear: that is, whether at the declaration of my intention to withdraw from the service of the public—or to let it be the closing Act of my Administration—which, will end with the next Session of Congress (the probability being that that body will continue sitting until March,) when the House of Representatives will also dissolve.

'Though I do not wish to hurry you (the cases not pressing) in the execution of either of the publications beforementioned, yet I should be glad to hear from you generally on both—and to receive them in time, if you should not come to Philadelphia until the Session commences, in the form they are finally to take. I beg leave to draw your attention also to such things as you shall conceive fit subjects for Communication on that occasion; and, noting them as they occur, that you would be so good as to furnish me with them in time to be prepared, and engrafted with others for the opening of the Session. With very sincere and Affectionate regard I am—ever Yours

To Marquis de Lafayette

Philadelphia, June 10, 1792.

My dear Sir: In the revolution of a great Nation we must not be surprized at the vicissitudes to which individuals are liable; and the changes they experience will always be in proportion to the weight of their public character; I was therefore not surprized, my dear Sir, at receiving your letter dated at Metz which you had the goodness to write me on the 22d of January. That personal ease and private enjoyment is not your primary object I well know, and until peace and tranquillity are restored to your Country upon permanent and honorable grounds I was fully persuaded, in my own mind, that you could not be permitted long to enjoy that domestic retirement, into which you had fondly entered.

Since the commencement of your revolution our attention has been drawn, with no small anxiety, almost to France alone; but at this moment Europe in general seems pregnant with great events, and to whatever nation we turn our eyes there appears to be more or less cause to believe, that an important change will take place at no very distant period. Those philanthropic spirits who regard the happiness of mankind are now watching the progress of things with the greatest solicitude, and consider the event of the present crisis as fixing the fate of man. How great! How important, therefore, is the part, which the actors in this momentous scene have to perform! Not only the fate of millions of the present day depends upon them, but the happiness of posterity is involved in their decisions.

You who are on the spot cannot, I presume, determine when or where these great beginnings will terminate, and for us, at this distance to pretend to give an opinion to that effect would at least be deemed presumptuous. We are however, anxious that the horrors of war may be avoided, if possible, and the rights of man so well understood and so permanently fixed, as while despotic oppression is avoided on the one hand, licentiousness may not be substituted for liberty nor confusion take place of order on the other. The just medium cannot be expected to be found in a moment, the first vibrations always go to the extremes, and cool reason, which can alone establish a permanent and equal government, is as little to be expected in the tumults of popular commotion, as an attention to the liberties of the people is to be found in the dark Divan of a despotic tyrant.

I assure you, my dear Sir, I have not been a little anxious for your personal safety, and I have yet no grounds for removing that anxiety; but I have the consolation of believing that, if you should fall it will be in defence of that cause which your heart tells you is just. And to the care of that Providence, whose interposition and protection we have so often experienced, do I chearfully commit you and your nation, trusting that he will bring order out of confusion, and finally place things upon the ground on which they ought to stand.

The affairs of the United States still go on in a prosperous train. We encrease daily in numbers and riches, and the people are blessed with the enjoyment of those rights which can alone give security and happiness to a Nation. The War with the Indians on our western frontier will, I hope, be terminated in the course of the present season without further effusion of blood; but, in case the measures taken to promote a pacification should fail, such steps are pursued as must, I think, render the issue by the sword very unfavorable to them.

Soon after the rising of Congress I made a journey to Mount Vernon, from whence I returned but a few days ago, and expect, (if nothing of a public nature should occur to detain me here) to go there again some time next month with Mrs. Washington and her two little grand children, where we shall continue 'till near the next meeting of Congress.

Your friends in this Country are interested in your welfare, and frequently enquire about you with an anxiety that bespeaks a warm affection. I am afraid my Nephew George, your old Aid, will never have his health perfectly re-established, he has lately been attacked with the alarming symptom of spitting large quantities of blood, and the Physicians give no hopes of a restoration unless it can be effected by a change of air, and a total dereliction of business, to which he is too anxiously attentive. He will, if he should be taken from his family and friends leave three fine childn. viz. two Sons and a daughter, the eldest of the boys he has given the name of Fayette to and a fine looking child he is.

Hamilton Knox Jay and Jefferson are well and remember you with affection. Mrs. Washington desires to be presented to you in terms of friendship and warm regard, to which I add my most affectionate wishes and sincere prayers for your health and happiness, and request you to make the same acceptable to Madm. le Fayette and your children. I am &c.

To Thomas Jefferson

Dear Sir   George Town July 17th. 1792.

I am extremely sorry to find by the enclosed letter that the affairs of France put on so disagreeable an aspect.

As I know it is your intention to proceed immediately on, I will not ask you to call at Mt. Vernon now but hope it is unnecessary to say that I shall be glad to see you on your way going or returning. I am sincerely & Affecy. Yrs.

To Alexander Hamilton

(Private & confidential)

My dear Sir,   Mount Vernon July 29th. 1792.

I have not yet received the new regulation of allowances to the Surveyors, or Collectors of the duties on Spirituous liquors; but this by the bye. My present purpose is to write you a letter on a more interesting and important subject. I shall do it in strict confidence, & with frankness & freedom.

On my way home, and since my arrival here, I have endeavoured to learn from sensible & moderate men—known friends to the Government—the sentiments which are entertained of public measures. These all agree that the Country is prosperous & happy; but they seem to be alarmed at that system of policy, and those interpretations of the Constitution which have taken place in Congress.

Others, less friendly perhaps to the Government, and more disposed to arraign the conduct of its Officers (among whom may be classed my neighbour, & quandom friend Colo M) go further, & enumerate a variety of matters, wch. as well as I can recollect, may be adduced under the following heads. Viz.

First   That the public debt is greater than we can possibly pay before other causes of adding new debt to it will occur; and that this has been artificially created by adding together the whole amount of the debtor & creditor sides of the accounts, instead of taking only their balances; which could have been paid off in a short time.

2d.   That this accumulation of debt has taken for ever out of our power those easy sources of revenue, which, applied to the ordinary necessities and exigencies of Government, would have answered them habitually, and covered us from habitual murmerings against taxes & tax gatherers; reserving extraordinary calls, for extraordinary occasions, would animate the People to meet them.

3d.   That the calls for money have been no greater than we must generally expect, for the same or equivalent exigencies; yet we are already obliged to strain the *impost* till it produces clamour, and will produce evasion, and war on our citizens to collect it, and even to resort to an *Excise* law, of odious character with the people; partial in its operation; unproductive unless enforced by arbitrary & vexatious means; and committing the authority of the Government in parts where resistance is most probable, & coercion least practicable.

4th   They cite propositions in Congress, and suspect other projects on foot, still to encrease the mass of the debt.

5th.   They say that by borrowing at ⅔ of the interest, we might have paid off the principal in ⅔ of the time; but that from this we are precluded by its being made irredeemable but in small portions, & long terms.

6th.   That this irredeemable quality was given it for the avowed purpose of inviting its transfer to foreign Countries.

7th.   They predict that this transfer of the principal, when compleated, will occasion an exportation of 3 Millions of dollars annually for the interest; a drain of Coin, of which as there has been no example, no calculation can be made of its consequences.

8th. That the banishment of our Coin will be compleated by the creation of 10 millions of paper money, in the form of Bank-bills now issuing into circulation.

9th. They think the 10 or 12 pr Ct. annual profit, paid to the lenders of this paper medium, are taken out of the pockets of the people, who would have had without interest the coin it is banishing.

10th. That all the Capitol employed in paper speculation is barren & useless, producing, like that on a gaming table, no accession to itself, and is withdrawn from Commerce and Agriculture where it would have produced addition to the common mass.

11th That it nourishes in our citizens vice & idleness instead of industry & morality.

12th. That it has furnished effectual means of corrupting such a portion of the legislature, as turns the balance between the honest Voters which ever way it is directed.

13th. That this corrupt squadron, deciding the voice of the legislature, have manifested their dispositions to get rid of the limitations imposed by the Constitution on the general legislature; limitations, on the faith of which, the States acceded to that instrument.

14th That the ultimate object of all this is to prepare the way for a change, from the present republican form of Government, to that of a monarchy; of which the British Constitution is to be the model.

15th. That this was contemplated in the Convention, they say is no secret, because its partisans have made none of it— to effect it then was impracticable; but they are still eager after their object, and are predisposing every thing for its ultimate attainment.

16th. So many of them have got into the legislature, that, aided by the corrupt squadron of paper dealers, who are at their devotion, they make a majority in both houses.

17th The republican party who wish to preserve the Government in its present form, are fewer even when joined by the two, three, or half a dozen antifederalists, who, tho' they dare not avow it, are still opposed to any general Government: but being less so to a republican than a Monarchical one, they naturally join those whom they think pursuing the lesser evil.

18th.   Of all the mischiefs objected to the system of measures beforementioned, none they add is so afflicting, & fatal to every honest hope, as the corruption of the legislature. As it was the earliest of these measures it became the instrument for producing the rest, and will be the instrument for producing in future a King, Lords & Commons; or whatever else those who direct it may chuse. Withdrawn such a distance from the eye of their Constituents, and these so dispersed as to be inaccessible to public information, and particularly to that of the conduct of their own Representatives, they will form the worst Government upon earth, if the means of their corruption be not prevented.

19th.   The only hope of safety they say, hangs now on the numerous representation which is to come forward the ensuing year; but should the majority of the new members be still in the same principles with the present—shew so much deriliction to republican government, and such a disposition to encroach upon, or explain away the limited powers of the constitution in order to change it, it is not easy to conjecture what would be the result, nor what means would be resorted to for correction of the evil. True wisdom they acknowledge should direct temperate & peaceable measures; but add, the division of sentiment & interest happens unfortunately, to be so geographical, that no mortal can say that what is most wise & temperate, would prevail against what is more easy & obvious; they declare, they can contemplate no evil more incalculable than the breaking of the Union into two, or more parts; yet, when they view the mass which opposed the original coalescence, when they consider that it lay chiefly in the Southern quarter—that the legislature have availed themselves of no occasion of allaying it, but on the contrary whenever Northern & Southern prejudices have come into conflict, the latter have been sacraficed and the former soothed.

20th.   That the owers of the debt are in the Southern and the holders of it in the Northern division.

21st. That the antifederal champions are now strengthened in argument by the fulfilment of their predictions, which has been brought about by the Monarchical federalists themselves; who, having been for the new government merely as a stepping stone to Monarchy, have themselves adopted the very construction, of which, when advocating its acceptance before the tribunal of the people, they declared it insuceptable; whilst the republican federalists, who espoused the same government for its intrinsic merits, are disarmed of their weapons, that which they denied as prophecy being now become true history. Who, therefore, can be sure they ask, that these things may not proselyte the small number which was wanting to place the majority on the other side—and this they add is the event at which they tremble.

These, as well as my memory serves me, are the sentiments which, directly and indirectly, have been disclosed to me.

To obtain light, and to pursue truth, being my sole aim; and wishing to have before me *explanations* of as well as the *complaints* on measures in which the public interest, harmony and peace is so deeply concerned, and my public conduct so much involved; it is my request, and you would oblige me in furnishing me, with your ideas upon the discontents here enumerated—and for this purpose I have thrown them into heads or sections, and numbered them that those ideas may apply to the corrispondent numbers. Although I do not mean to hurry you in giving your thoughts on the occasion of this letter, yet, as soon you can make it convenient to yourself it would—for more reasons than one—be agreeable, & very satisfactory to me.

The enclosure in your letter of the 16th. was sent back the Post after I received it, with my approving signature; and in a few days I will write to the purpose mentioned in your letter of the 22d. both to the Secretary of War & yourself. At present all my business—public & private—is on my own shoulders, the two young Gentlemen who came home with me, being on visits to their friends—and my Nephew, the Major, too much indisposed to afford me any aid, in copying or in other matters.

With affectionate regard   I am always—Yours

To Tobias Lear

Mount Vernon, July 30, 1792.

Dear Sir: Your letter from New York came duly to hand, and I was glad to find you had got that far in safety. I wish the remainder of your journey may prove equally pleasant and prosperous. My journey was not of this sort, for after I had parted with the Coach horses I was plagued with those which succeeded them, the following day; and the sick mare, by a dose of Physic which had been administered the night I reached Chester, was so weakened, and failed so much, that she was unable to carry Austin any farther than Susquehanna: from thence she was led to Hartford and left, and two days afterwards gave up the ghost.

I found the face of the Country here, and on the road this side Baltimore, much, very much indeed, parched by a severe drought; and the Corn in miserable plight; but the day and night we reached home there fell a most delightful and re-freshing rain, and the weather since has been as seasonable as the most sanguine farmer could wish; and if continued to us may make our Indian Corn Crop midling, great it is hardly possible to be, so much was it in arrears when the rains set in.

Great complaints were heard of the Hessian fly, and of the Rust and Mildew, as I travelled on; and in some places I be-lieve the damage has been great; but I conceive more is said than ought to be on this subject; and, that the Crop upon the whole will be abundent of Wheat: mine in quantity (and the quality is good) will, I expect, greatly exceed any I have made these several years past.

I found at George town many well conceived, and inge-nious plans for the Public buildings in the New City: it was a pleasure indeed, to find, in an infant Country, such a display of Architectural abilities. The Plan of Mr. Hoben, who was introduced to me by Doctr. Tucker, from Charleston, and who appears to be a very judicious Man, was made choice of for the Presidents House; and the Commissioners have agreed with him to superintend the building of it, and that of the Capitol also, if they should, thereafter, be disposed to put both under one management. He has been engaged in some of the first buildings in Dublin, appears a master workman, and has a great many hands of his own. He has laid out the foundation which is now digging and will be back in a month to enter heartily upon the work. The Plan for the Capitol was not fixed on when I left George Town, two or three very elegant ones (among a great many others of less merit) had been presented, but the draughtsmen, not being there, a postponement became necessary to receive explanations. The Bridge will be accomplished (it is said) by the time specified in the Contract; and everything that could be put in motion before the Plans for the public buildings were fixed on, is in as much forwardness as could be expected, and will now, I have no doubt, advance rapidly.

As you did not mention your having spoke to Mr. Morris about the house, I am under some apprehension that you omitted to do it; which will be unlucky. Give me an Acct. of what I suggested to you as a matter for indirect enquiry. All here are well, except the Major, whose situation I think is unpromising and precarious, growing worse, they all join me in best wishes for Mrs. Lear, yourself and the Child. I am etc.

To Thomas Jefferson

My dear Sir   Mount Vernon Augt. 23d. 1792.
    Your letters of the 12th. and 13th came duly to hand, as did that enclosing Mr. Blodgets plan of a Capitol. The latter I forwarded to the Commissioners, and the enclosures of the two first are now returned to you.

    I believe we are never to hear *from* Mr. Carmichael; nor *of him* but through the medium of a third person. His _____ I realy do not know with what epithet to fill the blank, is, to me, amongst the most unaccountable of all the unaccountable things! I wish much to hear of the arrival of Mr. Short at Madrid, and the result of their joint negotiations at that Court, as we have fresh, and much stronger Representations from Mr. Seagrove of the extraordinary interference of the Spaniards in West Florida, to prevent running the boundary line which had been established by treaty between the United States and the Creeks—of their promising them support in case of their refusal—and of their endeavouring to disaffect the four Southern tribes of Indians towards this Country. In the execution of these projects Seagrove is convinced McGillivray and his partner Panton are embarked, and have become principal agents and there are suspicions entertained, he adds, that the Capture of Bowles was a preconcerted measure between the said Bowles and the Spaniards. That the former is gone to Spain (and to Madrid I think) is certain. That McGillivray has removed from little Tellassee to a place he has within, or bordering on the Spanish line. That a Captn. Oliver, a Frenchman, but an Officer in a Spanish Regiment at New Orleans has taken his place at Tellassee and is holding talks with the Chiefs of the several Towns in the Nation. And that every exertion is making by the Governor of West Florida to obtain a full and general meeting of the Southern Tribes at Pensicola, are facts that admit of *no doubt*. It is also affirmed that five Regiments of about 600 men each, and a large quantity of Ordnance and Stores arrived lately at New Orleans, and that the like number of Regiments (but this can only be from Report) was expected at the same place from the Havanna. Recent accounts from Arthur Campbell (I hope without *much* foundation) speak of very hostile dispositions in the lower Cherokees, and of great apprehension for the safety of Govr. Blount and Genl. Pickens who had set out for the proposed meeting with the Chicasaws and Choctaws at Nashville, and for the Goods which were going down the Tenessee by Water, for that Meeting.

Our accounts from the Western Indians are not more favourable than those just mentioned. No doubt remains of their having put to death Majr. Trueman and Colo. Hardin; and the Harbingers of their mission. The Report from their grand Council is, that War was, or soon would be, decided on; and that they will admit no Flags. The meeting was numerous and not yet dissolved that we have been informed of. What influence our Indian Agents may have at it, remains to be known. Hendricks left Buffaloe Creek between the 18th. and 20th. of June, accompanied by two or three of the Six Nations; some of the Chiefs of those Nations were to follow in a few days—only waiting, it was said, for the Caughnawaga Indians from Canada. And Captn. Brandt would not be long after them. If these attempts to disclose the just and pacific disposition of the United States to these people, should also fail, there remains no alternative but the Sword, to decide the difference; and recruiting goes on heavily.

If Spain is really intrieguing with the Southern Indians as represented by Mr. Seagrove, I shall entertain strong suspicions that there is a very clear understanding in all this business between the Courts of London and Madrid; and that it is calculated to check, as far as they can, the rapid encrease, extension and consequence of this Country; for there cannot be a doubt of the wishes of the former (if we may judge from the conduct of its Officers) to impede any eclaircissment of ours with the Western Indians, and to embarrass our negotiations with them, any more than there is of their Traders and some others who are subject to their government, aiding and abetting them in acts of hostilities.

How unfortunate, and how much is it to be regretted then, that whilst we are encompassed on all sides with avowed enemies and insidious friends, that internal dissentions should be harrowing and tearing our vitals. The last, to me, is the most serious—the most alarming—and the most afflicting of the two. And without more charity for the opinions and acts of one another in Governmental matters, or some more infalible criterion by which the truth of speculative opinions, before they have undergone the test of experience, are to be forejudged than has yet fallen to the lot of fallibility, I believe it will be difficult, if not impracticable, to manage the Reins of Government or to keep the parts of it together: for if, instead of laying our shoulders to the machine after measures are decided on, one pulls this way and another that, before the utility of the thing is fairly tried, it must inevitably be torn asunder—And, in my opinion the fairest prospect of happiness and prosperity that ever was presented to man, will be lost—perhaps for ever!

My earnest wish, and my fondest hope therefore is, that instead of wounding suspicions, and irritable charges, there may be liberal allowances—mutual forbearances—and temporising yieldings on *all sides*. Under the exercise of these, matters will go on smoothly, and, if possible, more prosperously. Without them every thing must rub, the wheels of Government will clog—our enemies will triumph—and by throwing their weight into the disaffected Scale, may accomplish the Ruin of the goodly fabric we have been erecting.

I do not mean to apply these observations, or this advice to any particular person, or character—I have given them in the same general terms to other Officers of the Government—because the disagreements which have arisen from difference of opinions, and the Attacks which have been made upon almost all the measures of government, and most of its Executive Officers, have, for a long time past, filled me with painful sensations; and cannot fail I think, of producing unhappy consequences at home and abroad.

The nature of Mr. Seagroves communications was such, and the evidence in support of them so strong and corroborative that I gave it as my Sentiment to Genl. Knox that the Commissioners of Spain ought to have the matter brought before them again in the manner it was before, but in stronger (though not in committing) language, as the Government was embarrassed, and its Citizens in the Southern States made uneasy by such proceedings, however unauthorised they might be by their Court.

I pray you to note down, or rather to frame into paragraphs or sections such matters as may occur to you as fit and proper for general communication at the opening of the next Session of Congress—not only in the department of State, but on any other subject applicable to the occasion, that I may, in due time, have every thing before me. With sincere esteem & friendship I am, always, Your affectionate

To Alexander Hamilton

(Private)

My dear Sir,   Mount Vernon Augt. 26th. 1792
    Your letter of the 18th., enclosing answers to certain objections communicated to you in my letter of the 29th. Ulto.

came duly to hand; and although I have not, as yet, from a variety of causes, been able to give them the attentive reading I mean to bestow, I feel myself much obliged by the trouble you have taken to answer them; as I persuade myself, from the full manner in which you appear to have taken the matter up, that I shall receive both satisfaction and profit from the perusal.

Differences in political opinions are as unavoidable as, to a certain point, they may perhaps be necessary; but it is to be regretted, exceedingly, that subjects cannot be discussed with temper on the one hand, or decisions submitted to without having the motives which led to them, improperly implicated on the other: and this regret borders on chagrin when we find that Men of abilities—zealous patriots—having the same *general* objects in view, and the same upright intentions to prosecute them, will not exercise more charity in deciding on the opinions, & actions of one another. When matters get to such lengths, the natural inference is, that both sides have strained the cords beyond their bearing—and that a middle course would be found the best, until experience shall have pointed out the right mode—or, which is not to be expected, because it is denied to mortals—there shall be some *infallible* rule by which we could *fore* judge events.

Having premised these things, I would fain hope that liberal allowances will be made for the political opinions of one another; and instead of those wounding suspicions, and irritating charges with which some of our Gazettes are so strongly impregnated, & cannot fail if persevered in, of pushing matters to extremity, & thereby tare the Machine asunder, that there might be mutual forbearances and temporising yieldings *on all sides*. Without these I do not see how the Reins of Government are to be managed, or how the Union of the States can be much longer preserved.

How unfortunate would it be, if a fabric so goodly—erected under so many Providential circumstances—and in its first stages, having acquired such respectibility, should, from diversity of Sentiments, or internal obstructions to some of the acts of Government (for I cannot prevail on myself to believe that these measures are, as yet, the deliberate acts of a determined party) should be harrowing our vitals in such a manner as to have brought us to the verge of dissolution. Melancholy thought! But one, at the same time that it shows the consequences of diversified opinions, when pushed with too much tenacity; exhibits evidence also of the necessity of accommodation; and of the propriety of adopting such healing measures as will restore harmony to the discordant members of the Union, & the governing powers of it.

I do not mean to apply this advice to measures which are passed, or to any character in particular. I have given it in the same *general* terms to other Officers of the Government. My earnest wish is, that balsam may be poured into *all* the wounds which have been given, to prevent them from gangrening; & from those fatal consequences which the community may sustain if it is withheld. The friends of the Union must wish this—those who are not, but wish to see it rended, will be disappointed—and all things I hope will go well.

We have learnt through the medium of Mr. Harrison to Doctr. Craik, that you have it in contemplation to take a trip this way. I felt pleasure at hearing it, and hope it is unnecessary to add that it would be considerably encreased by seeing you under this roof, for you may be assured of the sincere and affectionate regard of   Yours

PS. I pray you to note down whatever may occur to you, not only in your own department but other matters also of general import that may be fit subjects for the speech at the opening of the ensuing Session.

To Edmund Randolph

(Private)

Mount Vernon, August 26, 1792.
My dear Sir: The purpose of this letter is merely to acknowledge the receipt of your favors of the 5th. and 13th. instt., and to thank you for the information contained in both without entering into the details of either.

With respect, however, to the interesting subject treated on in that of the 5th., I can express but one sentiment at this time, and that is a wish, a devout one, that whatever my ultimate determination shall be, it may be for the best. The subject never recurs to my mind but with additional poignancy; and from the declining State in the health of my Nephew, to whom my concerns of a domestic and private nature are entrusted it comes with aggrivated force. But as the allwise disposer of events has hitherto watched over my steps, I trust that in the important one I may soon be called upon to take, he will mark the course so plainly, as that I cannot mistake the way. In full hope of this, I will take no measure, yet a while, that will not leave me at liberty to decide from circumstances, and the best lights, I can obtain on the Subject.

I shall be happy in the mean time to see a cessation of the abuses of public Officers, and of those attacks upon almost every measure of government with which some of the Gazettes are so strongly impregnated; and which cannot fail, if persevered in with the malignancy they now teem, of rending the Union asunder. The Seeds of discontent, distrust, and irritations which are so plentifully sown, can scarcely fail to produce this effect and to Mar that prospect of happiness which perhaps never beamed with more effulgence upon any people under the Sun; and this too at a time when all Europe are gazing with admiration at the brightness of our prospects. and for what is all this? Among other things, to afford Nuts for our transatlantic, what shall I call them? Foes!

In a word if the Government and the Officers of it are to be the constant theme for News-paper abuse, and this too without condescending to investigate the motives or the facts, it will be impossible, I conceive, for any man living to manage the helm, or to keep the machine together. But I am running from my text, and therefore will only add assurances of the Affecte. esteem and regard with which I am &c.

To John Francis Mercer

Mount Vernon, September 26, 1792.

Sir: Your Letter of the 15th. inst: was presented to me by Mr. Corbin on his return from Philada.

As my object in taking your Land near Monocacy (in payment of the Debt due from the Estate of your deceased Father to me) is to convert it into Cash as soon as possible *without loss*, I can have no other objection to an advantageous partition of the Tract than what might result from the uncertainty of the price that may be affixed to it, and the consequent possibility that the amount of a moiety may exceed the sum which is due to me by the last Settlement of the Accts.; thereby occasioning a payment of money, instead of receiving it. If these difficulties where removed, I have none other to your proposal of dividing the Tract into two equal parts, and fixing the property therein by lot. A mean of doing this, I will suggest. It is, if you have not heard the sentiments of the Gentlemen, or either of them, who were chosen to affix a *ready money* price on the Land (and I give you my honor I have not, and moreover that I have never exchanged a word on the subject with any one, except what I told you was Colo. Wm. Deakins's opinion of it's worth) I will allow you seven Dollars pr. acre for a moiety; to be ascertained in the manner before mentioned. I name seven dollars for the following reasons: 1st. because I have been assured by the above Gentleman (who professes to be well acquainted with the Land) that, in his judgment, it would not sell for more than six Dollars Cash, or seven dollars on credit; and 2d. because you have set it at eight dollars yourself, without being able to obtain that price. Five hundred and fifty acres (if the tract contains 1100) wou'd then be within the compass of my claim; and the surplus, if any, I would receive in young Cows, or full grown heifers from Marlborough at three pounds a head, if more agreeable to you than to pay the Cash. Your answer to this proposal, soon, would be convenient to me, as I shall be on my return to Philada. in a short time.

I come now to another part of your Letter, and in touching upon it, do not scruple to declare to you that I was not a little displeased to find by a letter from Captn. Campbell, to a Gentleman in this neighbourhood, that my name had been freely used by you or your friends, for electioneering purposes, when I had never associated your name and the Election together; and when there had been the most scrupulous and pointed caution observed on my part, not to express a sentiment respecting the fitness, or unfitness of any Candidate for representation, that could be construed, by the most violent torture of the words, into an interference in favor of one, or to the prejudice of another. Conceiving that the exercise of an influence (if I really possessed any) however remote, would be highly improper; as the people ought to be entirely at liberty to chuse whom they pleased to represent them in Congress. Having pursued this line of conduct *steadily*, my surprise, and consequent declaration can be a matter of no wonder, when I read the following words in the letter above alluded to:

I arrived yesterday from Philadelphia, since which I find Colo. Mercer has openly declared, that Mr. Richd. Sprigg, jur; informed him, that Bushrod Washington told him that the President in his presence declared, that he hoped Colo. Mercer would not be left out of the next representation in Congress; and added that he thought him the best representative that now goes or ever did go to that Body from this State.

I instantly declared to the person who shewed me the letter, "that, to the best of my recollection, I never had exchanged a word to, or before Bushrod Washington on the subject of your Election; much less to have given such a decided opinion. That such a measure would have been incompatible with the rule I had prescrib'd to myself, and which I had invariably observed, of not interfering directly, or indirectly with the suffrages of the people, in the choice of their representatives; and added, that I wished B. Washington might be called upon to certify what, or whether any conversation had ever passed between us on this subject, as it was my desire that every thing should stand upon its proper foundations." Other Sentiments have been reported as mine, that are equally erroneous.

Whether you have, upon any occasion, expressed yourself in disrespectful terms of me, I know not: it has never been the subject of my enquiry. If nothing impeaching my honor, or honesty, is said, I care little for the rest. I have pursued one uniform course for three score years, and am happy in *believing* that the world have thought it a right one: of it's being so, I am so well satisfied myself, that I shall not depart from it by turning either to the right or to the left, until I arrive at the end of my pilgrimage. I am etc.

To Elizabeth Washington Lewis

Mount Vernon, October 7, 1792.

My Dr. Sister: As Mrs. Washington and myself expect to set out tomorrow for Philadelphia, and the Major and Fanny the day after, if the vessel which is to carry him to Colo. Bassets, arrives in time, I have taken the advantage of the good opportunity afforded by Mr. Robert Lewis of sending Harriet to Fredericksburg. It is done at this time (notwithstanding your proposed visit to Albemarle), 1st. because it would be improper to leave her here after we are all gone; 2nd. because there would be no person to accompany her down afterwards; and 3d. because it might be inconvenient for her to travel alone.

She comes, as Mrs. Washington informs me, very well provided with everything proper for a girl in her situation: this much I know, that she costs me enough to place her in it. I do not however want you, (or any one else) to do more by her than merely to admit her into your family whilst this House is uninhabited by a female white woman, and thereby rendered an unfit place for her to remain at. I shall continue to do for her what I have already done for seven years past; and that is to furnish her with such reasonable and proper necessaries as she may stand in need of, notwithstanding I have had both her brothers upon my hands, and I have been obliged to pay several hundred pounds out of my own pocket, for their boards, schooling, clothing &c. &c. of them, for more than the period aforementioned; their father's estate being unable to discharge the Executions as fast as they are issued against it.

Harriet has sense enough, but no disposition to industry, nor to be careful of her clothes. Your example and admonition, with proper restraints may overcome the two last; and to that end I wish you would examine her clothes and direct her in their use and application of them; for without this they will be, I am told, dabbed about in every hole and corner, and her best things always in use. Fanny was too easy, too much of her own indolent disposition and had too little authority to cause, either by precept or example, any change in this for the better and Mrs. Washington's absence has been injurious to her in many respects: but she is young, and with good advice may yet make a fine woman. If, notwithstanding the suggestion that she is well provided with everything (except a Cloak which may not be had in Alexandria, and may be got at Fredericksburgh) a deficiency is found and you wish to supply it, there will be no occasion for your laying in advance more than ten days; as I could at any time remit a bank note in a letter, to you in four days after I was made acquainted with the amount. I do not mean by this to launch into expensiveness; she has no pretensions to it, nor would the state of my finances enable me to indulge her in that if she had.

Mrs. Washington joins me in best wishes for the perfect restoration of your health, and every other blessing. I am etc.

To Thomas Jefferson

My dear Sir   Phila. Octobr. 18th. 1792.

I did not require the evidence of the extracts which you enclosed me, to convince me of your attachment to the Constitution of the United States, or of your disposition to promote the general welfare of this Country. But I regret—deeply regret—the difference in opinions which have arisen, and divided you and another principal Officer of the Government; and wish, devoutly, there could be an accomodation of them by mutual yieldings.

A Measure of this sort would produce harmony, and consequent good in our public Councils; the contrary will, inevitably, introduce confusion, and serious mischiefs—and for what—because mankind cannot think alike, but would adopt different means to attain the same end. For I will frankly, and solemnly declare that, I believe the views of both of you are pure, and well meant; and that experience alone will decide with respect to the salubrity of the measures which are the subjects of dispute.

Why then, when some of the best Citizens in the United States—Men of discernment—Uniform and tried Patriots, who have no sinister views to promote, but are chaste in their ways of thinking and acting are to be found, some on one side, and some on the other of the questions which have caused these agitations, should either of you be so tenacious of your opinions as to make no allowances for those of the other?

I could, and indeed was about to add more on this interesting subject; but will forbear, at least for the present; after expressing a wish that the cup which has been presented, may not be snatched from our lips by a discordance of *action* when I am persuaded there is no discordance in your *views*. I have a great—a sincere esteem and regard for you both, and ardently wish that some line could be marked out by which both of you could walk. I am always—Yr. Affecte

Fourth Annual Message to Congress

November 6, 1792.

Fellow-Citizens of the Senate, and of the House of Representatives: It is some abatement of the satisfaction, with which I meet you on the present occasion, that in felicitating you on a continuance of the National prosperity, generally, I am not able to add to it information that the Indian hostilities, which have for some time past distressed our North Western frontier, have terminated.

You will, I am persuaded, learn, with no less concern than I communicate it, that reiterated endeavors, toward effecting a pacification, have hitherto issued only in new and outrageous proofs of persevering hostility, on the part of the tribes with whom we are in contest. An earnest desire to procure tranquillity to the frontier; to stop the further effusion of blood; to arrest the progress of expense; to forward the prevalent wish of the Nation, for peace, has led, through various channels, to strenuous efforts, to accomplish these desirable purposes: In making which efforts, I consulted less my own anticipations of the event, or the scruples, which some considerations were calculated to inspire, than the wish to find the object attainable; or if not attainable, to ascertain unequivocally that such is the case.

A detail of the measures, which have been pursued, and of their consequences, which will be laid before you, while it will confirm to you the want of success, thus far, will, I trust, evince that means as proper and as efficacious as could have been devised, have been employed. The issue of some of them, indeed, is still depending; but a favourable one, though not to be despaired of, is not promised by anything that has yet happened.

In the course of the attempts which have been made, some valuable citizens have fallen victims to their zeal for the public service. A sanction commonly respected even among savages, has been found, in this instance, insufficient to protect from Massacre the emissaries of peace. It will, I presume, be duly considered whether the occasion does not call for an exercise of liberality towards the families of the deceased.

It must add to your concern, to be informed, that besides the continuation of hostile appearances among the tribes North of the Ohio, some threatening symptoms have of late been revived among some of those south of it.

A part of the Cherokees, known by the name of Chickamagas, inhabitating five Villages on the Tennesee River, have been long in the practice of committing depredations on the neighbouring settlements.

It was hoped that the treaty of Holstin, made with the Cherokee nation in July 1791, would have prevented a repetition of such depredations. But the event has not answered this hope. The Chickamagas, aided by some Banditti of another tribe in their vicinity, have recently perpetrated wanton and unprovoked hostilities upon the Citizens of the United States in that quarter. The information which has been received on this subject will be laid before you. Hitherto defensive precautions only have been strictly enjoined and observed.

It is not understood that any breach of Treaty, or aggression whatsoever, on the part of the United States, or their Citizens, is even alleged as a pretext for the spirit of hostility in this quarter.

I have reason to believe that every practicable exertion has been made (pursuant to the provision by law for that purpose) to be prepared for the alternative of a prosecution of the war, in the event of a failure of pacific overtures. A large proportion of the troops authorized to be raised, has been recruited, though the number is still incomplete. And pains have been taken to discipline and put them in condition for the particular kind of service to be performed. A delay of operations (besides being dictated by the measures which were pursuing towards a pacific termination of the war) has been in itself deemed preferable to immature efforts. A statement from the proper department with regard to the number of troops raised, and some other points which have been suggested, will afford more precise information, as a guide to the legislative consultations; and among other things will enable Congress to judge whether some additional stimulus to the recruiting service may not be adviseable.

In looking forward to the future expense of the operations, which may be found inevitable, I derive consolation from the information I receive, that the product of the revenues for the present year, is likely to supersede the necessity of additional burthens on the community, for the service of the ensuing year. This, however, will be better ascertained in the course of the Session; and it is proper to add, that the information alluded to proceeds upon the supposition of no material extension of the spirit of hostility.

I cannot dismiss the subject of Indian affairs without again recommending to your consideration the expediency of more adequate provision for giving energy to the laws throughout our interior frontier, and for restraining the commission of outrages upon the Indians; without which all pacific plans must prove nugatory. To enable, by competent rewards, the employment of qualified and trusty persons to reside among them, as agents, would also contribute to the preservation of peace and good neighbourhood. If, in addition to these expedients, an eligible plan could be devised for promoting civilization among the friendly tribes, and for carrying on trade with them, upon a scale equal to their wants, and under regulations calculated to protect them from imposition and extortion, its influence in cementing their interests with our's could not but be considerable.

The prosperous state of our Revenue has been intimated. This would be still more the case, were it not for the impediments, which in some places continue to embarrass the collection of the duties on spirits distilled within the United States. These impediments have lessened, and are lessening in local extent, and as applied to the community at large, the contentment with the law appears to be progressive.

But symptoms of increased opposition having lately manifested themselves in certain quarters, I judged a special interposition on my part, proper and adviseable; and under this impression, have issued a proclamation, warning against all unlawful combinations and proceedings, having for their object or tending to obstruct the operation of the law in question, and announcing that all lawful ways and means would be strictly put in execution for bringing to justice the infractors thereof, and securing obedience thereto.

Measures have also been taken for the prosecution of offenders: and Congress may be assured, that nothing within Constitutional and legal limits, which may depend on me, shall be wanting to assert and maintain the just authority of the laws. In fulfilling this trust, I shall count intirely upon the full cooperation of the other departments of Government, and upon the zealous support of all good Citizens.

I cannot forbear to bring again into the view of the Legislature the subject of a revision of the Judiciary System. A representation from the Judges of the Supreme Court, which will be laid before you, points out some of the inconveniences that are experienced. In the course of the execution of the laws, considerations arise out of the structure of that System, which, in some cases, tend to relax their efficacy. As connected with this subject, provisions to facilitate the taking of bail upon processes out of the Courts of the United States, and supplementary definition of Offences against the Constitution and laws of the Union, and of the punishment for such Offences, will, it is presumed, be found worthy of particular attention.

Observations on the value of peace with other Nations are unnecessary. It would be wise, however, by timely provisions, to guard against those acts of our own Citizens, which might tend to disturb it, and to put ourselves in a condition to give that satisfaction to foreign Nations which we may sometimes have occasion to require from them. I particularly recommend to your consideration the means of preventing those aggressions by our Citizens on the territory of other nations, and other infractions of the law of Nations, which, furnishing just subject of complaint, might endanger our peace with them. And in general, the maintenance of a friendly intercourse with foreign powers will be presented to your attention by the expiration of the law for that purpose, which takes place, if not renewed, at the close of the present session.

In execution of the Authority given by the legislature, measures have been taken for engaging some artists from abroad to aid in the establishment of our mint; others have been employed at home. Provision has been made for the requisite buildings, and these are now putting into proper condition for the purposes of the establishment. There has also been a small beginning in the coinage of half-dismes; the want of small coins in circulation calling the first attention to them.

The regulation of foreign Coins in correspondency with the principles of our national coinage, as being essential to their due operation, and to order in our money concerns, will, I doubt not, be resumed and completed.

It is represented that some provisions in the law, which establishes the Post-Office, operate, in experiment, against the transmission of newspapers to distant parts of the Country. Should this, upon due inquiry, be found to be the case, a full conviction of the importance of facilitating the circulation of political intelligence and information, will, I doubt not, lead to the application of a remedy.

The adoption of a Constitution for the State of Kentucky has been notified to me. The Legislature will share with me in the satisfaction which arises from an event interesting to the happiness of the part of the Nation to which it relates, and conducive to the general Order.

It is proper likewise to inform you, that since my last communication on the subject, and in further execution of the Acts severally making provision for the public debt, and for the reduction thereof, three new loans have been effected, each for three millions of Florins. One at Antwerp, at the annual interest of four and one half per Cent, with an Allowance of four per Cent in lieu of all charges; and the other two at Amsterdam, at the annual interest of four per Cent, with an allowance of five and one half per Cent in one case, and of five per Cent in the other in lieu of all charges. The rates of these loans, and the circumstances under which they have been made, are confirmations of the high state of our Credit abroad.

Among the objects to which these funds have been directed to be applied, the payment of the debts due to certain foreign Officers, according to the provision made during the last Session, has been embraced.

Gentlemen of the House of Representatives: I entertain a strong hope that the state of the national finances is now sufficiently matured to enable you to enter upon a Systematic and effectual arrangement for the regular redemption and discharge of the public debt, according to the right which has been reserved to the Government. No measure can be more desireable, whether viewed with an eye to its intrinsic importance, or to the general sentiment and wish of the Nation.

Provision is likewise requisite for the reimbursement of the loan which has been made for the Bank of the United States, pursuant to the eleventh section of the Act by which it is incorporated. In fulfilling the public stipulations in this particular, it is expected a valuable saving will be made.

Appropriations for the current service of the ensuing year, and for such extraordinaries as may require provision, will demand, and, I doubt not, will engage your early attention.

Gentlemen of the Senate and of the House of Representatives: I content myself with recalling your attention, generally, to such objects, not particularized in my present, as have been suggested in my former communications to you.

Various temporary laws will expire during the present Session. Among these, that which regulates trade and intercourse with the Indian Tribes, will merit particular notice.

The results of your common deliberations, hitherto, will, I trust, be productive of solid and durable advantages to our Constituents; such as, by conciliating more and more their ultimate suffrage, will tend to strengthen and confirm their attachment to that constitution of Government, upon which, under Divine Providence, materially depend their Union, their safety and their happiness.

Still further to promote and secure these inestimable ends, there is nothing which can have a more powerful tendency, than the careful cultivation of harmony, combined with a due regard to stability, in the public Councils.

Passport for Jean Pierre Blanchard

Philadelphia, January 9, 1793.
To all to whom these presents shall come

The bearer hereof, Mr. Blanchard, a citizen of France, proposing to ascend in a balloon from the city of Philadelphia at 10 A.M. this day to pass in such direction and to descend in such place as circumstances may render most convenient.

These are there to recommend to all citizens of the United States and others that in his passage, descent, return, or journeying elsewhere, they oppose no hindrance or molestation to the said Mr. Blanchard: and that on the contrary, they receive and aid him with that humanity and good will which may render honor to their country and justice to an individual so distinguished by his efforts to establish and advance his art in order to make it useful to mankind in general.

To Henry Lee

Philadelphia, January 20, 1793.
Dear Sir: I have been favored with your letter of the 6th. instant, congratulatory on my re-election to the Chair of

Government. A mind must be insensible indeed, not to be gratefully impressed by so distinguished, and honorable a testimony of public approbation and confidence: and, as I suffered my name to be contemplated on this occasion, it is more than probable that I should, for a moment, have experienced chagreen if my re-election had not been by a pretty respectable vote. But to say I feel pleasure from the prospect of *commencing* another tour of duty, would be a departure from truth; for however it might savour of affectation in the opinion of the world (who by the bye can only guess at my sentimts. as it never has been troubled with them) my particular, and confidential friends well know, that it was after a long and painful conflict in my own breast, that I was withheld (by considerations which are not necessary to mention) from requesting, *in time*, that no vote might be thrown away upon me; it being my fixed determination to return to the walks of private life, at the end of my term.

I am sorry to be informed by your letter, that death has snatched from us my old acquaintance and friend Colo. Bassett. The manner of it, adds to the regret. We shall all follow, some sooner and some later; and, from accounts, my poor Nephew is likely to be amongst the first.

Mrs. Washington joins me in wishing you the return of many new and happy years. With very great esteem etc.

To the Members of the New Church in Baltimore

Gentlemen: It has ever been my pride to merit the approbation of my fellow Citizens by a faithful and honest discharge of the duties annexed to those stations in which they have been pleased to place me; and the dearest rewards of my services have been those testimonies of esteem and confidence with which they have honored me. But to the manifest interposition of an over-ruling Providence, and to the patriotic exertions of united america, are to be ascribed those events, which have given us a respectable rank among the nations of the Earth.

We have abundant reason to rejoice that in this Land the light of truth and reason has triumphed over the power of bigotry and superstition, and that every person may here worship God according to the dictates of his own heart. In this enlightened Age and in this Land of equal liberty it is our boast, that a man's religious tenets will not forfeit the protection of the Laws, nor deprive him of the right of attaining and holding the highest Offices that are known in the United States.

Your prayers for my present and future felicity are received with gratitude; and I sincerely wish, Gentlemen, that you may in your social and individual capacities taste those blessings, which a gracious God bestows upon the Righteous.

c. January 27, 1793

To Frances Bassett Washington

Philadelphia, February 24, 1793.
My dear Fanny: To you, who so well know the affectionate regard I had for our departed friend, it is unnecessary to describe the sorrow with which I was afflicted at the news of his death, although it was an event I had expected many weeks before it happened. To express this sorrow with the force I feel it, would answer no other purpose than to revive, in your breast, that poignancy of anguish, which, by this time, I hope is abated. Reason and resignation to the divine will, which is just, and wise in all its dispensations, cannot, in such a mind as yours, fail to produce this effect.

The object of the present letter is to convey to your mind the warmest assurances of my love, friendship, and disposition to serve you; These also I profess to have in an eminent degree, for your Children.

What plan you have contemplated, or whether in so short a time you have contemplated any, is unknown to me; and therefore I add, that the one which strikes me most favorably, by being best calculated to promote the interest of yourself and Children, is to return to your old habitation at Mount Vernon. You can go to no place where you will be more welcome, nor to any where you can live at less expence, or trouble; matters at Mount Vernn. are now so arranged as to be under the care of responsible persons, and so they may continue; which would ease you of that anxiety, which the care of so large a family, otherwise, would naturally involve you in. It is unnecessary to observe to you that Housekeeping, under *any* circumstances, and with the best œconomy, is expensive; and, where provision for it is to be made, will be found, I fear, beyond your means.

You might bring my niece, Harriet Washington with you for a Companion; whose conduct, I hear with pleasure, has given much satisfaction to my sister. I shall, under my present view of things, be at Mount Vernon about the first of April for, perhaps, a fortnight; But your Aunt and family will not, I expect, be there before the middle of July. My Affectionate regards attend you and your Children; and I shall always be your sincere friend.

Second Inaugural Address

March 4, 1793.

Fellow-Citizens: I am again called upon by the voice of my Country to execute the functions of its Chief Magistrate. When the occasion proper for it shall arrive, I shall endeavour to express the high sense I entertain of this distinguished honor, and of the confidence which has been reposed in me by the people of United America.

Previous to the execution of any official act of the President, the Constitution requires an Oath of Office. This Oath I am now about to take, and in your presence, that if it shall be found during my administration of the Government I have in any instance violated willingly, or knowingly, the injunction thereof, I may (besides incurring Constitutional punishmt) be subject to the upbraidings of all who are now witnesses of the present solemn Ceremony.

To Gouverneur Morris

(Private)

Philadelphia, March 25, 1793.

My Dear Sir: It was not 'till the middle of February that I had the pleasure to receive your letter of the 23d. of October. If you, who are at the fountain head of those great and important transactions which have lately engrossed the attention of Europe and America, cannot pretend to say what will be their event, surely we, in this distant quarter, should be presumptuous indeed in venturing to predict it. and unwise should we be in the extreme to involve ourselves in the contests of European Nations, where our weight could be but small; tho' the loss to ourselves would be certain. I can however with truth aver that this Country is not guided by such narrow and mistaken policy as will lead it to wish the destruction of any nation, under an idea that our importance will be encreased in proportion as that of others is lessened. We should rejoice to see every nation enjoying all the advantages that nature and it's circumstances would admit, consistent with civil liberty, and the rights of other nations. Upon this ground the prosperity of this Country would unfold itself every day, and every day would it be growing in political importance.

Mr. Jefferson will communicate to you such official information as we have to give, and will transmit the Laws, public papers &c.

I have thought it best, My Dr. Sir, not to let slip this opportunity of acknowledging the receipt of your Letter, lest no other should occur to me very soon, as I am called to Mount Vernon by the death of my Nephew, Major Washington, and am on the point of setting out for that place tomorrow. I need not tell you that this is of course a very busy moment with me, it will therefore account for the conciseness of this letter by which however you must not measure my regard.

You see me again entering upon the arduous duties of an important office I do it so contrary to my intention, that it would require more time than I have prescribed to myself, to assign the reasons and therefore I shall leave them for your own suggestion, aided by the publications which you will find in the Gazettes. I am etc.

To Thomas Jefferson

Dear Sir   Mount Vernon April 12 1793.
    Your letter of the 7 instant was brought to me by the last Post.

War having actually commenced between France and Great Britain, it behoves the Government of this Country to use every means in it's power to prevent the citizens thereof from embroiling us with either of those powers, by endeavouring to maintain a strict neutrality. I therefore require that you will give the subject mature consideration, that such measures as shall be deemed most likely to effect this desirable purpose may be adopted without delay; for I have understood that vessels are already designated as Privateers, and preparing accordingly.

Such other measures as may be necessary for us to pursue against events which it may not be in our Power to avoid or controul, you will also think of, and lay them before me at my arrival in Philadelphia, for which place I shall set out To-morrow; but will leave it to the advices which I may receive tonight by the Post, to determine whether it is to be by the most direct Rout, or by the one I proposed to have come—that is, by Reading, the Canals between the Rivers of Pennsylvania, Harrisburgh, Carlisle &ca. With very great esteem & regard I am, Dear Sir, Your mo: hble Servt.

To the Earl of Buchan

                              Philadelphia, April 22, 1793.
    My Lord: You might, from appearances, suspect me of in-attention to the honor of your corrispondence: and if you should, I can assure you it would give me pain. Or you might conceive that, I had rather make excuses than acknowledge in

time, the receipt of your favors as this is the second instance of considerable lapse between the dates of them and my acknowledgments, this also would hurt me, for the truth is, that your favor of the 22d. of last October, under cover of one from Doctr. Anderson of the 3d. of November, accompanying the 7th. 8th. 10th. and 11th. Volumes of the Bee, did not come to my hands until the 18th. of the prest. month.

Having by me the rough draught of the letter I had the honor of addressing to your Lordship in May, I do, agreeably to your request, transmit a copy thereof. It is difficult for me, however, to acct. for the miscarriage or delay of the original, as it was committed to the care of Mr. Robertson at his *own* request, to be forwarded along with the Portrait of me which (for the reasons therein assigned) a preference had been given of him to take, for your Lordship; both of which, I expected you had received long since.

The Works of Doctr. Anderson do him much credit, and when they are more extensively known will, I am persuaded, meet a very ready Sale in this Country. I have taken an occasion to mention his wish to a respectable member of the Philosophical Society of this City, who has promised to bring his name forward at the next meeting: entertaining no doubt of his being readily admitted; as his pretensions are known to stand on solid ground.

The favorable wishes wch your Lordship has expressed for the prosperity of this young and rising Country, cannot but be gratefully received by all its Citizens, and every lover of it. One mean to the contribution of which, and its happiness, is very judiciously portrayed in the following words of your letter "to be little heard of in the great world of Politics." These words I can assure your lordship are expressive of my sentiments, on this head; and I believe it is the sincere wish of United America to have nothing to do with the political intrigues, or the squabbles of European Nations; but on the contrary, to exchange commodities and live in peace and amity with all the inhabitants of the Earth. And this I am persuaded they will do, if rightfully it can be done. To administer justice to, and receive it from every power with whom they are connected will, I hope, be always found the most prominent feature in the Administration of this Country; and I flatter myself that nothing short of imperious necessity can occasion a breach with any of them. Under such a system, if we are allowed to pursue it; the agriculture and Mechanical Arts; the wealth and population of these States will increase with that degree of rapidity as to baffle all calculation and must surpass any idea your Lordship can, hitherto, have entertained on the occasion.

To evince that our views, whether realized or not, are expanded; I take the liberty of sending you the Plan of a new City, situated about the centre of the Union of these States, which is designed for the permanent Seat of the Government; and we are at this moment deeply engaged and far advanced in extending the inland navigation of the River (Potomack) on which it stands and the branches thereof through a tract of as rich Country for hundreds of miles as any in the world. Nor is this a solitary instance of attempts of the kind, although it is the only one which is near completion, and in partial use. Several other very important ones are commenced and little doubt is entertained that in 10 years if left undisturbed we shall open a communication by water with all the Lakes Northward and Westward of us with which we have territorial connexion; and an inland navigation in a very few years more from Rhode Island to Georgia inclusively; partly by Cuts between the Great Bays and sounds and partly between the Islands and Sand banks and the Main; from Albemarle Sound to the River St. Marys. To these may also be added the erection of Bridges over considerable Rivers, and the commencement of Turnpike roads as further indications of improvements in hand.

The family of Fairfax in Virginia of whom you speak are also related to me by several intermarriages, before it came to this Country, (as I am informed) and since; and what remain of the old stock are near neighbours to my estate of Mount Vernon. The late Lord (Thomas) with whom I was perfectly acquainted, lived at the distance of Sixty miles from me after he had removed from Belvoir (the seat of his kinsman) which adjoins my estate just mentioned, and is going to be inhabited by a young member of the family as soon as the house, wch. some years ago was burnt down can be rebuilt. With great esteem &c.

Proclamation of Neutrality

Philadelphia, April 22, 1793.

Whereas it appears that a state of war exists between Austria, Prussia, Sardinia, Great Britain, and the United Netherlands, on the one part, and France on the other; and the duty and interest of the United States require, that they should with sincerity and good faith adopt and pursue a conduct friendly and impartial towards the belligerent powers:

I have therefore thought fit by these presents, to declare the disposition of the United States to observe the conduct aforesaid towards those powers respectively; and to exhort and warn the citizens of the United States carefully to avoid all acts and proceedings whatsoever, which may in any manner tend to contravene such disposition.

And I do hereby also make known, that whosoever of the citizens of the United States shall render himself liable to punishment or forfeiture under the law of nations, by committing, aiding or abetting hostilities against any of the said powers, or by carrying to any of them, those articles which are deemed contraband by the modern usage of nations, will not receive the protection of the United States against such punishment or forfeiture; and further that I have given instructions to those officers to whom it belongs, to cause prosecutions to be instituted against all persons, who shall, within the cognizance of the Courts of the United States, violate the law of nations, with respect to the powers at war, or any of them.

To Henry Lee

(Private)

Philadelphia, July 21, 1793.

Dear Sir: I should have thanked you at an earlier period for your obliging letter of the 14th. ulto. had it not come to my hands a day or two only before I set out for Mount Vernon; and at a time when I was much hurried, and indeed very much perplexed with the disputes, memorials and what not, with which the Government were pestered by one or other of the petulant representatives of the powers at War: and because, since my return to this City (nine days ago) I have been more than ever overwhelmed with their complaints. In a word, the trouble they give is hardly to be described.

My journey to and from Mount Vernon was sudden and rapid, and as short as I could make it. It was occasioned by the unexpected death of Mr. Whitting (my manager) at a critical season for the business with wch. he was entrusted. Where to supply his place, I know not; of course my concerns at Mount Vernon are left as a body without a head; but this by the bye.

The communications in your letter were pleasing and grateful; for, although I have done no public act with which my mind upbraids me, yet it is highly satisfactory to learn that the things which I do (of an interesting tendency to the peace and happiness of this Country) are generally approved by my fellow Citizens. But, were the case otherwise, I should not be less inclined to know the sense of the people upon every matter of great public concern; for, as I have no wish superior to that of promoting the happiness and welfare of this Country, so, consequently, it is only for me to know the means to accomplish the end, if it be within the compass of my powers.

That there are in this, as well as in all other Countries, discontented characters, I well know; as also that these characters are actuated by very different views: Some good, from an opinion that the measures of the General Government are impure: some bad, and (if I might be allowed to use so harsh an expression) diabolical; inasmuch as they are not only meant to impede the measures of that Government generally, but more especially (as a great mean towards the accomplishment of it) to destroy the confidence, which it is necessary for the people to place (until they have unequivocal proof of demerit) in their public servants; for in this light I consider myself, whilst I am an occupant of office; and, if they were to go further and call me their slave, (during this period) I would not dispute the point.

But in what will this abuse terminate? The result, as it respects myself, I care not; for I have a consolation within, that no earthly efforts can deprive me of, and that is, that neither ambitious nor interested motives have influenced my conduct. The arrows of malevolence, therefore, however barbed and well pointed, never can reach the most vulnerable part of me; though, whilst I am *up* as a *mark*, they will be continually aimed. The publications in Freneau's and Beeche's papers are outrages on common decency; and they progress in that style, in proportion as their pieces are treated with contempt, and are passed by in silence, by those at whom they are aimed. The tendency of them, however, is too obvious to be mistaken by men of cool and dispassionate minds, and, in my opinion, ought to alarm them; because it is difficult to prescribe bounds to the effect.

The light in which you endeavored to place the views and conduct of this Country to Mr. G——; and the sound policy thereof, as it respected his own, was, unquestionably the true one, and such as a man of penetration, left to himself, would most certainly have viewed them in; but mum on this head. Time may unfold more, than prudence ought to disclose at present. As we are told, that you have exchanged the rugged and dangerous field of Mars, for the soft and pleasurable bed of Venus, I do in this, as I shall in every thing you may pursue like unto it good and laudable, wish you all imaginable success and happiness being, with esteem &c.

To Edmund Pendleton

Mount Vernon, September 23, 1793.

My dear Sir: With very sincere pleasure I received your private letter of the 11th. instant. This pleasure was not a little enhanced by your reiterated assurance of my still holding that place in your estimation which, on more occasions than one, you have given me the most flattering testimony, highly gratifying to my mind. This assurance came opportunely, as I had begun to conceive (though unable to assign a cause) that some part of my public conduct, however well meant my endeavors, had appeared unfavorable in your eyes, for you will please to recollect that, formerly you promised me, and I always expected, an annual letter from you. It is now (if my memory has not failed me) at least four years since I have had that pleasure.

Sequestered you say you are, from the World, and know little of what is transacting in it but from Newspapers. I regret this exceedingly. I wish you had more to do on the great theatre; and that your means of information were co-equal to your abilities, and the disposition I know you possess to judge properly of public measures. It would be better perhaps for that public it should be so; for be assured we have some infamous Papers, calculated for disturbing if not absolutely intended to disturb, the peace of the community.

With respect to the fiscal conduct of the S—t—y of the Tr—s—y I will say nothing; because an enquiry, more than probable, will be instituted next Session of Congress into some of the Allegations against him, which, eventually, may involve the whole; and because, if I mistake not, he will seek, rather than shrink from, an investigation. A fair opportunity will then be given to the impartial world to form a just estimate of his Acts, and probably of his motives. No one, I will venture to say, wishes more devoutly than I do that they may be probed to the bottom, be the result what it will.

With the most scrupulous truth I can assure you, that your free and unreserved opinion upon any public measure of importance will always be acceptable to me, whether it respects men, or measures; and on no man do I wish it to be expressed more fully than on myself; for as I can conscientiously declare that I have no object in view incompatible with the Constitution, and the obvious interests of this Country, nor no earthly desire *half* as strong as that of returning to the walks of private life, so, of consequence I only wish whilst I am a Servant of the public, to know the Will of my masters, that I may govern myself accordingly.

You do me no more than Justice when you suppose that from motives of respect to the Legislature (and I might add from my interpretation of the Constitution) I give my Signature to many Bills with which my Judgment is at variance. In declaring this, however, I allude to no particular Act. From the nature of the Constitution, I must approve all the parts of a Bill, or reject it in toto. To do the latter can only be

Justified upon the clear and obvious ground of propriety; and I never had such confidence in my own faculty of judging as to be over tenacious of the opinions I may have imbibed in doubtful cases.

Mrs. Washington who enjoys tolerable good health joins me most cordially in best wishes to you and Mrs. Pendleton. I wish you may live long, continue in good health, and end your days as you have been waring them away, happily and respected. Always, and most affectionately I am &c.

To William Pearce

Mount Vernon, October 6, 1793.

Mr. Pearce: Enclosed is a copy of our agreement with my signature to it.

Since you were here, Mrs. Washington the Widow of my Nephew, who formerly lived at this place, has resolved as soon as we leave it, to remove to her Brother's in the lower part of this State, and will not, I believe, return to reside at it again. This will make it more convenient and agreeable, both for yourself and me, that you should live the Winter, at least, at my Mansion house; as it will allow more time for my carpenters to provide for Mr. Crow, and to put the place he lives at in better repair than it now is for yourself, if there should be occasion for you to go there; and this too, under your own inspection.

The right wing to my dwelling house as you possibly may have noticed, and heard called the Hall, (being kept altogether for the use of Strangers) has two good rooms below (with tiled floors) and as many above, all with fire places. This will accomodate your family (being a larger house) better than Crow's; and by being here, you will have the use of my Kitchen, the Cook belonging thereto, Frank the House Servant, a boy also in the House. The Stable, Garden, &ca. &ca. without any additional expence to me; at the same time that it will, by placing you in the centre of the business, ease you of much trouble; for otherwise, the frequent calls from the Farms, from workmen of different descriptions for Tools,

Nails, Iron, &ca., from the Store, and the particular attention which matters abt. the Mansion house will require, would have occasioned you many an inconvenient ride here, the necessity for which will be entirely superceded, as your mornings and evenings will, of course, be spent where your presence will be most wanting.

As I am never sparing (with proper œconomy) in furnishing my Farms with any, and every kind of Tool and implement that is calculated to do good and neat work, I not only authorize you to bring the kind of ploughs you were speaking to me about, but any others, the utility of which you have proved from your own experience; particularly a kind of hand rake which Mr. Stuart tells me are used on the Eastern Shore of Maryland in lieu of Hoes for Corn at a certain stage of its growth, and a Scythe and Cradle different from those used with us, and with which the grain is laid much better. In short I shall begrudge no reasonable expence that will contribute to the improvement and neatness of my Farms; for nothing pleases me better than to see them in good order, and every thing trim, handsome, and thriving about them; nor nothing hurts me more than to find them otherwise, and the tools and implements laying wherever they were last used, exposed to injuries from Rain, sun, &ca.

I hope you will endeavor to arrange your own concerns in such a manner as to be here as much before the time agreed on as you conveniently can. Great advantages to me will result from this, by putting the business in a good train before the Fall operations are closed by the frosts of Winter, and all improvements are thereby at an end for that season. On the other hand, inconveniences to yourself may arise from delay on account of the Weather, Navigation, &ca; there having been instances of this River's closing with Ice several days before Christmas which might prevent the removal of your things in time. That your living at the Mansion may be attended with no more expence to you than if you had gone to the other place (at which Crow now lives) on account of Gentlemen, who now and then call here out of curiosity, as they are passing through the Country, I shall lay in such things as will be necessary for this purpose, and the occasions (which are but rare) may require.

I expect to leave this place about the 28th of the Month for Philadelphia, or the neighbourhood of it; any letter therefore which shall arrive before that time will find me here, afterwards it will have to go to Philadelphia where it had better be directed. I am etc.

Fifth Annual Message to Congress

Philadelphia, December 3, 1793.

Fellow Citizens of the Senate,
and of the House of Representatives

Since the commencement of the term, for which I have been again called into office, no fit occasion has arisen for expressing to my fellow Citizens at large, the deep and respectful sense, which I feel, of the renewed testimony of public approbation. While on the one hand, it awakened my gratitude for all those instances of affectionate partiality, with which I have been honored by my Country; on the other, it could not prevent an earnest wish for that retirement, from which no private consideration should ever have torn me. But influenced by the belief, that my conduct would be estimated according to its real motives; and that the people, and the authorities derived from them, would support exertions, having nothing personal for their object, I have obeyed the suffrage which commanded me to resume the Executive power; and I humbly implore that Being, on whose Will the fate of Nations depends, to crown with success our mutual endeavours for the general happiness.

As soon as the War in Europe had embraced those Powers, with whom the United States have the most extensive relations; there was reason to apprehend that our intercourse with them might be interrupted, and our disposition for peace, drawn into question, by the suspicions, too often entertained by belligerent Nations. It seemed therefore to be my duty to admonish our Citizens of the consequences of a contraband trade, and of hostile Acts to any of the parties; and to obtain by a declaration of the existing legal state of things, an easier admission of our right to the immunities, belonging to our situation. Under these impressions the Proclamation, which will be laid before you, was issued.

In this posture of affairs, both new and delicate, I resolved to adopt general rules, which should conform to the Treaties, and assert the priviledges, of the United States. These were reduced into a system, which will be communicated to you. Although I have not thought myself at liberty to forbid the Sale of the prizes, permitted by our treaty of Commerce with France to be brought into our ports; I have not refused to cause them to be restored, when they were taken within the protection of our territory; or by vessels commissioned, or equipped in a warlike form within the limits of the United States.

It rests with the wisdom of Congress to correct, improve or enforce this plan of procedure; and it will probably be found expedient, to extend the legal code, and the Jurisdiction of the Courts of the United States, to many cases, which, though dependent on principles already recognized, demand some further provisions.

Where individuals shall within the United States, array themselves in hostility against any of the powers at war; or enter upon Military expeditions, or enterprizes within the jurisdiction of the United States; or usurp and exercise judicial authority within the United States; or where the penalties on violations of the law of Nations may have been indistinctly marked, or are inadequate; these offences cannot receive too early and close an attention, and require prompt and decisive remedies.

Whatsoever those remedies may be, they will be well administered by the Judiciary, who possess a long established course of investigation, effectual process, and Officers in the habit of executing it. In like manner; as several of the Courts have *doubted*, under particular circumstances, their power to liberate the vessels of a Nation at peace, and even of a citizen of the United States, although seized under a false colour of being hostile property; and have *denied* their power to liberate certain captures within the protection of our territory; it would seem proper to regulate their jurisdiction in these points. But if the Executive is to be the resort in either of the two last mentioned cases, it is hoped, that he will be authorized by law, to have facts ascertained by the Courts, when, for his own information, he shall request it.

I cannot recommend to your notice measures for the fulfilment of *our* duties to the rest of the world, without again pressing upon you the necessity of placing ourselves in a condition of compleat defence, and of exacting from *them* the fulfilment of *their* duties towards *us*. The United States ought not to endulge a persuasion, that, contrary to the order of human events, they will for ever keep at a distance those painful appeals to arms, with which the history of every other nation abounds. There is a rank due to the United States among Nations, which will be withheld, if not absolutely lost, by the reputation of weakness. If we desire to avoid insult, we must be able to repel it; if we desire to secure peace, one of the most powerful instruments of our rising prosperity, it must be known, that we are at all times ready for War.

The documents, which will be presented to you, will shew the amount, and kinds of Arms and military stores now in our Magazines and Arsenals: and yet an addition even to these supplies cannot with prudence be neglected; as it would leave nothing to the uncertainty of procuring a warlike apparatus, in the moment of public danger. Nor can such arrangements, with such objects, be exposed to the censure or jealousy of the warmest friends of Republican Government. They are incapable of abuse in the hands of the Militia, who ought to possess a pride in being the depositary of the force of the Republic, and may be trained to a degree of energy, equal to every military exigency of the United States. But it is an inquiry, which cannot be too solemnly pursued, whether the act "more effectually to provide for the National defence by establishing an uniform Militia throughout the United States" has organized them so as to produce their full effect; whether your own experience in the several States has not detected some imperfections in the scheme; and whether a material feature in an improvement of it, ought not to be, to afford an opportunity for the study of those branches of the Military art, which can scarcely ever be attained by practice alone?

The connexion of the United States with Europe, has become extremely interesting. The occurrences, which relate to it, and have passed under the knowledge of the Executive, will be exhibited to Congress in a subsequent communication.

When we contemplate the war on our frontiers, it may be truly affirmed, that every reasonable effort has been made to adjust the causes of dissension with the Indians, North of the Ohio. The Instructions given to the Commissioners evince a moderation and equity proceeding from a sincere love of peace, and a liberality, having no restriction but the essential interests and dignity of the United States. The attempt, however, of an amicable negotiation having been frustrated, the troops have marched to act offensively. Although the proposed treaty did not arrest the progress of military preparation; it is doubtful, how far the advance of the Season, before good faith justified active movements, may retard them, during the remainder of the year. From the papers and intelligence, which relate to this important subject, you will determine, whether the deficiency in the number of Troops, granted by law, shall be compensated by succours of Militia; or additional encouragements shall be proposed to recruits. An anxiety has been also demonstrated by the Executive, for peace with the Creeks and the Cherokees. The former have been relieved with Corn and with clothing, and offensive measures against them prohibited during the recess of Congress. To satisfy the complaints of the latter, prosecutions have been instituted for the violences committed upon them. But the papers, which will be delivered to you, disclose the critical footing on which we stand in regard to both those tribes; and it is with Congress to pronounce what shall be done.

After they shall have provided for the present emergency, it will merit their most serious labours, to render tranquillity with the Savages permanent, by creating ties of interest. Next to a rigorous execution of justice on the violators of peace, the establishment of commerce with the Indian nations in behalf of the United States, is most likely to conciliate their attachment. But it ought to be conducted without fraud, without extortion, with constant and plentiful supplies; with a ready market for the commodities of the Indians, and a stated price for what they give in payment, and receive in exchange. Individuals will not pursue such a traffic, unless

they be allured by the hope of profit; but it will be enough
for the United States to be reimbursed only. Should this recommendation accord with the opinion of Congress, they will
recollect, that it cannot be accomplished by any means yet in
the hands of the Executive.

Gentlemen of the House of Representatives

The Commissioners, charged with the settlement of Accounts between the United and individual States, concluded
their important functions, within the time limited by Law; and
the balances, struck in their report, which will be laid before
Congress, have been placed on the Books of the Treasury.

On the first day of June last, an instalment of one million
of florins became payable on the loans of the United States in
Holland. This was adjusted by a prolongation of the period
of reimbursement, in nature of a new loan, at an interest at
five per cent for the term of ten years; and the expences of
this operation were a commission of three pr Cent.

The first instalment of the loan of two millions of dollars
from the Bank of the United States, has been paid, as was
directed by Law. For the second, it is necessary, that provision
should be made.

No pecuniary consideration is more urgent, than the regular redemption and discharge of the public debt: on none
can delay be more injurious, or an œconomy of time more
valuable.

The productiveness of the public revenues hitherto, has
continued to equal the anticipations which were formed of it;
but it is not expected to prove commensurate with all the
objects, which have been suggested. Some auxiliary provisions
will, therefore, it is presumed, be requisite; and it is hoped
that these may be made, consistently with a due regard to the
convenience of our Citizens, who cannot but be sensible of
the true wisdom of encountering a small present addition to
their contributions, to obviate a future accumulation of
burthens.

But here, I cannot forbear to recommend a repeal of the
tax on the transportation of public prints. There is no resource
so firm for the Government of the United States, as the affections of the people guided by an enlightened policy; and

to this primary good, nothing can conduce more, than a faithful representation of public proceedings, diffused, without restraint, throughout the United States.

An estimate of the appropriations, necessary for the current service of the ensuing year, and a statement of a purchase of Arms and Military stores made during the recess, will be presented to Congress.

Gentlemen of the Senate, and of the House of Representatives

The several subjects, to which I have now referred, open a wide range to your deliberations; and involve some of the choicest interests of our common Country. Permit me to bring to your remembrance the magnitude of your task. Without an unprejudiced coolness, the welfare of the Government may be hazarded; without harmony, as far as consists with freedom of Sentiment, its dignity may be lost. But, as the Legislative proceedings of the United States will never, I trust, be reproached for the want of temper or candour; so shall not the public happiness languish, from the want of my strenuous and warmest cooperations.

To Arthur Young

Philadelphia, December 12, 1793.

Sir: I wrote to you three months ago, or more, by my late secretary and friend, Mr. Lear; but as his departure from this Country for Great Britain, was delayed longer than he or I expected, it is at least probable that that letter will not have reached your hands at a much earlier period than the one I am now writing.

At the time it was written, the thoughts which I am now about to disclose to you were not even in embryo; and whether, in the opinion of others, there be impropriety, or not, in communicating the object which has given birth to them, is not for me to decide. My own mind reproaches me with none, but if yours should view the subject differently, burn this letter and the draught which accompanies it, and the whole matter will be consigned to oblivion.

All my landed property East of the Apalachian Mountains
is under Rent, except the Estate called Mount Vernon. This,
hitherto, I have kept in my own hands; but from my present
situation; from my advanced time of my life; from a wish to
live free from care, and as much at my ease as possible during
the remainder of it; and from other causes which are not necessary to detail, I have, latterly, entertained serious thoughts
of letting this estate also, reserving the Mansion house farm
for my own residence, occupation, and amusement in agriculture; provided I can obtain what in my own judgment, and
in the opinions of others whom I have consulted the low Rent
which I shall mention hereafter; and provided also I can settle
it with *good* farmers.

The quantity of ploughable land (including meadow); the
relative situation of the farms one to another; and the division
of these farms into seperate inclosures; with the quantity and
situation of the Woodland appertaining to the tract, will be
better delineated by the sketch herewith sent (which is made
from actual surveys, subject nevertheless to revision and correction) than by a volume of words.

No estate in United America is more pleasantly situated
than this. It lyes in a high, dry and healthy Country 300 miles
by water from the Sea, and, as you will see by the plan, on
one of the finest Rivers in the world. Its margin is washed by
more than ten miles of tide water; from the bed of which, and
the enumerable coves, inlets and small marshes with wch. it
abounds, an inexhaustible fund of rich mud may be drawn as
a manure; either to be used seperately, or in a compost, according to the judgment of the farmer. It is situated in a latitude between the extremes of heat and cold, and is the same
distance by land and water, with good roads and the best
navigation (to and) from the Federal City, Alexandria, and
George town; distant from the first twelve, from the second
nine, and from the last sixteen miles. The federal City in the
year 1800 will become the seat of the general Government of
the United States. It is encreasing fast in buildings, and rising
into consequence; and will, I have no doubt, from the advantages given to it by nature, and its proximity to a rich interior
country, and the western territory, become the emporium of
the United States. The Soil of the tract I am speaking, is a

good loam, more inclined however to Clay than Sand. From use, and I might add abuse, it is become more and more consolidated, and of course heavier to work. The *greater* part is a greyish clay; some part is a dark mould; a very little is inclined to sand; and scarcely any to stone. A husbandman's wish would not lay the farms more level than they are, and yet some of the fields (but in no great degree) are washed into gullies, from which all of them have not, as yet, been recovered.

This River, which encompasses the land the distance abovementioned, is well supplied with various kinds of fish at all Seasons of the year; and in the Spring with the greatest profusion of Shad, Herring, Bass, Carp, Perch, Sturgeon &ca. Several valuable fisheries appertain to the estate; the whole shore in short is one entire fishery.

There are, as you will perceive by the plan, four farms besides that at the Mansion house: these four contain 3260 acres of cultivable land; to which some hundreds more, adjoining, as may be seen, might be added, if a greater quantity should be required; but as they were never designed for, so neither can it be said they are calculated to suit tenants of either the first, or of the lower class; because those who have the strength and resources proportioned to farms of from 500 to 1200 acres (which these contain) would hardly be contented to live in such houses as are thereon; and if they were to be divided and subdivided, so as to accommodate tenants of small means, say from 50 to one or 200 acres, there would be none; except on the lots which might happen to include the present dwelling-houses of my Overlookers (called Bailiffs with you), Barns, and Negro Cabins. Nor would I chuse to have the woodland (already too much pillaged of its timber) ransacked, for the purpose of building many more. The soil, howevr, is excellent for Bricks, or for Mud walls; and to the buildings of such houses there wd. be no limitation, nor to that of thatch for the cover of them.

The towns already mentioned (to those who might incline to encounter the expence) are able to furnish scantling, plank, and shingles to any amount, and on reasonable terms; and they afford a ready market also for the produce of the land.

On what is called Union farm (containing 928 acres of

arable and Meadow) there is a newly erected Brick Barn equal perhaps to any in America, and for conveniences of all sorts, particularly for sheltering and feeding horses, cattle, &c., scarcely to be exceeded anywhere. A new house is now building in a central position, not far from the Barn, for the Overlooker; which will have two Rooms 16 by 18 feet below and one or two above nearly of the same size. Convenient thereto is sufficient accommodation for fifty odd Negroes (old and young) but these buildings might not be thought good enough for the workmen or day labourers of your Country.

Besides these, a little without the limits of the farm (as marked in the Plan) are one or two other houses very pleasantly situated; and which, in case this farm should be divided into two (as it formerly was) would answer well for the Eastern division. The buildings thus enumerated are all that stand on the premises.

Dogue run farm (650 acres) has a small but new building for the Overlooker; one room only below, and the same above, 16 by 20 each; decent and comfortable for its size. It has also covering for forty odd negroes, similar to what is mentioned on Union farm. It has a new circular barn now finishing on a new construction; well calculated, it is conceived, for getting grain out of the straw more expeditiously than in the usual mode of threshing. There are good sheds also erecting, sufficient to cover 30 work horses and Oxen.

Muddy hole farm (476 acres) has a house for the Overlooker, in size and appearance nearly like that at Dogue run; but older The same kind of covering for about thirty negroes, and a tolerably good barn, with stables for the work horses.

River farm which is the largest of the four, and seperated from the others by little hunting Creek, (contains 1207 acres of ploughable land), has an Overlookers Ho. of one large and two small rooms below, and one or two above; sufficient covering for 50 or 60 Negroes like those before mentioned. A large barn and stables (gone much to decay, but these will be replaced next year with new ones).

I have deemed it necessary to give this detail of the buildings that a precise idea might be had of the conveniences and inconveniences of them; and I believe the recital is just in all its parts. The Inclosures are precisely, and accurately delineated in the plan; and the fences now are, or soon will be, in respectable order.

I would let these four farms to four substantial farmers, of wealth and strength sufficient to cultivate them; and who would insure to me the regular payment of the Rents; and I would give them leases for seven or ten years, at the rate of a Spanish milled dollar, or other money current at the time, in this country, equivalent thereto, for every acre of ploughable and mowable ground within the Inclosures of the respective farms, as marked in the plan; and would allow the tenants during that period to take fuel; and use timber from the Woodland to repair the buildings and to keep the fences in order; until live fences could be substituted in place of dead ones; but in this case, no sub-tenants would be allowed.

Or if these farms are adjudged too large, and the Rents of course too heavy for such farmers as might incline to emigrate, I should have no insuperable objection against dividing each into as many small ones as a society of them, formed for the purpose, could agree upon among themselves; even if it shd. be by the fields as they are now arranged (which the plan would enable them to do), provided such buildings as they would be content with, should be erected at their own expence, in the manner already mentioned. In which case as in the former, fuel, and timber for repairs, would be allowed; but as an inducement to parcel out my grounds into such small tenements, and to compensate me at the same time for the greater consumption of fuel and timber, and for the trouble and expence of collecting small Rents, I should expect a quarter of a dollar pr. acre in addition to what I have already mentioned. But in order to make these small farms more valuable to the occupants, and by way of reimbursing them for the expence of their establishment thereon, I would grant them leases for 15 or 18 years; although I have weighty objections to the measure, founded on my own experience of the disadvantage it is to the Lessor, in a Country where lands are rising every year in value. As an instance in proof, about 20 years ago I gave leases for three lives, in land I held above the blue Mountains, near the Shanondoah River, Seventy miles from Alexandria or any shipping port, at a Rent of one shilling pr. Acre (no part being then cleared) and now land of similar quality in the vicinity, with very trifling improvements thereon, is renting currently at five and more shillings pr. acre, and even as high as 8/.

My motives for letting this estate having been avowed, I will add, that the whole, (except the Mansion house farm) or none, will be parted with, and that upon unequivocal terms; because my object is to fix my income (be it what it may) upon a solid basis in the hands of *good* farmers; because I am not inclined to make a medley of it; and above all, because I could not relinquish my present course without a moral certainty of the substitute which is contemplated: for to break up these farms, remove my Negroes, and dispose of the property on them upon terms short of this would be ruinous.

Having said thus much, I am disposed to add further, that it would be in my power, and certainly it would be my inclination (upon the principle above) to accommodate the wealthy, or the weak handed farmer (and upon reasonable terms) with draughthorses, and working mules and Oxen; with cattle, Sheep and Hogs; and with such impliments of husbandry if they should not incline to bring them themselves, as are in use on the farms. On the four farms there are 54 draughthorses, 12 working Mules, and a sufficiency of Oxen, broke to the yoke; the precise number I am unable this moment to ascertain, as they are comprehended in the aggregate of the black cattle. Of the latter there are 317. Of sheep 634. Of hogs many, but as these run pretty much at large in the Woodland (which is all under fence) the number is uncertain. Many of the Negroes, male and female, might be hired by the year as labourers, if this should be preferred to the importation of that class of people; but it deserves consideration how far the mixing of whites and blacks together is advisable; especially where the former, are entirely unacquainted with the latter.

If there be those who are disposed to take these farms in their undevided State, on the terms which have been mentioned; it is an object of sufficient magnitude for them, or one of them in behalf of the rest, to come over and investigate the premises thoroughly, that there may be nothing to reproh themselves or me with if (though unintentionally) there should be defects in any part of the information herein given;

or if a society of farmers are disposed to adventure, it is still more incumbent on them to send over an Agent for the purposes abovementioned: for with me the measure must be so fixed as to preclude any cavil or discussion thereafter. And it may not be malapropos to observe in this place, that our Overlookers are generally engaged, and all the arrangements for the ensuing crops are made before the first of September in every year; it will readily be perceived then, that if this period is suffered to pass away, it is not to be regained until the next year. Possession might be given to the New comers at the Season just mentioned to enable them to put in their grain for the next Crop; but the final relinquishment could not take place until the Crops are gathered; which, of Indian Corn (maiz) seldom happens 'till towards Christmas as it must endure hard frosts before it can be safely housed.

I have endeavoured as far as my recollection of facts would enable me, or the documents in my possession allow, to give such information of the actual state of the farms as to enable persons at a distance to form as distinct ideas as the nature of the thing is susceptible short of ones own view, and having communicated the motives which have inclined me to a change in my system, I will announce to you the origin of them.

First: Few Ships, of late, have arrived from any part of G: Britain or Ireland without a number of emigrants, and some of them, by report, very respectable and full handed farmers. A number of others they say, are desirous of following; but are unable to obtain passages; but their coming in that manner, even if I was apprised of their arrival in time, would not answer my views for the reason already assigned; and which, as it is the ultimatum at present, I will take the liberty of repeating, namely: that I must carry my plan into *complete* execution, or not attempt it; and under such auspices too as to leave no doubt of the exact fulfilment; and,

2dly: because from the number of letters which I have received myself (and as it would seem from respectable people) enquiring into matters of this sort, with intimations of their wishes and even intentions of migrating to this Country, I can have no doubt of succeeding. But I have made no reply to these enquiries, or if any, in very general terms, because I did not want to engage in corrispondences of this sort with persons of whom I had no knowledge, nor indeed leisure for them if I had been so disposed.

I shall now conclude as I begun, with a desire, that if you see any impropriety in making these sentiments known to that class of people who might wish to avail themselves of the occasion, that it may not be mentioned. By a law, or by some regulation of your government, Artisans I am well aware, are laid under restraints; and for this reason I have studiously avoided any overtures to Mechanics although my occasions called for them. But never having heard that difficulties were thrown in the way of Husbandmen by the Government, is one reason for my bringing this matter to your view; a 2d is, that having, yourself expressed sentiments which showed that you had cast an eye towards this Country, and was not inattentive to the welfare of it, I was led to make my intentions known to you, that if you, or your friends were disposed to avail yourselves of the knowledge, you might take prompt measures for the execution. and 3dly. I was sure if you had lost sight of the object yourself, I could, nevertheless rely upon such information, as you might see fit to give me, and upon such characters too as you might be disposed to recommend.

Lengthy as this epistle is, I will crave your patience while I add, that it is written in too much haste, and under too great a pressure of public business at the commencement of an important session of Congress to be correct or properly digested. But the season of the year, and the apprehension of Ice are hurrying away the last vessel bound from this Port to London. I am driven therefore to the alternative of making the matter known in this hasty manner, and giving a rude sketch of the farms, which is the subject of it, or to encounter delay, the first I preferred. It can hardly be necessary to add, that I have *no* desire that any formal promulgation of these sentiments should be made.

To accomplish my wishes, in the manner herein expressed, would be agreeable to me; and in a way that cannot be exceptionable wd be more so. With much esteem etc.

To William Pearce

Philadelphia, December 18, 1793.

Mr. Pearce: The paper, enclosed with this letter, will give you my ideas, generally, of the course of Crops I wish to pursue. I am sensible more might be made from the farms for a year or two; but my object is to recover the fields from the exhausted state into which they have fallen, by oppressive crops, and to restore them (if possible by any means in my power) to health and vigour. But two ways will enable me to accomplish this. The first is to cover them with as much manure as possible (winter and summer). The 2d a judicious succession of Crops.

Manure can not be had in the abundance the fields require; for this reason, and to open the land which is hard bound by frequent cultivation and want of proper dressings, I have introduced Buck Wheat in the plentiful manner you will perceive by the Table; both as a manure, and as a substitute for Indian Corn for horses &ca; it being a great ameliorater of the soil. How far the insufferable conduct of my Overseers, or the difficulty of getting Buck Wheat and Oats for seed will enable me to carry my plan into effect, I am unable at this moment to decide. You, possibly, will be better able to inform me sometime hence. Colo. Ball of Leesburgh has promised to use his endeavours to procure and send the first to Mount Vernon; but where to get as much of the latter as will answer my purposes (unless I send them from this City) I know not; but before I can decide on the quantity it may be necessary for me to purchase it is essential I should know the quantity grown on my own estate; and which after I went to Virginia in September last I directed should no longer be fed away. The common Oats which are brought from the Eastern Shore to Alexandria for sale, I would not sow, first, because they are not of a good quality; and 2dly. because they are rarely, if ever, free from Garlick and wild Onions: with which, unfortunately, many of my fields are already but too plentifully stocked from the source already mentioned; and that too before I was aware of the evil.

I have already said that the insufferable conduct of my

Overseers may be one mean of frustrating my plan for the next year. I will now explain myself. You will readily perceive by the rotation of Crops I have adopted that a great deal of Fall plowing is indispensible. Of this I informed every one of them, and pointed out the fields which were to be plowed at this season. So anxious was I, that this work should be set about early, that I made an attempt soon after you were at Mount Vernon in September to begin it; and at several times afterwards repeated the operation in different fields at Dogue run farm; but the ground being excessively hard and dry, I found that to persevere would only destroy my horses without effecting the object in the manner it ought to be, and therefore I quit it; but left positive directions that it should recommence at every farm as soon as ever there should come rain to moysten the earth, and to stick constantly at it, except when the horses were employed in treading out Wheat (which was a work I also desired might be accomplished as soon as possible). Instead of doing either of these as I ordered I find by the reports, that McKoy has, now and then, plowed a few days only as if it were for amusement. That Stuart has but just begun to do it. And that neither Crow, nor Davy at Muddy hole, had put a plow into the ground so late as the 7th. of this month. Can it be expected then, that frosts, Snow and Rain will permit me to do much of this kind of work before March or April? When Corn planting, Oats sewing, and Buck Wht for manure ought to be going into the grd., in a well prepared state, instead of having it to flush up at that season, and when a good deal of Wheat is to be got out with the same horses. Crow having got out none of his that was stacked in the field nor Stuart and McKoy much of theirs which is in the same predicament; the excuse being, as far as it is communicated to me, that their whole time and force since the month of October has been employed in securing their Corn. When God knows little enough of that article will be made.

I am the more particular on this head for two reasons, first to let you see how little dependence there is on such men when left to themselves (for under Mr. Lewis it was very little better), and 2dly. to shew you the necessity of keeping these Overseers strictly to their duty, that is, to keep them from running about, and to oblige them to remain constantly with their people; and moreover, to see at what time they turn out of a morning, for I have strong suspicions that this, with some of them is at a late hour, the consequence of which to the Negroes is not difficult to foretell. All these Overseers as you will perceive by their agreements, which I herewith send are on standing wages; and this with men who are not actuated by the principles of honor or honesty, and not very regardful of their characters, leads naturally to endulgences, as *their* profits, whatever may be *mine* are the same whether they are at a horse race or on the farm, whether they are entertaining company (which I believe is too much the case) in their own houses or are in the field with the Negroes.

Having given you these ideas, I shall now add, that if you find any one of them inattentive to the duties which by the articles of agreement they are bound to perform, or such others as may reasonably be enjoined, Admonish them in a calm, but firm manner of the consequences. If this proves ineffectual discharge them, at any season of the year without scruple or hesitation, and do not pay them a copper; putting the non-compliance with their agreemt. in bar.

To treat them civilly is no more than what all men are entitled to, but my advice to you is, to keep them at a proper distance; for they will grow upon familiarity, in proportion as you will sink in authority, if you do not. Pass by no faults or neglects (especially at first) for overlooking only serves to generate another, and it is more than probable that some of them (one in particular) will try, at first, what lengths he may go. A steady and firm conduct, with an inquisitive inspection into and a proper arrangement of everything on your part, will, though it may give more trouble at first, save a great deal in the end, and you may rest assured that in everything which is just, and proper to be done on your part shall meet with the fullest support on mine. Nothing will contribute more to effect these desirable purposes than a good example, unhapply this was not set (from what I have learnt lately) by Mr. Whiting, who, it is said, drank freely, kept bad company at my house and in Alexandria, and was a very debauched person, wherever this is the case it is not easy for a man to throw the first stone for fear of having it returned to him: and this I take to be the true cause why Mr. Whiting did not look more scrupulously into the conduct of the Overseers, and more minutely into the smaller matters belonging to the Farms; which, though individually may be trifling, are not found so in the agregate; for there is no addage more true than an old Scotch one, that "many mickles make a muckle."

I have had but little opportunity of forming a correct opinion of my white Overseers, but such observations as I have made I will give.

Stuart appears to me to understand the business of a farm very well, and seems attentive to it. He is I believe a sober man, and according to his own account a very honest one. As I never found him (at the hours I usually visited the farm) absent from some part or another of his people I presume he is industrious and seldom from home. He is talkative, has a high opinion of his own skill and management, and seems to live in peace and harmony with the Negroes who are confided to his care. He speaks extremely well of them, and I have never heard any complaint of him. His work however, has been behind hand all the year, owing he says, and as I believe to his having too much plowing to do, and the last omission, of not plowing when he knew my motives for wishing it, has been extremely reprehensible. But upon the whole, if he stirs early, and works late, I have no other fault to find than the one I have just mentioned. His talkativeness and vanity may be humoured.

Crow is an active man, and not deficient in judgment. If kept strictly to his duty would, in many respects, make a good Overseer. But I am much mistaken in his character if he is not fond of visiting, and receiving visits. This, of course, withdraws his attention from his business, and leaves his people too much to themselves which produces idleness, or slight work on one side and flogging on the other; the last of which besides the dissatisfaction which it creates, has, in one or two instances been productive of serious consequences.

I am not clear either, that he gives that due attention to his Plow horses and other stock which is necessary, although he is very fond of riding the former, not only to Alexandria &ca. but about the farm, which I did not forbid as his house was very inconvenient to the scene of his business.

McKoy appears to me to be a sickly, slothful and stupid

fellow. He had many more hands than were necessary merely for his Crop, and though not 70 acres of Corn to cultivate, did nothing else. In short to level a little dirt that was taken out of the Meadow ditch below his house seems to have composed the principal part of his Fall work; altho' no finer season could have happened for preparing the second lot of the Mill swamp for the purpose of laying it to grass. If more exertion does not appear in him when he gets into better health he will be found an unfit person to overlook so important a farm especially as I have my doubts also of his care and attention to the horses &ca.

As to Butler, you will soon be a judge whether he will be of use to you or not. He may mean well, and for ought I know to the contrary may, in some things have judgment, but I am persuaded he has no more authority over the Negroes he is placed, than an old woman would have; and is as unable to get a proper days Work done by them as she would unless led to it by their own inclination wch. I know is not the case.

Davy at Muddy hole carries on his business as well as the white Overseers, and with more quietness than any of them. With proper directions he will do very well and probably give you less trouble than any of them except in attending to his care of the stock of which I fear he is negligent as there are deaths too frequent among them.

Thomas Green (Overlooker of the Carpenters) will, I am persuaded, require your closest attention, without which I believe it will be impossible to get any work done by my Negro Carpenters, in the first place, because, it has not been in my power, when I am away from home, to keep either him, or them to any settled work; but they will be flying from one trifling thing to another, with no other design, I believe, than to have the better opportunity to be idle, or to be employed on their own business; and in the next place, because, although authority is given to him, he is too much upon a level with the Negroes to exert it from which cause, if no other every one works, or not, as they please and carve out such jobs as they like. I had no doubt when I left home the 28th. of Octr. but that the house intended for Crow would have been nearly finished by this time for in order to facilitate the execution I bought Scantling, Plank and Shingles for the building instead of this I do not perceive by his weekly report that a tool had yet been applyed in it, nor can I find out by the said report that the Barn at Dogue run is in much greater forwardness than when I left it.

To correct the abuses which have crept into all parts of my business, to arrange it properly and to reduce things to system; will require, I am sensible, a good deal of time and your utmost exertions; the last, from the character you bear, I entertain no doubt; The other, I am willing to allow, because I had rather you should probe things to the bottom, whatever time it may require to do it, than to decide hastily upon the first view of them as to establish good rules, and a regular system, is the life, and the soul of every kind of business.

These are general thoughts. In my next letter (which, if possible shall be by the next Post) I will go more into detail upon some particular matters. In the mean while I remain, etc.

To Thomas Jefferson

Philadelphia, January 1, 1794.

Dear Sir: I yesterday received, with sincere regret your resignation of the office of Secretary of State. Since it has been impossible to prevail upon you, to forego any longer the indulgence of your desire for private life; the event, however anxious I am to avert it, must be submitted to.

But I cannot suffer you to leave your Station, without assuring you, that the opinion, which I had formed, of your integrity and talents, and which dictated your original nomination, has been confirmed by the fullest experience; and that both have been eminently displayed in the discharge of your duties.

Let a conviction of my most earnest prayers for your happiness accompany you in your retirement; and while I accept with the warmest thanks your solicitude for my welfare, I beg you to believe that I always am &c.

To Tobias Lear

Philadelphia, May 6, 1794.
My dear Sir: Your letter of the 26th. of Jany. with a Postcript of the 30th. of the same month, by Captn. Truxton, and another of the 12th. of Feby. by a Vessel to New York, I have safely received. But neither the one from Glasgow (with the box) nor the other by the Peggy, referred to in the above letters, are yet come to hand.

The Watch, and Portrait of the Earl of Buchan, were received in very good order. The first pleases, and for your attention to it Mrs. Washington prays you to accept her thanks. The extra: cost, together with the prices of the other articles from Glasgow and London shall be paid so soon as I can find a person disposed to receive the amount; and this I shall know, probably, when I converse with Mr. Dalton; who, I believe is on a visit to the Federal City, as he proposed to set out for it on Monday last.

The reception you met with from the Earl of Buchan and Sir John Sinclair, gives me sincere pleasure, and I am glad to find they have introduced you to characters which may not only contribute to your present gratifications, but which, in the revolution of events, may be of service in a future walk of life; without a possible disservice that results not from imprudence; against which your own good sense will always secure you.

I am much obliged to you for the several communications in your letters which have come to hand. I place great reliance on them. The opportunity you derive from mixing with people in different walks, high and low, of different descriptions, and of different political sentiments, must have afforded you an extensive range for observation and comparison: more so, by far, than could fall to the lot of a Stationary character, who is always revolving in a particular circle.

I am equally well pleased to hear that the concerns in which you are more immediately interested, are in as promising a state as the peculiarly disturbed state of matters in Europe would allow you to expect. I hope they will continue, and that your plans may be accomplished to the fullest extent of your wishes.

Mr. Pearce, my present Manager at Mount Vernon, has been directed to send for your fruit Trees the moment he hears of the Peggy's arrival at George Town; and my Gardener is instructed to take particular care of them until they are otherwise disposed of by you; but as the Vessel had not arrived the 29th. Ulto. (when I heard from Mr. Pearce) there is too much reason to fear they will come too late, as a mild and placid March and pleasant April (except the first days of it) has caused a most luxurient vegatation this Spring, with us, from North to South.

Not knowing where you may be when this letter shall have reached London, nor the hazard it might run in following of you if you should have left that metropolis, I shall do little more than *touch* political Subjects.

To tell you that the order of his Britannic Majesty in Council of the 8th. of June last, respecting Neutral Vessels had given much discontent in the United States, and, that that of the 6th. of November, and its results had thrown them into a flame, will hardly be News to you when you shall have received this letter. The subsequent order of the 8th. of Januy. has, in a degree, allayed the violence of the heat; but will by no means satisfy them without reparation for the Spoliations on our Trade, and the injuries we sustain from the non-performance of the Treaty of Peace. To effect these, if possible, by temperate means, by fair, and firm negotiation, an Envoy extraordinary is appointed, and will, I expect, sail in a few days. Mr. Jay is chosen for this trust. Mr. John Trumbull goes as his private Secretary.

Many measures have been moved in Congress in consequence of the aforementioned orders of the British Cabinet. Some have passed into Acts, and others are yet pending. Those which have become Laws are; one for fortifying our principal Seaports (which is now in vigorous execution) and for raising an additional Corps of 800 Artillerymen for the defence of them, and for other purposes. The Bills which are pending are to complete our present military establishment. To raise an Army of 25,000 in addition thereto. and to organize, put in training, and to hold in readiness at a minute's warning, a select Corps of 80,000 Militia. Of the passing of the first and last of these, no doubt seems to be entertained on either side of the House; but those who are fearful of what they call a standing Army, will give all the opposition they can to the other. The result therefore none will predict in the present stage of the business.

Besides these, a Bill passed the House of Representatives by a large Majority, founded on the following preamble and resolution.

Whereas, the injuries which have been suffered, and may be suffered by the United States, from violations committed by Great Britain, on their neutral rights and commercial interests, as well as from her failure to execute the seventh article of the treaty of peace, render it expedient for the interests of the United States, that the commercial intercourse between the two Countries should not continue to be carried on in the extent at present allowed:

Resolved, That from and after the first day of November next, all commercial intercourse between the Citizens of the United States, and the subjects of the King of Great Britain, or the citizens or subjects of any other nation, so far as the same respects articles of the growth or manufacture of G: Britain or Ireland, shall be prohibited.

This measure was arrested in the Senate, at the third reading, by the casting vote of the Vice-President; not, as it is said, and generally believed, from a disinclination to the ulterior expediency of the measure, but from a desire to try the effect of Negotiation previous thereto. Sequestration of British property (exclusive of that in the funds) and other expedients of a similar kind, have been agitated in the House of Representatives; but seem I think to be talked off the Stage.

The Packet from Mr. Bartrand to Mr. Jefferson was forwarded by the first Post after it reached my hands. Mr. Jefferson resigned the Office of Secretary of State the first of January, and was succeeded by the late Attorney General Mr. Randolph whose place of Attorney General is filled by Judge Bradford of this State (Pennsyla.).

Enclosed I give you the trouble of receiving the copy of a letter which I wrote to Mr. Arthur Young, by Mr. Willm. Morris, on the 12th. of december last. At the time that letter was written I had no knowledge of Mr. Youngs late appointment, as Secretary of the National board of Agriculture, nor of the change of his political sentiments. It is not improbable but that he has, already, or will, make you acquainted with the purport of the above letter. Be this however, as it may, my inducement to send you a copy of it, is, that if the case should be otherwise, if there appears to be any dereliction on his part to comply with my wishes, and a *fair* occasion should occur of mentioning the matter in the course of your peregrinations through England, Scotland or elsewhere and you see no impropriety from circumstances, or your views of the subject at the moment I should be glad if you were to do it. My wish further is, to dispose of the lands I have had restored to me by Mr. De Barth, and in short my settled lands in the Western parts of this State, in the Counties of Fayette and Washington. I have raised the price of my lands on the Ohio and great Kanhawa to twenty shillings Virga. currency pr. Acre; the tract in Fayette (about 1700 acres) to forty, and that in Washington to thirty shillgs. pr. Acre Pennsylvania Curry.

I have no scruple to disclose to you, that my motives to these sales (as hath been, in part, expressed to Mr. Young) are to reduce my income, be it more or less, to specialties, that the remainder of my days may, thereby, be more tranquil and freer from cares; and that I may be enabled (knowing precisely my dependence) to do as much good with it as the resource will admit; for although, in the estimation of the world I possess a good, and clear estate, yet, so unproductive is it, that I am oftentimes ashamed to refuse aids which I cannot afford unless I was to sell part of it to answer the purpose. (Private) Besides these, I have another motive which makes me earnestly wish for the accomplishment of these things, it is indeed more powerful than all the rest. namely to liberate a certain species of property which I possess, very repugnantly to my own feelings; but which imperious necessity compels; and until I can substitute some other expedient, by which expences not in my power to avoid (however well disposed I may be to do it) can be defrayed You are so well acquainted with the situation and quality of the lands which are here mentioned for Sale, that it is almost unnecessary to go more into detail respecting them, with you. Those however on the Ohio, between the Mouths of the little and Great Kanhawa, are in three tracts; first containing 2314 Acres, laying on the Banks of the River abt. 12 Miles below Mariatte, the 2d. 2448. acres, still lower down (being the 4th. large bottom on the east side of the River), and the 3d. on the same side opposite to the Great Bend in the River, containing 4395 acres. all of which are of the first quality. The Lands on the Great Kanhawa are in no respect inferior. They are contained in four Patents, the first, beginning within two miles of the mouth of that river, and contains 10990 Acres of the richest bottom; stretching 17. or 18 Miles along the river. The next of 7276 Acres is a little above the last, on the opposite side of the River, and the other two are still higher up, at the Mouth of, and on Coal River, both of the first quality and containing about 5,000 Acres.

Although it is my wish to convert these lands into Cash on the terms, and for the purposes mentioned, yet, for reasons which will readily occur to you, I would not hawk them about as some do if they were never to be sold.

I wish most sincerely that some inducement could be offered Professor Anderson which would bring him to this Country. His labours are certainly ingenious and worthy of encouragement; but I fear it will not be in my power to avail these States of them. His communications however are under consideration.

Often through the medium of Mr. Langdon, we hear of your son Lincoln, and with pleasure that he continues to be the healthy and sprightly child he always was. He declared if his Ticket should turn up a prize he would go and live in the Federal City. He did not consider, poor little fellow, that some of the prizes would hardly build him a Baby house, nor foresee that one of these was to fall to his lot. Having drawn ten dollars only. Mr. Bl—ts Agency in this lottery will, it is feared, be more productive of thorns than roses; the matter is not yet wound up, and the Commissioners appear to be uneasy. In all others respects, matters, as far as the acct. of them have come to my knowledge are going on well.

My public avocations will not, at any rate, admit of more than a *flying* trip to Mount Vernon for a few days this Summer; this not suiting Mrs. Washington I have taken a house in Germantown to avoid the heat of this City in the months of July and August. She, Nelly and the rest of the family, unite with me in every good wish for your health, prosperity and safe return; than whom none, you may be assured, offers them with more sincerity. With Affection and regard I am and always shall be, Yours.

Proclamation Calling Forth the Militia

Philadelphia, August 7, 1794.

Whereas combinations to defeat the execution of the laws laying duties upon spirits distilled within the United States, and upon stills, have from the time of the commencement of those laws existed in some of the Western parts of Pennsylvania:

And whereas the said combinations, proceeding in a manner subversive equally of the just authority of Government and of the rights of individuals, have hitherto effected their dangerous and criminal purpose; by the influence of certain irregular meetings, whose proceedings have tended to encourage and uphold the spirit of opposition; by misrepresentations of the laws calculated to render them odious; by endeavors to deter those, who might be so disposed from accepting offices under them, through fear of public resentment and of injury to person and property, and to compel those who had accepted such offices, by actual violence to surrender or forbear the execution of them; by circulating vindictive menaces against all those who should otherwise directly or indirectly aid in the execution of the said laws, or who, yielding to the dictates of conscience, and to a sense of obligation, should themselves comply therewith; by actually injuring and destroying the property of persons who were understood to have so complied; by inflicting cruel and humiliating punishments upon private citizens for no other cause, than that of appearing to be friends of the laws; by intercepting the public officers on the highways, abusing, assaulting, and otherwise ill-treating them; by going to their houses in the night, gaining admittance by force, taking away their papers, and committing other outrages, employing for these unwarrantable purposes the agency of armed banditti disguised in such manner as for the most part to escape discovery:

And whereas the endeavors of the Legislature to obviate objections to the said laws, by lowering the duties and by other alterations conducive to the convenience of those whom they immediately affect (though they have given satisfaction in other quarters,) and the endeavors of the executive officers to conciliate a compliance with the laws, by explanations, by forbearance, and even by particular accommodations, founded on the suggestions of local considerations, have been disappointed of their effect by the machinations of persons whose industry to excite resistance has increased with every appearance of a disposition among the people to relax in their opposition and to acquiesce in the laws, insomuch that many persons in the said Western parts of Pennsylvania have at length been hardy enough to perpetrate acts which I am advised amount to treason, being overt acts of levying war against the United States; the said persons having on the sixteenth and seventeenth of July last past proceeded in arms (on the second day, amounting to several hundreds) to the house of John Neville, inspector of the revenue for the fourth survey of the district of Pennsylvania, having repeatedly attacked the said house with the persons therein, wounding some of them; having seized David Lenox, marshal of the district of Pennsylvania, who, previous thereto, had been fired upon while in the execution of his duty, by a party of armed men, detaining him for some time prisoner, till, for the preservation of his life and the obtaining of his liberty, he found it necessary to enter into stipulations to forbear the execution of certain official duties touching processes issuing out of a Court of the United States; and having finally obliged the said inspector of the revenue, and the said marshal, from considerations of personal safety, to fly from that part of the country, in order, by a circuitous route, to proceed to the seat of Government; avowing as the motives of these outrageous proceedings an intention to prevent by force of arms the execution of the said laws, to oblige the said inspector of the revenue to renounce his said office, to withstand by open violence the lawful authority of the Government of the United States, and to compel thereby an alteration in the measures of the Legislature and a repeal of the laws aforesaid.

And whereas, by a law of the United States, entitled "An

act to provide for calling forth the militia to execute the laws of the Union, suppress insurrections, and repel invasions," it is enacted,

that whenever the laws of the United States shall be opposed or the execution of them obstructed in any State by combinations too powerful to be suppressed by the ordinary course of judicial proceedings, or by the powers vested in the marshals by that act, the same being notified by an Associate Justice or the District Judge, it shall be lawful for the President of the United States to call forth the militia of such State to suppress such combinations, and to cause the laws to be duly executed. And if the militia of a State where such combinations may happen shall refuse, or be insufficient to suppress the same, it shall be lawful for the President, if the Legislature of the United States shall not be in session, to call forth and employ such numbers of the militia of any other State or States, most convenient thereto, as may be necessary; and the use of the militia so to be called forth may be continued, if necessary, until the expiration of thirty days after the commencement of the ensuing session: *Provided, always,* That whenever it may be necessary, in the judgment of the President, to use the military force hereby directed to be called forth, the President shall forthwith, and previous thereto, by proclamation, command such insurgents to disperse and retire peaceably to their respective abodes within a limited time.

And whereas James Wilson, an Associate Justice, on the fourth instant, by writing under his hand, did, from evidence which had been laid before him, notify to me that

in the counties of Washington and Alleghany, in Pennsylvania, laws of the United States are opposed, and the execution thereof obstructed by combinations too powerful to be suppressed by the ordinary course of judicial proceedings, or by the powers vested in the marshal of the district.

And whereas it is, in my judgment, necessary, under the circumstances of the case, to take measures for calling forth the militia, in order to suppress the combinations aforesaid, and to cause the laws to be duly executed, and I have accordingly determined so to do, feeling the deepest regret for the occasion, but withal the most solemn conviction that the essential interests of the Union demand it; that the very existence of Government, and the fundamental principles of social order, are materially involved in the issue, and that the patriotism and firmness of all good citizens are seriously called upon, as occasion may require, to aid in the effectual suppression of so fatal a spirit.

Wherefore, and in pursuance of the proviso above recited, I, GEORGE WASHINGTON, President of the United States, do hereby command all persons, being insurgents as aforesaid, and all others whom it may concern, on or before the first day of September next, to disperse and retire peaceably to their respective abodes. And I do moreover warn all persons whomsoever against aiding, abetting, or comforting the perpetrators of the aforesaid treasonable acts; and do require all officers and other citizens, according to their respective duties and the laws of the land, to exert their utmost endeavors to prevent and suppress such dangerous proceedings.

To Charles Mynn Thruston

(Private)

Philadelphia, August 10, 1794.

Dear Sir: Your favor of the 21st. of June came duly to hand. For the communications contained in it, I thank you; as I shall do for any other that is interesting to the Community and necessary for me to be informed of. That there should exist in this country such a spirit as you say pervades the people of Kentucky (and which I have also learnt through other channels) is, to me, matter of great wonder; and that it should prevail there, more than in any other part of the Union, is not less surprising to those who are acquainted with the exertions of the General government in their favor. But it will serve to evince whensoever, and to whomsoever facts are developed (and they are not unknown at this moment, to many of the principal characters in that State) that there must exist a pre-disposition among them to be dissatisfied under any circumstances, and under every exertion of government (short of a war with Spain, which must eventually involve one with Great Britain) to promote their welfare.

The protection they receive, and the unwearied endeavours

of the General government to accomplish (by repeated and ardent remonstrances) what they seem to have most at heart, viz, the navigation of the Mississipi, obtain no credit with them, or what is full as likely, may be concealed from them or misrepresented by those Societies who under specious colourings are spreading mischief far and wide either from *real* ignorance of the measures pursuing by the government, or from a wish to bring it, as much as they are able, into discredit; for what purposes, every man is left to his own conjectures.

That similar attempts to discontent the public mind have been practiced with too much success in some of the Western Counties in this State you are, I am certain, not to learn. Actual rebellion against the Laws of the United States exist at this moment notwithstanding every lenient measure which could comport with the duties of the public Officers have been exercised to reconcile them to the collection of the taxes upon spirituous liquors and Stills. What may be the consequences of such violent and outrageous proceedings is painful in a high degree even in contemplation. But if the Laws are to be so trampled upon, with impunity, and a minority (a small one too) is to dictate to the majority there is an end put, at one stroke, to republican government; and nothing but anarchy and confusion is to be expected thereafter; for Some other man, or society, may dislike another Law and oppose it with equal propriety until all Laws are prostrate, and every one (the strongest I presume) will carve for himself. Yet, there will be found persons I have no doubt, who, although they may not be hardy enough to justify such open opposition to the Laws, will, nevertheless, be opposed to coercion even if the proclamation and the other temperate measures which are in train by the Executive to avert the dire necessity of a resort to arms, should fail. How far such people may extend their influence, and what may be the consequences thereof is not easy to decide; but this we know, that it is not difficult by concealment of some facts, and the exaggeration of others, (where there is an influence) to bias a well-meaning mind, at least for a time, truth will ultimately prevail where pains is taken to bring it to light.

I have a great regard for Genl. Morgan, and respect his

military talents, and am persuaded if a fit occasion should occur no one would exert them with more zeal in the service of his country than he would. It is my ardent wish, however, that this Country should remain in Peace as long as the Interest, honour and dignity of it will permit, and its laws, enacted by the Representatives of the People freely chosen, shall obtain. With much esteem &c.

To Henry Lee

(Private)

German Town, August 26, 1794.

Dear Sir: Your favor of the 17th. came duly to hand, and I thank you for its communications. As the Insurgents in the western counties of this State are resolved (as far as we have yet been able to learn from the Commissioners, who have been sent among them) to persevere in their rebellious conduct untill what they call the excise Law is repealed, and acts of oblivion and amnesty are passed; it gives me sincere consolation amidst the regret with which I am filled, by such lawless and outrageous conduct, to find by your letter above mentioned, that it is held in general detestation by the good people of Virginia; and that you are disposed to lend your *personal* aid to subdue this spirit, and to bring those people to a proper sense of their duty.

On this latter point I shall refer you to letters from the War office; and to a private one from Colo. Hamilton (who in the absence of the Secretary of War, superintends the *military* duties of that department) for my sentiments on this occasion.

It is with equal pride and satisfaction I add, that as far as my information extends, this insurrection is viewed with universal indignation and abhorrence; except by those who have never missed an opportunity by side blows, or otherwise, to aim their shafts at the general government; and even among these there is not a Spirit hardy enough, yet, *openly* to justify the daring infractions of Law and order; but by palliatives are attempting to suspend all proceedings against the insurgents until Congress shall have decided on the case, thereby intending to gain time, and if possible to make the evil more extensive, more formidable, and of course more difficult to counteract and subdue.

I consider this insurrection as the first *formidable* fruit of the Democratic Societies; brought forth I believe too prematurely for their own views, which may contribute to the annihilation of them.

That these societies were instituted by the *artful* and *designing* members (many of their body I have no doubt mean well, but know little of the real plan,) primarily to sow the seeds of jealousy and distrust among the people, of the government, by destroying all confidence in the Administration of it; and that these doctrines have been budding and blowing ever since, is not new to any one, who is acquainted with the characters of their leaders, and has been attentive to their manœuvres. I early gave it as my opinion to the confidential characters around me, that, if these Societies were not counteracted (not by prosecutions, the ready way to make them grow stronger) or did not fall into disesteem from the knowledge of their origin, and the views with which they had been instituted by their father, Genet, for purposes well known to the Government; that they would shake the government to its foundation. Time and circumstances have confirmed me in this opinion, and I deeply regret the probable consequences, not as they will affect me personally, (for I have not long to act on this theatre, and sure I am that not a man amongst them can be more anxious to put me aside, than I am to sink into the profoundest retirement) but because I see, under a display of popular and fascinating guises, the most diabolical attempts to destroy the best fabric of human government and happiness, that has ever been presented for the acceptance of mankind.

A part of the plan for creating discord, is, I perceive, to make me say things of others, and others of me, wch. have no foundation in truth. The first, in many instances I *know* to be the case; and the second I believe to be so; but truth or falsehood is immaterial to them, provided their objects are promoted.

Under this head may be classed, I conceive, what it is reported I have said of Mr. Henry, and what Mr. Jefferson is reported to have said of me; on both of which, particularly the first, I mean to dilate a little. With solemn truth then I can declare, that I never expressed such sentiments of that Gentleman, as from your letter, he has been led to believe. I had heard, it is true, that he retained his enmity to the Constitution; but with very peculiar pleasure I learnt from Colo. Coles (who I am sure will recollect it) that Mr. Henry was acquiescent in his conduct, and that though he could not give up his opinions respecting the Constitution, yet, unless he should be called upon by official duty, he wd. express no sentiment unfriendly to the exercise of the powers of a government, which had been chosen by a majority of the people; or words to this effect.

Except intimating in this conversation (which to the best of my recollection was introduced by Colo. Coles) that report had made Mr. Henry speak a different language; and afterwards at Prince Edward Court house, where I saw Mr. Venable, and finding I was within eight or ten miles of Mr. Henry's seat, and expressing my regret at not seeing him, the conversation might be similar to that held with Colo. Coles; I say, except in these two instances, I do not recollect, nor do I believe, that in the course of the journey to and from the Southward I ever mentioned Mr. Henrys name in conjunction with the Constitution, or the government. It is evident therefore, that these reports are propagated with evil intentions, to create personal differences. On the question of the Constitution Mr. Henry and myself, it is well known, have been of different opinions; but personally, I have always respected and esteemed him; nay more, I have conceived myself under obligations to him for the friendly manner in which he transmitted to me some insidious anonymous writings that were sent to him in the close of the year 1777, with a view to embark him in the opposition that was forming against me at that time.

I well recollect the conversations you allude to in the winter preceeding the last; and I recollect also, that difficulties occurred which you, any more than myself, were not able to remove. 1st., though you believed, yet you would not undertake to *assert*, that Mr. Henry would be induced to accept *any appointment* under the General Government; in which case, and supposing him to be inemical to it, the wound the government would receive by his refusal, and the charge of attempting to silence his opposition by a place, would be great; 2d., because you were of opinion that *no* office which would make a residence at the Seat of government essential would comport with his disposition, or views; and 3dly., because if there was a vacancy in the supreme Judiciary at that time (of which I am not at this time certain) it could not be filled from Virginia without giving two Judges to that State, which would have excited unpleasant sensations in other States. Any thing short of one of the great Offices, it could not be presumed he would have accepted; nor would there (under any opinion he might entertain) have been propriety in offering it. What is it then, you have in contemplation, that you conceive would be relished? and ought there not to be a moral certainty of its acceptance? This being the case, there wd. not be wanting a disposition on my part; but strong inducements on public and private grounds, to invite Mr. Henry into any employment under the General Government to which his inclination might lead, and not opposed by those maxims which has been the invariable rule of my conduct.

With respect to the words said to have been uttered by Mr. Jefferson, they would be enigmatical to those who are acquainted with the characters about me, unless supposed to be spoken ironically; and in that case they are too injurious to me, and have too little foundation in truth, to be ascribed to him. There could not be the trace of doubt on his mind of predilection in mine, towards G. Britain or her politics, unless (which I do not believe) he has set me down as one of the most deceitful, and uncandid men living; because, not only in private conversations between ourselves, on this subject; but in my meetings with the confidential servants of the public, he has heard me often, when occasions presented themselves, express very different sentiments with an energy that could not be mistaken by *any one* present.

Having determined, as far as lay within the power of the Executive, to keep this country in a state of neutrality, I have made my public conduct accord with the system; and whilst so acting as a public character, consistency, and propriety as a private man, forbid those intemperate expressions in favor of one Nation, or to the prejudice of another, wch. many have indulged themselves in, and I will venture to add, to the embarrassment of government, without producing any good to the Country. With very great esteem &c.

To John Jay

Philadelphia, August 30, 1794.

My dear Sir: Your letter of the 23d of June from London (and the duplicate) have both been received; and your safe arrival after so short a passage gave sincere pleasure, as well on private as on public account, to all your friends in this Country; and to none in a greater degree, I can venture to assure you, than it did to myself.

As you will receive letters from the Secretary of States Office giving an official account of the public occurrences as they have arisen, and progressed, it is unnecessary for me to retouch any of them: and yet, I cannot restrain myself from making some observations on the most recent of them, the communication of which was received this morning *only*. I mean the protest of the Govr. of Upper Canada (delivered by Lieutt. Sheaffe, against our occupying Lands far from any of the Posts which, long ago, they ought to have surrendered; and far within the known, *and until now*, the acknowledged limits of the United States.

On this irregular, and high handed proceeding of Mr. Simcoe, which is no longer *masked*, I would rather hear what the Ministry of G. Britain will say, than pronounce my own sentimts. thereon. But can that government or will it attempt, after this *official* act of one of their governors, to hold out ideas of friendly intentions towds. the United States, and suffer such conduct to pass with impunity?

This may be considered as the most open and daring act of the British Agents in America, though it is not the most hostile or cruel; for there does not remain a doubt in the mind of any well informed person in this country (not shut against conviction) that all the difficulties we encounter with the

Indians, their hostilities, the murders of helpless women and innocent children along our frontiers, results from the conduct of the Agents of Great Britain in this Country. In vain is it then for its Administration *in Britain* to disavow having given orders which will warrant such conduct, whilst their Agents go unpunished; whilst we have a thousand corroborating circumstances and indeed almost as many evidences (some of which cannot be brought forward) to prove that they are seducing from our alliances (endeavouring to remove over the line) tribes that have hitherto been kept in peace and friendship with us, at a heavy expence, and who have no cause of complaint except pretended ones, of their creating; whilst they keep in a state of irritation the tribes who are hostile to us, and are instigating those who know little of us, or we of them, to unite in the War against us; and whilst it is an undeniable fact that they are furnishing the whole with Arms, Ammunition, cloathing, and even provisions to carry on the war; I might go further, and if they are not much belied, add men also, in disguise.

Can it be expected I ask, so long as these things are known in the United States, or at least firmly believed, and suffered with impunity by G. Britain, that there ever will, or can be any cordiality between the two Countries? I answer NO! and I will undertake, without the gift of prophecy, to predict, that it will be impossible to keep this Country in a state of amity with G. Britain long if the Posts are not surrendered. A knowledge of these being *my* sentiments, would have little weight I am persuaded with the British Admn; nor perhaps with the Nation, in effecting the measure: but both may rest satisfied that if they want to be in Peace with this Country, and to enjoy the benefits of its trade &ca. to give up the Posts is the only road to it. withholding them, and the consequences we feel at present, continuing, war will be inevitably.

This letter is written to you in extreme haste, whilst the Papers respecting this subject I am writing on are copying at the Secretary of States Office to go by Express to New York, for a Vessel which we have just heard Sails tomorrow: you will readily perceive therefore I had no time for digesting, and as little for correcting it. I shall only add that you may be assured always of the sincere friendship and Affection of your &c.

To Elizabeth Parke Custis

German Town, September 14, 1794.

My dear Betcy: Shall I, in answer to your letter of the 7th. instant say, when you are as near the *Pinnacle* of happiness as your sister Patcy conceives herself to be; or when your candour shines more conspicuously than it does in *that* letter, that I will *then*, comply with the request you have made, for my Picture?

No: I will grant it without either: for if the latter was to be a preliminary, it would be sometime I apprehend before *that* Picture would be found pendant *at* your breast; it not being within the bounds of probability that the contemplation of an inanimate thing, whatever might be the reflections arising from the possession of it, can be the *only* wish of your heart.

Respect may place it among the desirable objects of it, but there are emotions of a softer kind, to wch. the heart of a girl turned of eighteen, is susceptible, that must have generated much warmer ideas, although the fruition of them may, apparently, be more distant than those of your Sister's.

Having (by way of a hint) delivered a sentiment to Patty, which may be useful to her (if it be remembered after the change that is contemplated, is consummated) I will suggest another, more applicable to yourself.

Do not then in your contemplation of the marriage state, look for perfect felicity before you consent to wed. Nor conceive, from the fine tales the Poets and lovers of old have told us, of the transports of mutual love, that heaven has taken its abode on earth: Nor do not deceive yourself in supposing, that the only mean by which these are to be obtained, is to drink deep of the cup, and revel in an ocean of love. Love is a mighty pretty thing; but like all other delicious things, it is cloying; and when the first transports of the passion begins to subside, which it assuredly will do, and yield, oftentimes too late, to more sober reflections, it serves to evince, that love is too dainty a food to live upon *alone*, and ought not to be considered farther than as a necessary ingredient for that matrimonial happiness which results from a combination of causes; none of which are of greater importance, than that the object on whom it is placed, should possess good sense, good dispositions, and the means of supporting you in the way you have been brought up. Such qualifications cannot fail to attract (after marriage) your esteem and regard, into wch. or into disgust, sooner or later, love naturally resolves itself; and who at the sametime, has a claim to the respect, and esteem of the circle he moves in. Without these, whatever may be your first impressions of the man, they will end in disappointment; for be assured, and experience will convince you, that there is no truth more certain, than that all our enjoyments fall short of our expectations; and to none does it apply with more force, than to the gratification of the passions. You may believe me to be always, and sincerely Your Affectionate.

Proclamation Concerning the "Whiskey Rebellion"

Philadelphia, September 25, 1794.
Whereas, from a hope that the combinations against the Constitution and laws of the United States, in certain of the Western counties of Pennsylvania, would yield to time and reflection, I thought it sufficient, in the first instance, rather to take measures for calling forth the militia than immediately to embody them; but the moment is now come, when the overtures of forgiveness, with no other condition than a submission to law, have been only partially accepted; when every form of conciliation not inconsistent with the being of Government has been adopted, without effect; when the well-disposed in those counties are unable by their influence and example to reclaim the wicked from their fury, and are compelled to associate in their own defence; when the proffered lenity has been perversely misinterpreted into an apprehension that the citizens will march with reluctance; when the opportunity of examining the serious consequences of a treasonable opposition has been employed in propagating principles of anarchy, endeavoring through emissaries to alienate the friends of order from its support, and inviting enemies to per-

petrate similar acts of insurrection; when it is manifest, that violence would continue to be exercised upon every attempt to enforce the laws; when, therefore, Government is set at defiance, the contest being whether a small proportion of the United States shall dictate to the whole Union, and, at the expense of those who desire peace, indulge a desperate ambition;

Now, therefore, I, GEORGE WASHINGTON, President of the United States, in obedience to that high and irresistible duty, consigned to me by the Constitution, "to take care that the laws be faithfully executed;" deploring that the American name should be sullied by the outrages of citizens on their own Government; commiserating such as remain obstinate from delusion; but resolved, in perfect reliance on that gracious Providence which so signally displays its goodness towards this country, to reduce the refractory to a due subordination to the laws; do hereby declare and make known, that, with a satisfaction which can be equalled only by the merits of the militia summoned into service from the States of New Jersey, Pennsylvania, Maryland, and Virginia, I have received intelligence of their patriotic alacrity, in obeying the call of the present, though painful, yet commanding necessity; that a force, which, according to every reasonable expectation, is adequate to the exigency, is already in motion to the scene of disaffection; that those who have confided or shall confide in the protection of Government, shall meet full succor under the standard and from the arms of the United States; that those who having offended against the laws have since entitled themselves to indemnity, will be treated with the most liberal good faith, if they shall not have forfeited their claim by any subsequent conduct, and that instructions are given accordingly.

And I do, moreover, exhort all individuals, officers, and bodies of men, to contemplate with abhorrence the measures leading directly or indirectly to those crimes, which produce this resort to military coercion; to check, in their respective spheres, the efforts of misguided or designing men to substitute their misrepresentation in the place of truth, and their discontents in the place of stable government; and to call to mind, that as the people of the United States have been permitted, under the Divine favor, in perfect freedom, after solemn deliberation, in an enlightened age, to elect their own Government, so will their gratitude for this inestimable blessing be best distinguished by firm exertions to maintain the Constitution and the laws.

And, lastly, I again warn all persons, whomsoever and whersoever, not to abet, aid, or comfort the insurgents aforesaid, as they will answer the contrary at their peril; and I do also require all officers and other citizens, according to their several duties, as far as may be in their power, to bring under the cognizance of the law all offenders in the premises.

To Burges Ball

Philadelphia, September 25, 1794.
Dear Sir: Your letter of the 10th. instt. from the Sulpher Springs has been recd.

When General Knox (who for several days has been expected) returns, I will deliver your letter to him, and from him (in whose department the business lyes) you will receive an answer to your proposition.

I hear with the greatest pleasure of the spirit which so generally pervades the Militia of every State that has been called upon, on the present occasion; and of the decided discountenance the Incendiaries of public peace and order have met with in their attempt to spread their nefarious doctrines, with a view to poison and discontent the minds of the people against the government; particularly by endeavouring to have it believed that their liberties were assailed, and that all the wicked and abominable measures that cod. be devised (under specious guises) are practiced to sap the Constitution, and lay the foundation of future Slavery.

The Insurrection in the Western counties of this State is a striking evidence of this; and may be considered as the first *ripe fruit* of the Democratic Societies. I did not, I must confess; expect their labours would come to maturity so soon; though I never had a doubt, that such conduct would produce some such issue; if it did not meet the frown of those who were well disposed to order and good government, in time; for can any thing be more absurd, more arrogant, or more pernicious to the peace of Society, than for self created bodies, forming themselves into *permanent* Censors, and under the shade of Night in a conclave, resolving that acts of Congress which have undergone the most deliberate, and solemn discussion by the Representatives of the people, chosen for the express purpose, and bringing with them from the different parts of the Union the sense of their Constituents, endeavouring as far as the nature of the thing will admit, to form *that will* into Laws for the government of the whole; I say, under these circumstances, for a self created, *permanent* body, (for no one denies the right of the people to meet occasionally, to petition for, or to remonstrate against, any Act of the Legislature &ca) to declare that *this act* is unconstitutional, and *that* act is pregnant of mischief; and that all who vote contrary to their dogmas are actuated by selfish motives, or under foreign influence; nay in plain terms are traiters to their Country, is such a stretch of arrogant presumption as is not to be reconciled with laudable motives: especially when we see the same set of men endeavouring to destroy all confidence in the Administration, by arraigning all its acts, without knowing on what ground, or with what information it proceeds and this without regard to decency or truth. These things were evidently intended, and could not fail without counteraction, to disquiet the public mind; but I hope, and trust, they will work their own cure; especially when it is known, more generally than it is, that the Democratic Society of this place (from which the others have emanated) was instituted by Mr. Genet for the express purpose of dissention, and to draw a line between the people and the government, after he found the Officers of the latter would not yield to the hostile measures in which he wanted to embroil this Country.

I hope this letter will find you, Mrs. Ball and the family in better health than when you wrote last. remember me to them, and be assured that I remain Your Affectionate.

To Edmund Randolph

(Private)

Fort Cumberland, October 16, 1794.
Dear Sir: Your letters of the 11th. instt. were received this morning at my stage 15 miles short of this place. We arrived here in the afternoon of this day; and found a respectable force assembled from the States of Virginia and Maryland; and I am informed that about 1500 more (from the former state) either is or will be at Frankfort (ten miles on our left) this evening or tomorrow at farthest. Nothing more precise, than you were informed of in my last, from Carlisle, has been heard from the Insurgent counties. All accts. agree however, that they are much alarmed at the serious appearance of things: The truth of which I expect to be better informed of to morrow, or next day, by persons whom I have sent amongst them and whose return may be looked for about that time.

I do not expect to be here more than two days; thence to Bedford, where, as soon as matters are arranged, and a plan settled, I shall shape my course for Philadelphia; but not because the impertinence of Mr. Bache, or his corrispondents has undertaken to pronounce, that I cannot, constitutionally, command the Army whilst Congress are in Session.

I believe the eyes of all the *well* disposed people of this Country will soon be opened, and that they will clearly see, the tendency if not the design of the leaders of these self created societies. As far as I have heard them spoken of, it is with strong reprobation. I should be extremely sorry therefore if Mr. M——n *from any cause whatsoever* should get entangled with them, or their politics.

As the Speech will be composed of several distinct subjects, my wish was that each of these shd. receive its final dress; subject however to revision; that part especially which relates to the insurrection and the proceedings thereupon. The subjects themselves, will naturally point to the order, in which they ought to follow each other; and the throwing them into it cannot, at any time, be more than the work of a few minutes after the materials are all provided. It will appear evident, on a moments reflection, that the continual interruptions in a militia camp, where every thing is to be provided, and arranged, will allow no time to clothe the speech in a correct or handsome garb; nor will there be time to do it after my return.

My mind is so perfectly convinced, that if these self created societies cannot be discountenanced, that they will destroy the government of this Country that I have asked myself whilst I have been revolving on the expence and inconvenience of drawing so many men from their families and occupations as I have seen on their march where wd. be the impropriety of glancing at them in my Speech by some such idea as the following;

That however distressing this Expedition will have proved to individuals, and expensive to the Country, the pleasing spirit which it has drawn forth in support of Law and Govt. will immortalize the American character and is a happy presage, that future attempts of a certain description of people will not, tho' accompanied by the same industry, sow the seed of distrust and disturb the public tranquillity will prove equally abortive.

I have formed no precise ideas of what is best to be done or said on this subject, nor have I time to express properly what has occurred to me, as I am now writing at an hour when I ought to be in bed; because all the day, from business or ceremonious introductions I have been unable to do it sooner. I am, &c.

Sixth Annual Message to Congress

United States, November 19, 1794.
Fellow Citizens of the Senate and of the House of Representatives: When we call to mind the gracious indulgence of Heaven, by which the American People became a nation; when we survey the general prosperity of our country, and look forward to the riches, power, and happiness, to which it seems destined; with the deepest regret do I announce to you, that during your recess, some of the citizens of the United

States have been found capable of an insurrection. It is due, however, to the character of our government, and to its stability, which cannot be shaken by the enemies of order, freely to unfold the course of this event.

During the session of the year one thousand seven hundred and ninety, it was expedient to exercise the legislative power, granted by the constitution of the United States, "to lay and collect excises." In a majority of the States, scarcely an objection was heard to this mode of taxation. In some, indeed, alarms were at first conceived, until they were banished by reason and patriotism. In the four western counties of Pennsylvania, a prejudice, fostered and embittered by the artifice of men, who labored for an ascendency over the will of others, by the guidance of their passions, produced symptoms of riot and violence. It is well known, that Congress did not hesitate to examine the complaints which were presented, and to relieve them, as far as justice dictated, or general convenience would permit. But the impression, which this moderation made on the discontented, did not correspond, with what it deserved. The arts of delusion were no longer confined to the efforts of designing individuals.

The very forbearance to press prosecutions was misinterpreted into a fear of urging the execution of the laws; and associations of men began to denounce threats against the officers employed. From a belief, that by a more formal concert, their operation might be defeated, certain self-created societies assumed the tone of condemnation. Hence, while the greater part of Pennsylvania itself were conforming themselves to the acts of excise, a few counties were resolved to frustrate them. It was now perceived, that every expectation from the tenderness which had been hitherto pursued, was unavailing, and that further delay could only create an opinion of impotency or irresolution in the government. Legal process was, therefore, delivered to the marshal, against the rioters and delinquent distillers.

No sooner was he understood to be engaged in this duty, than the vengeance of armed men was aimed at *his* person, and the person and property of the inspector of the revenue. They fired upon the marshal, arrested him, and detained him for some time, as a prisoner. He was obliged, by the jeopardy of his life, to renounce the service of other process, on the west side of the Allegeny mountain; and a deputation was afterwards sent to him to demand a surrender of that which he *had* served. A numerous body repeatedly attacked the house of the inspector, seized his papers of office, and finally destroyed by fire, his buildings, and whatsoever they contained. Both of these officers, from a just regard to their safety, fled to the seat of government; it being avowed, that the motives to such outrages were to compel the resignation of the inspector, to withstand by force of arms the authority of the United States, and thereby to extort a repeal of the laws of excise, and an alteration in the conduct of government.

Upon the testimony of these facts, an associate Justice of the Supreme Court of the United States notified to me, that "in the counties of Washington and Allegeny, in Pennsylvania, laws of the United States were opposed, and the execution thereof obstructed by combinations, too powerful to be suppressed by the ordinary course of judicial proceedings, or by the powers vested in the marshal of that district." On this call, momentous in the extreme, I sought and weighed, what might best subdue the crisis. On the one hand, the judiciary was pronounced to be stripped of its capacity to enforce the laws; crimes, which reached the very existence of social order, were perpetrated without controul, the friends of government were insulted, abused, and overawed into silence, or an apparent acquiescence; and the yield to the treasonable fury of so small a portion of the United States, would be to violate the fundamental principle of our constitution, which enjoins that the will of the majority shall prevail. On the other, to array citizen against citizen, to publish the dishonor of such excesses, to encounter the expense, and other embarrassments of so distant an expedition, were steps too delicate, too closely interwoven with many affecting considerations, to be lightly adopted. I postponed, therefore, the summoning of the militia immediately into the field. But I required them to be held in readiness, that if my anxious endeavours to reclaim the deluded, and to convince the malignant of their danger, should be fruitless, military force might be prepared to act, before the season should be too far advanced.

My Proclamation of the 7th of August last was accordingly

issued, and accompanied by the appointment of Commissioners, who were charged to repair to the scene of insurrection. They were authorized to confer with any bodies of men, or individuals. They were instructed to be candid and explicit, in stating the sensations, which had been excited in the Executive, and his earnest wish to avoid a resort to coercion. To represent, however, that without submission, coercion *must* be the resort; but to invite them, at the same time, to return to the demeanor of faithful citizens, by such accommodations as lay within the sphere of the executive power. Pardon, too, was tendered to them by the government of the United States, and that of Pennsylvania, upon no other condition, than a satisfactory assurance of obedience to the laws.

Although the report of the commissioners marks their firmness and abilities, and must unite all virtuous men, by shewing, that the means of conciliation have been exhausted, all of those who had committed or abetted the tumults, did not subscribe the mild form, which was proposed, as the atonement; and the indications of a peaceable temper were neither sufficiently general, nor conclusive, to recommend or warrant, a further suspension of the march of the militia.

Thus, the painful alternative could not be discarded. I ordered the militia to march, after once more admonishing the insurgents, in my proclamation of the 25th of September last.

It was a task too difficult to ascertain with precision, the lowest degree of force, competent to the quelling of the insurrection. From a respect, indeed, to œconomy, and the ease of my fellow citizens belonging to the militia, it would have gratified me to accomplish such an estimate. My very reluctance to ascribe too much importance to the opposition, had its extent been accurately seen, would have been a decided inducement to the smallest efficient numbers. In this uncertainty, therefore, I put in motion fifteen thousand men, as being an army, which, according to all human calculation, would be prompt, and adequate in every view; and might perhaps, by rendering resistance desperate, prevent the effusion of blood. Quotas had been assigned to the states of New-Jersey, Pennsylvania, Maryland, and Virginia; the governor of Pennsylvania having declared on this occasion, an opinion which justified a requisition to the other states.

As commander in chief of the militia, when called into the actual service of the United States, I have visited the places of general rendezvous, to obtain more exact information, and to direct a plan for ulterior movements. Had there been room for a persuasion, that the laws were secure from obstruction; that the civil magistrate was able to bring to justice such of the most culpable, as have not embraced the proffered terms of amnesty, and may be deemed fit objects of example; that the friends to peace and good government were not in need of that aid and countenance, which they ought always to receive, and I trust, ever will receive, against the vicious and turbulent; I should have caught with avidity the opportunity of restoring the militia to their families and home. But succeeding intelligence has tended to manifest the necessity of what has been done; it being now confessed by those who were not inclined to exaggerate the ill-conduct of the insurgents, that their malevolence was not pointed merely to a particular law; but that a spirit, inimical to all order, has actuated many of the offenders. If the state of things had afforded reason for the continuance of my presence with the army, it would not have been withholden. But every appearance assuring such an issue, as will redound to the reputation and strength of the United States, I have judged it most proper, to resume my duties at the seat of government, leaving the chief command with the governor of Virginia.

Still, however, as it is probable, that in a commotion like the present, whatsoever may be the pretence, the purposes of mischief and revenge may not be laid aside; the stationing of a small force for a certain period in the four western counties of Pennsylvania will be indispensable; whether we contemplate the situation of those, who are connected with the execution of the laws; or of others who may have exposed themselves by an honorable attachment to them.

Thirty days from the commencement of this session, being the legal limitation of the employment of the militia, Congress cannot be too early occupied with this subject.

Among the discussions, which may arise from this aspect of our affairs, and from the documents which will be submitted to Congress, it will not escape their observation, that not only the inspector of the revenue, but other officers of the United

States in Pennsylvania have, from their fidelity in the discharge
of their functions, sustained material injuries to their property.
The obligation and policy of indemnifying them are strong
and obvious. It may also merit attention, whether policy will
not enlarge this provision to the retribution of other citizens,
who, though not under the ties of office, may have suffered
damage by their generous exertions for upholding the constitution and the laws. The amount, even if all the injured
were included, would not be great; and on future emergencies, the government would be amply repaid by the influence
of an example, that he, who incurs a loss in its defence shall
find a recompense in its liberality.

While there is cause to lament, that occurrences of this nature should have disgraced the name, or interrupted the tranquillity of any part of our community, or should have diverted
to a new application, any portion of the public resources,
there are not wanting real and substantial consolations for the
misfortune. It has demonstrated, that our prosperity rests on
solid foundations; by furnishing an additional proof, that my
fellow citizens understand the true principles of government
and liberty: that they feel their inseparable union: that notwithstanding all the devices which have been used to sway
them from their interest and duty, they are now as ready to
maintain the authority of the laws against licentious invasions,
as they were to defend their rights against usurpation. It has
been a spectacle, displaying to the highest advantage, the value
of Republican Government, to behold the most and least
wealthy of our citizens standing in the same ranks as private
soldiers; pre-eminently distinguished by being the army of the
constitution; undeterred by a march of three hundred miles
over rugged mountains, by the approach of an inclement season, or by any other discouragement. Nor ought I to omit to
acknowledge the efficacious and patriotic co-operation, which
I have experienced from the chief magistrates of the states, to
which my requisitions have been addressed.

To every description, indeed, of citizens let praise be given.
But let them persevere in their affectionate vigilance over that
precious depository of American happiness, the constitution
of the United States. Let them cherish it too, for the sake of
those, who from every clime are daily seeking a dwelling in

our land. And when in the calm moments of reflection, they shall have retraced the origin and progress of the insurrection, let them determine, whether it has not been fomented by combinations of men, who, careless of consequences, and disregarding the unerring truth, that those who rouse, cannot always appease a civil convulsion, have disseminated, from an ignorance or perversion of facts, suspicions, jealousies, and accusations of the whole government.

Having thus fulfilled the engagement, which I took, when I entered into office, "to the best of my ability to preserve, protect, and defend the constitution of the United States," on you, Gentlemen, and the people by whom you are deputed, I rely for support.

In the arrangements, to which the possibility of a similar contingency will naturally draw your attention, it ought not to be forgotten, that the militia laws have exhibited such striking defects, as could not have been supplied but by the zeal of our citizens. Besides the extraordinary expense and waste, which are not the least of the defects, every appeal to those laws is attended with a doubt of its success.

The devising and establishing of a well regulated militia, would be a genuine source of legislative honor, and a perfect title to public gratitude. I, therefore, entertain a hope, that the present session will not pass, without carrying to its full energy the power of organizing, arming, and disciplining the militia; and thus providing, in the language of the constitution, for calling them forth to execute the laws of the union, suppress insurrections, and repel invasions.

As auxiliary to the state of our defence, to which Congress can never too frequently recur, they will not omit to enquire whether the fortifications, which have been already licensed by law, be commensurate with our exigencies.

The intelligence from the army, under the command of general Wayne, is a happy presage to our military operations against the hostile Indians north of the Ohio. From the advices which have been forwarded, the advance which he has made must have damped the ardor of the savages, and weakened their obstinacy in waging war against the United States. And yet, even at this late hour, when our power to punish them cannot be questioned, we shall not be unwilling to cement a lasting peace, upon terms of candor, equity, and good neighborhood.

Towards none of the Indian tribes have overtures of friendship been spared. The Creeks in particular are covered from encroachment by the interposition of the General Government and that of Georgia. From a desire also to remove the discontents of the Six Nations, a settlement, meditated at Presqu'isle on Lake Erie, has been suspended; and an agent is now endeavoring to rectify any misconception, into which they may have fallen. But I cannot refrain from again pressing upon your deliberations, the plan which I recommended at the last session, for the improvement of harmony with all the Indians within our limits, by the fixing and conducting of trading houses, upon the principles then expressed.

Gentlemen of the House of Representatives: The time, which has elapsed, since the commencement of our fiscal measures, has developed our pecuniary resources, so as to open a way for a definitive plan for the redemption of the public debt. It is believed, that the result is such, as to encourage Congress to consummate this work, without delay. Nothing can more promote the permanent welfare of the nation, and nothing would be more grateful to our constituents. Indeed whatsoever is unfinished of our system of public credit, cannot be benefited by procrastination; and as far as may be practicable, we ought to place that credit on grounds which cannot be disturbed, and to prevent that progressive accumulation of debt which must ultimately endanger all governments.

An estimate of the necessary appropriations, including the expenditures into which we have been driven by the insurrection, will be submitted to Congress.

Gentlemen of the Senate, and of the House of Representatives: The mint of the United States has entered upon the coinage of the precious metals; and considerable sums of defective coins and bullion have been lodged with the director by individuals. There is a pleasing prospect that the institution will, at no remote day, realize the expectation which was originally formed of its utility.

In subsequent communications, certain circumstances of our intercourse with foreign nations, will be transmitted to

Congress. However, it may not be unseasonable to announce that my policy in our foreign transactions has been, to cultivate peace with all the world; to observe treaties with pure and absolute faith; to check every deviation from the line of impartiality; to explain what may have been misapprehended, and correct what may have been injurious to any nation; and having thus acquired the right, to lose no time in acquiring the ability, to insist upon justice being done to ourselves.

Let us unite, therefore, in imploring the Supreme Ruler of nations, to spread his holy protection over these United States: to turn the machinations of the wicked to the confirming of our constitution: to enable us at all times to root out internal sedition, and put invasion to flight: to perpetuate to our country that prosperity, which his goodness has already conferred, and to verify the anticipations of this government being a safe guard to human rights.

To William Pearce

Philadelphia, November 23, 1794.
Mr. Pearce: Your letter of the 16th. with the reports, except the Carpenters which I have been without for several weeks, came to my hands yesterday.

As I expected, so it happened, my letters to Colo. Willm. Washington of Westmoreland, did not reach him until a few days ago. As you seem to be of the same opinion wch. I entertained at first, namely, that from the easy and simple manners of Donaldson, he wd. not be a fit overlooker of Negros, I have again written to my Nephew concerning the Carpenter in his neighbourhood; and put the letter under cover to you, open, that if you have engaged a person for this business, or have one in contemplation for it that you think will answer well, you may accompany it by a line from yourself to stop his application, otherwise let it go, and wait the result of Colo. Washington's answer which agreeably to my request, I expect you will receive; before you engage any other. In case you should get any one in the place of Donaldson as an overlooker of the Carpenters let him, Isaac and the boy Jem, be kept to the making and repairing of Carts of different sorts, Wheels, Plows, Harrows, Rakes, Wheelbarrows, and all kinds of farming impliments; and tell him, as from me, that I hope, and expect, that he will take pains to instruct both Isaac and the Boy in the *principles* of the work; that I may derive benifit hereafter from his instruction of them.

If you should succeed in getting an Overlooker for the out-doors Carpenters, you will direct the execution of such work as appears to be most wanting; but whether he be a married, or a single man, he must not occupy the rooms in the store house; these, while you remain in what is called the Servants Hall, must be kept for Gentlemens servants, and my own while I am on a visit to Mount Vernon. When you remove to the Ferry (if you mean to do so) and the house you are now in, is restored to its former use, a single man might, in that case, occupy the rooms in the store house in the manner Mr. Whitting did, but it would not be very convenient for a married man (especially one with children) to be there.

Speaking of Gentlemens Servts. it calls to my mind, that in a letter from Mrs. Fanny Washington to Mrs. Washington (her Aunt) she mentions, that since I left Mount Vernon she has given out four dozn. and eight bottles of wine. Whether they are used or not she does not say; but I am led by it to observe, that it is not my intention that it should be given to every one who may incline to make a convenience of the house in travelling; or who may be induced to visit it from motives of curiosity. There are but three descriptions of people to whom I think it ought to be given: first my *particular* and intimate acquaintances, in case business should call them there, such for instance as Doctr. Craik. 2dly. some of the *most* respectable foreigners who may, perchance, be in Alexandria or the federal city; and be either brought down, or introduced by letter from some of my particular acquaintance before mentioned; or thirdly to persons of some distinction (such as members of Congress &ca) who may be travelling through the Country from North to South or from South to North; in the first of which, I should not fail to give letters where I conceive them entitled. Unless some caution of this sort governs I should be run to an expence as improper as it would be considerable; for the duty upon Madeira wine makes it one of the most expensive liquors that is now used; while my stock of it is small and old wine (of which that is) is not to be had upon any terms for which reason, and for the limited purposes already mentioned, I had rather you would provide Claret, or other wine on which the duty is not so high than to use my Madeira unless it be on extraordinary occasions.

I have no objection to any sober or orderly person's gratifying their curiosity in viewing the buildings, Gardens &ca. about Mount Vernon; but it is only to such persons as I have described that I ought to be run to any expence on account of these visits of curiosity, beyond common civility and hospitality. No gentleman who has a proper respect for his own character (except relations and intimates) would use the house for the sake of conveniency (as it is far removed from the public roads), unless invited to do so by me or some friend; nor do I suppose any of this description would go there without a personal, or written introduction.

I have been thus particular, that you may have a full view of my ideas on this subject, and conform to them; and because the knowledge I have of my servants is such, as to believe, that if opportunities are given them they will take off two glasses of wine for every one that is drank by such visitors, and tell you they were used by them without such a watch over them as the other business you are employed in would not allow you to bestow.

I observe what you say respecting the Hogs for Porke, and have to add that so many as are necessary to furnish all those who, by your agreements are entitled to be served with Porke with a moderate allowance for Bacon for the use of the Mansion house should be put up, whether they be old or young; and I wish pains may be taken to cure the latter, as the most of that which was sent to this place was spoiled. The principal reason why I requested that none but full grown Hogs might be put up this fall was that my stock of them another year might be the better for it: but as I do not mean to buy porke, the necessity of breaking in upon the young hogs is unavoidable.

It was an omission of McKoy not to measure his Potatoes when, and as they were taken from the fields; and it is the more to be regretted, as I wanted to know the quantity which grew in each lot, and in a *particular* manner, the quantity that grew among the Corn at that place; that I might see and compare the Crop of Corn and the Crop of Potatoes together; but it would seem as if my blundering Overseers would forever put it out of my power to ascertain facts from the accuracy of experiments. Make your estimate (as I observed in my last) of the quantity of Potatoes required for seed next year, allowing for waste and spoilage, before you use, or sell many. It being my wish that many shd. be planted.

In making the calculation whether it is better to sell Wheat in grain, or in flour, it will be necessary to learn previously whether the first is sold by measure or by the weight, for if 60 lbs. is called a bushel, and the wheat weighs not more than 55 lbs. the difference will be very great when a 100 bushls. by measure is reduced to the bushels it will yield by weight at 60 lbs.

You have never informed me what precise measures have been taken with respect to the trespasses on my land on four mile run, neither of what has passed, or prevention. I wish you would see Mr. Minor and converse with him on this subject and act according to circumstances. If it be necessary to survey the land in order to ascertain the trespasses and the boundaries let it be done by some skilful person; the Papers I left with you; the wood is the most valuable part of the tract.

You did very right in putting the amount of Colo. Lyles bond into the bank of Alexandria. Let me know the precise amount thereof. as also of what you deposited there before that I may debit the Bank for it. With this letter you will receive another, enclosing money to discharge my bond to Mr. Lund Washington; my donation to the charity school in Alexandria and subscription towards the Salary of Mr. Davis which I desire may be done without delay. I wish you well and remain etc.

To Alexander Spotswood

Philadelphia, November 23, 1794.

Dear Sir: It has not been in my power to acknowledge, with convenience, the receipt of your letter of the 14th. Ulto. until now; first, because it did not get to my hands until my return from the Westward; and 2dly., because my attention ever since, to the present moment, has been occupied in examining the various papers on which my communications to Congress were to be founded.

I do not see how any one can decide so well on the project you have in contemplation as yourself, who has a view of all the circumstances of the case, before you; and who know how far so important a change in the scene, as that of transplanting yourself and family into a new country, is reconcilable to your feelings and dispositions. And because, from the enquiries you have undoubtedly made, you must better know than any other who has not turned his thoughts to the subject, what you can sell for *here*, and buy at *there*.

It has always been my opinion, that new countries (by this I mean the interior of our own) are the best to lay the foundation of wealth, inasmuch as lands which, comparatively speaking, are to be had there cheap, rise in a four fold ratio to what they do in the Atlantic States. and it is to this circumstance, and the opportunities of acquiring them (by being in the scene) that the advantages consist, as, until the navigation of the Mississippi can be obtained, or communication between the Eastern and western waters is made more easy, than is the case at present, the principal demand for the produce of the land is found in the emigrants who resort to it. To this cause also, is to be ascribed the rapidly encreasing prices of those lands.

In one part of your letter, you talk of removing to Kentucky; and in another, of vesting money in lands No. West of the Ohio, which creates a doubt as to your principal view. You are not uninformed, I presume, that there is no land office open at this time in the last named district; and that there is no means by which land can be obtained there, at present, except by purchase of Army rights, or from some of those companies to whom Congress have sold large tracts: and in the present stage of our disputes with the Indians, that no settlement is thought safe from the scalping knife, that is not under the protection of some fort. The same indeed may be said of the *frontiers* of Kentucky, while the central lands in that State are, as I have been informed, very high. But of these facts you must be better informed than I am.

I should think it perfectly expedient, so soon as you shall have resolved to sell your land on Rappahanock, to advertise it in all the *principal* Gazettes from Richmond to New York inclusively; and not to be too hasty in disposing of it, except for a very good price; as there are reasons to believe that in the course of this winter, and the ensuing Spring and Summer, many men of property from Europe will remove to this country, or send over their property, with a view to invest it, either in our funds, or in lands.

With respect to the other species of property, concerning which you ask my opinion, I shall frankly declare to you that I do not like to even think, much less talk of it. However, as you have put the question I shall, in a few words, give you *my ideas* of it. Were it not then, that I am principled agt. selling negros, as you would do cattle in the market, I would not, in twelve months from this date, be possessed of one, as a slave. I shall be happily mistaken, if they are not found to be a very troublesome species of property 'ere many years pass over our heads; (but this by the bye). For this reason, and because there is but little sale for what is raised in the western country, it remains for you to consider whether, their value would not be more productive in lands, reserving enough for necessary purposes than to carry many there. My love to Mrs. Spotswood and the family. I am etc.

To Eleanor Parke Custis

Philadelphia, January 16, 1795.
Dear Nellie: Your letter, the receipt of which I am now acknowledging, is written correctly and in fair characters, which is an evidence that you command, when you please, a

fair hand. Possessed of these advantages, it will be your own fault if you do not avail yourself of them, and attention being paid to the choice of your subjects, you can have nothing to fear from the malignancy of criticism, as your ideas are lively, and your descriptions agreeable. Let me touch a little now on your Georgetown ball, and happy, thrice happy, for the fair who were assembled on the occasion, that there was a man to spare; for had there been 79 ladies and only 78 gentlemen, there might, in the course of the evening, have been some disorder among the caps; notwithstanding the apathy which *one* of the company entertains for the *"youth"* of the present day, and her determination "never to give herself a moment's uneasiness on account of any of them." A hint here; men and women feel the same inclinations to each other *now* that they always have done, and which they will continue to do until there is a new order of things, and *you*, as others have done, may find, perhaps, that the passions of your sex are easier raised than allayed. Do not therefore boast too soon or too strongly of your insensibility to, or resistance of, its powers. In the composition of the human frame there is a good deal of inflammable matter, however dormant it may lie for a time, and like an intimate acquaintance of yours, when the torch is put to it, *that* which is *within you* may burst into a blaze; for which reason and especially too, as I have entered upon the chapter of advices, I will read you a lecture drawn from this text.

Love is said to be an involuntary passion, and it is, therefore, contended that it cannot be resisted. This is true in part only, for like all things else, when nourished and supplied plentifully with aliment, it is rapid in its progress; but let these be withdrawn and it may be stifled in its birth or much stinted in its growth. For example, a woman (the same may be said of the other sex) all beautiful and accomplished, will, while her hand and heart are undisposed of, turn the heads and set the circle in which she moves on fire. Let her marry, and what is the consequence? The madness *ceases* and all is quiet again. Why? not because there is any diminution in the charms of the lady, but because there is an end of hope. Hence it follows, that love may and therefore ought to be under the guidance of reason, for although we cannot avoid first impressions, we may assuredly place them under guard; and my motives for treating on this subject are to show you, while you remain Eleanor Parke Custis, spinster, and retain the resolution to love with moderation, the propriety of adhering to the latter resolution, at least until you have secured your game, and the way by which it may be accomplished.

When the fire is beginning to kindle, and your heart growing warm, propound these questions to it. Who is this invader? Have I a competent knowledge of him? Is he a man of good character; a man of sense? For, be assured, a sensible woman can never be happy with a fool. What has been his walk in life? Is he a gambler, a spendthrift, or drunkard? Is his fortune sufficient to maintain me in the manner I have been accustomed to live, and my sisters do live, and is he one to whom my friends can have no reasonable objection? If these interrogatories can be satisfactorily answered, there will remain but one more to be asked, that, however, is an important one. Have I sufficient ground to conclude that his affections are engaged by me? Without this the heart of sensibility will struggle against a passion that is not reciprocated; delicacy, custom, or call it by what epithet you will, having precluded all advances on your part. The declaration, without the *most indirect* invitation of yours, must proceed from the man, to render it permanent and valuable, and nothing short of good sense and an easy unaffected conduct can draw the line between prudery and coquetry. It would be no great departure from truth to say, that it rarely happens otherwise than that a thorough-paced coquette dies in celibacy, as a punishment for her attempts to mislead others, by encouraging looks, words, or actions, given for no other purpose than to draw men on to make overtures that they may be rejected.

This day, according to our information, gives a husband to your elder sister, and consummates, it is to be presumed, her fondest desires. The dawn with us is bright, and propitious, I hope, of her future happiness, for a full measure of which she and Mr. Law have my earnest wishes. Compliments and congratulations on this occasion, and best regards are presented to your mamma, Dr. Stuart and family; and every blessing, among which a good husband when you want and deserve one, is bestowed on you by yours, affectionately.

To Edmund Pendleton

Philadelphia, January 22, 1795.

Dear Sir: From a long acquaintance with, and a sincere regard for you, I always feel pleasure in hearing from you, and of you, consequently, your letter of the 30th. ult was an acceptable annuity.

Notwithstanding you have passed your 73 year, whilst you enjoy tolerable health, and retain your faculties in the vigor they are, I wish as well on public, as on private account, that length of days may be added to those which you have already numbered. A month from this day, if I live to see the completion of it, will place me on the wrong (perhaps it would be better to say, on the advanced) side of my grand climacteric; and altho' I have no cause to complain of the want of health, I can religiously aver that no man was ever more tired of public life, or more devoutly wished for retirement, than I do.

I hope, and believe, that the spirit of anarchy in the western counties of this State (to quell which the force of the Union was called for) is *entirely* subdued; and altho' to effect it, the community has been saddled with a considerable expence, yet I trust no money could have been more advantageously expended; both as it respects the internal peace and welfare of *this* country, and the impression it will make on *others*. The spirit with which the Militia turned out, in support of the Constitution, and the laws of our country, at the sametime that it does them immortal honor, is the most conclusive refutation that could have been given to the assertions of Lord Sheffield, and the prediction of others of his cast, that without the protection of G. Britain, we should be unable to govern ourselves; and would soon be involved in anarchy and confusion. They will see that republicanism is not the phantom of a deluded imagination: on the contrary, that under no form of government, will laws be better supported, liberty and property better secured, or happiness be more effectually dispensed to mankind.

The successes of our Army to the westward has, already, been productive of good consequences. They have dispelled a cloud which lowered very heavily in the northern hemisphere (the six nations); and tho' we have received no direct advices from General Wayne since November, there is reason to believe that the Indians with whom we are, or were, at war in that quarter, together with their abetters, begin to see things in a different point of view; but what effect these favorable changes may have on the Southern Indians, it is not easy, at this moment, to decide.

I accord fully in my opinion with you, that the plan of annual presents in an abstract view, unaccompanied with other measures, is not the best mode of treating ignorant Savages, from whose hostile conduct we experience much distress; but it is not to be overlooked, that they, in turn, are not without serious causes of complaint, from the encroachments which are made on their lands by our people; who are not to be restrained by any law now in being, or likely to be enacted. They, poor wretches, have no Press thro' which their grievances are related; and it is well known, that when one side only of a Story is heard, and often repeated, the human mind becomes impressed with it, insensibly. The annual presents however, which you allude to, are not given so much with a view to purchase peace, as by way of retribution for injuries, not otherwise to be redressed. These people are very much irritated by the continual pressure of land speculators and settlers on one hand; and by the impositions of unauthorised, and unprincipled traders (who rob them in a manner of their hunting) on the other. Nothing but the strong arm of the Union, or in other words, energetic laws, can correct these abuses; but here! jealousies, and prejudices (from which I apprehend more fatal consequences to this government than from any other source) aided by local situations, and perhaps by interested considerations, always oppose themselves to efficient measures.

My communications to Congress at the last and present Session, have proceeded upon similar ideas with those expressed in your letter, namely, to make *fair* treaties with the Savage tribes, (by this I mean, that they shall *perfectly* understand every article and clause of them, from correct and repeated interpretations); that these treaties shall be held sacred, and the infractors on either side punished exemplarily; and to furnish them plentifully with goods under wholesome regulations, without aiming at higher prices than is adequate to cover the cost, and charges. If measures like these were adopted, we might hope to live in peace and amity with these borderers; but not whilst our citizens, in violation of law and justice, are guilty of the offences I have mentioned, and are carrying on unauthorised expeditions against them; and when, for the most attrocious murders, even of those of whom we have the least cause of complaint, a Jury on the frontiers, can hardly be got to listen to a charge, much less to convict a culprit.

The madness of the European powers, and the calamitous situation into which all of them are thrown by the present ruinous war, ought to be a serious warning to us, to avoid a similar catastrophe, as long as we can with honor and justice to our national character. What will be the result of Mr. Jay's mission, is more than I am able, at this moment, to disclose. Charged as he has been with *all* matters in dispute between the two countries (not, as has been insinuated in some of the Gazettes, *merely* to that of spoliation) it may easily be conceived that there would be a large field of discussion; but upon what principle (except that of piracy) to account for the conduct of the Bermudian privateers, at this stage of the negotiation, is beyond my comprehension on any fair ground of conjecture; as it *must* swell the bill. With very great esteem and regard I am &c.

To the Commissioners of the District of Columbia

Philadelphia, January 28, 1795.

Gentlemen: A plan for the establishment of an University in the federal City, has frequently been the subject of conversation; but in what manner it is proposed to commence this important institution; on how extensive a scale, the means by which it is to be effected; how it is to be supported; or what progress is made in it; are matters altogether unknown to me.

It has always been a source of serious reflection and sincere regret with me, that the youth of the United States should be sent to foreign countries for the purpose of education. Altho' there are doubtless many under these circumstances who escape the danger of contracting principles, unfriendly to republican government; yet we ought to deprecate the hazard attending ardent and susceptible minds, from being too strongly, and too early prepossessed in favor of other political systems, before they are capable of appreciating their own.

For this reason, I have greatly wished to see a plan adopted by which the arts, Sciences and Belles lettres, could be taught in their *fullest* extent; thereby embracing *all* the advantages of European tuition with the means of acquiring the liberal knowledge which is necessary to qualify our citizens for the exigencies of public, as well as private life; and (which with me, is a consideration of great magnitude) by assembling the youth from the different parts of this rising republic, contributing from their intercourse, and interchange of information, to the removal of prejudices which might perhaps, sometimes arise, from local circumstances.

The federal City, from its centrality, and the advantages which, in other respects it must have over any other place in the U: States, ought to be preferred, as a proper site for such a University. And if a plan can be adopted upon a scale as *extensive* as I have described; and the execution of it shall commence under favorable auspices, in a reasonable time, with a fair prospect of success; I will grant, in perpetuity, fifty shares in the navigation of Potomac River towards the endowment of it.

What annuity will arise from these fifty shares, when the navigation is in full operation, can, at this time, be only conjectured; and those who are acquainted with the nature of it, can form as good a judgment as myself.

As the design of this University has assumed no form with which I am acquainted; and as I am equally ignorant who the persons are that have taken, or are disposed to take, the maturation of the plan upon themselves, I have been at a loss to whom I should make this communication of my intentions. If the Commrs. of the federal city have any particular agency in bringing the matter forward, then the information I now

give to them, is in its proper course; If, on the other hand,
they have no more to do in it than others, who may be desirous of seeing so important a measure carried into effect,
they will be so good as to excuse my using them as the medium for disclosing these intentions; for as much, as it appears
necessary, that the funds for the establishment and support of
the Institution, should be known to the promoters of it; and
because I saw no mode more eligible of making known mine.
For these reasons I give you the trouble of this Address, and
the assurance of being Gentlemen, &c.

To Charles Carter

Philadelphia, March 10, 1795.
Dear Sir: Your favor of the 23d ulto. came duly to hand. I
wish, sincerely, it was in my power to comply with your request in behalf of your son; but it really is not, to the extent
of it.

My friends entertain a very erroneous idea of my pecuniary
resources, when they set me down for a money lender, or one
who (now) has a command of it. You may believe me, when
I assert that the Bonds which were due to me before the Revolution, were discharged during the progress of it, with a few
exceptions in depreciated paper (in some instances as low as
a shilling in the pound). That such has been the management
of my estate, for many years past, especially since my absence
from home, now six years, as scarcely to support itself. That
my public allowance (whatever the world may think of it) is
inadequate to the expence of living in this city; to such an
extravagant height has the necessaries as well as the conveniences of life, arisen. And, moreover, that to keep myself out
of debt; I have found it expedient, now and then, to sell lands,
or something else to effect this purpose.

These are facts I have no inclination to publish to the world,
nor should I have disclosed them on this occasion, had it not
been due to friendship, to give you some explanation of my
inability to comply with your request. If, however, by joining
with nine others, the sum required can be obtained, notwith-

standing my being under these circumstances, and notwithstanding the money will be withdrawn from another purpose,
I will contribute one hundred pounds towards the accommodation of your sons wants, without any view to the receipt
of interest therefrom. With very great esteem &c.

To Thomas Jefferson

Philadelphia, March 15, 1795.
Dear Sir: I received your letter of the 23d. Ulto.; but not
at so early a period as might have been expected from the date
of it. My mind has always been more disposed to apply the
shares in the inland navigations of Potomac and James Rivers
(which were left to my disposal by the legislature of Virginia)
towards the endowment of a *University* in the U States, than
to any other object it had contemplated. In pursuance of this
idea, and understanding that other means are in embryo, for
establishing so useful a seminary in the federal city; I did, on
the 28th. of Jany. last, announce to the Commrs. thereof, my
intention of vesting, in perpetuity, the fifty shares I hold under
that act in the navigation of Potomac; as an additional mean
of carrying the plan into effect; provided, it should be adopted
upon a scale so liberal, and so extensive, as to embrace a *compleat* system of education.

I had but little hesitation in giving the federal dist. a pref-
errence of all other places for this Institution, and for the
following reasons. 1st. on account of its being the permanent
Seat of the government of this Union, and where the laws and
policy of it must be better understood than in any local part
thereof. 2d, because of its centrality. 3d, because one half (or
near it) of the district of Columbia, is within the Commonwealth of Virginia; and the whole of the State not inconvenient thereto. 4th, because as *part* of the endowment, it would
be useful; but *alone*, would be inadequate to the end. 5th,
because many advantages, I conceive, would result from the
Jurisdiction which the general government will have over it,
wch. no other spot would possess. And, lastly, as this Seminary
is contemplated for the *completion* of education, and study of

the sciences (not for boys in their rudiments) it will afford the Students an opportunity of attending the debates in Congress, and thereby becoming more liberally, and better acquainted with the principles of law, and government.

My judgment and my wishes point equally strong to the application of the James River shares to the same object, at the same place; but considering the source from whence they were derived, I have, in a letter I am writing to the Executive of Virginia on this subject, left the application of them to a Seminary, *within the State*, to be located by the Legislature.

Hence you will perceive that I have, in a degree, anticipated your proposition. I was restrained from going the whole length of the suggestion, by the following considerations: 1st, I did not know to what extent, or when any plan would be so matured for the establishment of an University, as would enable any assurance to be given to the application of Mr. D'Ivernois. 2d, the propriety of transplanting the Professors in a *body*, might be questioned for several reasons; among others, because they might not be all good characters; nor all sufficiently acquainted with our language; and again, having been at variance with the levelling party of their own country, the measure might be considered as an aristocratical movement by more than those who, without any just cause that I have been able to discover, are continually sounding the alarm bell of aristocracy. and 3d, because it might preclude some of the first Professors in other countries from a participation; among whom some of the most celebrated characters in Scotland, in this line, I am told might be obtained.

Something, but of what nature I am unable to inform you, has been written by Mr. Adams to Mr. D'Ivernois. Never having viewed my intended donation as more than a part of the means, that was to set this establishment afloat; I did not incline to go too far in the encouragement of Professors before the plan should assume a more formal shape; much less to induce an entire College to migrate. The enclosed is the answer I have received from the Commissioners: from which, and the ideas I have here expressed, you will be enabled to decide on the best communication to be made to Mr. D'Ivernois.

My letter to the Commissioners has bound me to the ful-

filment of what is therein engaged; and if the legislature of
Virginia, in considering the subject, should view it in the same
light I do, the James River shares will be added thereto; for I
think one good Institution of this sort, is to be preferred to
two imperfect ones; which, without other aids than the shares
in *both* navigations, is more likely to fall through, than to succeed upon the plan I contemplate. Which, in a few words, is
to supercede the necessity of sending the youth of this country
abroad, for the purpose of education (where too often principles and habits not friendly to republican government are
imbibed, which are not easily discarded) by instituting such
an one of our own, as will answer the end; and by associating
them in the same seminary, will contribute to wear off those
prejudices, and unreasonable jealouses, which prevent or
weaken friendships and, impair the harmony of the Union.
With very great esteem &c.

PS. Mr. Adams laid before me the communications of Mr.
D'Ivernois; but I said nothing to him of my intended donation towards the establishment of a University in the Federal
District. My wishes would be to fix this on the Virga. side of
the Potomac, therein; but this would not embrace, or accord
with those other means which are proposed for this establishment.

To William Pearce

Philadelphia, May 10, 1795.
Your letter of the 3d. instt, with the Reports of the preceeding week, was received yesterday; and I am glad to find
by it that the Wheat and grass continues to mend. I hope the
warm days we have had, and the showers of rain (if they have
extended to you) have also brought on the Oats. It is high
time they were advancing, if much is to be expected from
them.

Considering the quality of my flour this year, and the smal-
ness of the quantity, I am very well satisfied that you have got
it off your hands at the prices it sold; altho' flour at this market

is at 12 dollars a barrel and rising. In short, the scarcity of this article in Europe, and demand for it; added, to the failure of the last wheat crop in this Country will enable the holders to get any price they please. Let me know the quantity of Midlings and Ship-stuff you disposed of. And tell Davenport to make out, and to have sent to me, the Mill acct. for last year, that I may see what Wheat has gone into, and what flour has come out of, the Mill. I have no reason to suspect that Davenport is otherwise than an honest man; but regular and fair accts. should be stated, and rendered by all Men. In doing this with him, the Overseers accts. of the Wheat sent to, and his of what is received in the Mill, should agree; so likewise ought his charges of the flour, Bran &ca. sent to Mansion house, the Overseers, &ca. to agree with what is reported and credited. This being done, and added to the different kinds of flour that are sold, and the shorts and Bran used, will (accounting also for the Toll Wheat) show the state of the Manufacturing business which is not only satisfactory, but absolutely necessary; for I strongly suspect, notwithstanding it would appear by the experimts. which have been made of an hundred bushels that the balance is in favor of flour, that the case is otherwise on the aggregate quantity which is ground. That it is so this year, can admit of no doubt; it would be inconceivable otherwise that the [   ] of my last years crop of Wheat, and [   ] that of the year before, should yield only [   ] barrls. of flour, besides what was consumed in the family.

If the boy at the Mill is to go into the Garden, at Mansion house, the sooner it happens the better; and I really (considering the little work my Mill does) see no reason why he should not. I am sorry to find by your last reports that there has been two deaths in the family since I left Mount Vernon; and one of them a young fellow. I hope every necessary care and attention was afforded him. I expect little of this from McKoy, or indeed from most of his class; for they seem to consider a Negro much in the same light as they do the brute beasts, on the farms; and often times treat them as inhumanly.

If I recollect rightly, it appears in some of the weekly reports, that Posts and rails were getting at Dogue-run to inclose the Barn yard at that place. I forgot when I was at home, and on the spot with you, to fix on the manner of doing it. I once pointed out my plans to Green and Davis, and I think to McKoy, but little attention seems to have been paid to these things afterwards by either of them. To the best of my recollection, it was intended to run, from each end of the sheds, a Post and rail to the railing leading into the Barn, or treading floor of it, for the stable yard; on one side of which to have a gate, through which to pass into the yard which incloses the Barn on the other sides and into No. 5 also; then back of the two sheds at sufficient distances therefrom allowing full room to receive the litter, dung, &ca. from the Stables, to run Post and Rail fences from the lane South of the Barn, to the fence of No 5, which is back of the lots. Fences run straight, in the manner here described, and at sufficient distances from the back parts of the sheds or stables, would afford ample room for the grain in stacks; and I believe it would be sufficiently capacious also for cow yards, but it would have a bad exposure; and besides, is in low ground; therefore a yard, or yards for this purpose (cattle and Sheep) might adjoin (one on each side the Stable yard) the Lane between No 3 and the lots and the Stable yard fences; as will appear more distinctly in the sketch enclosed.

The number of Bricks which will be required for the Barn in the Neck (River farm) will fall very little short of 140,000 of those that are sound and good, as you will see by the calculation herewith. And that no other than hard [   ] bricks may be put into the Walls, letting it as soon as it is burnt, and cool, be immediately taken down and the

To Alexander Hamilton

(Private, & perfectly confidential)

My dear Sir,   Philadelphia 3d July 1795

The treaty of Amity, Commerce and Navigation, which has lately been before the Senate, has, as you will perceive, made its public entry into the Gazettes of this city. Of course the merits, & demerits of it will (especially in its unfinished state) be freely discussed.

It is not the opinions of *those* who were determined (before it was promulgated) to *support*, or *oppose* it, that I am sollicitous to obtain; for *these* I well know rarely do more than examine the side to which they lean; without giving the reverse the consideration it deserves; possibly without a wish to be apprised of the reasons, on which the objections are founded. My desire is to learn from dispassionate men, who have knowledge of the subject, and abilities to judge of it, the genuine opinion they entertain of *each* article of the instrument; and the *result* of it in the aggregate. In a word, placed on the footing the matter now stands, it is, more than ever, an incumbent duty on me, to do what propriety, and the true interest of this country shall appear to require at my hands on so important a subject, under such delicate circumstances.

You will be at no loss to perceive, from what I have already said, that my wishes are, to have the favorable, and unfavorable side of *each* article stated, and compared together; that I may see the bearing and tendency of them: and, ultimately, on which side the balance is to be found.

This treaty has, I am sensible, many relations, which, in deciding thereon, ought to be attended to; some of them too are of an important nature. I know also, that to judge with precision of its commercial arrangements, there ought likewise to be an intimate acquaintance with the various branches of commerce between this Country and Great Britain as it *now* stands; as it will be placed by the treaty; and as it may affect our present, or restrain our future treaties with other nations. All these things I am persuaded you have given as much attention to as most men; and I believe that your late employment under the General government afforded you more opportunities of deriving knowledge therein, than most of them who had not studied and practiced it scientifically, upon a large & comprehensive scale.

I do not know how you may be occupied at present; or how incompatible this request of mine may be to the business you have in hand. All I can say is, that however desirous I may be of availing myself of your sentiments on the points I have enumerated, and such others as are involved in the treaty,

& the resolution of the Senate; (both of which I send you, lest they should not be at hand) it is not my intention to interrupt you in that business; or, if you are disinclined to go into the investigation I have requested, to press the matter upon you: for of this you may be assured, that with the most unfeigned regard—and with every good wish for your health & prosperity

I am Your Affecte friend and Obedient Servant

PS. Admitting that his B. Majesty will consent to the suspension of the 12th. article of the treaty, is it necessary that the treaty should again go to the Senate? or is the President authorized by the Resolution of that body to ratify it without?

To Alexander Hamilton

(Private)

My dear Sir,   Mount Vernon 29th July 1795
    Your letters of the 20th and 21st. Instt found me at this place, after a hot & disagreeable ride.

As the measures of the government, respecting the treaty, were taken before I left Philadelphia, something more imperious than has yet appeared, must turn up to occasion a change. Still, it is very desirable to ascertain, if possible, after the paroxysm of the fever is a little abated, what the real temper of the people is, concerning it; for at present the cry against the Treaty is like that against a mad-dog; and every one, in a manner, seems engaged in running it down.

That it has received the most tortured interpretation, & that the writings agt. it (which are very industriously circulated) are pregnant of the most abominable mis-representations, yet, there are to be found, so far as my information extends, many well disposed men who conceive, that in the settlement of *old* disputes, a proper regard to reciprocal justice does not appear in the Treaty; whilst others, also well enough affected to the government, are of opinion that to have had *no* commercial treaty would have been better, for this country, than the restricted one, agreed to; inasmuch, say they, the nature of our Exports, and imports (without any extra: or violent measures) would have forced, or led to a more adequate intercourse between the two nations; without any of those shackles which the treaty has imposed. In a word, that as our *exports* consist chiefly of *provisions* & *raw materials*, which to the manufacturers in G. Britain, & to their Islands in the West Indies, affords employment & food; they must have had them on *our* terms if they were not to be obtained on their *own*; whilst the *imports* of this country, offers the best mart for their fabricks; &, of course, is the principal support of their manufacturers: But the string which is most played on, because it strikes with most force the popular ear, is the violation—as they term it—of our engagements with France; or in other words, the predilection shewn by that instrument to G. Britain at the expence of the French nation. The consequences of which are more to be apprehended than any, which are likely to flow from other causes, as ground of opposition; because, whether the fact is, in *any* degree true, or not, it is the interest of the French (whilst the animosity, or jealousies betwn. the two nations exist) to avail themselves of such a spirit to keep *us* & *G. Britain* at variance; and they will, in my opinion, accordingly do it. To what *length* their policy may induce them to carry matters, is too much in embryo at this moment to decide: but I predict much embarrassment to the government therefrom—and in my opinion, too much pains cannot be taken by those who speak, or write, in favor of the treaty, to place this matter in its true light.

I have seen with pleasure, that a writer in one of the New York papers under the Signature of Camillus, has promised to answer—or rather to defend the treaty which has been made with G. Britain. To judge of this work from the first number, which I have seen, I auger well of the performance; & shall expect to see the subject handled in a clear, distinct and satisfactory manner: but if measures are not adopted for its dissimination a few only will derive lights from the knowledge, or labour of the author; whilst the opposition pieces will spread their poison in all directions; and Congress, more than probable, will assemble with the unfavorable impressions of their constituents. The difference of conduct between the friends, and foes of order, & good government, is in nothg. more striking than that, the latter are always working like bees, to distil their poison, whilst the former, depending, often times *too much*, and *too long* upon the sense, and good dispositions of the people to work conviction, neglect the means of effecting it. With sincere esteem & regard

I am your Affecte.

To Henry Knox

Mount Vernon, September 20, 1795.

My dear Sir: I received with great pleasure the letter you wrote me from Boston, dated the 2d. instant; as I always shall do any others you may favor me with. This pleasure was encreased by hearing of the good health of Mrs. Knox and the rest of your family, and the agreeableness of your establishment at St. George's in the Provence of Maine. I may add also, that the account given of the favorable disposition of the people, generally, in your hemisphere, relatively to the Treaty with Great Britain, contributed not a little to the satisfaction I derived in hearing from you.

Next to a conscientious discharge of my public duties, to carry along with me the approbation of my Constituents, would be the highest gratification my mind is susceptible of; but the latter being subordinate, I cannot make the former yield to it; unless some criterian more infallible than partial (if they are not party) meetings, can be discovered as the touch stone of public sentiment. If any power on earth could, or the great power above would, erect the standard of infallibility in political opinions, there is no being that inhabits this terrestrial globe that would resort to it with more eagerness than myself, so long as I remain a servant of the public. But as I have found no better guide hitherto than upright intentions, and close investigation, I shall adhere to these maxims while I keep the watch; leaving it to those who will come after me to explore new ways, if they like; or think them better.

The temper of the people of this State, particularly the Southern parts of it, of South Carolina and Georgia, as far as it is discoverable from the several meetings and resolutions which have been published, is adverse to the Treaty with Great Britain; and yet, I doubt much whether the great body of Yeomanry have formed any opinion on the subject; and whether, if their sense could be fairly taken under a plain and simple statement of facts, nine tenths of them would not advocate the measure. But with such abominable misrepresentations as appear in most of the proceedings, is it to be wondered at that uninformed minds should be affrighted with the dreadful consequences which are predicted, and are taught to expect, from the ratification of such a diabolical instrument, as the treaty is denominated. From North Carolina we hear little concerning it, and from Kentucky nothing.

The moment I received your letter, with one from young Fayette (which was not until the evening preceeding my departure for this place) I wrote to Mr. Cabot, the Senator, requesting, without letting my name appear, that the young gentleman might be provided (at my expence) with every thing that he and his Tutor might stand in need of. And as his coming to Philadelphia, immediately at least, might, the French Minister being there, occasion embarrassments and be productive of no essential good, I proposed, until something more eligable could be devised, to have him entered at the University in Cambridge, with his Tutor. I did not write to the youth myself, for reasons which will readily occur to you; but entreated Mr. Cabot to explain them to him in the most affectionate and consoling manner; and to assure him in the strongest terms, that I would be to him as a friend and father; and that he might to all intents and purposes count upon me as such.

If your mind is still balancing between Philadelphia and Boston for Winter quarters, I sincerely wish it may fix on the former. Mrs. Washington and the rest of my family are well, and unite in best regards for you, Mrs. Knox &ca.; with Dear Sir Your etc.

To Patrick Henry

Mount Vernon, October 9, 1795.

Dear Sir: Whatever may be the reception of this letter; truth and candour shall mark its steps. You doubtless know that the Office of State is vacant, and no one can be more sensible than yourself of the importance of filling it with a person of abilities, and one in whom the public would have confidence.

It would be uncandid not to inform you that this office has been offered to others, but it is as true that it was from a conviction in my mind that you would not accept it (until Tuesday last in a conversation with Genl. (late Governor,) Lee he dropped sentiments which made it less doubtful) that it was not offered first to you.

I need scarcely add, that if this appointment could be made to comport with your own inclination it would be as pleasing to me, as I believe it would be acceptable to the public. With this assurance, and under this belief I make you the offer of it. My first wish is, that you would accept it; the next is that you would be so good as to give me an answer as soon as you conveniently can, as the public business in that departt. is now suffering for want of a Secretary.

I persuade myself, Sir, it has not escaped your observation, that a crisis is approaching that must if it cannot be arrested soon decide whether order and good government shall be preserved or anarchy and confusion ensue. I can most religiously aver I have no wish, that is incompatible with the dignity, happiness and true interest of the people of this country. My ardent desire is, and my aim has been (as far as depended upon the Executive Department,) to comply strictly with *all* our engagemts. foreign and domestic; but to keep the U States free from *political* connexions with *every* other Country. To see that they *may be* independent of *all*, and under the influence of *none*. In a word, I want an *American* character, that the powers of Europe may be convinced we act for *ourselves* and not for *others*; this in my judgment, is the only way to be respected abroad and happy at home and not by becoming the partizans of Great Britain or France, create dissensions, disturb the public tranquillity, and destroy, perhaps for ever the cement wch. binds the Union.

I am satisfied these sentiments cannot be otherwise than congenial to your own; your aid therefore in carrying them into effect would be flattering and pleasing to Dr. Sir &c.

Seventh Annual Message to Congress

United States, December 8, 1795.

Fellow-Citizens of the Senate, and House of Representatives: I trust I do not deceive myself, while I indulge the persuasion, that I have never met you at any period, when more than at present, the situation of our public affairs has afforded just cause for mutual congratulation; and for inviting you, to join with me, in profound gratitude to the Author of all good, for the numerous, and extraordinary blessings we enjoy.

The termination of the long, expensive and distressing war in which we have been engaged with certain Indians North west of the Ohio, is placed in the option of the United States, by a treaty, which the Commander of our Army has concluded, provisionally, with the hostile tribes in that Region.

In the adjustment of the terms, the satisfaction of the Indians was deemed an object worthy no less of the policy, than of the liberality of the United States, as the necessary basis of durable tranquility. This object, it is believed, has been fully attained. The articles agreed upon, will immediately be laid before the Senate, for their consideration.

The Creek and Cherokee Indians, who alone of the Southern tribes had annoyed our frontier, have lately confirmed their pre-existing treaties with us; and were giving evidence of a sincere disposition to carry them into effect, by the surrender of the prisoners and property they had taken: But we have to lament, that the fair prospect in this quarter, has been once more clouded by wanton murders, which some Citizens of Georgia are represented to have recently perpetrated on hunting parties of the Creeks; which have again subjected that frontier to disquietude and danger; which will be productive of further expense; and may occasion effusion of blood. Measures are pursuing to prevent, or mitigate, the usual consequences of such outrages; and with the hope of their succeeding, at least to avert general hostility.

A letter from the Emperor of Morocco, announces to me his recognition of our Treaty made with his father, the late Emperor; and, consequently the continuance, of peace with that Power. With peculiar satisfaction I add, that information has been received from an Agent, deputed on our part to Algiers, importing, that the terms of a Treaty with the Dey and Regency of that country, had been adjusted in such a manner, as to authorise the expectation of a speedy peace; and the restoration of our unfortunate fellow-citizens from a grievous captivity.

The latest advises from our Envoy at the Court of Madrid, give moreover, the pleasing information, that he had received assurances of a speedy, and satisfactory conclusion of his negociation. While the event, depending upon unadjusted particulars, cannot be regarded as ascertained, it is agreeable to cherish the expectation of an issue, which securing amicably, very essential interests of the United States, will at the same time lay the foundation of lasting harmony with a power, whose friendship we have uniformly, and sincerely desired to cultivate.

Though not before officially disclosed to the House of Representatives, you, Gentlemen, are all apprized, that a Treaty of Amity, Commerce and Navigation has been negotiated with Great Britain; and that the Senate have advised and consented to its ratification, upon a condition which excepts part of one article. Agreeably thereto, and to the best judgment I was able to form of the public interest, after full and mature deliberation, I have added my sanction. The result on the part of His Britannic Majesty, is unknown. When received, the subject will, without delay be placed before Congress.

This interesting summary of our affairs, with regard to the foreign powers, between whom and the United States controversies have subsisted, and with regard also to those of our Indian neighbours, with whom we have been in a state of enmity or misunderstanding, opens a wide field for consoling and gratifying reflections. If by prudence and moderation on every side, the extinguishment of all the causes of external discord, which have heretofore menaced our tranquillity, on terms compatible with our national rights and honor, shall be the happy result; how firm and how precious a foundation will have been laid for accelerating, maturing and establishing the prosperity of our country!

Contemplating the internal situation, as well as the external relations of the United States, we discover equal cause for contentment and satisfaction. While many of the nations of Europe, with their American Dependencies, have been involved in a contest unusually bloody, exhausting and calamitous; in which the evils of foreign war have been aggravated by domestic convulsion and insurrection; in which many of the arts most useful to society have been exposed to discouragement and decay; in which scarcity of subsistence has embittered other sufferings; while even the anticipations of a return of the blessings of peace and repose, are alloyed by the sense of heavy and accumulating burthens, which press upon all the departments of industry, and threaten to clog the future springs of Government: Our favored country, happy in a striking contrast, has enjoyed general tranquility; a tranquility the more satisfactory, because maintained at the expense of no duty. Faithful to ourselves, we have violated no obligation to others. Our Agriculture, Commerce and Manufactures, prosper beyond former example; the molestations of our trade (to prevent a continuance of which, however, very pointed remonstrances have been made) being over-balanced by the aggregate benefits which it derives from a Neutral position. Our population advances with a celerity, which exceeding the most sanguine calculations, proportionally augments our strength and resources, and guarantees our future security. Every part of the union displays indications of rapid and various improvement, and with burthens so light as scarcely to be perceived; with resources fully adequate to our present exigencies; with Governments founded on genuine principles of rational liberty, and with mild and wholesome laws; is it too much to say, that our country exhibits a spectacle of national happiness never surpassed if ever before equalled?

Placed in a situation every way so auspicious, motives of commanding force impel us, with sincere ackowledgment to heaven, and pure love to our country, to unite our efforts to preserve, prolong, and improve, our immense advantages. To co-operate with you in this desirable work, is a fervent, and favorite wish of my heart.

It is a valuable ingredient in the general estimate of our welfare, that the part of our country, which was lately the scene of disorder and insurrections, now enjoys the blessings of quiet and order. The misled have abandoned their errors, and pay the respect to our Constitution and laws which is due from good citizens, to the public authorities of the society. These circumstances, have induced me to pardon, generally, the offenders here referred to; and to extend forgiveness to those who had been adjudged to capital punishment. For though I shall always think it a sacred duty, to exercise with firmness and energy, the Constitutional powers with which I am vested, yet it appears to me no less consistent with the public good, than it is with my personal feelings, to mingle in the operations of government, every degree of moderation and tenderness, which the national justice, dignity and safety may permit.

Gentlemen: Among the objects which will claim your attention in the course of the session, a review of our Military establishment is not the least important. It is called by the events which have changed, and may be expected still further to change, the relative situation of our frontiers. In this review, you will doubtless allow due weight to the considerations, that the questions between us, and certain foreign powers, are not yet finally adjusted; that the war in Europe is not yet terminated; and that our Western Posts, when recovered, will demand provision for garrisoning and securing them. A statement of our present military force will be laid before you by the department of war.

With the review of our army establishment, is naturally connected that of the Militia. It will merit inquiry, what imperfections in the existing plan, further experience may have unfolded. The subject is of so much moment, in my estimation, as to excite a constant solicitude that the consideration of it may be renewed, till the greatest attainable perfection shall be accomplished. Time is wearing away some advantages for forwarding the object, while none better deserves the persevering attention of the public councils.

While we indulge the satisfaction, which the actual condition of our Western borders so well authorizes, it is necessary that we should not lose sight of an important truth, which continually receives new confirmations, namely, that the provisions heretofore made with a view to the protection of the Indians, from the violences of the lawless part of our frontier inhabitants are insufficient. It is demonstrated that these violences can now be perpetrated with impunity. And it can need no argument to prove, that unless the murdering of Indians can be restrained, by bringing the murderers to condign punishment, all the exertions of the government to prevent destructive retaliations, by the Indians, will prove fruitless; and all our present agreeable prospects illusory. The frequent destruction of innocent women and children, who are chiefly the victims of retaliation, must continue to shock humanity; and an enormous expence to drain the Treasury of the Union.

To enforce upon the Indians the observance of Justice, it is indispensable that there shall be competent means of rendering justice to them. If these means can be devised by the wisdom of Congress; and especially if there can be added an adequate provision for supplying the necessities of the Indians on reasonable terms, (a measure the mention of which I the more readily repeat, as in all the conferences with them they urge it with solicitude) I should not hesitate to entertain a strong hope, of rendering our tranquility permanent. I add with pleasure, that the probability even of their civilization is not diminished, by the experiments which have been thus far made under the auspices of Government. The accomplishment of this work, if practicable, will reflect undecayed lustre on our national character, and administer the most grateful consolations that virtuous minds can know.

Gentlemen of the House of Representatives: The state of our revenue with the sums which have been borrowed and reimbursed, pursuant to different acts of Congress, will be submitted from the proper Department; together with an estimate of the appropriations necessary to be made for the service of the ensuing year.

Whether measures may not be advisable to reinforce the provision for the redemption of the public debt, will naturally engage your examination. Congress have demonstrated their sense to be, and it were superfluous to repeat mine, that whatsoever will tend to accelerate the honorable extinction of our Public Debt, accords as much with the true interest of our country, as with the general sense of our Constituents.

Gentlemen of the Senate, and House of Representatives: The Statements, which will be laid before you relative to the Mint, will shew the situation of that institution; and the necessity of some further Legislative provisions for carrying the business of it more completely into effect; and for checking abuses which appear to be arising in particular quarters.

The progress in providing materials for the Frigates, and in building them; the state of the fortifications of our harbours; the measures which have been pursued for obtaining proper sites for Arsenals, and for replenishing our Magazines with military stores; and the steps which have been taken towards the execution of the law for opening a trade with the Indians; will likewise be presented for the information of Congress.

Temperate discussion of the important subjects, which may arise in the course of the Session, and mutual forbearance where there is a difference of opinion, are too obvious, and necessary for the peace happiness and welfare of our country, to need any recommendation of mine.

To Gouverneur Morris

(Private)

Philadelphia, December 22, 1795.

My dear Sir: I am become so unprofitable a corrispondent, and so remiss in my corrispondencies, that nothing but the kindness of my friends in overlooking these deficiencies, could induce them to favor me with a continuance of their letters; which, to me, are at once pleasing, interesting, and useful. To a man immersed in debt, and seeing no prospect of extrication but by an act of insolvency (perhaps absolvency would be a better word) I compare myself: and like him too, affraid to examine the items of the account, I will, at once, make a lumping acknowledgment of the receipt of many interesting private letters from you, previous to your last arrival in England; and will begin with those of the 3d. of July and 22d. of Augt. subsequent thereto.

As the British government has repealed the order for seizing our Provision Vessels, little more need be said on that head than that it was the *principle* which constituted the most obnoxious and exceptionable part thereof; and the predicament in which this country was thereby placed in her relations with France. Admitting therefore that the compensation to *some* individuals was adequate to what it might have been in another quarter, yet the exceptions to it on these grounds, remained the same.

I do not think Colo. Innes's report to the Govr. of Kentucky was entirely free from exceptions; but let the report be accompanied with the following remarks. 1, That the one which Lord Grenville might have seen published, was disclaimed by Colo. Innes as soon as it appeared in the public Gazettes, on account of its incorrectness. 2. An irritable spirit at that time pervaded all our people at the Westward, arising from a combination of causes (but from none more powerful than the analogous proceedings of Great Britain in the North, with those of Spain in the South, towards the United States and their Indian borderers) which spirit required some management and soothing. But 3. and principally, Lord Grenville if he had adverted to the many remonstrances which have gone from this country against the conduct of his own; which I will take the liberty to say has been as impolitic for their Nation (if Peace and a good understanding with this, was its object) as it has been irritating to us. And that it may not be conceived that I am speaking at random, let his Lordship be asked if we have not complained, that some of their naval Officers have insulted and menaced us in our *own Ports?* That they have violated our national rights, by searching Vessels, and impressing Seamen within our acknowledged Jurisdiction? and in an outrageous manner have seized the latter by *entire crews* in the West Indies, and done the like, but not so extensively, in all parts of the World? That the Bermudian Privateers, or to speak more correctly, Pirates; and the Admiralty Court of that Island, have committed the most atrocious depredations and violences on our Commerce in capturing, and in their adjudications afterwards, as were never tolerated in any well organized or efficient government? That their Governor of Upper Canada has ordered, in an official, and formal manner, Settlers within our own territory (and far removed from the Posts they have withheld from us) to withdraw, and forbid others to settle on the same? That the persons to whom their Indian Affairs are entrusted, have taken unwearied pains, and practiced every deception to keep those people in a state of irritation and disquietude with us; and, to the *last* moment, exerted every nerve to prevent the Treaty which has lately been concluded between the United States and them, from taking effect?

These complaints were not founded in vague and idle reports, but on indubitable facts. Facts not only known to the government, but so notorious as to be known to the people also; who charge to the last item of the above enumeration, the expenditure of a million, or more dollars annually, for the purpose of self defence against Indian tribes thus stimulated, and for chastising them for the ravages and cruel murders which they had committed on our frontier Inhabits. Our Minister at the Court of London has been directed to remonstrate against these things, with force and energy. The answer, it is true, has been (particularly with respect to the interferences with the Indians) a disavowal. Why then are not the Agents of such unauthorised, offensive, and injurious measures, made examples of? For wherein, let me ask, consists the difference *to us* between their being the acts of government, or the acts of unauthorised Officers, or Agents of the government; if we are to sustain all the evils which flow from such measures?

To this catalogue may be added, the indifference, nay more than indifference, with which the government of Great Britain received the advances of this country towards a friendly intercourse with it; even after the adoption of the present Constitution, and since the operation of the government; and also, the ungracious and obnoxious characters (rancorous refugees, as if done with design to insult the country) which they have sent among us as their Agents; who retaining all their former enmity, could see nothing through a proper medium, and becoming the earwigs of their Ministers (who bye the by does not possess a mind capacious enough, or a temper sufficiently conciliatory, to view things and act upon a great and liberal scale) were always labouring under some unfavorable information and impression; And, probably not communicating them in a less exceptionable manner than they received, or conceived them themselves.

I give you these details (and if you should again converse with Lord Grenville on the subject, you are at liberty, unofficially, to mention them, or any of them, according to circumstances) as evidences of the impolitic conduct, for so it strikes me, of the British government towards these United States; that it may be seen how difficult it has been for the Executive, under such an accumulation of irritating circumstances, to maintain the ground of neutrality which had been taken; at a time when the remembrance of the aid we had received from France in the Revolution, was fresh in every mind, and when the partizans of that country were continually contrasting the affections of that people with the unfriendly disposition of the *British government.* and that too, as I have observed before, while the recollection of their *own* sufferings during the War with the latter, had not been forgotten.

It is well known that Peace has been (to borrow a modern phraze) the order of the day with me, since the disturbances in Europe first commenced. My policy has been, and will continue to be, while I have the honor to remain in the administration of the government, to be upon friendly terms with, but independant of, all the nations of the earth. To share in the broils of none. To fulfil our own engagements. To supply the wants, and be carriers for them all: being thoroughly convinced that it is our policy and interest to do so; and that nothing short of self respect, and that justice which is essential to a national character, ought to involve us in War; for sure I am, if this country is preserved in tranquillity twenty years longer, it may bid defiance, in a just cause, to any power whatever, such, in that time, will be its population, wealth, and resource.

If Lord Grenville conceives that the United States are not well disposed towards Great Britain, his candour, I am persuaded, will seek for the causes; and his researches will fix them as I have done. If this should be the case, his policy will, I am persuaded, be opposed to the continuance, or renewal of the irritating measures which I have enumerated; for he may be assured, tho' the assurance will not, it is probable, carry conviction with it from me to a member of the British administration, that a liberal policy will be one of the most effectual means of deriving advantages to their trade and manufactures from the people of the United States; and will contribute more than any thing else, to obliterate the impressions which have been made by their late conduct towards it.

In a government as free as ours where the people are at liberty, and will express their sentiments, oftentimes imprudently, and for want of information sometimes unjustly, allowances must be made for occasional effervescences; but after the declaration which I have here made of my political creed, you can run no hazard in asserting, that the Executive branch of this government never has, nor will suffer, while I preside, any improper conduct of its officers to escape with impunity; or will give its sanctions to any disorderly proceedings of its citizens.

By a firm adherence to these principles, and to the neutral policy which has been adopted, I have brought on myself a torrent of abuse in the factious papers in this country, and from the enmity of the discontented of all descriptions therein: But having no sinister objects in view, I shall not be diverted from my course by these, nor any attempts which are, or shall be made to withdraw the confidence of my constituents from me. I have nothing to ask, and discharging my duty, I have nothing to fear from invective. The acts of my Administration will appear when I am no more, and the intelligent and candid part of mankind will not condemn my conduct without recurring to them.

The Treaty entered into with G. Britain has (as you have been informed) undergone much, and severe animadversion; and tho' a more favorable one were to have been wished, which the policy perhaps of Great Britain might have granted, yet the demerits thereof are not to be estimated by the opposition it has received; nor is the opposition sanctioned by the great body of the yeomanry in these States: for they (whatever their opinion of it may be) are disposed to leave the decision where the Constitution has placed it. But an occasion was wanting, and the instrument by those who required it, was deemed well calculated for the purpose of working upon the affections of the people of this country, towards those of France; whose interests and rights under our treaty with them, they represented as being violated; and with the aid of the Provision order, and other irritating conduct of the British Ships of War, and agents, as mentioned before, the means were furnished, and more pains taken, than upon any former occasion, to raise a general ferment with a view to defeat the Treaty.

But knowing that you have other corrispondents who have more leizure, and equally capable of detailing these matters, I will leave you to them, and the Gazettes, for fuller information thereon; and for a more minute account of the prevailing politics. And thanking you for the interesting information, and opinions contained in your letter of the 22d. of August, I shall only add that with sincere esteem etc.

PS. We have not heard through any other channel than your letter, of the intended resignation of Mr. Skipwith, and of the proposed recommendation of Mr. Montflorence.

To the Cabinet

Philadelphia, March 25, 1796.
Sir: The resolution moved in the House of Representatives, for the papers relative to the negotiation of the Treaty with G. Britain having passed in the affirmative, I request your opinion,

Whether that branch of Congress hath, or hath not a right, by the Constitution, to call for those papers?

Whether, if it does not possess the right, it would be expedient under the circumstances of this particular case, to furnish them?

And, in either case, in what terms would it be most proper to comply with, or to refuse the request of the House?

These opinions in writing, and your attendance, will be expected at ten o'Clock tomorrow.

To the House of Representatives

United States, March 30, 1796.
Gentlemen of the House of Representatives: With the utmost attention I have considered your resolution of the 24th. instant, requesting me to lay before your House, a copy of the instructions to the Minister of the United States who negotiated the Treaty with the King of Great Britain, together with the correspondence and other documents relative to that Treaty, excepting such of the said papers as any existing negotiation may render improper to be disclosed.

In deliberating upon this subject, it was impossible for me to lose sight of the principle which some have avowed in its discussion; or to avoid extending my views to the consequences which must flow from the admission of that principle.

I trust that no part of my conduct has ever indicated a disposition to withhold any information which the Constitution has enjoined upon the President as a duty to give, or which could be required of him by either House of Congress as a right; And with truth I affirm, that it has been, as it will continue to be, while I have the honor to preside in the Government, my constant endeavour to harmonize with the other branches thereof; so far as the trust delegated to me by the People of the United States, and my sense of the obligation it imposes to "preserve, protect and defend the Constitution" will permit.

The nature of foreign negotiations requires caution; and their success must often depend on secrecy: and even when brought to a conclusion, a full disclosure of all the measures, demands, or eventual concessions, which may have been proposed or contemplated, would be extremely impolitic: for this might have a pernicious influence on future negotiations; or produce immediate inconveniences, perhaps danger and mischief, in relation to other powers. The necessity of such caution and secrecy was one cogent reason for vesting the power of making Treaties in the President, with the advice and consent of the Senate, the principle on which that body was formed confining it to a small number of Members.

To admit then a right in the House of Representatives to demand, and to have as a matter of course, all the Papers respecting a negotiation with a foreign power, would be to establish a dangerous precedent.

It does not occur that the inspection of the papers asked for, can be relative to any purpose under the cognizance of the House of Representatives, except that of an impeachment, which the resolution has not expressed. I repeat, that I have no disposition to withhold any information which the duty of my station will permit, or the public good shall require to be disclosed: and in fact, all the Papers affecting the negotiation with Great Britain were laid before the Senate, when the Treaty itself was communicated for their consideration and advice.

The course which the debate has taken, on the resolution of the House, leads to some observations on the mode of making treaties under the Constitution of the United States.

Having been a member of the General Convention, and knowing the principles on which the Constitution was formed, I have ever entertained but one opinion on this subject; and from the first establishment of the Government to this moment, my conduct has exemplified that opinion, that the power of making treaties is exclusively vested in the President, by and with the advice and consent of the Senate, provided two thirds of the Senators present concur, and that every treaty so made, and promulgated, thenceforward became the Law of the land. It is thus that the treaty making power has been understood by foreign Nations: and in all the treaties made with them, *we* have declared, and *they* have believed, that when ratified by the President with the advice and consent of the Senate, they became obligatory. In this construction of the Constitution every House of Representatives has heretofore acquiesced; and until the present time, not a doubt or suspicion has appeared to my knowledge that this construction was not the true one. Nay, they have more than acquiesced: for till now, without controverting the obligation of such treaties, they have made all the requisite provisions for carrying them into effect.

There is also reason to believe that this construction agrees with the opinions entertained by the State Conventions, when they were deliberating on the Constitution; especially by those who objected to it, because there was not required, in *commercial treaties*, the consent of two thirds of the whole number of the members of the Senate, instead of two thirds of the Senators present; and because in treaties respecting territorial and certain other rights and claims, the concurrence of three fourths of the whole number of the members of both houses respectively, was not made necessary.

It is a fact declared by the General Convention, and universally understood, that the Constitution of the United States was the result of a spirit of amity and mutual concession. And it is well known that under this influence the smaller States were admitted to an equal representation in the Senate with the larger States; and that this branch of the government was invested with great powers: for on the equal participation of those powers, the sovereignty and political safety of the smaller States were deemed essentially to depend.

If other proofs than these, and the plain letter of the Constitution itself, be necessary to ascertain the point under consideration, they may be found in the journals of the General Convention, which I have deposited in the office of the department of State. In these journals it will appear that a proposition was made, "that no Treaty should be binding on the United States which was not ratified by a Law"; and that the proposition was explicitly rejected.

As therefore it is perfectly clear to my understanding, that the assent of the House of Representatives is not necessary to the validity of a treaty: as the treaty with Great Britain exhibits in itself all the objects requiring legislative provision; And on these the papers called for can throw no light: And as it is essential to the due administration of the government, that the boundaries fixed by the constitution between the different departments should be preserved: A just regard to the Constitution and to the duty of my Office, under all the circumstances of this case, forbids a complyance with your request.

To Alexander Hamilton

(Private)

My dear Sir,   Philadelphia 31st Mar: 1796

I do not know how to thank you sufficiently, for the trouble you have taken to dilate on the request of the House of Representatives for the Papers relative to the British Treaty; or how to apologize for the trouble (much greater than I had any idea of giving) which you have taken to shew the impropriety of that request.

From the first moment, and from the fullest conviction in my own mind, I had resolved to *resist the principle* wch. was evidently intended to be established by the call of the House of Representatives; and only deliberated on the manner, in which this could be done, with the least bad consequences.

To effect this, three modes presented themselves to me— 1. a denial of the Papers in toto, assigning concise, but cogent reasons for the denial; 2 to grant them in whole; or 3. in part; accompanied with a pointed protest against the rights of the House to controul Treaties, or to call for Papers without specifying their object; and against the compliance being drawn into precedent.

I had as little hesitation in deciding that the first was the most tenable ground, but from the peculiar circumstances of *this case* It merited consideration, if the *principle* could be saved, whether facility in the provisions might not result from a compliance. An attentive examination however of the Papers and the subject, soon convinced me that to furnish *all* the Papers would be highly improper; and that a *partial* delivery of them would leave the door open for as much calumny as the entire refusal—perhaps more so—as it might, and I have no doubt would be said, that all such as were essential to the purposes of the House, were withheld.

Under these impressions, I proceeded, with the heads of Departments and the Attorney General, to collect materials; & to prepare an answer, subject however to revision, & alteration, according to circumstances. This answer was ready on Monday—and proposed to be sent in on Tuesday but it was delayed until I should receive what was expected; not doing it definitively on that day, the delivery of my answer was further postponed till the next; notwithstanding the anxious solicitude which was visible in all quarters, to learn the result of Executive decision.

Finding that the draft I had prepared, embraced most, if not all the principles which were detailed in the Paper I received yesterday; though not the reasonings—That it would take considerable time to copy the latter—and above all, having understood that if the Papers were refused a fresh demand, with strictures might be expected; I sent in the answer wch. was ready; reserving the other as a source for reasoning if my information proves true.

I could not be satisfied without giving you this concise acct. of the business. To express again my sincere thanks for the pains you have been at to investigate the subject, and to assure you, over & over, of the warmth of my friendship and of the affectionate regard with which

I am Your Affectionate

To Alexander Hamilton

(Private & confidential)

My dear Sir,   Philadelphia 8th. May 1796.
Your note of the 5th. instant accompanying the information given to you by G.—— M.—— on the 4th. of March, came safe on friday. The letter he refers to, as having been written to me, is not yet received; but others from Mr. Monroe of similar complexion, and almost of as imperious a tone from that government, have got to hand.

That justice & policy should dictate the measures with which we are threatned, is not to be conceived; and one would think that even folly & madness on their part, would hardly go such lengths, without supposing a stimulus of a more serious nature than the Town meetings, & the partial resolutions which appeared in the course of last Summer & Autumn on ours. Yet, as it seems to be the Æra of strange vicissitudes,

& unaccountable transactions; attended with a sort of irresistable fatality in many of them, I shall not be surprized at any event that may happen, however extraordinary it may be; and therefore, it may not be amiss to ruminate upon the information which has been received in its fullest latitude; and be prepared to answer the demands on the extensive scale wch has been mentioned.

What then do you think ought to be said in case G.——M——s information should prove true, *in all its parts*? And what, if the proceedings, & Instructions of the French Directory should not exceed my conjecture, which is, that encouraged by the proceedings of last Summer on the Treaty (as already mentioned) and aided perhaps by communications of influencial men in *this* country, thro' a medium which ought to have been the last to engage in it, that that government *may*, and I believe *will* send out an Envoy extraordinary, with Instructions to make strong remonstrances against the unfriendliness (as they will term it), and the tendency of our Treaty with Great Britain; accompanied probably, and expectedly, with discretionary powers to go farther, according to circumstances, and the existing state of matters when he shall have arrived here. Perhaps these Instructions may extend to a releasement from that part of our Treaty with *them*, which claims exemption from the seizure of Enemies goods in *our* Vessels. Perhaps, to demand the fulfilment of our guarantee of their West India Islds. as the most likely means of affording them relief, under the circumstances they labor at present. Perhaps too, to endeavor to render null & void our Treaty with G. Britain. Possibly *all of them*, or the dissolution of the Alliance. But I cannot bring my mind to believe that they seriously mean, or that they could accompany this Envoy with a Fleet, to *demand* the annihilation of the Treaty with G. Britain in fifteen days; or that War, in case of refusal, must follow as a consequence.

Were it not for the unhappy differences among ourselves, *my* answer wd. be short & decisive, to this effect. We are an Independent Nation, and act for ourselves. Having fulfilled, and being willing to fulfil, (as far as we are able) our engagements with other nations, and having decided on, and strictly observed a Neutral conduct towards the Belligerent Powers, from an unwillingness to involve ourselves in War—We will not be dictated to by the Politics of any Nation under Heaven, farther than Treaties require of us.

Whether the *present*, or any circumstances should do more than *soften* this language, may merit consideration. But if we are to be told by a foreign power (if our engagements with it are not infracted) what we *shall do*, and what we shall *not do*, we have Independence yet to seek, & have contended hitherto for very little.

If you have communicated the purport of G—— M——s letter to Mr. Jay, I wish you would lay this also before him, *in confidence*, and that you & he would be so good as to favor me with your sentiments, & opinions on both; and on the measures which you think would be most advisable to be taken, in case we should have to encounter the difficulties with which we are threatned: which, assuredly, will have been brought on us by the misconduct of some of our own intemperate people; who seem to have preferred throwing themselves into the arms of France (even under the present circumstances of that Country) to that manly, & Neutral conduct which is so essential, & would so well become us, as an Independent Nation.

Before, I close this letter, I will mention another subject, which, tho' in a smaller degree, is nevertheless embarrassing. This also is communicated in confidence. It respects the wishes of young Fayette, relative to his father. As is very natural, & what might have been expected, he is extremely solicitous that something should be attempted to obtain the liberation of him; and has brought forward several plans (suggested by Doctr Ballman; who, it is to be feared will be found a troublesome guest among us) to effect it.

These will be better understood by the Enclosures now sent, than by any details I could give, when I add to them— the supposition of Fayette & Frestal, that the Doctor is without funds, and will be more embarrassing *to them* the longer he remains here. No mention, however, that has come to my knowledge of his going away.

The result of my reflection on this subject, and which I have communicated to the two young Men, is, that altho' I am convinced in my own mind that Mr. La Fayette will be held in confinement by the combined Powers until Peace is established; yet to satisfy them, & their friends of my disposition to facilitate their wishes, as far as it can be done with any propriety on my part, I would *as a private person*, express in a letter to the Emperor, my wish, and what I believe to be the wishes of this Country towards that Gentleman; viz, that the liberation of him, conditioned on his repairing hither, would be a grateful measure. That this letter I would put under cover to Mr. Pinckney, to be forwarded or not, according to the view he might have of its success; after conversing indirectly with the Diplomatic characters of the combined Powers in London. But that I could not, while in Public Office, have any Agency in, or even knowledge of, any projects that should require concealment, or that I should be unwilling to appear openly & avowedly in. That as Doctr. Ballman had committed an act (however meritorious & pleasing it might be to the friends of Mr. de la Fayette) which was viewed in a very obnoxious light by the Power in whose possession the prisoner was—Had narrowly excaped condign punishment for it himself—and was released upon the express condition that he should never again appear in those Dominions, that I could neither shew him countenance—nor could I furnish him with money to extricate himself from difficulties (if he was in any). Seeing but little difference between giving before, or after, to a man who stands in the light he does between that Power & the Executive of the U States; but that, if he was disposed to quit the latter, I had no doubt, & he might be so assured, that the friends of Mr. de la Fayette would raise a sufficient sum to enable him to do this, and to defray his expences since he has been in this Country. What they will say to him, or he do in this matter, I know not.

If you & Mr. Jay see no impropriety in such a letter as I have mentioned, to be used at the discretion of Mr. Pinckney—I would thank either of you for drafting it. Mr. Jay in particular having been in the habit, & better acquainted with the stile and manner of addressing these sort of characters than I am, would be able to give it a better shape. To return the papers now sent, with the draught required, as soon as convenient, would be acceptable to

Dear Sir   Your Affecte Servt.

To Alexander Hamilton

My dear Sir,   Philadelphia 15th May 1796

On this day week, I wrote you a letter on the subject of the information received from G—— M——, and put it with some other Papers respecting the case of Mr. De la Fayette, under cover to Mr Jay: to whom also I had occasion to write. But in my hurry (making up the dispatches for the Post Office next morning) I forgot to give it a Superscription; of course it had to return from N: York for one, & to encounter all the delay occasioned thereby, before it could reach your hands.

Since then, I have been favored with your letter of the 10th. instt.; & enclose (in its rough State) the paper mentioned therein, with some alteration in the first page (since you saw it) relative to the reference at foot. Having no copy by me (except of the quoted part)—nor the notes from wch it was drawn, I beg leave to recommend the draught now sent, to your particular attention.

Even if you should think it best to throw the *whole* into a different form, let me request, notwithstanding, that my draught may be returned to me (along with yours) with such amendments & corrections, as to render it as perfect as the formation is susceptible of; curtailed, if too verbose; and relieved of all tautology, not necessary to enforce the ideas in the original or quoted part. My wish is, that the whole may appear in a plain stile; and be handed to the public in an honest; unaffected; simple garb.

It will be perceived from hence, that I am attached to the quotation. My reasons for it are, that as it is not only a fact that such an Address *was written*, and on the point of being published, but *known also to one or two* of those characters who are now stronger, & foremost in the opposition to the Government; and consequently to the person Administering of it contrary to their views; the promulgation thereof, as an evidence that it was much against my inclination that I continued in Office, will cause it more readily to be believed, that I could have *no* view in extending the Powers of the Executive beyond the limits prescribed by the Constitution; and will serve to lessen, in the public estimation the pretensions of that

Party to the patriotic zeal & watchfulness, on which they endeavor to build their own consequence at the expence of others, who have differed from them in sentiment. And besides, it may contribute to blunt, if it does not turn aside, some of the shafts which it may be presumed will be aimed at my annunciation of this event; among which—conviction of fallen popularity, and despair of being re-elected, will be levelled at me with dexterity & keeness.

Having struck out the reference to a *particular character* in the first page of the Address, I have less (if any) objection to expunging those words which are contained within parenthesis's in pages 5, 7 & 8 in the quoted part, and those in the 18th page of what follows. Nor to the discarding the egotism (however just they may be) if you think them liable to fair criticism, and that they had better be omitted; notwithstanding some of them relate facts which are but little known to the Community.

My object has been, and must continue to be, to avoid personalities; allusions to particular measures, which may appear pointed; and to expressions which could not fail to draw upon me attacks which I should wish to avoid, and might not find agreeable to repel.

As there will be another Session of Congress before the Political existence of the *present* House of Representatives, or my own, will constitutionally expire, it was not my design to say a word to the Legislature on this subject; but to withhold the promulgation of my intention until the period, when it shall become indispensably necessary for the information of the Electors, previous to the Election (which, this year, will be delayed until the 7th. of December). This makes it a little difficult, and uncertain what to say, so long beforehand, on the part marked with a pencil in the last paragraph of the 2d page.

All these ideas, and observations are confined, as you will readily perceive, to *my draft* of the validictory Address. If you form one anew, it will, of course, assume such a shape as you may be disposed to give it, predicated upon the Sentiments contained in the enclosed Paper.

With respect to the Gentleman you have mentioned as Successor to Mr. P—— there can be no doubt of his abilities, nor in *my mind* is there any of his fitness. But you know as well as I, what has been said of his political sentiments, with respect to another form of Government; and from thence, can be at no loss to guess at the Interpretation which would be given to the nomination of him. However, the subject shall have due consideration; but a previous resignation would, in my opinion, carry with it too much the appearance of Concert; and would have a bad, rather than a good effect.

Always, & sincerely   I am Yours

Draft of the Farewell Address

Friends and Fellow Citizens:

The quotation in this Address was composed, and intended to have been published, in the year 1792; in time to have announced to the Electors of the President and Vice President of the United States, the determination of the former previous to the sd Election but the solicitude of my confidential friends added to the peculiar situation of our foreign affairs at that epoch induced me to suspend the promulgation; lest among other reasons my retirement might be ascribed to political cowardice. In place thereof I resolved, if it should be the pleasure of my fellow citizens to honor me again with their suffrages, to devote such services as I could render, a year or two longer: trusting that within that period all impediments to an honorable retreat would be removed.

In this hope, as fondly entertained as it was conceived, I entered upon the execution of the duties of my second administration. But if the causes wch produced this postponement had any weight in them at that period it will readily be acknowledged that there has been no diminution in them since, until very lately, and it will serve to account for the delay wch has taken place in communicating the sentiments which were then committed to writing, and are now found in the following words.

"The period which will close the appointment with which my fellow citizens have honoured me, being not very distant, and the time actually arrived, at which their thoughts must be designating the citizen who is to administer the Executive Government of the United States during the ensuing term, it may conduce to a more distinct expression of the public voice, that I should apprize such of my fellow citizens as may retain their partiality towards me, that I am not to be numbered among those out of whom a choice is to be made.

I beg them to be assured that the Resolution which dictates this intimation has not been taken without the strictest regard to the relation which as a dutiful citizen I bear to my country; and that in withdrawing that tender of my service, which silence in my situation might imply, I am not influenced by the smallest deficiency of zeal for its future interests, or of grateful respect for its past kindness: but by the fullest persuasion that such a step is compatible with both.

The impressions under which I entered on the present arduous trust were explained on the proper occasion. In discharge of this trust, I can only say that I have contributed towards the organization and administration of the Government the best exertions of which a very fallible judgment was capable. For any errors which may have flowed from this source, I feel all the regret which an anxiety for the public good can excite; not without the double consolation, however, arising from a consciousness of their being involuntary, and an experience of the candor which will interpret them. If there were any circumstances which could give value to my inferior qualifications for the trust, these circumstances must have been temporary. In this light was the undertaking viewed when I ventured on it. Being, moreover still further advanced into the decline of life, I am every day more sensible that the increasing weight of years, renders the private walks of it in the shade of retirement, as necessary as they will be acceptable to me. May I be allowed to add, that it will be among the highest as well as the purest enjoyments that can sweeten the remnant of my days, to partake in a private station, in the midst of my fellow citizens, of that benign influence of good laws under a free Government, which has been the ultimate object of all my wishes, and in wch I confide as the happy reward of our cares and labours. [May I be allowed further to add as a consideration far more important, that an early example of rotation in an office of so high and delicate a nature, may equally accord with the republican spirit of our Constitution, and the ideas of liberty and safety entertained by the people.]

In contemplating the moment at which the curtain is to drop forever on the public scenes of my life, my sensations anticipate and do not permit me to suspend, the deep acknowledgments required by that debt of gratitude which I owe to my beloved country for the many honors it has conferred on me, for the distinguished confidence it has reposed in me, and for the opportunities I have thus enjoyed of testifying my inviolable attachment by the most steadfast services which my faculties could render. All the returns I have now to make will be in those vows which I shall carry with me to my retirement and to my grave, that Heaven may continue to favor the people of the United States with the choicest tokens of its beneficence; that their union and brotherly affection may be perpetual; that the free Constitution which is the work of their own hands, may be sacredly maintained; that its administration in every department, may be stamped with wisdom and with virtue; and that this character may be ensured to it, by that watchfulness over public servants and public measures, which on the one hand will be necessary, to prevent or correct a degeneracy; and that forbearance, on the other, from unfounded or indiscriminate jealousies which would deprive the public of the best services, by depriving a conscious integrity of one of the noblest incitements to perform them; that in fine the happiness of the people of America, under the auspices of liberty, may be made compleat, by so careful a preservation, and so prudent a use of this blessing, as will acquire them the glorious satisfaction of recommending it to the affection; the praise; and the adoption of every Nation which is yet a stranger to it.

And may we not dwell with well grounded hopes on this flattering prospect; when we reflect on the many ties by which the people of America are bound together, and the many proofs they have given of an enlightened judgment and a magnanimous patriotism.

We may all be considered as the Children of one common Country. We have all been embarked in one common cause. We have all had our share in common sufferings and common successes. The portion of the Earth allotted for the theatre of our fortunes, fulfils our most sanguine desires. All its essential interests are the same; while the diversities arising from climate, from soil, and from other local and lesser peculiarities, will naturally form a mutual relation of the parts, that may give the whole a more entire independence than has perhaps fallen to the lot of any other nation.

To confirm these motives to an affectionate and permanent Union, and to secure the great objects of it, we have established a common Government, which being free in its principles; being founded in our own choice; being intended as the guardian of our common rights; and the patron of our common interests; and wisely containing within itself a provision for its own amendment, as experience may point out its errors, seems to promise every thing that can be expected from such an institution; [and if supported by wise Councils, by virtuous conduct, and by mutual and friendly allowances, must approach as near to perfection as any human work can aspire, and nearer than any which the annals of mankind have recorded.]

With these wishes and hopes I shall make my exist from civil life; and I have taken the same liberty of expressing them, which I formerly used in offering the sentiments which were suggested by my exit from military life. If, in either instance, I have presumed more than I ought, on the indulgence of my fellow citizens, they will be too generous to ascribe it to any other cause, than the extreme solicitude which I am bound to feel, and which I can never cease to feel for their liberty, their prosperity, and their happiness."

Had the situation of our public affairs continued to wear the same aspect they assumed at the time the foregoing address was drawn I should not have taken the liberty of troubling you my fellow citizens, with any new sentiments or with a repition, more in detail, of those which are therein contained; but considerable changes having taken place both at home and abroad, I shall ask your indulgence while I express with more lively sensibility, the following most ardent wishes of my heart.

That party disputes, among all the friends and lovers of their country may subside, or, as the wisdom of Providence has ordained that men, on the same subjects, shall not always think alike, that charity and benevolence when they happen to differ may so far shed their benign influence as to banish those invectives which proceed from illiberal prejudices and jealousy.

That as the allwise dispensor of human blessings has favored no Nation of the Earth with more abundant, and substantial means of happiness than United America, that we may not be so ungrateful to our Creator; so wanting to ourselves; and so regardless of Posterity, as to dash the cup of beneficence which is thus bountifully offered to our acceptance.

That we may fulfil with the greatest exactitude *all* our engagements: foreign and domestic, to the *utmost* of our abilities whensoever, and in whatsoever manner they are pledged: for in public, as in private life, I am persuaded that honesty will forever be found to be the best policy.

That we may avoid connecting ourselves with the Politics of any Nation, farther than shall be found necessary to regulate our own trade; in order that commerce may be placed upon a stable footing; our merchants know their rights; and the government the ground on which those rights are to be supported.

That every citizen would take pride in the name of an American, and act as if he felt the importance of the character by considering that we ourselves are now a distinct Nation the dignity of which will be absorbed if not annihilated, if we enlist ourselves (further than our obligations may require) under the banners of any other Nation whatsoever. And moreover, that we would guard against the Intriegues of *any* and *every* foreign Nation who shall endeavor to intermingle (however covertly and indirectly) in the internal concerns of our country; or who shall attempt to prescribe rules for our policy with any other power, if there be no infraction of our engagements with themselves, as one of the greatest evils that can befal us as a people; for whatever may be their professions, be assured fellow Citizens and the event will (as it always has) invariably prove, that Nations as well as individuals, act for their own benefit, and not for the benefit of others, unless both interests happen to be assimilated (and when that is the case there requires no contract to bind them together). That all their interferences are calculated to promote the former; and in proportion as they succeed, will render us less independant. In a word, nothing is more certain than that, if we receive favors, we must grant favors; and it is not easy to decide beforehand under such circumstances as we are, on which side the balance will ultimately terminate; but easy indeed is it to foresee that it may involve us in disputes and finally in War, to fulfil political alliances. Whereas, if there be no engagements on our part, we shall be unembarrassed, and at liberty at all times, to act from circumstances, and the dictates of Justice, sound policy, and our essential Interests.

That we may be always prepared for War, but never unsheath the sword except in self defence so long as Justice and our *essential* rights, and national respectability can be preserved without it; for without the gift of prophecy, it may safely be pronounced, that if this country can remain in peace 20 years longer: and I devoutly pray that it may do so to the end of time; such in all probability will be its population, riches, and resources, when combined with its peculiarly happy and remote Situation from the other quarters of the globe, as to bid defiance, in a just cause, to any earthly power whatsoever.

That whensoever and so long as we profess to be Neutral, let our public conduct whatever our private affections may be, accord therewith; without suffering partialities on one hand, or prejudices on the other to controul our Actions. A contrary practice is not only incompatible with our declarations, but is pregnant with mischief, embarrassing to the Administration, tending to divide us into parties, and ultimately productive of all those evils and horrors which proceed from faction, and above all,

That our Union may be as lasting as time; for while we are encircled in one band, we shall possess the strength of a Giant and there will be none who can make us affraid. Divide, and we shall become weak; a prey to foreign Intriegues and internal discord; and shall be as miserable and contemptible as we are now enviable and happy. And lastly:

That the several departments of Government may be preserved in their utmost Constitutional purity, without any attempt of one to encroach on the rights or privileges of another; that the Genl and State governmts may move in their propr Orbits; And that the authorities of our own constituting may be respected by ourselves as the most certain means of having them respected by foreigners.

In expressing these sentiments it will readily be perceived that I can have no other view now, whatever malevolence might have ascribed to it before, than such as result from a perfect conviction of the utility of the measure. If public servants, in the exercise of their official duties are found incompetent or pursuing wrong courses discontinue them. If they are guilty of mal-practices in office, let them be more exemplarily punished; in both cases the Constitution and Laws have made provision, but do not withdraw your confidence from them, the best incentive to a faithful discharge of their duty, without just cause; nor infer, because measures of a complicated nature, which time, opportunity and close investigation alone can penetrate, and for these reasons are not easily comprehended by those who do not possess the means, that it necessarily follows they must be wrong; This would not only be doing injustice to your Trustees, but be counteracting your own essential interests; rendering those Trustees (if not contemptible in the eyes of the world) little better at least than ciphers in the Administration of the government and the Constitution of your own chusing would reproach you for such conduct.

As this Address, Fellow citizens will be the last I shall ever make you, and as some of the Gazettes of the United States have teemed with all the Invective that disappointment, ignorance of facts, and malicious falsehoods could invent, to misrepresent my politics and affections; to wound my reputation and feelings; and to weaken, if not entirely destroy the confidence you had been pleased to repose in me; it might be expected at the parting scene of my public life that I should take some notice of such virulent abuse. But, as heretofore, I shall pass them over in utter silence; never having myself, nor by any other with my participation or knowledge, written, or published a scrap in answer to any of them. My politicks have been unconcealed; plain and direct. They will be found (so far as they relate to the Belligerent Powers) in the Proclamation of the 22d of April 1793; which, having met your approbation, and the confirmation of Congress, I have uniformly and steadily adhered to, uninfluenced by, and regardless of the complaints and attempts of *any of those* powers or their partisans to change them.

The Acts of my Administration are on Record. By these, which will not change with circumstances, nor admit of different interpretations, I expect to be judged. If they will not acquit me, in your estimation, it will be a source of regret; but I shall hope notwithstanding, as I did not seek the Office with which you have honored me, that charity may throw her mantle over my want of abilities to do better; that the gray hairs of a man who has, excepting the interval between the close of the Revolutionary War, and the organization of the new governmt. either in a civil, or military character, spent five and forty years, *All the prime of his life,* in serving his country, be suffered to pass quietly to the grave; and that his errors, however numerous; if they are not criminal, may be consigned to the Tomb of oblivion, as he himself soon will be to the Mansions of Retirement.

To err, is the lot of humanity, and never for a moment, have I ever had the presumption to suppose that I had not a full proportion of it. Infallibility not being the attribute of Man, we ought to be cautious in censuring the opinions and conduct of one another. To avoid intentional error in my public conduct, has been my constant endeavor; and I set malice at defiance to charge me, justly, with the commission of a wilful one; or, with the neglect of any public duty, which, in my opinion ought to have been performed, since I have been in the Administration of the government. An Administration which I do not hesitate to pronounce, the infancy of the government, and all other circumstances considered, that has been as delicate, difficult, and trying as may occur again in any future period of our history. Through the whole of which I have to the best of my judgment, and with the best information and advice I could obtain, consulted the true and permanent interest of my country without regard to local considerations, to individuals, to parties, or to Nations.

To conclude, and I feel proud in having it in my power to do so with truth, that it was not from ambitious views; it was not from ignorance of the hazard to which I knew I was exposing my reputation; it was not from an expectation of pecuniary compensation, that I have yielded to the calls of my country; and that, if my country has derived no benefit from my services, my fortune, in a pecuniary point of view, has received no augmentation from my country. But in delivering this last sentiment, let me be unequivocally understood as not intending to express any discontent on my part, or to imply any reproach on my country on that account. [The first wd be untrue; the other ungrateful. And no occasion more fit than the present may ever occur perhaps to declare, as I now do declare, that nothing but the principle upon which I set out, and from which I have, in no instance departed, not to receive more from the public than my expences, has restrained the bounty of several Legislatures at the close of the War with Great Britain from adding considerably to my pecuniary resources.] I retire from the Chair of government no otherwise benefitted in this particular than what you have all experienced from the increased value of property, flowing from the Peace and prosperity with which our country has been blessed amidst tumults which have harrassed and involved other countries in all the horrors of War. I leave you with undefiled hands, an uncorrupted heart, and with ardent vows to heaven for the welfare and happiness of that country in which I and my forefathers to the third or fourth progenitor drew our first breath.

May 15, 1796

To Alexander Hamilton

My dear Sir,   Mount Vernon 26th June 1796.

Your letter without date, came to my hands by Wednesdays Post; and by the first Post afterwards I communicated the purport of it (withholding the names) to the Secretary of State; with directions to bestow the closest attention to the subject, and if the application which had been made to the Minister of France, consequent of the Capture of the Ship Mount Vernon, had not produced such an answer as to supercede the necessity, then to endeavor to obtain such explanation of the views of the French government relatively to our Commerce with Great Britain, as the nature of the case appeared to require.

That the fact is, as has been represented to you, I have very little, if any doubt. Many, very many circumstances are continually happening in confirmation of it: among which, it is evident Bache's Paper, which *receives* and *gives* the hope, is endeavouring to prepare the Public mind for this event, by representing it as the *predicted*, and *natural* consequence of the Ratification of the Treaty with Great Britn.

Let me ask therefore.

Do you suppose that the Executive, in the recess of the Senate, has power in such a case as the one before us—especially if the measure should not be *avowed* by authority—to send a special character to Paris, as Envoy Extraordinary, to give, & receive explanations? And if there be a doubt, whether it is not probable—nay more than probable, that the French Directory would, in the present state of things, avail themselves of the unconstitutionallity of the measure, to decline receiving him? The policy of delay, to avoid explanations, would induce them to adopt any pretext to accomplish it. Their reliance upon a party in this country for support, would stimulate them to this conduct; and we may be assured they will not be deficient in the most minute details of every occurrence, and every opinion, worthy of communication. If then an Envoy cannot be sent to Paris without the Agency of the Senate, will the information you have received, admitting it should be realized, be sufficient ground for convening that body?

These are serious things; they may be productive of serious consequences; and therefore require very serious & cool deliberation. Admitting, however, that the Powers of the President during the recess, were adequate to such an appointment, where is the character who would go, that unites the proper qualifications for such a Mission; and would not be obnoxious to one party or the other? And what should be done with Mr. M—— in that case?

As the affairs of this country in their administration, receive great embarrassment from the conduct of characters among ourselves; and as every act of the Executive is mis-represented,

and tortured with a view to make it appear odious, the aid of
the friends to government is peculiarly necessary under such
circumstances; and at such a crises as the present: It is unnecessary therefore to add, that I should be glad upon the present, and all other important occasions, to receive yours: and
as I have great confidence in the abilities, and purity of Mr.
Jays views, as well as in his experience, I should wish that his
sentiments on the purport of this letter; and other interesting
matters as they occur, may accompany yours; for having no
other wish than to promote the true and permanent interests
of this country, I am anxious, always, to compare the opinions
of those in whom I confide with one another; and these again
(without being bound by them) with my own, that I may
extract all the good I can.

Having from a variety of reasons (among which a disinclination to be longer buffitted in the public prints by a set of
infamous scribblers) taken my ultimate determination "to seek
the Post of honor in a private Station" I regret exceedingly
that I did not publish my valedictory address the day after the
Adjournment of Congress. This would have preceeded the
canvassing for Electors (wch. is commencing with warmth, in
this State). It would have been announcing *publicly*, what
seems to be very well understood, and is industriously propagated, *privately*. It would have removed doubts from the
minds of *all*, and left the field clear for *all*: It would, by having
preceeded any unfavorable change in our foreign relations (if
any should happen) render my retreat less difficult and embarrassing. And it might have prevented the remarks which,
more than probable will follow a late annunciation—namely—
that I delayed it long enough to see, that the current was
turned against me, before I declared my intention to decline.
This is one of the reasons which makes me a little tenacious
of the draught I furnished you with, to be modified & corrected.

Having passed, however, what *I now* conceive would have
been the *precise* moment to have addressed my Constituents,
let me ask your opinion (under a full conviction that nothing
will shake my determination to withdraw) of the *next* best
time, considering the present, and what may, probably, be the
existing state of things at different periods previous to the

Election; or rather, the middle of Octr, beyond which the promulgation of my intentions cannot be delayed. Let me hear from you as soon as it is convenient; and be assured always of the sincere esteem, and affecte. regard of

To Thomas Jefferson

Mount Vernon, July 6, 1796.

Dear Sir: When I inform you, that your letter of the 19th. Ulto. went to Philadelphia and returned to this place before it was received by me; it will be admitted, I am persuaded, as an apology for my not having acknowledged the receipt of it sooner.

If I had entertained any suspicions before, that the queries, which have been published in Bache's Paper, proceeded from you, the assurances you have given of the contrary, would have removed them; but the truth is, I harboured none. I am at no loss to *conjecture* from what source they flowed; through what channel they were conveyed; and for what purpose they and similar publications, appear. They were known to be in the hands of Mr. Parker, in the early part of the last Session of Congress; They were shown about by Mr. Giles during the Cession, and they made their public exhibition about the close of it.

Perceiving, and probably, hearing, that no abuse in the Gazettes would induce me to take notice of anonymous publications, against me; those who were disposed to do me *such friendly Offices*, have embraced without restraint every opportunity to weaken the confidence of the People; and, by having the *whole* game in their hands, they have scrupled not to publish things that do not, as well as those which do exist; and to mutilate the latter, so as to make them subserve the purposes which they have in view.

As you have mentioned the subject yourself, it would not be frank, candid, or friendly to conceal, that your conduct has been represented as derogatory from that opinion *I* had conceived you entertained of me. That to your particular friends and connextions you have described, and they have denounced me, as a person under a dangerous influence; and that, if I would listen *more* to some *other* opinions, all would be well. My answer invariably has been, that I had never discovered any thing in the conduct of Mr. Jefferson to raise suspicions, in my mind, of his insincerity; that if he would retrace my public conduct while he was in the Administration, abundant proofs would occur to him, that truth and right decisions, were the *sole* objects of my pursuit; that there were as many instances within his *own* knowledge of my having decided *against*, as in *favor of* the opinions of the person evidently alluded to; and moreover, that I was no believer in the infallibility of the politics, or measures of *any man living*. In short, that I was no party man myself, and the first wish of my heart was, if parties did exist, to reconcile them.

To this I may add, and very truly, that, until within the last year or two ago, I had no conception that Parties would, or even could go, the length I have been witness to; nor did I believe until lately, that it was within the bonds of probability; hardly within those of possibility, that, while I was using my utmost exertions to establish a national character of our own, independent, as far as our obligations, and justice would permit, of every nation of the earth; and wished, by steering a steady course, to preserve this Country from the horrors of a desolating war, that I should be accused of being the enemy of one Nation, and subject to the influence of another; and to prove it, that every act of my administration would be tortured, and the grossest, and most insidious mis-representations of them be made (by giving one side *only* of a subject, and that too in such exaggerated and indecent terms as could scarcely be applied to a Nero; a notorious defaulter; or even to a common pick-pocket). But enough of this; I have already gone farther in the expression of my feelings, than I intended.

The particulars of the case you mention (relative to the Little Sarah) is a good deal out of my recollection at present, and I have no public papers here to resort to. When I get back to Philadelphia (which, unless I am called there by something new, will not be 'till towards the last of August) I will examine my files.

It must be pleasing to a Cultivator, to possess Land which will yield Clover kindly; for it is certainly a great Desiderata in Husbandry. My Soil, without very good dressings, does not produce it well: owing, I believe, to its stiffness; hardness at bottom; and retention of Water. A farmer, in my opinion, need never despair of raising Wheat to advantage, upon a Clover lay; with a single ploughing, agreeably to the Norfolk and Suffolk practice. By a misconception of my Manager last year, a field at one of my Farms which I intended shd. have been fallowed for Wheat, went untouched. Unwilling to have my crop of Wheat at that place so much reduced, as would have been occasioned by this omission, I directed, as soon as I returned from Philadelphia (about the middle of September) another field, not in the usual rotation, which had lain out two years, and well covered with mixed grasses, principally white clover, to be turned over with a good Bar-share; and the Wheat to be sown, and harrowed in at the tail of the Plough. It was done so accordingly, and was, by odds, the best Wheat I made this year. It exhibits an unequivocal proof to my mind, of the great advantage of Clover lay, for Wheat. Our Crops of this article, hereabouts, are more or less injured by what some call the Rot; others the Scab; occasioned, I believe, by high winds and beating rain when the grain is in blossom, and before the Farina has performed its duties.

Desirous of trying the field Peas of England, and the Winter Vetch, I sent last fall to Mr. Marray of Liverpool for 8 bushels of each sort. Of the Peas he sent me two kinds (a white and dark, but not having the letter by me, I am unable to give the names). They did not arrive until the latter end of April; when they ought to have been in the ground the beginning of March. They were sown however, but will yield no Seed; of course the experiment I intended to make, is lost. The Vetch is yet on hand for Autumn Seeding. That the Albany Peas will grow well with us, I know from my own experience: but they are subject to the same bug which perforates, and injures the Garden Peas, and will do the same, I fear, to the imported Peas, of any sort from England, in this climate, from the heat of it.

I do not know what is meant by, or to what uses the Caroline drill is applied. How does your Chicorium prosper? Four years since I exterminated all the Plants raised from Seed sent me by Mr. Young, and to get into it again, the seed I purchased in Philadelphia last Winter, and what has been sent me by Mr. Murray this Spring, has cost me upwards of twelve pounds Sterling. This, it may be observed, is a left handed way to make money; but the first was occasioned by the manager I then had, who pretended to know it well in England and pronounced it a noxious weed; the restoration of it, is indebted to Mr. Strickland and others (besides Mr. Young) who speak of it in exalted terms. I sowed mine broad-cast; some with and some without grain. It has come up well; but there seems to be a serious struggle between *it* and the grass and weeds; the issue of which (as I can afford no relief to the former) is doubtful at present, and may be useful to know.

If you can bring a moveable threshing Machine, constructed upon simple principles to perfection, it will be among the most valuable institutions in this Country; for nothing is more wanting, and to be wished for on our farms. Mrs. Washington begs you to accept her best wishes, and with very great esteem etc.

To Alexander Hamilton

Private

My dear Sir,   Philadelphia 25th. Augt. 1796
I have given the Paper herewith enclosed, several serious & attentive readings; and prefer it greatly to the other draughts, being more copious on material points; more dignified on the whole; and with less egotism. Of course less exposed to criticism, & better calculated to meet the eye of discerning readers (foreigners particularly, whose curiosity I have little doubt will lead them to inspect it attentively & to pronounce their opinions on the performance).

When the first draught was made, besides having an eye to the consideration above mentioned, I thought the occasion was fair (as I had latterly been the subject of considerable invective) to say what is there contained of myself—and as the Address was designed in a more especiall manner for the Yeomanry of this Country I conceived it was proper they should be informed of the object of that abuse; the silence with which it had been treated; and the consequences which would naturally flow from such unceasing & virulent attempts to destroy all confidence in the Executive part of the Government; and that it was best to do it in language that was plain & intelligable to their understanding.

The draught now sent, comprehends the most, if not all these matters; is better expressed; and I am persuaded goes as far as it ought with respect to any personal mention of myself.

I should have seen no occasion myself, for its undergoing a revision. But as your letter of the 30th. Ulto. which accompanied it, intimates a wish to do this—and knowing that it can be more correctly done after a writing has been out of sight for sometime than while it is in hand, I send it in conformity thereto—with a request, however, that you wd. return it as soon as you have carefully re-examined it; for it is my intention to hand it to the Public before I leave this City, to which I came for the purpose of meeting General Pinckney—receiving ministers from Spain & Holland—and for the dispatch of other business which could not be so well executed by written communications between the heads of Departments & myself as by oral conferences. So soon as these are accomplished I shall return; at any rate I expect to do so by or before the tenth of next month for the purpose of bringing up my family for the Winter.

I shall expunge all that is marked in the paper as unimportant &ca. &ca. and as you perceive some marginal notes, written with a pencil, I pray you to give the sentiments so noticed mature consideration. After which, and in every other part, if change or alteration takes place in the draught, let them be so clearly interlined—erazed—or referred to in the Margin as that no mistake may happen in copying it for the Press.

To what Editor in *this* City do you think it had best be sent for Publication? Will it be proper to accompany it with a note to him, expressing (as the principal design of it is to remove doubts at the next Election) that it is hoped, or expected, that the State Printers will give it a place in their Gazettes—or preferable to let it be carried by my private Secretary to that Press which is destined to usher it to the World & suffer it to work its way afterwards? If you think the first most eligable, let me ask you to sketch such a note as you may judge applicable to the occasion. With affectionate regard

I am always   Yours

Address to the Cherokee Nation

City of Philadelphia, August 29, 1796.

Beloved Cherokees: Many years have passed since the White people first came to America. In that long space of time many good men have considered how the condition of the Indian natives of the country might be improved; and many attempts have been made to effect it. But, as we see at this day, all these attempts have been nearly fruitless. I also have thought much on this subject, and anxiously wished that the various Indian tribes, as well as their neighbours, the White people, might enjoy in abundance all the good things which make life comfortable and happy. I have considered how this could be done; and have discovered but one path that could lead them to that desirable situation. In this path I wish all the Indian nations to walk. From the information received concerning you, my beloved Cherokees, I am inclined to hope that you are prepared to take this path and disposed to pursue it. It may seem a little difficult to enter; but if you make the attempt, you will find every obstacle easy to be removed. Mr. Dinsmoor, my beloved agent to your nation, being here, I send you this talk by him. He will have it interpreted to you, and particularly explain my meaning.

Beloved Cherokees,

You now find that the game with which your woods once abounded, are growing scarce; and you know when you cannot meet a deer or other game to kill, that you must remain hungry; you know also when you can get no skins by hunting, that the traders will give you neither powder nor cloathing; and you know that without other implements for tilling the ground than the hoe, you will continue to raise only scanty crops of corn. Hence you are sometimes exposed to suffer much from hunger and cold; and as the game are lessening in numbers more and more, these sufferings will increase. And how are you to provide against them? Listen to my words and you will know.

My beloved Cherokees,

Some among you already experience the advantage of keeping cattle and hogs: let all keep them and increase their numbers, and you will ever have a plenty of meat. To these add sheep, and they will give you cloathing as well as food. Your lands are good and of great extent. By proper management you can raise live stock not only for your own wants, but to sell to the White people. By using the plow you can vastly increase your crops of corn. You can also grow wheat, (which makes the best bread) as well as other useful grain. To these you will easily add flax and cotton, which you may dispose of to the White people, or have it made up by your own women into cloathing for yourselves. Your wives and daughters can soon learn to spin and weave; and to make this certain, I have directed Mr. Dinsmoor, to procure all the necessary apparatus for spinning and weaving, and to hire a woman to teach the use of them. He will also procure some plows and other implements of husbandry, with which to begin the improved cultivation of the ground which I recommend, and employ a fit person to shew you how they are to be used. I have further directed him to procure some cattle and sheep for the most prudent and industrious men, who shall be willing to exert themselves in tilling the ground and raising those useful animals. He is often to talk with you on these subjects, and give you all necessary information to promote your success. I must therefore desire you to listen to him; and to follow his advice. I appointed him to dwell among you as the Agent of the United States, because I judged him to be a faithful man, ready to obey my instructions and to do you good.

But the cares of the United States are not confined to your single nation. They extend to all the Indians dwelling on their borders. For which reason other agents are appointed; and for the four southern nations there will be a general or principal agent who will visit all of them, for the purpose of maintaining peace and friendship among them and with the United States; to superintend all their affairs; and to assist the particular agents with each nation in doing the business assigned them. To such general or principal agent I must desire your careful attention. He will be one of our greatly beloved men. His whole time will be employed in contriving how to do you good, and you will therefore act wisely to follow his advice. The first general or principal agent will be Colonel Benjamin Hawkins, a man already known and respected by you. I have chosen him for this office because he is esteemed for a good man; has a knowledge of Indian customs, and a particular love and friendship for all the Southern tribes.

Beloved Cherokees,

What I have recommended to you I am myself going to do. After a few moons are passed I shall leave the great town and retire to my farm. There I shall attend to the means of increasing my cattle, sheep and other useful animals; to the growing of corn, wheat, and other grain, and to the employing of women in spinning and weaving; all which I have recommended to you, that you may be as comfortable and happy as plenty of food, clothing and other good things can make you.

Beloved Cherokees,

When I have retired to my farm I shall hear of you; and it will give me great pleasure to know that you have taken my advice, and are walking in the path which I have described. But before I retire, I shall speak to my beloved man, the Secretary of War, to get prepared some medals, to be given to such Cherokees as by following my advice shall best deserve them. For this purpose Mr. Dinsmoor is from time to time to visit every town in your nation. He will give instructions to those who desire to learn what I have recommended. He will see what improvements are made; who are most industrious in raising cattle; in growing corn, wheat, cotton and flax; and in spinning and weaving; and on those who excel these rewards are to be bestowed.

Beloved Cherokees,

The advice I here give you is important as it regards your nation; but still more important as the event of the experiment made with you may determine the lot of many nations. If it succeeds, the beloved men of the United States will be encouraged to give the same assistance to all the Indian tribes within their boundaries. But if it should fail, they may think it vain to make any further attempts to better the condition of any Indian tribe; for the richness of the soil and mildness of the air render your country highly favorable for the practice of what I have recommended.

Beloved Cherokees,

The wise men of the United States meet together once a year, to consider what will be for the good of all their people. The wise men of each separate state also meet together once or twice every year, to consult and do what is good for the people of their respective states. I have thought that a meeting of your wise men once or twice a year would be alike useful to you. Every town might send one or two of its wisest counsellors to talk together on the affairs of your nation, and to recommend to your people whatever they should think would be serviceable. The beloved agent of the United States would meet with them. He would give them information of those things which are found good by the white people, and which your situation will enable you to adopt. He would explain to them the laws made by the great council of the United States, for the preservation of peace; for the protection of your lands; for the security of your persons; for your improvement in the arts of living, and for promoting your general welfare. If it should be agreeable to you that your wise men should hold such meetings, you will speak your mind to my beloved man, Mr. Dinsmoor, to be communicated to the President of the United States, who will give such directions as shall be proper.

Beloved Cherokees,

That this talk may be known to all your nation, and not forgotten, I have caused it to be printed, and directed one, signed by my own hand, to be lodged in each of your towns. The Interpreters will, on proper occasions, read and interpret the same to all your people.

Beloved Cherokees,

Having been informed that some of your chiefs wished to see me in Philadelphia, I have sent them word that I would receive a few of the most esteemed. I now repeat that I shall be glad to see a small number of your wisest chiefs; but I shall not expect them 'till November. I shall take occasion to agree with them on the running of the boundary line between your lands and ours, agreeably to the treaty of Holston. I shall expect them to inform me what chiefs are to attend the running of this line, and I shall tell them whom I appoint to run it; and the time and place of beginning may then be fixed.

I now send my best wishes to the Cherokees, and pray the Great spirit to preserve them.

To Alexander Hamilton

Private

My dear Sir,   Philadelphia 1st. Septr. 1796

About the middle of last Week I wrote to you; and that it might escape the eye of the Inquisitive (for some of my letters have lately been pried into) I took the liberty of putting it under a cover to Mr. Jay.

Since then, revolving on the Paper that was enclosed therein; on the various matters it contained; and on the just expression of the advice or recommendation which was given in it, I have regretted that another subject (which in my estimation is of interesting concern to the well-being of this country) was not touched upon also: I mean Education *generally* as one of the surest means of enlightening & givg. just ways of thinkg to our Citizens, but particularly the establishment of a University; where the Youth from *all parts* of the United States might receive the polish of Erudition in the Arts, Sciences & Belle Letters; and where those who were disposed to run a political course, might not only be instructed in the theory & principles, but (this Seminary being at the Seat of the General Government) where the Legislature wd. be in Session half the year, and the interests & politics of the Nation of course would be discussed, they would lay the surest foundation for the practical part also.

But that which would render it of the highest importance, in my opinion, is, that the Juvenal period of life, when friendships are formed, & habits established that will stick by one; the Youth, or young men from different parts of the United States would be assembled together, & would by degrees discover that there was not that cause for those jealousies & prejudices which one part of the union had imbibed against another part: of course, sentiments of more liberality in the general policy of the country would result from it. What, but the mixing of people from different parts of the United States during the War rubbed off these impressions? A century in the ordinary intercourse, would not have accomplished what the Seven years association in Arms did: but that ceasing, prejudices are beginning to revive again, and never will be eradicated so effectually by any other means as the intimate intercourse of characters in early life, who, in all probability, will be at the head of the councils of this country in a more advanced stage of it.

To shew that this is no *new* idea of mine, I may appeal to my early communications to Congress; and to prove how seriously I have reflected on it since, & how well disposed I have been, & still am, to contribute my aid towards carrying the measure into effect, I enclose you the extract of a letter from me to the Governor of Virginia on the Subject, and a copy of the resolves of the Legislature of that State in consequence thereof.

I have not the smallest doubt that this donation (when the Navigation is in complete operation, which it certainly will be in less than two years) will amount to twelve or £1500 Sterlg a year, and become a rapidly increasing fund. The Proprietors of the Federal City have talked of doing something handsome towards it likewise and if Congress would appropriate some of the Western lands to the same uses, funds sufficient, and of the most permanent and increasing sort might be so established as to invite the ablest Professors in Europe, to conduct it.

Let me pray you, therefore, to introduce a Section in the Address expressive of these sentiments, & recommendatory of the measure—without any mention, however, of my proposed personal contribution to the plan.

Such a Section would come in very properly after the one which relates to our religious obligations, or in a preceding part, as one of the recommendatory measures to counteract the evils arising from Geographical discriminations.

With Affecte regard   I am always Yours

Farewell Address

United States, September 19, 1796.

Friends, and Fellow-Citizens: The period for a new election of a Citizen, to Administer the Executive government of the United States, being not far distant, and the time actually arrived, when your thoughts must be employed in designating the person, who is to be cloathed with that important trust, it appears to me proper, especially as it may conduce to a more distinct expression of the public voice, that I should now apprise you of the resolution I have formed, to decline being considered among the number of those, out of whom a choice is to be made.

I beg you, at the same time, to do me the justice to be assured, that this resolution has not been taken, without a strict regard to all the considerations appertaining to the relation, which binds a dutiful citizen to his country, and that, in with drawing the tender of service which silence in my situation might imply, I am influenced by no diminution of zeal for your future interest, no deficiency of grateful respect for your past kindness; but am supported by a full conviction that the step is compatible with both.

The acceptance of, and continuance hitherto in, the office to which your Suffrages have twice called me, have been a uniform sacrifice of inclination to the opinion of duty, and to a deference for what appeared to be your desire. I constantly hoped, that it would have been much earlier in my power, consistently with motives, which I was not at liberty to disregard, to return to that retirement, from which I had been reluctantly drawn. The strength of my inclination to do this, previous to the last Election, had even led to the preparation of an address to declare it to you; but mature reflection on the then perplexed and critical posture of our Affairs with foreign Nations, and the unanimous advice of persons entitled to my confidence, impelled me to abandon the idea.

I rejoice, that the state of your concerns, external as well as internal, no longer renders the pursuit of inclination incompatible with the sentiment of duty, or propriety; and am persuaded whatever partiality may be retained for my services, that in the present circumstances of our country, you will not disapprove my determination to retire.

The impressions, with which I first undertook the arduous trust, were explained on the proper occasion. In the discharge of this trust, I will only say, that I have, with good intentions, contributed towards the Organization and Administration of the government, the best exertions of which a very fallible judgment was capable. Not unconscious, in the outset, of the inferiority of my qualifications, experience in my own eyes, perhaps still more in the eyes of others, has strengthened the motives to diffidence of myself; and every day the encreasing weight of years admonishes me more and more, that the shade of retirement is as necessary to me as it will be welcome. Satisfied that if any circumstances have given peculiar value to my services, they were temporary, I have the consolation to believe, that while choice and prudence invite me to quit the political scene, patriotism does not forbid it.

In looking forward to the moment, which is intended to terminate the career of my public life, my feelings do not permit me to suspend the deep acknowledgment of that debt of gratitude wch. I owe to my beloved country, for the many honors it has conferred upon me; still more for the stedfast confidence with which it has supported me; and for the opportunities I have thence enjoyed of manifesting my inviolable attachment, by services faithful and persevering, though in usefulness unequal to my zeal. If benefits have resulted to our country from these services, let it always be remembered to your praise, and as an instructive example in our annals, that, under circumstances in which the Passions agitated in every direction were liable to mislead, amidst appearances sometimes dubious, viscissitudes of fortune often discouraging, in situations in which not unfrequently want of Success has countenanced the spirit of criticism, the constancy of your support was the essential prop of the efforts, and a guarantee of the plans by which they were effected. Profoundly penetrated with this idea, I shall carry it with me to my grave, as a strong incitement to unceasing vows that Heaven may continue to you the choicest tokens of its beneficence; that your Union and brotherly affection may be perpetual; that the free constitution, which is the work of your hands, may be sacredly maintained; that its Administration in every department may be stamped with wisdom and Virtue; that, in fine, the happiness of the people of these States, under the auspices of liberty, may be made complete, by so careful a preservation and so prudent a use of this blessing as will acquire to them the glory of recommending it to the applause, the affection, and adoption of every nation which is yet a stranger to it.

Here, perhaps, I ought to stop. But a solicitude for your welfare, which cannot end but with my life, and the apprehension of danger, natural to that solicitude, urge me on an occasion like the present, to offer to your solemn contemplation, and to recommend to your frequent review, some sentiments; which are the result of much reflection, of no inconsiderable observation, and which appear to me all important to the permanency of your felicity as a People. These will be offered to you with the more freedom, as you can only see in them the disinterested warnings of a parting friend, who can possibly have no personal motive to biass his counsel. Nor can I forget, as an encouragement to it, your endulgent reception of my sentiments on a former and not dissimilar occasion

Interwoven as is the love of liberty with every ligament of your hearts, no recommendation of mine is necessary to fortify or confirm the attachment.

The Unity of Government which constitutes you one people is also now dear to you. It is justly so; for it is a main Pillar in the Edifice of your real independence, the support of your tranquility at home; your peace abroad; of your safety; of your prosperity; of that very Liberty which you so highly prize. But as it is easy to foresee, that from different causes and from different quarters, much pains will be taken, many artifices employed, to weaken in your minds the conviction of this truth; as this is the point in your political fortress against which the batteries of internal and external enemies will be most constantly and actively (though often covertly and insidiously) directed, it is of infinite moment, that you should properly estimate the immense value of your national Union to your collective and individual happiness; that you should cherish a cordial, habitual and immoveable attachment to it; accustoming yourselves to think and speak of it as of the Palladium of your political safety and prosperity; watching for its preservation with jealous anxiety; discountenancing whatever may suggest even a suspicion that it can in any event be abandoned, and indignantly frowning upon the first dawning of every attempt to alienate any portion of our Country from the rest, or to enfeeble the sacred ties which now link together the various parts.

For this you have every inducement of sympathy and interest. Citizens by birth or choice, of a common country, that country has a right to concentrate your affections. The name of AMERICAN, which belongs to you, in your national capacity, must always exalt the just pride of Patriotism, more than any appellation derived from local discriminations. With slight shades of difference, you have the same Religion, Manners, Habits and political Principles. You have in a common cause fought and triumphed together. The independence and liberty you possess are the work of joint councils, and joint efforts; of common dangers, sufferings and successes.

But these considerations, however powerfully they address themselves to your sensibility are greatly outweighed by those which apply more immediately to your Interest. Here every portion of our country finds the most commanding motives for carefully guarding and preserving the Union of the whole.

The *North*, in an unrestrained intercourse with the *South*, protected by the equal Laws of a common government, finds in the productions of the latter, great additional resources of Maratime and commercial enterprise and precious materials of manufacturing industry. The *South* in the same Intercourse, benefitting by the Agency of the *North*, sees its agriculture grow and its commerce expand. Turning partly into its own channels the seamen of the *North*, it finds its particular navigation envigorated; and while it contributes, in different ways, to nourish and increase the general mass of the National navigation, it looks forward to the protection of a Maratime strength, to which itself is unequally adapted. The *East*, in a like intercourse with the *West*, already finds, and in the progressive improvement of interior communications, by land and water, will more and more find a valuable vent for the commodities which it brings from abroad, or manufactures at home. The *West* derives from the *East* supplies requisite to its growth and comfort, and what is perhaps of still greater consequence, it must of necessity owe the *secure* enjoyment of indispensable *outlets* for its own productions to the weight, influence, and the future Maritime strength of the Atlantic side of the Union, directed by an indissoluble community of Interest as *one Nation.* Any other tenure by which the *West* can hold this essential advantage, whether derived from its own seperate strength, or from an apostate and unnatural connection with any foreign Power, must be intrinsically precarious.

While then every part of our country thus feels an immediate and particular Interest in Union, all the parts combined cannot fail to find in the united mass of means and efforts greater strength, greater resource, proportionably greater security from external danger, a less frequent interruption of their Peace by foreign Nations; and, what is of inestimable value! they must derive from Union an exemption from those broils and Wars between themselves, which so frequently afflict neighbouring countries, not tied together by the same government; which their own rivalships alone would be sufficient to produce, but which opposite foreign alliances, attachments and intriegues would stimulate and imbitter. Hence likewise they will avoid the necessity of those overgrown Military establishments, which under any form of Government are inauspicious to liberty, and which are to be regarded as particularly hostile to Republican Liberty: In this sense it is, that your Union ought to be considered as a main prop of your liberty, and that the love of the one ought to endear to you the preservation of the other.

These considerations speak a persuasive language to every reflecting and virtuous mind, and exhibit the continuance of the UNION as a primary object of Patriotic desire. Is there a doubt, whether a common government can embrace so large a sphere? Let experience solve it. To listen to mere speculation in such a case were criminal. We are authorized to hope that a proper organization of the whole, with the auxiliary agency of governments for the respective Sub divisions, will afford a happy issue to the experiment. 'Tis well worth a fair and full experiment With such powerful and obvious motives to Union, affecting all parts of our country, while experience shall not have demonstrated its impracticability, there will always be reason, to distrust the patriotism of those, who in any quarter may endeavor to weaken its bands.

In contemplating the causes wch. may disturb our Union, it occurs as matter of serious concern, that any ground should have been furnished for characterizing parties by *Geographical* discriminations: *Northern* and *Southern*; *Atlantic* and *Western*; whence designing men may endeavour to excite a belief that there is a real difference of local interests and views. One of the expedients of Party to acquire influence, within particular districts, is to misrepresent the opinions and aims of other Districts. You cannot shield yourselves too much against the jealousies and heart burnings which spring from these misrepresentations. They tend to render Alien to each other those who ought to be bound together by fraternal affection. The Inhabitants of our Western country have lately had a useful lesson on this head. They have seen, in the Negociation by the Executive, and in the unanimous ratification by the Senate, of the Treaty with Spain, and in the universal satisfaction at that event, throughout the United States, a decisive proof how unfounded were the suspicions propagated among them of a policy in the General Government and in the Atlantic States unfriendly to their Interests in regard to the Mississippi. They have been witnesses to the formation of two Treaties, that with G: Britain and that with Spain, which secure to them every thing they could desire, in respect to our Foreign relations, towards confirming their prosperity. Will it not be their wisdom to rely for the preservation of these advantages on the Union by wch. they were procured? Will they not henceforth be deaf to those advisers, if such there are, who would sever them from their Brethren and connect them with Aliens?

To the efficacy and permanency of Your Union, a Government for the whole is indispensable. No Alliances however strict between the parts can be an adequate substitute. They must inevitably experience the infractions and interruptions which all Alliances in all times have experienced. Sensible of this momentous truth, you have improved upon your first essay, by the adoption of a Constitution of Government, better calculated than your former for an intimate Union, and for the efficacious management of your common concerns. This government, the offspring of our own choice uninfluenced and unawed, adopted upon full investigation and mature deliberation, completely free in its principles, in the distribution of its powers, uniting security with energy, and containing within itself a provision for its own amendment, has a just claim to your confidence and your support. Respect for its authority, compliance with its Laws, acquiescence in its measures, are duties enjoined by the fundamental maxims of true Liberty. The basis of our political systems is the right of the people to make and to alter their Constitutions of Government. But the Constitution which at any time exists, 'till changed by an explicit and authentic act of the whole People, is sacredly obligatory upon all. The very idea of the power and the right of the People to establish Government presupposes the duty of every Individual to obey the established Government.

All obstructions to the execution of the Laws, all combinations and Associations, under whatever plausible character, with the real design to direct, controul counteract, or awe the regular deliberation and action of the Constituted authorities are distructive of this fundamental principle and of fatal tendency. They serve to organize faction, to give it an artificial and extraordinary force; to put in the place of the delegated will of the Nation, the will of a party; often a small but artful and enterprizing minority of the Community; and, according to the alternate triumphs of different parties, to make the public administration the Mirror of the ill concerted and incongruous projects of faction, rather than the organ of consistent and wholesome plans digested by common councils and modefied by mutual interests. However combinations or Associations of the above description may now and then answer popular ends, they are likely, in the course of time and things, to become potent engines, by which cunning, ambitious and unprincipled men will be enabled to subvert the Power of the People, and to usurp for themselves the reins of Government; destroying afterwards the very engines which have lifted them to unjust dominion.

Towards the preservation of your Government and the permanency of your present happy state, it is requisite, not only that you steadily discountenance irregular oppositions to its acknowledged authority, but also that you resist with care the spirit of innovation upon its principles however specious the pretexts. one method of assault may be to effect, in the forms of the Constitution, alterations which will impair the energy of the system, and thus to undermine what cannot be directly overthrown. In all the changes to which you may be invited, remember that time and habit are at least as necessary to fix the true character of Governments, as of other human institutions; that experience is the surest standard, by which to test the real tendency of the existing Constitution of a country; that facility in changes upon the credit of mere hypotheses and opinion exposes to perpetual change, from the endless variety of hypotheses and opinion: and remember, especially, that for the efficient management of your common interests, in a country so extensive as ours, a Government of as much vigour as is consistent with the perfect security of Liberty is indispensable. Liberty itself will find in such a Government, with powers properly distributed and adjusted, its surest Guardian. It is indeed little else than a name, where the Government is too feeble to withstand the enterprises of faction, to confine each member of the Society within the limits prescribed by the laws and to maintain all in the secure and tranquil enjoyment of the rights of person and property.

I have already intimated to you the danger of Parties in the State, with particular reference to the founding of them on Geographical discriminations. Let me now take a more comprehensive view, and warn you in the most solemn manner against the baneful effects of the Spirit of Party, generally

This spirit, unfortunately, is inseperable from our nature, having its root in the strongest passions of the human Mind. It exists under different shapes in all Governments, more or less stifled, controuled, or repressed; but, in those of the popular form it is seen in its greatest rankness and is truly their worst enemy.

The alternate domination of one faction over another, sharpened by the spirit of revenge natural to party dissention, which in different ages and countries has perpetrated the most horrid enormities, is itself a frightful despotism. But this leads at length to a more formal and permanent despotism. The disorders and miseries, which result, gradually incline the minds of men to seek security and repose in the absolute power of an Individual: and sooner or later the chief of some prevailing faction more able or more fortunate than his competitors, turns this disposition to the purposes of his own elevation, on the ruins of Public Liberty.

Without looking forward to an extremity of this kind (which nevertheless ought not to be entirely out of sight) the common and continual mischiefs of the spirit of Party are sufficient to make it the interest and the duty of a wise People to discourage and restrain it.

It serves always to distract the Public Councils and enfeeble the Public administration. It agitates the Community with ill founded jealousies and false alarms, kindles the animosity of one part against another, foments occasionally riot and insurrection. It opens the door to foreign influence and corruption, which find a facilitated access to the government itself through the channels of party passions. Thus the policy and the will of one country, are subjected to the policy and will of another.

There is an opinion that parties in free countries are useful checks upon the Administration of the Government and serve to keep alive the spirit of Liberty. This within certain limits is probably true, and in Governments of a Monarchical cast Patriotism may look with endulgence, if not with favour, upon the spirit of party. But in those of the popular character, in Governments purely elective, it is a spirit not to be encouraged. From their natural tendency, it is certain there will always be enough of that spirit for every salutary purpose. And there being constant danger of excess, the effort ought to be, by force of public opinion, to mitigate and assuage it. A fire not to be quenched; it demands a uniform vigilance to prevent its bursting into a flame, lest instead of warming it should consume.

It is important, likewise, that the habits of thinking in a free Country should inspire caution in those entrusted with its administration, to confine themselves within their respective Constitutional spheres; avoiding in the exercise of the Powers of one department to encroach upon another. The spirit of encroachment tends to consolidate the powers of all the departments in one, and thus to create whatever the form of government, a real despotism. A just estimate of that love of power, and proneness to abuse it, which predominates in the human heart is sufficient to satisfy us of the truth of this position. The necessity of reciprocal checks in the exercise of political power; by dividing and distributing it into different depositories, and constituting each the Guardian of the Public Weal against invasions by the others, has been evinced by experiments ancient and modern; some of them in our country and under our own eyes. To preserve them must be as necessary as to institute them. If in the opinion of the People, the distribution or modification of the Constitutional powers be in any particular wrong, let it be corrected by an amendment in the way which the Constitution designates. But let there be no change by usurpation; for though this, in one instance, may be the instrument of good, it is the customary weapon by which free governments are destroyed. The precedent must always greatly overbalance in permanent evil any partial or transient benefit which the use can at any time yield.

Of all the dispositions and habits which lead to political prosperity, Religion and morality are indispensable supports. In vain would that man claim the tribute of Patriotism, who should labour to subvert these great Pillars of human happiness, these firmest props of the duties of Men and citizens. The mere Politician, equally with the pious man ought to respect and to cherish them. A volume could not trace all their connections with private and public felicity. Let it simply be asked where is the security for property, for reputation, for life, if the sense of religious obligation *desert* the oaths, which are the instruments of investigation in Courts of Justice? And let us with caution indulge the supposition, that morality can be maintained without religion. Whatever may be conceded to the influence of refined education on minds of peculiar structure, reason and experience both forbid us to expect that National morality can prevail in exclusion of religious principle.

'Tis substantially true, that virtue or morality is a necessary spring of popular government. The rule indeed extends with more or less force to every species of free Government. Who that is a sincere friend to it, can look with indifference upon attempts to shake the foundation of the fabric

Promote then as an object of primary importance, Institutions for the general diffusion of knowledge. In proportion as the structure of a government gives force to public opinion, it is essential that public opinion should be enlightened

As a very important source of strength and security, cherish public credit. One method of preserving it is to use it as sparingly as possible: avoiding occasions of expence by cultivating peace, but remembering also that timely disbursements to prepare for danger frequently prevent much greater disbursements to repel it; avoiding likewise the accumulation of debt, not only by shunning occasions of expence, but by vigorous exertions in time of Peace to discharge the Debts which unavoidable wars may have occasioned, not ungenerously throwing upon posterity the burthen which we ourselves ought to bear. The execution of these maxims belongs to your Representatives, but it is necessary that public opinion should cooperate. To facilitate to them the performance of their duty, it is essential that you should practically bear in mind, that towards the payment of debts there must be Revenue; that to have Revenue there must be taxes; that no taxes can be devised which are not more or less inconvenient and unpleasant; that the intrinsic embarrassment inseperable from the selection of the proper objects (which is always a choice of difficulties) ought to be a decisive motive for a candid construction of the Conduct of the Government in making it, and for a spirit of acquiescence in the measures for obtaining Revenue which the public exigencies may at any time dictate.

Observe good faith and justice towds. all Nations. Cultivate peace and harmony with all. Religion and morality enjoin this conduct; and can it be that good policy does not equally enjoin it? It will be worthy of a free, enlightened, and, at no distant period, a great Nation, to give to mankind the magnanimous and too novel example of a People always guided by an exalted justice and benevolence. Who can doubt that in the course of time and things the fruits of such a plan would richly repay any temporary advantages wch. might be lost by a steady adherence to it? Can it be, that Providence has not connected the permanent felicity of a Nation with its virtue? The experiment, at least, is recommended by every sentiment which ennobles human Nature. Alas! is it rendered impossible by its vices?

In the execution of such a plan nothing is more essential than that permanent, inveterate antipathies against particular Nations and passionate attachments for others should be excluded; and that in place of them just and amicable feelings towards all should be cultivated. The Nation, which indulges towards another an habitual hatred, or an habitual fondness, is in some degree a slave. It is a slave to its animosity or to its affection, either of which is sufficient to lead it astray from its duty and its interest. Antipathy in one Nation against another, disposes each more readily to offer insult and injury, to lay hold of slight causes of umbrage, and to be haughty and intractable, when accidental or trifling occasions of dispute occur. Hence frequent collisions, obstinate envenomed and bloody contests. The Nation, prompted by illwill and resentment sometimes impels to War the Government, contrary to the best calculations of policy. The Government sometimes participates in the national propensity, and adopts through passion what reason would reject; at other times, it makes the animosity of the Nation subservient to projects of hostility instigated by pride, ambition and other sinister and pernicious motives. The peace often, sometimes perhaps the Liberty, of Nations has been the victim.

So likewise, a passionate attachment of one Nation for another produces a variety of evils. Sympathy for the favourite nation, facilitating the illusion of an imaginary common interest, in cases where no real common interest exists, and infusing into one the enmities of the other, betrays the former into a participation in the quarrels and Wars of the latter, without adequate inducement or justification: It leads also to concessions to the favourite Nation of priviledges denied to others, which is apt doubly to injure the Nation making the concessions; by unnecessarily parting with what ought to have been retained; and by exciting jealousy, ill will, and a disposition to retaliate, in the parties from whom eql. priviledges are withheld: And it gives to ambitious, corrupted, or deluded citizens (who devote themselves to the favourite Nation) facility to betray, or sacrifice the interests of their own country, without odium, sometimes even with popularity; gilding with the appearances of a virtuous sense of obligation a commendable deference for public opinion, or a laudable zeal for public good, the base or foolish compliances of ambition corruption or infatuation.

As avenues to foreign influence in innumerable ways, such attachments are particularly alarming to the truly enlightened and independent Patriot. How many opportunities do they afford to tamper with domestic factions, to practice the arts of seduction, to mislead public opinion, to influence or awe the public Councils! Such an attachment of a small or weak, towards a great and powerful Nation, dooms the former to be the satellite of the latter.

Against the insidious wiles of foreign influence, (I conjure you to believe me fellow citizens) the jealousy of a free people ought to be *constantly* awake; since history and experience prove that foreign influence is one of the most baneful foes of Republican Government. But that jealousy to be useful must be impartial; else it becomes the instrument of the very influence to be avoided, instead of a defence against it. Excessive partiality for one foreign nation and excessive dislike of another, cause those whom they actuate to see danger only on one side, and serve to veil and even second the arts of influence on the other. Real Patriots, who may resist the intriegues of the favourite, are liable to become suspected and odious; while its tools and dupes usurp the applause and confidence of the people, to surrender their interests.

The Great rule of conduct for us, in regard to foreign Nations is in extending our commercial relations to have with them as little *political* connection as possible. So far as we have already formed engagements let them be fulfilled, with perfect good faith. Here let us stop.

Europe has a set of primary interests, which to us have none, or a very remote relation. Hence she must be engaged in frequent controversies, the causes of which are essentially foreign to our concerns. Hence therefore it must be unwise in us to implicate ourselves, by artificial ties, in the ordinary vicissitudes of her politics, or the ordinary combinations and collisions of her friendships, or enmities:

Our detached and distant situation invites and enables us

to pursue a different course. If we remain one People, under an efficient government, the period is not far off, when we may defy material injury from external annoyance; when we may take such an attitude as will cause the neutrality we may at any time resolve upon to be scrupulously respected; when belligerent nations, under the impossibility of making acquisitions upon us, will not lightly hazard the giving us provocation; when we may choose peace or war, as our interest guided by our justice shall Counsel.

Why forego the advantages of so peculiar a situation? Why quit our own to stand upon foreign ground? Why, by interweaving our destiny with that of any part of Europe, entangle our peace and prosperity in the toils of European Ambition, Rivalship, Interest, Humour or Caprice?

'Tis our true policy to steer clear of permanent Alliances, with any portion of the foreign world. So far, I mean, as we are now at liberty to do it, for let me not be understood as capable of patronising infidility to existing engagements (I hold the maxim no less applicable to public than to private affairs, that honesty is always the best policy). I repeat it therefore, let those engagements be observed in their genuine sense. But in my opinion, it is unnecessary and would be unwise to extend them.

Taking care always to keep ourselves, by suitable establishments, on a respectably defensive posture, we may safely trust to temporary alliances for extraordinary emergencies.

Harmony, liberal intercourse with all Nations, are recommended by policy, humanity and interest. But even our Commercial policy should hold an equal and impartial hand: neither seeking nor granting exclusive favours or preferences; consulting the natural course of things; diffusing and deversifying by gentle means the streams of Commerce, but forcing nothing; establishing with Powers so disposed; in order to give to trade a stable course, to define the rights of our Merchants, and to enable the Government to support them; conventional rules of intercourse, the best that present circumstances and mutual opinion will permit, but temporary, and liable to be from time to time abandoned or varied, as experience and circumstances shall dictate; constantly keeping in view, that 'tis folly in one Nation to look for disinterested favors from another; that it must pay with a portion of its Independence for whatever it may accept under that character; that by such acceptance, it may place itself in the condition of having given equivalents for nominal favours and yet of being reproached with ingratitude for not giving more. There can be no greater error than to expect, or calculate upon real favours from Nation to Nation. 'Tis an illusion which experience must cure, which a just pride ought to discard.

In offering to you, my Countrymen these counsels of an old and affectionate friend, I dare not hope they will make the strong and lasting impression, I could wish; that they will controul the usual current of the passions, or prevent our Nation from running the course which has hitherto marked the Destiny of Nations: But if I may even flatter myself, that they may be productive of some partial benefit, some occasional good; that they may now and then recur to moderate the fury of party spirit, to warn against the mischiefs of foreign Intriegue, to guard against the Impostures of pretended patriotism; this hope will be a full recompence for the solicitude for your welfare, by which they have been dictated.

How far in the discharge of my Official duties, I have been guided by the principles which have been delineated, the public Records and other evidences of my conduct must Witness to You and to the world. To myself, the assurance of my own conscience is, that I have at least believed myself to be guided by them.

In relation to the still subsisting War in Europe, my Proclamation of the 22d. of April 1793 is the index to my Plan. Sanctioned by your approving voice and by that of Your Representatives in both Houses of Congress, the spirit of that measure has continually governed me; uninfluenced by any attempts to deter or divert me from it.

After deliberate examination with the aid of the best lights I could obtain I was well satisfied that our Country, under all the circumstances of the case, had a right to take, and was bound in duty and interest, to take a Neutral position. Having taken it, I determined, as far as should depend upon me, to maintain it, with moderation, perseverence and firmness.

The considerations, which respect the right to hold this conduct, it is not necessary on this occasion to detail. I will only observe, that according to my understanding of the matter, that right, so far from being denied by any of the Belligerent Powers has been virtually admitted by all.

The duty of holding a Neutral conduct may be inferred, without any thing more, from the obligation which justice and humanity impose on every Nation, in cases in which it is free to act, to maintain inviolate the relations of Peace and amity towards other Nations.

The inducements of interest for observing that conduct will best be referred to your own reflections and experience. With me, a predominant motive has been to endeavour to gain time to our country to settle and mature its yet recent institutions, and to progress without interruption, to that degree of strength and consistency, which is necessary to give it, humanly speaking, the command of its own fortunes.

Though in reviewing the incidents of my Administration, I am unconscious of intentional error, I am nevertheless too sensible of my defects not to think it probable that I may have committed many errors. Whatever they may be I fervently beseech the Almighty to avert or mitigate the evils to which they may tend. I shall also carry with me the hope that my Country will never cease to view them with indulgence; and that after forty five years of my life dedicated to its Service, with an upright zeal, the faults of incompetent abilities will be consigned to oblivion, as myself must soon be to the Mansions of rest.

Relying on its kindness in this as in other things, and actuated by that fervent love towards it, which is so natural to a Man, who views in it the native soil of himself and his progenitors for several Generations; I anticipate with pleasing expectation that retreat, in which I promise myself to realize, without alloy, the sweet enjoyment of partaking, in the midst of my fellow Citizens, the benign influence of good Laws under a free Government, the ever favourite object of my heart, and the happy reward, as I trust, of our mutual cares, labours and dangers.

Eighth Annual Message to Congress

December 7, 1796.

Fellow Citizens of the Senate and House of Representatives:
In recurring to the internal situation of our Country, since I
had last the pleasure to Address you, I find ample reason for
a renewed expression of that gratitude to the ruler of the Universe, which a continued series of prosperity has so often and
so justly called forth.

The Acts of the last Session, which required special arrangements, have been, as far as circumstances would admit, carried
into operation.

Measures calculated to insure a continuance of the friendship of the Indians, and to preserve peace along the extent of
our interior frontier, have been digested and adopted. In the
framing of these, care has been taken to guard on the one
hand, our advanced Settlements from the predatory incursions
of those unruly Individuals, who cannot be restrained by their
Tribes; and on the other hand, to protect the rights secured
to the Indians by Treaty; to draw them nearer to the civilized
state; and inspire them with correct conceptions of the Power,
as well as justice of the Government.

The meeting of the deputies from the Creek Nation at Colerain, in the State of Georgia, which had for a principal object
the purchase of a parcel of their land, by that State, broke up
without its being accomplished; the Nation having, previous
to their departure, instructed them against making any Sale;
the occasion however has been improved, to confirm by a new
Treaty with the Creeks, their pre-existing engagements with
the United States; and to obtain their consent, to the establishment of Trading Houses and Military Posts within their
boundary; by means of which, their friendship, and the
general peace, may be more effectually secured.

The period during the late Session, at which the appropriation was passed, for carrying into effect the Treaty of Amity,
Commerce, and Navigation, between the United States and
his Britannic Majesty, necessarily procrastinated the reception
of the Posts stipulated to be delivered, beyond the date assigned for that event. As soon however as the Governor

General of Canada could be addressed with propriety on the subject, arrangements were cordially and promptly concluded for their evacuation; and the United States took possession of the principal of them, comprehending Oswego, Niagara, Detroit, Michelimackina, and Fort Miami; where, such repairs, and additions have been ordered to be made, as appeared indispensible.

The Commissioners appointed on the part of the United States and of Great Britain, to determine which is the river St. Croix, mentioned in the Treaty of peace of 1783, agreed in the choice of Egbert Benson Esqr. of New York, for the third Commissioner. The whole met at St. Andrews, in Passamaquoddy Bay, in the beginning of October; and directed surveys to be made of the Rivers in dispute; but deeming it impracticable to have these Surveys completed before the next Year, they adjourned, to meet at Boston in August 1797, for the final decision of the question.

Other Commissioners appointed on the part of the United States, agreeably to the seventh Article of the Treaty with Great Britain, relative to captures and condemnations of Vessels and other property, met the Commissioners of his Britannic Majesty in London, in August last, when John Trumbull, Esqr. was chosen by lot, for the fifth Commissioner. In October following the Board were to proceed to business. As yet there has been no communication of Commissioners on the part of Great Britain, to unite with those who have been appointed on the part of the United States, for carrying into effect the sixth Article of the Treaty.

The Treaty with Spain, required, that the Commissioners for running the boundary line between the territory of the United States, and his Catholic Majesty's Provinces of East and West Florida, should meet at the Natchez, before the expiration of six Months after the exchange of the ratifications, which was effected at Aranjuez on the 25th. day of April; and the troops of his Catholic Majesty occupying any Posts within the limits of the United States, were within the same period to be withdrawn. The Commissioner of the United States therefore, commenced his journey for the Natchez in September; and troops were ordered to occupy the Posts from which the Spanish Garrisons should be withdrawn. Information has been recently received, of the appointment of a Commissioner on the part of his Catholic Majesty for running the boundary line, but none of any appointment, for the adjustment of the claims of our Citizens, whose Vessels were captured by the Armed Vessels of Spain.

In pursuance of the Act of Congress, passed in the last Session, for the protection and relief of American Seamen, Agents were appointed, one to reside in Great Britain, and the other in the West Indies. The effects of the Agency in the West Indies, are not yet fully ascertained; but those which have been communicated afford grounds to believe, the measure will be beneficial. The Agent destined to reside in Great Britain, declining to accept the appointment, the business has consequently devolved on the Minister of the United States in London; and will command his attention, until a new Agent shall be appointed.

After many delays and disappointments, arising out of the European War, the final arrangements for fulfilling the engagements made to the Dey and Regency of Algiers, will, in all present appearance, be crowned with success: but under great, tho' inevitable disadvantages, in the pecuniary transactions, occasioned by that War; which will render a further provision necessary. The actual liberation of all our Citizens who were prisoners in Algiers, while it gratifies every feeling heart, is itself an earnest of a satisfactory termination of the whole negotiation. Measures are in operation for effecting Treaties with the Regencies of Tunis and Tripoli.

To an active external Commerce, the protection of a Naval force is indispensable. This is manifest with regard to Wars in which a State itself is a party. But besides this, it is in our own experience, that the most sincere Neutrality is not a sufficient guard against the depredations of Nations at War. To secure respect to a Neutral Flag, requires a Naval force, organized, and ready to vindicate it, from insult or aggression. This may even prevent the necessity of going to War, by discouraging belligerent Powers from committing such violations of the rights of the Neutral party, as may first or last, leave no other option. From the best information I have been able to obtain, it would seem as if our trade to the mediterranean, without a protecting force, will always be insecure; and our Citizens exposed to the calamities from which numbers of them have but just been relieved.

These considerations invite the United States, to look to the means, and to set about the gradual creation of a Navy. The increasing progress of their Navigation, promises them, at no distant period, the requisite supply of Seamen; and their means, in other respects, favour the undertaking. It is an encouragement, likewise, that their particular situation, will give weight and influence to a moderate Naval force in their hands. Will it not then be adviseable, to begin without delay, to provide, and lay up the materials for the building and equipping of Ships of War; and to proceed in the Work by degrees, in proportion as our resources shall render it practicable without inconvenience; so that a future War of Europe, may not find our Commerce in the same unprotected state, in which it was found by the present.

Congress have repeatedly, and not without success, directed their attention to the encouragement of Manufactures. The object is of too much consequence, not to insure a continuance of their efforts, in every way which shall appear eligible. As a general rule, Manufactures on public account, are inexpedient. But where the state of things in a Country, leaves little hope that certain branches of Manufacture will, for a great length of time obtain; when these are of a nature essential to the furnishing and equipping of the public force in time of War, are not establishments for procuring them on public account, *to the extent of the ordinary demand for the public service*, recommended by strong considerations of National policy, as an exception to the general rule? Ought our Country to remain in such cases, dependant on foreign supply, precarious, because liable to be interrupted? If the necessary Articles should, in this mode cost more in time of peace, will not the security and independence thence arising, form an ample compensation? Establishments of this sort, commensurate only with the calls of the public service in time of peace, will, in time of War, easily be extended in proportion to the exigencies of the Government; and may even perhaps be made to yield a surplus for the supply of our Citizens at large; so as to mitigate the privations from the interruption of their trade. If adopted, the plan ought to exclude all those branches which are already, or likely soon to be, established in the Country; in order that there may be no danger of interference with pursuits of individual industry.

It will not be doubted, that with reference either to individual, or National Welfare, Agriculture is of primary importance. In proportion as Nations advance in population, and other circumstances of maturity, this truth becomes more apparent; and renders the cultivation of the Soil more and more, an object of public patronage. Institutions for promoting it, grow up, supported by the public purse: and to what object can it be dedicated with greater propriety? Among the means which have been employed to this end, none have been attended with greater success than the establishment of Boards, composed of proper characters, charged with collecting and diffusing information, and enabled by premiums, and small pecuniary aids, to encourage and assist a spirit of discovery and improvement. This species of establishment contributes doubly to the increase of improvement; by stimulating to enterprise and experiment, and by drawing to a common centre, the results everywhere of individual skill and observation; and spreading them thence over the whole Nation. Experience accordingly has shewn, that they are very cheap Instruments, of immense National benefits.

I have heretofore proposed to the consideration of Congress, the expediency of establishing a National University; and also a Military Academy. The desirableness of both these Institutions, has so constantly increased with every new view I have taken of the subject, that I cannot omit the opportunity of once for all, recalling your attention to them.

The Assembly to which I address myself, is too enlightened not to be fully sensible how much a flourishing state of the Arts and Sciences, contributes to National prosperity and reputation. True it is, that our Country, much to its honor, contains many Seminaries of learning highly respectable and useful; but the funds upon which they rest, are too narrow, to command the ablest Professors, in the different departments of liberal knowledge, for the Institution contemplated, though they would be excellent auxiliaries.

Amongst the motives to such an Institution, the assimilation of the principles, opinions and manners of our Country men, but the common education of a portion of our Youth from every quarter, well deserves attention. The more homogeneous our Citizens can be made in these particulars, the greater will be our prospect of permanent Union; and a primary object of such a National Institution should be, the education of our Youth in the science of *Government*. In a Republic, what species of knowledge can be equally important? and what duty, more pressing on its Legislature, than to patronize a plan for communicating it to those, who are to be the future guardians of the liberties of the Country?

The Institution of a Military Academy, is also recommended by cogent reasons. However pacific the general policy of a Nation may be, it ought never to be without an adequate stock of Military knowledge for emergencies. The first would impair the energy of its character, and both would hazard its safety, or expose it to greater evils when War could not be avoided. Besides that War, might often, not depend upon its own choice. In proportion, as the observance of pacific maxims, might exempt a Nation from the necessity of practising the rules of the Military Art, ought to be its care in preserving, and transmitting by proper establishments, the knowledge of that Art. Whatever argument may be drawn from particular examples, superficially viewed, a thorough examination of the subject will evince, that the Art of War, is at once comprehensive and complicated; that it demands much previous study; and that the possession of it, in its most improved and perfect state, is always of great moment to the security of a Nation. This, therefore, ought to be a serious care of every Government: and for this purpose, an Academy, where a regular course of Instruction is given, is an obvious expedient, which different Nations have successfully employed.

The compensations to the Officers of the United States, in various instances, and in none more than in respect to the most important stations, appear to call for Legislative revision. The consequences of a defective provision, are of serious import to the Government. If private wealth, is to supply the defect of public retribution, it will greatly contract the sphere within which, the selection of Characters for Office, is to be made, and will proportionally diminish the probability of a choice of Men, able, as well as upright: Besides that it would be repugnant to the vital principles of our Government, virtually to exclude from public trusts, talents and virtue, unless accompanied by wealth.

While in our external relations, some serious inconveniences and embarrassments have been overcome, and others lessened, it is with much pain and deep regret I mention, that circumstances of a very unwelcome nature, have lately occurred. Our trade has suffered, and is suffering, extensive injuries in the West Indies, from the Cruisers, and Agents of the French Republic; and communications have been received from its Minister here, which indicate the danger of a further disturbance of our Commerce, by its authority; and which are, in other respects, far from agreeable.

It has been my constant, sincere, and earnest wish, in conformity with that of our Nation, to maintain cordial harmony, and a perfectly friendly understanding with that Republic. This wish remains unabated; and I shall persevere in the endeavour to fulfil it, to the utmost extent of what shall be consistent with a just, and indispensable regard to the rights and honour of our Country; nor will I easily cease to cherish the expectation, that a spirit of justice, candour and friendship, on the part of the Republic, will eventually ensure success.

In pursuing this course however, I cannot forget what is due to the character of our Government and Nation; or to a full and entire confidence in the good sense, patriotism, self-respect, and fortitude of my Countrymen.

I reserve for a special Message a more particular communication on this interesting subject.

Gentlemen of the House of Representatives: I have directed an estimate of the Appropriations, necessary for the service of the ensuing year, to be submitted from the proper Department; with a view of the public receipts and expenditures, to the latest period to which an account can be prepared.

It is with satisfaction I am able to inform you, that the Revenues of the United States continue in a state of progressive improvement.

A reinforcement of the existing provisions for discharging our public Debt, was mentioned in my Address at the opening of the last Session. Some preliminary steps were taken towards it, the maturing of which will, no doubt, engage your zealous attention during the present. I will only add, that it will afford me, heart felt satisfaction, to concur in such further measures, as will ascertain to our Country the prospect of a speedy extinguishment of the Debt. Posterity may have cause to regret, if, from any motive, intervals of tranquillity are left unimproved for accelerating this valuable end.

Gentlemen of the Senate, and of the House of Representatives: My solicitude to see the Militia of the United States placed on an efficient establishment, has been so often, and so ardently expressed, that I shall but barely recall the subject to your view on the present occasion; at the same time that I shall submit to your enquiry, whether our Harbours are yet sufficiently secured.

The situation in which I now stand, for the last time, in the midst of the Representatives of the People of the United States, naturally recalls the period when the Administration of the present form of Government commenced; and I cannot omit the occasion, to congratulate you and my Country, on the success of the experiment; nor to repeat my fervent supplications to the Supreme Ruler of the Universe, and Sovereign Arbiter of Nations, that his Providential care may still be extended to the United States; that the virtue and happiness of the People, may be preserved; and that the Government, which they have instituted, for the protection of their liberties, may be perpetual.

To John Greenwood

Philadelphia, January 20, 1797.

Sir: I must again resort to you for assistance. The teeth herewith enclosed have, by degrees, worked loose and, at length, two or three of them have given way altogether. I send them to you to be repaired, if they are susceptible of it; if not, then for the purpose of substituting others. I would thank you for, returning them as soon as possible for although I now make use of another sett, they are both uneasy in the mouth and bulge my lips out in such a manner as to make them appear considerably swelled.

You will perceive at the first view, that one cause of these teeth giving way is for want of a proper socket for the root part of them to rest in, as well for the purpose of keeping them firm and in place at bottom, as to preserve them against the effect of the saliva, which softens the part that formerly was covered by the gums and afforded them nourishment. Whether this remedy can be applied to the present sett I know not; for nothing must be done to them which will, in the *least* degree force the lips out more than *now* do, as it does this too much already; but if both upper and lower teeth were to incline inwards more, it would shew the shape of the mouth better, and not be the worse in any other respect.

Send with the teeth, springs about a foot in length, but not cut; and about double that length of a tough gold wire, of the size you see with the teeth, for fastening the springs. Accompany the whole with your Account, and the amount shall be immediately sent by Post in a bank note. I am etc.

To Henry Knox

Philadelphia, March 2, 1797.

My dear Sir: Amongst the last Acts of my political life, and before I go hence into retirement, *profound*, will be the acknowledgment of your kind and affectionate letter from Boston, dated the 15th. of January.

From the friendship I have always borne you, and from the interest I have ever taken in whatever relates to your prosperity and happiness, I participated in the sorrows which I know you must have felt for your late heavy losses. But is not for man to scan the wisdom of Providence. The best he can do, is to submit to its decrees. Reason, religion and Philosophy, teaches us to do this, but 'tis time alone that can ameliorate the pangs of humanity, and soften its woes.

To the wearied traveller who sees a resting place, and is bending his body to lean thereon, I now compare myself; but to be suffered to do *this* in peace, is I perceive too much, to be endured by *some*. To misrepresent my motives; to reprobate my politics; and to weaken the confidence which has been reposed in my administration, are objects which cannot be relinquished by those who, will be satisfied with nothing short of a change in our political System. The consolation however, which results from conscious rectitude, and the approving voice of my Country, unequivocally expressed by its Representatives, deprives their sting of its poison, and places in the same point of view both the weakness, and malignity of their efforts.

Although the prospect of retirement is most grateful to my soul, and I have not a wish to mix again in the great world, or to partake in its politics, yet, I am not without my regrets at parting with (perhaps never more to meet) the few intimates whom I love, among these, be assured you are one.

The account given by Mr. Bingham and others, of your agreeable Situation and prospects at St. George's, gave me infinite pleasure; and no one wishes more sincerely than I do, that they may increase with your years. The remainder of my life (which in the course of nature cannot be long) will be occupied in rural amusements, and though I shall seclude myself as much as possible from the noisy and bustling crowd, none more than myself, would be regaled by the company of those I esteem, at Mount Vernon: more than 20 Miles from which, after I arrive there, it is not likely I ever shall be.

As early in next week as I can make arrangements for it, I shall commence my journey for Mount Vernon. To morrow, at dinner, I shall, as a servant of the public, take my leave of the President Elect, of the foreign characters, heads of Departments, &ca. And the day following, with pleasure, I shall witness the inauguration of my Successor to the Chair of government.

On the subject of Politics I shall say nothing; you will have an opportunity of seeing and conversing with many of the Legislators; from whom, so far as it relates to the proceedings of their own body, they can give you the details. The Gazettes will furnish the rest.

Mrs. Washington unites with me in every good wish for you, Mrs. Knox and family, and with unfeigned truth, I am yours always, and affectionately.

To Jonathan Trumbull, Jr.

Philadelphia, March 3, 1797.

My dear Sir: Before the curtain drops on my political life, which it will do this evening, I expect for ever; I shall acknowledge, although it be in a few hasty lines only, the receipt of your kind and affectionate letter of the 23d. of January last.

When I add, that according to custom, all the Acts of the Session; except two or three very unimportant Bills, have been presented to me within the last four days, *you* will not be surprised at the pressure under which I write at present; but it must astonish *others* who know that the Constitution allows the President ten days to deliberate on *each Bill* that is brought before him that he should be allowed by the Legislature less than half that time to consider *all* the business of the Session; and in some instances, scarcely an hour to revolve the most important. But as the scene is closing, with me, it is of little avail *now* to let it be with murmers.

I should be very unhappy if I thought my relinquishing the Reins of government wd. produce any of the consequences which your fears forebode. In all free governments, contention in elections will take place; and, whilst it is confined to our own citizens it is not to be regretted; but severely indeed ought it to be reprobated when occasioned by foreign machinations. I trust however, that the good sense of our Countrymen will guard the public weal against this, and every other innovation; and that, altho we may be a little wrong, now and then, we shall return to the right path, with more avidity. I can never believe that Providence, which has guided us so long, and through such a labirinth, will withdraw its protection at this Crisis.

Although I shall resign the chair of government without a single regret, or any desire to intermeddle in politics again, yet there are many of my compatriots (among whom be assured I place you) from whom I shall part sorrowing; because, unless I meet with them at Mount Vernon it is not likely that I shall ever see them more, as I do not expect that I shall ever be twenty miles from it after I am tranquilly settled there. To tell you how glad I should be to see you at that place is unnecessary; but this I will add, that it would not only give me pleasure, but pleasure also to Mrs. Washington, and others of the family with whom you are acquainted; and who all unite in every good wish for you, and yours, with Dear Sir, Your sincere friend and Affectionate Servant.

RETIREMENT
1797–1799

To James McHenry

(Private)

Mount Vernon, April 3, 1797.

Dear Sir: Your letter of the 24th. Ulto. has been duly received, and I thank you for the information given in it: Let me pray you to have the goodness to communicate to me, occasionally, such matters as are interesting, and not contrary to the rules of your official duty to disclose. We get so many details in the Gazettes, and of such different complexions that it is impossible to know what credence to give to any of them.

The conduct of the French government is so much beyond calculation, and so unaccountable upon any principle of justice or even of that sort of policy wch. is familiar to plain understanding that I shall not *now* puzzle my brains in attempting to develop their motives to it.

We got home without accident, and found the Roads drier, and better than I ever travelled them at that Season of the year. The attentions we met with on our journey were very flattering, and to some whose minds are differently formed from mine would have been highly relished, but I avoided in every instance where I had any previous knowledge of the intention, and cd. by earnest entreaties prevail, all parade, or escorts. Mrs. Washington took a violent cold in Philadelphia, which hangs upon her still but not as bad as it did.

I find myself in the situation, nearly, of a young beginner; for although I have not houses to build (except one, which I must erect for the accommodation and security of my Military, Civil and private Papers which are voluminous, and may be interestg) yet I have not one or scarcely anything else about me that does not require considerable repairs. In a word I am already surrounded by Joiners, Masons, Painters &ca &ca. and such is my anxiety to get out of their hands, that I have scarcely a room to put a friend into or to set in myself, without the Music of hammers, or the odoriferous smell of Paint.

I will make no apology for putting the enclosed under cover to you. If General Lee should have left Philadelphia, let me request the favor of you to open the letter to him and cause the one under *that* cover to be delivered to Messrs. Reed & Ford by a person who you can inform me *certainly has done so*, that I may know to what cause to ascribe (should it happen) any delay in their answer, and add, if you please, whether there be any cause to suspect a failure in these Gentlemen.

You will readily perceive that what is said of them, and what I write to Genl. Lee is of a private nature, and not to be mentioned unless the reports respecting Reed & Ford are facts of notariety. Mrs. Washington and Miss Custis thanks you for your kind remembrance of them and joins in best regards for Mrs. McHenry and yourself with Dear Sir etc.

To William Heath

Mount Vernon, May 20, 1797.

Dear Sir: Your kind and friendly letter of the 17th. Ulto. has been duly received and I beg you to accept my sincere thanks for the affectionate sentiments you have been pleas'd to express for me, therein.

I can assure you, Sir, I never ascribed a motive to the letter you wrote me, on my Election to the Chair of Government, so unworthy of you as to suppose it was written with a view of "Pressing yourself into notice, or seeking for a Place." On the contrary, I was led to believe that domestic enjoyments in rural pursuits, had more charms for you, and were more congenial to your inclination, than any appointment that would draw you from home.

I hope, as you do, that, notwithstanding our Political horison is much overcast, the wisdom, temper and firmness of the Government (supported by the great mass of the People) will dispel the threatning clouds, and that all will end without any shedding of Blood. To me, this is so demonstrable that not a particle of doubt would dwell on my mind relative thereto if our Citizens would advocate their own cause instead of that of any other Nation under the Sun; that is instead of being Frenchmen, or Englishmen, in Politics, they would be Americans; indignant at every attempt of either, or any other power to establish an influence in our Councils, or that should pre-

sume to sow the seeds of distrust or disunion among ourselves. No policy, in my opinion, can be more clearly demonstrated, than that we should do justice to *all* but have no
political connexions with *any* of the European Powers, beyond those which result from and serve to regulate our Commerce with them. Our own experience (if it has not already
had this effect) will soon convince us that *disinterested* favours,
or friendship from any Nation whatever, is too novel to be
calculated on; and there will always be found a wide difference
between the words and actions of any of them.

It gives me great pleasure to hear from yourself, that you
are writing *Memoirs* of those transactions which passed under
your notice during the Revolution war. Having always understood, that you were exact and copious in noting occurrances
at the time they happened, a work of this kind will, from the
candour and ability with which I am persuaded they were
taken, be uncommonly correct and interesting. Whether you
mean to publish them at your own expence, or by Subscription, is not intimated in yr. letter. If the latter, I pray you to
consider me as a subscriber. and in any event as a purchaser
of your production. That you may enjoy health to complete
the work to your entire satisfaction, I devoutly pray, and that
you may live afterwards to hear it applauded (as I doubt not
it will be) I as sincerely wish. If I should live to see it published, I shall read it with great avidity. Retired from noise
myself, and the responsibility attached to public employment
my hours will glide smoothly on. My best wishes however for
the prosperity of our country will always have the first place
in my affections, while to repair buildings (gone much to
ruin) and to cultivate my farms (which require close attention)
will occupy the few years (perhaps days) I may be a sojourner
here, as I am now in the Sixty sixth year of my peregrination
through life. Mrs. Washington is very thankful for your kind
remembrance of her, and joins cordially with me in a tender
of best regards for you. With assurances of great esteem etc.

To James McHenry

Mount Vernon, May 29, 1797.

Dear Sir: I am indebted to you for several unacknowledged letters; but ne'er mind that; go on as if you had them. You are at the source of information, and can find many things to relate; while I have nothing to say, that could either inform or amuse a Secretary of War in Philadelphia.

I might tell him that I begin my diurnal course with the Sun; that if my hirelings are not in their places at that time I send them messages expressive of my sorrow for their indisposition; then having put these wheels in motion, I examine the state of things further; and the more they are probed, the deeper I find the wounds are which my buildings have sustained by an absence and neglect of eight years; by the time I have accomplished these matters, breakfast (a little after seven Oclock, about the time I presume you are taking leave of Mrs. McHenry) is ready. This over, I mount my horse and ride round my farms, which employs me until it is time to dress for dinner; at which I rarely miss seeing strange faces; come, as they say, out of respect to me. Pray, would not the word curiosity answer as well? and how different this, from having a few social friends at a cheerful board? The usual time of sitting at Table; a walk, and Tea, brings me within the dawn of Candlelight; previous to which, if not prevented by company, I resolve, that, as soon as the glimmering taper, supplies the place of the great luminary, I will retire to my writing Table and acknowledge the letters I have received; but when the lights are brought, I feel tired, and disinclined to engage in this work, conceiving that the next night will do as well: the next comes and with it the same causes for postponement, and effect, and so on.

This will account for *your* letter remaining so long unacknowledged; and having given you the history of a day, it will serve for a year; and I am persuaded you will not require a second edition of it: but it may strike you, that in this detail no mention is made of any portion of time allotted for reading; the remark would be just, for I have not looked into a book since I came home, nor shall I be able to do it until I have discharged my Workmen; probably not before the nights grow longer; when possibly, I may be looking in doomsday book. On the score of the plated ware in your possession I will say something in a future letter. At present I shall only add, that I am always and affectionately yours.

To David Humphreys

Mount Vernon, June 26, 1797.

My dear Humphreys: Since I did myself the pleasure of writing to you by Captain O'Brian, I have been favoured with your letters of the first of Jany. and 18th. of Feby. The last in date was the first received; but neither came to hand until long after I had left the chair of Government, and was seated in the shade of my own Vine and Fig-tree.

The testimony of your politeness and friendship to Mrs. Washington and myself, which accompanied the latter, are accepted with the same cordiality and chearfulness with which I am sure they were presented. Presents however, to me, are of all things the most painful; but when I am so well satisfied of the motives which dictated yours, my scruples are removed; and I receive the Buckles (which are indeed very elegant) as a token of your regard and attachment; and will keep, and wear them occasionally for your sake.

As the Gazettes of this Country are transmitted from the Department of State to all our Diplomatic characters abroad, you will, of course, have perceived that the measure advised by you, relative to the disavowal of the forged letters (attempted to be imposed on the public, as written by me in 1776) had been previously adopted; without any of the accompaniments contained in your draught, wch was received long after the publication of it.

I am clearly in sentiment with you, that every man who is in the vigor of life, ought to serve his country, in whatsoever line it requires, and he is fit for; it was not my intention therefore to persuade you to withdraw your Services whilst inclination, and the calls of your country demanded your service. but the desire of a companion in my latter days, in whom I could confide, might have induced me to express myself too strongly on the occasion. The change however, which I presume has 'ere this taken place in your domestic concerns, would of itself, have annihilated every hope of having you as an inmate if the circumstance had been known at the time.

On this event, which I persuade myself will be fortunate and happy for you, I offer my congratulations, with all the sincerity and warmth you can desire; and if ever you should bring Mrs. Humphreys to the U. States, no roof will afford her and you a more welcome reception than this, while we are the Inhabitants of it.

To the Department of State, and the Gazettes which will be transmitted from thence, I shall refer you for the political State of our affairs; but in one word I might have added, that nothing short of a general Peace in Europe will produce tranquillity in this country, for reasons which are obvious to every well informed, observant man, among us. I have a confidence, however, in that Providence, which has shielded the U. States from the Evils which have threatened them hitherto: and as I believe the major part of the people of this country are well affected to the Constitution and government of it, I rest satisfied that if ever a crisis should arise to call forth the sense of the Community it will be strong in support of the honor and dignity of the Nation. Therefore, however much I regret the opposition which has for its object the embarrassment of the Administration, I shall view things in the "Calm light of mild Philosophy" and endeavour to finish my course in retirement and ease.

An absence from home of eight years, except short occasional visits to it (which allowed no time to investigate or look into the real state of my private concerns) has very much deranged them; and occasioned such depredations upon buildings, and all things around them, as to make the expence of repairs almost as great, and the employment of attending to Workmen almost as much, as if I had commenced an entire new establishment.

The Public buildings in the Federal City go on well: one wing of the Capitol (with which Congress might make a very good shift) and the Presidents house, will be covered in this autumn, or to speak more correctly perhaps, the latter is *now* receiving its cover, and the former will be ready for it by that epoch. An elegant bridge is thrown over the Potomack at the little Falls, and the navigation of the River above will be completed, nearly, this season; through which an immensity of Produce must flow to the Shipping Ports thereon.

Alexandria you would scarcely know; so much has it increased since you was there; two entire Streets where Shallops then laded and unladed are extended into the River, and some of the best buildings in the Town erected on them. What were the Commons, are now all inclosed, and many good houses placed on them.

As my circle is *now small*, my information will be, of course, contracted; as Alexandria and the federal City will, probably, be the extent of my perambulations. If you have entered the Matrimonial list, I pray you to present me in respectful terms to your lady, and at all times, and under all circumstances, that you would believe me to be, as I really am, etc.

To the Earl of Buchan

Mount Vernon, July 4, 1797.

My Lord: Under cover from Mr. Cambbell of New York, about the time of my bidding adieu to the Walks of public life, I had the honour to receive your Lordships letter of the 1st of July 1796 from Kirkhill.

Congress being then near the close of an important Session, many matters of a public, and some of private concern (preparatory to the change which was on the eve of taking place) engrossed so much of my time and attention as to induce me to suspend the acknowledgment of all letters not of a public nature, or requiring immediate answers, under an idea that when I should be fixed in my retreat abundant leizure would be afforded to discharge all my epistolary obligations. In this however I have found myself mistaken, for at no period have I been more closely employed, than within the three months I have been at home, in repairing the ravages which an eight years absence (except occasional short visits which were inadequate to investigation) have produced on my Farms, buildings, and everything around them.

I have taken the liberty of troubling your Lordship with these details to avoid the imputation of being inattentive to your favours; which I should be unwilling to incur, and ungrateful if I deserved to be so charged.

At the age of 65 I am recommencing my Agricultural pursuits and rural amusements; which at all times have been the most pleasing occupation of my life, and most congenial with my temper, notwithstanding a small proportion of it has been spent in this way.

I was not sanguine in my hope of obtaining tenants from Great Britain, for my Farms of the estate on which I reside, although the experiment was made. It appeared to me more probable that Capitalists, and such as would answer my purpose would rather become Proprietors than tenants; although the latter, in reality, might prove the best medium to attain the former; experience having shewn, in many instances, that *some* by making precipitate purchases, have made injudicious establishments; while *others*, by holding off too long, have expended their means, when small, before they had decided on the part of the Country, or on the plan to be adopted.

It was my constant endeavour whilst I had the honour to Administer the Government of these United States, to preserve them in Peace and friendship with all the World. Humanity, interest and policy all combined to dictate the measure; and I have reasons to believe that the Gentleman who has succeeded to the Chair of State will pursue a similar policy; and if to stop the further effusion of human blood; the expenditure of National wealth; and the cries, and distresses of fatherless children and widows made so by the most destructive Sword that has ever been drawn in modern times, are sufficient inducements for returning it to the Scabbard, a general Peace must surely be at hand. Be these things however as they may, as my glass is nearly run, I shall endeavour in the shade of my Vine and Fig tree to view things in the "Calm light of mild Philosophy." With Mrs. Washington's compliments to Lady Buchan to which I beg leave respectfully to add mine, I am etc.

To Samuel Washington

Mount Vernon, July 12, 1797.

Dear Sir: I perceive by your letter of the 7th Instant that you are under the same mistake that many others are, in supposing that I have money always at Command.

The case is so much the reverse of it, that I found it expedient before I retired from public life to sell all my Lands (near 5000 Acres) in Pennsylvania in the Counties of Washington and Fayette, and my lands in the Great Dismal Swamp in Virginia, in order to enable me to defray the expences of my station, and to raise money for other purposes.

That these lands might not go at too low a rate (for they sold much below their value) I was induced after receiving prompt payment for part, to allow credit for the remainder, of the purchase money, in obtaining payment of which from two of the purchasers, I find much difficulty; but a third having within these few days paid me an installment of three thousand Dollars, I will rather than you should be compelled to sell your land, lend you a third of them, altho' it will be inconvenient for me to do so; and may be the means of retarding my purchase of wheat for my mill: which for want of it, has been very unproductive to me for several years; I might indeed say an expence to me.

It is because you have assured me that misfortunes have brought on your present difficulties (tho' by the by let me observe if you had inspected as you ought, the staking of your wheat more closely, the spoiling thereof might have been avoided) and because I have heard that you are industrious and sober that I put myself to the inconvenience, of parting with the above sum; for I wou'd not lend it for the purpose to enable you to indulge in any thing that is not strictly œconomical and proper; and I shall add further, that it will be my expectation that the money be immediately applied to the uses for which you have required it, for you may be assured that there is no practice more dangerous than that of borrowing money (instance as proof the case of your father and uncles) for when money can be had in this way, repayment is seldom thought of in time; the interest becomes a moth; exertions to raise it by dint of Industry ceases, it comes easy and is spent freely: and many things indulged in that would never be thought of, if to be purchased by the sweat of the brow. in the mean time the debt is accumulating like a Snow ball in rolling.

I mention these things to you, because your inexperience may not have presented them to your mind; but you may rely on it, that they are indubitable facts, and have proved the ruin of thousands, before suspected. Great speculations and sometimes trade may be benefitted of obtaining money on Interest, but no landed Estate will bear it.

I do not make these observations on account of the money I have purposed to lend you, because all that I shall require is, that you will return the nett Sum when in your power, without Interest. It may and at any rate as it was

To Lawrence Lewis

Mount Vernon, August 4, 1797.

Dear Sir: Your letter of the 24th ulto has been received, and I am sorry to hear of the loss of your servant; but it is my opinion these elopements will be MUCH MORE, before they are LESS frequent: and that the persons making them should never be retained, if they are recovered, as they are sure to contaminate and discontent others. I wish from my soul that the Legislature of this State could see the policy of a gradual Abolition of Slavery; It would prevt. much future mischief.

Whenever it is convenient to you to make this place your home I shall be glad to see you at it for that purpose and that there may be no misunderstanding in the matter, I shall inform you beforehand, that you, servant (if you bring one) and horses, will fare in all respects as we and mine do, but that I shall expect no Services from you for which pecuniary compensation will be made. I have already as many on wages as are sufficient to carry on my business, and more indeed than I can find means to pay, conveniently. As both your aunt and I are in the decline of life, and regular in our habits, especially in our hours of rising and going to bed, I require some person (fit and Proper) to ease me of the trouble of entertaining company; particularly of nights, as it is my inclination to retire (and unless prevented by very particular company, always do retire) either to bed, or to my study, soon after candle-light. In taking these duties (which hospitality obliges one to bestow on company) off my hands, it would render me a very acceptable service, and for a little time only, to come, an hour in the day, now and then, devoted to the recording of some Papers which time would not allow me to complete before I left Philadelphia, would also be acceptable. Besides there is nothing at present, that would require any portion of your time, or attention; both of which, if you have inclination for it, might be devoted to Reading, as I have a great many instructive Books, on many subjects, as well as amusing ones, &c. &c &c

Your Aunt unites with me in best regards for you, and I am your sincere friend and Affectionate Uncle.

To Sarah Cary Fairfax

Mount Vernon, May 16, 1798.
My dear Madam: Five and twenty years, nearly, have passed away since I have considered myself as the permanent resident at this place; or have been in a situation to endulge myself in a familiar intercourse with my friends, by letter or otherwise.

During this period, so many important events have occurred, and such changes in men and things have taken place, as the compass of a letter would give you but an inadequate idea of. None of which events, however, nor all of them together, have been able to eradicate from my mind, the recollection of those happy moments, the happiest in my life, which I have enjoyed in your company.

Worn out in a manner by the toils of my past labour, I am again seated under my Vine and Fig tree, and wish I could add that, there are none to make us affraid; but those whom we have been accustomed to call our good friends and Allies, are endeavouring, if not to make us affraid, yet to despoil us of our property; and are provoking us to Acts of self-defence, which may lead to War. What will be the result of such measures, time, that faithful expositor of all things, must disclose. My wish is, to spend the remainder of my days (which cannot be many) in rural amusements; free from those cares which public responsibility is never exempt.

Before the War, and even while it existed, altho' I was eight years from home at one stretch, (except the *en passant visits* made to it on my March to and from the Siege of Yorktown) I made considerable additions to my dwelling house, and alterations in my Offices, and Gardens; but the dilapidation occasioned by time, and those neglects which are co-extensive with the absence of Proprietors, have occupied as much of my time, within the last twelve months in repairing them, as at any former period in the same space. and it is matter of sore regret, when I cast my eyes towards Belvoir, which I often do, to reflect that the former Inhabitants of it, with whom we lived in such harmony and friendship, no longer reside there; and that the ruins can only be viewed as the memento of former pleasures; and permit me to add, that I have wondered often, (your nearest relations being in this Country), that you should not prefer spending the evening of your life among them rather than close the sublunary Scene in a foreign Country, numerous as your acquaintances may be, and sincere, as the friendships you may have formed.

A Century hence, if this Country keeps united (and it is surely its policy and Interest to do so) will produce a City, though not as large as London, yet of a magnitude inferior to few others in Europe, on the Banks of the Potomack; where one is now establishing for the permanent Seat of the Government of the United States (between Alexandria and Georgetown, on the Maryland side of the River). A situation not excelled for commanding prospect, good water, salubrious air, and safe harbour by any in the world; and where elegant buildings are erecting and in forwardness, for the reception of Congress in the year 1800.

Alexandria, within the last seven years, (since the establishment of the General Government) has increased in buildings, in population, in the improvement of its Streets by well executed pavements, and in the extension of its Wharves, in a manner, of which you can have very little idea. This shew of prosperity, you will readily conceive, is owing to its commerce, the extension of *that trade* is occasioned in a great degree by opening of the Inland navigation of the Potomack River; now cleared to Fort Cumberland, upwards of 200 miles, and by a similar attempt to accomplish the like up the Shenandoah, 150 miles more. In a word, if this Country can steer clear of European politics, stand firm on its bottom, and be wise and temperate in its government, it bids fair to be one of the greatest and happiest nations in the world.

Knowing that Mrs. Washington is about to give you an account of the changes wch have happened in the neighbourhood, and in our own family I shall not trouble you with a repetition of them; [   ] receive accurate information [   ] from *particular* friends, from [   ] and having only one [   ] miles [   ] I have not been as far as Occoquan these seven years; [   ] from hoping it. Be that as it may, [   ] and under all circumstances, I shall [   ] be [   ]

To John Adams

Mount Vernon, July 13, 1798.
Dear Sir: I had the honour on the evening of the 11th. instant to receive from the hands of the Secretary of War, your favour of the 7th. announcing, that you had, with the advice and consent of the Senate appointed me "Lieutenant General and Commander in Chief of all the Armies raised, or to be raised for the Service of the U. S."

I cannot express how greatly affected I am at this New proof of public confidence, and the highly flattering manner in which you have been pleased to make the communication; at the sametime I must not conceal from you my earnest wish, that the choice had fallen on a man less declined in years, and better qualified to encounter the usual vicissitudes of War.

You know, Sir, what calculations I had made relative to the probable course of events, on my retiring from Office, and the determination I had consoled myself with, of closing the remnant of my days in my present peaceful abode; you will therefore be at no loss to conceive and appreciate, the Sensations I must have experienced, to bring my mind to any conclusion, that would pledge me, at so late a period of life, to leave Scenes I sincerely love, to enter upon the boundless field of public action, incessant trouble, and high responsibility.

It was not possible for me to remain ignorant of, or indifferent to, recent transactions. The conduct of the Directory of France towards our Country; their insidious hostility to its Government; their various practices to withdraw the affections of the People from it; the evident tendency of their Arts and those of their Agents to countenance and invigorate opposition; their disregard of solemn treaties and the laws of Nations; their war upon our defenceless Commerce; their treatment of our Minister of Peace, and their demands amounting to tribute, could not fail to excite in me corresponding sentiments with those my countrymen have so generally expressed in their affectionate Addresses to you. Believe me, Sir, no one can more cordially approve of the wise and prudent measures of your Administration. They ought to inspire universal confidence, and will no doubt, combined with the state of things, call from Congress such laws and means as will enable you to meet the full force and extent of the Crisis.

Satisfied therefore, that you have sincerely wished and endeavoured to avert war, and exhausted to the last drop, the cup of reconciliation, we can with pure hearts appeal to Heaven for the justice of our cause, and may confidently trust the final result to that kind Providence who has heretofore, and so often, signally favoured the People of these United States.

Thinking in this manner, and feeling how incumbent it is upon every person, of every description, to contribute at all times to his Countrys welfare, and especially in a moment like the present, when every thing we hold dear and Sacred is so seriously threatned, I have finally determined to accept the Commission of Commander in Chief of the Armies of the United States, with the reserve only, that I shall not be called into the field until the Army is in a situation to require my presence, or it becomes indispensable by the urgency of circumstances.

In making this reservation, I beg it to be understood that I do not mean to withhold any assistance to arrange and organize the Army, which you may think I can afford. I take the liberty also to mention, that I must decline having my acceptance considered as drawing after it any immediate charge upon the Public, or that I can receive any emoluments annexed to the appointment, before entering into a Situation to incur expence.

The Secretary of War being anxious to return, to the seat of Government, I have detained him no longer than was necessary to a full communication upon the several points he had in charge. With very great respect and consideration I had the honor etc.

To John Adams

Mount Vernon, September 25, 1798.

Sir: With all the respect which is due to your public station, and with the regard I entertain for your private character, the following representation is presented to your consideration. If in the course of it, any expression should escape me which may appear to be incompatible with either, let the purity of my intentions; the candour of my declarations; and a due respect for my own character, be received as an apology.

The subject on which I am about to Address you, is not less delicate in its nature, than it is interesting to my feelings. It is the change which you have directed to be made in the relative rank of the Major Generals, which I had the honor of presenting to you, by the Secretary of War; the appointment of an Adjutant General *after* the first nomination was rejected; and the *prepared* state you are in to appoint a third, if the second should decline, without the least intimation of the matter to me.

It would have been unavailing, *after* the nomination and appointment of me to the Chief command of the Armies of the United States (without any previous consultation of my sentiments) to have observed to you the delicate situation in which I was placed by that act. It was still less expedient, to have dwelt more than I did, on my sorrow at being drawn from my retirement; where I had fondly hoped to have spent the few remaining years which might be dispensed to me, if not in profound tranquillity, at least without public responsibility. But if you had been pleased, previously to the nomination, to have enquired into the train of my thoughts upon the occasion, I would have told you with the frankness and candour which I hope will ever mark my character, on what terms I would have consented to the nomination; you would then have been enabled to decide, whether they were admissible or not.

This opportunity was not afforded, *before* I was brought to public view. To declare them *afterwards*, was all I could do, and this I did, in explicit language to the Secretary of War, when he honoured me with your letter of the 7th. of July; showed me his powers; and presented the Commission. They were, that the General Officers, and General Staff of the Army should not be appointed without my concurrence. I extended my stipulations no farther, but offered to give every information, and render every service in my power, in selecting good Officers for the Regimts.

It would be tedious to go into all the details which led to this determination; but before I conclude my letter, I shall take the liberty of troubling you with some of them. Previously to the doing of which, however, let me declare, and I do declare in the most unequivocal manner, that I had nothing more in view in making this stipulation than to insure the most eligible characters for these highly responsible Offices; conceiving that my opportunities both in the Civil and Military administration of the affairs of this Country, had enabled me to form as correct an opinion of them as any other could do.

Neither the Secretary of War nor myself, entertained any doubt from your letters to me, and Instructions to him, that this was the meaning and object of his Mission. Unwilling however, to let a matter of such serious importance to myself remain upon uncertain ground, I requested *that* Gentleman to declare this in *his official letter to you* (supposing, as was the case) that the one I should have the honor of writing to you, might be laid before the Public, and that to incumber it with stipulations of that sort, would be improper. Nay more, as the acceptance was conditional, and you might, or might not be disposed to accede to the terms, I requested him to take the Commission back, to be annulled, or restored, according to your conception of the propriety, or impropriety of them. His remark upon this occasion was, that it was unnecessary, inasmuch as, if you did not incline to accept my services upon the condition they were offered, you would be under the necessity of declaring it, whilst on the other hand silence must be construed into acquiescence. This consideration, and believing that the latter mode would be most respectful, as the other might imply distrust of your intentions arrested that measure.

This, Sir, is a true, candid and impartial statement of facts. It was the ground on which I *accepted* and *retained* the Commission; and was the authority on which I proceeded to the arrangement that was presented to you by the Secretary of War.

Having *no idea* that the General Officers for the Provisional army would be nominated at the time they were, I had not even contemplated characters for those appointments.

I will now respectfully ask, in what manner these stipulations on my part have been complied with?

In the arrangement made by me, with the Secretary of War, the three Major Generals stood, Hamilton, Pinckney, Knox; and in this order I expected their Commissions would have been dated. This, I conceive, must have been the understanding of the Senate. And certainly was the expectation of all those with whom I have conversed. But you have been pleased to order the last to be first, and the first to be last. Of four Brigadiers for the Provisional army, one whom I never heard of as a Military character, has been nominated and appointed; and another is so well known to all those who served with him, in the Revolution, as (for the appointment) to have given the greatest disgust, and will be the means of preventing many valuable officers of that army from coming forward. One Adjutant General has been, and another is ready to be appointed in case of the nonacceptance of Mr. North, not only without any consultation with me, but without the least intimation of the intention; although in the letter I had the honor to write you on the 4th of July in acknowledgment of your favour of the 22d of June preceding, and still more strongly in one of the same date to the Secretary of War which (while here) his Clerk was, I know, directed to lay before you I endeavored to show you in a strong point of view, how important it was that this officer (besides his other qualifications) should be agreeable to the Commander in Chief, and possess his *entire* confidence.

To encrease the Powers of the Commander in Chief, or to lessen those of the President of the United States, I pray you to be persuaded was most foreign from my heart. To secure able Coadjutors in the arduous task I was about to enter upon, was my *sole* aim. This the public good demanded, and this must have been equally the wish of us both. But to accomplish it, required an intimate knowledge of the *Componant* parts of the characters among us, in the higher grades of the late army. and I hope (without incurring the charge of presumption) I may add that the opportunities I have had to judge of these, are second to none. It was too interesting to me, who had staked every thing which was dear and valuable upon the issue, to trust more to chance than could be avoided. It could not be supposed that I was insensible to the risk I was about to run, knowing that the chances of losing, was at least equal to those of encreasing that reputation which the partiality of the world had been pleased to bestow on me. No one then acquainted with these circumstances; the sacrifices I was about to make; and the impartiality of my conduct in the various walks of life, could suppose that I had any other object in view than to obtain the best aids the country afforded, and my judgment could dictate.

If an Army had been in actual existence, and you had been pleased to offer the command of it to me, my course would have been plain: I should have examined the Constitution of it; looked into the organization, and enquired into the character of its Officers &ca. As the army was to be raised, and the Officers to be appointed, could it be expected (as I was no Candidate for the Office) that I would be less cautious, or less attentive to secure these advantages?

It was not difficult for me to perceive that if we entered into a serious contest with France, that the character of the

War would differ materially from the last we were engaged in. In the latter, time, caution, and worrying the enemy until we could be better provided with arms, and other means, and had better disciplined Troops to carry it on, was the plan for us. But if we should be engaged with the former, they ought to be attacked at every step, and, if possible, not suffered to make an establishment in the Country, acquiring thereby strength from the disaffected and the Slaves, whom I have no doubt they will arm, and for that purpose will commence their operations South of the Potomack.

Taking all these circumstances into view, you will not be surprised at my sollicitude to intrench myself as I did; nor is it to be supposed that I made the arrangement of the three Major Generals without an eye to possible consequences. I wished for time, it is true, to have effected it, hoping that an amicable adjustment might have taken place; and offered, at a very short summons, (inconvenient as it would have been) to proceed to Philadelphia for that purpose; but as no subsequent notice was taken thereof, I presumed there were operative reasons against the measure, and did not repeat it.

It is proper too I should add, that, from the information which I received from various quarters, and through different channels, I had no doubt in my mind that the current sentiment among the members of Congress, and particularly among those from New England, was in favor of Colonel Hamilton's being second in command, and this impression has been since confirmed in the most unequivocal manner by some respectable members of that body, whom I have myself seen and conversed with on the subject.

But if no regard was intended to be had to the *order* of my arrangement, why was it not altered before it was submitted to the Senate? This would have placed matters upon simple ground. It would then have been understood as it is at present, namely, that the Gentlemen would rank in the order they were named; but the change will contravene this, and excite much conversation, and unpleasant consequences.

I cannot lay my hand readily upon the resolves of the old Congress, relative to the settlement of Rank between Officers of the same grade, who had been in service and were disbanded, while a part of the Army remained in existence; but if I have a tolerable recollection of the matter they are totally irrelevant to the present case. Those resolves passed, if I am not mistaken, at a time when the proportion of Officers to men was so unequal as to require a reduction of the former: and when the Army was about to undergo a reduction in part, and the officers might be called upon again. But will a case of this sort apply to Officers of an Army which has ceased to exist for more than fourteen years? I give it frankly as my opinion (if I have not entirely forgotten the principle on which the Resolves took place) that they will not: and I as frankly declare, that the only motive I had for examining a list of the Officers of that Army was to be reminded of names.

If the rule contended for was to obtain, what would be the consequences, and where would the evil end? In all probability resort would be had to the field officers of the Revolutionary Army to fill similar grades in the augmented and Provisional Corps which are to be raised. What then is to be done with General Dayton, who never ranked higher than Captain in it? The principle will apply with equal force in that case as in the case of Hamilton and Knox. The injury (if it is one) of putting a junr. over the head of a Senr. Officer of the last war, is not ameliorated by the nominations or appointments of them on different days. It is the act itself, not the manner of doing it, that affects.

I have dwelt longer on this point than perhaps was necessary, in order to show, that in my opinion, former rank in the Revolutionary Army ought to have no influence in the present case, farther than may be derived from superior experience, brilliant exploits, or general celebrity of character. And that, as the Armies about to be raised are commencing de novo, the President has the right to make Officers of Citizens or Soldiers at his pleasure; and to arrange them in any manner he shall deem most conducive to the public weal.

It is an invidious task, at all times, to draw comparisons; and I shall avoid it as much as possible; but I have no hesitation in declaring, that if the Public is to be deprived of the Services of Colo. Hamilton in the Military line, that the Post he was destined to fill will not be easily supplied; and that this is the sentiment of the Public, I think I can venture to pronounce. Although Colo. Hamilton has never acted in the character of a General Officer, yet his opportunities, as the principal and most confidential aid of the Commander in chief, afforded him the means of viewing every thing on a larger scale than those whose attentions were confined to Divisions or Brigades, who knew nothing of the correspondences of the Commander in Chief, or of the various orders to, or transactions with, the General Staff of the Army. These advantages, and his having served with usefulness in the Old Congress; in the General Convention; and having filled one of the most important departments of Government with acknowledged abilities and integrity, have placed him on high ground; and made him a conspicuous character in the United States, and even in Europe.

To these, as a matter of no small consideration may be added, that as a lucrative practice in the line of his Profession is his *most certain* dependence, the inducement to relinquish it, must, in some degree, be commensurate. By some he is considered as an ambitious man, and therefore a dangerous one. That he is ambitious I shall readily grant, but it is of that laudable kind which prompts a man to excel in whatever he takes in hand. He is enterprising, quick in his perceptions, and his judgment intuitively great: qualities essential to a Military character, and therefore I repeat, that his loss will be irrepairable.

With respect to General Knox, I can say with truth, there is no man in the United States with whom I have been in habits of greater intimacy; no one whom I have loved more sincerely, nor any for whom I have had a greater friendship. But, esteem, love, and friendship, can have no influence on my mind when I conceive that the subjugation of our Government and Independence, are the objects aimed at by the enemies of our Peace; and, when, possibly, our all is at stake.

In the first moments of leisure, after the Secretary of War had left this place, I wrote a friendly letter to Genl Knox, stating my firm belief that if the French should invade this Country with a view to the conquest or to the division of it, their operations would commence to the Southward, and endeavoured to show him, in that case, how all important it was to engage General Pinckney, his numerous family, friends and influential acquaintances heartily in the cause. Sending him at the sametime a copy of the arrangement, which I supposed *to be final*; and in a subsequent letter, I gave him my opinion fully with respect to the relative situation of himself and Colo. Hamilton, not expecting, I confess, the difficulties which have occurred.

I will say but little, relatively to the appointment of the Brigadiers before alluded to; but I must not conceal, that after what had passed, and my understanding of the compact, that my feelings were not a little wounded by the appointment of any, much more such characters, without my knowledge.

In giving these details, I have far exceeded the limits of a letter, but I hope to be excused for the prolixity of it. My object has been, to give you a clear and distinct view of my understanding of the terms, on which I received the Commission with which you were pleased to honor me.

Lengthy as this letter is, there is another subject, not less interesting to the Commander in Chief of the Armies (be him whom he may) than it is important to the United States, which I beg leave to bring respectfully to your view. We are now, near the end of September, and not a man recruited, nor a Battalion Officer appointed, that has come to my knowledge. The consequence is, that the spirit and enthusiasm which prevailed a month or two ago and would have produced the *best* men in a short time, is evaporating *fast*, and a month or two hence may induce but few, and those perhaps of the *worst* sort to Inlist. Instead therefore of having the augmented force in a state of preparation, and under a course of discipline, it is now to be *raised* and possibly may not be in existence when the Enemy is in the field; we shall have to meet veteran Troops inured to conquest with Militia or raw recruits; the consequence of which is not difficult to conceive or foretell.

I have addressed you, Sir, with openness and candour, and I hope with respect, requesting to be informed whether your determination to reverse the order of the three Major Generals is final, and whether you mean to appoint another Adjutant General without my concurrence. With the greatest respect and consideration I have the honor &c.

To Landon Carter

Mount Vernon, October 5, 1798.
Dear Sir: Your favour of the 1st. instt. has been received, and if it had been convenient, I should have been glad of your company as you travelled to Annapolis. As you propose however to send in your Servant, and I am generally on horse back between breakfast and dinner, that he may not be delayed, or disappointed, you will receive, enclosed, one letter for the Govr. of Maryland (an old acquaintance of mine), and another for Mr. McDowall President of the College. which, I hope may answer your purposes. They will be left, under this cover, for whomsoever you may send, in case I should be out.

I thank you for the trouble you have taken in delivering your thoughts on the means of preserving health. Having, through life, been blessed with a competent share of it, without using preventatives against sickness, and as little medicine as possible when sick; I can have no inducement now to change my practice. against the effect of time and age, no remedy has ever yet been discovered; and like the rest of my fellow mortals, I must (if life is prolonged) submit, and be reconciled, to a gradual decline. With esteem etc.

Please to put wafers on the letters before delivery.

To Alexander Spotswood

Philadelphia, November 22, 1798.
Dr. Sir: Your letter of the 13th. Inst. enclosing a publication under the signature of Gracchus, on the Alien and Sedition laws, found me at this place deeply engaged in business.

You ask my opinion of these Laws, professing to place Confidence in my judgment for the Compliment of wch. I thank you. But to give Opinions unsupported by reasons, might appear dogmatical, especially as you have declared that Gracchus has produced "the rough conviction in your mind of the unconstitutionality and inexpediency of the acts above mentioned." To go into an explanation on these points, I have neither leisure nor inclination, because it would occupy more time than I have to spare.

But I will take the liberty of advising such as are not "thoroughly convinced" and whose minds are yet open to conviction to read the pieces and hear the arguments which have been adduced in favor of as well as those against the Constitutionality and expediency of those laws before they decide. And Consider to what lengths a Certain description of men in our Country have already driven and even resolved to further drive matters and then ask themselves if it is not time and expedient to resort to protecting Laws against aliens (for Citizens you certainly know are not affected by that law) who acknowledge no allegiance to this Country, and in many instances are sent among us (as there is the best Circumstantial evidence to prove) for the express purpose of poisoning the minds of our people and to sow dissentions among them, in order to alienate their affections from the Government of their Choice, thereby endeavoring to dissolve the Union, and of Course the fair and happy prospects which were unfolding to our view from the Revolution. But as I have observed before I have no time to enter the field of Politicks, and therefore shall only add my best Respects to the good family at New Post, and the assurances of being, Dr. Sir etc.

To Patrick Henry

(Confidential)

Mount Vernon, January 15, 1799.

Dear Sir: At the threshold of this letter, I ought to make an apology for its contents; but if you will give me credit for my motives, I will contend for no more, however erroneous my sentiments may appear to you.

It would be a waste of time, to attempt to bring to the view of a person of your observation and discernment, the endeavors of a certain party among us, to disquiet the Public mind among us with unfounded alarms; to arraign every act of the Administration; to set the People at variance with their Government; and to embarrass all its measures. Equally useless would it be to predict what must be the inevitable consequences, of such policy, if it cannot be arrested.

Unfortunately, and extremely do I regret it, the State of Virginia has taken the lead in this opposition. I have said the *State*, Because the conduct of its Legislature in the Eyes of the world, will authorise the expression; because it is an incontrovertable fact, that the principle leaders of the opposition dwell in it; and because no doubt is entertained, I believe, that with the help of the Chiefs in other States, all the plans are arranged; and systematically pursued by their followers in other parts of the Union; though in no State except Kentucky (that I have heard of) has Legislative countenance been obtained, beyond Virginia.

It has been said, that the great mass of the Citizens of this State are well affected, notwithstanding, to the General Government, and the Union; and I am willing to believe it, nay do believe it: but how is this to be reconciled with their suffrages at the Elections of Representatives; both to Congress and their State Legislature; who are men opposed to the first, and by the tendency of their measures would destroy the latter? Some among us have endeavoured to account for this inconsistency, and though convinced themselves, of its truth, they are unable to convince others; who are unacquainted with the internal policy of the State.

One of the reasons assigned is, that the most respectable, and best qualified characters amongst us, will not come forward. Easy and happy in their circumstances at home, and believing themselves secure in their liberties and property, will not forsake them, or their occupations, and engage in the turmoil of public business, or expose themselves to the calumnies of their opponents, whose weapons are detraction.

But at such a crisis as this, when every thing dear and valuable to us is assailed; when this Party hangs upon the Wheels of Government as a dead weight, opposing every measure that is calculated for defence and self preservation; abetting the nefarious views of another Nation, upon our Rights; prefering, as long as they durst contend openly against the spirit and resentment of the People, the interest of France to the Welfare of their own Country; justifying the first at the expence of the latter: When every Act of their own Government is tortured by constructions they will not bear, into attempts to infringe and trample upon the Constitution with a view to introduce monarchy; When the most unceasing, and the purest exertion; were making, to maintain a Neutrality which had been proclaimed by the Executive, approved unequivocally by Congress, by the State Legislatures, nay, by the People themselves, in various meetings; and to preserve the Country in Peace, are charged as a measure calculated to favor Great Britain at the expence of France, and all those who had any agency in it, are accused of being under the influence of the former; and her Pensioners; When measures are systematically, and pertinaciously pursued, which must eventually dissolve the Union or produce coercion. I say, when these things are become so obvious, ought characters who are best able to rescue their Country from the pending evil to remain at home? rather, ought they not to come forward, and by their talents and influence, stand in the breach wch. such conduct has made on the Peace and happiness of this Country, and oppose the widening of it?

Vain will it be to look for Peace and happiness, or for the security of liberty or property, if Civil discord should ensue; and what else can result from the policy of those among us, who, by all the means in their power, are driving matters to extremity, if they cannot be counteracted effectually? The views of Men can only be known, or guessed at, by their words or actions. Can those of the *Leaders* of Opposition be mistaken then, if judged by this Rule? That they are *followed* by numbers who are unacquainted with their designs, and suspect as little, the tendency of their principles, I am fully persuaded. But, if their conduct is viewed with indifference; if there is activity and misrepresentation on one side, and supineness on the other, their numbers, accumulated by Intriguing, and discontented foreigners under proscription, who were at war with their own governments; and the greater part of them with *all* Government, their numbers will encrease, and nothing, short of Omniscience, can foretel the consequences.

I come now, my good Sir, to the object of my letter, which is, to express a hope, and an earnest wish, that you wd. come forward at the ensuing Elections (if not for Congress, which you may think would take you too long from home) as a candidate for representation, in the General Assembly of this Commonwealth.

There are, I have no doubt, very many sensible men who oppose themselves to the torrent that carries away others, who had rather swim with, than stem it, without an able Pilot to conduct them; but these are neither old in Legislation, nor well known in the Community. Your weight of character and influence in the Ho. of Representatives would be a bulwark against such dangerous sentiments as are delivered there at present. It would be a rallying point for the timid, and an attraction of the wavering. In a word, I conceive it of immense importance at this Crisis, that you should be there; and I would fain hope that all minor considerations will be made to yield to the measure.

If I have erroneously supposed that your sentiments on these subjects are in unison with mine; or if I have assumed a liberty which the occasion does not warrant, I must conclude as I began, with praying that my motives may be received as an apology; and that my fear, that the tranquillity of the Union, and of this State in particular, is hastening to an awful crisis, has extorted them from me.

With great, and very sincere regard, and respect, I am &c.

To James McHenry

(Private)

Mount Vernon, January 27, 1799.

My dear Sir: The enclosed letter for Mr. McAlpin (my Tayler in Philadelphia) left open for your perusal, may be delivered, or not, as you shall judge best. And if the former takes place, to be accompanied with your sentiments on the doubtful parts of it.

It is predicated first, on the supposition that the Uniform for the different grades of Officers, is conclusively fixed, and to be established as a standing regulation. and secondly, on

the presumption that no attempts will be made *this* Session of
Congress, to repeal the Law for augmenting the army of the
United States, or to reduce it below its present establishment.
If the first is liable to no change, and there is no indication
of an attempt to effect the latter, I would go to the expence
of providing a uniform previously to the spur of the occasion;
conformably to the regulations Ordered by the War Department, agreeably to the Presidents Command. On the other
hand, if either of the above things is likely to happen, I shall
suspend doing it.

On re-considering the Uniform for the Commander in
Chief, it has become a matter of doubt with me (although, as
it respected myself, *personally*, I was against *all* Embroidery),
whether embroidery on the Cape, Cuffs and Pockets of the
Coat, and none on the *Buff* waistcoat, would not have a disjointed, and aukward appearance. It is neither required, nor
forbidden. Which then, in your judgment, or that of Con-
noisseurs, if you should converse with any on the subject,
would be most eligable in itself, and accordent to what is
expected. To *you* I submit the matter. As I also do whether
the Coat shall have slash Cuffs (with blue flaps passing
through them) and slash pockets, or both to be in the usual
manner.

These, apparently, are trifling matters to trouble you with;
but, as it is the commencement of a New Scene, it is desirable
that the thing should take a right direction. I have therefore,
upon the whole, and since I began this letter, determined to
direct Mr. McAlpin to apply to, and follow your directions in
making the Uniform. I should not prefer a heavy embroidery,
or one containing much work. a light and neat one, would,
in my opinion be more elegant, and more desirable; as well
for the Coat, as for the Waistcoat, if the latter is to receive
any. If there are workers in this way in Philadelphia (and the
French are most likely to understand it) they will, no doubt,
have a variety of Patterns to chuse from. and I pray you to
examine them.

The Eagle too, having become part of the American Cock-
ade; has any of them been brought into use yet? My idea of
the size is, that it ought not to be larger than would cover a
quarter of a dollar at most and should be represented (for the

Officers) as clothed with their feathers. this any ingenious Silver Smith can execute; and if four were sent to me, I would thank you; and would remit the cost, as soon as known to me.

I must further beg, that proper Stars for the Epaulets (the latter I possess) may be sent to me with the other articles, that I may be equipped in dress *at least*; and if there are any tasty Cockades (but not whimsically foolish) in wearg., or any one, who can make them, I should be glad if they were sent with the Eagles fixed thereon, ready to be placed in the hats. Does the Presidt. and yourself wear them? Excuse this scrawl and trouble, as I wish to set out right; and be assured of the sincere esteem and regard of Dear Sir etc.

To James Welch

Mount Vernon, April 7, 1799.

Sir: I have received your letters of the 10th. of March from Rockingham County, and although I have no expectation of deriving any payment from your Kentucky Expedition, yet, I will (inconvenient as it is to me) wait a while longer to know the result of it: desiring you to be persuaded, in the meantime, that you have not got a person *now*, that will be trifled with in your dealings.

It would be uncandid, Mr. Welch, not to inform you, that I have heard too much of your character lately, not to expect tale after tale, and relation after relation, of your numerous disappointments, by way of excuses for the non-compliance of your agreement with me: but this I can assure you will not answer your purposes.

It is not difficult for a person who has no ground on which to expect a thousand cents, to talk with facility and ease of his expectation of receiving ten times as many dollars; the relation of disappointments in which, according to his account, he conceives is quite sufficient to ward off the payment of his own solemn Contracts, and to satisfy his Creditors.

I am not unacquainted, Sir, with your repeated declarations of your having purchased my Lands on the Great Kanawa, and endeavouring by that means, and such like impositions, and misrepresentations, to obtain extensive credit where you were not known. Letters, to enquire into the truth of these things, have been written to me on the Subject. Be cautious therefore how you provoke explanations that must, inevitably, end in your disgrace and entire loss of character. A character is valuable to all men, and not less so to a Speculator.

I will, before I conclude, assure you in the most unequivocal terms of two things.

First, that I am in extreme want of the money which you gave me a solemn promise I should receive the first of January last; and secondly, that however you may have succeeded in imposing upon, and deceiving others, you shall not practice the like game with me, with impunity.

To contract new Debts, is not the way to pay old ones. Nor is it a proof that you have any disposition to do it, when you are proposing to buy lands &ca. &ca. on credit (or partial advances) which can answer no other purpose that that of speculation; or (if you have them) of withholding the means which ought to be applied in the discharge of engagements, and debts, proceeding therefrom, which you are bound by every tie to do.

Consider this letter well; and then write without any deception to Sir, Your etc.

Last Will and Testament

In the name of God amen

I GEORGE WASHINGTON of Mount Vernon, a citizen of the United States, and lately President of the same, do make, ordain and declare this Instrument; which is written with my own hand and every page thereof subscribed with my name, to be my last Will and Testament, revoking all others.

Imprimus. All my debts, of which there are but few, and none of magnitude, are to be punctually and speedily paid; and the Legacies hereinafter bequeathed, are to be discharged as soon as circumstances will permit, and in the manner directed.

Item. To my dearly beloved wife Martha Washington I give and bequeath the use, profit and benefit of my whole Estate, real and personal, for the term of her natural life; except such parts thereof as are specifically disposed of hereafter: My improved lot in the Town of Alexandria, situated on Pitt and Cameron Streets, I give to her and her heirs forever, as I also do my household and Kitchen furniture of every sort and kind, with the liquors and groceries which may be on hand at the time of my decease; to be used and disposed of as she may think proper.

Item   Upon the decease of my wife, it is my Will and desire that all the Slaves which I hold in *my own right*, shall receive their freedom. To emancipate them during her life, would, tho' earnestly wished by me, be attended with such insuperable difficulties on account of their intermixture by Marriages with the Dower Negroes, as to excite the most painful sensations, if not disagreeable consequences from the latter, while both descriptions are in the occupancy of the same Proprietor; it not being in my power, under the tenure by which the Dower Negros are held, to manumit them. And whereas among those who will recieve freedom according to this devise, there may be some, who from old age or bodily infirmities, and others who on account of their infancy, that will be unable to support themselves; it is my Will and desire that all who come under the first and second description shall be comfortably cloathed and fed by my heirs while they live; and that such of the latter description as have no parents living, or if living are unable, or unwilling to provide for them, shall be bound by the Court until they shall arrive at the age of twenty five years; and in cases where no record can be produced, whereby their ages can be ascertained, the judgment of the Court upon its own view of the subject, shall be adequate and final. The Negros thus bound, are (by their Masters or Mistresses) to be taught to read and write; and to be brought up to some useful occupation, agreeably to the Laws of the Commonwealth of Virginia, providing for the support of Orphan and other poor Children. And I do hereby expressly forbid the Sale, or transportation out of the said Commonwealth, of any Slave I may die possessed of, under any pretence whatsoever. And I do moreover most pointedly, and most solemnly enjoin it upon my Executors hereafter named, or the Survivors of them, to see that *this* clause respecting Slaves, and every part thereof be religiously fulfilled at the Epoch at which it is directed to take place; without evasion, neglect or delay, after the Crops which may then be on the ground are harvested, particularly as it respects the aged and infirm; Seeing that a regular and permanent fund be established for their Support so long as there are subjects requiring it; not trusting to the uncertain provision to be made by individuals. And to my Mulatto man William (calling himself William Lee) I give immediate freedom; or if he should prefer it (on account of the accidents which have befallen him, and which have rendered him incapable of walking or of any active employment) to remain in the situation he now is, it shall be optional in him to do so: In either case however, I allow him an annuity of thirty dollars during his natural life, which shall be independent of the victuals and cloaths he has been accustomed to receive, if he chuses the last alternative; but in full, with his freedom, if he prefers the first; and this I give him as a testimony of my sense of his attachment to me, and for his faithful services during the Revolutionary War.

Item   To the Trustees (Governors, or by whatsoever other name they may be designated) of the Academy in the Town of Alexandria, I give and bequeath, in Trust, four thousand dollars, or in other words twenty of the shares which I hold in the Bank of Alexandria, towards the support of a Free school established at, and annexed to, the said Academy; for the purpose of Educating such Orphan children, or the children of such other poor and indigent persons as are unable to accomplish it with their own means; and who, in the judgment of the Trustees of the said Seminary, are best entitled to the benefit of this donation. The aforesaid twenty shares I give and bequeath in perpetuity; the dividends only of which are to be drawn for, and applied by the said Trustees for the time being, for the uses above mentioned; the stock to remain entire and untouched; unless indications of a failure of the said Bank should be so apparent, or a discontinuance thereof should render a removal of this fund necessary; in either of these cases, the amount of the Stock here devised, is to be vested in some other Bank or public Institution, whereby the interest may with regularity and certainty be drawn, and applied as above. And to prevent misconception, my meaning is, and is hereby declared to be, that these twenty shares are in lieu of, and not in addition to, the thousand pounds given by a missive letter some years ago; in consequence whereof an annuity of fifty pounds has since been paid towards the support of this Institution.

Item Whereas by a Law of the Commonwealth of Virginia, enacted in the year 1785, the Legislature thereof was pleased (as a an evidence of Its approbation of the services I had rendered the Public during the Revolution; and partly, I believe, in consideration of my having suggested the vast advantages which the Community would derive from the extension of its Inland Navigation, under Legislative patronage) to present me with one hundred shares of one hundred dollars each, in the incorporated company established for the purpose of extending the navigation of James River from tide water to the Mountains: and also with fifty shares of one hundred pounds Sterling each, in the Corporation of another company, likewise established for the similar purpose of opening the Navigation of the River Potomac from tide water to Fort Cumberland; the acceptance of which, although the offer was highly honorable, and grateful to my feelings, was refused, as inconsistent with a principle which I had adopted, and had never departed from, namely, not to receive pecuniary compensation for any services I could render my country in its arduous struggle with great Britain, for its Rights; and because I had evaded similar propositions from other States in the Union; adding to this refusal, however, an intimation that, if it should be the pleasure of the Legislature to permit me to appropriate the said shares to *public uses*, I would receive them on those terms with due sensibility; and this it having consented to, in flattering terms, as will appear by a subsequent Law, and sundry resolutions, in the most ample and honourable manner, I proceed after this recital, for the more correct understanding of the case, to declare:

That as it has always been a source of serious regret with me, to see the youth of these United States sent to foreign Countries for the purpose of Education, often before their minds were formed, or they had imbibed any adequate ideas of the happiness of their own; contracting, too frequently, not only habits of dissipation and extravagence, but principles unfriendly to Republican Governmt, and to the true and genuine liberties of mankind; which, thereafter are rarely overcome. For these reasons, it has been my ardent wish to see a plan devised on a liberal scale which would have a tendency to sprd. systematic ideas through all parts of this rising Empire, thereby to do away local attachments and State prejudices, as far as the nature of things would, or indeed ought to admit, from our National Councils. Looking anxiously forward to the accomplishment of so desirable an object as this is (in my estimation) my mind has not been able to contemplate any plan more likely to effect the measure than the establishment of a UNIVERSITY in a central part of the United States, to which the youth of fortune and talents from all parts thereof might be sent for the completion of their Education in all the branches of polite literature; in arts and Sciences, in acquiring knowledge in the principles of Politics and good Government; and (as a matter of infinite Importance in my judgment) by associating with each other, and forming friendships in Juvenile years, be enabled to free themselves in a proper degree from those local prejudices and habitual jealousies which have just been mentioned; and which, when carried to excess, are never failing sources of disquietude to the Public mind, and pregnant of mischievous consequences to this Country: Under these impressions, so fully dilated,

Item   I give and bequeath in perpetuity the fifty shares which I hold in the Potomac Company (under the aforesaid Acts of the Legislature of Virginia) towards the endowment of a UNIVERSITY to be established within the limits of the District of Columbia, under the auspices of the General Government, if that government should incline to extend a fostering hand towards it; and until such Seminary is established, and the funds arising on these shares shall be required for its support, my further WILL and desire is that the profit accruing therefrom shall, whenever the dividends are made, be laid out in purchasing Stock in the Bank of Columbia, or some other Bank, at the discretion of my Executors; or by the Treasurer of the United States for the time being under the direction of

Congress; provided that Honourable body should Patronize the measure, and the Dividends proceeding from the purchase of such Stock is to be vested in more stock, and so on, until a sum adequate to the accomplishment of the object is obtained, of which I have not the smallest doubt, before many years passes away; even if no aid or encouraged is given by Legislative authority, or from any other source

Item   The hundred shares which I held in the James River Company, I have given, and now confirm in perpetuity to, and for the use and benefit of Liberty-Hall Academy, in the County of Rockbridge, in the Commonwealth of Virga.

Item   I release exonerate and discharge, the Estate of my deceased brother Samuel Washington, from the payment of the money which is due to me for the land I sold to Philip Pendleton (lying in the County of Berkeley) who assigned the same to him the said Samuel; who, by agreement was to pay me therefor. And whereas by some contract (the purport of which was never communicated to me) between the said Samuel and his son Thornton Washington, the latter became possessed of the aforesaid Land, without any conveyance having passed from me, either to the said Pendleton, the said Samuel, or the said Thornton, and without any consideration having been made, by which neglect neither the legal nor equitable title has been alienated; it rests therefore with me to declare my intentions concerning the Premises; and these are, to give and bequeath the said land to whomsoever the said Thornton Washington (who is also dead) devised the same; or to his heirs forever if he died Intestate: Exonerating the estate of the said Thornton, equally with that of the said Samuel from payment of the purchase money; which, with Interest; agreeably to the original contract with the said Pendleton, would amount to more than a thousand pounds. And whereas two other Sons of my said deceased brother Samuel, namely, George Steptoe Washington and Lawrence Augustine Washington, were, by the decease of those to whose care they were committed, brought under my protection, and in conseqe. have occasioned advances on my part for their Education at College, and other Schools, for their board, cloathing, and other incidental expences, to the amount of near five thousand dollars over and above the Sums furnished by their Estate wch. Sum may be inconvenient for them, or their fathers Estate to refund. I do for these reasons acquit them, and the said estate, from the payment thereof. My intention being, that all accounts between them and me, and their fathers estate and me shall stand balanced.

Item   The balance due to me from the Estate of Bartholomew Dandridge deceased (my wife's brother) and which amounted on the first day of October 1795 to four hundred and twenty five pounds (as will appear by an account rendered by his deceased son John Dandridge, who was the acting Exr. of his fathers Will) I release and acquit from the payment thereof. And the Negros, then thirty three in number) formerly belonging to the said estate, who were taken in execution, sold, and purchased in on my account in the year   and ever since have remained in the possession, and to the use of Mary, Widow of the said Bartholomew Dandridge, with their increase, it is my Will and desire shall continue, and be in her possession, without paying hire, or making compensation for the same for the time past or to come, during her natural life; at the expiration of which, I direct that all of them who are forty years old and upwards, shall receive their freedom; all under that age and above sixteen, shall serve seven years and no longer; and all under sixteen years, shall serve until they are twenty five years of age, and then be free. And to avoid disputes respecting the ages of any of these Negros, they are to be taken to the Court of the County in which they reside, and the judgment thereof, in this relation, shall be final; and a record thereof made; which may be adduced as evidence at any time thereafter, if disputes should arise concerning the same. And I further direct, that the heirs of the said Bartholomew Dandridge shall, equally, share the benefits arising from the Services of the said negros according to the tenor of this devise, upon the decease of their Mother.

Item   If Charles Carter who intermarried with my niece Betty Lewis is not sufficiently secured in the title to the lots he had of me in the Town of Fredericksburgh, it is my Will and desire that my Executors shall make such conveyances of them as the Law requires, to render it perfect.

Item   To my Nephew William Augustine Washington and

his heirs (if he should conceive them to be objects worth prosecuting) and to his heirs, a lot in the Town of Manchester (opposite to Richmond) No 265 drawn on my sole account, and also the tenth of one or two, hundred acre lots, and two or three half acre lots in the City, and vicinity of Richmond, drawn in partnership with nine others, all in the lottery of the deceased William Byrd are given; as is also a lot which I purchased of John Hood, conveyed by William Willie and Samuel Gordon Trustees of the said John Hood, numbered 139 in the Town of Edinburgh, in the County of Prince George, State of Virginia

Item   To my Nephew Bushrod Washington, I give and bequeath all the Papers in my possession, which relate to my Civel and Military Administration of the affairs of this Country; I leave to him also, such of my private Papers as are worth preserving; and at the decease of my wife, and before, if she is not inclined to retain them, I give and bequeath my library of Books, and Pamphlets of every kind.

Item   Having sold Lands which I possessed in the State of Pennsylvania, and part of a tract held in equal right with George Clinton, late Governor of New York, in the State of New York; my share of land, and interest, in the Great Dismal Swamp, and a tract of land which I owned in the County of Gloucester; withholding the legal titles thereto, until the consideration money should be paid. And having moreover leased, and conditionally sold (as will appear by the tenor of the said leases) all my lands upon the Great Kanhawa, and a tract upon Difficult Run, in the county of Loudoun, it is my Will and direction, that whensoever the Contracts are fully, and respectively complied with, according to the spirit, true intent and meaning thereof, on the part of the purchasers, their heirs or Assigns, that then, and in that case, Conveyances are to be made, agreeably to the terms of the said Contracts; and the money arising therefrom, when paid, to be vested in Bank stock; the dividends whereof, as of that also wch. is already vested therein, is to inure to my said Wife during her life; but the Stock itself is to remain, and be subject to the general distribution hereafter directed.

Item   To the Earl of Buchan I recommit "the Box made of the Oak that sheltered the Great Sir William Wallace after the battle of Falkirk" presented to me by his Lordship, in terms too flattering for me to repeat, with a request "to pass it, on the event of my decease, to the man in my country, who should appear to merit it best, upon the same conditions that have induced him to send it to me." Whether easy, or not, to select *the man* who might comport with his Lordships opinion in this respect, is not for me to say; but conceiving that no disposition of this valuable curiosity can be more eligable than the recommitment of it to his own Cabinet, agreeably to the original design of the Goldsmith Company of Edenburgh, who presented it to him, and at his request, consented that it should be transfered to me; I do give and bequeath the same to his Lordship, and in case of his decease, to his heir with my grateful thanks for the distinguished honour of presenting it to me; and more especially for the favourable sentiments with which he accompanied it.

Item To my brother Charles Washington I give and bequeath the gold headed Cane left me by Doctr. Franklin in his Will. I add nothing to it, because of the ample provision I have made for his Issue. To the acquaintances and friends of my Juvenile years, Lawrence Washington and Robert Washington of Chotanck, I give my other two gold headed Canes, having my Arms engraved on them; and to each (as they will be useful where they live) I leave one of the Spy-glasses which constituted part of my equipage during the late War. To my compatriot in arms, and old and intimate friend Doctr. Craik, I give my Bureau (or as the Cabinet makers call it, Tambour Secretary) and the circular chair, an appendage of my Study. To Doctor David Stuart I give my large shaving and dressing Table, and my Telescope. To the Reverend, now Bryan, Lord Fairfax, I give a Bible in three large folio volumes, with notes, presented to me by the Right reverend Thomas Wilson, Bishop of Sodor and Man. To General de la Fayette I give a pair of finely wrought steel Pistols, taken from the enemy in the Revolutionary War. To my Sisters in law Hannah Washington and Mildred Washington; to my friends Eleanor Stuart, Hannah Washington of Fairfield, and Elizabeth Washington of Hayfield, I give, each, a mourning Ring of the value of one hundred dollars. These bequests are not made for the intrinsic value of them, but as mementos of my esteem and regard. To

Tobias Lear, I give the use of the Farm which he now holds, in virtue of a Lease from me to him and his deceased wife (for and during their natural lives) free from Rent, during his life; at the expiration of which, it is to be disposed as is hereinafter directed. To Sally B. Haynie (a distant relation of mine) I give and bequeath three hundred dollars. To Sarah Green daughter of the deceased Thomas Bishop, and to Ann Walker daughter of Jno. Alton, also deceased, I give, each one hundred dollars, in consideration of the attachment of their fathers to me, each of whom having lived nearly forty years in my family. To each of my Nephews, William Augustine Washington, George Lewis, George Steptoe Washington, Bushrod Washington and Samuel Washington, I give one of the Swords or Cutteaux of which I may die possessed; and they are to chuse in the order they are named. These Swords are accompanied with an injunction not to unsheath them for the purpose of shedding blood, except it be for self defence, or in defence of their Country and its rights; and in the latter case, to keep them unsheathed, and prefer falling with them in their hands, to the relinquishment thereof.

AND NOW

Having gone through these specific devises, with explanations for the more correct understanding of the meaning and design of them; I proceed to the distribution of the more important parts of my Estate, in manner following:

First   To my Nephew Bushrod Washington and his heirs (partly in consideration of an intimation to his deceased father while we were Bachelors, and he had kindly undertaken to superintend my Estate during my Military Services in the former War between Great Britain and France, that if I should fall therein, Mount Vernon (then less extensive in domain than at present) should become his property) I give and bequeath all that part thereof which is comprehended within the following limits, viz: Beginning at the ford of Dogue run, near my Mill, and extending along the road, and bounded thereby as it now goes, and ever has gone since my recollection of it, to the ford of little hunting Creek at the Gum spring until it comes to a knowl, opposite to an old road which formerly passed through the lower field of Muddy hole Farm; at which, on the north side of the said road are three red, or Spanish

Oaks marked as a corner, and a stone placed.—thence by a line of trees to be marked, rectangular to the back line, or outer boundary of the tract between Thomson Mason and myself. thence with that line Easterly (now double ditching with a Post and Rail fence thereon) to the run of little hunting Creek. thence with that run which is the boundary between the Lands of the late Humphrey Peake and me, to the tide water of the said Creek; thence by that water to Potomac River. thence with the River to the mouth of Dogue Creek. and thence with the said Dogue Creek to the place of beginning at the aforesaid ford; containing upwards of four thousand Acres, be the same more or less; together with the Mansion house and all other buildings and improvemts. thereon.

Second In consideration of the consanguinity between them and my wife, being as nearly related to her as to myself, as on account of the affection I had for, and the obligation I was under to, their father when living, who from his youth had attached himself to my person, and followed my fortunes through the viscissitudes of the late Revolution; afterwards devoting his time to the Superintendence of my private concerns for many years, whilst my public employments rendered it impracticable for me to do it myself, thereby affording me essential Services, and always performing them in a manner the most felial and respectful: for these reasons I say, I give and bequeath to George Fayette Washington, and Lawrence Augustine Washington and their heirs, my Estate East of little hunting Creek, lying on the River Potomac; including the Farm of 360 Acres, Leased to Tobias Lear as noticed before, and containing in the whole, by Deeds, Two thousand and Seventy seven acres, be it more or less. Which said Estate it is my Will and desire should be equitably, and advantageously divided between them, according to quantity, quality and other circumstances when the youngest shall have arrived at the age of twenty one years, by three judicious and disinterested men; one to be chosen by each of the brothers, and the third by these two. In the meantime, if the termination of my wife's interest therein should have ceased, the profits arising therefrom are to be applied for thir joint uses and benefit.

Third And whereas it has always been my intention, since

my expectation of having Issue has ceased, to consider the Grand children of my wife in the same light as I do my own relations, and to act a friendly part by them; more especially by the two whom we have reared from their earliest infancy, namely: Eleanor Parke Custis, and George Washington Parke Custis. And whereas the former of these hath lately intermarried with Lawrence Lewis, a son of my deceased Sister Betty Lewis, by which union the inducement to provide for them both has been increased; Wherefore, I give and bequeath to the said Lawrence Lewis and Eleanor Parke Lewis, his wife, and their heirs, the residue of my Mount Vernon Estate, not already devised to my Nephew Bushrod Washington, comprehended within the following description. viz: All the land North of the Road leading from the ford of Dogue run to the Gum spring as described in the devise of the other part of the tract, to Bushrod Washington, until it comes to the Stone and three red or Spanish Oaks on the knowl. thence with the rectangular line to the back line (between Mr. Mason and me) thence with that line westerly, along the new double ditch to Dogue run, by the tumbling Dam of my Mill; thence with the said run to the ford aforementioned; to which I add all the Land I possess West of the said Dogue run, and Dogue Crk. bounded Easterly and Southerly thereby; together with the Mill, Distillery, and all other houses and improvements on the premises, making together about two thousand Acres, be it more or less.

Fourth   Actuated by the principal already mentioned, I give and bequeath to George Washington Parke Custis, the Grandson of my wife, and my Ward, and to his heirs, the tract I hold on four mile run in the vicinity of Alexandria, containing one thousd. two hundred acres, more or less, and my entire Square, number twenty one, in the City of Washington.

Fifth   All the rest and residue of my Estate, real and personal, not disposed of in manner aforesaid. In whatsoever consisting, wheresoever lying, and whensoever found, a schedule of which, as far as is recollected, with a reasonable estimate of its value, is hereunto annexed: I desire may be sold by my Executors at such times, in such manner, and in such credits (if an equal, valid, and satisfactory distribution of the specific property cannot be made without), as, in their judgment shall be most condusive to the interest of the parties concerned; and the monies arising therefrom to be divided into twenty three equal parts, and applied as follows, viz:

To William Augustine Washington, Elizabeth Spotswood, Jane Thornton, and the heirs of Ann Ashton; son, and daughters of my deceased brother Augustine Washington, I give and bequeath four parts; that is, one part to each of them.

To Fielding Lewis, George Lewis, Robert Lewis, Howell Lewis and Betty Carter, sons and daughter of my deceased Sister Betty Lewis, I give and bequeath five other parts, one to each of them.

To George Steptoe Washington, Lawrence Augustine Washington, Harriot Parks, and the heirs of Thornton Washington, sons and daughter of my deceased brother Samuel Washington, I give and bequeath other four parts, one part to each of them.

To Corbin Washington, and the heirs of Jane Washington, Son and daughter of my deceased Brother John Augustine Washington, I give and bequeath two parts; one part to each of them.

To Samuel Washington, Frances Ball and Mildred Hammond, son and daughters of my Brother Charles Washington, I give and bequeath three parts; one part to each of them. And to George Fayette Washington Charles Augustine Washington and Maria Washington, sons and daughter of my deceased Nephew Geo: Augustine Washington, I give one other part; that is, to each a third of that part.

To Elizabeth Parke Law, Martha Parke Peter, and Eleanor Parke Lewis, I give and bequeath three other parts, that is a part to each of them.

And to my Nephews Bushrod Washington and Lawrence Lewis, and to my ward, the grandson of My wife, I give and bequeath one other part; that is, a third thereof to each of them. And if it should so happen, that any of these persons whose names are here ennumerated (unknown to me) should now be deceased, or should die before me, that in either of these cases, the heirs of such deceased persons shall, notwithstanding, derive all the benefits of the bequest; in the same manner as if he, or she, was actually living at the time.

And by way of advice, I recommend it to my Executors not

to be precipitate in disposing of the landed property (herein directed to be sold) if from temporary causes the Sale thereof should be dull; experience having fully evinced, that the price of land (especially above the Falls of the Rivers, and on the Western Waters) have been progressively rising, and cannot be long checked in its increasing value. And I particularly recommend it to such of the Legatees (under this clause of my Will) as can make it convenient, to take each share of my Stock in the Potomac Company in preference to the amount of what it might sell for; being thoroughly convinced myself, that no uses to which the money can be applied will be so productive as the Tolls arising from this navigation when in full operation (and this from the nature of things it must be 'ere long) and more especially if that of the Shanondoah is added thereto.

The family Vault at Mount Vernon requiring repairs, and being improperly situated besides, I desire that a new one of Brick, and upon a larger Scale, may be built at the foot of what is commonly called the Vineyard Inclosure, on the ground which is marked out. In which my remains, with those of my deceased relatives (now in the old Vault) and such others of my family as may chuse to be entombed there, may be deposited. And it is my express desire that my Corpse may be Interred in a private manner, without parade, or funeral Oration.

Lastly I constitute and appoint my dearly beloved wife Martha Washington, My Nephews William Augustine Washington, Bushrod Washington, George Steptoe Washington, Samuel Washington, and Lawrence Lewis, and my ward George Washington Parke Custis (when he shall have arrived at the age of twenty years) Executrix and Executors of this Will and testament, In the construction of which it will readily be perceived that no professional character has been consulted, or has had any Agency in the draught; and that, although it has occupied many of my leisure hours to digest, and to through it into its present form, it may, notwithstanding, appear crude and incorrect. But having endeavoured to be plain, and explicit in all the Devises, even at the expence of prolixity, perhaps of tautology, I hope, and trust, that no disputes will arise concerning them; but if, contrary to expectation, the case should be otherwise from the want of legal expression, or the usual technical terms, or because too much or too little has been said on any of the Devises to be consonant with law, My Will and direction expressly is, that all disputes (if unhappily any should arise) shall be decided by three impartial and intelligent men, known for their probity and good understanding; two to be chosen by the disputants, each having the choice of one, and the third by those two. Which three men thus chosen, shall, unfettered by Law, or legal constructions, declare their Sense of the Testators intention; and such decision is, to all intents and purposes to be as binding on the Parties as if it had been given in the Supreme Court of the United States.

In witness of all, and of each of the things herein contained, I have set my hand and Seal, this ninth day of July, in the year One thousand seven hundred and ninety and of the Independence of the United States the twenty fourth.

*Schedule of property comprehended in the foregoing Will, which is directed to be sold, and some of it, conditionally is sold; with discriptive, and explanatory notes relative thereto.

In Virginia

Loudoun County

	acres	price	dollars
Difficult run	300	. . . . .	6,666 (a)

(a) This tract for the size of it is valuable, more for its situation than the quality of its soil, though that is good for Farming; with a considerable portion of grd. that might, very easily, be improved into Meadow. It lyes on the great road from the City of Washington, Alexandria and George Town, to Leesburgh and Winchester; at Difficult bridge, nineteen miles from Alexandria, less from the City and George Town, and not more than three from Matildaville at the Great Falls of Potomac.

There is a valuable seat on the Premises, and the whole is conditionally sold, for the sum annexed in the Schedule

Loudoun and Fauquier

Ashbys Bent	2481 . .	$10 . . .	24,810	(b)
Chattins Run	885 . .	8 . . .	7,080	

(b) What the selling prices of lands in the vicinity of these two tracts are, I know not; but compared with those above the ridge, and others below them, the value annexed will appear moderate; a less one would not obtain them from me.

Berkeley

So. fork of Bullskin	1600
Head of Evans's M	453
On Wormeley's line	183

2236 . . .20 . . .44.720 (*c*)

(*c*) The surrounding land, not superior in Soil, situation or properties of any sort, sell currently at from twenty to thirty dollars an Acre. The lowest price is affixed to these

Frederick

Bought from Mercer . . . . . .   571 . . .20 . . . 11.420 (*d*)

(*d*) The observations made in the last note applies equally to this tract; being in the vicinity of them, and of similar quality, altho' it lyes in another County

Hampshire

On Potk River above B . . . .   240 . . . 15 . . . 3.600 (*e*)

(*e*) This tract, though small, is extremely valuable. It lyes on Potomac River about 12 miles above the Town of Bath (or Warm springs) and is in the shape of a horse Shoe; the river running almost around it. Two hundred Acres of it is rich low grounds; with a great abundance of the largest and finest Walnut trees; which, with the produce of the Soil, might (by means of the improved Navigation of the Potomac) be brought to a shipping port with more ease, and at a smaller expence, than that which is transported 30 miles only by land.

Gloucester

On North River . . . .   400 . . abt. . . . 3.600 (*f*)

(*f*) This tract is of second rate Gloucester low grounds. It has no improvement thereon, but lyes on navigable water, abounding in Fish and Oysters. It was received in payment of a debt (carrying interest) and valued in the year 1789 by an impartial Gentleman to £800. N B. it has lately been sold, and there is due thereon, a balance equal to what is annexed the Schedule

Nansemond

Near Suffolk ⅓ of 1119 acres . .   373 . . . 8 . . . 2.984 (*g*)

(*g*) These 373 acres are the third part of undivided purchases made by the deceased Fielding Lewis Thomas Walker and myself; on full conviction that they would become valuable. The land lyes on the Road from Suffolk to Norfolk; touches (if I am not mistaken) some part of the Navigable water of Nansemond River; borders on, and comprehends part of the rich Dismal Swamp; is capable of great improvement; and from its situation must become extremely valuable.

Great Dismal Swamp

  My dividend thereof . . . . abt . . 20.000 (*h*)

(*h*) This an undivided Interest wch. I held in the Great Dismal Swamp Company; containing about 4000 acres, with my part of the Plantation and Stock thereon belonging to the company in the sd Swamp.

Ohio River

  Round bottom   587
  Little Kanhawa   2314
  16 miles lowr down   2448
  Opposite Big Bent   4395

                            9744 . . . 10 . . .97.440 (*i*)

(*i*) These several tracts of land are of the first quality on the Ohio River, in the parts where they are situated; being almost if not altogether River bottoms.

  The smallest of these tracts is actually sold at ten dollars an acre but the consideration therefor not received; the rest are equally valuable and will sell as high, especially that which lyes just below the little Kanhawa and is opposite to a thick settlement on the West side the Rivr.

  The four tracts have an aggregate breadth upon the River of Sixteen miles and is bounded thereby that distance.

Great Kanhawa

  Near the Mouth West 10990
  East side above   7276
  Mouth of Cole River   2000
  Opposite thereto   2950
  Burning Spring   125

                            23341 . . . . . . 200.000 (*k*)

(*k*) These tracts are situated on the Great Kanhawa River, and the first four are bounded thereby for more than forty miles. It is acknowledged by all who have seen them (and of the tract containing 10990 acres which I have been on myself, I can assert) that there is no richer, or more valuable land in all that Region; They are conditionally sold for the sum mentioned in the Schedule; that is $200.000 and if the terms of that sale are not complied with they will command considerably more. The tract of which the 125 acres is a moiety, was taken up by General Andrew Lewis and myself for, and on account of a bituminous Spring which it contains, of so inflamable a nature as to burn as freely as spirits, and is as nearly difficult to extinguish

Maryland

Charles County	600 . . . 6 . . . 3.600	(*l*)
Montgomery Do	519 . . . 12 . . . 6.228	(*m*)

(*l*) I am but little acquainted with this land, although I have once been on it. It was received (many years since) in discharge of a debt due to me from Daniel Jenifer Adams at the value annexed thereto, and must be worth more. It is very level, lyes near the River Potomac

(*m*) This tract lyes about 30 miles above the City of Washington, not far from Kittoctan. It is good farming Land, and by those who are well acquainted with it I am informed that it would sell at twelve or $15 pr. acre.

Pennsylvania

Great Meadows	234 . . . .6 . . . 1.404 (*n*)

(*n*) this land is valuable on account of its local situation and other properties. It affords an exceeding good stand on Braddocks road from Fort Cumberland to Pittsburgh, and besides a fertile soil, possesses a large quantity of natural Meadow, fit for the scythe. It is distinguished by the appellation of the Great Meadows, where the first action with the French in the year 1754 was fought.

New York

Mohawk River . . . . abt.1000 . . . .6 . . . 6.000 (*o*)

(*o*) This is the moiety of about 2000 Acs. which remains unsold of 6071 Acres on the Mohawk River (Montgomery Cty) in a Patent granted to Daniel Coxe in the Township of Coxeborough and Carolana, as will appear by Deed from Marinus Willet and wife to George Clinton (late Governor of New York) and myself. The latter sales have been at Six dollars an acr; and what remains unsold will fetch that or more

North Westn. Territy

On little Miami	839
Ditto	977
Ditto	<u>1235</u>
	3051 . . . . 5 . . . 15.251 (*p*)

(*p*) The quality of these lands and their Situation, may be known by the Surveyors Certificates, which are filed along with the Patents. They lye in the vicinity of Cincinnati; one tract near the mouth of little Miami, another seven and the third ten miles up the same. I have been informed that they will readily command more than they are estimated at.

Kentucky
> Rough Creek   3000
> Ditto adjoing   2000

                                     5000 . . . .2 . . .10.000 (*q*)

(*q*) For the description of these tracts in detail, see General Spotswoods letters, filed with the other papers relating to them. Beside the General good quality of the Land, there is a valuable Bank of Iron Ore thereon: which, when the settlement becomes more populous (and settlers are moving that way very fast) will be found very valuable; as the rough Creek, a branch of Green River affords ample water for Furnaces and forges.

Lots—viz.

City of Washington
> Two, near the Capital, Sqr 634 Cost $963; ⎫
>   and with Buildgs   ⎬ . . 15000 (*r*)
>   ⎭
> No. 5. 12. 13. and 14: the 3 last, Water lots on ⎫
>   the Eastern Branch, in Sqr. 667. containing ⎬ . . 4.132 (*s*)
>   together 34.438 sqr. feet a 12 Cts   ⎭

(*r*) The two lots near the Capital, in square 634, cost me 963$ only; but in this price I was favoured, on condition that I should build two Brick houses three Story high each: without this reduction the selling prices of those Lots would have cost me about $1350. These lots, with the buildings thereon, when completed will stand me in $15000 at least.

(*s*) Lots No. 5. 12. 13 & 14 on the Eastn. branch, are advantageously situated on the water, and although many lots much less convenient have sold a great deal higher I will rate these at 12 Cts. the square foot only.

Alexandria
> Corner of Pitt and Prince Stts. half an   ⎫
>   Acre; laid out into buildgs. 3 or 4 of wch. ⎬ . . 4.000 (*t*)
>   are let on grd. Rent at $3 pr. foot   ⎭

(*t*) For this lot, though unimproved, I have refused $3500. It has since been laid off into proper sized lots for building on; three or 4 of which are let on ground Rent, forever, at three dollars a foot on the Street. and this price is asked for both fronts on Pitt and Princes Street.

Winchester
> A lot in the Town of half an Acre and   ⎫
>   another in the Commons of about   ⎬ . . . . 400 (*u*)
>   6 Acs. supposed   ⎭

(*u*) As neither the lot in the Town or Common have any improvements on them, it is not easy to fix a price, but as both are well situated, it is presumed the price annexed to them in the Schedule is a reasonable valun.

Bath—or Warm Springs

Two Well situated, and had buildings to the amt of £150 }... 800 (*w*)

(*w*) The Lots in Bath (two adjoining) cost me, to the best of my recollection, betwn. fifty and sixty pounds 20 years ago; and the buildings thereon £150 more. Whether property there has increased or decreased in its value, and in what condition the houses are, I am ignorant. but suppose they are not valued too high

Stock

United States 6 pr Cts 3746
   Do   defered . . . . 1873 } ..2500 6.246 (*x*)
          3 pr Cts . . . . 2946 } ——

(*x*) These are the sums which are actually funded. And though no more in the aggregate than $7.566; stand me in at least ten thousand pounds Virginia money. being the amount of bonded and other debts due to me, and discharged during the War when the money had depreciated in that ratio, and was so settled by public authoy.

Potomack Company

24 Shares, cost ea £100 Sterg . . . . .20.666 (*y*)

(*y*) The value annexed to these sha: is what they have actually cost me, and is the price affixed by Law: and although the present selling price is under par, my advice to the Legatees (for whose benefit they are intended, especialy those who can afford to lye out of the money) is that each should take and hold one; there being a moral certainty of a great and increasing profit arising from them in the course of a few years.

James River Company

5 Shares, each cost $100 . . . . 500 (*z*)

(*z*) It is supposed that the Shares in the James River Company must also be productive. But of this I can give no decided opinion for want of more accurate informatn.

Bank of Columbia

170 Shares, $40 each . . . . 6.800 }
Bank of Alexandria, besides } . . . . .1.000 } (&)
   20 to the Free School 5 }

(&) These are nominal prices of the Shares of the Banks of Alexandria and Columbia, the selling prices vary according to circumstances. But as the Stock usually divided from eight to ten percent per annum, they must be worth the former, at least, so long as the Banks are conceived to be Secure, though from circumstances may, some times be below it.

Stock, living, viz:

1 Covering horse, 5 Coh. horses; 4 riding do; Six brood Mares; 20 working horses and mares; 2 Covering Jacks, and 3 young ones; 10 she Asses, 42 working Mules; 15 younger ones 329 head of horned Cattle 640 head of sheep, and a large Stock of Hogs, the pricise number unknown ☞ My Manager has estimated this live Stock at £7,000 but I shall set it down in order to make rd sum at   15.653

Agregate amt $530.000

The value of livestock depends more upon the quality than quantity of the different species of it, and this again upon the demand, and judgment or fancy of purchasers.

Mount Vernon
9th. July 1799

To Jonathan Trumbull, Jr.

Mount Vernon, July 21, 1799.

My dear Sir: Your favour of the 22d. Ulto got to my hands yesterday, *only*. It came safe, and without any apparent marks of violence; but whence the length of its passage, I am unable to inform you.

To you, and to your brother Colo. Jno Trumbull, I feel much indebted for the full, frank, and interesting communication of the political sentiments contained in both your letters.

The project of the latter is rash and under any circumstances would require very mature consideration; but in its extent, and an eye being had to the disorganizing Party in the United States, I am sure it would be impracticable in the present order of things.

Not being able to convey my ideas to you on this subject in more concise terms than I have already done to your brother in answer to the letter he informs you he has written to me I shall take the liberty of giving you an extract thereof, as follow.

For the political information contained in it (that is his letter) I feel grateful, as I always shall for the free and unreserved communication of your Sentiments upon subjects so important in their nature, and tendency. No well informed and unprejudiced man, who has viewed with attention the conduct of the French Government since the Revolution in that Country, can mistake its objects or the tendency of the ambitious plans it is pursuing. Yet, strange as it may seem, a party, and a powerful one too, among us, affect to believe that the measures of it are dictated by a principle of self preservation; that the outrages of which the Directory are guilty, proceeds from dire necessity; that it wishes to be upon the most friendly and amicable terms with the United States; that it will be the fault of the latter if this is not the case; that the defensive measures which this Country have adopted, are not only unnecessary and expensive, but have a tendency to produce the evil which, to deprecate, is mere pretence, because War with France they say is the wish of this Government; that on the Militia we should rest our Security; and, that it is time enough to call these when the danger is imminent, &ca. &ca. &ca.

With these, and such like ideas, attempted to be inculcated upon the public mind (and prejudices not yet eradicated) with all the arts of sophistry, and no regard to truth, decency or respect to characters, public or private, who happen to differ from themselves in Politics, I leave you to decide on the probability of carrying such an extensive plan of defence as you have suggested in your last letter, into operation; and in the short period you propose may be allowed to accomplish it in.

I come now, my dear Sir, to pay particular attention to that part of your Letter which respects myself.

I remember well the conversation which you allude to, and have not forgot the answer I gave you. In my judgment it applies with as much force *now*, as *then*; nay more, because at that time the line between Parties was not so clearly drawn, and the views of the opposition, so clearly developed as they are at present; of course, allowing your observation (as it respects myself) to be founded, personal influence would be of no avail.

Let that party set up a broomstick and call it a true son of Liberty; a Democrat, or give it any other epithet that will suit their purpose, and it will command their votes in toto! as an analysis of this position, look to the pending Election of Governor in Pennsylvania. Will not the Federalists meet them or rather defend their cause, on the opposite ground? Surely they must, or they will discover a want of Policy, indicative of weakness, and pregnant of mischief which cannot be admitted. Wherein then would lye the difference between the present Gentleman in Office, and myself?

It would be matter of sore regret to me if I could believe that a serious thot. was turned towards me as his successor; not only as it respects my ardent wishes to pass through the vale of life in retiremt., undisturbed in the remnant of the days I have to sojourn here, unless called upon to defend my Country (which every citizen is bound to do), but on Public ground also; for although I have abundant cause to be thankful for the good health with whh. I am blessed, yet I am not insensible to my declination in other respects. It would be criminal therefore in me, although it should be the wish of my Countrymen, and I could be elected, to accept an Office under this conviction, which another would discharge with more ability; and this too at a time when I am thoroughly convinced I should not draw a *single* vote from the Anti-federal side; and of course, should stand upon no stronger ground than any other Federal character well supported; and when I should become a mark for the shafts of envenomed malice, and the basest calumny to fire at; when I should be charged not only with irresolution, but with concealed ambition, which waits only an occasion to blaze out; and, in short, with dotage and imbecility.

All this I grant, ought to be like dust in the balance, when put in competion with a *great* public good, when the accomplishment of it is apparent. But as no problem is better defined in my mind than that principle, not men, is now, and will be, the object of contention; and that I could not obtain a *solitary* vote from that Party; that any other respectable Federal character would receive the same suffrages that I should; that at my time of life, (verging towards three score and ten) I should expose myself without rendering any essential service to my

Country, or answering the end contemplated: Prudence on my part must arrest any attempt at the well meant, but mistaken views of my friends, to introduce me again into the chair of Government.

Lengthy as this letter is, I cannot conclude it without expressing an *earnest* wish that, some intimate and confidential friend of the Presidents would give him to understand that, his long absence from the Seat of Government in the present critical conjuncture, affords matter for severe animadversion by the friends of government; who speak of it with much disapprobation; while the other party chuckle at and set it down as a favourable omen for themselves. It has been suggested to me to make this Communication; but I have declined it, conceiving that it would be better received from a private character, more in the habits of social intercourse and friendship. With the most sincere friendship, and Affectionate regard, etc.

To James McHenry

(Private)

Mount Vernon, August 11, 1799.
My dear Sir: Your private letters of the 29th. Ulto. and 5th. instant, have been duly received. Mr. Bordley for presenting, and you for forwarding his Essays on Husbandry, are entitled to, and, accordingly receive, my thanks for these instances of both your kindnesses.

(Confidential)

I think you Wise men of the East, have got yourselves into a hobble, relatively to France, Great Britain, Russia and the Porte, to which, Allow me the priviledge of adding our worthy Demos. All cannot be pleased! Whom will you offend? Here then is a severe trial for your Diplomatic skill, in which the Editor of the Aurora says you are great adepts. But to be serious, I think the nomination, and appointment of Ambassadors to treat with France would, in any event, have been liable to unpleasant reflections (after the Declarations wch have been made), and in the present state of matters, in Europe, must be exceedingly Embarrassing. The President has a choice of difficulties before him, in this business; If he pursues the line he marked out, *all* the consequences cannot be foreseen: If he relinquishes it, it will be said to be of a piece with all the other Acts of the Administration; unmeaning if not wicked, deceptious, &ca., &ca, &ca.; and will arm the opposition with fresh weapons to commence new attacks upon the Government, be the turn given to it, and reasons assigned, what they may. I come now, to the Scene of Bribery.

And pray, my good Sir, what part of the $800,000 have come to your share? As you are high in Office, I hope you did not disgrace yourself in the acceptance of a paltry bribe. a 100,000 $ perhaps. But here again I become serious. There can be no medium between the reward and punishment of an Editor, who shall publish such things as Duane has been doing for sometime past. On what ground then does he *pretend* to stand in his exhibition of the charges, or the insinuations which he has handed to the Public? Can hardihood, itself be so great, as to stigmatise characters in the Public Gazettes for the most heinous offences, and when prosecuted, pledge itself to support the alligations unless there was something to build on? I hope and expect that the Prosecutors will probe this matter to the bottom. It will have an unhappy effect on the public mind if it be not so.

But how stands the charge, in verity and truth with respect to the Consul General (Stephens) purchase of Coffee, and breach of trust; or in other words taking advantage of his official knowledge to monopolise that article at a low price? This thing made a good deal of noise among the friends as well as the enemies of government; and if true, proves him unworthy, altogether, of public confidence; and denominates him a mercenary [   ] one who would do anything for lucre.

Is the President returned to the seat of Government? When will he return? His absence (I mention it from the best motives) gives much discontent to the friends of government, while its enemies chuckle at it, and think it a favourable omen for them. I am always your affecte.

To Robert Lewis

Mount Vernon, August 18, 1799.

Dear Sir: Your letter of the 7th. instant came duly to hand, but being received with many other letters, it was laid by, and entirely forgotten, until I came across it yesterday again. Mr. Ariss's draught on Mr. James Russell for £42 pounds shall be presented to him, but if he is indisposed to pay it, or wants time to do it, he has a good pretext for delay, as you have sent it without your Endorsement, although made payable to *you.*

Of the facts related in the enclosed letter, relative to the loss of his Crop, by the Hessian fly, I know nothing. If it should appear to you evident, that Kercheval has used his true endeavour to raise the means to discharge his Rent, and is deprived thereof by an Act of Providence, I am willing, however illy I can afford to do it, to make some reasonable abatement therefrom; of wch. you, from enquiry, will be the best judge.

It is demonstratively clear, that on this Estate (Mount Vernon) I have more working Negros by a full moiety, than can be employed to any advantage in the farming system, and I shall never turn Planter thereon.

To sell the overplus I cannot, because I am principled against this kind of traffic in the human species. To hire them out, is almost as bad, because they could not be disposed of in families to any advantage, and to disperse the families I have an aversion. What then is to be done? Something must or I shall be ruined; for all the money (in addition to what I raise by Crops, and rents) that have been *received* for Lands, sold within the last four years, to the amount of Fifty thousand dollars, has scarcely been able to keep me a float.

Under these circumstances, and thorough conviction that half the workers I keep on this Estate, would render me greater *nett* profit than I *now* derive from the whole, has made me resolve, if it can be accomplished, to settle Plantations on one of my other Lands. But where? with going to the Western Country I am unable, as yet to decide; as the *best* if not *all* the Lands I have on the East of the Alliganies, are under Leases, or some kind of incumbrance or another. But as you can give me correct information relative to this matter, I now *early* apply for it.

What then is the State of Kerchavals lot, and the other adjoining? are they under Leases? If not, is the Land good? and how many hands would it work to advantage? Have I any other good Land in Berkeley that could be obtained on reasonable terms? Is that small tract above the Warm Springs engaged for the ensuing year? How much cleared Land is there on it? and what kind of buildings? How many hands could be usefully employed thereon? Information on these points, and on others relative thereto, would be acceptable to me.

The drought has been so excessive on this Estate, that I have made no Oats, and if it continues a few days longer I shall make no Corn. I have cut little or no Grass, and my meadows, at this time, are as bear as the pavements, of consequence no second Crop can be expected. These things will compel me, I expect, to reduce the Mouths that feed on the Hay. I have two or three young Jacks (besides young Royal Gift) and several She Asses, that I would dispose of. Would Fauquier, or where else, be a good place to dispose of them?

I am glad to hear that your brother Lawrence is so much amended, as your letter indicates, whether it be from Sulpher application, or other causes: but if Doctr. Ingraham under whose hands he was, was unable to effect a radical cure, I should not place much confidence in Voss's Spring, as the disorder must be deep rooted.

Your Aunt unites with me in best wishes for Mrs. Lewis, yourself and family and I am etc.

To Jonathan Trumbull, Jr.

Mount Vernon, August 30, 1799.

My Dear Sir: Your favor of the 10th instant came duly to hand. It gave me pleasure to find by the contents of it, that your sentiments respecting the comprehensive project of Colo. Trumbull, coincided with those I had expressed to him. A very different state of Politics must obtain in this Country, and more unanimity prevail in our Public councils than is the case at present, 'ere such a measure could be undertaken with the least prospect of success. By unanimity *alone* the plan could be accomplished: while then a party, and a strong one too, is hanging upon the Wheels of Government, opposing measures calculated solely for Internal defence, and is endeavouring to defeat all the Laws which have been passed for this purpose, by rendering them obnoxious, to attempt anything beyond this, would be to encounter *certain* disappointment. And yet, if the Policy of this Country, or the necessity occasioned by the existing opposition to its measures, should suffer the French to Possess themselves of Louisiana and the Floridas, either by exchange or otherwise, I will venture to predict, without the gift of *"second sight"* that there will be "no peace in Israel." Or, in other words, that the restless, ambitious, and Intrieguing spirit of that People, will keep the United States in a continual state of Warfare with the numerous tribes of Indians that inhabit our Frontiers. For doing which their "Diplomatic skill" is well adapted.

With respect to the other subject of your letter, I must again express a strong, and ardent wish and desire that, no eye, no tongue, no thought, may be turned towards me for the purpose alluded to therein. For, besides the reasons which I urged against the measures in my last, and which, in my judgment, and by my feelings, are insurmountable, you, yourself, have furnished a cogent one.

You have conceded, what before was self-evident in my mind, namely, that not a single vote would, thereby, be drawn from the anti-federal Candidate. You add, however, that it might be a means of uniting the federal Votes. Here then, my dear Sir, let me ask, what satisfaction, what consolation, what safety, should I find in support, which depends upon caprice?

If *Men*, not *Principles*, can influence the choice, on the part of the Federalists, what but fluctuations are to be expected? The favorite today, may have the Curtain dropped on him tomorrow, while steadiness marks the conduct of the Anti's; and whoever is not on *their* side must expect to be loaded with all the calumny that malice can invent; in addition to which, I should be charged with inconsistency, concealed ambition, dotage, and a thousand more et ceteras.

It is too interesting not to be again repeated, that if principles, instead of men, are not the steady pursuit of the Federalists, their cause will soon be at an end. If *these* are pursued, they *will not divide* at the next Election of a President; If they do divide on so *important* a point, it would be dangerous to trust them on any other; and none except those who might be solicitous to fill the Chair of Government would do it. In a word, my dear Sir, I am too far advanced into the vale of life to bear such buffiting as I should meet with, in such an event. A mind that has been constantly on the stretch since the year 1753, with but short intervals, and little relaxation, requires rest, and composure; and I believe that nothing short of a serious Invasion of our Country (in which case I conceive it to be the duty of every citizen to step forward in its defence) will ever draw me from my present retirement. But let me be in that, or in any other situation, I shall always remain your sincere friend and Affectionate &c.

To Burges Ball

Mount Vernon, September 22, 1799.
Dear Sir: Your letter of the 16th. instt. has been received, informing me of the death of my brother.

The death of near relations always produces awful and affecting emotions, under whatsoever circumstances it may happen. That of my brother's has been so long expected, and his latter days so uncomfortable to himself, must have prepared all around him for the stroke; though painful in the effect.

I was the *first*, and am now the *last*, of my fathers Children by the second marriage who remain. when I shall be called upon to follow them, is known only to the giver of life. When the summons comes I shall endeavour to obey it with a good grace.

Mrs. Washington has been, and still is, very much indisposed, but unites with me in best wishes for you, Mrs. Ball and family. With great esteem, &c.

To Alexander Hamilton

Sir,   Mount Vernon, December 12th: 1799.

I have duly received your letter of the 28th ultimo, enclosing a Copy of what you had written to the Secretary of War, on the subject of a Military Academy.

The Establishment of an Institution of this kind, upon a respectable and extensive basis, has ever been considered by me as an Object of primary importance to this Country; and while I was in the Chair of Government, I omitted no proper opportunity of recommending it, in my public Speeches, and otherways, to the attention of the Legislature: But I never undertook to go into a *detail* of the organization of such an Academy; leaving this task to others, whose pursuits in the paths of Science, and attention to the Arrangements of such Institutions, had better qualified them for the execution of it.

For the same reason I must now decline making any observations on the details of your plan; and as it has already been submitted to the Secretary of War, through whom it would naturally be laid before Congress, it might be too late for alterations, if any should be suggested.

I sincerely hope that the subject will meet with due attention, and that the reasons for its establishment, which you have so clearly pointed out in your letter to the Secretary, will prevail upon the Legislature to place it upon a permanent and respectable footing.

With very great esteem & regard, I am, Sir, Your most Obedt. Servt.

To James Anderson

Mount Vernon, December 13, 1799.

Mr Anderson: I did not know that you were here yesterday morning until I had mounted my horse, otherwise I should have given you what I now send. As Mr. Rawlins was going to the Union Farm, to lay off the Clover lots, I sent by him the Duplicate for that Farm to his brother; and as I was going to River Farm myself, I carried a copy for that Farm to Dowdal. Both of them have been directed to consider them attentively, and to be prepared to give you their ideas of the mode of arrangeing the Work when they are called upon.

Such a Pen as I saw yesterday at Union Farm, would, if the Cattle were kept in it one Week, destroy the whole of them. They would be infinitely more comfortable in this, or any other weather, in the open fields; Dogue run Farm Pen may be in the same condition. It did not occur to me as I passed through the yard of the Barn to look into it. I am, etc.

CHRONOLOGY

NOTE ON THE TEXTS

NOTES

INDEX

Chronology

1732   Born February 22 (February 11, Old Style) on plantation
        on Potomac River between Bridges Creek and Popes
        Creek in Westmoreland County, Virginia, first child of
        Mary Ball and Augustine Washington. (Great-grandfather
        John Washington immigrated to Virginia from England in
        1657. Father, born 1694, married Jane Butler in 1715; they
        had three surviving children—Lawrence, Augustine, and
        Jane—before her death in 1729. In 1731 father married
        Mary Ball, born c. 1708.) Father is a planter, land specu-
        lator, part owner of an ironworks located near Fredericks-
        burg, Virginia, and county justice of the peace.

1733   Sister Betty born.

1734   Brother Samuel born.

1735   Half sister Jane dies. Family moves to Epsewasson, plan-
        tation on the Potomac near Little Hunting Creek in Staf-
        ford County (Fairfax County after 1742).

1736   Brother John Augustine born.

1738   Brother Charles born.

1739   Family moves to Ferry Farm on Rappahannock River in
        King George County, near Fredericksburg. Washington
        begins schooling. Sister Mildred born.

1740   Half brother Lawrence (born c. 1718) serves as officer with
        Virginia troops in the Caribbean during unsuccessful Brit-
        ish attempt to capture Cartagena from the Spanish. Sister
        Mildred dies.

1743   Father dies on April 12, leaving estate of 10,000 acres and
        50 slaves. Largest portion is bequeathed to Lawrence; at
        age 21, Washington is to receive 260-acre Ferry Farm, four
        other tracts of land, and ten slaves. On July 19 Lawrence
        marries Ann Fairfax, daughter of William Fairfax, cousin
        and land agent of Thomas, Lord Fairfax, proprietor of the

Northern Neck, a tract of over five million acres in northern Virginia.

1744–45   Lives with mother at Ferry Farm, with half brother Augustine at Westmoreland County plantation, and with Lawrence at Mount Vernon (Epsewasson plantation, now renamed in honor of Admiral Edward Vernon, commander of the Cartagena expedition). Lawrence becomes Washington's mentor and introduces him to the influential Fairfax family, whose house, Belvoir, is four miles from Mount Vernon. Washington studies mathematics, surveying, and geography along with legal forms and accounting methods used in plantation business.

1746–47   Considers joining the Royal Navy, but mother's opposition forces him to abandon the idea. Becomes proficient surveyor. Ends formal education.

1748   Joins George William Fairfax, son of William Fairfax, on surveying expedition of Fairfax lands in the Shenandoah Valley, March–April. Meets frontier settlers and Indians.

1749   With help from Fairfax family, Washington becomes surveyor of Culpeper County on July 20 (holds position until summer of 1750). Performs over 190 professional surveys between July 1749 and October 1752, mostly of Fairfax lands in the Shenandoah Valley.

1750   Buys total of 1,459 acres in Shenandoah Valley, first of many western land acquisitions.

1751   Sails to Barbados in September with Lawrence, who is suffering from chronic lung illness (probably tuberculosis). Arrives in November and is stricken with smallpox, but recovers by early December and gains lifelong immunity to the disease, a major cause of death in 18th-century army camps. Leaves Barbados in late December.

1752   Returns to Virginia in January. Lawrence Washington dies at Mount Vernon July 26, leaving the bulk of his estate to his wife, Ann, and infant daughter, Sarah. Washington joins Fredericksburg Masonic Lodge. On November 6 Virginia Council appoints him adjutant of militia for the Southern District, with rank of major.

1753   Volunteers to carry ultimatum demanding French with-
        drawal from the Ohio Valley from Lieutenant Governor
        Robert Dinwiddie (the highest-ranking British official re-
        siding in Virginia) to the commander of the French forces
        in the Valley. Receives orders from Dinwiddie to assess
        French strength and intentions and confer with leaders of
        the Iroquois Six Nations. Leaves Williamsburg on October
        31 and travels to the Forks of the Ohio (now Pittsburgh).
        Meets with Iroquois chiefs at Logstown on the Ohio, then
        goes to Fort Le Boeuf, French outpost near shore of Lake
        Erie. Delivers ultimatum on December 12 to Le Gardeur
        de Saint-Pierre, French commander in the Ohio Valley,
        who declines to comply. Begins return to Williamsburg on
        December 16.

1754   Reaches Williamsburg on January 16. Writes account of his
        journey, published in Williamsburg as *The Journal of Ma-
        jor George Washington* and reprinted in Maryland and
        Massachusetts newspapers and in London as a pamphlet.
        Commissioned lieutenant colonel of militia and adjutant
        of the Northern Neck District. Ordered to occupy Forks
        of the Ohio; sets out from Winchester on April 18 with
        force of 160 men. Learns that the French have seized the
        Forks of the Ohio. Surprises and defeats small French
        force on May 28 near present-day Uniontown, Pennsyl-
        vania, in first skirmish of what becomes the French and
        Indian War (1754–1763). Among the ten French dead is
        Ensign de Jumonville, the force's commander; although
        captured survivors insist de Jumonville was on a diplo-
        matic mission to deliver ultimatum demanding British
        evacuation of Ohio country, Washington informs Dinwid-
        die that French were engaged in a military reconnaissance.
        Writes in letter to brother John Augustine: "I heard Bul-
        letts whistle and believe me there was something charming
        in the sound." (When letter is printed in the London
        press, George II reportedly remarks: "He would not say
        so, if he had been used to hear many.") Builds Fort Ne-
        cessity at Great Meadows, Pennsylvania. French and In-
        dians attack fort on July 3; after several hours of fighting,
        Washington surrenders on terms allowing the garrison to
        withdraw to Virginia. Signs capitulation document written
        in French, which he cannot read, containing admission
        that de Jumonville had been "assassinated." (French cap-
        ture Washington's diary of the 1754 campaign; it is pub-

lished in France in 1756 and in England and the colonies in 1757, though Washington will dispute the accuracy of the printed English text.) Returns to Williamsburg on July 17. Resigns commission in October rather than accept reduction in rank to captain brought about by Dinwiddie's reorganization of the Virginia militia. Leases Mount Vernon from Ann Fairfax Lee, Lawrence's widow (now remarried), on December 17.

1755   Volunteers in spring to serve as aide, without rank or pay, to General Edward Braddock, commander in chief of British forces in North America. Despite severe attacks of illness (probably dysentery), accompanies expedition of British regulars and colonial militia against Fort Duquesne at the Forks of the Ohio. On July 9 Braddock's advance force of 1,450 men is attacked and defeated by 900 French and Indians after crossing the Monongahela seven miles from the fort. Although two horses are shot from under him and four bullets pierce his clothing, Washington is not wounded during the battle and helps command the withdrawal of surviving troops after Braddock is mortally wounded. Buries Braddock in secret grave along the retreat route on July 14. Commissioned as colonel and commander of the Virginia Regiment on August 14 with orders to defend frontier, left exposed to attack by Braddock's defeat and the withdrawal of surviving British regulars to Pennsylvania. Entered as candidate in December election for seat in House of Burgesses from Frederick County, possibly without his knowledge, but is defeated.

1756   Travels to Boston in February to confer with Massachusetts governor William Shirley, the acting British commander in chief in North America. Seeks royal commissions for himself and his officers and resolution of disputes concerning seniority of royal and colonial commissions. Returns to Virginia in March without royal commission. Struggles to defend 350 miles of frontier with inadequate resources and undisciplined militiamen.

1757   Travels to Philadelphia in February to see Lord Loudoun, new British commander in chief. Advocates mounting a new expedition against Fort Duquesne and unsuccessfully seeks royal commission. Returns to Virginia in April. Defeated again in election for House of Burgesses from Frederick County. Forced by severe dysentery to return to Mount Vernon in November for prolonged convalescence.

1758   Returns to active duty in March. Proposes marriage to Martha Dandridge Custis (b. 1731), wealthy widow of Daniel Parke Custis and mother of two young children, John Parke Custis (b. 1754) and Martha Parke Custis (b. 1756). Elected to House of Burgesses from Frederick County on July 24 (will be reelected through 1774, after 1765 from Fairfax, his home county). Commands Virginia troops in expedition against Fort Duquesne led by British brigadier John Forbes. Argues with Forbes over route expedition should use in advance to the Forks of the Ohio. Writes love letter to Sally Cary Fairfax, wife of his friend George William Fairfax. Nearly killed on November 12 when two lines of Virginia troops mistakenly exchange musket fire. British and colonial forces occupy Forks of the Ohio on November 25 after French burn and abandon Fort Duquesne. Resigns commission in December.

1759   Marries Martha Custis on January 6; Custis estate includes thousands of acres and hundreds of slaves. Attends his first session of Virginia Assembly in Williamsburg. Expands Mount Vernon estate, buying more land and slaves and enlarging mansion house; imports luxury goods from England. Orders books on agriculture and farm management. Engages in active social life, visiting and entertaining neighbors; enjoys riding, shooting, fox-hunting, and playing cards.

1761   Inherits Mount Vernon after death of Ann Fairfax Lee, Lawrence's widow (Lawrence's daughter Sarah had died in 1754).

1762   Becomes vestryman of Anglican church for Truro Parish.

1763   French and Indian War ends with Britain in possession of Canada but burdened with heavy war debt. Washington joins company of investors in plan to drain Great Dismal Swamp on Virginia–North Carolina border.

1764–67   Washington's debt to British merchants increases due to high spending on imported goods and continued difficulty in growing tobacco profitably in poor Mount Vernon soil. Plants more wheat and corn and experiments with growing hemp and flax. Makes wheat his main crop in 1767 and stops planting tobacco on his Potomac farms, though he continues to receive tobacco from tenants as rent. Stamp Act, passed by British Parliament in 1765, is repealed in 1766 after meeting with widespread colonial resistance, but in 1767 Parliament passes Townshend Acts, levying new taxes on the American colonies.

1768   Stepdaughter suffers first in series of epileptic seizures. Washington becomes a justice of the Fairfax County Court.

1769   Joins in growing colonial opposition to the Townshend Acts. Writes privately to neighbor George Mason that he would use arms as a last resort to defend American freedom. Mason drafts plan for boycott of imported British goods which Washington circulates among members of the Assembly in Williamsburg. Votes for resolutions asserting rights of Virginia colonists, including the right of self-taxation. When Governor Botetourt responds by dissolving the Assembly on May 17, delegates hold extralegal session in tavern. Washington serves on committee that drafts Nonimportation Association, which is adopted by majority of the burgesses on May 18. (Parliament repeals Townshend Acts, except for tax on tea, in 1770, and Virginia Association is dissolved in 1771.) Enlarges frontier land holdings by patenting land in western Pennsylvania and by campaigning for fulfillment of proclamation promising 200,000 acres of bounty land in Ohio Valley to members of the Virginia Regiment who participated in the 1754 campaign against the French. Takes leading role in securing fulfillment of proclamation and directs selection, surveying, and division of land among eligible officers and men. Receives 15,000 acres as a field officer; buys up rights of others (will gain title by 1773 to 24,000 acres on Ohio and Kanawha rivers in western Virginia).

1770   Joins Maryland attorney Thomas Johnson in promoting plan for improving navigation on the upper Potomac. Travels in the autumn by canoe down the Ohio from Pittsburgh to the mouth of the Kanawha River in search of land to claim under proclamation of 1754.

1771   Opens commercial flour mill at Mount Vernon; other plantation ventures designed to reduce debt owed to British merchants include weaving and commercial fishing.

1772   Has portrait painted by Charles Willson Peale at Mount Vernon in May; poses wearing uniform of colonel of the Virginia Regiment.

1773   Travels to New York City in May to enroll stepson John Parke Custis at King's College (now Columbia University). Stepdaughter Martha Parke Custis dies during epileptic seizure on June 19. Martha Washington inherits £8,000 from her daughter's share of Custis estate, which Washington uses to pay British debts.

1774   Learns while attending Assembly in May that Parliament has closed Boston harbor in retaliation for the Boston Tea Party. Votes for resolution calling for day of prayer and fasting to protest Boston Harbor Act. After Governor Dunmore responds by dissolving the Assembly on May 26, joins other delegates in adopting resolution calling for the appointment of delegates to a "general congress" of "the several Colonies of British America." Presides at Fairfax County meeting on July 18 that adopts "Fairfax Resolves," influential series of resolutions drafted by George Mason asserting colonial right of self-government and calling for a boycott of British trade. Attends Virginia Convention, extralegal session of Assembly held in Williamsburg, and is elected as one of seven Virginia delegates to the First Continental Congress. Travels to Philadelphia to attend Congress in September. Supports measures adopted by the Congress, including resolution declaring that colonial legislatures have an "exclusive power of legislation . . . in all cases of taxation and internal policy" in the colonies; a boycott of British imports; and a call for delegates to be elected to a Second Continental Congress. Returns to Mount Vernon at the end of October.

1775   Elected as one of seven Virginia delegates to Second Continental Congress at Virginia Convention, held in Richmond March 20–27. Revolutionary War begins with fighting between Massachusetts militia and British army at Lexington and Concord, April 19. New England forces besiege British in Boston. Washington is chosen as field

commander of five independent Virginia militia companies. Leaves Mount Vernon for Philadelphia on May 4
(will not see his home again until 1781). Attends sessions
of Congress in Philadelphia wearing buff and blue militia
uniform. Congress creates Continental Army on June 14;
seeking to unite colonies by appointing a southerner to
command predominately New England army, Massachusetts delegate John Adams nominates Washington to be
commander in chief. Receives unanimous vote of Congress on June 15 and accepts commission on June 16; declines salary but asks for reimbursement of expenses. Takes
command of Continental Army, numbering about 14,000
men, at Cambridge, Massachusetts, on July 3. Works to
equip, train, and reorganize army; is dismayed by lack of
discipline among New England troops and inability of
their elected officers to exercise authority. Dispatches
1,000 men under command of Benedict Arnold to join
with American forces in northern New York in attack on
Quebec (invasion of Canada ends in American defeat in
June 1776). Martha Washington arrives in Cambridge on
December 11 (she will continue to share winter quarters
with Washington throughout the war). Enlistments of
most Continental soldiers expire in December; although
many reenlist, strength of army falls to 10,000 men by end
of year.

1776   Washington becomes convinced by British policy and by
reading Thomas Paine's pamphlet *Common Sense* that
American independence is inevitable. Holds council of war
on February 16 and proposes launching assault on Boston,
but abandons plan when it is unanimously opposed by his
generals. Moves artillery brought from Fort Ticonderoga
onto Dorchester Heights overlooking the city on March
4. British evacuate Boston on March 17 and sail to Nova
Scotia. Washington marches Continental Army to New
York City in April in anticipation of British attack. British
fleet anchors off New York on June 29 and begins landing
troops on Staten Island on July 3. Washington orders Declaration of Independence read to entire army on July 9.
By mid-August Washington has 19,000 inexperienced
Continental soldiers and state militia under his command
at New York, facing 32,000 regular troops under command of General William Howe (the largest expeditionary
force in British history). British begin landing at western

end of Long Island, August 22, and defeat Americans in battle of Long Island, August 27. Washington withdraws army from Brooklyn Heights to Manhattan on August 30. Howe lands troops at Kip's Bay on east side of Manhattan on September 15, forcing Americans to retreat northward to Harlem Heights. Washington evacuates Harlem Heights on October 18 and moves army to White Plains. British attack at White Plains, October 28, forcing Americans to withdraw several miles further north. Washington divides Continental Army between New Jersey and New York banks of Hudson River and considers evacuating Fort Washington, remaining American outpost in Manhattan. British capture Fort Washington and take 2,800 prisoners on November 16, then cross Hudson on November 20 and force evacuation of Fort Lee. Washington retreats Continental Army across New Jersey and crosses Delaware River into Pennsylvania on December 8. Fears army will dissolve when enlistments of most soldiers expire at end of year. Howe abandons attempts to capture Philadelphia and disperses his army into garrisons across New Jersey. Washington leads 2,400 men across Delaware on night of December 25 and defeats Hessian garrison at Trenton, New Jersey, on morning of December 26, capturing over 900 prisoners. On December 27 Congress grants Washington extraordinary powers for six-month period, including authority to raise troops, appoint officers, requisition supplies, and arrest disloyal persons.

1777   Orders attack on British force at Princeton, New Jersey, on January 3; during battle Washington rides within 30 yards of the enemy line while leading successful assault. Victories at Trenton and Princeton strengthen American morale. Continental Army goes into winter quarters at Morristown, New Jersey, on January 6. Howe evacuates most British garrisons from New Jersey and takes his army into winter quarters in New York City. Washington pardons New Jersey citizens who swore loyalty to the crown during British advance in late 1776 on condition that they now declare allegiance to the United States. Alexander Hamilton joins Washington's military "family" (staff) in March and becomes trusted aide. By late May army at Morristown numbers 9,000 men, now equipped with arms covertly supplied by France. British and American armies maneuver inconclusively in New Jersey during

June. Howe decides to attack Philadelphia rather than move up Hudson Valley to meet British army advancing south from Canada and sails from New York with 18,000 men on July 23. British begin disembarking at Head of Elk, Maryland, on August 25 as Washington moves to defend Philadelphia. British defeat Continental Army at Brandywine Creek, Pennsylvania, September 11, and occupy Philadelphia on September 26 as Congress flees to York, Pennsylvania. Washington attacks British at Germantown, Pennsylvania, on October 4 but is forced to retreat after initial success. After series of defeats, General John Burgoyne surrenders army of 5,700 men to Americans under General Horatio Gates at Saratoga, New York, on October 17, ending British attempt to split New England off from other colonies by seizing Hudson Valley. Washington becomes alarmed by rumors of "Conway Cabal," alleged plot by General Thomas Conway to have Gates replace him as commander of the Continental Army. Congress submits proposed Articles of Confederation to states for ratification on November 15 (ratification is not completed until March 1, 1781). Washington takes army into winter quarters at Valley Forge, Pennsylvania, on December 21.

1778   Appeals to Congress for money and supplies as army suffers through winter at Valley Forge. France and the United States sign treaties of alliance and commerce in Paris on February 6; under their terms, France recognizes the independence of the United States and pledges to fight until American independence is won if the treaties lead to war between France and Britain. (News of French alliance reaches Washington at Valley Forge on May 3.) Washington wins renewed support of leaders in Congress; has army trained and drilled by Friedrich Steuben, a former Prussian officer. Sir Henry Clinton replaces Howe as British commander in chief in May. Anticipating arrival of French fleet in Delaware Bay, Clinton evacuates Philadelphia on June 18 and begins withdrawing army to New York City. Washington attacks British at Monmouth Court House, New Jersey, on June 28; battle is intense but inconclusive, and British complete march to New York. Continental Army moves to White Plains. French fleet with expeditionary force of 4,000 men under Comte d'Estaing arrives off Delaware Bay on July 8. Combined French and American attack on Newport, Rhode Island, in August fails, in part due to poor coordination between d'Estaing and American commander, General John Sullivan; failure causes mistrust between new allies. French fleet sails for West Indies on November 11. Washington establishes winter headquarters at Middlebrook, New Jersey, on December 11. British capture Savannah, Georgia, on December 29.

1779   Continues to appeal to Congress for support of army. Discouraged by desertion, rapid depreciation of Continental currency, corruption, and failure to sustain army with new enlistments ("too many melancholy proofs of the decay of public virtue"). Spain concludes alliance with France and declares war on Britain on June 21, but does not recognize American independence. Washington orders daring night attack led by General Anthony Wayne that recaptures Stony Point, New York, and takes 500 British prisoners on July 16, raising American morale and halting attempt by Clinton to extend British outposts up the Hudson Valley. Principal armies in north remain largely inactive through campaigning season while fighting continues in Georgia and South Carolina. Washington dispatches strong force under Sullivan on punitive mission against the Six Nations, British allies who have been raiding frontier settlements; expedition burns dozens of Iroquois villages in central New York. Takes army into winter quarters at Morristown, New Jersey, on December 1. Leaving garrison of 10,000 men to hold New York City, Clinton sails for South Carolina with army of 8,500 on December 26.

1780   Massachusetts troops at West Point briefly mutiny over terms of enlistment, January 1. Army at Morristown suffers from severe cold and hunger. Clinton captures Charleston, South Carolina, with over 5,000 prisoners on May 12, inflicting worst American defeat of Revolutionary War. Connecticut troops at Morristown mutiny over pay and rations, May 25, but are persuaded to return to duty. Clinton returns to New York in June, leaving behind 8,000 men under Lord Charles Cornwallis to continue campaign in the South. French expeditionary force of 5,500 men under Comte de Rochambeau lands at Newport, Rhode Island, on July 10. Cornwallis routs American army in South commanded by General Horatio Gates at Camden, South Carolina, on August 16. Washington meets with Rochambeau at Hartford, Connecticut, September 20, to discuss strategy; conference is inconclusive. Discovers treachery of General Benedict Arnold on September 25 while inspecting West Point, New York, key Hudson River fortress that Arnold has been conspiring to surrender to the British (Arnold escapes). Appoints General Nathanael Greene to succeed Gates as American commander in the South and advises him on strategy (Greene will successfully command troops in the Carolinas during 1781 campaign). Establishes winter headquarters at New Windsor, New York.

1781 Over 2,000 Pennsylvania soldiers at Morristown mutiny on January 1 and begin marching on Philadelphia. Mutiny ends January 8 after Congress makes concessions regarding pay and terms of enlistments. When New Jersey troops at Pompton mutiny on January 20, Washington sends troops from West Point to suppress mutiny by force; two ringleaders are summarily executed by firing squad on January 27. Cornwallis begins major campaign in Virginia on May 20. Washington and Rochambeau meet at Wethersfield, Connecticut, May 21–22, to plan attack on New York City. Clinton orders Cornwallis to establish strong base on Chesapeake Bay, and Cornwallis occupies Yorktown, Virginia, on August 2. American and French armies are concentrated outside New York when news arrives on August 14 that powerful French fleet under Admiral de Grasse is on its way from the West Indies to Chesapeake Bay. Washington perceives opportunity "to strike the enemy in the most vulnerable quarter" and orders march on Virginia while feinting attack on Staten Island. Directs rapid movement of more than 7,000 men, with stores and equipment, over 450 miles by land and water to Yorktown. (While traveling south with Rochambeau, Washington stops at Mount Vernon for three days in September, his first visit home since 1775.) French victory in naval battle of Chesapeake Capes on September 5 deprives Cornwallis of hope of reinforcement or evacuation by sea. Washington begins siege of Yorktown on September 30, commanding army of 9,000 American and 7,800 French soldiers. Cornwallis asks for terms on October 17; his army of 7,250 men marches out and surrenders on October 19. Cornwallis declines to attend surrender ceremony and sends a subordinate; Washington declines to accept subordinate's sword. Yorktown surrender ends British hopes of winning decisive military victory in America and brings an end to major fighting in the Revolutionary War. Stepson John Parke Custis joins staff during Yorktown siege; stricken with "camp fever," he dies November 5, leaving a widow and four young children (the two youngest will be raised by the Washingtons at Mount Vernon). Travels to Philadelphia to confer with Congress, arriving on November 26; remains for four months, while Continental Army goes into winter quarters at Newburgh, New York.

1782 Rejoins Continental Army at Newburgh on March 31. British open peace negotiations with Americans in April. Washington is outraged by May 22 letter from Colonel Lewis Nicola recommending that the army overthrow Congress and establish military rule with Washington serving as king. Orders Nicola never to speak of scheme again. American peace commissioners in Paris sign preliminary treaty with Britain on November 30.

1783 Britain, France, and Spain sign preliminary peace treaty on January 20. Anonymous papers circulated among officers at Newburgh, March 10–12, condemn Congress and exhort officers to rebel if their demands for pay are not met (discontented officers may have been working in collusion with Congressional proponents of stronger national government). Washington fears officers are "wavering on a tremendous precipice" above "a gulph of Civil horror" that threatens to "deluge our rising Empire in Blood." In dramatic meeting of March 15, wins over officers, who declare subordination to civil authority. Sets April 19, eighth anniversary of battles of Lexington and Concord, as official date for end of hostilities. Sends lengthy farewell address to state governors and legislatures on June 8, announcing intention to retire and calling for "indissoluble Union of the States under one federal Head." Elected president of Society of the Cincinnati, a fraternal organization of former Continental and French officers, on June 19. Final peace treaty is signed in Paris on September 3. British evacuate New York on November 25, and Washington leads army into city later that day. Bids emotional farewell to his officers on December 4. In carefully arranged ceremony, appears before Congress in Annapolis, Maryland, on December 23 and declares that he will never again hold public office, then hands over commission as commander in chief given him in Philadelphia in June 1775. Returns to Mount Vernon as a private citizen on December 24.

1784   Finds Mount Vernon run down after his eight-year absence. Persuaded by Thomas Jefferson and others that Society of the Cincinnati, with hereditary membership suggestive of European aristocracy, has anti-republican tendencies. Attends general meeting of the Society in May and urges abolition of hereditary membership; thereafter tries to distance himself from the organization. Revives project of improving Potomac navigation. Travels across Alleghenies in September to inspect his western lands and scout route for canals and roads designed to link tributaries of the Ohio with the Potomac.

1785   Serves as host for conference held at Mount Vernon, March 25–28, by commissioners appointed by Virginia and Maryland legislatures to resolve disputes regarding trade and navigation of common waterways. (Success of Mount Vernon conference leads to call for a general meeting of the states to discuss interstate trade.) Named president on May 17 of Potomac Navigation Company, chartered by Virginia and Maryland to build canal and road system joining Potomac and Ohio. Advocates opening of navigation as means to bind Ohio Valley settlements politically to United States. Begins correspondence with leading English agronomists, hires English agricultural workers, and imports seeds, plants, agricultural equipment, and livestock, including a Spanish jackass used to breed mules.

1786   Conducts census of 216 slaves living on Mount Vernon farms in February; about half belong to him, others to Custis estates. Declares privately that it is "among my first wishes to see some plan adopted, by which slavery in this country may be abolished by slow, sure, and imperceptible degrees." Grows increasingly concerned that weakness of Congress, state rivalries, and local unrest may sink American experiment in republican self-government into anarchy or despotism. Annapolis Convention meets September 11–14 to continue negotiations on interstate trade; delegates approve resolution calling for meeting of representatives from all states in Philadelphia on May 14, 1787, "to devise such further provisions as shall appear to them necessary to render the constitution of the Federal Government adequate to the exigencies of the Union." Washington is dismayed by reports of "Shays' Rebellion," outbreak of civil unrest by debt-burdened farmers in Massachusetts. Initially declines election by Virginia legislature on December 4 as delegate to Philadelphia convention, believing acceptance would violate 1783 pledge not to hold public office; is also wary of expending prestige on a potentially unsuccessful attempt to establish stronger national government.

1787   Urged by James Madison and Virginia governor Edmund Randolph to attend convention. Reluctantly agrees on March 28 to join Virginia delegation. Arrives in Philadelphia May 13. Unanimously elected president of the convention when quorum is reached on May 25. As presiding officer, does not take part in debates, but exerts influence by his presence (South Carolina delegate Pierce Butler later writes: "many of the members cast their eyes towards General Washington as President; and shaped their Ideas of the Powers to be given to a President, by their opinions of his Virtue"). During recess from July 26 to August 6, goes fishing and visits site of Continental Army's wartime encampment at Valley Forge. Observes local agricultural practices, poses for portraits, and visits William Bartram's botanical garden and Charles Willson Peale's museum. Convention votes September 15 to adopt Constitution. Document is presented for signing on September 17, final day of the convention. When three delegates propose changing apportionment of the House of Representatives so that the number of representatives not exceed one for every 30,000 persons instead of the 40,000 previously agreed upon, Washington speaks in debate for the first time, supporting the change in the hope that it will remove a possible objection to the Constitution. Change is adopted without opposition, and convention votes to deposit its official records in Washington's custody. Constitution is then signed by 39 delegates and forwarded to Congress and the states. Washington returns home on September 22. Closely follows ratification struggle from Mount Vernon (ratification by nine states is necessary to put Constitution into effect). Constitution is ratified in Delaware, December 7; Pennsylvania, December 12; New Jersey, December 18; and Georgia, December 31.

1788   Ratification is approved in Connecticut, January 9; Massachusetts, February 6; Maryland, April 26; and South Carolina, May 23. New Hampshire becomes ninth state to ratify, June 21, and is followed by key states of Virginia, June 27, and New York, July 26, ensuring that Constitution will go into effect. Washington remains reluctant to return to public life, but indicates in private correspondence that he would accept election to the presidency. Faced with chronic shortage of cash, tries unsuccessfully to sell or rent his Ohio lands.

1789   Presidential electors meet on February 4 and vote for two candidates in balloting for president. Washington receives votes from all 69 electors and is unanimously elected president; John Adams, with 34 votes, is elected vice-president. First Federal Congress achieves quorum in New York City on April 6, and electoral votes are officially counted. Washington is notified of his election at Mount Vernon on April 14. Borrows £600 to pay debts and for trip to New York. Greeted with pageantry and public acclaim along route. Takes oath of office at Federal Hall in New York on April 30. Offers to serve without pay, but Congress approves presidential salary of $25,000 a year. Lives in lavish style in rented New York mansion, staging elaborate weekly receptions criticized by some as monarchical in tone. Stricken in June with painful carbuncle on left leg, accompanied by high fever; recovers slowly after abscess is incised. Appears in person before the Senate on August 22 and August 24 to seek its "advice and consent" on treaty negotiations with Creek Indians; finds experience frustrating, and never again appears before the Senate to seek its advice (a precedent followed by all subsequent presidents). Mother Mary Ball Washington dies, August 25. Congress creates executive departments of State, War, and Treasury, and Washington appoints Alexander Hamilton as secretary of the treasury, Henry Knox as secretary of war, and Thomas Jefferson as secretary of state. Judiciary Act, creating federal court system and office of the attorney general, becomes law on September 24; Senate confirms appointments of Chief Justice John Jay, five associate Supreme Court justices, and Attorney General Edmund Randolph on September 26. Washington makes presidential tour of Connecticut, Massachusetts, and New Hampshire in October and November.

1790   Delivers first annual message to Congress on January 8. Hamilton submits report on public credit to Congress on January 14. Plan provides for funding of national debt of $54 million dollars through taxes and new borrowing, and for federal assumption of $25 million of debt incurred by the states during the Revolutionary War. James Madison leads successful opposition in the House to federal assumption of state debts, arguing that it unfairly discriminates against states, such as Virginia, that have already paid much of their war debt. Washington falls seriously ill with pneumonia in May; predicts after his recovery that another serious illness will kill him. Jefferson, Hamilton, and Madison agree in late June that in exchange for southern support of the assumption measure, northern members of Congress will support moving the capital to Philadelphia for ten years and then permanently establishing it along the Potomac in 1800. In November Washington arrives in Philadelphia, where the house of wealthy financier Robert Morris has been rented as presidential mansion. Hamilton submits plan to Congress on December 14 calling for chartering a national bank.

1791   Washington chooses ten-mile square area on the Potomac near Mount Vernon as site for national capital (new city is officially named "Washington" in September). Bank bill passes Congress but is opposed as unconstitutional by Madison, who urges Washington to veto it. Unsure of its constitutionality, Washington asks Randolph, Jefferson, and Hamilton for advisory opinions. Jefferson and Randolph also oppose measure as unconstitutional, but after reading Hamilton's opinion, Washington signs bill into law on February 25. Makes presidential tour of Virginia, North Carolina, South Carolina, and Georgia, April–June. Sends expedition under General Arthur St. Clair against hostile Indians in the Northwest Territory, and cautions him against being taken by surprise. Angered when St. Clair's army is routed in surprise attack on November 4 and suffers over 900 casualties. (Indians resisting American settlement in the Northwest are supplied and encouraged by the British, who continue to occupy forts in territory ceded to the United States in the 1783 peace treaty.) Washington begins meeting with Jefferson, Hamilton, Knox, and Randolph to discuss policy (term "cabinet" comes into use by 1793).

1792   Uses presidential veto power for the first time, April 5, disapproving a bill apportioning representatives on the grounds that it unconstitutionally gives some states more than one representative for every 30,000 persons; Congress sustains veto. (Washington believes veto should be used only against legislation president considers unconstitutional.) Appoints General Anthony Wayne to replace St. Clair as military commander on the Northwest frontier. Tired of public life and certain that age is diminishing his powers, intends to retire when term ends in 1793. Prepares draft of farewell address and on May 20 asks Madison to put it in final form. Madison, Jefferson, Randolph, Hamilton, Knox, and others urge him to serve another term. Dismayed by deepening personal bitterness between Hamilton and Jefferson and growing discord within the cabinet, Congress, and press as two political parties emerge—Federalists, who support Hamilton and his fiscal policies, and Republicans, whose leadership includes Jefferson and Madison. Attempts unsuccessfully to reconcile Hamilton and Jefferson. Persuaded that he must remain in office, does not announce intention to retire. Receives votes of all 132 presidential electors on December 5 and is unanimously reelected; Adams receives 77 votes and is reelected vice-president.

1793   Inaugurated for second term on March 4. When news that France has declared war on Britain arrives in April, holds cabinet meetings at which Hamilton and Jefferson disagree over proper response. Issues proclamation of neutrality on April 22 while maintaining 1778 treaty of alliance with France (action establishes important precedent regarding presidential power to make foreign policy decisions without consulting Congress). Controversy regarding relations with France increases bitterness between Republicans, who sympathize with revolutionary French republic, and Federalists, many of whom admire British constitutional monarchy. Becomes alarmed by enthusiastic public reception given to Edmond Genêt, new French minister to the United States, and rise of Democratic Societies formed by supporters of France. Refuses to allow outfitting of French privateers in American ports and asks French government to recall Genêt (will later grant Genêt asylum in the United States during the Jacobin terror).

Growing repugnance for slavery results in plan to rent Mount Vernon to capable farmers and then free his slaves, who could stay on as hired hands. Searches without success for suitable tenants. Jefferson resigns as secretary of state December 31.

1794   Names Edmund Randolph secretary of state, January 2; William Bradford becomes attorney general. Resists demands for commercial retaliation against Britain in response to British seizures of American ships trading with the French West Indies. Appoints Chief Justice John Jay, a leading New York Federalist, as special envoy to Britain on April 16 in effort to avert Anglo-American war. Wayne defeats Indian coalition at Battle of Fallen Timbers on August 20 (Indians will be forced to yield much of Ohio territory in 1795 treaty). Farmers in western Pennsylvania violently resist collection of federal excise tax on distilled spirits adopted in 1791 as part of Hamilton's plan for funding the national debt. Washington issues proclamation on August 7 calling for the insurgents to disperse and summoning 15,000 militia into service, then issues a second proclamation on September 25, calling for suppression of the insurrection. "Whiskey Rebellion" collapses without further bloodshed when Washington leads 12,000 troops into region in October (later pardons two men convicted of treason for their role in disorders). Creates controversy by accusing Democratic Societies of having fomented Whiskey Rebellion. Finds buyer for Pennsylvania frontier land (will realize $50,000 from sales of western tracts over next five years).

1795   Appoints Timothy Pickering as secretary of war and Oliver Wolcott, Jr., as secretary of the treasury after Knox and Hamilton resign in January; Hamilton continues to serve as his principal adviser. Receives on March 7 text of treaty signed by Jay in London on November 19, 1794. Treaty provides for evacuation of British garrisons from frontier posts in the Northwest but contains few British concessions regarding neutral maritime rights or terms of Anglo-American commerce. Senate ratifies treaty on June 24 after secret debate. Treaty is published on July 1 and is furiously attacked for failing to secure American rights. Despite his serious misgivings about its terms, Washington signs treaty on August 18. Forces Randolph to resign on August 19 after intercepted French diplomatic dispatch causes him to suspect Randolph of having solicited a bribe from the French. Names Pickering as secretary of state and James McHenry as secretary of war, making cabinet entirely Federalist. Appoints Charles Lee as attorney general after death of Bradford.

1796   Submits for Senate ratification treaty with Spain granting right of Mississippi River navigation to Americans; Senate ratifies treaty on March 3. House of Representatives votes on March 24 to request secret papers relating to Jay Treaty. Washington replies on March 30, withholding the papers on the grounds that the House has no constitutional role in ratifying treaties and asserting an executive right to maintain the confidentiality of diplomatic correspondence. After an intense debate, House narrowly votes on April 30 to appropriate money for implementation of Jay Treaty. Distressed by continuing attacks on his character and competence in the Republican press. Drafts farewell address and sends it to Hamilton in May for his revision. Makes public decision to retire on September 19, when farewell address is published in *American Daily Advertiser*, a Philadelphia newspaper. Delivers last annual message to Congress on December 7. In the presidential election, Federalist candidate John Adams receives 71 electoral votes and is elected president, while Jefferson, the Republican candidate, receives 68 electoral votes and becomes vice-president.

1797   Adams is inaugurated on March 4. Washington returns to Mount Vernon on March 15, gratefully taking up routine on his farms. Allows some of his household slaves to remain behind in Philadelphia, thereby giving them their freedom. Finds mansion house at Mount Vernon in need of repair. Plans new building "for the accomadation & security of my Military, Civil & private Papers." Continues revision of his French and Indian War correspondence, a task he had begun in the 1780s.

1798   Congress votes to expand army as relations with France worsen. President Adams commissions Washington as lieutenant general and commander in chief of the army on July 4. Washington insists on naming Hamilton as his second-in-command, and Adams reluctantly agrees. Travels to Philadelphia in November to direct planning of new army; returns to Mount Vernon on December 19.

1799   Supports diplomatic initiative by Adams that splits Federalist party but succeeds in preventing a full-scale war with France. Dismisses renewed suggestions that he seek third term. Drafts lengthy will in July, with detailed provisions for emancipating his slaves after Martha's death. Stipulates that his heirs provide pensions for freed slaves who are aged or infirm, and that freed slave children without parents capable of caring for them be apprenticed, taught to read and write, and "be brought up to some useful occupation" in accordance with the Virginia laws for poor white children and orphans. In schedule of property appended to will, inventories his 50,000 acres and calculates net worth at $530,000. Chilled by rain and snow during customary five-hour horseback inspection of Mount Vernon farms on December 12. Stricken with suffocating respiratory infection in early morning hours of December 14, and is treated by three physicians, who administer copious bleedings. Attended by Martha and his secretary Tobias Lear, dies while taking his own pulse sometime after 10 P.M. on the night of December 14. Buried in family vault at Mount Vernon on December 18.

Note on the Texts

This volume prints the texts of 446 documents—official and private letters, military orders, addresses, proclamations, memoranda, and diary entries—that were written by George Washington, or written at his direction, between 1747 and 1799. Most of these documents were not written for publication, and almost all of them existed only in manuscript form at the time of Washington's death in 1799.

For over 40 years Washington carefully attended to the organization, copying, and preservation of his papers. He began making copies of his outgoing correspondence in letter books while serving as a Virginia militia officer during the French and Indian War in the 1750s and continued keeping letter-book copies of both personal and business letters while living at Mount Vernon in the 1760s and early 1770s. As commander of the Continental Army, Washington wrote many letters in his own hand, but he also used the secretaries and aides who served in his military "family," including Joseph Reed, Thomas Mifflin, Robert Hanson Harrison, Tench Tilghman, Alexander Hamilton, John Laurens, and Jonathan Trumbull, Jr., to help him conduct his official correspondence. Typically Washington would give a written memorandum or an oral directive to an aide regarding the particular letter or order to be written. The aide would then prepare a draft, which Washington would review and often revise. A fair copy would be made for Washington's signature and then sent, and the revised draft would be retained at headquarters as a copy; in cases where no changes were made to the draft, it was often signed and sent after a copy was made from it. (At the beginning of the war a separate letter-book copy was often made in addition to the retained draft, but in 1776 this procedure became increasingly impracticable and fell into disuse.) In 1781–83 Washington ordered Lieutenant Colonel Richard Varick to arrange the records at Continental Army headquarters systematically; while doing so, Varick had a new transcription made of Washington's wartime correspondence, which eventually filled 44 volumes. Thus there are often three extant forms of a Washington letter sent between 1775 and 1783: the signed copy sent to the recipient; the draft retained at Continental Army headquarters; and the copy made for the Varick transcripts. (In some cases there is also a contemporary letter-book copy and in a few instances, such as letters received by the Continental Congress, a copy made by the recipient.)

At the close of the Revolutionary War Washington moved his Continental Army papers into the office wing at Mount Vernon. Sometime during the 1780s, possibly in 1786–87, he began to make revisions in letter-book copies of the letters and orders he wrote during the French and Indian War with the apparent intention of improving their clarity and diction. Washington appears not to have finished making these revisions until after his retirement from the presidency in 1797; once done, he then had the revised texts copied, possibly by his nephew Lawrence Lewis, into a new set of letter books. Only two of the original letter books from the French and Indian War, covering March 2–August 14, 1755, and June 14–September 12, 1758, are known to be extant.

During his presidency Washington continued to have copies of his correspondence and official papers recorded in letter books. At times he would ask his advisers, including Alexander Hamilton and, in his first term, James Madison and Thomas Jefferson, for assistance in drafting official papers. In his will Washington bequeathed his official and private papers to his nephew, Supreme Court justice Bushrod Washington. After Bushrod Washington's death in 1829, possession of the papers passed to Bushrod's nephew and heir, George Corbin Washington, who sold them in two lots to the United States government in 1834 and 1849 for the sum of $45,000. In 1903 the Washington papers were moved from the custody of the Department of State to the Library of Congress.

Three major editions of Washington's writings have appeared: *The Writings of George Washington*, edited by Jared Sparks (12 volumes, 1833–37); *The Writings of George Washington*, edited by Worthington Chauncey Ford (14 volumes, 1889–93); and *The Writings of George Washington from the Original Manuscript Sources, 1745–1799*, edited by John C. Fitzpatrick (39 volumes, 1931–44). A fourth edition, *The Papers of George Washington*, edited by W. W. Abbot, Dorothy Twohig, and others, is ongoing; 32 volumes have been published since 1976, and when complete this edition will be the most comprehensive edition so far.

Sparks began work on his edition in 1827 with the cooperation of Bushrod Washington and eventually included approximately 2,500 documents in it. He freely revised texts, correcting spelling and grammar, altering phrasing, omitting material he thought inconsequential, and in some instances rewriting passages. During the several years in which Sparks had custody of the Washington papers, he also mutilated or dispersed many manuscripts in order to produce souvenir autographs. Much of this material has not been subsequently located and either has never been printed or has been printed only in the form in which it appeared in the Sparks edition. Worthington Chauncey Ford exercised greater editorial restraint in preparing his edition, but he added only about 500 documents to those already published by Sparks.

The most complete edition to date is *The Writings of George Washington from the Original Manuscript Sources, 1745–1799*, edited by John C. Fitzpatrick of the Library of Congress and published under the auspices of the United States George Washington Bicentennial Commission. It contains the texts of some 17,000 Washington documents, mostly taken from the Washington papers in the Library of Congress, although in some cases Fitzpatrick was able to use the recipient's copy of a Washington letter as his text. In presenting these documents, Fitzpatrick frequently altered punctuation and paragraphing and in some instances regularized spelling, often by spelling out words that Washington had written in contracted form (e.g., printing "about" for "abt"). Fitzpatrick also printed in abbreviated form the formal closings Washington habitually used in his correspondence; for example, the closing "I have the honor to be With great respect & esteem Your Excellency's Most Obedt Humble Servt" appears in the Fitzpatrick edition as "I have the honor etc."

In 1969 work began on *The Papers of George Washington*, a new edition sponsored by the Mount Vernon Ladies' Association of the Union and the University of Virginia and published by the University Press of Virginia. The editors of *The Papers of George Washington* initiated a worldwide search for manuscript material, including both documents sent by and received by Washington, and have located, cataloged, and transcribed over 100,000 documents. Under the editorship of W. W. Abbot, Dorothy Twohig, and others, publication of *The Papers of George Washington* has proceeded in five series, of which three are still ongoing: *The Diaries of George Washington* (6 vols., 1976–79), *Colonial Series* (10 vols., 1983–95), *Revolutionary War Series* (6 vols. to date, 1985–94), *Confederation Series* (4 vols. to date, 1992–95), and *Presidential Series* (6 vols. to date, 1987–96). Whenever possible, *The Papers of George Washington* prints the recipient's copy of a Washington letter. Documents are transcribed and printed without alteration in their spelling, capitalization, paragraphing, and punctuation, except for the omission of dashes in instances where a dash appears together with another mark of punctuation.

The present volume prints 204 documents from *The Papers of George Washington*, its preferred source of texts. Another 28 documents are printed from a variety of sources, either because they were not included in the Fitzpatrick edition, or because more recent editions of the papers of Washington's correspondents (Alexander Hamilton, Thomas Jefferson, James Madison, George Mason) present texts of Washington letters with fewer editorial alterations than are present in the Fitzpatrick edition. The remaining 214 documents are taken from *The Writings of George Washington from the Original Manuscript Sources, 1745–1799,* edited by John C. Fitzpatrick.

This volume prints texts as they appeared in these sources, but with a few alterations in editorial procedure. Bracketed editorial conjectural readings in the source texts, in cases where the original manuscript text was damaged or difficult to read, are accepted without brackets in this volume when that reading seems to be the only possible one; but when it does not, or when the editor made no conjecture, the missing words are indicated by a bracketed space, i.e., [   ]. Where the editors of a source text use a bracketed space to indicate a space left blank in the manuscript, this volume uses a blank two-em space without brackets. Bracketed editorial insertions used in the source texts to expand contractions, abbreviations, or place names have been deleted in this volume. The editorial *sic* used in the Fitzpatrick edition after repeated words has been omitted in this volume and the indicated corrections accepted. In his edition, Fitzpatrick also used brackets to indicate which portions of a document were in Washington's handwriting, as opposed to that of an aide or secretary; this volume omits the brackets. In cases where the draft of a letter in Washington's handwriting contains alternate wordings supplied by an aide seeking to improve Washington's diction, Fitzpatrick printed the aide's emendations within brackets. This volume does not print these emendations and presents Washington's original version as its text. *The Papers of George Washington* presents documents from the French and Indian War letter book covering the period March 2–August 14, 1755, in texts in which material deleted by Washington while making his revisions in the 1780s and 1790s is printed with lines through the deleted material, and material added by Washington during his revisions is printed in the form of interlinear interpolations. This volume prints the deleted words without cancellations and omits the revisions printed as interpolations, presenting a clear text of the document as it was written by Washington in 1755. (*The Papers of George Washington* presents documents from the letter book for June 14–September 12, 1758, as they were originally written by Washington and indicates his subsequent revisions in footnotes.)

The following is a list of the documents included in this volume, in the order of their appearance, giving the source of each text. The most common sources are indicated by these abbreviations:

Writings   *The Writings of George Washington from the Original Manuscript Sources, 1745–1799,* edited by John C. Fitzpatrick (39 vols., Washington: United States Government Printing Office, 1931–44).

PGW: *The Diaries of George Washington* (6 vols., Charlottes-
Diaries   ville: University Press of Virginia, 1976–79). Volume I,
                edited by Donald Jackson (1976); Volume III, edited by
                Donald Jackson (1978); Volume V, edited by Donald
                Jackson and Dorothy Twohig (1979). Copyright © 1976,
                1978, 1979 by the Rectors and Visitors of the University
                of Virginia. Reprinted courtesy of the University Press
                of Virginia.

PGW: *The Papers of George Washington: Colonial Series*, vols.
Colonial   1–6, edited by W. W. Abbot, vols. 7–9, edited by W. W.
                Abbot and Dorothy Twohig, vol. 10, edited by Beverly
                H. Runge (10 vols., Charlottesville: University Press of
                Virginia, 1983–95). Volumes 1, 2 (1983), Volume 3, 4
                (1984), Volume 5, 6 (1988), Volume 7 (1990), Volume 8
                (1993), Volume 9 (1994), Volume 10 (1995). Copyright
                © 1983, 1984, 1988, 1990, 1993, 1994, 1995 by the Rectors
                and Visitors of the University of Virginia. Reprinted
                courtesy of the University Press of Virginia.

PGW: *The Papers of George Washington: Revolutionary War Se-*
Revolu-   *ries*, vols. 1–5, edited by Philander D. Chase, vol. 6, ed-
tionary   ited by Philander D. Chase and Frank E. Grizzard, Jr.,
                vol. 7 (forthcoming), edited by Philander D. Chase (6
                vols. to date, Charlottesville: University Press of Virginia,
                1985–94). Volume 1 (1985), Volume 2 (1987), Volume 3
                (1988), Volume 4 (1991), Volume 5 (1993), Volume 6
                (1994), Volume 7 (forthcoming). Copyright © 1985,
                1987, 1988, 1991, 1993, 1994 by the Rectors and Visitors
                of the University of Virginia. Reprinted courtesy of the
                University Press of Virginia.

PGW: *The Papers of George Washington: Confederation Series*,
Confed-   edited by W. W. Abbot (4 vols. to date, Charlottesville:
eration   University Press of Virginia, 1992–95). Volumes 1, 2
                (1992), Volume 3 (1994), Volume 4 (1995), Volume 5
                (forthcoming). Copyright © 1992, 1993, 1995 by the Rec-
                tors and Visitors of the University of Virginia. Reprinted
                courtesy of the University Press of Virginia.

PGW: *The Papers of George Washington: Presidential Series*, vols.
Presi-   1–4, edited by Dorothy Twohig, vol. 5, edited by Dor-
dential   othy Twohig, Mark A. Mastromarino, and Jack D.
                Warren, vol. 6, edited by Mark A. Mastromarino (6 vols.
                to date, Charlottesville: University Press of Virginia,

1987–96). Volumes 1, 2 (1987), Volume 3 (1989), Volume 4 (1993), Volumes 5, 6 (1996). Copyright © 1987, 1989, 1993, 1996 by the Rectors and Visitors of the University of Virginia. Reprinted courtesy of the University Press of Virginia.

PAH   *The Papers of Alexander Hamilton* (27 vols., New York: Columbia University Press, 1961–81). Volumes 3, 4, 5, (1962), Volume 12 (1967), edited by Harold C. Syrett and Jacob Ernest Cooke, Volume 18 (1973), Volume 20 (1974), Volume 24 (1976), edited by Harold C. Syrett. Copyright © 1962, 1967, 1973, 1974, 1976 by Columbia University Press. Reprinted with permission of the publisher.

PTJ   *The Papers of Thomas Jefferson* (26 vols. to date, Princeton: Princeton University Press, 1950–93). Volume 6 (1952), Volume 12 (1955), edited by Julian P. Boyd, Volume 24 (1990), Volume 25 (1992), edited by John Catanzariti. Copyright © 1952, 1955, 1990, 1992 by Princeton University Press. Reprinted with permission of the publisher.

THE COLONIAL PERIOD, 1747–1775

"Rules of Civility & Decent Behaviour In Company & Conversation," 1747. Charles Moore, *George Washington's Rules of Civility* (Cambridge: Houghton, Mifflin, 1926).

"A Journal of my Journey over the Mountains began Fryday the 11th. of March 1747/8," March 11–April 13, 1748. *PGW: Diaries*, vol. 1, 6–23.

Robin, c. 1749–1750. *PGW: Colonial*, vol. 1, 40–41.

Design for a Coat, c. 1749–1750. *PGW: Colonial*, vol. 1, 45–46.

Journey to the French Commandant, January 16–17, 1754. *PGW: Diaries*, vol. 1, 130–60.

Richard Corbin, January 28, 1754. *PGW: Colonial*, vol. 1, 70.

Robert Dinwiddie, April 25, 1754. *PGW: Colonial*, vol. 1, 87–90.

Robert Dinwiddie, May 18, 1754. *PGW: Colonial*, vol. 1, 98–100.

Robert Dinwiddie, May 29, 1754. *PGW: Colonial*, vol. 1, 107–13.

Robert Dinwiddie, May 29, 1754. *PGW: Colonial*, vol. 1, 116–17.

John Augustine Washington, May 31, 1754. *PGW: Colonial*, vol. 1, 118.

William Fitzhugh, November 15, 1754. *PGW: Colonial*, vol. 1, 225–26.

Mary Ball Washington, May 6, 1755. *PGW: Colonial*, vol. 1, 268–69.

John Augustine Washington, May 14, 1755. *PGW: Colonial*, vol. 1, 271–72.

John Augustine Washington, May 28, 1755. *PGW: Colonial*, vol. 1, 289–92.

Sarah Cary Fairfax, June 7, 1755. *PGW: Colonial*, vol. 1, 308–9.

John Augustine Washington, June 28, 1755. *PGW: Colonial*, vol. 1, 319–24.

Robert Dinwiddie, July 18, 1755. *PGW: Colonial*, vol. 1, 339–40.

John Augustine Washington, July 18, 1755. *PGW: Colonial*, vol. 1, 343.

Mary Ball Washington, August 14, 1755. *PGW: Colonial*, vol. 1, 359–60.

General Orders, October 6, 1755. *PGW: Colonial*, vol. 2, 75–76.

Christopher Gist, October 10, 1755. *PGW: Colonial*, vol. 2, 98–99.

Robert Dinwiddie, October 11, 1755. *PGW: Colonial*, vol. 2, 101–7.

Robert Dinwiddie, December 5, 1755. *PGW: Colonial*, vol. 2, 200–2.

Robert Hunter Morris, April 9, 1756. *PGW: Colonial*, vol. 2, 345–46.

Robert Dinwiddie, April 18, 1756. *PGW: Colonial*, vol. 3, 13–15.

Robert Dinwiddie, April 22, 1756. *PGW: Colonial*, vol. 3, 33–34.

General Orders, May 3, 1756. *PGW: Colonial*, vol. 3, 79–80.

General Orders, May 21, 1756. *PGW: Colonial*, vol. 3, 169.

Robert Dinwiddie, May 23, 1756. *PGW: Colonial*, vol. 3, 171–73.

General Orders, June 1, 1756. *PGW: Colonial*, vol. 3, 188–89.

The Earl of Loudoun, July 25, 1756. *PGW: Colonial*, vol. 3, 293–94.

Robert Dinwiddie, October 10, 1756. *PGW: Colonial*, vol. 3, 430–34.

Robert Dinwiddie, March 10, 1757. *PGW: Colonial*, vol. 4, 112–15.

Richard Washington, April 15, 1757. *PGW: Colonial*, vol. 4, 132–34.

John Stanwix, July 15, 1757. *PGW: Colonial*, vol. 4, 306–7.

Robert Dinwiddie, September 17, 1757. *PGW: Colonial*, vol. 4, 411–12.

John Stanwix, April 10, 1758. *PGW: Colonial*, vol. 5, 117–18.

James Wood, c. July 28, 1758. *PGW: Colonial*, vol. 5, 349.

Francis Halkett, August 2, 1758. *PGW: Colonial*, vol. 5, 360–1.

Sarah Cary Fairfax, September 12, 1758. *PGW: Colonial*, vol. 6, 10–12.

Farewell Address to the Virginia Regiment, January 10, 1759. *PGW: Colonial*, vol. 6, 186–87.

Robert Cary & Company, May 1, 1759. *PGW: Colonial*, vol. 6, 315–16.

Richard Washington, September 20, 1759. *PGW: Colonial*, vol. 6, 358–59.

Diary Entry, May 22, 1760. *PGW: Diaries*, vol. 1, 283.

Reward for Runaway Slaves, August 11, 1761. *PGW: Colonial*, vol. 7, 65–66.

Richard Washington, October 20, 1761. *PGW: Colonial*, vol. 7, 80–81.

Robert Cary & Company, May 28, 1762. *PGW: Colonial*, vol. 7, 135–37.

Charles Lawrence, April 26, 1763. *PGW: Colonial*, vol. 7, 201–2.

Robert Stewart, April 27, 1763. *PGW: Colonial*, vol. 7, 205–7.

Robert Cary & Company, August 10, 1764. *PGW: Colonial*, vol. 7, 323–26.

Robert Cary & Company, September 20, 1765. *PGW: Colonial*, vol. 7, 398–402.

Joseph Thompson, July 2, 1766. *PGW: Colonial*, vol. 7, 453–54.

John Posey, June 24, 1767. *PGW: Colonial*, vol. 8, 1–4.

Capel and Osgood Hanbury, July 25, 1767. *PGW: Colonial*, vol. 8, 14–15.

William Crawford, September 17, 1767. *PGW: Colonial*, vol. 8, 26–29.

Jonathan Boucher, May 30, 1768. *PGW: Colonial*, vol. 8, 89–90.

Robert Cary & Company, June 6, 1768. *PGW: Colonial*, vol. 8, 92–93.

William Ramsay, January 29, 1769. *PGW: Colonial*, vol. 8, 167–68.

George Mason, April 5, 1769. *PGW: Colonial*, vol. 8, 177–80.

Robert Cary & Company, July 25, 1769. *PGW: Colonial*, vol. 8, 229–30.

Charles Washington, January 31, 1770. *PGW: Colonial*, vol. 8, 300–3.
Thomas Johnson, July 20, 1770. *PGW: Colonial*, vol. 8, 357–60.
Jonathan Boucher, July 9, 1771. *PGW: Colonial*, vol. 8, 494–97.
Jonathan Boucher, May 21, 1772. *PGW: Colonial*, vol. 9, 49.
Benedict Calvert, April 3, 1773. *PGW: Colonial*, vol. 9, 209–10.
Burwell Bassett, June 20, 1773. *PGW: Colonial*, vol. 9, 243–44.
George Muse, January 29, 1774. *PGW: Colonial*, vol. 9, 460–61.
George William Fairfax, June 10, 1774. *PGW: Colonial*, vol. 10, 94–98.
Bryan Fairfax, July 4, 1774. *PGW: Colonial*, vol. 10, 109–10.
Bryan Fairfax, July 20, 1774. *PGW: Colonial*, vol. 10, 128–31.
Bryan Fairfax, August 24, 1774. *PGW: Colonial*, vol. 10, 154–56.
Robert McKenzie, October 9, 1774. *PGW: Colonial*, vol. 10, 171–72.
John West, January 13, 1775. *PGW: Colonial*, vol. 10, 234–35.
John Connolly, February 25, 1775. *PGW: Colonial*, vol. 10, 273–74.
George William Fairfax, May 31, 1775. *PGW: Colonial*, vol. 10, 367–68.

COMMANDER OF THE CONTINENTAL ARMY, 1775–1783

Address to the Continental Congress, June 16, 1775. *PGW: Revolutionary*, vol. 1, 1.
Martha Washington, June 18, 1775. *PGW: Revolutionary*, vol. 1, 3–5.
Burwell Bassett, June 19, 1775. *PGW: Revolutionary*, vol. 1, 12–15.
John Augustine Washington, June 20, 1775. *PGW: Revolutionary*, vol. 1, 19–20.
To the Officers of Five Virginia Companies, June 20, 1775. *PGW: Revolutionary*, vol. 1, 16–17.
Martha Washington, June 23, 1775. *PGW: Revolutionary*, vol. 1, 27.
Address to the New York Provincial Congress, June 26, 1775. *PGW: Revolutionary*, vol. 1, 41.
General Orders, July 4, 1775. *PGW: Revolutionary*, vol. 1, 54–56.
Richard Henry Lee, July 10, 1775. *PGW: Revolutionary*, vol. 1, 98–100.
John Augustine Washington, July 27, 1775. *PGW: Revolutionary*, vol. 1, 183–84.
Thomas Gage, August 11, 1775. *PGW: Revolutionary*, vol. 1, 289–90.
Thomas Gage, August 19, 1775. *PGW: Revolutionary*, vol. 1, 326–27.
Lund Washington, August 20, 1775. *PGW: Revolutionary*, vol. 1, 334–37.
To the Inhabitants of Bermuda, September 6, 1775. *PGW: Revolutionary*, vol. 1, 419–20.
To the Inhabitants of Canada, September 14, 1775. *PGW: Revolutionary*, vol. 1, 461–62.
William Woodford, November 10, 1775. *PGW: Revolutionary*, vol. 2, 346–47.
Lund Washington, November 26, 1775. *PGW: Revolutionary*, vol. 2, 431–33.
Benedict Arnold, December 5, 1775. *PGW: Revolutionary*, vol. 2, 493–94.
Joseph Reed, December 15, 1775. *PGW: Revolutionary*, vol. 2, 551–53.
General Orders, January 1, 1776. *PGW: Revolutionary*, vol. 3, 1–3.
Joseph Reed, January 4, 1776. *PGW: Revolutionary*, vol. 3, 23–25.

Joseph Reed, January 14, 1776. *PGW: Revolutionary*, vol. 3, 87–91.

Joseph Reed, January 31, 1776. *PGW: Revolutionary*, vol. 3, 225–29.

Joseph Reed, February 1, 1776. *PGW: Revolutionary*, vol. 3, 237–39.

John Hancock, February 9, 1776. *PGW: Revolutionary*, vol. 3, 274–76.

Joseph Reed, February 10, 1776. *PGW: Revolutionary*, vol. 3, 286–90.

Phillis Wheatley, February 28, 1776. *PGW: Revolutionary*, vol. 3, 387.

John Hancock, March 19, 1776. *PGW: Revolutionary*, vol. 3, 489–91.

John Augustine Washington, March 31, 1776. *PGW: Revolutionary*, vol. 3, 566–70.

John Augustine Washington, May 31, 1776. *PGW: Revolutionary*, vol. 4, 411–13.

General Orders, July 2, 1776. *PGW: Revolutionary*, vol. 5, 179–81.

General Orders, July 9, 1776. *PGW: Revolutionary*, vol. 5, 245–47.

John Hancock, July 14, 1776. *PGW: Revolutionary*, vol. 5, 304–7.

Adam Stephen, July 20, 1776. *PGW: Revolutionary*, vol. 5, 408–9.

General Orders, August 1, 1776. *PGW: Revolutionary*, vol. 5, 534–35.

Lund Washington, August 19, 1776. *PGW: Revolutionary*, vol. 6, 82–86.

General Orders, August 23, 1776. *PGW: Revolutionary*, vol. 6, 109–10.

John Hancock, September 8, 1776. *PGW: Revolutionary*, vol. 6, 248–52.

John Augustine Washington, September 22, 1776. *PGW: Revolutionary*, vol. 6, 371–74.

John Hancock, September 24, 1776. *PGW: Revolutionary*, vol. 6, 387–88.

Lund Washington, September 30, 1776. *PGW: Revolutionary*, vol. 6, 440–43.

To the Massachusetts General Court, November 6, 1776. *PGW: Revolutionary*, vol. 7 (forthcoming), 100–1.

John Augustine Washington, November 6, 1776. *PGW: Revolutionary*, vol. 7 (forthcoming), 102–5.

John Hancock, December 5, 1776. *PGW: Revolutionary*, vol. 7 (forthcoming), 262–64.

Lund Washington, December 10, 1776. *PGW: Revolutionary*, vol. 7 (forthcoming), 289–92.

John Hancock, December 27, 1776. *PGW: Revolutionary*, vol. 7 (forthcoming), 454–56.

Robert Morris, George Clymer, and George Walton, January 1, 1777. *Writings*, vol. 6, 463–65.

John Hancock, January 5, 1777. *Writings*, vol. 6, 467–71.

Proclamation Concerning Loyalists, January 25, 1777. *Writings*, vol. 7, 61–62.

Benedict Arnold, April 3, 1777. *Writings*, vol. 7, 352–53.

Alexander Spotswood, April 30, 1777. *Writings*, vol. 7, 494–95.

James Warren, May 23, 1777. *Writings*, vol. 8, 101.

John Hancock, September 11, 1777. *Writings*, vol. 9, 207–8.

Richard Henry Lee, October 17, 1777. *Writings*, vol. 9, 387–90.

John Augustine Washington, October 18, 1777. *Writings*, vol. 9, 397–99.

Israel Putnam, October 19, 1777. *Writings*, vol. 9, 400–1.

Thomas Conway, c. November 5, 1777. *Writings*, vol. 10, 29.

General Orders, December 17, 1777. *Writings*, vol. 10, 167–68.

Henry Laurens, December 23, 1777. *Writings*, vol. 10, 192–98.
Henry Laurens, January 2, 1778. *Writings*, vol. 10, 249–50.
Horatio Gates, January 4, 1778. *Writings*, vol. 10, 263–65.
William Howe, January 30, 1778. *Writings*, vol. 10, 408–9.
Henry Laurens, January 31, 1778. *Writings*, vol. 10, 410–11.
William Gordon, February 15, 1778. *Writings*, vol. 10, 462–63.
George Clinton, February 16, 1778. *Writings*, vol. 10, 469–70.
Bryan Fairfax, March 1, 1778. *Writings*, vol. 11, 2–5.
General Orders, March 1, 1778. *Writings*, vol. 11, 8–12.
John Banister, April 21, 1778. *Writings*, vol. 11, 284–93.
John Augustine Washington, May 1778. *Writings*, vol. 11, 500–2.
General Orders, May 5, 1778. *Writings*, vol. 11, 353–56.
Robert Morris, May 25, 1778. *Writings*, vol. 11, 453.
Landon Carter, May 30, 1778. *Writings*, vol. 11, 492–6.
Henry Laurens, July 1, 1778. *Writings*, vol. 12, 139–46.
Thomas Nelson, August 20, 1778. *Writings*, vol. 12, 341–43.
Comte d'Estaing, September 11, 1778. *Writings*, vol. 12, 423–28.
Gouverneur Morris, October 4, 1778. *Writings*, vol. 13, 21–23.
Henry Laurens, November 14, 1778. *Writings*, vol. 13, 254–57.
Benjamin Harrison, December 18, 1778. *Writings*, vol. 13, 462–68.
Lund Washington, February 24, 1779. *Writings*, vol. 14, 147–49.
Thomas Nelson, March 15, 1779. *Writings*, vol. 14, 246–47.
Henry Laurens, March 20, 1779. *Writings*, vol. 14, 263–64.
George Mason, March 27, 1779. *The Papers of George Mason*, vol. 2, edited by
    Robert A. Rutland (Chapel Hill: University of North Carolina Press, 1970),
    491–94. Copyright © 1970 by the University of North Carolina Press. Used
    by permission of the publisher.
James Warren, March 31, 1779. *Writings*, vol. 14, 311–14.
Elias Boudinot, May 3, 1779. *Writings*, vol. 14, 478–79.
William Maxwell, May 7, 1779. *Writings*, vol. 15, 13–16.
Gouverneur Morris, May 8, 1779. *Writings*, vol. 15, 23–26.
Speech to the Delaware Chiefs, May 12, 1779. *Writings*, vol. 15, 53–56.
Circular to State Governments, May 22, 1779. *Writings*, vol. 15, 122–24.
Marquis de Lafayette, July 4, 1779. *Writings*, vol. 15, 369–70.
John Cochran, August 16, 1779. *Writings*, vol. 16, 116–17.
Lund Washington, August 17, 1779. *Writings*, vol. 16, 123–25.
John Jay, September 7, 1779. *Writings*, vol. 16, 246–49.
Marquis de Lafayette, September 30, 1779. *Writings*, vol. 16, 368–76.
Benjamin Harrison, October 25, 1779. *Writings*, vol. 17, 20–23.
Robert Howe, November 20, 1779. *Writings*, vol. 17, 144–46.
Joseph Jones, May 14, 1780. *Writings*, vol. 18, 356–58.
Joseph Reed, May 28, 1780. *Writings*, vol. 18, 434–40.
Joseph Jones, May 31, 1780. *Writings*, vol. 18, 452–54.
John Augustine Washington, June 6, 1780. *Writings*, vol. 18, 482–85.
Benedict Arnold, August 3, 1780. *Writings*, vol. 19, 309–11.
Joseph Jones, August 13, 1780. *Writings*, vol. 19, 366–69.

Circular to State Governments, August 27, 1780. *Writings*, vol. 19, 449–51.
Samuel Huntington, September 26, 1780. *Writings*, vol. 20, 91–93.
Henry Clinton, September 30, 1780. *Writings*, vol. 20, 103–4.
Instructions to Spies Going into New York, c. September 1780. *Writings*, vol. 20, 104–5.
John Cadwalader, October 5, 1780. *Writings*, vol. 20, 121–23.
John Laurens, October 13, 1780. *Writings*, vol. 20, 172–74.
Circular to State Governments, October 18, 1780. *Writings*, vol. 20, 204–11.
William Fitzhugh, October 22, 1780. *Writings*, vol. 20, 246–47.
George Mason, October 22, 1780. *Writings*, vol. 20, 241–42.
Benjamin Franklin, December 20, 1780. *Writings*, vol. 20, 507–8.
James Duane, December 26, 1780. *Writings*, vol. 21, 13–16.
Circular to New England State Governments, January 5, 1781. *Writings*, vol. 21, 61–63.
John Laurens, January 15, 1781. *Writings*, vol. 21, 105–10.
Sarah Bache, January 15, 1781. *Writings*, vol. 21, 101–2.
Robert Howe, January 22, 1781. *Writings*, vol. 21, 128–29.
Circular to State Governments, January 22, 1781. *Writings*, vol. 21, 129–31.
General Orders, January 30, 1781. *Writings*, vol. 21, 158–60.
John Parke Custis, February 28, 1781. *Writings*, vol. 21, 318–21.
Lund Washington, April 30, 1781. *Writings*, vol. 22, 14–15.
Journal of the Yorktown Campaign, May 1–November 5, 1781. *Papers: Diaries*, vol. 3, 356–436.
Charles Cornwallis, October 17, 1781. *Writings*, vol. 23, 236–37.
Thomas McKean, October 19, 1781. *Writings*, vol. 23, 241–44.
Thomas Nelson, October 27, 1781. *Writings*, vol. 23, 271–72.
Thomas McKean, November 15, 1781. *Writings*, vol. 23, 342–43.
Lewis Nicola, May 22, 1782. *Writings*, vol. 24, 272–73.
John Price Posey, August 7, 1782. *Writings*, vol. 24, 485–87.
Thomas Paine, September 18, 1782. *Writings*, vol. 25, 176–77.
Benjamin Lincoln, October 2, 1782. *Writings*, vol. 25, 226–29.
James McHenry, October 17, 1782. *Writings*, vol. 25, 267–70.
Benjamin Franklin, October 18, 1782. *Writings*, vol. 25, 272–73.
William Gordon, October 23, 1782. *Writings*, vol. 25, 287–89.
Joseph Jones, December 14, 1782. *Writings*, vol. 25, 430–31.
Tench Tilghman, January 10, 1783. *Writings*, vol. 26, 27–30.
Bushrod Washington, January 15, 1783. *Writings*, vol. 26, 38–40.
Nathanael Greene, February 6, 1783. *Writings*, vol. 26, 103–5.
Thomas Jefferson, February 10, 1783. *PTJ*, vol. 6, 233–34.
Lund Washington, February 12, 1783. *Writings*, vol. 26, 126–27.
Alexander Hamilton, March 4, 1783. *PAH*, vol. 3, 277–79.
General Orders, March 11, 1783. *Writings*, vol. 26, 208–9.
Alexander Hamilton, March 12, 1783. *PAH*, vol. 3, 286–88.
Joseph Jones, March 12, 1783. *Writings*, vol. 26, 213–16.
Elias Boudinot, March 12, 1783. *Writings*, vol. 26, 211–12.
Speech to the Officers of the Army, March 15, 1783. *Writings*, vol. 26, 222–27.

Elias Boudinot, March 16, 1783. *Writings*, vol. 26, 228.
Joseph Jones, March 18, 1783. *Writings*, vol. 26, 232–34.
Lund Washington, March 19, 1783. *Writings*, vol. 26, 245–46.
Nathanael Greene, March 31, 1783. *Writings*, vol. 26, 275.
Alexander Hamilton, March 31, 1783. *PAH*, vol. 3, 309–11.
Theodorick Bland, April 4, 1783. *Writings*, vol. 26, 285–91.
Marquis de Lafayette, April 5, 1783. *Writings*, vol. 26, 297–301.
Guy Carleton, April 9, 1783. *Writings*, vol. 26, 307–8.
General Orders, April 18, 1783. *Writings*, vol. 26, 334–37.
Tench Tilghman, April 24, 1783. *Writings*, vol. 26, 358–59.
Circular to State Governments, June 8, 1783. *Writings*, vol. 26, 483–96.
John Augustine Washington, June 15, 1783. *Writings*, vol. 27, 11–13.
Elias Boudinot, June 17, 1783. *Writings*, vol. 27, 16–18.
William Gordon, July 8, 1783. *Writings*, vol. 27, 48–52.
Robert Stewart, August 10, 1783. *Writings*, vol. 27, 88–90.
James Duane, September 7, 1783. *Writings*, vol. 27, 133–40.
Lund Washington, September 20, 1783. *Writings*, vol. 27, 157–58.
Farewell Address to the Armies of the United States, November 2, 1783. *Writings*, vol. 27, 222–27.
Thomas Mifflin, December 20, 1783. *Writings*, vol. 27, 277–78.
Address to Congress on Resigning Commission, December 23, 1783. *Writings*, vol. 27, 284–85.

THE CONFEDERATION PERIOD, 1783–1789

George Clinton, December 28, 1783. *Writings*, vol. 27, 287–88.
Benjamin Harrison, January 18, 1784. *PGW: Confederation*, vol. 1, 56–57.
Marquis de Lafayette, February 1, 1784. *PGW: Confederation*, vol. 1, 87–89.
Tench Tilghman, March 24, 1784. *PGW: Confederation*, vol. 1, 232.
James Craik, March 25, 1784. *PGW: Confederation*, vol. 1, 234–36.
Marquise de Lafayette, April 4, 1784. *PGW: Confederation*, vol. 1, 257–58.
William Gordon, May 8, 1784. *PGW: Confederation*, vol. 1, 376–77.
Benjamin Harrison, October 10, 1784. *PGW: Confederation*, vol. 2, 89–9
Richard Henry Lee, December 14, 1784. *PGW: Confederation*, vol. 2, 181–3.
William Gordon, December 20, 1784. *PGW: Confederation*, vol. 2, 196–97.
Benjamin Harrison, January 22, 1785. *PGW: Confederation*, vol. 2, 282–84.
George William Fairfax, February 27, 1785. *PGW: Confederation*, vol. 2, 386–90.
Francis Hopkinson, May 16, 1785. *PGW: Confederation*, vol. 2, 561–62.
Tench Tilghman, June 2, 1785. *PGW: Confederation*, vol. 3, 33–34.
William Goddard, June 11, 1785. *PGW: Confederation*, vol. 3, 50.
David Humphreys, July 25, 1785. *PGW: Confederation*, vol. 3, 148–151.
Marquis de Lafayette, July 25, 1785. *PGW: Confederation*, vol. 3, 151–55.
Edmund Randolph, July 30, 1785. *PGW: Confederation*, vol. 3, 163–64.
James McHenry, August 22, 1785. *PGW: Confederation*, vol. 3, 197–99.
George Mason, October 3, 1785. *PGW: Confederation*, vol. 3, 292–93.
James Warren, October 7, 1785. *PGW: Confederation*, vol. 3, 298–301.

Robert Morris, April 12, 1786. *PGW: Confederation*, vol. 4, 15–16.

Marquis de Lafayette, May 10, 1786. *PGW: Confederation*, vol. 4, 41–44.

William Fitzhugh, May 15, 1786. *PGW: Confederation*, vol. 4, 52.

John Jay, May 18, 1786. *PGW: Confederation*, vol. 4, 55–56.

Thomas Jefferson, August 1, 1786. *PGW: Confederation*, vol. 4, 183–85.

Arthur Young, August 6, 1786. *PGW: Confederation*, vol. 4, 196–98.

John Jay, August 15, 1786. *PGW: Confederation*, vol. 4, 212–13.

John Francis Mercer, September 9, 1786. *PGW: Confederation*, vol. 4, 243–44.

Henry Lee, October 31, 1786. *PGW: Confederation*, vol. 4, 318–20.

Comments on David Humphreys' Biography of Washington, October 1786. *Writings*, vol. 29, 36–50.

James Madison, November 5, 1786. *PGW: Confederation*, vol. 4, 331–32.

James Madison, November 18, 1786. *PGW: Confederation*, vol. 4, 382–83.

James Madison, December 16, 1786. *PGW: Confederation*, vol. 4, 457–59.

Edmund Randolph, December 21, 1786. *PGW: Confederation*, vol. 4, 471–72.

Henry Knox, December 26, 1786. *PGW: Confederation*, vol. 4, 481–84.

David Humphreys, December 26, 1786. *PGW: Confederation*, vol. 4, 477–80.

Henry Knox, February 3, 1787. *PGW: Confederation*, vol. 5 (forthcoming), 8–9.

Mary Ball Washington, February 15, 1787. *PGW: Confederation*, vol. 5 (forthcoming), 33–36.

Henry Knox, February 25, 1787. *PGW: Confederation*, vol. 5 (forthcoming), 52–53.

Henry Knox, March 8, 1787. *PGW: Confederation*, vol. 5 (forthcoming), 74–75.

John Jay, March 10, 1787. *PGW: Confederation*, vol. 5 (forthcoming), 79–80.

Edmund Randolph, March 28, 1787. *PGW: Confederation*, vol. 5 (forthcoming), 112–14.

James Madison, March 31, 1787. *The Papers of James Madison*, vol. 9, edited by Robert A. Rutland and William M. E. Rachal (Chicago: University of Chicago Press, 1975), 342–44. Copyright © 1975 by the University of Chicago. Reprinted by permission.

Edmund Randolph, April 9, 1787. *PGW: Confederation*, vol. 5 (forthcoming), 135–36.

Contract with Philip Bater, April 23, 1787. *Writings*, vol. 29, 206–7.

Marquis de Lafayette, June 6, 1787. *PGW: Confederation*, vol. 5 (forthcoming), 221–22.

Alexander Hamilton, July 10, 1787. *PAH*, vol. 4, 225.

John Cannon, September 16, 1787. *PGW: Confederation*, vol. 5 (forthcoming), 325–26.

To the Continental Congress, September 17, 1787. *The Debate on the Constitution, Part One*, edited by Bernard Bailyn (New York: The Library of America, 1993), 965–66.

Diary Entry, September 17, 1787. *PGW: Diaries*, vol. 5, 185.

Patrick Henry, September 24, 1787. *PGW: Confederation*, vol. 5 (forthcoming), 339–40, headed "To Benjamin Harrison."

David Humphreys, October 10, 1787. *PGW: Confederation*, vol. 5 (forthcoming), 365–66.

Henry Knox, October 15, 1787. *PGW: Confederation*, vol. 5 (forthcoming), 375–76.

Bushrod Washington, November 9, 1787. *PGW: Confederation*, vol. 5 (forthcoming), 421–24.

Thomas Jefferson, January 1, 1788. *PTJ*, vol. 12, 488–91.

Edmund Randolph, January 8, 1788. *Writings*, vol. 29, 357–58.

Marquis de Lafayette, February 7, 1788. *Writings*, vol. 29, 409–12.

John Armstrong, April 25, 1788. *Writings*, vol. 29, 464–67.

Marquis de Lafayette, April 28, 1788. *Writings*, vol. 29, 475–80.

Marquis de Chastellux, April 25, 1788. *Writings*, vol. 29, 483–86.

Marquis de Lafayette, May 28, 1788. *Writings*, vol. 29, 506–8.

Marquis de Lafayette, June 19, 1788. *Writings*, vol. 29, 522–26.

Richard Henderson, June 19, 1788. *Writings*, vol. 29, 519–22.

Benjamin Lincoln, June 29, 1788. *Writings*, vol. 30, 11–12.

Noah Webster, July 31, 1788. *Writings*, vol. 30, 26–28.

Alexander Hamilton, August 28, 1788. *PAH*, vol. 5, 206–8.

Edward Newenham, August 29, 1788. *Writings*, vol. 30, 70–74.

Alexander Hamilton, October 3, 1788. *PGW: Presidential*, vol. 1, 31–33.

Benjamin Lincoln, October 26, 1788. *PGW: Presidential*, vol. 1, 70–73.

Reflection on Slavery, c. 1788–1789. *David Humphreys' "Life of General Washington" with George Washington's "Remarks"*, edited by Rosemarie Zagarri (Athens: University of Georgia Press, 1991), p. 78. Copyright © 1991 by the University of Georgia Press. Reprinted by permission of the publisher.

Fragments of a Draft of the First Inaugural Address, c. January, 1789. *PGW: Presidential*, vol. 2, 158–73.

Marquis de Lafayette, January 29, 1789. *PGW: Presidential*, vol. 1, 262–64.

Richard Conway, March 4, 1789. *PGW: Presidential*, vol. 1, 361–62.

George Steptoe Washington, March 23, 1789. *PGW: Presidential*, vol. 1, 438–41.

James Madison, March 30, 1789. *PGW: Presidential*, vol. 1, 464–65.

Thomas Green, March 31, 1789. *PGW: Presidential*, vol. 1, 467–69.

Henry Knox, April 1, 1789. *PGW: Presidential*, vol. 2, 2.

PRESIDENT, 1789–1797

Reply to Charles Thomson, April 14, 1789. *PGW: Presidential*, vol. 2, 56.

John Langdon, April 14, 1789. *PGW: Presidential*, vol. 2, 54.

Diary Entries, April 16 and 23, 1789. *PGW: Diaries*, vol. 5, 445–47.

First Inaugural Address, April 30, 1789. *PGW: Presidential*, vol. 2, 173–77.

James Madison, May 5, 1789. *PGW: Presidential*, vol. 2, 216–17.

Edward Rutledge, May 5, 1789. *PGW: Presidential*, vol. 2, 217–18.

Reply to the House of Representatives, May 8, 1789. *PGW: Presidential*, vol. 2, 232.

John Adams, May 10, 1789. *PGW: Presidential*, vol. 2, 245–47.

To the United Baptist Churches in Virginia, May 1789. *PGW: Presidential*, vol. 2, 423–24.

Betty Washington Lewis, September 13, 1789. *PGW: Presidential*, vol. 4, 32–35.

Arthur St. Clair, October 6, 1789. *PGW: Presidential*, vol. 4, 140–42.

Gouverneur Morris, October 13, 1789. *PGW: Presidential*, vol. 4, 176–79.

First Annual Message to Congress, January 8, 1790. *PGW: Presidential*, vol. 4, 543–46.

Catharine Macaulay Graham, January 9, 1790. *PGW: Presidential*, vol. 4, 551–54.

Thomas Jefferson, January 21, 1790. *PGW: Presidential*, vol. 5, 29–31.

David Stuart, March 28, 1790. *PGW: Presidential*, vol. 5, 286–87.

Comte de la Luzerne, April 29, 1790. *PGW: Presidential*, vol. 5, 358–60.

David Stuart, June 15, 1790. *PGW: Presidential*, vol. 5, 524–27.

Marquis de Lafayette, August 11, 1790. *PGW: Presidential*, vol. 6, 233–35.

To the Hebrew Congregation in Newport, Rhode Island, August 18, 1790. *PGW: Presidential*, vol. 6, 284–86.

Henry Knox, November 19, 1790. *PGW: Presidential*, vol. 6, 668–70.

Second Annual Message to Congress, December 8, 1790. *Writings*, vol. 31, 164–69.

To the Chiefs of the Seneca Nation, December 29, 1790. *Writings*, vol. 31, 179–84.

Message to Congress Concerning the Seat of Government, January 24, 1791. *Writings*, vol. 31, 202–4.

David Humphreys, July 20, 1791. *Writings*, vol. 31, 317–21.

Marquis de Lafayette, July 28, 1791. *Writings*, vol. 31, 324–26.

Gouverneur Morris, July 28, 1791. *Writings*, vol. 31, 326–30.

Jean Baptiste Ternant, September 24, 1791. *Writings*, vol. 31, 375–76.

Tobias Lear, October 14, 1791. *Writings*, vol. 31, 387–88.

Third Annual Message to Congress, October 25, 1791. *Writings*, vol. 31, 396–404.

Harriot Washington, October 30, 1791. *Writings*, vol. 31, 407–9.

Alexander Martin, November 14, 1791. *Writings*, vol. 31, 415–16.

Arthur Young, December 5, 1791. *Writings*, vol. 31, 436–40.

Gouverneur Morris, January 28, 1792. *Writings*, vol. 31, 468–70.

David Stuart, April 8, 1792. *Writings*, vol. 32, 18–19.

Isaac Heard, May 2, 1792. *Writings*, vol. 32, 31–33.

Comte de Ségur, May 4, 1792. *Writings*, vol. 32, 33.

James Madison, May 20, 1792. *The Papers of James Madison*, vol. 14, edited by Robert A. Rutland and Thomas A. Mason (Charlottesville: University Press of Virginia, 1983), 310–12. Copyright © 1983 by the Rectors and Visitors of the University of Virginia. Reprinted courtesy of the University Press of Virginia.

Marquis de Lafayette, June 10, 1792. *Writings*, vol. 32, 53–55.

Thomas Jefferson, July 17, 1792. *PTJ*, vol. 24, 238.

Alexander Hamilton, July 29, 1792. *PAH*, vol. 12, 129–34.

Tobias Lear, July 30, 1792. *Writings*, vol. 32, 100–2.

Thomas Jefferson, August 23, 1792. *PTJ*, vol. 24, 315–18.

Alexander Hamilton, August 26, 1792. *PAH*, vol. 12, 276–77.

Edmund Randolph, August 26, 1792. *Writings*, vol. 32, 135–37.

John Francis Mercer, September 26, 1792. *Writings*, vol. 32, 164–66.

Betty Washington Lewis, October 7, 1792. *Writings*, vol. 32, 175–77.

Thomas Jefferson, October 18, 1792. *PTJ*, vol. 24, 499–500.

Fourth Annual Message to Congress, November 6, 1792. *Writings*, vol. 32, 205–12.

Passport for Jean Pierre Blanchard, January 9, 1793. *Writings*, vol. 32, 296–97.

Henry Lee, January 20, 1793. *Writings*, vol. 32, 309–10.

To the Members of the New Church in Baltimore, c. January 27, 1793. *Writings*, vol. 32, 314–15.

Frances Bassett Washington, February 24, 1793. *Writings*, vol. 32, 354–55.

Second Inaugural Address, March 4, 1793. *Writings*, vol. 32, 374–75.

Gouverneur Morris, March 25, 1793. *Writings*, vol. 32, 402–3.

Thomas Jefferson, April 12, 1793. *PTJ*, vol. 25, 541.

To the Earl of Buchan, April 22, 1793. *Writings*, vol. 32, 427–30.

Proclamation of Neutrality, April 22, 1793. *Writings*, vol. 32, 430–31.

Henry Lee, July 21, 1793. *Writings*, vol. 33, 22–24.

Edmund Pendleton, September 23, 1793. *Writings*, vol. 33, 94–96.

William Pearce, October 6, 1793. *Writings*, vol. 33, 110–12.

Fifth Annual Message to Congress, December 3, 1793. *Writings*, vol. 33, 163–69.

Arthur Young, December 12, 1793. *Writings*, vol. 33, 174–83.

William Pearce, December 18, 1793. *Writings*, vol. 33, 188–95.

Thomas Jefferson, January 1, 1794. *Writings*, vol. 33, 231.

Tobias Lear, May 6, 1794. *Writings*, vol. 33, 353–60.

Proclamation Calling Forth the Militia, August 7, 1794. *Writings*, vol. 33, 457–61.

Charles Mynn Thruston, August 10, 1794. *Writings*, vol. 33, 464–66.

Henry Lee, August 26, 1794. *Writings*, vol. 33, 474–79.

John Jay, August 30, 1794. *Writings*, vol. 33, 483–85.

Elizabeth Parke Custis, September 14, 1794. *Writings*, vol. 33, 500–1.

Proclamation Concerning the "Whiskey Rebellion," September 25, 1794. *Writings*, vol. 33, 507–9.

Burges Ball, September 25, 1794. *Writings*, vol. 33, 505–7.

Edmund Randolph, October 16, 1794. *Writings*, vol. 34, 2–4.

Sixth Annual Message to Congress, November 19, 1794. *Writings*, vol. 34, 28–37.

William Pearce, November 23, 1794. *Writings*, vol. 34, 40–44.

Alexander Spotswood, November 23, 1794. *Writings*, vol. 34, 46–48.

Eleanor Parke Custis, January 16, 1795. *Writings*, vol. 34, 91–93.

Edmund Pendleton, January 22, 1795. *Writings*, vol. 34, 98–101.

To the Commissioners of the District of Columbia, January 28, 1795. *Writings*, vol. 34, 106–8.

Charles Carter, March 10, 1795. *Writings*, vol. 34, 139–40.

Thomas Jefferson, March 15, 1795. *Writings*, vol. 34, 146–49.

William Pearce, May 10, 1795. *Writings*, vol. 34, 191–94.

Alexander Hamilton, July 3, 1795. *PAH*, vol. 18, 398–400.

Alexander Hamilton, July 29, 1795. *PAH*, vol. 18, 524–25.

Henry Knox, September 20, 1795. *Writings*, vol. 34, 310–11.

Patrick Henry, October 9, 1795. *Writings*, vol. 34, 334–35.

Seventh Annual Message to Congress, December 8, 1795. *Writings*, vol. 34, 386–93.

Gouverneur Morris, December 22, 1795. *Writings*, vol. 34, 398–403.

To the Cabinet, March 25, 1796. *Writings*, vol. 34, 505.

To the House of Representatives, March 30, 1796. *Writings*, vol. 35, 2–5.

Alexander Hamilton, March 31, 1796. *PAH*, vol. 20, 103–5.

Alexander Hamilton, May 8, 1796. *PAH*, vol. 20, 162–66.

Alexander Hamilton, May 15, 1796. *PAH*, vol. 20, 174–78.

Draft of the Farewell Address, May 15, 1796. *Writings*, vol. 35, 51–61.

Alexander Hamilton, June 26, 1796. *PAH*, vol. 20, 237–40.

Thomas Jefferson, July 6, 1796. *Writings*, vol. 35, 118–22.

Alexander Hamilton, August 25, 1796. *PAH*, vol. 20, 307–9.

Address to the Cherokee Nation, August 29, 1796. *Writings*, vol. 35, 193–98.

Alexander Hamilton, September 1, 1796. *PAH*, vol. 20, 311–14.

Farewell Address, September 19, 1796. *Writings*, vol. 35, 214–38.

Eighth Annual Message to Congress, December 7, 1796. *Writings*, vol. 35, 310–20.

John Greenwood, January 20, 1797. *Writings*, vol. 35, 370–71.

Henry Knox, March 2, 1797. *Writings*, vol. 35, 408–10.

Jonathan Trumbull, Jr., March 3, 1797. *Writings*, vol. 35, 411–12.

RETIREMENT, 1797–1799

James McHenry, April 3, 1797. *Writings*, vol. 35, 430–31.

William Heath, May 20, 1797. *Writings*, vol. 35, 448–50.

James McHenry, May 29, 1797. *Writings*, vol. 35, 455–56.

David Humphreys, June 26, 1797. *Writings*, vol. 35, 480–82.

To the Earl of Buchan, July 4, 1797. *Writings*, vol. 35, 486–88.

Samuel Washington, July 12, 1797. *Writings*, vol. 35, 497–98.

Lawrence Lewis, August 4, 1797. *Writings*, vol. 36, 2–3.

Sarah Cary Fairfax, May 16, 1798. *Writings*, vol. 36, 262–65.

John Adams, July 13, 1798. *Writings*, vol. 36, 327–29.

John Adams, September 25, 1798. *Writings*, vol. 36, 453–62.

Landon Carter, October 5, 1798. *Writings*, vol. 36, 484.

Alexander Spotswood, November 22, 1798. *Writings*, vol. 37, 23–24.

Patrick Henry, January 15, 1799. *Writings*, vol. 37, 87–90.

James McHenry, January 27, 1799. *Writings*, vol. 37, 109–11.

James Welch, April 7, 1799. *Writings*, vol. 37, 176–78.

Last Will and Testament, July 9, 1799. *Writings*, vol. 37, 275–303.

Jonathan Trumbull, Jr., July 21, 1799. *Writings*, vol. 37, 312–14.

James McHenry, August 11, 1799. *Writings*, vol. 37, 327–28.

Robert Lewis, August 18, 1799. *Writings*, vol. 37, 338–40.

Jonathan Trumbull, Jr., August 30, 1799. *Writings*, vol. 37, 348–50.

Burges Ball, September 22, 1799. *Writings*, vol. 37, 372.

Alexander Hamilton, December 12, 1799. *PAH*, vol. 24, 99–100.

James Anderson, December 13, 1799. *Writings*, vol. 37, 473–74.

This volume presents the texts of the editions chosen as sources here but does not attempt to reproduce features of their typographic design. Some headings have been changed and George Washington's name at the end of letters has been omitted. The texts are printed without alteration except for the changes previously discussed and for the correction of typographical errors. (Two transcription errors have also been corrected: at 481.13 "pill" replaces "work" and at 865.30 "must" replaces "much.") Spelling, punctuation, and capitalization are often expressive features, and they are not altered, even when inconsistent or irregular. The following is a list of typographical errors corrected, cited by page and line number: 9.3, tof; 36.12, or our; 63.37–38, sumbitted; 89.13, scrace; 170.9, it; 189.10, porvide; 198.3, strenght; 236.5, think; 249.1, may prove; 274.2, Setember; 301.28, intersting; 339.30, hostitlities; 351.19, Brethen; 395.33, dimished; 406.13, through; 449.17, Strain; 466.15, conored; 478.24, inpection; 484.21, whole; 489.10, conincides; 524.26, (who; 527.15, bested; 558.35, them; 577.27, of Sixty; 579.13, esteeem; 620.35, Is it is; 649.5, if offered; 652.25, willfind; 655.1, existence,; 701.8, it as; 703.16, hositlity; 717.30, though; 759.20, nothern; 769.35, frontrier; 791.25, Gentlement; 858.12, in in; 860.7, weer; 884.24, within; 887.7, socities; 888.18, permit,; 897.15, roads,; 902.11, fool?; 907.1, course,; 908.2, be to be; 917.16, PLACE I; 925.26, (and; 933.22, was to; 957.6, meet; 963.10, strengthned; 963.17, patriotim; 966.9, foregin; 1006.34, it so; 1025.2, certainty; 1029.7, Bryd; 1037.14, tract tract.

Notes

In the notes below, the reference numbers denote page and line of this volume (the line count includes headings). No note is made for material included in standard desk-reference books such as Webster's *Collegiate, Biographical,* and *Geographical* dictionaries. Biblical quotations are keyed to the King James Version. Quotations from Shakespeare are keyed to *The Riverside Shakespeare,* ed. G. Blakemore Evans (Boston: Houghton Mifflin, 1974). For further biographical background, references to other studies, and more detailed notes, see Douglas Southall Freeman, *George Washington* (7 vols., New York: Charles Scribner's Sons, 1949–57; volume 7 by John A. Carroll and Mary Wells Ashworth); *The Writings of George Washington from the Original Manuscript Sources, 1745–1799,* edited by John C. Fitzpatrick (39 vols., Washington: United States Government Printing Office, 1931–44); *The Diaries of George Washington,* edited by Donald Jackson (6 vols., Charlottesville: University Press of Virginia, 1976–79); *The Papers of George Washington: Colonial Series,* edited by W. W. Abbot (10 vols., Charlottesville: University Press of Virginia, 1983–95); *The Papers of George Washington: Revolutionary War Series,* edited by Philander D. Chase (6 vols. to date, Charlottesville: University Press of Virginia, 1985–94); *The Papers of George Washington: Confederation Series,* edited by W. W. Abbot (4 vols. to date, Charlottesville: University Press of Virginia, 1992–95); and *The Papers of George Washington: Presidential Series,* edited by Dorothy Twohig (6 vols. to date, Charlottesville: University Press of Virginia, 1987–96).

THE COLONIAL PERIOD, 1747–1775

3.1–2 *"Rules. . . Conversation"*]   The rules derive from a 1595 Jesuit treatise, "Bienséance de la Conversation entre les Hommes." Washington's text was probably based on the translation by Francis Hawkins (1628–81), which was published in England in more than ten editions between 1640 and 1672.

11.5 George Fairfax]   George William Fairfax (1742–87) was a cousin of Lord Fairfax; he and his wife, Sally Cary Fairfax (c. 1730–1811), were close friends of Washington.

11.10 his Lordships]   Thomas Fairfax, sixth Baron Fairfax (1693–1781), was proprietor of the Northern Neck, a tract of over five million acres in Virginia between the Potomac and Rapidan-Rappahannock rivers.

16.8 my Brothers]   Lawrence Washington's estate, Mount Vernon.

16.22–23   George Fairfax's Wife's sister]   Probably Mary Cary (1733–81).

17.17   Commission'd]   Dinwiddie's commission, dated Williamsburg, October 30, 1753, ordered Washington to deliver Dinwiddie's letter to the French commandant and wait no more than a week for an answer before returning to Virginia. Dinwiddie's letter to the French commandant, also dated October 30, declared that all the Ohio country was the "Property of the Crown of Great Britain" and demanded the "peaceable Departure" of all French forces therein. Washington wrote an account of the 1753 journey and the 1754 campaign in his commentary on David Humphreys' biography; see pp. 611–13 in this volume.

17.23   Jacob Vanbraam]   Jacob Van Braam (b. 1729) would also accompany Washington on the Fort Necessity campaign in 1754. He was responsible for the faulty translation of the Fort Necessity surrender document, July 3, 1754, in which Washington unwittingly admitted to having "assassinated" a French officer.

17.28   Mr. Gist]   Christopher Gist (c. 1706–59) made several early explorations of the Ohio region.

18.5   the General's Death]   Pierre Paul de La Malgue, sieur de Marin (1692–1753), was the leader of the French expedition into the Ohio which had aroused Dinwiddie's protest. He had died on October 29.

19.8   Half King]   English name for the important Seneca chief Tanacharison. Allied with the British, he would also accompany Washington during the Fort Necessity campaign in 1754.

20.37   Morail]   Montreal.

21.39   Lead]   Robert Cavelier, sieur de La Salle, who had explored the Ohio Valley in the 17th century.

26.27   La Sol]   La Salle.

28.25   the Commander]   Jacques Le Gardeur, sieur de Saint-Pierre (1701–55), became commandant of the French forces in the Ohio country after the death of the sieur de Marin.

28.29   Monsieur Riparti]   Louis Le Gardeur de Repentigny.

34.17   Belvoir]   Plantation of William Fairfax on the Potomac near Mount Vernon.

34.31   *Richard Corbin*]   Richard Corbin (1708–90) served as receiver general of Virginia from 1754 to 1776.

35.19   Forks of the Monongehele]   The Forks of the Ohio, where the Allegheny and Monongahela come together to form the Ohio River. The French seized the forks on April 17, 1754, and built Fort Duquesne on the site. It fell to the British in November 1758 and was renamed Fort Pitt. Now Pittsburgh, Pennsylvania.

36.37   Connotaucarious]   The name given by Indians to Washington's great-grandfather John Washington. Connotaucarious meant "town taker" or "devourer of villages." The Half King applied the name to Washington.

38.27   Committee's resolves]   The pay of officers engaged in the expedition to the Ohio had been set by a committee of the Virginia House of Burgesses.

40.32   Belhaven]   Alexandria, Virginia.

43.38   De Jumonville]   The French officer Joseph Coulon de Villiers, sieur de Jumonville (1718–54), was ordered to carry to the British a message demanding their withdrawal from the Ohio. He had left Fort Duquesne on May 23, 1754, with about 35 men.

47.24   *John Augustine Washington*]   Washington's brother John Augustine (1736–87).

48.19   something charming . . . sound.]   A version of this letter was published in the *London Magazine* for August 1754. Horace Walpole wrote that George II remarked: "He would not say so, if he had been used to hear many."

48.32   the General]   Maryland governor Horatio Sharpe was at the time commander of colonial forces in the Ohio country, including Washington's Virginia regiment.

50.27   Generals Family]   Major General Edward Braddock's personal staff.

58.10–11   our late Engagemt]   "Braddock's Defeat," July 9, 1755. Washington wrote an account of the battle in his commentary on David Humphreys' biography; see pp. 614–17 in this volume.

66.36   Rects]   Recruits.

69.15   General Shirley]   Massachusetts governor William Shirley (1694–1771) was commissioned major general and commander in chief of British forces in North America in 1755. In March 1756, Washington rode from Virginia to Boston to appeal to Shirley for a resolution of the conflict in seniority between royal and colonial military commissions.

69.17–18   Dagworthy]   Washington clashed with Captain John Dagsworthy over rank. Dagsworthy, an officer serving at Fort Cumberland, Maryland, in 1755, had held a temporary royal commission in 1746, and maintained that his royal commission gave him authority over all officers with colonial commissions. Governor Shirley ruled in Washington's favor on March 5, 1756.

71.21   *Robert Hunter Morris*]   Morris (c. 1700–64) was governor of Pennsylvania from 1754 to 1756.

73.3   Behaviour of the Officers]   Dinwiddie had written Washington on April 8, 1756, about a report that officers of the Virginia Regiment had been guilty of "the greatest Immoralities & Drunkenness," charges Washington angrily rejected.

80.29   *Earl of Loudoun*]   John Campbell, 4th Earl of Loudoun (1705–82), was commander in chief of British forces in North America, 1756 to 1758.

88.13   *Richard Washington*]   A London merchant to whom George Washington believed himself distantly related. He would visit Mount Vernon in 1774.

89.16   Carlyle]   John Carlyle (1720–80) was a prominent Alexandria merchant.

89.16–17   Fielding Lewis]   Fielding Lewis (1725–82), a Fredericksburg, Virginia, merchant, had married Washington's sister Betty (1733–97) in 1750.

89.30   *John Stanwix*]   Colonel John Stanwix (c. 1690–1765), a British officer serving in America, was commissioned brigadier general on December 27, 1757.

91.20   report of this nature]   In a letter of August 22, 1757, William Peachey had described rumors then circulating in Williamsburg that Washington had exaggerated the Indian threat on the frontier to persuade the Assembly to authorize greater support for the Virginia Regiment.

93.10   Ft L]   Fort Loudoun.

93.21   General Forbes]   General John Forbes (1707–59) was given command of the 1758 expedition against Fort Duquesne.

95.1   *James Wood*]   Wood (died c. 1777) was, from 1743 to 1760, clerk of the court for Frederick County, from which Washington won election to the House of Burgesses on July 24, 1758.

95.28   *Francis Halkett*]   Halkett was General Forbes's brigade major (staff officer); both his father and brother had been killed at Braddock's defeat.

95.33   New way to the Ohio]   Washington was unable to persuade Forbes to use Braddock's Road to the Forks of the Ohio for the expedition against Fort Duquesne. It was the route that Washington himself had laid out and had its beginnings in Virginia. The road Forbes chose began in Pennsylvania.

97.21   A—— B—s]   Usually rendered as Assembly Balls.

98.21   10th Janry 1759]   Washington had married Martha Dandridge Custis on January 6.

100.1   *Robert Cary & Company*]   A London firm trading with Virginia, the company had managed the Custis accounts; after his marriage Washington gave most of his business to the firm.

106.26   Miss Custis's]   Martha Washington's daughter, Martha Parke Custis (1756–73).

108.9   *Robert Stewart*]   Stewart had served as a captain in the Virginia Regiment.

110.28   Master Custis]   Martha Washington's son, John Parke Custis (1754–81).

116.18–19   Hemp . . . Act of Parliament]   The British government provided incentives for the production of hemp, essential for the manufacture of naval stores.

116.30   Stamp Act]   The Stamp Act, passed by Parliament on March 22, 1765, imposed a tax in the colonies on the paper used in formally written and printed documents, including newspapers, almanacs, broadsides, pamphlets, and legal and commercial papers. It provoked widespread protest from the American colonists, many of whom believed that taxation without the consent of the taxed was unconstitutional. The Act proved unenforceable and was repealed on March 18, 1766.

118.1   *Josiah Thompson*]   Thompson was captain of the schooner *Swift*. The ship sailed from Alexandria to St. Christopher's in July 1766.

118.28   *John Posey*]   Posey was a friend and neighbor of Washington. His plantation, Rover's Delight, eventually became part of Mount Vernon.

123.24   *William Crawford*]   Crawford (1732–82) had served under Washington as an ensign in the Virginia Regiment.

123.27   Brother Vale]   Valentine Crawford (d. 1777).

125.2   Proclamation]   The royal Proclamation of 1763 forbade colonists to claim or settle land west of the Appalachians.

126.23   *Jonathan Boucher*]   Boucher (1738–1804), an English clergyman, was tutor to John Parke Custis.

129.10   Jersey College]   College of New Jersey, now Princeton University.

133.1   Association]   Washington served on the committee that drafted the Nonimportation Association, an agreement calling for a boycott of goods imported from Britain, in Williamsburg on May 18, 1769.

134.14   *Charles Washington*]   Washington's brother Charles (1738–99).

134.18   Br. Saml]   Washington's brother Samuel (1734–81).

134.26   Kings Proclamation]   The Proclamation of 1763.

137.17   *Thomas Johnson*]   Johnson (1732–1819) would become governor of Maryland in 1777.

143.34   Mr Peale]   Charles Willson Peale (1741–1827), artist and Continental Army officer, painted Washington from life at least seven times, more than any other artist. The portrait that resulted from this sitting is the earliest-known likeness of Washington.

144.18   *Benedict Calvert*]   Calvert (c. 1724–88) was a wealthy Maryland planter.

144.23   Second Daughter]   Eleanor (Nelly) Calvert (1758–1804) married John Parke Custis in 1774.

146.12   *Burwell Bassett*]   Bassett (1734–93) was the husband of Martha Washington's sister Anna Maria Dandridge.

146.27   College of New York]   King's College, now Columbia University.

146.31   Mrs Dandridge]   Frances Jones Dandridge (1710–85) was Martha Washington's mother.

147.5   *George Muse*]   Muse (1720–90) had served as a lieutenant colonel in the Virginia Regiment.

148.8   *George William Fairfax*]   Fairfax and his wife, Sally Cary Fairfax, had sailed for England in 1773; they would never return to America. Washington had agreed to manage their affairs in Virginia.

149.10   Act of Parliament]   The Boston Port Act, passed March 31, 1774, was one of the four laws—known in the colonies as the Intolerable or Coercive Acts—enacted by Parliament to punish Massachusetts for the Boston Tea Party of December 16, 1773.

153.5–7   for depriving . . . offenders]   Two of the Intolerable Acts. The Massachusetts Government Act, signed May 20, 1774, abrogated the colony's 1691 charter, giving greater power to the king and his appointed governor. The Administration of Justice Act, also signed on May 20, allowed persons accused of committing capital crimes in Massachusetts while enforcing the law or collecting revenue to be transported to Britain for trial.

153.29   *Bryan Fairfax*]   Fairfax (1737–1802) was half brother of George William Fairfax.

159.1   *Robert McKenzie*]   McKenzie, a British officer, had served in the Virginia Regiment.

161.1   *John West*]   West, a Virginia planter, died in 1777.

162.22   *John Connolly*]   Connolly was a Pittsburgh land speculator.

COMMANDER OF THE CONTINENTAL ARMY, 1775–1783

167.28   *To Martha Washington*]   This letter and the letter dated June 23, 1775 (p. 173 in this volume) are the only letters from Washington to his wife known to be extant. Martha Washington is believed to have burned all of the other letters sometime after Washington's death in 1799.

181.1   *Thomas Gage*]   Gage (1721–87) was royal governor of Massachusetts and commander of British forces in North America until late 1775. Washington had served with him during the Braddock expedition in 1755.

183.23   *Lund Washington*]   Lund Washington (1737–96) was a distant cousin to George Washington. He managed Mount Vernon during the Revolutionary War.

189.22   *William Woodford*]   Woodford (1734–80) was the commander of a Virginia regiment. He later became a Continental Army brigadier general and died in British captivity after the surrender of Charleston, South Carolina, in 1780.

195.22   Lord Dunmore]   John Murray, Earl of Dunmore (1732–1809), was appointed governor of Virginia in 1770; Washington was frequently in his company in Williamsburg. He angered Virginia patriots by dissolving the House of Burgesses in 1773 and 1774. Dunmore took up arms for the Crown in 1775, promising freedom to slaves who joined his army. On December 9, 1775, Virginia militia defeated Loyalist forces led by Dunmore at Great Bridge, near Norfolk, Virginia.

196.9   the new-army]   Enlistments in the old army expired with the year 1775; by December 31 only 9,650 men had enlisted in the new army, less than half the 20,000 authorized by Congress.

198.23–24   his Majesty's . . . Speech]   In his speech of October 26, 1775, George III declared his determination to crush the American rebellion. On August 23, 1775, the king had proclaimed the colonies to be in rebellion.

203.39–40   Genl Lee]   Major General Charles Lee.

206.5   Norfolk]   After withdrawing his forces onto ships in Chesapeake Bay, Dunmore burned Norfolk, Virginia, on January 1, 1776.

206.13   Common Sense]   Thomas Paine's widely read pamphlet *Common Sense* was published in Philadelphia on January 10, 1776.

208.31   *John Hancock*]   Hancock (1737–93) was president of Congress from May 1775 to November 1777.

212.29   cast of a Dye]   The decisive attack on the British in Boston that Washington favored in early 1776.

216.5   *Phillis Wheatley*]   Phillis Wheatley (c. 1753–84), the African-American poet, had written a 42-line poem in praise of Washington. It was published in *The Pennsylvania Magazine: or, American Monthly Museum* in April 1776.

223.22–23   Virginia Convention . . . vote]   On May 15, 1776, the Virginia convention passed a resolution instructing its delegates to the Continental Congress to propose a declaration of American independence.

232.15   *Adam Stephen*]   Stephen (c. 1718–91) had served as lieutenant colonel in the Virginia Regiment; in February 1776 he was appointed colonel of the 4th Virginia Regiment, Continental Line.

233.15   Meadows . . . Monongahela]   The battles of Fort Necessity, July 3, 1754, and Braddock's defeat, July 9, 1755.

248.29   by ——]   The omitted word is "Congress."

249.5   I assured ——]   The omitted word is "Congress."

256.1–2   vine & fig Tree]   Cf. 1 Kings 4:25.

265.33–34   powers . . . unlimited in extent]   On December 27, 1776, Congress voted Washington extraordinary powers for six months to sustain the Continental Army, including the power to raise troops, gather provisions, and "to arrest and confine Persons who refuse to take the Continental Currency, or are otherwise disaffected to the American Cause."

271.1   *Alexander Spotswood*]   Spotswood (1751–1818) was a colonel in the 2nd Virginia Regiment.

271.26   *James Warren*]   Warren (1726–1808) was president of the Provincial Congress of Massachusetts.

280.1   *Thomas Conway*]   General William Alexander had informed the commander in chief of the damaging statement that Washington quoted back to Conway in this letter. In December 1777, Congress appointed Major General Thomas Conway (1735–c. 1800) inspector-general of the army over Washington's objections. In the winter of 1777–78, Conway was allegedly involved in a movement, known as the "Conway Cabal," to elevate Horatio Gates, victor at Saratoga, to the command of the Continental Army in Washington's place. The effort to oust Washington owed its beginnings to the dissatisfaction of some delegates in Congress with his military leadership, but his detractors blundered repeatedly and the plot, if there was one, collapsed. Completely discredited, Conway resigned in April 1778. See the letters to Henry Laurens, January 2, 1778 (pp. 286–87); to Horatio Gates, January 4, 1778 (pp. 287–89); to Henry Laurens, January 31, 1778 (pp. 290–91), and to Landon Carter, May 30, 1778 (pp. 310–13).

281.33   *Henry Laurens*]   Laurens (1724–92) was president of the Continental Congress from November 1777 to December 1778.

290.21   anonymous paper]   The paper, dated January 17, 1778, and titled "The Thoughts of a Freeman," was critical of Washington's leadership.

291.8   *William Gordon*]   Gordon (1728–1807), a Massachusetts clergyman, was collecting material for a history of the American Revolution. It was published in 1788 as *The History of the Rise, Progress, and Establishment of the Independence of the United States of America.*

292.1   *George Clinton*]   Clinton (1739–1812) was governor of New York.

298.13   *John Banister*]   Banister (1734–88) was a Virginia delegate to the Continental Congress.

302.23   Lord North's Speech]   The Prime Minister's conciliatory speech of February 19, 1778, had held out the offer of a negotiated settlement to the war.

305.13   forged Letters]   A series of letters purportedly written by Washington were published in London in 1776 in a pamphlet titled *Letters of General Washington to several of his Friends in the year 1776*; by 1778 the spurious
letters had been reprinted in America. The aim of the deception was to discredit Washington's leadership by depicting him as an opponent of independence and a critic of those who favored the break with England.

310.12   *Landon Carter*]   Carter (1738–1801) had served in the Virginia
Regiment.

311.29   gentleman at Sabine Hall]   Landon Carter of Sabine Hall (1710–
78) was a wealthy Virginia planter and father of the recipient of the letter.

311.31   G—s]   Horatio Gates.

311.38   three men]   Gates, Conway, and Thomas Mifflin.

318.10   General Wayne]   Anthony Wayne (1745–96).

318.30   General Lee]   General Charles Lee was convicted by a court-
martial in August 1778 and suspended from the service for a year. He was dismissed from the army in 1780 after he sent an insulting letter to Congress.

319.8   *Thomas Nelson*]   Nelson (1738–89) became governor of Virginia in
1781. He had given Washington a fine horse, which Washington named Nelson
and rode during much of the Revolutionary War. Washington returned the
horse after the war ended.

319.20   discontinuance of your Corps]   Nelson had raised a troop of volunteer Virginia cavalry that Congress subsequently declined to authorize.

319.27   the French Fleet]   A French fleet, carrying an expeditionary force
of 4,000 men commanded by Comte Jean Baptiste Charles Henri Hector
d'Estaing (1729–94), arrived off Delaware Bay on July 8, 1778.

321.12–13   best concerted enterprise]   The unsuccessful Franco-American
attack on the British garrison at Newport, Rhode Island, July 29 to August 31, 1778.

334.8–9   Mason . . . another]   George Mason, George Wythe, Thomas
Jefferson, Wilson Cary Nicholas, Edmund Pendleton, Thomas Nelson, and
Benjamin Harrison.

338.3   arming Slaves]   Laurens had written to Washington on March 16,
1779: "had we Arms for 3000 such black Men, as I could select in Carolina I
should have no doubt of success in driving the British out of Georgia."

338.20   Mr. Laurens]   Lieutenant colonel John Laurens (1754–82), son of
Henry Laurens, served on Washington's staff.

340.35   C——]   Congress.

342.34–35   Our cause is . . . the cause of Mankind!]   Cf. Thomas Paine,

Common Sense, "Introduction": "The cause of America is in a great measure the cause of all mankind."

344.11   means of ——]   Washington's prospective spy was New York merchant Lewis Pintard (1732–1818).

345.6   *William Maxwell*]   Maxwell (1733–96) was a Continental Army brigadier general from New Jersey.

347.26   great undertaking]   The attack on New York City proposed by Morris in his April 26, 1779, letter to Washington.

348.18   the *event expected*]   The arrival of French reinforcements.

354.37   Sullivan . . . Expedition]   General John Sullivan led a successful campaign against the Iroquois in New York State, May–November, 1779.

355.6–7   take up their Beds and Walk]   Cf. Mark 2:9.

355.20   *John Cochran*]   Dr. Cochran (1730–1807) was director-general of the Continental Army hospitals.

358.1   *John Jay*]   Jay (1745–1829) was president of Congress from December 1778 to September 1779.

359.26   person you recommended]   Elijah Hunter. Jay had recommended his employment as a spy.

361.29–30   Swords . . . pruning hook]   Cf. Isaiah 2:4.

363.22   declaration of Spain]   Allied with France, Spain had declared war on Britain on June 21, 1779.

364.38   G.]   Garrison.

369.32   *Robert Howe*]   Howe (1732–86) was a Continental Army major general.

369.34–35   Mr. Pulteney's lucubrations]   William Pulteney, *Thoughts on the Present State of Affairs with America, and the Means of Conciliation* (London, 1778).

371.19   *Joseph Jones*]   Jones (1727–1805) was a Virginia delegate to Congress.

378.1   Charles Town]   On May 12, 1780, Clinton captured Charleston, South Carolina, with its garrison of 5,000 troops commanded by Major General Benjamin Lincoln.

387.1   *Samuel Huntington*]   Huntington (1731–96) was president of Congress from September 1779 to July 1781.

389.2   to suffer death]   Major John André was hanged on October 2, 1780.

390.7   *John Cadwalader*]   Cadwalader (1742–86) was a brigadier general in the Pennsylvania militia.

392.2–3   a member of my family] A member of Washington's staff.

397.39   Battle of Campden] American forces under Horatio Gates were defeated by Cornwallis at Camden, South Carolina, on August 16, 1780.

400.12   *William Fitzhugh*] Fitzhugh (1741–1809) was a wealthy Virginian. His son Robert, a lieutenant in the 3rd Continental Dragoons, had been captured at Tappan, New York, in September 1778.

404.1   *James Duane*] Duane (1733–97) was a New York delegate to Congress.

404.11   Ct. of V——] Court of Versailles.

406.35–407.2   mutiny . . . Pennsylvania Line] The mutiny by enlisted men of General Anthony Wayne's Pennsylvania Line broke out at winter quarters in Morristown, New Jersey, on January 1, 1781. The mutineers marched under arms to Princeton, where they presented their grievances over back pay, terms of enlistment, and supplies to representatives of Congress. Washington, who took no part in the negotiations, feared that mutiny would spread through the Continental Army's main winter encampment at his headquarters at New Windsor, New York. Joseph Reed, president of the Pennsylvania executive council, negotiated a settlement on January 8 that made significant concessions to the mutineers.

408.20–21   your commission] Laurens had been named special envoy to France in December 1780.

411.21   minutes of a conference] Washington and Rochambeau had met at Hartford, Connecticut, on September 20, 1780.

412.30   *Sarah Bache*] Sarah Franklin Bache (1743–1808) was the daughter of Benjamin Franklin.

417.26   so young a Senator] Custis had been elected to the upper house of the Virginia Assembly.

420.13   the Plantation in ruins] A British warship (probably the armed sloop *Actaeon*) had threatened Mount Vernon while on a raid up the Potomac. Lund Washington's letter describing the incident is not known to be extant; in a letter of April 23, 1781, Lafayette wrote: "Mr Lund Washington Went on Board the Ennemy's vessels and Consented to give them provisions. This Being done By the Gentleman who in Some Measure Represents you at your House will certainly Have a Bad effect, and Contrasts with Spirited Answers from Some Neighbours that Had their Houses Burnt Accordingly."

420.33   my Negroes] Eighteen Mount Vernon slaves escaped to the British vessel; seven were eventually recaptured.

421.20   *Journal . . . Yorktown Campaign*] Washington also discussed allied strategy in 1781 in a letter to Noah Webster, July 31, 1788; see pp. 689–91 in this volume.

422.36–37   C——s Senr. & Junr.]   Samuel Culper, Sr., and Jr., were the code names of two American spies operating against the British in New York. The senior Culper was Abraham Woodhull (c. 1750–1826); junior was Robert Townsend (1753–1838).

424.1   The D . . . Ct House]   The Deputy Quarter Master at Sussex Court House.

425.17   R. Isld.]   The main French land force of about 4,000 was stationed at Newport, Rhode Island, where the French fleet was anchored.

426.10   dated 729]   729 was code for Setauket, Long Island, where the spy Abraham Woodhull ("Samuel Culper, Sr.") operated.

426.24   R & F]   Rank & File.

427.29–30   Govr. Trumbull]   Jonathan Trumbull, Sr., (1710–85) was governor of Connecticut from 1769 to 1785. He was the father of Washington's aide Jonathan Trumbull, Jr., (1740–1809) and of the painter John Trumbull (1756–1843).

427.34–35   Chevr. de Chastellux]   François Jean le Beauvoir, marquis de Chastellux (1734–88), was a major general in Rochambeau's army.

432.19   the Govr. of Virginia]   In a letter dated May 28, 1781, Governor Thomas Jefferson had urged Washington to move against British forces in Virginia.

433.16   Q. M. G.]   Quarter Master General.

435.18   the Minister of France]   Anne-César, chevalier de la Luzerne (1741–91), was French minister to the United States from 1779 to 1784.

436.4   Yk. Island]   York Island, or Manhattan.

448.13   Mr. Morris (Financier)]   Robert Morris (1734–1806) was appointed superintendent of finance by Congress in February 1781.

450.24   The Invalids]   A Continental Army corps of sick and disabled soldiers fit only for guard duty.

456.2–3   Barras . . . had done before]   A pages or pages, perhaps containing entries for September 23 and 24, 1781, may be missing from the diary at this point.

456.6   remr.]   remainder.

457.37   French opened a battery]   According to a contemporary account, "his Excellency General Washington put the match to the first gun, and a furious discharge of cannon and mortars immediately followed, and Earl Cornwallis has received his first salutation."

459.9   royals]   A royal was a small mortar that fired an explosive shell.

462.38   some 50s. & 44s.]   Warships armed with 50 and 44 cannon each.

463.3   Sailing for Chesapeak]   Sir Henry Clinton dispatched a large force to reinforce Cornwallis at Yorktown. The fleet left New York on October 19, 1781, the day Cornwallis surrendered.

464.10   Regiments at]   Washington's Yorktown journal ends here, in midsentence.

464.24   *Thomas McKean*]   McKean (1734–1817) was president of Congress from July to November in 1781.

466.25   Your State]   Nelson was governor of Virginia.

468.20–21   new Choice . . . President]   John Hanson had been elected to succeed McKean as president of Congress on November 5, 1781.

468.28   *Lewis Nicola*]   Nicola (1717–1807) was a Continental Army colonel.

468.31   Sentiments you have submitted]   In his letter of May 22, 1782, Nicola wrote: "This war must have shewn to all, but to military men in particular the weakness of republicks, & the exertions the army has been able to make by being under a proper head, therefore, I little doubt, when the benefits of a mixed government are pointed out & duly considered, but such will be readily adopted; in this case it will, I believe, be uncontroverted that the same abilities which have led us, through difficulties apparently unsurmountable by human power, to victory & glory, those qualities that have merited & obtained the universal esteem & veneration of an army, would be most likely to conduct & direct us in the smoother paths of peace." He continued: "Some people have so connected the ideas of tyranny & monarchy as to find it very difficult to seperate them, it may therefore be requisite to give the head of such a constitution as I propose some title apparently more moderate, but if all other things were once adjusted I believe strong arguments might be produced for admitting the title of king, which I conceive would be attended with some material advantages. . . ."

469.20   *John Price Posey*]   Posey (d. 1788) was the son of Washington's old friend and neighbor John Posey.

469.23   deceased Mr. Custis]   John Parke Custis, Martha Washington's last surviving child, had died on November 5, 1781.

471.9   your last publication]   Probably *Letter Addressed to the Abbé Raynal*, a pamphlet published in August 1782.

471.15   Your Observation on the *Period of Seven Years*]   On September 7, Paine had written Washington expressing his belief that after fighting an unsuccessful war for seven years, the British would soon abandon their attempts to subdue America. Paine observed: "The British have accustomed themselves to think of the term of seven years in a manner different to other periods of time. They acquire this partly by habit, by religion, by reason and by superstition. They serve seven years apprenticeship—They elect their parliament for seven years—They punish by seven years transportation, or the duplicate or triplicate of that term—Their leases run in the same manner; and they read that Jacob served seven years for one wife and seven years for another; and the same term, likewise, extinguishes all allegations (in certain cases) of debt or matrimony; and thus, the particular period, by a variety of concurrences has attained an influence in their minds superior to that of any other number."

471.35   case of Capt Asgill] Washington had ordered the selection of a British officer for possible retaliation after Loyalists hanged an American prisoner, militia Captain Joshua Huddy, in New Jersey in April 1782. Captain Charles Asgill (c. 1762–1823), who had surrendered at Yorktown, was chosen by lot in May 1782. On August 19, 1782, Washington referred the matter to Congress with the recommendation that Asgill not be hanged. Congress ordered his release on November 7, 1782, after learning that Asgill's mother had appealed to Louis XVI and Marie Antoinette.

480.14   no Peace would be concluded] On November 30, 1782, the American negotiators in Paris, Benjamin Franklin, John Adams, John Jay, and Henry Laurens, had signed a preliminary treaty of peace with Britain. The treaty recognized American independence, gave the United States borders extending north to the Great Lakes and west to the Mississippi, and provided for an end to hostilities, payment of American debts to British creditors, British recognition of American fishing rights in Canadian waters, and an American promise to consider the restoration of rights and properties of the Loyalists. News of the preliminary treaty reached Washington at Newburgh on March 19, 1783. The definitive Treaty of Paris was signed on September 3, 1783.

482.10   *Bushrod Washington*] Bushrod Washington (1762–1829) was the son of Washington's brother John Augustine. He would inherit Mount Vernon and Washington's papers. Appointed by President Adams in 1798, Bushrod Washington served as an associate justice of the Supreme Court until his death.

490.13   the Newbuilding] A meeting house built at the Continental Army's Newburgh encampment for the use of the officers; it was also called the "Temple of Virtue."

490.13–14   paper . . . circulated yesterday] The anonymous paper circulated on March 10, 1783, was written by Continental Army officer John Armstrong (1758–1843), later secretary of war (1813–14) under President James Madison. In his address, Armstrong described himself as "A fellow soldier whose interest and affection bind him strongly to you, whose past sufferings, have been as great & whose future fortune may be as desperate as yours" who until recently had "believed in the Justice of his Country." Armstrong concluded: "After a pursuit of seven long Years, the object for which we set out, is at length brot within our reach—Yes, my friends, that suffering Courage of yours, was active once, it has conducted the United States of America, thro' a doubtfull and bloody War—it has placed her in the Chair of Independancy—and peace returns again to bless—Whom? a Country willing to redress your wrongs? cherrish your worth—and reward your Services—a Country courting your return to private life, with Tears of gratitude & smiles of Admiration—longing to divide with you, that Independancy, which Your Gallantry has given, and those riches which your wounds have preserved. Is this the case? or is it rather a Country that tramples upon your rights, disdains your Cries—& insults your distresses? have you not more than once suggested your wishes—and made known your wants to Congress (wants and wishes, which gratitude and policy should have anticipated, rather than evaded)—and have you not lately, in the meek language of intreating Memorials, begged from their Justice, what you would no longer expect from their favor. How have you been answered? let the Letter which you are called to consider tomorrow, make reply, If this then be your treatment while the swords you wear are necessary for the Defence of America, what have you to expect from peace; when your voice shall sink, and your strength dissipate by division—when those very swords, the Instruments and Companions of your Glory, shall be taken from your sides—and no remaining mark of Military distincion left, but your wants, infirmities & Scars—can you then consent to be the only sufferers by this revolution—and retiring from the field, grow old in poverty, wretchedness, and Contempt; can you consent, to wade thro' the vile mire of dependency, and owe the miserable remnant of that life to Charity, which has hitherto been spent in honor? If you can—Go—and carry with you the jest of Tories, & the Scorn of Whigs—the ridicule—and what is worse—the pity of the world—go—Starve and be forgotten. But if your spirits should revolt at this—if you have sense enough to discover, and spirit enough to oppose Tyranny, under whatever Garb it may assume—whether it be the plain Coat of Republicanism—or the splendid Robe of Royalty—if you have yet learned to discriminate between a people and a Cause—between men & principles—Awake—attend to your Situation & redress yourselves; If the present moment be lost, every future Effort, is in vain—and your threats then, will be as empty, as your entreaties now—I would advise you therefore, to come to some final opinion, upon what you can bear—and what you will suffer—If your determination be in any proportion to your wrongs—carry your appeal from the Justice to the fears of government—Change the Milk & Water stile of your last Memorial—assume a bolder Tone, decent, but lively, spirited and determined—And suspect the man, who would advise to more moderation, and longer forbearance. Let two or three Men, who can feel as well as write, be appointed to draw up your last Remonstrance (for I would no longer give it the sueing, soft, unsuccessfull Epithet of Memorial) Let it be represented in language that will neither dishonor you by its Rudeness, nor betray you by its fears—what has been promised by Congress and what has been performed—how long and how patiently you have suffered—how little you have asked, and how much of that little, have been denied—Tell them, that tho' you were the first, and would wish to be the last to encounter Danger—tho' dispair itself can never drive you into dishonor, it may drive you from the field—That the wound often irritated and never healed, may at length become incurable—and that the slightest mark of indignity from Congress now, must operate like the Grave, and part you forever—That in any political Event, the Army has its alternative—if peace, that nothing shall seperate you from your Arms but Death—If War—that courting the Auspicies, and inviting the direction of your Illustrous Leader, you will retire to some unsettled Country, Smile in your Turn, and 'mock when their fear cometh on'—But let it represent also, that should they comply with the request of your late Memorial, it would make you more happy; and them more respectable—That while War should continue, you would follow their standard into the field, and When it came to an End, you would withdraw into the shade of private Life—and give the World another subject of Wonder & applause, An Army victorious over its Enemies, Victorious over itself."

491.5   a certain Gentleman] Walter Stewart (c. 1756–96), a colonel of the Pennsylvania Line.

493.3   second address] The address of March 12, 1783, also written by John Armstrong, asserted that Washington's general order of March 11 (p. 490) demonstrated that the commander in chief sympathized with the aims and methods of the disaffected officers.

495.20   *Elias Boudinot*] Boudinot (1740–1821) was president of Congress from November 1782 to November 1783.

495.28   No 2] See note 490.13–14.

496.11   No. 4] See note 493.3.

496.12   *Speech to the Officers of the Army*] In the meeting with the disgruntled officers held in the Temple of Virtue on March 15, 1783, Washington first read this speech and then began to read a letter from congressional delegate Joseph Jones promising justice to the army. Washington paused, produced a pair of spectacles—which very few of the officers had ever seen him wear—and said: "Gentlemen, you must pardon me. I have grown gray in your service and now find myself growing blind." (This remark has also been reported: "Gentlemen, you will permit me to put on my spectacles, for I have not only grown gray, but almost blind, in the service of my country.") Some of the formerly rebellious officers were moved to tears. Washington then left the building and major generals Henry Knox and Israel Putnam introduced and carried a resolution strongly repudiating the anonymous address of March 10 and pledging the army's obedience to civil authority.

498.8   Emissary . . . from New York] From the British high command (New York City remained under British occupation until November 1783).

500.29   Report of the Meeting] See note 496.12.

504.8   General Peace] Britain, France, and Spain signed a preliminary peace agreement on January 20, 1783.

506.1   *Theodorick Bland*]   Bland (1742–90) was a Virginia planter and physician who served as a colonel in the Continental Army.

507.26–27   clothing . . . to have]   The text printed in this volume, taken from *The Writings of George Washington from the Original Manuscript Sources, 1745–1799*, edited by John C. Fitzpatrick, is based on the autograph manuscript of the letter. A contemporary transcript made at Continental Army headquarters gives the end of the sentence as: "clothing and other exps were to have made a Part?"

509.11–12   from whence . . . return]   Cf. *Hamlet*, III.i.78–79.

510.25   The scheme . . . which you propose]   On February 5, 1783, Lafayette had written: "Permit me to propose a plan to you Which Might Become Greatly Beneficial to the Black part of Mankind—Let us Unite in Purchasing a small Estate Where We May try the Experiment to free the Negroes, and Use them only as tenants—Such an Example as Yours Might Render it a General Practice, and if We succeed in America, I Will chearfully devote a part of My time to Render the Method fascionable in the West indias." In the 1790s, Washington considered freeing his Mount Vernon slaves and establishing them as paid agricultural laborers.

514.23   Discharges to be printed]   Washington personally signed the discharges of thousands of Continental Army soldiers.

526.20   deceased Brothers]   Samuel Washington had died in 1781.

526.27   our Nephew Ferdinand]   Ferdinand Washington (1767–88), son of Samuel.

536.25   motives of Compn]   motives of Compassion.

541.22–25   Mrs. Custis . . . attachment to D.S.]   In 1783, Eleanor Calvert Custis, widow of John Parke Custis, would marry Dr. David Stuart (1753–c. 1814).

546.29   *Thomas Mifflin*]   Mifflin (1744–1800) was president of Congress from November 1783 to November 1784.

THE CONFEDERATION PERIOD, 1783–1789

555.11   the bust]   A bust of Lafayette by Jean-Antoine Houdoun intended for the Virginia State Capitol, Richmond.

556.12   *James Craik*]   Dr. James Craik (1730–1814) was Washington's friend and personal physician.

559.33   the western Country]   Washington had made his last visit to the Ohio country from September 1 to October 4, 1784.

560.18–21   Evans . . . Hutchins]   Lewis Evans, *A General Map of the Middle Colonies of Virginia* (London, 1755); Thomas Hutchins, *A Topographical*

Description of Virginia, Pennsylvania, Maryland, and North Carolina (London, 1778).

563.31   the Posts . . . Oswego &c.]   The British refused to give up forts in the Northwest Territory ceded to the United States by the 1783 Treaty of Paris, maintaining that the Americans had not honored their treaty obligations to bring about payment of debts owed British creditors and to compensate Loyalists for seized property.

565.28   the Great Kanhawa]   Washington owned 30,000 acres near the confluence of the Great Kanawha and the Ohio.

566.36   Rumsey's discovery]   James Rumsey (1743–92) developed an early steamboat.

567.20–21   treaty . . . Fort Stanwix]   The Iroquois Six Nations ceded all territory west of the Niagara River to the United States in the Treaty of Fort Stanwix, October 22, 1784.

568.6–7   On this event]   Richard Henry Lee (1732–94) was elected president of Congress on November 30, 1784.

568.14   repealed . . . British debts]   In 1782 the Virginia Assembly passed a law forbidding British citizens to sue for the recovery of debts contracted before April 19, 1775. The repeal measure introduced during the 1784 session did not pass.

570.6   Colo. Ward]   Joseph Ward was 47 years old at the time of his marriage.

570.18   Miss Custis]   Martha Washington's granddaughter Eleanor (Nelly) Parke Custis (1779–1852) was raised by the Washingtons.

572.28   Fanny Bassett]   Frances Bassett Washington (1767–96) was a niece of Martha Washington who began living at Mount Vernon in 1784. In 1785 she married George Augustine Washington (1763–93), son of Washington's brother Charles, and manager of Mount Vernon from 1785 until his death. In 1795 Fanny married Tobias Lear (1762–1816), George Washington's private secretary.

577.2   Mr Pine]   Robert Edge Pine (1730–88) was an English-born portraitist.

578.2   a girl of six, & a boy of 4]   Nelly Custis and her brother George Washington Parke Custis (1781–1857), who was also brought up by the Washingtons.

578.21   *William Goddard*]   Goddard (1740–1817) published the *Maryland Journal* in Baltimore.

578.27   the work]   Goddard planned to print the papers of General Charles Lee, the officer court-martialed for misconduct at Monmouth, and

NOTES

had written Washington on May 30, 1785, advising him that some of the documents to be included in the work would point up the "unhappy differences" that had existed between the two commanders.

581.2–3   an Ordinance]   The Land Ordinance of 1785, adopted by Congress on May 20, provided for the surveying and sale of Ohio lands. It was the basis for the Northwest Ordinance of 1787.

585.36–37   matrimonial . . . Frigate F. Bassett]   George Augustine Washington married Fanny Bassett on October 15, 1785.

588.1   Longchamp]   Charles Julien Longchamps, a French citizen living in Philadelphia, had assaulted the French chargé d'affaires to the United States in May 1784. The French government demanded that he be returned to France for trial, but eventually he was tried in Pennsylvania.

590.8–9   memorial . . . assessment Bill]   Virginia had disestablished the Anglican Church in 1779, ending the long-standing obligation of citizens to be taxed for the support of the Church of England. In 1784, the Virginia Assembly considered a new bill for a general assessment to support all Christian denominations, dissenting sects as well as the old established church. The bill had the support of Patrick Henry, Edmund Pendleton, and Richard Henry Lee; it was opposed by James Madison. In June 1785 Madison wrote a "Memorial and Remonstrance" against the assessment bill, a copy of which Mason sent Washington. The assessment bill was defeated in late 1785, and in January 1786 the Assembly adopted a statute on religious freedom, originally drafted by Thomas Jefferson in 1777, forbidding taxation to support any religion.

593.18   law-suit . . . slave]   Philip Dalby of Alexandria, Virginia, had traveled to Philadelphia in February 1785 with his servant, a young slave named Frank. According to Dalby, a committee of Quakers approached Frank, persuaded him seek his freedom, and brought a writ of habeas corpus on his behalf. Dalby won the case and returned to Virginia with Frank, who then ran away early in 1787.

600.35–601.1   the Statue in question]   The state of Virginia commissioned Jean-Antoine Houdoun to create the statue of Washington that still stands in the Virginia State Capitol in Richmond. Houdoun had come to Mount Vernon in October 1785 to model his subject from life. As Washington suggested, the finished statue was garbed in modern dress.

601.10   Mr West]   Benjamin West (1738–1820).

601.14   Majr L'Enfant]   Pierre Charles L'Enfant (1754–1825), a native of France, was a Continental Army major and designer of the master plan for the city of Washington, D.C.

602.24   *Arthur Young*]   Young (1741–1820) was a noted British agronomist who began a correspondence with Washington after the Revolutionary War.

610.16–17   *Comments . . . Washington*]   Humphreys worked on his life of Washington while living at Mount Vernon in the summer of 1786. Although he never completed the work, Humphreys did publish an anonymous sketch surveying the period from Washington's birth through his retirement in 1783 as commander of the Continental Army in Jedidiah Morse's *The American Geography; or, a View of the Present Situation of the United States of America* (1789).

610.19   Page 1st (1)]   Washington's comment on Humphreys' passage: "As it was the design of his Father that he should be bred for an Officer in the British navy, his mental acquisitions & exterior accomplishments were calculated to give him distinction in that profession."

610.23   (2)]   Washington's comment on Humphreys' passage: "The Father of General Washington had three sons by a former wife. The eldest, a young man of the most promising talents, after having been appointed Adjutant General of the Militia of Virginia, commanded the Colonial troops in the expedition against Carthagena."

610.32   (3)]   Washington's comment on Humphreys' passage: "and on his return called his patrimonial Mansion Mount Vernon, in honour of the Admiral of that name with whom he had contracted a particular intimacy."

610.34   (4)]   Washington's comment on Humphreys' passage: "On the death of all the children by the first marriage, George Washington acceded to a large landed property."

611.3   Page 2. (1)]   Washington's comment on Humphreys' passage: "the future hero of America began his military career by a principal appointment in that Department, with the rank of Major."

611.4–14   (2) . . . (2)]   Washington's comments on Humphreys' account of his journey to the French commandant in 1753–54.

611.20   Page 4th. (1)]   Washington's response to Humphreys' memorandum asking him to comment on his service in the French and Indian War.

612.26   Captn. (McKay]   James Mackay (d. 1785), an officer from Georgia.

615.4   James's powder]   An 18th-century fever remedy developed by Dr. Robert James.

617.32   Prals]   Provincials, the colonial militia.

618.13–14   the established Corps]   The regular British Army.

619.37   G W . . . imminent danger]   This episode occurred on November 12, 1758.

620.18   Page 8 (1)]   Washington's estimate of grain production at Mount Vernon before the Revolution.

620.21   Page 11 (2)]   Washington's comment on Humphreys' passage describing the "demonstrations of affectionate esteem" given by Virginians after Washington's retirement from the army in 1783.

620.29   Page 14 (1)] Washington's comment on Humphreys' passage: "He keeps a pack of hounds, & in the season indulges himself with hunting once in a week, at which diversion the gentlemen of Alexandria often assist."

620.31   (2)] Washington's comment on Humphreys' passage: "Agriculture is the favorite employment of General Washington, in which he wishes to pass the remainder of his days. To acquire practical knowledge, he corresponds with Mr Arthur Young, who has written so sensibly on the subject."

620.32   (3)] Washington's comment on Humphreys' passage: "He also makes copious Notes in writing relative to his own experiments the state of the seasons, nature of soils, effect of different kinds of manure & everything that can throw light on the farming business."

621.31   commotion in that State] "Shays' Rebellion," in which debt-burdened Massachusetts farmers resisted tax collection and foreclosures in an uprising that broke out in the late summer of 1786 and was finally suppressed by state militia in February 1787. Nine men were killed during the suppression of the insurrection.

623.14–15   the Convention at Annapolis] Commissioners from five states met at Annapolis, Maryland, September 11–14, 1786, to discuss interstate commercial regulations. They adopted a report calling for a convention of delegates from all 13 states to meet in Philadelphia on May 14, 1787, to "devise such further provisions as shall appear to them necessary to render the constitution of the Federal Government adequate to the exigencies of the Union."

624.9–12   Colo. Lee. . . . new choice] The Virginia Assembly had declined to reelect Henry "Light-Horse Harry" Lee (1756–1818) as a delegate to the Congress. Madison was reelected.

626.2–3   the honor . . . the Assembly] The Virginia Assembly had elected Washington a delegate to the Constitutional Convention on December 4.

627.8   *Edmund Randolph*] Randolph (1753–1813) was governor of Virginia from 1786 to 1788. He would serve as President Washington's attorney general (1789–94) and secretary of state (1794–95).

631.8–9   Captn. Asgill] See note 471.35. Humphreys' essay "The Conduct of General Washington Respecting the Confinement of Captain Asgill" was published in the November 16, 1786, number of the *New-Haven Gazette and Connecticut Magazine.*

631.31   old frd of yours] The old friend was Washington himself: Humphreys had warned in his letter of November 1, 1786, that "in case of civil discord . . . you could not remain neuter—and that you would be obliged, in self-defence, to take part on one side of the other: or withdraw from this Continent."

636.28–29   to George Washington]   George Augustine Washington.

641.15–16   the enclosed letters]   The Comtesse d'Anterroche had asked Washington to help her son, who had come to America in 1777 and settled in Elizabethtown, New Jersey. She also wrote appeals to Lafayette, Benjamin Franklin, and Thomas Jefferson.

645.33–34   *attending* delegates]   The Virginia delegates to the Convention were George Washington, George Mason, James Madison, George Wythe, Edmund Randolph, James McClurg, and John Blair. McClurg was chosen after Patrick Henry, Thomas Nelson, and Richard Henry Lee declined to serve.

653.9   *John Cannon*]   Cannon (d. 1799) was a justice of the peace in Washington County, Pennsylvania, where Washington owned land.

660.31   nine other States]   Article VII of the Constitution stipulated: "The Ratification of the Conventions of nine States, shall be sufficient for the Establishment of this Constitution between the States so ratifying the Same."

670.27   *John Armstrong*]   Armstrong (1717–95) had served as a Continental Army major general and as a delegate to Congress from Pennsylvania. His son, John Armstrong, was the author of the Newburgh Address (see note 490.13–14).

673.2   the pieces . . . Publius]   *The Federalist*, written by Alexander Hamilton, James Madison, and John Jay.

680.22   Mr. Barlow]   American poet Joel Barlow (1754–1812) went to France in 1788 as an agent for the Ohio Company, selling land in the Ohio Valley.

685.33   *Richard Henderson*]   Henderson was a resident of Bladensburg, Maryland, who operating an ironworks near Antietam Creek.

687.29–39   The Abbe Raynal . . . Mr. Crevecœur]   Guillaume Thomas François, Abbé Raynal, *A Philosophical and Political History of the British Settlements and Trade in North America* (Edinburgh, 1779); William Guthrie, *New Geographical, Historical and Commercial Grammar* (London, 1777); Jedidiah Morse, *The American Geography; or, a View of the Present Situation of the United States of America* (1789); and Michel-Guillaume Jean de Crèvecœur, *Letters of an American Farmer* (1782).

688.34   declaratory of the rights]   The Virginia convention ratified the Constitution on June 27, 1788, with the recommendation that 40 amendments, including 20 forming a bill of rights, be subsequently adopted.

690.26   late Quartermaster General]   Timothy Pickering had told Webster that "a combined attack was intended to be made upon New York, and that the arrival of the French fleet in the Bay of Chesapeake was unexpected, and changed the plan of operations," an interpretation Washington disputed.

692.13   Circular Letter . . . Convention]   The New York convention voted to ratify the Constitution, 30–27, on July 26, 1788. To secure ratification, the Federalists agreed to sending a circular letter from the New York convention to the other states calling for a second general convention to consider amendments.

693.1   *Edward Newenham*]   Sir Edward Newenham (1732–1814) represented Dublin in the Irish Parliament.

701.33   *Reflection on Slavery*]   This statement was transcribed by David Humphreys, who lived with the Washingtons at Mount Vernon from November 1787 to April 1789.

702.8–9   *Fragments . . . Inaugural Address*]   In January 1789 Washington sent to James Madison for his review a lengthy draft of the presidential inaugural address that Washington expected to be called upon to deliver in a few months. Washington told Madison that the draft was the work of a "gentleman under this roof," presumably David Humphreys, then living at Mount Vernon. Madison convinced Washington that he should not deliver the speech. In 1827 Jared Sparks found the 73-page manuscript, entirely in Washington's hand, among the papers at Mount Vernon. After corresponding with Madison, Sparks decided not to publish the draft in his edition of Washington's writings, and then cut it into fragments which he dispersed to those who sought an example of Washington's autograph. The fragments printed in this volume on pp. 702–16 are presented in the order assigned to them by the editors of *The Papers of George Washington: Presidential Series*, volume 2 (1987).

In 1996 a sheet from the manuscript, believed to have been given by Sparks to the geologist Charles Lyell, was discovered and sold at auction in England. It contains two additional distinct fragments from the draft; their intended position in the address has not been established. The first fragment reads:

> But until the people of America shall have lost all virtue; until they have become totally insensible to the difference between freedom & slavery; until they shall have been reduced to such poverty of spirit as to be willing to sell that pre-eminent blessing, *the birthright of Freemen*, for a mess of pottage; in short, until they shall have been found incapable of governing themselves and ripe for a Master—those consequences, I think, can never arrive.—But it is time

The second fragment reads:

> To advert to the system of policy, which ought, in my opinion, to be pursued to secure our public credit & secure our public felicity.—I have already just glanced upon the superior advantages of a natural kind, which America possesses.—My present object is to point out the means of encreasing & perpetuating the happiness of the people of that Coun-

try.—To embrace this object the mind must dilate with the dimensions of a Continent, and extend with the revolutions of futurity.—The New World is now becoming a stage for wonderful exhibitions.—The discovery of another Continent, in some unknown Seas, could alone afford a Theatre for political action, which could extend in their influence to so large a portion of the earth, or affect so great a multitude of its inhabitants.—It may not then be improper (the more clearly to comprehend our abilities & duties) to make some remarks on our moral, political and relative situation.—

The preliminary observation that a free government ought to be built on the information and virtue of the people will here find its proper place.—Happily our Citizens are remarkably instructed by education, docile to duty & ingenious for making improvements.—I believe, that more knowledge is, at this moment, diffused among them, than among almost any

718.22–23   Hartford fabric] In an endorsement of domestic manufactures, Washington wore a suit of this material at his inauguration on April 30, 1789.

719.27   *George Steptoe Washington*] George Steptoe and his brother Lawrence Washington were the sons of George Washington's brother Samuel (1734–81). They moved into Dr. Craik's house in Alexandria in April 1789.

724.5   *Thomas Green*] Green was head carpenter at Mount Vernon from about 1783 to 1793.

PRESIDENT, 1789–1797

729.1   *Charles Thomson*] Thomson (1729–1824) served as secretary of the Continental Congress, 1774–89. The new Senate asked him on April 6, 1789, to travel to Mount Vernon and formally notify Washington of his election to the presidency.

729.27   *John Langdon*] Langdon (1741–1819), a senator from New Hampshire, had been elected president pro tempore of the Senate when it met on April 6, 1789, to count the electoral votes for president.

733.14–15   Fifth article of the Constitution] The article providing for amendment. Madison opened debate on amendments in the House of Representatives on June 8, 1789, and Congress proposed 12 amendments to the states on September 25, 1789. Ratification of 10 of the amendments—the "Bill of Rights"—was completed on December 15, 1791.

733.36   pecuniary compensation] Washington requested that he receive no presidential salary; as during the Revolutionary War, he asked only that his expenses be reimbursed. Congress, however, voted him an annual salary of $25,000.

734.23   short reply . . . Address] Madison had composed the address of the House of Representatives to the new president and would also draft Washington's May 8, 1789, reply to that address (p. 736 in this volume).

735.1   *Edward Rutledge*]   Rutledge (1749–1800) was a member of the South Carolina House of Representatives.

737.37   tour of the United States]   Washington made presidential tours in New England, October–November 1789, and in the South, April–June 1791.

740.3–4   my Mother's death]   Mary Ball Washington had died August 25, 1789.

743.16   *Arthur St. Clair*]   St. Clair (1736–1818) was governor of the Northwest Territory from 1787 to 1802. He commanded the federal army that was routed by Indians on November 4, 1791.

751.24   *Catharine Macaulay Graham*]   Graham (1731–91), an English-woman, was the author of *History of England from the Accession of James I to That of the Brunswick Line* (8 vols., 1763–83). She had visited Washington at Mount Vernon in 1785.

754.29   your Office abroad]   Jefferson had been serving as American minister to France since 1785.

756.10   such jealousies]   Stuart had written: "A spirit of jealousy which may be dangerous to the Union, towards the Eastern States, seems to be growing fast among us. It is represented, that the Northern phalanx is so firmly united, as to bear down all opposition, while Virginia is unsupported."

757.37   question of discrimination]   During the debate in Congress over Hamilton's plan for funding the national debt, Madison had proposed making a distinction in the rates of repayment between the original holders of Continental securities and the speculators who had bought up the securities at reduced prices. The House voted against discrimination, 36–13, on February 22, 1790.

758.3   Memorial of the Quakers]   Stuart had written that the "late applications to Congress, respecting the slaves, will certainly tend to promote" Southern suspicions. He added: "It gives particular umbrage, that the Quakers should be so busy in this business." On February 11, 1790, Quakers had presented a petition to the House calling for Congress to take action against the slave trade, notwithstanding the prohibition in the Constitution against abolition of the slave trade before 1808. The House considered the petition and eventually adopted a report declaring that Congress could not prohibit the importation of slaves before 1808 or interfere with the treatment of slaves within the states.

761.8–9   questions of assumption—Residence]   Federal assumption of the states' war debts and the permanent location of a national capital.

764.12   the token of victory]   Lafayette had sent Washington the key to the Bastille. In his letter, Lafayette wrote: "give me leave, my dear general, to present you with a picture of the Bastille, just as it looked a few days after

I ordered its demolition, with the main key of the fortress of despotism. It is a tribute which I owe as a son to my adoptive father—as a missionary of liberty to its patriarch." Both the key and the picture still hang in the central passage at Mount Vernon.

778.13–14   law imposing a duty on home made spirits] A federal excise tax on distilled spirits, proposed by Hamilton as part of the 1790 funding plan, was passed by Congress on March 3, 1791. Resistance to the tax in western Pennsylvania in 1794 resulted in the outbreak of lawlessness known as the "Whiskey Rebellion."

785.9   *Jean Baptist Ternant*] Ternant was French minister to the United States.

793.1   *Harriot Washington*] Harriot Washington (1776–1822) was the orphaned daughter of Washington's brother Samuel.

800.30–31   The letter . . . of the] The letter was dated March 28, 1792.

801.23   Major L'Enfant] L'Enfant had been dismissed from his post as chief designer of the new national capital in February 1792 after others involved in the project had found him too difficult to work with. David Stuart was one the commissioners of the federal city.

802.1   *Isaac Heard*] Sir Isaac Heard (1730–1822) was master of the Royal College of Arms.

803.10   *Comte de Ségur*] The Comte de Ségur had bought an estate in Delaware.

804.6–7   subject . . . conversed upon] Madison prepared memoranda recording his conversations with Washington on May 5 and 9, 1792, regarding the President's hope to retire from office in 1793. Madison had urged Washington to stay on, insisting "that in the great point of conciliating and uniting all parties under a Govt which had excited such violent controversies & divisions, it was well known that his services had been in a manner essential."

806.31   furnish me with them] Madison responded on June 20, 1792, enclosing a draft of a brief valedictory speech. Washington consulted Madison's draft in 1796 and incorporated it into the draft of the Farewell Address that he sent Hamilton on May 15, 1796; for the text of Madison's draft, see pp. 940.34–943.29 in this volume.

810.3–4   Other . . . Officers] The enumerated points in Washington's letter (pp. 810.9–813.14) were copied almost verbatim from a letter Thomas Jefferson had written to Washington on May 23, 1792.

810.5   Colo M] George Mason.

814.33   The Plan of Mr. Hoben] Washington's favor helped architect James Hoban (c. 1762–1831) win the commission to design the President's House, later called the White House.

815.28   Mr. Carmichael]   Peter Carmichael (d. 1795) was an American diplomat in Spain, 1782–92.

820.34   the interesting subject]   In his letter of August 5, 1792, Randolph had urged Washington to continue to serve as president.

832.14   *Jean Pierre Blanchard*]   The French balloonist ascended from Philadelphia on January 9, 1793. According to an account in Dunlap's *American Daily Advertiser*, the balloon traveled about 15 miles before coming to earth near Woodbury, New Jersey.

832.29   *Henry Lee*]   Henry "Light-Horse Harry" Lee (1756–1818) was governor of Virginia from 1792 to 1794.

835.18   *Second Inaugural Address*]   Washington's speech remains the shortest inaugural address ever delivered by an American president.

837.27   *Earl of Buchan*]   David Stuart Erskine (1742–1829), eleventh earl of Buchan, who earlier had sent Washington a box supposedly made from the oak tree in which Scottish patriot William Wallace had hid after his defeat at Falkirk in 1298.

842.6   Freneau's and Beeche's]   Philip Freneau's *National Gazette* and Benjamin Franklin Bache's *General Advertiser* were two Philadelphia newspapers that regularly attacked administration policy.

842.15   Mr. G——]   Edmond Charles Genêt (1763–1834) arrived in Philadelphia in May 1793 as the first minister to the United States from the new French republic. His refusal to respect American neutrality in the Anglo-French war led the Washington administration to ask for his recall in August 1793, and he was replaced in February 1794.

844.10   *William Pearce*]   Pearce was manager of Mount Vernon from 1793 to 1796.

850.37   public prints]   Newspapers.

852.6–7   other causes . . . necessary to detail]   Washington hoped that renting his farms to competent English farmers would permit him to free his slaves and establish them as paid agricultural laborers (see the passage marked "(Private)" in Washington's letter to Tobias Lear, May 6, 1794, p. 868.27–35 in this volume). Young responded to this letter on June 2, 1794, asking whether it was Washington's intention to rent the slaves with the farms at which they worked and lived. Washington replied on November 9, 1794, apologizing that "my intention, respecting the Negros which reside on my farms, did not sufficiently appear to you. It was not my meaning (if it was so understood) to make it a *condition* that they should be annexed as an appendage thereto. I had something better in view for them than that. To accomodate—not to incumber the farmer, was the idea I meant to convey to you—that is—that he might, or might not as his inclination or interest should dictate, hire them, as he would do any other labourers which his necessity wd require him to employ."

852.18   sketch herewith sent]   The map of Mount Vernon enclosed in this letter has not been found. Another copy of the December 1793 map of the five Mount Vernon farms, the only example known to survive, is in the Huntington Library in San Marino, California.

863.19   Davy at Muddy hole]   Davy, a slave born about 1743, was overseer at Muddy Hole, one of the five Mount Vernon farms. Davy was married to Molly, a woman at the Mansion House farm. The overseers on the other farms were white.

866.18–22   8th. of June . . . 8th. of Januy.]   On June 8, 1793, the British government ordered the Royal Navy to stop and seize neutral ships carrying grain and flour to French ports. A second order, issued on November 6, 1793, imposed a total blockade on the French West Indies; within a few months more than 250 American ships were captured and their cargoes confiscated. The British government revoked the November 1793 order on January 8, 1794, allowing Americans to resume trade in non-military items with the French West Indies.

869.30   Mr. Bl—ts]   Samuel Blodget.

873.15   *Charles Mynn Thruston*]   Thruston (1738–1812) was an Anglican minister who had served as a lieutenant in the Virginia militia during the French and Indian War.

873.22–23   the people of Kentucky]   Thruston had written "there is existing at Kentuckey a powerful faction for placing that Country under the protection of the British Government, & of seperating from the Union of the States."

874.5   those Societies]   Democratic Societies. At least 11 Democratic Societies were founded in the United States in 1793, and approximately 24 more were organized in 1794. Inspired by the French Revolution, the Societies championed the cause of the French republic in its war with monarchical Britain.

874.40   Genl. Morgan]   In his letter to Washington, Thruston had recommended that former Continental general Daniel Morgan (1736–1802) be entrusted with the defense of the frontier in the event of a British or Spanish invasion.

877.1   Mr. Henry . . . Mr. Jefferson]   Lee had written that Patrick Henry believed that Washington considered him to be "a factious seditious character." Lee also reported that Jefferson, when recently asked if Washington had attached himself to Britain and was being "governed by British influence," had replied " 'that there was no danger of your being biassed by consideration of that sort so long as you was influenced by the wise advisers or advice which you at present had.' "

877.34   opposition . . . against me]   The so-called "Conway Cabal." See note 280.1.

879.9–10   your safe arrival]   Washington had nominated Jay, chief justice of the Supreme Court, as special envoy to Britain on April 16, 1794, in an effort to avoid Anglo-American war. Jay sailed on May 12 and landed June 8. His instructions, largely drafted by Hamilton, directed him to seek a commercial treaty with England and to secure the evacuation of the British posts in the Northwest Territory, compensation for captured American shipping, and compensation for the slaves liberated by the British during the Revolutionary War.

879.25–26   Mr. Simcoe]   John Graves Simcoe (1752–1806), lieutenant governor of Canada from 1792 to 1794.

881.1   *Elizabeth Parke Custis*]   Martha Washington's granddaughter Elizabeth Custis (1776–1834) would marry Thomas Law in 1796.

881.5   your sister Patcy]   Martha Washington's granddaughter Martha Parke Custis (1777–1854) had become engaged to Thomas Peter; they married on January 16, 1795.

886.1   *Edmund Randolph*]   Washington named Attorney General Randolph secretary of state on January 2, 1794. Jefferson had resigned December 31, 1793.

886.25–26   these self created societies]   The Democratic Societies.

886.28   Mr. M——n]   James Madison.

887.12   my Speech]   The forthcoming Annual Message to Congress.

893.34   general Wayne]   An American army in the Northwest Territory commanded by Anthony Wayne had decisively defeated an Indian coalition at Battle of Fallen Timbers on August 20, 1794.

895.22–23   Colo. Willm. Washington]   William Augustine Washington (1757–1810), son of Washington's half-brother Augustine, had commanded American cavalry with distinction at the Battle of Cowpens, fought in South Carolina on January 17, 1781.

903.28–29   Lord Sheffield]   John Baker Holroyd, Earl of Sheffield, had made his prediction in *Observations on the Commerce of the American States* (1783).

907.11   *Charles Carter*]   Charles Carter, Jr., (1733–96) had asked Washington for a loan of $1,000 to help his son, William Carter, whose carriage-making business had fallen on hard times.

912.32–34   treaty of Amity . . . Gazettes]   Jay had signed a treaty with Britain in London on November 19, 1794, and a copy had reached Washington on March 7, 1795. Although he had yet to decide whether to sign the treaty, Washington submitted it to the Senate, which ratified it on June 24 after a secret debate. Republican journalist Benjamin Franklin Bache obtained the text of the treaty and published it his *Philadelphia Aurora* on July 1, 1795, arousing intense public controversy.

913.37   this request of mine]   Hamilton responded on July 11, 1795, to
Washington's request for a review of the Jay Treaty with a 53-page commentary, concluding with the recommendation that the president should sign the
treaty.

914.1   resolution of the Senate]   The Senate had ratified the treaty with
the provision that its 12th article, limiting the size of American merchant ships
trading in the British West Indies to 70 tons, be suspended.

915.30   Camillus]   A series of 38 essays defending the Jay Treaty were pub-
lished by "Camillus" in New York newspapers between July 22, 1795, and
January 9, 1796. Hamilton wrote 28 of the essays and Massachusetts Federalist
Rufus King wrote the remainder.

917.14–15   young Fayette]   George Washington Motier Lafayette (1779–
1849), the son of Marquis de Lafayette, had arrived in the United States as a
refugee from revolutionary France. (His father, a supporter of constitutional
monarchy, had fled France in August 1792 following the overthrow of Louis
XVI and had been captured and imprisoned by the Austrians.) In April 1796
Washington invited the young man to join the presidential household in
Philadelphia.

918.9   offered to others]   Following the forced resignation of Edmund
Randolph on August 19, 1795, Washington had offered the position of Sec-
retary of State to William Paterson, Thomas Johnson, and Charles Cotesworth
Pinckney; all three had declined.

925.16   Colo. Innes's report]   In his letter of July 3, 1795, Morris had alluded to the report of Harry Innes "to the Governor of Kentucky in which
he states that the withholding an acknowledgement of our Right to a free
Navigation of the River Mississippi by the Court of Spain must be attributed
in part to british influence."

929.26   papers relative . . . the Treaty]   The House resolution requesting
the papers had passed on March 24, 1796. All of Washington's cabinet had
responded to this note by March 26, and all advised against complying with
the request from Congress.

931.22   the General Convention]   The Constitutional Convention of 1787.

934.23–24   information . . . G.—— M.——]   Hamilton had sent Washington a copy of a letter written by Gouverneur Morris in London on March
4, 1796. In his letter, Morris wrote that a trusted confidential source in Paris
had informed him that the French government, angered by the Jay Treaty,
would soon annul the 1778 Franco-American treaty of alliance and send a fleet
to America to deliver a diplomatic ultimatum.

934.26   Mr. Monroe]   James Monroe, American minister to France.

937.5   a letter to the Emperor]   On May 15, 1796, Washington wrote a
private letter to Francis II, the Austrian Emperor, pleading for Lafayette's
release from prison. Lafayette was freed in the summer of 1797.

938.12–13   the paper mentioned therein]   Washington's first draft of the Farewell Address (pp. 940–48 in this volume).

938.14   the reference at foot]   On the first page of the draft, after the phrase "solicitude of my confidential friends" (p. 940.16 in this volume), Washington had written and then crossed out "'(particularly in one who was privy to the draught)'"; an asterisk referred to the identification "Mr. Madison" at the foot of the page, which Washington also crossed out.

938.27–28   the quotation]   The text of the farewell address Washington and Madison had prepared in 1792; see pp. 940.34–943.29 in this volume.

938.30   *one or two . . . characters*]   Madison and Jefferson.

939.9   *particular character*]   Madison.

939.12–13   pages 5, . . . 18th page]   The three passages marked by Washington are printed within square brackets in this volume on pp. 941.38–942.3, p. 943.16–20, and p. 948.8–16.

939.39–40   Successor to Mr. P——]   Hamilton had recommended Rufus King to succeed Thomas Pinckney as American minister to Britain.

940.34–943.29   The period . . . their happiness.]   These paragraphs contain the text of the valedictory message Madison had submitted to Washington on June 20, 1792.

948.29   letter without date]   In a letter probably written on June 16, 1796, Hamilton told Washington that a French merchant in New York had informed him of a French plan to seize American ships trading with British ports.

948.34–35   the Ship Mount Vernon]   The American ship *Mount Vernon* was seized by a French privateer off the coast of Delaware on June 9, 1796.

949.37   Mr. M——]   James Monroe.

951.13   Bache's Paper]   The questions concerning American neutrality that Washington had submitted in writing to his cabinet on April 18, 1793, had been obtained surreptitiously and published by Benjamin Franklin Bache.

952.10–11   person evidently alluded to]   Alexander Hamilton.

952.33–34   the Little Sarah]   In July 1793 French envoy Edmond Charles Genêt had outfitted a captured British merchant ship, the *Little Sarah*, in Philadelphia and sent it to sea as a privateer in defiance of the Washington administration's neutrality policy.

954.22   Paper herewith enclosed]   Hamilton submitted drafts of the Farewell Address to Washington on July 30 and August 10, 1796. Washington preferred the July 30 draft and followed it closely in preparing the final version.

961.30–31   introduce a Section in the Address]   Hamilton replied September 5, 1796, recommending that Washington present his proposal regarding a national university in his forthcoming Annual Message to Congress, not in the Farewell Address.

962.1   *Farewell Address*]   The Farewell Address first appeared in the September 19, 1796, number of the Philadelphia newspaper *American Daily Advertiser*, published by David C. Claypoole.

978.37–38   date assigned . . . event]   The posts were to have been surrendered by June 1, 1796.

985.26   *John Greenwood*]   Greenwood was a New York City dentist who constructed several sets of false teeth for Washington.

988.19–20   consequences . . . fears forebode]   On January 23, 1797, Trumbull had written: "Some of the consequences while I have heretofore ventured to present to your View in contemplation, have already been experienced, in the late hardly contested Election for your Successor. Would to Heaven! that this might be the only Evil we shall have to encounter in this Event—circumstances however, almost forbid us the Hope."

RETIREMENT, 1797–1799

993.11   conduct . . . French government]   McHenry had written to Washington on March 24, 1797, that the French government had refused to recognize or receive Charles Cotesworth Pinckney, the new American minister to France.

994.12   *William Heath*]   Heath (1737–1814) had been a Continental Army major general.

997.34   withdraw your Services]   Washington had offered Humphreys, then American minister to Spain, a position as his private secretary at Mount Vernon.

998.3   your domestic concerns]   Humphreys married Ann Frances Bulkeley in 1797.

998.26–27   the "Calm light . . . Philosophy"]   A line from Washington's favorite play, Joseph Addison's *Cato* (1713): "Thy steady temper . . . can look on guilt, rebellion, fraud, and Caesar, in the calm light of mild philosophy."

1001.1   *Samuel Washington*]   Samuel Washington (c. 1765–1832) was the son of Washington's brother Charles.

1001.26–27   your wheat . . . spoiling thereof]   Samuel Washington had written on July 7, 1797, asking his uncle for a loan. He had lost most of his wheat crop because an inexperienced harvester had stacked the grain in such a way that it was ruined by rain.

1002.16   *Lawrence Lewis*]   Lewis (1767–1839) was the son of Washington's sister Betty Washington Lewis. He had agreed to serve as his uncle's secretary. On Washington's last birthday, February 22, 1799, Lawrence Lewis married Nelly Custis, Martha Washington's granddaughter.

1002.19   the loss of your servant]   Lewis had written that his departure for Mount Vernon had been delayed by the escape of a slave.

1005.21   the Secretary of War]   James McHenry.

1015.23   *Alexander Spotswood*]   Spotswood (1751–1818), a Continental Army veteran, was married to Elizabeth Washington, daughter of Washington's half brother Augustine.

1015.25–27   letter of the 13th. . . . Sedition laws]   On December 9, 1798, Spotswood wrote Washington to declare that the letter "dated the 13th, bearing my signature, is an infamous forgery . . ." In June and July 1798 the Federalist Congress had passed, and President Adams signed into law, three alien acts and a sedition act. The alien acts extended the period required for naturalization from five to 14 years and gave the president power to expel or, in time of declared war, to imprison dangerous aliens; the sedition act made publication of "false, scandalous, and malicious writing" attacking the federal government, the president, or the Congress a crime punishable by up to two years in prison and a fine not exceeding $2,000.

1019.3   candidate . . . General Assembly]   Henry agreed to become a candidate for the Virginia House of Delegates and was elected, but his death in June 1799 prevented his taking office.

1021.14   *James Welch*]   In December 1797 Welch had contracted to lease 23,000 acres Washington owned on the Great Kanawha River. Welch planned to divide the land into smaller parcels that he would rent to tenant farmers. That rent was to be the source of the payments the speculator would make to Washington, for Welch himself had no money, though he did hold title to some 99,995 acres on the Elk River in Randolph County, Virginia. Welch was unable to meet his obligations and his contract with Washington lapsed.

1023.12   Slaves which I hold]   In the summer of 1799, Washington drew up a detailed census of the Mount Vernon slaves, a document he titled "Negros Belonging to George Washington in his own right and by Marriage." The census listed 317 slaves on the five Mount Vernon farms. Washington owned 124 of these people, 40 were leased from another owner, and the remaining 153 "Dower" slaves were the property of the Custis estate. The Custis slaves could not be freed by Washington or his wife; they were to be inherited by Martha Washington's grandchildren after her death. At the time of Washington's death, there were 314 slaves at Mount Vernon; 122 of them were freed under his will. The executors of Washington's estate continued to support the freed people who chose to remain as pensioners at Mount Vernon after the death of Martha Washington. The last pensioner died in 1833.

1023.34   taught to read and write]   Subsequent legislation made it illegal to educate blacks in Virginia.

1024.11   William Lee]   Washington had bought his personal servant Billy, or William Lee, in 1768 from Mrs. Mary Lee, widow of Col. John Lee of

Westermoreland County, Virginia, for £68 15s. He served Washington throughout the Revolutionary War. By 1799 William Lee, who had broken both knees, was crippled and employed as a shoemaker at Mansion House farm. He died at Mount Vernon in 1810.

1027.10   Liberty-Hall Academy]   Now Washington and Lee University.

1043.36   the answer I gave you]   In his letter of June 22, 1799, Trumbull had urged Washington to enter the presidential election in 1800. Washington continued to refuse to consider the suggestion.

1044.9–10   present Gentleman in Office]   President John Adams.

1045.22–23   Mr. Bordley . . . Essays on Husbandry]   John Beale Bordley, *Essays and Notes on Husbandry and Rural Affairs . . .* (Philadelphia, 1799). A copy of the book was in the library at Mount Vernon when Washington died.

1046.12   part of the $800,000]   Republican newspaper editor William Duane had charged in the *Philadelphia Aurora* that the Adams administration was under corrupt British influence. Secretary of State Pickering moved to have Duane indicted under the Sedition Act, but the case was dropped after Duane announced that he would introduce as evidence a letter critical of the Washington administration that Adams had written while serving as vice-president.

1047.1   *Robert Lewis*]   Lewis (1769–1829) was the son of Fielding Lewis and Washington's sister Betty. He was employed as a secretary to Washington in the late 1790s.

1049.20   other subject of your letter]   Trumbull had again urged Washington to become a candidate for the presidency.

1050.21   death of my brother]   Charles Washington.

1051.28   *James Anderson*]   Anderson was farm manager and operator of the distillery at Mount Vernon. This is the last letter Washington is known to have written before his death on December 14, 1799.

Index

Adam, Robert, 129, 149

Adam & Campbell, 149

Adams, Daniel Jenifer, 184, 236, 1039

Adams, John, 205, 403, 475, 477, 909, 910; letters to, 736, 1005, 1007

Adams, Peter, 455

Agriculture, Society for the Promotion of (Philadelphia), 592

Albany, N.Y., 231, 232, 233, 423, 424, 431, 434, 435, 438, 446, 447, 448, 454, 510, 561

Albemarle, Va., 84, 824

Albemarle Sound, 839

Alexander, Gerald, 52

Alexander, Robert, 756

Alexander, William. *See* Stirling, Lord

Alexander the Great, 681

Alexandria, Va., 17, 40, 63, 66, 68, 75, 78, 127, 153, 168, 184, 432, 565, 577, 593, 611, 612, 614, 626, 644, 663, 719, 776, 785, 789, 825, 852, 855, 859, 861, 862, 896, 898, 999, 1004, 1023, 1024, 1033, 1040

Alferd, Thomas, 185

Algiers, 920, 980

Alien and Sedition Acts, 1015–16

Aliquippa (Delaware woman), 33

Allegheny County, Pa., 872, 889

Alleghany Mountains, 12, 18, 29, 134, 150

Alleghany River, 432, 561, 612

Allen Town, N.J., 315

Alton, John, 57, 1031

Amboy, N.J., 257

Amelia County, Va., 446

Amherst, Lord Jeffrey, 305

Anderson, Ephraim, 231

Anderson, James, letter to, 1051

Anderson, Dr. James, 838

Anderson (New York merchant), 390

André, John, 387–89

Annapolis, Md., 400, 554, 570, 633, 663, 1015

Anne, Queen of England, 681

Annual Addresses to Congress: first, 748–51; second, 768–72; third, 786–92; fourth, 826–32; fifth, 846–51; sixth, 887–95; seventh, 919–24; eighth, 978–85

Anstey, John, 642

Antwerp, 831

Appalachian Mountains, 530, 611, 852

Aquia Creek, Va., 277

Aranjuez, Spain, 979

Arbuthnot, Marriot, 359, 364, 368, 427

Ariss, John, 1047

Armstrong, John, 124, 274; letter to, 670

Arnold, Benedict, 206, 208, 387, 388, 392, 431; letters to, 192, 270, 381

Articles of Confederation, 224, 505, 509, 515, 519–20, 525, 531–32, 552–53, 588–89, 595–96, 600, 605–06, 629, 648, 703

Asgill, Charles, 471, 481, 631

Ashby, John, 11, 66, 75

Ashby's Bent, Va., 16

Ashford family, 336

Ashton, Ann, 1034

Athawes, Samuel, 107

Atkin, Edmund, 106

Augusta, Ga., 67, 68, 82, 150, 438

Augusta County, Va., 83

Augustus, Emperor, 681

Austria, 585, 840

Bache, Benjamin Franklin, 842, 949

Bache, Richard, 413, 886

Bache, Sarah, letter to, 412

Badlam, Ezra, 426

Bahamas, 585

Baldwin, Jonathan, 239

Balfour & Barraud. *See* Barraud, Daniel

Ball, Blackall William, 297

Ball, Burges, 740, 742, 859; letters to, 884, 1050

Ball, Mrs. Burges, 885, 1050

Ball, Frances, 1034

Ballman, Dr., 936, 937

Baltimore, Md., 454, 455, 456, 482, 555, 685, 814

Banister, John, letter to, 298

Bank of Alexandria, 1041

Bank of Columbia, 1041

Bank of the United States, 778, 784, 787, 831, 850

Barbé-Marbois, François, Marquis de, 362

Barber, Francis, 510

Barère de Vieuzac, Bertrand, 867

Barlow, Joel, 680, 684, 687

Barras Saint Laurent, Jacques Melchoir, Comte de, 425, 427, 429, 431, 442, 446, 451, 455–56

Barraud, Daniel (Balfour & Barraud), 184

Barrett, Nathaniel, 594

Barth, John Joseph de, 868

Bartrand, Mr. *See* Barère de Vieuzac, Bertrand

Barwicks, Thomas, 12

Bassett, Anna Maria Dandridge, 147, 170

Bassett, Burwell, 824, 833; letters to, 146, 169

Bassett, Frances, 572

Bater, Philip, 650

Bath, England, 604

Bayard, Samuel, 653

Bayard, William, 389

Baylor, George, 264

Beaver Dam Creek, Va., 456

Bedford, N.Y., 436

Bedford, Penn., 886

Bedford, Va., 82, 83

Belhaven. *See* Alexandria, Va.

Bell, David, 66, 68

Belvoir, Va. (Fairfax plantation), 34, 52, 97, 98, 148, 149, 573, 839, 1004

Benson, Egbert, 979

Bergen County, N.J., 240

Berkeley County, Va., 148, 797, 1027, 1037, 1048

Berkeley Springs, Va., 12, 149

Berkshire County, Mass., 435, 448

Bermuda, 585, 925–26

Berrien, John, 227

Bevan, David, 307

Bicker, Henry, 307

Big Beaver Creek, 564, 663, 664

Bingham, Mr., 987

Birney, Thomas, 40

Bishop, Thomas, 1031

Black Islands (mistranslation of "Illinois"), 19–20

Bladensburg, Md., 129, 786

Blaine, Ephraim, 670

Blair, John, 678

Blanchard, Jean Pierre, 832

Bland, Humphrey, 190

Bland, Theodorick, 762; letter to, 506

Bland (privateer), 107

Block Island, R.I., 427, 429

Blodgett, Samuel, 810, 815, 869

Blount, William, 816

Blue Mountains, 855

Blue Ridge, 11

Bocker, Phillip, 297

Bordentown, N.J., 263, 266

Bordley, John Beale, 1045

Boston, 150, 153, 155, 158, 159, 160, 168, 170, 172, 173, 176, 179, 189, 195, 198, 199, 200, 202, 204, 205, 206, 207, 213, 214, 215, 217, 219, 220, 221, 222, 239, 324, 360, 362, 428, 429, 435, 450, 475, 569, 631, 916, 917, 979

Boston Harbor, 179, 180

Boston Neck, 178, 217, 219

Boston Port Act, 149, 150

Boucher, Rev. Jonathan, letters to, 126, 140, 143

Boucher, Miss, 144

Boudinot, Elias, 289; letters to, 344, 495, 500, 528

Bound Brook, N.J. *See* Middlebrook, N.J.

Bouquet, Henry, 95, 96

Bowie, John, 556, 557

Bowles, William Augustus, 816

Boyes (shipmaster), 110, 112, 115

Bracken, Rev. John, 573

Braddock, Edward, 50, 51, 55, 56, 59, 614, 617; defeat of, 220

Bradford Hall, 602

Bradford, William, 867

Bradstreet, Lyonel, 163

Brandywine Creek, battle of, 274, 283

Brant, Joseph, 354, 817

Brattle, William, 176

Brenton's Point, R.I., 435

Brissot de Warville, Jean Pierre, 753

Bristol, Pa., 263

Briston, Mary, 573

Briston, Robert, 573

Bristow. *See* Briston

British East India Company, 153

Broadwater, Charles, 152
Brown, James, 137
Brown, Dr., 663
Brown (Indian trader), 20
Bronx River, 437, 443, 445, 448
Buchan, David Stuart Erskine, Earl of, 865, 1029; letters to, 837, 999
Buchan, Lady, 1000
Buchanan, James, 587
Buchanan, John, 82, 83, 84, 85
Buffalo River, 56, 816
Bullions Tavern, N.J., 453
Bullitt, Thomas, 223
Bulls Ferry, N.J., 426
Bunker Hill, Mass., 203, 217, 220; battle of, 178–180, 184–85, 213, 219
Bunner, Rudolph, 318
Burgoyne, John, 219, 279, 283
Burlington, N.J., 267–68
Burnett, Icabod, 485
Burr, Aaron, 297
Burton, Ralph, 56, 59, 615
Bushfield, Va., 305
Butler, James, 863
Butler, Richard, 316, 354
Byrd, William, 1029
Byron, John, 320, 322, 325, 389

Cabell, Buchanan & Southall (James Navigation Company), 587, 1025, 1027, 1041
Cabot, George, 917
Cacapon River, 15, 71
Cadiz, 504, 508, 509, 584
Cadwalader, John, 263, 266; letter to, 390
Cadwalader, Mrs. John, 392
California, 582
Calvert, Benedict, 184; letter to, 144
Calvert, Mrs. Benedict 146
Calvert, Eleanor, 144–46
Cambridge, Mass., 178
Camden, S.C., 433; battle of, 397, 399
Camillus (pseud. of Alexander Hamilton), 915
Campbell, Alexander (pseud.), 207
Campbell, Alexander, 999
Campbell, Andrew, 12
Campbell, Archibald, 337
Campbell, Arthur, 816
Campbell, Henry, 78, 80

Campbell, James, 459
Campbell, John, 823
Campbell, Joseph, 32
Campbell, Mungo, 279
Canada, 22, 220, 311, 312, 396, 539, 560, 649, 879, 978–79; as American military objective, 187–89, 192–93, 195, 206, 224, 327–30; as destination, 213; British troops from, 355, 427, 432; Canada Act, 158; Canada Expedition, 41, 42; French interests in, 328–29
Cannon, John, letter to, 653
Cape Fear, N.C., 224
Cape François, Haiti 451
Cape Henry, Va., 455
Carey's American Museum, 687
Carleton, Guy, 311, 475, 554; letter to, 511
Carlisle, Pa., 124, 837, 886
Carlyle, John, 53, 70, 89, 91
Carmichael, Peter, 584, 815
Carolina, 70, 81, 92, 451
Carolina Brigade, 317
Caroll, Daniel, 482
Carrington, Edward, 649
Carroll, Margaret, 556
Carter, Charles, 598, 742, 1028; letter to, 907
Carter, Landon, letters to, 310, 1015
Carter, Elizabeth (Lewis), 740, 743, 1034
Cary, Miles, 151
Cary, Robert & Co., 108, 109, 169
Cassey, Peter, 15
Catawba Creek, Va., 82, 85
Cates Marsh, Va., 11
Catharine II, of Russia, 683
Caudy, James, 15
Caunotaucarius (Indian name for George Washington), 36, 611
Cayenne, Colony of, 597
Cazneau, Isaac, 217
Chads Ford, Pa., 274
Chambly, Quebec, 229
Chapman, Russell, 56
Charles III, of Spain, 584, 599
Charles County, Md., 1039
Charleston, S.C., 348, 355, 360, 364, 378, 435, 445, 447, 585, 690, 814
Charlestown, Mass., 164, 179, 180, 183, 239

Charlottesville, Va., 432, 436
Chastelleux, Jean François, Marquis de, 579; letter to, 678
Chastelleux, Madame de, 674
Chatham, N.J., 452, 453
Cheat River, 565, 664
Chesapeake Bay, 435, 448, 449, 451, 454, 463
Chester, Pa., 274, 814
Chesterfield Court House, Va., 423
Chittendens Hill, N.Y., 437
Choisy, Claude Gabriel, Marquis de, 455
Chota (Indian town), 90
Christiana Bridge, Del., 454
Cincinnati, Ohio 1039
Cincinnati, Societies of the, 601, 623, 624, 625, 632, 634, 642, 645, 650
City Tavern (Philadelphia), 655
Clark, George Rogers, 432
Clark, Joel, 227
Claverack, N.Y., 382
Cleveland, James, 184, 185
Clinton, George, 229, 435, 436, 608, 773, 1029, 1039; letters to, 292, 551
Clinton, Mrs. George, 551
Clinton, Sir Henry, 205, 213, 224, 258, 279, 314, 322, 348, 353, 354, 367, 691; letter to, 388
Clinton, James, 423, 427, 429, 431, 434, 435, 446
Clymer, George, letter to, 264
Coal River, 869
Cochran, Dr. John, letter to, 355
Cochran, Mrs., 355
Cocks, William, 57
Coddy. See Caudy, James
Coffin & Alexander (N.Y. merchant), 390
Cogswell, Nathaniel, 428
Colerain, Ga., 978
Coles, Isaac, 877
College Creek, Va., 455, 456
College of New Jersey, 129
Collier, Sir George, 354
Collins, John, 15
Colombe, M. de la, 360, 362
Colvill, Thomas, 143, 161
Common Sense (Paine), 206
Concord, Mass., 164, 183, 198
Connecticut: and Constitution, 664, 669, 675, 698; Assembly, 434; British military in, 367; manufacturing, 718; provisions, 424, 428; recruitment, 204, 368, 434; troops of, 199, 215, 239, 244, 270, 425, 436, 443, 446, 447, 450, 452, 514
Connecticut River, 324, 428
Connolly, Dr. John, letter to, 162
Conococheague (Maidstone), Md., 79
Conococheague River, 797
Constitution, 622, 654–62, 664, 666–73, 675, 677–79, 681, 684, 688–89, 692, 695, 698–99, 706, 708, 732, 733, 739, 748, 750, 756, 787, 805, 810, 829, 830, 835, 843, 877, 882, 883, 884, 893, 931–32; Constitutional Convention, 531, 596, 599–600, 627, 629, 632–35, 641–46, 648, 650–52, 654–58, 664, 676, 695, 705, 708–10, 712, 739, 811
Contee, Thomas, 163
Contrecoeur, Claude Pierre Pécardy, Sieur de, 35, 44
Conway, Henry, 204
Conway, Richard, letter to, 719
Conway, Thomas, 275, 276, 286, 287, 288, 289; letter to, 280
Cooke, Joseph Platte, 239
Corbin, Francis, 822
Corbin, Richard, 69, 91, 92; letter to, 34
Cornell, Ezekiel, 422
Cornplanter (Seneca chief), 772, 775
Cornwallis, Charles, 403, 431, 432, 433, 436, 438, 445, 446, 451, 452, 462, 464, 465; letter to, 464
Cortland. See Van Courtland
Coryell's Ferry (Delaware River), 314
Courtland. See Van Courtland
Couzens, Capt. (shipmaster), 105, 106, 112
Cox, Friend, 61
Cox Hill, N.Y., 440, 444
Coxe, Daniel, 1039
Coxen. See Couzens
Craik, Dr. James, 147, 185, 613, 722, 820, 896, 1030; letter to, 556
Craik, Mrs. James, 722
Cranbury, N.J., 314–15
Crawford, Valentine, 123
Crawford, William, letter to, 123
Cresap, Thomas, 12, 13, 61

Crèvecoeur, Hector St. John, 687
Crompond, N.Y., 452
Cross, Jacob, 297
Crosswicks, N.J., 266
Croton Point, N.Y., 425, 437
Crow, Hyland, 844, 860, 862
Crown Point, N.Y., 229, 429, 431, 433
Culpeper County, Va., 136
Culper, Samuel Jr., (pseud. of Robert Townsend), 429
Culper, Samuel Sr., (pseud. of Abraham Woodhull), 429, 430
Cupid (slave), 102
Currin, Barnaby, 17, 18, 29
Custaloga, Chief, 25, 28
Custis, Daniel Parke, 100, 469, 470, 578
Custis, Eleanor Parke, 419, 541–42, 869, 901, 1033; letter to, 900. See also Lewis, Eleanor Parke
Custis, Elizabeth Parke, 1034; letter to, 881
Custis, George Washington Parke, 578, 808, 1033, 1035
Custis, John Parke, 110–14, 122, 126, 127, 132–34, 140, 141, 145, 313, 336, 237; letter to, 417
Custis, Martha, 96, 100, 106. See also Washington, Martha
Custis, Martha Parke ("Patsy"), 112, 113, 132, 140, 146
Custis, Martha Parke (granddaughter of Martha Washington), 808, 994. See also Peter, Martha Parke
Cuyahoga River, 564, 663
Cuzzens, Capt. See Couzens

Dagsworthy, John, 69
Dalby, Philip, 593, 594
Dalton, John, 53, 57, 70, 76
Dalton, Tristram, 865
Danbury, Conn., 323
Dandridge, Bartholemew, 470, 585, 1028
Dandridge, Frances Jones, 146, 147, 170
Dandridge, Francis, 117
Dandridge, John, 636, 1028
Dandridge, Mary, 1028
Daniel, Capt., 84
Darby, Samuel, 433
D'Arendt, Baron, 287
Davenport, Joseph, 911

D'Avilion, Capt., 458
Davis, Thomas, 898, 912
Davison, John, 19, 20, 28
Davy (slave, overseer), 860, 863
Dayton, Jonathan, 414, 423, 424, 425, 1012
De Beville, Pierre François, 439
De Broglie, Prince, 476
De Chatteleaux, Chevr., 402, 427, 455
De Eponsien, Maj., 309
De Haven, Joseph, 297
De Lancy, James, 389, 436, 437, 443
De Repentigny, Louis Le Gardeur, 28, 30
Deakins, William, 822
Dean, John, 68
Declaration of Independence, 737
Delaware: and Constitution, 664, 669, 675, 698; circular to, 399; provisions, 292, 376; troops of, 256, 399
Delaware River, 192, 256, 266, 267, 278, 313, 314, 319, 395
Demeré, Paul, 49
Demmarree. See Demeré, Paul
Denmark, 358
Derby, Conn., 282
Detroit, 432, 539, 540, 560, 564, 979
Deux-Ponts Regiment, 453
Dick, Charles, 68, 80
Dickinson, Edmund B., 318
Dickinson, Philemon, 315, 316
Dieppe, 748
Difficult Run, Va., 1029, 1036
Dinsmoor, Silas, 956, 957, 958, 959
Dinwiddie, Robert, 17, 22, 23, 24, 32, 34, 36, 49; letters to, 35, 38, 40, 46, 58, 62, 69, 72, 74, 77, 81, 85, 91
District of Columbia, 797, 852, 998–99, 1004, 1026, 1033, 1040, 865, 869, 908; establishment of Federal City, 776, 779, 786, 789–90, 801, 814, 839, 852, 865, 998–99, 1004; establishment of university in, 905–07, 908–10, 982–83
Dobbs, William, 439
Dobbs Ferry, N.Y., 426, 437, 438, 439, 441, 443, 446, 474
Dogue Run Farm, 102, 854, 860, 864, 911. See also Mount Vernon
Donaldson, James, 895
Donville, Alexandre d'Agneau, 71–72
Dorchester Hill, Mass., 215

Dorchester Point, Mass., 219
Druillon, Pierre Jacques, 43, 46, 47
Du Pont, M., 680
Du Portail, Louis le Bèque, 439, 455, 480, 554
Duane, James, letters to, 404, 535
Duane, William, 1045
Dublin, Ireland 815
Duke de Burgoyne (ship), 431
Dulany, Lloyd, 143
Dumfries, Va., 148
Dunbar, Thomas, 54, 56, 59, 614, 616
Dundas, Thomas, 401
Dunmore, John Murray, Earl of, 149, 162, 184, 195, 198, 236, 305, 331
Dupont's Regiment. *See* Deux-Ponts Regiment
Dutchess County, N.Y., 229

East Indies, 685
East River, 253
Easton, Capt. *See* Esten, James
Eden, Caroline, 144
Eden, Robert, 143, 144
Edinburgh, Va., 1029
Elizabeth, N.J., 257, 258, 319, 380, 423, 641
Elk River, 463
Englishtown, N.J., 315
Enoch, Henry, 61
Erie, Pa., 611, 612, 894
Essay on War (de Crissé), 190
Esscruniata. *See* Monacatoocha
Estaing, Charles Henri Hector, Comte d', 320, 363, 364, 368, 504; letter to, 321
Esten, James, 122
Euclid, 552
Evans, John, 227
Evans, Lewis, 560, 797
Ewing, George, 263

Fairfax, Bryan, 54; letters to, 152, 153, 157, 293
Fairfax, George William, 11, 14, 15, 16, 39, 40, 42, 52, 55, 57, 107, 129, 157, 161, 573, 604; letters to, 148, 163, 572
Fairfax, Hannah, 54
Fairfax, Sarah Cary, 16, 52, 151, 573, 576; letters to, 53, 96, 1003
Fairfax, Thomas, 63, 66, 75, 839

Fairfax County, Va., 16, 63, 102, 139, 650, 756
Fairfax family, 839
Falconer, William, 577, 578
Fairfield, Conn., 364
Falmouth, Va., 206
Farewell Address, 962–77; draft of, 940–48
Farmington, Conn., 427, 428
Fauquier County, Va., 1036, 1048
Fayette County, Pa., 653, 868, 1001
Federal City. *See* District of Columbia
Fish, Nicholas, 450
Fishkill, N.Y., 381, 427, 530
Fitzgerald, John, 583
Fitzhugh, William, 599; letters to, 48, 400, 598
Fitzhugh, Mrs. William, 400
Flagg, Ebenezer, 427
Fleury, François Louis Teisseydre, Marquis de, 364
Flood, John, 424
Floridas, 343, 766, 815, 979
Forbes, John, 93, 94, 96, 619
Forman, David, 427, 442, 462
Fort Augusta, Pa., 337, 443
Fort Charles, N.Y., 444
Fort Cumberland, Md., 57, 58, 60, 61, 66, 67, 68, 70, 73, 74, 75, 78, 80, 91, 94, 139, 613, 614, 617, 797, 1005
Fort Dinwiddie, Va., 67, 85
Fort Duquesne (Ohio Company fort), 55, 56, 58, 88, 91, 615, 618, 619. *See also* Fort Pitt, Pittsburgh
Fort Frederick, Md., 94, 462, 464
Fort George, N.Y., 430, 441–44
Fort Granby, S.C., 433
Fort Harmar, Ohio, 745
Fort Independence, N.Y., 441, 443
Fort Lee, N.J., 254, 426, 436
Fort Miami, Ohio, 979
Fort Montgomery, N.Y., 279
Fort Mott, S.C., 433
Fort Necessity, Pa., 613
Fort Oswego, N.Y., 27
Fort Pitt, Pa., 125, 135, 561, 565, 568. *See also* Fort Duquesne, Pittsburgh
Fort Schuyler, N.Y., 423, 427. *See also* Fort Stanwix
Fort Stanwix, N.Y., 567; treaty of, 773, 774. *See also* Fort Schuyler

Fort Ticonderoga. *See* Ticonderoga

Fort Trial, Va., 83

Fort Tryon, N.Y., 440, 441–44

Fort Vass, Va. (Vause's fort), 618

Fort Washington (Knyphausen), N.Y., 253, 254, 430, 439, 440, 441, 444

Fowey, H.M.S., 200

Fox, Charles James, 480

France, 306, 327–29, 358, 363, 570, 601, 674, 676, 682, 683, 694, 753, 759, 765, 780–81, 809, 832, 915, 918, 936, 948, 949, 984, 993, 1006, 1010–11, 1017, 1018, 1043, 1045, 1049; Cabinet of, 330; Court of, 371, 404, 411, 481, 559, 585, 670, 775, 799, 588; fleet, 319, 326, 374, 453, 463, 475; military aid to U.S., 381, 390, 411; people of, 534; Revolution in, 746, 753, 779, 807; settlers in western territories, 837; treaty of alliance with, 301–2, 322, 370, 412, 737, 927; treaty of commerce with, 847; troops of, 36, 37, 42, 48, 51, 55, 58, 71, 88, 403, 423, 425, 428, 435, 437, 439, 442, 451–56, 458–61; war with Great Britain, 363, 375, 475, 670, 838, 840

Frankfort, Va., 886

Franklin, Benjamin, 338, 360, 423, 687; letters to, 402, 476

Franklin County, Pa., 797

Frazier, John, 17–18, 24, 26, 33, 34, 58

Frederick II, of Prussia, 595, 683

Frederick County, Va., 13, 139, 143, 611, 1037

Frederick Town. *See* Winchester, Va.

Fredericksburg, Va., 17, 63, 66, 68, 69, 75, 78, 127, 186, 218, 423, 432, 433, 451, 464, 740, 742, 743, 824, 825, 1028

Frelinghuysen, Frederick, 414

French and Indian War, 71–72, 75–76, 85, 162

French Creek, Pa., 22, 26, 27, 29

Freneau, Philip, 842

Frestal, Felix, 936

Frogs Point, N.Y. *See* Throgs Neck.

Frogs Neck, N.Y. *See* Throgs Neck.

Fry, Joshua, 41, 46, 48

Gage, Thomas 56, 72, 155, 158, 164, 615, 616; letters to, 181, 182

Gardner, Thomas, 176

Gardoqui, Diego de, 779

Gates, Horatio, 171, 173, 280, 288, 401; letter to, 287

General Washington (ship), 438

Gênet, Edmond Charles, 864, 876, 885

Genn, James, 11

George III, of Great Britain, 198–200, 234–35, 471, 480, 481, 485, 866

Georges Creek, Md., 54, 55

Georgetown, Md., 435, 776, 786, 789, 814, 815, 852, 866, 901, 1004

Georgia, 796, 839, 916; and Constitution, 669, 675, 699; and Creek Indians, 765, 894, 919; as destination, 631; British military in, 348, 395, 445

Gérard de Rayneval, Conrad Alexandre, 338, 347, 360, 361, 362

Germain, Lord George, 364

Germantown, 869

Germany, 450, 594, 694

Gerry, Elbridge, 655

Gibraltar, 363, 685

Gildart, James, 113

Giles, William, 951

Gilpin, George, 583

Gist, Christopher, 17, 28, 32, 33, 34, 43, 67, 98; letter to, 62

Gist, Nathaniel, 462, 464

Glasgow, 128, 865

Gloucester County, Va., 259, 531, 1037

Gloucester Town, Va., 452, 461, 464, 468

Glover, John, 176, 265

Goddard, William, letter to, 578

Gordon, Samuel, 1029

Gordon, Mrs. William, 291, 478, 533

Gordon, Rev. William, letters to, 291, 477, 530, 556, 559, 569, 587

Gouch, Sir William, 610

Gouvion, Jean Baptiste, 480, 510

Graham, Catharine Macaulay, letter to, 751

Grafton, Augustus Henry Fitzroy, third duke of, 204

Granchain de Sémerville, Guillaume Jacques Constant Liberge de, 458

Grasse, François, Comte de, 442, 446, 447, 448, 451, 453, 454, 455, 456, 458, 463, 464, 689, 690

Gratton, Henry, 693

Graves, John, 607

Graves, Thomas, 455

Great Britain, 36, 42, 86, 93–94, 101, 108, 143, 174, 187–88, 222, 223, 279, 280, 294, 295, 301, 306, 312, 329, 358, 359, 363, 375, 403, 411, 412, 419, 480, 509, 511, 512, 536, 539, 589, 595, 600, 603, 605, 660, 670, 676–77, 681, 683, 694, 702, 737, 765, 766, 798, 851, 857, 867, 873, 878, 879, 880, 903, 913, 915, 916, 917, 918, 920, 949, 1018; as naval power, 328, 390; Cabinet, 467, 866; colonial grievances against, 116–17, 151, 153–58; colonial support for, 221, 269; commerce with America, 130–32, 139, 589, 677, 913, 915, 920, 928–33, 949 (*see also* Jay Treaty); Court, 397, 474, 817; fleet, 450, 475; Parliament, 116, 117, 130, 132, 149, 152, 154, 155, 157–58, 160, 163, 480, 484; postwar relations with U.S., 630, 867, 873, 925–33, 880, 935, 949; relations with France, 328, 363, 375, 475, 670, 837–38, 840, 918

Great Cacapehon River. *See* Cacapon River

Great Cunnaway River. *See* Kanawha River

Great Dismal Swamp, Va., 1001, 1029, 1037

Great Kanhawa River. *See* Kanawha River

Great Meadows, Pa., 617, 1039

Great Miami River, 540

Greaton, John, 514

Green, Rev. Charles, 53, 120

Green, John, 425, 426

Green, Sarah, 1031

Green, Thomas, 863, 912; letter to, 724

Green Spring, Va., 34

Greenbrier River, 575

Greene, George, 485

Greene, Nathanael, 225, 248, 254, 270, 316, 317, 383–85, 400, 401, 433, 438, 445, 462, 463, 467, 602, 629; letters to, 484, 504

Greene, Mrs. Nathanael, 485

Greene, William, 432, 449, 484

Greenwood, John, letter to, 985

Grenville, Thomas, 475

Grenville, Lord William Wyndham, 925, 927

Griffin, Samuel, 176

Gulph Mills, N.J., 307

Guthrie, William, 687

Hackensack, N.J., 253, 256, 257

Hague, the, 475

Half-King. *See* Tanacharison

Halifax, N.S., 199, 204, 364

Halkett, Francis, letter to, 95

Halkett, Sir Peter, 56, 59, 615

Hall, George Abbott, 735

Hamilton, Alexander, 450, 655, 782, 809, 875, 1009, 1011, 1012–13; letters to, 487, 491, 504, 652, 691, 696, 809, 818, 843, 912, 914, 933, 934, 938, 948, 954, 960, 1051

Hamilton, James, 38

Hammond, Sir Andrew Snape, 364, 368

Hammond, Mildred, 1034

Hampshire County, Mass., 435, 448

Hampshire County, Va., 68, 139, 150, 1037

Hampton, Va., 97, 151, 235

Hampton Roads, Va., 451, 452

Hanbury, Capel and Osgood, 108; letter to, 122

Hancock, John, 435, 466; letters to, 208, 216, 228, 240, 248, 256, 262, 266, 274

Hanover Court House, Va., 432

Hanson, John, 722

Harden, Martin, 61

Hardin, Capt. John (Virginia militia), 66

Hardin, Col. John (Kentucky militia), 816

Harlem, N.Y., 430, 440, 445; heights of, 247, 252, 253

Harlem River, 438, 441, 444, 445

Harmar, Josiah, 767

Harrisburg, Pa., 837

Harrison, Benjamin, letters to, 330, 366, 551, 559, 570

Harrison, Elizabeth, 553, 572

Harrison, Richard, 584

Harrison, Robert Hanson, 333

Harrison, Capt., 68, 75

Harrison, Mr., 820

Hartford, Conn., 387, 434, 447, 814

Hartnet, Thomas, 307

Harvard University, 917

Havana, 816
Hawkins, Benjamin, 958
Haynie, Sarah Ball, 1031
Hays Gazette, 624
Hazard, Ebenezer, 229
Hazen, Moses, 400, 417, 431, 438, 450, 452–54
Head of Elk (Elkton), Md., 452, 454, 455, 457, 463
Heard, Sir Isaac, letter to, 802
Heard, Nathaniel, 225
Heath, William, 298, 424, 425, 433, 995; letter to, 994
Hedges, Solomon, 13
Hell Gate (Horns Hook), N.Y., 244, 430
Hempstead Plains, N.Y., 430
Henderson, Richard, letter to, 685
Hendricks (Indian agent), 816
Henley, David, 240
Henry, Patrick, 664, 678, 689, 699, 877, 878; letters to, 656, 918, 1016
Henry, Prince of Prussia, 595
Herbert, William, 251
Hessians, 223, 234, 263, 265, 364 429, 430, 437, 441
Hill & Co., Messrs., 106
Hinchliffe, John, Bishop of Peterborough, 204
Hinman, Benjamin, 239
Hispaniola, 785
Hite, Jost, 11, 15
Hite family, 121
Hoban, Charles, 814
Hogg, Peter, 82, 83, 84, 85
Holland. *See* Netherlands
Holston, treaty of, 827, 959
Homer, 681
Hood, John, 1029
Hooper, Capt., 110
Hopewell Township, N.J., 314
Hopkinson, Francis, letter to, 576
Hopkinson, Mrs. Francis, 577
Horns Hook, N.Y. *See* Hell Gate, N.Y.
Horseneck, Conn., 437
Houdon, Jean Antoine, 601
House of Burgesses. *See* Virginia Assembly.
Howe, Richard, Viscount, 209, 213, 230, 232, 234, 252, 254, 255, 258, 260, 261, 267, 268, 269, 294, 306, 319, 320, 325, 443
Howe, Robert, 414–15; letters to, 369, 413
Howe, Sir William, letter to, 289
Hubbard, Edward, 61
Hudson River, 220, 242, 255, 322–23, 429, 561
Hughes, Edward, 475
Hull, William, 417
Humphreys, David, 601, 620, 621, 723, 730, 765; letters to, 579, 631, 656, 777, 997
Humphreys, Mrs. David, 998
Hunt, Capt., 83
Huntington, Countess of, 572–3
Huntington, Samuel, letter to, 387
Hutchins, Thomas 560, 568

Inaugural Addresses: draft for first, 702–16; first, 730–34; second, 835
Indians, 12–13, 14, 20–23, 26, 51, 62, 63, 65, 66, 67, 71, 73, 74, 75, 82, 88, 93, 94, 125, 150, 162, 224, 529, 535–40, 562, 567, 569, 580, 597, 598, 611–15, 617–18, 648, 686, 743, 749, 769, 778–79, 781, 787–88, 808, 826–29, 832, 893, 904–05, 920, 923, 926, 978; Arundack, 24; Catawba, 37, 84; Caughnawaga, 817; Cayuga, 365; Cherokee, 37, 71, 81, 90, 135, 765, 790, 816, 827, 849, 919, 954–60; Chickamaga, 827; Chicasaw, 37, 816; Chippewa, 24, 37; Choctaw, 816; Creek, 71, 337, 765, 816, 849, 894, 919, 978; Delaware, 23, 24, 36, 45, 349–51; "French Indians," 22–23, 32, 33, 47, 58; Illinois, 743; Miami, 540, 568, 775; Mingo, 23, 24, 45, 48, 90; "Northern Indians," 567; Oneida, 365, 541; Onondaga, 350, 365; Ottway, 24, 33, 37; Seneca, 775, 776; Shanoah, 36; Shawnesse, 20, 21, 23, 25, 45, 765; Six Nations, 19, 22, 25, 36, 38, 90, 365, 367, 537, 567, 773, 775, 776, 790, 816, 894, 904; "Southern Indians," 96, Wabash, 46, 743, 744–45, 767; Wyandotte, 745
Information for those who would wish to remove to America (Franklin), 687
Ingraham, Dr., 1048
Innes, Harry, 678

Innes, James, 975
Innes, Gov. James, 57, 73, 74, 78
Ireland, 199, 204, 312, 363, 614, 857, 867
Isaac (carpenter, slave), 895
Ivernois, François d', 909, 910

Jack (slave), 102, 103
Jackson, Henry, 307
Jackson's River, Va., 82, 85
Jagers. *See* Hessians
Jamaica, N.Y., 430
James River, 69, 82, 159, 423, 431, 436, 445, 446, 457, 463, 564, 565, 568, 570, 575, 581, 583, 586, 587, 592, 620, 659, 663, 908, 909, 910, 1025
James River Company. *See* Cabell, Buchanan & Southall (James Navigation Company)
Jameson, John, 387, 392
Jamestown, Va., 423, 445, 454
Jaudennes, José de, 779
Jay, John, 334, 597, 782, 809, 866, 905, 936–38, 950, 960; letters to, 358, 599, 605, 642, 879
Jay, Mrs. John, 600
Jay Treaty, 912–16, 920, 928–33, 935, 978–79
Jefferson, Thomas, 334, 341, 584, 597, 670, 678, 679, 687, 779, 782, 785, 800, 809, 836, 867, 877, 878; letters to, 485, 600, 663, 754, 809, 815, 825, 837, 864, 908, 951
Jeffreys Rock, N.Y., 440
Jem (carpenter), 895
Jenkins, William, 17
Jeskakake (Shawnesse chief), 25, 26
Johnson, Thomas, 583; letter to, 137
Johnson, John, 118
Johnson, Joshua, 795
Johnstone, Abram, 13
Johnstoun, John, 127, 128, 132
Joncaire, Phillippe Thomas de, 24, 26, 27, 28, 32
Jones, John Paul, 664
Jones, Joseph, 678; letters to, 371, 377, 382, 478, 493, 501
Julian, Isaac, 65
Julius Caesar, 681
Jumonville, Joseph Coulon de Villiers, sieur de, 43, 47

Kalb, Johann, Baron de, 275, 309, 362
Kanawha River, 33, 136, 222, 565, 581, 663, 868, 869, 1029, 1038
Kaskaskies, the (Kaskaskia, Ill.), 745
Keith (ship), 128
Kentucky, 585, 769, 788, 830, 873, 899, 900, 917, 1017, 1040
Keppel, Augustine, 305
Kercheval. *See* Kirchwald, William
King, John, 68
King William County, Va., 103
Kings Bridge, N.Y., 225, 242, 243, 436, 437, 438, 441, 443, 444
King's College, 146
Kings Ferry, N.Y., 354, 364, 367, 381, 426, 452
Kingston, N.J., 314
Kirchwald, William, 1047, 1048
Kirkpatrick, John, 68, 73
Knowlton, Thomas, 203, 247
Knox, Henry, 406, 442, 448, 455, 601, 621, 628, 718, 782, 802, 813, 818, 884, 1009, 1013; letters to, 628, 634, 640, 641, 658, 726, 767, 916, 986
Knox, Mrs. Henry, 630, 636, 641, 659, 726, 916, 917, 987

La Force (Michel Pépin), 43, 45, 46, 47
La Luzerne, Anne César, Chavalier de, 360, 362, 579
La Peyronie, William, 46, 58
La Sol (La Salle), 26
Lafayette, Marchioness de, 355, 361, 365, 366
Lafayette, Marie Adrienne François, Marquise de, 510, 555, 582, 586, 598, 652, 680, 718, 809
Lafayette, Marie Joseph, Marquis de, 274, 288, 309, 314, 315, 330, 338, 355, 371, 423, 432, 433, 436, 438, 445, 446, 448, 450, 451, 454, 455, 458, 462, 474, 480, 504, 505, 560, 570, 579, 587, 601, 753, 759, 1030; letters to, 354, 360, 508, 553, 557, 582, 594, 651, 667, 674, 680, 682, 716, 764, 780, 807
Lafayette, George Washington, 355, 917, 936–37, 938
Lake Erie, 19, 20, 22, 27, 540, 564, 568, 611, 663, 664, 745, 894
Lake Huron, 540
Lake Michigan, 540, 568, 745

Lake St. Clair, 540
Lancashire, England, 802
Lanfant. *See* L'Enfant
Langdon, John, 869; letter to, 729
Lanphier, Going, 238
Laurel Hill, N.Y., 430, 441, 444, 566, 612
Laurel Hill, Pa., 96, 135
Laurens, Henry, letters to, 281, 286, 290, 313, 327, 337
Laurens, John, 338, 429, 461, 466; letters to, 392, 408
Lauzun, Armand Louis de Gonlaut Biron, Duc de, 431, 435, 436, 437, 443, 453–54, 676; letter to, 758
Law, Elizabeth Parke. *See* Custis, Elizabeth Parke
Law, Thomas, 902
Lawrence, Charles, letter to, 107
Lawrence, Jonathan, Jr., 426
Lear, Lincoln, 869
Lear, Tobias, 634, 723, 851, 1031, 1032; letters to, 785, 814, 865
Lear, Mrs. Tobias, 786, 815. *See also* Bassett, Frances; Washington, Frances (Bassett)
Lebeauf River, 612
Ledyard, Benjamin, 227
Lee, Charles, 171, 173, 174, 203, 206, 222, 224, 256, 258, 260, 315, 316, 318, 578, 583, 918, 993
Lee, Henry ("Light Horse Harry"), 365, 399, 891; letters to, 608, 832, 840, 875
Lee, Mrs. Henry, 610
Lee, Richard Henry, 218, 304–05, 624, 664, 699; letters to, 177, 275, 567
Lee, William, 429
Lee, William (slave), 1024
Leitch, Andrew, 247
L'Enfant, Pierre Charles, 309, 601, 779, 786
Lenox, David, 771
Leslie, Alexander, 432, 433
Letters of an American Farmer (Crèvecoeur), 687
Lewis, Andrew, 61, 66, 68, 81, 222, 1038
Lewis, Betty Washington, 1028, 1033, 1034; letters to, 740, 824
Lewis, Eleanor Parke, 1033, 1034. *See also* Custis, Eleanor Parke

Lewis, Fielding, 89, 151, 259, 1034
Lewis, George, 1031, 1034
Lewis, Howell, 1034
Lewis, Lawrence, 860, 1033, 1034, 1035, 1048; letter to, 1002
Lewis, Nathan, 76, 78
Lewis, Mrs. Robert, 1048
Lewis, Robert, 740, 824, 1034; letter to, 1047
Lewis, Warner, 259
Lexington, Mass., battle of, 183
Liberty Hall Academy (Rockbridge, Va.), 1027
Lincoln, Benjamin, 251, 436, 437, 443, 448, 453, 640; letters to, 472, 688, 698
Lisbon, 779
Litchfield, Conn., 427, 428
Litchmores Point, Mass., 195, 215
Little Beaver Creek, 19
Little-falls Plantation, Va., 742
Little Kanawha River, 663, 664, 868, 1038
Little Meadows, Pa., 55
Littlepage, Lewis Jay, 597, 599
Liverpool, England, 113
Livingston, James, 70, 381
Livingston, Jolin, 773
Livingston, Robert R., 229, 505
Livingston, Mrs., 355
Logstown, Pa., 18, 19, 28, 30
Lomax, Lumsford, 61
London, 101, 109, 113, 116, 160, 163, 204, 586, 534–35, 603, 687, 747, 765, 795, 858, 865, 866, 879; Court of, 926, 937
Long Island, N.Y., 67, 200, 205, 239, 240, 244, 245, 430, 445
Long Marsh, Va., 11
Longchamps, Charles-Julien, 588
Loudoun, John Campbell, Earl of, 89, 618
Loudoun County, Va., 139, 1036
Louis XIV, of France, 681
Louis XVI, of France, 350, 429, 508, 683, 764
Low Countries, 694
Lloyds Neck, N.Y., 430
Lunenburg, Va., 83
Luneys Ferry, Va., 82
Lyles, William, 898
Lynch, John, 474

McAlpin, James, 1019, 1020
McCarty, Daniel, 53
McCleod, Norman, 290
McClocklan, James, 30
McDougall, Alexander, 227, 298, 602
McDowell, John, 1015
McGillivray, Alexander, 765, 816
McGowans Heights, N.Y., 441
McGuier, John, 17
McHenry, James, letters to, 474, 587, 993, 996, 1019, 1045
McHenry, Mrs. James, 994
McKay, Henry. *See* McKoy, Henry
McKay, James, 612
McKean, Thomas; letters to, 464, 468
McKenzie, Robert, 68; letter to, 159
McKonkey's Ferry, Penn., 262
McKoy, Henry, 860, 862, 897, 911, 912
McLean, Laughlin, 133
McMillan, John, 77
McNeil, John, 82, 83
McQueen, Capt., 360
McWilliams, William, 287
Mad River, 540
Madeira, 106, 896
Madison, James, 632, 678, 699, 754, 757, 886; letters to, 621, 623, 624, 646, 723, 734, 804
Madrid, 509, 815, 816, 817, 920
Magaw, Robert, 254
Magowan, Walter, 113, 126, 134
Maidenhead, N.J., 267
Maine, 916
Malcom, William, 381
Malden, Mass., 176
Malta, 584
Malvin Hill, Va., 446
Manchester, Va., 1029
Manley, John, 206, 215
Marblehead, Mass., 164
Marbois. *See* Barbé-Marbois
Mariatte. *See* Marietta, Ohio
Marietta, Ohio, 869
Marray, Mr., 953
Marshall, Thomas, 585
Martin, Alexander, letter to, 794
Martin, Thomas Bryan, 63
Mary (ship), 693
Maryland, 113, 134, 143, 149, 292, 675, 795, 796, 845; and Constitution, 664, 675, 680–81, 684, 698–99; Assembly,

38, 568, 575, 629, 640; borders of, 125, 617; circular to, 399; establishment of Federal City, 776; George Washington's property in, 1039; regiments in Ohio Expedition, 70, 73, 614; river navigation, 139, 561, 565, 583, 663–64; troops of, 171, 244, 252, 283, 376, 455, 464, 514, 883, 886, 890
Mason, George, 152, 251, 298, 334, 609, 655, 658, 664, 678; letters to, 129, 338, 401, 590
Mason, Thomson, 53, 1032, 1033
Massachusetts, 368, 422, 621, 630, 700, 718; and Constitution, 634, 655, 664, 670, 675, 698; General Court of, 222, 640; insurgents, 609, 622, 628, 631, 634, 640–41, 648; troops of, 199, 381–82, 386, 417, 428, 432, 442, 446, 448, 450, 490, 514
Massachusetts Bay Colony, 153, 155, 158, 159, 160, 164
Matthews, Capt., 693
Matthews, David, 389
Matthews, Edward, 354
Maxwell, William, 274, 307, 314; letter to, 345
Mediterranean Sea, 771
Mellish, Samuel, 514
Menonville, François, Comte de, 423, 597
Mercer, George, 60, 68, 69, 70, 74, 98, 143 (?), 235, 260
Mercer, Hugh, 160, 161, 169, 223, 225, 235, 267, 356, 619, 823
Mercer, James, 143 (?), 236, 740
Mercer, John Francis, letters to, 607, 822
Merryland (Maryland property), 143
Michilimackinac, 979
Middlebrook, N.J., 333, 354, 454
Middlesex County, Va., 103
Middletown, N.J., 315
Mifflin, Thomas, 175, 225, 228, 229, 266, 620, 890; letter to, 546
Milanberger, Michael, 297
Miles, John, 439
Milford Haven, Wales, 204
Miller, Charles, 226
Millstone River, N.J., 268
Milner, Nathaniel, 68
Milnor, William, 185

Minisink, N.Y., 424

Minor, George, 898

Minorca, 363

Mississippi River, 19, 20, 563, 565, 581, 583, 609, 629, 745, 766, 967

Mohawk River, 429, 541, 1039

Molleson, William, 163

Monacatoocha, 19, 24, 25, 36, 43

Monckton, Robert, 314

Monmouth, N.J., 442–43; battle of, 314–19

Monocasy River, 797, 822

Monongahela River, 18, 19, 34, 35, 37, 58, 87, 121, 233, 565, 612, 614–15, 616, 663

Montflorence, James Cole, 929

Montgomery, Richard, 193, 207, 209, 232, 396

Montgomery County, Md., 1039

Montour, Andrew, 62, 67

Montreal, 561

Morail, 20, 26–27

Mores Mill, N.Y., 457

Morgan, Daniel, 314, 315, 319, 691, 874

Morocco, 694

Morrel, John, 307

Morris, Gouverneur, 716; letters to, 325, 347, 745, 782, 799, 836, 924

Morris, Robert Hunter, 264, 266, 448, 450, 747, 782, 815; letters to, 71, 264, 309, 593

Morris, Mrs. Robert, 594

Morris, Roger, 615

Morris, William, 867

Morris's Heights, N.Y., 440

Morrisania, N.Y., 443

Morristown, N.J., 268, 407, 424, 446, 453

Morse, Jedidiah, 631, 687

Morton, Mrs. Andrew, 574

Mount Vernon, 100, 340, 379, 434, 533, 730, 753, 754, 760, 763, 808, 809, 839, 841, 852, 866, 988, 1047; as destination, 455, 764, 836, 840, 869, 896, 987; as possible British objective, 420–21; estate management, 190–92, 250–51, 486–87, 650–51, 724–26, 740–44, 814–15, 844–45, 859, 910–912, 993, 995, 1048, 1051–52; in last will and testament, 1031, 1033–35; invitations to, 170, 172, 482, 511, 535, 559, 573, 834–35;

mill at, 184–86, 910–11; overseers, 861–64, 895–96; 911–12; plans to rent, 852–57; planting at, 186, 259, 261, 487, 637, 845, 857, 859–62, 866, 897, 910–11, 953–54, 1048, 1051–52

Mount Vernon (ship), 948

Mount Washington, 242

Moylon, Stephan, 371

Muddy Hole farm, 854, 860, 863

Mulay Suleiman, Sultan of Morocco, 920

Murford's Bridge, Va., 456

Murdering Town, Penn., 32

Murray, John. See Dunmore, John Murray, Earl of

Murray, John (gardener), 954

Muse, George, letter to, 147

Muskingum River, 564, 663, 664, 687

Mutiny Bill, 69, 71

Nansemond County, Va., 1037

Nash, Francis, 278

Nash, John, 82

Nashville, Tenn., 816

Natchez River, 979

Neales Grant (land grant), 125

Neavels, George, 11

Nelson, Thomas, 334; letters to, 319, 336, 466

Nelson's Ferry, S.C., 433

Neptune (slave), 102

Netherlands, 358, 488, 683, 694, 761, 769, 790, 840, 850

Neutrality; policy of, 694, 840, 867, 878, 927–28, 935–36, 944–45, 972–77, 994–95; proclamation of, 840

Nevil, Joseph, 61

Neville, John, 362, 871

New Brunswick, N.J., 256, 257, 258, 268, 454

New Hampshire, 796; and Constitution, 684, 688; insurgents, 622; troops of, 119, 215, 381–82, 425

New Haven, Conn., 364, 687

New Jersey, 248, 253, 256, 261, 284, 313, 314, 338, 368, 395, 403, 653, 795, 796; and Constitution, 664, 669, 675, 698; troops of, 204, 225, 257, 266, 278, 292, 319, 345–46, 376, 413–415, 438, 439, 446, 452, 512, 514, 883, 890

New Kent, Va., 184

New Orleans, La. 19, 20, 328, 581, 816
New Windsor, Conn., 428
New York (city), 80, 203, 205, 206, 223, 244, 252, 253, 261, 320, 348, 352, 354, 364–65, 376, 382, 387, 388, 423, 430, 451, 475, 477, 481, 498, 509, 530, 551, 554, 561, 570, 585, 596, 601, 608, 641, 646, 648, 651, 655, 664, 684, 687, 699, 726, 729, 730, 745, 795, 796, 814, 865, 880, 900, 915, 938; British troops at, 320, 323–24, 364, 368, 395, 403, 425, 427, 430; British evacuation of, 554; harbor of, 368, 462, 554; planned campaign (American), 428–29, 435–51, 690; preparations for British attack on, 200, 220, 224
New York (state), 261, 278, 567, 568, 596, 601, 648, 655, 687, 699, 795–96, 1039; Assembly of, 334, 369; Convention, 684; provisions, 368, 376, 382; troops of, 438, 446, 447, 448, 450, 452, 453, 454, 514
Newberry (Newbury), Roger, 239
Newell, Eliphilet, 244
Newenham, Edward, letter to, 693
Newenham, Lady, 696
Newfoundland, 328, 451
Newks Hill, Mass., 217
Newport, R.I., 200, 428, 433, 435, 446, 449, 766
Newtown, N.Y., 430
Niagara, N.Y., 365, 773, 979
Nicholas, Wilson Cary, 334, 678
Nicola, Lewis, letter to, 468
Ninety Six, S.C., 445
Nisbet, Dr. Charles, 673
Nixon, John, 176
Noailles, Louis Marie, Viscount de, 461, 466
Norfolk, Va., 206, 648
Norfolk County, Va., 224
North, Frederick, Earl of Guilford, 198, 302, 312, 304, 305, 364
North, William, 1009
North Anna River, 433
North Carolina: 224, 917; and Constitution, 688, 699, 746, 748; and excise laws, 778; circular to, 399; regiments in Ohio Expedition, 611–14; George Washington's lands in, 794
North (Hudson) River, 245–46, 256,

312, 318, 323, 324, 354, 360, 381, 382, 428, 439, 440, 441, 443, 447, 448, 449, 463
Northcastle, N.Y., 437, 452
Norwalk, Conn., 364
Notes on the State of Virginia (Jefferson), 687

Obaish River, 20, 26
O'Brien, Richard, 997
Occoquan River, Va., 1004
Ogden, Aaron, 307
Ohio Company, 18, 125
Ohio River, 18, 29, 30, 37, 40, 42, 51, 60, 69, 88, 95, 125, 135, 140, 564–68, 581, 583, 598, 611, 620, 663, 664, 670, 686, 687, 745, 769, 775, 827, 849, 868, 893, 899, 919
Oliver, Robert, 816
Orange County, N.Y., 229
Orangeburg, S.C., 433
Orangetown (Tappan), N.Y., 243
Orléans, Duchess of, 674
Orme, Robert, 57, 59, 615
Oswald, Richard, 481
Oswego Lake, 26, 27
Oswego, N.Y., 979
Ottoman Empire, 670, 676, 693
Outasitta (Cherokee), 90
Outawaies River, 560

Paine, Thomas, letter to, 471
Panton, William, 816
Paramus, N.J., 453
Paris, 475, 486, 555, 558, 582, 747, 780, 949
Paris, Treaty of (1783), 511, 527, 534, 536, 596, 646, 979
Paris, Richard. *See* Pearis, Richard
Parker, Josiah, 951
Parks, Harriot, 1034. *See also* Washington, Harriot
Parsippany, N.J., 453
Parsons, Samuel Holden, 417, 443, 670
Pasavent, Mrs., 112
Passaic Falls, N.J., 403
Passamaquoddy Bay, 979
Paterson's Creek, Va., 13, 75
Paulus Hook. *See* Powles Hook
Peacey, William, 604

Peachy, William, 91

Peake, Humphrey, 1032

Peale, Charles Willson, 144

Pearce, William, 866; letters to, 844, 859, 895, 910

Pearis, Richard, 71

Peekskill, N.Y., 433, 434, 437

Peggy (ship), 865, 866

Pendleton, Edmund, 169, 334; letters to, 842, 903

Pendleton, Mrs. Edmund, 844

Pendleton, Philip, 1027

Pennington, Isaac, 11

Pennsylvania, 124, 149, 260, 261, 284, 405, 561, 564, 795, 796; and Constitution, 664, 669, 675, 698; Assembly of, 49; borders of, 540, 744; circular to, 400; George Washington's lands in, 1001, 1039; newspapers, 149, 367; manufacturing, 718; provisions for Revolutionary War effort, 292, 366–67, 438; recruitment, 368; transportation through, 566; troops and provisions for Ohio Expedition, 63, 70; troops of, 123, 171, 258, 368, 400, 407, 414, 415, 883, 890; Whiskey Rebellion, 870–73, 882–84, 887–93

Pennsylvania Academy, 38

Pennsylvania Mercury (newspaper), 798

Pensacola, Fl., 816

Percy, Lord Hugh, 164

Peros (slave), 102, 103

Peter, Martha Parke, 1034. *See also* Custis, Martha Parke

Peters, Richard, 450

Peterson, Jacob, 133

Petersburg, court of, 429

Petersburg, Va., 431

Peyrouney. *See* La Peyronie

Peyton, Craven, 163

Peyton, Francis, 235

Phelps, Oliver, 773

Philadelphia, 91, 190, 193, 237, 270, 278, 281, 284, 297, 305–06, 321, 341, 360, 361, 437, 442, 448, 480, 482, 485, 491, 493, 494, 509, 515, 530, 533, 561, 565, 566, 649, 652, 653, 658, 670, 772, 775, 786, 822, 823, 832, 837, 914, 953, 959, 993; as destination, 59, 157, 158, 319, 351, 362, 371, 407, 434, 454, 504, 554, 617, 768, 846, 886, 917; as probable

British objective, 253, 258; as site of Constitutional Convention, 625, 627, 629, 632, 634, 642, 644–46; as site of Societies of the Cincinnati General Meeting, 623–25, 632, 634, 642, 645; British troops at, 284, 278, 312, 395; militia, 268

Philadelphia Aurora (newspaper), 1045

Philip's Hill, N.Y., 449

Phoenix (ship), 233, 235

Philosophical Society (Philadelphia), 838

Pickering, Timothy, 772, 774, 775

Picket, William, 61

Pidgein Hill, 452

Pierce, William, 227

Piercy, Lord. *See* Percy, Lord Hugh

Pinckney, Charles Cotesworth, 955, 1009, 1013

Pinckney, Thomas, 937

Pine, Robert Edge, 577

Piscataway, Md., 183

Pittsburgh, Pa., 125, 432, 433, 653. *See also* Fort Duquesne, Fort Pitt

Pittstown, N.J., 405

Plater, Elizabeth, 599

Plater, George, 599

Plymouth, Mass., 206

Point Shirley, Mass., 196

Poland, 779

Polk, Charles, 12

Polson, John, 58

Pompton, N.J., 413, 453

Poor, Enoch, 317

Port Tobacco, Md., 183

Portsmouth, N.H., 204

Portsmouth, Va., 354

Portugal, 358

Posey, John, letters to, 118

Posey, John Price, letter to, 469

Posey, Milly, 238, 421

Posey, Thomas, 331

Potomac Navigation Company, 587, 597, 1026, 1034, 1041

Potomac River, 12, 44, 89, 100, 105, 106, 112, 113, 114, 449, 551, 553, 587, 664, 999; establishment of university on, 910; extension of inland navigation, 137–39, 564–65, 568, 570, 575, 583, 586, 592, 620, 797, 801, 839, 906, 908, 999, 1025; military operations on, 67,

449, 451, 1011; seat of government on, 1004. *See also* Potomac Navigation Company

Potomack Run, 277

Potsdam, 585

Powell, Ambrose, 136

Powell, Leven, 235

Powell, Mr., 659, 663

Powles Hook, N.J., 248, 365

Prescott, Richard, 208

Presidency, 636, 668, 699–701, 706–07, 709, 723, 732, 734, 735, 736–38, 752, 755, 765, 835, 846, 847, 850, 872, 878, 883, 922, 930–32, 1010

Presque Isle, Pa. *See* Erie, Pa.

Preston, William, 82

Prince, Capt., 183

Prince Edward Court House, Va., 877

Prince William County, Va., 11, 63

Princess Anne County, Va., 224

Princeton, N.J., 256, 258, 263, 266, 267, 268, 314, 454, 485

Prospect Hill, Mass., 176, 178, 179

Providence, R.I., 428, 430

Prussia, 594, 595, 694, 840

Publius (pseud. author of *The Federalist*), 673, 691

Pugh, Jesse, 61

Pulteney, William, 369

Putnam, Israel, 171, 173, 174, 193, 670; letter to, 279

Putnam, Mrs. Israel, 279

Quakers, 593, 758, 761

Quebec, 199, 206, 209, 329

Queen Charlotte (ship), 455

Rack, Edmund, 604

Raleigh Tavern (Williamsburg, Va.), 150

Rall, Johan Gottlieb, 263

Ramsay, William, 53, 157; letter to, 129

Ramsay, William, Jr., 129

Rand, Dr. Isaac, 176

Randolph, David Meade, 432

Randolph, Edmund, 655, 664, 867; letters to, 586, 627, 644, 649, 666, 820, 886

Rappahannock River, 89, 100, 900

Raritan River, 256

Rawden, Lord Francis, 433, 435

Rawlings, Moses, 254

Rawlins, Mr., 1051

Ray, John Jr., 227

Raynal, Abbé Guillaume Thomas François, 687

Read, Joseph, 227

Reading, Pa., 277, 837

Red Stone Creek, 37

Redeisel, Friedrich Adolf von, 425

Reed, Esther (de Berdt), 195, 207, 216, 377

Reed, Joseph, 175, 230; letters to, 193, 198, 200, 205, 207, 211, 373

Reed & Ford, 994

Rhode Island, 425, 431, 435, 455, 456, 484, 839; and Constitution, 660, 664, 689, 746; British military in, 320, 322, 352, 368; insurgents, 622; troops of, 199, 449, 452, 453

Rice, Hopkins, 227

Richardson, Francis, 204

Richmond, Va., 419, 431, 436, 570, 573, 587, 607, 689, 900

Ridgebury, N.Y., 436

Ridout, Thomas, 585

Ringwood, N.J., 413

Riparti, Capt. *See* De Repentigny, Louis Le Gardeur

Rittenhouse, David, 480

Ritzema, Rudolphus, 227

River Farm, 854, 912. *See also* Mount Vernon

Roanoke, Va., 82

Roberts, William, 185

Robertson, Archibald, 838

Robin, letter to, 16

Robinson, Sir Thomas, 49

Rochambeau, Jean Baptiste Donatien de Vimeur, Comte de, 411, 423, 425, 427, 428, 429, 431, 434, 435, 436, 439, 443, 444, 446, 452, 454, 455, 465

Rock Creek, Va., 800

Rockingham, Charles Watson-Wentworth, Marquis of, 477

Rodney, George Brydges, 450, 451

Ronald, William, 662

Roots, John, 331

Rose, H.M.S., 233

Ross, Alexander, 461

Ross, Dr. David, 129, 130

Rough Creek, Ky., 1040

Rousby Hall, 48

Roxbury, Mass., 177, 178, 179, 215
Rumsey, James 566
Rush, S., 112
Russel (London agent), 113
Russell, James, 1047
Russia, 341, 358, 390
Rutherford, Robert, 151
Rutledge, Edward, letter to, 735
Rutledge, Mrs. Edward, 736
Rutledge, James, 13
Rutledge, John, 432, 651
Rutledge, John, Jr., 651

S. G. *See* Smith, George
Sabine Hall, Va. (home of Landon Carter), 311
Sackett, William, 436
St. Andrews, Maine, 979
St. Clair, Arthur, 384, 428, 463, 687; letter to, 743
St. Clair, Sir John. *See* Sinclair, Sir John
St. Croix River, 979
St. George's, Me., 916, 987
St. James, Court of, 86
St. Johns, Quebec, 229
St. Joseph River, 540, 568
St. Lawrence River, 561
St. Louis, Military Order of, 28
St. Mary's River, 839
St. Pierre, Jacques Le Gardeur, Sieur de, 17, 19, 20, 22, 26, 28, 30, 34
St. Simon-Montblérn, Claude Anne de Rouvroy, Marquis de, 457, 597
St. Vincennes (town on Mississippi), 745
Salem, Mass., 164
Sandwich, John Montagu, Earl of, 164, 364
Sandy Hook, N.J., 318, 453, 455
Sanpinck Creek, N.J., 267
Sarah (privateer), 107
Saratoga, N.Y., 435
Sardinia, 840
Savage, Margaret, 161
Savage River, 664
Savannah, Ga., 445
Saw Mill River, N.Y., 449
Sayre, Stephen, 204
Scammell, Alexander, 417, 425, 427, 436, 443, 452
Scarborough, H.M.S., 200

Schuyler, Philip, 171, 173, 174, 188, 372, 384, 427, 429, 431, 435, 438, 446, 447, 535, 536, 537, 541
Schuylkill River, 277, 561, 565
Scioto River, 37, 564
Scotland, 687, 868
Scott, John Morin, 225, 314
Seagrove, James, 815–18
Sears, Isaac, 200
Ségur, Louis Philippe, Comte de, 476; letter to, 803
Semple, John, 143
Shanapin's Town, Va., 29, 32, 33
Sharpe, Horatio, 38, 48, 49, 50
Shays' Rebellion, 609, 622, 628, 631, 634, 640–41, 648
Sheaffs, Roger, 879
Sheffield, John Holyrod, Earl of, 903
Shelburne, William Petty, Earl of, 477, 480
Shelby, Isaac, 925
Sheldon, Elisha, 438, 439, 443
Shenandoah River, 11, 107, 797, 855, 1005
Sherman, Isaac, 417, 670
Shippen, Dr. William, 179
Shirley, William, 69, 71, 618
Shirley, Va., 446
Short, William, 815
Shreve, Israel, 414
Shrewsbury, N.J., 315
Shuldan, Molyneaux, 199
Simcoe, John Graves, 879
Simpson, Gilbert, Jr., 184, 185, 186
Sinclair, Sir John, 59, 614, 615, 865
Singess (Delaware chief), 18, 19, 24, 25, 45
Singsing, N.Y., 452
Six Nations. *See* Indians, Six Nations
Skipwith, Fulwar, 929
Slaves and Slavery, 102–103, 109, 110, 118, 120, 121, 140, 145, 149, 150, 156, 158, 164, 195, 224, 259, 335–36, 338, 420–21, 470, 510, 593–94, 607–08, 637–39, 701–02, 726, 740, 741, 742, 761, 785, 853, 854, 856, 861, 862, 863, 900, 1002, 1047
Smallwood, William, 399
Smith, Charles, 147
Smith, Francis, 164
Smith, George, 430

Smith, Jeth, 239
Smith, Joshua, 388
Smith, Dr. Patrick, 431
Smith, Thomas, 587
Smiths Clove, N.Y., 362
Somerset, N.J., 454
Somerset Court House (Somerville), N.J., 453–54
South Amboy, N.J., 313
South Carolina, 348, 355, 395, 651, 675, 681, 698, 756, 916; ratifying convention, 684
Southall, James, 587
Spain, 326, 328, 329, 341, 343, 358, 363, 374, 375, 390, 584, 597, 599, 610, 683, 765, 766, 817, 873, 925; treaties with, 967, 979–80
Sparke, William, 56
Spearing, Ann, 52
Spencer, Joseph, 225
Spikendevil River, 436, 439, 440
Spiltdorf, Carolus Gustavus de, 46
Spotswood, Alexander, 1040; letters to, 271, 898, 1015
Spotswood, Elizabeth Washington, 900, 1034
Spotswood, Mary, 97
Sprigg, Richard, 823
Sprilldorph. See Spiltdorf, Carolus Gustavus de
Springfield (Short Hills), N.J., 452, 453
Sprout, Ebenezer, 670
Stafford, Va. 134
Stamp Act, 116, 117, 123
Stanislaw II, King of Poland, 779
Stanley, Lord Edward, 219
Stanwix, John, letters to, 89, 93
Stapleton, John, 511
Stark, John, 435
Staten Island, N.Y., 232, 236, 240, 430, 452
Stephen, Adam, 68, 71, 80, 256; letter to, 232
Stephenson, Hugh, 254
Steuben, Frederick, Baron von, 309, 392, 393, 423, 436, 506
Steward, Henry, 17, 18
Stewart, Robert, 70, 76, 79, 82, 133, 160, 514; letters to, 108, 553
Stirling, Lord, 245, 256, 258, 287, 288, 309, 316, 510

Stony Brook, N.J., 267
Stony Point, N.Y., 364, 367, 368, 382, 387, 388
Street, Mr., 773
Strong, Simeon, 239
Stuart, Dr. David, 570, 902, 1030; letters to, 756, 760, 800
Stuart, Mrs. David, 570
Stuart, Eleanor, 1030
Stuart, William, 860, 862
Stump, Michael, 13
Suffolk, England, 602
Suffolk, Va., 354
Suffrans, N.J., 453
Sullivan, John, 229, 321, 354, 365
Sullivan's Bridge (Schuylkill River), 307
Sumner, Job, 490
Supreme Court, 829, 889
Susquehanna River, 139, 355, 561, 565, 814
Sussex Court House, N.J., 424
Swift, Heman, 514

Talcott, Matthew, 239
Tallahassee, Florida, 816
Tallmadge, Benjamin, 422, 430
Talman, Henry, 100
Tanacharison, 19, 20, 22, 23, 24, 25, 26, 27, 30, 31, 35, 36, 43, 44, 45, 611
Tappan Bay, N.Y., 229, 233
Tarlton, Va., 446
Tarrytown, N.Y., 388, 437, 439
Taupon Bay. See Tappan Bay
Tayloe, John, 161, 235, 236
Tea Act, 294
Tellasee. See Tallahassee
Tellers Point (Hudson River), 439
Ten Broek, Abraham, 435
Tennessee River, 816, 827
Ternant, Jean Baptiste, 779; letter to, 785
Ternay, Charles Louis d'Arsac, Chevalier de, 411
Thomas, James, 78, 80
Thomas, John, 218
Thompson, Ensign, 417
Thompson, Joseph, letter to, 118
Thomson, Charles, 729, 730; reply to, 729
Thornton, Francis, 802
Thornton, Jane, 1034

Thornton, Mary, 190
Throgs Neck, N.Y., 253, 443, 445
Thruston, Charles Mynn, 135, 137; letter to, 873
Ticonderoga, 264, 384
Tilghman, Anna, 556
Tilghman, Tench, 406, 466, 602; letters to, 480, 515, 555, 577
Tilton, Philip, 239
Tioga Point, N.Y., 772, 774, 775
Tippell, William, 163
Tippets Hill, N.Y., 444
Toby Creek, Pa., 561, 565
Tom (slave), 118
Town Taker (Indian name for GW), 611
Townsend, Robert. *See* Culper, Samuel Jr.
Treasury, Department of, 738, 755, 769, 785, 791, 843, 850
Trebells Landing, Va., 457
Trent, William, 35, 41
Trenton, N.J., 232, 263, 406, 454; battle of, 262–268
Trenton Ferry, 263
Tripoli, 980
Triumph, H.M.S., 504
Trotter, John, 30
Trueman, Alexander, 816
Trumbull, Jonathan, Jr., 866, 1042, 1048; letters to, 988, 1042, 1048
Trumbull, Jonathan, 427, 434, 438, 447
Truro, Parish of, Va., 650
Truxton, Thomas, 865
Tryon, William, 206, 207
Tucker, Dr. Thomas, 814
Tunis, 980
Tupper, Benjamin, 630, 670
Turtle Creek, Pa., 18
Twigtwees. *See* Indians, Wabash
Tyler, John, 227
Tyler, John Steel, 307, 308

Ulster County, N.Y., 229
Union Farm (Mount Vernon), 853
Unity (ship), 105

Valentine, Joseph, 113, 116
Valentine Hill, N.Y., 437, 443, 449
Valley Forge, Pa., 395, 487
Van Braam, Jacob, 17, 32, 46

Van Courtland, Philip, 225, 297, 448, 450, 464
Van Courtland, Pierre, 435
Van Schaik, Goose, 429, 431
Vandenburg, James, 427, 428–29
Vanderkemp, Rev. Francis Adrian, 680
Vanmetris, Henry, 13, 14, 15
Vanscaik. *See* Van Schaik
Varnum, James Mitchell, 670
Vass, Ephraim, 82, 83, 84
Vaux, Noël de Jourda, Comte de, 361
Venable, Abraham Bedford, 877
Venango, Pa., 20, 22, 24, 25, 26, 28, 29, 30, 31, 35, 56
Vergennés, Charles Gravier, Comte de, 481
Vermont, 648
Verplanks Point, N.Y., 367, 368, 382, 387, 388
Versailles. *See* France, Court of
Vienna, 594, 595
Ville de Paris (French flagship), 455, 462
Vioménil, Antoine Charles du Houx, Baron de, 459
Virgil, 126
Virginia, 22, 39, 72, 149, 179, 198, 206, 319, 354, 357, 360, 361, 363, 426, 436, 447, 448, 451, 453, 482, 526, 531, 536, 561, 574, 610, 614, 617, 621, 690, 749, 756, 760, 769, 795, 796, 797, 859, 1017; and Constitution, 223, 655, 664, 678, 681, 757; as destination, 200, 203, 434, 455, 599; Assembly, 72, 73, 135, 136, 332, 368, 369, 418, 436, 466, 568, 575, 618, 677, 908, 909; borders of, 617, 744; pre-Revolutionary troops of, 58, 59, 60, 61, 64, 72, 73, 77, 79, 81, 85, 86, 87, 89, 99, 610, 614; relation to District of Columbia, 776, 910–12; river navigation, 138, 561, 563, 663; troops of, 171, 256, 260, 298, 304, 311, 376, 400, 433, 464, 466, 744, 883, 86, 890; George Washington's lands in, 357, 1001, 1036–39
Vulture, H.M.S., 388

Wabash River, 568, 769
Wadsworth, James, 427
Waggener, Thomas, 41, 45, 48, 66, 67, 68

Wales, 204

Walker, Ann (Alton), 1031

Walker, Benjamin, 309, 551

Wallace, Sir William, 1029

Wallop, Henry, 393

Walton, George, letter to, 264

Wappings Creek, N.Y., 438, 447

War, Department of, 755, 770, 775, 785, 813, 875

Ward, Artemas, 171, 173, 174

Ward, Edward, 35

Ward, Joseph, 570

Warm Spring Mountain, Va., 74

Warm Springs. *See* Berkeley Springs

Warren, James, letters to, 271, 341, 591

Warren, Mercy Otis, 343, 593

Warville, Jean Pierre. *See* Brissot de Warville

Washington, Augustine (brother), 101, 1034

Washington, Bushrod (nephew) 638, 742, 823 1029, 1031, 1033, 1034, 1035; letters to, 482, 659

Washington, Charles (brother), 740, 1030, 1034, 1050; letter to, 134

Washington, Charles Augustine (great-nephew), 1034

Washington, Corbin (nephew), 1034

Washington, Elizabeth ("of Hayfield"), 1030

Washington, Fanny Bassett, 793, 824, 896; letter to, 834. *See also* Bassett, Frances

Washington, George Fayette (great-nephew), 1032, 1034

Washington, George Steptoe (nephew), 1031, 1035

Washington, George Augustine (nephew), 808, 813, 815, 821, 824, 833, 856, 1027, 1034; letter to, 719

Washington, Hannah (sister-in-law), 1030

Washington, Hannah ("of Fairfield"), 1030

Washington, Harriot, 824, 835; letter to, 793

Washington, Jane (niece), 1034

Washington, John Augustine (brother), 134, 161, 637, 638, 740; letters to, 47, 51, 54, 59, 171, 179, 218, 223, 244, 252, 276, 305, 379, 526

Washington, Lawrence (grandfather), 803

Washington, Lawrence Augustine (nephew), 1027, 1032, 1034

Washington, Lawrence ("of Chotanck"), 1030

Washington, Lund, 135, 137, 168, 251, 637, 741, 898; letters to, 183, 190, 234, 248, 258, 334, 356, 420, 486, 502

Washington, Maria (daughter of nephew), 1034

Washington, Martha, 112, 140, 144, 146, 184, 193, 205, 207, 216, 225, 259, 261, 307, 310, 313, 336, 338, 361, 366, 377, 406, 433, 481, 482, 541, 551, 558, 576, 577, 585, 598, 649, 658, 736, 763, 808, 824, 825, 835, 865, 896, 989, 993, 995, 1005, 1023; letters to, 167, 173; sends regards, 291, 343, 413, 421, 485, 510, 515, 528, 535, 553, 555, 556, 559, 572, 573, 586, 590, 593, 594, 599, 610, 630, 634, 636, 641, 659, 680, 696, 748, 753, 780, 809, 825, 833, 869, 917, 987, 994, 1003, 1048, 1050. *See also* Custis, Martha

Washington, Mary Ball (mother), 161, 740–743; letters to, 50, 60, 636

Washington, Mildred (sister-in-law), 1030

Washington, Milly (Mrs. Lund), 336, 570

Washington, Mrs. (widow of Maj. George Washington), 844

Washington, Richard, letters to, 88, 100, 103

Washington, Robert ("of Chotanck"), 1030

Washington, Samuel (brother), 134, 740, 1027, 1031, 1034, 1035; letter to, 1001

Washington, Thornton (nephew), 1027, 1034

Washington, William, 895

Washington, William Augustine (nephew), 1028, 1031, 1034, 1035

Washington County, Md., 797

Washington County, Penn., 653, 868, 872, 889, 1001

Washington family, 802

Waterbury, David, 436, 437, 443, 447

Watertown, Mass., 178

Watson, Robert, 110

Wayne, Anthony, 260, 274, 314, 317, 318, 365, 407, 445, 446, 451, 462, 893, 904

Webb, Joseph, 427

Webster, Noah, letter to, 689

Weedon, George, 247, 260, 378

Welch, James, letter to, 1021

Welch, Wakelin, 603, 604

West, Benjamin, 601

West, John, 53, 152, 161

West, William, 16, 46, 48

West Indies, 363, 364, 390, 451, 477, 585, 687, 694, 915, 925, 935, 980, 984

West Point, N.Y., 381, 382, 386, 387, 390, 392, 395, 403, 424, 425, 426, 429, 433, 434, 450, 514

Westchester, N.Y., 417

Westover, Va., 431, 433

Wethersfield, Conn., 425, 427, 428, 442, 446

Wharton, John, 359

Wharton, Thomas, 266

Wheatley, Phillis, 215; letter to, 216

"Whiskey Rebellion," 882–95

White, John, 176

White Plains, N.Y., 253, 437

Whitehaven, Mass., 206

Whiting, Anthony, 841, 861, 896

Wilkinson, James, 287, 288

Willet, Marinus, 541, 1039

Williams, Mr., 585

Williams Bridge, N.Y., 443

Williams Gap, Va., 16

Williamsburg, Va., 19, 34, 53, 62, 69, 71, 72, 73, 78, 105, 132, 140, 144, 145, 157, 162, 223, 438, 455, 573, 611, 617

Williamson, Mr., 154

Williamson, Andrew, 337

Willie, William, 1029

Willis, Francis, 43, 148

Wills Creek (Ohio Company Post), 19, 34, 46, 50, 51, 55, 613

Wilmington, Del., 283, 462, 463

Wilmot, Henry, 227

Wilson, James, 678, 872

Wilson, Rev. Thomas, 1030

Wilton, Va., 431

Winchester, Va., 11, 12, 15, 17, 37, 39, 48, 51, 57, 61, 67 82, 85, 462, 464, 611, 613, 1040

Windham, Conn., 434

Winter Hill, Mass., 178, 179

Witherspoon, Dr. John, 557

Wood, James, 330; letter to, 95

Wood, Mary, 95

Woodford, William, 254, 274, 311, 317, 377; letter to, 189

Woodford, Mrs. William. See Thornton, Mary

Woodhull, Abraham. See Culper, Samuel Sr.

Woodward, Henry, 80

Worcester, Mass., 206

Worcester County, Mass., 531

Worrell, Joseph, 298

Wright, Samuel, 226

Wrisst. See Wright, Samuel

Wyllys, Samuel, 226

Wythe, George, 334, 678

Yagers. See Hessians

York Island (Manhattan), N.Y., 252, 436, 438, 439

York River, 113, 115, 132, 452

Yorkshire, England, 802

Yorktown, 286, 468, 569, 1004; campaign, 421–66

Youghiogheny River, 33, 56, 57, 58, 565

Young, Arthur, 867, 868, 953; letters to, 602, 795, 851

CATALOGING INFORMATION

Washington, George, 1732–1799.
    [Selections. 1997]
    Writings / George Washington ; [selected by John H.
Rhodehamel].
        p.   cm. — (The Library of America ; 91)
    Includes index.
    1. Washington, George, 1732–1799—Archives.
2. Virginia—History—Colonial period, ca. 1600–1775—
Sources. 3. United States—History—Revolution, 1775–
1783—Sources. 4. United States—Politics and government—
1775–1783—Sources. 5. United States—Politics and
government—1783–1809—Sources.   I. Title.   II. Series.
E312.72   1997
973.4'1'092—dc20
    [B]   96-9665
    ISBN 1-883011-23-X (alk. paper)   CIP

THE LIBRARY OF AMERICA SERIES

1. Herman Melville, *Typee, Omoo, Mardi* (1982)
2. Nathaniel Hawthorne, *Tales and Sketches* (1982)
3. Walt Whitman, *Poetry and Prose* (1982)
4. Harriet Beecher Stowe, *Three Novels* (1982)
5. Mark Twain, *Mississippi Writings* (1982)
6. Jack London, *Novels and Stories* (1982)
7. Jack London, *Novels and Social Writings* (1982)
8. William Dean Howells, *Novels 1875–1886* (1982)
9. Herman Melville, *Redburn, White-Jacket, Moby-Dick* (1983)
10. Nathaniel Hawthorne, *Collected Novels* (1983)
11. Francis Parkman, *France and England in North America* vol. I, (1983)
12. Francis Parkman, *France and England in North America* vol. II, (1983)
13. Henry James, *Novels 1871–1880* (1983)
14. Henry Adams, *Novels, Mont Saint Michel, The Education* (1983)
15. Ralph Waldo Emerson, *Essays and Lectures* (1983)
16. Washington Irving, *History, Tales and Sketches* (1983)
17. Thomas Jefferson, *Writings* (1984)
18. Stephen Crane, *Prose and Poetry* (1984)
19. Edgar Allan Poe, *Poetry and Tales* (1984)
20. Edgar Allan Poe, *Essays and Reviews* (1984)
21. Mark Twain, *The Innocents Abroad, Roughing It* (1984)
22. Henry James, *Essays, American & English Writers* (1984)
23. Henry James, *European Writers & The Prefaces* (1984)
24. Herman Melville, *Pierre, Israel Potter, The Confidence-Man, Tales & Billy Budd* (1985)
25. William Faulkner, *Novels 1930–1935* (1985)
26. James Fenimore Cooper, *The Leatherstocking Tales* vol. I, (1985)
27. James Fenimore Cooper, *The Leatherstocking Tales* vol. II, (1985)
28. Henry David Thoreau, *A Week, Walden, The Maine Woods, Cape Cod* (1985)
29. Henry James, *Novels 1881–1886* (1985)
30. Edith Wharton, *Novels* (1986)
31. Henry Adams, *History of the United States during the Administrations of Jefferson* (1986)
32. Henry Adams, *History of the United States during the Administrations of Madison* (1986)
33. Frank Norris, *Novels and Essays* (1986)
34. W. E. B. Du Bois, *Writings* (1986)
35. Willa Cather, *Early Novels and Stories* (1987)
36. Theodore Dreiser, *Sister Carrie, Jennie Gerhardt, Twelve Men* (1987)
37. Benjamin Franklin, *Writings* (1987)
38. William James, *Writings 1902–1910* (1987)
39. Flannery O'Connor, *Collected Works* (1988)
40. Eugene O'Neill, *Complete Plays 1913–1920* (1988)
41. Eugene O'Neill, *Complete Plays 1920–1931* (1988)
42. Eugene O'Neill, *Complete Plays 1932–1943* (1988)
43. Henry James, *Novels 1886–1890* (1989)
44. William Dean Howells, *Novels 1886–1888* (1989)
45. Abraham Lincoln, *Speeches and Writings 1832–1858* (1989)
46. Abraham Lincoln, *Speeches and Writings 1859–1865* (1989)
47. Edith Wharton, *Novellas and Other Writings* (1990)
48. William Faulkner, *Novels 1936–1940* (1990)
49. Willa Cather, *Later Novels* (1990)
50. Ulysses S. Grant, *Personal Memoirs and Selected Letters* (1990)
51. William Tecumseh Sherman, *Memoirs* (1990)
52. Washington Irving, *Bracebridge Hall, Tales of a Traveller, The Alhambra* (1991)
53. Francis Parkman, *The Oregon Trail, The Conspiracy of Pontiac* (1991)
54. James Fenimore Cooper, *Sea Tales: The Pilot, The Red Rover* (1991)
55. Richard Wright, *Early Works* (1991)

56. Richard Wright, *Later Works* (1991)
57. Willa Cather, *Stories, Poems, and Other Writings* (1992)
58. William James, *Writings 1878–1899* (1992)
59. Sinclair Lewis, *Main Street & Babbitt* (1992)
60. Mark Twain, *Collected Tales, Sketches, Speeches, & Essays 1852–1890* (1992)
61. Mark Twain, *Collected Tales, Sketches, Speeches, & Essays 1891–1910* (1992)
62. *The Debate on the Constitution: Part One* (1993)
63. *The Debate on the Constitution: Part Two* (1993)
64. Henry James, *Collected Travel Writings: Great Britain & America* (1993)
65. Henry James, *Collected Travel Writings: The Continent* (1993)
66. *American Poetry: The Nineteenth Century,* Vol. 1 (1993)
67. *American Poetry: The Nineteenth Century,* Vol. 2 (1993)
68. Frederick Douglass, *Autobiographies,* (1994)
69. Sarah Orne Jewett, *Novels and Stories* (1994)
70. Ralph Waldo Emerson, *Collected Poems and Translations* (1994)
71. Mark Twain, *Historical Romances* (1994)
72. John Steinbeck, *Novels and Stories 1932–1937* (1994)
73. William Faulkner, *Novels 1942–1954* (1994)
74. Zora Neale Hurston, *Novels and Stories* (1995)
75. Zora Neale Hurston, *Folklore, Memoirs, and Other Writings* (1995)
76. Thomas Paine, *Collected Writings* (1995)
77. *Reporting World War II: American Journalism 1938–1944* (1995)
78. *Reporting World War II: American Journalism 1944–1946* (1995)
79. Raymond Chandler, *Stories and Early Novels* (1995)
80. Raymond Chandler, *Later Novels and Other Writings* (1995)
81. Robert Frost, *Collected Poems, Prose, & Plays* (1995)
82. Henry James, *Complete Stories 1892–1898* (1996)
83. Henry James, *Complete Stories 1898–1910* (1996)
84. William Bartram, *Travels and Other Writings* (1996)
85. John Dos Passos, *U.S.A.* (1996)
86. John Steinbeck, *The Grapes of Wrath and Other Writings 1936–1941* (1996)
87. Vladimir Nabokov, *Novels and Memoirs 1941–1951* (1996)
88. Vladimir Nabokov, *Novels 1955–1962* (1996)
89. Vladimir Nabokov, *Novels 1969–1974* (1996)
90. James Thurber, *Writings and Drawings* (1996)
91. George Washington, *Writings* (1997)
92. John Muir, *Nature Writings* (1997)

This book is set in 10 point Linotron Galliard,
a face designed for photocomposition by Matthew Carter
and based on the sixteenth-century face Granjon. The paper is
acid-free Ecusta Nyalite and meets the requirements for permanence
of the American National Standards Institute. The binding
material is Brillianta, a woven rayon cloth made by
Van Heek-Scholco Textielfabrieken, Holland.
The composition is by The Clarinda
Company. Printing and binding by
R.R.Donnelley & Sons Company.
Designed by Bruce Campbell.